PENGUIN BOOKS

THE GREEN FLAG

Robert Kee is the author of thirteen books, including *A Crowd is Not Company*, an account of his time in a German prisoner-of-war camp, and his monumental history of Irish nationalism, *The Green Flag*, which is also published by Penguin in three separate volumes: *The Most Distressful Country*, *The Bold Fenian Men*, and *Ourselves Alone*. His highly acclaimed history of Charles Stewart Parnell and Irish Nationalism, *The Laurel and the Ivy*, is published by Penguin too. His other books include *1939: The World We Left Behind*; *1945: The World We Fought For*, and *Munich: The Eleventh Hour*, published in 1988 to commemorate the fiftieth anniversary of the Munich Agreement. His book, *Trial and Error*, about the Maguire Seven and Guildford Four cases, played a significant part in helping to right those miscarriages of justice.

He is also a freelance journalist and broadcaster, and has worked for many years on radio and television for both the BBC and ITV, making many documentaries, including a thirteen-part series based on *The Green Flag* for BBC television entitled *Ireland: A History*, which received great critical acclaim and was widely shown both here and in the United States. He began his journalistic career on *Picture Post*, became a special correspondent for the *Sunday Times* and the *Observer*, and was at one time literary editor of the *Spectator*. He is at present employed on a life of François Mitterrand.

THE
GREEN
FLAG

*A History of
Irish Nationalism*

ROBERT KEE

PENGUIN BOOKS

PENGUIN BOOKS

Published by the Penguin Group
Penguin Books Ltd, 80 Strand, London WC2R 0RL, England
Penguin Putnam Inc., 375 Hudson Street, New York, New York 10014, USA
Penguin Books Australia Ltd, 250 Camberwell Road, Camberwell, Victoria 3124, Australia
Penguin Books Canada Ltd, 10 Alcorn Avenue, Toronto, Ontario, Canada M4V 3B2
Penguin Books India (P) Ltd, 11 Community Centre, Panchsheel Park, New Delhi – 110 017, India
Penguin Books (NZ) Ltd, Cnr Rosedale and Airborne Roads, Albany, Auckland, New Zealand
Penguin Books (South Africa) (Pty) Ltd, 24 Sturdee Avenue, Rosebank 2196, South Africa

Penguin Books Ltd, Registered Offices: 80 Strand, London WC2R 0RL, England

www.penguin.com

This omnibus first published by Weidenfeld and Nicolson 1972
Published in three volumes by Penguin 1989
This omnibus published in Penguin Books 2000

021

Copyright © Robert Kee, 1972
All rights reserved

Permission to quote from the Collected Works of W. B. Yeats
from the executors of W. B. Yeats and from Macmillan and Co.

The moral right of the author has been asserted

Printed in England by Clays Ltd, St Ives plc

ISBN-13: 978-0-14-029165-0

www.greenpenguin.co.uk

MIX
Paper from
responsible sources
FSC
www.fsc.org   FSC® C018179

Penguin Books is committed to a sustainable
future for our business, our readers and our planet.
This book is made from Forest Stewardship
Council™ certified paper.

To the memory of my father,
Robert Kee (1880–1958),
and of my mother,
Dorothy Frances Kee
(1890–1964)

Contents

PART FOUR THE TRAGEDY OF HOME RULE

PART FIVE OURSELVES ALONE

Contents

Contents

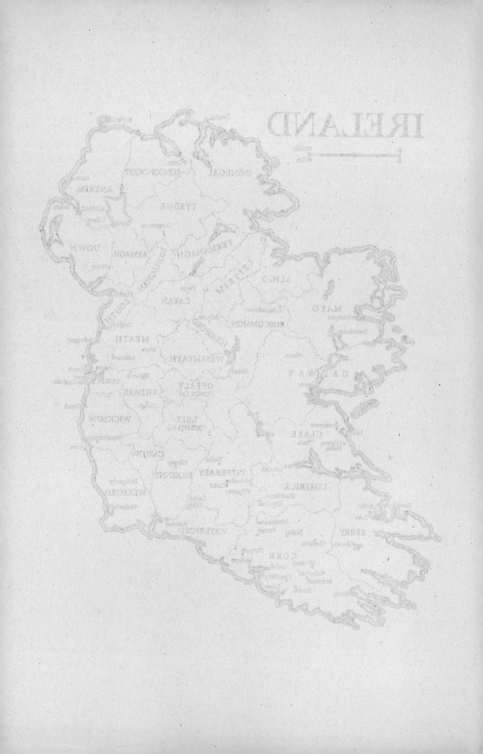

A standard to be got for each company ten
feet long with a pike in the end, the flag to be
of green stuff, about two feet square.
    Military instructions from the Leinster
    Provincial Committee of the United
    Irishmen, 19 April 1798

QUESTION: You say that the predisposition to
discontent which prevails generally is partly
to be attributed to the recollections of ancient
times?
ANSWER: I think so. I have heard and I
believe that that feeling is kept alive in the
minds of the people and is one of the causes. . .
    Evidence of Mr George Bennett, K.C., before
    a *Select Committee appointed to enquire into*
    the Disturbances in Ireland, given 18 May 1824
    (Minutes of Evidence, p. 94)

Nearly a million of our countrymen have fixed
their homes in England and Scotland. Every
family in the Kingdom is linked by domestic
connexion with England – every British colony
teems with the children of our soil. . . . Deep
indeed must be the wounds inflicted upon our
national pride, and upon our national interests,
before we can consent to deplore the
associations which belong to identity of
language, similarity of constitutions, connexion
of kindred, and community of glory. . .
    William Smith O'Brien, Letter to *The Nation*,
    30 December 1843

The National Flag is an uncrowned gold harp
on a plain green background.
    The Irish Volunteer, 18 March 1916

...My God, I thought that I would never live to see what is happening today under an Irish government. When we look back on the days when we were oppressed by England it would look like Paradise if we could get the same sort of oppression now.

John Dillon, 9 January 1925

...The study of Irish history does not excite political animosity but leads to the very opposite result. Thoroughly to appreciate the history of this or any country it is necessary to sympathise with all parties...

A. G. Richey. From *A Short History of the Irish People*, 1869

Preface

When the original complete volume of *The Green Flag* appeared in 1972 I wrote in the Preface that it was an attempt to illuminate for the general reader part of the dark and confusing ground of Irish history. Events in the intervening years have made that ground no less dark or confusing.

Here, in the course of a narrative running in detail from the end of the eighteenth century to 1925, when the last fine points of the 1921 Treaty as it affected Northern Ireland were agreed between London and Dublin, I have tried to unfold, as dispassionately as possible, earlier events of which some knowledge is essential for the understanding of anything that has happened, or may happen in Ireland. Knowledge and understanding do not in themselves provide solutions, but there can be no solutions without them.

The first inspiration for *The Green Flag* came from a magical valley in Co. Wicklow to whose resident spirit I send across many years gratitude and affection.

ROBERT KEE
March 2000

Part One

Who were Irishmen?

1
Treaty Night

In London, during the night of Monday, 5 December 1921, there occurred one of those sudden changes in the weather which Londoners come to accept as part of their long inconclusive battle against the winter. A week before there had been three days of fog. This was followed by a very cold spell. Then on this Monday night there came a quick rise in temperature so that, according to the newspapers, those who had slept with their windows shut set out next morning unaware of what had happened and arrived at their offices sweating in overcoats and mufflers.[1] Otherwise it must have seemed a night much like any other in the dying year.

But it was during this night that seven centuries of British history came to an end. For at 2.20 a.m., after some last-minute motoring between 10 Downing Street and 22 Hans Place, SW1, where a delegation of men from Ireland had been staying, a document was signed at 10 Downing Street that has come to be known as the Anglo-Irish Treaty. Viewed in the grand perspective of history, England's long attempt to rule all Ireland, begun in the reign of Henry II, was over.

For more than forty years after that night in December 1921 Englishmen gradually allowed themselves to forget that there had ever been an Irish question. Ireland became a country which, if it held English interest at all, held it largely for pleasant amiable reasons. It was – and still is – a beautiful, quiet, rainy country in which, as the Irish Tourist Board once put it with a touch of genius, 'it is easy to take things easy'; a country of good racehorses and stout and an eccentric writer or two, where the Englishman can combine the pleasures of being on unfamiliar ground with the pleasures of feeling thoroughly at home.

But in the late 1960s Britain and the rest of the world were startled by events in Northern Ireland which, violent, unpredictable and sometimes incomprehensible, seemed to most people to strike like a bolt from the blue. But they had not come from the blue. They had come out of Irish history.

Forty odd years before, Englishmen had let themselves think that they had solved the Irish question. Inasmuch as the Anglo-Irish Treaty had removed from England the most complex emotional problem in her long domestic history, this was true. But it had solved the problem for England, not for

Ireland. The chief fault of English government in Ireland had always been not that it had oppressed her but that it had ignored her problems until too late. Now the untied ends of England's 'Treaty' settlement have returned to trouble her.

It is already difficult, fifty years later, to realize what a momentous change, despite its failings, that settlement of 6 December 1921 brought about. In 1921, for more generations than anyone would normally stop to consider, there had been living in Ireland men who thought of themselves as indistinguishably British and Irish and whose lives made the two islands to them one country. Such men would take pride in being 'Irishmen' as Welshmen or men from Yorkshire today take pride in their backgrounds, regarding their love of Ireland as part of a wider loyalty. Others who lived in Ireland shared the experience but with a different emphasis: they thought of themselves as primarily 'Irish', but since 'Irish' was an identity which had so long existed only within the framework of the British Empire, that framework was part of the identity. When such men joined the British Army or Navy, as they did in great numbers, or came to England to build for themselves careers which welded them almost indistinguishably to the people among whom they lived, they developed a more positive wider loyalty without in any way excluding a great love for the country in which they had been born.

Politically England and Ireland had long seemed inextricably entangled. The basic political connection of the two islands through the Crown had until only a very few years before been taken for granted by the vast majority of both Irishmen and Englishmen for many centuries. Until the end of the eighteenth century the two islands had had separate Parliaments under the Crown, but for over a hundred years after that the connection had been closer still, with Ireland sending to a joint British House of Commons roughly one-sixth of that House's representation.

The problems of government in Ireland had preoccupied British statesmen throughout the nineteenth century. For some fifty years before 6 December 1921, that is to say for the entire adult life of a whole generation of Englishmen, 'the Irish Question' had repeatedly dominated English politics in time of peace. A British Prime Minister, Gladstone, had once described it as 'leading to the utter destruction of the mind of Parliament, to the great enfeebling and impeding of its proper working'.[2]

Now, quite suddenly, on the night of 5–6 December 1921, all this was ended. It was ended by a few strokes of the pen – by the signatures on one side of the British government of the day, and on the other of five men all but one of whom had been quite unheard of a few years before. One had had a price of £10,000 set on his head by the British Government earlier in the year. Another had been educated at Rugby, one of the best known of English public schools.

It is easy to see now that what took place that night was the first crack in the disintegration of the British Empire as it had been known for over a century – a disintegration (transformation is a more comfortable word) which has steadily continued and been so much a part of our own day. But this was a separation far more painful than any of those which were to follow, involving as it did a rupture at the very heart of the Empire itself. The British Empire never recovered from it. Some would say that Ireland has never recovered either.

2
Contradictions of
Irish Nationality

In a letter to a friend in February 1918, Eamon de Valera wrote that for seven centuries England had held Ireland 'as Germany holds Belgium to-day, by the right of the sword'.[1] This is the classical language of Irish separatism and can be very misleading.

An Irish nationalism of this sort, which saw England and Ireland as two separate and hostile countries, had itself then only been in existence for a little over a hundred years. From its origin at the end of the eighteenth century until the very year in which Mr de Valera was writing, it had been not so much a normal patriotic faith as an intellectual theory held by idealists who were trying, with little success, to make their theory materialize in practice. Inevitably they used many synthetic and unreal concepts as if they were facts. Chief of these was the notion that England 'held' Ireland by force. Its corollary was that the undoubted ills from which Ireland suffered over the centuries were those inflicted by a strong oppressor over a weak and subject alien people. Both of these notions are a large enough distortion of events to amount to a historical untruth. Between 1845 and 1919, the period during which this view of Irish nationalism laid what foundations it could among the ordinary Irish people, Ireland was in fact 'held' by twelve thousand Catholic Irishmen of the Royal Irish Constabulary, drawn largely from among the younger sons of the suffering peasantry. In these circumstances to talk of Ireland as being 'held' at all in a military sense is patently ridiculous.

It is perhaps a virtue of the British that, often so arrogant when the star of their power was at its zenith, they cheerfully accept almost any interpretation of their former behaviour now that that star has grown dim. They have thus come to accept almost without reserve that what took place in Ireland between the years 1916 and 1922 was a bitter struggle by a small subject nation battling for its independence against British imperialist might in a conflict which the British morally deserved to lose. But perhaps the British like to see it this way because the truth is even more difficult to face. For Britain can take little credit for the way in which she managed that part of herself that was Ireland for seven centuries.

Though the sword indeed played its dreadful part there as savagely as in any other country of Europe, to see Irish history in the plain, uncompromisingly nationalistic terms of Mr de Valera's statement is to miss, together with the truth, much of the poignancy and drama of the strange relationship that persisted between the two islands for so long. It is also the surest way to become bewildered and confused by the very events in which Mr de Valera was then embroiled, as certain obvious facts about these events make plain enough.

For example, the Commander-in-Chief of the Irish forces in the heroic Dublin Rebellion of 1916 was not strictly an Irishman at all, but the son of a Birmingham man. The rebellion itself was unpopular with the great majority of the Irish people at the time, and, after the rebels' surrender, some of the prisoners being marched away through the streets of Dublin by the British were jeered at by the local population. By contrast, one of the British officers who guarded those prisoners was, just over five years later, to be a member of the very Irish delegation which signed the Anglo-Irish treaty on behalf of Ireland.*

The first problem, in fact, is to define an Irishman at all. An English civil servant, Erskine Childers, was one of the most steadfast of all supporters of the Irish republican cause between 1919 and 1922 and was reviled as an Englishman by both English and Irish alike for his pains. He even met his death before a firing squad in the end – and an Irish firing squad at that. One of the bravest of all the many other brave men who died during these years, Cathal Brugha, at first sight an authentic enough Gaelic hero, is on closer examination just plain Charles Burgess, also shot to death by uniformed Irish soldiers for his loyalty to an Irish Republic.

On the other hand Sir Henry Wilson, British Chief of the Imperial General Staff in 1918, was as much an Irishman by his own or Sinn Fein's standards as the members of the Irish Republican Brotherhood who killed him with revolver bullets on the door-step of his home, 36 Eaton Place, SW3 in 1922. And Sir Edward Carson, an equally implacable enemy of Irish independence, was proud to be able to refer to Ireland as 'my country'. Equally an Irishman, by descent at any rate, was the British General Sir Nevile Macready, who on 10 July 1921 walked up the steps of the Dublin Mansion House to negotiate a truce with the leaders of the Irish Republican Army. Many thought then and have thought since that he went unarmed, but, complimenting himself in a peculiarly English sort of way that he knew the Irish too well for that, he put a revolver in the right-hand pocket of his tunic where it can be discerned to this day in the photograph of him taken as he made his way through applauding Dublin crowds to that historic meeting.[2]

The confusing contradictions multiply indefinitely. The leader of the Ulster Volunteers, Carson, was a Dubliner, the leader of the Irish Volunteers

* The Old Rugbeian, Robert Barton.

in the south, MacNeill, an Ulsterman. At the conclusion of the story 'Ulster'
is no longer Ulster,* and the most northerly point of Ireland, Malin Head,
is in 'Southern Ireland'. But the most serious proof of the complexity of
what is still sometimes so simply called the 'War of Independence' can be
seen in a study of the judicial executions which took place during and after
it. For, between 1919 and 1921, the British Government shot in cold blood
or hanged twenty-four Irishmen who had taken up arms for an independent
sovereign Irish Republic. Between 1922 and 1923, in the so-called 'Civil
War', the new Irish Government executed over three times that number of
Irishmen who had taken up arms for exactly the same cause.

Part of the explanation of all this is that the whole struggle was really
something of a civil war from the start. But how it came about, and how
it was possible for some people to regard it sincerely, however self-consciously or even half-heartedly, as a national struggle, can only be understood
if it is seen in the wider context of the Irish history to which it provided such
an unexpected climax. For on both sides of this struggle men were sometimes
self-consciously, sometimes unconsciously, in the grip of forces other than
those of the time in which they lived. For over seven centuries the history
of the people who lived in Ireland had been a folk-trauma comparable in
human experience perhaps only to that of the Jews. In these years of the
twentieth century a haphazard series of events finally exorcized that trauma
for ever.

---

* The historic province of Ulster consists of the nine counties of Antrim, Down,
Armagh, Derry, Tyrone, Fermanagh, Donegal, Monaghan and Cavan, and the state
of Northern Ireland consists only of the first six of these.

3
Strongbow (1170)
to the Ulster Plantation (1609)

There is a fairly close limit in time beyond which it is pointless to go back and try to trace nationality. An Englishman proud of being an Englishman today is himself the product of many warring races. If Mr de Valera in 1918 could identify the Irish who fought the English in our own century with those who fought 'the English' seven centuries earlier, there was no logical reason to stop there. He could have gone back further still and seen the only true Irish as the small dark race called the Firbolg who were in Ireland when the Celts, or Gaels, came to conquer them from the mainland of Europe a few centuries BC.

However, it was the Gaels, bringing from Europe an elegantly ornamental civilization based on a loose tribal structure, who laid a foundation for Irish life and character which was to colour all succeeding influences for some two thousand years. The failure of the Romans to reach Ireland and the survival through the dark ages after the Roman withdrawal from Britain of Celtic civilization in Ireland, christianized by the legendary St Patrick and enriched by trading contacts with the mainland of Europe, ensured that there was left on Ireland a mark of difference from the rest of Britain that even in the latter half of the twentieth century has still not wholly faded.

And yet if one decides to begin with the Gaels as the first 'Irish' and see their High King Brian Boru as the first Irish national hero after his defeat of invading Norsemen at Clontarf in 1014, a problem arises over all the Norsemen who even before that battle had become absorbed into the population of Ireland and all the Norsemen and other 'invaders' who were absorbed soon afterwards.

Seven centuries later the Irish were a too complicated and subtle amalgam of conquered and conquerors for historical racialism to be of much value in explaining events.

It was not in any case 'the English' whom the Gaels, or some of them, fought in the twelfth century. Invaders like Robert Fitzstephen and Richard 2nd Earl of Pembroke, known as Strongbow, who first crossed to Ireland from England in 1169 and 1170 were Norman adventurers, speaking Norman French. They came not in England's interests but their own, in search of land, power and wealth. Moreover, they came at the express invitation of an Irish chief, Dermot MacMurrough, to help him in his quarrel with other Irish chiefs. Such Normans built themselves into the ever-changing pattern of Gaelic tribal alliances in Ireland, and in the process often intermarried with the Irish, adopted their language and customs and became Irish too. It has often been pointed out that many of the names we think of today as most typically Irish – Joyce, Burke, Costello, Prendergast, Fitzgerald, etc. – are in fact the names of these early Norman 'conquerors'.*

For centuries afterwards men who owed a nominal feudal loyalty to the English king continued to settle in Ireland and become, in the medieval phrase, *hiberniores hibernis ipsos* – 'more Irish than the Irish'. Many became indistinguishably Gaelic. The term Old English was later applied to them if their identity had remained in some ways distinct from Gaelic tribal society. But the distinction between the Old English and the other Catholic Irish was, as far as the royal authority was concerned, often only one between the king's rebels and the king's enemies.

The original claim to authority by the English king in Ireland derived from the automatic feudal obligations of his subjects who acquired land there. Henry II had been so alarmed by Strongbow's independent self-aggrandizement in Ireland that he had visited the country almost at once to try and assert these feudal ties, and his royal authority was strengthened by an obscure commission apparently given him by Pope Adrian IV to reform the Irish Church.† But the practical difficulties of medieval communications across a large expanse of sea made the Crown's task of supervision impossible. Over the years the effective authority of the English Crown in Ireland shrank further and further to a small area round Dublin known as the Pale – and was not even always to be found there. The first real sign of any sort of 'national' independent spirit to appear in Ireland came from the Old English themselves – from the Norman Fitzgeralds, who, though nominally the king's deputies, built up for themselves in the second half of the fifteenth and first half of the sixteenth centuries a formidable power which defied the king, and was itself known quasi-regally as that of the House of Kildare.

The Gaelic chiefs themselves had no scruples about submitting to the authority of an English king when this proved tactically necessary. Their one concern was to be left free to pursue their private interests and ambitions by their subtle system of tribal alliances, and to look after their lands with the minimum of outside interference.

* De Jorz, de Burgo, etc. Edmund Curtis's *History of Ireland* (London, 1936), makes this point.

† The medieval historian Giraldus Cambrensis says the Commission was made in the form of the Papal Bull *Laudabiliter* of 1155. The authenticity of this Bull has been doubted. It does not exist in the Papal Archives. However, there is other evidence that Adrian IV made some sort of grant of Ireland to Henry II. (See Curtis, *History of Ireland*, pp. 56–7.)

In 1541 Henry VIII, having finally succeeded in breaking the power of the House of Kildare, determined to turn nominal feudal ties into effective administrative ones. He had himself proclaimed in Dublin 'King of this land of Ireland as united, annexed and knit for ever to the Imperial Crown of the Realm of England'. So many of the Gaelic chiefs attended the ceremony that the bill was read over to them in Irish and they expressed their 'liberal consents'. Five years later the Earls of Tyrone, Desmond and Thomond with the Fitzpatrick, O'Connor, O'Murphy, O'Carrol, MacGeoghan and other native chiefs wrote to the king in Latin: 'We call God to witness that we acknowledge no other king or lord on earth except your Majesty.'[1]

As it happened, this sort of talk was no longer to do them any good. The new Tudor state was out to replace not only the independent power of Old English nobles but also the power of Gaelic tribal organization by the authority of a central administration. A peaceful system of submission was offered to the Gaelic chiefs by which they could surrender their lands to the king and immediately receive them back again, 'regranted'. In this way they acknowledged that their only title to the land they held was through the king.

Some accepted willingly. But such a system, assuming, as it did, acceptance of English laws of succession, clashed directly with Gaelic tradition. By Gaelic, or Brehon law, land was the property of the tribe, and the chief, who was elected, held his title only for life. In cases where the chiefs themselves were ready enough to accept the new English laws, the lesser Irish whose interests were thus disregarded often refused to asquiesce so obligingly. Sometimes the situation was reversed. A native chief, defying the new attempt at control of his affairs, would take to arms to resist it and at the same time try to strengthen his position with his lesser chiefs by forcing them into a closer obedience than was traditional. In such cases, as one historian was put it, 'the lesser chiefs ... sought only to maintain their local independence and hailed the English as deliverers'.[2] One way or another, violent conflict between the new system and the interests it challenged was inevitable. And where the principle of 'surrender and re-grant' broke down it was replaced by the Tudors with conquest and confiscation. But this was not a conflict between one nation and another. It was a conflict between an old system of government and a new one, and men of Gaelic and Old English origin were to be found motivated by self-interest on both sides.

When resistance was encountered, whether from Old English or Gaelic Irish, the Tudors dealt with it with a ferocity which, in the words of the great historian Lecky, 'has seldom been exceeded in the pages of history'.[3] The fiercest of the great Gaelic chiefs to challenge the new system was Shane O'Neill, and if any chief had been thinking in modern terms of national leadership it would have been he. But 'no Irish chiefs had learnt to look beyond the limits of his tribe',[4] and the battle which finally brought about Shane O'Neill's downfall was fought not against the English but against another Gaelic chief, the O'Donnell.

If this war, like all Ireland's wars, was a civil war and not a national one, it brought, as all were to do, terrible suffering to the people who lived in Ireland. An eye-witness description by the poet Spenser of a contemporary scene from these Tudor wars, was from one cause or another, to become all too representative of the experience of the common people of Ireland for the next three centuries: 'Out of every corner of the woods and glens', writes Spenser, 'they came creeping forth upon their hands, for their legs could not bear them. They looked like anatomies of death; they spoke like ghosts crying out of their graves ...'[5] And the English sixteenth-century historian, Fynes Morison, who witnessed the campaigns in Ulster, also uncannily pre-echoes scenes of later centuries when he writes of the multitudes of dead 'with their mouths all coloured green by eating nettles, docks and all things they could rend above ground'.[6]

The lands of those, of whatever origin, who resisted the new centralization process were confiscated and planted where possible with settlers from England or Scotland. The first of such plantations had actually been carried out with settlers from the Pale in the reign of the Catholic sovereigns Philip and Mary in the counties Leix and Offaly, then re-named King's and Queen's Counties.* However, plantations often failed to take root and where this happened those who had been dispossessed drifted back on to their former lands without any precise legal status. It was this lack of any right to be on the land on any other terms than those of mere sufferance, in contrast with a certain sense of post-feudal mutual obligation which characterized relations between landlord and occupier elsewhere in Europe, that was to determine the condition of the Irish peasant for three centuries.

The most successful of all 'plantations' was completed in the reign of James I, principally in six of the nine counties of Ulster. These had been the lands of Hugh O'Neill, Earl of Tyrone. He was the last of those great Gaelic chiefs who, though acknowledging in theory the sovereignty of the English monarchy, tried to resist the new Tudor administrative machine. Despite help from Spain, O'Neill was defeated decisively at the battle of Kinsale in 1601. Finally, in 1607 he abandoned all hope of recovering his former position and sailed from Ireland for ever with his ally the Earl of Tyrconnell. The event became nostalgically enshrined in Irish folk-memory as 'the Flight of the Earls'. Their lands were confiscated and 'planted' with new settlers.

With these Ulster plantations a profoundly significant addition was made to the Irish population. For the new inhabitants of Ireland were Protestants.

---

* Although Mary was a Catholic she pursued the policy of establishing the central government's authority with the same purpose as Protestant Tudors.

The Reformation itself had not made much impression on Ireland. This was partly because the Gaelic population was often physically inaccessible and largely intellectually inaccessible behind the language barrier, and partly because at a time when Ireland could so easily provide a base for England's Catholic enemy Spain, it was important not to antagonize the Old English unnecessarily by forcing on them an unwelcome change of faith. So the new Protestant inhabitants of Ireland set about their lives among other Irish, who, whether Gaelic, Gaelicized or Old English, were largely Catholics. Very few of the old families, Gaelic or Old English, changed to the new Protestant faith, although among those that were eventually to do so were names of both types: the O'Briens, for instance, already Earls of Thomond and later of Inchiquin from among the Gaelic Irish, and the Butlers, ancient Earls of Ormond, from among the Old English. But racial origins in themselves were now becoming less and less important. This was an age in which religion determined political thinking. With the Protestant plantations, a cleavage between two sections of the Irish population was established which, though it was to make no distinction between who was an Irishman and who was not, set a pattern for the social and political development of Ireland for many centuries.

By the early seventeenth century, the people who lived in Ireland were a people of mixed racial origins and differing interests and could hardly be said to form any single distinct nation. Certainly Gaelic language and traditions surviving from an older form of society and often acquired by those to whom they had not been native gave the majority of them a very distinctive character. But even for these there was no single political or constitutional identity. The monarch of England was universally accepted as the monarch of Ireland. The only dispute was about the effectiveness with which he was to wield his power. Neither in groups nor as a whole did this mixed people want to assert a political national independence. All that could be said was that a tradition had been established by which the stretch of water between Ireland and the rest of Britain induced a remarkable independence of spirit in whoever crossed it.

Certainly, too, the deliberate winding-up of formal Gaelic tribal society had left a deep confused nostalgia among the majority of the population. In fact, Gaelic society, even in the days of its High Kings, had never been more than a loose association of tribal kingdoms, sharing common laws, customs and a language under the High King's symbolic leadership. By the very nature of its individualistic organization it could never have been nor could have aspired to be a nation state, and clearly the Gaelic chiefs had no patriotic objections to the *theory* of submission to an English king. O'Neill himself, the Earl of Tyrone, had been brought up in London as an Elizabethan gentleman. He fought for his own local, if considerable, self-interest and ambition. But he did leave behind a very powerful legend of resentment for myth to work on, a legend about individual resistance to central authority and particularly to the new ownership of land.

In that beautiful country of mountain, bog and fern the legend would have lingered a long time in any case, preserved and ornamented as it was in a Gaelic language of its own. But the subsequent repetition of great personal suffering by the majority of the people of Ireland for the next three centuries kept this resentful nostalgia very much alive. As late as 1824, a Catholic priest from County Cork told a Parliamentary Committee how the peasantry among whom he lived still talked frequently of the days of Elizabeth and Tyrone, having, he said, 'recollections of the liberty and what they conceive the privileges they enjoyed formerly compared with their present degraded state'.[7] And a writer early in the twentieth century met a shepherd near Luggala in the Wicklow Hills dreaming of Ireland before the battle of Kinsale.[8]

But this was an emotional rather than a political legacy. Politically important for the future was the fact that the Gaelic resistance to central authority had had no coordinated national expression. The difficulty of effectively coordinating such feeling was to bedevil the efforts of those trying to create Irish nationalism until well into the twentieth century.

4

Great Rebellion (1641) to Penal Laws (1703)

In 1641 a great rebellion broke out in Ireland. It began simply as an attempt on the part of the dispossessed Gaelic Irish of Ulster to recover their confiscated lands. But it was not just the dispossessed Gaelic Irish of Ulster who felt they had a grievance. For years, all Catholics in Ireland had been agitating for the redress of grievances. These were embodied principally in their status as 'recusants', or citizens who refused to acknowledge the Crown's spiritual as well as temporal supremacy over the Pope. Particularly this penalized recusant status gave those Catholics who still held land (and Catholics at this date still held two-thirds of the cultivable land of Ireland) a feeling of uneasiness and insecurity about their rights to that land; for the monarch, who proclaimed himself the source of all land ownership, held in his hands the ultimate weapon of dispossession for uncooperative subjects.

In 1641 the Puritan Parliament of England actually went so far as to decree the absolute suppression of the Catholic religion in Ireland. But by then the rebellion which had begun as a local Gaelic uprising for the return of lost lands in the North had become an alliance of all Catholics in Ireland, whatever their origin, determined to preserve their religion and defend their rights and property under the monarchy and within the Constitution. Gaelic Irish and Old English joined together to form what later historians called 'The Confederation of Kilkenny'.

The history of this 'confederation' was confused. The alliance between its Gaelic Irish and Old English wings was not always easy.* There was a further complication in that it became in time a third force in Charles I's own war against his Parliament. But the effect of the rebellion's final suppression by the Parliamentary forces under Cromwell in 1652 was devastatingly clear. The terrible suffering which Cromwell inflicted in the name of God on all Catholic rebels in Ireland, regardless of racial origin, forged for them

* The attractive leader of the Gaelic wing was Owen Roe O'Neill, nephew of the great Hugh O'Neill, Earl of Tyrone, who had fled abroad in 1607. Owen Roe O'Neill arrived in Ireland from Spain in 1642.

something very like a single identity and strengthened still further the cleavage between them and the other (Protestant) part of Ireland's population. Fynes Morison, the Elizabethan historian, had once drawn a distinction between 'the Irish in general' and 'the mere Irish' (by which he meant the Gael or Gaelicized).[1] 'The Irish of English race' was how the Old English had been referred to officially a generation before Cromwell's war.* From the time of Cromwell onwards, native Irish and Old English Catholics became increasingly indistinguishable.

The eleven years of fighting in the civil war that began with the rebellion of 1641 cost the lives of about one-third of the Catholic Irish, and many of those who were neither killed nor transported by slave-dealers to the West Indies were sentenced in their own country to a life of social ignominy and handicap. Most of the best land of Ireland was now confiscated from its owners and divided among more new Protestant settlers and adventurers, many of them Cromwellian soldiers who were in this way compensated for arrears of pay. Whereas, even after the plantation of Ulster in James I's time, two-thirds of the cultivable land of Ireland had remained in the hands of Catholics, now, after Cromwell's settlement, rather more than three-quarters of the cultivable land was to be found in the hands of the small minority of Protestants.

But though down the retrospect of history it is reasonable enough to give to these people who fought and suffered and died at this time a common identity as 'the Irish', the Protestants who had been settled in Ireland could, by now, also reasonably be called 'Irish' too. And there is one all-important fact about the Catholics which was later often forgotten. Both the Gaelic and the Old English elements in the rebellion constantly proclaimed their loyalty to the Crown – indeed it was exactly this which accounted for much of the Republican Cromwell's savagery. The first leader of the Ulster Gaelic rebels to take the field, Sir Phelim O'Neill, had insisted in his opening call to arms that the rebellion was in no way directed against the king. And even before the Old English had properly joined the rebellion the leaders of the Gaelic Irish had introduced an oath of association which contained the words: 'I further swear that I will bear faith and allegiance to our sovereign lord King Charles, his heirs and successors, and that I will defend him and them as far as I may, with my life power and estate ...'[2] The confederation fought under the slogan: *'Pro Deo, Pro Rege, Pro Hibernia Unanimis'* – 'One for God, King and Ireland'. And by 'King' they meant the man who was king of both England and Ireland simultaneously. A separatist nationalism was no part of their outlook; they were fighting only for what they regarded as their rights under the British Crown. Patriotic love of Ire-

* e.g., at a council meeting at Southampton in 1625. (Aidan Clarke, *The Old English in Ireland, 1625–1642*, London, 1966, p. 33.)

land was, and was long to remain, wholly compatible with loyalty to a British monarch.

The restoration of the monarchy in 1660 indeed automatically raised Irish Catholic hopes that Cromwell's settlements would be reversed and that they would get back their family lands. But Charles II owed his restoration more to the wily compromise he had worked out with Protestant parliamentarians than to the individual loyalties of Catholics. He could hardly afford to alienate the interests of his new Protestant supporters in the Irish House of Commons. And although Catholics were able to enjoy a more tolerant religious atmosphere, there was no change in the law in so far as the land was concerned and the Restoration Act of Settlement with minor modifications virtually confirmed the land settlement of Cromwell.

It was when Charles's Catholic brother James II succeeded him as King of England and Ireland in 1685 that the moment of the Catholics in Ireland seemed at last to have arrived. A Catholic was appointed Viceroy; Catholics were placed in key administrative positions and a new Catholic-dominated Parliament in Ireland actually passed an Act reversing the Cromwellian land settlement, ousting the new Protestant occupiers (though not without compensation) and returning the land confiscated by Cromwell to its former owners.*

This Act, like the rebellion of 1641 itself, had a traumatic effect on later generations. For though it never had time to come into force, the idea that the Catholics might one day try to reassert their ancient titles to land taken from them, and long held by Protestants, was the nightmare that seemed to justify the Protestant Irish in their assumption of total ascendancy in Irish society. Two hundred years later one of the Land Commissioners of 1841 was to report:

> The Repeal of the Irish Act of Settlement by the Parliament of James II gave the Protestant proprietors a fright from which they have not properly recovered even to this day.... They seem to think that they only garrison their estates, and therefore they look upon the occupiers – I cannot call them tenants – as persons ready to eject them on a favourable opportunity.[3]

What prevented the Irish Catholic Parliament's reversal of the land settlement from coming into force was the military defeat of James II by the English Parliament's new Protestant champion, William of Orange. This took place at the battles of the Boyne and Aughrim in 1690 and 1691, and these defeats were followed by the capitulation of James's army under the Catholic Irish General, Patrick Sarsfield, after William's siege of Limerick.

The words 'Remember the Boyne' are still periodically chalked up on the

---

* The separate existence of an Irish Parliament and its constitutional relations with that of England are discussed below, on pp. 29–31.

walls of Belfast today, and 12 July,* the anniversary of this victory which took place over 280 years ago, is still celebrated in Northern Ireland as if it had some real significance for the present. And so, in the curious political anomaly that is Northern Ireland, it has. For the Boyne and other disasters suffered by the Catholics of Ireland between 1689 and 1692 marked the beginning of a long period, fading slowly in intensity over the centuries but not yet in the North wholly ended, in which to be Catholic in Ireland meant automatically to be the under-dog. To be Protestant meant, whatever one's status, and by no individual effort of one's own, to be automatically superior. Ireland became a place where, as the Protestant historian Lecky was to put it, 'many who would never have sought ascendancy if it had not been established, wished to preserve the privileges they had inherited, and the most worthless Protestant, if he had nothing else to boast of, at least found it pleasing to think that he was a member of a dominant race'.[4]

'After Aughrim's great disaster . . .' runs an Irish song commemorating the significance of this and the other defeats of the period for the majority of the people of Ireland. Indeed, they now joined Kinsale and the Flight of the Earls as further ingredients of popular myth. And yet in view of the separatist slant that was to be given to this myth in the twentieth century it must be remembered that at Aughrim James's troops were rallied by appeals to their religion, not to their race,[5] and that this and the other disasters of the time were suffered by Irishmen fighting for a man who had ascended the throne as an English king and whom they wanted as their king too.

The Catholic Irish soldiers who fought for James II were allowed under the Treaty of Limerick to leave for France and large numbers of them did so. For over a hundred years these 'Wild Geese' and their later followers and descendants were to be found fighting under the banners of the Irish Brigade in the armies of France on every major battlefield of Europe. They at least became members of a separate race, though not an Irish one. Some drifted into the service of other foreign states besides France, and within a generation or two Irish families were to be found dispersed throughout Europe speaking French or Spanish or German or Russian as their first language.† Sarsfield himself, a personification of the merged Catholic Irish people, descended as he was from Gaelic chieftains on one side and an Old English Catholic family on the other, was killed in 1693 at the battle of Landen in Flanders with, so it is said, the words: 'Would it were for Ireland!' on his lips.

In Ireland itself the Irish Protestants now proceeded to turn their victory

* By the new style calendar introduced in 1752. Before this date 1 July was the day of celebration.
† Among the many descendants of the 'Wild Geese' who achieved international fame or notoriety in later times were Macmahon, the French general of the war of 1870, and Taafe, the Foreign Minister of the Austro-Hungarian Empire.

to personal advantage. Still more confiscations directly transferred an even greater proportion of the land into the hands of the Protestant minority. In 1688 the Catholic share of the land had been just under a quarter, or twenty-two per cent. In 1703, after the Williamite settlement, it was only fifteen per cent.[6] Moreover, in the course of the next two decades a body of severely discriminatory legislation was passed against all Catholics in Ireland, which apart from inflicting crippling social handicaps reduced the proportion of land held by Catholics further still.

This new legislation is known in history as the 'penal laws'. The injustice and inhumanity of these laws (there was actually one curious legislative proposal to castrate Catholic priests) is here less relevant than their effect on the country's social future. For many years they excluded Catholics from all public life and much normal private social activity. They made any form of Catholic education illegal. Most important of all was the effect they had on the system of land ownership and tenure. They made it illegal for Catholics to buy land, obtain a mortgage on it, rent it at a reasonable profit or even inherit it normally. When a Catholic land-owner died his estate could not descend to his elder son by the normal law of primogeniture, but had to be divided equally among all his sons. On the other hand, if any of the sons were to turn Protestant he automatically inherited the whole estate over the heads of any elder brothers. Similarly, if the wife of a Catholic turned Protestant she automatically acquired part of her husband's estate. While a Catholic was legally allowed to rent land on a lease not exceeding thirty-one years, if he made a profit of more than one-third of his rent he might lose the lease to the first Protestant who could inform against him. In this way not only did the penal laws prevent Catholics from acquiring land by purchase or lease, they also saw to it that such land as was still left in the hands of the Catholic majority after all the confiscations dwindled with the years. By the mid-eighteenth century the fourteen per cent of the land of Ireland still held by Catholics after the Williamite settlement of 1703 had been halved to seven per cent.

By dealing these and other social and economic blows at the old Catholic landed class and their tenants, the penal laws isolated the vast majority of the people of Ireland in an inferior identity. They became segregated from the rest of society and the normal processes of law. Both the Lord Chancellor and the Lord Chief Justice in fact declared at one time that 'the law does not presume any such person to exist as an Irish Roman Catholic'.*

* Catholics could not now join the army or navy, vote or be elected to Parliament or enjoy any offices of state, and those who had previously been able to lead the lives of country gentlemen found themselves subject to the penalty of whipping for keeping a sporting gun or a horse worth more than £5. The Catholic priesthood had to leave the country and were liable to be hanged, drawn and quartered if they returned. A system of registering ordinary Catholic priests was at first introduced, but the terms proved almost impossible for a priest to reconcile with his conscience. Mass had to be celebrated in bog or forest as an outlawed conspiracy. The only education for

This division between Protestant and Catholic which was to shape for so
long the whole character of Irish society heightened an even more fundamental and obvious division common to every society: the division between
rich and poor. Certainly some Catholic gentry did manage to avoid sub-
mergence into the lowest classes, clinging to what land they could by good
luck or ingenious circumvention of the law. Others switched interests and
even sometimes made fortunes in trade. But, in general, Catholicism and all
the older traditions of Ireland, including the Gaelic language, now coloured
poverty with a special identity, making the poor, more even than in most
countries, a nation of their own.

Catholic children which did not involve their exposure to Protestant proselytism was
in illicit schools in hedgerows and byways. The degree to which these laws were strictly
applied varied greatly. In time many came to be tacitly circumvented or were allowed
to fall into abeyance.

5
Majority Living (1703–1880)

Since long before Henry VIII had become King of Ireland as well as England, Ireland had had her own Parliament under the Crown. Here, as in the English Parliament, grants of money and supplies were made to the Crown in return for consideration of the interests of those inhabitants who made them. But use of this Irish Parliament by the Old English as an instrument for establishing independent strength in Ireland had led to its powers being curbed considerably and by the mid-seventeenth century it was partly *de jure* and wholly *de facto* subservient to the Parliament of England.

The later English Parliament took advantage of this constitutional subservience to see that local economic interests in the Kingdom of Ireland should present no threat to those in the Kingdom of England. Irish trading and manufacturing opportunities were severely restricted to protect England's own trade manufactures. For instance, in 1699 the export of woollen goods from Ireland – one of the island's principal manufactures at the time – was totally forbidden to everywhere but England where English import duties were themselves prohibitive. This and earlier restrictive measures had the most profound effect not just on the trading class but on the majority of the population. For them, who were in any case precariously placed on the land, the land now became virtually the only source of livelihood available.

On the land, without any surviving vestige of a feudal link between peasant and landlord that elsewhere involved at least some unwritten status, the Irish peasant lived on sufferance, paying the highest possible rent that could be extracted from him. He had neither rights against extortionate rent, nor against arbitrary eviction whether paying rent or not, nor rights to any improvements he might carry out. In fact, to carry out improvements at all was undesirable because to do so only raised the value of the land and thus the rent. All this, to a people among whom there were dim folk-memories of a Gaelic system in which the common people had certain rights of common ownership in the soil, and whose landlord was an elected chief, was doubly painful.

Only in North-West Ulster where tenants had been 'planted' with the landlords on confiscated land were they awarded a certain status. What came to

be known as the 'Ulster custom' prevailed there – a custom which gave certain basic rights to a tenant such as security of tenure provided he paid the
rent, and a financial interest in such improvements as he might make to his
land. But even in Ulster the once privileged status of tenants often became
partially obscured by the passage of time and excessive competition for land
there led to excessive rents and caused distress.

The Protestant Dean Swift described in 1720 the condition of the Irish
tenant of his day as being worse than that of English beggars.[1]

The landlords, he said, 'by unmeasurable screwing and racking their rents
all over the kingdom, have already reduced the poor people to a worse condition than the peasants in France, or the vassals in Germany or Poland'.[2]
'Whoever travels this country,' he declared, 'and observes the face of nature,
or the faces and habits and dwellings of the natives will hardly think himself
in a land where law, religion, or common humanity is professed.'[3] Swift's
contemporary, the Protestant Bishop of Derry, wrote of a journey he made
through Ireland in 1723 : 'Never did I behold even in Picardy, Westphalia or
Scotland such dismal marks of hunger and want as appeared in the coun-
tenances of the poor creatures I met on the road.'[4] And another Protestant
bishop, the philosopher Berkeley, asked in his publication *The Querist:*
'whether there be upon earth any Christian or civilised people so beggarly
wretched and destitute as the common Irish', and he repeated the question in
a new edition in 1750.[5]

A gentleman living in Dublin in 1764 sent a friend near Dover an account
of the conditions of the Irish peasantry in which he drew attention to the
numbers of middlemen exploiting the desperate need for land, saying that
holdings were being sold by private tender to the highest bidder, 'in small
parcels of £20 or £30 a year at third, fourth and fifth hand from the first
proprietor'. The condition of the lower class of farmer, he wrote, was 'little
better than a state of slavery'.[6]

The Viceroy himself wrote in 1770 : 'I hoped to be excused for representing to His Majesty the miserable situation of the lower ranks of his subjects
in this kingdom. What from the rapaciousness of their unfeeling landlords
and the restrictions on their trade, they are amongst the most wretched people
on earth.'[7] In 1787, even the Protestant Attorney-General Fitzgibbon described the poor of Munster as 'being in a state of oppression, abject poverty,
sloth, dirt and misery not to be equalled in any part of the world'.[8] As for the
sloth, a Frenchman who travelled through Ireland in the 1790s, and found
himself shocked by the nakedness of the poor and by their huts which did
not seem made for human beings at all, remarked shrewdly that they might
well have been industrious and hard-working had there been any hope of
work improving their lot. But if they produced more the landlord only put
up the rent. 'When reduced to starvation, is it not better to do nothing if
the most assiduous labour can do nothing to prevent it?' The excessive drink-

ing to which the peasantry were given was simply a form of Lethe and their apathy and indifference 'no more than the habit of despair'.[9]

Descriptions of the living conditions of the Irish peasantry vary astonishingly little over the whole vast period that spans the defeat of James II and the land reforms of Gladstone. Yet to paint only a tragic and bleak picture of the lives of the Irish common people over such a great expanse of time is to miss the real poignancy of their suffering. Some years were, in the course of nature, less rigorous than others, and in any case the everyday poetry of these people's language, their love of music, their simple gifts of resourcefulness, charm and wit always coloured a natural easy-going and tenacious love of life, if life could only somehow be supported. 'As we went along' and eye-witness was to write of conditions during the Great Famine of the next century, 'our wonder was not that people died but that they lived: and I have no doubt whatever that in any other country the mortality would have been far greater: that many lives have been prolonged, perhaps saved, by the long apprenticeship to want in which the Irish peasant has been trained, and by that lovely touching charity which prompts him to share his scanty meal with his starving neighbour.'[*]

Nor did the Irish people always accept their condition docilely. Another witness of the next century also gives a glimpse of something more than their misfortune, when he describes before the government's Devon Commission a typical 'agrarian crime' of the period in which twenty of a landlord's cows had been driven up on to the top of a cliff and then 'clifted', or thrown over. A financial reward was offered for the apprehension of the culprit and the whole village then came forward to claim it, having persuaded a convenient small boy to confess. The Devon Commission witness commented: 'They were a very desperate people at this period with all this degree of courtesy, hospitality and cleverness among them.'[10]

Their desperation had in fact long expressed itself at the one level at which it could find an outlet – crudely and locally, in the form of intimidation and violence on the land. After the confiscations and massacres of Cromwell, the more enterprising and desperate of the persecuted had taken to the hills in marauding bands of 'Tories' and 'Rapparees'. Now, under the permanent social persecution which crystallized as the land system of Ireland at the time of the penal laws and long outlasted them, the Irish poor resorted to primitive self-help in the one obvious form that was available. A rough justice of the common people's own making took the place of the law which gave them so little.

* W. E. Forster, from the transactions of the Central Relief Committee of the Society of Friends, quoted in Gavan Duffy, *Fours Years of Irish History* (p. 431). Nearly forty years later Forster was to become a Chief Secretary for Ireland in Gladstone's government, and to earn the nickname 'Buckshot' for carrying out the planned humanitarianism of arming the Royal Irish Constabulary with buckshot rather than ball cartridges. (See below, p. 382 fn.)

Lawlessness was no more a natural trait of the Irish common people's character (as has occasionally been suggested) than it is of any other social grouping, the majority of whom are always instinctively law-abiding. It was just that in Ireland for nearly two centuries there were two different sets of law in existence: the one, established by a society and government which did nothing to alleviate the common people's plight; and the other seeking to supply the deficiency, administered by the secret societies with which Ireland became riddled.

Both sets of law had their disadvantages and inconveniences; both could be inexorable and powerful. The punishments exacted by the secret societies were more often than not exacted from the persons and property of the peasantry themselves – on incoming occupiers of land from which a man had been evicted, or simply on unfortunates who out of land hunger were paying extortionate rents when a secret decree had gone out against doing so. Nevertheless, when the mass of people looked at the two sets of law available, the one clandestine and crude, the other official and aloof, the former at least had the advantage that it proclaimed itself to be on their side.

A prototype of this sort of violence which was to dominate Irish life for so long had first made an appearance in Ireland as early as 1711. Bands of armed men, with blackened faces and wearing white shirts over their clothes for easier mutual recognition at night, started to roam the countryside mutilating cattle and carrying out other reprisals for the tyranny and rapacity of harsh landlords or the subservience of those who played along with them. Threatening letters to landlords and others appeared signed by a mysterious 'Captain Eaver'.[11] But that there was no fundamental political outlook in such outbreaks, no purpose so constructively serious as that of overthrowing the government, was soon proved in a most convincing fashion. For both in 1715 and in 1745 when at least some stirring might have been expected in Ireland in favour of a Catholic Pretender to the throne of Great Britain and Ireland, nothing of the sort occurred. The country remained loyal and quiet. And this lack of sophisticated wider political purpose, this concentration on local day to day conditions, was long to remain a consistent feature of Irish agrarian violence, and be the bane of those who later sought to mobilize it for nationalism.

It was in 1760 that the Whiteboy movement, as it came generally to be called, broke out on a large scale. Bodies of armed men, numbering anything from half a dozen or so to five hundred, again took to riding about the countryside at night with white shirts over their clothes, tearing down fences which enclosed land for pasturage rather than tillage, punishing those who collected tithes for the Protestant Church, preventing the payment of extortionate rents, intimidating would-be tenants from taking land from which another had been evicted, and generally asserting the existence of a rough and ready justice to redress the grievances of the poor. For the next hundred years and more, similar organizations, with names that vary with the years and the locality, conducted similar operations with similar objectives and a surprisingly similar degree of cruel detail.

Thus men assembling by night with white shirts over their clothes later called themselves Rightboys, and in the early 1800s Thrashers. They are Rockites and Ribbonmen in the 1820s and subsequent years. 'Ribbonmen' in fact tended to become the generic term for the secret-society phenomenon in the nineteenth century, as 'Whiteboys' had done in the eighteenth, but there were also groups calling themselves Whitefeet, Blackfeet, the Lady Clares, the Terry Alts and other names. Finally, there was a curious survival of Ribbonism which functioned under the more respectable official cover of the Land League in the late 1870s and early 1880s.*

All were secret, oathbound organizations of a rather primitive nature in which the swearing of the oath (often forcibly exacted) was an important part of the ritual. Their leaders were shadowy men whose names, though occasionally found in police reports, reach the history books only in the form in which they struck awe and terror into the countryside, the 'Captains' Rock, Right, Starlight and Moonlight of whom there would usually be a number operating under the same pseudonym at any given time.† The methods by which they practised their rough justice hardly vary across two centuries: the ham-stringing of cattle, the levelling of houses, the burning of ricks and barns, the firing of shots through windows, the delivery of threatening letters and many other violations of the government's law which were to become a commonplace in constabulary reports from Ireland. Even the actual physical details of the savage tortures inflicted on offenders against the code, such as the branding of flesh, the lacerations with wool cards, and the particular addiction to cutting off small pieces of the ear, are all found over and over again in records that run from the early eighteenth century to the 1880s.

'Wool-carding', for instance, the drawing of a steel tooth comb through the flesh of the victim, had become frequent in the early nineteenth century and had even given its name to a secret society of the time: the Carders. But by 1832 a contemporary witness was able to say that it had 'not been used at all latterly'.[13] However, nearly fifty years later in Land League days in 1880 a man named Costello was dragged from his bed at 1.30 a.m. by about twenty men, who made him swear he would not fence in some grazing land then in

---

* These secret societies should not be confused with the simple 'factions' such as the Shanavists, Caravats, Ruskavallas and others who were little more than rival gangs disturbing the peace with often lethal 'faction fights' at fairs and elsewhere. A most important late eighteenth-century peasant secret society, the Defenders, though its details often followed the familiar pattern of agrarian societies, was in fact somewhat different in character from all others, expressing political and national aims of a crude but positive nature. It is examined at length below on pp. 44–5, and 57–6.

† Sometimes it was 'General' Rock.

common use and then 'drew a wool card down his hip lacerating his flesh'.[13]
Mutilation of the ears, frequent in the eighteenth century, survived not only
into the time of the Land League but even into the twentieth century.

At times these secret societies held certain areas of Ireland largely at their
mercy. The warning to children: 'The fairies will get you' once carried
sinister undertones. In Tipperary in 1762 parties of more than five hundred
men were described as doing 'whatever mischief they please by night under
sanction of being fairies as they call themselves', and it was said that no one
dared take the place of a dismissed servant or shepherd in the county unless
'he had more interest with the fairies'.[14] In parts of County Cork in 1824 the
gentry had their houses permanently barricaded and posted sentries on them
during the daytime. Some houses were dark almost all day long because the
barricades, being bullet-proof and of considerable thickness, were so heavy
that it was too much of a business to move them daily; and sometimes for the
same reason there was only one sitting-room where light was admissible at
all in daytime and then not even through all the windows.[15]

All this activity was either wholly unpolitical or politically very crude.
Even when, as happened from time to time, attempts were made to enlist it
for political purposes it tended to remain most stubbornly what it had
always been: the simplest form of war that the poor can wage against the
rich or those who play the rich man's game.

When, for instance, the first Whiteboys were executed in 1762 – for being
present at the burning down of the cabin of a peasant who would not combine with them – they declared categorically, when past all hope of reprieve,
that 'in all these tumults it never entered into their thoughts to do anything
against the King and government'.[16] And a government commission which
reported on the disturbances in the *London Gazette* of May 1762 confirmed
that 'no marks of disaffection to His Majesty's person or government appeared in any of those people'.[17] An Irish gentleman on a tour of Ireland in
1764 who met with a band of Whiteboys in arms between Waterford and
Carrick-on-Suir, was told by them that they were not motivated by 'any
disposition to rebel against their King or the peace of their country', but
only by their resentment of their everyday conditions.[18] When on the occasion of the revolt of the American colonies in 1775, the Catholic gentry
expressed their loyalty to the Crown in fulsome terms, they probably, as they
claimed, expressed the *political* thinking of all their co-religionists quite
truthfully when they wrote: 'We humbly presume to lay at his (Majesty's)
feet two millions of loyal, faithful and affectionate hearts and hands, unarmed indeed, but zealous, ready and desirous to exert themselves strenuously in defence of his Majesty's most sacred person and government.' Their
address described Irish Catholic loyalty as 'a loyalty which we may justly
say is and always was as the dial to the sun, true, though not shone upon'.[19]
Many years later, in 1832, a witness of the very considerable agrarian tumults

that occurred in Ireland in the second and third decades of the nineteenth century stated: 'I never knew a single instance of hostility or combination against the government.'[20]

By that date a most important further development had taken place in Irish society: the Penal Laws preventing Catholics from owning, leasing and inheriting land had been repealed in 1778 and 1782, and Catholics were land-owners again on a quite considerable scale. All contemporary witnesses including Daniel O'Connell agree that not only were attacks directed proportionately as much against Catholic as Protestant land-owners but also that the Catholic gentry were equally active in putting disturbances down.[21] In the sphere that mattered most to the Irish peasantry, that of their economic status on the land, members of their own religion and blood were to be found in the nineteenth century increasingly on the other side of the fence, or the landlord's wall, with the Protestant. Thus non-political in character, these Whiteboy and other organizations were not predominantly sectarian in motive. Most of the activists were, of course, Catholics simply because most of the poor who were trying to live off the land were Catholics, and this common basis of identity often proved a useful rallying cry. But in the eighteenth century in the Presbyterian North, where, in spite of the 'Ulster custom', there were harsh landlords prepared to exploit land hunger by the excessive raising of rents as elsewhere in Ireland, secret societies known as Oakboys and Steelboys developed as Protestant counterparts of the Whiteboys.

For nearly two centuries such secret societies regularly absorbed much of the natural political energy of the Irish masses. The spirit of protest and concern remained focused there at a primitive level, just below that of the higher public politics which were a normal part of this as of any other organized society.

6
Minority Politics, Eighteenth Century

For much of the eighteenth century, after the defeat of James II and the Catholic Irish, the public political life of Ireland had flowed placidly and steadily, almost, it seemed, dissociated altogether from the currents in the depths below. This public political life was confined by the Penal Laws to the Irish Protestant minority and, in an era before the reform of Parliament and the widening of the franchise, even to a minority of them. But in the second half of the eighteenth century, this small oligarchic Irish political world developed an exciting dynamic of its own which was to have an influence on the whole subsequent course of Irish history.

An 'Irishman' by the eighteenth century meant simply anyone who had by now taken root in Ireland. The rigorous Protestant ascendancy established by the victories of William of Orange and confirmed by the Penal Laws was an Irish one. Ireland alone gave it personality and coherence. It is true that in the main it consisted of those who had become Irish more recently than the rest of the population, but even this was not wholly the case. Any Catholic, by changing his religion, automatically became eligible for the ruling class. And though only about four thousand such converts were actually registered in the eighteenth century, many of them were ancient Gaelic or Gaelicized nobility re-seeking their inborn sense of superiority in the terms of a new society. Among the names to be hated most of all as symbols of oppression over the next two hundred years, the vast majority were those of Irishmen. Some were the most Irish of all, with long-blended Norman and Gaelic blood in their veins.*

This mixed Irish Protestant ascendancy of the eighteenth century eventually asserted their Irishness in a pattern made familiar by the past. Emphasizing their nominal loyalty to the joint Crown of the two Kingdoms, they gradually developed a spirit of independence towards the English Government.

* For example, in the late eighteenth century, the Lord Chancellor John Fitzgibbon, Earl of Clare, and in the nineteenth century those Burkes who, having turned Protestant and been created Earls of Clanrickarde long before, were responsible for some of the harshest evictions.

Colonists throughout history have felt an ambivalence towards their mother country like that with which all adolescents regard their parents, seeking somehow to reconcile an affection for the ties which bind them with impatience at the restraint these place on freedom of action. Nowhere was this colonists' ambivalence ever more intensely felt than in Ireland where even geography conspired to emphasize it by making the two islands quite separate and yet not too far apart.

Early in the eighteenth century the spirit of Irish colonists' independence began to be vigorously expressed in the writings of two men. One was William Molyneux, a scientist and a member of Trinity College, Dublin, who clearly put forward a political theory that the Irish colonists' Parliament alone had the right to legislate for Ireland; the other was Jonathan Swift, the Irish-born Protestant Dean of St Patrick's, Dublin, who emphasized his allegiance to the king not as King of England but as King of Ireland and told his fellow Irishmen to burn 'everything English except their coal'. Both men attacked the unfairness of the commercial restrictions on Irish manufacture and trade which had been imposed by the English Parliament in the interests of English manufacturers and traders, and claimed that such legislation was an interference with ancient Irish colonists' rights.

The exact constitutional status and power of the Irish Parliament had in fact always been vague. In the late Middle Ages the Old English had consistently used the Irish Parliament to assert their own interests against the King's Government, and it was to curb such use of it that an Act passed by Sir Richard Poynings, a Viceroy of the day, had made the Irish Parliament's right to legislate subject to previous approval of Bills by the English Government. But with this important proviso, the Crown in the Irish Parliament was still theoretically regarded in matters that were of Irish concern as being the sovereign authority for Ireland. It was where matters of Irish concern were of English concern as well, as for instance in commerce and trade, that these had usually been judged to be the affair of the English Parliament. But in attacking the unfairness of all the restrictive commercial measures both Molyneux and Swift claimed that the English Parliament had usurped the Irish Parliament's sovereign rights and had no right to legislate for Ireland.

In fact, whatever the original constitutional theory of the Irish Parliament's rights may have been, practice had long established its virtual insignificance. Of the hundred and six years between 1586 and 1692 the Irish Parliament had only sat for fifteen. In 1719 the English Parliament finally tried to forestall further constitutional ambiguity or awkward insistence on Irish Parliamentary sovereignty with a so-called Declaratory Act, which categorically stated that the English Parliament had a full right to legislate for Ireland if it wanted to.

But the ideas first put forward by Molyneux and Swift slowly began to find wider acceptance. By the second half of the eighteenth century, the

'Protestant nation' of Ireland, as it was called by one of its political leaders, the lawyer Henry Flood, had already established its Irish social individuality in the life and architecture of its capital. Dublin had become in the eighteenth century one of the finest and most sophisticated cities in Europe, and many streets and squares still stand in Dublin today as monuments to that 'nation's' elegance. It was inevitable that such a Protestant nation, irked by commercial restrictions from England, should in the end stake political claims to dignify its social individuality – just as it was inevitable that the American colonists under similar provocation should do the same.

The links of sympathy between Ireland and America were obvious. In the first place there was a physical bond. During the eighteenth century Presbyterians had emigrated in large numbers from Ulster to the American colonies in times of agricultural distress and in protest against the disabilities imposed on them by law as Nonconformists. These emigrants were now some of the fieriest spirits among the American colonists. Secondly, the growing commercial and political aspirations in both countries were very similar.

By 1760 Protestant Ireland was developing a general unwillingness to recognize the dependence of the Irish Parliament on the British Parliament. 'To be uneasy in their present state', wrote a contemporary, 'and to express among themselves this uneasiness is the turn and fashion of the upper sort of the people, and is caught from them downwards.'[1]

But a most important practical consideration seemed to make the Irish Parliament's subservience a permanent reality. The machinery of government in Ireland was theoretically a replica of that in England. That is to say, a Viceroy with the title of Lord Lieutenant, worked through the Irish Parliament with Irish Ministers of the Crown and against such opposition as presented itself, as in England. The Irish Protestant Earl of Charlemont, in defining his view of his country's (i.e. Ireland's) Constitution in 1760, spoke optimistically of this machinery as a 'distinct' executive of the Kingdom of Ireland. But, given the facts of eighteenth-century political life, it could not really be distinct at all, however attractive to Irish Protestant self-esteem the theory might be.

In the eighteenth century the system by which a small number of individuals could influence up to the point of total control the result in a number of constituencies was common to both the English and Irish Parliaments.* The person who thus controlled the constituency could ensure, in return for suitable rewards by those with patronage at their disposal, that the vote of his constituency's representative went whichever way the patron thought was the right one.

The eighteenth-century political system was thus often a battle of patronage rather than of votes. This practice which the twentieth century sees as

---

* The so-called rotten or pocket boroughs often had only one or two voters.

corrupt can also be seen less pejoratively as simply the machinery by which the political system happened to function at that time. But certainly the system was very much more corrupt, or mechanical, in Ireland than in England.

According to the contemporary Irish historian, Plowden, a moderate and objective man, 128 of the 300 members of the Irish House of Commons could by the most generous estimate be reckoned to have been freely chosen by such electorate as there was. The remaining 172 seats – a comfortable majority – were the property of less than a hundred individuals, some thirty of whom controlled a sufficient number to provide a majority of the House. In these circumstances it was obviously very easy for the Crown to deploy its powerful patronage to effect. As many as one-third of the entire House were in fact direct pensioners or placemen of the Crown. In England only one-ninth of the House of Commons were reckoned Crown placemen or pensioners and there such members had to submit themselves for re-election on receipt of their benefits – which was not the case in Ireland.

In both countries Ministers of the Crown worked through Parliament with a majority secured as far as possible by the Crown's patronage. But in Ireland, since so many of the seats were in the control of such a small number of individuals, the Crown, with easily the largest single source of patronage at its disposal, could command the support of most of these controllers and thus count on an almost automatic majority in the House.* And, since Crown patronage in Ireland and in England emanated from a single source in England, whoever controlled the source in England – that is to say, the English Government of the day – controlled Ireland as well.

After Henry Flood, the early leader of 'the Protestant Nation' in the Irish House of Commons, had been induced to join the administration for seven years, another lawyer, Henry Grattan, emerged as the most effective orator of a so-called Protestant 'Patriot' party in Parliament.

When the clash with the American colonists came, the loyalty of the Irish Protestants to the Crown was full of ambiguous undertones which the Patriots exploited and which the administration was shrewd enough to see must be kept to undertones by concession. Both sides played the situation skilfully. The successes of the American colonists considerably strengthened the hands of the Irish Protestants in their own restiveness, drawing attention both to what could happen if colonists were pushed too far and to the value in the circumstances of the Irish loyalty to the Crown. Reciprocally, the American colonists' successes made the English Government readier for concession in Ireland to avoid a second imperial disaster.

The formation of 'Irish Volunteers', originally to defend Ireland against

* Where these individuals gave the support of the seats they controlled to the Crown they were known as Undertakers because they 'undertook' to get the government's business through the House.

possible French invasion after regular troops had been withdrawn for the American war, began in 1778. These companies of Volunteers in their various uniforms of brilliant scarlet, blue, orange and green had at first been raised locally by private subscription, but before long welded themselves into something like a national force, well armed – partly, though with some misgivings, by the government – and even in possession of artillery. They were all imbued with the now widespread public theory that the Irish Parliament should by right have full legislative sovereignty under the Crown of Ireland and that this had been usurped in times past by the English Parliament. The point of their existence now subtly altered. Instead of simply being there to defend the coastline, these Volunteers became a fashionable and extremely effective expression of the Protestants' political aspirations. Their very presence enormously strengthened the hand of men like Grattan, and Charlemont and other leading Protestant 'Patriots' in their attempts in Parliament to get the commercial restrictions rescinded and the Irish claim to legislative independence acknowledged. By the end of 1778 the Volunteers numbered some forty thousand men.*

With that force behind them, the independent minority in Parliament concentrated first on attacking the commercial restrictions. Within a year they had brought the administration to abandon the entire system of restrictive commercial legislation. Ireland obtained complete freedom to trade in anything with anybody.

But the basic loyalty to the Crown underlying the new spirit of independence was well demonstrated in 1779 when a motion in the Irish Parliament to give Ireland complete legislative independence of England was withdrawn out of deference to the government's feelings on the arrival of the news of military disasters from America.

In 1780 Grattan for the first time tried to get the Irish House of Commons to vote an Irish Declaration of Independence. He was then unsuccessful, owing to the Crown's effective control of the majority in Parliament, through the system of patronage. By the end of the following year, however, the Volunteers outside Parliament had become much stronger. They were said now to number some eighty thousand men, and early in 1782 a convention of democratically elected Volunteer delegates was held at Dungannon, a sort of parliament outside Parliament, backed by potential physical force for the first but by no means the last time in Irish history. This Volunteer convention unanimously resolved that 'a claim of any body of men, other than the King, Lords and Commons of Ireland, to bind this kingdom is unconstitutional, illegal and a grievance'. Before the end of the year the government

---

* All were Protestants at this stage. Catholics' offers to raise companies were initially rejected, but wealthy Catholics did contribute liberally to the funds from the start. Although still technically disqualified from bearing arms, Catholics eventually joined the Volunteers in considerable numbers.

yielded to the implied armed threat and Grattan was able to persuade the Irish Parliament to pass his Declaration of Independence unanimously.

This Declaration of Independence was accepted by the English Government. There were then repealed: both that Act of George I which categorically affirmed the English Parliament's right to legislate for Ireland and also that part of Poyning's law which proclaimed that the Irish Parliament must first submit its legislation to the English Parliament for approval. To complete the apparent triumph, in 1783 Flood, who had now rejoined the opposition, insisted on ramming the Protestant Irish victory home by pressing the English Government for a specific Act of Renunciation of English legislative rights in Ireland.* This was eventually agreed to and the Act declared, in words to be much quoted thereafter in Irish history, that the 'right claimed by the people of Ireland, to be bound only by laws enacted by His Majesty and the Parliament of the Kingdom in all cases whatever – shall be, and it is hereby declared to be, established and ascertained for ever, and shall at no time hereafter be questioned or questionable'.

Thus there came into existence for nineteen years what is usually known as Grattan's Parliament, though in it Grattan himself never took office. The Irish Protestants had won for 'Ireland' in the abstract an explicitly free and sovereign constitution, complicated only by a limitation which seemed neither a complication nor a limitation at the time: namely, the inalienable identity of the Irish Crown with that of England.

This connection of two independent 'nations' – one Irish, one English – under a joint Crown and within one British Empire had always been a cardinal principle of Grattan's political thought. He saw in the very connection itself a sort of guarantee of the purity of the Irish independence achieved. The society of Ireland had, he said, asserted 'her liberty according to the form of the British Constitution, her inheritance to be enjoyed in perpetual connection with the British Empire. . . . Connected by freedom as well as by allegiance, the two nations, Great Britain and Ireland, form a constitutional confederacy as well as an Empire.' And the emotional tie, now that it was, nominally, no more than that, was unashamedly acknowledged: '. . . the people of this kingdom have never expressed a desire to share the freedom of England without declaring a determination to share her fate likewise, standing or falling with the British nation.'²

The concept of a totally independent country under a joint British Crown was a fine inspiring one for men like Grattan. Ironically, it might have made good political sense in terms of the twentieth century. Constitutional monarchy, as evolved in the framework of a reformed Parliament and a widened franchise, would have permitted a true sovereign independence for Ireland under a joint Crown. Later constitutional practice has made it quite

---

* Since his position as opposition leader had been taken over by Grattan, he made a bid to reassert himself by putting forward more strongly radical views.

possible for the same monarch to have different faces in different situations. But in Grattan's time, with Parliament still unreformed, the nominal independence inevitably remained nominal only. For the old flaw in the status of the Irish Parliament survived legislative independence intact. The actual government of the 'King of Ireland' was still carried on by an Irish executive who were dependent in the end not so much on what happened in Ireland as on the power to influence the Irish Parliament made available to them in the form of Crown patronage by changing English ministers.

In an unreformed Irish Parliament, with such power at their disposal, the Irish ministers were a permanent professional department of the British Government. Certainly they had to work through the Irish Parliament and certainly the will of that Parliament was now technically sovereign. But that will could still be manipulated freely by English-controlled influence and patronage. Moreover, in the period after 1782 the government in London made a deliberate practice of extending their parliamentary influence in Ireland by the sale of honours, places and pensions. The only way to get round this and make 'Irish legislative independence' into something more than a nominal phrase was, as Grattan and the Patriots saw, to reform the whole parliamentary system and make seats in Parliament dependent on the true will of the electorate.

On the issue of legislative independence itself, the true will of the electorate and of the Irish House of Commons had been able to assert itself. But this was only because behind it there had been really effective pressure in the threat of armed force from the Volunteers. On that occasion the system tactfully allowed itself to lose face in order to maintain power. But there was not to be the same unanimity among Irish Protestants on the new issue of reform. Moreover, there was a further important question which now had to be confronted squarely if the new independent Ireland were really to be a country at all in anything but theory. All the talk about 'Ireland' and 'Irish legislative independence' had proceeded as if 'the Irish' were the Irish Protestants. But of course they were only a small minority of the Irish. The vast majority of the population were Catholics. And yet all Catholics were still excluded from the entire political system.

These two issues of parliamentary reform and Catholic Emancipation now dominated the Irish Parliament's life until the end of the century.

The Patriots' argument for reform was clear enough. If Ireland were to be in practice as well as in theory a genuinely distinct country, confederate with Britain, then obviously she must have control over her own affairs. This could only be achieved by such a reform of the parliamentary system as would make two-thirds of the seats in the Irish Parliament no longer the property of a few men who could always be bought by the English Government.

But apart from this national constitutional argument there was more down-to-earth pressure for reform. Those Protestants who were not part of the small oligarchy involved in the system of patronage and the rotten borough, were beginning to clamour on their own account for the power from which it permanently excluded them.

A similar clamour was also arising from similar classes in England for a reform of the English Parliament. But the clamour in Ireland was more acute. For not only was the Irish Parliament much more exclusive and corrupt, but it owed its present proud and independent 'national' status to the pressure through the Volunteers of this very Protestant yeomanry and middle class which was still virtually unrepresented in it.

The argument for Catholic emancipation was equally clear. If Ireland were to be truly an independent nation under the Crown, then the three-quarters of the nation who were Catholics would have to be eligible for the same rights in their identity as Irishmen as the quarter who were Protestant. Again, the admission of Catholics to political life was also an issue in England. But again a far greater urgency applied in Ireland, where Catholic Emancipation meant not, as in England, political recognition for a small minority, but for the vast majority of the country.

In 1778 the first Catholic Relief Bill had been passed enabling Catholics to start buying property again. Edmund Burke had written to an Irish Protestant: 'You are now beginning to have a country. . . . I am persuaded that when that thing called a country is once found in Ireland, quite other things will be done than were done when the zeal of men was turned to the safety of a party.'[3] (By which he meant the Protestant party.) Now, in 1782 that country had been found and the Volunteers who had done most to find it were not only chafing for representation but had to some extent at least shown themselves ready for new thinking about Catholics. At Dungannon, referring to the recent changes in the land laws, they had resolved, with only two dissentient voices in an assembly of 143 delegates, that 'as men and as Irishmen, as Christians and as Protestants, we rejoice in the relaxation of the penal laws against our Roman Catholic fellow-subjects, and . . . conceive the measure to be fraught with the happiest consequences to the union and the prosperity of the inhabitants of Ireland'.[4] Grattan had taken tolerance further in the Irish House of Commons with the words, 'the question is now whether we shall be a Protestant settlement or an Irish nation . . . for so long as we exclude Catholics from natural liberty and the common rights of man we are not a people'.[5] In this year 1782 a further Relief Act was passed admitting Catholics fully to exactly the same rights of property and leasehold in land as Protestants.

All the same there was still so much disagreement, even among the old Patriot party, on the issue of admitting Catholics to *political rights* that Reform assumed more convenient priority. Both Charlemont and Flood, for

instance, were opposed to admitting Catholics to full political rights. Charlemont even believed that Catholics could not safely be admitted to political
power for a hundred years. On the issue of Reform, on the other hand, all
those at least who had led the parliamentary struggle for independence were
agreed on the desirability of the goal.

The only difficulty was how to achieve it – how those two-thirds of the
House of Commons who depended one way or another on the government
for place and patronage were to be brought to abandon the whole structure
of their personal advantage and aggrandizement.

The logic of the situation was certainly that the instrument of force present
in the Volunteers, which had been so useful in the background when legislative independence was won, might be used again. But some of the old leaders
of the Patriot party were squeamish at the prospect of putting extra-parliamentary pressure on that very independent Parliament which they had
created. Thus the concentration of the drive for Reform was nothing like so
great as it had been for legislative independence.

Flood, most radical of the leaders on the issue of reform, believed in
using the Volunteers, sitting as they were by 1783 in a democratically elected
Convention of the whole country in Dublin, as the necessary external pressure on Parliament. It is difficult in retrospect not to think that he was tactically right in wanting to apply the same method again. But Charlemont
and even Grattan himself, whose pleasure in the more nebulous ties of the
connection somewhat clouded his daring, disapproved of unconstitutional
threats to the new sovereign legislature by a sort of alternative legislative
assembly of armed men. When Flood, ostentatiously wearing Volunteer uniform, brought a Reform Bill from the Convention to put before the House of
Commons it was overwhelmingly rejected. Even Flood himself was not so
radical as to try and push the Volunteers' pressure to its logical extreme in
face of this defeat and resort to force, though in Belfast the Volunteers had
their artillery ready with round shot and grape shot and five hundred of them
waited hourly for the order which never came, to march on the Dublin
Parliament. The Convention disbanded. And though the Volunteers continued nominally in being for many years as a nostalgic association, and a few
companies were to develop a very special character several years later, their
effective political power as a body was now really dispersed for ever.

A century or so later lofty nostalgia was often evoked by politicians on
behalf of 'Grattan's Parliament' or 'the old house on College Green'. The
constitution of 1782 came to be thought of by many as compatible with the
highest aspirations of Irish 'nationality'. But though it may have been good
politics, such talk was poor history. For, once the independence of the Irish
Parliament had been technically granted, the English government's hold over
it was actually tightened by its systematic ever-increasing outlay of Crown
patronage in Ireland.

That the constitution of 1782 was in practice a sham, and Ireland's claim to enjoy full independence within the Empire a romantic illusion, eventually became clear enough even to Grattan himself. On 2 February 1790 he castigated the Ministers of the Irish Crown in the Irish House of Commons in a speech which not only demonstrates the simple mechanism by which the 'independent' legislature was officially undermined, but also already carried significant if gentlemanly echoes of the great revolution that had begun in France the year before. Grattan declaimed, of the Irish ministers :

We charge them publicly in the face of their country, with making corrupt agreements for the sale of peerages, for doing which we say they are impeachable; we charge them with corrupt agreements for the disposal of the money arising from the sale, to purchase for the servants of the Castle, seats in the assembly of the people, for doing which we say they are impeachable; we charge them with committing these offences, not in one, not in two, but in many instances, for which complication of offences we say they are impeachable; guilty of a systematic endeavour to undermine the constitution in violation of the laws of the land . . .[6]

The only answer Grattan got from the Ministers was that the disposal of Crown patronage was a matter of the royal prerogative and therefore above debate. In the latter days of this Parliament Grattan was driven to refer to the 'base condition of our connection and allegiance' which the corrupt structure of Parliament necessitated – though he never wavered from his deep emotional conviction that an honourable British connection was the only conceivable framework for true Irish independence. But the falsity of Ireland's 'national' position had been faced earlier with even bleaker frankness by another member of the Irish House of Commons who was emotionally just as loyal to the principle of the connection as Grattan himself.

'Boast', said Sir Lawrence Parsons, in the Irish House of Commons in 1790,

Boast of the prosperity of your country as you may, and after all I ask : what is it but a secondary kingdom? An inferior member of a great Empire without any movement or orbit of its own. . . . We may pride ourselves that we are a great kingdom, but the fact is that we are barely known beyond the boundaries of our shores. Who out of Ireland ever hears of Ireland? Who respects us? Where are our ambassadors? What treaties do we enter into? With what nation do we make peace or war? Are we not a mere cipher in all these, and are not these what give a nation consequence and fame? All these are sacrificed to the connection with England. . . . A suburb to England we are sunk in her shade. True we are an independent kingdom; we have an imperial Crown distinct from England; but it is a metaphysical distinction, a mere sport for speculative men. . . . It is asked why, after all the acquisitions of 1782, there should be discontent? To this I say that when the country is well-governed the people ought to be satisfied but not before. . . . It has been the object of English ministers ever since to countervail what we obtained at that period, and substitute a surreptitious and clandestine influence for the open power which the English legislature was then obliged to relinquish . . .

All this was undeniably true. What then of the future? Parsons outlined it with prophetic clarity:

> Those concessions on the part of the English Parliament I grant were as ample as they well could be for they were everything short of separation. Let ministers then beware of what conclusions they may teach the people if they teach them this, that the attainment of everything short of separation will not attain for them the good government. . . . Where, or when, or how is all this to end? Is the Minister of England himself sure that he sees the end? Can he be sure that this system, which has been forming for the coercion of Ireland, may not ultimately cause the dissolution of the Empire?[7]

A friend of Sir Lawrence Parsons at this time was a young Protestant middle-class lawyer, already showing a slightly erratic interest in politics, whose name was Theobald Wolfe Tone. Meanwhile, in France, a country with which Ireland had long been associated by ties less explicit but in some ways as strong as those which bound her to England, an event was taking place which was gradually shaking all existing political thought everywhere to its foundations.

Part Two

The First Irish Republicans

1
Ireland and the French Revolution

The French Revolution had a remarkable message for all peoples, to the effect that an apparently deadlocked society was not necessarily deadlocked at all, and that a new order of society based on the theory of the people's participation rather than just on their acceptance of their lot was a practical possibility. This excited the minds of political thinkers all over the world, particularly in Britain, and most particularly of all in Ireland, where even more acutely than elsewhere in the British Isles, an urgent need for the reform of the political system along more popular lines was already being widely felt and discussed.

To the more independent-minded, even among the aristocracy and gentry, the deadlock of a Parliament in which a few individuals controlled the majority of the representatives, whose support the English Ministry could always secure by extending the Crown's patronage, made nonsense of the nominal legislative independence won in 1782. Grattan, himself the most enthusiastic and loyal architect of that independence, had become increasingly disillusioned, and had already used the term 'a creeping union' to describe the relationship between the two countries.[1] As for the commercial and professional middle classes, who by their self-organization and external pressure in the hey-day of the Volunteers had helped to win the independence of '82, they found that the goal of parliamentary reform and thus their own share and influence still eluded them; whereas in France they saw their class in the seats of power overnight. Now therefore in Ireland, merchants, lawyers and doctors, often wealthy and almost always Protestants, banded together to provide most of the intellectual leaders of a new radical movement.

At the same time, the peasantry, the vast majority of the common people of Ireland, lived in conditions a good deal harder than those suffered by the peasantry of France. An English traveller through Tipperary in 1790 found his mind 'filled with melancholy on contemplating these poor creatures who drag on a miserable existence under an accumulation of woes that it is hard to think human nature can sustain....'[2] Their situation was 'not better than a beast of burden,'³ and the last straw in the burden was the tithe, a tax in the form of about one-tenth of the peasant's produce which he was by law compelled to pay for the upkeep of a Protestant Church to which he did not belong.

A folk memory of the outlawry of the peasant's own religion, of the legal oppression of himself and his fellows simply for being the sort of people they were, went back well over a hundred years in aggravation of all this. Every Catholic's legal position had in fact improved out of all recognition in the recent past with the Catholic Relief Acts of 1778 and 1782. But folk memories are inordinately long when any grievances at all remain, and to the average Irish peasant everyday life was itself grievance enough. There were in any case still some legal humiliations to which all Catholics were subject. Under the surviving penal laws Catholics of every class were still prevented from voting, sitting in Parliament or occupying any of the offices of state. It was the Catholic middle class and gentry who felt the deprivation of this and all it symbolized most directly, but reaction to the anachronism was one which could and did usefully unite many radical men of every type and class, while to the peasantry it provided an obvious symbol of their total grievance.

Parliamentary reform, Catholic Emancipation and the need to improve the lot of the peasantry particularly with regard to the injustice of tithe – these were the political thoughts circulating in Ireland at the moment when all political thought received a sudden stimulus from the sensational developments in France.

The politically articulate among the reformers in Irish society had few direct contacts with the peasantry. And though an acknowledgement of the peasantry's condition was fairly widespread among all classes, people interested in reform and change inevitably concentrated on those issues that seemed closest and most real to them. Reformist and radical circles in Belfast and Dublin concerned themselves with Parliamentary reform or Catholic relief and sometimes the two together, persuading themselves that once the system of government was reformed at source and made more representative, the necessary change in the condition of the peasantry would follow automatically.

As a result, the stimulus which the French Revolution gave to the hopes of the peasantry worked in isolation from the rest of society at first. In the years just before the French Revolution, secret societies had been particularly active in the South and West of Ireland. There, in 1786 and 1787, a society known as Rightboys had been accumulating large numbers of adherents by oath-taking ceremonies in Catholic chapels, each chapel when sworn sending on representatives to swear in the next. The oaths taken were to obey the laws of 'Captain Right', and not to pay more than a certain amount of rent per acre of land. Apart from this regulation of rent their objects were the raising of the price of labour and the abolition of hearth and other taxes and, in particular, tithes. Before long Captain Right's boys had spread over the whole of Munster and were sometimes to be met with openly in parties of five hundred or so at a time. They were usually unarmed, but busied themselves with the infliction of savage punishments on any peasant who refused to join them, dragging him from his bed in the middle of the night and burying him alive in a grave lined with thorns, or setting him naked on horseback tied to a saddle of thorns and perhaps sawing his ears off as well.[4]

Meanwhile, similar secret society activity, but with one important difference, was developing simultaneously in the North.

In North-East Ulster the mainly Protestant tenantry had, ever since the great plantation of the seventeenth century, benefitted from the so-called 'Ulster custom', which allowed fairly extensive rights to tenants, such as freedom from eviction, so long as they paid their rents, and compensation on departure for any improvements they might have made to their land. They were thus on the whole a good deal more prosperous than the Catholics in the South. (Catholics in North-East Ulster were chiefly labourers without any land at all.) Nevertheless, throughout the eighteenth century the Presbyterian tenantry in the North had suffered not only from certain social and civil penalties inflicted on them as nonconformists, but also, like any other tenantry in Ireland, from the rapaciousness of landlords and middlemen. Rents, as elsewhere in Ireland, were determined solely by the inexorable law of supply and demand. And under pressure of these high rents and nonconformist civic disadvantages, many Presbyterians in the eighteenth century, better able to afford emigration than the peasantry of the South, had left for America.

In 1779 and 1782 by the Catholic Relief Acts, Catholics were again permitted to purchase and hold leases on land on an equal footing with Protestants. Many of them moved on to land in Ulster left vacant by the Presbyterian emigrants. Such Catholics, long acclimatized to a lower standard of living, were prepared to bid the price of land up to heights to which Presbyterians refused to go. But for years agrarian secret societies among the Presbyterians, with names like 'Oakboys' and 'Steelboys', had fought successfully to keep the price of land down. In 1763, for instance, the 'Hearts of Oak boys', who forced land-owners to promise on oath not to raise rents above seven shillings an acre, had been described as 'absolute masters' of Armagh, Cavan and other counties. At Belturbet in Donegal they had entered the town, headed by a man on horseback in soldier's clothes, with drums beating, horns blowing and a fife playing, and flying red and white colours, and compelled several gentlemen to take their oath, threatening to remove their wives and daughters if they refused.[5] It was this spirit of local solidarity which the new eager Catholic tenants in Ulster now threatened to undermine, introducing as they did a new element of undisciplined competition for land. And the Protestant secret societies began to array themselves against the Catholics just as effectively as they had already arrayed themselves against the landlords.

It was around 1785 that this specifically anti-Catholic form of secret society first made its appearance in the North. It was known simply as 'the Protestant Boys', sometimes expressively as 'the Wreckers', but most often as 'the Peep o' Day Boys', because it was at dawn that its members took to appearing at the houses of Catholics and burning them or otherwise terrorizing their occupants into removing to some other part of Ireland. The Catholics in these districts soon formed a rival protection society, which, while assuming the traditional pattern of former agrarian secret societies, also had a new emphasis in that it was formed for the defence of Catholics solely as Catholics and against Protestants. Its members called themselves, appropriately enough, the Defenders.

At first these Defenders did exist simply for local defence against a real threat from the Ulster Protestants. But as they were driven from their homes in Ulster into neighbouring counties like Meath and Louth, where Catholics were in a majority, the Defenders continued and developed their organization on the assumption that the whole Catholic peasant identity in Ireland required defence on principle, and that the best form of defence was often attack. It was on just such an organization on the brink of a crude political attitude, primitive and ill-coordinated and yet expressing incoherently the everyday grievances and resentments of over a century, that the French Revolution inevitably worked a powerful influence.

For a hundred years close ties between France and Catholic Ireland had made Ireland sensitive to anything that happened there. Ever since the Wild Geese had flown to France after the Treaty of Limerick,* adventurous Catholics, frustrated by the penal laws, had been crossing the seas to put on the uniform of France, fight in her armies and become her citizens. French boats arriving at lonely points off the southern and south-western Irish coasts to take off these recruits, or to carry priests to and from their training or the sons of gentry to and from their education or simply smuggling out wool and smuggling in claret and brandy, had been a permanent feature of popular Irish life. If the people of France felt overcome by a sudden sense of emancipation it was inevitable that the people of Ireland should be strongly affected by it too, particularly when one of the first acts of the Revolution in France had been to abolish tithes. A powerful democratic influence at work in both countries was Tom Paine's *Rights of Man*, which was being so generally distributed in Ireland in 1791 that people were hired to read it to those who could not read themselves.[6]

The earliest oaths of the Defenders' societies began with a straightforward expression of allegiance to the king and his successors, together with general

* See above, p. 18.

expressions of mutual aid and support. The idea was plainly much influenced by Freemasonry, which had enjoyed a great revival in the North of Ireland at the time of the Volunteers some years before,[7] and from which many of the forms of the Defenders' Society were copied. The rules of a local Defender Committee in County Louth in 1789 declared that no Defender was 'to strike another upon any account' or to come to the monthly meeting drunk. There was to be 'no swearing or speaking loud', and secrecy about membership and passwords was strictly enjoined.[8] But it was soon clear that the Defenders were determined, even when not under direct pressure, to be something more than a mere Masonic brotherhood of Catholics.

In this County Louth Defender Committee's oath of April 1789, some months even before the outbreak of the French Revolution, there is already a significant variation in the phrasing of the oath which, in Masonic tradition, expresses allegiance to the king. For, after swearing to be true to one another, and to obey the committee in all things that are lawful, the Louth Defenders swear that 'as in our former oath we are bound to his Majesty King George III and his successors, so for this present year 1789 we promise faithfully the same obedience and also while we live subject to the same government . . .'[9] As an experienced Defender organizer was later to remark, this form of the oath was very useful in getting those with loyalist misgivings to join the society for, as he put it, 'if the King's head were off tomorrow we were no longer under his government'.[10]

The Catholic Irish peasantry had traditionally drawn strength from looking back to better times in the past. They were natural conservatives and the idea of anything but allegiance to the traditional form of monarchical government had never been heard in Ireland. There was also another important conservative factor at work. Though the Revolution in France attracted the Irish peasantry with its abolition of tithes and its general appeal for emancipation of the suffering common man, and though a certain amount of fashionable free-thinking had been discernible among the Rightboys, yet the anti-clerical character which the Revolution assumed in France was generally confusing to a people who had for so long seen in their religion the only popular symbol of their identity.

With such confusing trends at work among the peasantry, and the interests of the peasantry in any case uncoordinated with those of the middle class, the organization of the potentially revolutionary forces in Ireland into a successful revolution on the French model could never have been an easy task. Even so, it must be said of the men into whose hands the manipulation of the new revolutionary spirit now fell, that though they proved themselves men of great courage and integrity, they hardly showed that outstanding political and organizational ability which the occasion demanded.

2
Wolfe Tone
and Samuel Neilson

At the beginning of the French Revolution there had been many members of the ruling class in Ireland with a poor opinion of the way things were done in their country and who thought that they should be changed. 'If', the lord lieutenant wrote some years later, 'the French Revolution had taken a humane and genial turn, and had not degenerated into such a rapid succession of tyranny upon tyranny, the speculative minds among the educated and superior classes of this kingdom would have hearkened eagerly to democratic novelties.'[1] But the course of the French Revolution, with its ruthlessness and its radical republicanism, antagonized conservative democrats and left even Patriot reformers like Grattan and Sir Laurence Parsons helpless between their wish for political freedom and their refusal to try and achieve it by endangering the whole equilibrium of society. Leadership of the new spirit fell more and more into the hands of men who had no inhibitions about being as radical and, in the long run, if needs be as republican and violent as the revolutionaries across the water.

The names of these men are, with the exception of a very few – notably Wolfe Tone – largely forgotten today even in Ireland. One of them, a few nights before his death on the scaffold, wrote in a letter from prison to his family: '... justice will yet be done to my memory, and my fate be mentioned rather with pride than with shame ... if I did not expect the arrival of this justice to my memory, I should be indeed afflicted at the nominal ignominy of my death.'[2] His death was in fact to be peculiarly ignominious, for by some clumsiness on the part of the executioner he was hauled up on the rope for nearly a minute before being lowered again to the platform for his final drop.[3] He has a small street named after him in Cork but otherwise his name, John Sheares, has little popular appeal in modern republican Ireland. Thomas Emmet, Samuel Neilson, William MacNevin, Arthur O'Connor, Oliver Bond, Thomas Russell, Napper Tandy, John Lawless, John and Henry Sheares, Beauchamp Bagenal Harvey – these are some of the names who deserve to share with Wolfe Tone and the romantic Lord Edward Fitzgerald the fame of founding the separatist republican movement.

Among them Napper Tandy alone has become popularly known, though few who sing the opening verse of the 'Wearing of the Green' probably have any idea who he was or what he did.*

Most of these men were of considerable bourgeois standing in society – Fitzgerald was an aristocrat – and all but one were Protestants. Of them all Wolfe Tone is the best known, being usually described as 'leader' of the Society of United Irishmen which finally in 1798 tried to carry out a republican revolution in Ireland. Tone was in fact out of Ireland during almost the whole time in which the movement took on its characteristically violent and conspiratorial form. His contribution to events lay in the persistent and effective personal pressure he put on the French Government to give military aid to Irish conspirators with whom he was largely out of touch and in many cases unacquainted. He shares with Lord Edward Fitzgerald the honour of being the most celebrated figure of the rebellion, partly because like Fitzgerald he suffered a brave and pathetic death in the course of 1798, partly because as a shadowy figure behind the scenes, in league with the enemy, he took on a legendary quality for his opponents even in his own lifetime, and partly because he left behind him memoirs of considerable shrewdness and charm, in which he now shines through history by contrast with some of the other revolutionary figures.

The first Tone to settle in Ireland more than a century before had been a soldier of Oliver Cromwell's. Both by antecedence and upbringing Tone could hardly have had fewer connections with Gaelic Ireland, nor would this have seemed to him at any stage of his career a matter of the slightest relevance. His father, a respectable Protestant, had succeeded to the leasehold of a farm near Naas in County Kildare and later moved to Dublin to become a coachbuilder. His mother, whose name was Lamport, was the daughter of a sea captain in the East India trade. Tone himself, after a good Protestant schooling in the city, was sent to Trinity College where he studied logic. His real wish was to be a soldier, and he longed to be allowed to join the British Army then fighting the colonists in America. But his father insisted that he should complete his education, and he took his degree. At Trinity Tone enjoyed himself and always retained 'a most sincere affection' for his old university to the end of his life, though it was a pillar of that establishment which he came to oppose. An attractive and spirited young man who loved the material pleasures of life, particularly eating and drinking in good company, Tone is, in his account of his early activities in Ireland, always more a student prince of politics than any sort of national hero in the making.

---

* Oh, I met with Napper Tandy and he took me by the hand,
   And he says how's poor oul' Ireland and how does she stand?
   'Tis the most distressful country that ever yet was seen
   For they're hanging men and women for the wearing of the green.

Tone married at the age of twenty-two and tried to take his responsibilities seriously by going to London to study law. But in this, by his own admission, he had little success, finding the rest of life more enjoyable than the law itself. He did, however, apply himself seriously to one political scheme: a plan for establishing a British colony in Captain Cook's newly discovered islands in the South Seas, in order, as he wrote, to 'put a bridle on Spain in time of peace and annoy her grievously in time of war'.[4] It was an odd political debut for one usually thought of as first practitioner of the principle that England's difficulty was Ireland's opportunity. He actually went round to Downing Street and handed in a copy of this plan personally to the porter there, but Pitt, the Prime Minister, did not even acknowledge it. He took the affront in reasonably good part and his next move was to try and volunteer with his brother for the East India Company's military service. But calling at their offices one day in September he found that no ships were sailing until the following March, so he gave up the idea and returned to Dublin on 23 December 1788.[5]

Called to the Irish bar early in 1789 Tone's interests again turned instinctively to politics. The two fashionable progressive issues of parliamentary reform and Catholic Emancipation made an obvious appeal to a young man of his spirit. He joined a political club, the Whig club, which had been founded by Grattan and Charlemont to obtain a reform of Parliament, made friends with Sir Lawrence Parsons and other 'patriot' members of the opposition, and even entertained some hopes of sitting in Parliament himself. But before long he was playing with political ideas that were a good deal more progressive and shocking altogether.

His first important publication in fact was a pamphlet written when the British Government was on the point of breaking off relations with Spain, and this time he took up a very different attitude from that which had taken him to Downing Street. He now suggested that Ireland as an independent nation would not in fact necessarily be bound to go to war with Spain at all, even if Britain did. Hanging about the Dublin bookshops on the first day of this pamphlet's publication, Tone was delighted to hear bishops and other Establishment figures express their outrage and indignation at its seditious contents. But his political ideas were still immature, for soon afterwards he was once again advocating his old South Sea colony scheme for thwarting Spain on Britain's behalf. This time he not only got an acknowledgement from the government but approbation from the Foreign Secretary, Grenville.[6] However, an improvement in relations between Britain and Spain soon made both points of view irrelevant. In any case the shock waves were by now beginning to be felt of that great developing political event in France which finally directed Tone's thinking towards the separatist and eventually republican lines for which he became famous.

Tone later wrote that the Revolution 'changed in an instant the politics of Ireland' and that within twelve months when its implications for monarchy and aristocracy had become clear it had divided political thinkers clearly into 'aristocrats' and 'democrats'.[7] Given the compressive tendencies of hindsight – Tone himself was, after all, still toying with his Imperial South Sea project in the summer of 1790, because he 'had nothing better to do'[8] – this is a fair enough definition of the Revolution's effect on Ireland.

To one group of Irishmen in particular the Revolution had acted like a clarion call and in the light of later Irish history this makes a strange paradox. Protestant Ulster, and particularly Belfast, from which most of the anti-British American colonists had come, had long been a centre of popular republican ideas. Presbyterianism, with its dislike of bishops, was in any case a religion cast in a republican mould. In Belfast in the early 1790s the remnants of the old Volunteers of ten years before still survived to a much more positive extent than in Dublin. They were now proud companies of radical political thinkers sticking devotedly to the great cause of reform which had received such a setback when Flood failed to force it through the Irish Parliament, wearing his Volunteer uniform, in 1783. On that occasion the Belfast Volunteers had been prepared to march on Dublin, and something of the same spirit still survived, much stimulated by recent events in France.

A close friend of Tone's, a twenty-three-year-old officer in the British Army called Thomas Russell who had served in India and who had spent the summer of 1790 on half-pay with Tone and his wife at their 'little box of a house' by the sea at Irishtown, was posted to join his regiment in Belfast in the autumn. Russell, who had a radical turn of mind himself, was soon in touch with the surviving groups of Volunteers there who elected him to one of their political clubs. He discovered that political thought in these clubs and among the Volunteers was being actively directed and influenced by a secret committee headed by the thirty-year-old son of a Presbyterian clergyman, one Samuel Neilson. Neilson more than any other single figure can be said to be the founder of the society soon to be known as the United Irishmen.

Russell wrote to Tone in the summer of 1791 to tell him of his new friends. It seemed that, in one most important respect, the thought of some of these clubs was developing on parallel lines to some recent discussions he and Tone had been having earlier. These had concerned the possibility of getting Protestant Dissenters to overcome their prejudices against Catholics and to unite with Catholics to realize a joint strength for Ireland in the cause of change and reform. There was nothing particularly original in such an idea. It had been put forward years before in the hey-day of volunteering by the *Volunteer Journal*, which had proclaimed for a while : 'When the men of Ireland forget their destructive religious prejudices, and embrace each other with the warmth of genuine religious philanthropy, then, and not until then, will they eradicate the baneful English influence, and destroy the aristocratic tyrants of the land.'⁹ But though there had been a certain amount of such thinking among the more radical Volunteers it was not on the whole typical of the Protestant attitude of the day. And, in any case, the objective of the Volunteers on that occasion – legislative independence – had been won without the need fully to resolve ancient prejudices.

To apply the principle of united effort to the new issue of reform was logical and reasonable enough. Russell, writing to Tone, asked him to draw up a suitable declaration for his new friends in the North, and on 14 July 1791, the second anniversary of the storming of the Bastille, Tone sent three resolutions 'suited to this day' to Belfast for adoption.

These were: (1) that English influence in Ireland was the great grievance of the country; (2) that the most effective way to reform it was by a reform of Parliament; and (3) that no reform could be any use unless it included the Catholics.¹⁰ In a covering letter to his new contacts in Belfast he added: 'I have not said one word that looks like a wish for separation, though I give it to you and your friends as my most decided opinion that such an event would be a regeneration of their country.'¹¹

It was the third of Tone's open resolutions – the key one, that a union of all the people of Ireland, Protestant and Catholic, was indispensable to achieve reform – that was treading on the most dangerous ground in the North. For some years clashes between Peep o' Day Boys and Defenders there had been growing more and more ugly, and it was in many ways the worst possible time to try and put forward such an otherwise intelligent proposition. Tone himself admitted to his diary that this last resolution 'in concession to prejudices, was rather insinuated than asserted'. But only three days later he was told by Neilson that in spite of his care it had had to be dropped altogether. The news made him note bitterly that in that case he would devote himself solely to the Catholic cause from then on because clearly the people in the North who were nominally most anxious for reform were really just seeking 'rather a monopoly than an extension of liberty ... contrary to all justice and expediency'.¹²

Tone was in fact always too excited by the desirability of a union between Catholics and Dissenters to pay lasting attention to the practical obstacles to it with which he was constantly presented. He, and many United Irishmen later, fell too easily into the assumption that the reconciliation could be brought about almost as easily as it could be wished for.

In any case encouraging evidence had appeared in Dublin itself, quite independently of Tone and his new friends in Belfast, that similar ideas to theirs were stirring in other radical minds. As early as June 1791 – even before Tone had sent his heads of proposals to Belfast – a broadsheet had been circulated in Dublin which outlined proposals for a future separatist nationalism with a prophetic touch.

It is proposed at this juncture [the broadsheet ran] that a SOCIETY shall be instituted in this City, having much of the secrecy and somewhat of the ceremonial attached to Freemasonry ... Let one benevolent, beneficent conspiracy arise, one Plot of Patriots, pledged by solemn adjuration to each other in the service of the people ... let its name be the Irish Brotherhood ... What are the rights of Roman Catholics, and what are the immediate duties of Protestants regarding these rights? Is the independence of Ireland nominal or real, a barren right or a fact regulative of national conduct and influencing national character? ... Is there any middle state between the extremes of union with Britain and total separation, in which the rights of the people can be established and rest in security? ... By the Brotherhood are these questions and such as these to be determined.[13]

Tone's own thoughts concentrated more and more on the absurdity of Protestants trying to think and act as Irish patriots while at the same time regarding Catholics, the vast majority of the people of Ireland, as somehow not involved with them in Irish patriotism. In September of this year, 1791, he published under the pseudonym of 'A Northern Whig' a well-reasoned pamphlet entitled *An Argument on behalf of the Catholics of Ireland.* It was addressed to the Presbyterians of the North, urging them to 'forget all former feuds, to consolidate the entire strength of the whole nation and to form for the future but one people'.[14]

This pamphlet attracted immediate approval and interest in its author by an organization called the Catholic Committee, a respectable and hitherto conservative body of Catholic gentry founded in the middle of the eighteenth century to represent Catholic views with the minimum of offence to the Establishment. Stimulated, like every organisation in Ireland, by the French Revolution, the Catholic Committee had recently been showing new life under the guidance of a middle-class Catholic radical named John Keogh, who soon split the Committee in two and assumed leadership of the radical half which from then on was the only part that effectively counted. It was natural that Keogh should want to get in touch with Tone at once and he did so. But the pamphlet excited an equally immediate response from the quarter to which it was directly addressed, namely, the Protestants of the North.

For Tone's argument was exactly the sort of message that Neilson and the more sophisticated radicals of his secret committee in the North had been trying to get across to the ordinary Presbyterian members of the various Volunteer bodies and clubs there. Neilson and his friends invited Tone to Belfast in the following month. He met the secret committee formally for the first time at dinner at four o'clock on 14 October and there helped argue out the final resolutions of a new and quite open reforming organization to be officially launched under the name of the Society of United Irishmen. Tone found that the political temperature of Belfast had risen noticeably since his first proposals had had to be watered down in the summer. The secret committee in their turn were delighted to hear from him and his friend Russell of developments within the Catholic Committee. But there were plenty of indications that the desirable Union was still more easily wished for than achieved.

For instance, at this very inaugural secret meeting which Tone attended it had to be agreed that the North was 'not yet ripe to follow' to the full the lead they were being given.[15]

Some days later Tone found himself engaged in an argument after dinner in which individuals took up the relative positions of Peep o' Day Boys and Defenders. The Peep o' Day Boys, wrote Tone, were 'ashamed of their own positions'.[16] At another dinner some days later there was another 'furious battle, which lasted two hours, on the Catholic question, as usual neither party convinced'.[17] A dissenting clergyman of some prominence, the Reverend William Bruce, was particularly anti-Catholic. Tone noted that almost all the company were of the same opinion, citing the prevalent fear that the Catholics might revive their claims to ancient estates. Bruce declared that thirty-nine out of forty Protestants were opposed to the liberation of the Catholics.[18] It was an ill-omened start to a movement whose chief tactic was to try and gain strength by bringing Catholics and Dissenters together.

But on this first visit to the North, Tone also heard a lot that he found stimulating and reassuring. Walking in the Belfast Mall with Russell and an American named Digges, one of the inner circle of the Belfast club, Tone asked Digges whether he thought Ireland could exist independent of England and was told yes, decidedly. Nothing could be done, said Digges, until all the religious sects were united and England engaged in a foreign war, but 'if Ireland were free ... she would in arts, commerce and manufactures spring up like an air balloon and leave England behind at an immense distance'. There was, continued Digges, 'no computing the rapidity with which she would rise'. 'Digges', wrote Tone in his diary, 'promised to detail all this, and much more, on paper.'[19]

The important immediate result for Ireland of Tone's visit was that the first open meeting of the United Irishmen took place in Belfast on 18 October 1791. The agreed resolutions were unanimously adopted: namely, that a union of Irishmen of all religious persuasions was required to counteract the weight of English influence in the country and secure a reform of Parliament.

Returning to Dublin ten days later after a good deal of convivial hospitality, Tone got in touch with a prominent Dublin radical and former stalwart of the Volunteers of 1782 named Napper Tandy whom he had been commissioned to contact by the Belfast secret committee. Tandy found the approach much to his liking. On 9 November 1791 a similar club of United Irishmen to that in Belfast was founded in the capital and Tandy took charge of it from the start. Signing the Dublin Society's declaration at its inaugural meeting Tandy wrote:

> In the present great era of reform when unjust governments are falling in every quarter of Europe ... we think it our duty as Irishmen to come forward and state what we feel to be our heavy grievance, and what we believe to be its effectual remedy. We have no National Government. We are ruled by Englishmen and the servants of Englishmen whose object is the interest of another country, whose instrument is corruption, whose strength is the weakness of Ireland, and these men have the whole power and patronage of the country as means to subdue the honesty and the spirit of her representatives in the legislature.[20]

There was nothing in this with which Grattan and other members of the Whig club would not theoretically agree, though the very radical nature of the language might suggest eventual extremes which would be too much for them. Even the simple open affirmation which all members of the United Irish Society were called upon to make – at this stage no oath was required – was constitutional, and technically inoffensive:

> I, A.B., in the presence of God, do pledge myself to my country that I will use all my abilities and influence in the attainment of an adequate and impartial representation of the Irish nation in Parliament, and as a means of absolute and immediate necessity in the attainment of this chief good of Ireland, I will endeavour as much as lies in my ability, to forward a brotherhood of affection, an identity of interests, a communion of rights, and a union of power among Irishmen of all religious persuasions ... the freedom of this country.[21]

Contrary to the proposal in the Dublin broadsheet earlier in the year, the society was an open one and as yet adopted none of the paraphernalia of Freemasonry. The United Irishmen did not become a secret society until three years later, when its character changed altogether. Now it set itself up as little more than a radical reform club or debating society, though already convinced republicans like Tandy in Dublin and Neilson in Belfast held secret designs in reserve.

Before the end of 1791 Tandy issued a circular letter signed by himself in which he declared: 'The object of this institution is to make a United Society of the Irish Nation; to make all Irishmen Citizens, all Citizens Irishmen ...' And he added that for a century past there had been tranquillity 'but to most of our dear countrymen it has been the tranquillity of a dungeon'.[22] In other words the Irish patriotic principles which had so often been so eloquently invoked by the Protestant gentry and middle classes on their own behalf were now taken to their logical conclusion in a patriotism which all Irishmen might invoke equally. A new comprehensive Irish patriotism was on offer to all.

3

United Irishmen
and Defenders

Tone himself almost at once ceased to play any active part in the Society of United Irishmen. He concerned himself more and more with the agitation for Catholic rights by Keogh's Catholic Committee of which he became a salaried official in the course of 1792. In his own words he sank 'into obscurity'[1] in the affairs of the United Irishmen which were conducted by men like Napper Tandy and William Drennan, a doctor, who probably wrote the Dublin broadsheet of the summer and certainly coined for Ireland the phrase 'the Emerald Isle'. Other active members of the Society at this stage were two young lawyer brothers from Cork, Henry and John Sheares, and a wealthy Wexford land-owner named Beauchamp Bagenal Harvey. All of them, like Tone, were Protestants, though Catholics did in fact join the Society in considerable numbers.

However, Tone kept up his personal links with Neilson and the branch of the United Irishmen in Belfast, and visited them twice during the summer of 1792. Each time he was again confronted by the gap between United Irish aspirations and the realities of the situation in Ireland.

He went to Belfast, for instance, to celebrate the third anniversary of the storming of the Bastille, an occasion on which he was to address some of the Northern Volunteer corps. '... Expect sharp opposition to-morrow,' he wrote in his diary the day before. 'Some of the country corps no better than Peep o' Day Boys ...' Neilson, returning to his hotel that evening, and passing a half-open door behind which he heard a voice he recognized, pushed it open to discover one of the Volunteer Captains haranguing against the Catholics.[2]

Soon afterwards Tone journeyed from Belfast to the small town of Rathfriland to investigate personally the scenes of recent clashes between Peep o' Day Boys and Defenders. Several people had been killed on both sides. Great offence was being taken by the Protestants at the Catholics 'marching about in military array and firing shots at unseasonable times'.[3] Tone claimed to find that the Protestants were universally the aggressors, and that on the whole the Catholics seemed not to 'do anything worse than meet in large bodies and fire powder; foolish certainly but not wicked'.[4] Some days later a gentleman of Sligo gave Tone 'a most melancholy account' of the depression and insult under which Catholics of that town were labouring. '. . . Every Protestant rascal breaks their heads and windows for his amusement . . . the Catholic spirit quite broken.'[5]

On a third visit to Belfast, in August 1792, travelling to Rathfriland again with John Keogh of the Catholic Committee, he found that the landlord in the inn would not even give them rooms there when he knew who they were. And that day he saw some 150 Peep o' Day Boys exercising within a quarter of a mile of the town. The boisterous optimism with which he countered such evidence is revealed by a diary entry he made only three days later, on 14 August, after visiting the shipyards with an industrialist member of the United Irishmen named Henry Joy McCracken:

> Walk out and see McCracken's new ship, the Hibernia. Hibernia has an English Crown on her shield. We all roar at him. . . . The Co. Down getting better everyday on the Catholic question. Two of the new companies applied to be admitted in the Union regiment * . . . were refused membership on the ground of their holding Peep O' Day principles. *Bon* . . . Lurgan† green as usual. Something will come out of all this. Agree to talk the matter over to-morrow when we are all cool. Huzza: Generally drunk. Vive la Nation! . . . Generally very drunk. Bed. God knows how.[6]

Tone's optimistic frivolity was far more damaging to his constructive political thought than his drinking, which was probably no more than any spirited young man of his background engaged in. He was not an alcoholic but he was a chronic optimist. Finding that a new Volunteer corps which had been raised in Ballinahinch had actually been raised on Peep o' Day principles, he pondered less the long-term implications of such an incident than the short-term success of one McClockey who, temporarily at any rate, converted them to the principles of the United Irish Society and was chosen lieutenant of the company in return. 'All well,' wrote Tone cheerfully, '. . . Both parties now in high affection with each other, who were before ready to cut each other's throats.'[7]

In Dublin in November 1792, together with Tandy, Tone set about the formation of a new corps of city Volunteers, devoted to United Irish principles. They were to wear a uniform with buttons embossed with the Irish harp without the Crown above, and similar to that of the National Guard of Paris, after whom it was to be called.

'Is that quite wise?' commented Tone in his diary. 'Who cares?'[8]

He had to note that there was not all that much enthusiasm for the idea, and indeed owing to the lack of sufficient support for such a republican manifestation this National Guard never paraded in public.[9] Tone, however,

---

* i.e., the United Irishmen.
† A town in County Armagh.

took comfort from the fact that it was becoming fashionable for Dubliners to address each other as 'Citizen' in the French fashion, and that 'trifling as it is, it is a symptom'.[10] An even more encouraging symptom was that on the anniversary of William of Orange's birthday the remnants of the old Dublin Volunteers had not paraded as usual round his statue on College Green, but had simply held a normal parade wearing 'national' green cockades instead of the traditional orange ones. 'This is striking proof', wrote Tone optimistically, 'of the change of men's sentiments when "Our Glorious Deliverer" is neglected. This is the first time the day has passed uncommemorated since the institution of the Volunteers. Huzza! Union and the people for ever!'[11]

However, the Dublin Volunteers by this time numbered no more than 250 men,[12] and the Great Deliverer's birthday was hardly neglected by others, as *The Times* newspaper recorded. After 'a splendid appearance' at noon of the nobility and other persons of distinction to compliment the lord lieutenant on the anniversary, the lord lieutenant himself, attended by the nobility and gentry and escorted by a squadron of horse, went in procession round King William's statue. Guns in the Phoenix Park fired a salute which was answered by volleys from regiments of the garrison drawn up on College Green, and at night there were bonfires, illuminations 'and other demonstrations of joy'.[13] If Tone's concept of an Irish Union* was to progress beyond the Huzzas of his own diary, or the parochial deliberations of intellectual societies in Dublin and Belfast, this formidable establishment and the automatic respect it commanded had somehow to be assaulted.

In fact, Tone in his capacity as an official of the Catholic Committee was already on the point of breaching one bastion in the Establishment's position. He and Keogh, besides making intensive propaganda for the Catholic cause, had, in this year 1792, succeeded in bringing about a Convention of elected Catholic delegates sitting in Dublin, the first representative body of Catholics to meet in Ireland since the Parliament of James II over a century before. And together Tone and Keogh played an important part in applying pressure which in 1793 helped lead to the admission of Catholics to the vote on exactly the same terms as Protestants.

The passing of this further Catholic Relief Act in 1793 was in itself testimony to the sycophancy and impotence of the so-called independent Irish Parliament. For the year before, this Parliament had overwhelmingly rejected exactly the same measure, because the government in England had not been in favour of it. Now, in 1793, the English Government under Pitt was prepared to accept the measure and it was passed on 9 April. Also,

---

* Anyone studying the years preceding the Parliamentary Union of 1801 will be struck by the extent to which the terms 'the Union' and 'the Irish Union' were then in current usage to express a sense very different from that which eventually became so familiar. Throughout these years 'the Union' is constantly used to mean that union of all Irishmen, independent of Britain, at which the United Irishmen were aiming.

early in 1793 occurred an event of the greatest importance which was to colour the attitudes of both government and would-be reformers in Ireland for many years to come. This was the outbreak in February 1793 of war between England and France.

On the outbreak of war, the English Prime Minister's immediate concern over Ireland was to prevent the country from becoming a seat of disaffection which France could exploit. And in this respect the recently passed Catholic Relief Act was distinctly helpful. Tone had more than once noted with some apprehension that the Catholics might not be interested in any political aim beyond their own sectarian Emancipation. Once when Grattan had said to him that he thought of the Catholic question only as a means of advancing the general good, Tone had commented: 'Right! But do the Catholics consider it so? The devil a bit except one or two of them.'[14]

Pitt did not grant full Emancipation and there was, as Tone pointed out, a ludicrous inconsistency in granting the vote to the peasant Catholic forty-shilling freeholder and yet continuing to disallow Catholic gentry to sit in Parliament.* So that some grounds for resentment remained. But the Act was undoubtedly a major concession encouraging Catholics to look no further than their own sectarian interests when contemplating political goals.

Meanwhile, almost entirely dissociated from the middle-class reformers represented in the Society of United Irishmen and the Catholic Committee, the peasantry had been stirring on its own account. For the first time in Irish history the Irish common people had begun to take something like primitive political action of their own. In Louth and Meath, counties adjacent to Ulster where Catholics were in the majority, the Defenders were assuming a more and more aggressive role. Their activities were still very like those of the agrarian secret societies already so long a feature of Irish rural life, and for many who took part in the raiding of gentlemen's houses for arms and horses there can have been little distinction in their minds between these and the familiar Whiteboy raids of the past. However, the vague political innuendoes in the Defender oath for those who chose to see them, and the general revolutionary infection of the time, gave a rather more generalized attitude to protests which in the past had been limited and localized. In the South, where the Defender Society as such had not yet superimposed itself on the old Whiteboy system as it was soon to do, raids when they occurred were described as simple Whiteboy activities, as for instance on the night of 17 September 1792 when arms, horses, bridles and saddles were taken from

---

* 'During the whole progress of the Catholic question', Tone wrote, 'a favourite and plausible topic with their enemies was the ignorance and bigotry of the multitude ... If the Catholics deserved what has been granted, they deserved what has been withheld; if they did not deserve what has been withheld, what has been granted should have been refused.' (op. cit., i, p. 100.)

houses near Cork.[15] But in other parts of Ireland a new organized pattern of such activity under the banner of the Defenders was becoming unmistakable.

Defenders, acting more and more on the principle that attack was the best form of defence, had started appearing in armed bodies in Louth in April 1792 and by the end of the year they had spread to Meath, Cavan, Monaghan and other predominantly Catholic counties adjacent to the Protestant areas of Ulster, and had attacked some forty houses for arms in County Louth alone, mostly successfully. In the last week of December they assembled in very large numbers first at Dunleer and then at Dundalk, armed with guns and pitchforks. Their exact purpose was not clear, but it was thought that they would possibly try to liberate a large number of convicts then collected in that area from all over the North on their way to transportation. There were no military available to deal with them, but *The Times* reported that 'the respectable inhabitants of the town, principally Roman Catholics, went among them, and having conferred with them for some time they dispersed'.[16]

On 9 January 1793 *The Times* again referred to 'those infatuated and deluded people', the Defenders, being involved in an engagement with troops at Carrickmacross. The 'insurrection' was reported to be spreading, and the insurgents' aims were variously described as sometimes the abolition of tithes, sometimes the Towering of rents. '... In Louth,' said *The Times*, 'the first object seems to be to get arms and ammunition.'[17] There was another engagement with the military later in January, this time at Kells, in County Meath, and eighteen Defenders were killed.[18]

A correspondent from the Bishop of Meath's palace at Ardbracken wrote in February 1793: 'Not a night passes that the Defenders do not assemble and break open houses in some part or other of this country', and he recounted how 150 of them on foot and horseback with a drum and three sledges had raided Lord Maxwell's house, where, however, 'they had behaved with some degree of politeness'. After taking three double-barrelled guns, two muskets and two cases of pistols, his Lordship, who was particularly fond of one of the cases of pistols, asked if he could buy it back from them. The Defenders complimented him on his taste and returned it to him, refusing the money. 'This house', wrote the correspondent, 'now looks more like a Bastille than a Bishop's Palace, from the quantity of bolts, bars and cross barricades on the doors and windows of the house and offices.'[19]

On 22 February 1793 *The Times* drew attention to what was different about this outbreak of disturbances from previous Whiteboy activities. 'The disturbances in Ireland', it wrote – much too sweepingly in fact – 'are not on account of any complaint of grievances. They arise from the pure wantonness of a set of desperadoes called Defenders ... encouraged and abetted by a secret Junto, that like the French Jacobins, wish to throw all government into confusion ...'[20]

Retribution of course was not long in catching up with such a primitively organized movement, and the Defenders were soon being hanged in droves. In the months of March and April 1793 alone, sixty-eight Defenders were reported by *The Times* as being sentenced to death while a further seventy-seven were sentenced to transportation for administering or taking the Defender oath. But the cheapness with which the Defenders regarded life right up to the final bloodbath of 1798 was always the most impressive tribute to the desperation with which they pursued their confused cause. And though the sentence of capital punishment was at this period a particularly savage one, including as it did the phrase '... but being yet alive, should be cut down, but being alive their bowels be taken out and burned before their faces',[21] it seems to have had surprisingly little force as a deterrent. More than two years later an Irish government official was writing to the English Prime Minister: 'Defenderism puzzles me more and more; but it certainly grows more alarming daily, as the effect of the executions seems to be at an end and there is an enthusiasm defying punishment.'[22]

The intensity of Defender activity varied from time to time, but as a crudely organized secret system, controlled apparently by a shadowy and probably rather ineffectual central committee, it was throughout the 1790s superimposing itself on all already existing secret society organizations in Catholic Ireland, giving them for the first time some appearance of uniformity and at least a primitive political tinge. Where any particular grievance was uppermost the Defenders now organized crude protest. Their significance lay in the fact that they were expressing, however incoherently, for the first time in Irish history, something like a national resentment of the long general grievance of the Irish common people's everyday suffering.

Soon after the outbreak of war between England and France, Pitt began to balance his conciliatory approach to Irish Catholics with strictly defensive measures. At almost the same time as the Catholic Relief Act, an Act went through the Irish Parliament creating an Irish militia whose rank and file were to be drawn by ballot from among the peasantry. The government's refusal at first to allow substitutes for those drawn for this militia led to widespread resistance which was organized by the Defenders. By June 1793 reports of anti-militia riots were coming in from all over Ireland.

The Times reported from Sligo: 'The abstracts of the Militia Act which have been lately circulated through this country operated like electric fire on the weak understanding of the poor uninformed multitude.'[23] Reports, possibly exaggerated, spoke of bands of six or seven thousand men roving the Sligo countryside, and it was noted that two Catholic country gentlemen in particular, one actually a delegate to the recent Catholic Convention in Dublin, had been treated with uncommon cruelty when their houses had been raided by the Defenders for arms. Nineteen Defenders were killed and several prisoners taken at a battle at Boyle in County Roscommon; eight more were killed at Manor Hamilton in County Leitrim, and a further large anti-militia assembly was reported from Baltinglass in County Wicklow, all within a few days.

In July 1793 the most serious engagement of all took place just outside the town of Wexford, where fifty of the recruited militia under a Major Valloton confronted some two thousand Defenders, armed with guns, scythes and picks. The Defenders demanded the return of two men taken prisoner a few days earlier. While a parley was taking place between the two sides the Major was suddenly struck down and killed, whereupon the militia fired, killing some eighty Defenders and putting the rest to flight. The leader of the Defenders, a young farmer of twenty-two named John Moore, whose legs were broken by the militia's first volley, fought on his stumps until his men fled. He himself was then shot out of hand. Five prisoners taken were executed two days later.

Grievances over the enrolment of the militia were largely met by government concessions which allowed voluntary enlistment as well as conscription by ballot, and at the same time permitted substitutes to be found for those upon whom the ballot fell. But one significant feature had emerged from these events: the loyal behaviour of those militia whom the Defenders had engaged in the Wexford incident. For it was to be by the Catholic militia itself, drawn from exactly the same class as the Defenders, that the Defenders were eventually to be crushed.

The Defender system, which continued to grow dramatically after the particular grievance of the militia had abated, was almost as much of a puzzle to the radical middle-class members of the Society of United Irishmen and the Catholic Committee as it was to the government. Certainly they seem to have known little about the Defenders for a long time, though a Committee of the (Irish) House of Lords which reported in 1793 claimed that there was a liaison between the leaders of the Catholic Committee and the Defenders.[24] However, the experiences suffered by the Catholic gentry at the Defenders' hands makes this improbable, and the allegation seems to have been based solely on the fact that the Catholic Committee had subscribed funds for some of the unfortunate peasants facing trial. The Catholic Committee, besides refuting the House of Lords committee's charge, issued a strong condemnation of the Defenders on their own account, describing them, like The Times, as 'deluded people', expressing their 'utmost detestation and abhorrence of such illegal and criminal proceedings' and calling upon 'these unhappy men ... to desist from such unwarrantable acts of violence ... and to return to their obedience to the laws and the laudable pursuits of honest industry'.[25] The Catholic Bishops in Dublin also issued a strong condemnation of Defenderism.

Tone described the Defenders contemptuously as 'rabble',[26] though he had some correspondence with them. Nevertheless, for middle-class Protestant radicals already thinking in terms of a republican attempt at revolution, the Defenders were clearly a force of great significance about whom it was necessary to become better informed. Napper Tandy, in the summer of 1793, met some Defender leaders at Castlebellingham in County Louth and took the Defender oath, but he was betrayed by an informer and fled for his life, first to America and then to France. Such knowledge of the Defenders as was held in middle-class reforming and radical circles at this time was later summed up by the United Irishman, Thomas Emmet, as follows: 'The Defenders were bound together by oaths obviously drawn up by illiterate men, different in different places, but all promising secrecy and specifying whatever grievance was, in each place, most felt and understood. ... The views of these men were in general far from distinct.'[27] There was, he continued, some sort of 'national notion that ... something ought to be done for Ireland' but nothing more precise than that, except that arms would be necessary and therefore had to be procured.

Meanwhile, in Dublin and Belfast, the Society of United Irishmen, that more sophisticated and articulate body which also held the notion that 'something ought to be done for Ireland', was making singularly little progress. In Dublin it had continued to issue stirring addresses to the Irish nation and particularly to the remnants of the Volunteers.

'Citizen Soldiers to Arms!' it had proclaimed in December 1792, desperately trying to animate the old Volunteering spirit with the new principles of revolutionary France on behalf of parliamentary reform. 'Fourteen long years are elapsed since the rise of your associations, and in 1782 did you imagine that in 1792 this nation would still remain unrepresented ...?'[28]

While the Catholic Convention was still sitting in Dublin the Society of United Irishmen made its theoretical position clear:

'The Catholic cause is subordinate to our cause and included in it, for as United Irishmen we adhere to no sect but to society.... In the sincerity of our souls do we desire catholic emancipation, but were it obtained tomorrow, to-morrow we would go on, as we do to-day, in the pursuit of that reform as well as our own.'[29] And on 25 January 1793 with a cry of 'Ireland! O! Ireland!' the society put forward its plan for reform which consisted of universal male adult suffrage with annual parliaments.

In spirit the society resembled very much those democratic clubs and societies which had become so much a feature of the radical scene in England: the London Corresponding Society, the Constitutional Society and the 'Friends of the People' to the last of which a member of the Irish House of Commons, Lord Edward Fitzgerald, younger son of the Duke of Leinster, already belonged. There was even in England a society of United Englishmen. What aggravated an otherwise similar situation in Ireland to such a dangerous pitch for the government was the combination of such activity with a French threat of invasion and such a significant quantity of open peasant unrest. The Society of United Irishmen itself was at this time hardly one to give the government much concern. But in the prevailing circumstances they could not afford to take any chances with it. Not long after the outbreak of war early in 1793, all the remaining Volunteer corps in Ireland were suppressed. And in Dublin the government had already begun a long and successful tradition of informers when they started receiving inside information of the proceedings of the Dublin Society of United Irishmen within six weeks of its foundation[30]* Their informer's news was reassuring. He reported that the affairs of the society were in fact at a low ebb, and attendance had sunk to around thirty. Its most energetic and uncompromising leader, Napper Tandy, was in exile; another official, Hamilton Rowan, had been found guilty of seditious libel and was in prison. Tone himself was preoccupied with agitation for full Catholic Emancipation.

Thomas Emmet, a barrister who was already a member of the society and in a later phase was to become one of its principal leaders, wrote of this period: 'The expectations of the reformers had been blasted, their plans had been defeated, and decisive means had been taken by government to prevent their being resumed. It became necessary to wait for new events, from which might be found new plans. Nor did such events seem distant, for now the French arms were again emblazoning their cause with success and hiding in the splendour of their victories the atrocities of their government.'[31]

* From a linen merchant, Thomas Collins.

French Contacts

With France successful in arms all over Europe, and England emerging as her chief enemy, the war sharpened all attitudes in Ireland to extremes.

The French, in spite of, indeed partly because of, the presence of large numbers of *émigré* Irish families in Paris, were not particularly up to date in their information about Ireland. But they had begun to show a new interest in her since the very beginning of the Revolution. An agent sent to Dublin in 1789, discerning new trends, had reported in 1790: 'A few years more and the Irish may form a nation which they have not been for 600 years.'[1] In December 1792 another agent, impressed presumably by the renewed activities of the old Volunteer companies in Ulster and by contacts with the United Irishmen in Dublin and Belfast, had reported dramatically if prematurely that under the guidance of six or seven daring conspirators an Irish revolution was being prepared and France might find a powerful ally in Ireland in the coming struggle.[2] In the following year, 1793, another special emissary from France appeared, this time with an introduction to the now notoriously radical Irish aristocrat, Lord Edward Fitzgerald.

Fitzgerald, who was twenty-nine, had been for many years an officer in the British Army, and had served with heroism in action against the American colonists. He was now one of those Irishmen who were most sympathetic to the French revolutionary cause. From Paris he had written enthusiastic letters to his mother dated '1st Year of the Republic', signing himself 'le citoyen Edouard Fitzgerald'.[3] In November 1792 he had attended a dinner in Paris to celebrate the great French victory at Jemappes and had there proposed a toast that the Marseillaise might 'soon become the favourite music of every army'. This was too much for the British Army and shortly afterwards he was dismissed from its service. The following January, 1793, Fitzgerald shocked the Irish House of Commons by declaring that the lord lieutenant and the majority of the House were the worst subjects the king had. He must have seemed a natural contact for the French. In fact, Fitzgerald, who was not then a member of the United Irishmen, passed the new agent on to the society but they would have nothing to do with him. Next year, however, the French sent another agent to Ireland whose mission was to have much more widespread repercussions.

This new agent was an Anglican clergyman of Irish descent named Jackson who had lived in France professing radical views for the past three years. He now came to Dublin as a secret emissary of the French Committee of Public Safety. He was an inexpert choice, and displayed little skill for the subtlety and security demanded by his new profession. However, his mission to Ireland became a sensation for he was accompanied throughout it by an old friend from London, a solicitor called Cockayne, now acting, unknown to Jackson, as a counter-spy for the British Government. Cockayne reported to London everything that happened, though he found his assignment a considerable strain, complaining to his masters that Jackson would never let him go to bed before 2 a.m. without at least three bottles of claret, whereas he was used to no more than a pint of wine. '. . . Besides,' he added, 'the expense is enormous.'⁴ It may have been this that caused Cockayne to turn out little more competent as a counter-agent than the man on whom he was keeping watch. Though Jackson himself was arrested, little hard evidence of treason had been acquired against those with whom he had been in contact. The government had to admit to themselves that Cockayne would 'not speak positively to the different conversations of these persons, but only caught the substance by hints and accidental words'.⁵ And when after nearly a year's delay Jackson was eventually brought to trial in 1794 the nature of Cockayne's evidence must have proved exasperating to the Crown. Asked if he had heard a certain conversation he replied:

'Yes.'
'Did you understand it?'
'Yes, in part.'
'How do you mean, in part?'
'They were at one corner of the room and I in another with a book in my hand and I did not hear enough to hear what they said.'⁶

The two men whose conversation he had in part overheard were Jackson himself and Wolfe Tone.

Tone was at this time disillusioned both with the incomplete nature of the Catholic Relief Act of 1793 and with the Catholics themselves for not pressing for total Emancipation more forcefully. He was reluctantly coming to the conclusion that the only hope of making his theory of a united Irish nation materialize was revolution. He was not by nature a violent or bloodthirsty man and had, for instance, deprecated in his diary the need for Louis XVI's execution. But now a fellow lawyer, Leonard Macnally, introduced Jackson to him as an emissary from the Committee of Public Safety who held out the hope that if the state of Ireland were properly known in France she would be prepared to help the Irish win their independence. Tone replied that 'it would be a most severe and grievous remedy for our abuses' but that he saw no other.⁷

The day after the meeting with Jackson, Tone rashly committed to paper his view on the state of Ireland and the likelihood of the country's favourable response to a French invasion. He showed the paper to Jackson. It was a typically optimistic document inspired more by a regard for the facts as they might have been than as they were. 'In a word,' summarized Tone, 'from reason, reflection, interest, prejudice, the spirit of change, the misery of the great bulk of the nation, and above all the hatred of the English name, resulting from the tyranny of near seven centuries, there seems little doubt that an invasion in sufficient force would be supported by the people. There is scarcely an army in the country, and the militia, the bulk of whom are Catholics, would to a moral certainty refuse to act, if they saw such a force as they could look to for support.'[8] The resolute performance of the militia against the Defenders at Wexford was something he appeared to ignore.

Though the desirability of sending someone back to France to urge Tone's point of view in person was also discussed, Tone made it clear that he himself could not go because of family ties. However, even by this degree of contact with the French agent, he was most seriously compromised. And a few days later a copy of his paper came into the government's hands. As Tone himself put it, his situation was 'a very critical one'.[9]

The immediate effect of Jackson's arrest was to cause the flight of some of those United Irishmen with whom he had been in contact. Hamilton Rowan, for instance, escaped from the prison where he was serving his sentence for libel and where Jackson had been able to visit him, and fled romantically by horseback and fishing vessel to France. But the effect of Jackson's arrest on another United Irishman, Macnally, the lawyer who had introduced Jackson to Tone and others, was of greater importance. For Macnally, scared by the treasonable implications of his own association with Jackson, agreed in return for immunity from prosecution and certain sums of money, to turn informer for the government. For many years he was to remain one of the government's most valuable sources of information, high as he was in the councils of the United Irishmen and other radicals, and quite unsuspected of perfidy, even defending them consistently in court on charges of the very treason from which he had been made immune. Tone himself entered into a compact with the government of a more honourable, though still rather curious sort. Making use of his aristocratic friends' influence with the government he agreed that he was in an awkward spot and declared that he would neither fly the country nor give evidence against anyone else, and would stand trial if necessary. But he added that if the government decided not to prosecute him he would voluntarily undertake to exile himself to America. The bargain was agreed to, though Tone kept his part of it in leisurely enough fashion, not leaving for America until Jackson's trial had ended a year later and, thereafter, it might be argued, breaking the spirit of the agreement if not the letter.[10]

Jackson himself, the first important contact between revolutionary

France and the potential revolutionary forces in Ireland, died a most dramatic death. The case against him was amply proved. Before the pronouncement of the inevitable sentence a legal argument took place in court about whether or not the indictment was to be read in full, as requested by Macnally, his defence counsel. The judge drew attention to the prisoner's apparent ill state of health and said that in view of it he 'would not wish to increase his labour by waiting. But do as you please . . .'.[11] During the course of the long ensuing argument between Macnally and the Attorney General it was noticed that the prisoner had grown very faint, and the court ordered the windows to be opened so that he could get some fresh air. Later still it was noticed that 'the prisoner having sunk upon his chair appeared to be in a state of extreme debility'. And when the judge came to pronounce sentence he declared:

'If the prisoner is in a state of insensibility it is impossible that I can pronounce the judgement of the court on him . . . humanity and common-sense would require that he should be in a state of sensibility.'

A doctor, called to remedy this unsatisfactory state of affairs, himself pronounced of the prisoner that 'there was every apprehension that he would go off immediately'. A juryman, who was a chemist, then stepped down from the box and declared the prisoner 'verging to eternity with every symptom of death about him'. The slumped figure was about to be carried from the court when the Sheriff finally pronounced him dead. An inquest was ordered and the body left in the dock until nine o'clock next morning when a surgeon found nearly a pint of 'some acrid and mortal matter . . . a metallic poison' in his stomach, which had been the cause of death. It is said that on entering court on the last day Jackson had whispered to Macnally a cryptic suicide line from Otway's *Venice Preserved* – 'We have deceived the Senate' – and certainly in his pocket was found a verse from the Psalms which read 'O keep my Soul and deliver me. Let me be not ashamed, for I put my trust in thee.'

Jackson's arrest and subsequent trial and suicide mark a watershed in the series of events which were to reach their bloody climax in 1798. Immediately on his arrest, the hitherto legal and constitutional Society of United Irishmen was suppressed. At the same time, would-be reformers had to face the fact that every attempt at achieving parliamentary reform by constitutional means, such as those initiated by Grattan and his friends, seemed permanently doomed to founder hopelessly in the Irish House of Commons.

To confirm this sense of hopelessness there had taken place, just before the trial itself, a curious political incident. After a political change in England by which a Whig element joined forces with Pitt's administration, a new viceroy, Lord Fitzwilliam, was appointed to Ireland. Fitzwilliam was prepared to recommend total Catholic Emancipation to the Irish House of Commons. But as a result not so much of this attitude – though it caused difficulties enough for Pitt with the king and the Irish executive – but of Fitzwilliam's attempt at some parliamentary reforming from within by dismantling the hereditary grip held on the Irish parliamentary system by one of the leading Irish families, the Beresfords, the new Viceroy was recalled. Tone himself in February 1795 accompanied a last desperate delegation of the Catholic Committee to London to try and prevent the recall. Six weeks after Fitzwilliam's departure and ten days after Jackson's death, he kept his compact with the government and sailed from Belfast for America.

Before leaving he learnt of the existence of a new secret organization which had come into being in Belfast in 1794 when the old open Society of United Irishmen was suppressed. Its existence was until then as unknown to him as it was to the government. Its nucleus was one of the Belfast United Irish societies which had somehow escaped the government's attention and had continued to meet in secret. Merged together with some members of another political club as a secret society they had decided to resume the former name of United Irishmen, but to replace the old test of membership by an oath which left room for republican sentiments. Samuel Neilson was once again one of the prime movers of the organization, which consisted in its early days principally of mechanics, petty shop-keepers and farmers, though as it grew it embraced members higher and higher up in the middle-class social scale. At a meeting on 10 May 1795, seventy-two secretly elected delegates met in Belfast to coordinate a planned system of district, county and eventually pro- vincial and national committees, though at that time the organization in fact extended little further than the two Ulster counties of Antrim and Down. After business the chairman asked every delegate what he stood for and got the answer: 'A republican government and separation from England.'[12]

Tone was asked by Neilson to pass information about the growing strength of this new organization on to the French Government through its Minister in Philadelphia, the port to which he was sailing. A most important part of the new United Irishmen's secret plans to which Tone had been introduced was their intention of contacting and coordinating their efforts with the Defenders.

5
Defenders and Orangemen

Jackson's trial, apart from anything else, had had the effect of publicizing the serious interest the French now had in Ireland. Fitzwilliam's recall and the denial of total emancipation, though of little practical relevance to the peasantry, made for a hardening of their emotional attitudes.

The Defender organization had in any case continued to be active throughout 1794 and was now spreading over the whole of Ireland. In March, at Kinsale, County Cork, a body of Defenders was dispersed with ten killed – again significantly by the (Catholic) Carlow militia.[1] There were as many as 185 Defenders under arrest in Cork gaol that month alone, while on the North-East circuit some three hundred more were awaiting trial at Trim, Dundalk and Drogheda.[2] On 21 May an engagement was reported from County Cavan in which between one hundred and two hundred Defenders were killed.[3] And in the same month seventy were killed in Ballina, County Mayo.[4] By the summer of 1795, when the new secret society of United Irishmen was still only just completing its skeleton organization, there were already thirteen different Irish counties from which armed bodies of Defenders, usually numbering hundreds and sometimes thousands at a time, were being reported.[5]

In several counties the Defenders, who held their own primitive courts, were sufficiently strong to intimidate juries in the normal courts of law and secure acquittals against all the evidence. In return the government embarked for the first time on its own course of rough justice by rounding up the peasantry in those parts of the country where the Defender movement was strong and transporting them without trial into the navy.

Lord Camden, the new Viceroy who replaced Fitzwilliam, commented on the way in which blacksmiths everywhere were being organized by the Defenders to make pikes.[6] But the structure of the Defender system, though widespread, seems to have been a very loose one, varying from county to county with different oaths and recognition signs. Objectives too were still often local: the lowering of rent or the increase of wages. Nevertheless, pervading always what was often no more than old-fashioned Whiteboy activity were the new fashions of French liberty and the doctrines of Tom Paine – 'the whiskey of infidelity and treason' as the Solicitor General once described them.[7] Indeed, the vague feeling that 'something ought to be done for Ireland', and that the opportunity would come when the French landed, was spreading very like some cloudy intoxication.

Such feelings were actively encouraged by Defender organizers who moved from county to county, often with only the most rudimentary regard for security. Known as 'committee men', they received a shilling for each new Defender they enrolled, a fact which may well have accounted for the rashness and eagerness of their approach. Public houses were a favourite place for the transaction. 'Where are you going?' a man might be asked.

'To the Defender maker,' would come the reply, as readily as if he were off to the shoemaker.[8]

The new recruit might be asked to swear, as in one Defender oath of 1795, 'to be true to the present United States of France and Ireland and every other kingdom now in Christianity'.[9] He would follow this with a number of equally solemn expressions of Masonic brotherly obligation. At other times the old ambiguous formula of swearing loyalty to the king '. . . whilst I live under the same government . . .' still did service. After a glass of punch, perhaps,[10] and the oath on the prayer book, the new Defender would be instructed in a strange sort of catechism.

'What is your designs?'
'On freedom.'
'Where is your designs?'
'The foundation of it is grounded upon a rock.'
'What is the password?'
'Eliphismatis.'[11]

(Asked in court the meaning of the word 'eliphismatis' one sworn Defender said he didn't know but that it was Latin. Counsel dismissed it as mere 'trash of enigmatical or rather nonsensical import'.)

Another similar Defender catechism ran:

'Are you a Christian?'
'I am.'
'By what?'
'By baptism . . .'
'Are you consecrated?'
'I am.'
'By what?'
'To the National Convention – to equal all nations – to dethrone all Kings, and plant the tree of liberty on our Irish land – whilst the French Defenders will protect our cause and the Irish Defenders pull down the British laws . . .'[12]

There would be instruction in recognition signs: 'Two hands joined backwards on top of the head and pretend to yawn, then draw the hands down upon the knee or on the table. Answer by drawing the right hand over the forehead and return it to the back of the left hand.' A less complicated form of greeting seems to have been, on shaking hands, to press the thumb of the right hand on the back of the other's – 'and not be afraid to hurt the person' – coupled with pronunciation of the magic password 'Eliphismatis'.[13]

There would be talk of the need to get arms to help the French, and if, as frequently happened, through the action of an informer, the novitiate soon afterwards fell into the hands of the law, he would be tried with full solemnity for associating '. . . with several false traitors associated under the name of Defenders, to aid, assist and adhere to persons exercising the powers of government in France in case they should invade Ireland'.[14]

Yet the crude nature of many of the Defenders' proceedings make it clear that in so far as it was a national conspiracy it was a very clumsy one and ill-organized. Such practical projects as came to light involving anything more than arming in preparation for a French landing seem to have been of the most primitive sort. In 1793 a society called the Philanthropic Society, which later merged with the Defenders, had a theoretical plan to take Dublin Castle, the seat of government, by sending in a hundred of its members disguised in the scarlet coats of soldiers, but nothing came of it.[15] When, early in 1794, Jackson finally came up for trial, the same society had a plan to kidnap Cockayne the British counter-spy, the night before the trial opened – but this plan too came to nothing.[16] The next year some Dublin Defenders had a plan to take the powder magazine in the Phoenix Park and seize Dublin Castle, and 'to put all the nobility to death there',[17] but again nothing happened. The carelessness endemic in many Defender proceedings is revealed by one ardent Defender who failed to prevent his wife being seen hiding sixty musket balls 'in a dirt hole' and who himself openly asked his lodging-house keeper if he could let him have a room where a society could meet.[18]

Some of the Defender oaths were of the wildest sort and often contained ominous portents for the future. Thus, as early as February 1795, a group of Defenders declared that they would have no king, would recover their estates, 'sweep clean the Protestants, kill the Lord Lieutenant and leave none alive'.[19] The gap which was later to prove so fatal between the semi-literate mass Defender movement and the more sophisticated world of the Belfast and Dublin radicals is here well illustrated by the fact that while Defenders were taking this oath the Lord Lieutenant was still Lord Fitzwilliam, the centre of sophisticated Catholic hopes. Indeed, the crude sectarian spirit of the Defenders, which though little more at first than a defensive mark of identity was the very opposite of the goal at which the United Irishmen were aiming, was on the increase. At least one Protestant Defender in 1795 who had been passing himself off as a Catholic among his colleagues turned informer on hearing that 'as soon as the harvest was in' the Defenders would rise against the Protestants and put them all to death.[20]

This sectarian element in the Defender system was heightened and developed by the continual feuding between Defenders and Peep o' Day Boys which was now more than ever a feature of the North. The tension in these areas, growing as it did from economic competition, had understandably been aggravated by the recent political progress of the Catholics. Catholic forty-shilling freeholders had been admitted to the vote in 1793. Now total Emancipation itself, raising Catholics to full equal status with Protestants, had become a burning issue of the day and at one time looked like becoming a reality at any moment. The Protestants felt themselves more than ever threatened.

The new outbreak of feuding in the North reached its climax in September 1795 at the so-called Battle of the Diamond, a piece of ground near the town of Armagh. A large party of Defenders attacked a party of Peep o' Day Boys there and got the worst of it, leaving twenty or thirty corpses on the field. The incident, which in itself constituted nothing new, is a historical landmark since it led the Peep o' Day Boys to reorganize under a name which was to play an increasingly significant role in the future of Ireland: the Orange Society – the colour orange having long been a popular symbol with which to celebrate the victory of William of Orange over James II a century before.

For the time being the Orangemen remained a crude organization, successors to the Peep o' Day Boys, turning Catholics out of their homes with great brutality that often ended in murder. An alternative was to affix to the doors of Catholics such threats as 'To Hell – or Connaught' or 'Go to Hell – Connaught won't receive you – fire and faggot. Will Thresham and John Thrustout.'[21] Those Catholics thus 'papered', as it was called, seeing the barbarous punishments inflicted on those who did not obey, usually took the hint and left for Connaught. At the end of 1795, at a famous meeting of northern magistrates, all but one of whom were Protestants, the Orangemen were described by Lord Gosford, Governor of Armagh, as 'a lawless banditti' carrying out a ferocious persecution of Roman Catholics simply because they professed that faith. Sending the unanimous resolutions of his magistrates, condemning the Orangemen, to the Chief Secretary, Gosford wrote: 'Of late no night passes that houses are not destroyed, and scarce a week that some dreadful murders are not committed. Nothing can exceed the animosity between Protestant and Catholic at this moment in this county...'[22]

But though the Defenders in other parts of Ireland were inflamed by news of these atrocities, the driving force behind their own organization still remained the poverty which so often went together with their religion, rather than their religion for its own sake. Catholicism was the mark of their identity. Their increasingly sectarian spirit denoted not proselytizing zeal but assertion of rights for that identity. They continued to be strongly condemned by the Catholic Church, and some of the worst Defender outrages were committed against Catholic magistrates. Where the Defenders were opposed by members of their own class and religion, as in the various county militias, they found themselves regarded not primarily as Catholics but as rebellious trash, and as such were fought and defeated.

In 1795 a Kildare schoolmaster called Laurence O'Connor was tried for administering a Defender oath 'to be loyal to all brother Defenders and the French'. The judge declared astonishingly before passing the inevitable death sentence that 'there was no country in Europe where a poor man had more advantages than in Ireland'. The prisoner was asked if he had anything to say. After listing the grievances of the poor, chief of which were the fantastically high rents, O'Connor concluded that 'prosecutions were not the means of bringing about peace in the country; but if the rich would alleviate the sufferings of the poor, they would hear no more of risings or Defenders, and the country would rest in peace and happiness'.[23]

The man's head, which was severed from his body 'with no great dexterity',[24] ended up on a seven-foot spike outside the gaol at Naas. His words were echoed a few months later by a very different sort of Irishman, Lord Edward Fitzgerald, who, speaking almost for the last time in the Irish House of Commons in February 1796, attacked the Insurrection Act which the government then introduced in an attempt to break the Defenders and tranquillize the country. Nothing, said Lord Edward, would in fact tranquillize the country but the sincere endeavour of the government to redress the grievances of the people. If that was done the people would return to their allegiance.[25]

This Insurrection Act, which was passed in March 1796, was the first of the severe measures by which the government now set about trying to counteract the danger which the Defenders presented. Though the severity of these government measures was to increase steadily over the next two years and finally reach a brutal crescendo which did much to provoke the very rebellion they were designed to prevent, it is important to understand the extreme gravity of the situation as the government now saw it. It was not just a question of establishing public order in conditions of growing anarchy. The kingdoms of Ireland and of Great Britain were at war with France, whose armies in Europe, particularly in the years 1795 and 1796, were sweeping all before them. The final logical step for France was the defeat of her one unbeaten enemy, Britain, by an invasion of England, either direct, or through Ireland.

England itself was at this time full of radical clubs, founded originally to promote a return of Parliament, but in many cases now imbued with French republican principles of an extreme sort. Many of them were arming themselves with pikes and drilling. In Sheffield alone in 1797 there were forty to fifty such small clubs; and in every important town in the north of England the picture was similar.[26] In London the Constitutional Society and the London Corresponding Society carried on near-treasonable activity, run by a secret committee of five persons. By 1797 there were more than seventy United Corresponding Societies in Great Britain. Yet the government knew that in England, in the event of French invasion, the probability was overwhelming that the majority of the British people, for all their grievances, would stand firmly and patriotically behind the government.

In Ireland the situation was very different. In the Defenders, a massive though ill-coordinated and unsophisticated conspiracy already existed, which for all its political incoherence linked a hazy pro-French republicanism to real everyday grievances, and was daily acquiring more supporters throughout the country. And this was the country open to French invasion from Atlantic ports much less easily supervised by the British Navy than those in the Channel. The government's chief force for dealing with the danger, apart from the normal processes of law, was the militia, which apart from a proportion of Protestant officers and other officers of the Catholic gentry consisted almost entirely of those very Catholic peasants and artisans who were filling the ranks of the Defenders. The Defenders were already making a bid to seduce the militia from their allegiance, and numbers were known to be taking the Defender oaths. The crime of O'Connor, the executed schoolmaster, had been that of administering a Defender oath to a private of the North Mayo militia.

The government's situation was in fact even worse than the Defender disturbances and their seduction of the militia made it seem. For the Defenders were not the only potential rebels they had to face. In the North, though not yet widely organized into any effective military conspiracy, a ready-made traditional body of radical middle-class Protestant opinion was profoundly disaffected. Disappointed for the last ten years or more in their efforts to give Parliament that broader base which would include themselves, these northern radicals had been strengthened in their natural republican instincts by the successful republican progress of the French. Here – and to a much smaller extent in the Protestant radical circles of Dublin – organized in the Society of United Irishmen was that sophisticated political approach noticably lacking in the clumsy but much more powerful organization of the Defenders. If the two hitherto distinct forces were to come together no force of government would be able to stop them. And in August 1796 Camden, the Viceroy, wrote to the British Home Minister, Portland, that the recent endeavours of the Belfast Clubs to form a junction with the Defenders had 'been attended with much success'.[27]

We have the word of the members of the Directory of United Irishmen that they themselves had no military organization, 'until the latter end of 1796'.[28] Even then, for a time its only existence was in Ulster. But plans at least for eventual revolution had begun to be formed earlier in the year. Ever since the formation of the new secret United Irish Society its members had for obvious reasons wanted to make contact with the Defenders. In 1795 and early in 1796 the northern United Irishmen sent emissaries among the Defender leaders in Meath, Dublin and elsewhere to explain the advantages of a proper unified organization with coherent political aims. The Defenders also sent deputations to Belfast.

As a result of these meetings an agreement was reached by which the Defenders undertook to incorporate their societies within the 'Union' and to take the United Irish oath. From then on United Irish organizers appeared more and more among the Defenders, explaining the political advantages of their ideas. In particular, they spread alarm about the outrages of the Orangemen in the North and made inflammatory suggestions that it was the Orangemen's intention to deal similarly with Catholics throughout Ireland. The rumour was spread that the Orangemen had entered into a solemn league and covenant 'to wade up to their knees in Papist blood'. The United Irish leaders wrote later: 'To the Armagh persecution is the Union of Irishmen most exceedingly indebted.'[29] On a short-term view they were correct, though their exploitation of it had much to do with their failure in the end. Catholics did in fact begin to think that they had no alternative but to join 'the Union'. But by inciting Catholics to join a non-sectarian organization with threats of sectarianism from another quarter, the United Irish agents were playing with fire. Inevitably they turned the higher political principles of 'the Union' into something of secondary importance, and themselves encouraged a crude sectarian hate.

Evidence of these successful overtures to the Defenders by the United Irishmen caused the government great concern, particularly as the United Irishmen were simultaneously known to be strengthening their links with France.

6

Bantry Bay

The leaders of the United Irishmen always had some reservations about seeking aid from France. This was due partly to a natural pride which made them want to achieve independence by their own efforts, and partly to a practical fear that the French might dominate Ireland once they arrived. Wolfe Tone himself wrote that he would never be accessory to 'subjecting my country to the control of France merely to get rid of that of England. We are able enough to take care of ourselves, if we were once afloat, or if we are not, we deserve to sink.'[1]

The matter of pride was resolved by what, in the circumstances, may seem a curious reference to historical precedent: namely, the acceptance of foreign intervention from William of Orange over a century before. 'We were of the opinion,' wrote one of the United Irish leaders, 'that if the people were justified in calling for foreign aid to rescue the liberties and constitution from James's government it was infinitely more justifiable in us to call in foreign aid.'[2] The statement shows the deeply Protestant radical cast of mind of even the most sophisticated leaders of the United Irishmen.

The danger of domination implicit in acceptance of French aid was dealt with by asking the French only for a suitably limited number of troops in any expedition.

By 1796 it had been accepted by the United Irishmen that French help was required. This very acceptance did much to harden the separatist and republican strain in United Irish political thinking, for the only *quid pro quo* the Irish could offer the French for their support was a guarantee of the total separation of the two islands in the future.

The first local societies in Ulster had been agitating for some mission to the French since 1795. However, since Tone had then only just set sail for his exile in America, under a definite obligation to press the Irish cause on the French minister in Philadelphia, it was decided at first merely to send Tone a letter stressing the increased discontent in Ireland since he had left and the progress being made by the new organization of United Irishmen. Tone received this letter in America towards the end of November 1795 at a crucial psychological moment.

He had arrived there in August after a six weeks' voyage during which he narrowly escaped being press-ganged by three British naval frigates which stopped his ship off Newfoundland – a fairly routine procedure of the day. Most of the crew and fifty or so of Tone's fellow passengers were taken off and he himself had already been ordered into one of the boats when the screams of his wife and sister softened a British officer's heart.[3] On arrival in Philadelphia itself he met with what seemed to him only a lukewarm response from the French Minister there. In fact we know that the Minister wrote to his government warmly commending Tone and his project of French intervention in Ireland.[4] But, waiting in America, Tone grew despondent. Far from being the single-minded driving force of the United Irishmen, as he has sometimes been supposed, he was making preparations to settle down for good as a farmer on a 180-acre farm near Princeton when in November 1795 the letter from Belfast arrived, signed by his old friends Keogh and Russell. He changed his plans and on 1 January 1796 set sail from New York for France where he landed a month and a day later at Le Havre. He carried letters of introduction from the French Minister in Philadelphia, but came, as he admitted a few months afterwards, more to discharge a duty than with much expectation of success.[5]

Tone's day-to-day record of his next few months in France is of the greatest interest not only for its vivid picture of life in Paris in the hey-day of the Directory, but also because of his most realistic and convincingly unheroic account of the way in which the French came to mount their great expedition to Ireland of 1796. Tone, acting with something of the quiet forcefulness of a good journalist trying to see those people who matter, eventually penetrated to the top of the French government hierarchy. He clearly impressed those he met there. But he was long kept in the dark as to whether or not the expedition he urged so strongly both verbally and in written memoranda was really being seriously considered. The French Directory had many other preoccupations besides an expedition to Ireland and Tone often became depressed and felt he was getting nowhere. As late as 2 May 1796 he wrote: '... I am utterly ignorant whether there is any design to attempt the expedition or not; I put it twice to Carnot (the Minister for War) and could extract no answer. My belief is, that as yet, there is no one step taken in the business, and that, in fact, the expedition will not be undertaken ...'[6]

Tone began to think again of retiring to the backwoods of America. Carnot had told him to work through a young General named Clarke, the son of an Irish Catholic *émigré*, whose ideas about Ireland seemed far astray. Clarke even asked Tone if Fitzgibbon, the Lord Chancellor, might not prove useful to them. 'Anyone who knows Ireland,' commented Tone, 'will readily believe that I did not find it easy to make a serious answer to this question.'[7] Clarke earned further scorn from Tone later when, apparently thinking that Ireland was still devoted to the House of Stuart, he suggested that a new Pretender might be found.*⁸ Tone even began to suspect Clarke of being a traitor, for he worked out that he was remotely related by marriage to Fitzgibbon himself.

But in fact the French were taking the idea of an expedition to Ireland quite seriously and Clarke was a faithful enough bureaucrat in the service of Carnot.⁹ Tone had impressed the French with his sincerity and ability but, as Clarke explained to an agent whom he decided to send to Ireland for further information, it was several months since Tone had left Ireland and things might have changed considerably in that time. Moreover, he said, Tone urged the Irish cause so earnestly that the French could not help feeling he might be heightening the picture a little, though without any conscious intention to deceive.¹⁰

During the summer of 1796 the French began seriously to plan an expedition to Ireland to be led by the brilliant young General Hoche, then second in repute only to Bonaparte. In July, Tone, sitting in his hotel studying a French cavalry manual (for he was about to be given the rank of colonel in the French Army), received a summons to Carnot's War Ministry in the Luxemburg Palace. He waited in an office there for two hours 'when the door opened, and a handsome young man in a brown coat and yellow pantaloons, entered and said:

'*Vous êtes le citoyen Smith?*' ('Smith' was the *nom de guerre* under which Tone had been living since his arrival in France in an ineffectual attempt to avoid the attention of Pitt's spies.)

The young man had a sabre cut right down his forehead, eyebrow and one side of his nose, which did not, however, disfigure him. Tone thought he was an official of the War Ministry.

'*Oui, citoyen, je m'appelle Smith.*'

'*Vous vous appelez, aussi, je crois, Wolfe Tone?*'

'*Oui, citoyen, c'est mon véritable nom.*'

'*Eh bien,*' replied the stranger. '*Je suis le Général Hoche.*'¹¹

That evening Tone dined with Hoche, Carnot, Clarke and others. ('Very well served without being luxurious.' Two courses, dessert and coffee.) During dinner it was made unmistakably clear that preparations for a strong expedition to Ireland were under way. It was to consist of ten to fifteen thousand men with great quantities of arms, ammunition and stores.

Yet the French continued to keep Tone in the dark about some of their contacts with Ireland. Less than a fortnight later, by which time Tone had received his commission as a colonel in the French Army, he was discussing future arrangements with Hoche, when the conversation took a strange turn.

---

* Clarke was an exception among *émigrés* descended from the Wild Geese in not emigrating from France after the Revolution. Most of the old Irish Brigade, aristocratic and monarchical by temperament, did so. There was actually a project for merging the Brigade with the British Army. Some Irish Brigade French officers even went on a recruiting visit to Ireland for this very purpose but met with a poor response.

Hoche suddenly asked him if he knew a man called Arthur O'Connor, and a little later what he thought of Lord Edward Fitzgerald.

O'Connor was the thirty-six-year-old youngest son of a rich Protestant land-owner in County Cork.[12] He had sat in the Irish House of Commons since 1790 and had at first shown no radical tendencies whatever. He had actually spoken against a bill intended to reduce the number of government pensioners in 1791 – a year in which he was High Sheriff of Cork – and had been quite silent when the Catholic Relief Bills came before the House in 1792 and 1793. But he had visited France just before war broke out, had been deeply impressed by the Revolution, and had come back an ardent republican. He acted out his conversion in the Irish House of Commons, where in 1795 he spoke out vigorously in favour of Grattan's bill for total Catholic Emancipation.

O'Connor had good contacts with the Whig opposition in England, though he concealed from them the extreme, treasonable position he soon reached. He was also a close friend of that other wealthy convert to republican radicalism in Ireland, Lord Edward Fitzgerald, from whom there was by this time no need to conceal anything. For both O'Connor and Fitzgerald, if not themselves already technically members of the United Irishmen, were by now in close contact with them and assuming among them positions of leadership. O'Connor also seems to have been in the inner councils of the Defenders in the south, and certainly before the year was out his brother Roger was one of the chief nominal organizers of that society.[13]

To Hoche's question, which Tone assumed to have been put on the strength of O'Connor's speech in the Irish House of Commons of 1795, Tone replied that he did know O'Connor, thought highly of his talents, principles and patriotism, and hoped that he would undoubtedly join them. He made a mental note if he ever met O'Connor to tell him that he seemed to be well thought of in France. But really Hoche had made rather a fool of Tone, being in close personal contact with O'Connor at the time.

Two months earlier, while Tone still imagined himself to be struggling alone in an attempt to get the French to mount an expedition to Ireland, Lord Edward Fitzgerald had gone to Hamburg and opened his own line of approach to the French. He had soon afterwards gone back to Ireland and returned to the Continent a month later, in June 1796, with Arthur O'Connor. He and O'Connor then started detailed negotiations with the French Directory.

O'Connor, who took the lead, presented a rosy picture of the state of revolutionary affairs in Ireland. He emphasized the extent to which secret societies had now sworn Irishmen both North and South into a conspiracy for a separate republic and that the country was ripe for insurrection. The militia, he said, would go with the people. Cork, Waterford and even Dublin could easily be captured. And a successful insurrection in Ireland would knock England out of the war. All that was needed was guns, artillery, officers and a few troops. 'We only want your help in the first moment,' O'Connor continued. 'In two months we should have 100,000 men under arms; we ask your assistance only because we know it is your own clear interest to give it, and only on condition that you leave us absolute masters to frame our government as we please.'[14]

But when the French, taking him at his word, suggested that perhaps the rising could then take place before the landing, O'Connor emphasized the severity of the measures the government were taking to disarm the people under the Insurrection Act and entered a certain caution about the militia. Although, he said, the great majority of them were certainly in favour of revolution they were scattered about the country, they had had no munitions and their officers were anti-revolutionary. The Irish leaders, he insisted, were resolved that the arrival of French aid must be the signal for the rising.[15]

In September 1796, when the French plans were progressing and Tone had joined Hoche at his headquarters at Rennes, convenient for the port of Brest, Hoche one day in conversation with Tone referred obscurely to 'somebody here who wished to see me, but I did not press him for an explanation and he did not offer it'.[16] In fact this person was none other than Arthur O'Connor who had actually been in conference with Hoche close by. But for some reason best known to the French, Tone was left in ignorance of what he called his 'invisible cooperators' right up to the time he sailed. He took his exclusion from the full secret amiably enough, remarking to himself that at least it divided the responsibility and didn't leave the whole thing 'resting on my single assertion'.[17]

In view of this September check-up between the French and the actual revolutionary leadership in Ireland it is strange that final coordination between them turned out so imperfect. For when Hoche's expedition finally sailed for Ireland on 16 December, neither O'Connor nor Fitzgerald seem to have known.[18]

Bad luck was to play a very large part in the events that followed, but the misunderstanding and lack of closer cooperation between the two sides was remarkable. The French had definitely told the United Irish societies of Belfast to expect an expedition shortly.[19] But then there had arrived another message saying that the expedition had been postponed.[20] The efficient channels of communication so necessary between the two major parties in such a hazardous enterprise were clearly inadequate. Equally dangerous was the fact that Fitzgerald and O'Connor had conveyed a false picture of the revolutionary organization in Ireland. It was nothing like so well coordinated or under their control as they had represented.

In the first place, incorporation of the vast and fragmented Defender organization within the United Irish system was often more nominal than real. Second, even among the United Irish societies of the North themselves there was a good deal of independence and autonomy. It was during this winter that the final Executive Directory of the United Irishmen took shape, consisting of O'Connor, Fitzgerald, Thomas Emmet, the barrister, Dr William MacNeven, a doctor of medicine, and Oliver Bond, a wealthy wool merchant. But the degree of authority the Directory held over the subordinate societies is problematical. Signs of insubordination from local committees in Ulster itself were not infrequent.

At the secret meeting of the Down County Committee on 13 October 1796, for instance, the 'Reporter' from the Ulster provincial committee told the members that foreign aid was expected immediately and that the United Irishmen were to hold themselves in readiness. Whereupon 'a person at the meeting desired to know what they should rise with?'

The Reporter answered:

'With pikes and guns and with any other weapons they could in any way get,' reassuring them further that 'the United Business was going well in England and Scotland.'[21]

In December 1796 a lower committee poured cold water on much of the big talk that was going on, complaining indignantly of a County Committee report which, it said, was 'unworthy of men who are fit to represent a county and an insult to our understandings'. They were being rushed into things, they continued. It was impossible to hide registered arms as they were ordered to '... We are called upon to learn to march well, as if a knowledge of military tactics could be acquired in a closet or by night.' And, warning against any rash attempt at rebellion, they added: '... although we are well aware that oppression greatly abounds and abuses exist, yet it is evident that a few counties in Ulster would be unable by force of arms to accomplish an object of such magnitude until our principles are more generally known and understood.'[22]

The truth was that for all Tone's fine words to the French Government about an Ireland ripe for liberation, and all the more up-to-date enthusiastic confirmation provided by O'Connor and Fitzgerald, no sort of properly coordinated rebellious system, let alone a revolutionary system, covered the whole of Ireland.

If, however, the United Irish conspiracy, for all its vast potential, was an amateurish affair at this stage – and indeed largely remained so to the end – the other participants in the situation, the French and British governments, were professionals.

The British government had at its disposal a militia of eighteen thousand men (though as a largely Catholic body its loyalty was open to doubt); about fifteen thousand regular troops most of them also Catholic Irish troops but well-trained and disciplined; and finally, a new force of yeomanry raised late in 1796 officered by local gentry and predominantly Protestant, though where the units were Catholic they outdid the Protestants in keenness and loyalty. On the legal side the government had the benefit of the Insurrection Act which greatly assisted the military's natural impatience in its search for arms, and in November 1796 a further impediment to over-nice procedure was removed by the suspension of Habeas Corpus.

The French, too, were poised for action. Tone, who now held the rank of a General in the French Army, had spent the last weeks before setting sail from Brest in a state of some anxiety, first for his family who were somewhere on the high seas on their month-long journey between America and France, and secondly for his friends Neilson and Russell who he learned had been arrested and imprisoned in Ireland. His mind, he wrote, was 'sixty times more troubled than the ocean on which I am going'.[23] To add to his troubles Hoche disappeared from Brest altogether for two days to pursue an affair with a local girl.[24] However, by 16 December everyone was ready. Hoche issued an order of the day:

Jaloux de rendre à la liberté un peuple digne d'elle, et mûr pour une révolution, le Directoire nous envoie en Irlande, a l'effet d'y faciliter la révolution que d'excellents Républicains viennent d'y entreprendre ...

A sharp injunction followed to avoid rape and pillage and to treat the Irish as allies rather than enemies. The weather, wrote Tone, was delicious, the sun as warm and bright as May. All were in high spirits, and the French troops – about fourteen thousand of them altogether – 'as gay as if they were going to a ball'.[25] The fleet of forty-three sail must indeed have presented, as Hoche's biographer maintained, 'a most majestic spectacle'. *'Aussi fière que la flotte romaine,'* he expanded, *'qui, commandé par Scipion, portait la ruine de Carthage, l'escadre est rassemblée, les voiles deployées – il part.'*[26]

It was in trouble at once.

On the passage out of Brest during the night one of the French ships struck a rock and all but thirty-seven of the 550 troops aboard were drowned. The next day a violent storm partially dispersed the fleet and drove another ship of the line ashore with the loss of a thousand men. The flagship, the *Fraternité*, with the Admiral and Hoche himself aboard, parted company with the main body, and, after a series of appalling adventures in the course of which it once found itself undetected in the middle of the English fleet, finally succeeded in returning to France three weeks later. Meanwhile fog, succeeding the storm, brought further confusion to the rest of the fleet. By 21 December, however, all but eight or nine had reassembled off the southwest coast of Ireland and were making their way into Bantry Bay, a magnificent piece of water, twenty-six miles long, seven miles broad and with a draught of forty fathoms in the middle. A head wind was blowing strongly against them and their progress was extremely slow. They cast anchor off Bear Island, half-way up the Bay, some time after six on the evening of 21 December 1796.

A heavy gale blew throughout the night so that when Tone woke next morning he found the mountains on the northern shore covered with snow. He also found that twenty of the thirty-four ships which had arrived had been blown out to sea again. Though there had been absolutely no sign that the enemy was yet aware of their existence, spirits on board the French fleet, which was now reduced to less than half its strength, were low. Tone himself, now so close to his native land that he felt he could have thrown a biscuit on to the shore, was still uncertain whether in this gale he would ever set foot on it again. He was surprised to find that he felt no emotion at all. 'I expected I should have been, at returning in these circumstances after an absence of more than a year, violently affected,' he wrote. 'Yet I look to it as if it were the coast of Japan.'[27] He added that if they did not take some action soon the enemy would have collected a superior force and they would be in serious trouble.

It was in fact only on the evening of the previous day that a messenger, riding desperately hard over the snow-covered roads between Bantry and Cork, and covering over forty miles on a single horse in four hours, had managed to bring to the government news of the appalling danger that now threatened. That the French were in strength was clear, although their precise numbers were unknown and it could not even be said for certain whether this was the main force or only a diversion. The only troops able to oppose them at once were some four hundred men of the Galway militia stationed at Bantry, together with the local yeomanry, who were mobilized by the principal local land-owner, a Mr Richard White, later rewarded with the title of Lord Bantry for his part in these events. Only about three thousand men stood between Bantry and Cork altogether, and the British General Dalrymple wrote to Pelham, the Chief Secretary for Ireland, that he could not possibly concentrate more than eight thousand before the French reached Cork. Even then he could not hope for anything better than a holding action while he fell back on main positions on the River Blackwater near Kilworth and Fermoy.

If the French had indeed arrived in Bantry Bay with the fourteen thousand troops with which they had set out, the future history of Ireland might have been very different. But the French had arrived not only with less than half their troops, but without their commander. The continuing gale prevented them both from landing where they were and also from making any further progress to more sheltered waters up the Bay. Grouchy, the military second-in-command of the expedition, was determined to try and land at almost all costs, but when on Christmas Day the storm grew even worse and the French ships were making almost no progress towards Bantry (about fifty yards in eight hours, Tone says) the naval second-in-command, Admiral Bouvet, decided he could no longer be responsible for his ships under such conditions and gave orders to cut cables and make for the open sea before the gale.

   His signals were either not received or else not properly understood, so that the other ships which remained at anchor during the night found on the following day that they were now without even secondary commanders on land or sea, for both Bouvet and Grouchy had been aboard the same frigate and, mistakenly imagining themselves to have been followed by the rest of the fleet, were already far out to sea on their way back to Brest. For those ships still in the Bay which just managed to hold their anchors the weather worsened. Visibility came down to barely more than a ship's length, which added to the confusion. Finally, one by one the great ships found it impossible to hold on any longer and, cutting their cables, ran down the Bay and out to sea again. Tone's ship, the *Indomptable*, weighed anchor on the 28th, or rather, having had considerable difficulty in pulling up one anchor, cut the other and put to sea followed by about eight or nine others. Tone noted that he didn't wonder at all at Xerxes whipping the sea; he felt like doing the same. Even this small squadron was now dispersed and after failing to rendezvous as agreed at the mouth of the Shannon, where they had hoped to make some last-minute desperate attempt on that part of Ireland, they returned one by one to France which Tone himself reached again on the first day of 1797.

   Some ships remained in the Bay a few days longer and as late as 31 December there was even an alarm on shore when some boats were seen to put off from a French ship with the intention, it was supposed, of landing. The Galway militia drew themselves up in their full strength on the beach, thus hoping to deceive the French into thinking there were greater numbers in reserve behind them. But it was a false alarm. The French were merely boarding an American ship in the Bay and soon afterwards returned to their own ship. Three days later they had all left Bantry Bay for good. The only Frenchmen who had actually set foot on Irish soil were an officer who landed from an open boat on Bear Island and was taken prisoner, some patrols which had reconnoitred Whiddy Island off Bantry itself and others who had collected some sheep off an island in the Shannon. Tone noted reasonably in his diary that England had not had such an escape since the days of the Spanish Armada.

   Yet perhaps the most significant feature of the incident lay after all in the behaviour not of the elements, but of man. For in the ten days that the French had lain in the Bay, molested only by the weather, the Catholic peasantry of the district, far from rising in disaffected multitudes to greet their liberators, had displayed a remarkable lack of enthusiasm for them. Although the French patrols which landed on Whiddy Island met with a civil enough reception, being informed, as was no more than the truth, that they had been expected for some months,[28] all government reports agreed that the loyal spirit of the peasantry in general was exemplary. 'Their good will, zeal and activity exceeds all description,' wrote General Dalrymple to the King.[29] In

Limerick the peasants were boiling their potatoes for the soldiers.[30] And a correspondent from Mayo wrote revealingly that the local inhabitants had associated the French with the Protestants of the North, who, they understood, had invited the French over. Since their chief memory of the Protestants of the North was of Orangemen and Peep o' Day Boys, they had consequently transferred part of their hatred to the enemy 'who, they are persuaded, are coming with their northern allies to drive them from their habitations and properties'.[31] No comment could reveal more plainly the deep confusion of Irish radical emotions at that time.

In the North the United Irishmen showed no particular disappointment over the failure of the French at Bantry. This was hardly surprising since they had had so very little precise information about their arrival from the start. The net result was on the whole probably encouraging for the Bantry expedition at least proved beyond doubt that the French were in earnest. Activity in the North intensified ahead of the next French attempt. And before long a vast new invasion fleet for Ireland was indeed being assembled at Texel by France's new ally, the Dutch Republic, with Tone once more in attendance.

Though the rebellious preparations in the North still remained largely a matter of individual local societies drilling and organizing – a central military committee for the whole of Ireland did not come into existence until 1798 – yet these local preparations were now being conducted on such a scale as to cause the government the greatest concern. Nightly drillings, the cutting down of trees to make pike handles, raids on gentlemen's houses for arms, the seduction of the militia by the United Irish oath – all this was now commonplace and continuous in Ulster in the early months of 1797.

After the fright the government had received at Bantry and with another French invasion in the offing it was inevitable that they should resort to the harshest policies. Backed by the Insurrection Act, and equipped with specific instructions to disarm the North, the British commander, General Lake, set about his task with vigour, and by March 1797 most of Ulster was virtually under martial law. But something more than normal military firmness was required to deal effectively with the situation. Political concessions – which meant some measure of parliamentary reform – would, according to one of the United Irish leaders, still have prevented rebellion as late as the middle of 1797.[32] However, parliamentary reform did not enter into the government's calculations and certainly was of no concern to the military. As the population of the North grew more and more skilful at concealing their arms, only the sternest methods of repression seemed to offer any chance of success. A vicious spiral of terror soon began which led within a year to the worst display of savagery Britain had witnessed since the wars of Cromwell.

7

United Irishmen in Trouble

For all General Lake's zeal in Ulster during the early spring of 1797, the situation there continued to worsen. Virtually all 'the lower order of the people', as Lake himself told the government in March, and most of the middle classes were by now determined Republicans, imbued with French principles and set on revolution.[1] And in case the government should think that this was just the sort of sweeping militarist conclusion any general in charge might be expected to form, he emphasized that he had been talking to a lot of men who were still keen on parliamentary reform but were now scared out of their wits because the tenants and labourers they had first introduced to the idea had now got completely out of control. Magistrates from many different localities confirmed the situation. One wrote from Newry in the same month that nearly the whole population round about had been sworn into the United Irishmen and that every tree in his neighbourhood had been cut down for the making of pike handles.[2] 'The game is nearly up in Ulster,' he concluded. The French were expected again by I May.

In County Monaghan, on the pretext of planting potatoes, gangs of several hundred men roamed the countryside, carrying the white flags which were the characteristic emblem of the Defender corps among the United Irishmen and singing republican songs.[3] Part of the country near Omagh in County Tyrone was wholly in the hands of the United Irishmen. A hundred men, well-armed and officered, openly paraded the streets of Dromore. 'The insurgents', as the local clergyman already called them, were going about in great gangs, swearing, plundering, burning, maiming. 'Yesternight', he wrote, 'the hills between this and Clogher exhibited a striking scene. The summits topped with bonfires – bugle horns sounding and guns occasionally firing, no doubt as signals to the marauding parties who were employed seeking for weapons in the neighbourhood.... The populace are now so powerful and desperate, that for any individual to attempt resistance would be both imprudent and romantic ..."[4]

At Ballyclare in County Antrim a large leaden statue of Neptune which had stood in a mill-dam for over a hundred years was spirited away by the United Irishmen during the night to be recast into bullets.[5] Engagements with the troops were soon taking place; fourteen United Irishmen were killed and ten taken prisoner in a skirmish near Dundalk in May.

The United Irish leaders, who were high-minded, educated men, later protested strongly that they had never countenanced the use of murder or terror to enforce support. It is reasonable to believe them. But the nature of their control over the multitude of lower committees, with their cruel peasant tradition derived from the agrarian secret societies, was so tenuous that the leaders clearly often had very little idea of what was going on at the popular level. The many magistrates' accounts of murder and terror must certainly also be believed. 'You can have no idea', wrote a magistrate from Donegal, 'of the terror that pervades the whole country.'[6] Another correspondent from Antrim wrote: '. . . they are all uniting and threatening anyone who will not join them; the Murphys are in a dreadful situation, dare not stir out at night, particularly Sam.'[7]

Counter-terror seemed the only answer. It did not immediately become official policy, but brutality and excesses by troops not much interested in distinguishing between the guilty and the innocent became increasingly frequent, and the search for arms was conducted with ever increasing ruthlessness. It was this ruthlessness which, one way and another, was to determine the whole future course of events.

It is easy enough to read into what now took place the interpretation placed on events by later nationalists, and to see the undoubtedly brutal troops who acted against the ill-organized peasantry and others as 'British' troops putting down 'the Irish'. But the terms are very misleading, for the troops though British were also mainly Irish and of Catholic labouring stock. In the rebellion that was about to break out, the fighting was between groups of Irish subjects wishing desperately to overthrow or at least protest against the established form of government by which they did so badly, and other Irish subjects remaining loyal to that establishment. A small caucus of intellectuals and political aspirants gave the rebels an ambitious separatist political theory, which the masses apprehended only dimly and with little coherence.

The burning of cabins by troops in Ulster in the course of their searches for arms rapidly became normal practice, both as a punishment and a warning to others. The wounding and killing of the cabins' inhabitants also soon became an inevitable part of the process and, in this too, the difficult business of distinguishing between guilty and innocent went increasingly by default. A captain of the Dublin militia carrying out searches for arms in the County of Down in June 1797 found a sort of competition in brutality going on between a notorious Welsh yeomanry regiment known as the Ancient Britons and the local yeomen of the district. He described how he made his way to the scene of one disturbance by the smoke and flames of burning houses and by the dead bodies of boys and old men killed by the Ancient Britons, though there had been no opposition at all. The only shooting had come from the yeomanry themselves though '. . . I declare there was nothing to fire at, old men, women and children excepted'.[8]

General Lake, like all high military commanders in such situations, stood by his men as charges of brutality and outrage piled up against them. 'Considering their powers and provocations,' he said, they had acted well and he had tried on all occasions 'to prevent as much as possible any act of violence on the part of the troops.'[9] But a more humane British general in Ireland, Sir John Moore, referring to what happened in the North of Ireland in 1797 wrote that 'undoubtedly enormities had been committed entirely disgraceful to the military as well as prejudicial to their discipline'.[10] In March of the following year a newly appointed Commander-in-Chief, Sir Ralph Abercromby, resigned soon after his appointment because the government would not support him in his efforts to improve the army's conduct. In a private letter to relatives he wrote of the 'violence and oppression' which had been employed in Ireland for more than twelve months, adding that within that time 'every crime, every cruelty that could be committed by Cossacks or Calmucks has been transacted here'.[11] Before he resigned he explained to his subordinate Sir John Moore the attitude of the government which, he said, wanted the Commander-in-Chief and the army to take the responsibility of acting 'with a violence which they did not choose to define, and for which they would give no public authority'.[12] With the one slightly embarrassing hitch of Abercromby's own resignation, this formula in fact worked well enough from the government's point of view over the whole period in question.

In March and in May 1797 the government made successive proclamations in Ulster, demanding the surrender of all arms within a certain period, coupled with offers of pardon and 'protection' if these were complied with. In the first proclamation General Lake had exhorted the people 'instantly' to 'rescue themselves from the severity of military authority'.[13] Arms, he added, would be paid for. In the orders given to him he was allowed, rather naïvely, 'the greatest latitude, relying at the same time on your prudence and discernment in the exercise of it, so that the peaceable and well-affected may be protected . . .'.[14] The combination of toughness with pardon was soon working so successfully and so many former United Irishmen began to come in to surrender their arms and take the oath of allegiance that the time limit on the second proclamation was extended. How much sincerity was involved in such oaths of allegiance is obviously questionable. A government informer, who was the United Irishmen's chief legal adviser in the North, afterwards declared that many people took the oath after the first proclamation as a mere cloak of protection for themselves, and that most of them on that occasion did not deliver up their arms.[15] As late as June a loyalist making the journey between Belfast and Dublin said he found almost everyone he met among the people on his journey an open well-wisher to the

United Irishmen's cause and expecting an early rising *en masse* with French support.[16] But the back of the movement in the North was slowly being broken. Neilson's radical newspaper, the *Northern Star*, which had achieved very wide popularity, was suppressed. And even though many arms were being held back the surrender of them under the military counter-terror was soon on a very considerable scale. By August 1797 the government had been successful enough in Ulster to be able to restore civil law there.

An important force in achieving this success, but one which also considerably aggravated the savagery, had been the participation on the government side of the Orangemen, the former Peep o' Day Boys, either in independent groups or incorporated in units of yeomanry. The Orangemen needed to be handled by the government with great delicacy and care. In 1795 authorities had not hesitated to describe them as the 'lawless banditti' they undoubtedly then were.[17] As late as mid 1796 the government had been criticizing the 'supine' and 'partial' conduct of magistrates in Armagh who favoured the Orangemen as opposed to the Defenders in the continuous disorderly feuding between the two. But threatened now by foreign invasion and a secret society whose avowed aim was to unite all Catholics and Protestants in support of the invader, the government would have been unrealistic not to make use of this other secret society whose principle was to keep Catholics and Protestants at enmity. A magistrate writing to the government in May 1797 summed it up: 'The enemies of our Establishment have reduced us to the necessity of making "divide" a justifiable measure.'[18] Already, in the course of 1796, an officially more respectable, propertied element, including some of the previously partial magistrates, had taken over the machinery of the Orange Society, disavowing its vicious sectarian trend and converting this, so they claimed, into no more than an emotionally charged loyalty to the establishment.

That the Orangemen were still emotionally charged is beyond doubt. It was the Orangemen in the yeomanry who in 1797 were responsible for the worst excesses of that year in Ulster, and the terror they spread throughout the countryside was duly amplified by the United Irishmen to rally the masses throughout Ireland in a Union, if not of political principle, as had originally been intended, at least of self-defence.

The wearing of some piece of green clothing had become a symbol of identification with the United Irish cause, and it was taken to be such whether so intended or not. One lady's maid in a loyalist party travelling from the North to Dublin, inadvertently wearing a green ribbon in her bonnet, was so pursued by waiters at the inns crying 'Success to your colours, ma'am!' that her employer made her remove it in a great hurry.[19] The Orangemen invariably made the wearing of green a cause for provocation and reprisals, and there were many incidents recorded of women having green articles of clothing torn from them and being humiliated for the effrontery of displaying them. The Frenchman De Latocnaye touring Armagh in 1797 met a party of Orangemen on the road with Orange cockades in their hats, and shortly afterwards went into some of the peasants' cabins which he had visited on an earlier tour. He found the inhabitants cowed and frightened and not nearly so pleased to see him as they had been before. Eventually an old woman said to him: 'You are come, sir, perhaps from some distant place – perhaps your umbrella on account of the string of it may bring you into trouble.' Realizing that the string of his umbrella was indeed a greenish colour, he laughed at first but on second thoughts, remembering the Orangemen on the road, cut it off.[20]

One loyalist eye-witness of the Orangemen's activity about this time wrote to the government: 'Were I to enumerate the robberies, murders and shameful outrages committed on the Catholics of this place, by those Orange Boys, headed by officers in full yeomanry uniforms, it would be an endless business ...'[21] A slightly less squeamish government supporter who conceded that the excursions of the yeomanry, when headed by their officers, had at first had a happy effect 'in bringing in arms and returning the country to its allegiance', nevertheless deplored that, without officers, they should be 'permitted at their pleasure day after day, and what is worse, night after night, to scour whole tracts of country, destroy houses, furniture, etc., and stab and cut in a most cruel manner numbers that, from either private resentment or any other cause, they may take a dislike to ...'.[22]

The hitherto local feud between Peep o' Day Boys and Defenders was turning to something on a national scale. Catholics fled from Ulster into other parts of Ireland where the Defender societies were widely organized, carrying tales of the terror with them. The ground was being prepared for the crude and desperate rebellion that was to take place in the South in the following year.

So successful, however, were the various measures in Ulster in 1797 and so soon did it become apparent that the whole movement there was in danger of disintegration, that the Ulster Directory of the United Irishmen even put forward a desperate project to start the rebellion without waiting for French help any longer. But the proposal was over-ridden by the recently formed Leinster Directory in Dublin, dominated by an Executive consisting of Arthur O'Connor, Lord Edward Fitzgerald, Thomas Emmet, Oliver Bond and W. J. MacNeven – the latter incidentally being the only Catholic in the group.

The decision not to act at this moment brought accusations of cowardice against the Leinster Directory, but dependence on French help had long been regarded as an indispensable part of United Irish plans. Macneven even paid a secret visit to France in June 1797 to make sure it was coming. It was coming all right, but not yet, and it was this further failure of the French to arrive this year that proved virtually the last straw for the Protestant

Republican movement in Ulster. It was already strained almost to breaking point by the vigorous severity of the government's measures. Now, with the chances of French help and ultimate successes receding fast, the offers of pardon became more and more attractive. And the heart began to go out of the Republican movement in the North.

In any case, the old rivalry between Protestant and Catholic, continually kept alive by the spilling of fresh blood, proved far more durable than any new theoretical alliance. As early as May 1797 it had been noted by the government that the Protestants of Armagh, who had for some time been deluded by the United Irishmen, were renouncing the societies and returning to their loyalty.[23] The wishful thinking about reconciliation between Presbyterians and Catholics which Tone and others had indulged in so easily in spite of so much deep-seated evidence to the contrary, was now revealed for what it was. Under the first serious strains, the divisions which the United Irishmen had partially papered over re-appeared.

In 1798 a clergyman wrote to the old Earl of Charlemont, who had been proud President of the Volunteers in the great days of the late seventies and early eighties, and confirmed what had been taking place:

> Your old Ballymascanlan (Co. Louth) Volunteers [he said] who six months ago were all United Irishmen, are now complete Orangemen, which is more congenial with their feelings.... In speaking of the astonishing increase of Orangemen, I forgot to mention the most wonderful part of it, that immense numbers of them are in Belfast.

When rebellion did break out in Ireland in this May of 1798 the contribution of the North – the centre of the conspiracy the year before – was to be negligible.

8

New French Preparations

The failure of the French to arrive in 1797 had a profoundly depressing effect on the North. But the French, as in the year before, had been serious enough in their intentions. As at Bantry they were once again thwarted by the elements. This time the first stage of their expedition had been mounted on behalf of France by her new ally, the Dutch Republic. 'They venture no less than the whole of their army and navy,' wrote Tone, who by July 1797 was assisting with the preparations at the North Sea port of Texel.[1] He was much impressed by the scale of the preparations and the condition of the Dutch fleet, which he considered superior to that of the French the year before. But even as late as this he had reservations about accepting any help at all from the French and their allies. In a conversation with Hoche on 1 July he had raised the whole question of the amount of control the French might want to claim for themselves in Ireland, saying that he feared it would be greater than the Irish might want to allow them.[2] Tone cited Bonaparte's proclamation to the Government of Genoa published in that day's *Gazette*, which he thought 'most grossly improper and indecent as touching on the indispensable rights of the people'. He added that in Italy such dictation might pass, but never in Ireland where they understood their rights too well to submit to such treatment.

'I understand you,' said Hoche. 'But you may be at ease in that respect; Bonaparte has been my scholar, but he shall never be my master.'

Tone was not wholly reassured for he rightly discounted some of this as jealousy of Bonaparte.

Perhaps it was reservations and hypothetical fears, together with natural personal anxieties about his own fate and that of his family, which produced in Tone the same curious apathy he had noted in himself the year before when anchored in Bantry Bay. He even used the same image to describe it. For, with fifteen sail of the line, ten frigates and sloops, and twenty-seven transports all ready and waiting for a fair wind for Ireland he wrote: 'For our expedition I think no more of it than if it were destined for Japan.'[3]

It was not in fact destined for anywhere at all. Once more and at an even more critical moment than the year before the elements came to England's rescue. This time the wind blew not too hard but in the wrong direction.

For weeks, while the British fleet had been largely paralysed by mutinies at the Nore and at Spithead, the Dutch had not been ready. Now at last the great fleet lay ready at the Texel but no wind blew which would enable it to put to sea. 'Eighteen days aboard and we have not had eighteen minutes of fair wind,' wrote Tone, in whom desperate impatience alternated with apathy and despair. 'Hell! Hell! Hell! Allah! Allah! Allah!'[4]

On 30 July 1797 the wind seemed set fair at last, and the ships were just about to get under way when it suddenly changed again and left them. A few days later messages arrived from Ireland bringing news of the loss of confidence in Ulster and the despair that was setting in with the continuing success of Lake's disarming measures and the continuing failure of the French to arrive. A month later, Tone's hopes and those of all revolutionaries in Ireland received a severe blow. Hoche, the one man in France who was as enthusiastic about the expedition to Ireland as the Irish themselves, died suddenly of consumption. The blow was capped by an even greater one in October when the Dutch fleet ventured out of Texel roads for the first time, and was totally defeated by the British in a bloody battle off Camperdown.

In December Tone had his first meeting with Bonaparte whom he found 'perfectly civil' though not very well informed about Ireland whose population he believed to be only two millions, less than half its actual figure.[5] It was extremely difficult to assess what the great man's attitude to Ireland was going to be and how important he would consider it, although early in January 1798 Tone took some encouragement from the fact that Bonaparte told him personally that he was assigned with the rank of Adjutant General to the Army of England.[6]

Another French expedition was indeed collected for Ireland in 1798. It was to be the only one of the three mounted in three successive years actually to land there.

Paradoxically it was not until after the real strength of the United Irishmen had begun to disintegrate in the North that they began to organize themselves on something like a national scale. Only right at the end of 1797 were delegates secretly elected to a National Directory for the first time. The head of the society became in fact more and more active as its control over its limbs became less and less coordinated.

But the cause of the political revolutionaries appears much more desperate in retrospect at this point than it must have seemed to the conspirators themselves at the time. In the first place, although the French expeditions had failed to materialize, news arrived in February 1798 that the third was being prepared.[7] France was now unquestionably the greatest military power in Europe. Secondly, the huge uncoordinated bodies of the Defenders in the three other provinces of Leinster, Munster and Connaught were still largely untouched by the government's measures. It was among the Defenders with their promising contacts with the militia that the United Irishmen who had nominally incorporated them within their system made increasing efforts to stimulate enthusiasm and exert control.. The new National Directory centred on Dublin sent emissaries throughout Ireland spreading tales of the Orange terror in the North. They embroidered them with extravagant details such as the Orangemen's 'oath of extermination' and generally promoted the idea that on top of all the grievances which the Defenders were combined to protest against was now the threat of a general massacre of all Catholics in Ireland.

Lord Edward Fitzgerald was now the chief organizer of the United Irishmen's military efforts. His experience in action with the British Army in America made him a plausible focus for the hopes of the new revolutionary patriotism. The peasantry retained from their inherited Gaelic traditions a mystical respect for aristocratic chieftains, and this plumpish, brave and energetic, if not particularly subtle, aristocrat fitted the bill very well. There was even talk among the ignorant rebels later at Wexford that he was to be their king. A song called the Shan Van Vocht (the name of the legendary poor old crippled woman who is Ireland) relates him to the excitement of the time :

Oh the French are on the sea
Says the Shan Van Vocht,
The French are on the sea,
Says the Shan Van Vocht ...

And where will they have their camp?
Says the Shan Van Vocht,
Where will they have their camp?
Says the Shan Van Vocht.
On the Curragh of Kildare,
The boys will all be there,
With their pikes in good repair
Says the Shan Van Vocht.

To the Curragh of Kildare
The boys they will repair
And Lord Edward will be there,
Says the Shan Van Vocht ...

The military organization of the United Irishmen, such as it was, had been superimposed on their pyramid-like political structure late in 1796 and early in 1797.[8] The secretaries of the lowest-level committees were made sergeants. Groups of five committees sent delegates to a higher committee with the rank of captain, and ten of those committees sent delegates to a still higher committee with the rank of colonel. All these ranks were elected. Colonels had to submit to the Executive the names of three men to be considered by them for the rank of general. Each member of a society who could afford to was supposed to provide himself with a musket, bayonet and ammunition, while the rest were to provide themselves with pikes and, if possible, a pair of pistols. Hence the incessant raids for arms on gentlemen's houses, although the leaders, probably sincerely but certainly unrealistically, always claimed that they disapproved of these.

Fitzgerald himself seems to have recognized that his organization existed more effectively in theory than in practice. In a conversation in November 1797 with someone who had expressed doubts about the ability of the United Irishmen to stand against the king's troops, he had replied that this would not be altogether necessary in view of the French help that was expected. Some of the United Irishmen, he replied, would be incorporated in the French army where they would learn discipline soon enough, but by far the greater part would be engaged in harassing ammunition trains, cutting off foraging parties, and generally making the king's troops feel themselves in enemy country, while the actual battles would be left to the French.[9]

Nevertheless, it was Fitzgerald's chief concern to extend as much discipline and control as he could over the ranks of the Defenders incorporated within the United Irishmen. And in this winter and spring of 1797-8, while United Irishmen from Dublin worked up enthusiasm for the cause among the Defenders with their tales of impending terror and massacre, some such extension was nominally achieved. By February 1798 Fitzgerald's secret returns showed him that theoretically he had some 280,000 men he could call on − 170,000 of them from counties outside Ulster.[10] Once again a dispute took place, this time within the Supreme Directory of the United Irishmen itself, as to whether or not to take the field before the French came. Fitzgerald himself was personally in favour of this, but the belief that a French invasion was imminent was running so strongly that it hardly seemed like hesitation to delay a little longer. The latest messenger from France had spoken of the invasion taking place by the middle of May at the latest. The British Government too was receiving, through its intelligence, news of extensive invasion preparations at four Channel ports.

Tone himself, apart from Bonaparte's assurance that he was assigned to the Army of England under the command of a general of Irish descent named Kilmaine, had been told almost nothing about the actual preparations. A friend of his, Edward Lewins, who had been sent to France in 1797 by the United Irishmen to act as permanent diplomatic representative there, was informed on 1 April 1798 by the President of the French Directory that the timing and placing of the newest French expedition could not be divulged because it was a State secret. Lewines was, however, reassured that there would never be any question of France making peace with England on terms which did not include the independence of Ireland.*[11]

On 4 April Tone set off for the third time in three years to an invasion headquarters, this time making for Rouen, the headquarters of the Army of England. But before then news had reached him of two successive blows which had struck the United Irishmen at home. The first was the arrest at the end of February of Arthur O'Connor at Margate while trying to embark clandestinely for France – presumably to coordinate final arrangements between the new expedition and the rebels. The second was far worse. In fact. Tone described it in his diary as 'the most terrible blow which the cause of liberty in Ireland has yet sustained'.[12] This was no less than the arrest on 12 March 1798 of the entire Leinster Provincial Committee of the United Irishmen, containing as it did most of the members of the Supreme National Directory. Lord Edward Fitzgerald alone escaped.

It was not only intelligence of the French that the British Government had been getting. Their penetration of the Society of United Irishmen itself by informers at a reasonably high level had long been extensive. Among the principal informers, apart from the lawyer Macnally, was a former member of the Ulster Provincial Committee, a young Protestant gentleman named Samuel Turner, who had provided the information for the arrest of Arthur O'Connor at Margate. Thanks to such informers the government had in fact long been aware of the identity of most of the leaders of the United Irishmen.

It is a curious reflection on the contradictory nature of the political morality of the time that they had not felt able to arrest any of them earlier. For while prepared passively to condone, in the interests of the State, barbarities when practised on the peasantry in the course of a relentless hunt for arms, the government could not bring itself while the civil law still applied throughout most of Ireland to arrest political opponents without bringing them to trial. The normal processes of the law were, of course, always open to them, but for this sufficient evidence had to be available to make conviction certain. It was a condition of service made by most top-level informers, out of an understandable instinct of self-preservation, that they should not have to come forward in open court to give evidence. The government also had an interest in their not doing so, since even if the informer survived retaliation, he would be of little use as an informer in the future. And there was still a great deal of information they wanted. Whereas the United Irishmen's own knowledge of its associated Defender corps was vague enough, the government's view of the relationship was wrapped in mystery. All they knew was

* Both Tone and Lewins had had to spend a great deal of their time in Paris coping with the sort of jealousy invariably found among any groups of political exiles. Napper Tandy, claiming great military expertise on the strength of his membership of the old Volunteers corps, seems to have been the chief source of this. But of the Irishmen in Paris at this time, clearly it was Tone and Lewins whom the French trusted. Indeed, this fact was probably the main cause of the jealousy.

that considerable bodies of the discontented peasantry, organized as Defenders, were now affiliated to the United Irishmen's political conspiracy.
And they had to assume there was still much to discover before they could
have the situation under control.

However, early in March 1798, soon after O'Connor's arrest red-handed
at Margate, a new informer of great importance approached the government
with information on which, in the mounting tension, it was decided to take
action against the whole Directory. This new informer was a young silk-
merchant named Thomas Reynolds, a colonel in the United Irishmen's
military organization and a friend of Fitzgerald himself. He now revealed
to the government that the Leinster Provincial Committee of the United
Irishmen, including as it did members of the Supreme National Directory,
would be meeting in the house of the woollen merchant Oliver Bond on
12 March. Out of last-minute personal loyalty Reynolds seems to have
warned Fitzgerald to keep away. Fifteen members of the Directory were
taken that day, including Emmet, Bond and MacNeven.

Fitzgerald remained at large, but only for another few weeks. He spent
this time in feverish last-minute organization of military revolt. But before
it could break out he was caught in the house of a rich Dublin leather merchant, betrayed by yet another informer named Magan. Lying on a bed at
the moment the police entered the room, he fought furiously, stabbing an
officer many times with a knife and inflicting wounds which proved fatal.
Fitzgerald himself was shot through the shoulder in the struggle but the
wound was not thought to be serious at first. He died from it in prison six
weeks later. His arrest took place on the very day his uniform as commander-
in-chief of the rebel army, with its coat, jacket and trousers of dark green
edged with red, together with a conical military cap, was delivered to his
hiding place from the tailor.[13]

9

Repression, 1798

Military technique in Ulster had not been confined to the burning of houses and the periodical slaughter of guilty and innocent. It also included torture, though the methods were more or less the standard military punishments of the day. These involved picketting, or the suspension of a man by one arm with one pointed stake below his feet on which alone he could rest his weight, and, much more commonly, flogging, both applied as inducements to the victims to supply information. A clergyman living near Ballymena in County Antrim reported to his patron as early as May 1797 that the soldiers were not hesitating to strip men, tie them to a tree and flog them with bits and bridles.[1] In June 1797 he himself saw 'a country fellow' given seventy lashes, which was all he could take without fainting, and which would have rendered him useless for further information. A few days later, he watched an old man of over seventy stripped naked and given forty lashes while being held down by two soldiers.[2] A Belfast doctor confirmed that this sort of procedure was general when he wrote in October 1797: 'Many are the military outrages which have been committed in the north, such as inflictions of military punishment on poor people in no way subject to martial law.'[3]

But what had happened in the North was nothing to the severity with which the military – regulars, yeomanry and militia – soon applied their systems of punishments to suspects in Leinster, particularly after the arrests of the leading United Irish conspirators at Bond's house. The advanced state of the conspiracy was now openly revealed and the government set out to break it by the harshest methods possible.

The army's official view of what constituted harsh methods can be gauged from its own standard of punishment at the time. Thus, in the previous year, when a number of militia and dragoons in a camp at Bandon near Cork were found to have taken the local Defender oath, they were given sentences which, when other than death, consisted of from 500 to 999 lashes. Only between 200 and 425 of these were in fact administered – the remainder being remitted on the culprit's agreement to serve abroad for the rest of his life. General Coote, no sentimentalist, who witnessed this particular flogging, described it in a letter to the lord lieutenant as 'a dreadful business'.[4] A man who as a boy of ten witnessed floggings of his neighbours by the army in 1798 described how one of them had begged to be shot while his flesh was being torn to shreds and how another, before he had received a hundred lashes, had cried out: 'I'm a-cutting through.' There had been a very heavy shower of rain at the time, he remembered.[5] Numerous accounts of such floggings which were now to play a most important part in Irish history confirm their bestiality with descriptions of flesh torn in lumps from the body by the cat o' nine tails, and the baring of bones and even internal organs.

On 30 March 1798, many districts in Leinster were officially proclaimed as areas in which the military could thenceforth live at free quarters and search for arms. Discipline among the militia and the yeomanry was poor at the best of times. General Sir John Moore had already noted in his diary in January 1798 that the system of proclaiming areas simply meant 'to let loose the military, who were encouraged in acts of great violence against all who were supposed to be disaffected'.[6] Now, in April and the first weeks of May 1798, there were virtually no restraints at all on the troops living at free quarters in the proclaimed districts. Their one task was to obtain the surrender of arms and procure information as to the identities of local sergeants, captains and colonels of the United Irishmen.

Other forms of torture besides flogging were introduced. All were applied fairly indiscriminately to both guilty and innocent since torture itself was the speediest method of distinguishing between the two. So-called 'half-hanging' became common: the pulling of a rope tight round the victim's neck from which it was slackened every time he lost consciousness. A fiercely loyal Protestant of New Ross in County Wexford described with some disapproval how about this time he began to hear of 'very many punishments put in execution in the barracks yard to exort confessions of guilt'.[7] One man, named Driscol, a hermit-like figure who was taken in a wood outside the town with two Roman Catholic prayer-books in his pocket on which he was suspected of swearing United Irishmen, was half-strangled three times and flogged four times during confinement 'but to no purpose'.[8] In other districts, the torment of the pitch-cap was introduced. This was a brown paper cap filled with molten pitch which was jammed on to the head of the victim and, after it had been allowed to set a little, was then set fire to. As the frantic wearer tried to tear it off, burning pitch fell into his eyes and down his face and the cap itself could usually only be removed with the accompaniment of much hair and scalp as well. The practice was inspired by a recent fashion of cropping the hair short adopted in imitation of the French republicans. A song, 'Croppies Lie Down', popular among the Orange yeomanry, acquired a sinister ring for all who either rashly or just unwittingly adopted the fashion.

> Oh, Croppies ye'd better be quiet and still
> Ye shan't have your liberty, do what ye will,
> As long as salt water is found in the deep

Our foot on the neck of the Croppy we'll keep.
Remember the steel of Sir Phelim O'Neill
Who slaughtered our fathers in Catholic zeal
And down, down, Croppies, lie down ...

But it was the floggings which inspired the greatest terror and which proved the most effective method of obtaining quick information and a surrender of arms. After the proclamation of 30 March, the wooden triangle, on which the victim was spreadeagled, seems first to have been set up in the town of Athy in County Kildare. A captain of the United Irishmen wrote many years later an account of the terror which first-hand news of this immediately inspired in his own town of Carlow, some ten miles away.

There was no ceremony used in choosing victims, the first to hand done well enough. ... They were stripped naked, tied to the triangle and their flesh cut without mercy and though some men stood the torture to the last gasp sooner than become informers, others did not, and to make matters worse, one single informer in the town was sufficient to destroy all the United Irishmen in it.[9]

General Sir John Moore came across one of these routine flogging sessions a few weeks later. The High Sheriff of Tipperary, a man named Fitzgerald, was at work. Already, by his severity he had most effectively broken the United Irish movement altogether in that county.

We found a great stir in Clogheen, [wrote Moore, who arrived there about ten o'clock on a hot fine morning]. A man tied up and being flogged, the sides of the streets filled with country people on their knees and hats off. ... The rule was to flog each person till he told the truth and gave the names of other rebels. These were then sent for and underwent a similar operation. Undoubtedly several persons were thus punished who richly deserved it. The number flogged was considerable. It lasted all forenoon. That some were innocent is I fear equally certain.[10]

A loyalist Quaker lady, a schoolteacher, already experiencing the 'unchecked robbery' which free quarters meant in her village of Ballitore, in County Kildare, now heard her once peaceful village street ring with the shrieks of those who were being flogged and the cries of their loved ones looking on. Guards were placed at every entrance to the village to prevent people entering or leaving. 'The torture,' she wrote later, 'was excessive, and the victims were long in recovering.'[11]

It is, however, necessary to remember that this whole system of torture was being carried out on the Irish population largely by Irish soldiers, a great proportion of them Catholics of the poorest class in the militia, who were ready enough to do their duty against their fellow-countrymen as unworthy rebels. Of all the troops available for the government in Ireland before and during the coming rebellion, over four-fifths were Irish.*

* On 8 December 1797 Sir John Moore listed 76,791 men as available to the government in Ireland out of whom 11,193 were English or Scots (Maurice Moore (ed.), *Diary of Sir John Moore*, vol. ii, p. 270). Additional English and Scots troops were not brought into Ireland in any quantity until after the rebellion was over.

Soon the terror of the floggings, the burning of houses, of pitch-capping, half-hanging and indiscriminate shooting was so great that all over Leinster people started sleeping out in the fields at night for safety. 'No one slept in his own house,' wrote a man who himself soon became a rebel though he had never been a United Irishman. 'The very whistling of the birds seemed to report the approach of an enemy.'[12] And although he was then writing some thirty years after the event he added that the memory of the wailings of the women and the cries of the children still awoke in his mind, even at that distance of time, feelings of deep horror.

On 29 May 1798 a Lady Sunderlin living in Sackville Street, Dublin, wrote to her friend, Mrs Roper, in Berkhamsted: 'Our long threatened rebellion has at length broken out in various parts about Dublin.'[13]

She made no mention of any other part of Ireland. She was safe, she said, and the rebellion appeared to be premature. The rebels were out in very great numbers, but wherever they had been engaged they had been defeated with great loss. The Lord Mayor's butler had been arrested as a United Irishman and the servants in the country were said to be letting the Defenders into their masters' houses.

Lady Sunderlin's account was fairly accurate. The rebellion which had now indeed erupted was to prove a haphazard, desperate and pathetically unco-ordinated affair.

After the arrests at Bond's house on 12 March the United Irishmen claimed that they had filled the vacancies on the Leinster Committee immediately and, five days later, on St Patrick's Day, they confidently announced in a handbill that the organization of the capital was 'perfect'.[14] A new National Directory had in fact been set up under the leadership of a young Protestant barrister of some brilliance, named John Sheares. Though born into the Establishment (his father had been a member of the Irish House of Commons) he had been deeply impressed by the French Revolution and had become a member of the Society of United Irishmen in its open and legal days. His respectability in fact was to prove a source of distress and embarrassment to the judge who was eventually to sentence him and his brother Henry to death for high treason, for he knew their parents well.[15]

The Sheares brothers were arrested only five weeks after the arrest of the previous Directory at Bond's, and two days after Lord Edward Fitzgerald himself had been caught. They had been working together with Fitzgerald and with Samuel Neilson on details of a plan to take Dublin, which involved the capture of the military barracks at Loughlinstown, theoretically undermined from within by the swearing in of many of the troops there as United Irishmen. The government had been watching them all the time. A young captain of the King's County militia, whom they had mistakenly and most rashly assumed to be sympathetic to their plans, simply because in earlier times he had expressed himself as a radical, was daily giving in a detailed report of all their preparations. This captain, whose name was Armstrong, has gone down in legend among the execrable informers of Irish history, but he was hardly an informer in any dishonourable sense and his first utterance on cross-examination at the Sheares' trial was the proud statement that he was an Irishman.[16] He made just as sincere though less flamboyant a claim to patriotic motives as the Sheares themselves, in whose house was found a premature address to the people, beginning: 'The National Flag, the Sacred Green, is at this moment flying over the Ruins of Despotism ...'[17]

The control of the original Directory over the United Irishmen's unwieldy component parts had been inadequate enough. That of the Sheares brothers was even more so. Whatever powerful mystique Fitzgerald himself might have been able to substitute for effective organization disappeared with his arrest on 19 May. By 21 May the Sheares brothers were in gaol. Whoever replaced them must have been going blindly through the motions of setting off the rebellion planned for 23 May. Matters had gone too far to be stopped. Among the peasantry the tension could hardly be contained any longer. The basic sense of injustice which had first driven them into the Defender organizations was now inflamed to desperation by the military terror. At the same time, this had very nearly broken their spirit. They were at a point where the alternatives of total despair or a desperate gesture were perilously close together.

William Farrel, a United Irish captain from Carlow, gives a vivid account of the way in which the local attempt at rebellion in that town finally came about. It may serve as an individual representative example of the experience of many localities in and about the Irish midlands at this time. Everything was expected from the great men in Dublin, but when it came to fighting 'everyone wished most earnestly to see it done but none cared to do the job himself'.[18] Government posters had been up in Carlow town for several days, demanding the surrender of arms and threatening the full rigour of martial law at free quarters if they were not forthcoming. Only ten miles from Athy and its flogging triangle everyone now knew what that meant. In the absence of any word from 'the great men behind the curtain in Dublin' the United Irishmen of Carlow themselves debated as to whether to surrender the arms or not. Farrel himself was in favour of doing so, but the majority were not, and on 24 May orders came down from Dublin to rise.

The United Irishmen's military organizer in the district was a man named Heydon, actually a member of a local yeomanry corps. After alerting as many sympathizers in the town as he could, he rode off to raise the countryside. He found the country people reluctant to move, saying that they were 'heart-sick of the business and would much rather give it up and have peace'.[19]

They implored him not to lead them into the town unless he could guarantee that he could take it with the support he had there anyway. With a wild optimism which was often typical of future Irish conspiracies, Heydon replied that he had nearly all the yeomanry with him, nearly all the militia and a considerable number of the Ninth Dragoons who were stationed in the town. All the country people would have to do would be to march into the town at a given signal, raise a great shout and all would be over.

As evening came on it began to be whispered in Carlow town that the country people were coming in and that boats were ready on the River Barrow to ferry other contingents of rebels over from the neighbouring Queen's County. Farrel himself stole out of the town to check on this last report, but finding it to be false became even more determined to have nothing to do with what he was now convinced must be a disastrous rising. In the darkness, though, about a thousand of the Carlow men were already gathering. A famous ballad written many years later immortalizes another Farrel of this time, a man of at least more ballad-worthy mettle:

'Oh, then, tell me Sean O'Farrel, tell me where you hurry so?'
'Hush my boucal, hush and listen' – and his cheeks were all aglow –
'I bear orders from the Captain; get you ready quick and soon
For the pikes must be together by the rising of the Moon.'

'Oh then, tell me Sean O'Farrel, where the gathering is to be?'
'In the old spot, by the river, right well known to you and me.
One word more: for token signal whistle up the marching tune
With your pike upon your shoulder by the rising of the Moon.'

Out from many a mud-walled cabin, eyes were watching through the
    night:
Many a manly heart was throbbing for that blessed warning light;
Murmurs passed along the valley, like the banshee's lonely croon;
And a thousand pikes were flashing by the rising of the Moon.

Down along yon singing river, that dark mass of men was seen;
High about their shining weapons floats their own beloved green
Death to every foe and traitor! Forward strike the marching tune,
And hurrah, my boys, for Freedom! 'Tis the Rising of the Moon.

The rebels started moving towards Carlow at two o'clock in the morning of 25 May. A Catholic parish priest called O'Neill whose house they passed came out and went on his knees imploring them to turn back. They pressed on. But a little later doubts seem to have beset them and they were only rallied by a man called Murray with a blunderbuss who threatened to blow out the brains of the first man to turn back. One contemporary says that a man was shot as an example, thus giving timely warning to the garrison of their approach.[20] Heydon repeated his assurances that the town was as good as won. They marched into Carlow through one of the four main gates without opposition and halted when they came to the potato market. There they raised the great shout which was to deliver the town into their hands. It died away into the silence of the night.

They had hardly time to sense panic before the first shot rang out. The yeomanry, the militia and the Ninth Dragoons had indeed been waiting for them and now opened a murderous fire. They flew, wrote Farrel long afterwards, 'like frightened birds'.[21] But there was virtually nowhere to fly to for they had been neatly trapped. Those who escaped the firing from the ends of the streets and from the windows of the houses managed to force their way into a cluster of poor peasant cabins on the edge of the town. The soldiers poured volley after volley into the cabins, setting them alight. Those who tried to escape the flames were bayonetted or shot or immediately hanged from signposts and gateways. Between four and five hundred people may have died altogether. The government troops had no losses at all. It was a massacre. Many bodies were thrown, when daylight came, into a sand-pit called 'the croppy hole'.

Heydon, who had vainly tried to rally his panic-stricken followers for a time, had eventually decided to escape as best he could. He succeeded in doing this by putting on his yeomanry uniform and mingling with his former comrades. He made his way out into the country but was caught three miles from Carlow and hanged the next day from a lamp-iron, going to his death, as Farrel who witnessed it declared, 'seemingly as unconcerned as if he was going to some place of amusement'. The rope broke, and after lying insensible on the ground for a few moments he had to go through the business of mounting the ladder and being 'turned off' all over again. This time the rope held.

Retribution was only just beginning. The triangle was now set up in the barrack square at Carlow and scenes of incredible brutality took place as men were stripped and flogged and their flesh cut to shreds by the cat o' nine tails in attempts to extract information from them. Some who refused to talk were finally hanged, naked, bleeding and insensible as they were. Gordon, the loyalist historian, reckons that some two hundred people were executed in Carlow by hanging or shooting, as a result of courts-martial alone.[22]

A dozen or more such 'risings' of ill-organized groups of peasantry armed with many pikes and some firearms took place in the counties round Dublin between 23 and 25 May. Sometimes these amounted to little more than demonstrations. Mary Leadbeater, the Quaker lady who had heard her village street ringing with the cries of those flogged by the soldiers, was now to have experience of the rebels.[23] After the withdrawal of the military to deal with the situation nearer Dublin, certain people in the village who had been lying low suddenly appeared in the streets dressed in green, and in the afternoon about two or three hundred men came in from the surrounding country armed with pikes, knives and pitchforks and carrying poles with green flags flying. They were accompanied by young girls wearing green ribbons and carrying pikes and were headed by a man riding a white horse. A number of the rebels crowded into her kitchen demanding food and drink, but otherwise behaved quite respectfully. She was cutting bread for them a little apprehensively when a small elderly man relieved her of the task telling her not to worry and that they would be 'out in a shot'. She told them that she felt unable to wear anything green since as a Quaker she could not join any party. 'What?' they asked her, 'not the strongest?'

'None at all,' she replied.

Among them she noticed a young farmer named Horan whom she had seen unhappily getting a 'protection' slip from an officer only a few days before. His whole face was now quite changed and radiant with excitement.

The man on the white horse did what he could to prevent bloodshed and 'showed as much courage as humility'. But at least one yeoman who had been taken prisoner by the rebels was piked and shot. They took a number of horses which they galloped about unmercifully, making her feel glad that she had lent hers to a yeomanry officer and thus could not give it to a rebel who demanded it from her with a drawn sword. Her other bad moment was when one rebel, brandishing a pistol, demanded her husband, though another persuaded him to leave her alone.

The real horror of these Quakers' experience only took place when the loyalist military descended on the village a few days later. The rebels had by then wisely fled, leaving only peaceable loyalists behind. Nevertheless, for two hours the village was delivered over to what Mary Leadbeater called 'the unbridled licence of a furious soldiery'. Houses were burned, windows smashed, and one soldier on learning that she had given food and drink to the rebels placed a musket against her breast and seemed about to shoot her when he changed his mind and simply swept pans and jugs off the kitchen table with his musket and broke the kitchen window. Another soldier lolling in one of her chairs boasted of having just burned a man in a barrel. She saw the grisly remains in the village a little later.

Outside, terrible scenes were being enacted. The village blacksmith, who had actually been acquitted of the charge of making pikes by a court-martial a few days before, was taken out and shot. The village carpenter who had hidden himself in terror with his family in the graveyard was unearthed there and quickly done to death. The widow of a yeoman who had actually been killed fighting on the loyalist side in a battle against rebels at Kilcullen had her house sacked while her brother, her son, and her servant were all murdered. The local doctor, himself a yeoman, a much loved man who had taken control of the village when the army left, and had had his horse and all his instruments taken by undisciplined rebels with whom he finally made terms, was now given a peremptory court-martial in the course of which he was several times slashed by dragoons' sabres and finally clumsily shot. 'Such', wrote the Quaker lady, 'are the horrors of civil war.'

It was the sort of pattern that was repeating itself in these days in many of the counties round Dublin. Only at one point, at Prosperous in County Kildare, where some twenty-eight men of the Cork militia were trapped in a burning barracks and slaughtered either in the flames or on the ends of pikes as they jumped from the blazing windows, did the rebels have anything that might be called a victory. The leader of the rebels on this occasion was a Catholic lieutenant of yeomanry named Esmond, who after his victory went back to his unit and nonchalantly reappeared there, as if nothing had happened, to take part on the loyalist side in the defence of Naas. He was recognized by a soldier who had escaped from Prosperous, sent to Dublin and hanged.

At all the other points the rebels were finally routed with great slaughter, though at a few points they first inflicted some casualties on the troops, and the scale of the rebel movements in Kildare caused Dublin Castle considerable anxiety for a time. The rebels' own casualties were said to be enormous, running, so the army claimed, into several hundred after each battle. It seems likely that the majority of these rebel casualties took place after the battle itself was over. William Farrel, the United Irishman of Carlow, described how, after the events there, 'any person seen flying through the country could be shot on the spot, without any ceremony, and no more thought of it than shooting a sparrow'.[24] Lord Cornwallis, who became both viceroy, replacing Camden, and commander-in-chief after some weeks of rebellion, wrote to the British Prime Minister that the numbers of enemy given as destroyed were 'greatly exaggerated', adding that he was sure anyone found in a brown coat (i.e. civilian clothes) within miles of the action was 'butchered without discrimination'.[25] Though this was perhaps to be expected in the circumstances from the loosely disciplined units of yeomanry, particularly where they were composed of Orangemen, it is clear that the same barbaric ferocity was displayed by the Catholic militia itself, of whom Cornwallis indeed wrote that they were 'ferocious and cruel in the extreme when any poor wretches either with or without arms came within their power'.[26] 'In short,' he added, 'murder appears to be their favourite pastime.' Burnings of houses, floggings and summary executions now began to take place on a far greater and more violent scale even than before.

Even before the inevitable retribution had made itself felt in its full horror, such desperate heart as the local rebel leaders had managed to put into their disordered bands in Kildare and the neighbouring counties was showing signs of disappearing. An assembly of some two thousand rebels, under the leadership of a man named Perkins, surrendered their arms on the Curragh of Kildare on condition that Perkins himself should be delivered up and the rest of them be allowed to return home unmolested, which they did, 'dispersing homewards in all directions with shouts of joy, and leaving thirteen cart-loads of pikes behind'.[27] A few days later an attempt by another large collection of rebels to repeat this performance foundered when somebody discharged his firearm by mistake and the military seized the excuse to massacre several hundred of them.

A fight on the hill of Tara, ancient seat of the High Kings of Ireland, which resulted in the death of some 350 rebels for the loss of relatively few loyalist troops, was remarkable for the effective part played in the action on the loyalist side by the Catholic Lord Fingall and his Catholic yeomanry.[28] Not that there was any real fear of Catholics, simply as Catholics, being favourable to the rebels. A few days after the desultory rebellion had erupted a loyal address, signed by the entire Roman Catholic college of Maynooth, four Catholic peers and some two thousand other members of the gentry, was presented to the lord lieutenant. This ran:

We, the undersigned, his Majesty's most loyal subjects, the Roman Catholics of Ireland, think it necessary at this moment publicly to declare our firm attachment to His Majesty's person, and to the constitution under which we have the happiness to live. . . . We cannot avoid expressing to Your Excellency our regret at seeing, amid the general delusion, many, particularly of the lower orders, of our own religious persuasion engaged in unlawful associations and practices.[29]

Nevertheless, some doubts about the possible delusion of the Catholic militia were understandable, for they themselves were drawn from the lower orders. The Defenders had made a good deal of nominal progress in seducing the militia from their allegiance the previous year. Courts-martial in the summer of 1797 alone had shown that soldiers from at least eleven different county militias had taken the Defender oath and that the 2nd Fencible Dragoons stationed near Cork were also seriously tainted.[30] And though the deterrent effect of the savage punishments meted out to the culprits can hardly have been nil, it was natural for the government to be apprehensive when rebellion finally broke out.* However, from the start the militia showed remarkable loyalty, earning rebuke only for the very ferocity they displayed against those of their own class they met as rebels.

'You will have observed,' a correspondent wrote to the Chief Secretary, Pelham, after a week of the '98 rebellion, 'that our militia, even the King's County regiment, have all behaved very well,' though he added that there had been 'instances of disaffection among the yeomanry'.[31]

Lord Castlereagh, who substituted for Pelham during the latter's ill-health, and was eventually to replace him as Chief Secretary, wrote, referring to the militia's regrettable excesses among the civilian population, that they were 'in many instances defective in subordination, but in none have they

---

* As late as July 1798, twelve privates of the Westmeath militia were tried and sentenced for taking the United Irish oath. Report of Secret Committee of House of Commons (Dublin 1798), 297.

shown the smallest disposition to fraternize, but on the contrary, pursue the insurgents with the rancour unfortunately connected with the nature of the struggle'.[32]

It might of course have been argued that the real test of the militia's loyalty could not be made until the French had landed. But there was no sign whatsoever of the French. Tone, who had spent most of the month before the outbreak of the rebellion 'deliciously with my family at Paris',[33] was now back with the Army of England at Le Havre, but he was soon doing his best to get sent to India to join his brother Will, recognizing, as he said, 'that there is no more question or appearance here of an attempt on England than of one on the Moon'.[34] On that same day about three o'clock in the morning Lady Louisa Connolly, sister of Lord Edward Fitzgerald, watched about two hundred rebels force their way through her gates at Castletown in County Kildare and pass quietly across her front lawn.[35] Writing about it soon afterwards she said they did not seem to know what they were fighting for. To the North, South and West, she reported, everything was perfectly quiet. Yet to the South, unknown to her as yet, the most serious threat the rebels were to mount was already under way.

10

Rebellion in Wexford

Dublin itself, which had remained firmly under government control, assumed proudly for a time something of a siege mentality. A United Irish attempt to undermine the city from within by getting the lamplighters to withhold their services was summarily countered by sending them to work with, as the Bishop of Dromore wrote gleefully to his wife in England, 'a bayonet in the breach'.[1] Men of sixty and seventy put on uniforms and joined any corps that would have them.[2] A young yeomanry captain arriving in the capital on 4 June, the day after Fitzgerald's death from his wounds in prison, found 'every man in the city a soldier'.[3] The law courts were shut and all business was at a standstill. The Castle was barricaded and gunners stood on the alert outside it with lighted matches ready beside their guns. The same was true of St Stephen's Green – then on the outermost limits of the city. Express messengers were arriving every moment with accounts of what was happening to the rebels and the army. Communication with Cork and Limerick had been cut off for several days and had only just been re-opened.

The next day, this particular captain was to join his yeomanry unit in the Queen's County, where 11,500 men were said to have been sworn into the United Irishmen, although, as he wrote in his letter, 'by flogging and co. such information had been gained as to enable the officers and magistrates of the county to get possession of many of the Captains and to break in upon their organization'.[4] However, news from the South was bad. Wexford Town and most of that county were in rebel hands and 'matters seemed to wear a serious aspect'.

An organization of the Defenders had existed in County Wexford for many years. In 1793 they had fought the celebrated battle outside the town of Wexford itself over the raising of the new militia.* But since then they had not been particularly active. In 1797 some United Irish emissaries had been in the county, circulating what seemed increasingly plausible rumours among the peasantry that the Orangemen were about to rise and murder all Papists. But beyond strengthening an already natural sense of Catholic peasant solidarity, they do not seem to have created anything like a really active conspiracy. Wexford was in no sense the county where anyone expecting rebellion

* See above, p. 60.

in this year would have expected it to appear particularly menacing. The number of sworn United Irishmen in the county – as distinct from Defenders – was only around three hundred.[5] And yet it was only in Wexford, so feebly organized, that the rebellion in fact took on any menacing proportions at all.

The explanation of this lies partly in accident – the cause of much important history – and partly in a number of special factors local to the county. One such local factor was this very absence of serious rebellious organization, and the consequent lack of concern on the part of the government until almost the last moment. The number of militia or regular troops garrisoning the county was small. As a result, when the government happened to find a note of Fitzgerald's which mentioned the port of Wexford as possibly suitable for French disembarkation, a last-minute alarm was raised about the state of the county. The task of searching for arms was left to the local yeomanry, who were mainly Protestants, and by their amateur nature less concerned with the niceties of disciplined behaviour even than other troops. Here another special local factor operated. For the Protestants of Wexford had long been more sectarian in their outlook than those of most other counties of Leinster. In the days of the original Volunteers it had been the one county in Ireland not to permit Catholics to enrol in the corps.[6] And in 1798 itself a private attempt to raise a yeomanry corps composed largely of Catholics had collapsed because of official disapproval.[7] Thus when the Protestant yeomanry now began their forays round the country in a last-minute search for arms they employed a sectarian viciousness which much aggravated the sense of apprehension and terror already there. In 1797 only 16 out of 142 parishes had been 'proclaimed' as Defender-tainted areas subject to special military regulations. As late as 9 April 1798 Lord Mountnorris, one of the most influential Protestant landowners of the county, who for some time had been sucessfully exhorting the people to give up arms and make declarations of allegiance to the government, forwarded one such declaration to the government signed by a local priest and 757 of his flock from the small Wexford parish of Boulavogue.[8]

The chief signatory of this declaration of 9 April was a curate named Father John Murphy. Since he was soon to take a prominent part in the insurrection, there has been an assumption by some commentators, chiefly Protestant, that the declaration represented merely deception on the part of a cunning priesthood and peasantry. But other commentators, usually Catholic, maintain that this and other similar declarations were genuine and made in good faith at the time; and this in fact seems more probable. The completely haphazard nature of the insurrection in Wexford when it did break out, with its lack of considered strategy or design, and its precarious and largely aimless gyrations round the country as it gathered force, suggests not artifice and cunning but an act of desperation undertaken at the last moment in the belief that neither declarations of allegiance nor written 'protections' were any longer of use against the burnings, floggings, shootings and general depredations of the military. Certainly a Protestant clergyman, the Reverend James Gordon, who lived in the heart of the affected area at the time and afterwards wrote an intelligent and balanced history of the whole rebellion, thought that but for the floggings and half-hangings and other 'acts of severity' the rebellion there might possibly never have broken out at all.[9]

To supplement the yeomanry and make matters worse, the troops the government sent to Wexford were the North Cork militia who, though predominantly Catholic, were the very troops popularly credited with the invention of the pitch-cap method of torture. One of their sergeants named Heppenstal had acquired the nickname of 'the walking gallows' for his peculiar skill in half-hanging men over his shoulder. And the Reverend James Gordon, emphasizing the fear which gripped the people of Wexford in these last days of May 1798, tells of a man who having subscribed for a pike which he had not yet received and which he was therefore unable to surrender, actually dropped dead from fright.[10]

The yeomanry and the North Cork militia were already at work in Wexford when the rebellion broke out in the counties round Dublin. The sense of terror naturally rose accordingly. News of the sadistic slaughter at Carlow must have travelled fast to the adjoining county. Certainly news of the shooting of twenty-eight prisoners at Carnew in Wicklow and the killing of others at Dunlavin in the same county reached Wexford, where the country people were already sleeping out in the fields at night in fear, on 26 May.

The day before, a party of men had been cutting turf near Boulavogue, the very parish which had sent in its massive declaration of allegiance to the Crown six weeks before. The curate, Father John Murphy, was with the men on the top of a bank when a troop of yeoman cavalry came galloping up to them. After wheeling round they came galloping back again and again drew up in front of them in menacing fashion.[11] Murphy, who had been playing an important part in getting the people to surrender their arms in return for 'protections', decided that the situation was too menacing for them to remain at work and recommended them to return home.

The Arms Proclamation in Wexford had allowed a period of fourteen days for the surrender of arms. But the local magistrates and troops had shown no inclination to wait that long but had begun floggings and other tortures immediately.

An eye-witness of the Boulavogue incident said of the mood of the time: 'A portion of the men in this district had now become spiritless. They saw that a Proclamation issued with all the formality and apparent binding of an Act of Parliament was despised and made no account of ... Their arms in a great measure surrendered, they became silent, sullen and resolved to meet their fate with such arms as they were in possession of.'[12] He adds that even now such thoughts were not generally entertained but were only being put forward as far as he knew by individuals in this one locality.

Murphy, who was constantly being asked for advice, was himself becoming more and more desperate. On the evening of the next day, 26 May, accompanied by a number of men in similar mood, some of whom were carrying arms, he had just visited the house of a neighbouring farmer when he encountered a troop of cavalry similar to that on the day before. The cavalry either fired a volley and demanded the surrender of the group's arms, or simply made the demand. In either case they were met with shots and a shower of stones. While the main body of the cavalry then withdrew with some circumspection, the lieutenant in charge, named Bookey, and one other man pressed through the crowd and set fire to the farm. The thatch caught alight easily, for Ireland was experiencing an unusually long period of hot dry weather that summer.

About ten minutes later, attempting to rejoin the main body of his men, Bookey and his companion found themselves surrounded by Murphy's group. Someone stabbed Bookey with a pike on the side of his neck. He fell from his horse and was grimly finished off on the ground. His horse, which had also received a pike thrust in the flank, plunged so violently in its agony that it wrenched the pike from the pikeman's hand and galloped all the way into the nearest village, trailing the ugly weapon behind it.* In the words of an eye-witness of this event: 'The first blow of the insurrection in Wexford was now struck and they immediately proceeded to rouse their neighbours – a thing easily done, as scarcely any of them had slept in their houses on that, or the preceding night.'[13]

The next day, as a reprisal, houses were in flames all over the countryside. Bookey's cavalry unit burned over 170 on that day by their own admission, including Father Murphy's chapel at Boulavogue.[14] They also slaughtered a number of people who seemed as if they were collecting in a rebel body on Kiltomas Hill. The group with Father Murphy, gathering strength to about a thousand men, camped on Oulart Hill. They had only about forty to fifty firearms among them and virtually no commander. Father Murphy and the only other man with any sense of leadership, a sergeant of the local yeomanry named Roache who had joined them, were principally occupied in trying to decide what to do next and in preventing desertion. However, when they were attacked by a detachment of about 110 men of the North Cork militia, the rebels courageously held their ground and finally drove the troops from the hill, killing many of them for the loss of only about six of their own men.

As when the situation was reversed, most of the slaughter seems to have

---

* The detail book of the yeomanry unit involved merely records that Bookey, on meeting Murphy's party, ordered them to deliver their arms but was received with shots and a shower of stones which knocked him from his horse. The fuller account is the later record of an eye-witness.

taken place after the battle was over. The defeated men of the North Cork militia, being Catholics, presented Catholic prayer books to prove it and called out for mercy but received none, or none at least from the rebel pikes. One of the last to die, when asked his name, replied in Irish: 'Thady Illutha'. But since the Wexford rebels did not understand Irish they had to have this translated for them as Thady, the Unfortunate. Whereupon they appropriately ran the man through with a pike. He did not die immediately but struggled helplessly, calling for mercy for some time.[15]

Flushed with this victory at Oulart Hill, and equipped now with a valuable addition of arms from the slaughtered militia, the rebels went on a round-about march through the countryside and finally attacked the town of Enniscorthy. A clergyman who watched their assault through a telescope noticed a man on a bright bay horse who seemed to be some sort of leader. He was wearing a scarlet coat which glittered in the sun and had probably been taken from one of the officers of the North Cork killed the day before, but he was without boots. 'Yet,' noted the clergyman, 'he rode along the rising ground with some address, and the mass of the people moved in whatever direction he waved or pointed a drawn sword by the gleam of which I could observe with my glass that it was a long sabre.' He could also discern two or three white standards and one green flag.[16] After a three-hour fight the rebels took Enniscorthy, virtually burning it to the ground in the process. They then set up what was to be their most permanent base camp in the rebellion on a prominence beside the town called Vinegar Hill.

On the Sunday morning on which Enniscorthy was taken the young Catholic farmer, Thomas Cloney, who had found even the whistling of the birds so sinister* and who had himself never been either a United Irishman or a Defender, still knew nothing of this startling course of events though he a Defender, still knew nothing of this startling course of events though he lived not far away. He and his neighbours were simply filled with gloomy forebodings for their own safety in anticipation of the fury of the soldiers then known to be rampaging round the countryside. They had been listening for some time to the sounds of battle from Enniscorthy when a roughly-dressed horseman galloped up crying 'Victory! Victory!'[5] His neighbours immediately recovered sufficient spirit at least to search the houses of the neighbouring yeomanry and commit a certain number of 'excesses'.

Two days later, large bodies of rebels rode up to Cloney's house on two separate occasions to urge him to join them. He finally agreed to do so on the principle that this part of the country was now a prey to the military whether it resisted or not, so he might as well resist. He rode off to Vinegar Hill. There he found some thousands of people in a state of total disorder and confusion, relating their sufferings at the hands of the military to each other and calling blood-thirstily for revenge. The only concept of future strategy seemed to be that they should march off towards whichever place seemed

* See above, p. 100.

most likely next to find itself at the mercy of the troops. But there was such difficulty in determining which this would be, each man putting forward the claims of his own district as paramount, that no final decision could be reached. Revenge was more easily come by, and had indeed already begun.

Vinegar Hill was topped by the remains of a windmill on which a green flag had been planted. Inside this mill some thirty-five Protestants from Enniscorthy, suspected in the most general and haphazard way of Orange sympathies, had been collected and on the very Tuesday of Cloney's arrival some fourteen or fifteen of them were clumsily put to death by an execution squad of rebels armed with pikes and guns, lined up in front of the windmill door and commanded by a man with a drawn sword named Martin.[17] One of their victims, severely wounded, was found next morning insensible but still alive by his wife, just as an old man with a scythe was going round the silent forms finishing off those that showed any signs of life.[18]

Another man, a glazier of Enniscorthy called Davies, had even greater luck. The Protestant clergyman, Gordon, relates how, after hiding in a privy for four days 'during which he had no other sustenance than the raw body of a cock, which had by accident alighted on the seat, he fled from this loathesome abode', but was found, taken to Vinegar Hill, shot through the body, piked in the head and thrown into a grave where he remained covered with earth and stones for twelve hours.[19] His faithful dog discovered him, scraped away the earth and revived him by licking his face. The man came to, dreaming that pikemen were about to stab him again and moaning the name of a local Catholic priest whom he hoped might save him. This priest, one Father Roche, happened to have become one of the rebel leaders, and the pikemen, who were indeed in the offing, were so impressed by what seemed their victim's conversion to Catholicism in near-miraculous circumstances that they took him to a house where he recovered.

A Protestant lady, a Mrs White, who bravely came to Vinegar Hill in search of a 'protection' from this same Father Roche for herself and her family, also described the scene there. The camp

> ... presented a dreadful scene of confusion and uproar. ... Great numbers of women were in the camp. Some men were employed in killing cattle, and boiling them in pieces in large copper brewing-pans; others were drinking, cursing and swearing; many of them were playing on various musical instruments, which they had acquired by plunder in the adjacent Protestant houses ...[20]

Besides musical instruments the rebels also brought Wilton carpets and fine sheets to Vinegar Hill, and to other such hill camps which became a standard feature of their movements round the Wexford countryside during the next few weeks.[21] However, they had few tents and mostly lay out in the open at nights in the astonishingly fine weather which they took as a favourable omen, saying that it would not rain again until final victory was theirs.[22]

Mrs White got her protection. 'No man to molest this house, or its inhabitants, on pain of death.' However, while she was still on the hill trying to obtain it '... the pikemen would often show us their pikes all stained with blood, and boast of having murdered our friends and neighbours'.[23] Though there is plenty of evidence that such vengeance – which was to be repeated elsewhere – was deplored by all the more intelligent and sensitive rebels like Cloney himself, it was difficult to restrain because it was the one form of positive action easily available to the mob in the general frustration. The discipline which the senior officers were able to maintain among the rebels was always tenuous. Otherwise, quite apart from humanitarian considerations, it would clearly have been in their interest to have employed the energies wasted on such brutalities in some more strictly military design.

The lack of almost any coherent strategic plan, or indeed of any true leadership, was to be the rebels' undoing. Their determination and bravery in the field, already displayed effectively enough at their first two victories at Oulart Hill and Enniscorthy, was to prove remarkable on many subsequent occasions, stemming as it did from the sense of desperation with which they had finally taken up arms. But their discipline even in battle was poor. The Reverend James Gordon wrote: 'As they were not, like regular troops, under any real command of officers, but acted spontaneously, each according to the impulse of his own mind, they were watched in battle one of another, each fearing to be left behind in case of retreat, which was generally swift and sudden.'[24] For the same reason, they were reluctant to take part in actions at night when it was less easy to tell what was going on and who was doing what. Cloney, the young farmer, although he had no previous military or organizational experience, soon found himself in a position of authority among the rebels. He described them as often 'ungovernable'. Since it was everyone's ambition to get hold of a firearm, in which few in fact had any experience, and since there was a good deal of drunkenness, they were constantly letting off their guns and exposing themselves and their comrades to danger.[25]

The rebels' clothes were usually those of the ordinary Wexford farmer or labourer of the day: felt flowerpot hats, swallow-tailed coats, corduroy knee-breeches, stockings and shoes with a buckle. Sometimes they carried raw wheat in their pockets as an iron ration. This, it is said, was often to be seen in the following year sprouting from the crude and nameless graves.[26] Some of the captains, colonels and generals wore a sort of uniform; Roache, the yeomanry sergeant who went over to the rebels before the battle of Enniscorthy, and became a general, is described by an eye-witness as wearing ordinary clothes except for 'two most enormous epaulettes and a silk sash and a belt in which he carried a large pair of horse pistols'.[27] He carried a sword by his side. The same witness says that the only proper uniform he ever saw was worn by a shoe-black named Monk who was a United Irish captain. This consisted of a light horse-man's jacket of green, with silver lace cross banded in front; pantaloons to match with silver seams; and a green helmet cap, with a white ostrich feather on top. The lower ranks wore white bands round their hats, while those with some authority had a green ribbon either with a gold harp surrounded by the words *Erin Go Bragh* ('Ireland for Ever'), or the words Liberty and Equality. Whenever they could, they decorated themselves with green feathers and green handkerchiefs. They carried flags and standards in profusion – generally green, but where enough green material could not be found any colour except orange did service. Their total numbers always seem to have been exaggerated by the loyalists, partly probably through natural apprehension, and partly because in military reports exaggeration of the enemy's numbers is equally convenient both in victory and defeat. Probably the total number of rebels who took arms in the entire Wexford insurrection did not exceed thirty thousand men, and may have been much less.[28]

The confusion and indecision to which the rebels on Vinegar Hill had immediately succumbed was temporarily resolved by the arrival there of emissaries from the loyalists in the town of Wexford. These were two Catholic gentlemen who had been imprisoned by the authorities for suspected United Irish sympathies, but had now been sent on parole to entreat the rebels to disperse. The entreaty had no other effect than to put the idea of capturing Wexford into the rebels' heads.

If there had been any sort of overall coordinated rebel plan, it would undoubtedly have involved an attempt to link up with the rebels in Kildare and the other counties near Dublin. In this case, the Wexford rebels would have marched north, rather than southwards to Wexford town, for already the town of Gorey on the northern route had been abandoned in anticipatory panic by the loyalists. In preparation indeed for the rebels' arrival, the middle-class Catholics of Gorey had been apprehensively forming themselves into guard companies to protect the houses of their Protestant neighbours. If the rebels had marched straight to Gorey, Arklow still further north would have been threatened and possibly also abandoned, whereupon the road into Wicklow and Dublin itself would have lain open. But this was no strategically designed rebellion. In fact, several days later, after further victories in the south, the rebels did eventually move northwards with some of their forces, but by that time the loyalist troops had had time to make their dispositions.

Before that, however, the rebels drawn quixotically towards Wexford had established another camp on a hill called Three Rocks just outside the town itself. There they spent the night, and in the stillness of the summer darkness the calls of rebel stragglers trying to find the men of their own locality could be heard clearly by the loyalists' outposts down below.[29] The next morning, on this site of Three Rocks, the rebels defeated and killed or captured some seventy men of the Meath militia and shortly afterwards entered Wexford itself from which the garrison had hastily withdrawn.

A genteel Protestant lady, a Mrs Brownrigg, who in panic had just taken passage with her family for Wales on a ship in the harbour, watched them pouring down in great hordes into the town. The captain of her ship promptly declared himself a United Irishman and prepared to land her again. Coming ashore, she was filled with terror to find the streets crowded with rebels shouting and firing their guns. She and her family took refuge in a Catholic friend's house where, however, they expected to be murdered hourly. The rebels held a sort of parade twice a day outside the house with fifes, fiddles and drums. 'It was,' she wrote in her diary, 'a kind of regular tumult, and everyone was giving his opinion.'[30]

A Quaker family, the Goffs, who lived in the country just outside Wexford, had heard the morning thunder of the cannon from Three Rocks and soon afterwards had their first contact with the rebels. These came in search of two Goff cousins who had been with the defeated militia in the battle and had taken refuge in the house. But the cousins managed to escape and the worst that happened to the Goffs that day was that two of their Catholic servants were made to join the rebel force and given pikes – 'the first we had seen'.[31] Mrs Goff, on hearing of this, was deeply shocked and insisted that 'she could not allow anything of the kind to be brought into the house'. Whereupon the offensive weapons were always left outside the door at nights when the servants returned home from their work with the rebel army. Some 250 other Protestants, however – men, women and children – were taken from all over the neighbourhood and confined as prisoners in a barn at Scullabogue House, about a mile and a half away, where a grisly fate awaited them.

The Goffs, who were respected by the country people like most of the Quakers in Ireland, suffered only from a continual massing of rebels on their lawn, asking for food. Large tubs of butter-milk and water were placed outside the door and the servants frequently had to stay up all night baking bread while the women of the house made their hands bleed cutting up bread and cheese.[32] The men were so impatient that they sometimes carried away whole loaves of bread and cheeses on the ends of their pikes. And though some of the pikemen had such savage tales to tell of their prowess that one of the girls wept as she was handing round the food, there were always others who rebuked such manners and won the Goff family's admiration and respect.

The absence of resolute stratagem and decision, which had so far marked the triumphant progress of the rebels round County Wexford, was now theoretically remedied by the appointment of a most curious commander-in-chief. This was Beauchamp Bagenal Harvey, a Protestant land-owner with the then considerable income of some £3,000 a year. A sophisticated radical by temperament, he had been a United Irishman in the early days of

the society, while it was still open and legal, but seems to have had no connection with it in its later clandestine phase, though his radical sympathies
clearly remained unchanged. He had made no secret of them and had been
arrested as a precaution by the authorities in Wexford on the outbreak of the
rebellion. He was immediately released by the insurgents when they entered
the town, and accepted the post of commander-in-chief, hoping, it seems,
that he might at least be able to bring some sort of order into their confused
ranks, though he had no military experience whatsoever. Another Protestant
gentleman of radical political inclinations, Matthew Keogh, who had at one
time been a captain in the British Army, was put in charge of the town of
Wexford itself by the rebels. Whether or not as a result of these appointments, some signs of stratagem now appeared in the rebel army – numbering by this time perhaps some sixteen thousand men. It split into three
columns, one moving westwards under its new commander-in-chief to the
important town of New Ross, whose capture would open the way to the
large bodies of Defenders known to exist in Kilkenny and Waterford. Another
column moved north to the town of Bunclody (or Newtownbarry) in an
attempt to penetrate into County Wicklow. A third moved north-west
towards Gorey and Arklow and the road to Dublin.

On 5 June one of the three decisive battles of the rebellion in Wexford
took place at New Ross. The rebel army of about three thousand men,
under Bagenal Harvey, had already delayed in camp for three days on the
nearby hill of Carrickburne, behind which it had spent some time trying out
artillery captured from the military at Three Rocks and elsewhere. Now,
on the 5th it finally attacked in force, driving before it, in antique Irish
military style, herds of cattle which most successfully overran the loyal outposts and enabled the rebels themselves to penetrate into the heart of the
town. There the battle raged backwards and forwards through the streets
for thirteen hours. An officer of the garrison, writing next day, said the rebel
attack was as severe as could possibly have been made by men fighting with
such primitive weapons, and that they gave proofs of 'very extraordinary
courage and enthusiasm'.[33] Thomas Cloney, who now held a position of
command over some five hundred men, described it as a battle fought entirely without tactics on both sides: '. . . two confused masses of men,
struggling alternately to drive the other back by force alone'.[34]

The rebels, who suffered from some desertions before the assault, were,
as Cloney admits, unamenable to discipline throughout, and the initial
attack, which had been intended simply to be a shock assault, turned into
a tumultuous uncontrolled advance of everyone who felt like joining in.
Once in the town the rebels displayed a fatal tendency to be distracted by
liquor. Cloney has a particular rebuke for one small group who made a cask
of port their base in an entrenched position just outside the town, from which
they occasionally sallied forth to inquire, 'How goes the day, boys?' before

safely retreating again to their source of courage. He singles out for praise a woodcutter's daughter named Doyle, who was always in the thick of the fight, distinguishing herself particularly by cutting off with a small billhook the cross belts of twenty-eight fallen dragoons and distributing their cartridge boxes to her friends. Cloney also pays tribute to the fighting qualities of his enemies in the Clare militia, almost all of whom must have been Catholics and who held their positions against him throughout the day. A young United Irish colonel, who led the first rebel assault, was John Kelly, a blacksmith from Killan. He was to become the hero of a popular ballad in later times when these bloody events acquired the rather fusty veneer appropriate to the drawing-room heroics of purely political warfare.

After thirteen hours, in which they had more than once looked like gaining the town, the rebels withdrew. Their losses were heavy, though probably nowhere near the figure of two thousand which some loyalist writers suggest. Among those killed on the rebel side was a Mr John Boxwell, a Protestant gentleman of some property. Among the hundred or so loyalist troops killed was Lord Mountjoy who, as Luke Gardiner twenty years before, had carried through the Irish House of Commons the first Catholic Relief Bill, permitting Catholics once again to own land.

On the same day as the battle of New Ross a massacre of Protestant prisoners took place in the barn at Scullabogue. It is thought that rebels flying from the battle with news of slaughter and defeat helped to work up a hysterical frenzy against them. The barn was set on fire and men, women and children inside it burned to death while others were executed on the lawn with pikes. Dinah Goff, the fourteen-year-old daughter of the local Quaker family, heard the screams and smelled the appalling stench a mile and a half away. The number said to have perished varies in different accounts but was possibly around two hundred.

Again, given the crude simplicity of the average Irish peasant of the day, it is not difficult to see how such atrocities came about. For weeks they had either experienced at first hand, or heard from those who had, examples of the most brutal physical cruelty on the part of the military. These were quite enough to sustain all the wild rumours of Orange atrocities and plots to annihilate all Catholics. What was surprising was not that such massacres occurred but that they did not occur more often. The crude state of mind of the average rebel is well illustrated by evidence from the various trials which eventually followed massacres such as that at Scullabogue. One of those responsible for the murders there, on hearing the cries and lamentations of the bereaved in a nearby village, came up to one of the women and threatened her that if he heard any more they would all go the way of their husbands. A few days later he solemnly gave the same woman a pass to have herself baptized a Catholic, for, he said, 'they must all be of one religion, it was that they were fighting for'.[35]

The other two rebel columns met with no more final success than the one which, under Harvey, had tried to take New Ross. But the Arklow column rambling in the general direction of Dublin gave the government at least one fright, at Tuberneering, before it was turned back. Here, as whenever they fought at all, the rebels fought with courage and tenacity, and, though displaying a typical characteristic of inexperienced troops in frequently firing too high, they made good tactical use of hedges and other natural cover. They decisively defeated a body of the king's troops, killing or taking prisoner over a hundred of them, largely through the skilful exploitation of a good ambush position. What, however, was even more typical of the rebels was their delay after their victory of several days spent looting and drinking before pressing on to attack the key town of Arklow on 9 June.

Yet when they did finally attack, they not only disposed themselves skilfully but fought with almost absurd dash and bravado. One young Irish loyalist who fought at Arklow thus described them:

... about 4 o'clock all of us at our posts I first saw in a moment thousands appear on the top of ditches forming one great and regular circular line from the Gorey road through the fields quite round to the Sand Banks near the sea as thick as they could stand. They all put their hats on their pikes and gave most dreadful yells. I could clearly distinguish their leaders riding through their ranks with flags flying ...[36]

Among these leaders was Father Michael Murphy, who two months before, like his namesake Father John from Boulogne had been prepared to swear allegiance to the Crown.

Grape shot among the rebels 'tumbled them by twenties'. But the gaps in their ranks were immediately re-filled and they came on like madmen.

Another of the king's soldiers at Arklow also describes the rebels coming at him with green flags flying and how one of their officers galloped ahead waving his hat and shouting: 'Blood and wounds, my boys! Come on, the town is ours!'[37] until, turning a corner into the mouth of a cannon, he and his horse were sent sprawling into the dust by a volley of muskets and bayonets and a final bullet in the head finished him off. The priest, Michael Murphy, was killed within thirty yards of the loyalist lines.

Bravery was not enough. The rebel tactics in anything like an open battle were unsubtle, their marksmanship inaccurate and their weapons inferior. Though they had some cannon of their own at Arklow, captured from the North Antrim militia at Tuberneering, it seems to have fired too high for much of the time, since the rebels had no artillerymen of their own and had to force prisoners taken with the guns to operate them, which they seem to have done to minimum effect. By eight o'clock in the evening the loyalist army still stood their ground, though there had already been some talk of their retreat. But the rebels, now short of ammunition, themselves

withdrew, with what one of them afterwards described as 'a sulky reluctance'.[38] The battle, regarded by the contemporary historian Gordon as the
most important in the whole rebellion, was over.

A third strong rebel column, consisting of about 2,500 men, had set out for
Bunclody (Newtownbarry) in County Wicklow under the command of another redoubtable priest, called Father Kearns. He was a man so physically
enormous that when, years before, in the course of a visit to France during
the Terror he had been hanged from a lamp-post, the lamp-iron had bent
under his weight and he had been saved from strangulation by his toes touching the pavement. His strength was, however, of little avail at Newtownbarry.
There his followers drove the King's County militia from the town, then
abandoned themselves to plunder and drunkenness on such a scale that
they proved an easy prey to the counter-attack which expelled them with
much slaughter.

Meanwhile, such coherent leadership as Beauchamp Bagenal Harvey had
temporarily represented had collapsed. His bizarre command had only lasted
a few days. Returning to his camp on Carrickbyrne Hill after the battle of
New Ross he was appalled to hear the news of what had happened at
Scullabogue. He immediately issued an edict from his headquarters which
reveals the true state of that army over which he was trying to exercise discipline. After laying down that all 'loiterers' found still at home should be
brought to join the army on pain of death, and equally threatening death to
all officers who deserted their men, all who left their respective quarters
when 'halted by their commander-in-chief ... unless they shall have leave
from their officers for doing so' and all who did not turn in plunder to
headquarters, he finally dealt with the appalling event that had taken place
that day, declaring that 'any person or persons who shall take upon them
to kill or murder any person or prisoner, burn any house, or commit any
plunder, without special written orders from the commander-in-chief, shall
suffer death'.[39] Though it could be maintained that this order came late in
the day and that the event at Scullabogue might have been foreseen, at least
one body of Protestant prisoners had reason to be grateful for it. It seems
certain that twenty-one Protestants would have been massacred at Gorey
after the battle of Arklow but for the arrival in time there of the order from
Carrickbyrne. Since there was, however, nothing in the order about applying
the torture of the pitch-cap to prisoners, this was proceeded with – a significant enough comment in itself on the motive of revenge behind such atrocities. Even at this simple level, however, the lust for vengeance was by no
means always indulged. On one occasion, when a Quaker found a group
of rebels about to flog a man suspected of being an informer they agreed
to desist, declaring that 'though they had received very grievous treatment
they ought not to return evil for evil'.[40] And the clergyman who had watched
the battle for Enniscorthy through his spy-glass later commented : 'In justice

I must allow that the rebels often displayed humanity and generosity deserving of praise and admiration.'[41]

Whether on account of the excessive humanitarianism of his edict or simply because he had lost the battle of New Ross the day before, the rebels now deposed Harvey from his rank of military commander-in-chief, and his place was taken by Father Roche, who had been the victor at Tuberneering. Harvey continued to head the rather tenuous apparatus of rebel civic government which had its seat in Wexford town, but he was becoming a desperate man. Only two days after his deposition, when a fellow-Protestant wrote to him beseeching a 'protection', Harvey replied:

I from my heart wish to protect all property; I can scarce protect myself. ... I took my present situation in hopes of doing good and preventing mischief and had my advice been taken by those in power the present mischief would never have arisen. ... God knows where the business will end, but end how it will the good men of both parties will inevitably be ruined.[42]

And according to Mrs Brownrigg, the genteel Protestant lady who had failed to escape from Wexford town, he told her that 'he had no real command and that they were a set of savages exceeding all descriptions'.[43]

In the short run, there could now only be one end to the rebellion: inexorable destruction of the rebel forces by loyalist troops. This took place in the course of a few weeks. After one particularly frightful scene of last-minute massacre on the wooden bridge at Wexford, in the course of which perhaps a hundred Protestants were either shot or piked and tossed writhing from the ends of pikes into the waters of the River Slaney below, the rebels withdrew from the town to face a concerted government attack on their main camp at Vinegar Hill on 21 June. It was a strong position, with what a loyalist eye-witness described as the rebels' 'green flag of defiance' flying from the remains of the old windmill.[44] Another witness recounts how the rebels themselves began the battle while the Crown forces under General Lake were still waiting for reinforcements. Lake then fired eighty or ninety 'bomb-shells' into their ranks, carrying 'death in a variety of awful forms to the terrified and wondering multitude' who, according to this witness, were soon crying out, 'We can stand anything but those guns which fire twice.'[45] An assault was then ordered and after a two-hour climb, during which the rebels kept up a smart but irregular fire on the attackers, the summit was stormed with shouts of 'Long Live King George!' and 'Down with Republicanism!' The rebel standard was seized and trampled underfoot. The cannon were drawn up and brought into action and as the rebels retreated down the hill they 'fell like mown grass'.[46] A considerable number of rebels escaped owing to a gap in the Crown forces' ring of encirclement, but it was the beginning of the end.

11

Collapse of United Irishmen

Of those rebels who escaped from Vinegar Hill on 21 June 1798, one sizeable body, which included Father John Murphy, made its way into County Kilkenny, hoping to find fresh support there. But though they won a short engagement at Goresbridge and actually occupied the mining town of Castlecomer in that county for a few hours, there was small sign of the Kilkenny Defenders or anyone else rising to join them, and they even found themselves plundered and preyed on by the local inhabitants. They had no alternative but to withdraw again, and suffered a particularly bloody final rout when their base camp on Kilcomney Hill was stormed by government troops on 26 June. An officer in one of the yeomanry units, who helped to defeat them, has described how the remnants of this rebel force then made their way in disorder into Meath, Westmeath and Louth, 'harassed beyond all example' and leaving behind them a trail of half-eaten sheep and bullocks from which they often did not even have time to strip the skin or remove the entrails.[1] 'The people in the counties they marched into', he wrote, 'refuse to join them as they saw their cause was desperate.'[2]

The rest of the Wexford rebels were soon in an equally hopeless situation. They disintegrated into bands of varying sizes, mainly making their way northwards as best they could and taking refuge principally in the mountainous country of County Wicklow, under two powerful local leaders, Joseph Holt (a radical Protestant farmer) and Michael Dwyer (a Catholic). One group operated for a shorter time in Kildare under the leadership of William Aylmer, the twenty-two-year-old son of a Protestant gentleman of some property in that county. Though the latter force was quite soon suppressed and Aylmer himself came in to surrender on the promise that his life would be spared,* the bands in Wicklow were much more difficult to dislodge, and long presented a considerable nuisance to the government with their constant raids on houses for arms and occasional sorties against government troops. (Dwyer did not surrender until 1803.) Yet they presented no serious threat to the political stability of Ireland. All signs of that had disappeared within six weeks of the rebellion's outbreak. By 1 July Cornwallis, the lord

---

* He subsequently had an adventurous military career with Bolivar in South America.

lieutenant, was writing to one of his generals that there was not the least need for all the English regiments they were sending.³ The Buckinghamshire and Warwickshire militias which had already arrived were quite enough, provided there was no French invasion. Cornwallis added significantly: 'The violence of our friends, and their folly in endeavouring to make it a religious war, added to the ferocity of our troops who delight in murder, most powerfully counteract all pleas of conciliation.'

The behaviour of his own troops was now to present Cornwallis with almost as much of a problem as the rebels had done. It was his policy to issue written certificates of pardon (popularly known as 'Cornys') to all rank and file among the rebels who were prepared to surrender within fourteen days and accept them. But as Sir John Moore, engaged in mopping up operations in Wicklow, observed: 'They would have done this sooner had it not been for the violence and atrocity of the yeomen, who shot many after they had received protections and burned houses and committed the most unpardonable acts.'⁴ The whole mopping up procedure, in fact, was if anything an even bloodier business than anything that had taken place during or before the rebellion itself.

The officer who pursued the fugitives from Kilcomney Hill into Meath and beyond reported that the king's troops 'never gave quarter in the rebellion ... hundreds and thousands of wretches were butchered while unarmed on their knees begging mercy; and it is difficult to say whether [regular] soldiers, yeomen or militia men took most delight in their bloody work'.⁵ In such actions as he saw, all the male inhabitants of any house in which the rebels took refuge were put to death and the German contingent in the king's army, Hessians commanded by a Count Hompech, won fame for their rape and slaughter of women.* The same officer reckons that altogether 25,000 rebels and peaceable inhabitants were killed in this way, 'by the lowest calculation', and the Protestant historian, Gordon, in trying to assess the total number of people killed on both sides in the whole rebellion and reaching the tentative figure of 50,000, says he 'has reason to think that more men than fell in battle were killed in cold blood'.⁶

The more humane members of the government were appalled by what happened as the rebellion disintegrated. Cornwallis, the lord lieutenant and commander-in-chief, applied his strictures equally to foreigners, the militia and the yeomanry. Of the latter he wrote that they had 'saved the country, but ... now take the lead in rapine and murder'.⁷

At least for the leaders of the rebellion certain formalities of retribution were reserved, though these were often, in accordance with the custom of

---

* The government has been so universally reviled in nationalist historical tradition for its use of German troops in the rebellion of 1798 that it is interesting to note that Wolfe Tone himself had envisaged the use of German troops in Ireland as part of an invading army. (See Tone (ed.), *Tone*, ii, p. 235.)

the day, barbarous enough. Father John Murphy, taken soon after the rout at Kilcomney, was hanged at Tullow, his body burned in a tar barrel and his head set upon a spike in one of the main streets. In Wexford itself, courts-martial began their work immediately after the liberation of the town. Bagenal Harvey, the earnest intellectual radical of many years' standing, with long face and expressive eyes, who had so recently been sporting a pair of silver epaulettes on his ordinary clothes,[8] was now ignominiously hauled out of a cave on the Galtee islands in which he had taken refuge and given the inevitable death sentence. He pleaded in extenuation of treason the fact that he had hoped by his leadership to save lives and property. But this, as smaller fry were to find, was a dangerously double-edged plea, being accepted as often as not as conclusive proof of a rebel's authority and influence rather than of his humanity. Harvey can hardly have expected to be spared. He, together with Matthew Keogh, the rebel Wexford town governor who had once been a British Army officer, and Father Roche were all hanged on 1 July off Wexford Bridge, a place of grisly and vengeful associations which, when the loyalist army moved in ten days earlier, had been covered in human blood from the massacre of Protestants the previous day, its rails everywhere indented with bullet holes and vicious pike thrusts.[9] The bodies of Harvey, Keogh and Roche were thrown into the River Slaney below and their heads impaled upon the pikes over the court-house where they remained for several weeks.[10]

There was one rather remarkable exception to the general blood-letting. It illustrates the vast gap between those who planned the theory of the rebellion and those who gave it its crude unsophisticated reality. For in prison in Dublin were some seventy of the political élite of the United Irishmen, including all the members of the Leinster Executive taken in March at Oliver Bond's house and elsewhere, and among them Arthur O'Connor, Thomas Emmet, William MacNeven, Samuel Neilson and other leaders of the movement. Few had as yet been tried, but the execution of one man had already taken place and that of Bond himself was due shortly. The fate of the others against whom the government had massive evidence would in the course of time have been inevitable. However, seeing that the rebellion had wholly collapsed and hoping to avert all further bloodshed as well as their own, O'Connor, Emmet and MacNeven agreed, with the concurrence of the other prisoners, to divulge to the government all they knew of the origins of the United Irish movement. The conditions were, first, that they should not be obliged to name any individuals and, second, that they should thereafter be allowed to exile themselves to a country of their own choice outside the United Kingdom. The compact was agreed to by the government, and though there were to be mutual recriminations of breaches of faith over details, in its essentials it was kept. Bond himself was saved from the gallows just in time (though he died almost immediately afterwards of a heart attack).

The other prisoners were never brought to trial, but after a prolonged period of relaxed imprisonment in Fort George in Scotland (the cause of accusations of bad faith against the government on the part of the prisoners, who had anticipated immediate release) they were allowed in 1802, at the time of the Peace of Amiens, to go to France. From there, some, including Emmet and MacNeven, subsequently moved to America. Emmet became State Attorney of New York, MacNeven a distinguished American physician. O'Connor became a general in the French Army.

For those who had actually taken up arms and who may often not even have heard of their would-be political leaders, a very different sort of fate was in store, even if they did manage to escape the gallows or the unlicensed butchery that now raged in Ireland. Some were handed over, by government arrangement, as slaves to the King of Prussia; others, often after severe floggings, were transported to the fleet or to the new penal colonies in New South Wales.

The disclosures made to the British Government by the imprisoned conspirators revealed little it did not already know by means of its excellent informer network. But the government was at least enabled to make the information public for propaganda purposes, without jeopardizing its sources. The amount of light people like O'Connor and Emmet were able to throw on the primitive mass movement which had provided the main source of energy for the rebellion was of course minimal. Even such revelations as they could make about their connections with the Defenders were sketchy and vague in the extreme, for the simple reason that these connections themselves had always been sketchy and vague. The account of their negotiations with the French was much more explicit, though the details were already largely known to the government through its spies.

The United Irishmen's wary attitude to French help was emphasized by MacNeven, who declared that, 'faithful to the principle of Irish independence', the amount of French help the executive had worked for had been 'what they deemed just sufficient to liberate their country, but incompetent to subdue it'.[11] They also made other statements which throw a useful light on the nature of that Irish republican separatism which they now bequeathed as an idea to posterity. Thus, in MacNeven's evidence there is a sudden almost inspired glance into the future, and to one Irish crisis 123 years later in particular, when he says in his public examination before the House of Lords:

'... I am now and always have been of the opinion, that if we were an independent republic, and Britain ceased to be formidable to us, our interest would require an intimate connexion with her.'[12]

The unsectarian nature of republican theory as opposed to the rebel practice was spelt out by MacNeven who, when asked if it had not been the intention to establish the Roman Catholic Church in Ireland, replied that he would as soon establish Mahomedanism.[13]

Emmet, also before the Lords, faced up frankly enough to this gap between the theory and reality of the new Irish nationalism. Of the issue of Parliamentary Reform, which had after all been the mainspring of the whole United Irish movement, he said: 'I don't think the common people ever think of it, until it is inculcated into them that a reform would cause a removal of those grievances which they actually do feel.'[14] And as far as the poor were concerned, he put Catholic Emancipation, which by now meant little more than the fight for Catholics to sit in Parliament and occupy high offices of state, into the same category. He said he didn't think it mattered 'a feather' to the common people, or that they ever thought of it.[15] Asked by the Speaker if it were not so that 'the object next their hearts was a separation and a republic', Emmet replied: 'Pardon me, the object next their hearts was a redress of their grievances.' He said that if such an object could be accomplished peaceably, 'they would prefer it infinitely to a revolution and a republic'. This remains a sound enough definition of Irish 'nationalism' as it was to be found among the bulk of the Irish population for the next century and more.

Much heroic phrase and ballad-making later went to enshrine the memorable events of 1798 as a classic example of a small subject nation's struggle for freedom. But though often punctuated by heroism, these events can be seen on any objective reading to have grown out of a much more complex and subtle social situation than any plain heroic confrontation of nationalities. Perhaps the ballad of 1798 that best expresses the true mood of confusion and desperation in that pathetic year is one which significantly does not even mention the United Irishmen at all, but is entitled 'The Banished Defender'.

... For the sake of my religion I was forced to leave my native home,
I've been a bold defender and a member of the Church of Rome,
... They swore I was a traitor and a leader of the Papist band,
For which I'm in cold irons, a convict in Van Diemen's Land.

Right well I do remember when I was taken in New Ross
The day after the battle as the Green Mount Ferry I did cross,
The guards they did surround me and my bundle searched upon the spot,
And there they found my green coat, my pike, two pistols and some shot.

The reason that they banished me, the truth I mean to tell you here,
Because I was head leader of Father Murphy's Shelmaliers,
And for being a Roman Catholic I was trampled on by Harry's breed,
For fighting in defence of my God, my country and my creed.

Transubstantiation is the faith that we depend upon
Look and you will find it in the sixth Chapter of St John ...

And yet somewhere in the desperation that had made that simple Irish-man take up arms, driven either by the need for social self-justification or simple self-defence, there had developed through the organization of the Defenders a crude and confused notion of an independent Irish patriotism. Not only Tone and his friends, in the sophisticated style of the political theorist, but also the semi-literate Defender had learnt, in these years, to think of themselves for the first time as somehow fighting for their country when they opposed its established order.

On the Saturday after the battle of Arklow fifteen rebel prisoners were, so a contemporary writer records, 'all hanged together out of the same tree'. They were made to hang each other. Before this dance of death took place a young bandsman of the militia who was watching called out to the rebels: 'For decency's sake, for religion's sake, and for your precious souls' sake, reflect properly on your awful passage into eternity and be reconciled to your Saviour.'

Whereupon one of the rebels called back to him:

'You be damned! I die in a good cause: I die fighting for my country and shall go to heaven; and you will go to hell for fighting against it.'[16]

In this simple answer a new emerging patriotism in Ireland seems plain enough. Yet a confusing element, and one which these men had no time left to ponder, though it was to confuse other Irishmen for generations, was that the bandsman (probably as firm a believer in transubstantiation as any Defender) considered that in supporting the established order he was fighting for his country too.

On 8 July 1798, some six weeks only after the outbreak of the rebellion, Cornwallis had summed up the military situation for the benefit of the British minister, Portland. The only rebel forces still in arms were, he wrote, (1) in Wicklow, where parties of five thousand or so, armed mainly with pikes, were at large; (2) on the northern boundaries of Wexford (where die-hard deserters from the militia had taken to the woods); and (3) in Kildare and on the borders of Meath and County Dublin – the latter being small parties which burned and murdered and then retired to the shelter of the bogs. By the end of July he could report that the rebellion in Kildare was over. And by the middle of August, in spite of the continued existence of the Wicklow bands under Holt and Dwyer, he could report temporarily that the county now had 'a quiet and settled appearance'.[17] In fact, things were settling back into that fairly normal state of armed peasant lawlessness which Ireland had more or less taken for granted for half a century and which was to continue to pass for normality for almost a century more.

The absence of serious repercussions of the rebellion in other parts of Ireland had been one of its most curious and fortunate aspects for the govern-ment. On the day of Vinegar Hill, a small rising of sorts had taken place between Bandon and Clonakilty in County Cork, but, though it was to inspire a heroic monument of a pikeman in Clonakilty a hundred years later, the real event was concerned more with the rescue of some prisoners than any serious attempt to coordinate with the Wexford rebels, and, as Cornwallis remarked, the rescue of prisoners by bodies of Whiteboys or Defenders was 'a practice not unusual in this country'.[18]

As already seen, the calculated attempt by the force who escaped from Vinegar Hill to raise the country in Kilkenny was an ignominious failure. What Cornwallis called 'an appearance of insurrection'[19] in Tipperary, taking place in July, well after the main rebellion was over, was quickly crushed, and again significant, if of anything, of a return to normal unrest. In only one other part of Ireland, apart from Leinster, had there been any attempt at serious rebellion and that had been remarkable not for the fact that it took place but that it took place so half-heartedly and ineffectually. For it was, after all, in the North, in Ulster, that the whole concept of an Irish republican rebellion to be brought about by a union of Irishmen of every class and creed had first been planned.

'The quiet of the North is to me unaccountable,' the government Under-Secretary Cooke had written on 2 June,[20] as the full momentum of the Wexford rebellion began to reveal itself. And Wolfe Tone in France, where details of the events in Ireland only arrived late, wrote incredulously as the news at last began to pour in: 'In all this business I do not see one syllable about the North, which astonishes me more than I can express. Are they afraid? Have they changed their opinions? What can be the cause of their passive submission, at this moment, so little suited to their former zeal and energy?'[21]

In two respects the United Irishmen had always lived in a world of illusion. First, they had too gladly assumed that the union of Catholic and Protestant which their theory proclaimed was automatically achieved by proclaiming it. Second, their actual mechanism of conspiracy was similarly less effective in practice than in theory.

With the arrests at Oliver Bond's house in March, coordination between any National Executive in Dublin and the Provincial Committee in Ulster clearly became much more difficult, while between the higher and lower committees in Ulster itself coordination seems to have broken down altogether. A United Irishman, who later escaped to America, wrote, in his account of 'the Republican Army' of Down during May 1798:

In that month several communications from the Executive relative to the Insurrection had been communicated. Special orders with respect to the Counties had been given in the Commissions to the Adjutant Generals – these Orders on account of the supineness of the Adjutant Generals were not universally communicated, but in your county they were diffused and their good effect was lost by the ignorance or supineness of the subaltern officers . . .[22]

Also, he said, the procedure for filling gaps in the ranks after an arrest was inadequate, so that such arrests 'threw the whole battalion into disorder, and in the moment of embodying [i.e.mobilizing] proved of infinite disadvantage, for instead of the force meeting at any point in collected or organized bodies, they met more by accident than by design – and they were in no better order than a mere country mob ...'[23]

There was also little effective coordination between various county committees. In the end, the two strongest counties, Antrim and Down, conducted risings not only independent of what was happening in Wexford, but also independent of each other. The leaders of these only took up their commands at the very last moment. The originally designated leader in County Antrim, theoretically 'commander-in-chief' for all Ulster, actually resigned on 1 June, the day after the rebels in the South had taken Wexford, but before anything had happened in the North at all. His place was taken by Henry Joy McCracken, a Presbyterian cotton manufacturer who had helped found the first open society of United Irishmen with Neilson, Russell and Tone many years before, and at whose ship bearing the Crown above the Irish harp on its insignia they had once all jeered in such carefree fashion.*

In County Down, the designated leader was arrested on 5 June, also before he had taken the field, and his post was filled haphazardly by a prosperous Episcopalian draper, Henry Monro, only a day before the rising in that county finally broke out.

This sort of confusion did not augur well for the future, and in both Antrim and Down the risings ended quickly in disaster. McCracken's men in Antrim, after capturing Randalstown and looking for a while as if they might take Antrim town, were eventually driven out and bloodily dispersed. The dead and wounded were left on the streets for two days and were then cleared away together in carts and dumped into sand-pits near the lake. A land agent who watched one such cartload arriving at the pits heard an officer of the yeomanry ask the driver:

'Where the devil did these rascals come from?'

A feeble voice from the cart itself replied:

'I come frae Ballybofey.'

The entire load was buried together.[24]

Well might the historian Lecky, writing innocently long before the horrors of the twentieth century, comment on the events of this year in Ireland: 'In reading such narratives we seem transported from the close of the eighteenth century to distant and darker ages, in which the first conditions of civilized society had not yet been attained and to which its maxims and reasonings are unapplicable.'[25]

Three days after the defeat at Antrim, the Down rebels under Monro took the field. Arrayed on a hill-top like the Wexford rebels, armed mainly with

* See above, p. 55.

pikes and wearing their Sunday clothes with green ribbons and cockades in their hats, while some of the leaders wore green coats of military cut with yellow facings, and, like the Wexford rebels, depleted by wayward desertions on the eve of battle, they were routed by the king's troops after a fierce fight at Ballinahinch on 12 June.[26] There were a few other, uncoordinated appearances of rebels in arms (sometimes carrying only pitchforks) at different points in the counties of Down and Antrim, with skirmishes at Saintfield and Ballymena, but with the battle at Ballinahinch the rising in the North, for so long the great hope of Irish revolutionaries and the dread of the government, was over. It had given far less trouble than the simple protest of the desperate Wexford peasantry into whose heads the idea of a republican rebellion had barely entered a few short weeks before.

As in the South, great slaughter and savagery followed the northern rebels' defeat. In the town of Antrim after the battle there, a Quaker described the men of the Monaghan and Tipperary militia who cleared it as acting 'with great cruelty, neither distinguishing friends nor enemies.... Numbers who were not in any way concerned lost their lives, for the soldiers showed pity to none ...'[27] And when this awful ordeal of liberation was over, 'people were to be seen here and there saluting their neighbours, like those who survived a pestilence or an earthquake, as if they were glad to see each other alive after the recent calamity ...'[28] Both McCracken and Monro were soon taken and executed.

This almost unbelievably ineffectual performance by rebel Ulster, birth-place of the whole United Irish movement, must be explained by something more than mere haphazard organization and incompetence. To a large extent, certainly, the heart had already gone out of the movement in Ulster in 1797, when the severity of the government's military measures, coupled with conditional offers of pardon, had proved so effective. Another factor already operating then had been disillusionment with the French. France's increasingly unidealistic and cynical attitude to small nations like the Swiss and Genovese, together with their repeated inability to put in an effective appearance in Ireland, combined to make many republicans abandon hope of French support altogether, and without French support republican hope itself easily seemed unrealistic. But the most important factor of all in deter-mining the northern débâcle was the large-scale reversion to the standard Protestant–Catholic rivalry which had persisted as one of the ever-present factors of life in the North.

The rebellion in the South had, in a most acute form, laid bare that deep division between Dissenter and Catholic which the United Irishmen had so long done their best to paper over in the interests of new political strength. It had already been noted by observers that where Protestant United Irish-men in the North had been persuaded to give up the conspiracy, either by force or cajolement or a mixture of the two, they reverted easily to their former sectarian attitudes, and going to the other extreme tended to express their old radicalism in the new Orange Society. Now, the insurrection in the South had revealed from the start an almost exclusively Catholic character. Worse than that, it had revealed a distinctly anti-Protestant bias. News of some of the massacres of Protestants on Vinegar Hill and of the murders in the barn at Scullabogue had reached the North before either McCracken's or Monro's forces took to arms in Antrim and Down. Many of those old radical volunteer corps who had shocked Neilson and Tone in the early days with their 'Peep o' Day Boy' principles, but who had eventually been persuaded to sink these in the new principles of the United Irishmen, must now have felt that if Vinegar Hill and Scullabogue were what the United Irishmen stood for, then they were on the wrong side after all.

It is significant that even in those rebel forces in the North which did take the field there, dissension was reported between the regiments of the Defenders and those of the United Irishmen with whom they nominally associated. A song of the time which celebrates an unsuccessful attempt to take Glenarm Castle in Antrim expresses Defender resentment in terms which cast an odd light on the idealistic patriotic cause in which they were supposed to be united:

> Treachery, treachery, damnable treachery!
> Put the poor Catholics all in the front,
> The Protestants next was the way they were fixed
> And the black-mouthed Dissenters they skulked at the rump.

This was all a far cry from those edifying principles of united brotherhood for which the United Irishmen had nominally taken up arms, and on which Tone and others had relied to establish a new sense of Irish nationality and their country's independence.

12

The French Landing

A significant postscript to the rebellion was still to come. It revealed once again how little any coherent idea of nationality was as yet an indigenous Irish political force. It also brought to a sombre end the adventures of Wolfe Tone.

For all the United Irishmen's chronic optimism, they had generally regarded French military help as essential to a successful revolution in Ireland. All their other hopes had been built on it. And the failure of the French to appear in 1797 or in the early months of 1798 had done much to weaken such revolutionary enthusiasm as existed in a movement that in any case always contained more desperation than political consciousness. When the rebels finally did chaotically take the field, uncoordinated as they were with their own leaders, they had no contacts at all with the French. The men of Wexford thought of the French chiefly to revile them for leaving them in the lurch.

Tone himself had spent the early part of the summer with the immobile French invasion fleet at Le Havre, increasingly despondent. Now, in August 1798, such rebellion as had been able to gain momentum was crushed, and the slaughter of the rebels was proceeding so methodically that at least one gaoler felt the need to invent for himself a gallows which would hang thirty at a time.* It may therefore seem the final disastrous absurdity that at this, of all moments, the French should send another expedition to Ireland, and one which this time succeeded at last in landing on Irish soil.

Yet the idea of the expedition was in many ways a credit to the French. If the state of Irish national feeling had been as positive as Tone, O'Connor and others had repeatedly represented it, the plan would not have been unreasonable. For the events of May and June, though terrible and disappointing, could be expected to have inflamed the Irish national spirit still further. It was true that the resolution with which the Catholic militia had fought rebels of their own class and creed in the king's name had been disconcerting, yet even Tone, when insisting that the militia would come over to a man, had always made the arrival of a French force a necessary proviso.

* 'I hate this dribble drabble work', he told an English militia officer in Kilkenny, meaning hanging in ones and twos. (*Diary of Captain Hodges.* BM Add. MSS. 40,166.)

All the French did now was to put to a final test the theories of militant Irish nationality to which they had been converted.

Bonaparte, who after the death of Hoche had inherited the notion of an invasion of Ireland as part of the Directory's strategic outlook, had been at best non-committal about it when he met Tone in January 1798. But for the next few weeks at least most serious preparations were continued for a major assault on the British Isles. And though Kent and Sussex were clearly in Bonaparte's mind more than Ireland, it is unlikely that, had that assault been launched, some part of it would not have been concerned with Ireland if only as a diversion. In any case, even a descent on Kent and Sussex might have been expected to have important repercussions in Ireland. The preparations were on a vast scale. The whole of the Channel coast from Antwerp to Cherbourg had been turned into a vast naval area, and other work was proceeding in the Atlantic ports of Brest and La Rochelle.

Why then, knowing as the French did at this time that a rebellion of sorts was about to break out in Ireland, did they not strike immediately in support of it?

The answer is that just before the rebellion's haphazard outbreak, the French Directory, for whom Ireland was always only one factor in a vastly complex strategic situation, had been persuaded by Bonaparte to change their strategy altogether. An inspection of the Channel in February had convinced Bonaparte that France was not within sight of that mastery of the sea which he considered essential for a successful invasion.[1] He persuaded the Directory to switch their attention towards the East. An Army of the Orient was created in April, drawing its strength from the former Army of England, and late in May, as the Irish rebellion lumbered into the open, Buonaparte himself sailed for Egypt.

But, having completed this major readjustment of strategy, the Directory remained honourably true, at least in spirit, to their recent assurances to Tone and Lewins. In July they finally issued the orders containing plans 'to bring help to the Irish who have taken up arms to shake off the yoke of British domination'.[2] Three small separate expeditions were to carry troops, arms and ammunition to the help of the Irish simultaneously by different routes: some light vessels with *émigré* Irishmen on board were to sail from the Channel ports, another expedition was to leave from Rochefort (by La Rochelle) and a third – the largest, with about three thousand men – from Brest. The overall command of this 'Army of Ireland' was given to General Hardy, and of the naval arrangements to Admiral Bompard stationed at Brest. The instructions ended with an exhortation to do everything to encourage Irish morale by keeping up a hate for the name of England, and at the same time to preserve a discipline which would be a model to the Irish troops who, it must not be forgotten, were 'their persecuted brothers fighting in a common cause'.[3] No expedition, concluded the orders, could have greater influence on the political situation in Europe. Command of that part of the expedition which was to sail from Rochefort was given to a general named Humbert.

Humbert was a true son of the Revolution. Then a man of thirty, of peasant stock, he had risen from the ranks and had fought in Europe, in the Vendée and at Quiberon Bay. He had taken part in Hoche's Bantry Bay expedition of 1796, sailing in the ship *Les Droits de l'Homme* which was intercepted by the British on the return journey and wrecked with the loss of some 1,200 of its 1,800 men. In 1797 Humbert had put up to the Directory ideas for what would now be called commando-type expeditions to be landed in Scotland or Cornwall, and he may have been disappointed not to have been given overall command of the new expedition to Ireland. In any case, he seemed determined to seize the major share of whatever glory was to be had from the enterprise. Held up in port like the other two parts of the expedition for lack of cash, due to the bureaucratic delays of the French Treasury, Humbert succeeded in raising the money himself from local sources, and on 6 August 1798 set sail for Ireland independently with his three frigates, and just over a thousand officers and men, together with some five thousand stand of extra arms and a number of spare French uniforms.

Though audacious, his action was not as absurd as hindsight may make it seem. He knew that the other forces of the invasion were about to follow him to the north-west corner of Ireland. He knew that the force which was sailing from the Channel ports was specially designed to bring extra supplies to those Irish whom his own arrival should bring out in insurrection. Above all he assumed, and this was the premise on which the whole concept of the enterprise was based (for Tone and his friends had done their work well), that the Irish people, though they might have suffered a terrible setback two months earlier, must be only waiting for the chance to rise *en masse* again. After experience of the *chouannerie* in the Vendée his military thinking was particularly attuned to the idea of fast-moving commando-type forays behind the enemy lines. And personally he was a very brave man. In any case, the omens seemed on his side. For Humbert's expedition began with a brilliantly successful evasion of a large British squadron that was patrolling for the French ships just outside Rochefort.

Sixteen days later, on 22 August 1798, at about two o'clock in the afternoon, three men o' war flying the British flag appeared in the Bay of Killala, a small town in County Mayo which was the seat of both a Protestant and a Catholic bishopric. Two sons of the Protestant bishop were among those who eagerly pushed off in small boats to examine the new arrivals. One British Army officer who had himself only just arrived in Killala to take over command of the garrison there rowed out to offer them a catch of fish he had made on his way from Sligo. He arrived on board to find himself surrounded by Frenchmen and made their prisoner. By the ruse of flying the British flag, Humbert's expedition had achieved total surprise.⁴

The French, who on the last few days of their voyage had experienced rough weather and had been unable to get in at their first choice of landing point, Donegal Bay, must have had the disastrous anticlimax of Bantry Bay two years earlier very much in their minds. This small force of about a thousand men now disembarked immediately with efficiency and speed, hidden from the town of Killala itself by a chain of hills and the indentation of the bay.

The Protestant bishop was giving a dinner-party that fine summer evening for three or four visiting clergymen and some officers from Ballina. They were on the point of rising from their wine to join the ladies when a terrified messenger entered the room to say that three hundred Frenchmen were within a mile of the town. After a brief and not particularly heroic stand in the streets by the local yeomanry, the French themselves were in the house, headed by their general, a man of good height and shape, in the full vigour of life but with 'a small sleepy eye . . . the eye of a cat preparing to spring on its prey'.⁵ The bishop, though a liberal-minded man, could not help noticing that Humbert's 'education and manners were indicative of a person sprung from the lowest orders of society', but conceded that he knew how to assume the deportment of a gentleman when he wanted to. Humbert immediately made clear that the French intended to behave with total correctness, in accordance with his orders. Later, the bishop was to pay a glowing tribute to the impeccable discipline with which the French conducted themselves throughout the whole of their stay.⁶

The next morning a green flag was hoisted over the castle gate, bearing the inscription *'Erin go Bragh'*, or 'Ireland for Ever'. The moment that the United Irishmen and the Defenders had awaited with such desperate hope for so long, and which the government had so long dreaded, had come at last. A French Army was on Irish soil, calling upon the Irish to rise.

Humbert issued a proclamation headed 'LIBERTY, EQUALITY, FRATERNITY, UNION!'

Irishmen, you have not forgot Bantry Bay – you know what efforts France has made to assist you. Her affections for you, her desire for avenging your wrongs, and assuring your independence, can never be impaired.

After several unsuccessful attempts, behold Frenchmen arrived amongst you.

They come to support your courage, to share your dangers, to join their arms, and to mix their blood with yours in the sacred cause of liberty. They are the forerunners of other Frenchmen whom you shall soon infold in your arms . . .

We swear the most inviolable respect for your properties, your laws and all your religious opinions. Be free; be masters in your own country. We look for no other conquest than that of your own liberty – no other success than yours.

The moment of breaking your chains has arrived. ... Can there be any Irishman base enough to separate himself at such a juncture from the grand interests of his country? If such there be, brave friends, let him be chased from the country he betrays, and let his property become the reward of those generous men who know how to fight and die.

Irishmen ... recollect America, free from the moment she wished to be so.

The contest between you and your oppressors cannot be long.

Union! Liberty! the Irish Republic! – such is our shout. Let us march. Our hearts are devoted to you; our glory is in your happiness.[7]

A measure of the sort of response that Humbert had hoped for is shown by his treatment of the first two officer prisoners he took. One of these, a Lieutenant Sills, was sent on board his ships to be conveyed to France because he was an officer in an English regiment, the Leicester Fencibles. The other, a Captain Kirkwood of the local yeomanry unit, he released on parole because he was an Irishman. Indeed, on the very evening of his arrival Humbert made a vain attempt to get the bishop himself to join the Irish Republic, offering him a post in the Directory of Connaught which he was about to form and telling him that such powerful other forces would soon be on their way from French ports that Ireland would be free within a month.[8]

The French, as they admitted afterwards, had been led by the Irish in France to expect that 'a numerous and well-disciplined army, headed by the gentry and chief land-owners, would join them'.[9] Their hopes of the peasantry had, of course, been even higher, but these too were to be no less seriously disappointed.

It may be asked, as the Bishop of Killala asked himself, why the French should have landed in this particular north-west corner of Ireland at all, where so far there had been virtually no suspicion of disloyalty among the population. But they had received many assurances, such as one from MacNeven in the previous year in which he declared with typical over-optimism that ... 'Even in the places where the United Irish system has not been fully adopted, the cooperation of the poor and middle classes can be counted on.'[10] Moreover, in June 1798, Lewins, urging the Directory to take action, had given them details which may well have been accurate of the disposition of loyalist troops in Ireland and the fact that in the north-west these were thinly distributed. He had added assurances similar to MacNeven's about the Irish patriotism of the greater part of the militia and the *yeomanry* as well (Lewins's italics).

The reality of Humbert's reception was very different from what he had been led to expect. Certainly the peasantry turned out to welcome him rapturously on the roadside. And when on the very first day the French started distributing arms and uniforms in the castle yard at Killala, there was no shortage of customers. The bishop estimated they arrived in thousands to take part in the share-out. But campaign-toughened French republicans fresh from chasing the Pope out of Italy, were rather astonished to hear them say that they had come to take arms for France and the blessed Virgin. About a thousand were given complete blue uniforms, including helmets edged with spotted brown paper to make them look like leopard skins. A French naval officer stood on a barrel thumping the helmets down on to peasant heads to make them fit. Some 5,500 muskets were also distributed. Swords and pistols were reserved for rebel officers.

The distribution of the muskets together with ball and powder proved rash, for the peasantry were not naturally disciplined soldiers. In the course of experimentation with the new weapons Humbert himself narrowly escaped death from a clumsy recruit whose gun went off accidentally in the yard, sending a bullet past the general's ear as he stood at a window, to lodge in the ceiling just behind him. The French soon refused to hand out any more ammunition until the peasantry agreed to cease using it for shooting at ravens.[11]

Although the Irish who rallied to Humbert were occasionally, like the rebels in Wexford, to give proof of great quixotic courage and bravado, they proved a military disappointment. Their rapaciousness and lack of discipline appalled their French commander and he more than once had to deal with them severely. One senior officer later told the bishop that he would never trust himself to such a horde of savages again.[12] It seemed particularly inappropriate to the French, too, that these Irish should consider themselves as fighting primarily for their religion. As one officer remarked: 'God help these simpletons. If they knew how little we care about the Pope or his religion they would not be so hot in expecting help from us. .... We have just sent Mr Pope away from Italy, and who knows but that we may find him in this country?'[13]

He also commented that if it were up to him he would pick one-third of them and shoot the rest.

Humbert had been led to expect something like a national revolutionary organization at work in Ireland. He found only an ignorant, neglected peasantry. In them, a sometimes desperate sense of being on their own in society could be momentarily excited into a spirit of revolt, but at the same time their long hard training in individual survival at all costs made them individualists to the end.

The size of the French force was in any case hardly large enough to inspire any but the most foolhardy or dedicated to chance their new arms, particularly after the terrible retribution that had so recently overtaken those who took to arms in Wexford. When Humbert sent his first dispatch to the French Admiralty a few days later, he reported, in spite of the eager acceptance of arms and uniforms, that 'The Irish have until this day hung back.

The County of Mayo has never been disturbed and this must account for the slowness of our approach which in other parts would have been very different.'[14]

By then, in fact, about six hundred Irish had already been in battle with him, but they had fled at the first cannon shot, though, he wrote, 'I expected as much and their panic in no way deranged my operations.'[15] The final words of that sentence were no boast. By contrast with the rest of his news, this disappointing showing of the Irish seemed insignificant. For the dispatch also contained accurate details of a sensational success of French arms.

Leaving about a fifth of his small army behind at Killala as a garrison, Humbert quickly moved south, and within a week had met and totally defeated a much superior British force under General Lake at Castlebar. Lake lost more than fifty of his men killed and the rest fled in panic, some of them falling back as far as Athlone, a distance of sixty-three miles said to have been covered in twenty-seven hours. The battle has gone down to history as 'the races of Castlebar'.

Humbert immediately set up a Provisional Government, making its President a young Catholic Irish gentleman named John Moore, and 'in the name of the Irish Republic' required everyone between the ages of sixteen and forty inclusive to rally at once to the French camp and march *en masse* 'against the common enemy, the Tyrant of Ireland – the English; whose destruction is the only way of ensuring the independence and happiness of ancient Hibernia'.[16] He also incidentally declared traitors to their country all those who having received arms did not rejoin the army within twenty-four hours.

At the same time Humbert sent for the two hundred Frenchmen he had left to garrison Killala. The bishop and the Protestant citizens of that town now had only three French officers between themselves and the rough Irish levies Humbert had armed. Everything the Protestants had heard about the recent massacres in Wexford was naturally very much in their minds. But it is to the credit of the trio of French officers that nothing of the sort occurred in Mayo. They acted quickly as soon as any signs of unmilitary personal vengeance appeared among their Irish followers, and in this, on the bishop's evidence, had the support of some Irish officers among the rebels who, like their less successful counterparts in Wexford, wished to prevent any degradation of their cause. Sixty Protestants imprisoned in Ballina as alleged Orangemen had the narrowest escape. They were released on the immediate intervention of one of the three Frenchmen. Otherwise, though it proved impossible to prevent looting of Protestant houses which took place on a considerable scale, there was not a single attempt to kill Protestants in cold blood during the entire month in which Connaught – or more accurately the country round Killala – was under the nominal government of the 'Irish Republic'. Creditable as this was, both to the French and certain Irish rebel captains, it is difficult not to conclude that it was due as much to the absence so far of any government terror of the sort that had inspired such a desperate desire for revenge in Wexford.

In his dispatches after Castlebar Humbert wrote confidently to the French Directory that he hoped to link with Irish insurgents either in the North or in Roscommon, and then march on Dublin. At the same time he recommended a suitable anchorage for the fleet that was to follow him. But the Bishop of Killala noted in his diary that in spite of the early success the French officers with him were soon considering themselves a forlorn hope with little more than nuisance value and little other future than surrender. In fact, their fate still very much depended on whether or not the two eventualities for which Humbert was hoping took place: the rising of substantial bodies of rebels in Ireland and the arrival of the planned reinforcements from France.

From Castlebar he marched North again with his army – only just over eight hundred men now, for his losses at Castlebar had been proportionately high – in the direction of Sligo which he seemed to intend to seize as a suitable harbour for the eventual arrival of Bompard's fleet. But on coming into contact with a small British force close by he wrongly supposed it to be the vanguard of a much larger army and turned away eastwards into County Leitrim where he had hopes of being joined by a considerable body of rebels. Unpleasantly harassed, though from a respectful distance, by troops under Lake, the general he had defeated at Castlebar, Humbert knew now that Cornwallis himself, the lord lieutenant and commander-in-chief, was moving towards him with a great new army of some twenty thousand men against which even his hardened veterans of the Army of Italy, now of the Army of Ireland, could have little chance. As there was still no word of any of the other expeditions from France, his one hope lay with a major rising of Irish rebels. News of an important rising near Granard in Leitrim now came in, reported to the French as a success.

Humbert ordered an immediate march in the direction of Granard, telling his men that they would be in Dublin in two days.[17] At Cloon they were met by a rebel chief, armed, according to one of the French officers, from head to foot and looking like one of the knights errant of the thirteenth century.[18] He asked them to wait for a day while he mustered ten thousand men. But the very next day Humbert received a terrible blow. As his third-in-command put it, 'He was astonished to learn that the insurgents, informed of the state of our forces, and judging them too weak to resist Lord Cornwallis ... no longer wanted to swell our ranks and make common cause with us. The fear of seeing their women and children murdered, if they abandoned their homesteads, was another reason for deciding to play for safety and run no further risks.'[19]

In fact, the rising at Granard had been bloodily repulsed by the military, and equally disastrous failure met an attempted simultaneous rising in County Westmeath. So much for all the assurances Tone and the United Irishmen had been giving the French for so long. They had been given honestly enough. But they had been based on a concept of how they thought things ought to have been rather than of how they were. The only evidence Humbert had had of the national rising promised to the Directory had been utterly insignificant. The crude levies of peasantry who had presented themselves at Killala had fought bravely when they had fought at all, but they were unpredictable and ungovernable and in the long run more an embarrassment than an asset. More relevant had been the ninety-odd men of the Longford and Kilkenny militias who had deserted to the French after Castlebar. The Bishop of Killala had watched them come into his yard after the battle with their coats turned. But after all the French had been told about the state of mind of the militia such members were pitifully few.

With the collapse of all hopes of serious help from the Irish, and still no sign of the other expeditions from France, it was inevitably only a short time before Humbert was cornered. On 8 September 1798 he found himself trapped by Cornwallis at Ballinamuck and, after a short battle in which the French put up little more than a token fight, he surrendered. The French prisoners, consisting of 884 officers and men, were treated with the greatest respect by their captors, and their week's journey across Ireland to Dublin by mail coach and canal, during which they played cards, sang the Marseillaise and attended dances, had something of a triumphant progress about it. One of the officers of Humbert's escort was reported as saying that Humbert had little but contempt for the allies he had come to liberate, and complained that on the very first day of his landing they had immediately relieved him of £50 and his watch.[20] On arrival in Dublin, they were given a banquet in their honour before being put on a ship to England from which they were soon afterwards returned to France.*

A starker fate awaited the Irish. One French officer has recorded how, at least at Ballinamuck, some three hundred of them had 'fought bravely to the last and were cut to pieces, selling their lives dearly'.[21] The usual indiscriminate slaughter overtook most of those who fled. A fortnight later, a detachment of the loyalist army consisting of some Highlanders and the Queen's County, Downshire and Kerry militias (the latter under the command of Maurice Fitzgerald, the Knight of Kerry), marched inexorably

---

* Humbert afterwards took part in the suppression of Toussaint l'Ouverture's revolt on Haiti, but later fell out with Napoleon and found exile in the United States. There he took part in the War of 1812 in which, at New Orleans, he was opposed by a man who had also faced him at Ballinamuck, General Pakenham. He engaged in the Mexican rebellion against Spain of 1815, but after its failure returned to New Orleans where he died in 1823, 'passing the closing years of his life in comparative obscurity, and earning a modest competence as a teacher of French and fencing'. (V. Gribayedoff, *The French Invasion of Ireland in '98*, p. 182.)

against Killala itself. The town had remained throughout this fortnight in the hands of three French officers and the Irish rebels, a further 750 of whom had actually come to offer their services to the French *after* the battle of Ballinamuck. ('A great crowd of clowns came in this day, armed with pikes ...' was how the bishop reported their arrival.) There were in fact about nine hundred rebels in the town of Killala as the loyalist army approached it along the road from Ballina on 22 September.²² Some of these rebels ran away before any battle could take place, but others were soon 'running on death with as little appearance of reflection or concern as if they were hastening to a show'.²³ They posted themselves behind the low stone walls on either side of the road and awaited the assault of their fellow countrymen wearing the king's uniform.

They stood bravely for about twenty minutes, firing too high as usual, and then broke and ran. Some four hundred of them were killed during the fighting, and in the usual savage mopping-up operations that followed. The always fair-minded bishop commented of his deliverers: 'Their rapacity differed in no respect from that of the rebels, except that they seized upon things with somewhat less of ceremony or excuse, and that his Majesty's soldiers were incomparably superior to the Irish traitors in dexterity at stealing.'²⁴

Though Cornwallis issued 'protections' for those 'deluded' people who had served the French as rank and file, there followed the usual savage courts-martial for those who had served in any position of authority. Some ninety death sentences were carried out, and among the victims were Wolfe Tone's brother, Matthew, and another Irishman who had accompanied the expedition, Bartholomew Teeling. They had been taken wearing French officer's uniform but, in spite of the plea of their commander Humbert that they were entitled to be treated as prisoners under the laws of war, they were shown no mercy. As a passionate loyalist of the day remarked with approval in the context of loyalist severity throughout the rebellion as a whole: 'Where the sword of civil war is drawn, the laws are silent.'²⁵

But the year still held a few more surprises. For, unaware of what had happened to Humbert, except for the news of his early successes, two other components of the multiple French expedition to Ireland had already set sail.

The first had left Dunkirk on 4 September, four days before Humbert's surrender at Ballinamuck. This new expedition was a minute one, consisting solely of one of the fastest sailing corvettes in the French navy, the yellow-painted *Anacreon*, with some 180 men on board and a large supply of arms, including artillery, and saddles and bridles for Irish cavalry. The whole expedition in fact was prepared on the assumption that Ireland had risen in revolt. There were also a number of *émigré* Irishmen on board, including the remarkable Napper Tandy, now boasting the rank of a French general, while the overall command was held by a French American called Rey.[26]

They landed on Rutland Island off County Donegal at midday on 16 September, with Tandy one of the first ashore. Appeals to the population were immediately distributed. One of these, signed by Rey, was headed:

'Liberty or Death! Northern Army of Avengers. Headquarters, the first year of Irish Liberty.'

It began: 'United Irishmen ...' and declared that the French, with Napper Tandy at their head, sworn to lead them on to victory or die, had come 'to break your fetters, and restore you to the blessings of liberty.... The Trumpet calls ...' Another proclamation, similarly headed, and signed by Tandy himself, told the people that it was their duty 'to strike on their blood-cemented thrones the murderers of your friends' and 'to wage a war of extermination against your oppressors, the war of liberty against tyranny, and liberty shall triumph'.[27]

The number of Irish who could then read English in that part of Donegal must have been very few. In any case, the local population had fled to the mountains and showed no inclination to join the invaders at all.[28] Tandy and his allies who, as they told the local postmaster, had come expressly 'to try the pulse of the people', were shattered by the disappointment; their discomfort was completed by news of the fate of Humbert's army at Ballinamuck. After a meal, which they asked for politely, and paid for, they returned to their ship and sailed away again. Tandy, who was fond of drink, had to be carried on board and was in such a state that he made water on the shoulders of those carrying him.[29]

Their ship, the *Anacreon*, had an encounter with an armed merchantman off the Orkneys on the way back, in the course of which Tandy sat on deck drinking brandy with eight-pound cannon balls in his pockets, ready to leap overboard and drown himself if necessary rather than submit to capture.[30] But the French were victorious, and after escaping all pursuing British warships the corvette reached Hamburg. From there, however, the British Government managed to secure Tandy's extradition. He was brought to England, kept in prison a long time, but finally reprieved, partly thanks to the intercession of the lord lieutenant, Cornwallis, who stressed 'the incapacity of this old man to do further mischief'.[31] Tandy was eventually returned to France in 1802, during the short Peace of Amiens, and died soon afterwards.

Long before this, the British Government had at last caught up with the most attractive personality of all among the early United Irishmen, Wolfe Tone. Tone had set off for Ireland on the last instalment of the French invasion just two days before Tandy and co. made their dismal landfall on Rutland Island. The fleet which Tone accompanied was the largest to set sail for Ireland since the expedition to Bantry Bay nearly two years before. It was, however, considerably smaller than that, being composed of only ten ships altogether: of which only one was a ship of the line, appropriately named the *Hoche* of 74 guns with Admiral Bompard, General Hardy and Tone himself on board. The rest of the fleet consisted of eight heavy frigates of between 24 guns and 12 guns, and one fast schooner.[32] They carried some three thousand men in all and quantities of stores. It was at least better than the 'corporal's guard', which Tone had always said he was ready to go to Ireland with if necessary, and it was still not known what had happened to Humbert.

At 5.30 on the morning of 12 October, after a twenty-three day voyage, the French were intercepted off the northern coast of Donegal by a British squadron under Sir John Warren which, though numerically smaller, was much more heavily gunned, including as it did six ships of the line.[33] Seeing that a battle was inevitable, and defeat more than likely, the French tried to persuade Tone to leave the *Hoche* and escape to France in the fast sailing schooner. But, as one would expect from his character, he refused to go and commanded a battery on board during the fight.[34] An action began about 7.30 a.m. The *Hoche* suffered the handicap of being without her main top-mast which had been carried away in the rough weather of the previous days. Castlereagh's uncle, Sir James Stewart, watched the battle from Horn Head.[35] It took place too far out to sea for him to be quite certain of the outcome, but he thought it had gone favourably for the British. In fact, the *Hoche* put up a gallant defence, but after four hours struck her colours. The other nine ships all tried to make their escape back to France but six were eventually taken and found to be 'full of troops and stores'.[36]

Three weeks later, when several hundred prisoners were being landed from Lough Swilly to which the *Hoche* had been brought for repair, one of the first men to step out of one of the boats in the uniform of a French officer was Tone himself. The British Government had known he was on board the *Hoche*, but he seems to have made no attempt to conceal his identity. Recognizing a loyalist bystander on the shore, who had been at Trinity with him, he spoke to him at once.[37] He was taken to Dublin in irons, an insult to the French uniform which he much resented, and on Saturday, 10 November, appeared in court in that uniform: 'a large and fiercely cocked hat with broad gold lace and the tricoloured cockade, a blue uniform coat, with gold and embroidered collar and two large epaulettes, blue pantaloons with gold-laced garters at the knees, and short boots bound at the top with gold lace'.[38]

The result of the trial was a foregone conclusion. Tone admitted the charge of acting hostilely to the king, though he refused to use the word guilty himself, simply saying that he had admitted the charge 'and consequently the appellation by which I am technically described'.[39] He delivered a rather high-flown but dignified address to the court, which he was made to

abbreviate because of its inflammatory irrelevance, but he concluded with
the words:

> Success is all in this life; and, unfavoured of her, virtue becomes vicious in the
> ephemeral estimation of those who attach every merit to posterity. In the glorious
> race of patriotism, I have pursued the path chalked out by Washington in
> America and Kosciusco in Poland. Like the latter I have failed to emancipate my
> country; and unlike both I have forfeited my life. I have done my duty, and I
> have no doubt the Court will do theirs. I have only to add that a man who has
> thought and acted as I have done should be armed against fear of death.[40]

Except for a moment right at the beginning of the trial when he had asked
rather agitatedly for a glass of water, he seemed to some 'unmoved and
unterrified throughout'.[41] But the Marquis of Buckingham who was present
at the trial commented the same day that he thought Tone was 'much agitated
and I cannot help thinking that he means to destroy himself on Monday'
(the day appointed for his execution).[42] Cooke, the under secretary, expressed
the same fears to Cornwallis on the Saturday.

Tone's one request in court had been that instead of being hanged he
should, out of respect for the uniform he wore, be shot 'by a file of grenadiers'. The request was transmitted to Cornwallis. All weekend Tone lay in
prison listening to the gallows being erected outside his window and waiting
for an answer. On the Sunday evening he was told that his request had been
refused. The government's intention was to make as public an example of
him as possible.

Next morning, when the gaoler came to rouse Tone at about four o'clock,
he found him exhausted and weltering in his own blood with his throat cut.
He had in fact missed the main artery but cut through his windpipe with a
penknife he had kept concealed. 'I find then I am but a bad anatomist', he is
reported as saying.[43] His head was kept in one position and a sentry placed
over him to prevent him moving.[44]

While a legal wrangle proceeded as to whether or not Tone should have
been tried by a court-martial at all since he was not one of His Majesty's
soldiers and the normal processes of law were available, Cornwallis suspended the execution, though there were those, including the fellow student
from Trinity who had greeted him on landing, who thought his neck should
be sewn up immediately and he should be summarily hanged. After a week
of agony his condition deteriorated and it is said that on hearing a surgeon
remark that if he were to move or speak it would be fatal to him, he managed
to utter: 'I can yet find word to thank you, sir. It is the most welcome news
you could give me,' and died at once.[45]

Whether or not the story is mythical is unimportant, for it was as a
mythical figure that Tone was to make his greatest contribution to history.
For to this sympathetic young man, most remote of all the influential United

Irishmen from practical events in Ireland during the years of conspiracy and rebellion, but most articulate expounder of the theory that Ireland should be a sovereign independent country separate from England, there was to attach a legendary significance which long after his death did more for the cause in which he believed than he himself had ever been able to do during his lifetime.

After the great events of the decade to which Tone had been witness, political attitudes in Ireland could never be the same again. Up to this point in Irish history no Irishman, of whatever origin, when thinking of his country had considered it as being one that had to be made separate from the Crown that was shared with England. Now at least that idea had been planted. And with it had been planted that notion of a republic which, originally adopted as the desirable constitutional form in imitation of America and France, was long afterwards to become an Irish ark of the covenant in its own right.

From these years, at the end of the eighteenth century, dates much of the manner and style of a movement that was often to be mannered and stylized. A song of the period runs:

> See, Erin's song, you rising beam
> The eastern hills adorning,
> Now freedom's sun begins to gleam
> And break a glorious morning ...

Such a golden sunrise, literally depicted against an emerald green background, was to become the standard of the republican movement in the course of the nineteenth century. 'Sunburstry', as it came to be called, or the habit of talking of freedom with this sort of flourish without actually getting down to more practical politics, became one of its most popular vices. An increasingly rhetorical question was to arise: how far were separatists prepared to try to make separatism practical politics? How far was it practical politics at all?

'Plant, plant the tree, fair freedom's tree' – the song's chorus continues –

> Midst danger, wounds and slaughter,
> Erin's green fields its soil shall be,
> Her tyrants' blood its water.

In this decade after the French Revolution blood – though not so much of the tyrants – had flowed in plenty. And by blood too, for all the fanciful sunburstry, freedom of a sort was to be won in the end.

Part Three

The Union

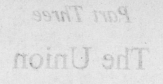

1
The Making of the Union

It is easy to see turning-points in history where turning-points later turned out to have been; but to do so often misrepresents the way things looked at the time. The events of the year 1798 proved a major turning-point in the history of Irish nationalism. They left an inspiration, however vague and emotional, for the future; and more important they led directly to a Parliamentary Union with Great Britain, the long-term effects of which seemed to confirm Ireland as a province and not a country at all. But the last defeat in October 1798 of French attempts to assist rebellion in Ireland that year seemed to contemporaries only the end of one immediate cause for anxiety. Even this was revived within days when the news reached Dublin that yet another French squadron had actually anchored again in Killala Bay.

These were the same three ships that had brought Humbert in the first place. They had been back to France in the meantime and had now returned with some three thousand more men and supplies. When they heard of the defeats of Humbert and Admiral Bompard, they made good their escape without attempting a landing. But their reappearance emphasized what, for contemporaries, was the most important fact of all about the Irish situation at the time: the constant possibility, even probability, of the arrival on those discontented shores of a force from the great land power in Europe which was England's enemy. The very real likelihood of invasion from France remained a most vivid threat at least until 1805.

In Ireland itself by the end of 1798 the original United Irish movement had been most effectively broken. Seventy of its most intelligent leaders were in prison, and others and many subordinate organizers were dead. But because of its obscure ties with the vast bodies of the Defenders, an internal as well as external threat appeared to pervade the situation in Ireland for a long time. While it was possible, on the one hand, to accept that the guerrilla activities of Holt and Dwyer and their men in the fastnesses of the Wicklow mountains were simply the dying echoes of an old convulsion, there were at first enough ominous new signs to keep alive a general apprehension too. So soon after the breaking of the rebellion as September 1798, a traveller on the mail coach between Cork and Dublin was stopped and held for thirteen hours while he was tried by a rebel court-martial consisting of two colonels, one major and four captains, and finally given a pass, permitting him to proceed to Dublin 'free and unmolested by any of the Friends of Liberty'.[1] The Quaker lady of Ballintore, County Kildare, who had herself experienced many of the terrible events of the early summer, felt that the business was by no means over that autumn. She could hear the sound of the trees being felled at night for pike handles and the creaking of the carts which took them away.[2] The darkness was frequently lit up by the fires of houses burned by insurgents, and the funeral of a man who had been hanged moved through the village 'with a kind of indiscreet solemnity'. During that winter of 1798–9, she wrote afterwards, 'the country was far from being settled; it was like the working of the sea after the storm'.[3]

In February 1799 an English militia captain serving in Ireland wrote in his diary that 'although this immediate neighbourhood and the Kingdom at large appears to wear a face of Tranquillity, it more resembles the Pause of Expectation and the silence of Fear . . .'.[4] Whole bodies of the lower orders of Catholics, he added, were sworn United Irishmen. On 24 February a strong party of mounted rebels were encountered by a detachment of yeomanry some twenty-five miles from Youghal in County Cork. The yeomanry pursued the rebels so hard that many jumped from their horses into the River Blackwater where they were supposed drowned.[5]

In other parts of Ireland the outlook was equally uncertain. The Member of Parliament for Mayo had already reported that Ireland was 'in a very precarious state that winter'[6] and in the middle of March 1799 none of the main roads into Dublin itself were passable except to large parties or military escorts.[7] In the North, though the short-lived alliance between Catholics and Dissenters continued to break up, Defenderism itself was again on the increase, particularly in Antrim, where many former United Irishmen were now absorbed into the Defenders. Nightly raids for arms were taking place there and a system of intimidation by flogging with the cat o' nine tails began in macabre imitation of established authority. A rising was confidently expected for 10 April 1799 and special messengers were said to have been sent to the French Directory to arrange assistance. Bonfires lit the hillsides at night both in Antrim and Derry, when orders were said to have been received from France to hold themselves in readiness.[8] Nor was the continuing threat of clandestine conspiracy confined to Ireland alone. Irishmen still composed a very large proportion of the seamen in the British fleet and late in 1798 and during 1799 numerous plots were uncovered among crews to seize British men-of-war in the name of the United Irishmen, run up the green flag and sail for French ports. Dozens of such prospective mutineers were hanged: others were flogged through the Fleet.

It is against this assumption of a continuously unresolved dangerous situation in Ireland for any foreseeable future that the political manoeuvrings which led to the Parliamentary Union between Great Britain and Ireland, and the abolition of a separate Irish Parliament after five hundred years, must be understood.

When the rebellion of 1798 took place, the concept of Irish nationality had twice been put forward, each time in much common nationalistic language but from different standpoints – that of the Protestant ascendancy, and that of the radical United Irishmen, also largely Protestants. Simultaneously with the United Irish movement, there had also sometimes emerged among the uncouth and ill-coordinated bodies of Defenders a vague awareness that the wants and grievances which were the source of their own political motivation could be thought of dramatically in terms of a green flag. Such dramatic coherence, however, containing perhaps the crude beginnings of a mass nationalism, had been abruptly and chasteningly shattered by the rebellion's failure.

The strongest and most effective expression of nationality to date – that of the Protestant ascendancy – had been analogous to the colonial nationalism of eighteenth-century America. Since in Ireland, however, a quarrel with the mother country had been avoided, Irish patriots of this type had been able to feel that they had the best of both worlds, always emphasizing, like Grattan, their pride in Ireland as an independent sovereign country simultaneously with their sense of connection with Britain in the wider British Empire. But the rebellion of 1798 had exposed the artificiality in such thoughts, painfully emphasizing that only in the most highflown theoretical sense could they claim to speak for Irishmen as a whole.

The United Irishmen had put forward a more democratic version of Irish patriotism, using the same nationalistic phrases by tying them to Republicanism and to a proposed separation from Britain and the Empire altogether. The easy defeat of the rebellion, notable for the failure of the Irish masses to respond coherently to the new Republican appeal, emphasized that this too was unrepresentative and ineffectual.

Neither form of nationalism looked particularly convincing immediately after the events of 1798, and though obviously this conclusion did not present itself to contemporaries with simple analytical clarity, their uncertainty is plainly expressed in the eighteen months of political groping that took place before the passing of the Parliamentary Union.

The British Government had a practical problem to solve. Unlike the Protestant ascendancy, they had been getting the worst of both worlds. They had total final responsibility for the situation in Ireland and yet only an indirectly geared and cumbersome machinery with which to deal with it. And the one thing the outbreak of 1798 had proved conclusively was that the situation in Ireland needed dealing with. As a former lord lieutenant wrote at the time with the sense of urgent desperation about Ireland that so many people were feeling: 'something new must be attempted'.[9]

Early in June 1798, even before the Wexford rebellion had reached its climax, Pitt, the British Prime Minister, was working on a plan for a union of the two countries' parliaments. It was to be a few months before the British cabinet concentrated on the problem of getting the project accepted by Irish opinion. But thereafter it never once relented in its determination to carry the Union through.

The idea of a legislative union between the English and Irish parliaments was not a new one. Such a union had even existed for a few years in the time of Cromwell's Commonwealth, but the *status quo* of two separate Parliaments had been restored with Charles II. Early in the eighteenth century before a sense of Irish Protestant nationality had developed very widely, the Irish House of Commons had actually unsuccessfully petitioned Queen Anne to extend the blessings of the new Anglo-Scottish Union to Ireland. In 1751, a pamphlet advocating a union had prophesied with some accuracy that the Irish (meaning the Protestant Irish) though not yet a nation, would soon be too vain and insolent to accept a union at all. One of the many replies to this pamphlet, which immediately expressed horror and contempt at the idea of a union, tried to formulate the mystical ambivalence which lay beneath the Protestant Irishman's developing sense of nationality. Unlike America, which was a simple colony, said the pamphleteer, 'Ireland should be looked on rather as a sister whom England has taken under her protection on condition she complies with the economy of the family, yet with such distinction and deference to show that they were once upon an equality'.[10] By the end of the 1770s the emphasis had shifted: it was the equality of the present that was being stressed, and Protestant Irishmen were considering themselves Irishmen as proudly as the English considered themselves English. The idea of a union was hardly ever broached and then only to be mistrusted.

When, therefore, towards the end of 1798, the subject of a legislative union again began to be seriously put forward, there was a situation which in the light of later events seems a paradox: it was among the Protestant Irish gentry that the great body of opposition to a union was to be found. However, their opposition to it was not so solid or coherent as, in the light of former events, one might have expected. For rebellion had delivered a profound social shock to their whole way of thinking. And the notion of joint sisterhood in the British connection was already so well-established at the back of their minds that a shift of ground towards closer connection was still at least something conceivable.

Later nationalists often extolled eighteenth-century opposition to the Union as activated by patriotic principles analogous to their own, but the analogy is imperfect. Even Foster, the Speaker of the Irish House of Commons, who emerged as the most implacable and influential of all the Protestant Irish leaders against the Union, was not unequivocally opposed to the measure on principle. Pitt, discussing the projected Union with him, found him 'strongly against the measure of an Union (*particularly at the moment*), yet perfectly ready to discuss the point fairly'.[11] And Protestants who had previously presented a single political front for legislative independence now divided not on principle but on how they assessed the chances of their own élite society surviving within the British connection in these troublous times.

Clare, the Chancellor (formerly Fitzgibbon) who had been urging Union since 1793, proclaimed predictably: '... it is utterly impossible to preserve this country to the British Crown, if we are to depend upon the precarious bond of union which now subsists between Great Britain and Ireland.'[12] But many who had previously been among the foremost protagonists of legislative independence agreed with him and opted for a union. Sir George Hill on the other hand, the loyalist who had felt so vindictive about Wolfe Tone that he wanted him hanged with his neck stitched up, was strongly against it. The Earl of Charlemont, founder of the Volunteers of twenty years before, was against a union, as might be expected, but the terms in which he expressed his opposition are revealing. 'Next to the liberty of my country,' he wrote, 'its perpetual connection with its beloved sister has ever been the dearest wish of my heart, the gratification of which could only have been endangered by the plan now in agitation, the disuniting union, a measure which I reprobate as an Irishman, and, if possible, still more as a member of the empire and an adorer of the British constitution.'[13]

Separation from the British connection was the last thing men like Charlemont and the Speaker, Foster, wanted; they opposed the Union just because they thought it was likely to bring that about. As Foster said: 'If a resident Parliament and resident gentry cannot soften manners, amend habits or promote social intercourse, will no Parliament and fewer resident gentry do it?'[14] J. C. Beresford, a man who had helped put down the rebellion with great savagery and from whose family riding school in Dublin the shrieks of the tortured had been clearly audible, was equally against the Union, whereas his father was strongly for it. In other words, the vast majority of opponents of the measure were not at odds with Unionists about the need for a connection. Their argument was that this was not the way to strengthen it. The Irish Parliament had shown itself impeccably loyal and resolute during the rebellion, and the rebellion had been broken militarily by Irish troops and the Irish militia. The withdrawal of most of the influential inhabitants which would inevitably follow a union 'would leave room for political agitators, and men of talents without principle or property, to disturb and irritate the public mind'.[15]

However, even the anti-Unionists in their certainty about the disadvantages of a legislative union did not conceal an uneasy awareness of the need for a new approach in Ireland after the events of 1798. Ideas such as a reform of the tithes system, or some financial provision for the Catholic clergy, or an increase in the amount Ireland should pay Britain for her protection within the Empire were all put forward as a tentative basis of some comprehensive new deal universally acknowledged to be necessary.

Opinion about a union did not run clearly down any political or social dividing line. The most solid opinion seems to have been among the Orangemen, who were very generally described as being against it. This too may seem a paradox in the light of later events, but it was a logical attitude at the time, for the Orangemen simply represented the most extreme expression of the Protestant point of view, namely, that they held a dominant position in Irish society and the legislature as things were, and what they held they wanted to hold. Even in later times, after they had identified their interests with the Union they were always to make clear that, in the event of a clash between those interests and the Union, it was the Union they were prepared to sacrifice. But even the Orangemen were not now unanimous, for a Unionist supporter while accepting that they were chiefly against the measure thought they could be brought to be neutral though it was the utmost the friends of the Union could hope.[16] The Masters of the Orange Lodge did in the end opt for neutrality.

The lawyers and bankers of Dublin, whose particularist interests were threatened, were outspoken against a Union. 'We look with abhorrence,' declared the bankers, 'on any attempt to deprive the people of Ireland of their Parliament and thereby of their constitution ...' And they added that, '... impressed with every sentiment of loyalty to our King and affectionate attachment to the British connection', to propose a union was 'highly dangerous and impolitic'.[17] For the Dublin poor, the Union did not seem an urgent issue one way or the other, though as Castlereagh wrote they might 'easily be set in motion, should their cooperation become of importance to the leading opposers of the measure'.[18] Indeed, siding with the bankers, they were within a short time to be triumphantly drawing the Union's opponents in carriages from the Irish House of Commons and pelting Clare, its leading protagonist, with mud.

The mixture and confusion of opinions was observable not only in social and political groupings but geographically. Dublin, for instance, since it was going to lose its special status as an independent capital and the seat of the national legislature, was strongly against the Union. Cork, because it might hope by the Union to achieve something like parity with Dublin, was strongly for it. Elsewhere in Ireland opinion divided geographically in an arbitrary fashion, determined often by the individual opinions of whoever exercised great influence in any particular county. Sligo, Limerick, Waterford, Wexford, Derry, Antrim and Cork were all reported as being in varying degrees for; Carlow, Cavan, Fermanagh, Roscommon, Kildare, Louth and Wicklow against.[19] In the North, though the Orangemen were broadly against, the division of opinion was often determined by a straight conflict of view as to what the Union would or would not do to the linen trade. Thus some argued that within a union the linen trade would now all go to England, and since the linen trade in the North was flourishing this argument was said to be having some effect in promoting anti-Unionism. Others countered that the very security of their trade was bound up with the security of the British connection, and that only a union could ensure that. Linen merchants themselves were said to be too busy to take part in the argument very actively one way or the other, but on the whole they inclined to this latter view and favoured a union.

In short, the real argument about the Union was not over any major issue of national principle at all but over what its effects were going to be on certain interests. The largest single set of interests involved was that of the Catholics, who still had much to gain and many recent gains to lose.

All laws penalizing Catholics for the exercise of their religion or excluding them from ownership or other acquisition of land had long been abandoned. In 1793 they had been admitted to the vote on exactly the same terms as Protestants. However, no State or municipal offices were yet open to them (though they could be magistrates) and above all they were disqualified from entering Parliament by the need to make a formal abjuration of their beliefs in order to do so. The claim for rights of full equal citizenship with Protestants was obviously a matter of real concern only to the better-off Catholics, who incidentally had proved themselves zealously loyal to the Crown in the rebellion, with many fewer exceptions than among well-to-do Protestants. For the Catholic peasant masses Catholic Emancipation was, as it had always been, at best only a remote symbol of their own far more down-to-earth aspirations, and, as Thomas Emmet the United Irish leader had already remarked, they did not 'give a feather for it'.* Deprived, by the defeat of the rebellion, of more dramatic hopes of seeing their down-to-earth aspirations realized, symbols were all that was left to them. But Emancipation was such an oblique one that, without anyone consciously to make it a part of their lives, as Daniel O'Connell was eventually to do, the strange rituals of the secret societies seemed to provide more satisfying evocations of their hearts' desires.

Since the better-off Catholics all identified themselves as strongly as Protestants with the maintenance of the British connection, and yet had been admitted to a much smaller share of the pride in independent Irish nationality, they saw no objections to a union in itself. Their concern with the issue confined itself largely to whether or not it would make Emancipation more or less probable. But this was an extremely difficult question to

* Cf. above, p. 42 (Emmet, *Pieces of Irish History*, p. 221.)

decide. On the one hand, it might be said that if the Orangemen were mainly against the Union as likely to undermine their dominant position then Catholics should be for it. And on the whole this was the attitude which the majority of Catholics took up. It seemed to them that they were more likely to obtain from a united kingdom, in which they would be only a minority, those concessions at present withheld from them through fear of their majority in Ireland. On the other hand, this argument could be turned the other way round. It could and was argued by some Catholics that their numerical preponderance in Ireland gave them greater power to wring concessions either now or later out of an Irish Parliament alone. And certainly, if the future development of parliamentary institutions on democratic lines could have been foreseen, the argument for Catholic interests opposing a union would have been overwhelming. But, as things were, their best chance seemed to lie with the generosity of a united parliament in which they would escape from the narrow bigotry of the apprehensive Protestant minority which had so often thwarted them in an Irish one. The vote itself had, after all, only been given to Catholics because the British Government had put pressure on the Irish Parliament.

Pitt's earliest ideas for a union had indeed been drafted on the assumption that the project would include Catholic eligibility for Parliament and all offices of state.[20] He himself was in favour of this, but was not prepared to press it if it should make for difficulties. Difficulties in fact threatened on all sides from the king downwards. And when Clare went to London in October 1798 to add his weight to the argument against immediate Emancipation he was soon able to write back to Ireland that the Union was to go forward 'unencumbered' by it.[21] Cornwallis, the lord lieutenant, though he also personally thought that Emancipation should have been part of the deal, accepted the decision. In order to convey some hint of flexibility for the future the stipulation in the Union arrangements that Irish parliamentary representatives must take the Protestant oath of supremacy was qualified by the phrase 'unless it shall be otherwise provided for by Parliament'.

This rather vague and distant prospect of undefined hope suited the Catholic gentry and priesthood well enough. They were opposed to any further pressure for Catholic Emancipation at present on the very grounds that it would be 'injurious to the Catholic claims to have them discussed in the present temper of the Irish Parliament'.[22] And they officially decided to play things coolly. A meeting of influential Catholics just before Christmas 1798 to discuss the projected union decided it would be 'inexpedient to publish any resolution at present' and adjourned *sine die*.[23]

Responding to this careful attitude of the Catholics, both pro- and anti-Unionists set about wooing them. The prospects of Emancipation which the anti-Unionist Foster could offer were necessarily limited since the solid bulk of his support against the Union came from those who wanted to maintain the Protestant ascendancy. The government, on the other hand, though they could not offer immediate Emancipation, dropped vaguely encouraging hints about the future more and more frequently. As Castlereagh, the Chief Secretary, had put it quite candidly: 'I conceive the true policy is by a steady resistance of their [the Catholics'] claims, so long as the countries remain separate, to make them feel that they can only be carried with us, through an union.'[24] And Pitt's speech for the Union in the British House of Commons was full of general hints that concessions to the Catholics could be discussed more safely within the constitution of a united kingdom than within that of Ireland alone. Of the lower orders of Catholics he said: '... A united legislative body promises a more effectual remedy for their grievances than could be likely to result from any local arrangements.'[25]

Since, not only with the Catholics but with all groups, it was a matter of persuading people that the Union would benefit their interests, the government embarked on a series of similar persuasive tactics in other directions. The chief material cause for complaint about the re-arrangements required by the Union was of course the inevitable reduction in the number of Irish parliamentary seats and in the power and influence that went with them. The three hundred seats in the Irish Parliament were now to be reduced to one hundred in the Imperial Parliament.*

But before Cornwallis and Castlereagh could start effectively deploying every technique of persuasion and compensation to placate the interests which controlled these seats, the strength of the opposition to the Union in the Irish House of Commons revealed itself. A motion to reject any discussion of the Union as projected in the king's speech for the session of January 1799 was passed by 111 votes to 106. 'We are yet a nation,' wrote Charlemont to a friend. 'The abominable project is defeated; I can think or talk of nothing else.'[26] But within a week he was sounding more cautious: 'I now begin to perceive that our victory though glorious is not absolutely decisive.'[27]

It was not only 'not absolutely decisive'; eventual defeat was almost certain. The British Government had always ultimately held the Irish Parliament in its power through its control of the patronage system. The full range of patronage was now deployed by Cornwallis and his Chief Secretary, Castlereagh, to secure the objective on which the British Government had set its mind.

There were certain steps they could not take. For instance, when the Marquis of Downshire, an opponent of the Union, showed some signs of wavering if the Irish representatives in the new House of Commons were to be kept at their present figure of three hundred, it was clearly impracticable to meet him on the point. But where individuals might be influenced by rewards of title or office to support the Union every possible effort was made to make them do so. And since the chief arguments *against* a union were

* These became 105 after the Reform Act of 1832.

that it would work out against individual interests, to make it in individual interests to vote for the Union was not perhaps as despicable as it has sometimes been made to seem. Altogether, as a result of Cornwallis's and Castlereagh's ceaseless activity, sixteen important borough-owners were given English peerages, twenty-eight Irish peerages were created, and twenty Irish peerages were increased in rank. As a further general inducement to the Irish peers to seek their prestige within a union rather than outside it, twenty-eight of them were to be virtually nominated by the government as representative Irish peers in the British House of Lords.

This trade in inducements to vote was certainly a two-way one, and was conducted by the opposition just as vigorously as by the government, though clearly the same resources were not available to them. But direct money bribes were undoubtedly offered by the opposition; one man who had voted for the Union in the debate in 1799 voted against it in 1800 in return for a sum of £4,000, though even this man's venality had its limits, for an attempt by the government to win him back once again by a still larger bribe is said to have been unsuccessful.[28] Few direct bribes seem in fact to have been made by the government, though this accusation was often levelled afterwards. Financial compensation, on the other hand, was certainly offered to and taken by the owners of the close boroughs on the straightforward principle that such boroughs were private property like any other. It is illustrative of the inadequacy of the word 'corruption' for the whole procedure that one-third of those to whom such compensatory payments were made actually voted against the Union.[29] Lord Downshire, who received the largest single payment of this sort, maintained his opposition to the Union to the end.

The government's most effective single measure to secure the passage of the Union was the creation of vacant seats in the Irish Parliament, which were then filled with Union supporters before the crucial final debate. This was done partly by approaching men who, though they were not prepared openly to vote for the Union, were willing to accept rewards for vacating their seats – perhaps the most dishonest individual attitude to be found in all the various Union transactions. Exploitation of such moral dishonesty proved very effective. Altogether, including vacancies from deaths and other causes, one-fifth of the Irish House of Commons changed its representation in the eighteen months before the crucial debate took place in 1800 and many of the newcomers thus brought in for what proved to be the death throes of the Irish Parliament were Englishmen. Indeed, the very thoroughness with which Cornwallis and Castlereagh pursued their task itself converted many people in the end to the inevitability of the Union. Already by the end of June 1799 a correspondent was writing to Castlereagh that the impression that the Union would be passed was itself helping to do the trick. 'Little alternative is left to people but to reconcile their minds to its advantages, and which they seem to do with a very good will.'[30] And towards the end of September one of the under secretaries told him that even in Dublin the talk of the coffee houses was that the Union would be carried.[81]

Although Cornwallis and Castlereagh did their work extremely well – almost too well, for the king and the British Cabinet were slightly appalled when they realized the scale on which the Irish ministers had been offering rewards for support[82] – Cornwallis himself had felt distinctly squeamish at times. 'I despise and hate myself every hour for engaging in such dirty work,' he wrote, but he added that what kept him going was the thought that without a union the British Empire must be dissolved.[83] Castlereagh was less emotional. 'The Irish government,' he wrote, after the Union had been carried, 'is certainly now liable to the charge of having gone too far in complying with the demands of individuals; but had the Union miscarried, and the failure been traceable to a reluctance on the part of the Government to interest a sufficient number of supporters in its success, I am inclined to think we should have met with, and in fact deserved, less mercy.'[84] The final voting in the Irish House of Commons was conclusive: a majority of forty-six for the Union where only the year before there had been a majority of five against it. It was to come into force on 1 January 1801. And so, what one member of the British Cabinet described as 'the greatest and most desirable measure which ever was in contemplation' was brought into being. Something of this extravagant mysticism continued to surround the Union for the 120 years of its existence.

At once exaltation on the part of the British Government and the pro-Unionists achieved almost religious dimensions. According to Cornwallis, the Empire was now so completely united that the Union would remain 'in all future ages, the fairest monument of His Majesty's reign already distinguished by so many and such various blessings conferred upon every class and description of his subjects'.[85] What had been achieved, Unionist supporters felt, was the almost magical formula which Pitt had expressed in a speech in the House of Commons: 'the voluntary association of two great countries, which seek their common benefit in one Empire, in which each will retain its proportionate weight and importance, under the security of equal laws, reciprocal affection, and inseparable interests, and in which each will acquire a strength that will render it invincible'.[86]

Grattan, however, in his last speech in the Irish House of Commons opposing the Union, had struck a very different note.

The Constitution may, for a time, be lost – the character of the country cannot be so lost. The Ministers of the Crown may at length find that it is not so easy to put down for ever an ancient and respectable nation by abilities however great, by power and corruption, however irresistible. Liberty may repair her golden beams, and with redoubled heart re-animate the country. . . . I do not give up the country. I see her in a swoon, but she is not dead; though in her tomb she lies helpless and motionless, still there is on her lips a spirit of life and on her cheek a glow of beauty ...[37]

Both attitudes were misleadingly rhetorical. What golden beams of liberty, it might have been asked, had the wretched masses intoxicating themselves with the mumbo-jumbo of the Defenders ever known? The Constitution as it had existed for nineteen years was indeed going down but no 'ancient and respectable nation' had been truly identified with it – only the propertied classes, and many of these, even, without the right to function within it. The country in the sense that Grattan was talking about was indeed helpless and motionless but not in her tomb, or even in a swoon, for she had still to have life breathed into her.

The challenge to Pitt's rhetoric lay in the future. It was not by any means inconceivable that the Union might turn out to benefit Ireland in the way he foretold. But whether or not she would acquire the promised invisible strength would depend entirely on the reality given to phrases like 'common benefit' and 'equal laws', and how exactly an attempt was going to be made to meet those 'interests' which were now to be 'inseparable' from the rest of Britain's.

The fact that the Union was to fail the challenge of reality was not, as has sometimes been maintained, the result of treacherous English villainy. The Union was not intended as a trap for Ireland although it turned out afterwards to have been one. What was to make it fail was not villainy, or even neglect, but inability to understand until almost too late the fundamental problem of Irish society. This problem, so long evaded not only by the British Government but by Irish patriots themselves, was the historically conditioned land system which covered the greater part of the country. This system's injustice, its lack of acknowledgement of any rights for those who worked the land and lived by it – as distinct from those who owned it – was the result of the ancient religious conflict between Protestants and Catholics long conceded to be irrelevant where land was concerned. The injustice was magnified by another historically conditioned factor: the absence of any alternative form of livelihood but land. The land system had to be changed, even at the cost of interfering with the rights of property, if the population of the country was ever to come within sight of the decent satisfactions of normal everyday life. When eventually understanding did break through and relevant action was taken, it was still just not too late to save the Union in its widest form and certainly not too late in any case to save the British connection through a joint Crown. That both were eventually lost was due to another failure, not this time of understanding, but of imagination.

informer, the government ordered his arrest. They found that he had already
fled.

Robert Emmet's whereabouts for the next year or so are obscure though
he undoubtedly had some contact with the prisoners in Fort George,
where conditions, though far from intolerable, were harsher than they had been in
Kilmainham. Early in 1800 he went to France where for about a year he
seems to have been trying to organize some form of United Irish directory
as was functioning in Ireland. But the apparent half-heartedness of the
French towards the cause made it an unrewarding post. Certainly it seems
that Bonaparte was more interested in making the British fear an invasion
of Ireland than in actually carrying one out. Emmet optimistically studied

2
Robert Emmet's
Fall and Rise

The actual passing of the Union turned out to be something of an anti-
climax at the time. The issue had always given rise to more calculation than
passion and such passion as had been generated was spent. From all over
the country, including Dublin, came reports of perfect tranquillity.[1] Even
those forces which by definition existed to disturb Irish tranquillity seem
hardly to have been affected one way or the other. Agrarian disturbances
came and went, as they had done for decades, in Lecky's phrase 'like the
passing storms that sweep so rapidly over the inconstant Irish sky'.[2] Part of
the pro-Union argument had in any case always been that it would in time
work to eradicate such disaffection. As for the United Irishmen, they had
been opposed not particularly to the Union but to the British connection
which existed whether there were a union or not. They had been broken
not by the Union but by their own incompetence and lack of effective
organization three years before, and by the consequent military defeats both
of the rebels and the French. But there was to be one last attempt to revive
their cause. And total failure and puny in scale though it was, it was to echo
through history with almost as much effect as the convulsion of 1798 itself.

While the Union arguments had been proceeding in the course of 1799
the government had received information that a new United Irish executive
had been formed in Dublin and that one of its guiding spirits was the
Protestant Robert Emmet, youngest son of a sometime physician to the
Vice-Regal Lodge and younger brother of Thomas Addis Emmet, then a
state prisoner in Fort George in Scotland. The year before, Robert had
been a noticeably brilliant student at Trinity College where he had studied
science, but he had been expelled for holding radical political views like
those for which his brother had got himself into much more serious trouble.
Robert had visited his brother and MacNeven, O'Connor and the rest in Kilmainham gaol before they were moved to Scotland. The prisoners had had
considerable latitude and freedom of association in Kilmainham, and Robert
had taken out instructions from them to such members of the United Irish
executive as were still at large, and had himself become a member of the
executive. Now, in 1799, on receipt of information about his activity from an

informer, the government ordered his arrest. They found that he had already fled.

Robert Emmet's whereabouts for the next year or so are obscure though he undoubtedly had contacts with his brother and the others in Fort George, where conditions were even more lax and civilized than they had been in Kilmainham. Early in 1801 he went to France, where for about a year he seems to have been the Paris representative of such United Irish directory as was functioning in Ireland. But the apparent half-heartedness of the French towards the cause made it an unrewarding post. Certainly it seems that Bonaparte was more interested in making the British fear an invasion of Ireland than in actually carrying one out. Emmet optimistically studied military textbooks, including a history of the Seven Years War.[3] Among acquaintances he made was the American engineer and armaments specialist, Robert Fulton, who was then trying to sell the idea of a submarine to Bonaparte and who imparted to Emmet his fascination with rockets and explosives. But the chances of putting theory into practice receded further than ever when France concluded the Peace of Amiens with England in 1802.

The United Irish prisoners were now released from Fort George in delayed implementation of their compact with the British Government, and it was Robert Emmet's first wish to join his brother in exile in America. But the loneliness of his ageing parents in Ireland troubled him and he eventually decided with some reluctance to return there.[4] Presumably he felt free to do so because Habeas Corpus, which had been suspended when the government wanted to arrest him earlier, had now been restored, and there was probably little solid evidence against him which would have held up in front of a jury. The private letter in which he writes of the difficulty this decision caused him also makes clear that he was not then contemplating anything in the way of radical conspiracies, but rather reluctantly considering them a thing of the past.[5]

He returned to Ireland in October 1802, leading for a time a purely social life, dining out in merchants' houses in Dublin and emphasizing that he had come about private and not public affairs.[6] But there was in fact already a conspiracy on foot in Dublin, with which in its first stage he apparently had no connection. This was a curious affair timed to coincide with a three-part rising of radical republicans in the British Isles – in England, Scotland and Ireland simultaneously. The chief branch of the conspiracy was in England, where it was headed by an eccentric military figure of previous good standing named Colonel Despard. Despard had had a respectable public career up to a point but had developed a bitter sense of grievance against the British Government when they dismissed him from a post in the West Indies, and this sense of grievance transformed him into a violent republican. The London end of the plot, which was to begin by blowing George III to bits with a cannon aimed at him from the park, was foiled in plenty of time. Despard was arrested, tried with six other conspirators, found guilty and hanged in a row with them, in spite of a recommendation to mercy by the jury on account of past services to the nation and personal testimony to his character from Lord Nelson. Altogether, Despard in fact appears as a rather absurd and pathetic figure in history who only keeps his place there thanks to his tenuous connection with another conspiratorial failure to whom myth was kinder: Robert Emmet.

It seems unlikely that Emmet had any part in the Irish end of the conspiracy while Despard was alive, but it must have been soon after Despard's execution that he once again became entangled in United Irish activity in Dublin. In his Proclamation of July 1803, headed very like another more famous proclamation of over a century later, 'The Provisional Government to the People of Ireland', Emmet declared that such a government had been organizing for eight months and referred to the 'failure of a similar attempt in England', clearly meaning Despard's.[7] It must therefore have been around the end of 1802 that he entered into his plan for a new United Irish rising in Dublin. Certainly the police began to show an interest in him again about that time, because they paid a visit to his father's house where he was living at the end of December 1802, but he evaded them by means of an elaborate series of trap-doors, ropes, pulleys and concealed hiding-places which he had constructed there.[8]

Emmet does not appear to have been the prime mover in the new conspiracy at first, though it is not clear who was. Certainly, by the time his ill-assorted band took to the streets in the following July he, in his general's uniform of green and lace with gold epaulettes on each shoulder, was the chief person in authority – though authority is an inappropriate word in the circumstances.

In spite of past disappointments with France, the conspirators had been plainly encouraged by the renewal of the war in May 1803, and a messenger was sent to France, to Robert's brother Thomas, with the familiar sort of wildly optimistic assertions about the state of affairs in Ireland. There was 'a new and closer plan' ... communication between North and South had been thoroughly established ... respectable men had come forward ... Kildare, Wicklow and Dublin were in a very forward state ... one depot in Dublin alone held 2,500 pikes already fitted with handles ... the government did not seem to have the slightest suspicion, etc.[9] Thomas Emmet was to procure arms and money and officers from Bonaparte, but in this he proved unsuccessful, being unable even to obtain personal access to Bonaparte, a problem aggravated by a split among the exiled revolutionaries in Paris.*

---

* Arthur O'Connor, who seems more to have enjoyed the First Consul's favour, and was made a French general, was the leader of the rival group to T. A. Emmet.

In any case, after past experience the Dublin men do not seem to have been relying too heavily on the French, stressing in their application for help that they were disgusted with France and would not take her assistance if they could do without it.[10] In Emmet's excited proclamation, it was positively stated that the conspiracy had been conducted 'without the hope of foreign assistance'.[11] Certainly, whether hoped for or not, French help was not forthcoming, for, in what was to become the tradition of Irish nationalist rebellions, the rising went off at half-cock.

The plan itself was reasonable and practical, its execution lamentable to the point of farce. Bad luck played its part but need not have played such a disastrous one if organization and leadership had been efficient. The chief objective was Dublin Castle, the seat for centuries of the Irish executive which had been retained intact after the Union, though responsible now directly to the British Parliament. The Pigeon House fort in the harbour and the Artillery Barracks at Islandbridge were to be captured first. Meticulous care had been given to the planning of this operation. Points in between the main objectives where loyalist forces might be expected to give trouble were detailed, and an elaborate defensive system worked out whereby certain streets were to be chained and padlocked and strategic nearby houses occupied. The bridges over the Liffey were to have boards covered with long nails fixed into the roadway to impede entry. A special feature of the rising was to be the ingenuity of weapons employed. In secret arms depots in Dublin men had for weeks been manufacturing not only the conventional pikes in use five years before but also an improved version which folded in half so that it could be carried concealed under a man's greatcoat, and, more revolutionary still, a great quantity of explosives including rockets, grenades and fixed wooden blocks full of explosive and shrapnel which could be set to go off in the street like mines. It was in fact the preoccupation with explosives that set off the disastrous sequence of events in which Emmet's attempt ended. On 16 July 1803 an accidental explosion took place in one of the depots in Patrick Street, Dublin, drawing the attention of the police to the house.

One of the most remarkable features of Emmet's ill-starred attempt was that, unlike the business of five years before, the secret of the conspiracy had been kept very close. This part at least of the message to his brother in France had been no boast. Although the government had some general uneasy feelings that something was afoot they had no suspicion of what it was, or who was involved in it. Even after the explosion in Patrick Street the police were unable to discover anything like the real nature or extent of what had been going on there. Many of the remaining arms had been removed before the police arrived; others were stored in specially prepared hiding-places which were not discovered. But Emmet reasonably concluded that it would only be a matter of time before the government were on to him and decided not to postpone the date of the rising already fixed for the following Saturday, 23 July 1803. Thomas Russell, Tone's old friend, the only one of the exiled prisoners from Fort George to come over from France to join him, was sent off to alert the North which, he assured Emmet, was all ready to rise.

It had been a conscious part of Emmet's strategy not to try to organize the country outside Dublin to any large extent. He thus hoped to avoid the pitfalls of conspiratorial bureaucracy which had helped undo the men of '98. His assumption was that large areas of the country were ready to rise in any case if given the proper signal, and that there could be no more proper signal than the taking of the Castle and victory in Dublin. This replaced the old previously awaited signal of a French landing.

In his Proclamation Emmet said he was counting on the support of nineteen counties. When he finally launched his abortive attempt that Saturday, the country so conspicuously failed to rise that it is easy to say his assumptions were ludicrous. But then, no signal was given. Not only did Emmet fail to take Dublin; he came nowhere near any success at all. And the cautious and individualistic nature of the discontent in the country was such that without any very clear indication of success it inevitably remained inert.

The trail of disasters after the accident of the Patrick Street explosion was almost continuous. There was a remarkable lack of any firm leadership or preparedness to deal with them. Apart from sending Russell off to the North, the only practical arrangements Emmet had made with forces other than his own were with the men of Kildare and those remnants of the '98 rebellion still holding out under Michael Dwyer in Wicklow. But these arrangements, and Emmet's entire system of communications, proved highly unreliable. Through a failure of the messenger sent to summon Dwyer's men from Wicklow, they never arrived at all. The men from Kildare did come into Dublin, principally on the evening before, but did not like what they found. Emmet had to spend hours arguing with them not only about whether the arms provided were sufficient but also, at this absurdly late stage, about whether or not the rising ought to wait for a French landing. These Kildare men spent much of the day itself waiting for the zero hour of 9 p.m. in the Dublin public houses, and many actually moved out of the city about 5 p.m. on receipt of a false report that Dublin was not going to rise after all. A message had been circulated by some treacherous or cowardly person, wrote Emmet later, that the rising was off till the following Wednesday.[12] The Wexford men who did assemble at the right place in Dublin waited in vain on the night for their prearranged signal – the firing of a rocket. It was never fired, because by then Emmet had been so overwhelmed by the magnitude of the other disasters that he had decided to call the whole adventure off.

'There was failure in all,' Emmet wrote afterwards, 'plan, preparation and men.' [13] Until as late as five o'clock on the day of the rising he was desperately trying to find money to buy more blunderbusses. The last two days, which should have been spent in perfection of plans, had to be devoted to making good the shortage of pikes after losses in the Patrick Street explosion. '... Even this, from the confusion occasioned by men crowding into the Depot, from the country, was almost impossible.' The man who was to make the fuses for the wooden explosive devices forgot about them. The man in charge of the depot 'mixed, by accident, the slow matches that were prepared with what were not, and all our labour went for nothing. The fuses for the grenades he had also laid by, where he forgot them, and could not find them in the crowd. The cramp irons could not be got in time from the smiths, to whom we could not communicate the necessity of dispatch; and the scaling ladders were not finished (but one).'

At Dublin Castle itself the government had had many indications to supplement their vague suspicions of the past few weeks. On the morning of 23 July itself a publican came in to report that he had heard some men discussing over breakfast a rising due for that evening, and an employer arrived to say that some of his men had asked to be paid off early that night so that they could take part in it.[14] A state of increased alert was maintained but no positive move made and the government was afterwards heavily criticized for not having taken the situation more seriously.

Meanwhile, the Proclamation of the Provisional Government was arriving wet from the presses* in the depot where Emmet in his general's green uniform and his feathered cocked hat was assembling his men. Three hours – from six to nine – had been allotted for the assembly of two thousand men. By nine o'clock eighty had arrived.[15] 'You are now called upon,' began the Proclamation, 'to show the world that you are competent to take your place among the nations; that you have a right to claim their recognisance of you as an independent country. ... We have now, without the loss of a man, with our means of communication untouched, brought our plans to the moment when they are ripe for execution. ... We therefore solemnly declare that our object is to establish a free and independent republic in Ireland ...'[16] The 'Provisional Government of the Republic' appended to the Proclamation a list of thirty decrees, abolishing tithes, making Church lands the property of the nation, and suspending all transfers of land and securities until the formation of a national government. A new sovereign assembly was to be elected on universal suffrage by secret ballot, to consist of three hundred representatives as in the old Parliament but now elected in proportion to the population of the thirty-two counties.[17]

Over such matters at least considerable care had been taken, and this evidence of it may at the last moment have given some confidence to the

* So described by the soldiers who arrived on the scene shortly afterwards.

group assembled round their small uniformed general in the confusion of the Thomas Street depot. If so, it could not have lasted long. News suddenly arrived that the horses pulling the coaches on which they had been counting to carry the assault force under cover to Dublin Castle had bolted on their way there, after an incident in which one of the escorting rebels had fired his pistol at a patrol. Soon after, a near panic ensued when word came that the military were approaching. The news was to prove false but there and then Emmet drew his sword and, accompanied by about a hundred men, sallied forth into the night in the name of the Irish Republic. The streets were filled with the usual Saturday night crowds, many of them drunk.

An indeterminate mob was soon rampaging through the streets with pikes and blunderbusses. It eventually found itself, quite fortuitously, surrounding the coach of Lord Kilwarden, the Lord Chief Justice, and a remarkably humane man, who with his son-in-law was now savagely piked to death. Emmet, striding on with a band of followers which soon dwindled to about twenty, was quite unaware of this grisly occurrence, and afterwards wholeheartedly deplored it. But the catastrophic nature of his failure was already plain to him, and, refusing to give the signal for the Wexford men to move to the now useless shedding of blood, he took himself off into hiding. As he himself conceded, what had happened did not even have the respectability of insurrection.[18] About thirty lives were lost in the course of the desultory rioting that completed the night.

Elsewhere in Ireland, almost nothing happened at all. The faithful Russell, as 'General of the Northern District', issued a proclamation that 'vast multitudes in all parts of the country were engaged',[19] but this was quickly recognized as untrue and treated accordingly. One claim Emmet could, and did, justifiably make for the whole disastrous undertaking. It had always been predicted that any new attempt at a rising would fail, but for quite different reasons. It was impossible, it was said, to hatch a conspiracy that was not known at the Castle. This at least Emmet had proved to be not so. When the government afterwards discovered the scale on which preparations had been made, unknown to them, they took considerably more fright than the actual events of the rising seemed to justify. There was an internal political row and the army commander was rather unfairly made the scapegoat.

But Emmet's real contribution to the cause in which he had so far cut such a forlorn and ludicrous figure was still to come. Under the name of Mr Ellis, his *nom-de-guerre* throughout the whole affair, he remained at large for nearly a month but, once caught, the result of his trial was a foregone conclusion. His speech from the dock must have had considerable effect in the darkening court room even at the time, for a number of his fellow students from Trinity days who were in court wearing the king's uniform went up and shook him by the hand afterwards, and the judge who sentenced him to be hanged, drawn and quartered, a notoriously callous man, is said to have been profoundly moved.[20] But the effect of the speech at the time was as nothing compared with the force it was to have as, with increasingly romantic persistence, it echoed through the history of the next hundred years into our own time. Since it was as a legend that this speech took wings it seems unimportant that the exact text is probably not wholly accurate. Certainly Emmet's words must have been close to the form in which they so popularly and effectively survived. He concluded:

I have but one request to ask at my departure from this world. It is the charity of its silence. Let no man write my epitaph; for as no man who knows my motives dare now vindicate them, let not prejudice or ignorance asperse them. Let them rest in obscurity and peace, my memory be left in oblivion and my tomb remain uninscribed, until other times and other men can do justice to my character. When my country takes her place among the nations of the earth, then and not till then, let my epitaph be written.

There is said to have been a curious delay at the scaffold. Emmet, who was allowed by the hangman to give the signal for his own drop by letting go of a handkerchief, continually replied, 'Not yet' to the hangman's repeated question: 'Are you ready, sir?' Finally, the hangman lost patience and tipped him into eternity in mid-sentence. The incident gave rise to some speculation as to whether or not Emmet was hoping for a last-minute rescue by some of Dwyer's men from Wicklow. But no rescue could have achieved the dramatic effect of the execution itself. After hanging for half an hour his unconscious form was cut down and, in accordance with the judicial custom of the day, his head was cut off with a butcher's knife. It was exhibited by the hangman who strode about the scaffold crying, 'This is the head of Robert Emmet, a traitor'. Dogs were seen licking up the blood. Handkerchiefs were dipped in the blood and jealously prized and preserved. Metaphorical handkerchiefs were dipped in it for over a century.

A few years later Emmet's old friend and fellow student at Trinity, the poet Tom Moore, wrote some lines which he included in his *Irish Melodies* without a title:

Oh! breathe not his name, let it sleep in the shade,
Where cold and unhonoured his relics are laid;
Sad, silent and dark be the tears that we shed,
As the night dew that falls on the grass o'er his head.

But the night dew that falls, though in silence it weeps,
Shall brighten with verdure the grave where he sleeps,
And the tear that we shed, though in secret it rolls,
Shall long keep his memory green in our souls.

Moore's poem, picking up Emmet's own last words from the dock, set the tone for the future of the legend.

The reason why exactly the Emmet débâcle should have become transformed into a myth of such powerful emotive force, and thus indirectly of political importance, is not immediately easy to see. His failure could hardly have been more ignominious and complete. It is true that the myth gained incidental colour from Emmet's romantic attachment to Sarah Curran, the daughter of the prominent barrister John Philpot Curran. Letters compromising her in his treason were found on Emmet at the time of his arrest. She was disowned by her father and there is a story of her waiting down a street in a closed carriage and waving a last farewell to him as he proceeded to the scaffold. But what still needs explaining is why it should be such a romantic ethereal figure so much closer to the sentimental balladist's heart than to practical politics who was to become Ireland's noblest hero. Why was it Robert Emmet's portrait above all others that was to go up along with the crucifix in countless small homes in Ireland for over a century and may even be seen there still?

The proximity of the crucifix may provide a clue. The success of the Emmet myth lay in the very need to ennoble failure. For tragic failure was to become part of Ireland's identity, something almost indistinguishable from 'the cause' itself.*

* Compare the speech made by Padraic Pearse, who was to be Commander of the Republican forces in the Easter Rising of 1916, at Wolfe Tone's grave the year before. 'No failure,' he said, 'judged as the world judges these things, was ever more complete, more pathetic than Emmet's. And yet he has left us a prouder memory than the men of Brian victorious at Clontarf or of Owen Roe victorious at Benburb. It is the memory of a sacrifice Christ-like in its perfection.'

3
The Failure of the Union

If the Union were to be a political success, it had to bring about some definite change in Irish life. Its justification lay in ushering in a new era. The one thing it could not afford to be in everyday terms was meaningless. Yet, for the vast majority of Irishmen clinging with unceasing precariousness to their small holdings of land, the Union made no practical difference at all; if anything, by making them more remote from government, it made things worse. The ground swell of social discontent remained as before, a vast unwieldy incoherent force, available to any political skill that might be bold enough to try to harness it.

There is an uncanny similarity about the way in which all eye-witnesses describe the conditions of the majority of the population of Ireland over a vast span of nearly two centuries. In the middle of these two centuries stands the Union of 1801, an almost irrelevant landmark. The commonest feature of all such descriptions is the comparison between Ireland and other countries to the detriment of Ireland, and this is stressed even more heavily after the Union.[1]

'I have seen several countries,' said a Resident Magistrate of Cork in 1824, 'and I never saw any peasantry so badly off.'[2] Richard Cobden, the Free Trader, told a friend that once after spending three months in Ireland he had gone direct to Egypt and that, taking the difference of climate into consideration, the condition of the fellaheen was infinitely better than that of the Irish cottier, or labouring class.[3]

'The wretchedness in some of the western parts of the County of Clare,' stated a Constabulary Inspector in 1824, 'is as great as human nature can almost be subjected to.'[4] And Sir Walter Scott visiting Ireland a year later noted in his diary: 'Their poverty has not been exaggerated: it is on the extreme verge of human misery.'[5] Nor were the years 1824–5 years of famine as 1817 and 1822 had been. Nor had anything like the worst yet been seen.

In 1844 a German traveller echoed many earlier comments with the words: 'To him who has seen Ireland no mode of life in any other part of Europe however wretched will seem pitiable.'[6] And a year later the Devon Commission, the last government inquiry to report on Ireland before the

Great Famine, confirmed this with a reference to 'the patient endurance which the labouring classes have generally exhibited under sufferings greater we believe than the people of any other country have to sustain'.[7] But by that time the greatest disaster of all in the Irish common people's long history of suffering was already befalling them. It was a disaster which everyone, including the government, had in one sense been able to see coming for decades, but which, since they felt quite powerless to do anything about it, they had preferred to treat as if it might never materialize.

A Frenchman, De Latocnaye, who toured Ireland fifty years before in 1796 had confirmed the continuation of the middleman system that had even then long been in existence.*

... A rich man, unwilling to be at any trouble, lets a large tract of country to one man, who does not intend to cultivate it himself, but to let it out to three or four others; those who have large shares farm them to about a score, who again let them to about a hundred comfortably situated peasants, who give them at an exorbitant price to about a thousand poor labourers, whom necessity obliges to take their scanty portion at a price far beyond its real value ...[8]

Fifty years later this situation had become a nightmare. The early years of the nineteenth century saw a great surge of agricultural prosperity in Ireland, started partly by earlier government corn bounties to farmers in the days of the Irish Parliament, but accelerated by the high farm prices obtainable as a result of the Napoleonic War. Yet in Ireland, where land was virtually the only source of livelihood, and competition for land therefore unlimited, agricultural prosperity meant prosperity only for those who received rents. For the rest of the population, who would pay any price that gave them a minimum subsistence, prosperity meant only that subsistence was at least for a time not in doubt, and that more such subsistence was available for more such people.

More such people soon appeared by the normal processes of nature to take advantage of the fact. The census of 1841 gave a population of just over eight million, probably double what it had been at the beginning of the century.† Middlemen on the land, taking a natural commercial advantage of the multiplying masses' desire and indeed absolute need for land, themselves multiplied accordingly on the pattern described by Latocnaye. Holdings were increasingly subdivided and sub-let to others who increasingly subdivided and sub-let in turn. Soon tenants on any sizeable piece of land were increasing at a terrifying rate of progression, and it became common enough to find a chain of succession on any one piece of land going down four or five times from the initial landlord. In the early 1820s when the

* See above, p. 22.
† This census also revealed that Irish was still the common speech of the majority. The Irish population was at this time just about half that of Great Britain – then sixteen million.

simple lease of one of the Duke of Leinster's 500-acre farms fell in, he found that on some parts of it there were tenants at seven removes from himself.[9] And the Catholic barrister Daniel O'Connell said he knew of farms, where he remembered only two farmhouses, supporting, in 1825, nearly two hundred families.[10]

All this was possible because land was the only means by which a man could procure a living for his family. The vast majority of the population naturally found themselves at the end of these series of middlemen; almost half the total number of holdings being less than five acres, and, by 1841, only seven per cent of them more than thirty acres.[11]

As each middleman in each series had to take his profit, the rent paid by those at the end of the series was all that a man could possibly afford to pay and continue to survive. Indeed, the series only came to an end in any given piece of land when that point had been reached.

The competition for land had 'attained something like the competition for provisions in a besieged town or in a ship that is out at sea'.[12] Whatever the size of a holding (and few were more than fifteen acres) the tenant-farmers lived almost entirely on potatoes, selling their crops to pay the extortionate rent. Frequently they could not even afford salt for their potatoes, which themselves were of the coarsest quality.

The Irish [wrote a desperate tenant farmer to the lord lieutenant] are reduced to the necessity of entirely subsisting on the lumper potato – a kind that grows something better in the poor man's impoverished land than the potatoes of good quality. The lumper is not indeed human food at all. Mix them with any other kind of potatoes and lay them before a pig, and she will not eat one of them until all the good kind are devoured. . . . People like you cannot have the least idea of our misery. The great governors of nations ought to go in disguise through the country and enter the hovels of the peasantry to make themselves acquainted with the kind of food they live on and how they must labour for that food.[13]

Bread itself was hardly eaten by the average Irishman from one year's end to the other. Nor was this only true of the poorest. A farmer with a holding of above average size on the Marquis of Conyngham's estate in 1846 declared: 'Not a bit of bread have I eaten since I was born, nor a bit of butter. We sell all the corn and the butter to give to the landlord' [for rent] 'yet I have the largest farm in the district and am as well off as any man in the county.'[14]

During the first half of the nineteenth century a number of most thorough inquiries were made by Parliament into the state of Ireland, and all reveal clearly this wretched life lived by the majority of the inhabitants, paying rents, 'by which it was impossible for the tenant at any time to pay, reserving the means of decent subsistence', living huddled together without distinction of age or sex, usually in the company of their livestock, on the bare floor of cabins through which ran open sewage, possessing hardly any bedding except straw, and often only able to go to Mass on alternate Sundays because there were not enough clothes to go round.[15] The lowest class of all could not even afford to pay rent, but in return for a minimum plot on which to grow enough potatoes for survival gave their labour for nothing all the year round like serfs. Some families of this type occupied as little as a quarter of an acre (though not less than two to three acres was regarded as necessary for the proper support of a large family).* So far down the economic scale were many of them that they hardly ever handled money at all.

Moreover, with a drop in agricultural prices after the Napoleonic War and the general trend for grazing land to become more profitable than tillage, landlords, appalled by the number of poor people they found multiplying on their land, understandably enough began to try and consolidate their property. A parish priest described what happened when they did.

'About three weeks or a month ago,' he said in May 1824, he had seen 'a certain farm (about 500 acres) that had 40 families residing on it, thinned in this manner. These 40 farms consisted of 200 individuals. When the lease fell in ... 28 or 30 of these farms, consisting of 150 individuals, were dispossessed; they were allowed to take with them the old roofs of the cabins, that is the rotten timber and the rotten straw; and with these they contrived to erect stands upon the highway. The men could get no employment, the women and children had no resource but to go and beg; and really it was a most affecting scene to behold them upon the highway, not knowing where to go.'[16] Some, thus evicted, moved to the towns where they crowded into small apartments and perhaps four or five families would live huddled together in a garret without proper clothes or bedding or food, while the men scavenged for casual labour, which was seldom to be had.

In all these circumstances it needed no social or economic genius to foretell what would happen if the potato crop, which alone was keeping the vast majority of the population alive, were to fail. In any case, the potato crop had failed quite frequently before, and history had already recorded the terrible famines which then ensued. There had been famines with particularly appalling spectacles of misery and death in 1720, 1739, 1741, 1800, 1817 and 1822. The great famine of the years 1845–8 was only the worst because by that time the population had grown to such a size that the pressure on land was that much greater, and the whole precarious system that much more disastrously balanced. A little over twenty years before, a parliamentary inquiry had asked a witness: 'Looking ahead to 15 or 20 years or more, what must this increase in population without employment end in?' and he had replied, 'I do not know; I think it is terrible to reflect upon.'[17]

Terrible indeed it proved to be, killing probably about a million people altogether and reducing the population of Ireland by death or agonizing

---

* An Irish acre was slightly larger than a normal British acre, being in the relation of about 1⅗ : 1.

emigration by as much as a quarter in six years. Men found that the scenes long spoken of with awe as characterizing earlier famines were now taking place, on an even more horrifying scale, before their eyes. The dead were already lying unburied six or eight days in the streets of Skibbereen and it was possible to plead on behalf of a sheep-stealer that his wife was so hungry that she had been eating the thigh of her own daughter who had died from famine fever.[18] And since starving and dying people had not the strength to till the soil to pay the rent – only the potato was affected by blight: other crops were good in the famine years – eviction on an unprecedented scale now took place in horrifying circumstances. One eye-witness described the eviction of 143 families (700 persons) from an estate in Tipperary as 'the chasing away of 700 human beings like crows out of a cornfield'.[19] Often they were too weak to be chased or had to be evicted dead. In either case, their corpses were found soon afterwards littering the hedgerows.

The opportunity was also seized of clearing *all* unwanted people off land, even those who were managing to pay their rent regularly. In one such case, seventy-six families, or about three hundred persons, were evicted from the estate of a Mr and Mrs Gerard in County Galway in spite of having the rent ready, and they were even driven from the ditches to which they had fled to try to fix up some sort of shelter with sticks and mud.[20] A bizarre individual instance of an eviction where no rent was owing was that of James Brady, cleared with his family from a holding near Kells in the rich farming county of Meath, though he had always paid his rent regularly. After spending nine days and nights with his wife and four little girls in a ditch, he dug the family a living grave in a churchyard on the plot of a man called Newman. Newman then served him with an eviction order but, before it could be enforced, himself died of famine fever and was buried in the grave beside the squatters, who thus continued to defy him into eternity.[21]

Sir Robert Peel, who had been Prime Minister when the potato crop first failed in 1845, said of one set of evictions at Kilrush in County Mayo involving the clearance of some fifteen thousand people like rubbish over a period of twelve months, that he did not think the records of any country, civil or barbarous, presented materials for such a picture.[22] And he went on to quote a government inspector's account of one significant but poignant incident involving a man employed breaking stones.

He [the inspector] saw that man suddenly seize on the remnant of a pair of shoes and run across a heath. He followed the direction the man took and saw a fire blazing. On making inquiry as to the cause of it, he was told that upon the man being driven from his home, he had occupied a still more wretched hovel of his own construction and that it was this last place in which he had sought shelter that had been set fire to in order to get rid of him.[23]

There are countless descriptions of what happened in those years on such a vast scale in the workhouses and fever hospitals, in the prisons to which people chose entry by the most direct means only to find the packed cells riddled with typhus, in the lonely derelict cabins where families of dying and dead were stretched out one above the other in layers, in the cramped emigrant ships in which as many as one-fifth of all the passengers sometimes had to be buried at sea, and in the fever-ridden camps on the other side of the Atlantic. But it was in millions of individual memories, often incoherent and inarticulate, handed down in America and Ireland from one suffering generation to the next, and from them to men and women who were young in the twentieth century, that the sense of fundamental outrage and resentment at this monstrous thing that had happened under civilized government to the humble people of Ireland lived on.[34]

It is easy, over a hundred years later and after the successful establishment of an Irish Republic, to look back and say, quite correctly, that the accusations of genocide made by some Irish writers at the time and since were unjust and absurd; that the government was the prisoner of the economic philosophy of the day, which taught that economic laws had a natural operation and that to interfere with them was to breed chaos and anarchy; that, far from looking on callously, the government looked on with an increasing sense of dismay at what it regarded as its helplessness before irresistible economic and social forces; that, eventually, by what seemed a superhuman effort at the time, it succeeded in abandoning at least some of the principles it held most sacred and brought itself to distribute government charity, expecting only in return that its recipients should continue to live. All this is true.

It is also true, as the appalling conditions from which the English working classes suffered at the same time make clear, that there was no specifically anti-Irish callousness in the government's outlook. The agricultural lower classes of Ireland were of no less theoretical concern to the government than the industrial working classes of England. The trouble was simply that in neither case was the concern great enough. Complex situations had developed within both patterns of lower-class living with which government had never contemplated having to deal. In Ireland the problems, besides being physically more remote, were also more complex, being bound up with a historical land system that went much further back than the industrial revolution; and the sufferings of the lower classes there were correspondingly greater. But the government were dealing 'with their own people' in both cases, however ironic the phrase may seem in the circumstances.

It is also necessary to say that the rigidity of the formula from which the government of the day had to escape in order to govern better is, at this distance of time, very difficult to appreciate. A Poor Law Commissioner of the famine time declared that he had heard the opinion stated both implicitly and explicitly that 'it was desirable to allow things to take their normal course; not to assist the people in their suffering but to permit disease and want to go to their natural termination'. And he added that 'many individuals even of superior minds, who seemed to have steeled their hearts to the suffering of the people of Ireland, justify it to themselves by thinking it would be going contrary to the provision of nature to render assistance to the destitute of that country'.[25] And this was at the height of the disaster when the government were in fact already distributing free soup. It was held then and continued to be held even for long afterwards that 'the economic laws which govern all human society are fixed by divine wisdom, and that any attempt to struggle with them by human legislation invariably results in making matters worse'.[26]

In the current of such a social philosophy clearly the government of the famine time showed some courage and enterprise in grappling with the disaster even to the inadequate extent it did. Yet it must finally be said of men who, when faced by the manifold unmistakable warnings they had received, had felt unable to grapple with the situation earlier or more effectively, that there was about them a lack of imagination and a fear of acting outside the civilized conventions of their time that amounted to a blot on civilization itself. Certainly it made nonsense of all the fine phrases about 'common benefit ... equal laws ... reciprocal affection ... inseparable interests and invincible strength' with which Pitt had ushered in the Union over forty years before.

There was also a flaw in their economic philosophy which amounted to something very like hypocrisy. For this society had no scruples about interfering by human legislation with 'natural' economic laws where the interests of property demanded it. It was only where the demand was in the interests of the poor that their principles were so sternly unyielding. As a future Prime Minister, Gladstone, was to comment, the law was amended over and over again in favour of the landlord but there was not to be, until 1870, a single act on the statute book in favour of the tenant.

If, then, it must be the calm judgement of history that the government which could allow such a thing to happen stands condemned, it is easy to imagine how bitter and outraged was the reaction at the time of those who survived and who understood only the pain they and their loved ones suffered. This deep resentment was to take on a profound historical importance.

For the famine and its after-effects played a role in Irish history long after the grass had grown over the mass graves and the unwanted roads and pointless earthworks which the starving had had to construct in return for the first attempts at relief. In the late forties and early fifties well over a million Irish of the poorer class, hating what passed for government in Ireland, became literally physically separate from that government when they emigrated to the other side of the Atlantic. Given the conditions under which their class had lived ever since the penal laws, there had obviously never been much enthusiasm for government as such but, in a primitive struggle like theirs, the real enemy had appeared not so much in the form of the government itself as in the more get-at-able form close at hand of a landlord or his agent, or, most frequently, of another member of the Irish peasant class refusing to combine in the common interest. Moreover, hostile as the government had been felt to be, it had been the only government there was; there had been no real conceivable alternative. Now, for a considerable section of the Irish people this was no longer so. They had separated from it. And since they and their descendants and followers to America long continued to be very Irish, for the first time in Irish history a very large body of Irish common opinion, often retaining close personal links with Ireland, could feel itself politically anti-British without the confusing factor of being somehow British too.

In Ireland itself the situation was less clear. The famine and its evictions had been only the worst in a long series of cruelties to which the humble people of Ireland had been exposed for centuries. Over and over again they had suffered and died, and society had been shocked, or had 'steeled their hearts', and the dead had been buried and society had continued as before, with more fine laments simply added to the stock of legend. In one sense the famine could be seen as the last straw, demanding at last some form of political atonement to the nameless millions who had suffered for centuries and, for the living, a better future. Yet to think, in Ireland itself, of creating a 'separate' Ireland demanded a much greater effort of the imagination than it did on the other side of the Atlantic. For the whole external fabric of society in Ireland was British, and, more confusing still, this British society in Ireland was Irish too.

One of the British Government's nineteenth-century Chief Secretaries for Ireland, the Earl of Mayo, a descendant of one of the most ancient Norman–Gaelic families, spoke no more than the truth when, in 1868, he declared that he had considerably less Anglo-Saxon blood in his veins than 'many of the gentlemen in green uniforms flourishing about New York' at that time.[27] And by then, too, religious divisions in Ireland, though more obvious than racial ones, were themselves becoming of less and less social or political significance. By the 1820s Catholics had once again accumulated considerable landed property in Ireland. By 1834 they owned about one-fifth of the land of Ireland outright – compared with one-fourteenth at the height of the penal laws – and a further half was held by Catholics on long lease, compared with almost none under the penal laws.[28] Thus, though the land system itself had not changed, Catholic landlords now exploited it together with Protestants. When, immediately after the famine, one-third of the land of Ireland changed hands as bankrupt estates were sold off, ninety per cent of the new landlords were Irishmen of one religion or the other, and particularly harsh in increasing rent and effecting clearances they proved to be. The important divisions in Irish society were no longer those of race or religion, but those of class.

In such circumstances the idea of Irish nationalism, never precise for the masses, took on a blurred image, and, inasmuch as it came to mean something positive at all, meant different things to different people.

4
Daniel O'Connell
and Catholic Emancipation

Some years before the famine a new form of Irish nationalism, rejecting republican separation altogether, had taken shape under the leadership of the lawyer Daniel O'Connell, one of the great pioneers of popular democracy. It had in fact, until swamped by the famine, acquired the power of the people behind it unlike anything put forward in the name of Irish nationalism before; being the first real effective organization of Irish mass opinion since the days of James II.

The new movement had different names at different times depending on O'Connell's immediate political objective, but its real objective, under whatever label, was the improvement of the lot of the Irish common people as a national aim in itself. Nationalism, or Irish-consciousness, with its heavy and romantic sense of the past and its love of the beautiful landscape in which this flourished, became primarily a powerful emotive auxiliary in the drive towards political goals which were to mean better times for all.

For the rest of the century and beyond, this was what Irish nationalism was to represent for the majority of the Irish population. Republican separatism, though it could often call on wide passive sympathy, became only a small minority movement, and remained so until almost the final moment of its surprise success in the next century. Only the swelling numbers of separate Irishmen in the great republic across the Atlantic, nursing the bitterest memories of government in Ireland, gave it a significance out of proportion to its Irish presence.

Daniel O'Connell was twenty-five at the time of the Union. He was by then a promising lawyer, born of a prosperous Catholic family from one of the remote promontories of County Kerry in south-west Ireland. As a Catholic, he had been rather untypical of his faith in strongly opposing the Union in 1800, declaring that if offered the alternatives of Union and the re-enactment of the penal laws in their full severity he would choose the latter. Certainly his own family history showed how some well-to-do Catholics could survive through long years of difficulty and darkness.

The O'Connells had been High Sheriffs of Kerry in the sixteenth century, but had suffered setbacks in the seventeenth when the head of the family was transplanted under Cromwell's anti-Catholic measures to Connaught. However, another O'Connell, by not joining in the rebellion of 1641, had managed to retain his own land. Throughout the eighteenth century the O'Connells had continued to cling to a nucleus of their ancient estates in Kerry and even before the repeal of the penal laws had been adding to them by the fairly common device of buying land in the name of a cooperative and friendly Protestant. One of O'Connell's uncles had emigrated to reach high rank in the French Army, another to become chamberlain to three Emperors of Austria. But another, after the abolition of the penal land laws, had added further to the family estates in Kerry and become an owner of grazing cattle on a considerable scale. He had also carried on a productive sideline in the smuggling trade with France for which the innumerable wild bays and inlets of Kerry made it so suitable. He virtually took over his nephew's upbringing.

O'Connell, like better-off Catholics throughout the eighteenth century, was educated in France where he stayed during the early part of the Revolution, leaving on the day of Louis XVI's execution. After studying law in London he was called to the Irish bar in May 1798, on the day Lord Edward Fitzgerald was arrested. Appalled by the bloodshed of the rebellion of that year, he was, by the time of Emmet's fiasco, a member of the loyalist Lawyers Artillery Corps.

But although O'Connell rejected the United Irishmen's ideas of separatist nationalism, he had a very strong emotive Irish-consciousness rooted in his own family history and he was successfully to take over much of the United Irishmen's rhetorical thunder and convert it to his own uses. A lot of his language was to be often almost indistinguishable from that of separatist nationalists. Thus, although he attached his own constitutional limitation to what he meant by 'liberate', he echoed Tone when he declared in 1810: 'The Protestant alone could not expect to liberate his country – the Roman Catholic alone could not do it – neither could the Presbyterian – but amalgamate the three into the Irishman, and the Union is defeated.'[1] Again, later in his career he said: 'In the struggle for nationality I recognize no distinction of creed or party. Every man who joins with me for Ireland is my sworn brother.'[2] And he could talk about 'the desire for National Independence' or 'the want of Nationhood'[3] with as much emotive power as anyone.

But for O'Connell the British connection and acceptance of the Crown were never questioned. Late in his life he insisted that he would abandon all his political aims overnight if he thought them in any way 'dangerous to the connection between the two countries, or dangerous to our allegiance to our sovereign'.[4] More than twenty years earlier, when George IV had visited Ireland in 1821 and the port of Dunleary was renamed Kingstown in his honour, O'Connell presented the king with a laurel crown on bended knee on his departure.[5] The address from the citizens of Dublin on that occasion referred to the king uniting 'six millions of a grateful people in a bond of brotherly love to one another, and of affectionate attachment to your Majesty's person and throne'.[6] O'Connell afterwards suggested the formation of a Royal Georgian club to dine six times a year, wearing cloth of Irish manufacture and rosettes of blue. 'Loyalty,' he declared, 'is not the peculiar prerogative of one sect or another, but it is the legitimate and appropriate characteristic of all His Majesty's subjects of every class, every rank, every denomination."[7]

In other words, the sort of Irish nationality and Irish independence in which O'Connell believed was an extension to all the people of Ireland of that very sort of independence within the Empire which Protestant Irishmen had so proudly insisted on for themselves in the eighteenth century. What he meant by liberating the Irish people was liberating them all to this equality of rightful national pride within the connection. Ultimately this would bring about their liberation from the whole tyranny of their everyday conditions. The reason why he stuck so firmly to the British connection was not from any profound mystical convictions about it such as Grattan had had. O'Connell had simply learnt from recent history that any attempt to break the connection not only got the Irish people nowhere, but actually increased their dreadful suffering a thousandfold. On the other hand, anything on the right side of treason might theoretically be obtained. Thus the only insuperable obstacle to his aims became treason itself.

It was in the 1820s that the first stage of O'Connell's political career opened with his great campaign for Catholic Emancipation. This issue had simmered on for some twenty years after the Union, as a middle- and upperclass affair of polite petitions to Parliament. It was of direct interest only to those Catholics who might aspire to the relatively few high offices and functions, including membership of Parliament, from which they were still debarred. The peasantry concentrated on their own immediate interests through the network of the secret societies. Even as a symbol Emancipation had lost much of its force, for the major concession to Catholics had been made in the 1790s, when they received the vote on the same terms as the Protestants.

Yet it was precisely by managing to organize the masses so effectively in a campaign for the little that remained that O'Connell succeeded in raising a new issue of national political principle altogether. The real issue now, and for the first time in modern Irish politics, was this: were the masses, wellorganized, but acting constitutionally, to be allowed to have their way against the government? It was this new subtle threat that accounted for the bitterness with which the government now fought Emancipation thirty years after Pitt had been prepared to concede it.

Although O'Connell had long been in favour of more vigorous action on Emancipation, it was only in 1823 that he began to give his full energies to the cause. Many sophisticated Catholics that year felt that the prospect of Emancipation had never been so dim. One wrote afterwards: 'I do not exaggerate when I say that the Catholic question was nearly forgotten.'[8] But that year O'Connell founded the Catholic Association for the purpose of adopting 'all such legal and constitutional measures as may be most useful to obtain Catholic Emancipation'.[9] The outstanding feature of the new organization was the broad democratic basis O'Connell gave it by introducing an associate membership, for which the subscription was only a shilling a year. The 'penny a month' became known as the Catholic Rent and soon vast sums, sometimes of £1,000 a week and more, were pouring in to the organization from all over Ireland, providing it with a regular campaign fund. The only immediate political objective for which the Association could campaign was the return to Parliament of Protestants who favoured Emancipation, but something like an embryonic political party apparatus on a democratic model had come into being.

The old oligarchic political system had survived the Union unreformed. But it did contain one odd democratic feature ready to hand for anyone with the will and determination to use it. When Catholics were enfranchised in 1793, the qualification had been the forty-shilling freehold. Almost any bit of property, sometimes even a bit of furniture, could be and often was spuriously dignified with the title of a forty-shilling freehold, for, with no secret ballot and the tradition still holding good that a tenant voted for his landlord, it was in a landlord's interest to have as many forty-shilling freeholders as possible. Anyone who voted against that interest could expect immediate eviction. But during the second decade of the nineteenth century evidence began to appear that Catholic forty-shilling freeholders could, if given support and encouragement by their priests, be brought to defy their landlords at the polls. The numerous forty-shilling freeholders were thus potentially a considerable democratic force. Some years even before the appearance of the Catholic Association the forty-shilling freeholders of Leitrim, Wexford and Sligo, mobilized by their priests, had successfully defied their landlords and obtained the election of liberals favourable to Catholic Emancipation. And just before the foundation of the Association the landed proprietors in County Dublin itself had also seen themselves outvoted.

O'Connell seems to have been slow to realize the powerful instrument made available to him by this new trend. A picture had long ago impressed itself on his mind of freeholders being driven by their landlords to the polls, like so many cattle to market. In spite of recent evidence he thought they were more a political liability as automatic landlord votes than an asset, and was even prepared to see their disfranchisement. Thus the initiative to overthrow the entrenched Tory landlord interests in a new election pending in Waterford in 1826 did not actually come from him.

Waterford was the property of the Beresford family, the most powerful in Ireland for influence and patronage. Only ten days before the actual election, for which preparations had been going on for months, O'Connell and the Catholic Association finally decided to throw themselves into the fight against the Beresfords' nominee. But they did so with a masterly organization which immediately struck fear into the government. The frightening thing was not the expected disorder, but the reverse. The police major in charge in Waterford reported to Dublin Castle that, quite unlike normal Irish elections, there was very little drunkenness and no rioting.[10] The Catholic Association itself patrolled the town to keep order. Green handkerchiefs, sashes, cockades and ribbons were being worn everywhere and green flags flew in all parts of the city.

The Emancipation candidate at Waterford was elected. It was a staggering blow to the landed proprietors, one of whom emphasized what to him was the really ominous feature, namely that all those very Catholics who had most loyally helped him put down rebellion in 1798 had now voted contrary to his wishes. The prospect of an organized mass political opinion which could no longer be dealt with as treason was thoroughly alarming. An equally sensational result took place soon afterwards at Louth, where a man whose family had controlled the county for half a century was defeated by an Emancipation candidate.

One of the ways in which Association funds were used was to give help to tenants evicted in reprisal for voting against their landlord's wishes. Publicity given by the Association to such acts of vindictiveness also discouraged the use of this ultimate landlord's sanction against the rebellious Catholic freeholder. Further elections followed, in which the Association continued to be successful.

The government, alarmed by this new democratic phenomenon, had already passed one act which made the Catholic Association illegal. But O'Connell always boasted that with his lawyer's skill he could drive a coach and six through any act of Parliament. He soon founded a New Catholic Association, 'merely for the purposes of public and private charity ... promoting public peace and tranquillity as well as private harmony among all classes of His Majesty's subjects throughout Ireland'.[11] Peel, the Home Secretary, and Wellington, the Prime Minister, strongly pressed the law officers of the Crown to prosecute the new organization. They were advised that, although the Association had technically broken the Convention Act of 1793 which had been specifically designed to prevent Catholics organizing extra-parliamentary power, it would be 'hazardous' in the present climate of Ireland to risk a prosecution by bringing the case before a jury. The climax of the Association's campaign came when O'Connell himself decided to stand for County Clare in 1828.

There was nothing illegal about a Catholic actually standing at an election, though none had done so for nearly 150 years. It was only after election that the test of his suitability to sit in Parliament was made. On presenting himself at the House of Commons he had not only to take the oaths of allegiance and supremacy, but also to testify that 'the invocation or adoration of the Virgin Mary or any other saint and the sacrifice of the Mass, as they are now used in the Church of Rome, are superstitious and idolatrous'.[12] If, in full knowledge of this, an electorate voted for a Catholic it was clearly as arrogant a defiance of the political establishment as could constitutionally be made. The Clare election presented the government with the most serious challenge it had had to face since the passing of the Act of Union.

There was a threat, too, behind the challenge, which, though largely unspoken, was a real consideration to the government and an essential, if risky, aspect of the tactics of O'Connell and the Catholic Association. The bloody horrors of 1798, though now some thirty years old, were very much a part of living memory. Any organization of the Irish masses in their incredible poverty and misery and their fierce resentment of their conditions could not help conjuring up the old spectre of violent and terrible insurrection. Though all leadership for political insurrection had disappeared, the masses' instinct for violence as a last resort had continued to manifest itself in the activities of the agrarian secret societies, particularly in the period between 1815 and 1824, which had seen two serious potato famines. In the circumstances, the government and the established order made no nice distinction between agrarian and political activity, between the masses collected in night bands of Rockites and Ribbonmen and the masses collected in their constitutional organization under O'Connell. One Orangeman, the Earl of Clancarty, thought that in 1824 Ireland was in a more dangerous state than on the eve of the rebellion of 1798, and in letters to the government there was exaggerated talk similar to that of the 1790s, of nightly meetings and arming with pikes and firearms.[13]

O'Connell's own horror of bloodshed was founded in recent Irish history. He had made technical legality and a constitutional attitude the cornerstone of his political faith. But he was not beyond implying that but for him and the Catholic Association violence would gain the upper hand. And in thus drawing attention to the threat he was averting, he uttered a sort of threat himself. The vivid and emotive metaphorical language of his speeches heightened the effect. His technique was to use those very dark forces of violence, which he was holding back, as a force obscurely at the back of him. This was to become even more blatantly his tactic in his later campaign for Repeal of the Union.

There was a good deal of substance in O'Connell's and the Catholic Association's claim that by the broad democratic nature of their own appeal they kept the violence of the agrarian secret societies harnessed and under control. O'Connell boasted that they and they alone prevented 'civil war', at the same time warning Wellington: 'Why, even in London if Pat took it into his head, he would go near to beat the guards; but for efficient strength at home it is but folly not to appreciate us justly.'[14] Sheil, another prominent member of the Association, sailed even closer to the wind by drawing attention in public to the 'vast body of fierce, fearless and desperate peasantry, who would be easily allured into a junction with an invader'.[15]

Certainly agrarian violence diminished after 1824 and the government reluctantly had to admit that this was due to the Association and its ability to assert discipline. 'We are in that happy state in Ireland,' wrote Peel to Wellington, bitterly, 'that it depends upon the prudence and discretion of the leader of the Roman Catholic Association whether we shall have a rebellion there or not in the next few months.'[16] And O'Connell continuously reminded the British Government of their predicament, playing sometimes too on their fear of French and even American[17] intervention. In his address to the people of England early in 1825, he stressed that 'Those who are labouring under oppression ... will be exposed to the strong temptation of receiving (if they can obtain it) assistance from any part of the world', and he talked of 'the possibility of seeing foreign fleets or bands the deliverers of Ireland'.[18] Moreover, by 1828, the year of O'Connell's own candidacy in the Clare election, the government were beginning to have serious doubts about the reliability in any emergency of the Irish troops.

Thus in the Clare election of 1828 the Irish bogey loomed almost as large as if rebellion had broken out, with the additional disadvantage that it could not be dealt with as if it had.

O'Connell stood in Clare as 'Man of the People'. The discipline of the crowds was again uncanny for an Irish election. Drunkenness was actually made a subject for mob punishment, offenders being thrown into the river, where they were kept for two hours and subjected to repeated duckings.[19] The commander of the troops described how the people marched in regular columns under officers who gave orders like 'keep in step' and 'right shoulders forward' which were immediately obeyed.[20] Peel himself wrote of the 'fearful exhibition of sobered and desperate enthusiasm'.[21]

O'Connell won the election by an overwhelming majority.

'Such a scene we have had!' wrote Peel. 'Such a tremendous prospect it opens to us! ... no man can contemplate without alarm what is to follow in this wretched country.'

With reports coming in that columns of men wearing green sashes and carrying green flags were parading in the West of Ireland,[22] Wellington and Peel, who even before the election had been facing up to the need to accept the inevitable, were in no doubt about one thing that had to follow. 'No one can answer for the consequences of delay,' wrote Wellington to the king in November.

A Catholic Emancipation Bill was introduced early in 1829 and received a pained and angry royal assent on 13 April of that year. It was immediately followed by an act which did something to reduce O'Connell's political power in Ireland for the immediate future by raising the franchise qualification from a forty-shilling to a ten-pound freehold. But, dazzled by his victory, O'Connell does not seem to have thought this important.

His victory meant much more than that Catholics could now sit in Parliament and become judges. The real victory consisted in the fact that for the first time ever the down-trodden Catholic masses had taken on the government and won. They had won by organization and discipline, by courage and leadership, by keeping just on the right side of the law and a long way on the right side of loyalty. There was a lesson to be learnt from this victory in contrast with the disastrous defeat into which the far cruder methods of the Defenders and the United Irishmen had led them. And in the first flush of this first victory, it either escaped them or seemed unimportant that the victory brought no real change to their everyday lives. In any case, the new strength by which they had won Emancipation could presumably be brought to bear on other issues too.

O'Connell, whose election had taken place before the passing of the Emancipation Act, now tried to take his seat in the Commons. But by a piece of government spite the act had not been made retrospective. Though O'Connell knew what the outcome of an attempt to take his seat must be in the circumstances, he made the most of the occasion for political ends. He went down to the House and, putting on his spectacles, laboriously read through to himself the wording with which he must have been perfectly familiar, of the oath of royal ecclesiastical supremacy together with the passage about the superstitious and idolatrous nature of the adoration of the Virgin and of the Mass.

'I see,' he declared aloud, 'in this oath, an assertion as a matter of opinion which I know to be false. I see in it another assertion as a matter of fact which I believe to be false. I therefore refuse to take this oath.'[23]

O'Connell had to travel all the way back to Clare to re-submit himself to the electorate. But again he made the most of the occasion, travelling much of the road in triumph and entering Ennis, the county town, escorted by a procession of forty thousand people with bands and banners.[24] This time he was elected unopposed, and under the Emancipation Act could now take his seat. The government's spite had deprived him of a personal ambition to be the first Catholic to enter Parliament, for the Duke of Norfolk and other peers had already been able to take their seats in the House of Lords.

A great triumph was behind O'Connell. He immediately set out in pursuit of a greater one. His next campaign would be Repeal of the Union itself.

5
The Repeal Debate

It was O'Connell's unforgettable campaign for Repeal of the Union, which consolidated for Ireland a strong mass national feeling that was political but not separatist. The important part of the campaign took place in the early 1840s; but it was to be preceded by a false start ten years earlier.

The outlook had seemed promising. O'Connell founded a popular organization similar to that which had just won Emancipation, and the government was soon suitably alarmed by its proportions. But the very different nature of the difficulties which confronted O'Connell on this new issue equally soon became plain.

In the Parliament that met after the great Reform Act of 1832 O'Connell found himself able to muster something very like a parliamentary party of his own in the House of Commons from among those Irish members who supported Repeal. There were thirty-nine Repealers out of a total Irish representation of 105 (the remainder being Tories and Liberal-Whigs). But the earlier issue of Catholic Emancipation had been supported by many more than thirty-nine members of the Union Parliament, for its supporters were not confined to Irish members. The mass agitation in Ireland and the election results had acted on a live political situation inside the Union Parliament. But Repeal was a dead issue in the Union Parliament. There were virtually no supporters for it other than the thirty-nine Irish Repeal members.

When in 1834 O'Connell first moved the Repeal of the Union in the House of Commons, the futility of his position on the new issue was revealed at once. The great debate that followed was notable not for its actual outcome, which was a foregone conclusion, but for a first parade of arguments for and against the Union which were to become more or less standard for the rest of the century.

O'Connell stated clearly the exact constitutional position he was aiming at. Ireland, he said, should be regarded 'not as a subordinate province, but as a limb of the empire – as another and distinct country, subject to the same King, but having a Legislature totally independent of the Legislature of Great Britain'.[1] He put this forward as a simple call to restore Ireland to the station she occupied 'when I was born'.

But it was of course naif to pretend, as he thus did, that what he sought was no different from the old Protestant Ascendancy's idea of national sovereignty, something traditional and normal and in no way revolutionary. Political circumstances had changed out of all recognition since 1782. Catholic Emancipation and the Reform Act had altered the whole balance of political power in Ireland. Irish national sovereignty under the Crown now meant not an oligarchic but an increasingly democratic 'nation'. However sweepingly O'Connell asserted that it was the Union which was 'the great source of Ireland's wrongs' he would have been doing no great service to Ireland in simply returning her to the conditions prevailing just before it. After all, there had been wrongs enough then to bring about the desperate catastrophe of 1798. His claim for independent Irish legislative power made little sense unless he intended to use it.

Irish national sovereignty within the Empire would now mean something like a social revolution in Ireland, however constitutionally it might be proposed. In the circumstances his conservative claim made little appeal to conservatives, particularly in the British House of Commons. Put forward as an old national claim, it was in reality something new. Given, however, a prior concern for the fate of the Irish masses rather than that of the landlords, it was a new claim which made good political sense.

There was sense too in O'Connell's final political argument. 'Repeal', he said, 'cannot endanger the connection – continuing the Union may . . .'[2] This was to remain the central point of debate for the rest of the century. The arguments would apply whether the issue at stake was Repeal (a wholly independent Irish legislature under the Crown) or, as later, Home Rule (an Irish legislature under the Crown with limited domestic powers only). Opponents of Irish legislative freedom of either kind always argued that it would lead to still further Irish national demands and eventually total separation. Conversely, Repealers and Home Rulers always argued that the only danger of separation arose from a refusal to grant Irish demands within the connection. This, they said, would play into the hands of the small minority of separatists.

In this first Repeal Debate in the Commons of April 1834, the chief government spokesman was the Secretary for War and the Colonies, Spring Rice, a Protestant Irishman. He argued as an Irishman whose national pride was satisfactorily fulfilled by the theory of the Union. His argument was ingenious to the point of absurdity.

'Why,' he declaimed, 'who contends that England has or ever had a right of domination over Ireland, either derived from conquest or concession? England exercised such a right, it is true, and strongly contended in its defence, but the claim was founded on usurpation alone. . . . Who governs Ireland? Who legislates for Ireland? Why the Parliament of the United Kingdom, not the Parliament of England . . .'[3] The 'usurpation' had been rectified in 1782 and 1783, and the Union had merely been a fresh development of the rights which Ireland had then won for herself. He actually cited the Union as a fruit of the Renunciation Act of 1783 by which the English Parliament abandoned all claim to legislate for Ireland. English members, he maintained, were as much charged with the maintenance of Irish interests and the protection of Irish rights, 'as if you had Irish constituents at your backs.' ... I deny that Ireland is a province of Great Britain. ... We are all parts of the United Empire, and I [Spring Rice, the Irishman] as much belong to England and have as much right to all the privileges of an Englishman as the proudest Howard who walks the earth; and in like manner the Howard belongs to Ireland as fully as if born there. We are all subjects of one King – we live under the protection of one and the same law – we belong to one United Empire ...'[5]

The argument in theory was impeccable, but it depended in practice wholly on the manner in which the Union Parliament did in fact protect Irish rights. Unfortunately, the privileges of the Howards and Spring Rices were hardly relevant to the Irish peasant of the day.

Spring Rice made an attempt to meet the obvious charge that England had in fact done nothing for Ireland. His soundest point lay in what he called 'the industry set in motion in the North'.[6] But the very truth of this claim weakened the rest of his argument. For the North of Ireland, with the industry it already had, had been able to enter England's industrial revolution and was the one part of Ireland in which something like a real union of interests had come about. Since 1801 the town of Belfast had been utterly transformed. Its population rose from around 20,000 in 1803 to little short of 100,000 by 1851.[7] With the Reform Act of 1832, the core of the Protestant North's original revolutionary grievance had been removed and from now on it associated its interests as closely with the Union as in earlier days it had associated them with the cause of revolution.

But no such change had been wrought in the daily lives of people in the South. When Spring Rice came to refer, in the same tone, to the 'agricultural improvement developed in the South',[8] such a ludicrous gloss on the true facts could only be explained by the government's ignorance. Indeed, it was this ignorance which was the real indictment of the Union. Spring Rice proudly drew attention to the remarkable fact that between 1801 and 1833 there had been sixty government Committees of Inquiry into Ireland, and 114 Reports of Commissioners, making 174 altogether bearing on Irish interests. Then, anticipating the objection that these in themselves did not necessarily constitute the fulfilment of Ireland's wants, he cited as an instance of practical results: free trade between the two islands in butter and corn. That he could do so showed total misunderstanding of the message which these reports conveyed. For what they made clear was that the average Irish peasant lived so far below the poverty line that he could not afford to eat butter or bread however cheap. He produced it to pay the rent with. To lower the price actually struck him a blow because it meant he had to work harder and produce more to pay the rent. As the English radical, Hume, said in answer to Spring Rice's claims of agricultural improvement: 'It was but of little consequence what a country produced, if the inhabitants of that country partook not of that produce.'⁹

As further high points in the Union's achievements for Ireland, and equally irrelevant to the central problem of Irish agricultural poverty, Spring Rice proudly cited administrative acts such as one for the Assimilation of the Currency and another – marginally more relevant – for the Encouragement of Fisheries by the Construction of Piers and Harbours. The Union had also doubled the number of schools, made possible the charitable provision of dispensaries for the sick and 'built noble asylums for the lunatic poor'.¹⁰ That a Union government could talk with such complacency at a time of such universal distress as continued to prevail in Ireland in the 1830's was final total refutation of the Union's claim to concern itself with Irish interests.

On the purely political front Spring Rice's argument in this debate of 1834 was sounder. Voicing what was to become the traditional fear that Repeal would lead to a total separation, he cited O'Connell's use of ambivalent menace at its crudest: 'The United States of America', the Liberator had said, ' – the western boundary of Ireland – threw off the British yoke, and gained freedom by the sword; they were three million and we are eight million.'¹¹ And it was on this constitutional point of the danger of separation that pro-Union arguments increasingly concentrated. To simplify the whole Irish question into a political issue conveniently glossed over the real problems of government in Ireland. 'I feel and know,' declared Peel sweepingly, 'that the Repeal [of the Union] must lead to the dismemberment of this great empire; must make Great Britain a fourth-rate power of Europe, and Ireland a savage wilderness.'¹²

But if one eye in the Unionist attitude remained exaggeratedly wide open to constitutional dangers, the other remained obstinately closed to those on the economic front.

'Of what grievance did the people of Ireland complain?' asked a member of the House of Lords. 'They [their Lordships] knew not. Of the book of Ireland's wrongs little now remained, except one or two chapters which would speedily by the wisdom and justice of Parliament be erased out of its pages.' Everything was the fault of agitators who preferred trouble-making to honest industry.¹³ And this was some years before that great famine which all who had any knowledge of Irish conditions were already dreading.

The 1834 motion for Repeal was lost in the House of Commons by 529–38, and O'Connell had to recognize that to attempt a Repeal of the Union by conventional parliamentary methods was not in the realm of practical politics. Later, he said that he would never have introduced the issue in this manner at this time, had he not been pressed to do so by hot-headed colleagues.* His immediate reaction to failure was not to try and obtain Repeal by unconventional methods, as he later did, but to use conventional parliamentary methods to try and obtain benefits for Ireland in other ways. In the following year, 1835, O'Connell, dropping his demand for Repeal, gave the support of his members in the House of Commons to the Whig government in return for a policy of concessions to Ireland. The alliance was sealed in the so-called Lichfield House compact between O'Connell's party and the Whigs. It introduced a short period when Ireland was certainly administered more sympathetically – that is to say, with less immediate recourse to 'Coercion' Acts suspending the constitutional rights of the individual – than at any other time since the Union. Thanks for this were largely due to a remarkable Under-Secretary in Dublin Castle, Thomas Drummond, who enunciated the, for Ireland, revolutionary principle that 'property has its duties as well as its rights'. But nothing was done to strike at the roots of Irish agricultural poverty, for to do this would mean striking, in a way that seemed inconceivable, at the whole system of land-ownership.

Some well-intentioned governmental measures were passed. The tithe problem, which had reached its climax during the 1830s in a savage war between the secret societies and the authorities, was nominally solved by an Act of 1838. The tithe was in future to be paid by the landlord, but he was entitled to add a corresponding charge to the existing rent. All this really did was to simplify the sense of economic oppression felt by the tenant farmer. It was easier now for his hatred to concentrate wholly against rents.

A Whig Irish Poor Law and a Municipal Reform Act for Ireland proved equally rather tame compromises. O'Connell acquiesced in them despite his stated objections, for the sake of preserving the political alliance and as being at least better than nothing. But increasing criticism from Ireland that he was sacrificing what should be Ireland's real goals in order to maintain the alliance at all costs was inevitable. O'Connell often went far out of his way to be moderate, in order not to embarrass his political allies. He used, for instance, the full weight of his political machine to oppose the Protestant Irish liberal member for County Down, Sharman Crawford, an Ulster landlord who though not himself a Repealer had actually proposed the abolition of tithes altogether, and who at this time was concentrating much more single-mindedly on the real issue of tenant rights than O'Connell. On matters outside Ireland, O'Connell's attitude to the government even bordered on the sycophantic, and he appalled even many English radicals by his conservative attitude to both Canada's struggle for freedom within the Empire and the movement for a ten-hour day in factories.[14]

* Chiefly Feargus O'Connor, the Chartist leader of the forties and son of Roger O'Connor; see above, p. 78. See O'Connell's later speeches on Repeal at Monster Meetings, *The Nation*, 1843.

In Ireland his final political objective was still theoretically Repeal, but he had stated more than once that if he could get justice for Ireland by other means he would be prepared to drop it. 'A real Union or no Union' was his motto at this stage.[15] His trouble was that he was getting neither. When in 1838 a new Association was formed in Dublin to Repeal the Union, all reference to Repeal itself was omitted in order not to embarrass O'Connell's Whig allies, and it was called the Precursor Society. In 1840, with the probable end of the Whig Administration already in sight, an avowed 'Repeal Association' was formed, but it made no difference to O'Connell's continued support of the government and the new Association's first two principles hastened to make clear its constitutional aspect. These were:

1. 'Most dutiful and ever inviolate loyalty to our most gracious and ever beloved Sovereign Queen Victoria and her heirs and successors for ever.'

2. 'The total disclaimer of, and the total absence from all physical force, violence or breach of the law.'[16]

These two principles represented no retreat on O'Connell's part, for they had always been at the foundation of all his political ideas. However, the reality of any repeal movement at all was inevitably in question with O'Connell so devoted to alliance with a government which would always oppose Repeal as relentlessly as the Conservative opposition. The power of his party had in any case been seriously weakened during the course of the alliance, for ten of its thirty-nine members had accepted places, titles or offices under the government.

From this awkward dilemma of trying to alter the course of the ship of state without rocking the boat O'Connell was finally released by the results of the General Election of 1841.

The Whigs, who had been almost continuously in office for ten years, were swept away and Peel and the Conservatives returned to power. O'Connell himself, as the Whigs' ally, understandably suffered a personal setback in the elections; only eighteen repealers were now returned instead of the previous thirty-nine. But important as he was to be in Parliament the net result of the election was not to restrain his political power but to release it. For with the Whigs out of office, O'Connell could now clamour for Repeal without embarrassment. By the nature of the situation it had to be a clamour outside Parliament altogether.

6

O'Connell and Davis

To win Catholic Emancipation more than ten years earlier, O'Connell had mobilized mass opinion to a point where it became a national movement. But the movement had lost its momentum since Emancipation had been won, and since O'Connell had become linked with the Whigs' own inability radically to change Irish society. The local secret societies had resumed their hold, contributing effectively to the bloody battles fought against tithe-collectors and police in the early 1830s. From November 1841, however, when the Whigs lost office, O'Connell set about rebuilding a national political movement similar to that which had won emancipation.

The Repeal Association founded in 1840 while the Whigs were still in power, with an old Protestant Volunteer of the '82 period as a symbolic chairman, had made little headway. But in the following year, renamed the Loyal National Repeal Association, it was effectively re-organized on the model of the old Catholic Association. Its principal democratic feature, as with the Catholic Association earlier, was the penny a month subscription which bought Associate Membership and now became known as the Repeal Rent.

The Association was firmly under the control of O'Connell, who addressed its meetings week after week, hammering home his basic argument that only a native Irish Parliament under the Crown could bring about those measures which were necessary to change the conditions of everyday life in Ireland. Though always inclined to use 'Repeal' as an emotive inspiration, and careful not to commit himself in much detail to the practical measures required to change society, he did definitely commit himself to the general principle of fixity of tenure for the tenant, making it clear that he was prepared to interfere with the basic structure of the landlord–tenant relationship.

This was enough to make his high-sounding claims for Repeal ('... fraught with the richest benefits to our common country ... in an eminent degree calculated to advance the interests of all classes ...' etc.)[1] seem plausible. It meant that a native Parliament would be different from the British one, which regarded the landlord–tenant relationship as virtually sacrosanct. At a time when the British Home Secretary was solemnly able to write that the most difficult problem of practical government in Ireland was that of financing the Maynooth priests' college and of Roman Catholic education in general,² and when even the future Irish rebel Smith O'Brien thought it impossible to intervene directly between landlord and tenant,³ the Repeal movement's continuous insistence on the need to do so made Repeal seem a practical alternative as well as a rousing slogan. Repeal itself thus began to assume something of the nature of a mystical goal for the ordinary Irishman. When several hundred labourers on the Shannon works defied their overseers to attend a Repeal meeting in 1842, one of them remarked: 'If we lost our work for it, do you think we would have skulked away from the day's meeting? Oh no, we love the Repeal too well for that!'⁴

But the problem of how the Repeal of the Union was actually to be brought about in the face of the British Parliament's uncompromising refusal to consider it was another question. O'Connell was fond of brushing this fundamental problem aside, sometimes by saying that it was only necessary for the Queen to sign the requisite writs for the Irish Parliament's summons,⁵ and at other times drawing attention to earlier causes such as Reform, which had received slender support in Parliament almost up to the moment of their acceptance.⁶ But the weakness of the Repeal movement was that there was no prospect whatever of support from anyone in the British Parliament save the small handful of Irish Repealers. In the prevailing parliamentary situation, with one English party holding a large majority over the other, the Repeal movement had no means of putting pressure on the government, except by the threat of armed rebellion which O'Connell made clear he would not countenance. All he could do was to bluff, leaving the government to wonder whether or not he was as opposed to armed rebellion as he maintained, or, alternatively, whether he would always be able to control the vast numbers whose support he commanded. This tactic of openly playing on the government's fear had worked with Emancipation. Moreover, the size of the demand for Repeal which he was about to call forth was to prove even more imposing than anything Emancipation had produced.

In his great Repeal campaign, which reached its first climax in the autumn of 1843, O'Connell was immeasurably assisted by new allies, who though very different in age, background and temperament from himself were eventually to have an equally profound influence on nationalism in Ireland. This was a group of middle-class young men, half of them Protestants, who later came to be known as Young Ireland, but who for the present simply acted as a strong pressure group inside the Repeal Association. The nucleus of this group, consisting of Thomas Davis, John Blake Dillon and Charles Gavan Duffy, had come together in 1842 to found on their own initiative a new newspaper, *The Nation*. The first copy of *The Nation* appeared on 8 October 1842, and, though selling at sixpence, it had within a very short time a higher circulation than any other newspaper in Ireland. Its editor, Gavan Duffy, calculated that because of its wide distribution through reading rooms and from hand to hand it was read by a quarter of a million Irishmen.[7]

Duffy, a Catholic from Ulster and the only one of the three with much journalistic experience, was the official editor and manager of the paper. But the greater part of the editorial writing was done at first by Thomas Davis, a Protestant, who was to prove one of the key formative figures in the development of Irish nationalism.

Just as O'Connell had been the first man to mobilize Irish opinion effectively on a national scale, so Davis was the first man to construct for such national opinion a coherent theory of nationality. Irishness was something which the Catholic O'Connell did not need to think about intellectually for it was such a recognizable part of him and his long family tradition. But for Davis, the son of an English army surgeon and an Irish mother whose maiden name was Atkins (though with both Gaelic and English settlers' blood in her veins), Irishness was something which he found he consciously needed to work out and acquire for his own self-respect. He became, as it were, the grammarian of Irish nationality.

Trained as a barrister, though he never practised regularly, Davis, who had been born in County Cork in 1814, was considered by a man who knew him in 1838 as 'more like a young Englishman than a young Irishman'.[8] He had at first looked to England and made some attempt to concern himself with English radical politics, but had become disillusioned and after about a year turned back to his native land.[9] It was the very sense of provincialism thrust upon him in the country of his birth that he felt undignified and that he set out to overcome by elevating into a sense of nationality.*

A sense of Irish nationality was still very much something that seemed to need justification.

'Surely,' Davis wrote in December 1840, 'the desire of nationality is not ungenerous, nor is it strange in the Irish (looking to their history); nor, considering the population of Ireland, and the situation of their home, is the expectation of it very wild.'[10]

But it was still something to be hoped for and formed as nationality in Europe was being formed among the Czechs, or the Italians. Davis had spent some time in Europe after studying at Trinity College, Dublin, and his concept of what Irish nationality should be like was something all-embracing and creative in the new romantic European tradition, a conscious spiritual launching of the self into patriotism. Though Mazzini, the Italian nationalist and leader of Young Italy, was to maintain that Irish nationalism could not in fact be equated with Italian or any other conventional nationalism because the Irish were not sufficiently distinctive from the English,[11] the whole of Davis's short life's work was devoted to assertion of the opposite.

* Cf. Davis: 'Verily, we repeat, we are provincials.' (February 1841, quoted Duffy, *Thomas Davis*, p. 49.)

When in 1840, as outgoing President of the Historical Society, Dublin, he addressed a gathering of his young contemporaries from Trinity, he used the occasion to exhort them to seek out a national identity for themselves in Ireland. Speaking to 'what are called the upper classes of Ireland', he told them, as if opening their eyes to what was around them:

'Gentlemen, you have a country. ... Reason points out our native land as the field for our exertions. ... The country of our birth, our education of our recollections, ancestral, personal, national; the country of our loves, our friendships, our hopes, our country. ... You are Irishmen, she relies on your devotion.' [12] And he reminded his audience, the majority of whom were young Protestants, of the great days of 1782.

It was exactly among Protestants that the most difficult part of Davis's creative nationalist task lay. Protestants were to be brought into an all-embracing definition of Irish nationality that included both themselves and the Catholic peasantry. Yet the only Protestant national tradition that had existed, and to which he was appealing, had been one which emphasized their ascendancy over Catholics. Davis's appeal for a united front was similar to that which Wolfe Tone had made fifty years earlier. But Tone had been able to stress the need for it in utilitarian political terms. Protestants had then been seeking something the British Government refused to give them, namely Reform. But now Davis could only make a vaguer and more general utilitarian appeal to Protestants about the future prosperity of the country as a whole and had to rely vainly on the appeal of his doctrine as a spiritual end in itself.

In the prospectus which he wrote for *The Nation*, he put forward a prospectus for nationality itself. Nationality, he said, was the paper's first object,

... a Nationality which will not only raise our people from their poverty, by securing to them the blessings of a DOMESTIC LEGISLATURE, but inflame and purify them with a lofty and heroic love of country – a Nationality of the spirit as well as the letter ... which may embrace Protestant, Catholic and Dissenter – Milesian and Cromwellian – the Irishman of a hundred generations and the stranger who is within our gates ... [13]

Over and over again Davis spelt out this same doctrine.

'We must sink,' he wrote, 'the distinctions of blood as well as sect. The Milesian, the Dane, the Norman, the Welshman, the Scotsman and the Saxon, naturalized here, must combine regardless of their blood – the Strong-bownian must sit with the Ulster Scot and him whose ancestor came from Tyre or Spain must confide in and work with the Cromwellian and the Williamite ...' If a union of all Irish-born men ever be accomplished Ireland will have the greatest and most varied materials for an illustrious nationality and for a tolerant and flexible character in literature, manners, religion and life of any nation on earth.[14]

In order to give this nationality substance Davis industriously reinforced his argument with a wealth of historical and cultural research into Ireland's past. Articles on Irish antiquities, Irish music, Irish art, Irish ballad poetry, Irish scenery, Irish ethnology and the Irish language poured from his pen in great profusion, appearing week after week in the columns of *The Nation* and always related to the cult of nationality. A few Irish Protestant patriots of the eighteenth century had shown an interest in Irish antiquities and the Irish language as part of their national consciousness, as had also some of the radicals of the 1790s. But such studies had been the prerogative of scholars and amateur specialists even though spoken Irish was still the vernacular for almost half the population. Davis was the first man to try to make such matters of popular concern, to try to link the past with the present as a continuing relevant force.

That a country is without national poetry [he wrote] proves its hopeless dullness or its utter provincialism. National poetry is the very flowering of the soul – the greatest evidence of its wealth, the greatest excellence of its beauty . . .[15]

Soon romantic stanzas of trite but often stirring quality, written largely by Davis himself who had hardly written a line of verse before, were resounding through the columns of *The Nation*, and being repeated all over Ireland.

> When boyhood's fire was in my blood,
>   I read of ancient freemen
> For Greece and Rome who bravely stood
>   Three Hundred men and Three men.
> And then I prayed I yet might see
>   Our fetters rent in twain
> And Ireland, long a province, be
> A NATION ONCE AGAIN.

The original attitude of Young Ireland to force as a solution to political problems was the same as O'Connell's and was made clear in a typical poem in the very first number of *The Nation*. Entitled 'We Want No Swords' it began

> We want no swords, no savage swords,
>   Our fetters vile to shatter . . .

and ended:

> With conquering mind alone we fight –
> 'Tis all we need for freedom!

But from the start, also like O'Connell, *The Nation* had the best of both worlds by use of ambivalent metaphor. Inspiration for the political present

was continually being drawn from ancient war-like deeds, and its Poets'
Corner at least was not shy of the clash of steel.

> For often, in O'Connor's van
> To triumph dash'd each Connaught clan –
> Sing oh! how fleet the Normans ran
> Through Corlieu's Pass and Ardrahan!
>
> And later times saw deeds as brave
> And glory guards Clanricarde's grave –
> Sing on! they died their land to save
> At Aughrim's slopes and Shannon's wave.
>
> And if, when all a vigil keep
> The West's asleep, the West's asleep –
> Sing oh! poor Erin well may weep;
> That men so sprung are still asleep.
>
> But – Hark! – some voice like thunder spake:
> 'The West's awake, the West's awake' –
> Sing oh! hurra; let England quake,
> We'll watch till death for Erin's sake.

Of the Irish language Davis wrote: 'A people without a language is only
half a nation';[16] and he vigorously urged a revival until 'the brighter days
shall surely come, and the green flag shall wave on the towers, and the
sweet old language be heard once more in college, mart and senate'.[17]

Often an admonitory note was to enter these national exhortations.

'We have Irish artists, but no Irish art,' he complained. 'This ought not
to continue; it is injurious to the artists and disgraceful to the country.'[18] And
with the constructive diligence which characterizes all Davis's writing he
proceeded to suggest a number of suitable subjects that truly national
painters might get down to right away: Brian Boru, for instance, reconnoit-
ring the Danes before Clontarf; James II entering Dublin; Wolfe Tone with
Carnot; the Battle of Oulart Hill and 'The Lifting of the Flags of a National
Fleet and Army'.[19]

In an article on Foreign Travel, Davis recommended that those who
travelled abroad should 'carry a purpose for Ireland in their hearts'.[20] Celtic
words mixed in classical French or the patois of Brittany or Gascony should
be noted and compared with Irish; Irish saints should be tracked down
wherever possible, and monuments and museums in France, Spain, Italy and
Scandinavia studied with reference to the antiquities of Ireland to make a
summer both pleasant and profitable. Useful tips might also be collected
abroad to help serve Ireland's defective agriculture and her untapped
mineral resources and waterpower, while encouragement might be derived
for that cultivation of the fine arts and design that was so sadly neglected in
Ireland. 'Our Irish cities,' wrote Davis, 'must be stately with sculptures,

pictures and buildings, and our fields glorious with peaceful abundance.'
This was not, he maintained, just a Utopian dream. '... To seek it is the
solemn, unavoidable duty of every Irishman.'[21]

It was in this emphasis on the spiritual dimension of what was otherwise
basically the same as O'Connell's view of nationality that the special contribution of Davis and the rest of *The Nation* writers lay. Yet *The Nation*
also from the start closely concerned itself with practical politics and like
O'Connell and the Repeal Association, of which Davis, Duffy and Dillon
were all committee members, concentrated specifically on the land question.
Fixity of tenure was a basic objective, and an early issue of *The Nation*
had a neat epigram about rents.

> 'Well, Pat, my boy,' said I, 'I've heard some chat
> With the ground landlord of this wilderness.'
> 'The *grinding* one your Honour means,' grinned Pat.
> 'It is the tenants that are ground, I guess.'[22]

An article headed 'Rents the Question of the Day' quoted with approval
the Ulster Liberal Protestant landlord, Sharman Crawford, who, while
agreeing that a landlord had a right to do what he willed with his own, denied
that land was a landlord's own except subject to the principle that those who
tilled it should get a fair and honest living out of it. Like O'Connell, Davis
and his friends publicly proclaimed that there was only one major political
remedy which would enable all Ireland's thousand grievances to be put
right, and that was Repeal of the Union and an Irish legislature. And just
as they spiritualized O'Connell's concept of nationality, so they turned
Repeal into something like a moral principle in words which were to have
an echo in the twentieth century.

> The work that should today be wrought
>   Defer not till tomorrow;
> The help that should within be sought
>   Scorn from without to borrow.
> Old maxims these -- yet stout and true --
>   They speak in trumpet tone,
> To do at once what is to do
>   And trust OURSELVES ALONE.*

Not only did *The Nation* bequeath a slogan to later nationalists, but also
specific tactics. A correspondent in *The Nation* of 19 November 1842
proposed that the sixty Irish Liberal Members of Parliament should not
go to Westminster at all, but should join with two hundred and forty other
'Irish gentlemen' to form a Parliament of their own. (Three hundred had
previously been the number of representatives in the Irish Parliament.) The

* *The Nation*, 3 December 1842. 'Ourselves alone' is an accepted translation of the
Irish words Sinn Fein.

idea was to be elaborated in the next year in O'Connell's plan for a Council of Three Hundred. He proposed circumventing the Convention Act of 1793, which made any extra-parliamentary convention of representatives in Ireland illegal, by turning the delegates nominally into mere bearers of special Repeal Rent contributions of £100 from their localities. Similarly, 'arbitration courts', or an indigenous Irish system of court-administered justice to supersede the work of the official Crown Courts, were put into operation for a time in 1843.

In none of this was there any suggestion of a constitutional break with the Crown itself. The Repeal Association and O'Connell himself continued to go out of their way to assert their essential loyalty to the queen.

'The political principles', wrote a prominent member of the Repeal Association in *The Nation*, 'that have struck their roots deepest in the Irish peasant's heart are, devoted allegiance to the Queen, and undying hatred of the execrable legislative union.'[23]

This was probably a fair enough statement of the truth. Certainly, O'Connell often thought it worth his while to play on a crowd's emotional feelings about the monarchy.

'I want you,' he said, at a public meeting at Trim in March 1843, 'I want you not to violate your allegiance to the lovely and beautiful being that fills the throne – our gracious Queen, long life to her [great cheers]. I want you to preserve your allegiance unbroken to her as I do mine; but I want you, at the same time, to remember that you have another allegiance equally dear and higher in its quality, though not so binding in law, but equally binding in an Irish heart, and that is the allegiance you owe to your country [cheers]. I call on you to be loyal men – loyal to the Queen and loyal to your country.'[24]

On another occasion, after bringing in mention of the queen, he cried: 'May heaven bless her! – three cheers for her [tremendous cheering]. ... She was the Queen of their affections, as she had invariably been the Queen of their unswerving loyalty and allegiance.'[25]

He argued that it was the queen's enemies who came between her and her devoted and loyal subjects in Ireland, and declared that when the Irish people had conquered these enemies the first use they would make of their victory would be 'to place the sceptre in the hands of her who has ever showed us favour, and whose conduct has ever been full of sympathy and emotion for our sufferings'.[26]

Triumphal arches at O'Connell's meetings were inscribed 'The Queen, O'Connell and Repeal', and fulsome toasts to the queen were drunk at Repeal banquets.

There was little of this fulsomeness towards the monarchy in Davis's writing. He even at times seems to have used words associated with Tone intentionally to blur Young Ireland's precise constitutional image.

'Once,' he wrote in *The Nation* in December 1842, 'once the Irish People declare the disconnection of themselves, their feelings and interests from the men, feelings and interests of England, they are in the march for freedom. Ireland must bid all whom it concerns to know that her interests are separate and her rights peculiar.'[27]

Yet it was made positively clear elsewhere in *The Nation* that although the Irish Parliament was to be independent and separate, there would be a unity of the two kingdoms under a joint Crown. A parallel was drawn between the future relationship of the two countries and the relationship then existing between Norway and Sweden, in which the Norwegians had complete control of their affairs, with their own flag and navy, but shared a common crown and foreign policy with Sweden.[28] Davis was quite prepared to accept that England should have the chief say in affairs that concerned the Empire as a whole.

'It is right', he wrote, 'that England should have the preponderance in matters of Imperial interest; it is wrong that she should have it where those interests are not at all involved.'[29] On imperial matters he was content that decisions should be taken by a joint vote of both Parliaments and that the majority of the combined vote should prevail.

These words were written in *The Nation* in the course of an objective examination of a new proposal being made in some quarters for something less than total Repeal of the Union. This was the idea known as Federalism being urged by that same Liberal Ulster landlord, Sharman Crawford, who had already shown enlightened views on the land question. Federalists stood for an independent domestic legislature for Ireland, to be concerned with Irish interests only, while all wider responsibilities were to be assumed by the Imperial Parliament, in which Ireland should have a reduced representation. This in essence was that solution to the Irish problem which was to be put forward in the late nineteenth and early twentieth centuries as Home Rule.

Davis himself, though he saw the wider claim of total repeal as the only one consistent with the elevating doctrine of nationality, was by no means hostile to Federalists and thought that they should be supported as advocating a step in the right direction.[30] Realistically he admitted, in a private letter to a friend late in 1842, that Federalism was in fact all that Ireland stood a chance of getting out of the present political situation.

'Things have come to that pass,' he wrote, 'that we must be disgraced and defeated, or we must separate by force, or we must have a Federal Government.'[31]

In another letter to the same friend he made a hopeful appraisal of the Repeal movement's resources. He concluded: 'I think we can beat Peel (the British Prime Minister). If we can quietly get a Federal Government, I for one shall agree to it and support it. If not, then anything but what we are.'[32]

7

'Monster Meetings'

O'Connell had declared that 1843 was going to be 'Repeal year'. Though his young colleagues thought this a rash declaration, they threw their entire energy into his new campaign, acting for him as a sort of general staff and infusing the movement with their own particular flavour of historic national consciousness. 'To the work then, ye millions of Irish people,' *The Nation* exhorted. 'To the work! Catholic – Dissenter – Protestant band together under the green standard of your common country! Bear aloft that proud, stainless banner; and with the blessing of the great and just God, it will soon wave over your heads in the temple of the Irish constitution!'[1]

By March 1843 a new card for Members of the Repeal Association had been issued. It was green, and had four key battles of Irish history in the four corners and a flag in the middle, displaying the symbolic rays of a sun bursting over the horizon, together with a shamrock with 'Catholic', 'Dissenter' and 'Protestant' in each leaf and *'Quis separabit?'* up the stalk.

The chief feature of the campaign was the series of vast public demonstrations addressed in the open air all over Ireland by O'Connell, often at places of historic emotive appeal selected by Davis. *The* (London) *Times* in its indignation came to dub these demonstrations Monster Meetings, and the appellation stuck. In spite of the size of the crowds the meetings were conducted with a disciplined order which frightened the government much as the self-imposed discipline at elections had done in the Emancipation era.

The alliance between O'Connell and his young supporters worked harmoniously and effectively in this year. O'Connell himself preached nationality as proudly as *The Nation* itself, if in a less sophisticated style.

'Irish patriotism is alive,' he proclaimed at a public dinner. '. . . It is not buried, it only sleeps and I am the cock that shall crow for its morning.'[2] Though already a man in his middle sixties he crowed through the spring, summer and early autumn of 1843 to such effect that Peel and the Duke of Wellington felt the Empire shaken to its foundations.

In his speeches O'Connell continually repeated his abhorrence of violence and his belief in constitutional action, but, like the writers of *The Nation*, he often employed an ambivalent language which enabled him to raise the maximum amount of public emotional enthusiasm at all levels.

'I came here to recruit,' were the words with which he began his monster meeting at Trim, and as the cheers died away he continued: 'I want you to enlist with me; and reversing the old method of enlisting, where they give the recruit a shilling, I want you to enlist by giving the shilling to me ... [a reference to the penny a month of Repeal Rent].'

Later in the same speech he referred to himself as 'one who would give the last drop of his life's blood, and smile to see it flow to do any good for Ireland'.

The words were followed by loud cheers and cries of 'Long life to you', and O'Connell went on: 'I would wish to have life to make Ireland free, to get that without which she can never be prosperous or happy, to get Ireland for the Irish and the Irish for Ireland.'³

The following week *The Nation* published a poem which, though not by Davis himself, expressed in verse Davis's strong feeling that the actions of the United Irishmen and others, who had been under a polite historical cloud for nearly half a century, were nothing for Ireland to be ashamed of.

> Who fears to speak of '98?
>   Who blushes at the name?
> When cowards mock the patriots' fate
>   Who hangs his head for shame?
> He's all a knave or half a slave
>   Who slights his country thus:
> But a true man, like you, man,
>   Will fill your glass with us ...
>
> Then here's their memory – may it be
>   For us a guiding light
> To cheer our strife for liberty,
>   And teach us to unite!
> Though good and ill be Ireland's still
>   Though sad as theirs, your fate,
> And true men, be you, men,
>   Like those of '98.*

O'Connell's own disapproval of the methods of '98 had not changed, but he was not beyond infusing his own national appeal with martial ardour. At an open-air meeting at Roscrea in County Limerick he asked, to the cheers of the crowd, whether there was any man among them who would not, if necessary, die for Ireland, and himself immediately supplied the answer:

'There was not a man amongst them that would not brunt the battle's blaze, and glory in achieving victory for Ireland.'⁴

* The author was John Kells Ingram, who died, a forgotten scholastic recluse, in Dublin in 1907.

He continued in a vein that was always to play as powerful a part in Irish nationalist sentiment as any intellectual theory of nationality or inspiration from history – an appeal to the deep emotions aroused by the physical beauty of the land in which Irishmen lived. Small blame to them, he said, if they wanted to die for Ireland:

... there is not a lovelier land on the face of the earth – a more fruitful or fertile land the sun never shone upon [hear, hear, hear, and cheers]. I will repeat that the sun never shone upon a lovelier, or greener, or brighter land [hear, hear, hear, and great cheering]. Oh, it is a land to fill one with patriotism – its picturesque beauties please and delight the eye – its majestic mountains rise to the heavens – its limpid waters irrigate the plains, and its harbours are open to the commerce of the entire world, asserting for Ireland the great prerogative of being the first nation on the earth; and the period is coming, when standing forth in their native dignity, the people will be prosperous and free [cheers].[5]

The year 1843, not 1798, was the real emotional storehouse on which future Irish nationalism would always draw for its reserves.[5]

In the course of this year, in a long series of such monster meetings, O'Connell touched on every patriotic note in the vast range of rhetoric he commanded. Some contemporaries, drawn to Ireland to hear him because of his world-wide reputation as a national orator, were disappointed and found only crude demagoguery. But all testified to the magic spell he was able to cast over the crowds themselves. Bulwer Lytton, the English novelist and poet, wrote of him:

> Once to my sight the giant thus was given:
> Walled by wide air and roofed by boundless heaven,
> Beneath his feet the human ocean lay,
> And wave on wave flowed into space away.
> Methought no clarion could have sent its sound
> Even to the centre of the hosts around;
> But, as I thought, there rose the sonorous swell,
> As from some Church tower swings the silvery bell.
> Aloft and clear, from airy tide to tide
> It glided, easy as a bird may glide;
> To the last verge of that vast audience sent,
> It played with each wild passion as it went;
> Now stirred the uproar, now the murmur stilled,
> And sobs or laughter answered as it willed.

And a peasant said of O'Connell's voice: 'You'd hear it a mile off as if it was coming through honey.'[6]

At a great open-air meeting at Cork in May 1843 half a million people were estimated to be present, many of them having travelled great distances from other parts of Ireland to hear him. The streets of the city were packed, as a long procession of trade groups with banners (printers, rope-makers, chandlers, etc.) made its way past O'Connell's carriage. Every house-top, every lamp-post even, was occupied, and the procession took three hours and five minutes to file past. After the meeting nine hundred Repealers sat down to dinner, including many priests, one of whom said grace in Irish.[7]

The active support of the Catholic priesthood and many of the bishops demonstrated the true national impetus of the movement. The Catholic gentry and middle classes, together with a few Protestants, also appeared regularly on Repeal platforms emphasizing that what was by nature a mass movement was also deeply respectable. By midsummer 1843 Repeal Rent had topped the then enormous sum of £2,000 in a single week.

The British Government played the situation on the whole skilfully. One short-sighted action had been the dismissal from office of twenty-four Catholic gentry for attending Repeal meetings. This offended the sort of non-political Irish pride that was by no means necessarily committed to the agitation for Repeal. A number of other gentry resigned their commissions of the peace in sympathy with the dismissed magistrates, among them the Liberal Member of Parliament for Limerick, William Smith O'Brien, an old Harrovian who liked to trace his descent from Brian Boru, and another Protestant, Henry Grattan, the son of the great orator patriot. An attempt was also made by the government to introduce a new Arms Bill, facilitating the search for privately held arms, but it was held up by an early example of Irish 'obstruction' in the House of Commons. Otherwise the government did not try to check O'Connell by coercive measures. Reasonably, Peel had accepted the advice of his officials in the Irish administration and was letting O'Connell have his head, in the belief that he must in the end either commit himself to plain illegality or beat an ignominious retreat.

But the more conservative element in Peel's Conservative ministry were unhappy, and becoming increasingly convinced that Ireland was on the brink of civil war. 'Ireland,' wrote the Duke of Wellington, 'is in truth no longer in a social state.'[8]

Even the moderate Peel himself and his Home Secretary, Graham, soon became anxious. Graham expected the situation to 'lead to bloodshed and convulse the empire'.[9] Peel had already declared that in the long run there were no steps he would not take to maintain the Union and that even civil war would be preferable to 'the dismemberment of the Empire'.

At a meeting at Longford, O'Connell promised the crowd that they would be getting back their Parliament in College Green whatever Peel might say. He went on:

'They tell us there will be civil war if we attempt to get the Repeal – bah!'

The crowd cheered loudly and laughed.

'We will put them in the wrong, and if a civil war should break out it must be of their making ... and I tell you what, it they attack us then' – here

O'Connell slapped his breast and the crowd went wild with enthusiasm – 'who will then be the coward?' (More cheers.) 'We will put them in the wrong, and if they attack us, then in your name I set them at defiance.' (Great applause.)[10]

He repeated the defiance more solemnly at a dinner in Mallow later in the month, declaring again that though he and his supporters would never resort to force so long as they were left 'a rag of the constitution' to stand on, it was a mistake to think that the enemy would not attack them, and if that were to happen, then it was his dead body England would have to trample on, not the living man.[11]

O'Connell was pushing his old strategic bluff further and further towards the point where it would either have to succeed or be called in question.

At Ennis, capital of County Clare, the scene of his great victory of fifteen years before, he recalled that an ancestor of his who had led a battalion for James II at the battle of Aughrim was killed and buried nearby and he quoted the lines:

> We tread the land that bore us,
> Our green flag flutters o'er us,
> The friends we tried are by our side
> And the foes we hate before us ...

'Yes,' he concluded, 'the green flag of Clare is flying again.'[12]

At Murroe he caused a sensation by suddenly crying: 'I want you to get arms', but added typically: 'Now, mind me, do you know the arms I want you to get? – the Repeal Society's cards! Everyone who has that is well armed ...'[13]

Military images appeared increasingly in his speeches, while the crowds themselves, marshalled by Repeal 'wardens', preserved a well-ordered discipline. At Donnybrook, Dublin, before a crowd estimated at between 150,000 and 200,000, he said:

'It has never happened to me to behold such an assemblage as I have congregated here today. No; it is impossible to have more power. I have power enough – the only question is how to use it. I have more strength and more physical force than gained the battle of Waterloo – I have more physical force than ever monarch commanded or general led – I have abundance of physical force ...'[14]

The Nation criticized some of the 'Cockney and Italian' tunes played at this meeting as insufficiently national. It also complained that too many people had been marching out of step and that there had not been that minute subdivision into twelves and sixties, or tens and hundreds, 'which is essential to the permanent ordering and handling of arrayed men'.[15]

At Wexford O'Connell addressed crowds which, he declared, the Emperor of Russia himself did not have the power to put down. *The Nation* wrote:

'Never was organization more complete than it is in this noble county ...'[16]
And when the county sent in a remittance of over £600 to the Loyal National
Repeal Association, O'Connell commented that Wexford had done its duty,
but then 'it was an old truth for Wexford to do its duty'.[17]

O'Connell and his young supporters now commanded by far the most
comprehensive national movement in Irish history. They had woven together
the traditions of the Wild Geese, of the Protestant Patriots of '82, of the
Defenders and United Irishmen themselves, into one ideal. All the many
different and often conflicting causes that had been fought for in Ireland
in the past were now recognized as 'Ireland', a mystical cause which must
continue to be fought for in the future.

But for all the unmistakable national character of the movement, O'Connell continually insisted that this was not a movement to separate England
from Ireland:

'We encourage loyalty,' he said. 'We preach attachment to the Crown and
submission to the laws ...' The only rebels in sight, he continued, were those
who instigated the public against the queen, and maligned the loyal people
of Ireland who were actually striving to uphold the security of the throne by
basing it on the rights, the liberty and the prosperity of the entire nation.[18]

For the Repeal meeting at Tuam, where crowds estimated at 300,000
collected, with 400 gentry and over 100 clergy on the platform, the green flag
on the Market House was overshadowed by a Union Jack flying from the
top of the cathedral 'to mark the true character of the Repeal movement'.[19]
It was the first object, viewable from an immense distance, seen by the
multitudes coming from far and wide to hear O'Connell.

Yet, in spite of all the protestations of loyalty by Repealers, and all the
undoubtedly sincere arguments of Federalists that their main concern was the
preservation of the connection, it was not unreasonable for Unionists to take
the view that *any* form of concession meant the thin end of the wedge of
separation. To the Unionist the very blurring of the distinctive lines between
Repealer and Federalist was itself ominous, for the Repealers themselves
often blurred the lines between Repeal and separatism. And while renouncing ultimate separation O'Connell and his supporters continued to play on
fears of it adroitly. A Wexford priest, criticizing the enemies of Repeal for
continually harping on the danger of separation, commented that it was not
wise thus 'to be throwing temptation' in the people's way. The sort of
emotions which O'Connell and the Young Irelanders of *The Nation* were
stirring delved deep into a past in which ancient hostilities and resentments
lurked dangerously. In the same week as both O'Connell and *The Nation*
expressed approval of Federalism, John Blake Dillon, who had founded
the paper with Davis and Duffy, made a speech at Castlebar. The country,
he said, had been visited with many sorrows, but even the sorrows it had
endured were now playing their part in the work of regeneration. '... Even

now from the graves which the tyrants have opened like wounds upon her
bleeding breast, there comes a voice instructing, encouraging, purifying the
people for the trial through which they have to pass. It searched the depths
of the nation's memory.'[20] Powerful confused emotions were being played
upon. No one could reasonably be certain how this would end.

'War harps of Erin!' sang *The Nation*'s Poets' Corner,

> I strike thee again,
> To echo the challenge of mountaineer men,
> While they climb the tall summits, and gazing afar,
> Shout aloud for the foemen and pant for the war.[21]

The largest of all O'Connell's monster meetings took place at Tara, the
seat of the old Irish High Kings. A correspondent of *The Nation* claimed
'without the slightest fear of exaggeration' that there were three-quarters of
a million people present.[22] O'Connell himself, never worried by fear of
exaggeration, put it at a million and a half.[23] A contemporary ballad-maker
gives as good an idea of its vast size as any.

> On the 15th day of August in the year of '43,
> This glorious day I well may say, recorded it shall be,
> On the Royal Hill of Tara, Irish thousands did prevail,
> In Union's bands to join their hands with Dan, for the Repeal.

> Such a good sight was never seen nor will till times no more,
> His lasting fame will long remain around Hibernian shore,
> No pen or talent can describe the glories of that day,
> As there was seen on Tara's Green a matchless grand display.

> There was Wexford, Wicklow and Kildare, sweet Dublin and Ardee,
> Westmeath, King's County and Dundalk most glorious for to see
> Cork, Limerick, Tuam, and Waterford, Strabane and sweet Kinsale,
> On the Royal Hill of Tara stood to sign for the Repeal.

> I topt the hill with heart and will – and cast my eyes around,
> With alarming consternation I viewed from the rising ground,
> The approaching legions of the Earth advancing from afar –
> With floating Flags and beating Drums like thundering claps of War.

> It baffles my description to portray the sight I seen,
> From Tara to Dunseeny and the lofty hill of Screen
> Ballinter, Trim and Bectivet with Kells, Navan and Altboy
> Came as one man for to see Dan their hearts' delight and joy.

> To see the flags of Drogheda with each harmonious band,
> Which with sacred pious music round the Croppies' graves did stand,
> Where is the heart that could not feel or eye refuse a tear,
> To see those noble heroes, for their country sleeping there.*[24]

* The last three lines refer to the graves of rebels slaughtered at Tara in 1798. See
above, p. 106.

O'Connell began his speech with a pardonable romanticization of history.
'We are at Tara of the Kings,' he cried, '... emphatically the spot from
which emanated then the social power – the legal authority – the right to
dominion over the furthest extremes of this island ...'

He went on: 'The strength and majority of the national movement was
never exhibited so imposingly as at this great meeting. The numbers exceed
any that ever before congregated in Ireland in peace or war. ... It is a sight,
not grand alone, but appalling – not exciting merely pride but *fear*. Such an
army – for you have the steadiness and order of trained men – no free state
would willingly see in its bosom, if it were not composed of its choicest
citizens. ... The great review of the Volunteers was the precursor of
Ireland's independence – the Repealers at Tara outnumber as three to one
the Citizen Army of '82. Step by step we are approaching the great goal itself;
but it is at length with the strides of a giant.'[25]

The real question was whether the giant had a giant's strength. The closer
O'Connell got to his goal the nearer came the moment when the question of
how exactly he hoped to get Repeal if the government continued to stand
firm would have to be answered. This critical moment was in fact just seven
weeks away.

At the end of August O'Connell published his nine-point plan for a restoration of Irish parliamentary activity in Ireland. It included the ballot, household suffrage and a restoration of the Irish House of Lords. Of the rest of
the nine points three were concerned with constitutional questions and in
themselves could not have been objected to by the most die-hard Unionist.
The first laid down that 'the Irish people recognize, acknowledge, maintain
and will continually preserve and uphold for the throne of Ireland

HER MAJESTY QUEEN VICTORIA
WHOM GOD PROTECT',

and that they would give true allegiance to her heirs and successors for ever.
Another stipulated that the Monarch and Regent *de facto* in England was
the Monarch or Regent *de jure* in Ireland. The last ran: 'the connection
between Great Britain and Ireland, by means of the power, authority and
prerogatives of the Crown, to be perpetual and incapable of change or any
severance or separation'.[26]

The picture of a new form of Irish nationalism commanding the enthusiastic support of the vast majority of the country was now complete. It had
been evolved by the joint talents of an Irishman of the old Catholic and
Gaelic strain, O'Connell, and an Irishman of the Protestant colonists' strain,
Davis. It had its emotional roots in the glories and sorrows of the people
of Ireland of both strains in the past, and derived its political dynamic from
the misery and degradation of the majority of the population in the present.
Both as part of its heritage from the past and as the acknowledged necessary
condition for its existence in the present, it recognized an unalterable tie.

with the sister island on the other side of the Irish Sea. But it asked to be granted, in the now more democratic political circumstances of the mid-nineteenth century, the same sovereign right to manage Ireland's own affairs as Ireland had been granted constitutionally in the late eighteenth. As a slogan displayed at a great meeting at Lismore at the end of September 1843 had it: 'The rose of England shall never fade as long as it is entwined with the shamrock of Ireland; the only way to entwine it is by justice to Ireland.'[27]

The monster meetings continued as successfully as ever, even when as at Loughrea on 10 September they were deluged in torrential rain.[28] They became more and more brazen in their display of discipline.

At Clifden on 16 September green flags flew outside every home though sometimes there was a green, white and blue [sic] tricolour. Some six hundred men came to the meeting on horseback. They were drawn up in troops of what *The Nation* called 'peasant cavalry', five deep, with Repeal cards in their hats bound with green ribbons, and they answered with implicit obedience to the commands of farmers. O'Connell singled out these 'mountaineer cavalry' for special praise, admiring the precision with which they manoeuvred and declaring that no field-marshal was ever more punctually and willingly obeyed by his troops.[29] And he indulged himself in a particularly provocative version of his usual ambivalent language: 'He had demonstrated, to England,' he said, 'that more men of an adult age – why should he hesitate to say it? – that more men of fighting age [cheers] than had ever made a declaration for any other country in the world, had met together in Ireland to denounce the legislative Union [loud cheers] and yet they made no attack, nor allowed any threat of attack against their enemies . . .'[30]

A fortnight later, yet another monster meeting took place at Mullaghmast. At it for the first time, men with the words, 'O'CONNELL POLICE' printed on tickets in their hats and armed with staves marshalled the crowd.[31] Truly, as O'Connell himself had said, he had dared the government to their teeth.

The issue of *The Nation* of that week, beginning 30 September, contained a leading article headed 'The Coming Struggle', which declared: 'The clouds are thickening – Heaven only knows with what they are charged.' Its front page carried an advertisement for yet another monster meeting to be held at Clontarf, scene of Brian Boru's victory over the Danes, on 5 October. The notice was headed 'Repeal Cavalry' and continued:

'Muster and March of the Repeal Volunteers ! ! ! [sic] . . . each troop to consist of 25 Horsemen, to be led by an officer in front, followed by 6 ranks 4 abreast, half distance, each bearing a wand and cockade . . .' It ended '. . . God Save The Queen. March for Repeal! March for Clontarf!'[32]

The government waited until the day before and then prohibited the meeting. The bluff was called. The question was now whether O'Connell and the Repealers would go ahead all the same and defy the troops sent to Clontarf to prevent them assembling?

Fully supported by his young allies on *The Nation* O'Connell called off the meeting.

Going in to dinner that night in England after hearing of the ban, the Duke of Wellington remarked contentedly to a neighbour: *'Pour la canaille, faut la mitraille.'*

8

Biding Time After Clontarf

Many years later, Gavan Duffy maintained that he and his Young Ireland friends on *The Nation* had been dismayed by O'Connell's capitulation after Clontarf, regarding it as a craven act, and his power as thereby 'recklessly squandered', his policy 'practically relinquished'.[1] However, an examination of the contemporary files of *The Nation* shows that Duffy and his Young Ireland colleagues in fact gave O'Connell immediate and unhesitating support on the decision.*

'The man who dares adopt any policy not sanctioned by O'Connell will deserve the deepest execration ...' proclaimed *The Nation* in a leading article the week after Clontarf. 'Trust in O'Connell and fear not.'[2] A few weeks later Davis expressed the prescribed attitude for the Repeal movement in verse:

> Bide your time – one false step taken
> Perils all ye yet have done.
> Undismayed, erect, unshaken,
> Watch and wait and all is won.
>
> 'Tis not by one rash endeavour
> Men or states to greatness climb –
> Would you win your rights for ever
> Calm and thought bids bide your time.[3]

O'Connell now bided his time. The bluff of the monster meetings had been called. But, with the bluff called, what was future policy to be? How, practically, was the goal of Repeal, for which they were biding their time, in the fullness of time to be attained?

The one unmistakable asset remaining after the monster meetings was the fact that the Irish masses and the Catholic clergy (whose influence was always so closely linked with mass opinion) were overwhelmingly behind O'Connell. The government ban on Clontarf had brought further proof of

* Randall Clarke, *Irish Historical Studies*, vol. iii, p. 21 (1940), was the first historian to draw public attention to the inaccuracy of Duffy in this respect. But even he seems unaware of the full extent to which Gavan Duffy in his two books *Young Ireland* and *Four Years of Irish History* distorted the history of the post-Clontarf period. See below, pp. 219 and 225.

this, for, at less than twenty-four hours' notice, O'Connell and the Repeal Association had been able to prevent the assembly of perhaps half a million people, many of whom were already on their way to the meeting from many different parts of Ireland. Additional proof that the setback itself did not diminish O'Connell's authority with the Irish people was immediately forthcoming in the shape of the Repeal Rent, which rose sharply in the third week of October to the then record sum of £2,287.[4] However, evidence of popular support was of only limited advantage in a political situation which, before the great extensions of the franchise later in the century, was only in a limited sense democratic. The Irish upper and middle classes, a considerable proportion of whom were Protestants, were still widely opposed to Repeal just because of its character as a powerful popular movement, although the support of the Catholic Church made the movement seem more respectable to Catholic than to Protestant gentry.

As for support for Repeal in the British Parliament, where in the end Repeal had to be won, there was as little sign of it as when the issue had been debated there ten years before. The analogy with Catholic Emancipation which O'Connell was fond of drawing was still far from realistic. All in all, despite the past success of the monster meetings, the future for Repeal now looked bleak. And Peel's Tory government displayed its confidence when, within a week of Clontarf, it instigated a prosecution against O'Connell, Duffy and five others for 'conspiracy'.

Now, however rashly O'Connell and others had indulged in the ambivalent use of martial language during the year's campaign, there had never been anything conspiratorial about the Repeal movement. O'Connell had expressed *ad nauseam* his hatred and contempt for secret societies – partly a matter of genuine principle and partly because the agrarian secret societies were an unfathomable menace to his own influence over the Irish people. The Association's meetings had always been careful to assert their character as legal attempts by citizens of the Crown humbly and constitutionally to petition for a change in the law. So that it was possible at least that, by a prosecution, Peel was carrying his new confidence too far, and might arouse English Liberal sympathy for O'Connell.

While waiting to be brought to trial O'Connell embarked on the long laborious campaign that inevitably lay ahead if he were to win over to Repeal enough of the Irish gentry and, still more important, enough English support to give him a realistic force to manoeuvre with in the House of Commons. The arguments put forward in these years, and the arguments used to refute them, like those in the Repeal debate of the decade before dominated the question of constitutional Irish nationalism for the next seventy-five years.

In November 1843 O'Connell publicly examined the two evils which he said must be avoided if Repeal were to be obtained. The first was the separation of Ireland from the rest of Great Britain, which would be a great calamity'.[5] The other was the danger of what he called 'a Catholic ascendancy'.[6]

As far as separation was concerned, O'Connell insisted once again that not only was there not the least danger of separation in Repeal, but that Repeal would actually consolidate the connection between the two islands by removing all cause of further strife. To which Unionists could reply that they only had O'Connell's word for this, and that even he at times was careful to point out that he could not bind posterity beyond his lifetime.

As to the danger of a Catholic ascendancy, O'Connell made an interesting point that was relevant enough for his own day, but which would be less valid for the future. Catholic ascendancy, he maintained, could never come about because, although in an Irish House of Commons Catholics might well outnumber Protestants, yet in an Irish House of Lords Catholics would always be in a minority and there was therefore a cast-iron constitutional safeguard against the passing of any anti-Protestant measures.*[7]

Some encouraging signs were to be found that the Protestant gentry of Ireland were at this time not automatically wed to the inevitable continuation of the Union. It was, after all, a Protestant, the progressive landlord Sharman Crawford, who had already put forward Federalism – the proposal for an Irish legislature for domestic affairs only – as an important compromise between orthodox Unionism and total Repeal. It was a compromise of which Davis himself had already noted the tactical attractions.† Ten days after Clontarf, the Repeal Association declared Federalists eligible for membership; though Sharman Crawford himself did not in fact join. O'Connell made it clear that he himself, in accepting Federalism, was accepting no compromise, but that, in so far as an arrangement such as a Federalist might suggest would literally require the repeal of the Act of Union, he would consider such a man a Repealer.[8] 'We will not require him,' he continued, 'to go to the full length with us in every particular – we will go to that length ourselves and never give it up; but we will take the assistance of every man that is for a domestic legislature of any kind in Ireland.'[9]

The Nation, while also stressing its own more uncompromising aim, equally saw no reason to fear that a Federal Union could impede the march of nationality.[10] What it rightly did fear was what it called 'the deadly bane of Ireland – DIVISION . . .'[11] and it welcomed Federalists with the words: 'They strike for nationality; they honour Ireland; they demand self-government; they ask part of what we ask – nothing against it.'[12]

But even Federalism was very much a minority creed among Protestants,

---

* In the Home Rule Bills later in the century, special Irish Upper Houses were envisaged which would not have had the same total veto on legislation which the House of Lords had in O'Connell's time.

† See above, p. 201.

and O'Connell's main problem, that of bringing Protestants into the fold of any sort of Irish nationalism, remained as formidable as ever. The government had, however, helped him acquire one Protestant recruit of considerable standing.

The ban on Clontarf and the prosecution of O'Connell had been too much for a forty-year-old Protestant landlord, named William Smith O'Brien, a man of some distinction and moral standing who had already resigned his commission of the peace in sympathy with those magistrates dismissed for attending Repeal meetings.*[13] O'Brien had been a member of Parliament for many years, first representing Ennis, in County Clare, and then County Limerick. Educated in England, like all the Protestant Irish upper classes of his day, he had the speech and mannerisms of an English gentleman and was often regarded by the Irish as stiff and stilted in a typically English fashion. One of his new Repeal associates remarked of him soon after he had joined the Repeal Association that the amalgam was unskilfully made: there was too much of the Smith and not enough of the O'Brien.[14] But these very characteristics were what made him such a sensationally imposing addition to the Repealers' ranks. For Smith O'Brien was a living embodiment of that nationalist theory first put forward by Tone and reiterated and substantiated by O'Connell and Davis that the Protestants of Ireland could and should make common cause with Catholics as Irishmen first and foremost in their allegiance. Moreover, he was a particularly suitable example of the theory, for although his family had been long of the ascendancy in style, and his new political views were to lead to painful difficulties with his mother, Lady O'Brien, yet he also traced his descent from Brian Boru, while a more recent ancestor had been one of the Wild Geese, had fought for the French at the battle of Ramillies and fathered a future Marshal of France.[15]

Again, although Smith O'Brien had been in favour of Catholic Emancipation in the twenties and had consistently taken up an attitude sympathetic to the Irish common people in the House of Commons, he had actually first been elected as a Tory. As a Whig-Liberal from 1835 onwards he had continued to oppose Repeal. As late as the summer of 1843, when moving in the House of Commons that the House should 'examine the causes of discontent in Ireland with a view to the redress of grievances and the establishment of a just and impartial government', he had used as one of his arguments for doing so the desirability of consolidating the legislative Union.[16] His decision now to join the Association was a powerful advertisement for the Repealers' argument that for all true Irishmen of whatsoever creed or class the Union was no longer supportable. Before the end of 1843, Smith O'Brien was taking part in the discussions on Federalism in the columns of *The Nation*, and agreeing that even a mere Federal constitution

* See above, p. 205.

would be better than 'the present miscalled Union which carries eternal weakness into the heart of the Empire, and which to Ireland is fraught with ruin and danger'.[17]

In the general desire to welcome all men of goodwill, particularly Protestant gentry, to the cause of the Repealers' Irish nationalism, there was certainly a tendency to skate rather optimistically over the sort of problems that Federalism would give rise to. For instance, with a domestic Irish Parliament concerned only with internal Irish affairs, and an Imperial Parliament which contained only a minority of Irish members, decisions on such questions as foreign treaties and the issue of peace or war would inevitably be those of the British and not of the Irish Government. Yet this hardly fitted the concept of Irish nationality which Davis and the other writers of *The Nation* and even O'Connell had been preaching. Certainly, they all emphasized that they would accept Federalism only as an experiment rather than as a final solution, but the half-way solution had to seem fairly stable if the British Parliament were ever to be brought to consider it seriously.

In a letter to *The Nation* at the end of the year Smith O'Brien faced up to the real problem with typical straightforwardness though not with altogether convincing arguments. He admitted that under Federalism there might theoretically be head-on conflicts over foreign treaties and peace or war, but the very danger of this would, he thought, be likely to prevent England from acting rashly on such matters. There would, O'Brien continued, be a two-way check on either England or Ireland allowing such conflicts to develop to a point where total separation threatened. When the Union was repealed England would have everything to lose and Ireland, if wisely governed, nothing to gain by separation. And in stating this he elaborated on an aspect of Irish life which was always to be a complicating, it not downright confusing, factor in the majority of Irishmen's national thinking.

'Nearly a million of our countrymen,' he continued, 'have fixed their homes in England and Scotland. Every family in the kingdom is linked by domestic connection with England – every British colony teems with the children of our soil.'[18] In these circumstances he held it very unlikely that Ireland would 'wantonly, without cause – nay, contrary to her own interest – desire to overthrow that majestic fabric of Imperial greatness on which she has lavished her energies to rear, and which she has profusely cemented with her blood. Deep indeed must be the wounds inflicted upon our national pride, and upon our national interests, before we can consent to deplore the associations which belong to identity of language, similarity of institutions, connection of kindred, and community of glory.'

The Nation, in spite of its own reservations about Federation, applauded this letter from its new star recruit and welcomed Federalists with equal enthusiasm. Since *The Nation* group were to have their first major public difference of opinion with O'Connell almost a year later on the very subject of Federalism, this earlier agreement is of some interest.

At the beginning of the new year, 1844, the problem of what tactics to adopt were still the Repeal cause's principal concern. *The Nation* itself had nothing practical to suggest beyond general consolidation of the movement. It reiterated the two main principles of the cause: 'Ourselves Alone' and non-violence. 'Ireland must attempt nothing which can fail,' it wrote. 'Our fathers failed because they yielded to passion. . . . Hoard your passions as though they were coined gold. . . . Your policy is clear – organization, union, order.'¹⁹ 'Bide your time', in fact, as Davis had put it earlier. A week later, *The Nation* had the grace to quote, from *Blackwood's Magazine*, a parody on Davis's poem.

'Bide your time,' wrote *Blackwood's*,

> . . . bide your time,
> Patience is the true sublime;
> Heroes, bottle up your tears –
> Wait for ten, or ten-score years;
> Shrink from blows, but rage in rhyme –
> Bide your time, bide your time.

'But,' commented *The Nation*, 'neither scolding, or jibbing bayonets or proclamations shall push us a hair's breadth from the track on which prudence beckons us. We will bide our time and to some purpose.'²⁰

In February 1844 something happened which increased the element of caution in O'Connell's natural pragmatism. The State trial of himself and the six other repealers which had dragged on throughout the winter came to an end and he and his co-defendants were found guilty of conspiracy. The actual sentence was postponed until the following law term, which meant a respite of three months or so on bail, but the verdict made the most profound impression on O'Connell.

His whole policy to date had been based on the necessity of keeping within the law. Its premise, rooted in his memory of '98, had been that illegal activity brought disaster. His determination and ability to make legality itself work for the Irish cause had so far been his most redoubtable asset. Now suddenly as a convicted conspirator he found himself virtually bracketed with the United Irishmen after all. An even greater sensitivity to the dangers of illegality was to characterize his political speech and behaviour for the rest of his life.

He at first considered dissolving the Repeal Association altogether and establishing some new organization quite uncompromised by the verdict. But dissuaded from such a drastic step by *The Nation* group, he turned his thoughts to the practical possibilities of the political situation in England.

There, a movement for a quite different sort of repeal – that of the Corn Laws – was under way and though this was not in itself of primary concern to Ireland, it opened up the possibilities of greater manoeuvrability for O'Connell on the English political scene, because the ruling Tory party was split on the issue. Conversely, the Whigs, united and energized by it, were already looking towards the end of the Tories' natural term of parliamentary office.

The bluff of the monster meetings had failed principally because the degree of English support for Repeal of the Union had been nothing like what it had been for Emancipation. But in the new political situation O'Connell had something to offer. His own parliamentary support became infinitely more valuable to British politicians. To trade one form of support for the other now became the underlying tactical principle of all his political action.

O'Connell had to wait between law terms for the pronouncement of sentence against him and his fellow 'conspirators' and used the interval to proceed to England to try to condition at least the English middle classes in favour of the Repeal cause. He went, in *The Nation's* words, 'with the approval of the warmest Repealers'[21] and the Repeal Association soon afterwards passed with acclamation a resolution conveying their gratitude towards the Liberals and the sympathetic section of the British people whom O'Connell was meeting.[22]

But behind the scenes in Ireland there were already signs of that disquiet and even distaste with which the Young Irelanders were increasingly to view O'Connell's whole style of political activity. As yet it was more a question of differences of attitude rather than of policy. O'Connell, after years of political in-fighting, was the professional politician, with the professional's intuitive ability to adjust between the idealistic and the pragmatic approach to political problems. Davis, Duffy, Dillon, and the other young men whom they were begining to collect round them were unburdened by experience in politics. They were filled with the iconoclasm of the intelligent young for whom politics is a field for idealistic integrity, a practical extension of the written word, rather than a different element altogether. Even in the great monster meetings' the year before there had been *sotto voce* disapproval for some of O'Connell's cheaper flights of demagogic oratory and now too, even before O'Connell's departure for England, Davis had already expressed some irreverent doubts about his firmness on Repeal to Smith O'Brien, who at this stage still stood aside both from the Liberator and Young Ireland in the Repeal movement. 'If O'Connell were firmer,' Davis wrote to O'Brien, 'I would say he ought not to go to England; but fancy his speeches at ten meetings here with the State trial terror on him! I fear we must keep him out of that danger by an English trip till Parliament meets, and then all will be well.'[23]

Biding Time After Clontarf

The Nation too had hinted at some doubts, when in the week of O'Connell's departure for England it published a leading article headed 'No Compromise'. The article's apparently innocuous intention was to disabuse any members of the Whig opposition of any idea they might have that all O'Connell was seeking in England was a political alliance on the model of the old Lichfield House Compact of the 1830s. If the Whigs were thinking this, then, said *The Nation*, speaking as if on O'Connell's behalf, they were making a mistake.[24] But what *The Nation* really meant was that if O'Connell himself were thinking this then he was making a mistake.

A still clearer public glimpse of such doubts appeared two days later in a meeting of the Repeal Association. A brief exchange of words took place between O'Connell's son John – his favourite of four, and always the acknowledged deputy of his father in his absence – and one Young Irelander, M. J. Barry, on what exactly the Lichfield House Compact had amounted to. John O'Connell showed himself very anxious to expunge any possible inference that might be drawn from Barry's words to the effect that O'Connell had compromised the full Repeal goal at that time and therefore might be supposed to be about to do so in the future.[25] The matter was at once cleared up to everyone's apparent satisfaction, but this fear that O'Connell might settle permanently for something less than Repeal, and a reciprocal resentment of this suspicion on his part, was to become a more and more painful feature of the O'Connell–Young Ireland relationship and finally seriously to damage the whole Repeal movement.

Modern historians, while rejecting some earlier detail of Gavan Duffy's account of this period,* have acquiesced in his general contention that soon after Clontarf O'Connell lost interest in Repeal and was overcome by physical debility. The very writer who first exposed Duffy's lapse in claiming to have opposed the Clontarf decision, himself declared that from the time of the trial verdict onwards O'Connell 'seems to have lost all faith in the Repeal movement'.[26] Thereafter, he continues, O'Connell had no real hope of achieving Repeal and only continued the agitation because the Young Irelanders and O'Brien forced him to do so. In fact, any close study of O'Connell's activity in the years 1844 to 1846 makes it impossible to accept that he could have carried an interest in Repeal to such impressive lengths or with such energy and enthusiasm if he had been as disingenuous or as senile as Duffy implies.

The imaginative technique of the monster meetings had proved by itself inadequate. While not, in fact, as will be seen, abandoning the moral power which massed displays of Irish popular opinion lent his other efforts, he now combined this with more conventional pragmatic manoeuvres in the political field. Before, however, such manoeuvres could be effective, the entire Irish scene was overshadowed by the appalling catastrophe of the famine.

* See above, p. 212.

Pragmatic politics suddenly meant simply trying to preserve life itself for the starving common people of Ireland. And only when overwhelmed by the relative failure to do even this in which all politicians were to be involved did O'Connell succumb quite rapidly to debility and advancing age.

9

O'Connell's Imprisonment
and After

In the very week of March 1844 in which the exchange of words took place
in the Repeal Association between the Young Irelander, Barry, and John
O'Connell about his father's intentions in England, Thomas Davis himself
wrote John O'Connell a private letter expressing his own anxiety. He
suggested that the success which the Liberator was soon enjoying in England
was 'embarrassing' and even contradictory to the Repeal policy. There was
an almost panicky note in Davis's letter.

'I do not, and cannot suppose,' he wrote, 'that your father ever dreamt of
abandoning Repeal to escape a prison, yet that is implied in all the Whig
[newspaper] articles.'[1]

Yet when the record of this short campaign of O'Connell's in England is
examined, it seems that Davis was paying an almost obsessional attention
to what the Whig newspapers were saying, rather than to what O'Connell
himself was saying. And in view of the fact that no alternative to O'Connell's
practical attempt to win English support had been suggested by anyone else,
Davis's implied suspicions seem unworthy of him.

In O'Connell's public references to Repeal on this visit he usually made
clearer than was strictly necessary his intention to seek, in the long run,
nothing short of full Repeal. But his chief concern was to make Repeal
acceptable to English ears. Thus, at Birmingham, where on 9 March 1844
he spoke on the same platform as the Federalist Sharman Crawford, he
admitted openly that if the Union had been a fair bargain between Britain
and Ireland it ought to be preserved, but denied that it was a fair bargain.
(The emphasis was different from that of the thirties when he had talked
openly about 'testing' the Union.) At the same time he denied that Repeal
of the Union meant separation, maintaining that he would be against it if
it did and insisting that one of his chief reasons for being in favour of 'a just
and equitable Repeal' was that it alone could prevent eventual separation.
(His tactful use of the adjectives 'just' and 'equitable' in Sharman Crawford's
presence made it unnecessary to go into any precise distinctions between
Federalism and full Repeal.) His way of putting things was not that of the

Young Irelanders, but then their more aggressively expressed nationalism would not have won many voices for Repeal of the Union within the British political system. In fact, O'Connell's argument was to become the basic argument of the vast majority of nationalist Irishmen for the rest of the nineteenth century and the first sixteen years of the twentieth.

The day after this Birmingham meeting another large meeting took place in Manchester – this time without O'Connell – to direct the government's attention to 'the public grievances under which the people of Ireland labour'.[2] The Mayor presided. Professors, bankers and clergy were among the sponsors. There was enthusiastic applause at the mention of O'Connell's name. Certainly, it was primarily a Whig rally. But it was also a valuable part of that necessary process of softening up English opinion if Repeal were ever to be won by constitutional means. And no Young Irelander was then in favour of it being won by any other.

In the following week a great dinner was given to O'Connell in the theatre at Covent Garden, where the auditorium was entirely boarded over and made level with the stage.[3] A number of Whig notables were present, including the Earl of Shrewsbury who proposed the toast of 'The People', and particularly 'The Irish People', though in a rather confused and dated way he seemed to mean by this the Irish country gentlemen. However, he announced the opening of a new era in history, and the toast of 'O'Connell' was received with immense cheering, the whole audience rising *en masse* and cheering and waving handkerchiefs for several minutes on end.

But though playing for British support, O'Connell was aware of the anxiety of the young men who were his political élite in Ireland, and was careful to consider them too. At Coventry on the following Monday he took up the remark of an earlier speaker who had said, in an over-accommodating manner, that what O'Connell was looking for was not in fact really Repeal of the Union at all, but simply justice for Ireland.

'Now,' said O'Connell of this speaker, 'he was mistaken in his views of my objects for although it is true that I am looking for justice to the Irish people, yet I see no prospect of justice. I believe there is none in any other means than by a restoration of her domestic legislature to Ireland. ... If,' he went on in familiar vein, 'by looking for Repeal of the Union I sought a separation of the two countries, I would be wrong in seeking it – but a Repeal of the Union would not produce separation – it would unite the two countries more closely.'[4] He refused to leave his audience with any comforting sense of ambiguity about his final purpose: 'You can never convince me that any other than an Irish Parliament will give justice to Ireland, and I will go to the grave with that feeling.' But he compensated by concluding in his woolliest vein with a call for 'a strong pull and a long pull for England and Ireland – for Ireland and for England; a strong pull and a long pull, and a pull altogether'. He sat down amid loud and renewed cheering.

Before leaving England for Ireland at the end of March 1844 O'Connell told a great indoor meeting at Liverpool, for which tickets had been changing hands at treble their official price, that if justice were not done to Ireland and the Union repealed there would be 'a bloody revolution and separation between the two countries'.[5] After a night at the Adelphi Hotel he sailed for Ireland, where Smith O'Brien was quick to approve his visit and wholly refute any suggestion that it had been nothing but a Whig manoeuvre.[6]

The date was approaching on which O'Connell and his six co-defendants were due for sentence on the conspiracy charge. Temporary loss of O'Connell's leadership would inevitably be a serious tactical blow for the Repeal Association. He made clear how he wished its affairs to be conducted in his absence. At a dinner at Cork on 8 April 1844, at which a letter of support from MacHale, the Archbishop of Tuam, was read, O'Connell laid down the principle that 'the Repeal must continue', adding: 'If you want to confer on me comfort when in my dungeon, you will rally for Old Ireland and Repeal.'[7]

On 30 May 1844 he was sentenced with the others to a year's imprisonment. *The Nation* protested between black borders: 'He, the King of your hearts, cannot step this land which he has so served, beyond the walls of his gaol.'[8] Smith O'Brien, at the first meeting of the Repeal Association after the sentence, swore to vehement applause that he would not allow a drop of intoxicating liquor to pass his lips until O'Connell was released.[9]

O'Connell's dungeon in fact turned out to be a luxurious one. The Dublin prison in which he was confined was under the control of the Dublin Corporation and the Governor graciously vacated his own house for O'Connell's use. He was allowed as many visitors as he liked. Food was sent in from outside and very large dinner parties of twenty-four people or more were frequent, sometimes held in a special dining tent in the garden from which a tricolour flag was flown until over this at least the Governor put his foot down.*[10] Smith O'Brien, who now assumed something of the position of O'Connell's deputy in the Association, was able to consult with him continually, while Davis, who ran *The Nation* while Gavan Duffy served his sentence, was equally able to consult with him as much as he liked. Nevertheless, a great wave of sympathy and protest at the sentences was felt all over Ireland, and the additional enthusiasm for the Repeal cause in which it resulted was immediately signalled in a sudden prodigious rise in the Repeal Rent. The weekly sum had been drifting sluggishly around the £500 mark until O'Connell's imprisonment, but it rose sharply to over £2,500 in the week in which he was sentenced and climbed still higher to over £3,000 a week for several weeks afterwards.[11] These amounts, which in the money values of the mid-nineteenth century were considerable, were subscribed

---

* There is no indication as to the nature of the tricolour. It was probably the French red, white and blue, a symbol of progressive defiance. The orange, white and green as an Irish variant of this first appeared in 1848. See below, p. 265.

almost entirely in small sums by people in all walks of life – carmen, coach-lace weavers, solicitors, stockbrokers, priests, peasants, etc. Almost all of it came from Ireland itself. Of the tally of £3,389 14s 8d recorded in *The Nation* of 22 June 1844, only £34 came from America. More progress, wrote Davis in *The Nation* of 15 June, heading his leader 'Third Week of the Captivity', had been made in the previous fortnight than in any other quarter of the agitation.[12]

Davis now gave his mind to the question of how this favourable situation was to be turned to more practical advantage. He stressed particularly the need for internal unity and, on the principle that any sort of domestic legis-lature would at least give nationality 'a temple', he added that a Federalist was 'a Repealer of the Union as decidedly as if he never called himself a Federalist'.[13] He made it clear that *The Nation* itself thought that a claim in the government of the Empire and consent to contribute taxes and soldiers towards its upkeep 'seems to us unwise' but that this was 'not such a difference as should make us divide'.[14]

Signs of a broad, if vague, sort of Irish unity were indeed coming from some unexpected quarters. In July 1844 an Irish National Society was formed in London to bring peers and gentlemen together for the promotion of social and intellectual intercourse among Irishmen, irrespective of political differ-ences. The Earl of Clanrickarde and Lord Castlereagh were listed among its members, together with one of O'Connell's sons, Maurice. This was the first of a number of such attempts made in these years to bring Irishmen of all parties together in London on the basis of nothing but their Irishness. Such groupings never led to anything very positive or constructive, but in retrospect they can be seen as a residual flickering of that sense of Protestant gentry nationalism which had partly inspired the more broadly based Irish nationalism now at work. At the time, to the young men of *The Nation*, they seemed more like the flickering of a reviving than a dying fire, a first faint sign of their vision being fulfilled.

Late in August 1844 a development in foreign affairs suggested a much more promising analogy with the years of the Volunteers. France became engaged in a series of actions against the Sultan of Morocco to which the British Government reacted with traditional sensitivity. *The Nation* declared that if war were to come between England and France then Repeal must be made to follow. There was no specific proposal as to how exactly this might be done beyond increased nationalist efforts to acquire knowledge and improve organization. But the inference was obvious. At the end of the month the paper spelt things out. The Prince de Joinville had bombarded the island and town of Mogador, while on land Marshal Bugeaud had defeated twenty-four thousand Moorish cavalry. 'We heave a sigh for Morocco,' wrote Davis in *The Nation*. 'We rejoice for Ireland. There is hope for us in every volley ...' He drew the parallel with 1779. 'The opportunity

of 1779 may come again – our garrisons empty – an invader on the horizon.'
He addressed himself to Peel, telling him how rapidly he should endeavour
to conciliate the people by releasing their leaders and yielding Ireland to the
Irish; for 'nationality consecrates a coast'. How too he 'should accept their
volunteer battalions, and strengthen their Patriotism by arsenals and
discipline'.[15]

Yet even in this prospective concrete situation *The Nation* offered no
practical scheme to nationalists. There was no call for the formation of
volunteers, merely one to strengthen the Association by forming Repeal
Reading Rooms and increasing contributions to the Repeal Rent. The
furthest Davis went was to exhort Repealers to 'carefully study every book
and map that may qualify them for the defence of their soil'.[16]

The war did not materialize, but within a fortnight something happened
which gave almost as much hope to the Repeal movement. Against all
expectation, the judgement on O'Connell and his fellow prisoners was
reversed in the House of Lords. They were released the same day, but
chose to return to the prison for the night so that a triumphal procession of
some 200,000 citizens could make the most of the event on the following day.
Similar rejoicing took place all over Ireland. In Cork there was 'the very
ecstasy of joyous delirium'.[17] The bands turned out. Bonfires were lit. Houses
were decked with laurel. Torchbearers and blazing tar barrels turned night
into day and beacons flared from hill to hill across the countryside.[18]

But when the first natural excitement was over, the same question which
had faced Repealers before O'Connell's imprisonment still remained: what
was the next step to be?

Duffy's retrospective account of events, coloured by Young Ireland's subsequent quarrel with O'Connell, tries to establish that a physical and mental
deterioration of O'Connell set in after his release from imprisonment.[19] But
there is no evidence of this at the time. There is no contemporary comment
on a physical deterioration in O'Connell until November 1846. Then it is his
friend, W. J. O'Neill Daunt, who notes specifically that while 'his physical
energies are plainly decaying' he displays 'unimpaired intellectual power'.[20]
Even in the following year, only a few months before O'Connell's death,
Daunt records that, though complaining of the feebleness of age, O'Connell
declared himself otherwise 'very well'.[21] And Daunt was no sycophant, like
Tom Steele, O'Connell's so-called 'Head Pacificator' and others of his supporters in the Association. Certainly Duffy's implication of O'Connell's
rapid decline into enfeeblement and senility after his release cannot be sustained, though his need to find some explanation that was not too painful
for events which even forty years later were painful to look back upon is
understandable.

In his first speech to the Association a few days after his release, O'Connell
faced up to the problem of what the next step was to be without claiming to

be able to supply the answer. Though he maintained that the Clontarf meeting had been legally summoned and illegally prohibited, he was on the whole against risking another challenge of that sort. Pre-eminent in his mind was the need to preserve what had always given his movement its strength: namely, the fact that, unlike the United Irishmen's demand for nationality, it was not treasonably expressed.

The trial and the original legal decision against him had plainly given him a fright, and something like an obsession with this fright can be seen in his first suggestion – soon dropped – to prosecute those British authorities who had brought about his imprisonment; the Attorney General, the Judges and the British Ministers themselves. His other positive proposal was to proceed with the plan for the summons of a Council of Three Hundred (the same number of members as had sat in the old Irish Parliament). Since this plan had been actively under review when the prosecution was instigated he approached the subject now with extreme caution, and emphasized that it was full of legal difficulty. The fifty-year-old Convention Act, expressly designed to prevent any such extra-parliamentary body from meeting, was still on the Statute Book and O'Connell's old confidence in his ability to drive a coach and six through any Act of Parliament had been rudely shaken. However, he was in favour of summoning the Council 'as a Preservative Society' which, while initiating nothing, should act as the supreme sanctioning and consultative body for the Association itself.[22]

Duffy, in his later history, suggests that Young Ireland's reaction to this speech of O'Connell's was one of disappointment bordering on dismay. But the issue of *The Nation* which reported it does not bear him out. The leading article appearing under its regular heading, 'Remember the 30th May',* in summarizing the Association's prospects said: 'the Preservative Society must be made a reality, though we concur with O'Connell that it must be done slowly and carefully'.[23] It also agreed with O'Connell in deprecating a Clontarf meeting. Further, it advised a renewal of those arbitration courts which in the previous years had heard something like four thousand cases in an indigenous Irish process altogether outside the machinery of British law, and had obtained acceptance for their verdicts in all but a minute percentage of cases.[24]

O'Connell himself was in favour of these courts, though again he was anxious to keep their activities separate from the Association lest their possible illegality should endanger it.[25] Nor was there anything in the rest of *The Nation*'s article with which O'Connell would not have agreed. Better organization was needed. The Reading Rooms should be extended. The men of the North should be educated, and England must be taught that it was in her interest to have Ireland a friendly neighbour helping her in danger, rather than a discontented province. In general the paper struck a most

* The date of O'Connell's imprisonment.

realistic note: '... while legally we are in the same position as on the day they [O'Connell and the other defendants] were impeached, politically we are far stronger. We have rallied good and generous men in our adversity. ... We are far stronger than we were a year ago. ... We have got where we are by organization, conciliation and peace. Our peace cannot be improved – the People cannot do better than adhere to their present obedience to the law.' [26]

In a speech at a banquet in his honour a few days later O'Connell echoed *The Nation's* general tone. Their first duty, he said, was 'to combine together the Irish of every sect and persuasion – to unite and combine Irishmen of every gradation of opinion who agree with us in thinking one thing necessary – the Repeal of the Union'. [27]

Many hopeful portents for such a combination were in the air. The Federal idea was becoming increasingly popular among men who had been previously opposed to the Repeal movement, and Sharman Crawford had actually sent a letter to this very banquet in O'Connell's honour, apologizing for his absence. O'Connell took up an inference in this letter that Repealers ruled out Federalism, which he said was quite incorrect. It was true that most members of the Association preferred 'simple Repeal, but there is not one of us that would not be content to Repeal the Act of Union and substitute a Federal Parliament, not one. I don't think Federalism to be the best, but I was never one of those who had such an overweening opinion of the infallibility of my own judgement as not readily to yield to argument, and cooperate with anyone that thinks better. I am ready to join with Federalists to repeal the Act of Union.' [28] He even went so far as to propose that he should hand over leadership of a combined movement to a new Protestant recruit for Federalism, a former Orangeman who was now High Sheriff of County Fermanagh, named Grey Porter.

Though such extravagant and uncharacteristic humility can be discounted as oratorical display, O'Connell was again undoubtedly sounding the one note which seemed likely to promise real advance for the Repeal movement, namely conciliation of those forces which were in any case moving towards it. Some time before this banquet a high Tory of distinction on the Dublin Corporation, a Dr Maunsell, had written to him with a proposal which while not going so far as Federalism was significant enough of a general shift in opinion. This proposal was that while the Act of Union itself should not be altered, the Imperial Parliament should meet in Dublin every three years. In this case O'Connell could only reply politely that much though the prospect of working together for Ireland with such men as Dr Maunsell delighted him in principle, he could not support this particular measure as it was clearly intended as a substitute for Repeal. Nevertheless, as Davis himself pointed out, the proposal did represent at least a 'loosening of ideas, an abandonment of the old superstition that all was right'. [29]

That the general conciliatory line of tactics was a promising one seems confirmed by the British Government's own reaction to these straws in the wind. Graham, the Home Secretary, wrote to Peel, the Prime Minister, voicing his suspicion that 'the Federal arrangement will be the middle term on which for the moment opposite parties will agree: and some scheme of national representation will be devised, to which the Whigs will agree'.[30] And the fact that the proposal for occasional Imperial Parliaments in Dublin should come from such a high Tory as Dr Maunsell alarmed him still further.[31] Even Lord John Russell, the leader of the Whigs, seemed frightened by the way things were going and wrote to the Duke of Leinster asserting his determination to maintain the Union and reject any Federal solution.[32]

All this makes the breach that was about to take place between O'Connell and Young Ireland on the subject of Federalism difficult to understand. For *The Nation*, under both Davis's and Duffy's editorship, at first appeared wholly to endorse O'Connell's tactic. 'Mr O'Connell,' it wrote, two days after his banquet speech, 'is prepared to welcome Federalism. .... We too will hail the concession of Irish supremacy in Ireland and will give this plan a fair trial.'[33] And a week later, in another leading article headed 'Conservative Repealers', it drew attention to the fact that the Protestants felt sold out by the government and were therefore ready to listen to new suggestions that might be in their interests.[34] 'Federalism is making such way,' *The Nation* continued, 'both among Tories and Whigs, here and in England, as to lead us to hope that that great object will be gained without a shot being fired.'[35]

The new spirit among Conservatives derived partly from the developing political split between Peelites and anti-Peelites within the party. And it was not just wishful thinking to suppose that this internal split might be turned to advantage by advocates of the Repeal cause. An anti-Repeal English journal, the *London Examiner*, commented on the advance of the Repeal cause as moderate and sensible men came to see that in their own interests some new parliamentary organization was necessary 'to adjust appropriate legal capacity and attention to the peculiar needs of different parts of the country'. 'Affairs,' continued the *London Examiner*, 'have become too complex for the careless scrambling legislation in a mob of six hundred members ... a very considerable portion of the thinking classes ... are of opinion that the duties of the legislature have outgrown its means of performing them.'[36]

At the weekly meeting of Belfast repealers in those days it was no unusual thing now for Protestants and Orangemen to be proposed as members or associates. And the ultra-Tory *Belfast Newsletter*, in commenting that there were now many distinguished Conservatives openly supporting Federalism, wrote of 'most extraordinary times' and that the crisis of Ireland's fate was approaching.[37] No wonder *The Nation* felt optimistic. 'Let the people go on as they had begun,' it wrote, '– growing more thoughtful, more temperate, more educated, more resolute – let them complete their parish organization, carry out their registries, and above all establish those Reading Rooms which will inform and strengthen them into liberty; and 'ere Many Years Work, the Green Flag will be saluted by Europe, and Ireland will be a Nation.' None of this fits in with the 'silent discontent and dismay' which Duffy nearly forty years later remembered to have greeted O'Connell's utterances on his release.

After the necessary three weeks or so of speech-making and celebration O'Connell retired to his home, Darrynane Abbey in County Kerry, for a short holiday. This was reasonable enough for a man of seventy who had just emerged from three months' confinement, even of a comfortable sort. He found his farm in excellent shape with the richest crop of hay of anyone in the district, and he was soon out on the hills delightedly hunting hares with his pack of beagles. Acknowledging his debt to 'my merciful God for my health and strength' he concluded a letter to one of his closest friends, 'I am becoming very impatient to hear authentically from "the Federalists".'[38] Ten days later, he wrote a letter to the Repeal Association almost ten thousand words long containing his thoughts on future policy.

In this letter O'Connell started from two premises. First, it would be 'criminal' not to exploit their great legal victory 'to achieve the great object of our desires – the restoration of an Irish Parliament'.[39] Secondly, the conciliation of a sizeable body of Protestants was necessary in order to do so. Having demonstrated from ancient and recent history that Protestants had nothing to fear from a Catholic ascendancy, he proceeded to examine that movement which, for the first time since the Union, seemed to show Protestants again moving towards the idea of an Irish Parliament, namely Federalism. He recommended some alliance with it, and in terms of political tactics in the prevailing situation it was a realistic enough recommendation to make. Although O'Connell already knew enough of *The Nation* group to realize that political realism was not their strong point, it was not unreasonable to expect their support in this policy in view of their frequent editorial blessings on Federalism in *The Nation* in the past, and in particular in view of the fact that Davis himself was even at that moment in Belfast conducting negotiations with prominent Federalists.[40]

In fact the only practical difficulty O'Connell appeared to see was that the Federalists were not yet themselves precisely agreed on how their scheme was to work. But while admitting this reservation and making clear that no such precise scheme could be expected to come from him he went so far as to declare: 'For my own part, I will own, I do at present feel a preference for the Federative plan, as tending more to the utility of Ireland, and to the maintenance of the connection with England than the mode of simple Repeal.'[41]

The qualification 'at present' seems to denote plainly the waiting game on which he was embarking. Davis himself had specifically approved such a game, writing of O'Connell the day after he had left for Darrynane: 'He is wisely playing a slow game to let the Federalists ... show themselves.'[42]

In the end O'Connell's attempt at a new tactical move came to nothing for the Federalists remained unable to agree publicly on a precise formula. Indeed, his rather transparent eagerness to embrace them may have scared some of them off altogether. But their failure to respond gave him a way of escape from an even greater embarrassment. For O'Connell's statement on Federalism rather surprisingly led to the first major public disagreement between *The Nation* and himself, a portent of disastrous things to come.

Duffy alone of those prominent in *The Nation* group had been in Dublin when O'Connell's letter to the Association was inserted in the minutes.[43] Without consulting any of the other Young Irelanders he published in the leader column of *The Nation* an open letter to O'Connell, signed by himself, repudiating the idea of any compromise on pure and total Repeal of the Act of Union.

It is possible to read between the lines of Duffy's later writings that Davis himself did not approve of Duffy's action.[44] It would have been odd if he had approved, since he was then negotiating with Federalists in Belfast. And at the time Davis even described O'Connell's letter as 'very able of its kind', though he thought his gesture of embrace towards the Federalists was too precipitate.[45] Federalism could never be a final settlement, but it deserved a fair trial and toleration; in any case, whether they went through Federation or not, he believed there would be no limit to Irish nationality in twenty years.[46] However, once Duffy in *The Nation* had made his purist stand for principle regardless of political expediency, Davis could only back him up. A fortnight later in *The Nation* he himself was stressing that Ireland's aspiration was 'for UNBOUNDED NATIONALITY'.

O'Connell seems to have been genuinely surprised, and not without reason, at the sudden indignation of his young supporters. He quickly seized on the Federalists' failure to agree a detailed scheme as justification for reappearing as 'a simple Repealer' again, literally snapping his fingers in public at Federalism, as something that had let him down.[47] But though *The Nation* soon radiated a conciliatory tone, reassuring its readers that all was going well with Ireland and that cordiality and resolution were perfectly restored,[48] the situation was in two senses unalterably different after the incident. In the first place, the relationship between O'Connell, the experienced politician, and those literary idealists who were the intellectual élite of his movement, had taken an open turn for the worse. Secondly, a possible new tactic by which the Repeal movement might break through the post-Clontarf political deadlock had disintegrated. Though public enthusiasm for Repeal remained as great as ever, it was now again as difficult as ever to use that enthusiasm to effect.

In this frustrating situation the differences of temperament and outlook between O'Connell and Young Ireland grew more and more inescapable,

and were increasingly reflected within the transactions of the Repeal Association. Contempt for many of the sycophants and provincial time-servers
by whom the Liberator was surrounded, including his favourite son John;
embarrassment about the lack of sound accountancy with which the Repeal
Rent and other funds were administered; a dislike, though many Young
Irelanders were themselves Catholics, of a routine sectarian flag-waving
which even O'Connell was inclined to fall back on in the absence of other
emotive material; but above all youth's natural leanings towards uncompromising political puritanism in a power vacuum which O'Connell alone was
seriously committed to fill – all these things made Young Ireland more and
more impatient with the undoubted fact that O'Connell was the only conceivable leader who commanded the affections and loyalty of the Irish
people.

Reciprocally, O'Connell, shouldering all political responsibility in a
power situation which by the nature of the Union Parliament was heavily
loaded against him, and in any case inevitably feeling something of an older
man's natural resentment for the cocksureness and intransigence of youth,
found his particular style of pragmatic manoeuvre increasingly cramped by
Young Ireland's independent spirit, and longed to be able to contain it
within the confines of what today would be called party discipline. The
mutually irritant effect of the two parties on each other was only exacerbated
by mutual recognition of the fact that each needed the other badly. Without
O'Connell's power of leadership over the Irish people, Young Ireland knew
that they were only a minority middle-class group who commanded virtually
no following at all. Without the practical drive and energetic intelligence of
Young Ireland, and particularly its effective propagandizing influence
through the columns of *The Nation* newspaper, O'Connell knew that the
movement was in danger of acquiring a hack Catholic sectarian image
against which the Protestants of Ireland and even some of the Catholic
gentry would remain steadfastly united. When the break finally came the
worst fears of each party were to be realized, to the sole benefit of the Union
they had combined to repeal. Whether or not the internal stresses in any
case made the final break inevitable is uncertain. What they could not stand
was the additional dislocation of the political situation by the appalling
consequences of the potato disease which settled on Ireland in the autumn
of 1845.

10

More 'Monster Meetings'

In spite of increasing internal strains, the Repeal movement for the greater part of 1845, though not breaking new ground as in the sensational days of '43, was certainly not retreating. And for the first ten months of 1845 O'Connell continued to commit himself energetically and unequivocally to Repeal and the restoration of an Irish Parliament.[1]

The central problem remained: how to bring majority Irish opinion to make an impact on government. Hope of building and bargaining for English support for Repeal within the House of Commons had become, after Clontarf, the only solution that seemed realistic to O'Connell. But this inevitably seemed a very long-term affair, although O'Connell continued to draw analogies with both Emancipation and Reform to show that the House of Commons could change its mind very suddenly.

On the whole, feeling was consolidating among Repealers that they would have to wait for some sort of situation analogous to that of 1778–82. They must be ready for some external threat to Britain to arise which would enable them to show their strength while nominally organizing to help meet it.

In December 1844 *The Nation*, in supporting a public demand that had been made for Irish Volunteers, had written: '... it is our right by God's ordinance and the old constitution of both realms to link our citizens into an army, and therewith to smite all who invade our land or our liberties'.[2] The next week *The Nation* drew a parallel between Ireland, within the British connection, and Hungary, that 'loyal province of Austria', which not only had her national Parliament but her own army, voted by that Parliament and dressed in national Hungarian uniform.[3]

In January 1845 an '82 club was formed in Ireland with O'Connell as its president and the veteran Protestant Volunteer of 1782, Cornelius McLoughlin, as one of its vice-presidents. In emulation of the splendours of the old Volunteers the uniform, designed by Davis, was a green coat with a velvet collar, white lining and gilt buttons (inscribed 1782, in a wreath of shamrocks), green trousers with patent leather boots, white kid gloves and a black satin cravat.[4] In response to some criticism that this all seemed rather too military, Smith O'Brien, who hoped that the club might prove a sort of

alternative to the Council of Three Hundred until the legal difficulties surrounding that body could be overcome, declared: 'I am not sorry that the
government should feel that the dress we wear wants nothing but the sword
attached to it to constitute us officers of the Irish people.'[5] It was as an
officer class, too, that Davis seemed to envisage its membership, for he had
accepted that the uniform should cost a minimum of twelve guineas.[6] When
a banquet for 'the Repeal martyrs' was held at Kilkenny at the end of
March, attended by the Mayor and Corporation in their municipal robes
preceded by outriders dressed in orange and green, '82 club members
appeared in their uniform for the first time in public, and *The Nation* held
out high hopes of it for 'the people'.[7] While admitting that the uniform was
'yet to be decorated by achievements and honour', it continued: 'Incon-
siderate men may ask what it will accomplish – let them for that take the
words of the very practical men who have assumed it – time will show its
uses.'[8]

Within a month *The Nation* was hailing what it called 'Our First
Triumph':[9] Peel's decision to increase very substantially the annual grant
made by the British Government to the Roman Catholic priests' training
college at Maynooth.

In comparison with the sort of triumphs for Irish national pride on which
The Nation had set its sights, this may today hardly seem anything of great
significance. But within the context of the time it was an imaginative and
courageous step, and one which very considerably increased Peel's own
difficulties within the Conservative Party. Its remarkable welcome in Ireland
was a measure of the Repeal movement's frustration on the main count of
Repeal itself. *The Nation* exulted in one particular remark of Peel's in the
House of Commons to the effect that, when trouble came to a head with the
United States that month over the annexation of Texas and Oregon, he had
been able to recollect 'with satisfaction and consolation, that the day before
I had sent a message of peace to Ireland' – namely, the proposal for the increase in the Maynooth grant. Thus, claimed *The Nation*, Ireland's foreign
policy had been recognized and the Repeal Association had shown itself 'a
permanent nation within the Union'.[10] But the Repeal Association had
come into business for more substantial proofs of nationhood than the
Maynooth grant.

In fact, the Maynooth grant was part of a series of conciliatory measures
with which Peel hoped to weaken the Irish nationalist demand. Concessions
intended to placate Catholic feelings in Ireland were made in other fields
too, principally that of education, where Peel proposed to found and endow
three regional university colleges for Ireland which, unlike Trinity, Dublin,
should be equally open to Catholics and Protestants alike and wholly undenominational in character.

The effect of these conciliatory measures on some Irish ultra-Conservatives was paradoxical in the extreme. For, in their blind fury at any concessions to Catholics at all, they became ready to assert Irish independence themselves. And it is one of the strange ironies in which Irish history abounds that it was a right-wing Protestant newspaper which first proposed for Ireland in 1845 the underlying conception of that flag which is today the emblem of the Irish Republic. Arguing that the Protestants of the North might very well be able to get better terms out of the Repealers than the government themselves proposed, the *Dublin Evening Mail* on 2 August 1845 wrote that 'the Repeal banner might then be orange and green, flying from the Giant's Causeway to the Cove of Cork and proudly look down from the walls of Derry upon a newborn nation'. Nevertheless, the total effect of these measures was, in general, as Peel had intended, to consolidate rather than disrupt the Union. In the words of a modern Irish historian, 'they certainly made it easier for a Catholic to be a conservative and an anglophile and so facilitated the growth of a quiet but influential body, the Catholic 'Unionists'.[11] And to do that was to strike at the very heart of Repeal.

One of Peel's measures – the proposal to create three undenominational regional university colleges – was the immediate cause of the next public clash between O'Connell and the Young Irelanders, a further portent of disastrous quarrels to come. For some time temperamental differences between the two groups in the Association had been polarizing round the issue of Catholic sectarianism. Disputes usually took the form of indignant denials by each side of the attitude of which the other was accusing it. O'Connell continually, and plainly sincerely, reiterated his determination to have no Catholic ascendancy in an independent Ireland. 'I would rather die upon the scaffold,' he declared in April 1845, 'and I say it with all the solemnity of truth – than consent to a Catholic ascendancy in Ireland.'[12] And he was always quick to resent any Protestant criticism of what appeared to Young Ireland as Catholic sectarian tendencies. Yet it would have been unreasonable to expect O'Connell and his intimates, who derived the great bulk of their support from a people whose chief identifying feature was their Catholic religion, not to make that identity an occasional rallying cry.

Davis, on the other hand, a Protestant himself, whose nationalism was based wholly on the belief that religion was irrelevant where an Irishman's nationality was concerned, deplored any attempt to accentuate Catholic views as part of the movement. Once, in 1844, he had even written to Smith O'Brien threatening to withdraw altogether from politics because he thought exclusively Catholic interests were being pushed to excess.[13] And as he went out of his way to issue private and public warnings against Catholic bigotry in the movement, the chief O'Connellite newspaper, *The Pilot* (over which, however, O'Connell always insisted rather disingenuously that he had no control) responded in kind. It accused Young Ireland and *The Nation* of being not only anti-Catholic but even godless and irreligious.

In Peel's university colleges Davis and the other Young Irelanders welcomed at least a step in the right direction of extending educational facilities to Catholic Irishmen. But the Catholic hierarchy was uneasy about the idea of an education that was not specifically a Catholic education and decided to reject the proposal unless provisions were made to protect the faith and morals of Catholics. Quite apart from a natural pleasure at reemphasizing his identity with the Catholic Church – a far more indispensable ally to him than Young Ireland for all their value as an élite – O'Connell seems to have decided from the first to make an issue of the matter as a means of keeping Young Ireland in their place. To these colleges, in which Davis and the rest saw so much hope for the Ireland of the future, O'Connell applied the epithet 'godless'.[14] When on 26 May the question was publicly debated in the Repeal Association he went out of his way to provoke the Young Irelanders, and a remarkable incident took place.

The Young Irelander, M. J. Barry, a Protestant, applauded the likely educational effects of the proposal and declared himself 'utterly indifferent' to the fact that their character was undenominational. The next speaker, a young Catholic named Conway, assailed this statement with indignation, drawing somewhat florid attention to the traditional Christianity of Ireland and exclaiming ' "Utterly indifferent!" What a sentiment for a Catholic!' The Young Irelanders, he maintained, understood nothing of the Irish character or Irish heart.

At this O'Connell took off his cap, waved it repeatedly over his head, and cheered vociferously in approval.

Davis then rose to speak in reply, as he put it, to 'my old college friend, my Catholic friend, my very Catholic friend, Mr Conway'.[15]

O'Connell interrupted him:

'It is no crime to be a Catholic, I hope?'

'No,' said Davis, 'Surely no, for —'

'The sneer with which you used the word would lead to the inference.'

Davis quickly did his best to disavow the inference, declaring that some of his best friends were Catholics and making it clear that he thought that the proposals of the Catholic bishops (which included the appointment of Catholic chaplains to the colleges) would actually improve the bill. But O'Connell was determined to humiliate him. He emphasized that Young Ireland and *The Nation* had approved of the bill from the start, before the Catholic amendments were proposed, and launched into a broad attack on what he called 'the section of politicians styling themselves the Young Ireland party'.

'There is no such party as that styled "Young Ireland",' he continued. 'There may be a few individuals who take that denomination on themselves. I am for Old Ireland. 'Tis time that this delusion should be put an end to. Young Ireland may play what pranks they please. I do not envy them the name they rejoice in, I shall stand by Old Ireland. And I have some slight notion that Old Ireland will stand by me.'

There was general consternation. Then O'Connell rose to withdraw the nickname Young Ireland since he had been told by those sitting near him that they did not call themselves this. Davis also got to his feet and in avowal of the affection in which he held O'Connell burst suddenly into tears of emotion.[16]

O'Connell was equally overcome and the two men shook hands. 'The result,' declared *The Nation* in its next issue, 'was a better understanding and closer amity than ever', and it emphasized that differences were bound to occur from time to time in a confederacy such as theirs, but hoped that in future they would be confined to a committee and not aired in public.[17]

But *The Pilot* was less conciliatory, revealing the intense feeling that lay behind the incident and which any further political pressures were bound to exacerbate. The Young Irelanders, it wrote, were 'a party of young men, actuated by a morbid self-esteem, who have latterly been assuming an un-earned and fancied importance among us ... but their temerity has been checked, and their presumption chastised in a manner that will be, if they bear it in mind, of essential service to them'.[18]

Smith O'Brien, who had for some time now been getting confidential letters from the Young Irelanders expressing their exasperation with O'Connell, was not yet, in any way, their leader. His central position at this time is best ex-plained by an appeasing joke he made after the emotional scene over the 'Queen's Colleges'. He, he said, personally belonged to 'Middle-Aged Ireland'.[19]

After the row, the movement outwardly again proceeded on what seemed its continuing even course. Large open-air meetings reminiscent of 1843 were again held. One at Dundalk, in the North, on 1 May 1845, was described by *The Nation* as 'characterized by all the zeal and enthusiasm which the people manifested during the progress of the monster meetings of 1843. In truth it was a monster meeting in the full sense of the word.'[20] The paper added that it was even of a 'much more important character than any that occurred that year [1843]' because addresses were sent to it from some of the most remote and Orange districts of the North. After a procession through evergreens and triumphal arches which included 'every variety of vehicle from the dashing barouche to the humble car', O'Connell told the men of the North that he had come there to meet them half-way. Let the Protestants of the North, he proclaimed, join them, and the Union would not last a month. He hoped there were some of them listening to him.

A voice called out from the crowd:

'There are thousands of us.'

Above the chairman's seat at the ensuing banquet, which was rather a crush because the stewards had sold seven hundred tickets for six hundred places, hung a shield optimistically inscribed:

> If again the sword we draw,
> True men that none may sever,
> For Ireland's right and Ireland's law
> We'll cross the Boyne together.
> Each for the altar of his love
> But all for Ireland's glory.

But this claim to be uniting Protestant and Catholic, North and South, at last was to prove, as so often in Irish history, dream rather than reality.

'Repeal – No Compromise – Repeal' was another slogan on the walls of this banqueting hall at Dundalk, and O'Connell at the beginning of his speech drew attention to it, saying, 'I repeat again: Repeal, no compromise, and nothing but Repeal.' There was loud and long continued cheering and O'Connell then added: 'All that I say, all that could be written is comprehended in that short sentence.' He returned to the theme again later when he insisted: 'We are disciples of a political faith which we will never for one moment abandon.'[21]

Week after week now O'Connell repeated this same refrain – a fortnight later at Navan, where 200,000 people had come to hear him, some 50,000 of them assembling first on the Hill of Tara; and in the Association itself when Smith O'Brien, asking rhetorically whether they would ever abandon Repeal, however many other concessions might be made to Ireland, was answered by O'Connell with great emphasis:

'Never.'[22]

At a great meeting in Dublin on the anniversary of his release from prison on 30 May, O'Connell declared:

'They are now offering us a price for not agitating. They say that if we don't agitate they will give us something good. ... Let them make the experiment. I give them the fullest opportunity to do so; and when they are done with experiments, I will have one answer to the entire lot – THE REPEAL OF THE UNION.'[23] And a pledge was taken by all participants to continue the campaign for Repeal until final victory.

A few days later, in describing to the Association the pleasure he had felt at this anniversary meeting, he let loose the full flood of his oratory to convey his emotional commitment to the cause.

'I never,' he said, 'felt such ineffable delight as I felt on Friday last. I never before so completely perceived that the Repeal of the Union is inevitable – that its progress is irresistible.... Yes, from north to south – from east to west the voice for Repeal is spread abroad – it is borne on the wild winds of heaven – it careers throughout our sea-girt land – it is heard

in the resounding of the waves, and all nature seems to cry out with me
Repeal! Repeal!'[24]

Although O'Connell in a difficult political situation could be as full of
tricks as any good politician, he was fundamentally an honest man. It is
inconceivable that he can have so constantly repeated the refrain of
No Compromise all over Ireland throughout the greater part of 1845 if he
had not then meant what he was saying. The political situation was then
neither more nor less difficult than it had been since Clontarf, and according to *The Nation* the Repeal movement had made more progress in self-
organization since O'Connell's release from prison than in the whole of the
monster meetings year of 1843.[25]

The situation was made even more promising by the prospect of a change
of ministry in England. When O'Connell said in one of these speeches that
no candidate for Parliament should get endorsement from him or the votes
of Repealers unless he became a member of the Repeal Association, and actually named his friend Sheil, Liberal member for Dungarvan, as a man
whose personal friendship with O'Connell would not win him exception from
the rule, there seems no reason to doubt that he then meant what he said.

Although over seventy, he continued the series of vast open-air meetings
with which he had begun the summer. At Cork on 10 June he addressed a
crowd estimated at half a million. Tar barrels, sugar hogsheads and other
improvised torches blazed through the night.[26] On 12 June he addressed five
open-air meetings in the county in one day.[27]

'I am told I will not carry Repeal,' he declared on Sidney Hill outside Cork.
'Did I not carry Emancipation against the most cunning minister England ever
had, Sir Robert Peel, and against the greatest General she ever had, the Duke of
Wellington [loud cheers] ... Repealers, then, stand together in union, in firmness,
in continuation, in undoubted allegiance to our gracious Sovereign – God bless
her – in firm attachment to the value of the connection with Great Britain, but
with a more inviolable determination to have our parliament in College Green
[loud cheers]. ... Who without feeling the glow of patriotism within him, could
stand on the spot I now occupy and view that superb scene before him – that
beautiful landscape now before my eye – the placid waters of the Lee rolling
among the green fields and cultivated demesnes, and the distant mountains rising in
fertility, grandeur and beauty? Ireland! Land of my fathers – Ireland! birth-
place of my children – Ireland! that shall hold my grave – Ireland! that I love
with the fondest aspirations, your men are too brave, your women are too beautiful and good – you are too elevated among the nations of the earth, too moral, too
religious to be slaves. I promise you that you shall be free!

His words were, as usual, followed by loud and continuous cheering.[28]

Although the Young Irelanders had a certain sophisticated disdain for
O'Connell's demagogy, they seem often to have been carried away on his
moods of general optimism that summer. A leader in *The Nation* in July

headed 'Growth of an Irish Nation' began: '... In our days Ireland under-goes a marvellous change.'[29]

In the middle of this month there was another monster meeting, this time at Wexford, where some quarter of a million people listened to O'Connell in a field. One of the flags in the procession was green with orange binding and inscribed with the slogan 'Tenant Right and No Mistake'.[30] On 27 July O'Connell was in the West, where his reception 'exceeded anything of the kind ever before attempted in the province of Connaught'.[31] He had been given an enthusiastic reception along the entire line of the route from Dublin to Galway, and was greeted on the platform with the strains of 'See the Conquering Hero Comes'. He promised the crowd of a quarter of a million Repeal for 1846.

Retiring to his Kerry home at Darrynane for a well-earned summer holi-day, O'Connell wrote to the Repeal Association telling them how impressed he had been by the demonstrations in Wexford and Galway, and, on the analogy of Emancipation and the Clare election, declared that sixty members of the Repeal Association returned to the House of Commons would 'demon-strate irresistibly to the present government the still greater necessity of repealing the Union'.[32] The voting registry must be carefully attended to, and proper candidates for Parliament elected.

The Nation backed up this call by O'Connell for Repealers to get their names on the registry. Smith O'Brien wrote to the paper agreeing that the most important thing that could possibly be done for the cause was to get a large majority of Irish members returned as Repealers to Westminster. Then on 16 September 1845, the movement was dealt an unexpected blow.

On the 9th Duffy had received a note from Davis, who was at home, to say that he had had an attack of some sort of cholera and perhaps had slight scarlatina.[33] There was no cause for alarm, but he could not be relied on to write for the paper for a while. Two days later Duffy received another note to say that Davis hoped to be able to do some light business in four days. In reply Duffy passed on a bantering message from a friend to the effect that Davis now had the opportunity of rivalling Mirabeau by dying, but begging him not to 'be tempted by the inviting opportunity'. Four days later Davis was dead. He was not quite thirty-one.

It is impossible to say whether or not future history would have been different if he had lived, though his death was the sort of event which auto-matically raises such a question. Certainly, in him, the movement lost the most imaginative and generous mind among the Young Irelanders at a time when imagination and generosity of mind were to be badly needed. Yet it seems unlikely that the presence of Davis could have altered the subsequent course of political events. For a disaster far greater than that of Davis's death and with far more inexorable consequences for the Repeal movement was about to break over Ireland.

O'Connell, still on holiday at Darrynane, wrote in a moving letter to a friend that his mind was so bewildered and his heart so afflicted by the news of Davis's death that he didn't know what to say.[34] He paid an honourable tribute to his qualities, declaring that his death was an irreparable loss and that there was no one who could be so useful to Ireland in the present stage of her struggles.

As yet no indication had reached him of the desperate phase of Ireland's troubles that lay immediately ahead. A few days earlier he had actually written from Darrynane in another letter: 'The poor man's harvest in particular is this year excellent ...' His only complaint was that in the hot weather the scent would not lie for his beagles, even though he had been getting up at six in the morning while the dew was still on the ground.[35] He concluded with the cry: 'Register! Register! Register!', for in a consolidation of the Repeal vote at the polls he still had high hopes of winning the Irish independence for which he stood.

The Nation was in equally optimistic mood, despite its natural sense of shock at the news of Davis's death. The leading article which preceded the obituary of Davis was entitled 'Our Future Prospects' and declared: 'The autumn is waning sunnily and cheerfully. It is a busy and hopeful time ...'[36]

Some days later, O'Connell went to address a new monster meeting in Tipperary. According to *The Nation* 'the Liberator was never in more robust health or better spirits'.[37] His progress from Limerick to Cashel was a triumph and he was met outside the town itself by the Young Irelander, Michael Doheny, with whom he was to stay. A Repeal Band dressed in green uniforms with gold lace also awaited him together with thousands of people carrying green boughs whose acclamations were taken up as he entered the city by well-dressed ladies crowding the windows of the houses. An address from the Cashel Juvenile Reading Class proclaimed:

'Welcome, welcome, not to Cashel, not to Tipperary, for these we own not and cannot give, but welcome, ten thousand times welcome to our green hearts.'[38]

The procession, accompanied by bands and groups representing various trades, proceeded to Thurles. In the countryside the ditches were full of cheering people and the fields were darkened by the crowds crossing them to catch a glimpse of their Liberator.[39] A meeting of some 100,000 people, it was estimated, assembled half-way at the fair green in Holycross and the procession was two miles long as it finally passed through a triumphal arch into Thurles where the streets were packed to suffocation. At another vast open-air meeting held just outside the town O'Connell summed up in a few sentences what this massed display of public opinion stood for:

'Let England give us liberty and I will stand by her to the death.... Ireland for the Irish is my motto.... Repeal! Repeal! ...' He had carried Emancipation, he said, against Peel and Wellington, but this had been partly in the interests of the gentry ... 'what I am now working for, what I ask for now, will be for the benefit of the working man'.[40]

At a banquet in honour of O'Connell, attended by about a thousand people that evening, Michael Doheny asked in his speech: 'Who that saw or will read of the multitude today and hears of physical force that will not smile? There is no power from Hindustan to the Pole that could crush that great multitude.'[41]

The Repeal Rent for the week was, at £600, nearly three times the figure it had been running at for some time. But a letter, tucked away in the issue of *The Nation* that announced this heartening fact, drew attention to an event soon to loom larger in Irish minds that all enthusiasm for Repeal: 'the lamentable and nearly universal rot in the potato'.[42]

Oblivious of the significance of such news, the series of monster meetings continued. In the first week of October they were extended to Kerry, O'Connell's own home county which so far, oddly, had shown little enthusiasm for the idea of nationality. Now, as *The Nation* put it, it was 'as if touched with an enchanter's wand'.[43] But here, too, reality broke in awkwardly for a moment. O'Connell rhapsodizing about Kerry and Repeal in the open air, was interrupted unusually by a voice in Irish crying: 'Our houses are tumbled about us every day.'[44]

Still, the significance of what was happening was not apparent. *The Nation* could see 'victory wooing the people of Ireland and not from afar', and O'Connell wheeling his triumphant progress up the West of Ireland through County Sligo to County Mayo spoke of 'the near and approaching prospect of success'.[45] At a banquet for five hundred attended by MacHale, the Archbishop of Tuam, O'Connell's mind was wholly concentrated on the issue of Repeal. He put the constitutional part of his case in a nutshell, when he said:

'I tremble for the connection unless we place it on such a footing that it will be the interest of both countries to maintain it, and never violate it ... on a footing that is limited to the wants and wishes, to the virtues of the Irish people. If we don't succeed in placing the connection on such a footing I defy any rational man to assert that ten years after my death the countries will be connected at all.'[46] He had, he thought, sufficient influence to promise that nothing would happen in his lifetime, but he could not promise beyond that.[47]

John MacHale, the Archbishop of Tuam, also made a strong speech asking for legislative independence for the Irish people 'to secure Her Majesty's throne in peace, prosperity and freedom of religion'. And though the exact details of the future connection had not been worked out any more clearly than in the year before, its indispensability was still wholly taken for granted by all Irish Nationalists in 1845. That autumn Smith O'Brien, drawing attention to the number of friends he had in England, again said he had no wish to see the great British Empire of which Irishmen formed so glorious a part broken up.[48]

Meanwhile, 'the State of the Crops,' wrote the *Farmer's Journal*, 'is still the subject of much anxiety. . . . Regarding the potato failures we still continue to receive the most melancholy accounts.'[49]

The last of the 1845 monster meetings took place on 23 October at Rathkeale in County Limerick. A hundred thousand people were said to be present, and the procession, which started from Smith O'Brien's house at Cahermoyle, where O'Connell had been staying, stretched for three miles.[50] Prominent banners in the procession, inscribed 'Repeal and No Surrender' and 'No Compromise', reflected the impending political change in England, where it was becoming clear that Peel's ministry, increasingly at odds with a section of its own Conservative Party, could not last much longer. Repealers were about to be wooed for political support by Whigs under Lord John Russell.

But the potato disease was at last attracting attention. Dublin Corporation appointed a special committee of inquiry, and a priest from Kells reported of his parish his 'inexpressibly painful conviction that one family in twenty would not have a potato left on Christmas Day'.[51] The situation was soon to be much worse than that, though conservative newspapers were at first quick to insist that it was not nearly so bad as 'alarmists' made out and that there was a great deal of exaggeration. *The Nation* summed things up more accurately:

'It may now be stated,' it declared on 25 October 1845, 'that fully one half of the crop on which millions of our countrymen are half-starved every year is, this season, totally destroyed or in progress to destruction.'[52]

The inexorable approach of these two events – what Smith O'Brien called 'the awful calamity . . . impending'[53] and the fall of Peel's Tory ministry – now dominated O'Connell's mind.

In normal times a political situation in which the Whigs needed Irish support would have been ripe for exploitation in the Repeal interest by a man of O'Connell's skill and experience. But now his room for wider political manoeuvre was almost totally restricted by the famine, which made Ireland desperate for any sort of help at all.

He himself had been one of the first publicly to appreciate the enormity of the crisis and his mind was soon largely concentrated on the business of getting the, then still Tory, Government to carry out any government's most elementary duty, and prevent its citizens from dying of starvation. In the circumstances Repeal inevitably became a second priority.

For the famine, it was already clear, was going to be the most terrible of all the terrible disasters in Irish history.

11

Repeal, Famine
and Young Ireland

In December 1845, when it was thought (prematurely as things turned out) that Lord John Russell and the Whigs were about to take over from Peel, O'Connell had explained to the Repeal Association something of the political dilemma which faced him, and his proposed attitude towards it. After announcing as a dramatic gesture that he was doubling his subscription to the Association, he came to the business of the day:

'Hurra for the Repeal,' he began orthodoxly, being received with orthodox cheers. 'No compromise – no surrender – no postponement ... let parties shift and scenes vary – let their view of politics be changed by others – we are firm and immovable [cheers], the high heart of Ireland beats for Ireland ... come weal, come woe, we will struggle for the Repeal.'[1]

He then quoted a letter he had received from Smith O'Brien, in which O'Brien pledged him his support and declared that if the incoming Whig ministry were to succeed in winning the Irish people from Repeal in the course of a mere struggle for party ascendancy, 'indescribable would be the scorn with which the people of Ireland would be named'.[2] After reading this O'Connell repeated three times the slogan 'Repeal and No Compromise!'.

He then went on to explain the nature of his present difficulty: 'While we seek Repeal without compromise and without postponement, it is our business, our sacred duty to look into the present awful state of the Irish people, and to see what is to be done for their relief ... while I desire Ireland's liberty, I desire also the preservation of her people.'[3]

He asked the prospective ministry to give them food and to come forward with finance for public undertakings, such as the immediate construction of railways in Ireland. He had, he said, hopes of such things from Lord John Russell, though not from the Duke of Wellington.

'And when,' he went on, 'I promise conditional support to Lord John Russell, it may be asked if I purpose to compromise Repeal?'

There were loud cries of 'No! No!' and O'Connell responded:

'I thank you for that "No", but I had the very same in my own mouth.

[Cheers and laughter.] There shall be no compromise. But I tell Lord John Russell I will act fairly by him.'

He then named two things he wanted for the Irish peasant, which, in the light of the immediate situation, were even more relevant than cash for the purchase of food to be earned through public works. First, he wanted the law of property amended so that it would become illegal to evict a tenant without giving him compensation for the improvements he had wrought on the land. And in the course of making this proposal he enunciated a theory of property which, to landlords at least, then seemed revolutionary. The land, he said, was by right the property of the landlord; but the labour which went into the land was equally by right the property of the tenant, 'and his claim to that right came from a higher source than the landlord's title to his estate. If the landlord wanted his land given up, he must pay the tenant in cash the full and fair value of the tenant's expenditure.'[5]

This doctrine was to remain a fundamental part of Irish nationalist thinking on the land question for the rest of the century, though O'Connell himself is seldom given credit for subscribing to it.

O'Connell also wanted the law amended to prevent any evictions taking place at all except where the tenant held by twenty-one year lease.

Thus, as the first evictions of hungry people unable to pay rent began on a serious scale, O'Connell rightly named as the most necessary immediate terms for Ireland two of those 'three Fs', – Free Sale and Fixity of Tenure – which were not finally to be conceded by a British Government until another land crisis nearly thirty years later.* In pressing at the same time also for a supply of cash to be earned by public works, O'Connell was putting forward an altogether coherent plan for dealing with the famine. Everyone knew that Ireland was short only of the potato and otherwise full of food in the form of oats, wheat, butter, eggs, sheep and pigs, all of which continued to be exported to England on a considerable scale throughout the famine.[5] And all these measures were what O'Connell hoped for immediately from the new ministry in return for his parliamentary support.

'I will get all I can for Ireland,' he declared, 'and when I can I will take the rest.'[6]

Finally, so that there should be absolutely no doubt about where he stood on the constitutional issue, he restated his basic position:

'I believe you understand me distinctly. I am totally against any compromise and postponement, or any surrender of the Repeal Cause. Repeal is the great object of my existence – it is the first and last thought of my heart – it is the entire text of my life and if there are marginal notes upon it they

---

* The third 'F' was to be 'Fair Rent', a truly revolutionary principle, implying the government's right to tell a landlord what rent he could charge for his own property, and conceded by Gladstone's Land Act of 1881. See pp. 378–9 following.

are mere appendages to the great cause of Repeal. Repeal is all we desire and with the blessing of Providence we shall obtain that Repeal."

There were loud cheers as he sat down.

The Nation's own position was, at this stage, not so far apart from O'Connell's. A leading article in the paper on 20 December 1845 stated that a Whig ministry, resting its right wing on the anti-Corn Law League and its left on the Repealers in Ireland, making Repeal itself an open question and giving the lord lieutenancy and chief secretaryship to Irishmen, and office to Repealers as Repealers, would unquestionably command *The Nation*'s allegiance.

'We would be bound to sustain them by every sacrifice and every labour that a people can offer to their country,' *The Nation* added.

But new divisions were about to appear between O'Connell and the Young Irelanders of *The Nation* at this critical time. Since the death of Davis, Duffy had brought on to *The Nation* a handsome and iconoclastic young Protestant solicitor from County Down called John Mitchel. His father, a Unitarian minister, had been 'out in '98'. Mitchel himself was now imparting a fresh, strident and aggressive note to the paper, and in November 1845 had suddenly caused O'Connell considerable alarm.

A government newspaper had just published an article urging that the agitation for Repeal should itself be made high treason. The paper congratulated itself on the fact that the new system of railways then being built in Ireland would make it easy to put down such treason by bringing troops from Dublin to any point in Ireland within six hours. The article itself must have been unpleasant enough for O'Connell, containing as it did insulting references to him and other 'convicted conspirators'.[8] But Mitchel's reply in *The Nation* upset him still further.

'As the Dutch dealt with the French by laying land under water,' wrote Mitchel, 'ruining their fertile plains of waving corn – so Ireland's railways, though most valuable to her, were better dispensed with for a time than allowed to become a means of transport for invading armies. Every railway within five miles of Dublin could in one night be totally cut off from the interior of the country. To lift a rail, fill a perch or two of any cutting or tunnel, to break down a piece of embankment seems obvious and easy enough.'[9] He added that it should hardly be necessary to point out the uses to which railway material such as good hammered iron and wooden sleepers might be put. As if this evocation of the now traditional Irish rhetorical symbol of the pike were not enough to dismay O'Connell, Mitchel recommended that Repeal Wardens should be familiarized with the best ways of 'dealing with railways in case of any enemy daring to make a hostile use of them'.[10]

O'Connell at once went round to *The Nation* office to protest against linking the Repeal Association with such militant policy in this way. He demanded that Duffy should in the next issue of the paper make clear that neither *The Nation* nor its editor had any official connection with the Association[11] – which was true, for the separation of identity had been made for tactical purposes after *The Nation* had been cited in the general indictment of the year before. In the next issue Duffy obligingly pointed out the lack of connection between *The Nation* and the Repeal Association. But O'Connell observed in the Association that, though he bore no ill feeling towards the paper, 'he had admired its talents more in the time of the illustrious dead' – meaning, of course, Davis.[12]

Smith O'Brien's political position within the Repeal movement still remained somewhere between Young Ireland and O'Connell. He agreed within the Association that subjects like Mitchel's railways article should not be pressed into discussion, since they might 'endanger the safety of the Association'.[13] Temperamentally, however, he was closer to Young Ireland, if for no other reason than that he, like them, was less a practical politician than a man for whom politics meant primarily the pursuit of high principles often in somewhat rhetorical attitudes. He had already been emphasizing strongly his own mistrust of any prospective deal with a Whig government. In January 1846 he declared that 'complete neutrality' between the contending British political parties should be observed; and concluded this speech with the words '. . . we shall prove ourselves steadfast to the cause for which we are ready if necessary to lay down our lives'.[14]

'I trust,' he said in the Repeal Association the following month, '. . . that the time is not far distant when men of all parties in this country will see that it is in vain to place any trust save in ourselves – ourselves alone is the motto I would wish the Irish people to assume . . .'[15]

But such ambitious thoughts were becoming increasingly irrelevant to the immediate condition of the Irish people. From almost every county in Ireland more and more alarming reports were coming in as the earthed-up potatoes were uncovered and found to be masses of loathsome rottenness. Agrarian outrages in the old Whiteboy tradition, which had long been diminishing in proportion with the success of the Repeal movement, became commoner again as Repeal itself now seemed of less immediate urgency. As the two million-odd of the rural population who lived even in normal times on the verge of starvation,* now faced the reality of total famine, they began to take such desperate action against landlords and their agents as their strength still allowed. The peasantry's enthusiasm for Repeal and *The Nation*'s ennobling principles of nationality had been rooted in the hope that conditions on the land would thereby be changed for the better. O'Connell had always acknowledged this with his prominent insistence on tenant right. Now, as the people began to struggle with the basic problem of physical survival, thoughts of nationality became middle-class luxuries. The Repeal Rent which had been running at a fairly steady level of between

* The figure of 2,300,000 was given by the Poor Law Commissioners of 1835.[16]

£300 to £400 a week for eighteen months began a slow and fairly steady decline from which, under the full impact of the famine, it never recovered.

Young Ireland meanwhile tended to consolidate its position of detachment, meeting as a group from time to time in the gold and green uniforms of the '82 club, often with Smith O'Brien in the chair while O'Connell, the titular president, was away in London. Gavan Duffy, John Mitchel, M. J. Barry and Michael Doheny were joined by other bright young men, mainly Catholics, often dandified in their dress and speech [17] and drawn with the others from the middle classes but making up for their lack of contact with the Irish people by the zeal with which they held the principles of nationality in trust for them. Prominent among the newcomers were Thomas Meagher (pronounced Maher), son of a Mayor of Waterford, and Richard O'Gorman, son of another prosperous merchant. Speaking with an English accent derived from his education at Stonyhurst in England,[18] Meagher made a strong 'No Compromise' speech in the Association in February 1846;[19] and Richard O'Gorman in the same month made oblique references to 'others choosing the sword' but himself at present preferring 'the might of mind' as they were not yet driven to 'the last resource'.[20] But the signs of a vast social catastrophe were now unmistakable. The Duke of Cambridge as late as January 1846 subscribed to the view that talk of famine was greatly exaggerated, adding 'they all knew Irishmen could live upon anything, and there was plenty of grass in the fields, even though the potato crop should fail'.[21] But the following month O'Connell was telling the House of Commons that hope had now quite vanished.[22] He also emphasized strikingly the very special character of this freak famine, which was in one sense no famine at all. More wheat, barley and wheat meal flour, he pointed out, had in fact been imported into Great Britain from Ireland in 1845 than in any other of the three previous years, and between 10 October 1845 and 5 January 1846 over 30,000 oxen, bulls and cows, over 30,000 sheep and lambs, and over 100,000 pigs had sailed from Ireland to English ports.[23]

Impotence before the overwhelming catastrophe sharpened people's sense of political frustration. Attitudes became more desperate; quarrels developed more quickly. *The Nation* began nagging at the Repeal Association more openly for not publishing its accounts. *The Pilot*, the specifically O'Connellite paper, replied that *The Nation* was trying to subvert Christianity. John Mitchel expressed a growing restlessness within the Association in words which indicated still further the direction in which his thoughts were heading. He had, he said, been a member of the Association for three years and would continue to remain so until the policy it had been originated to try had been fully tried, and until he saw 'whether the peaceful and moral organization could effect the good it was intended to effect for Ireland'.[24]

In April 1846 Smith O'Brien wrote from London to the Repeal Association, declaring that the proceedings of Parliament convinced him daily more and more that the affairs of Ireland could only be dealt with properly in an Irish legislature.[25] And a leading article in *The Nation* that week, commenting on the situation in Poland, declared meaningfully: 'Better a little blood-letting to show that there is blood, than a patient dragging of chains and pining beneath them slowly for generations leading to the belief that all spirit is fled.'[26]

A display of militancy on the part of Smith O'Brien provoked a further scene of public dissension between O'Connell and Young Ireland, and as a result of it O'Brien began to gravitate from his central position in Repeal politics towards Young Ireland.

As long ago as 1844 Davis had proposed that one tactic for the Repealers might be for their Members of Parliament to refuse to sit at Westminster but meet instead as a body in Ireland. The proportion of Ireland's total number of representatives who were Repealers was small, and a more suitable method of convening a specifically Irish representative body seemed to lie in the idea of a Council of Three Hundred. There was also a constitutional difficulty in the proposal for non-attendance. Repeal Members of Parliament had already attended the House of Commons and taken the oath.* There was some legal doubt as to whether non-attending Repealers summoned, for instance, to attend Committees of the House of Commons might not be committing an offence in refusing to respond to the Speaker's writ. However, O'Connell himself had decided in the middle of 1845, before the famine, that such action would be perfectly legal and certainly there was no greater stickler for legality in the Association than he. It had therefore been agreed as policy that when a summons for any committees on which they were serving should arrive for either John O'Connell or Smith O'Brien, they should reject the summons and announce their intention of attending to the needs of their constituents in Ireland instead. In June 1845 such summonses duly arrived and were duly rejected by both John O'Connell and O'Brien. But the session ended before the House of Commons had decided what appropriate action to take.

By the next session of Parliament the situation had been transformed by the famine. In April 1846, when O'Brien decided on his own account to renew the gesture of defiance and refuse to serve on the railways committee to which he was summoned, O'Connell was already in London, accompanied by his son John, devoting himself to measures of famine relief and engaged in fighting, together with the Whigs, the Coercion Bill introduced by Peel's government to deal with the recent rapid increase in agrarian violence.† John

---

* The Sinn Feiners of the twentieth century elected to Westminster never went there at all.

† Between 1 January and 16 May 1846 there had been eighty cases of murder in Ireland, in only seven of which convictions had been obtained (*The Nation*, 20 June 1846). It was to deal with such a state of affairs that the government proposed a suspension of the normal rights and processes of law in the new Coercion Bill.

O'Connell was actually already attending the railways committee. It is testimony as much to poor coordination of Repeal tactics as to O'Brien's undoubtedly high sense of principle and integrity that he nevertheless decided to defy the Speaker alone by refusing to attend the committee. He was rewarded with a month's imprisonment in a cellar beneath the clock tower of Westminster, the first Member of Parliament to be imprisoned by the House of Commons for two hundred years. His sense of betrayal and disillusion was naturally increased when he heard that O'Connell had taken steps to see that the Association should not too strongly associate itself with his gesture for fear of compromising its legality. O'Brien even drafted from his prison a bitter letter of resignation to his constituents in Limerick.

Both in *The Nation* and in the meetings of the Association itself, the Young Irelanders supported O'Brien valiantly. *The Nation*'s leading articles still appeared under the two-year-old banner heading 'REMEMBER THE 30TH MAY' (the date of O'Connell's own imprisonment), but one such article on 16 May appeared under the further heading: 'The Man in Jail for Ireland', and meant O'Brien. It described him as 'an Irishman intensely Irish' and not one of the 'pretended Irishmen – luke-warm, milk-and-water ... small-beer lovers of their country', to whom it applied the derogatory term 'West Britons'.[27] The Young Irelanders not only spoke up for O'Brien in the Association, where Michael Doheny described him as a man who 'dared to stand forth as the Defender of Ireland's rights',[28] but also summoned the '82 club, in which they outnumbered O'Connellites by two to one, and passed a resolution in O'Brien's support. A deputation of the '82 club, including Mitchel, O'Gorman, Doheny, Meagher and a new recruit T. B. McManus, then went to Westminster where, in their gold and green uniforms, they conveyed the club's respect and admiration to O'Brien in his cellar in the House of Commons, and persuaded him not to send the letter of resignation to his constituents after all.

On Smith O'Brien's discharge from imprisonment at the end of May, O'Connell immediately wrote him a handsome tribute in the form of a letter to the Association. It was impossible, he said, to estimate too highly O'Brien's services in the sacred cause of Irish nationality, adding: 'I am convinced that if necessary he would sacrifice his life to preserve union and harmony amongst the supporters of the cause ...'[39] Reciprocally, the Young Irelanders, M. J. Barry and Michael Doheny, then strongly expressed their gratitude to O'Connell, but with a gentle and firm reminder that they could not be expected to betray themselves or the memory of Thomas Davis. Michael Doheny concluded:

'Let me sincerely hope from this day forth we will be agreed in all things ... and that steps will be taken, under the guidance of the Liberator of Ireland [cheers] – to do honour to the martyr of the House of Commons and receive him upon the shores of this kingdom as the descendant of one of her Kings ought to be received.'[30]

When O'Brien 'the martyr' himself appeared at a great demonstration in his honour in Limerick, he too made a point of emphasizing ties with O'Connell, in spite of what had passed. At the same time he, too, affirmed nationalistic principles which in his case seemed to have hardened perceptibly in the course of his imprisonment. Arriving in a triumphal chariot in a field outside Limerick, through which the Shannon flowed, to address tens of thousands of people assembled from all over the West of Ireland, he declaimed that he could not contemplate 'that noble river without remembering that the flag of our country – the green flag, bearing the harp of our native land – cannot be hoisted lest it be pulled down with ignominy and disgrace'.[31]

'The mighty multitude,' which, according to *The Nation*, had marched to the field 'with waving flags and martial music through the country of the Wild Geese, proclaiming their hatred of British misrule', let out a great roar. 'For a hundred and fifty years,' wrote *The Nation*, 'the grey Shannon has not heard such a chorus of triumph.'

And though the evening banquet for two thousand guests was a decorous affair, with portraits of the queen and Prince Albert above the chair and attended largely by the middle classes, O'Brien was greeted there too with ten minutes of such thunderous applause that it 'actually pained the ear'.[32] After suitable expressions of gratitude, he declared that the occasion marked the most important day of his life and the opening of an era in the history of Ireland.

'I have appealed,' he said, rightly emphasizing the significant aspect of his imprisonment, 'from the British House of Commons to the Irish Nation.'[33]

In his speech that evening O'Brien hailed O'Connell as 'the undoubted leader of the Irish people' and said that although there were 'stories of a disposition to overthrow his leadership ... as long as O'Connell lives he shall have the guidance of the Irish nation'. But he also made a point of stressing the danger of trying to barter advantages for the country in return for a compromise on Repeal.[34]

Neither side in fact wanted a breach with the other, yet as the return to power of a Whig ministry became more and more certain, so a breach became inevitable. It was O'Connell's unalterable intention to work with the Whigs. Indeed, he replied to O'Brien's compliment from Limerick with the slightly testy remark that while Smith O'Brien had been very properly receiving a tribute of gratitude from his constituents, he himself had been in London busy trying to defeat the Tory Coercion Bill and could have done with his support.[35] But Thomas Meagher, who had hailed O'Connell's successful obstruction of the Coercion Bill in alliance with the Whig opposition generously enough, spoke for Young Ireland when he made clear in the Association that he regarded any sort of alliance with a Whig *ministry* as fatal.[36] Young Ireland was as determined to insist that alliance with the Whigs meant betrayal of Repeal as O'Connell was adamant that it meant no more than a temporary but necessary shifting of political priorities.

In June 1846 wordy public disputes between the two halves of the movement became frequent in the Association's meetings. These often took place in O'Connell's absence, and certainly his henchmen, Tom Steele and others, were by no means as sophisticated and flexible in debate as he himself could be, but the eventual parting of the ways began to look more and more inevitable. Speaking of a Whig alliance – and incidentally reminding his audience that Lord John Russell had actually voted for the first reading of the Coercion Bill – Meagher told the Association:

It is not for this that ... you looked back to the Church of Dungannon, and embraced the principles, though you could not unsheath the sword of the patriot soldiers of '82; that you gathered in thousands upon the Hill of Tara, and hailed your leader upon the Rath of Mullaghmast. ... There you swore that Ireland should be called a free nation.'[37]

The implication was clear: a Whig alliance meant that Ireland would never be a free nation. In O'Connell's absence Steele replied indignantly. He took particular exception to a reference by Meagher to Davis as 'our prophet and our guide', and himself insisted that the people of Ireland had never had as prophet and guide any other than O'Connell, 'the crownless, sceptreless monarch of the hearts of the people – the lay pontiff of his religion, Catholicity.'[38]

The following week O'Connell wrote to the Association of 'the bitterest regret and deepest sorrow' with which he had witnessed 'the efforts which are made by some of our juvenile members to create dissension and circulate distractions amongst the Repealers'. He emphasized yet again that he had 'nailed the colours of Repeal to the mast and would not be taking them down until there was an Irish Parliament again on College Green'.[39] He reminded the Association of the pledges he had already taken to this effect and recommended that they be framed and glazed and hung on the walls of Conciliation Hall. 'This,' he added, 'may take away some claptraps from juvenile orators.'[40]

At the meeting at which this letter was read one of O'Connell's supporters again reiterated the substance of the Liberator's case, namely that it was quite possible to be a good Repealer and yet take what advantages you could get from the Whigs. But the Young Irelanders were angered by O'Connell's letter. M. J. Barry now raised the possibility that they might soon no longer be able to remain with the Association.[41] Meagher denied that they had suspicions of the integrity of their leader – a disingenuous statement, to say the least, for if they did not suspect O'Connell's integrity, it was difficult to see what the fuss was about. At the same time Meagher was intransigent. 'As we have united,' he continued of the Young Irelanders, 'thus shall we continue to act. You may exclude us from this Hall, but you will not separate us from the country.'[42]

It is unlikely that O'Connell actually wanted to exclude the Young Irelanders from the Repeal Association, though, being an emotional and sometimes impatient man, he must have known many moments when he longed to be rid of them. But when the Whig ministry finally did come into office in July 1846 it was imperative for him to have control of this brilliant but erratic element in his own party. The issue on which he decided to assert discipline was one he had chosen carefully. On 13 July 1846 two acrimonious debates took place in the Association. The first concerned the selection by O'Connell of his friend Sheil as parliamentary candidate for Dungavan in spite of the fact that Sheil had still not come out for Repeal and in spite of the fact that O'Connell had, before the famine, said that Sheil would not be selected unless he did. On this point O'Connell now successfully carried the Association with him. The second debate concerned the hypothetical issue of physical force and took the form of a discussion of a special committee's report. This contained declarations to the effect that the Association should call the country's attention to its policy of 'seeking amelioration of political institutions by peaceable and legal means *alone*, disclaiming all attempts to improve and augment constitutional liberty by means of force, violence and bloodshed'.[43]

Now this report really only stressed what had long been known to be the Association's attitude. The implication, that under no circumstances whatever was force justifiable, was not very strong; and the resolution elsewhere explicitly allowed the use of self-defence against unjust aggression. Indeed, Mitchel, who was the first of the Young Irelanders to discuss the report, began mildly enough. Though he and Meagher had been on the committee and had there voted against the resolutions, he accepted that they had been sanctioned by a majority of the committee and declared that it would not therefore be right to contest them in the hall, nor, he added, was there any necessity or disposition to do so. However, he could not resist just adding that he personally did not accept the abstract principle stated, namely that force was never justified. He did not, for instance, abhor the Volunteers of '82, nor his ancestor who had fought in '98.

O'Connell immediately jumped up and with some justification accused Mitchel of pretending to be with him when he was really against him. If, he said, Mitchel was not opposing the resolutions as he claimed, then he should not go on as he was doing, for the resolutions under discussion were not concerned with past events.

And at this point O'Connell too began to overstep the mark. The resentment and mistrust of many months were soon animating the debate. Sanctimoniously he announced that 'the greatest political advantages are not worth one drop of blood'.

It is often said that in this matter of 'physical force' O'Connell went out of his way unnecessarily to force an issue out of a purely abstract principle. Inasmuch as he was looking for an issue on which to assert his control over Young Ireland this is true. But it is equally true that the Young Irelanders, who themselves were all agreed at this stage that peaceful means alone should achieve Repeal, also went out of their way to make the question of abstract principle an outright challenge to O'Connell. Since they renounced physical force for the forseeable future there was an intellectual dishonesty in pretending that the question was of such immediate importance.

The debate was adjourned for nearly a fortnight and *The Nation*, appearing in the interval, argued the case more sincerely. The present, it maintained, was a bad moment for the introduction of the 'peace resolutions'. To say that they would never use force now was 'to deliver themselves bound hand and foot to the Whigs'. It would make nonsense of what after all was O'Connell's dictum that England's weakness was Ireland's opportunity.[44]

The adjourned debate on the 'peace resolutions' took place on 27 and 28 July. This time O'Connell himself was not present. He sent a letter to the Association declaring that his spirit was 'sad, my heart heavy at the miserable dissensions', but he made his attitude uncompromisingly clear: 'The advocacy of the physical force doctrine renders it impossible for those who stand on the constitution to cooperate with those who will not adhere.'[45] But this of course was unfair. To say that Young Ireland were actually advocating the physical force doctrine was a travesty of their attitude. And now it was that Smith O'Brien finally decided to abandon his self-appointed role of 'umpire' between O'Connell and Young Ireland and commit himself wholly to the Young Ireland side. He stated bluntly that he was afraid the real object of the resolutions was to drive *The Nation* group from the Association altogether. If such an attempt to exclude them were to be made he himself would feel it impossible to cooperate with the Association until they had been restored to it.

The bitterness of the renewed debate was heightened by the fact that O'Connell's elder son John, much despised by the Young Irelanders, officially dominated the proceedings. An insolent 'little frog', Dillon, co-founder of *The Nation*, had once called him, '... There is no man or country safe from his venom.'[46] And another Young Irelander, MacNeven, had described him as 'the most mischievous public man in Ireland'.[47] Certainly much of his interest at this stage was to ensure his own final inheritance of the role of Irish leader and therefore to have Young Ireland crushed or at least conveniently out of the way in time.

As when the resolutions had first been debated, the nominal argument centred on the purely metaphysical point of whether or not at any time past, present or future in any situation, phyical force was a justifiable means for anybody to use. Everyone continued to agree that moral force was the only viable instrument for the Repeal movement.

And during the last day's debate the line of division between the two parties on the ostensible issue became fainter and fainter. The discussion was about whether offensive rebellion was hypothetically as acceptable as defensive rebellion – for the O'Connellites were always prepared to concede the principle of the latter. But John Mitchel expressed the true point at issue when he declared: 'The real complaint against us is that we cannot endure any tampering with these Whigs.'

For a time the debate reached a creditable level as both sides argued the actual point of difference cogently. John O'Connell made the reasonable point that it was better for Repealers than enemies of the national cause to have places under a Whig Government because they could be 'eminently useful in situations in which details are carried on'.

'Do you think,' replied Mitchel putting the case against this in a nutshell, 'do you think that the men who have been begging one day at the gate of an English minister will come down here the next day to help you get rid of English ministers altogether? If some of the legal gentlemen now in this box accept commissionerships and assistant barristerships from Lord John Russell, will they be so eloquent afterwards in this Hall, denouncing English tyranny and English rapacity?'

But in the light of what was happening in the Irish countryside all hypothetical propositions were increasingly irrelevant. For the ravages of the potato blight had appeared for the second year in succession and this time the entire potato crop of Ireland seemed likely to be consumed. Unity at all costs in the face of the impending disaster was the only reasonable policy.

However, Meagher raised the argument back to a highly-charged emotional level, on which there could be no hope of settlement. Contending rightly that there was no need for the peace resolutions, he continued to argue dramatically against them as if there were a need to oppose them.

'Then, my Lord Mayor,' he said, addressing the chair in the speech's most famous passage, 'I do not disclaim the use of arms as immoral nor do I believe it is the truth to say that the God of Heaven withholds His sanction from the use of arms. . . . Be it for the defence, or be it for the assertion of a nation's liberty, I look upon the sword as a sacred weapon. And if, my lord, it has sometimes reddened the shroud of the oppressor, like the anointed rod of the high priest, it has, at other times, blossomed into flowers to deck the freeman's brow. . . . Abhor the sword and stigmatize the sword? No, my lord, for at its blow a giant nation sprang up from the waters of the Atlantic, and by its redeeming magic the fettered colony became a free republic . . .' He cited also the winning of Belgium's freedom from the Dutch Republic 'by effusion of generous blood'.

This was too much for John O'Connell and his supporters. They immediately declared that Meagher and themselves could no longer belong to the same Association. There were shouts and scenes of confusion as Smith O'Brien protested at Meagher being 'put down'. John O'Connell rose and replied that the question was not whether a young man should be put down in the Association but whether the young man should put down the Association. He played his trump card, saying they could try to turn Daniel O'Connell himself out of the Association if they wanted to. It was simply a question between him and them. O'Connell had founded the Association on the basis of these resolutions. Would they stand by them? If not, let them adopt other resolutions and another leader.

Emotional tension had now reached such a pitch that while the hall rang with enthusiastic cheering and loud cries of 'O'Connell! O'Connell!', Smith O'Brien abruptly got up and left, followed by Meagher, Mitchel, Duffy and other Young Irelanders. An eye-witness saw most of the ladies then leave the gallery while many people rushed to the doors to follow O'Brien and his companions. An impromptu enthusiastic reception took place for them in the street outside, but inside the hall the cries still resounded for 'O'Connell! O'Connell!'

It was an impulsive gesture rather than a calculated decision. It is unlikely that any of the seceders intended their secession to be permanent. Each side recognized that the split was harmful to them. The damage proved irrevocable.

12

The Irish Confederation

The rest of the history of the Repeal movement and Young Ireland is a dismal one.

By the end of August 1846, the month after the split between O'Connell and Young Ireland,' the failure of the potato crop was total in almost every part of Ireland. Each half of the Repeal movement heaped invective on the other. O'Connell mocked 'the paltry Young Ireland party' who 'while vapouring about physical force and vindication by the sword ... would be afraid to look at a poker'.² But he himself became increasingly helpless before the appalling fact of starvation spreading over the entire island. O'Brien and the Young Irelanders, aware of the fatal effect the split had had on Ireland's 'self-reliant' political strength, oscillated between attempts at reconciliation with O'Connell and uninspired efforts to regroup. For all the talk of physical force Smith O'Brien laboriously redefined his own constitutional position as non-separatist. He could advocate no newer policy than a Davis-like refurbishing of the literary and historical springs of Irish nationality.

Meanwhile, the common people of Ireland were being carried far out of reach of Repeal politics altogether. They were staggering into the towns and dying as they begged for food, or collapsing on the mountainsides either on their way back from work or before they could bring back to their starving families whatever they had managed to beg from the towns. 'No language,' wrote a curate in Mayo that winter, 'can describe the awful condition of the people – they are to be found in thousands, young and old, male and female, crawling in the streets, and on the highways, screaming for a morsel of food.'³ A priest wrote to the *Cork Examiner:* 'No description that I could give would for a moment adequately tell the misery, the wretchedness and the suffering of my poor people – they are in the most frightful state of destitution that can possibly be imagined.'⁴ Such people were living – when they lived – almost entirely on seaweed. From every port in Ireland cargoes of oats, barley, bacon, eggs, butter and other foodstuffs continued to sail out to England.

To all this the Young Irelanders replied with rhetoric, which, though often moving, was politically useless. 'I feel by the teachings of history,' Doheny prophesied hopefully in December 1846, 'that there is such a thing as an avenging angel – that he may sleep long and watch a wicked power until it is doomed – that he often springs all around from the maddened brain of a suffering people.'[5] It was mere wishful thinking.

In January 1847 O'Brien and the Young Irelanders founded a new organization known as the Irish Confederation, and O'Brien himself, dubbed by the Young Irelander D'Arcy Magee, 'as kingly a king as the most eminent among the number of his ancestors',[6] addressed it in April 1847 in tones of the deepest despondency. He pointed out in horror that what was happening in Ireland was being done in an Empire that called itself the most civilized, most powerful and most Christian in the world. Yet he himself had no new thought to break the spell in which all seemed gripped. When, eleven months after its foundation, the Irish Confederation issued its first major exposition of its principles, there was only the inevitable proclamation of the right of self-government, the disavowal of separation and physical force, the need to get the same sort of support from the upper classes for the principle of nationality as in 1872, and a reiteration of Davis's principle of self-reliance, with a special emphasis on home manufacture.[7] None of this was different from the policy of the old Repeal Association. None of it was relevant to the Irish peasant in his agony. Moreover, even if the large assumption were correct that Repeal itself would prove a political and social panacea, there was still no hint of how Repeal, so elusive hitherto, was to be achieved. What was to be *done* became the more and more insistent question in people's minds.

The only answer O'Connell thought relevant was relief from England. But he was soon forced to accept that there was no prospect of this, or at least not 'on that enormously large scale which is absolutely necessary to prevent hundreds of thousands of the Irish people from perishing of famine and pestilence'.[8] He was now seventy-one, and at last feeling the feebleness of age upon him. Ordered by his doctors to the south of Europe in March in the hope of restoring his strength for the coming autumn, he decided to make a pilgrimage to Rome. The horrors of the famine and his own relative impotence to obtain really effective relief from the Whig government had taken a terrible toll of him. Before leaving, he went down to the House of Commons at the start of the new session. Disraeli described his appearance:

... of great debility and the tones of his voice very still ... it was a strange and touching spectacle to those who remembered the form of colossal energy and the clear and thrilling tones that had once startled, disturbed and controlled senates ... to the House generally it was a performance of dumb show, a feeble old man muttering from a table; but respect for the great parliamentary personage kept all as orderly as if the fortunes of a party hung on his rhetoric.

The words O'Connell could be heard muttering were both a tragic admission of the failure of his campaign for Repeal of the Union, and at the same time total justification of the principle on which it had been based.

'Ireland is in your hands,' he told the House of Commons. 'If you do not save her, she cannot save herself. I solemnly call on you to recollect that I predict with the sincerest conviction that one-fourth of her population will perish unless you come to her relief.'

He had always been inclined to hyperbole. In fact, only about one-eighth of the population died. But before the decade was over more than another eighth had emigrated to the United States, and as a direct result of the famine the population of Ireland was almost halved in twenty years.

O'Connell himself did not live to know the worst. He died at Lyons on 15 May 1847. An autopsy revealed a brain severely damaged, its membranes inflamed and thickened with blood. His heart, in accordance with his wishes, was taken to Rome. The rest of him, the first man ever to give one voice to the mass of the Irish people, was buried in Ireland.

His death clarified nothing, actually adding to the sense of impotence and ineffectualness on the political scene. For although *The Nation* appeared edged with black borders for three successive issues, Young Ireland was said to have killed him by its opposition, and when Smith O'Brien asked with typical gentlemanly tact if he and his supporters might attend the funeral it was made plain to him that they would not be welcome. Bitterness between O'Connell's supporters and the Young Irelanders continued particularly at mob level for many months. When later in the year the Irish Confederation tried to hold a meeting in Belfast, it was not the Orangemen but the O'Connellites who broke it up.

An attempt to break out of the total impasse was made when a so-called Irish Council was formed of people from all sections of the Irish political spectrum, to represent at least that unanimity in horror which all Irishmen felt in face of the famine, whatever their class or political belief. It was to be above party, and followed the abortive attempt a few months earlier to get all Irish Members of Parliament to agree to act together at Westminster, an attempt which had predictably disintegrated the moment the members had been put to the first severe test of party loyalties. But though the Irish Council – composed of some Conservatives, some Federalists, John O'Connellites and the Young Irelanders of the new Irish Confederation – effectively expressed its unanimous sense of horror, and sponsored some worthy committees of investigation into social conditions, it was hardly surprising that it failed to achieve a break-through where those not handicapped by party differences could find none. Such non-party groupings were little more than gestures of self-respect in a situation of general impotence.

The Irish Confederation's own single practical step lay in the field of organization: the founding of so-called Confederate clubs in different parts of the country to fill the need for more knowledge and understanding of the principles of Repeal and self-reliance. But though a mere twenty persons were required to form the nucleus of a Confederate club, only twenty-three such clubs had been formed by November 1847, four of which were in Dublin and some of the rest in Great Britain.[9] As the different parts of the country entered on yet another winter of famine the majority of the population were wholly absorbed by the more practical need to keep alive. At Skibbereen in County Cork a workhouse designed by no very generous standards for 800 persons was holding over 1,300, and hordes of others besieged the doors waiting for those inside to die and yield them a place.[10] The *Cork Examiner* described similar scenes from Bantry and Killarney while the *Galway Vindicator* reported from further up the west coast that nothing could exceed the frightful conditions of the poor of that district.[11] Two eleven-year old boys in Enniskillen had been sentenced to seven years' transportation each for stealing a pint of Indian meal porridge from a workhouse.[12] The queen's speech for the winter session of 1847 promised only a bill for the better prevention of crime and outrage.

The situation had deteriorated to the point where only original or revolutionary thinking was relevant. All the 'national' talk was now grotesquely out of touch with reality. Most of the Young Irelanders were in varying degrees trapped in the ineffectualness of their own familiar rhetoric. But one serious attempt was made to carry nationalist thinking forward into new areas. In keeping with events, it introduced a harsh, unconciliatory note which in time led to a further split in the movement.

This new thinking was provided by the hitherto unknown eldest son of a prosperous Protestant farmer of Queen's County, named Lalor. The father had himself helped organize the peasant resistance to tithes in the thirties, and had been an O'Connellite Member of Parliament. His son, Fintan Lalor, suffered from a disease of the spine and was almost a hunchback. He was an ardent reader of *The Nation* and his physical handicap had given him time in which to brood over the political and social impasse in which Ireland seemed trapped. When the Irish Confederation was founded in January 1847, he immediately wrote to Gavan Duffy with some fundamental suggestions which Duffy, impressed, passed on to the other leading Young Irelanders.

Even today, to come across some of Lalor's words suddenly in the middle of a history of the Young Ireland movement is to experience a breath of fresh air. His argument was that the Confederation, with its old slogan of Repeal, was based only on a collection of vague impulses and emotional generalities. 'Men,' he wrote, 'keep theorizing and dreaming too long – and building up, or restoring an airy and ideal nationality, which time is wearing down, and wasting away faster than they can work it up; and when they awake from their dreams they will find, I fear, that one other people has gone out of the world, as nations and races have gone ere now.'[13]

Repeal, he said, as an objective in itself must now be abandoned as 'an impracticable absurdity'. It had been shown by the events of past years to be unattainable by constitutional means. Military means were out of the question not so much because of the inevitable superiority of government strength but chiefly because, with the events of the famine, Repeal had become a remote and meaningless abstraction to the Irish peasant. The only thing the peasant could be roused about was the land.

In any case, to try and establish two independent sovereign legislatures within one framework was 'an arrangement repugnant alike to common sense and experience'. The analogy of 1782 was invalid; it was, after all, this very arrangement which Tone and Lord Edward Fitzgerald had found it necessary to try and dissolve. Therefore, total national independence must be the objective. And this the peasant was to help achieve.

Lalor had nothing in principle against the idea of the peasant arming himself, but to bring the government to its knees more immediately and with less general suffering he proposed another way, which he defined as 'moral insurrection'. And the area of this moral insurrection would be something the peasant really did care about, namely the land, specifically the landlord–tenant relationship. Rents were to be refused until the land-lords agreed to a quite new land system to be negotiated directly between the Irish people and their landlords, based on the principle that the people who worked the land held by right a co-equal ownership of that land with the landlord. All future rents and conditions of tenure would start from that premise. Any landlord who did not recognize this inalienable right of the Irish people to their land would receive no rent and forfeit his property. From such an assumption by the Irish people of sovereign authority with regard to land titles and land tenures would flow automatically all other law-making rights.

They were already half-way there, Lalor maintained, for the famine and its consequences had begun their work for them by demolishing the old land system for ever. In this he was to be proved unduly optimistic. Social systems are tougher and more resilient than the human beings who compose them. Though the famine was to remove one quarter of the population from the land altogether and change ninety per cent of the landlords, the system itself survived for over another thirty years.

There was much that was imprecise and much that was fanciful in Lalor's radical thinking. As practical policy it was itself unreal in pre-supposing that the peasantry were prepared to stand up to the landlords. In fact, whether or not they could or could not pay their rents the peasantry were allowing themselves to be driven, famished and submissive, off the land into the ditches and hedgerows in tens of thousands. As Gavan Duffy objected, Lalor's 'angry peasants, chafing like chained tigers, were creatures of the imagination – not the living people through whom we had to act'.[14]

Yet by linking, even in theory, the violent power and passion which the Irish peasant in more normal times had manifested for his land to loftier thoughts of Irish nationalism, Lalor at least made an attempt to bring Irish nationalism down to earth. O'Connell in the early days of Repeal had had an instinctive feeling for the same principle, emphasizing as he constantly did tenant right, together with the need for Repeal. But Fintan Lalor formulated it more positively as a radical political theory. Other men in other times were to try and turn it into practice.

In his own day Lalor failed to convert the Confederation to his ideas, but he did at least force them to acknowledge that they themselves were lacking in practical policies and must adopt a more positive attitude. He also made one important individual convert, John Mitchel, who, inspired by Lalor, was soon to adopt the spirit at least of his argument and add a page to that record of history which was itself always to influence Irish history. Even Duffy had been convinced that while rejecting Lalor's scheme it was necessary to substitute another as specific.[15] And *The Nation* itself, for which Mitchel was still writing, continually voiced the need. '... It is indeed full time that we cease to whine and begin to act.... Good heavens, to think that we should go down without a struggle.'[16]

When at the beginning of 1848 Duffy wrote in *The Nation* that the coming year would witness great changes, he himself echoed: 'But how?', adding immediately: 'Our readers will not long be ignorant now.'[17]

Duffy had a plan of a sort. But it was hardly revolutionary, depending as it did for its effectiveness on that old assumption of national unity of all classes which never materialized. His proposal was that from all the present legal institutional functions of the Irish people in corporations, grand juries, boards of guardians, and as town commissioners, and Members of Parliament, there should be constituted a new National Authority in Ireland. Representing this at Westminster, Irish members would make Englishmen listen to the justice of Irish national claims by 'making Irish interests cross and impede and rule the British senate'.[18] They would '... stop the entire business of Parliament till the constitution of Ireland was restored'.[19] If the Members of Parliament failed to achieve this then they would withdraw from Westminster and together with representatives from the other institutions and other elected delegates form a Council of Three Hundred and 'demand the reassembly of the Irish Parliament'.

It is significant that the proposal did not even go so far as to make such a Council of Three Hundred in itself a Constituent Assembly, but only empowered it to make a final 'demand'. Altogether, the plan expressed what was increasingly to become the Confederation's attitude: namely that of wanting a revolution without having to bring one about.

By the end of 1847 John Mitchel, stimulated by the radical nature of Lalor's thought but dissatisfied with Duffy's plan and maddened with frustration, at last came to the conclusion that constitutional methods should be abandoned altogether.

He left *The Nation* and soon afterwards seceded from the Confederation itself. From among the prominent Young Irelanders he took with him only the young journalist Devin Reilly, but the general mood of the rank and file was by now so desperate that two-fifths of those present at the debate which led to his secession voted for him. He immediately founded a new weekly, brazenly named *The United Irishman*, from which he preached in a sort of violent vacuum the general principle of revolution. In his very first issue he openly defied the viceroy, giving him what he called 'a true account of . . . the rules, signs and passwords of our new United Irish Society Lodge A 1'.[30]

Mitchel had in fact no organization whatsoever. He had only the sympathy of fanatical members in the new Confederate clubs in the towns, and virtually no support at all in the countryside. He simply assumed that the frenzied indignation he himself felt and expressed would somehow reproduce itself widely enough to generate revolution spontaneously. He hardly seemed to care what such a revolution's outcome might be.

'I hold it is a more hideous national calamity,' he wrote, 'for ten men to be cast out to die of hunger, like dogs in ditches, than for ten thousand to be hewn to pieces, fighting like men and Christians in defence of their rights.'[21]

It was not long before he was publishing articles on how to form hollow squares of pikemen against cavalry, and extolling the pike itself as 'the queen of weapons . . . the weapon of the brave'.[22]

Smith O'Brien and the rest of the prominent Young Irelanders had deprecated Mitchel's extremism as soon as it had become apparent within the Confederation. O'Brien had called it 'utterly fatal to the liberties of the country'.[23] Even Meagher ('of the sword') wrote to O'Brien in January 1848 that for all his own increasing sense of desperation he was convinced that 'the only policy which we can successfully conduct is the constitutional policy advised by Duffy'.[24] O'Gorman took the same line, writing of Mitchel and Devin Reilly as 'Infant Ireland', and dissociating himself altogether from 'opinions so dangerous'.[25] Doheny, who, though a barrister, had himself been bred on the soil and had actually helped Fintan Lalor form a Tenant Right Association in the previous year, maintained that with the priests against them they had no chance with the peasantry. Moreover, he continued: 'If the peasants do take to arms they'll be faced by England's disciplined soldiery and end as corpses on their native fields, or, if they did manage to have a local success, on the gibbet. . . . But even if that were not so, where are your peasantry? – sicklied, hungry, wasted, exiled or in their graves. If you want to arm – I tell you your best chance – go to Skibbereen, re-animate the corpses that are huddled there and bid them arm . . .'[26]

O'Brien finally made it clear that he would rather retire from the Confederation altogether than allow himself to be 'compromised by the reckless violence of men who care very little what is their destiny. . . . If I understand their policy,' he continued, 'I feel persuaded that it can lead to nothing but to confusion, anarchy and bloodshed, and must inevitably, for one generation at least, defeat all efforts for the attainment of our liberties.'[27] He moved finally in the Confederation that 'to hold out to the Irish population the hope that in the present broken and divided condition they can liberate their country by an appeal to arms ... would be in our opinion fatal misdirection of the public mind'.[28]

Within six months Smith O'Brien and the rest had all taken the field and every word they had said about the disastrousness of such an enterprise was proved correct.

The Young Ireland group were respectable, comfortably-situated, middle-class nationalists; the sort of men who even at the height of the famine could and did winter abroad for their health's sake.* They were men of unquestionable personal courage and integrity, as was soon to be shown. But for all their theoretical talk of physical force in the time of O'Connell, they were congenitally unfitted by temperament and tradition to abandon the safety of constitutionalism, particularly when the alternative was a desperate rebellion for which no preparation had been made and for which there was little positive inclination on the part of a starving and exhausted populace. O'Connell's cruel gibe that they were men afraid to look at a poker had a certain simple truth in it. It was a desperate determination to escape at all costs from their natural ambience in such desperate circumstances that had made Mitchel consciously adopt his wild course, and it is impossible not to admit the logic in his illogical gesture. The others were to allow themselves to be forced into such an attitude against their will.

It is, however, possible to sympathize both with the main body of the Confederation and with Mitchel. Each can be seen to be doing the wrong thing where no right thing was discernible. Cautious and sensible as was the main group, audacious as was Mitchel, both were utterly ineffectual. Mitchel was anxious to provoke a climax as quickly as possible. The others, in what now seemed a parody of Davis's motto, continued to 'bide their time'. What they were really waiting for was a miracle.

In February 1848 the miracle seemed to have arrived.

The Young Irelanders had been looking for inspiration to a number of developing nationalist movements on the continent of Europe. Speaking in 1847 of the movement then gaining force in Italy, Meagher had ended a Confederation meeting at Cork with the words: '... the beautiful, the brilliant and the gifted Italy is in arms! ... Glory! glory! to the citizens of Rome, patricians and Plebeians, who think that liberty is worth a drop of blood!'[29] and he had been received with tremendous cheering.

* Dillon, who suffered from tuberculosis, spent the winter of 1846–7 in Madeira; Richard O'Gorman spent it in London.

Now, in February 1848, with all Italy itself alight with nationalist fervour, there came on the 26th the astonishing news that an almost bloodless popular revolution had taken place in Paris. Louis Philippe had fled with barely a shot being fired. The thought of such a thing – a revolution achieved with no more than rhetorical blood, and with a poet and orator (Lamartine) himself one of the leading figures – went to the heads of the Irish Confederation. A revolution without the embarrassing task of making one had been shown to be possible. Many people now appeared to think that it only had to be hailed and glorified for a similarly painless reversal of the *status quo* to take place in Dublin.

The assumption was made that somehow the entire situation in Ireland had already changed overnight. At the next meeting of the Confederation Gavan Duffy, making one of his rare appearances on a public platform, declared:

'If we are no slaves and braggarts, unworthy of liberty, Ireland will be free before the coming summer fades into winter.... All over the world – from the frozen swamps of Canada to the rich corn-fields of Sicily – in Italy, in Denmark, in Prussia and in glorious France, men are up for their rights.'[30]

But they were not up for their rights in Ireland. Nothing in Ireland had in fact been changed by these events. The one small straw which many hurried to seize was the remote possibility of war between the new French Republic and England. The common-sense arguments by which members of the Confederation and Smith O'Brien himself had felt restrained hitherto and with which they had censured Mitchel only a few weeks before were now thrown to the winds. 'The day of our deliverance is at hand,' wrote Duffy in *The Nation* in positively Mitchel-like tones.[31] 'Ireland's opportunity has come at last.'[32]

As he himself was to admit much later: 'The men who a few weeks before had fearlessly resisted anarchy, now as fearlessly embraced revolution.'[33] They were to pay dearly for their euphoria.

O'Gorman, who had thought Mitchel's opinions so mischievous, foolish and dangerous in January, now declared that all honest men were bound to arm.[34] O'Brien himself thought that the moment of Ireland's liberation was at hand, though typically he counselled patience, still hoping to bring the gentry on to the right side of the barricades.[35]

All the previous arguments still held good. The British Government was as strong, the populace as weakened by starvation and disease, the gentry as disinclined to repeal the Union as ever. But at the first meeting of the Council of the Confederation after the February revolution it was officially decided that if one last effort to get a national Parliament by negotiation should fail then there should be a revolution within the year.[36]

The nature of the goal had not changed. The Confederates still wanted another and better '82. The only change consisted in the miraculous renewal of their hopes that they could achieve it, winning it bloodlessly by the same combination of moral and physical pressure with which the Protestants had won their victory in '82. 'If the English government give us our freedom we will fight for England,' declared a prominent Kilkenny Confederate only in March. 'If that freedom be withheld, I cannot answer for my country or myself.'[37] Mitchel, who was now somehow regarded as largely vindicated by the events in Paris, was brought back into the Confederation's discussions, though his paper, *The United Irishman*, was hardly counselling patience in the manner of O'Brien. Addressing Clarendon, the Viceroy, as 'Her Majesty's Executioner-General and General Butcher of Ireland', it declared openly that its object in publishing, as he did, treasonable articles about street-fighting and barricades was 'to sweep this island clear of British butchers and plant the green flag on Dublin Castle'.[38]

The excitement of the Dublin Confederates was echoed in other Irish cities. A new Irish flag made its appearance. French red, white and blue tri-colours had been widely hoisted in honour of the new young French republic from the start, but in the first week of March there appeared in the cele-brations at Enniscorthy in County Wexford a tricoloured flag of orange, green and white, hopefully 'expressive of the union of the parties'.[39] And at a dinner given in April by the Dublin Trades Committee to O'Brien, Meagher and other members of a deputation that had carried Ireland's con-gratulations to the new French republic, Meagher presented his hosts with a silken orange, white and green flag surmounted by an Irish pike which he had brought back from Paris. He explained that the centre signified a lasting truce between the 'Orange' and the 'Green'. Mitchel, speaking at the dinner, declaimed:

'Brighter days are coming to us; this noble weapon glittering above us, this majestic banner, are of good omen to us. Ah! the gleaming pike-head rises through our darkness like a morning star; this magnificent Irish tri-colour, with its orange, white and green, dawns upon us more glorious than ever Sunburst flashed over the field of Brunanburgh, or blazed thro' the battle haze of Clontarf. My friends, I hope to see the flag one day waving, as our national banner, over a forest of Irish pikes.' *

But if the mood of victory and optimism had been miraculously restored, the old question soon began to re-impose itself: what exactly, apart from

---

* The delegation's reception in Paris had been enthusiastic, but the British Govern-ment, through their Ambassador, had put pressure on Lamartine to state that the new republic did not wish to interfere in the internal affairs of the British Empire. This caused dismay to some extremists in Ireland who were hopefully thinking of an analogy with '98, but to O'Brien, thinking in terms of '82 and hoping for success without resort to war, it was only marginally disappointing. The general intoxication of the optimistic Paris scene, with everyone under arms and trees of liberty in every square, more than made up for it. (See O'Brien's *Personal Memorandum*, quoted Gwynn, *Young Ireland and 1848*, pp. 167–8.)

defying the government in the press, was to be done? Though the potato crop, or such as people had managed to plant, had not been so severely damaged by the blight in this winter of 1847–8, the ravages of starvation and disease after two years of famine were if anything worse than ever. People were dying daily in all parts of Ireland. Early in March 1848 the Mayo Constitution wrote: 'The streets of every town in the country are over-run by stalking skeletons.'[40] An inquest on a man found lying dead face downwards on the roadside near Westport revealed that his mouth was full of masticated turf and grass.[41] A Galway woman ate part of the legs and feet of her own daughter.[42] In Galway gaol, intended for 110 persons, there were 903 prisoners and 34 children, while 44 other people had died there in the previous week. In the prison hospital it was common to find three persons to a bed, one or more of them often dead.[43]

In the general revolutionary excitement, *The Nation* sounded a sobering warning note that Ireland's last chance had come.

'... If this be another roar of blank cartridge, if once again the passionate sobbing and straining of the people for liberty end in some shameful disappointments, hundreds of thousands of our truest hearts will fly from the land for ever, and the black hopeless darkness of slavery will settle down on it for a hundred years. For all the living race of Irishmen this is indeed the last chance.'[44]

Duffy issued a call for a 'National Guard' in imitation of the French revolutionaries. The Confederate clubs would provide a nucleus.

Even Smith O'Brien began to sound a new note of realism and urgency. He described how night after night he had sat in the House of Commons listening to the government and becoming more and more convinced that they were utterly indifferent to what was taking place in Ireland – '... never at any time did that Parliament seem to me to treat with more disdain than at present the claims of the Irish people'.[45] He thought it was time they bid the British Parliament 'good morning' and went home to take care of the Irish people. Yet none of the other Irish members would have followed him.

On 15 March 1848, speaking before a meeting of the Confederation three thousand strong, Smith O'Brien came out in his most theoretically rebellious mood to date. 'I trust,' he said, 'I speak in all true humility when I say that, if by surrendering my life, either upon the scaffold or the field, I could thereby secure the redemption of this land from the bondage under which it now suffers that life would be cheerfully given in my country's cause.'[46] He had, he said, the utmost possible horror of bloodshed, but an Irish parliament, an Irish army, an Irish national guard were what the vast majority of Ireland now wanted. Whether the final form of government were to be a republic or not, was at this stage unimportant. He personally believed that 'at present at least' the Irish people would be content to remain subject to the sovereignty of the British Crown.

O'Brien clearly envisaged the national guard as the principal lever to be used against the government, performing a similar function on behalf of the whole of Ireland to that which the Volunteers had performed on behalf of the Protestant ascendancy in 1782. To be composed of about 300,000 men, it would both be ready to protect social order and to act in defence of the country. It should enrol publicly and 'not by your night walkings, and by your ribbon societies, which have been the curse of the country'.[47] He recommended 'fraternizing' with the army and with the police, reminding his audience that the latter were Irishmen like themselves, 'as fine a body of men as ever held a musket; and if their energies were properly directed they would become the safeguard of this country . . .'.[48]

The Confederates indeed now resolved to draw up a roll of enlistment for a national guard and to summon a Council of Three Hundred. But almost nothing was actually done. The pulse of revolution was still quickening mainly in words. Mitchel drew attention to the fact.

'Speeches,' he said, 'or resolutions here never will avail or do one bit of good unless we all have arms and are ready to turn out.'[49]

But these were words too.

Increasingly aware of the need for some practical move, O'Brien decided to undertake a tour of inspection to discover the real state of the Confederate movement in other parts of the country. But the omens, even for a united front among Repealers, at once seemed poor. When he addressed his first meeting in his own home town of Limerick it was broken up by old O'Connellite supporters, angered by the presence at the meeting of Mitchel. Smith O'Brien, potential leader of an Irish revolution, was assaulted by other Irishmen with sticks and stones and received a black eye and bruised jaw and ribs for his pains. Though it was hurriedly pointed out to him that no offence had been intended to him personally, he was so disgusted that he threatened to retire altogether from public life.

It was the British Government which, understandably alarmed in such a year of revolutions by the talk in Ireland and unaware of how much effectiveness might or might not lie behind it, gave the revolutionary movement some apparent coherence by its counter-actions. In the circumstances these were not really excessive. A few counties had already been 'proclaimed' under the Crime and Outrage Act of the previous year, but in the others it was still quite legal to possess and even manufacture weapons including pikes, though little of this was going on.[50] Then in March the government instituted prosecutions against Smith O'Brien, Meagher and Mitchel for sedition in recent speeches and articles, though the three were allowed out on bail.*

'The war between the people and their English rulers has begun,' declared Duffy in *The Nation*, hopefully.[51] But it was not until the end of April that

---

* It was while out on bail that O'Brien and Meagher had been able to carry Dublin's congratulations to the new republic in France.

the viceroy issued a specific proclamation declaring any national guard and the summoning of the Council of Three Hundred illegal.

O'Brien, Meagher and Mitchel all came up for trial in May. The indictment itself did the mild O'Brien something of a service by describing him as 'a wicked, turbulent and seditious person'.[52] He was suitably escorted to the trial by a number of the Dublin Confederate clubs, one of which was called the Sheares Club after the unfortunate brothers of 1798.[53] In both his case and that of Meagher the juries failed to agree, in spite of intensive packing by the government with likely Unionist supporters. O'Brien and Meagher were released in triumph.

Mitchel himself was tried under a recent act creating the new offence of treason–felony, which allowed much severer penalties for sedition than hitherto, but did not demand the full rigours of treason. An article in *The United Irishman* – written in fact by Mitchel's young lieutenant Devin Reilly – had only recently advocated the throwing of vitriol into the eyes of soldiers in street fighting,[54] and this and the far more radical and violent republican tone Mitchel had long adopted made his conviction seem more certain. When some of the rank and file Confederates demanded that if Mitchel were convicted there should be an armed attempt to defy the government, rescue him and raise the country, the Confederate leaders took a desperate look round at their organization and resources.

They found there were only just over seventy Confederate clubs in Ireland altogether, almost half of which were in Dublin, containing between two and five hundred members each.[55] There was virtually no organization by the Confederates in country districts at all. The Dublin clubs themselves, probably the best organized, were, for all their enthusiasm, found by Meagher and O'Gorman after a rapid inspection to be unfit for any sort of action with a reasonable expectancy of success.[56] Against them the government had ten thousand police and troops in the city and forty thousand in the rest of Ireland. Though many in the Dublin clubs wanted to make a rescue bid all the same, they were restrained by Meagher and O'Gorman after O'Brien himself had advised very strongly against it.[57]

On 26 May 1848 Mitchel was found guilty and sentence was postponed till the following day.

One eye-witness described Dublin at midnight that night as wearing the aspect of a city on the eve of insurrection. Men walked the streets distractedly, as if they had forgotten all sense of time and weariness. Carriages drove constantly to and from the several military and police stations while large bodies of police patrolled the streets.[58] But the night passed off quietly, and the next day Mitchel came up for sentence. Many of his old friends were in court. The sentence was that he should be transported beyond the seas for a period of fourteen years.

'I do not regret anything I have done,' he cried from the dock, 'and I believe that the course which I have opened is only commenced. The Roman who saw his hand burning to ashes before the tyrant promised that three hundred should follow out his enterprises. Can I not promise for one' (and here he pointed at Meagher in the courtroom) – 'for two?' (at Reilly) – 'for three?' (at O'Gorman) – 'aye, for hundreds?'[59]

There was a rush of outstretched hands towards the dock and the judges withdrew in disorder while Mitchel was forcibly taken below. One man he could not promise for so confidently was Smith O'Brien, who had circumspectly withdrawn to Wicklow during the trial, still suffering from the battering he had received a month before at Limerick.[60]

Mitchel was taken aboard a warship in Dublin Harbour that afternoon, stumbling over the chain which fastened his hand to his right leg as he reached the deck.[61] Special instructions were given by the government that he should be treated without vindictiveness.[62] He was soon allowed to change his convict dress for his own clothes and the Governor of Spike Island outside Cork, where he was held for a few days, even bought him some shirts.[63] On his way to Bermuda, where he was to spend a year of close confinement, he took his meals at the Captain's table. Even in Bermuda, where he was lodged in one of the prison hulks offshore, he had a quite spacious room to himself with books. He was kept apart from the other convicts, could go ashore for exercise and did not have to work.

It is still sometimes said that Mitchel lived through 'appalling privations and physical sufferings'[64] during this period, but this is not strictly so. He was treated as a 'gentlemanly' prisoner with, relatively, considerable privileges, and the fact was more than once made the subject of angry comment in the House of Commons. Apart from the damp climate of Bermuda, which was bad for his asthma, the worst he had to endure was the shrieking of the ordinary convicts being flogged with the cat o' nine tails on the decks above.[65] But though he found this unpleasant, it did not trouble his sensibilities unduly for he was a stern man who did not disapprove of flogging as such and even thought it too good for most common criminals.[66] After a year he was sent to Tasmania where, immediately given his parole, and receiving a ticket of leave, he spent some years sheep-farming and kangaroo-hunting.[67] Then one day, having made his plans, he suddenly announced that he was giving up his parole and escaped to America.

But, for Ireland, Mitchel had become a martyr – a martyr second in that century only to Emmet. And, as with Emmet, the total ineffectualness of the defiance seemed no reflection on the individual, only an inspiring evocation of the hopelessness of the Irish people's plight.

13

Smith O'Brien's 'Rising', 1848

What is often described as the rising of 1848 in Ireland was not in any practical sense a rising at all, nor until the very last minute was it ever intended to be one. There was no previously drawn up military plan of campaign, no secret organization, and such conspiracy as there was had previously been overtaken by events and made irrelevant. Though a confrontation of sorts between the Young Irelanders and the government had been planned in theory for the autumn of 1848, the confused series of events which actually took place in July and August was no more than a desperate last-minute attempt by would-be Irish leaders to avoid arrest and thus force the government into a negotiating position. It failed hopelessly, for the same reason as the more positive effort vaguely proposed for the autumn would have failed. The gap between words and deeds, but above all between leaders and people, was too great. In such a situation the initiative remained throughout with the government.

Immediately after Mitchel's transportation one of the few priests who had come out not only in favour of the Irish Confederation but also of the extreme viewpoint expressed by Mitchel had arrived in Dublin to see Duffy. He was a Father Kenyon of Templederry in County Tipperary. Even before Mitchel's sentence he had expressed some impatience with mere histrionic gestures and talk. Addressing a crowd at Kilkenny in April 1848 he had said:

'You have often met before in crowds like this; you have been hitherto accustomed to shout and cheer and take off your hats, until shouting and cheering and taking off your hats has come to be worth a pinch of snuff. ... I ask you again, are you ready to die for Ireland?' And the crowd had replied: 'Yes, yes, all ready to die this minute', whereupon he had expressed himself content.[1]

Now he put it to Duffy that some positive preparations should be made for armed action if necessary. Duffy, all too aware how little had been done, agreed.[2]

But activity was largely restricted to sending agents to France and America to enlist general support, one of whom dramatically carried his commission to America smeared with gunpowder in a loaded pistol so that it could be blown to pieces in the event of arrest.[*]

O'Brien himself, only kept vaguely informed of the moves, remained brooding at home. He was still unable to 'stoop or stretch without pain' after his Limerick injuries, but he was also as late as June on his own admission still 'not one of those who wish to plunge recklessly' and this must have played its part in delaying his recovery.[4] However, he kept quite closely in touch by letter with developments, and one of the most important of these was a reunion at least between the Confederation and the old O'Connellite Repeal Association.

For the Confederation the benefit of this reunion was more psychological than organizational, for under the combined influence of the famine and John O'Connell's leadership the old Repeal organization had become moribund and inactive. The Repeal Rent, which had once run into thousands of pounds per week, had for a long time barely reached double figures. But the reunion did bring theoretically to the Confederation the potential sympathy of those masses for whom the name O'Connell was still the only one which held any political magic at all. The reunion also seemed to promise some tentative approval from the bulk of the Roman Catholic clergy, who had so far largely held aloof from the Confederation and were the key to all popular support in Ireland. Out of the reunion a new political body was formed to replace the Irish Confederation. It was named the Irish League.

O'Brien, still at home, wrote on 1 June a letter to *The Nation* approving the Irish League's formation, in some of his most committed language to date.

'Our controversy,' he wrote, 'will soon narrow itself into the single question how often uttered with impatience – When will the Irish Nation strike?',[5] though typically he also quoted the Young Ireland poet who had written:

> ... Your worst transgressions
> Were to strike, and strike in vain.

And it is clear that by 'striking' he still meant more the striking of a defiant attitude, backed by an armed organization, rather than literally taking the field.

The effectiveness of the new united front was soon reduced by two events. The first was a decision taken by John O'Connell to retire from public life. In making his decision known he also let it be known that the new note of militancy in O'Brien's letter had contributed to it. The second event was another revolution in Paris at the end of June. This, unlike that in February, was

---

[*] This was the conspiracy made irrelevant by subsequent events. The money raised in America for arms arrived in Ireland too late for anything but a defence fund for those members of the Confederation who were by then under arrest. (See Duffy, op. cit., pp. 693–5.)

extremely bloody, and openly socialistic and anti-clerical. It alarmed many wavering middle-class supporters of the Irish League and put a sharp brake on the clergy's approbation of radical methods.

Nevertheless, the spirit of optimism among the faithful of the Confederate clubs was running high. Meagher and O'Gorman in particular were busy travelling about the country working up enthusiasm. The press, in the shape not only of *The Nation* but of a new paper, the *Irish Felon*, which had replaced Mitchel's suppressed *United Irishman* and was edited by a close personal friend of his, John Martin, with help from Fintan Lalor, was striking a more and more openly revolutionary note.

Letters were appearing in *The Nation* on how to look after steel weapons, whether pikes, sword blades or daggers, and how to cast bullets.[6] Duffy was promising that one of the first duties of the Irish League would be to plant the country with clubs from end to end.[7] O'Brien himself, in his more militant mood, actually wrote that he was bound to tell the people of Ireland that injustices and wrongs were 'rapidly bringing us to that period when armed resistance to the oppressors of our country will become a sacred obligation, enforced by the highest sanctions of public duty.'[8] Meagher, fully extravagant again, declaimed: 'Generation transmits to generation the holy passion. From the blood which drenched the scaffolds of 1798 the felons of this year have sprung.'[9]

Duffy had been subtly encouraging the more militant side of O'Brien's nature and trying to goad him at least into committing himself to leadership. 'There is no half-way house for you,' he wrote to him probably on 17 June. 'You will be head of the movement, loyally obeyed, and the revolution will be conducted with order and clemency; or the mere anarchists will prevail with the people and our revolution will be bloody chaos. . . . If I were Smith O'Brien I would shape out in my own mind . . . a definite course for the revolution and labour incessantly to develop it that way.'

He blamed O'Brien for allowing the projects for a National Guard and the calling of a Council of Three Hundred to lapse, but thought it was now too late to try and revive them. The Confederate clubs were now the one real hope. 'Forgive me for urging this so anxiously upon you, but I verily believe the hopes of the country depend upon the manner in which the next two months are used.'[10]

And at the beginning of July O'Brien came out from his home at last and went on a tour of the country. In spite of the 'abject looks' rather than 'glad faces' he met among the peasantry,[11] he began, under the combined influence of the beauty of the Irish countryside and the enthusiasm he found in the Confederate clubs, to drift more and more positively towards a guarded revolutionary fervour. In Cork he held a sort of review by moonlight in a city park of some seven to ten thousand members of the clubs, many of whom marched past him in military order.[12] The next day he wrote to his wife that 'we shall be able to make the whole of this force available for good purposes ...'.[13]

But how exactly these good purposes were to be worked out was still left vague. There was no practical plan of rebellion such as Lord Edward Fitzgerald and even Robert Emmet had developed. It was clear that both O'Brien and Duffy too were still thinking primarily in terms of a display of armed organized clubs which, when the time came in the autumn, would stand as a challenge to the government behind the demand for Repeal and succeed in getting it to back down, much as the Volunteers had achieved their objectives in '82.

However, some awkward voices were beginning to be raised.

Another new radical paper had appeared, the *Irish Tribune*, edited by two students, Dalton Williams and Kevin O'Doherty. 'Why?' asked a letter in this on 1 July, echoing Duffy's private letter of a fortnight earlier, 'Why is not the Council of Three Hundred, which alone is required to save the country, proceeded with? ... We call upon Smith O'Brien – we call upon T. F. Meagher to rouse from his apathy.' The harvest, the letter continued, would be ready in two months and it must be prevented from leaving Dublin and other ports by the clubs. '... No faltering, no hesitating, no suspense. Ever keep before your minds the GREAT CAUSE. ... Think of those great victims whose names, still unappeased, cry out for vengeance – FITZGERALD, and EMMET and TONE. Think of MITCHEL. ... Think, think and BE COURAGEOUS.'[14]

A letter in the *Irish Felon*, also at the beginning of July, came even closer to the point when it stated that though the clubs were numerous they were not well-armed. There was too much braggartry, the writer complained. He discerned only the desire for freedom – not the energy to win it. Each club that was aware of its own deficiencies imagined that the others were better equipped. 'Cork looks to Dublin and Dublin looks to Cork.' Defeatism was spreading with 'each new postponement of the revolutionary drama which seems necessary to our cautious managers. ... The words you speak are meaningless, for you have spoken them so frequently already; and the attitudes you adopt are lifeless and unimpressive, because custom has exhausted passion. ... Our alternative now is ... the hillside or the court. I for one would rather die with the green flag for my shroud than pine into the grave with the insignia of felony on my limbs ...'[15]

Duffy himself had expressed similar reservations about the clubs only a short time before. Certainly the number of members in Dublin had doubled in three weeks after Mitchel's sentence, but there were still large blanks on the map of Ireland where there were no clubs at all.[16] This knowledge, however, did not prevent the issue of *The Nation* which revealed this from carrying an article entitled 'Night Thoughts on The Bayonet'.[17]

Then, while O'Brien was still down in Cork intending to continue his leisurely tour of inspection through Youghal and Dungarvan and up to

Dublin, the government struck. It arrested Gavan Duffy for sedition. He was joined in prison the same night by John Martin, Mitchel's friend and editor of the *Irish Felon*, for whom a warrant had been out for some time. Next day the two young students who had started the *Irish Tribune* were there too, having only been allowed to bring out three issues of their paper. Early the following week Doheny and Meagher, whose oratory had been becoming increasingly violent, were also arrested, as was D'Arcy Magee, Duffy's assistant editor on *The Nation*.

Doheny, Meagher and Magee were all allowed bail. Duffy and the others were not, though, as had been the case with O'Connell, the prison regime under the control of Dublin Corporation was lax. Both Duffy and Martin were able to keep in contact with their papers and, being allowed any visitors they liked, could continue to confer on general 'revolutionary' policy.

This remained as imprecise as ever, except for the principle that nothing rash or premature should be attempted. As Duffy himself was being taken to prison in a police van on the night of his arrest, a vast crowd had collected round it in the streets of Dublin, forcing it to walking pace in spite of a large police escort. Shouts of 'Take him out! Take him out!' had arisen, and the president of one of the Confederate clubs climbed up on the steps of the van and asked Duffy if he wanted to be rescued.

'Certainly not,' replied Duffy, and then at the request of the police officer appealed to the crowd to let him be taken to prison.[18]

Similar scenes had occurred the next week when Doheny was arrested in Cashel and Meagher in Waterford. Meagher had had to appeal to the clubs from the top of the vehicle on which he was being taken to gaol to remove a barricade blocking the bridge and to abandon their determination to occupy the town.

They agreed reluctantly, saying: 'We fear you will be sorry for it, sir.'[19]

But clearly not all initiative could be left to the government. Smith O'Brien cut short his tour and returned to Dublin by sea on 14 July to discuss what should be done. On the 15th a meeting of the council of the Confederation took place together with representatives of the clubs. It was a private meeting, but there was nothing secret or illegal about it, though the government had taken the precaution of infiltrating an informer.*

O'Brien, after going through the strength of the organization of the Dublin clubs with their representatives, gave an encouraging report on his experiences in Cork. But, as he truly said, they were not yet well-enough informed of the state of the clubs' organization in Ireland as a whole. When discussion arose as to the desirability of a rescue attempt on behalf of the new prisoners should they be convicted, he said that he personally would rather ascend the gallows himself than let anyone lose his life by a premature step on his

* James Stephenson Dobbyn. The bulk of his information as revealed in evidence in court was admitted afterwards by Meagher to have been accurate.

account. But the consensus of the meeting seems to have been that a rescue should be attempted in the event of the prisoners' conviction. Since the next law term in which convictions might be expected was not until October no thought of an immediate insurrection seems to have been contemplated by anyone.

A quite different situation had, however, arisen when the council met again four days later, with O'Brien again in the chair. For the government had again taken the initiative. On 18 July the lord lieutenant issued a proclamation declaring the holding of arms in Dublin and a number of other counties as illegal. At the Irish League council's meeting a resolution was immediately put forward that the clubs should no longer wait for the harvest in the autumn but should start an insurrection at once. This was proposed by the young man from Cork, Joseph Brenan, who had written the fiery letter to the *Irish Felon* earlier in the month.*

An amendment to Brenan's motion was moved by John Blake Dillon, to the effect that the clubs should merely conceal their arms and offer only passive resistance to the proclamation, refusing to open any door or lock voluntarily.[20] This was eventually carried by a small majority.[21] Brenan, arguing that the clubs were at the peak of their morale now, declared in exasperation that they were always waiting – till American or French aid came, 'till rifles are forged in heaven and angels draw the trigger'.[22]

During these days since his return to Dublin, O'Brien had been touring Confederate clubs in towns in the capital's vicinity. At Drogheda, Navan and Trim he had received great welcomes and told his audiences that the day might not be far distant when they would be called on 'to afford sterner indications of patriotism than mere cheers'.[23] But at a meeting of the League itself on the evening of 19 July (the day of the council's decision to offer passive resistance to the arms proclamation) he insisted that the organization would continue constitutional efforts 'until we find all constitutional efforts exhausted'.[24]

On 21 July a further meeting of the council took place which O'Brien purposely did not attend. The object of this was to elect a small inner executive to manage the clubs, a directory whose deliberations would be less unwieldy than those of the thirty-strong council, and both swifter to take any necessary emergency action and more secret. O'Brien refused even to let his name go up for election, objecting to the whole idea on the grounds that such a directory would be a source of pealousy and weakness.†[25] Those elected were Duffy, Meagher, Dillon, D'Arcy, Magee and Devin Reilly; three were to form a quorum. Pressed by the rest of the meeting to give a

---

* See above, p. 273.

† Both Duffy and Gwynn, following him, say that the directory never met; but since, on the evidence of the informer Dobbyn, three were to form a quorum, they are not strictly correct (see below, p. 277).

pledge that a rising would take place before 8 August Meagher refused, though he said he would do everything he could to expedite one even before that date. But the general feeling seems to have been that nothing would occur to precipitate a rising for three or four weeks, and the feeling was shared by O'Brien.

On the next day, 22 July, Smith O'Brien went down by invitation to stay near Enniscorthy in Wexford with an old friend, John Maher, Deputy Lieutenant for that county and formerly its Member of Parliament. There was a plan for them to go the following day to visit some mudlands then in process of reclamation in Wexford Harbour, a subject in which O'Brien, with his admirable civic sense, had expressed considerable interest.[26]

The same day, after O'Brien had left, the news reached Dublin that the government was rushing a suspension of the Habeas Corpus Act through the House of Commons.

O'Brien never visited the mudlands. Soon after six o'clock on the morning of 23 July he was woken to be told that Meagher and Dillon, whom he thought were in Dublin, were in the house and wanted to speak to him urgently. They were shown to his bedside where they told him that Habeas Corpus was being suspended and that a warrant was said to be out for his arrest. After consulting with them for over an hour he asked his host to come to his room and, while dressing, told him the news.[27]

'My dear Maher,' said O'Brien, 'I did not come to your house to disturb its peace; get us some breakfast, and send us on our way. I do not wish that any arrest should take place in your house. Send for a car, that we may go towards Kilkenny, where we have some friends with whom I wish to consult in this crisis.'[28]

With these unambitious words began the 'rising' of 1848.

O'Brien had rejected both the idea of submitting to arrest and that of flight. As he wrote soon afterwards:

'So much had been said by the Party with which I was associated and by myself, about the necessary preparation for conflict, that we should have been exposed to ridicule and reproach if we had fled at the moment when all the contingencies which we had contemplated as justifying the use of force were realized ...'[29] But he continued, '... In order to leave as little as possible to conjecture I resolved before I summoned the country to arms, still further to test the disposition of the people.'[30]

In other words, having come South without any idea of an immediate insurrection in mind, and having been forced by circumstances to recognize that the moment for some sort of decisive action had at last arrived, he decided to prolong that moment as long as possible.

The town of Kilkenny, with its historical associations from 1642, and its dominating position over much of southern Ireland, had for some time been

commanding the Confederates' attention. Only three days earlier, when positive action was still far from O'Brien's mind, he had been publicly looking
forward to holding the next meeting of the Irish League there.[31] A prominent
citizen of Kilkenny, Dr Cane, was an enthusiastic supporter of the League
and there had been a newspaper report to the effect that the Confederate
clubs there were organized to a strength of seventeen thousand men.[32] In the
adjacent county of Tipperary, at Templederry, lived Father Kenyon, the
fiery priest who had tried to jolt Duffy into some sort of action two months
earlier. On the other side lay Waterford, where in the county town Meagher
had his own personal Confederate stronghold. In deep support to the south-
west lay the city of Cork, where O'Brien himself had witnessed the militant
dash of the Confederate club members.

To Meagher, already thinking more single-mindedly of insurrection than
O'Brien, certain tactical military considerations reinforced the advantages of
Kilkenny as a base. The railway from Dublin still stopped fourteen miles
short of the town, and the undulating landscape and twisting roads flanked
by high walls and hedges made it suitable territory in which to confront
regular troops with spirited irregulars. An additional coincidental factor
thought to be of advantage was that the Annual Show of the Royal Agricultural Society was being held in Kilkenny that week in the presence of the
Duke of Leinster, the Marquis of Ormond, the Earl of Clancarty and other
gentry who might prove useful as hostages while the cattle themselves
could also be put to good purpose.[33]

Such thoughts had run through the minds of Meagher and Dillon the
day before, when they had taken a number of hurried decisions with D'Arcy
Magee, the only other member of the inner directory available in Dublin.
(In tune with the general feeling that nothing unexpected was likely to
happen for a few weeks, O'Gorman had left Dublin to continue the organization of the clubs in Limerick, and Doheny was in Cashel on a similar
errand.) Now, given the recent resolution of the clubs to offer only passive
resistance to the arms ban and the known effectiveness of the government's
Dublin garrison, it seemed mad to take responsibility for blood-letting in
the streets of the capital and call out the clubs.[34] The three looked naturally
to the areas of the South which were less heavily garrisoned, and in which
in any case the most respected figure of the movement was known to be
staying. Agreeing that D'Arcy Magee should go off to Glasgow where he had
connections and, with the help of the very large Irish population of the city,
try to organize a supply of arms by sea for the moment of insurrection,
Meagher and Dillon then themselves travelled all night down to O'Brien in
Wexford.

Soon after ten o'clock the next morning, Sunday the 23rd, after collecting
O'Brien, all three were on their way by coach to Kilkenny.

They stopped at a number of points en route to try to rally feeling. At

Enniscorthy, since it was Sunday, Meagher and Dillon went to Mass. Afterwards they were joined by O'Brien, and all three were soon surrounded by a large crowd who assured them that, though not prepared or organized for an insurrection, they would protect them if any attempt were made by the police to arrest them. O'Brien expressed some disappointment that a town of the size of Enniscorthy did not have more than one Confederate club. He did not call them out to insurrection, but told them that they had to prepare for an emergency. The townspeople were asked to pledge themselves to take the field should the people of a neighbouring county rise, and a ringing shout came back that they would 'and with God's blessing too'.[35] But in this they were over-stepping the mark. In the peasantry's eyes, at any rate, it was the priests who were the final arbiters of God's blessing.

It was raining heavily that Sunday and, stopping occasionally by the roadside for shelter, O'Brien, Meagher and Dillon were left in no doubt by the famished and dispirited peasantry they met that they had no enthusiasm for any rising. A longer stop at the small town of Graigue-na-mana was also discouraging, for the priest there would not commit himself to approval of an insurrection, remarking merely that 'the whole affair was a very difficult subject to decide upon'.[36] Spirits recovered a little, however, when it was remembered that Thomas Cloney, the old rebel of '98,* now a venerated citizen, lived in the town, and O'Brien, Meagher and Dillon went to see him.[37] Cloney, long popularly known as 'General' Cloney, threw his arms round O'Brien and wept with emotion. Speaking to a crowd of between three and four hundred from Cloney's house, Meagher told them the news of the suspension of Habeas Corpus and urged them to form a club, but also told them to beware of 'the claws of the law' and to commit no breach of it.[38] It may well have seemed unclear to the crowds whether they were actually being called to insurrection or not. The position roughly was that O'Brien and the others were saying they would take up arms if the people supported them while the people were saying they would support them if they took up arms.

The three arrived in Kilkenny at about eight o'clock that Sunday evening and went straight to the house of Dr Cane. There they received their first serious shock. There were not 17,000 members of the clubs in the town as reported, but 1,700. It had been a misprint in the newspapers. Only about one in four of the members had arms.[39]

Abandoning the idea of an immediate insurrection in the town, O'Brien, Meagher and Dillon proceeded next day on a tour of the surrounding countryside. They hoped to mobilize support for those ardent spirits in Kilkenny who, in spite of all, had encouraged Meagher and Dillon to think that within a week the green flag would be flying from Ormond Castle.

The travels of O'Brien, Meagher and Dillon now continued in the same

* See above, p. 112.

pattern as the day before, only with the difference that the longer such travels continued the more desultory and inconclusive they seemed. At Callan a party of the 8th Irish Hussars was in the town when they arrived, but they left O'Brien unmolested as he again asked a crowd, this time about nine hundred strong, if they would let him be arrested and the crowd replied emphatically: no. One Englishman among the Hussars, alarmed by the prevailing mood, prepared to leave the Market House where the troops were quartered. But Meagher reassured the men that there was no need to leave the building and that they and their arms were quite safe.[40]

'We know that, Sir,' replied a corporal of the Hussars. 'We know well you wouldn't take an unfair advantage of the poor soldiers; at any rate, you wouldn't do it to the Irish Hussars.'[41]

Again the gist of the message to the people was two-fold. They should help O'Brien resist arrest if arrest were attempted. They should also organize and be ready, for the time was at hand. It was still not made clear what the time was at hand for, other than being ready.

That evening on the road between Callan and Carrick-on-Suir, O'Brien, Meagher and Dillon stopped at a halt to change horses and chatted with the country people. They learned that though many were disposed to rise against the government even if they only had bill-hooks and pitchforks rather than guns, the priests were overwhelmingly against it. However, some of the more enthusiastic people they spoke to said that if only one priest could be found in favour of action that would do 'for the people were tired of keeping so quiet and dying from day to day'.[42]

Just short of Carrick itself they pulled up at some cross-roads to talk to some men digging in a field. On hearing that a young Catholic land-owner named John O'Mahony, who had done much to organize the local clubs, lived in the neighbourhood they asked to see him. Twenty minutes later O'Mahony himself came galloping up on a black horse to vouch personally for the local enthusiasm.[43]

In Carrick town itself therefore O'Brien, on being brought into the presence of the club leaders, asked for six hundred men with guns and ammunition to guard him and his companions while they raised the countryside. Since Tipperary was a proclaimed county, this was to propose an open act of war. But though O'Brien was beginning to commit himself his request met with dismay. One man asked pointedly why it was that the leaders should have come to Carrick of all places to start the rising. Was it because they had been rejected everywhere else?[44]

The most influential priest in the neighbourhood, a Father Byrne, who had in his day made inflammatory enough speeches, would have nothing to do with the project, saying that O'Brien 'must be mad', and that he should at least wait until the harvest had been brought in in a fortnight's time.[45]

That other well-known Tipperary priest, Father Kenyon at Templederry, was also backing out of any positive action on the grounds that an attempt now would be suicidal.

O'Mahony, ashamed for Tipperary, pledged himself to go out and raise the neighbourhood. He actually succeeded in collecting four hundred men from his own club with about eighty guns and a large number of pikes. But there was apparently no immediate work for them to do. For by next morning O'Brien had moved off in the direction of Cashel, hoping to get some encouragement from Michael Doheny, whose home town it was. Before leaving Carrick he addressed a crowd of some five thousand in the streets, telling them positively this time that he was calling them to the field. Meagher also spoke and was quite carried away by his own oratory, for after first appearing to contradict his leader and telling the crowd that they must all deliberate a little longer he also cried:

'What care I for all their force? They may threaten us with death; they may tear from us our lives; more they cannot do for they have already deprived us of all else besides. Death is the worst they can inflict. Death is the utmost bounds of their threats. They are again renewing the bloody deeds of '98 ...'[46]

It was half a century since '98, but memories of the appalling government brutalities that had followed its failure were still vivid. Any reminder of them was a doubtful rhetorical gambit, for apprehension of failure was growing daily.

The whole of the rest of the week was spent in similar dilatory and cumulatively demoralizing fashion. Day followed day without any very positive action being taken by anyone. O'Brien and his companions simply moved from place to place within a relatively small area of Tipperary, often visiting the same town or village more than once. Those who at first had had a certain amount of heart for a fight became understandably cautious, while those who were already pessimistic became even more determined not to involve themselves in the consequences of disaster. The priests did all they could to discourage premature audacity, coming out increasingly into the open to argue against O'Brien.[47]

Meagher went off to his own city of Waterford, hoping to raise the clubs there and return with a thousand men. He returned alone, having been unable to get the leaders to move against the advice of their own radical priest, Father Tracy. Meagher seems, however, to have accepted their reply a little too readily, for later in the week another young Confederate, Michael Cavanagh, found the boatmen of Waterford disappointed and feeling let down by Meagher who had sent them no word when 'thousands' of them were still waiting for a summons to the fight. They felt, they told Cavanagh, 'something was wrong somewhere'.[48]

Almost nothing was right.

O'Mahony, by force of his own local appeal and vigorous personality, continued to rally the countryside effectively for a time. He reckoned afterwards, probably with some exaggeration, that he had some twelve to fifteen thousand men ready to march by the night of Tuesday, 25 July, and Michael Doheny, who had by then joined him, substantiates at least the enthusiasm with which pikes were being forged in the area round the Slievenamon hills.⁴⁹ But O'Mahony, waiting for a signal from his leaders that never came, was unable himself to give his followers any very clear indication of the purpose for which they were being summoned.

A number of other enthusiastic middle-class young Irishmen had by now made their way south to swell the group round O'Brien. Among them were P. J. Smyth, son of a prosperous Dublin merchant, and a successful young shipping agent, named T. B. McManus, who had crossed over from Liverpool specially for the purpose. Also in this group was a twenty-five-year-old employee of the Limerick and Waterford Railway Company who, though he had never been a member of the Irish Confederation, had come to join O'Brien from Kilkenny. His name was James Stephens.

It was in the company of Stephens, armed with a double-barrelled gun, that on the morning of Wednesday, 26 July, O'Brien made his first overt move against the forces of the Crown. Wearing the gold and green cap of the '82 club, and with a number of pistols tucked into his coat, O'Brien, with Stephens and one other companion, marched into the police station at Mullinahone, in County Tipperary. It was garrisoned by a head constable and five others.⁵⁰

An enthusiastic crowd had gathered in the village the night before, but in the morning, under the influence of their priests, they had begun to have second thoughts. The presence of the police was given as an excuse for their new-found timidity. O'Brien decided to tackle the problem head on. He had been maintaining throughout the last three days that the police were as good Irishmen as any, and when the time came would know how to act. He proceeded to the police station to prove his point, and asked the police to surrender.

The head constable said afterwards in court that he replied: 'I would be unworthy of the name of Irishman if I gave up my arms.'⁵¹ And though O'Brien, who is probably more reliable, stated that the constable had by no means been so firm as he later pretended, the fact that this was at least thought to be the right answer to give is significant. O'Brien, like other Irish nationalists before and after, was up against the awkward fact that Irish nationalism was not the clear-cut cause he made it out to be.

Another eye-witness maintained, many years later, that while O'Brien and Stephens were inside the police station, a big policeman put his head out of an upper window and exclaimed to the crowd: 'Yerrah! sure the time isn't come yet to surrender our arms. D'ye wait till the right time comes!'⁵²

Whatever the truth of this, while O'Brien gave them further time in which
to deliberate, they worked out their own compromise and made off with
their arms to a stronger police post.

This new appearance of resolution on O'Brien's part had first taken shape
the night before, when he had sent P. J. Smyth off to Dublin with orders to
'start an insurrection there'.[53] Nevertheless, a man who saw O'Brien that
same night later described him as having been 'like a man in a dream'.[54] And
it was a fact that the secretary of the Dublin clubs, James Halpin, was
actually already in the South looking for O'Brien in order to get instructions
for his clubmen. These had been left 'disheartened and bewildered',[55] without
any indications of what was going on or how to communicate with their
leaders. Some isolated manoeuvres were carried out in a few parts of Ireland
on the initiative of a few individuals who hoped for news from the South
to give coherence to their movements. Richard O'Gorman, for instance,
began to raise the peasantry in Limerick, and D'Arcy Magee, after he had
had to fly from Glasgow to escape arrest, had landed in Sligo and organized
some qualified support from the agrarian secret societies there.[56] But by
then total fiasco had overtaken O'Brien's perambulations in Tipperary.

Without any proper organization, or even effective communications, with
the priests against him, and beset by failures such as that of Meagher's in
Waterford and his own before the police station in Mullinahone, O'Brien
must by mid-week already have begun to grasp that his chances were forlorn
in the extreme. Nevertheless, the same eye-witness who described him as
having been like a man in a dream at Mullinahone, also saw him not many
hours after looking dreamy still, but happy and smoking a cigar as he left
on a jaunty car.[57] He stubbornly refused to requisition private property for
supplies, as his companions urged him to, maintaining incongruously that
the last thing he wanted to start was a *jacquerie*.[58]

A certain amount of shambling drill seems to have taken place in Mullinahone itself and other villages where he appeared. But always the parties
of peasants, armed mainly with agricultural implements and a few muskets,
melted away after entreaties from their priests not to risk their lives without
hope of success, or on realizing that supplies of free food were not unlimited.
(O'Brien paid for more than 160 loaves of bread on one occasion out
of his own pocket, but another day solemnly issued an order that each
man among the starving peasantry should appear with at least four days'
rations.)[59]

However, on Friday, 28 July, at the small town of Killenaule, O'Brien had
the nearest thing to a victory that came his way during the whole week. A
party of dragoons was seen approaching the town and, it being assumed
that they had come to arrest O'Brien, barricades were thrown up in their
path. When the captain of dragoons, a Captain Longmore, halted before
the first barricade a rifle was presented at him by James Stephens, and he

was asked by Dillon if he had a warrant for O'Brien's arrest. On giving an assurance that he had not and that he had no intention of trying to arrest O'Brien, the barricades were lifted and he and his men were allowed through and out of the town.[60] It was a transaction from which on reflection neither party considered it had emerged with credit. O'Brien, after all, was a proclaimed outlaw, and it would have seemed Captain Longmore's duty to proceed against him whether he had a warrant or not. To this extent it was a victory for O'Brien. On the other hand, if O'Brien had really been wanting to start an insurrection and put heart into those thousands in the area who were understandably wavering, this had been an opportunity for forcing a body of government troops to surrender which had not been taken.

But it was still perhaps not wholly O'Brien's policy to commit himself to a fighting insurrection. Future policy was indeed the subject of a conference held that night in the small town of Ballingarry, the centre of a colliery district from which O'Brien hoped for support from the miners. Earlier that evening Meagher had told the miners that they were to be ready in three weeks' when the wisp would be lit over the hills'.[61] Another, unnamed, companion had stated more directly that they would 'hunt every English bugger to his own side, and let him live there'.[62]

The conference at Ballingarry was the nearest thing to a council of war the Confederates ever held. Doheny and O'Mahony, as well as Meagher, had managed to join O'Brien for it, along with Stephens, Dillon, McManus and the others already there. The conference lasted only an hour and a quarter. Everyone declared himself dissatisfied with the course which events had taken during the week. In the circumstances most people were in favour of going into hiding and waiting for the harvest. But O'Brien, whose strong personal sense of honour prevented him from becoming a fugitive at this stage, determined to try and continue to raise sufficient force to be effective. It was decided that Dillon, Meagher and Doheny should once more go off to rally the neighbouring districts while he stood firm where he was.[63]

Prospects had been doubtful enough before. Now nothing seemed in their favour. After so much delay already the only hope of rallying the countryside lay in the news of an outstanding success. As Father Kenyon, the former militant priest of Templederry in Tipperary, told Dillon and Meagher when they arrived: it was not becoming in a priest to start a hopeless struggle; they were perfectly at liberty as far as he was concerned to raise a green flag on a pole anywhere in his district and see just how many men would rally round it.[64]

And soon there came to Templederry and elsewhere news not of a success but of a particularly lamentable failure.

On Saturday, 29 July, the government forces slowly began to move towards O'Brien, penned up in his Tipperary box. He had spent the night writing a letter to the mining company, saying that if they withheld wages from the miners who joined him, then the colliery would be confiscated as national property in the event of the Irish Revolution succeeding.[65] It was the one truly revolutionary step he took in the whole week. Next morning McManus reviewed the local forces. Two days before few people in Ballingarry had even heard of O'Brien, let alone had any clear idea of his cause.[66] Now McManus counted twenty men armed with guns and pistols, and eighteen with crude pikes.[67] The decision was taken to try and join up with another more powerful force optimistically thought to be in the neighbourhood and attack the nearest police barracks.

Before they could move, a member of one of the Dublin clubs, named John Kavanagh, who had come South to join O'Brien, galloped up to say that on his way he had spotted a large body of police approaching Ballingarry.[68] He had come via Kilkenny, where incidentally the rumour was that the town of Callan was in rebel hands and O'Brien himself at the head of twenty thousand men. All the approaches to Kilkenny were now guarded by the military, but he thought the government were in a panic and urged O'Brien, who seemed elated by this news, to strike rapidly. At that moment another messenger came up to say that an even larger body of police was now approaching from Thurles. O'Brien and McManus decided to defend Ballingarry.

A barricade, manned by O'Brien himself, was thrown up. Stephens and some of those armed with guns occupied the houses immediately overlooking it. McManus and another party lay flat on their faces in a hollow about 250 yards ahead of the barricade, waiting to catch the police in the rear as they approached it.[69]

The police whom Kavanagh had spotted had now arrived within a mile or so of Ballingarry. But seeing the barricade and the large crowds assembled – the majority of whom can only have been sightseers – the police veered prudently away and made for cover in a solid one-storey stone house with a slate roof about a mile northwards at Farrinrory.[70] This house belonged to a widow, a Mrs McCormack. She was out at the time, but her five children, all under ten, were inside when Sub-Inspector Trant and forty-six men entered, and chorusing 'The British Grenadiers' started breaking up the furniture to put the house in a state of defence.[71]

Without waiting for orders the mob rushed towards the house, sweeping Smith O'Brien before them. McManus decided the best policy would be to try and smoke the police out by setting fire to some straw in the stables at the back, and was in the process of doing this when he was stopped by O'Brien who said that the widow herself had now arrived and was appealing to him to save her house and her children from destruction.[72]

She, O'Brien, McManus and a few others then went through a gate into the small cabbage garden that surrounded the house, and O'Brien boldly went up to one of the windows. Climbing up onto the sill he asked to speak to Sub-Inspector Trant, the police commander. Trant had taken up his post at an upstairs window and there was a delay while someone went to fetch him. Meanwhile, O'Brien talked to the policemen at his window telling them that he was an Irishman and a soldier too, and asking them to give up their arms. To this they replied: 'We would forfeit our lives rather than give up our arms.'[73]

Whereupon O'Brien said he would allow them five minutes in which to make up their minds, and got down from the window sill.

The next thing that happened was that, as O'Brien turned away, someone – clearly not O'Brien – shouted:

'Slash away, boys, and slaughter the whole of them!' or words to that effect.[74]

Some stones were thrown. Possibly a shot was fired from the crowd.

The police were in an unpleasant situation and very nervous. They fired a volley. They continued to fire intermittently for the next hour or so, expending some 230 rounds in all.[75] Two of the would-be besiegers were killed and a number wounded. None of the police were wounded.[76] There was a general retreat of the besiegers, including eventually even O'Brien, who had at first refused to leave the scene declaring formally that an O'Brien never turned his back on an enemy.[77]

The local priest, a Father Fitzgerald, now came on the scene. O'Brien enlisted his help in making one more attempt to persuade the police to lay down their arms. But the priest received only a harangue from the agitated Sub-Inspector, who conjured up visions of '98 and threatened martial law, the burning of houses and summary executions for this resistance to lawful authority. On his return to O'Brien Father Fitzgerald advised him to give up all notion of attacking the house and O'Brien seemed disposed to take the advice.[78]

Another policeman had arrived during the fighting with a message for Sub-Inspector Trant about reinforcements on the way but had been made prisoner by the mob and had his horse taken from him before being released. Some time later this policeman ran into O'Brien wandering about on this horse of his in a state of some distraction. O'Brien, thinking that the man had come to arrest him, produced a pistol and prepared to sell his life dearly. The policeman hurriedly reassured him, and when the misunderstanding had been cleared up they had something of a heart-to-heart conversation.

The policeman told O'Brien he had no hope of success with the clergy against him, and asked him how, in any case, he hoped to be able to take on regular troops. O'Brien's reply was that he had been working for his country for twenty years and his country could redeem itself if it liked. The policeman said the only way it could be redeemed was with blood. O'Brien said he wanted no blood and gave him his horse back.[79]

Two hours later another force of police arrived, and after a brief engagement with the mob, which James Stephens attempted to rally, they relieved the widow McCormack's house and its loyal defenders.* Further bodies of police followed. O'Brien, McManus and Stephens went off into hiding. They had little alternative since McManus's attempt to raise a force from the citizens of Ballingarry to avenge their fallen comrades produced only three volunteers.[80] The 'rising' was over.

As an eye-witness of Ballingarry declared a few days later: the idea that it had been a rebellion was ridiculous.[81] O'Brien himself called it an 'escapade' and added, echoing Emmet, 'it does not deserve the name of insurrection'.[82]

Large bodies of troops and police soon poured into the area round Ballingarry. There was no repetition of the horrors of '98. Many arrests were made and according to the local parish priest 'whole families were left mourning and desolate, for many died in captivity and exile, others perished from long concealment in bogs and mountains'.[83] But there were no executions.

None of the leaders were betrayed in hiding. O'Brien himself remained at large for over a week and was eventually captured on the platform at Thurles railway station, trying to make his way back to his home near Limerick.[84] He was wearing a black hat, a blue coat and light plaid trousers at the time, and had just bought himself a second-class ticket and forgotten to collect his sixpence change. An English railway guard named Hulme made the initial arrest and received the £500 reward.[85]

Others arrested while more conventionally on the run included McManus, taken on board a ship bound for America in Cork harbour, and Meagher, caught on the open road near Cashel after nights spent in ditches, haylofts and peasant cabins. James Stephens's death from a bullet at Ballingarry was reported in the *Kilkenny Moderator*. The paper, while regretting the loss of this 'most inoffensive young man, possessed of a great deal of talent', and lamenting 'his untimely and melancholy fate', nevertheless trusted it might prove a 'wholesome warning to the hot young blood of Kilkenny'.[86] However, the *Moderator*'s rival, the *Kilkenny Journal*, scooped it a couple of months later when it was able to announce that Stephens had written to a friend in Tipperary from Paris, where he had found sanctuary and where refugees were, he revealed, being received in the highest circles.[87] Stephens had made his escape to France via Bristol and London, after spending adventurous weeks in hiding together with Doheny who also got to France. O'Mahony, thanks to the local loyalties he commanded, kept some-

---

* More than thirty years later Stephens gave a rather fanciful account of this engagement in the *Irishman* newspaper, in which he claimed that several constables were killed. None of the Crown forces were killed that day at Ballingarry. Stephens's exaggerations have unfortunately been repeated in Desmond Ryan, *The Fenian Chief* (Dublin, 1907). There is little doubt, however, that Stephens acted bravely.

thing of a force in being in Tipperary for a few weeks. In September he un-successfully attacked a police barracks at Glenbar with the loss of two men, and another at Portlaw in County Waterford with the loss of one. He then escaped to join Stephens and Doheny in Paris.[88]

O'Brien's trial for high treason was by then over. He was found guilty and sentenced to be drawn on a hurdle to the place of execution, there hanged by the neck until dead and then decapitated and cut into four quarters to be disposed of as Her Majesty thought fit – the routine formula of the day*.[89] The same sentence awaited Meagher, McManus and others involved in the misfortunes of that last chaotic week in July. From the dock, McManus, who had been earning the large sum of £2,000 a year as a shipping agent in Liverpool only a few months before, stressed that he had been activated not by animosity towards Englishmen, among whom he had spent some of the happiest and most prosperous days of his career. 'It is not', he added, 'for loving England less but for loving Ireland more that I stand now before you.'[90] Meagher had declaimed with dignity: '... the history of Ireland explains my crime and justifies it ... judged by that history, the treason of which I have been convicted loses all guilt – is sanctified as a duty – will be ennobled as a sacrifice'.[91]

The jury in O'Brien's case had brought in a strong recommendation to mercy, and it was not thought that the death sentence would be carried out. However, O'Brien typically refused to apply for a pardon, which was the only legal means of granting him a reprieve, and a special act of Parliament had to be passed in the following year enabling the government to transport him for life instead. He was sent to Tasmania with Meagher, McManus and John Martin, who had meanwhile been convicted for sedition in his paper, the *Irish Felon*. In Tasmania they were joined by Mitchel, who after his year in Bermuda had spent a further eleven months on the high seas journeying via South America and the Cape.

In Tasmania O'Brien, again typically, alone refused to give his parole at first. He was confined to a solitary existence in and around a cottage on a small island off the coast of Tasmania, and made an abortive attempt to escape which was betrayed. Later, as his health deteriorated, he gave in and became a ticket-of-leave man like the others, with the run of a district about thirty-five miles long by ten miles wide.

McManus, Meagher and Mitchel all eventually escaped from Tasmania to America, having planned their escapes while on parole with the aid of the Young Irelander, P. J. Smyth, who had come specially from America for that purpose.[92] O'Brien was finally pardoned with Martin in 1854, and allowed to return to Ireland and the bosom of his embarrassed family in

* Earlier in the queen's reign the time-honoured passage about disembowelling the traitors while still alive and burning their entrails in front of them had been relinquished.

1856.[93] Though it is sometimes said that he 'took no further part in public life',[94] this is not strictly so. A curiously dignified figure, even to those political enemies who regarded his antics of 1848 as ridiculous, he continued to appear on the fringes of public life, writing letters to newspapers and identifying himself with aspirations for constitutional nationality until his death in 1864. 'Erratic' was the respectful term of opprobium Unionists reserved for him. In 1859 he visited America, where he met Mitchel, Meagher and O'Gorman again. The *New York Express* wrote: 'There is a hesitancy and diffidence about him which perhaps does not attract favourably at first, but ... there is something in him which rivets the hearer in spite of himself.'[95]

Mitchel, Meagher and O'Gorman were all to make new lives for themselves in the stimulating and demanding conditions of the still evolving nation on the other side of the Atlantic. The need to earn a living there, to establish a social identity in a strange society, to find both the material and psychological security necessary for day-to-day existence always set up a personal conflict between the demands of America and Ireland in the minds of even the most spirited and determined emigrant advocates of the Irish 'cause'. The very imprecision of this cause and its slightly theoretical nature in contrast with the hard facts of life in the States was part of this conflict. The conflict was resolved in many different ways, but usually so as to dilute the amount of energy directly applied to Ireland.

Some, like O'Gorman, chose the easy way out, abandoning all further serious thoughts of Irish nationalism. He died in 1895, a distinguished New York judge. D'Arcy Magee, though he retained an interest in Ireland, equally firmly renounced the rebelliousness of his youth, became postmaster-general of Canada, and was assassinated by an extreme Irish separatist in 1867.

Meagher continued to breathe fire and lived quite successfully off it in the form of lectures or journalism. When he did finally take the field it was not in Ireland at all but in the country of his adoption. In the early years of the American Civil War he fought in the three-thousand-strong Irish brigade of the Union Army at the great battles of Bull Run, Antietam, Fredericksburg and Chancellorsville, taking command with the rank of general after its commanding officer had been taken prisoner. Both the brigade and its general showed outstanding bravery and dash. At Fredericksburg, of the twelve hundred men Meagher led into action only 280 were fit for action the next morning.[96] An exasperated Confederate general burst out during the battle: 'There are those damned green flags again',[97] and a Confederate soldier wrote home to his wife: 'Why, my darling, we forgot they were fighting us, and cheer after cheer at their fearlessness went up all along our lines.'[98] But out of the battle line Meagher's military career seems to have been less distinguished. He left the army under something of a cloud, with accusations of drunkenness and incompetence and even talk of a court-martial hanging over him.[89] He died in 1866 when acting-governor of the district of Montana, which had not yet become a State. Drunk or ill, or possibly both, he fell overboard from a steamboat moored on the Missouri where he was spending the night and disappeared in the rapid current. His wife searched the river's banks for two months for his body without success.[100]

Of all the *émigrés* of this time Mitchel perhaps maintained the best balance in his attitude to Irish affairs. He lived by journalism, running a newspaper himself first in New York and then in the South where he lived during the Civil War. He became a stern advocate of the Confederate cause, and, as one might have expected from his remarks about his fellow convicts on the Bermuda hulks, indulged in no sentimental libertarianism towards the Negro slaves. He was prepared to involve himself in Irish affairs whenever prospects seemed to him realistic, which was less often than more bombastic Irish patriots preferred to assume. Mitchel actually ended his life in Ireland in 1875 in the very house in which he was born, having just been elected Member of Parliament for Tipperary, though unseated as a convicted felon.

Curiously, T. B. McManus was to prove the most effective Young Irelander in the long run, but as a corpse. Having settled in California, where he showed little further interest in the cause of Irish nationality, he died there in 1861. The return of his body to Ireland and its subsequent funeral in the streets of Dublin was made the occasion for a mass patriotic demonstration which inaugurated in Ireland the first hopeful phase of a new movement altogether.

14

The Corpse on the
Dissecting Table

'For the first time these many years,' declared the leading article in the *Kilkenny Journal* for Saturday, 19 August 1848, 'this country is without any popular political association. There is no rallying point.... A more prostrate condition no country was ever in ...'[1] It was true. The Irish Confederation and the subsequent Irish League had been proved by the events of July to be rallying-points of straw. Now even they were gone. There was not a single club left in Dublin.[2]

It was no use trying to find a convenient scapegoat in O'Brien. It was, as the *Kilkenny Moderator* put it, the 'absurd bravado and unmeaning rhodomontade' of the whole movement that had been exposed.[3] Those club leaders who did try and blame O'Brien's leadership conveniently forgot that 'by their grandiloquent ovations, by bragging of what they would do and what they could do, unfortunate O'Brien was led out absolutely under false pretences'.[4]

The ineffectualness of simply talking about nationality in the face of the realities of Irish life was most cruelly revealed. In the political silence that now prevailed, the sounds the Irish people heard were not the dying trumpets of a defeated cause, but the clanking of crowbars demolishing cabins, the cries of evicted women and children, and the moans of the starving, all of which had persisted for the past three years.[5] With the potato crop again blighted, the prospects for the autumn and winter of 1848 were as grim as they had ever been.[6] The ragged, barefoot crowds lucky enough to find outdoor relief still laboured ten hours a day on empty stomachs for food tickets, throwing themselves on the ground when the overseer's own dinner hour arrived, and staggering to their feet again like sea-sick men when he returned.[7] 'Travel where you would,' wrote a contemporary later, 'deserted and ruined cabins met the eye on every side. You frequently met large parties of emigrants proceeding to the ports.'[8]

Clearly the ideal of nationality had to be brought closer to the lives of the ordinary Irish people if it was to mean anything. A new sort of policy altogether was required.

For a year or so a few of the very young men who had been peripherally involved in the events of July 1848 tried to show that they could do better in the existing situation than their leaders. One was a former member of a Dublin Confederate club, a railway clerk named Philip Gray, one of whose uncles had been hanged in '98.[9] Gray had on his own initiative tried to rouse the peasantry in Meath while O'Brien was making his way round Tipperary at the end of July. Having totally failed, he had joined up with O'Mahony in the South in August and taken part the next month in the attack on Portlaw barracks. In November, with another Dublin ex-Confederate, an eighteen-year-old Protestant student of Trinity College, named John O'Leary, he planned to attack Clonmel gaol and rescue Smith O'Brien.

The rescue was arranged for the night of 8 November, but an informer gave away one of the assembly points, a piece of ground known as 'the Wilderness', and O'Leary and sixteen other young men under his command were arrested there and a few pikes and a large pistol found.[10] The matter was not treated very seriously by the authorities, presumably because of the youth of the apparent leader. Gray, the real leader, was not caught. O'Leary was released from gaol a few weeks later.

It is not quite so easy to dismiss Gray, and O'Leary's next moves as childish pranks. For although they too ended in fiasco they involved the formation of oath-bound secret societies to establish an Irish republic, and there were to be links at least in personnel between these and a later society of the same sort which finally altered the course of Irish history. The formation in 1848 by Gray and O'Leary of these secret societies in the South, and that of another by Joseph Brenan and Fintan Lalor in Dublin, showed at least a recognition, however amateurish, of the need to organize better in future. Their own particular deficiency in professional skill was revealed in the following year.

First, a bold plan of Brenan's to capture Queen Victoria on her visit to Dublin in the summer of 1849 came to nothing, though 150 men actually assembled one night for the purpose.[11] Then, when the different secret societies amalgamated under Fintan Lalor in September, they immediately embarked on a plan for a rising which was not only badly coordinated but also largely known beforehand to the authorities. On the night of 16 September 1849, an unsuccessful attack was made on the police barracks at Cappoquin by a force under Brenan, and the movement disintegrated. Lalor, and the son of a professor at Trinity named Thomas Luby, were imprisoned for a short time. Lalor, whose health had always been bad, died not long afterwards. O'Leary and Gray escaped arrest. Brenan fled to America. This abortive movement to assert Irish nationalism in a more openly aggressive manner than anything the Irish Confederation or Irish League had wished to undertake seemed only to confirm that all such purely nationalistic activities were doomed as unrealistic.

Of the realities of everyday Irish life two were paramount: the desperate hardship of trying to get a livelihood out of the land and the presence of the Catholic Church. The Church was, as it were, the only permanent form of national organization, or indeed true representation, the peasantry had. In Ireland, wrote a Catholic editor of this time, the priests occupied towards the people the role of a gentry or local aristocracy. They were the *only* educated class who truly sympathized with the people, and thus the only class to whom the poor Catholic farmer could turn for advice and guidance on matters temporal as well as spiritual.[12]

The Church was more important than any political association. It was more all-embracing than the agrarian secret societies, not only because it was open, but because it was both localized and universal at the same time. The only time the peasantry had shown themselves capable of being organized politically at all had been when political forces and the Church cooperated closely, in the days of O'Connell. At elections the extent of the priests' spiritual intimidation was often grossly exaggerated, but they exercised considerable influence.[13] Their general influence as day-to-day leaders was something no serious nationalist could leave out of account.

For the Irish farmer and labourer, national consciousness, such as it was, was an emotion rather than a doctrine, a powerful but vague adjunct to that identity of which the chief features were the passionate need to improve his material lot and his Catholicism. Irish nationality was not an end to be pursued for its own sake, as it had been for Davis. Any doctrinaire nationalist had to come to terms with this fact. It was not enough to appeal to national sentiment in order to assert it. If idealists wanted the Irish people to take the idea of Irish nationality seriously, they themselves must take the land situation seriously and must work if possible with the approval, or at worst the benevolent neutrality, of the Catholic Church.

This presented the doctrinaire exponent of nationalism with a dilemma. To work obliquely towards nationality was the only way of making it a reality; yet, by thus appealing primarily to other interests and other loyalties, the goal of nationality itself became secondary. It forfeited that overriding loyalty which should by definition be the essential characteristic of nationalism.

Thus for the rest of the nineteenth century and beyond – perhaps still even today – there remains a certain lack of distinctness about Irish nationality. Many questions have always lain, only half-asked, just below the surface of political life. What, for instance, really was nationality, in Irish terms, if it did not spontaneously and instinctively assert itself as a separate force? Was it something real enough to be pursued for its own sake at all? Or was it only a means to an end; a tactical slogan with which to achieve a better life for the majority of the people of Ireland? And if this could be achieved without pursuit of separate nationality, was there really a need for any positive nationality? Given the long historical tradition of political and racial entanglement with the rest of Britain, was there not something absurd about the idea of 'pure' nationality? Could there perhaps be such a thing as a half-way status between a nation and a province? If not, in view of the past, could Irish pride be satisfied with the status of a province? Events alone were to resolve these uncertainties, often with an arbitrary disregard for national considerations.

With the total humiliation in 1848 and 1849 of all grandiloquent attempts to assert Irish nationality, Irish political life proceeded to concern itself for a time with more down-to-earth affairs. Even a former ardent nationalist like Duffy saw no alternative but to rest his ardour and concentrate, in the appalling wake of the famine, on efforts to alter the land system and extend Ulster custom of tenant right by law to the whole of Ireland. At the same time, Catholic considerations inevitably figured prominently.

The Irish Catholic Church's attitude to the idea of Irish nationality was ambivalent. On the one hand, sympathizing with the people for whose material as well as spiritual welfare it was acutely concerned, it naturally favoured any emphasis on the people's identity which would help further an improvement in their appalling conditions. Similarly, there were specifically Catholic objectives which could be pursued and gained by an effective political rallying of the people. Emancipation itself had been one obvious example of this, and there were other outstanding Catholic issues in which the hierarchy had a political interest, not least of which were the disestablishment of the Protestant Church and the principle of separate denominational education for Catholics.

As far as the pursuit of nationality as an end in itself was concerned, the Church had inevitable reservations, which were not just confined to its spiritual need to assess the justifiability of violence. The Catholic Church itself was, after all, the supreme loyalty with which the hierarchy wanted the people to identify themselves. Any attempt to promote the spiritual idea of nationality must in some sense prove competitive with this. On the whole, therefore, the Church's attitude to nationality in the nineteenth and twentieth centuries proved pragmatic, being generally determined by tactical considerations. Inasmuch as Catholic interests seemed likely to be enhanced by nationality, it was in favour of it. Inasmuch as they seemed likely to be endangered by nationality, it tried to restrain it. In the last resort, where restraint eventually proved impossible, it was prepared to follow, for fear ultimately of losing the power to lead. All of which meant that individual members of the hierarchy, sometimes in conflict, were the forces that determined the Church's attitude to nationality at any given time.

The Irish Catholic Church in the fifties, sixties and seventies of the nineteenth century was dominated by two giant ecclesiastical personalities of

very different outlook and temperament: John MacHale, Archbishop of
Tuam, who had been a prominent supporter of O'Connell, and Paul Cullen,
who became Archbishop of Dublin in 1852. Though Cullen is usually
thought of – and rightly by comparison with the progressive MacHale – as
having been an extreme conservative, his appointment was from the point of
view of nationalists an improvement on his predecessor Archbishop Murray
who had been an out-and-out supporter of the government.[14] But Cullen's
approach to political developments was based on the cautious assumption
that they should be judged by the experience of a dangerous past rather
than in the light of an optimistic future. Whereas MacHale saw self-government as the eventual key to all other Irish political and social problems,
Cullen feared that an Irish government would be controlled by the Protestant
ascendancy. When something like an independent Irish party began to
operate in the British House of Commons during the early 1850s, with its
immediate objective a Tenants' Rights Bill, Cullen soon cooled towards it
because, he said, 'if all Catholics were to unite in adopting such principles I
am persuaded that the English government in self-defence would have to
expel them from Parliament and begin to renew the penal laws'.[15]

The appearance in the 1850s of an independent Irish party in the Commons is of interest chiefly as an indication of more effective things to come.
It eventually failed to obtain its objectives and had disintegrated by the end
of the decade. But it was for a time quite an impressive political force, a
working combination of the strongest feelings that dominated Irish opinion,
namely those concerning the Catholic religion and the land.

Over a hundred thousand persons had been officially evicted from their
holdings in 1849 and local tenants' organizations had sprung up in that year
as simple measures of self-defence. By 1850 there were twenty such organizations in ten different counties in Ireland. Simultaneously, Ulster tenants,
who though protected by the custom of tenant right had suffered hardship
trying to meet their rents in famine conditions and were anxious about
future security, agitated for legalization of the Ulster custom. A Tenants'
League of North and South was formed, and this public recognition of common interest even on a purely material plane seemed particularly hopeful to
a nationalist like Gavan Duffy.

Duffy had survived five attempts to convict him of treason felony in 1848
and 1849 when five successive juries failed to agree. He had returned to the
editorship of *The Nation*, and in 1852 he entered Parliament as one of forty-
eight Irish members of a so-called Irish Tenants' League. The members of
this League took a significant public pledge. This was, to be 'perfectly independent of, and in opposition to, all governments who do not make it a
part of their policy and a cabinet question to give to the tenants of Ireland
a measure embodying the principles of Mr Sharman Crawford's tenant right
bill'.[16]

In fact, the nationally unifying drive of the new political association was never very great, for relative agricultural prosperity began to return to Ireland with a series of good harvests beginning in 1851, and the Ulster share in the agitation became insignificant. To some extent the good harvests also lessened the impetus of the tenant right movement in the South. But here religious issues came to its aid.

Even before the election of 1852 Irish members in the House of Commons had been combining in the defence of Catholic interests, particularly against a bill to prevent Catholic bishops assuming territorial titles. In this way Irish Members in Parliament had already achieved some temporary solidarity, parading under the name of 'the Irish Brigade' or, as their opponents called them, 'the Pope's Brass Band'. They had assumed a position of obvious importance in the prevailing delicate balance of British political parties. One prominent member of the 'Brigade' (the Mayo Catholic land-owner G. H. Moore, father of the novelist George Moore) even proposed that they should employ methods of obstruction in the House, but was over-ruled by his colleagues. And it was the alliance of this parliamentary 'Irish Brigade' and the Tenant Right League which gave the forty-eight members elected in 1852 their appearance of independent strength. They took a public pledge to remain independent of any English party that did not commit them to Tenant Right.

But this notion of independence received a temporary shock soon after the new Parliament had assembled. For though the party's first action had been to help turn out Lord Derby's Tory government, yet when a new government under Lord Aberdeen was formed, also depending on the Irish vote for its majority, it was suddenly revealed that two members of the 'independent' Irish party, in spite of their pledge, had taken posts as ministers. These were John Sadlier, a junior Lord of the Treasury, and William Keogh, the new Solicitor General. No assurance of any kind had been given by Aberdeen that he would introduce a Tenant Right Bill. In the light of their public pledge, the behaviour of Sadleir and Keogh was cynical and undermining to the party. Both were men of over-riding personal ambitions.

The character of Sadleir in particular was soon afterwards shown to have been unsavoury by any standards. A gigantic financial swindle was uncovered in 1856, involving securities personally forged by himself, the collapse of the Tipperary Joint Stock Bank, the ruin of thousands of humble Irish farmers and his own suicide on Hampstead Heath. Something of the ill-repute thus attaching to him and Keogh, who though he was to become a judge, also in the end committed suicide, was often later extended by extreme nationalists to the whole principle of trying to work through the House of Commons at all. But at the time, the colleagues of Sadleir and Keogh, once they had recovered from their shock, hailed their departure as having a cleansing effect on the Irish party in the Commons. Ireland was stronger as a result, declared *The Nation*.[17] Frederick Lucas, editor of the *Catholic Tablet*, who had done much to bring the independent party alliance about, also thought that the prospects were good, or even better than they had been before the defection.[18] The term 'independent opposition' was in fact only used about the party after Keogh and Sadleir had left it in April 1853.[19]

A more serious threat to the party's effectiveness was the increasingly reserved attitude of Archbishop Cullen to the principle of 'independent opposition'. Cullen had originally shown some goodwill towards the Tenant Right League and had obviously been gratified by the mobilization in Parliament of pro-Catholic sentiment. But his fear of the possible consequences to Catholicism of too effectively thwarting the British Government was reinforced by the irrational obsession with which he viewed the activities of Gavan Duffy and any sort of national principle that stemmed from the Young Ireland tradition. Cullen had been at the Vatican during the Roman revolution of 1848, and the traumatic shock he had experienced there at the hands of Young Italy became indistinguishably associated in his mind with Young Ireland. Duffy, Cullen declared, was 'a wicked man ... the Irish Mazzini'.[20] Cardinal Newman related how Cullen always compared Young Ireland to Young Italy; and 'with the most intense expression of words and countenance assured me they never came right, never – he knew them from his experience in Rome'.[21]

It was partly due to the discouraging attitude of the Church that in 1855 Duffy decided to abandon hope for the Tenant Right movement and independent opposition altogether, and emigrate to Australia. Those, he said, who ought to have guided and blessed the people's cause had deserted it.[22] There was, he wrote in *The Nation*, no more hope for Ireland 'than for a corpse on the dissecting table'.

It so happened that this independent opposition did in the end achieve nothing. But its failure was not as foregone a conclusion at the time of Duffy's withdrawal as Duffy's own later history made out. His rival editor, Frederick Lucas of the *Tablet*, declared that Duffy's real reason for leaving Ireland was want of financial means, 'but he wants to go off in poetry rather than prose'.[23] The truth was that a number of different factors had made political life difficult for the 'independent party' – Sadleir, and Keogh's defection, the cold shoulder of Archbishop Cullen, Duffy's withdrawal itself, and above all perhaps the good harvests of the fifties which took the desperation out of the Tenant Right movement. But if the core of the party had been stronger, if there had been better organization and discipline, or if there had even been one figure of outstanding political ability to lead it, these setbacks might not have led to its disintegration.

By 1857, of the original forty-eight members who had emerged as 'independents' from the election of 1852 there were only fourteen left, the rest having drifted off into conventional party commitments. The party introduced a land bill every year until 1858, but without converting the government of the day to anything like the necessary radical reappraisal of the system of land-ownership. The greatest failure had been a tactical one: the party's incapacity to exploit the sort of political situation in the House of Commons most favourable to it. In February 1859, for instance, the Liberal Government fell and the Conservatives came into office with a minority vote. The Irish might have been expected to wring from them some major concession in return for their invaluable support. But all that was extracted from the government was a series of peripheral concessions to Catholics, such as the award to Catholic chaplains in the British Army of permanent rank and status along with Church of England chaplains. This concession, though long overdue considering that about one-third of the British Army were Irish Catholics, was of little relevance to the condition of the Irish tenant farmer and labourer. Admittedly, a government landlord and tenant bill was said to be in the course of preparation, but as yet only the intention had been stated. And when later in the year this bill actually appeared and became law it made virtually no difference to the existing situation on the land at all, inspired as it was still by the assumption that at all costs the rights of property must remain paramount. By then, however, the Irish party had already split on other issues and disintegrated.

The failure of this attempt to work through the Union Parliament even for limited Irish national interests was afterwards often taken to prove the hopelessness of trying to achieve Irish national goals through Parliament at all. But the collapse of the independent party of the fifties proved no such point. It proved only the inadequacy of one particular set of men in one set of circumstances. There was no intrinsic reason why in different circumstances, with the agrarian temperature rising and with more gifted men and better tactics, the principle of parliamentary action should not one day be highly successful. And with additional assistance from the widening franchise it was one day to be so, changing the face of Ireland and effectively deploying a widely based national movement for the first time in Irish history.

A potential nucleus of nominally independent Irish members remained, though long unorganized, in being in the House of Commons. The traditional aim of Repeal or some lesser restoration of Irish autonomy remained continually before the Irish people. In 1864 a National League was founded to recover Irish legislative independence, by constitutional means. It is now almost entirely forgotten because another contemporary movement, Fenianism, has retrospectively eclipsed it in Irish history. But it is remarkable that in the eyes of two contemporaries it was the constitutional movement and not Fenianism that then seemed the important national movement of the day. 'The Irish political movements since 1860,' wrote W. J. O'Neill Daunt, the old friend of O'Connell, in 1867, 'have been chiefly an attempt by John Martin [former editor of the *Irish Felon*, now a constitutionalist] and The O'Donoghue [a young ex-soldier MP for Tralee] to establish a National League for the recovery of our national cause of 1782.'[24] And the journalist A. M. Sullivan, himself to be a Member of Parliament, could write in 1878 the now seemingly incredible words: 'The men who led, or most largely influenced, Irish National politics from 1860–65 were William Smith O'Brien, John Martin and The O'Donoghue.'*[25] On the other hand it was the failure of such efforts to make progress that gave moral encouragement to other men, trying to promote a more effective way for nationalists to go about their business. These were the men soon popularly to be known as Fenians.

---

* Smith O'Brien, usually regarded as having withdrawn from public life after his release from exile, in fact afterwards engaged quite frequently in public controversy on national issues as a strict constitutionalist.

15

Beginnings of the
Fenian Movement

In the autumn of 1858 respectable Irishmen reading their newspapers were made unpleasantly aware of a new phenomenon on the Irish scene.

Secret societies had been a feature of Irish agrarian life for over a century and a half, fluctuating in virulence and intensity with the district and the season, a fact of life Ireland had grown to live with. So far, the nearest thing to a national character which such societies had assumed since the days of the Defenders had been through the loose federation of lodges of the so-called 'Ribbon' society first founded in 1826 and relatively flourishing at local levels ever since. The name derived from the wearing of a white ribbon round the hat for purposes of mutual recognition at night. Occasionally, as in the days of the Defenders, vague political aspirations had been discernible in Ribbon Society transactions: references to 'freeing Ireland', 'liberating our country' or just 'uniting all Roman Catholics'.[1] Once, ambitiously, in the late 1830s, the phrase had been bandied about: 'The hour of England's difficulty is at hand, the Russian bear is drawing near to her in India.'[2] But the Ribbon Society was principally an agrarian secret society, concerned as such societies had always been with dealing out rough justice on the land, a nineteenth-century form of Whiteboyism. The naïve political parlance of such Ribbon lodges could hardly be taken as an organized threat to the constitution.

Apart from the abortive and amateurish efforts of Gray, Lalor, Luby and O'Leary in 1849 there had been no attempt to organize a secret society primarily for political purposes since the days of the United Irishmen. Now, in this autumn of 1858, reports began to appear of a new type of secret society active in the south-west of Ireland.

The *Cork Constitution* of 4 November, while describing the new phenomenon as a Ribbon society and talking of nightly oath-taking, remarked on one rather untypical characteristic. The society apparently appealed mainly to labourers and farm servants, while the tenant farmers themselves held aloof, being 'not altogether at ease with the activists'.[3] An anonymous letter to the paper from someone in Macroom a few days later gave a clearer indication of what was up. Numbers, it said, had taken the oath, but others were not doing so 'because those who so acted before gained nothing by it but were shot down like dogs, hanged, transported and their families turned out of farms and became beggars'.[4] This was an unmistakable reference to '98.

On 29 November the *Cork Examiner*. speculating about the rumours, pronounced: 'If a secret club has been formed, it is in the furtherance of a national movement for the independence of Ireland.' It did its best to make light of the affair.

If it has sprung into life at all it is simply from the dreams of a few enthusiastic young men, who, not yet sufficiently experienced to read the lessons of the past, hope to make of this country a free nation ... they will before long not only see how utterly impracticable are their hopes, and how dead is all sympathy for such movements in this country, but they will find their organization falling asunder now, as it did before, in a more stirring time, like a rope of sand ...[5]

The lord lieutenant issued a proclamation on 3 December offering £100 reward for information about oath-taking, and the first arrests followed immediately. In fact, Dublin Castle had already been given much information by the parish priest of Kenmare, possibly first alerted in the confessional.[6]

The 'enthusiastic young men' turned out to be mainly clerks and National schoolteachers, with a shopkeeper or two. The name of one was to ring sporadically down Irish history for the next fifty years: Jeremiah Donovan (later O'Donovan) Rossa. The Cork newspapers commented that these young men were of a more respectable class than those usually associated with agrarian secret societies.[7] It appeared that the secret society had been functioning under the cover of an open and legal, if nationally-minded, club for self-improvement, the Phoenix National and Literary Society of Skibbereen. This had been founded at the beginning of 1857, with reading-room premises on the walls of which 'Ireland for the Irish' was inscribed in ivy-leaf lettering.[8] The flavour of the talk that had gone on there can be gauged from a letter found in the house of O'Donovan Rossa after his arrest, which ran:

'I am ever ready to do my utmost to promote the cause and acquire the reality of nationality ... but ... I don't believe the Saxon will ever relax his grip except by the persuasion of cold lead and steel ...'[9]

The oath administered to members of the secret society formed under cover of this literary club may have varied slightly from mouth to mouth, and was sometimes inaccurately recollected by informers, but appears to have run, then, along the following lines:

'I ... swear in the presence of God, to renounce all allegiance to the Queen of England, and to take arms and fight at a moment's warning, and to make

Ireland an Independent Democratic Republic, and to yield implicit obedience
to the commanders and superiors of this secret society . . .'*

The redoubtable O'Donovan Rossa (a member of the House of Lords
once thought he was two people, 'Donovan' and 'Rosser')[10] had been doing
his share of the swearing-in. When a soldier whom he attempted to suborn
declared that 'he was a Queen's man', Rossa replied, so the soldier said,
that there was no harm in that, and 'that there was many a Queen's man
joining, that no one would know it till the hop of the ball was up, and
everyone could turn to whatever side he liked then'.[11]

Another court witness at this time reported that he had been fed with
similar optimistic tidings. Someone, he said, had notified him in the summer
of 1858 that 'the Constables of Dublin Castle were in it, but that it would
not be prudent to depend on them, though . . . it was strongly hoped that
. . . the whole affair would be done without spilling a glass of blood, there
would be such good management'.[12]

Perhaps it was partly such language that helped mislead the authorities
into thinking they had no very serious threat to contend with. Moreover, in
their critical zeal and alarm they had unearthed a number of other oath-
taking societies, all at first supposed to be 'Phoenixes', but which in the end
turned out only to be old-style Ribbon Lodges operating with some political
flavour, but with no apparent connection with the men in the south-west.[13]
Some of these had been using a crude set of challenges and passwords, such
as 'We expect a new war between England and France', to be countered
by: 'Yes, the Irish Brigade is on the advance.' At night the correct words
were: 'The night is dark.' Answer: 'As black as heresy.' And again: 'That
the triumph of freedom may proclaim a war.' To which the correct reply
was: 'And hoist the French Eagle and American star.' The right hand was
then to be brought to the nose and the left hand to the ear.[14] A man arrested
in Westmeath with these passwords on him was, according to the police, so
drunk he didn't know what he was doing. He turned out to be a naturalized
Irish-born citizen of the United States named Fallon, with £38 and the
constitution of a so-called Shamrock Benevolent Society of New York in

* Another prescribed version of this famous oath of what later became the Irish
Republican Brotherhood seems at this date to have been: 'I . . . do solemnly swear, in
the presence of Almighty God, that I will do my utmost, at every risk, while life lasts, to
make Ireland an independent Democratic Republic; that I will yield implicit obedience,
in all things not contrary to the law of God to the commands of my superior officers;
and that I shall preserve inviolable secrecy regarding all the transactions of this
society that may be confided in me. So help me God! Amen.' See John O'Leary,
Recollections of Fenians and Fenianism (London 1896), p. 120; Ryan, *The Fenian
Chief*, p. 91. The form quoted in the text above was given in court in two separate
cases, see *Irishman*, 8 January 1859, 12 March 1859. A famous phrase about the Irish
Republic being 'now virtually established' first entered the oath when it was revised
in 1859.

his pocket. He had been in the country some ten or eleven months and now received a sentence of seven years' penal servitude.[15]

Of all the others arrested at this time only one other received a term of imprisonment and even he was respited within the year, for O'Donovan Rossa and the rest agreed to plead guilty and bind themselves over to be of good behaviour on condition that he was released. While they had been in prison Smith O'Brien had been one of those who subscribed to a Fair Trial Fund opened on their behalf, though he had at the same time strongly dissociated himself from all attempts to identify the national cause with secret organizations.[16]

Newspaper readers breathed a sigh of relief. But, for all the rather anti-climactic spirit of reassurance that now set in, the *Kilkenny Moderator* had been quite right when it had declared earlier: 'There cannot now be much, if any doubt, that secret and illegal societies, having a directing power or body in some particular place, and activated by a community of purpose, ramify throughout the country.'[17]

The 'directing power' had not been touched; the one really dangerous man had got away. He was in America at the time of the Phoenix trials and the authorities, who knew that he was out of the country, may have made the mistake of bracketing his abilities with those of the slipshod Fallon of Westmeath. If so it was a serious error, for they had out against them a determined and formidable, if himself by no means infallible, opponent.

This man had cropped up in evidence more than once in the course of the Phoenix trials, figuring sometimes under the mysterious name of Shook or Shooks and at others under his real name of Stephens.[18] 'Shook' was merely an anglicization of the Irish 'An Seabhac', or 'the Wandering Hawk', a pseudonym under which for two years now Stephens had been travelling, mainly on foot, sometimes alone, and sometimes with one or two companions, over large tracts of Ireland. Stephens was that same young Kilkenny railway engineer, James Stephens, who had joined Smith O'Brien in the week before Ballingarry, and after weeks of adventurous wanderings during which he was reported dead, had eventually escaped to France.

In Paris Stephens had been with other Irish refugees, principally Michael Doheny and John O'Mahony. He had become particularly friendly with O'Mahony and together with him had made the acquaintance of some of the French and other social revolutionaries then active in the capital. It seems that Stephens and O'Mahony fought together on the barricades in the popular resistance to Louis-Napoleon's *coup d'état* of 1851.[19] Certainly they had contact with, and Stephens made a study of, the international secret societies through which revolutionary democratic activity was then carried on. He was anxious, in the words of an approved panegyrist writing fifteen years later, to acquire 'those secrets by means of which an indisciplined mob can be most readily and effectually matched against a mercenary army'.[20] Certainly, when he again turned his attention to Ireland his political thought contained obvious traces of revolutionary socialist thinking, a small instance of which was the reference to an 'Independent Democratic Republic' in the early oaths quoted at the Phoenix trials. It had, however, been some time before Stephens in Paris again turned his active attention to Ireland. As with most exiles the business of day-to-day living absorbed most of his energies. He taught English, and learned French so well that he was able to join the staff of the *Moniteur* and translated Dickens's *Martin Chuzzlewit* for it in serial form.[21]

Stephens's friend, John O'Mahony, left France for America in 1853. Stephens himself left Paris late in 1855, and after a stay in London came to Ireland again early in 1856. He seems to have returned partly out of a natural wish to see his family and friends again, and partly with some deliberate desire to assess the state of Irish national feeling and see if some of the political lessons he had learnt in France might not be applicable there. His own thoughts for Ireland were based firmly on the need for total separation and republican independence. But he was not just a doctrinaire abstract nationalist, and soon after his arrival he declared in private conversation his general creed, which was to remain constant all his life, namely that '... unless the Irish land were given to the Irish people, Irish national independence was not worth the trouble and sacrifice of obtaining it'.[22] Since, however, his entire active life was to be spent on attempts at organization, political details of the independent Irish Republic for which he strove remained largely undeveloped.

The Ireland of 1856 to which Stephens returned was one in which virtually the only nationalist thinking was that represented in constitutional form by the 'independent opposition' in Parliament. An occasional radical voice cried in the wilderness. One such was Philip Gray's new paper the *Tribune*, which, analysing the demand for Tenant Right, maintained that the real demand was for something much more fundamental than that. It allowed that a landlord had a right to do what he would with his own but asked whether the land really was the landlord's own. 'The truth is,' it declared in italics, 'that all the land of Ireland belongs to the people of Ireland, in the aggregate, to be distributed and made use of just so as best may serve the happiness, prosperity, peace and security of the People of Ireland.'[23]

The *Tribune* went out of business after fifteen weekly issues. Before it did so it published another leader headed 'No True Idea of Nationality in Ireland'. In this it deplored Irishmen's 'existing incapability of comprehending the large idea of an Irish Nation. It is true they talk of their country very plausibly, and in the most high flown terms; but behind all this there is no clear and comprehensive idea of the universal Irish nation, taking in ...

the entire population. All notions of country in the popular mind are vague and confused . . .'[24]

The *Wexford Guardian* commented bitterly on the fact that when O'Connell was alive and had talked about 'England's difficulty being Ireland's opportunity' everyone had thrown their hats into the air and 'dinned the ear of heaven with our acclamations'. Now England's difficulty in the Crimean war had come and gone and they looked like mountebanks or fools or worse. 'Is it to be said that we are men of Gascony, who boasted what we dared not perform?'[25] It was certainly a question extreme Irish nationalists would often need to ask themselves, none more so than Stephens, the man about to try and remedy the situation.

'The ardour of Young Ireland', wrote Stephens later, 'had evaporated as if it had never existed.'[26] He made contact with the surviving members of the youthful secret societies of 1849, with Gray and, later, with Luby, but all reported that such societies had now collapsed for want of any unifying force and that the thoughts they represented were totally isolated. Abandoning a temporary inclination to leave Ireland altogether, Stephens decided to set out mainly on foot to feel Ireland's pulse for himself.

He must have made a curious figure with his slightly foreign appearance and cut of clothes acquired in Paris. In the course of what he later called his 'three thousand mile walk' over much of southern and western Ireland he was frequently mistaken for an actor.[27] He found much to make him pessimistic. A revenue officer in Athlone told him that all was now so quiet in the country, with the '48 men crushed or out of the way, that 'in a few years more Ireland will be as content and as happy as Scotland'.[28] He was shocked to find a sense of national unity so little developed in Connaught that they considered there that there was 'little or none of the Irish in the Leinsterman, he's like any other foreigner and we don't like them'.[29] More than once he asked himself bitterly, 'Did Christ ever die for such a people?'[30] The closest he got to any ground for hope on this tour in 1856 seems to have been in Longford where he came across the age-old 'prophecies' of St Columbille. These had long figured as a mystical untutored inspiration in Irish country life. 'After a time', so ran the legend, or 'when the right time comes', then, and not till then, would Ireland wake from her trance and liberate herself. It was never precisely known what such liberation would involve, but the prophecies in this form probably dated back to the days of the great Tudor confiscations of land, and it was the return of the lost lands that was enshrined in the legend.

But if Stephens found little external encouragement, his own sense of purpose and determination had somehow acquired strength from his long walk. His health, too, which had been poor when he first arrived in Dublin was now greatly improved. And though he lacked almost all the qualities required of a great revolutionary leader, being jealous and boastful, capable of small-mindedness and untruthful at least to the point of serious self-deception, his extraordinary egotism was always allied to an extraordinary capacity for organization and work.

By the end of this tour of 1856, though he was still 'feeling his way' politically, his mind was moving in favour of some secret oath-bound revolutionary organization with ramifications throughout the country which would be dedicated to separation from England and the establishment of an Irish republic.[31] There was, after all, a tradition for such a republican organization in Ireland older than those secret societies which had so caught his attention in Paris. 'Such a movement,' he wrote, on looking back many years later, 'had not been inaugurated in Ireland since '98; but did not the United Irish society give me hope that their attempt would be improved upon by our avoiding the errors they fell into, and by a close adhesion to more Continental clubs where traitors were "few and far between".'[32] And though much of his tour had been discouraging, he had at least become clear about certain realities, not all of which were unfavourable.

First, it was a waste of time to bother any longer about winning the upper classes for nationality. In a conversation he had had with Smith O'Brien, himself only just returned from exile, in his home near Limerick, O'Brien had told him bluntly: 'You see, Mr Stephens, the respectable people of the towns especially are quite indifferent to, if not hostile to, nationality.'[33] Stephens accepted the fact and thus disencumbered himself of the most fatally preoccupying illusions of Young Ireland. The tenant farmers also, Stephens acknowledged, were temporarily mainly interested in their better harvests and 'apathetic' towards nationality. But among the labourers, small tradesmen and the sons of peasants he had discovered a great deal of general 'disaffection', and saw that 'even now it would not be hard to stir them up into insurrection'.[34] To this end he devoted, with little consideration for his own material well-being, the next ten years of his life.

Apart from the needs of his ego, it was the socially radical nature of the task that was Stephens's inspiration as much as any emotional Irish patriotism. He was to write in his diary not long afterwards that it was the principle of liberty and right that he was fighting for: if, he said, England were a republic battling for human freedom against an Ireland in league with despots he would unhesitatingly take up arms against his native land.[35] And this unabashed linking of Irish republicanism with those at the lower end of the social scale – an affirmation in European terms of the native principles of Lalor – was thereafter to remain one of its permanent features, with important consequences long after Stephens's own death. Another factor in the Irish republican tradition, which Stephens consciously formulated, and which was also to be of great importance after his death, was that of the need for continuity in the tradition at all costs, even the cost of dismal failure. There was inevitably some *post hoc* rationalization in which Stephens was to write of his own efforts. But this rationalization was picked up and consciously adopted as a principle by a later generation of nationalists.

'I came to the resolve', Stephens wrote, reminiscing years later, 'that the attempt was not only worth trying, but should be tried in the very near future if we wanted at all to keep our flag flying; for I was sure as of my own existence that if another decade was allowed to pass without an endeavour of some kind or another to shake off an unjust yoke, the Irish people would sink into a lethargy from which it would be impossible for any patriot ... to arouse them ...'[36]

In fact, in 1856, to James Stephens contemplating a republican organization there were quite other favourable factors besides those he had been able to detect in Ireland. Across the Atlantic existed a vast potential of hitherto little organized Irish money and Irish manpower which might be brought to Ireland's aid. Some attempts had already been made to organize this Irish power realistically for Irish purposes, but so far to little effect. The poverty of the vast majority of American-Irish immigrants and their primary wish to settle down successfully in their new lives meant for a long time that far more eloquence and emotion was readily available for Ireland than hard cash and practical intent. Irish nationalism was often more important in what it did for the emigrants' status in America than in what it did for Ireland. Some Irish republican clubs had been first formed in New York in 1848, but had proved their military effectiveness not in Ireland but in their transformation into a regiment of the New York State militia.[37] Shortly after Mitchel's escape from Tasmania and arrival in New York there had been founded under his inspiration, in April 1854, an 'Irishmen's Civil and Military Republican Union' with the object of liberating Ireland from English oppression.[38] But it came to nothing, and at the end of the year Mitchel left New York for Tennessee.

Mitchel's 'Republican Union' had a number of successors forming themselves on similar lines, and a Massachusetts Emigrant Aid Society actually held a convention to discuss the speediest and most effective means of promoting action 'leading to ensure the success of the cause of liberty in our native land'.[39] Another such organization was the Emmet Monument Association, whose purpose was plainly expressed in its name, recalling Emmet's wish to have no epitaph until his country took its place among the nations of the earth. Stephens's friend, John O'Mahony, who had gone to America in 1853, had helped run the Emmet Monument Association together with Michael Doheny, the former Young Irelander and Stephens's old companion on the run. They had even sent an emissary of their own to Ireland in 1855, a man called Joseph Denieffe, who was given *carte blanche* to organize and to inform the faithful that 'they' – Doheny and co. – were ready to land thirty thousand men in Ireland in the autumn.[40] Given the wild improbability of such a boast it was as well for Denieffe he got little further than founding a small organization in the neighbourhood of Kilkenny, and, after meeting Gray, Luby and others in Dublin, found it more relevant for a while to concentrate on the practical business of earning a living.[41]

When Stephens on his return to Dublin at the end of 1856 heard again of his old friend O'Mahony, it was to the effect that O'Mahony was so disgusted with Irish political agitation in America that he was going to give it up altogether. 'I am sick of Young Ireland and its theatrical leaders', he had written, '... I am sick of Irish Catholics in America. I am sick of Yankee-doodle twaddle, Yankee-doodle selfishness and all Yankee-doodle-dum! ... It is refreshing to my heart to turn from Irish tinsel patriots, the people's leaders on gala days, and from American retrogression, to the stern front and untiring constancy of the continental apostles of liberty and the ceaseless preparation of their disciples.'[42]

A man possessed of less demonic and egotistical pertinacity than Stephens might have taken this letter as discouragement. But Stephens seems by now to have made up his mind that something could be done. 'I have no hesitation', he once said, 'in saying that I think very highly of myself. I have grasped more of the truth than almost any other man.'[43] In any case, he had himself long thought Irish America worthless for want of a proper organization.

It was [he wrote later] a wind-bag, or a phantom, the laughing stock of sensible men and the El Dorado of fools. For what was the sum total at that time of Irish-American patriotism. ... Speeches of bayonets, gala days and jolly nights, banners and sashes ... bunkum and fulsome filibustering. ... The oratory of the Young Irelanders was the immediate cause of this scandalous state of things. They introduced into the Irish-American arena the pompous phrases of the old Nation suppers and the gilded harangues of Conciliation Hall. ... Irish patriots sang songs and responded in glowing language to glowing toasts on Irish National Independence over beakers of fizzling champagne.[44]

To all this Stephens felt convinced that he could put a stop. He wrote back to John O'Mahony at once to dissuade him from giving up Irish agitation in America and presumably gave him some inkling of the organization at home that was in his own mind.

The Emmet Monument Association, which had been inactive since 1855, and the dispatch of Denieffe to Ireland, began to revive. Meanwhile, Stephens extended his contacts in Dublin and elsewhere, meeting Thomas Luby for the first time and attending with him and speaking at the funeral of Philip Gray who died early in 1857. Stephens also found himself a satisfactory means of earning a living by teaching French. Two of his pupils were the sons of John Blake Dillon, with whom nine years before he had faced Captain Longmore of the Dragoons on the barricade at Killenaule. Stephens apparently proved a satisfactory tutor to the sons, but wholly failed to convince the father that there was anything but futility in his proposal for a secret revolutionary organization.[45]

In the autumn of 1857 another Irish American from the Emmet Monument Association arrived in Ireland. His name, Owen Considine, is known to history only because of the historic message he brought. That message itself might have been grounds for no more than a historical footnote, and the Emmet Monument Association of no more significance than the Shamrock Benevolent Institution which had dispatched Fallon of Westmeath, but for the personality of the man to whom the message was addressed.

The message brought by Considine to Stephens came from O'Mahony and Doheny, and positively asked Stephens to set up a revolutionary organization with which they and other American exiles could cooperate. The available extent of the practical cooperation from America was not precisely stated, and Stephens, typically, seems either to have optimistically assumed it was adequate, or at least taken for granted his own ability to make it so. He sent a message to Doheny and O'Mahony to be carried by Denieffe, whom Stephens disinterred for the purpose from the tranquillity of a job in the North. Calmly Stephens stated that if, as suggested, he could be guaranteed money, and a spearhead force of some five hundred men from the States, preferably armed with Lee Enfield rifles, he would undertake, within three months of Denieffe's return to him with an official Yes, to have at least 10,000 men organized – 1,500 with firearms, the rest with pikes – ready to move at twenty-four hours' notice.[46]

It was the beginning of a near-decade of such optimistic statements. Stephens's message concluded with a warning which was equally characteristic of a whole future pattern of events.

'I believe it essential to success,' wrote Stephens, on this 6 January 1858, 'that the centre of this or any similar organization [i.e., himself] should be perfectly unshackled; in other words, a provisional dictator. On this point I can conscientiously concede nothing. That I should not be worried or hampered by the wavering or imbecile, it will be well to make this out in proper form with the signature of every influential Irishman of our union ...'[47] The man who was soon to be known as the Chief Organizer (sometimes Chief Executive) of the Irish Republic was beginning as he intended to go on.

Nearly three months later Stephens's messenger, Denieffe, returned from the States with the results of a fund-raising operation on the part of the American organization. This had brought in precisely £80 – the very minimum Stephens had stipulated as a necessary monthly income.[48] A man less obsessed by his own will than Stephens might have been daunted by such a puny result. Denieffe also had to make clear to Stephens that there was in New York as yet no proper organization, only a body of sympathizers. Nevertheless, the very evening of Denieffe's return, appropriately St

Patrick's Day, 17 March 1858, Stephens formally founded in his lodgings behind Lombard Street, Dublin, a secret society dedicated to the establishment in Ireland of an Independent Democratic Republic. This was the society later to be known as the Irish Republican Brotherhood, though it did not generally assume that name for some years.*[49]

Stephens, Denieffe, Thomas Luby and others who were present all swore themselves into the society. The very next day Denieffe was sent back to America for more money and Stephens and Luby set off on an organizing tour of the south and south-west of Ireland.

The organization of this new secret society was presumably partly modelled on what Stephens had learnt during his contacts with the international revolutionary societies in Paris. It was, however, also similar to the organization of the old United Irishmen. At the head of the society was the Chief Organizer, or Chief Executive, James Stephens himself, sometimes known as the Head Centre. Below him were four Vice-Organizers or 'Vs' – one for each province of Ireland – and below them came numerous Circles each of which had an A as 'Centre' or 'Colonel', with nine Bs or captains under him.[50] Under each B in turn came nine Cs or sergeants, and under each C, nine Ds or privates. The theory was that no member should be known to any other members except those in their own circles. This was not strictly adhered to, but Stephens's primary aim of establishing a system of security superior to that of the United Irishmen was for some time achieved. This was all the more remarkable since, as in the days of the United Irishmen and the Defenders, much of the oath-taking was conducted in and around public houses.

Although Stephens had many personal failings his ability as an organizer in the primitive and difficult conditions of rural Ireland was outstanding. All who in the course of time arrived from America to inspect the 'Home Organization', or 'men in the gap' as they came to be called, were impressed by the extent of the organization they found in Stephens's day and even those who, writing later, were fully alive to his defects as a leader continued to praise his qualities as an organizer. Luby and John O'Leary, the young student rebel of 1849, whom Stephens soon drew into his organization, were to come to refer to him as 'The Great Sir Hocus Pocus' and 'vain, arrogant, with a most inordinate belief in his own powers';[51] yet they retained to the end admiration for his organizing ability. And the French General Cluseret, who for a brief moment found himself caught up in Stephens's organization, described him as 'vain, despotic and overbearing beyond any

* In Devoy's *Recollections*, which was followed by Desmond Ryan in both his *Phoenix Flame* (1936) and his *The Fenian Chief* (1967), the exact place of the founding of the IRB is given as Peter Langan's timber yard in Lombard Street. But Devoy, who himself professed to be following Denieffe, more than once does so inaccurately and the versions of Denieffe, who was there, and of O'Leary who was merely repeating what he had been told by Luby who was also there, seem more reliable.

man I ever saw' but at the same time 'an organizer to the fingers' ends'.[52]

As yet, in the spring of 1858, the organization was in a totally embryonic state. The secret society had at this stage no official name, probably as an intentional feature of Stephens's security system. Members referred to it as 'Our Body', 'Our Movement' or 'Our Organization'.[53] And later in 1858 this certainly turned out to its advantage, for those corners of it that were revealed in the 'Phoenix' arrests were identified only with the name of the Phoenix societies thus put down.

It was in May of 1858 that Stephens and Luby had first made contact with the young men of the Phoenix Society of Skibbereen and had sworn in O'Donovan Rossa and his associates with promises of help coming from beyond the seas. However, Denieffe returned from America during the summer, this time with only £40, and Stephens thereupon undertook to go to America to put things on a better basis there himself. He sailed for the States in October 1858. Working there virtually from scratch he managed to collect some £600 in six months. This sum would have been larger, but for the discovery of the Phoenix societies and publication of details of the trials in the Irish American press during the winter. These reports induced a certain sudden wariness in the attitude of those whom Stephens had at first often impressed favourably. Thus he failed to get his hands on what was left of the sum of money collected on behalf of Gavan Duffy's tentative organization in 1848.* He also failed to secure the total confidence of the two Irishmen who were then still the most colourful patriots in the States, Meagher and Mitchel. But he left behind him in the States on his return to Ireland in March 1859 the embryo of an effective organization. This was to be headed by John O'Mahony and was soon to be known as the Fenian Brotherhood.

The name Fenian was given to the new organization by O'Mahony who, as a Gaelic scholar, found inspiration in the legend of the ancient Gaelic warrior Fiona MacCumhail and his élite legion, the Fianna.[54] Stephens, on sailing for Ireland, left O'Mahony in no doubt at all that he (Stephens) was in overall charge and that O'Mahony was subordinate to him. This O'Mahony reluctantly accepted. But the name under which those who worked in both halves of the movement – in America and in Ireland – were to go down to history was the one O'Mahony had given the American branch of the organization: the Fenians.

* See above, p. 271.

16

James Stephens at Work

For over a year after leaving America in the spring of 1859 Stephens did not return to Ireland at all but lived in Paris, out of reach of the British authorities. He sent O'Leary to America for a time to work with John O'Mahony, while Luby acted as his agent in Ireland, quickly re-organizing the South after the release of the Phoenix prisoners and creating for the first time an effective organization in Dublin.

Stephens himself in Paris soon began to show signs of enjoying the conspiracy for its own sake, rather than for the sake of its practical objective. The important thing for him was that he held the threads of the conspiracy in his own hands. The letter of introduction which he gave John O'Leary to take to America proclaimed that he expected for O'Leary 'the highest possible courtesy, respect and even deference, as my representative; and through me, the representative of the Irish cause'.[1] He protested continually to O'Mahony of the inadequate funds he was receiving from the States and strongly resented O'Mahony's dispatch of envoys to Ireland on his own initiative to see what progress the organization was making.

Stephens at this stage had no undue sense of urgency about planning a rising. He spent agreeable hours visiting picture galleries and pointing out the details of the bas relief on the Arc de Triomphe to other conspirators.[2] But though his main reason for not returning to Ireland was, sensibly, to avoid the authorities so soon after the Phoenix trials, he managed also to convince himself that he was not wasting time. He hoped to obtain help from the French Government, remembering undoubtedly the analogous situation of Wolfe Tone, who unlike Stephens had not had the advantage of knowing what was going on in Ireland.

But in an admittedly far less favourable international situation Stephens had no success with the French Government at all. He wrote to O'Mahony in America in lame self-justification: '... the very parties I relied on for putting me in touch with those I had to expect anything of consequence from, were not here, and the letters I addressed to each of them remained unanswered ...'[3] Even when Napoleon III embarked on his Italian campaign and Stephens's hopes of 'complicating' Franco–British relations were again raised, nothing came of them. He told O'Mahony: 'I succeeded in getting introduced to parties who, from the very first, showed a willingness to forward my views, of which disposition I found it impossible to avail myself, owing to my inability to meet the expenses incidental to important negotiations.'[4]

The curious strain of bombast and incompetence which was to mix with much that was idealistic and courageous in the Fenian movement was already at work. But at least there was in Stephens's thinking at this stage some appreciation of what was realistic and what was not. He wrote to O'Mahony from Paris in September 1859: 'I give you once more to understand that we cannot strike this year', adding that if anyone was suggesting that they ought to strike whatever happened they could never have got the idea from him.[5]

This was partly in response to some dissatisfaction with Stephens's leadership which had already been expressed in Ireland but which was quickly crushed by Luby and other supporters of Stephens. Among these was that eye-witness who had had such singular glimpses of Smith O'Brien smoking a cigar in his dreamy state in July 1848. This was Charles Kickham of Mullinahone. Kickham, though he had since become almost blind and totally deaf as a result of a shooting accident, had rallied to Stephens's organization early, and was one day himself to become its head centre. Now, as peacemaker, he tried to reduce the tension developing with O'Mahony as a result of Stephens's continual and often arrogant complaints of lack of financial support from America. Stephens had grounds for such complaints. Very little money was in fact sent from the States to the organization in Ireland for several years.[6] But O'Mahony's task was not easy, for a financial crisis in the United States in 1857 had depleted Irish emigrant savings and for a long time words remained easier to raise than money for the Irish cause. As Doheny himself was to remark frankly on one occasion: 'God knows, if eloquence could free or save a people we ought to be the freest and safest people on the face of the globe.'[7] In addition to this, however, many Irish in America in 1859 had to be convinced that there was anything realistic to subscribe for.

Stephens showed small patience with O'Mahony's difficulties. But O'Mahony, gentle and more likeable than Stephens, was a weaker personality. Moreover, O'Mahony's political future was for better or worse linked with Stephens. He had little alternative but to submit to the taunts and insults Stephens heaped on him. At the end of 1860 he came personally to Ireland for the first time since 1848 and to meet him there Stephens himself returned from Paris to Dublin. Personal relations were left little better as a result of the meeting, but some clarification of what was expected from America was agreed on. The arrival of five hundred men from America, with arms and officers, plus at least fifty thousand rifles, was accepted as the prerequisite of any rising of the Irish people. Stephens would continue to organize in Ireland itself. But the onus of making it possible for the Irish people to use their organization was placed squarely on the American half of the conspiracy.

An air of inactivity and apathy seemed to settle over the movement in Ireland for a while. John O'Leary allowed himself to get out of touch with it altogether and went off to make his life in London.[8] He lacked the willingness to dedicate himself professionally to the thankless and grinding tasks of humdrum revolutionary work. This was Stephens's own most notable quality. His presence in Ireland was a guarantee that the organization would not fade away. But the initiative for an event that was really to give the organization significance in Ireland came originally from outside Ireland altogether.

On 15 January 1861 there had died in a San Francisco hospital Terence Bellew McManus, the Young Irelander who at the prospect of a rising in 1848 had abandoned his very successful shipping agency in Liverpool, and rushed over to Ireland to join Smith O'Brien in his ineffectual progress round Tipperary. The gesture had ruined McManus's commercial career, for although he had escaped from Tasmania, where he had been transported, he had been unable to make a success of business life in America and had died in poverty. Little had been heard of McManus in a decade and he had not figured with any prominence in Irish American politics, despite a letter to Gavan Duffy soon after 1848, in which he had written: 'Whenever a death-blow is to be struck at this vile despotism that crushes our land, I trust in heaven I will be there to strike.' Now at last, in death, he was to be almost as good as his word.

The Fenian Brotherhood in America was an open and legal organization, keeping only its inner policies and contacts with Ireland as secret as possible. Some San Francisco Fenians proposed that McManus's body should be sent back to Ireland as a national gesture. The Brotherhood as a whole took to the project and the coffined body was brought with due Irish patriotic emphasis through a number of American cities to New York. There it was given a lying-in-state in St Patrick's Cathedral by the Catholic Archbishop Hughes, who reminded Catholics in his address that the Church in some cases found it lawful to resist and overthrow a tyrannical government.[9]

In Ireland, constitutional nationalists like A. M. Sullivan, the editor of *The Nation*, were hoping to acquire prestige from the mood of national solemnity evoked by McManus's return. But Stephens seized the opportunity to take control of the arrangements for the funeral himself and to work up national enthusiasm through his own organization. In doing this he challenged two groups of political opponents in Ireland: constitutional nationalists like Sullivan, and the Catholic hierarchy.

In a Lenten Pastoral as early as 1859 at the time of the Phoenix trials Archbishop Cullen had already made clear his interpretation of the Church's attitude to secret societies. He had not only condemned them along with 'improper dances, such as the polka' as repugnant to the Church. He had specifically stated that the Catholic Church solemnly excommunicated all her children who engaged in secret societies, and that no member of any secret society could receive absolution.[10] Although Cullen was to spend some years wresting from the Vatican a specific sentence of excommunication against Fenianism as such, his own clear attitude, expressed so early, presented Stephens with a formidable difficulty in his attempts to organize the Irish people. Though Stephens was to succeed in amassing much general popular sympathy for Fenianism, the Church's condemnation was always one additional telling reason why in the end people should be careful about committing themselves to it.

Cullen forbade the use of Dublin Cathedral for McManus's lying-in-state, and the coffin had to rest the day before the funeral at the Mechanics' Institute. But Stephens managed to score something of a triumph by reminding people that the Church did not always speak with one coherent voice. He secured for the funeral arrangements the cooperation of a radical priest named Patrick Lavelle, who was always to show sympathy with Fenianism and who, though more or less permanently embattled with Cullen, enjoyed a certain favour with the next most important member of the Catholic hierarchy, John MacHale, Archbishop of Tuam.

Stephens's practical organization of the funeral was an outstanding success. On the cold and cheerless morning of 10 November 1861, with the pavements deep in slush from the heavy sleet and rain of the night before and a drizzling rain which settled in by noon, an estimated crowd of between twenty and thirty thousand Dubliners turned out to watch the Young Irelander McManus brought to his final rest in Glasnevin cemetery, while the bands played the Dead March of Saul.[11] A measure of the whole manoeuvre's success had already been registered the day before when the very respectable constitutional paper, the *Freeman's Journal*, had commented of the crowds who attended the lying-in-state in the Mechanics' Institute the day before: 'the demonstration ... owed its origins and its magnitude to the cause with which he was identified.'

The whole event was an advertisement for 'the cause' of a dimension which Stephens could never have achieved by other legal, or even illegal means. His horsemen, wearing black scarves and armlets and carrying batons, kept the crowds in disciplined order. An official delegation from America, including Doheny and O'Mahony, were present. The four pall-bearers were all members of Stephens's organization and three thousand of an open 'front' organization, the National Brotherhood of St Patrick, followed close behind the coffin. There was not the slightest disorder or confusion in the procession. The formal funeral oration, rather starchily composed by Stephens, was delivered at Glasnevin by torchlight by a member of the American delegation. But before this, as night descended, Patrick Lavelle, the radical priest who was not afraid to risk Archbishop Cullen's anger, gave an impromptu address by the graveside. He seemed embarrassed by and deplored the occasional cheers by which he was interrupted. But he must have known he was inviting them.

'I am proud,' he said, 'to see that the people of Ireland and of Dublin are not dead – that they have hope – that though the prophet be dead the spirit he evoked will outlive him, and even in the present generation raise his country from degradation to the glory of a nation.'[12]

From the time of the McManus funeral Stephens's organization in Ireland began to flourish. Though referred to mysteriously rather in the same sort of way as people spoke of the fairies, it came eventually to be known popularly, from association with the open Brotherhood in the States, as 'the Fenians'.* Early in 1862 Stephens, accompanied by Luby, continued the series of organizational tours of Ireland which were to be a regular feature of his activity whenever he was in the country.[13] He kept up an active network in Dublin. In the summer of 1863, in an attempt to raise funds of which he was still desperately short, he started his own weekly newspaper, the *Irish People*, inducing John O'Leary to come back from London to help edit it, and installing O'Donovan Rossa as business manager.

The *Irish People* was not financially the success that had been hoped for and it never succeeded in Ireland in getting much circulation away from the constitutional nationalist paper, *The Nation*.†[14] But it was a propaganda platform for Stephens of major importance and wholly under his control, unlike the only other extreme nationalist paper, the *Irishman*. Though keeping within the bounds of legality the *Irish People* preached a much stronger message than *The Nation*, flirting continually with the language of violence and openly proclaiming that parliamentary agitation was a useless way of trying to achieve the Irish independence which was unequivocally its goal.[15] Like the old *Nation* under Davis it spoke of the need for 'National Self-Reliance'[16] and published patriotic songs and verses, which O'Leary, the editor, tried to keep to a certain literary standard, complaining bitterly on at least one occasion of the poor literary quality of many of the poems submitted – the endless repetitions of green, dear and poor Erin and the inevitable rhyming of sheen with green and crag with flag.[17] It kept constantly in front of the Irish people reminders of the existence of the open Fenian Brotherhood in the United States, and though the outbreak of the civil war there temporarily overshadowed the Irish American scene, there were

* This was true at least by the spring of 1864. See, e.g., *Irish People*, 26 March 1864, and thereafter Irish and British newspapers generally.

† Note, however, that in England and Scotland, where it would have been bought more, and passed from hand to hand or read aloud from less, it 'almost annihilated' *The Nation*.

continual hints of the eventual significance of that war for Ireland. A song published at Christmas 1863 entitled 'An Irish Maiden to her American soldier' concluded:

> Come home, come home, to your waiting bride – come home to your plighted vows, love,
>
> But never come back like a cringing slave, with the brand on your stainless brow, love.
>
> Come home with the heart you bore away – to your kindred and home and sire-land.
>
> But stay away if you bear not back your manhood's resolve for Ireland.[18]

And when some New York ladies presented a green silk flag specially made by Tiffany's to the 1st Regiment of the Phoenix brigade, commanded by John O'Mahony, the fact was reported in faithful detail.[19]

The outbreak of the American civil war had obviously been a set-back for Stephens, confining American Irish energies for several years primarily to the other side of the Atlantic. On the other hand, it did provide the American Irish, who were fighting for both North and South, with unequalled experience of modern war. If they could afterwards be persuaded to turn their attention to Ireland the delay might even prove to have been worth while. But they needed organization and Stephens was increasingly dissatisfied with O'Mahony as an effective leader, actually sending Luby to the States early in 1863 with powers to suspend or even depose him, if necessary.[20] He himself kept up a continual pressure on O'Mahony with accounts of his own success in Ireland, while deploring the small amount of financial support from the States. 'One Hundred and Thirteen Pounds from the whole American organization in a whole year!' he wrote in 1862, and continued '... our numbers are in all places I have heard from increasing, in some places the increase is next to incredible. Thus, a centre who, three months ago, did not count a hundred men, sent me last week a return for eight hundred.'[21]

As late as 1864 the Fenian Brotherhood in the States numbered only some ten thousand men, but in that year Stephens himself went to America, and carried out a most energetic and successful tour of the Union Armies recruiting for the Fenian Brotherhood. He wrote to O'Mahony in New York that there were a hundred thousand men ready to fight for Ireland, adding: 'Don't say any more that I exaggerate.'[22] And as the civil war moved towards its conclusion Stephens increasingly sounded a note of optimistic urgency. 'Let no man, for an instant, forget,' he wrote to O'Mahony in December 1864, 'that we are bound to action next year ... I ask you in the name of God to believe that no others, after us, can bring the cause to the test of battle and that our battle must be entered on sometime in the coming year.'[23]

In January 1865 the Fenians in the States themselves began to show signs of effective consolidation and firmness. At the Fenian Convention at Cincinnati in that month O'Mahony proclaimed that 'this Brotherhood is virtually at war with the oligarchy of Great Britain ... the Fenian Congress acts the part of a national assembly of an Irish Republic. Our organized friends in Ireland constitute its army ...'.[24] Supplies of money to Ireland increased considerably and a number of envoys were sent over to report back on whether in fact the organization there was in as good shape as Stephens maintained. Though the implied suspicion inevitably irritated Stephens, these envoys in fact all confirmed his own account, reporting back enthusiastically on the widespread nature of the organization.

One envoy, Captain T. J. Kelly (soon to be colonel), who had fought in the 10th Ohio Regiment of the US army, arrived in Ireland in March 1865.[25] He reported in June that everyone in Ireland was now ready, that property was being sold and rent withheld and that half the militia was Fenian-minded.[26] Only this inspection with its possibility of postponement implied is a dampener,' he added.[27]

The business of seducing the militia and other British soldiers from their loyalty to the queen and transferring it to the Irish Republic, which in terms of the 'The Brotherhood's' oath was 'now virtually established', had been in the hands of a young man named John Devoy, a member of Stephens's organization since the early days, who in 1861 had spent a year in the French Foreign Legion to acquire military experience which he hoped might one day be useful to Ireland.[28] Assisted effectively by a colourful character known as Pagan O'Leary and other agents, Devoy had managed to get a number of British soldiers to take the Fenian oath, though their eagerness to do so may often have owed more to the attractions of the public houses where the ritual was performed than to idealism. In addition to these successes Devoy had brought over from England some seventeen deserters from the British Army to act in Dublin as drill-masters for the Irish Republic in return for board and lodging and one shilling and sixpence a day – twopence more a day than they had been getting before.[29]

Meanwhile, Stephens himself, often known colloquially as 'the Captain', but operating under many different aliases (Power, Watson, Kelly, Wright, Daly, etc.),[30] had been perfecting his organization. Fenian meetings, held in fields under the cover of football matches, had proliferated.[31] Drilling proceeded regularly in groups of fifty to sixty in halls in the towns, while in the countryside and especially at night mysterious bodies of Fenians were parading and manoeuvring. A contemporary song ran

> See who comes over the red-blossomed heather,
> Their green banners kissing the pure mountain air,
> Heads erect! Eyes to front! Stepping proudly together ...
> Out and make way for the bold Fenian men.

> ... Pay them back woe for woe,
> Give them back blow for blow,
> Out and make way for the bold Fenian men.

> Side by side for the cause have our forefathers battled
> On our hills never echoed the tread of a slave,
> In many a field where the leaden hail rattled,
> Through the red gap of glory they marched to the grave.

> All those who inherit their name and their spirit
> Will march with the banners of liberty then
> All who love foreign law, native or Sassenach,
> Must out and make way for the bold Fenian men.

During 1864 some arrests had been made for illegal drilling associated with the Fenians. The Brotherhood was known to have ramifications over most of Ireland, but considering its extent remarkably little hard evidence about it had come publicly to light.[32] Altogether, by the beginning of 1865, Stephens reckoned that he had some eighty-five thousand men effectively organized in Ireland and the only difficulty he foresaw was in keeping them together while delay occurred in supplying them with arms. He had established schools of engineering and musketry, manufacturing percussion caps, cartridges and shells and even, so he said, founding cannon. 'Nothing shall be wanting,' he wrote to America, 'if our American brothers do their duty.'[33]

When, therefore, after the South's surrender the Union and Confederate armies began to disband in June 1865, the prospects for a rising in Ireland seemed good. Former American officers, recognizable from their felt hats and square-toed boots, were soon making their way across the Atlantic to Ireland.[34] In August, after further confirmation by Fenian envoys in Ireland of the readiness of the organization there, O'Mahony issued the 'final call' for money in the States, raising some $30,000 in two weeks.*[35] The idea of fitting out Irish privateers, 'to hoist the green flag and ... sweep English commerce from the seas' was openly advertised in the American press.[36] Ten Irish pilots arrived in New York to help bring Fenians into Ireland. But ominously O'Mahony found it 'maddening' that people in Ireland should think his plans so far advanced.[37]

A worrying incident of another kind had occurred in Ireland the month before. The last set of Fenian envoys, P. W. Dunne and Patrick J. Meehan, had on the very day of their arrival in Dublin lost some vital documents, including a letter from O'Mahony introducing them as plenipotentiaries to the Chief Executive of the Irish Republic.[38] This letter, together with another which compromised O'Donovan Rossa and a draft for £500, had been pinned to Meehan's underwear but had dropped out.[39] The whole day was spent looking for the documents, but in vain, and the possibility that they

---

* The total for 1865 was to top a quarter of a million dollars altogether.

might have fallen into the hands of the police was disconcerting. In fact this was exactly what had happened, for they were picked up by a small boy at Kingstown railway station about 4.30 that afternoon. But the authorities did not move.[40]

By September 1865 Ireland was tense. The gentry in Clare and Limerick were sending their plate in boxes to the Bank.[41] Boatmen on the Shannon saw large boatloads of men crossing silently by night from Clare to the Limerick side of the river, their arms glinting in the moonlight.[42] There was continued talk of the Fenians everywhere in the Irish and English press. Instances of Fenian drilling and marching became more and more blatant, the *Cork Herald* supposing correctly that 'some of those who have returned from America are disseminating the spirit of disaffection among the people'.[43] The police were said to be on the alert, but the *Dublin Evening Mail* warned against complacency. It reminded its readers that the authorities were not now dealing with hot-headed enthusiasts as in 1848, but with determined and clever men; 'and nothing has shown this more than the clever organization of the Fenians, which never leaves a password, paper or any other tangible means by which they can be discovered, and at the same time they appear to be under perfect control from some unseen authority'.[44] To Unionists there was certainly something sinister and mysterious about the quality of their opponents, but the *Mail* in fact was going too far. The loss of the documents from envoy Meehan's underwear had not been their only mistake.

On 8 September 1865 Stephens in Dublin wrote a letter on the subject of organization to the Fenians in Clonmel. It concluded: 'There is no time to be lost. This year – and let there be no mistake about it – must be the year of action. I speak with a knowledge and authority to which no other man could pretend and I repeat, the flag of Ireland – of the Irish Republic – must this year be raised.... Yours fraternally, J. Power.'[45]

The letter was to be taken to Clonmel by hand. But instead of proceeding there at once the messenger went and had a number of drinks. He then went to the *Irish People* office to sleep things off, and half-sleepy and half-drunk was making water into a chamber pot when the letter was taken from his pocket by a former folder of parcels and writer of labels at the office named Nagle. Nagle was a Fenian and former National schoolmaster. He had been giving detailed information to the authorities in return for money for the past eighteen months.[46]

17

Stephens In and Out of Trouble

Even the careful John O'Mahony in the States had succumbed to the wave of euphoria among the Fenians. 'Ere long,' he declared, 'there shall be an Irish Army on the Irish hillsides ready to do battle for Irish independence and drive back from the green and sacred Isle of Erin those ruthless tyrants who have desolated our homes and driven us wandering exiles over the whole earth.'[1]

Four days later A. M. Sullivan, the editor of *The Nation*, was woken in the morning in the northern suburbs of Dublin by his brother telling him excitedly to get up and hurry into town.

'Quick – quick. There is desperate work. The *Irish People* is suppressed; the office is seized; Luby, O'Leary and Rossa are arrested; telegraphic communication with the South is stopped . . .'[2]

All this was true. The government had struck during the night.

It had been a thorough operation, with only one disappointment. Stephens himself had not been caught. A. M. Sullivan thought this meant that there would be barricades up in the city by nightfall. But there were to be no barricades up in Dublin either that night or for many thousands of nights to come.

Though Stephens had begun his organization determined to improve on the security of the United Irishmen, and had succeeded in that, his security was by no means watertight. What was surprising in the circumstances was that it was as effective as it was.

The very openness with which the technically legal activity was carried on must in itself have been confusing to the authorities. Stephens himself, O'Donovan Rossa, O'Leary, Luby and others long associated with separatism and republicanism were regularly to be found in or around the *Irish People* office. And the paper always made the most of the fact that the Fenian Brotherhood in the United States was not a secret organization; it quoted with approval a contemporary weekly which with mock-naïvety declared that it had searched through the American papers for information about that society and discovered 'there is no more secrecy about it than there is about ordering a joint of meat from your butcher'.[3] In Ireland, too, a body calling itself the National Brotherhood of St Patrick was an open legal organization, which by its very unabashed avowal of the cause of separation and its sympathy with the Fenian Brotherhood in the United States must have added to the government's difficulty in deciding exactly how much more there was in all this than met the eye.

But though the authorities were often in the dark about details of Stephens's organization, the broad lines of what was going on in secret and the identities of all the important people involved had long been known to them through their system of informers. Nagle, who had been giving information since March 1864, was not the only source. A detective named Thomas Talbot passed himself off so successfully as a water-bailiff called John Kelly at Carrick-on-Suir that local Fenians, thinking he was the head centre for the South of Ireland, used to come to him for promotion. He attended many a Fenian meeting at which drinking and the singing of Fenian songs took place, though he was overcome by scruples when 'Out and Make Way for the Fenian Men' came up, simply letting on he was singing it, but only moving his mouth up and down.[4]

Just as important as the penetration of the organization in Ireland was the fact that very close to John O'Mahony in America was a man named James MacDermot ('Red' Jim, after his beard), who had been working for the British secret service for years, and in 1865 was selling every secret of the Fenian Brotherhood to the British Consul in New York. Many Fenians, including Stephens, strongly mistrusted MacDermot, but O'Mahony's trust in him could not be shaken and it was many years before he was finally exposed.

But though the government information net was fairly widely spread, the organization itself was so large that there were always many secrets unpenetrated. Stephens himself was able to remain free in Dublin for two months after the *Irish People* arrests, living as Mr Herbert with Kickham and two other leading Fenians in a house in Sandymount which they left only at night.[5] From his hiding-place he got a message out to America to the effect that the organization in Ireland was, despite the arrests, in all its essentials still intact. The arrests, he said, had only made its members more impatient than ever and men and supplies must be sent without delay.[6] And one of the American officers whom O'Mahony had sent over as yet another envoy, William Halpin, reported back that the determination to strike was as strong as ever.[7] Nevertheless, the rot was beginning to set in for those American rank and file who had now been hanging about Dublin for some months without anything to do. They were becoming hard-up and discouraged, and were applying to the American Consul in Dublin to send them home with a free passage.[8]

Then on the morning of 11 November the rented house in Sandymount in which Stephens had been living was surrounded while he was still in bed, and he, Kickham and the others were arrested. They had eventually been betrayed by yet another informer.[9] The reaction to the news by the average non-Fenian Dubliner was probably accurately summarized by A. M. Sullivan when he wrote, later: 'The dreaded Chief Organizer of the Irish Republic was now in custody. Now everyone might sleep with an easy mind. No "rising" need be apprehended. No lurid flame of civil war would redden the midnight sky.'[10] But Stephens still had some counter strokes in store.

The secret 'military council' of the Fenians – consisting of Kelly, Halpin, Devoy and others – now met and elected a temporary head for the movement, the American officer, General Millen, who at once sent a message to the States saying that they still intended to strike before the end of the year. Then Stephens made his most dramatic single contribution to the cause of Fenianism to date. With the help of two warders named Byrne and Breslin, who were sworn Fenians, he escaped from gaol. Breslin led him out of his cell in the middle of the stormy night of 24 November 1865, and with Byrne's help brought him to where an organized party, headed by Captain Thomas Kelly and John Devoy, threw a rope-ladder over the outer wall and got him away.[11]

Sometimes it seems that all the bungling during these years was on the Fenian side. But the escape was a masterly achievement. Nor was the government innocent of blunders. The governor of the prison remarked frankly at the subsequent inquiry that he had no confidence generally in any of his officers. And on more than twenty occasions since June 1861 the warder Byrne had been reprimanded, cautioned or fined for neglect of duty, once being temporarily suspended for allowing a prisoner to escape.[12] Stephens's escape gave a great boost to Fenian morale, and confirmed the worst fears of many loyalists that the tentacles of the conspiracy had spread everywhere.

In spite of the offer of a reward of £1,000 for Stephens's capture, or of £300 for information leading to his arrest, he remained in hiding in the centre of Dublin, just opposite the Unionist Kildare Street club, for nearly three months.[13] The fact is a tribute both to Fenian security when not already penetrated by an informer and to the unvenal idealism of the best Fenians, many of whom must have known of Stephens's whereabouts.

Before he finally left the country he was responsible for a decision only possible to a man whose reputation was at its height with his fellow conspirators. From the moment of his escape there had been strong pressure on Stephens both from the American and Irish Fenians in Dublin to keep the much repeated vow to strike before the year was out. But now on Stephens's part a distinct cooling-off suddenly became noticeable.

The later history of the Fenian movement is so full of personal quarrels and recriminations and charges of cowardice or other defects of character levelled against individuals – many of them centring on Stephens – that it is often difficult to sort out genuine charges from mere factional propaganda. Stephens's own motivation in the years 1865 and 1866 is particularly difficult to assess. For all the strain of self-aggrandizement in his activity to date there was much about it that was realistic. The organization was after all in being on a considerable scale, and was almost entirely the result of his own hard work. And at least until his arrest there had been a genuine note of urgency and determination about his final plans for a rising. Only in the field of coordination with the vast potential in America had there been something of a failure. There had been piece-meal help certainly with men and money, but given the number of men fresh from the civil war and the sums of money available it should have been possible to organize something much more like the well-supplied spearhead that Stephens had originally stipulated. For all the talk there was still no such well-organized expedition forthcoming.

The note of urgent determination in Stephens's statements about striking in 1865 may always have been partly a device for forcing O'Mahony and the American Fenians into more effective action. Partly, too, it was simply characteristic of Stephens's moral bombast. More than one factor may have been at work in his mind as he now decided to abandon hope of a rising for that year. But to give preponderance at this stage to the fright his arrest may have given him seems fair. His personal experience may have made him rather more cautious. But then there was plenty to be cautious about. For, in addition to other shortcomings, in America a serious disaster had just overtaken the Fenian cause. At the very moment when the concentration of all efforts for Ireland was more necessary than ever, the movement in America had split into two rival sections. One, the more powerful, led by a Colonel Roberts in opposition to O'Mahony, and therefore outside Stephens's control, now favoured the direction of all Fenian efforts against the more easily accessible territory of Canada in the first phase of the battle for Irish independence.

With only weeks of the year to go, Stephens with some political skill succeeded in bringing leading Fenians in Dublin, both Irish and Irish American, reluctantly to accept his view that the rising must be postponed. The most effective argument he had to overcome was a purely military one, presented with particular strength by John Devoy, who had had charge of the seduction of British soldiers. A considerable part of the British garrison then in the country, particularly that part in Dublin, had been, nominally at least, seduced from their allegiance to the queen by the Fenian oath. Stephens himself conceded that about one-third of the total garrison in Ireland were Fenians – some twelve thousand trained men to be added to the two hundred thousand Irishmen sworn altogether, fifty thousand of whom he maintained were 'thoroughly armed'.

The argument for immediate action, pressed by Devoy, but strongly supported by most of the Dublin 'centres' and the American-dominated military council of which Kelly, promoted now to colonel, was chief of staff, persisted until February 1866. Such action would have had a desperate quality about it, as its advocates recognized, but that desperation need not have made it unsuccessful. Looking back with hindsight, as many Fenians and particularly Devoy were later to do, it was easy to say that any action taken then would have been more successful than what finally happened. But Stephens's feelings at the time were probably dominated by a typical conviction that his own ability could straighten out the difficulties in America and bring about that properly coordinated rising which had always been planned and which, if achieved, would have had at least a better than desperate chance of success. A less charitable interpretation of Stephens's attitude, even leaving out of account considerations of personal safety, would be that his ego had become so wedded to the business of conducting and managing the conspiracy that he preferred to spin it out indefinitely on one rational excuse or another rather than bring it to a climax. Probably shades of these different motivations were at work in him simultaneously at different levels. Of course, the longer he remained in Dublin without taking action the weightier became the arguments for postponement. The elements of suddenness and surprise necessary to all desperate actions were fading all the time, and the government itself became better and better placed to meet the situation. Arrests of American officers had been taking place since before the end of the year. In February 1866 Habeas Corpus was once again suspended, and most of those whom the government had so far failed to lay their hands on were arrested too.

On 21 February 1866 Devoy himself was arrested with a number of his Fenian soldiers in a public house in Dublin. Those who had so far only accepted most reluctantly Stephens's argument for postponing action now had to agree that there was no longer any other immediate alternative left. Stephens himself was smuggled with Colonel Kelly on to a collier and took to the Irish Sea. Blown by adverse winds up to Scotland, they landed there and came down by train to London, where they spent a night at the Palace Hotel near Victoria. They then passed on to France, en route for America, where Stephens was determined to heal the disastrous split in the Fenian Brotherhood.

This split had originated squalidly, as did many quarrels in the Fenian movement, over the handling of money, but its real cause had been the normal political factor of personal ambition. O'Mahony's rival, Colonel John Roberts, now dominated what was called the 'Senate' or Roberts's wing of the Fenian Brotherhood, and his half of the movement was numerically the stronger. There had been superimposed on the personal rivalry and the quarrel over handling of the funds a serious division of opinion about strategy. Roberts and his followers now held the view that an attempt on Canada would be of more immediate advantage to the Irish cause than coordination with the movement in Ireland because it was more likely to achieve immediate success. Stephens, for all his old taunts against O'Mahony, naturally sided with him and did all in his power to restore his authority. But when he reached America the split had gone too far. In any case, now that the civil war was over, the whole movement had now grown too big an American phenomenon for the limited magic of Stephens's strong personality to be able to control it. All he could really do was to try to use his formidable energy to rally support for the O'Mahony wing and its policy of a rising in Ireland in 1866, while the Roberts wing went its own flamboyant way.

'We promise,' declared the Roberts-wing Fenian general in charge of the Canada plan, in February, 'that before the summer sun kisses the hilltops of Ireland, a ray of hope will gladden every true Irish heart. The green flag will be flying independently to freedom's breeze, and we will have a base of operations from which we can not only emancipate Ireland, but also annihilate England.'[14] The theory was that if only a foothold could be won on which the Irish flag could be raised, then independent Ireland would be recognized as reality.

Meanwhile, the O'Mahony wing, much to Stephens's disapproval, itself made an attempt in April to capture the island of Campo Bello off the coast of New Brunswick. This proved totally abortive, and the ship which had been purchased for the expedition for $40,000 never even set sail. The British Government had been kept informed of the project throughout by Red Jim MacDermot, who also reported that the idea of an expedition to Ireland was not totally exploded, and that six of the Irish pilots who had arrived the previous summer were still in the States.[15]

American Fenian energies now switched to the Vermont border with Canada where the 'Right Wing of the Army of Ireland' was soon poised. Some three thousand armed Fenians had assembled in Buffalo. On the night of 31 May 1866, eight hundred of them, commanded by a Colonel O'Neill, crossed the Niagara river and occupied the village of Fort Erie on the Canadian shore. On the morning of 2 June they won an engagement with some Canadian student volunteers at Lime Ridge, also known as Ridgeway, but with his rear threatened O'Neill retired on Fort Erie again hoping for reinforcements to reach him across the lake from Buffalo. But this was now being patrolled by the United States Government, which though it maintained a carefully ambivalent attitude towards the Fenians (finding their nuisance value against the British diplomatically too handy to throw away), felt obliged to enforce the neutrality laws now that an actual invasion had taken place. Cut off on the foothold he had won for the green flag O'Neill had no alternative but to withdraw again. In the skirmish at Ridgeway the Canadians had lost twelve dead and forty wounded, while the Fenian losses had been eight dead and twenty wounded. About sixty Fenians had been captured and there had been some desertions.[16] 'The Irish Republican Army', as Fenian headquarters described it, had been in action for the first time.[17] This fact alone gives the incident greater historical interest than it might otherwise merit.

Its sponsors seemed in no way dismayed by the failure. 'Arise, Irishmen,' proclaimed Roberts, 'a glorious career has opened for you. The Green Flag has waved once more in triumph over England's hated emblem...'[18] But as the US Government gently sent the Fenians home from the frontier with their passages paid – though seizing their arms which they later returned to them – the net effect of this rather empty demonstration in Canada was to lend force to Stephens's exhortations to the Brotherhood to strike in Ireland.

He had already been in the States, since his escape, for some months. In July and August 1866 he was promising that an army would be fighting on Irish soil before the year was out.[19] On 28 October he declared at a rally that they would next hear of him leading his troops against the Saxon aggressor.[20] A final appeal for arms and money was issued. But the response so far had not been good. Once again, as in the previous year, a situation had arisen in which Stephens was defiantly committed to rising in Ireland before the year was out with only a few more weeks of the year to run and the American end of the movement in disarray.

The moment of truth had again arrived. But how with any dignity or prestige left could Stephens face it for the second year running? The answer was that he could not.

In some ways, though accusations of personal cowardice were soon to multiply thick and fast, not least from Kelly,[21] the course he now took was a most courageous one, though the element of humbug present in so much of his activity should not be discounted.

It was in fact reasonable of him to urge as he now did, in the light of inadequate armament and American support, a further postponement of the rising. But it had not been reasonable of him to talk of the coming fight with such bombast and flourish if he had been unsure – as he had been throughout the seven months of his 1866 campaign in America – whether that support would materialize. In September in New York he had even hinted that whether or not the arrangements for a rising were adequate he would go to Ireland in any case for the men could be held back no longer. 'If I thought it would be any gain to delay, I would do so and risk all my popularity,' he had said. 'But I cannot for they are determined on fighting this year, and I am fully determined on being with them, come weal or woe. No matter what others say, take my word I will be in Ireland, and the people will strike a blow for liberty.'[22]

Having said that, he could not now, with any dignity or reasonable hope of being listened to, counsel his own Fenian officers in the States to postpone the rising. However, that was what he now tried to do and he paid the inevitable political penalty. At a series of meetings in his lodgings in New York beginning on 15 December 1866 they heard him detail as a reason for postponement the inadequate resources available for Ireland. There were, it appeared, only four thousand rifles out of the minimum of thirty thousand considered necessary.[23] His behaviour at these meetings, faced with charges of cowardice, seems sometimes to have approached hysteria. Once he even melodramatically offered to go to Ireland at once 'to get hanged' to prove his personal courage, a suggestion which no one took seriously.[24] Soon afterwards he was to confuse the issue, when justifying himself to the centres of the organization in Dublin, by writing that his health had been a reason for inaction, describing himself as having been 'apparently not long for this world'.[25] But in the same letter he urged his men, should Colonel Kelly call on them to rise, to do so '... and prove the stuff that is in you ...'.[26] He would, he said, be among them himself soon afterwards. He did not return to Ireland for almost another thirty years.

For all practical purposes the Fenian movement was taken out of Stephens's hands as a result of these meetings in New York. He was deposed from his recently assumed position of Head Centre of the Fenian Brotherhood in the States. To salve his pride the officers let him remain for a time the nominal civil head of the organization in Ireland, but Kelly became head of the all-important military sector, and was soon to be known as Acting Chief Executive of the Irish Republic.[27] The real control of the Fenians in Ireland passed into Kelly's hands, and Stephens, though he was to spend much of the rest of his life jockeying to regain position and was not to be without occasional supporters particularly in Ireland, passes out of Irish history as an effective force. Kelly's own appearance in the limelight was to be brief but sensational, and in one respect at least to have an indirect effect of enormous importance for the future, so that his name today is probably better known in Ireland than that of Stephens himself who virtually founded the Fenian movement.

Having deposed Stephens the next step taken by the officers assembled in his lodgings in New York was themselves to volunteer to cross the Atlantic and start a rising in Ireland. Thus the impetus for the dramatic events that were about to occur came from a group of tough, footloose Irish emigrant soldiers of fortune whose occupation had gone with the end of the civil war and was made good by the cause and livelihood provided by the Fenian Brotherhood. But that revolution happened to suit them was only one element in their motivation. After all, to be sustained by the hopes and funds of the Fenian Brotherhood there was no need to cross the Atlantic and risk their necks, as some of the Canadian or Roberts wing of the movement could demonstrate. Those who under Kelly now proceeded to engineer the Fenian rising of 1867 in Ireland were all – with one or two exceptions – idealists of one sort or another. Most had bitter first-hand memories of poverty and degradation in Ireland to avenge. All had been in battle. Many, like Kelly and Captain John McCafferty, a former Confederate soldier who had been particularly contemptuous of Stephens's prevarication in the New York meetings, had already risked their freedom in Ireland the year before and McCafferty had been actually arrested there as a suspect, though as an American-born US citizen he was released after American diplomatic intervention.*

Even John Mitchel, in Paris at the end of 1866 as an agent for Fenian funds, was opposed to a rising by this date on the grounds that it had no chance of success. But, without responsibility for any decision himself, he described the situation of any Fenian leader at the time as being like that of a man holding wolves by the ears.²⁸ The character of those who had escaped from Stephens's grasp justified the simile.

Among those who sailed with Kelly and McCafferty from New York to Europe in the second week of January 1867 was, for instance, Captain Richard O'Sullivan Burke of the 15th New York Engineers. He had been born in Macroom, County Cork, and had been a corporal in the South Cork militia before emigrating to the States in 1857. He, too, had spent part of the last year on British soil, negotiating, under different aliases, large commercial purchases of arms and ammunition with a Mr Kynoch of Birmingham.²⁹

Some officers now assumed with sometimes dubious entitlement the rank of general. General William Halpin, a close associate of Kelly's, who had been one of O'Mahony's envoy-inspectors in 1865, and was soon again to be operating in Ireland under the alias of Bird, seems to have been at least a colonel in the Union Army in the civil war. But a more questionable figure altogether was 'General' Gordon Massey, a native of County Limerick and a former corporal in the British Army, who had served in the Crimea and then emigrated to America. Illegitimate, he had been known then and throughout his service with the Confederates in the civil war under his mother's name of Condon – Patrick Condon. After joining the Fenians in Texas in 1865 he came to New York late in 1866, and, perhaps because there was another Patrick Condon active among the upper echelons of the Brother-

---

* The British law's attitude to Irish-American nationality was, however, severe. Those Irish who had become naturalized Americans and had thereby specifically renounced all earlier allegiance were nevertheless held by British law to be subject to the allegiance under which they were born, and as liable to charges of high treason as any Briton. American-born US citizens were in any case subject to the normal British criminal law.

hood, he began to be known as Gordon Massey, after his father.[30] But a more profound question mark still remains over his name to this day. Before many months were out he was to turn queen's evidence, but whether his defection dated only from his own arrest or earlier is unsure. What is certain is that when he sailed from New York on 11 January 1867 he was high in the Fenian military councils.

Though Kelly was the 'acting Chief Executive of the Irish Republic' after Stephens's deposition, he had at his service a purely military command headed by a man who was not an Irishman at all. This was an adventurous Frenchman named Cluseret, who at least had every right to call himself a general and became the Fenian 'Commander-in-Chief'.[31] Cluseret's military career had begun in 1848 in the Garde Mobile of the Second Republic when he was awarded the Legion of Honour for storming eleven barricades during the suppression of the June insurrection.[32] Thereafter in thought at least he had gravitated more and more to the revolutionary left. His fighting career had continued in Algeria, the Crimea, in Sicily under Garibaldi and finally in the Union Army during the civil war under McLellan, where he achieved the rank of brigadier general.[33] He had met and made friends with Stephens in the States during 1866 and felt drawn to Fenianism partly because he was a natural soldier of fortune, but also undoubtedly because its identification with the cause of the poor of Ireland, and its republicanism appealed to his own radical sentiments.[34] As a practical soldier, however, he had driven a bargain with Stephens. He would agree to take over all military command of the rising only when he could be guaranteed that ten thousand men had already taken the field in Ireland.[35]

Cluseret had attended the meetings in New York in December 1866 at which Stephens had been deposed, and had agreed to go along with Kelly on similar terms. He selected as his military adjutants two other foreign veterans of the American civil war, Fariola and Vifquain, shadowy figures whose names flicker momentarily across the brief scene of the Fenian Rising.

One more name among the band of 'wolves' now on their way to Europe deserves mention. It is that of Michael O'Brien, a native of Cork, who had taken a formal part in the arrangements for McManus's funeral in 1862, but had then emigrated and emerged from service with the Union Army in the American civil war with the rank of captain. His name, with that of two Fenian companions, was soon to assume a heroic position in the history of nineteenth-century Ireland beside those of Mitchel and Emmet.

18

1867: Bold Fenian Men

Kelly set up his operational headquarters in London where, since Habeas Corpus was not suspended as in Ireland, freedom of movement and general security was that much easier.[1] He and Halpin took rooms under the names of Coleman and Fletcher off the Tottenham Court Road, while Bourke and Massey, known as Wallace and Cleburne, took other rooms at 7 Tavistock Street.[2] The heads of the conspiracy were all lodged within a square mile of each other. General Cluseret and his adjutant Fariola took up residence at 137 Great Portland Street,[3] but they had no need to adopt aliases. They had obtained through Fenian political influences in America a commission to inspect British military organizations on behalf of the State of New York, and were furnished with documents to do so signed by the innocent American legation in London.[4] A directory, or provisional government of the Irish Republic, consisting half of civilians and half of military men was established.[5]

The military plan was for guerrilla warfare. In many respects it did not differ in general intention from the scheme of action finally adopted more than fifty years later by the Irish Republican Army of that day. The fighting of pitched battles was not contemplated. Bodies of fighting men were to assemble flexibly in different parts of Ireland, with a concentration round Dublin and the south-west. These were to destroy rail and telegraph communications, attack police barracks and have a general harassing effect on government movements until the army of the republic could be recognized as belligerents and substantial aid received from America.[6] This was the theory.

The speed with which the plotters moved into action after their arrival in London at the very end of January was a tribute both to their determination and the extent of the organization already existing in England and Ireland. The first intention was for the rising to start in Ireland on 11 February, preceded by a most daring action into which Kelly afterwards felt that McCafferty had too rashly precipitated them.*[7] This had as its objective no

---

* It was said by Kelly that the raid on Chester was attempted without agreement from London from him, but this was contradicted at the Trial of Flood (*Report of Dublin Special Commission*, p. 882).

less than the capture, with the aid of the man-power of the well-organized Fenians in the north of England, of the large British arms and ammunition store at Chester Castle, which was less a castle than a military barracks with a gaol attached.[8] Simultaneously, trains between Chester and Holyhead were to be seized and the arms rushed to Holyhead where the mail boat would also have been captured. With all rail and telegraph communications cut to prevent government intervention, the vast stock of supplies would then be rushed to Ireland for the rising which would have started the same day.*[9]

All this was to take place on Monday, 11 February, and early that morning strangers, mainly working men, began arriving at Chester station in large numbers by trains from Warrington, Crewe, Manchester and other towns of Lancashire and Cheshire. By the early afternoon there were well over a thousand in the town.[10] The day before, at Kelly's lodgings in London, an important meeting had taken place at which three of the four provincial 'centres' for the organization in Ireland were present and a number of military men. A statement of political aims had been drawn up. After the meeting 'General' Massey, who was to take charge of the first assembly phase of the rising under Cluseret felt conditions ready himself to take overall command, left for Ireland.[11]

It is not clear when the decision to postpone the rising was taken, but it seems at least likely that it was linked closely with what happened at Chester on the afternoon of 11 February. Certainly one Fenian close to the top of the organization believed this to be so.† In which case, the speed and efficiency with which news of the postponement was carried to every part of Ireland but one was commendable. For it was not until one o'clock on Monday afternoon, 11 February, when the trains crowded with strange working men from other towns were continuing to arrive at Chester, that McCafferty himself learnt that the authorities had been alerted to his plan.[12] The guard on the Castle had been strengthened; the Volunteers had been called out; a detachment of the Guards was on its way from London. It was too late to stop at least half the Fenians assembling. Most were already there. But with considerable skill McCafferty and his agents succeeded in calling the operation off and the police afterwards found large quantities of ammunition and revolvers dumped in the neighbourhood of the railway station and in the ponds and canals of the town.[13] Next day and for several days afterwards the police in Ireland met steamers arriving at Dublin and Dundalk and arrested dozens of young Irish working men who had been seen crowded together on the boats and, though without money in their pockets, had given up jobs in England to return to their native country.[14] McCafferty, calling himself William Jackson, was arrested on suspicion as

---

* 'If the Chester affair had succeeded, there was to have been a rising in Ireland.' (Corydon.)

† The informer, John Joseph Corydon. See, e.g., *The Times*, 30 April 1868.

he attempted to row away with a companion from a collier which had anchored in the Liffey after crossing the Irish Sea.[15] He continued to maintain he was William Jackson until those searching him found sewn into the lining of his coat a ring inscribed 'Erin I love thee and thy patriots – Presented to Captain John McCafferty IRB by the Detroit Circle of the Fenian Brotherhood, a token of esteem.'[16]

What McCafferty did not then know was how the authorities had learnt of his plan to raid Chester Castle. The information had been given them by one of his own men, John Joseph Corydon, a well-trusted Fenian who had acted as the principle carrier of dispatches between Ireland and America in 1865. A man of disreputable private life, he had been giving information to the authorities since September 1866 because, he said, he 'did not think the Fenian organization worth spilling one drop of blood for'.[17]

Only in Kerry did notice of the postponement of the rising fail to get through. Some men assembled in arms at Cahirciveen. But though a certain panic was caused among the gentry who flocked for refuge to the Railway Hotel, Killarney, the affair was more one of rumour than of real menace, for the Fenian Head Centre for Kerry, J. J. O'Connor, soon discovered his mistake and his men, estimated by the newspapers at anything between nine hundred and one hundred (including '20 Americans'), melted away.[18] James Stephens himself, chief Fenian bogeyman, of whose fall from grace the public were not yet aware, was widely reported to be in the district in person.[19]

Meanwhile, plans to bring the postponed rising to a new climax were being worked on. Massey, who had been in Ireland since 11 February, had conferred with the Irish centres, in Dublin, in the West and in the Cork district – where the most widespread effort was to be made – and returned to London on 24 February to report to Kelly and Cluseret.[20] On the strength of what he had learned of the available resources in Ireland he considered the prospect hopeless.

There was not, he thought, the least chance of the Fenians holding the field for a day.[21] Though there were fourteen thousand men organized in Dublin and twenty thousand in Cork, the proportion of arms to men, and of modern rifles to shot-guns and pikes, was absurdly low. Nevertheless, as Massey himself afterwards declared: 'I knew it would be destruction but I did not like to go back having gone so far.'[22] In any case, his seemed to be the only voice saying it was hopeless. A meeting of all the top military men, including Cluseret and Fariola, was held in London under Kelly and the decision was taken to rise on 5 March.

When Massey returned to Dublin to tell the centres there of the new date, he again told them frankly that he thought there was not a chance of success. 'To do them justice,' he said later, 'they were all for "shoving it on".'[23]

The Commander-in-Chief, Cluseret, had himself been unimpressed by his experiences with the Irish since arriving in London. Instead of receiving the news he wanted of adequate stocks of arms, he had to listen to endless discussions of an almost theological nature as to who should succeed James Stephens as Head Centre. He had been overwhelmed with complaints, recriminations and accusations. 'Everybody,' he recalled five years later, 'came to me with their personal grievances but with nothing else.'[24] He found many of the American-Irish Fenians too fond of drink, including Massey, on whom his verdict was that 'as captain or corporal he would do very well, but as a general he was deplorable'.[25] He himself thought there was not a chance in two thousand of success, but engaged as he was only to take the field once the rising had established itself in the field the prospect may not have appeared too personally disastrous. Cluseret, like Massey, paid tribute to the Irish 'centres' who took the decision with Kelly to strike on 5 March. He describes them as 'noble' and 'with fine natures'. They insisted to him that they would keep their word, even though Stephens may not have kept his. 'The people will know,' they told Cluseret, 'that, if there are some who deceive them, there are others who know how to die for them.'[26]

This iron, selfless dedication to a cause which, though often viewed with sympathy by the Irish people, was made consistently ludicrous by events, became an important feature of the Fenian movement. Tenacity to the extreme republican cause in spite of every failure, continued seriousness in the face of every absurdity, became a quality that won at least some respect, even if it gained little positive support.

When Massey went back to Ireland to inform the organization there of the new date for the rising, the informer Corydon went with him.[27] The commands for the various districts had been allotted in London. Halpin was to have the Dublin area, subordinate to Massey, whose own base would be the large railway centre just outside Tipperary, Limerick junction. There his only specific orders were to coordinate the various gatherings in the south-western districts. Halpin's orders from Massey were, in case of a reverse in the Dublin area, to withdraw to the Wicklow Mountains, like Holt and Dwyer seventy years before, and from there harass government communications. Vifquain, one of Cluseret's French aides, was to take command in the west of Ireland, but his arrival was held up at the last minute for lack of funds. Cluseret's other aide, however, Fariola, arrived in Cork on 1 March to put finishing touches with Massey to the arrangements with local commanders: Dunne and Moran for the county of Cork, William Mackey Lomasney and Michael O'Brien for the city of Cork, Deasy for Millstreet, McClure for Midleton. At last, on the evening before the rising, 4 March 1867, Massey set out by train from Cork to take up his command at Limerick junction.

In London the provisional government of the Irish Republic sent a copy of their proclamation to *The Times*. It began:

'We have suffered centuries of outrage, enforced poverty and bitter misery. Our rights and liberties have been trampled on by an alien aristocracy, who, treating us as foes, usurped our lands and drew away from our unfortunate country all material riches ...'[28]

The essential Fenian myth was thus established that the 'foes', the owners of the soil, were alien. In fact, most had been Irishmen for centuries, often of the same religion and racial extraction as the suffering multitudes. But making allowance for this political colouring, the description of what had actually happened in Ireland was acceptable enough.

'The real owners of the soil,' continued the proclamation, 'were removed to make room for cattle, and driven across the ocean to seek the means of living and the political right denied to them at home.... But we never lost the memory and hope of a national existence ...'

Again, the folk-memory of better times on the land was equated with modern nationalistic aspirations. A retrospective national gloss was given to the turmoil of '98, the Emmet débâcle, and the feeble gyrations of Smith O'Brien. But the desperate spirit of the proclamation rang tragically true:

'We appealed in vain to the reason and sense of justice of the dominant powers.... Our appeals to arms were always unsuccessful. Today, having no honourable alternative left we again appeal to force as our last resource. We accept the conditions of appeal, manfully deeming it better to die in the struggle for freedom than to continue an existence of utter serfdom.... All men are born with equal rights.'

The influences of international socialism with which Stephens and Cluseret had been in contact joined forces with the radical teachings of the United Irishmen, and of Fintan Lalor twenty years before:

'... We aim at founding a republic based on universal suffrage, which shall secure to all the intrinsic value of their labour. The soil of Ireland at present in the possession of an oligarchy belongs to us, the Irish people, and to us it must be restored. We declare also in favour of absolute liberty of conscience, and the complete separation of Church and state ...'

The final section had an unmistakably Marxist ring, for it was Marx's teaching, totally at variance with the facts of British life, that Irish freedom would be brought about by English workmen supporting their cause. Kelly had founded an English Republican Brotherhood, within two miles, as he liked to boast, of Buckingham Palace itself.[29]

'Republicans,' the proclamation concluded, 'Republicans of the entire world, our cause is your cause.... Let your hearts be with us. As for you, workmen of England, it is not only your hearts we wish but your arms. Remember the starvation and degradation brought to your firesides by the oppression of labour. Remember the past, look well to the future, and avenge yourselves by giving liberty to your children in the coming struggle for human freedom. Herewith we proclaim the Irish Republic.'

In Ireland the Army of the Irish Republic was about to go into action. Its senior commander on Irish soil, General Massey, stepped off the train from Cork at Limerick junction shortly after ten o'clock on the evening of 4 March to take up his secret command. Someone tapped him on the shoulder as he was walking along the platform.[30] He was under arrest, betrayed by the informer Corydon, together with all the Fenian plans.

Word got to Fariola, Cluseret's chief of staff, within hours. He fled from his hotel in Cork in the middle of the night, leaving behind him an unpaid bill for thirty-five shillings, and a revolver.[31] He was only arrested several months later, walking along Oxford Street, London.[32] But on the evening of the 5th, unaware as yet of the disaster that had overtaken its high command, the Irish Republican Army in Dublin, Drogheda, Cork, Tipperary, Clare and Limerick was on the march.

Considering the detailed information the government had received from Corydon, a curious feature of the affair was the relative state of unpreparedness of the police which was now revealed. It was a dark night and the moon was not yet up when a constable called McIlwaine in Stepaside barracks near Dublin, lying on his bed with his shoes off, heard what he afterwards described as 'the weighty tramp of a number of people ... going near the barracks'.[33] He had had some information that 'there might be a stir' but clearly so far he had not taken this very seriously. Now he hurriedly called his four men to arms and on investigation found himself required by a man wearing a green feather in his cap to surrender the barracks to the Irish Republic. This the Irish constable refused to do at first. There was an exchange of shots. Then, threatened that the barracks would be set on fire, he complied. Outside, he and his men were placed with some other police whom the rebels had captured en route. To one of these the local rebel 'captain' had remarked in an early moment of exaltation: 'I suppose you did not think we would rise as sudden as we did? You did not imagine we had so many arms concealed without your knowledge?'[34] This same leader, Peter Lennon, now reconnoitred the town of Bray, but, deciding it was too strong,[35] marched his men with his captives to the police barracks at Glencullen which he also called upon to surrender to the Irish Republic. It did so after the captured police had been placed as hostages in the line of fire between the rebels and the barracks. It was then about 6 a.m. Lennon told Constable McIlwaine that he hoped to have between fourteen and fifteen thousand men on the hill at Tallaght by midday.[36]

All through the night Halpin had been sending up signal rockets in the Green Hills round Tallaght to show the rebels where to rally.[37] Apart from Lennon's victorious column other bodies of men had marched out of Dublin in that direction but with less success. All seem to have arrayed themselves at first in fair military order, forming fours and marching off from their first assembly points with sloped arms, some of which at least were Lee Enfield rifles with fixed bayonets.[38] But discipline does not seem to have been good or morale particularly high. More than one group of men transporting ammunition fled at their first haphazard encounter with the police, and one rebel leader was heard calling out that he would shoot on the spot the first man who flinched from his duty.[39]

Marching into the small town of Tallaght itself, which Halpin had specifically wanted them to avoid, one body of several hundred rebels found themselves confronted by fourteen men of the Constabulary under the command of a Sub-Inspector Burke. He had already succeeded in forcing another such party to retreat by calling out to them: 'Disperse, or so help me God, I'll fire!'[40] It had withdrawn in disorder to the shelter of a stone wall some two hundred yards away. Now he called upon the second party to halt and surrender. Answered by a volley of stones, he threatened to fire. Thereupon a rebel leader himself called out: 'Now, boys, fire, fire.' There was a volley, estimated later by Sub-Inspector Burke at about fifty shots, but none of the police were hit. They then fired back. The rebels immediately fled, leaving one man wounded behind them.

The effect of this defeat seems to have been devastating, for it virtually ended the attempt to assemble in the neighbourhood of Tallaght. In any case, soon after first light, news of the arrest of Massey over twenty-four hours before and the collapse of the entire high command must have penetrated to Halpin and the victorious Lennon making clear to them the forlorn nature of their enterprise. They vanished underground and were not arrested for several months.

But many stragglers among the rank and file were picked up in the course of the night and next morning. Near Stepaside, where the barracks had been taken, a green flag was found on a broken staff. The flag bore the slogan 'God and Our Country', beneath which were the Irish Harp without the Crown and the words 'Remember Emmet'.[41]

There had been clashes elsewhere in Ireland on the night and morning of 6–7 March, but nowhere were the Fenians much more successful than round Dublin – in some places considerably less so. A body of about a thousand men assembling in the middle of the night in the Potato Market in Drogheda were totally routed after a brief exchange of shots with a force of less than forty police.[42] In County Limerick a party of fifteen police at Kilmallock barracks held off a strong Fenian attack under a captain wearing a dark green uniform and a slouch hat with a feather in it. The barracks were eventually relieved after a three-hour fight in which at least two Fenians were killed. One of the constables firing from a window had kept an open notebook beside him, in which, in the intervals between firing his gun, he noted down the names of those assailants he recognized.[43]

Elsewhere in County Limerick a party of some 250 Fenians had been unable to take the barracks at Ardagh, though they did succeed in breaking into the ground floor. In Clare a party assembled by Drumcliffe churchyard, where Yeats was one day to lie, but were easily dispersed.[44] In County Cork there was a Fenian success when some two thousand men headed by J. F. X. O'Brien, William Mackey Lomasney and Michael O'Brien captured the police barracks at Ballyknockane.* The same party also successfully carried out sabotage of the Great Southern and Western Railway, according to the guerrilla plan, tearing up rails, destroying points and cutting telegraph wires, and actually derailing the Dublin express but without injury to the passengers.[45]

In County Cork, too, a party of Fenians captured a coastguard station at Knockadoon and made off with the arms they found there. But the impossibility of any significant follow-up without orders from above meant that even where there had been a success there was little to do afterwards but disperse. (Cluseret packed his bags for France as soon as he heard of Massey's arrest.) In addition to which, military flying columns were soon busy over the whole of the south-west and west of Ireland, dispersing such bodies of Fenians as were still intact. A sudden bout of severe weather with heavy falls of snow made the plight of the scattering rebels more desperate still.

On the morning of 6 March itself one of the first of these military columns approached an old Danish earthwork named Ballyhurst just outside the town of Tipperary. It was circular and surrounded by a hawthorn hedge.[46] A force of Fenians had assembled there during the night and early morning under an Irish-American 'general' with a shrunken leg, T. F. Bourke. They had earlier destroyed some telegraph poles and torn up railway lines. They were better at sabotage than fighting in the open. They fired a volley at the approaching soldiers, but as soon as the fire was returned they fled in disorder. With a cry of 'To the mountains! To the mountains!', their commander, Thomas Bourke, galloped off in a different direction from the main body of his men, but a soldier spotted him and brought him down from his horse with a shot at about three hundred yards.[47] A quarter of an hour later he was arrested creeping along a bank with the aid of a stick. In his pocket, together with a Catholic prayer book, a prescription for an eye infection, three photographs of girls and a Bradshaw's Railway Guide map, was found a Fenian oath which differed from the usual formula. It ran:

'In the presence of Almighty God, I solemnly swear that I will not bear arms against, or by word or act give information, aid or comfort to the enemies of the Irish Republic until regularly relieved of this obligation. So help me God.'

It was one clearly designed to be administered to less than enthusiastic Irishmen in the tide of the Fenian advance.

* Lomasney eventually blew himself up in 1884 trying to destroy London Bridge. O'Brien was to end on the gallows in Manchester; see below, pp. 342–3.

But the tide of the Fenian advance was already past its peak. If anyone had taken that oath during the night the moment when they could feel relieved of the obligation was at hand.

Thomas Bourke, though he had not proved much of a field commander, made amends from the dock. Shortly before being sentenced to be hanged, beheaded and cut into four quarters he declared :

'I accept my doom and I hope that God will forgive me my past sins. I hope that inasmuch as He has for seven hundred years preserved Ireland, notwithstanding all the tyranny to which she has been subjected, as a separate and distinct nationality, He will also assist her to retrieve her fallen fortunes, and raise her in her beauty and mystery, the sister of Columbia, the peer of my nation in the end.'[48]

A quarter of a century later, even the miserable action at Ballyhurst had become part of heroic myth. At a time when physical force as a means of righting Ireland's wrongs or awarding her national pride appeared to have been abandoned for ever in favour of parliamentary and constitutional agitation, a poet, looking back to the Fenians, could write :

> Thus, handicapped on every side, what wonder that we failed,
> And none but knaves and cowards say our spirit ever quailed,
> And Ballyhurst did more that day to raise all England's fears,
> Than all the 'blatherskite' I've heard these five and twenty years ...
>
> It makes me sick to talk to you and those who agitate* –
> Oh, give us but ten thousand men with rifles up to date
> Then Saxon laws and Saxon rule may do their very worst
> To men behind the rifles like the men of Ballyhurst.[49]

Desultory mopping-up operations by the military flying columns continued for several weeks. The last dramatic action was fought on the last day of March, when the three leaders of the successful raid on Knockadoon coastguard station, Peter O'Neill Crowley, McLure and Kelly were surprised in Kilclooney Wood in County Tipperary. After a running action among the trees Crowley was killed and the other two arrested – one with a small green flag and a manual of military tactics in his pocket.[50] These were the sort of men who, if the Fenian military high command had not been obliterated by the betrayal of Massey, might have been able, in spite of local defeats, to have given the rising the persistently harassing, continuous character that had always been part of the main plan. The defeats in the actual engagements with the Constabulary were disappointing and humiliating, but need not have been totally decisive if there had been any central command available to coordinate further guerrilla warfare as intended. It is significant that, for all the immediate disaster, Kelly himself at the time did not consider all further opportunity for action lost. On 15 March, ten days after the catas-

---

* i.e., for concessions from England.

trophe of the rising's opening, he wrote from London to America: 'Aid before two weeks and Irish independence is a fixed fact.... Fit out your privateers.... A landing in Sligo at the present time would be of infinite service.'[51]

Such a privateer was in fact fitted out – the *Jacknell Packet*, a two-hundred-ton brig – but did not sail from New York until the following month. On board were thirty-eight officers holding commissions in the army of the Irish Republic, signed by Colonel Kelly.[52] In the hold packed in piano cases, sewing-machine cases and wine casks labelled for Cuba were about five thousand modern breech-loading and repeating rifles, and a million and a half rounds of ammunition.[53] There were also on board three unmounted cannon taking a 3 lb shot which were fired from time to time during the voyage.[54] The ship was under the command of General Nagle, though it also had on board General Millen, who had been in Ireland under Stephens in 1865.[55] Whenever they met another ship on the high seas they hoisted the English colours, but just before noon on Easter Sunday, 21 April, they hoisted a green flag with a sun bursting over the horizon and re-christened the ship the *Erin's Hope*.[56] A month later the *Erin's Hope* slipped warily into Sligo Bay.

To meet it there, disguised as an English tourist, was Richard O'Sullivan Burke, the Fenian armaments' organizer who had come to England with Kelly in January and was now his second-in-command. Burke rowed out in a small boat to the *Erin's Hope*, whose officers had already pressed a reluctant pilot called Gallagher into service, threatening him with a revolver and at the same time telling him that they had come with a cargo of fruit from Spain.[57] Burke's news was that there was not the slightest hope of getting any support from the people of Sligo by this date, so the *Erin's Hope* sailed southwards down the coast of Ireland, looking for somewhere more suitable to land.

It was a desperately inconclusive and unsatisfactory voyage. A senior member of the crew afterwards reported that he could have landed the arms anywhere if only there had been anyone to receive them.[58] The fact that they had sailed unmolested as far south as Dungarvan in County Waterford before taking any further decision seems to bear him out. By then it was the beginning of June. Provisions were running out and it was decided simply to land a few of the officers and sail the ship back to New York. A Waterford fisherman named Whelan, who came alongside, agreed to land two officers for £2, but twenty-eight men altogether jumped aboard his boat, and fearing intervention by the coastguards, he landed them all in three feet of water off a spit of land called Cunnegar. Four were arrested soon afterwards, soaked through to the waist, and all the rest were in gaol within twenty-four hours.[59]

Fenian fortunes could hardly have been at a lower ebb. Yet they retained a general sympathy among the people for all their failure, and for all the people's failure to support them more positively. In Waterford the police escorting some of those from the *Erin's Hope* to gaol were attacked by a mob of eight thousand, one of whom was killed in the subsequent fracas, while thirty-eight of the police were wounded.[60] Corydon, the informer, who came to give evidence, was stoned in the streets of the town. Elsewhere in Cork, Limerick and other towns of Munster there were demonstrations of sympathy with the rebels. Yet the sympathy was emotional and confused rather than expressive of identity with specific political aims. The crowds who stoned the police in Waterford calling out 'Hurrah for the Fenians' also called out in a fine upsurge of deeply preserved resentment of old injustices 'Hurrah for Carrickshock', the site of a famous victory over the police during the tithe war nearly forty years before.[61]

But the most effective Fenian action, one that was to have an immediate consequence for policy in Ireland, was still to come.

19

The Manchester Martyrs

In spite of all the débâcles of the spring and summer, the Fenian organization still existed on a formidable scale. Its headquarters remained in England and there towards the end of the year it made itself felt with greater impact than any it had been able to achieve in Ireland.

A Fenian convention had already unanimously elected Kelly chief executive of the Irish Republic. An intensive search for him by the authorities had yielded no results. With Corydon and Massey exposed and removed from Fenian councils the organization now maintained a much more effective level of security. Then, on 11 September, the police arrested two men for acting suspiciously in a doorway in Manchester.

They gave the names of Wright and Williams and were charged with loitering, but, possibly because they had already been recognized by the informer Corydon,[1] their real names were soon known to the police. The arrest was of major importance. The loiterers were none other than Kelly himself and that Captain Deasy who had had a command in County Cork on the night of the March rising. A week later, on 18 September, the most important Fenian action of the year was fought in the streets of Manchester.

As an unescorted prison van conveying Kelly and Deasy in handcuffs from the police court to Belle Vue Gaol passed under a railway arch it was stopped and surrounded by about thirty Fenians who had been lying in wait for it, some of them armed with revolvers. These forced the unarmed police on the outside of the van to get down, and kept them and anyone else who might intervene at bay, while others tried to batter open the locked van and rescue Kelly and Deasy from the cells inside.

Inside the van with the two Fenians and some common criminals was a Police Sergeant Brett. Called upon through the ventilator of the locked back door by the Fenians to surrender, he refused to do so. Attempts to batter in the roof with stones were only partially successful and, eventually aware that help for the beleaguered sergeant would soon be on its way from the nearby gaol, a Fenian named Peter Rice fired his revolver through the ventilator, whether with intent to kill or merely to frighten the sergeant or simply to break open the door will never be known. In any case the bullet mortally wounded Sergeant Brett. It has been said that the shot was fired through the lock of the door in order to break it and that the sergeant had his eye to it and was killed accidentally. But a gunsmith who examined the van afterwards found that there was no mark of a bullet on the door, though one appeared to have smashed the ventilator. In any case, the desired effect was achieved. One of the women criminals in the van was so frightened by the shooting of Brett that she took the keys out of the dying sergeant's pocket and passed them through the ventilator. In a minute Kelly and Deasy, still in their handcuffs, had been released from their cells and were down from the van. 'I'll die for you, Kelly,' one of the rescuers is said to have shouted in the confusion. Still in their handcuffs the two men made their way over a wall and across the railway line. They were never recaptured.

Large numbers of Irishmen in Manchester were soon rounded up. The identification procedure employed by the police was so questionable, and much of the eye-witnesses' evidence so doubtful, that the surprising thing was not that one of the five men eventually put on trial for their lives should have been entirely innocent, but that the other four were in fact all involved in one way or another in the rescue attempt. The five were Maguire (an Irish Marine on leave who had never been near the scene of the rescue in his life), Edward Condon (tried as 'Shore'), who later claimed to have master-minded the whole escape, William Allen, Philip Larkin and Michael O'Brien (tried under the alias of 'Gould'). In court it was repeatedly maintained and generally accepted that Allen had fired the fatal shot. In fact this was not so and the man, Rice, who did, eventually escaped along with Kelly and Deasy to America. But in English law it was immaterial who had fired the shot, for anyone taking part in an illegal act as a result of which someone is killed is guilty of constructive murder. In law, Allen, Larkin, O'Brien and Condon were undoubtedly guilty of murder. They were found so, together with the unfortunate Maguire who pathetically asserted to the end that he had not been present and knew nothing of Fenianism.

Allen, Larkin, O'Brien and Condon, denying that they had fired the shot, all regretted the death of Brett and made idealistic speeches from the dock, clearly raising the level of their action above that of common murder.

'I want no mercy – I'll have no mercy,' said Allen. 'I'll die as many thousands have died, for the sake of their beloved land and in defence of it. I will die proudly and triumphantly in defence of republican principles and the liberty of an oppressed and enslaved people.'[2]

Larkin referred to Kelly and Deasy as 'those two most noble heroes'.

O'Brien, after giving his true name and saying that he was proud to be a fellow parishioner of the man killed in Kilclooney wood in March, went on: 'Look to Ireland; see the hundreds of thousands of its people in misery and want. See the virtuous, beautiful and industrious women who only a few years ago – aye and yet – are obliged to look at their children dying for want of food. Look at what is called the majesty of the law on one side, and the long, deep misery of a noble people on the other. Which are the young men of Ireland to respect: the law that murders or banishes their people, or the means to restrict relentless tyranny and ending their miseries forever under a home government. I need not answer that question here. I trust the Irish people will answer it to their satisfaction soon.'

Condon made the most famous remark of all. 'I have nothing to regret, to retract or take back,' he declared. 'I can only say: God Save Ireland!' And, as *The Times* man in court reported, the other prisoners all called out 'in chorus and with great power: "God Save Ireland!"'

The last spoken words of any of them as they left the dock after being sentenced to death were Larkin's: 'God be with you, Irishmen and Irishwomen.'[3]

Anyone who knew anything of Ireland knew that, though the Irish people had not 'risen' to support the military projects of the Fenians any more than they had risen in 1798, 1803 or 1848, the sort of mood which Allen, Larkin, O'Brien and Condon had expressed in the dock had sufficient roots in Irish everyday reality to make an emotional appeal to the Irish people. One might have expected that the British Government's chief concern now would be to prevent any further identification of Fenianism with Irish disaffection. Instead, it saw as its highest priority only the need to carry out the letter of the law and avenge the killing of a brave member of the Manchester police force. With some embarrassment it had to recognize that in Maguire's case at least a miscarriage of justice had taken place and the bewildered marine was granted a free pardon. The decision inevitably cast doubt on the quality of the evidence in the other cases. Condon, who was an American citizen, was reprieved a few days before the date of execution after pressure from the American legation in London. Its intervention on behalf of O'Brien, however, was unsuccessful, as he had already been released from British justice as an American citizen once before, in 1866.[4]

Allen, Larkin and O'Brien were executed in public on the foggy morning of 24 November 1867, Larkin and O'Brien suffering much agony as a result of bungling on the part of the hangman.[5] The atmosphere was so tense that when, a few seconds after the triple drop two loud explosions were heard on the left of the gallows, everyone assumed it was a Fenian attack, and the riflemen of the 72nd Highlanders, who had been placed with fixed bayonets round the scaffold, got ready to use their arms. But it was only the detonation of two fog signals placed on the railway which passed close to the gaol.[6]

The reverberations of the execution in Ireland were heard for over half a century to come. Quite apart from any legal doubts about the fairness of the trial it was impossible for most people in Ireland, however critical of the Fenians, not to feel that Allen, Larkin and O'Brien had been executed because they were Irish rebels. They were the first Irishmen since Emmet to be executed for political action. In a country where even constitutional opinion had now accepted Emmet and the United Irishmen as legendary heroes, it was impossible that Allen, Larkin and O'Brien should not too become enshrined as martyrs for the nebulous cause that was Ireland's. Their names became words with which to heighten the emotion behind any particular aspect of Ireland's cause. A few days after the execution A. M. Sullivan, the constitutional nationalist who was editor of *The Nation* and had been one of the Fenians' most bitter Irish opponents, published some verses in his paper written by his brother, T. D. Sullivan, which soon attained a wide popularity:

> 'God save Ireland!' cried the heroes,
> 'God save Ireland!' say we all ...

Set to the American civil war tune of 'Tramp, tramp, tramp, the boys are marching' the song became virtually the national anthem of Ireland for the next fifty years.

When some years later, in June 1876, a British Home Secretary, Hicks-Beach, speaking in a debate on Home Rule made a reference in the House of Commons to 'the Manchester murderers' he was interrupted by a cry from the Irish benches of 'No! No!'

The interruption seems in fact to have been directed at the particular argument the Home Secretary was then elaborating rather than at the phrase. For Hicks-Beach was accusing an Irish member of saying that one of the first acts of an Irish parliament in Ireland would be to order the release of the Fenian prisoners in England. It was being denied that this was what the member had said.

Skilfully, however, Hicks-Beach turned the interruption with the remark: 'I regret that there is any Honourable member in this House who will apologize for murder.'

But the sally rebounded on him. For the member for County Meath, a Protestant land-owner who had been elected the year before and up to that moment had attracted little notice in the House, rose in his seat and declared: 'The Right Honourable member looked at me so directly when he said that he regretted that any member should apologize for murder, that I wish to say as publicly and as directly as I can that I do not believe, and I never shall believe, that any murder was committed at Manchester.'' This member's name was Charles Stewart Parnell, and he was soon to blend the emotional legacy of Fenianism with the procedures of a constitutional campaign in a manner that would change Anglo-Irish relations for ever.

The government's obtuseness in carrying out the Manchester executions seems in retrospect all the greater since they had confronted similar situations earlier in 1867 more wisely. Indeed, ever since the arrests of Rossa, Luby, O'Leary and others in September 1865 the government had dealt with the conspiracy to rise in arms against the queen relatively mercifully. All those convicted at the Irish People.trials had received substantial terms of penal servitude, but only Rossa was sentenced to life imprisonment because of his previous release on condition of good behaviour after the Phoenix trials. Penal servitude in English prisons of the mid-nineteenth century was a hard and often crushing experience, but it was noticeably more humane than the treatment that had been meted out to many of the conspirators of '98.

After the rising of March 1867 Burke, the Fenian commander at Bally-hurst, J. F. X. O'Brien, the victor of Ballyknockane barracks, and McCafferty, the organizer of the Chester raid, had all been sentenced to death, and for a time it had looked as if the government were determined to carry out the sentences. Burke was the test case. Balanced pleas for the commutation of his sentence came from all shades of political opinion in Ireland. One memorial from Trinity College, the stronghold of Unionism, carried 320 signatures, including those of 18 Fellows, 8 Professors, 13 QCs and 67 members of the outer bar.[8] Burke's execution, wrote the Irish correspondent of *The Times*, 'would be a terrible expiation, at this stage of the world, for a political crime committed by men of otherwise blameless life, who abstained in an impressive manner, from perpetrating outrages that were in their power'.[9] When, finally, the government changed its mind on the specific grounds that the deterrent effect intended would not be achieved by the execution, *The Times* man in Dublin reported with relief that the 'anxious angry feeling, which was deepening and spreading every hour, has given place to grateful expressions of loyalty to the queen'.[10]

All other death sentences imposed after the March rising were eventually commuted and the rank and file among the Fenians who had been picked up, cold and hungry, in the fields and on the highways in the days after the fiasco, had been treated with remarkable leniency. Most were tried only under the Whiteboy Acts and given sentences of from twelve to fifteen months' imprisonment, while others were discharged altogether on giving sureties to be of good behaviour.[11] It was an intelligent policy, the benefits of which were virtually obliterated by the Manchester executions.

One other Fenian incident in 1867, also in England, also had an effect on the future more profound than any of the haphazard skirmishes round Irish police barracks in March. This was an attempt to rescue Richard O'Sullivan Burke, the Fenian armaments' organizer, who had been arrested in London in December 1867, and placed on remand in Clerkenwell prison to await trial.

On the afternoon of Thursday, 12 December, Burke was being exercised with other prisoners in the prison yard when he was seen by a warder to go over to the wall and take off his boot as if looking for a stone in it and then knock his boot against the wall.[12] At about the same time a man in the street outside noticed two men stop by the wall with a truck out of which they tipped what looked like a barrel of paraffin. They seemed drunk and he went into his stables remarking to someone there: 'Here's two fools with a truck.'[13] When he came out again a few minutes later they and the barrel had gone and he thought no more about it. Inside the prison yard a warder saw a white indiarubber ball come over the wall, but as things were frequently coming over that wall from the street, particularly shuttlecocks and dead cats, he too thought no more about it.[14] In fact the barrel had contained gunpowder and an attempt had been made to blow up the wall, but failed owing to difficulty in getting the fuse to burn.[15] The white ball presumably was a prearranged signal for postponement.

So many warnings of a possible rescue attempt at Clerkenwell had already been received by the authorities that a state of alert had become a way of life in the prison, and Burke, though allowed to receive visitors, was moved constantly from one cell to another. It had even been rumoured that an attempt would be made to blow the prison up, but for some reason it was assumed only that the Fenians were trying to undermine the building, possibly by tunnelling through the sewers. Nevertheless, on the night of this Thursday the 12th, a special state of alert was ordered and half the prison officers remained on duty throughout the night, armed with revolvers. Those in the towers overlooking the prison yard were given carbines. Definite information had been received that an attempt was about to be made to free Burke and another Fenian, Casey, but not how it would be done. Next day the prisoners were exercised in the morning instead of the afternoon, and Burke, it was noticed, was particularly agitated by this change of routine.[16]

That afternoon some boys were playing much as usual in the street outside the wall, and a woman was talking to the milkman. Seeing two men come and place a barrel against the wall and try to light something sticking out of the top the woman said to a policeman who happened to be coming down the street: 'I wonder what sort of a game that is.' As the policeman moved towards them one man threw the other a second box of matches, from which he took one, struck it and applied it to the object at the top, which began to spark. The man turned and ran, and the policeman, who was then about five or six yards away, also prudently turned and ran in the opposite direction.[17] The ensuing explosion wrecked the prison wall, totally destroyed a number of houses in the street, and damaged others over a wide area. Altogether twelve Londoners were killed and some thirty others badly wounded, losing their limbs, their eyesight or being permanently disfigured.[18] The prison yard was, of course, empty. It was showered with bricks and rubble, but explosives experts testified afterwards that a man crouching just where Burke had crouched the day before to adjust his boot would have escaped injury.[19]

The combination of the Manchester rescue and the Clerkenwell explosion brought home to the English public a sense of Irish danger as nothing had ever quite done before. The very remoteness of Irish problems had always made failure to deal with them seem a somehow natural and acceptable state of affairs. Now, in the crudest way, the Irish situation had landed on the Englishman's own doorstep. It was something which had to be dealt with, if not on its own merits, at least for the sake of comfort. As if to compensate for previous neglect of Ireland, the Fenian menace now assumed hideous proportions in the English mind. In Worcestershire, Cumberland, Bedfordshire, Surrey, Derbyshire, Suffolk, Kent – all over the country – special constables were sworn in to defend life and limb and the British constitution. More than five thousand special constables were enrolled in the City of London alone, and even in the Channel Island of Jersey pensioners held themselves ready to spring to arms on hearing three guns fired from the fort.[20]

The English statesman, William Ewart Gladstone, in anticipation of the premiership which finally came his way in 1868, had long been turning over the problems of Ireland in the labyrinthine recesses of his remarkable mind. He now found public opinion prepared as never before to contemplate measures that might be necessary to give Ireland peace and justice. As he himself put it, Fenianism conditioned the British population 'to embrace in a manner foreign to their habits in other times, the vast importance of the Irish controversy'.

Part Four

The Tragedy of Home Rule

1
Beginnings of Home Rule

Popular national feeling in Ireland had so far been mainly a negative expression of resentment at intolerable living conditions reinforced by a law made beyond the Irish Sea. It had taken only the vaguest traditional patriotic form, because there was no realistic patriotic tradition for it to conform to. Available traditions dwelt either in the dim regions of Celtic legend or in the eighteenth century where, formulated by the Protestant ascendancy, Irish nationalism had even seemed remote from the majority of the Irish people altogether. Only O'Connell, with Repeal of the Union, had temporarily succeeded in giving a single political and patriotic shape to national demands, and he had been beaten by the famine. In any case, he had been at a serious disadvantage in an age before the widening of the vote when popular support was not automatically an effective political instrument. After him the Irish tenant farmer had again lowered his sights to the problems of escaping starvation and eviction and paying the rent.

The Fenians, it seemed, had failed to create a widely accepted national tradition almost as dismally as the United Irishmen, from whom they took part of their inspiration. They had accumulated popular sympathy but little positive popular support for republican separatism. Even this sympathy stemmed much less from political idealism than from the inherited tradition of resentment at a special time when harvests were bad and the number of evictions on the increase. Evictions had risen steeply from 1860 to 1864 when the number – nearly two thousand – was three times the average of the next ten years. In 1865 they dropped to 842, and thereafter continued to decline until the end of the decade.[1] 'The accompanying drop in emigration in the improved seasons 1865–7 probably also helped the Fenians.* More young Irishmen than usual, who had just been through a bitter experience and who in other seasons would have emigrated, were at large in the country.

Though the Fenians had strengthened the emotional heritage, even leaving popular martyrs, they had otherwise changed nothing. In fact, for the next decade even martyrs were less in demand than usual, for harvests were universally good until 1877 and evictions dropped to the lowest numbers recorded since records had been kept.[3]

* From 114,169 in 1864 to 72,000 in 1867. (*The Times*, 28 January 1868.)

And yet, looking ahead at Ireland some forty years after the Fenians – an Ireland entering the second decade of the twentieth century – a fantastic transformation is seen to have taken place. The two major features of the Irish scene have been irrevocably changed. First, the poverty-stricken insecurity of the great majority of the population on the land, with its attendant menace of starvation, eviction and enforced emigration, has disappeared for ever. The landlords have virtually vanished and the great majority of Irish holdings are actually owned by Irish peasant proprietors, sons and grandsons of men who had often been treated with less respect than cattle. Second, for the first time since O'Connell and in the setting of modern parliamentary democracy a coherent and well-organized nationalist movement exists on a popular basis. Its aim is much more modest than that of the Fenians, but unlike that of the Fenians it enjoys active popular support. The aim is Home Rule, or the establishment of an Irish Parliament to deal with internal Irish affairs within the British connection and under the Crown.

How has such a double transformation come about?

Partly it can be explained by the general progressive evolution in British democracy which took place during the period. Until 1867, the year in which Allen, Larkin and O'Brien were hanged at Manchester, the electorate had been virtually the same as at the time of the Reform Act of 1832. A new Reform Act in 1967, concerned primarily with the urban vote, was only of limited significance to Ireland compared with England, but the Irish borough vote went up about twenty-seven per cent altogether as a result of it.[3] in 1872 the secret ballot was introduced. This, in Ireland, had a double-edged effect, for intimidation at open elections had come from the popular as well as from the landlord's side; but, on balance, secrecy in the polling booth probably strengthened the ability of the tenant farmer to express his wish for a better life. The long-expected further extension of the vote to the agricultural labourer, which came in 1884, was to treble the Irish vote. That more consideration and attention should in such circumstances be given to the needs and wishes of the humbler classes of the community was inevitable. Yet the extent of the revolution brought about on behalf of the Irish peasant was far more sweeping than anything comparable achieved on behalf of the British industrial working man in the same period.

For this there were two principal causes. First, even before the implications of the evolving democratic process had fully made themselves felt in the British political arena, there came to office in Britain a man who combined in a way unique in the history of British democracy an eye for the main political chance with the highest moral principle and deep intellectual perception and understanding. This man was William Ewart Gladstone, who formed his first ministry in 1868. Until his final retirement in 1893 at the age of eighty-six he was to concern himself with the affairs of Ireland to a greater extent than any other English statesman since the making of the Union.

The second cause also lay in the impact of personality on events. For thanks primarily to the work of two Irish politicians, Isaac Butt and Charles Stewart Parnell, the latter a political genius, Gladstone's own natural inclination 'to do justice to Ireland' was allowed no rest. Where their pressure for this justice was resisted either by Gladstone himself or by his Conservative political opponents, that resistance was bitterly contested. The momentum of the vast social revolution thus set in motion was inexorable and was only fully implemented by the Conservatives themselves some years after Gladstone's death.

To help engineer this revolution a new practical nation-wide organization had to be created in Ireland, and it was this which was the work first of Butt, and then of Parnell. It found all the old powerful emotional traditions automatically at its disposal.

But the Fenians too made their contribution to the end result. For they left on the Irish political scene, after their own cause had failed, a small élite of diehard radicals, backed by financial resources in the United States. This élite, while dedicated in theory to militant republican separatism, provided an organizing spearhead of general radical national activity which Parnell in particular was to turn to most effective use. Perhaps more important still, their impact in advertising Irish disaffection so publicly had convinced large sections of opinion not only in England but in Ireland too that, after Fenianism, something much more than a mere return to the *status quo* was required.

As an indication of the way new winds were soon blowing in Ireland after the Fenian débâcle, a body of Roman Catholic clergy met in the George Hotel, Limerick, as early as January 1868 and announced that they already had 198 signatures from the clergy for what they called their Repeal Declaration.

'We simply ask,' they declared, 'the Repeal of Parliament; and we ask it by no other means than those consecrated by the long years of O'Connell's teaching – constitutional and legal means.... We feel certain that the restoration of Ireland's nationality will do more to conciliate the empire than the greatest power or the greatest severity which the government could employ.' And they passed a resolution 'that a national legislature means neither revolution, nor weakening of the power of the empire, but on the contrary its better consolidation and progress'.[4]

This was an expression of opinion in advance of the clergy as a whole. But later in the same month another powerful statement, though less ambitious in its political demands, came from an even more august source. Some of it might almost have been part of a Fenian manifesto.

'Our poor country,' it ran, 'has been reduced to a state of the greatest misery and destitution. Our towns and cities are filled with poor men, women and children half starved, without shoes or stockings or proper clothing to preserve them from the snows and frosts of winter. More squalid poverty of this kind is to be seen in Dublin alone than in all the great cities of France, Austria or Spain. The country has lost more than 3,000,000 of inhabitants who have been obliged to brave the dangers of the wide Atlantic in order to save themselves and their families from starvation. About 400,000 cottages of the poor have been levelled to the ground, lest they should ever again afford shelter to their former inmates . . .'[5]

But this was followed by a strong condemnation of Fenianism. For the statement was a Pastoral Letter from the ultra-conservative Archbishop Cullen of Dublin, to be read in all the churches and chapels of his diocese. He concluded by exhorting his flock to obtain redress of the many grievances from which they suffered by electing Members of Parliament who would defend their rights. The following immediate objectives were listed: the disestablishment of the Protestant Church, freedom of education and a law for the regulation of relations between landlord and tenant so that the fruits of their capital and labour might be secured to the agricultural classes.

From the extreme wing of the constitutional movement, the Dublin newspaper the *Irishman*, came more spectacular advice addressed to the Members of Parliament themselves. It cited the Dual Monarchy in which Hungary had just obtained equal partnership with Austria, and suggested that MPs should 'act like the Hungarians to win for their native land what Hungary rejoices in; let them, complying with all forms legal and constitutional, withdraw from London to their Irish homes'. There they should establish themselves as an Irish Parliament.[6]

In England, Gladstone had been coming to his own conclusions. He took office in 1868 with the declared intention of doing justice to Ireland. 'My mission,' he proclaimed, before proceeding to Windsor to kiss hands, 'is to pacify Ireland.'[7] To the extent that the Manchester rescue and the Clerkenwell explosion had prepared English opinion for the need to do some such thing his task was, as he conceded later, easier. But it was still not easy.

Gladstone seems at first to have imagined that he could solve the problem of Ireland for ever by two measures: first, by disestablishing the Irish Protestant Church and, second, legislating to compensate a tenant financially on eviction. That he should have thought like this is not the absurdity it now appears. Even in Ireland itself there were those, naturally mainly among the Catholic hierarchy, who thought that the grievance of the Established Church lay at the root of all others. And to begin to think at all of allowing the State to intervene in the relationship between landlord and tenant on behalf of the tenant was at that time itself a revolution.

To ridicule Gladstone, as it is tempting to do, for declaring that with Disestablishment of the Church 'the final hour' in Ireland was 'about to sound',[8] underestimates what seemed then the boldness of the step he was undertaking. In disestablishing the Protestant Church he was tampering with the Act of Union, and his Conservative opponents did not let him forget the fact. Before considering his proposal to go into a committee of the House of Commons on the subject, they insisted on the reading of the fifth article of that Act to the House:

'... The doctrine, worship, discipline and government of the said United Church,' members heard, 'shall be and shall remain in full force for ever.'[9] Conservatives declared that Disestablishment would mean 'the most violent shock to the Constitution since the Reformation'.[10]

Many fundamental and far-reaching political emotions were stirred by the introduction of the measure. To decide that the Church, which represented only one-sixth of the country's population, should no longer be that country's established Church might have seemed an overdue technical adjustment. But even the English radical Roebuck scented danger. There was no knowing where this would lead to, he said; nothing was going to content the Irish until they had total separation from Britain and Independence. '... Cut off Ireland from England and you cut off her right arm. As long as I have a voice in this great Assembly that voice shall be raised in maintenance of Imperial rule.... No sentimental talk about oppression to Ireland, and indeed nothing on earth shall move me from that position.'[11]

A Conservative member also sensed in Disestablishment the beginning of the end, declaring that they were making the concession 'to that very class of the Irish population who wilfully shut their eyes to the advantages of the incorporation of the two countries ... who rather choose to regard them-selves as members of a conquered race than of a triumphant united Empire'.[12] To this a Liberal presented the classic reasoned reply on which all Gladston-ian and indeed future Liberal policy was to be based, namely that 'it was a mistake to suppose that when symptoms of nationality arose they must either succeed in suppressing them or else must give them full sway and allow them to lead to absolute separation and independence'.[13]

Stanley, replying to Gladstone for the Conservatives in the Disestablish-ment debate, in a restrained and sensible speech merely warned Gladstone against 'that common and tempting fallacy of believing that certain political consequences will follow from what you are doing, merely because from your point of view you think it just and right that they should'.[14] And even some of Gladstone's Liberal supporters failed to share their leader's optimis-tic hopes that Disestablishment would eliminate Irish disaffection. 'I fear,' said one, 'that the youngest member of this house will never live to see Ire-land what she might have been if our ancestors in their dealings with her people had not read backwards every precept of Christianity and every postulate of policy.' But the measure, he thought, would at least 'purify the air'.[15]

It did more than that. It showed that the Union was not itself sacrosanct, and thus opened up the possibility of a fundamental re-adjustment of attitudes. It was in fact no part of Gladstone's intention to disrupt the Union, only to make it work. But that in itself was the beginning of a revolution.

The Act disestablishing the Protestant Church over the whole of Ireland became law in 1869. *The Nation* hailed it as 'the greatest victory ever won in the British Parliament',[16] and the statement is not the exaggeration it may seem. Of the sixty-seven years of the Union only just over half had seen a normal functioning of the British Constitution in Ireland at all. The other thirty had been marked by so-called coercion acts of every style, all restricting the normal liberties of the subject – Peace Preservation Acts, Arms and Insurrection Acts and Acts proclaiming Martial Law and the suspension of Habeas Corpus. Habeas Corpus itself had been suspended for rather more than one-sixth of the whole period. During that time the population had been depleted by a quarter. A million people had died of starvation and its after-effects. Another million had felt compelled to emigrate. Disestablishment of the Irish Protestant Church, though marginal to the Irish people's welfare, was the first measure the Union Parliament had passed solely because the majority of the Irish people wanted it. It was indeed, in a sense, the beginning of the end.

But the vital issue was the issue of the land. Gladstone's first Land Bill, introduced in 1870, was as inadequate as Church Disestablishment to do proper justice to Ireland. But it too was of the greatest significance as the beginning of another aspect of revolution. Introducing this Land Bill in the House of Commons, Gladstone said in a masterpiece of understatement: 'I sorrowfully admit that neglect is chargeable (upon Parliaments since 1832) in respect to the question of Irish land tenure', and he cited, from a quarter of a century before, the Devon Commission's recommendations for security of tenure which had never been acted on.[17] His own bill was not to go so far as those recommendations. But even so, one apprehensive member of the House, while prepared to vote for it in the hope that it would tie the Irish people to the Empire, saw in it 'the principles of communism' in the way in which it dealt with property.[18]

In the context of the time he was not far wrong. For the new Act made clear that, in defiance of laissez-faire tradition, a man no longer altogether had a right to do what he would with his own. Henceforth a landlord who wanted to evict a tenant for any other reason than non-payment of rent would have to pay over a sum of money to the tenant for the improvements his occupation had made to the property.

Almost every Irish member who spoke in the debate pointed out that this really missed the heart of the problem altogether. What the Irish tenant wanted was not compensation for eviction, but freedom from eviction. Gladstone, by imposing a sort of fine on the landlord, sought to discourage the landlord from eviction. But the competition for land in Ireland was still such that a landlord legally liable to pay compensation could always re-coup himself financially by making a new tenant pay either a premium or an increased rent, and could anyway insure himself against any future need to pay compensation by raising the rent immediately for the incumbent tenant. Finally, if he really wanted to evict without penalty all he had to do was to raise the rent to a level the tenant could not afford to pay and, provided that it was not what the law courts would define as 'exorbitant', he could evict the tenant for non-payment without the need to pay any compensation at all.*

Really to ensure security of tenure for the Irish tenant farmer, what was necessary was to establish by law rents which the tenant could afford to pay and to make any eviction illegal so long as he paid them. Twelve years later this was to become the principle embodied in Gladstone's second Land Act. But the inadequacies of the first Land Act did not immediately make themselves felt with any severity, for the early seventies saw continued agricultural prosperity. It was when that prosperity suddenly collapsed towards the end of the seventies that the Act's failure was to have immediate political repercussions.

Quite a wide section of opinion in Ireland reacted to Gladstone's policy of intended justice to Ireland in a cooperative manner at first. It was to be the contribution of Isaac Butt to Irish nationalism that, in spite of this cooperative atmosphere, he first organized Irish public opinion to reject the principle of piecemeal justice from a British Parliament. His theme, taking its cue from O'Connell, was that only an Irish Parliament itself could give Ireland the full justice she required.

In September 1870, a so-called Home Government Association held its first public meeting in Dublin. This was a curious alliance at first, embracing a number of Protestant supporters motivated by actual resentment of Gladstone's new measures, particularly a feeling of betrayal over the Disestablishment of the Protestant Church. Somewhat naturally, therefore, the Home Government Association in this first phase had little success in promoting any wide national movement. To be effective such a movement had to have the Catholic Church behind it and the Catholic Church was obviously not happy about the support of Conservative Protestants converted by spite, as the former Young Irelander, John Martin, put it.[19] The Archbishop of Cashel declared that the Protestant Home Rulers looked on the movement as identical with a movement against (sic) 'Rome Rule'.[20] Even in the following year, when Conservative Home Rulers, increasingly appreciating the inappropriateness of their liberal nationalist bedfellows, began to

* The original word in Gladstone's bill had been 'excessive', but this was amended by the House of Lords to 'exorbitant', thus giving the landlord greater latitude.

withdraw, the Church still disapproved of the movement. The imperial government, wrote Dr Moriarty, the Bishop of Kerry, was for the first time heading in the right direction and he feared that a barrage of agitation for Home Rule[21] would enable Gladstone to feel released from a sense of obligation to do something for specifically Catholic education in Ireland.

Although Home Rulers won a number of spectacular by-election victories in 1871 and 1872, Irish Catholic liberals willing to cooperate with Gladstone could still, as late as November 1872, trounce them at the polls. Moreover, there were other elements making for discord on the national scene. Between the remnants of the Fenians and those Irishmen agitating for a reform of the land system as the most important goal, there was even downright hostility.

In 1869 a wide section of Irish opinion had been mobilized in an amnesty campaign for the Fenian prisoners serving grim terms of penal servitude in English prisons. The drive in the amnesty movement came from those Fenians who had remained at liberty. It was an early example of their new spearhead activity on the political scene and was organized by a Fenian, John ('Amnesty') Nolan. This movement made the most of the undoubted severities to which Fenians were subjected by prison rules. It particularly publicized details of the sufferings of O'Donovan Rossa who, for throwing the contents of his chamber pot at the prison governor, had on one occasion spent thirty-five days with his hands manacled behind his back throughout the day except at meals, when they were manacled in front.[22] He had spent some of the time reading a copy of D'Aubigny's *History of the Reformation* by turning pages over with his teeth.[23] The government commission of inquiry, a consequence of the amnesty agitation, found the punishment to have been out of order, though as the governor of Chatham prison pointed out, Rossa was lucky by the standards of the day to have escaped a flogging for such an offence.

A further propaganda success of Nolan's, who organized vast mass meetings on behalf of the amnesty campaign – one of them at Cabra was said to have been attended by 200,000 people – was to put Rossa himself up as a candidate for the by-election in Tipperary at the beginning of 1870, while still in prison, and get him elected, although he was of course subsequently unseated as a convicted felon. But the amnesty movement, which in any case was disapproved of by the Catholic hierachy for its Fenian association, was very far from representing any politically coordinated national movement. The less heroic day-to-day issue of Tenant Right preoccupied many Irishmen. The amnesty men, being good orthodox Fenians, thought that no issue should be allowed to blur the single over-riding goal of an independent Irish Republic. Clashes actually took place between Amnesty meetings inspired by the Irish Republic Brotherhood – as the Fenians were now more and more commonly called – and Tenant Right meetings.[24] O'Donovan

Rossa had triumphed in Tipperary not over a Unionist but over a tenant righter.

The significance of Isaac Butt was that he was a figure common not only to the cause of Tenant Right but also to the Amnesty Movement of which he was the cover 'President', and at the same time to the Home Government Association with which he had been connected from the beginning. He was eventually to pull all three strands together into one Home Rule movement, and thus establish that movement in a position where it naturally acquired the support of the Church.

Butt was a distinguished QC who had defended both Smith O'Brien and Meagher in 1848, and the Fenians from 1865 onwards. He was himself a Protestant, and a Conservative by instinct, but even when early in his career he had opposed O'Connell on Repeal he had always shown a national pride in being born an Irishman. It was the famine which had begun his disenchantment with the Union. What alternative was there for any Irishman, he had asked in 1847, as the full horror of the calamity made itself felt, but to think that the Union Parliament had abdicated the functions of government for Ireland and to demand for his country a separate existence?[25]

Addressing himself now to the clashes between the IRB amnesty meetings and the tenant righters, he foreshadowed what in IRB parlance was later to be known as 'the new departure', namely a participation of the IRB, for all their iconoclastic separatism, in constitutional politics.

'I believe,' he said of tenant right and nationalism, 'that the two objects, so far from being antagonistic, help each other. . . . No proceeding,' he added, was 'more mischievous than any attempt to sever the cause of the Irish tenantry from the cause of the Irish nation.'[26]

Butt has been much disparaged by latter-day nationalists, and was indeed left behind by events even in his own lifetime. But the credit for first coordinating the movement from which latter-day nationalism was to draw its strength must be his.

'Bide your time,' Butt told the Amnesty Association in December 1869, echoing Davis. '. . . Next session will prove the utter impotency of the English Parliament to legislate for Ireland's people.' And by consciously working to discredit Gladstone's 'justice to Ireland' as inadequate, he eventually succeeded in substituting for it the more ambitious aspiration of Home Rule.

Like O'Connell's Repeal, Home Rule in the early stages combined the attractions of national sentiment with the attractions of a social panacea. But no movement in Ireland could effectively become a national movement without in the end securing at least the benevolence of the Catholic Church. And for a time Cardinal Cullen's satisfaction with the British Government for carrying the Protestant Church's Disestablishment made it difficult for the hierarchy to bestow this, however much individual priests might see that the

Home Rule movement was developing a popular dynamic of its own. The gradual withdrawal of Protestant support from the movement made things easier. Increased Catholic support made Protestant withdrawal faster. Instead of the movement being regarded as a movement against Home Rule, the belief that 'Home Rule means Rome Rule' now took root as the traditional basis of opposition to the movement. This in turn inevitably made it increasingly sympathetic to many Catholics.

In a famous election in Kerry in 1872, a Home Ruler, Blennerhassett, was elected with the support of many priests against a pro-Gladstone Liberal Catholic backed by the hierarchy. Butt himself, after one defeat, had been elected in September 1871 as a Home Ruler for Limerick, and as part of his attempt to polarize all demands round Home Rule he made a point of raising during the election not only the issues of tenant right but also those of a Catholic university and denominational education. It was actually Gladstone's failure to satisfy the Catholic Church with his provisions for education that finally turned conventional Catholic thought towards the need for something more than mere piecemeal 'justice'. Gradually the Church came to identify itself with Butt's Home Rule altogether. And the Bishop of Clogher was soon heard declaring that he had had enough of 'a Parliament that confessedly loathes our religion and loathes ourselves because of that religion'.[27]

On the other wing of national sentiment Butt secured at least the neutrality of the IRB for a trial period of three years. Thus under-cover Fenians took part in the first Home Rule Conference which met in Dublin in November 1873, together with twenty-five members of Parliament and fifty Catholic priests. The Fenians were 'determined that within certain limits, Mr Butt's projects should have fair play'.[28]

What Butt's 'projects' amounted to was simply separate parliaments for the domestic affairs of England, Scotland and Ireland. Details seemed at this stage hardly relevant. The likelihood of achieving any such goal seemed so remote that discussion among Home Rulers centred at this stage more on the tactics to be adopted and the extent of party discipline to be exerted than on the precise form Home Rule was to take. Butt's tactical proposal at the conference was that the only pledge which sitting Home Rule members should take should be to vote for an annual Home Rule motion in Parliament and otherwise vote as their consciences dictated. In discussion of such things there was inevitably recall of the Sadleir–Keogh fiasco of twenty years before. One of the Fenians at the Conference, Joseph Biggar, a Belfast pork butcher then a member of the Supreme Council of the IRB and soon to be Member of Parliament for Cavan, outlined the shape of things to come in what seemed to many a disturbing amendment. This was to the effect that Irish members should act compactly together by majority decision on all parliamentary issues.[29] But such a proposal was still regarded as unthinkable by the majority of Home Rulers at the conference, and Butt's original resolution was carried unanimously.

As a result of this conference in 1873, the Irish Home Rule League was founded, and at the General Election of 1874 a few weeks later fifty-nine nominal Home Rulers were elected for Ireland. This was really the peak of Butt's achievement. Though the driving forces in Irish politics were still primarily other than national, they were now incorporated in a Home Rule movement, and Home Rule as a national aspiration was at least on the political map. Only two out of thirty-eight non-Home Rule Liberal candidates at the election had thought it politic actively to oppose Home Rule.[30]

However, under Butt's leadership the performance of the Home Rule party in Parliament was ineffective. This was partly because Butt himself, caught in the personal trap of trying to lighten a long accumulated burden of heavy debt by increasing his burden of work at the bar, could not give the party more than part-time political leadership. But the party's ineffectualness was mainly due to the fact that its fifty-nine Home Rulers elected in 1874 were a far more disparate body than their nominal triumph then made them appear. The election had taken place only three weeks after the end of the Home Rule League's conference and long before it had been possible to get any professional coordination into the party, even of those who had any real disposition to accept it. Of the famous fifty-nine soon only between twenty and thirty acted in any way like a regular party when they got to the House of Commons.[31]

On 30 June the first Home Rule motion was put to the House of Commons. At the meeting of the party which had agreed the wording only thirty-two members had been present.[32] The motion was that the House should go into committee to consider parliamentary relations between England and Ireland. If this was accepted, Butt was to propose:

'That it is expedient and just to restore to the Irish nation the right and power of managing all exclusively Irish affairs in an Irish Parliament.

'That provision should be made at the same time for maintaining the integrity of the empire and the connection between the countries by reserving to the imperial parliament full and exclusive control over imperial affairs.'[33]

This set the framework of the Home Rule demand for the next forty years, during which it became the Irish nationalist creed for the vast majority of the Irish people. Compared with the ambitious phrases about national independence in which the United Irishmen and the Fenians or even the Young Irelanders had indulged, the demand may seem an almost absurdly modest national one for Ireland. Yet nothing re-emphasizes more clearly the irrelevance such earlier phrases had held for the majority of the Irish people than the fact that even for this modest demand enthusiasm was quite difficult to arouse. Any prospects of fulfilment seemed at this stage remote.

On this first occasion in 1874, fifty-one Irish members out of a total of

103 voted for the motion. Together with the tellers and those who were paired this comprised almost the whole of the so-called Home Rule party – not at all a bad turn-out considering that party's essentially flimsy structure. But only ten English members voted for the motion, whereas Butt had earlier claimed that twenty-nine were sympathetic to Home Rule.

Clearly, if the movement were to take hold more effectively, even to seem in Ireland something seriously worth going for, then a more active and vigorous procedure than merely presenting a similar motion once a year was required. The tenant farmers did not in any case have too much enthusiasm for a cause that might well push into the background of parliamentary affairs their more pressing immediate interests on the land. At the other extreme a small doctrinaire majority felt that Home Rule did not go far enough. The Fenians in particular soon became disillusioned by their experiment in cooperation with Butt, but other non-IRB nationalists also voiced their disapproval. John Mitchel, now allowed to return to Ireland, declared that he was 'savage against the helpless, driftless concern called "home rule" . . .'.[34]

Mitchel, as a nationalist seeking something more advanced than mere Home Rule, accepted nomination for a by-election in Tipperary. This embarrassed Butt who was unwilling to antagonize the Church by endorsing him but also unwilling to antagonize the Fenians by opposing him. Mitchel was elected, but immediately disqualified as an undischarged felon, an affront to national pride which made it easier for Butt to support him in a second campaign. In this Mitchel was also helped by young John Dillon – spirited son of John Blake Dillon, co-founder of *The Nation* in 1842 – who was himself later to occupy a major position in Irish national politics. Mitchel was again elected, but the seat was at once awarded to his Tory opponent, and Mitchel himself died a week later. The contemporary comment: 'Poor Mitchel's last legacy to Ireland is a Tory misrepresentation of Tipperary'[35] was literally true and in one sense justified as a caustic judgement on his whole erratic political career. But his true legacy was something more than that: the idea that there were times when Irish republicanism must defy reason to assert itself, and this idea, it might be said, passed into the Fenian subconscious.

The small handful of Fenians actually in Butt's parliamentary party soon showed their restlessness in the parliamentary dead end in which they found themselves. As early as 1874, Joe Biggar, the IRB pork butcher from Belfast, was already practising the technique of obstruction in the House of Commons by reading long extracts from previous Acts of Parliament to delay the passage of a bill to continue the government's special powers in Ireland. Butt's own distaste for such tactics was immediately apparent, but on the night of 22 April 1875, when Biggar spoke for four hours against a new coercion bill, reading extracts from newspapers and government blue books until finally sitting down because he was 'unwilling to detain the House any longer', a new member entered the House. He was soon to become Biggar's most powerful ally, eclipse Butt altogether and earn himself the popular title of the Uncrowned King of Ireland. This was the new member for County Meath, a tall, elegant, bearded man, a former high sheriff of County Wicklow which he had captained at cricket and in which he owned over four thousand acres: a Protestant, Cambridge educated, who spoke with the precise accents of an Englishman. His name was Charles Stewart Parnell. Four days later, in his maiden speech, he objected to a reference made by a former Chancellor of the Exchequer to Ireland as a 'geographical fragment'. Ireland, said Parnell, was 'not a geographical fragment but a nation'.

2

Parnell and the Land Crisis

It is unnecessarily melodramatic to suggest that any man in history may have been indispensable to events. By the time Parnell appeared on the scene a new economic inexorability was at work in Irish politics which would have brought about great political changes whatever the personalities involved. Yet to match that inexorability history could hardly have timed a better manipulator of events than Charles Stewart Parnell. It is relatively easy to see how other men who played important roles in the next decade could have been duplicated, even men of the stature of Michael Davitt and John Devoy. Parnell alone dominated events, forging from them a political movement from which there eventually grew at last a modern popular Irish nationalism.

1877 was a key year in the gradual revolution on which Ireland, thanks to Gladstone and the impact of the Fenians, was now embarked. Politically it saw a wider use of obstructionist methods in Parliament by that very small group of Irish MPs who were trying to draw forcible attention to the demand for Home Rule – methods of which Butt, the party's nominal leader, increasingly disapproved. Joseph Biggar and F. H. O'Donnell, the erratic and irascible member for Dungarvan, had been the pioneers of obstruction, but the new member for Meath, Charles Stewart Parnell, with an iron stamina, a cool indifference to the clubman's atmosphere of the House of Commons, and his concern only for the way in which what was said there would strike people in Ireland, soon made himself a master of the technique.

Descended on his father's side from a Protestant Irish patriot of the eighteenth century, a strain which in any case conferred a certain remoteness from the Ireland of his own day, Parnell had an American mother whose dislike of the British had not prevented her from having her daughters presented at Queen Victoria's court, or sending him to Cambridge. Her own father, Charles Stewart, nicknamed 'Old Ironsides', had been an American admiral and a scourge of the British in the war of 1812. And it was Parnell's emotional detachment from both England and in a way Ireland, too, that was to be his chief strength as an Irish politician. His least favourite colour was green: and during one critical period of three years in the next decade he never even visited Ireland at all. He had incorporated early into a natural aloofness a sympathy for the Irish peasantry in their distress and having once engaged in politics on their behalf treated the subsequent problems which arose rather like problems in engineering or science, of which he was an enthusiastic amateur.' He made inscrutability and unpredictability into political techniques which baffled colleagues and opponents alike. 'We feared him,' an English viceroy was to say, 'because we never knew what he was up to.'

Never before had there been a man who thus deployed the essentially English qualities of inborn superiority and arrogance in the cause of the Irish peasant. For this his colleagues forgave him much and his countrymen, after his tragic death, everything. 'An Englishman of the strongest type moulded for an Irish purpose', the Fenian Michael Davitt called him when he first met him in 1877.[3] And so he was to prove.

Not the least of Parnell's political merits was that he felt under no obligation towards any form of Irish national dogma. His definition of the Irish national goal was constantly criticized by Englishmen as equivocal, but that was its virtue: it was wholly pragmatic. 'I'm not sure he knows exactly where he is going,' observed another Fenian early in Parnell's career while saying that he had qualities which should endear him to Fenians.[3] Irish nationalism did not know where it was going either and had suffered from too many people trying to force it to go where it could not. Parnell never worried about where he was going. 'None of us,' he once said, 'whether we are in America or Ireland, or wherever we may be, will be satisfied until we have destroyed the last link which keeps Ireland bound to England.' But he was also quite happy to deny that he ever said it.*[4] He subsequently often categorically rejected a separatist republican goal but never made it clear whether he did so as a matter of principle or policy. In so far as he had a basic national position it was the infinitely flexible one now inscribed on his monument in O'Connell Street, Dublin: '... no man has the right to fix the boundary to the march of a nation. No man has the right to say to this country "Thus far shalt thou go and no further", and we have never attempted to fix the *ne plus ultra* to the progress of Ireland's nationhood and we never shall.'[5]

'They will do what we can make them do,' he said once of the British Government, and this was the only national principle on which he operated.[6]

In the summer of 1877, taking advantage of the generous rules of debate and the latitude then given by gentlemanly custom to individual members

---

* During the debate on the first Home Rule Bill in 1886 Parnell, challenged with these words by the then Liberal–Unionist, George Trevelyan, denied that he had ever uttered them. He had, he said, only been in Cincinnati once in his life and held verbatim accounts of the two speeches he made that day and neither contained the words in question (Hansard, iii, 306, 99). Trevelyan then correctly gave the *Irish World* reference, with its report of Parnell using the words in Cincinnati on 23 February 1880. This does not rule out the possibility that the *Irish World* may have misreported him, but it seems on the face of it improbable.

to assert their rights against the government machine, Parnell and his small group of half a dozen or so supporters began holding up government business to a point where ministers desperately sought the help of Butt himself in restraining them.

'I regret,' said Butt, dragged in from the smoking-room on the night of 12 April 1877 when Parnell was holding up the passage of the Mutiny Bill with innumerable amendments and unnecessary divisions, 'I regret that the time of the House has been wasted in this miserable and wretched discussion. . . . I am not responsible for the member for Meath and cannot control him. I have, however, a duty to discharge to the great nation of Ireland and I think I should discharge it best when I say I disapprove entirely of the conduct of the honourable member for Meath.'[7]

Though the House itself rang with cheers,[8] Butt could hardly have struck a more unsuitable note for Ireland. He was in fact sounding his own political death-knell. For while throughout that summer Parnell and his friends, equally contemptuous of Butt and the House of Commons, persisted in their obstruction, forcing the House on 31 July 1877 into its longest ever continuous session of twenty-six hours over the South Africa Bill, an agricultural slump was looming in Ireland and an imperative need was arising that the always discordant voice of the Irish peasant should be properly heard. The tenant farmers faced their gravest crisis since the great famine of the forties. To take political charge in such a crisis Parnell was ideally suited.

The season of 1877 had been disastrously wet in Ireland but a deeper economic cause underlay the Irish tenant farmer's troubles. The opening up of the corn-growing areas of the American West, together with the development of efficient transport by rail and fast steamship across the Atlantic, was flooding Europe with cheap grain with which the United Kingdom could not compete. Prices began to fall and with them went the Irish farmer's ability to pay his rent. Evictions loomed. The wet summer, and a consequent reduction in the potato crop to less than half the value of the previous year, complicated the prospect with the additional threat of famine.[9] The number of evictions more than doubled in 1878 to the highest figure for over a decade.[10] By 1880 they had more than doubled again and literally half the population of Ireland was living on private charity, with the proportion in the south-west of the country as high as nine-tenths.[11] 'Charity alone,' the Lord Mayor of Dublin's Mansion House Committee was later to report, 'stood between the vast masses of the population and a terrible death . . . a Famine . . . was stayed by the hand of private charity . . .'[12] As in the forties much of the private charity came from England. But that after eighty years of the Union the vast majority of the population should still be ultimately dependent for survival only on private charity, from whatever source, was a terrible condemnation of government, if not of the Union itself, and certainly of that mood of civilized self-satisfaction at Westminster which Parnell and his supporters had been so busily disturbing.

As early as August 1877 a natural Irish political alliance had begun to suggest itself. There were only two positive national forces in Irish politics: those extreme nationalist elements in Ireland represented by the IRB, isolated as they were from the great body of Irish opinion by their obsession with the dogma of armed national revolt, and the new force in the constitutional sphere first created by Butt but active only in the small group round Parnell.

The Irish Republican Brotherhood had been reorganized in 1873 under the leadership of the deaf and almost blind novelist Charles Kickham, who as a young man had observed Smith O'Brien's trance-like perambulations in Tipperary. But remoteness from political reality was now the IRB's own chief characteristic. Most of those IRB men, who had been at first prepared to cooperate with Butt, were disillusioned with the experiment. One critic had expressed his disappointment in Butt graphically but unkindly by saying he 'would not give the snuff of a farthing candlelight for all the nationality that existed in that man'.[13] The IRB leadership itself therefore had deduced that only total abstinence in future from any such parliamentary compromise could guarantee the purity of the republican separatist doctrine. But it was not unreasonable to question the point of preserving such a doctrine, however pure, in totally ineffective isolation.

Joseph Biggar and another Fenian member of Parliament, John O'Connor Power, together with other members of the Supreme Council of the IRB, recognized the absurdity of such an attitude and decided to continue to work through Parliament as the only avenue available. They were consequently expelled or forced to resign from the IRB for their heresy. But more and more former Fenians were, like them, becoming impatient with classical Fenian orthodoxy and looking round for ways in which they could at least be active. And though Fenians of any sort were relatively few, their political significance in Irish politics was always out of proportion to their numbers. The total membership of the IRB in Ireland in 1877 was only about nineteen thousand,[14] but because of their close affiliation with the wealthy Irish revolutionary organizations in the United States they were a political force which any more practical political operator in Ireland had to take seriously into account.

In the summer of 1877 an Irish-American journalist named James J. O'Kelly, a close friend of the exiled Fenian John Devoy who was now the most effective figure in Irish-American politics, came on a visit to Europe and, in the course of it, held two long conversations with Parnell. In the first of these Parnell told O'Kelly that he was thinking in terms of some political collaboration between the radical extremists and constitutional nationalists. O'Kelly, writing to John Devoy in August, commented approvingly: 'With the right kind of support behind him and a band of *real* nationalists in the House of Commons he would so remould Irish public opinion as to clear away many of the stumbling blocks in the way of progressive action.'[15]

The next month Parnell himself, speaking to one of those members of the Supreme Council of the IRB who had just been expelled from the organization, used a phrase which was soon to become famous. 'I think there must be quite a new departure in our party,' he said. 'We are only at the beginning of an active forward policy but it must be pushed to extremes. A few men in the House of Commons can do nothing unless they are well-supported in the country . . .'[16]

The New Departure' was the term soon to be given by extremist republicans in the United States, headed by Devoy, to a new public policy of their own. This consisted of temporarily shelving the single uncompromising goal of an Irish Republic to be won by force of arms, and substituting a more gradualist approach of short-term objectives to be won at Westminster under the leadership of Parnell. The theory was that this would help activate popular nationalist feeling, and parliamentarians were in turn to accept as a final goal a totally independent Ireland.

To make this compromise and work with parliamentarians demanded considerable heart-searching on the part of former Fenians. The IRB itself, under the leadership of Kickham, could not bring itself to do so and this in turn led to its further ineffectualness and a further splintering off of its members into would-be more active groups. Devoy, however, who had received favourable personal reports on Parnell and his attitude not only from his journalist friend J. J. O'Kelly, but also from his chief revolutionary collaborator in the States, Dr William Carroll, who saw Parnell during a long visit to Europe in 1878, finally swung the full force of his Irish-American organization, the Clan-na-Gael, over to the principle of such an alliance. He himself referred to it as a New Departure when he published details of a proposed offer of collaboration with Parnell in his paper the *New York Herald* on 26 October 1878. The chief terms were named as the substitution of 'a general declaration in favour of self-government' for the federal demand of Home Rule, and 'vigorous agitation of the land question on the basis of a peasant proprietary, while accepting concessions tending to abolish arbitrary eviction'.

Soon afterwards Devoy himself visited Europe, and in two meetings with Parnell came to an unwritten understanding about the sort of way in which the new alliance should work. It seems fairly clear that Devoy, who had also been corresponding with the old Fenian John O'Leary on the matter, thought of the alliance as soon leading to some sort of practical nationalist climax, if possible to coincide with the centenary of the 1782 meeting of the Protestant Volunteers at Dungannon.* It also seems fairly clear that Parnell, mak-

* See above, p. 35.

ing use throughout his life of any effective instrument to further immediate political advantages, encouraged Devoy to think in such ambitious terms, though his own eye was in fact set on down-to-earth political objectives. Later in his career it was to be in Parnell's interest to play down any suggestion that he had originally entered into collaboration with revolutionaries for revolutionary aims. But contemporary evidence suggests that at the time of the new departure, and even as late as 1881, to keep the extreme revolutionaries working for him, he certainly allowed them to think that he worked for the same goal of total separation as themselves.

According to Devoy, part of the undertaking agreed at his own meeting with Parnell was that the direction of their combined energies into the land crisis should not prevent preparations for an armed uprising from going forward. Dr Carroll in a later description of his first 1878 interview with Parnell wrote: 'I asked him if he was in favour of the absolute independence of Ireland. He replied that he was and that as soon as the people so declared he would go with them. . . . I met him several times afterwards in London, always on the most friendly terms and with the same understanding.'[17] And a contemporary letter of Carroll's to Clan-na-Gael, dated March 1878, seems to confirm this, saying that Parnell and his friends expressed themselves 'at the firm's service for anything they can do in their line'.[18] As late as February 1881, William Lomasney, a former Fenian who had helped capture Ballyknockane barracks in the '67 rising and within a few years was to blow himself up with dynamite in an attempt to destroy London Bridge, met Parnell in Paris. He wrote to Devoy that Parnell meant to go as far as both of them 'in pushing the business' of national independence, and that Parnell had told O'Leary 'as soon as he secured the means he would start in business with us and smash up the opposition firm'.[19] Finally, in June of this same year, 1881, Parnell was seen at the House of Commons by an Englishman living in America named Thomas Beach. Beach called himself Henri Le Caron, which was the name under which for years he had been posing as a French-American Fenian and supplying information to the British Government about American-Irish revolutionary circles, with which he had the highest contacts. He had been instrumental in frustrating the Fenian raid into Canada in 1868. Now, in 1881, writing to Devoy, he passed on to him a reassuring message from Parnell (having first passed it on to the British Government), to the effect that an armed rising was still his (Parnell's) ultimate goal.[20] Parnell, in fact, was having difficulty with the IRB in Ireland at the time and needed Devoy's and the Clan-na-Gael's support in preventing their hostility.

Such was the nature of Parnell's political pragmatism that it is of little value to try to assess how far he may or may not have meant what he said in such conversations. He himself avoided the need to inquire into his own sincerity. He was already making a political art out of not knowing precisely where he was going provided he went in a direction which he thought would help Ireland. He was content in his active plans to have his hands full with immediate political objectives. By instinct rather than by well-calculated intent he made use of the revolutionary extremists at this period as he was later to make use of both the great English parties, Liberal and Conservative, and, in the end, turn back again to make use of 'the hill-side men' with whom he had begun.

Whatever the degree of sincerity with which Parnell had managed to secure the support both of Devoy and his American financial resources, and that of many dissident IRB men in Ireland, two salient facts emerge in retrospect. First, he did secure their support, and, second he put it to a purpose which, whatever his continued assurances, reversed the priority of the terms on which the New Departure had been formally based. In those terms agitation on the land had been seen as a means to the end of fairly immediate nationalist revolution. What Parnell did was to turn the policy inside out. He used the energies of idealist nationalists to work the land problem into an urgent and overriding political consideration in national life. This he did, not out of any particular principle, but because to a politician like himself looking for an area in which to be effective, the land situation clearly presented itself as the more promising. Effectiveness alone was Parnell's political criterion; when he could not be effective he did nothing.

Much of his political skill lay in his ability to master forces which others had set in motion. It was largely thanks to the efforts of another man altogether that he found the critical situation on the land politically so promising: that very Fenian who, meeting Parnell in December 1877, had seen in him 'an Englishman of the strongest type moulded for an Irish purpose'. His name was Michael Davitt, and he had then just been released on ticket of leave from Dartmoor after seven years in prison.

Davitt had been born at the height of the famine and his mother and father had been evicted from their smallholding in County Mayo in 1852 when he was five. They had emigrated to Lancashire where, as a boy of eleven, he had lost an arm in a factory accident. Almost inevitably in such circumstances, being a young man of spirit and feeling, he had become a Fenian. He had gone to Chester on the morning of 11 February 1867 to take part in McCafferty's abortive raid on the castle. Later he had helped to run rifles and revolvers to Ireland, and in 1870 had been sentenced to fifteen years' penal servitude for his alleged part in an assassination plot. In prison, handicapped in his ability to work in the stone quarries by his one arm, he had been harnessed to a cart like an animal. He had thought much about the future of Ireland. Recognizing realistically, on his emergence from prison, that 'the vast mass of our population had grown politically indifferent or apathetic'[21] and that the Irish revolutionary movement as represented by the IRB needed a new outlook, Davitt felt immediately drawn towards

Parnell, whom he actually asked to join the IRB of which he himself remained for a time a member. Parnell refused. But he expressed much sympathy with Davitt's general ideas for future action, which largely coincided with his own, and included a proposal that a new type of parliamentary party drawn from men of strong nationalist convictions should make a reasoned demand in Parliament for Repeal of the Union and, if this was refused, withdraw in a body and form a national assembly in Ireland. Parnell immediately endorsed the proposal in a public speech.[22]

On a visit to America soon afterwards Davitt discussed at length with Devoy the prospects of future collaboration with Parnell. But Davitt was not himself party to the formal inauguration of Devoy's new departure, being apprehensive that too public an identification of Parnell with extremists might prejudice Parnell's opportunities for effectiveness. Davitt's own political preoccupation was with the relationship between nationalism and the problem of the land; and he was to become increasingly obsessed with land reform as an end in itself. Now, in a speech in Boston in December 1878, he had publicly asked himself the pertinent question: 'Why is the Irish farmer not an active nationalist?' and replied on behalf of that farmer: 'If the nationalists want me to believe in and labour a little for independence, they must first show themselves willing and strong enough to stand between me and the power which a single Englishman, a landlord, wields over me.'[23] With the reservation that the landlord was in fact far more likely to be an Irishman and that the nationalist element in the tenant farmer's mind was therefore even more remote than Davitt postulated, this was a reasonable diagnosis.

Back in Ireland in 1879 Davitt found that in his own home county of Mayo the situation on the land was nearing desperation. Under the pressure of the agricultural crisis the peasantry confronted the classical pattern of disaster. Unable to pay their rents because of the slump in prices they were threatened with eviction. There was nowhere for them to go except out of the country. Simultaneously, the failure of the potato crop meant that there was nothing to eat. The spectre of the Great Famine, for thirty years never far from the back of any Irish peasant's mind, was suddenly out in the open again.

The protection from eviction supposed to have been conferred on the tenant by Gladstone's Land Act of 1870 was revealed as useless. The would-be deterrent effect on the landlord of having to pay compensation for eviction did not apply because, under the Act, compensation only applied to cases of non-payment of rent where the rent demanded was 'exorbitant', and the tenant could not now pay even a normal rent.

On one estate in County Mayo administered by an Irish Catholic priest, Canon Burke, the tenants made a stand and called a protest meeting at Irishtown near Claremorris on 20 April 1879. The meeting, which Davitt himself helped to organize, demanded a general reduction of rents and denounced the landlord system. It had an immediate local effect, for the priest, Canon Burke, reduced his rents by twenty-five per cent within a few days. It also set the pattern for a whole new land agitation in the rest of Ireland where similar conditions of hardship were soon experienced.

Davitt proceeded to extend the Irishtown principles on a national scale. When he organized a similar meeting to take place at Westport, County Mayo, on 8 June 1879, he secured Parnell's promise to speak at it. Parnell, carefully weighing up the situation, had recognized the vast social forces that now stood ready to be harnessed to a political movement.

Intimidation and agrarian violence of the traditional Irish secret society type had already begun to manifest themselves. This was intensified by the participation of former Fenians who on the principle of the new departure now became active in the land movement. Because of this the venerable Archbishop of Tuam, John MacHale, O'Connell's former supporter, felt obliged publicly to criticize Parnell's decision to speak at the Westport meeting. Parnell displayed that bland indifference with which he was to confront all opposition whether from Church, State, Liberal, Conservative or his own party for the next eleven years.

'Will I attend?' he said to Davitt who went to see him at his Dublin hotel the day before the meeting and the day after the publication of the Archbishop's pronouncement. 'Certainly! Why not? I have promised to be there and you can count on me keeping that promise.'[24]

At the meeting itself he set the tone of the whole subsequent Land League agitation.

'A fair rent,' he declared, 'is a rent the tenant can reasonably afford to pay according to the times, but in bad times a tenant cannot be expected to pay as much as he did in good times.... Now, what must we do in order to induce the landlords to see the position? You must show them that you intend to hold a firm grip of your homesteads and lands. You must not allow yourselves to be dispossessed as your fathers were dispossessed in 1847. ... I hope ... that on those properties where the rents are out of all proportion to the times a reduction may be made and that immediately. If not, you must help yourselves, and the public opinion of the world will stand by you and support you in your struggle to defend your homesteads.'[25]

He was as good as his word. In August Davitt summoned an assembly of 150 tenant farmers of Mayo who founded the Land League of Mayo with no less an ultimate objective than the transference of the ownership of the soil from the landlords to the cultivators, with compensation payable to the landlord. It was the first open convention in Ireland for eighty-five years, for the Convention Act of 1793 had just been repealed. And that autumn, while men with blackened faces were increasingly shooting at or otherwise intimidating landlords and their agents – more particularly terrorizing those Irishmen who were prepared to occupy land from which another had been evicted – and while threatening letters were being received, signed this time not by Captain Right or Captain Rock but by Rory of the Hills ('who always warns before he kills'), the National Land League of Ireland was founded on 21 October 1879 with, as its president, Charles Stewart Parnell.

The Land League's object was, by promoting the organization of the tenant farmers, to bring about a reduction in rents, protect those threatened with eviction, and finally obtain 'such reform in the laws relating to the land as will enable every tenant to become the owner of his holding by paying a fair rent for a limited number of years'.[26]

This latter objective enshrined the principle known as 'land purchase' by which, in the course of the next fifty years, a complete transfer of the land-ownership of Ireland was to be brought about.

The principle of land purchase had been first introduced by Gladstone in his Church Disestablishment Act of 1869 and Land Act of 1870. Land purchase clauses in these acts made it possible for tenants to buy their holdings by putting up a proportion of the purchase price and paying off the remainder in annual instalments over a period of years, the whole of that remainder being meanwhile advanced to the landlord by the State. Little advantage had, however, so far been taken of these provisions because the proportion of the price which the tenant had to put up – as much as a third – was far beyond the means of the average Irish tenant, and the period over which repayment was to be made too short. But an extension of the principle on more and more generous terms over the fifty years that followed the foundation of the Land League meant that by the time of the Anglo-Irish Treaty in 1921 out of 470,000 holdings, 400,000 were owned by their occupiers, who were paying off the purchase price by an annual sum considerably less than their rent would have been and for a limited period only.*

However, this goal of full Irish peasant proprietorship seemed almost utopian at the time it was first formulated by the Land League in 1879. Starvation and large-scale evictions were then the immediate order of the day, and concessions to prevent these were the immediate objectives. Final victory on the land was only achieved after a so-called Land War which the Land League then inaugurated, and which was to be fought out in spasms for more than twenty years. Though it was to be fought out in many phases and by organizations with different names it was fought in the first formative and crucial phase by Parnell and Davitt, with twin offensives on the land in Ireland and in Parliament at Westminster.

A new generation of polite society had now to be reminded of what eviction meant in Ireland. An Irish Member of Parliament recalled a sight

---

* Vindication of those who had always maintained that it was the system itself and not the fecklessness of the Irish tenant that made land tenure in Ireland unworkable was found in the fact that out of a total of some £120,000,000 advanced to the Irish peasant in the course of the entire operation, only £12,000 was not repaid.

witnessed long ago by the Roman Catholic Bishop of Meath, who had seen seven hundred people evicted in one day with winnowing sheets placed over the forms of sick and unconscious people lying in bed while the roof was pulled down over their heads.[27] Nothing now prevented a repetition of such things for, as no less a patrician figure than Lord Hartington told the House, the exceptional circumstances of the time had placed in the hands of a bad landlord a power which enabled him absolutely to defeat the purpose of the Land Act of 1870. If he wanted to clear his estate, now was the time to do it without pecuniary loss.[28] The report of a Quaker committee from the West of Ireland insisted that it was absolute poverty alone that prevented payment of rent, for many of the people there had even pawned their shawls and were without any other food than that supplied by charity.[29] A case was cited of a small farmer in Kerry who in 1854 had been threatened with eviction if he did not take an additional ten acres of marsh land, and had agreed to do so. He had drained and fenced this land and for twenty-three years had regularly paid the rent but now, hit by the slump, had been unable to pay for two years and had been evicted. He and his wife and five children had taken shelter with a neighbour, but the landlord's agent then threatened the neighbour with eviction for sheltering them. Whereupon the man and his family in desperation had returned to the house from which they had been evicted and two days later had had the roof pulled down over their heads.[30]

A letter quoted in *The Times* in 1880 from that pillar of Empire, General Gordon himself, described the prevailing condition of the Irish peasantry in terms uncannily reminiscent of other witnesses over two centuries. He found them 'patient beyond belief. . . . Loyal, but at the same time broken-spirited and desperate, living on the verge of starvation in places where we would not keep our cattle. . . . The Bulgarians, Anatolians, Chinese and Indians are better off than many of them are . . .'[31]

Loyal, in a constitutional sense, most of them were, but this time they were not taking things lying down.

The popular power of the Land League, organized in Ireland largely by ex-Fenians, spread rapidly throughout the country. Mass demonstrations to secure reductions of rents were successfully mobilized. Many evictions were physically prevented. Where they could not be prevented, victims of eviction were sheltered and supported while private charity kept the majority of the people fed. The Land League operated by a combination of above-ground official action and underground violence. On the one hand there were the meetings, the speeches, even official Land League Courts replacing the normal administration of justice in some parts of the country – all largely financed by Devoy from America under the working of the New Departure. On the other hand there were the shots fired into windows, the threatening letters and the visits in the dead of night to those paying rents which the League regarded as excessive or taking holdings from which another had been evicted. Sometimes shots were fired into their thighs or pieces of ear removed from them or other physical torture applied. In this traditional agrarian activism many rank-and-file ex-Fenians of the New Departure school could now take part in the rather blurred conviction that they were in some way promoting that national uprising to which their original creed had been dedicated. On the official level, both the Secretary of the Land League, Thomas Brennan, and the Treasurer, Patrick Egan, were ex-Fenians.

The leadership of the Land League officially deplored violence, as of course did Parnell from his position in Parliament. But it was often a case of the Land League's right hand not being particular to inquire what its left hand was doing. And Parnell's ally in Parliament, the outspoken member for Belfast, Joseph Biggar, crudely summarized something of this ambivalent attitude when he opposed the shooting of landlords on the grounds that it was wrong because the assailant frequently missed and hit someone else. At the same time, the officially correct character of the movement, with its determination to right the poor man's wrongs, made it possible for the Land League to enlist that support of the parish priests without which no movement in Ireland could flourish. The priests worked almost to a man to help their people fight a possible repetition of the 1840s. Even some of the Catholic hierarchy and in particular the popular Archbishop Croke of Cashel proclaimed the Land League's principles of justice to the tenant to be moral and right. And the official organ of the Vatican itself declared that 'in consequence of the unsupportable state of the Irish peasantry the people must shake off their oppression. The crimes committed in Ireland are not attributable to the Land League . . .'[32]

By 1880 there were parts of Ireland where the queen's writ no longer ran. Reductions of rent from between ten and fifty per cent had been forced from many landlords, and where landlords refused to yield to pressure or to their own moral promptings in face of the Irish peasant's distress, it was made often physically impossible for them to carry out an eviction at all. The Irish correspondent of *The Times* described the Land League as 'a very distinct and potent government which is rapidly superseding the Imperial government. . . . It rules with an iron hand and with a promptitude which enforces instant obedience. Its code is clear, its executive resolute, its machinery complete and its action uniform. There is a Government *de facto* and a Government *de jure* – the former wielding a power which is felt and feared, the latter exhibiting the paraphernalia and pomp, but little of the reality of power.'[33]

This was the situation which Parnell now exploited to maximum political advantage in the British Parliament, elevating the Irish question to that Parliament's chief preoccupation for the first time since the Union, so that as one member complained soon it was 'occupying all minds to the exclusion of everything else'.[34]

3

Parnell and Home Rule

Butt had died in 1879, and his place as leader of the Home Rule party had been temporarily taken by another moderate, William Shaw. But a general election took place in April 1880 in which significantly it was not the still rather abstract question of Home Rule but that of the land that was the issue. This was the first election fought with the principles of the New Departure in operation, and former Fenians with advanced ideas sympathetic to Parnell not only took part in the electoral campaign but were elected in some constituencies. Joining Biggar and O'Connor Power in Parliament were now other former Fenians, such as John Barry, Thomas Sexton and T. P. O'Connor, together with other radicals of a new type, of whom the most striking was John Dillon, the son of the Young Ireland founder of *The Nation*, and already a pillar of the Land League. Though it was not until the election of 1885 that the Irish Party finally became a closely-knit and efficient radical machine with strict party discipline and officially paid members, yet some suggestion at least of this new radical phenomenon was felt after the election of 1880 and was almost immediately signalized by the election of Parnell himself to be the party's leader in May 1880. A few of its members had even probably received some clandestine financial support from Land League funds.[1] By the end of the year the party under Parnell had already taken the decision to sit in opposition to Gladstone's new Liberal government – itself a striking departure from the traditional Irish parliamentary practice of looking for what crumbs might come Ireland's way at the Liberals' table.

Yet at this stage Parnell's real source of strength was still the extent to which the Land League in Ireland was making Ireland ungovernable. And here he walked a political tightrope.

The parliamentary party was a relatively moderate force, and even the decision to sit in opposition to Gladstone had led to a rupture within it. Yet on his other wing, the Land League with its neo-Fenian elements and extravagant aims was a remarkably independent organization. And the most delicate consideration of all in the balance of forces he commanded was this: the government he was fighting was led by a man who in the past decade had shown a genuine concern to solve the problems of Ireland equitably. While pressing Gladstone, therefore, to do much more for Ireland than Gladstone saw his way clear to do, Parnell had to remember that up to a point Gladstone was a potential ally. Only while Gladstone did nothing but introduce special repressive legislation against the Land League, and before the good intent in his mind had had a chance to show itself, was an outright challenge to his safe tactics.

In such a situation, Parnell, while identifying himself with Land League policy, had to be careful to deplore violence in itself, merely explaining crimes where necessary, as the Vatican did, as the inevitably evil products of an evil system. In fact, the most extreme offensive measure which either he or the Land League ever officially sanctioned was the one he proposed in a famous speech at Ennis, in September 1880: that 'species of moral Coventry', as he called it, into which a proclaimed enemy of the Land League was to be placed by a rigid denial of all social or commercial contact on the part of his neighbours. The policy itself was not new and had been advocated as Land League technique by John Dillon in 1879. But its endorsement by the new leader in graphic phrases about isolating such a man from his kind 'as if he were a leper of old' and showing him 'your detestation of the crime he has committed' in bidding for a farm from which his neighbour had been evicted, gave Irishmen a firm new spirit of self-respect with which to gird themselves. The next month the technique was employed against a man whose name is still identified with it all over the world, a much disliked but courageous evicting land agent on Lough Mask, County Mayo, named Captain Boycott. Fifty volunteer Orangemen from Ulster crossed Ireland to help harvest Captain Boycott's crops when no one else would touch them, and seven thousand men, one-sixth of the entire British military force in Ireland, was required to protect them. It was, said a local carman, 'the queerest menagerie that ever came into Connaught'.[2] Boycott's crops were saved, but there was no slackening of the campaign against him, and when he tried to retire to a hotel in Dublin even the proprietor there refused to let him stay, and he had to withdraw temporarily from Ireland altogether.

But for all the Irish popularity Parnell won by speeches endorsing boycotting, the balance of forces he had to manipulate was soon to become almost intolerably delicate. The Land League agitation emboldened by success was growing increasingly wilder and demanding nothing less than the total compulsory buying-out, on terms favourable to the tenantry, of all landlords.

Gladstone's method of dealing with the crisis, which reached its climax in the winter of 1880–81, was to introduce a severe Coercion Bill to restore law and order before any land reform. Parnell and his supporters fought the Coercion Bill in the House of Commons with all the persistence and ingenuity in obstruction which past experience gave them, and his supporters were now many more than in the previous Parliament.

On the night of 31 January 1881 they far outdid the previous record of 1877, by forcing the House into a continuous session of forty-one hours in an attempt to hold up the Coercion Bill. Whereupon the Speaker on his own initiative arbitrarily suspended the time-honoured rules of the House and forced the closure of the debate. This called the bluff of obstruction, and a formal reorganization of the House's rules later in the year confirmed the eclipse of obstruction as an effective technique. But meanwhile, after a last gesture of defiance on the day following the Speaker's historic ruling, Parnell and thirty-five other Irish members were suspended from the House of Commons and temporarily ejected from the Chamber.

A situation had come about as envisaged in Parnell's conversation with Davitt a few years before, when the possiblity of a withdrawal from the British Parliament altogether and the establishment of some self-styled national assembly in Ireland discussed.* The decision Parnell now took against this was epoch-making one, though it would have been out of character if he had thought of it as such. It was based on a firm grasp of political realities: chief of which was the fact that at most one-third of the party would have followed him to Ireland.³ While keeping the radical wing among his New Departure supporters in the Land League as happy as possible, by being, as one historian has put it, 'adept at the cape-work of the pseudo-revolutionary gesture',⁴ Parnell directed his mind towards the future which included the all-important question of Gladstone's new Land Bill.

Two Royal Commissions on the tenure of land in Ireland had just reported. These were the Bessborough Commission, appointed by Gladstone himself to inquire into the working of the 1870 Land Act, and the Richmond Commission, appointed in the previous administration of Disraeli, to inquire into agricultural conditions in Great Britain and Ireland. In the light of these, quite apart from the pressure of the present crisis, the argument for some new measure to regulate relations between landlord and tenant was unanswerable. Gladstone's first attempt to devise one, a relatively tame affair, the principle of which was expressed in its title, the Compensation for Disturbance Bill, was thrown out by the House of Lords in August 1880.

Any land reform short of the total abolition of landlordism was going to dissatisfy the extremists among the Land League organizers. But their persisting intransigence made it easier for Gladstone to present and eventually get accepted by Parliament a Land Bill that was of much more revolutionary dimensions than the Compensation for Disturbance Bill and yet which could by then seem, if not moderate, at least acceptable by contrast with the Land League's increasingly violent demands. The new bill became the Land Act in August 1881.

Basically it granted the three F's, long demanded by tenant righters from the days of Sharman Crawford and O'Connell: fixity of tenure, provided the

* See above, p. 371.

rent was paid; free sale by the tenant of the tenant's interest and improvements in a holding on his vacating it; but above all, fair rents. The Act laid down that the definition of a fair rent no longer rested ultimately with the landlord but with a government Land Court to be especially appointed for the purpose. Given the prevailing notions of the rights of property, it was in the context of its time perhaps the most revolutionary social legislation any British Government has ever introduced.

Parnell, confronted with what he knew to be a relatively excellent measure, had to reconcile this with the knowledge that it would not satisfy his extreme friends in Ireland who wanted a total transfer of the land to the people. Above all, it would not satisfy his New Departure supporters in America with their all-important financial resources, who wanted an independent Irish republic. They, after all, had embarked on the New Departure intending land reform to be only a secondary consideration, the means by which the temperature was to be raised to white hot national heat. The temperature had in fact been raised to white heat but to fashion not a nationalist revolt but land reform. Nationalism, though thus partly aroused, was still a long way secondary in the peasantry's mind to concern for their own economic situation. How was Parnell to welcome and rest on the major success he and his supporters had won from Gladstone without giving many of those supporters the feeling that they had been sold or at least cynically exploited?

At first, in public and in the House of Commons, he refused to support the bill, on the grounds of its inadequacy, thereby going so far to please his extreme supporters that his more conservative supporters began to doubt his political wisdom. But he knew that while the Land League and even the more iconoclastic land reformers among his parliamentary group, like John Dillon, were assailing the bill for not abolishing the landlords outright, the benefits of the Act would be extended to Ireland whether he opposed it or not.

In fact, he played a classical political game of keeping the movement together by not altogether satisfying either wing. Croke, the nationalist Archbishop of Cashel, condemned Parnell's decision not to support the bill, and almost a third of the Home Rule members in the House of Commons even voted for Gladstone. Parnell, replying to the Archbishop's public criticism of himself, maintained that there had been a need to mark the imperfections of the bill by 'making a demonstration ... which ... will not affect the division'.[5] Those on the left, who rightly suspected from such remarks that Parnell was at heart inclining towards moderation and some eventual compromise with Gladstonian policy, were partly placated by his launching at this time a new newspaper, *United Ireland*, under the editorship of the ex-Fenian, William O'Brien. In *United Ireland*, O'Brien unleashed the wild and colourful verbal violence in which his journalistic talent revelled, backing the stern public policy of Parnell with papery battle cries and trumpet calls which were almost a parody of traditional Irish revolutionary language. The working of the Coercion Act, with sporadic arrests of prominent land leaguers like Dillon for rash speech-making, made this sort of reaction obligatory. But reality in the form of the passing of the Land Act and the practical prospect which this opened to tenant farmers of lowered rents secured through government Land Courts was an equally obligatory consideration. Parnell, a politician interested in concrete results, had to take up a concrete position. He finally devised the masterly formula of 'testing the Act', or letting the Land League put forward a number of selected cases to see what sort of reduction in rents the government was really prepared to give, thus skilfully placing the onus of cooperation on the government rather than on the Land League.

To the extremists, however, particularly in America, who thought the only policy for the tenant was to hold the harvest and refuse to pay rent until the government abandoned coercion altogether and transferred the land to the tenant, 'testing the Act' was a dangerously soft attitude. Parnell typically did his best to reassure them by the toughness of his speeches in Ireland. He talked of the hollowness of the Act and used increasingly militant language to denounce the British Government, reminding them that behind all this lay Ireland's national aspirations. Things were made easier for him by attacks on him from England, particularly a famous speech of Gladstone's at Leeds in October 1881 in which the Prime Minister reminded Parnell that 'the resources of civilization in Ireland were not yet exhausted'.

Finally, Gladstone rescued Parnell from his awkward spot altogether by putting the resources of civilization into action. As the contemporary balladmaker had it:

> ... Before this wrong all other wrongs of Ireland do grow pale,
> For they've clapped the pride of Erin's isle into cold Kilmainham jail.

Parnell was arrested.

It was the best thing that could have happened to him. William O'Brien, John Dillon and others prominent in the Land League agitation were soon in Kilmainham gaol with him. From there they issued at last a desperate and often envisaged call for 'a general strike against rent' in the form of a 'No Rent Manifesto'. On 20 October the government suppressed the Land League.

To subscribe to this No Rent Manifesto was in many ways Parnell's master-stroke. It was to make things impossibly difficult for his opponents on both sides: his own and the government's. It did so at the very moment he was himself withdrawn from the scene, thereby suggesting his own indispensability and the need for both sides to take him on something like his own terms. Parnell had already said that Captain Moonlight would replace him if he were imprisoned, meaning that the time-honoured methods of the secret societies, always at the back of the Land League agitation, would take over completely. And Captain Moonlight, unlike Parnell, was inaccessible to the government and could be dealt with only by unpopular methods of repression, leading to further bitterness and chaos. At the same time Captain Moonlight would not in fact get the average tenant farmer anywhere, for the resources of civilization were indeed quite adequate to deal with him, particularly since they also included the advantages of the new Land Act. Parnell 'on the shelf'* automatically became a catalyst who could make things easier for everyone.

In a private letter on the day he was imprisoned Parnell admitted that the Land League movement was already breaking up fast. The principal cause of this was the success of the new Land Act. Though he later blamed the clumsy repressive measures of the government for giving the agitation a longer lease of life than it would otherwise have had, the tenants were soon obtaining substantial reductions of rent from the Land Courts and often getting a fairer deal than many of them had dreamt of as possible. The extremists in Ireland and America were thus increasingly isolated from the majority of Irish opinion and Parnell could more cavalierly afford to disregard them. One practical problem remained. It concerned holdings on which considerable arrears of rent had accumulated. The Act had failed to make adequate allowance for such cases, and the need for further legislation on this score became an important item in the clandestine and unofficial negotiations between Parnell in Kilmainham and Gladstone, which were first tentatively entered into as early as November 1881† and seriously taken up in the New Year.

These negotiations were carried on through two sets of intermediaries. On Gladstone's side was Joseph Chamberlain, the young radical Birmingham politician who was one of the Liberal leader's brilliant young supporters. On Parnell's side there were two intermediaries. One was Captain Willie O'Shea, formerly of the 18th Hussars and now Liberal Home Rule MP for County Clare. O'Shea was a dashing and feckless character who hoped to achieve through politics that worldly wealth and influence which had so far eluded him in bloodstock breeding and company promotion. The other intermediary

* It was the tyrant Gladstone and he said unto himself,
'I nivir will be aisy till Parnell is on the shelf
So make the warrant out in haste and take it by the mail,
And we'll clap the pride of Erin's isle into cold Kilmainham Jail'.

The ballad is given in Jules Abels' *The Parnell Tragedy* (London and New York, 1966), p. 126.

Conditions for Parnell in Kilmainham were by no means as bleak as the ballad-maker envisaged. Like O'Connell some forty years before, he received privileged treatment.

† W. H. Duignan, a friend of Chamberlain's, went to Ireland in November 1881 with an introduction from Chamberlain to the Chief Secretary, Forster. He saw the 'suspects' in Kilmainham, but, he added later, rather disingenuously 'by no means on Mr Chamberlain's account'. (Letter from Duignan in *Freeman's Journal*, 8 July 1893.)

on this side was O'Shea's wife, Katharine, who had been carrying on a passionate love affair with Parnell since the winter of 1880. She was, in April 1882, about to bear him his first child.

The extent to which Captain O'Shea was or was not a complaisant husband at this stage is a complex one of considerable human interest but of no immediate significance to Irish history. Parnell's own personal involvement is more relevant.

The extent to which any personal considerations affect the decisions of professional politicians must always be difficult to assess. But the strength of Parnell's attachment to Mrs O'Shea and the fact that she was about to bear him a child must have made it at least easier for him to continue in the political direction in which he was already moving, and have confirmed an inclination away from revolutionary politics towards some sort of understanding with Gladstone.

The understanding eventually arrived at became known as the Kilmainham Treaty, though there was no document or even formal agreement of any sort. The terms were that in return for legislation to protect tenants with heavy arrears from eviction and a repeal of the Coercion Act together with the release of Parnell and his fellow detainees Parnell should call off the agitation on the land and cooperate in working the Land Act. The further implications of the understanding were that Parnell should in future use his strength in Ireland and in the House of Commons to collaborate with the Liberals in continuing Gladstone's whole policy of 'justice to Ireland'. And since the Irish party was after all a Home Rule party, even though the land and not Home Rule had so far been its chief preoccupation under Parnell's leadership, 'justice to Ireland' would inevitably one day include some recognition as yet unspecified by Gladstone of Ireland's aspiration to self-government.

The situation within the Liberal party on the one hand, and between Parnell and his extremist supporters on the other, was still much too delicate for any such prospective final development to be aired. But a grim fortuitous event occurred within a few days of Parnell's release to complicate and considerably set back the implementation of the new alliance at all levels.

The Chief Secretary for Ireland, W. E. 'Buckshot' Forster, had felt betrayed by Gladstone's decision to release Parnell and had resigned.* When Gladstone told the House of Commons that his place was to be taken by

---

* Forster had been a member of a Quaker Famine Relief Committee in 1847 (see above, p. 23). He earned the epithet 'Buckshot' because it was in his period of office as Chief Secretary that an earlier administrative decision was implemented by which the police on certain occasions were to be armed with buckshot rather than the more lethal ball cartridge. There has been so much injustice in Irish history that the anomaly by which this marginally humanitarian administrative gesture, which was not his, should have earned the well-meaning Forster an ineradicable reputation for brutality must seem of trifling importance. See *I.H.S.*, Vol. xvi, no. 62 (September 1968), p. 238.

Lord Frederick Cavendish, younger brother of Lord Hartington and his own nephew by marriage, the announcement was greeted with jeers and laughter. Though an agreeable and intelligent man, Cavendish had hardly made the sort of mark on politics that seemed to qualify him for such a post. 'We will tear him in pieces within a fortnight,' jocularly commented one of the Irish party's brightest newcomers, Tim Healy.[6] Before the week was out Cavendish was found at about half past seven on the evening of his arrival in Dublin lying outside the vice-regal lodge in Phoenix Park, hacked to death by twelve-inch long surgical knives. Killed with him was the Under-Secretary, a diligent Catholic Irishman named Thomas Burke. Their assassins, who had earlier hoped to kill Forster, were members of a recently formed secret society named the Irish National Invincibles. This was composed mostly of former IRB men operating independently of the IRB in the general atmo-sphere of the New Departure, though they seem to have modelled themselves on the IRB assassination committees for dealing with traitors, and the IRB itself issued a statement after the deed that the men who had carried out 'this execution ... deserve well of their country'.[7] The Invincibles' leader was the Irish-American ex-Fenian, McCafferty, who had made the attempt on Chester Castle. As head of the Invincibles he had the connivance of senior officials of the Land League itself, principally an organizer named P. J. Sheridan, the Treasurer Patrick Egan, and the Secretary, Frank Byrne. The man given the job of supervising the Dublin end of the operations, a com-mercial traveller named Tynan, had been recruited by Byrne in the Cham-bers in Westminster which the Land League shared with the Irish party.[8] The surgical knives for the deed had been purchased in Bond Street and brought over to Dublin by Mrs Byrne, then seven months pregnant, in her skirts.[9]

The Invincibles and their leaders in the Land League represented that very strain of idealist extremism from which Parnell was trying to extricate him-self before embarking on the new phase of collaboration with Gladstone. In this respect the assassination could not have come at a worse time and Parnell's immediate reaction was one of political despair. He thought for a moment of resigning his leadership of the Irish party, but was dissuaded by Gladstone himself. Parnell's denunciation of the murder – sincere enough because it made his own political task so very much more difficult – had on the whole a convincing effect on English opinion at the time, and was echoed from almost all quarters in Ireland except the IRB. But the murders post-poned the day when Gladstone and the majority of the Liberals on the one hand and Parnell and his party on the other could finally present a united front on Home Rule. Gladstone's first preoccupation inevitably was to ap-pease English opinion. This meant further coercion which Parnell equally inevitably had to oppose. Even without the consequent delay there were in any case considerable internal difficulties to be resolved on the Liberal side

before the full alliance implicit in the Kilmainham Treaty could be implemented. Gladstone, at the time of Kilmainham, was in his mind moving in
the general direction of Home Rule, but he was much too skilled a politician
to be explicit even to himself on such a point when finding himself, as he
did, so far ahead of his own party. His final public commitment to Home
Rule did not in any case come about until Parnell had once again applied
considerable political pressure.

In order to force Gladstone to realize his good intentions over the land,
Parnell had made use of crude violence in Ireland. The form of pressure
which he continually applied to help Gladstone manifest his conversion to
Home Rule was subtler and played out on the parliamentary scene in England.

No attempt was made to resurrect the suppressed Land League. Instead,
in October 1882, Parnell founded the Irish National League, the object of
which, now that the agricultural crisis had temporarily subsided, was no
longer agrarian but specifically national. It expressed a popular national
demand for Home Rule, which had been considerably stimulated by the
general anti-government feeling aroused during the recent land agitation.
The importance of the new National League in practical terms was that it
gave the Irish party for the first time its own national structure at constituency level, and with this structure the party went into the General Election of 1885.

This election of 1885 was the first fought with the new enlarged electorate
introduced by the Franchise Act of the year before, which had granted household suffrage to the country as well as the towns. It was also the first election
fought in Ireland mainly on the issue of Home Rule. From it Parnell
emerged triumphant, with Home Rulers victorious in 85 out of 103 Irish
seats, including an actual majority of 17 to 16 in Ulster itself. He also now
had at his disposal in the Irish Parliamentary Party a far more tightly disciplined and effectively fashioned instrument than ever before. It was the
first British democratic political machine of modern times.

In Parliament in the months before the election Parnell had manoeuvred
with tactical ingenuity. He had put the ultimate logical pressure on Gladstone by actually voting with the Conservatives to turn him out of office, thus
demonstrating to the Liberals that they could hardly afford in the end not to
implement the full implications of the Kilmainham Treaty. For seven months
of minority government the Conservatives under Lord Salisbury, dependent
on the Irish, themselves flirted obscurely with Parnell through their Viceroy
Carnarvon, a personal but unrepresentative convert to the idea of self-
government for Ireland. Deftly Parnell had suddenly made Home Rule the
principal issue in English politics.

At the General Election Parnell had called on his supporters in England
to vote for the Conservatives. It is reckoned that this cost the Liberals some

twenty seats. But the final result was ideally calculated to make Gladstone commit himself. The Conservatives won 249 seats, the Liberals 335 and the balance was held by 86 Irish Home Rulers.*

Gladstone, adroitly blending true statesmanship with political interest, had hoped that the Conservatives might raise Home Rule above party politics altogether, and would have supported them in conceding it. Quite apart from allowing Parliament to devote its time to other issues in the national interest, this would have spared himself the awkward task of trying to make Home Rule the special cause of his own party. Both the right wing of the Liberals, represented by the Whig Lord Hartington, and the left wing, represented by the radical Joseph Chamberlain, were deeply uneasy about Home Rule though prepared to concede a limited form of local government. But given the Conservatives' natural leanings towards imperial grandeur the chances of any agreed solution between the two parties was remote. The Conservatives were in any case at this time looking round for an issue on which to mould an effective political identity, and were soon to realize that they had found a good one in 'patriotic' opposition to Home Rule.

Gladstone, seeing the balance held in the Commons by the Irish and feeling in his own conscience the need for Home Rule, inevitably played for Irish support and introduced a bill to grant it. The Conservatives gratefully made the most of the role with which he had presented them. Quite apart from the solution to their identity problem it gave the Conservatives the immediate prospect of a return to power in alliance with the dissident Liberals, those followers of Hartington and Chamberlain who opposed Home Rule and were soon to be known as Liberal Unionists. When the vote came on the Home Rule Bill's second reading in June 1886, Hartington, Chamberlain and 91 other Liberals voted against it and the measure was rejected by 341–311. A new General Election followed and a Conservative–Liberal–Unionist alliance then held power for the next six years.

Paradoxically, this defeat of the first Home Rule Bill in the House of Commons was of less moment than the great victory which its introduction marked for Irish nationalism. It was the climax of a great achievement engineered by Parnell. He had not only effectively coordinated Irish nationalists feelings into a wide popular movement for the first time since O'Connell but, unlike O'Connell, had succeeded in securing for it at the centre of political power the nominal adherence of one of the great English parties.

The mood in Ireland, immediately after the defeat, did not reflect despair but rather a proud recognition of what had been achieved. The reaction of the *Cork Examiner* was typical:

'The progress of the cause of Irish Nationalism,' it wrote, 'has suffered a check, but it has at the same time reached a point at which five years ago

* The seat additional to the 85 in Ireland was won in Liverpool by T. P. O'Connor.

it would have been deemed simply impossible to reach within that period of time. The Irish question now is to the forefront of politics and the defeat of last night cannot relegate it to a minor place.'[10]

Ten days later the paper was talking about nationalists being actually 'on the eve of the triumph of their principles'.[11] Parnell, speaking at Manchester in the election campaign that followed Gladstone's inevitable dissolution of Parliament, spoke of the Irish having 'nothing before them now but the prospect of hope'.[12] Even when the new election results began to come in, showing a marked swing away from the Liberals in England, there was no Irish despondency. Tim Healy, the member for Cork and, together with John Dillon, one of Parnell's two most able lieutenants, declared the results 'a mere temporary set back'.[13] The general feeling was that a Conservative government could hardly last and that every effort must be concentrated on another great battle in a few months' time.[14]

Both inside and outside Parliament Irishmen went out of their way to emphasize that they were prepared to accept Home Rule as a full and final settlement of the national question. What then exactly did Home Rule mean?

Like the three subsequent Home Rule Bills which were to follow it over the course of the next thirty-five years, the first Home Rule Bill offered Ireland no more than a domestic legislature and executive for Irish affairs only, with such legislature and executive itself expressly subject to the supremacy of the British Parliament. In addition to this latter overall constitutional limitation, all matters affecting peace or war, foreign affairs or even customs and excise were specifically excluded from the Irish Parliament's powers.* Ireland was to have no army or navy of its own and even control of the police was reserved to the Imperial Parliament for a certain period. Unionist opponents of the bill who were worried that Ireland might nevertheless at some future date raise a body of Volunteers through her own legislature were immediately reassured that this would be a specific occasion for the Imperial Parliament to assert its supremacy. What the Imperial Parliament had granted, it was proclaimed by the bill's promoters, the Imperial Parliament could also take away.

This was a puny position compared with the aspirations of the United Irishmen or the Fenians or even the Young Irelanders of 1848. Much of the Unionist criticism of the bill was in fact based on the argument that it was so inadequate a fulfilment of the Irish national demands that Irishmen could not possibly accept it as a final settlement. Joseph Chamberlain taunted Gladstone and Parnell simultaneously by recalling a speech of Parnell's in which he had said he would never be satisfied until Ireland took her full

* It was to enjoy virtually the same status as is today enjoyed by the Government of Northern Ireland.

place among the nations of the world. 'How can Ireland,' asked Chamberlain, 'take her place among the nations of the world when her mouth is closed on every international question? Ireland is to have no part in the arrangement of Commercial Treaties by which her interests may be seriously affected … and Irishmen under this scheme are to be content to be sent to battle and to death for matters in which Irish members are to have no voice in discussing or determining. I say that Ireland under this scheme is asked to occupy a position of degradation.'[15] Lord Wolmer said he could not believe that a proud nation like Ireland 'would accept a back-seat like that';[16] while Lord Randolph Churchill declared that if he were an Irishman he 'would be deeply wounded and affronted'.[17]

And yet Irishman after Irishman got up in the House of Commons and solemnly declared that subject to such minor modifications as he hoped to gain in committee he did accept this bill in principle as a final settlement. 'We look upon the provisions of this bill,' said Parnell, 'as a final settlement of this question and I believe that the Irish people have accepted it as such a settlement. … Not a single dissentient voice has been raised against the bill by any Irishman … holding national opinions,'[18] J. F. X. O'Brien, who less than twenty years previously had been sentenced to be hanged, drawn and quartered for his attack on Ballyknockane barracks, County Cork, in the Fenian rising, assured the House that the bill would be 'loyally accepted as a settlement by the vast majority of the Irish people at home and abroad and will put an end to the strife of centuries'.[19] Another Irish member who had been a Fenian as a very young man, William O'Brien, the editor of *United Ireland*, was even more impressive by being more realistic. They did not pretend for an instant, he said, that the bill would satisfy every man of Irish race. O'Donovan Rossa, for instance, didn't like it and they did not altogether hope to conquer his objection. 'We do not even promise,' he said, 'that by any incantation you can eradicate the feelings [which were] the growth of many a sad year and many a sad century.' But he did think that the Irish people had never been so united or unanimous as in acceptance of the bill.[20] Ireland itself, both through the voice of the Church and of the Irish popular press, bore him out. O'Brien's own fiery paper *United Ireland* raised its circulation some thirty per cent in one week by presenting its readers with a coloured portrait of Gladstone.[21]

Many Unionists maintained that what was said in Parliament by the Irish party was simply a tactical device and that the Gladstonians were being deceived into allowing the thin end of the wedge of separation. Even those who were prepared to accept that the Irish party were acting in good faith expected to see its members swept aside in any Irish Parliament as part of a great wave of national disappointment with absurdly exaggerated hopes.[22] But experienced Irish politicians like Parnell, O'Brien and Healy would never have said the sort of things they were saying in the Commons if there had been any danger of that. The whole success of the Parnellite movement was based on its acute sense of what would or would not go down well in Ireland. In any case, such a supposition quite misread the history of the development of Irish nationalism. The really remarkable thing was not so much that the majority of the Irish people could now accept so little in the way of a national demand, but that they had again been sufficiently well-organized to make any coherent national demand at all.

For, unlike O'Connell's Repeal, the attraction of Home Rule did not lie principally in any economic panacea it seemed to offer, but in a pure if unambitious demand for national self-respect. As far as economic conditions were concerned, the Imperial Government itself had long ago begun reforms. A major breach in the injustice of the land system had been made by the Land Act of 1881 with its concession of the principle of protection from eviction and fair rents. Fair rents were actually being applied in practice by the Land Court. It was true that in times of bad harvest, such as those which once again visited Ireland in the mid-eighties, the inflexibility of the rents adjusted by the Land Courts could and did lead to hardship and exposed some tenants once again to the horrors of eviction; and undoubtedly it was believed that under an Irish Parliament such things would all be much easier. But it had been proved already that such battles could be fought out successfully by a combination of action on the land itself and action in the British Parliament. Equally, the principle of land purchase by which the State bought out the landlords and the tenant was enabled to buy the land from the State by a series of annual mortgage payments, though not yet operating to any large extent, had been established and was being slowly extended. This meant that 'national independence' was no longer an indispensable prerequisite if the tenant farmer was to obtain ownership of the land. Nationalism was thus to a considerable extent deprived of the force which had given it its vague dynamic. Left to itself it amounted to nothing very remarkable – a reasoned if not impassioned demand that Irish identity should to a limited extent be recognized in some political form.

Unionists were unable to realize what had happened. For decades they had consistently underestimated the demands of the common people of Ireland. Now they exaggerated them. For the greater part of the Union's history English Unionists had been content to know little about Ireland, dismissing its persistent calls for special attention as either irritating or mischievous. Similar ignorance now dominated their excessive attention to Home Rule. Appalled by the Fenians, Land League agitators and American-based dynamiters who had been the superficial product of the country's long neglect, they saw in Irish nationalism little else. For the thirty years in which Home Rule remained the Irish national demand, the majority of Unionists allowed themselves to be hypnotized by almost nameless fears of what would happen if Home Rule were granted. Predictions of inevitable calamity and disaster multiplied each time the subject came under debate.

Certainly it was understandable that, for many people, the Irish 'national' position should seem menacing. Irish politicians who had so often used wild, green-flag oratory about freedom in the past were themselves largely to blame for this. It needed a knowledge of the balance of political forces between the party and its American supporters and an appreciation of the need actually to work up emotive feeling for Home Rule in Ireland to fathom the currents of Irish political language. In the circumstances it was largely a question of personal political temperament whether an Englishman decided that Home Rule was likely to be the final goal of Irish nationalism or the beginning of something which would lead to the 'separation condemned by all parties'.

Joseph Chamberlain in 1884, while still a radical, had understandably confessed himself bewildered by the term Irish nationalist as then in use. 'I should like to know clearly what this word means', he wrote to a friend. He could not, he said, regard the Irish people as having the separate rights of an absolutely independent community any more than he could the people of Scotland or Wales ... 'or to take still more extreme instances, of Sussex, or of London'. Rather than agree to separation he would 'govern Ireland by force to the end of the chapter. But if nationalism means home rule I have no objection to grant it in principle, and am only anxious to find out what it means.'[23] Curiously, having found out that it did not mean separation, his fears of separation assumed precedence and he opposed it in principle and practice to the end at least of his own chapter.

Even accepting the good faith of the Irish, there was certainly a logical argument to be made that separation might be the final result. Parnell himself had said that no man 'could set a boundary to the march of a nation'. There was no knowing what might happen in future generations. In the light of our own knowledge of subsequent colonial and commonwealth development the possibility that Home Rule might eventually have led to separation can by no means be discounted. Chamberlain and other Unionists had a valid constitutional point when they met reassurances about the reserve supremacy of the Imperial Parliament with the objection that such supremacy was at that time still retained by the British Parliament over Canada, but that no one would ever realistically think of trying to assert it.[24]

Nevertheless, it is difficult now not to regard the failure to grant Home Rule in 1886 and for the next thirty years as a tragedy for both the Irish and the British peoples. Given the undoubted acceptance of Home Rule at the time by the great majority of Irishmen as a satisfaction of national demands, and given the continuing extension over the next thirty years of social and administrative reforms which did at times, in the Tory phrase, almost kill even the demand for Home Rule by kindness, it now seems probable that extreme separatist nationalism – so totally unrepresentative at the time – would certainly have been killed, and that Home Rule would have kept Ireland a part of the United Kingdom rather than have taken her or the greater part of her outside it. All a historian can definitely say, however, is that, whether or not Home Rule would in the end have led to separation, the refusal to grant it over the next thirty years certainly did so.

4
The Orange Card

For thirty years the political definition of Irish nationality, for the vast majority of Irishmen, remained that given by Home Rulers in the course of the Home Rule debates. One Irish member, Sir Thomas Esmonde, had expressed it neatly when he described the Irish as being 'a distinct though not a separate nationality'.[1] Gladstone himself had given as accurate a version as any:

'We stand,' he wrote, 'face to face with what is termed Irish nationality. Irish nationality vents itself in the demand for local autonomy, or separate and complete self-government in Irish, not in Imperial affairs. Is this an evil in itself? Is it a thing that we should view with horror or apprehension? ... I hold that there is such a thing as local patriotism, which, in itself, is not bad but good.' He cited the instances of Scotsmen and Welshmen, both 'full of local patriotism'. Misfortune and calamity had wedded the Irishman even more profoundly to his country's soil than the English, Welsh or Scotch, 'but it does not follow that because his local patriotism is keen, he is incapable of imperial patriotism ...'[2]

The numbers of Irishmen who were to fight under the British colours in the Boer and First World Wars were to confirm his point.

But there were two complications in this view of Irish nationalism as formulated in the Home Rule era. Two groups of Irishmen, both minorities, were left outside it. One was that tiny minority stemming from the old Fenian tradition who still felt that only complete separation from Britain and an independent republic was an adequate satisfaction for Irish national pride. This group was, at this time, virtually of no significance. Many old Fenians had become wholly absorbed by the now more successful parliamentary tradition, and though the Irish Republican Brotherhood continued to exist as a secret society, it was by the last decade of the nineteenth century a minute and isolated organization. That it could ever again be in a position to influence Irish affairs at all, let alone decisively, seemed then to the overwhelming majority of Irishmen unthinkable.

The other minority, which like the IRB was also to influence future events decisively, was then already of far greater significance. This was composed of the million or so Protestants of Ireland, slightly under half of whom lived in the north-east corner of Ulster.

To understand fully the action by which the Ulster Protestants were soon to change the course of Irish history it is indispensable momentarily to look back three centuries.

The ancestors of these twentieth-century Irishmen had been, in 1609, strangers to Ireland, brought over mainly from Scotland as settlers, on favourable terms, of lands confiscated from the Catholic Gaelic tribes which had owned them.* The newcomers were Protestants. But though the Chiefs of the Gaelic tribes, the Earls of Tyrone and Tyrconnell, had fled the country, the people of the tribes remained to a large extent surrounding the new occupiers. In such a situation, two salient considerations dominated the Protestants' everyday lives and everyday thinking: they were on their own and they were surrounded by enemies. This sense of isolation, combined with an originally rational fear that their Catholic neighbours would try to regain their lands and dispossess them, became as much a part of the Protestant Ulster heritage as the land itself. Ingrained in the ordinary Protestant Ulster mind was the thought that the Catholic represented a material threat to him. Ingrained, too, became the belief that when a crisis threatened the safest way of driving such a threat away was to drive the Catholic away physically, much as the armed warriors whom the earls had left behind had been driven by law, at the time of the Plantation, into Connaught.

The reasoning behind such thinking was long kept alive by history. The 1641 native rebellion in Ulster, a violent attempt by the Catholic Irish to recover their lands, seemed to provide full vindication of Protestant fears. Half a century later a Catholic monarch, James II, came to the throne of England and Ireland and actually carried out legally that same threat of dispossession which Protestants had hitherto successfully survived. Before, however, an attempt could be made to put the new laws into force, the English Revolution took place and dethroned James II, who made his last stand in Ireland. James's defeats at the battles of the Boyne and Aughrim saved the Ulster Protestant inheritance, and the sense of salvation imprinted itself so indelibly in the Ulster Protestant memory that it is common to this day to see crude portraits of William of Orange, the Protestant saviour, and the slogan 'Remember 1690' chalked up on the walls of Belfast. Celebrations of this famous victory on 12 July,† and similar ritualistic recollections of the siege of Derry when London apprentices shut the gates in the face of the advancing troops of the Catholic Earl of Antrim, became themselves bastions against a continuing sense of insecurity.

---

* See above, p. 12. Before this Plantation of Ulster, and before the Reformation, there had been intermittent small-scale Scottish settlement of this part of Ireland by clans from across the intervening water, but their religion was, of course, Catholic.

† 1 July, old-style calendar.

For nearly a century after the defeat of James II the fear of Protestants that Catholics would try to regain their lands remained in the background. It had indeed become an ineradicable part of Ulster Protestant tradition, but the rigour of the penal laws against the Catholics, particularly those which prevented Catholics from buying land, inheriting it, or even renting it as a commercial proposition, removed the old fear at least from the realm of immediate reality. But throughout the eighteenth century the other half of the Ulster Protestant personality was strangely accentuated: namely, its awareness of its isolated identity in Ireland. The penal laws themselves did not only contain the Catholics. They also set apart the Ulster Protestants from most of the rest of the Protestants of Ireland by inflicting certain religious tests and restrictions on them as Presbyterians, the sect to which the vast majority of Ulster Protestants belonged. This Presbyterian religion conditioned a state of mind different from that of other Irish Protestants, for its rejection of bishops and respect for the opinions of the meeting-house gave Ulster Protestants a radical attitude to politics ahead of their times, and even a potentially republican as opposed to a monarchical outlook.

Though most of the tenants of Protestant Ulster, descendants of the original planters, customarily held land on terms which gave them – centuries before Gladstone's Land Acts – a security of tenure provided they paid their rent, together with compensation for their improvements, rents had been high. Their own secret agrarian associations which they formed to protect their interests against landlords had not always been able to prevent distress and hardship. Thanks, however, to a higher standard of living than in the rest of Ireland, due to the Ulster custom, Ulster Protestants had often had the money to emigrate. Emigration from Presbyterian Ulster to America had been a feature of eighteenth-century Ireland and had contributed to some of the most fiery republican spirits of the American independence movement.

Much of the same radical Ulster Protestant spirit had manifested itself in Ireland in the Volunteer movement of the late 1770s and early 1780s, and in the movement which evolved from that to try to obtain a reform of the newly 'independent' Grattan's Parliament.* The stronghold of the Irish parliamentary reform movement had been in the North, and it was of course in Belfast that the first Society of United Irishmen had been formed in 1791 to try and secure reform by bringing Irishmen of all denominations together to act as Irishmen. Desirable, however, as was the objective of parliamentary reform to all Ulster Protestants, the methods proposed were for a special reason then particularly inappropriate. For with the relaxation of the penal laws as they affected land, Catholics had once again moved back into the North. Because of the lower standard of living to which Catholics were long accustomed, they were bidding up the price of land to levels which Ulster Protestant tenants found ruinous. This was a new version of the old threat,

* See above, p. 32.

and many Protestants reacted in the old style. Clashes between organized Protestant Peep o' Day Boys and reciprocally organized Catholic Defenders had been the result, culminating in the famous Battle of the Diamond and the formation of the Orange Society in 1795. Verbal and written threats, frequently carried out, to burn out Catholic families and drive them 'to Hell or Connaught' made their appearance – as indeed they have continued to do whenever Protestants have felt that Catholics in Ulster were getting above themselves, well into the second half of the twentieth century.

When the United Irishmen had eventually tried to organize themselves in arms for reform, the fact that most of the Ulster Protestants were by historical temperament more anti-Catholic than they were anti-government made it relatively easy for the government to break the revolt at least as far as its manifestation in Ulster was concerned. The only two counties of Ulster which rose at all in 1798 were, significantly, those of Antrim and Down, which had been outside the area of settlement in the early seventeenth century, having been already more gradually permeated by Scots over a longer period and therefore less traumatically involved in the classic Catholic–Protestant confrontation of the area. But here, too, Protestant United Irish Societies – full of strong anti-Catholic feeling from the start, as Tone had found – came out in their true Orange colours and were soon as identified with the government cause as they had been with the republican.

It would be a mistake to deduce from this that the Ulster Protestants' new-found loyalty to the government was the really characteristic feature of their new attitude. This was not so. What still moulded the Ulster Protestant Irish personality was its radical self-sufficiency. Anti-Catholic feeling, charged certainly with nearly two centuries of emotion but still predominantly of the traditional economic type, finally determined their attitude in 1798, but even today when 'loyalism' has long been the hallmark of Ulster it is only so because loyalism has long suited the interests of Ulster Protestants. It is no paradox that many a 'loyalist' today in Ulster is proud to claim that he had an ancestor out for an Irish Republic in 1798.

Environment had conditioned Ulster Protestants from the first to be self-protective and self-reliant in a potentially hostile situation. What motivated them was always their self-interest. Thus in 1800, loyal as most of them had in the end been in the crisis, they were opposed to the idea of the Union because they doubted whether a Union Parliament could maintain as strict an ascendancy over the Catholics as Protestants could themselves. Then, with the Union, new forces of self-interest developed to bind them to it fiercely.

One of the most astonishing social phenomena in the history of the Union was the growth in the course of it, both in population and prosperity, of the City of Belfast. A Belfast population of twenty thousand at the time of the Union had expanded more than ten times that number by the late

1880s to some 230,000. The population of Dublin in the same period only doubled. At the same time Belfast, also in contrast with Dublin, became one of the most thriving industrial cities of the United Kingdom. As a modern Irish historian has put it, Belfast, instead of being the solitary Irish industrial city, became an outpost of industrial Britain.[3]

This was principally due to the overwhelmingly successful development of the linen industry, which, unlike wool, had not been suppressed by the English Parliament in the late seventeenth century since there had been no English linen industry which it had threatened as a competitor. Linen, then a cottage industry in Ireland, had flourished, particularly in Ulster, partly because of the custom of tenant right which gave the farmer a security conducive to its practice, and partly because of an influx of skilled French Protestant refugees who settled near Belfast at the end of the seventeenth century and taught new techniques of spinning, weaving and bleaching. When at the beginning of the nineteenth century the industrial revolution began to gather momentum, North-East Ulster was the only area in Ireland in a position to take advantage of it.

Around 1800, with the development of new machines and new processes, cotton also temporarily took root and flourished in and around Belfast, and though it succumbed to competition from Lancashire after about twenty years its short period of success was of the utmost importance for the future, for it not only attracted labour into Belfast but also served as a model for the technical reorganization of the linen industry. Linen expanded rapidly as the industrial revolution gathered pace with the faster transport facilities provided by rail and steamship, and the Ulster linen industry finally consolidated its position as one of the major industries of the United Kingdom when, during the cotton famine caused by the American civil war, it was able to step into the gap as an alternative.

From the 1850s onwards another highly successful industry was started in Belfast, thanks primarily to the genius of one man, Edward Harland, who came as manager to a small shipyard on Queen's Island, Belfast, in 1853. Harland's revolutionary designs for iron and steel ships gave Belfast an international reputation for shipbuilding, and a flow of rewarding contracts for passenger and naval vessels, which by the end of the century had made shipbuilding as important in its own right as the flourishing linen trade.

Thus, by the time of the first Home Rule Bill, the Ulster Protestants felt wedded to the United Kingdom by something much stronger than mere traditional opposition to Catholic Ireland. Their livelihood was wholly bound up with the United Kingdom's prosperity, and any proposal which seemed to tamper with their bonds with it seemed also to tamper with that prosperity and that livelihood. The apprehension was particularly strong when the proposal did in fact come from the traditional source of all apprehension: Catholic Ireland.

The Orange Society had had some ups and downs in the course of the century, but was relatively flourishing by the early 1880s. It was now to become the nucleus round which the new mood of defensive militant Protestant self-interest consolidated.

The Orange Lodges had always operated on two levels. The first was that of a fairly crude Protestant working-class self-protection society operating in the linen mills and shipyards, the direct descendant of the Peep o' Day Boys with their tough anti-Catholic approach of the end of the eighteenth century. However, just as in the late 1790s the gentry had taken over leadership of the Orange Society in order to make its power respectable, so at later crises of Irish history the society had always been able to show a constitution expressed in unexceptionable terms about brotherly love, toleration and loyalty to the Crown, and to display an impressive string of eminent and respectable landed gentry as its higher functionaries. A Royal Commission had once drawn attention to this dichotomy, commenting that 'the educated and refined classes may possibly make such an organization to be compatible with brotherly love and toleration to those who differ from them, but the uneducated and unrefined, who act from feeling and impulse, and not from reflection, cannot be expected to restrain the passions excited by the lessons of their own dominancy and superiority over their fellow subjects whom they look upon as their conquered foes. In practice it is not as it is in the letter of its constitution . . .'*[4]

Because of this double edge, the Orange Society was always a potentially significant political element in the Ulster situation.

Banned by the government in 1836 after a curious conspiracy in which it had become part of a British political plot to set the Duke of Cambridge on the throne of the United Kingdom, it had been reconstituted in August 1845 at a meeting in the town of Enniskillen, with the Earl of Enniskillen himself in the chair. This was at the height of the last phase of O'Connell's Repeal campaign and the Orangemen were then particularly protesting against what they regarded as the thin end of the wedge of separation in the government's grant of a subsidy to the Roman Catholic seminary at Maynooth. Believing as they did that the Papacy was pursuing a systematic policy 'aiming at the subjugation of all nations beneath the sway and tyranny of the Roman pontiff', they resolved to combine under the old name, but, theoretically at least, without the old secret signs and passwords 'to preserve inviolate the Legislative Union, and the blessings of civil and religious liberty'.[5] Three years later, at the time of Smith O'Brien's foray into Tipperary, the government made a special arrangement with the Orangemen by which they should be allowed to buy arms even though an arms ban was then in force. Money for the purpose was actually handed over to

---

* Even the formal records of the society at this time showed regular expulsions for 'marrying a Papist'.

the Grand Master of the Orange Lodge, the Earl of Enniskillen, by the Viceroy's Master of the Horse, but O'Brien's half-hearted venture collapsed before anything could come of the project.[6] A tentative link between the Orangemen and the establishment, qualified by the Orangemen's fear that the establishment might sell them out, had become a part of Irish historical tradition.

It had been in 1868 with the prospect of Disestablishment for the Protestant Church that the true shape of things to come was first clearly outlined. For months militant clergymen in Ireland had been using the sort of fanatical language which was to become commonplace in the North over the next fifty years and more. 'We will fight,' declared the Reverend Thomas Ellis of Newbliss in County Monaghan, 'as men alone can fight who have the Bible in one hand and the sword in the other; we will fight – nay, if needs be we will die as our fathers died before us ... and this will be our dying cry, echoed and re-echoed from earth to heaven and from one end of Ulster to the other: "No Popery, no surrender".'[7] Such a mood was not of course confined to the North but to be found among Protestants all over Ireland, and a Reverend Ferrers of Rathmines, Dublin, also proclaimed that 'if the Church Establishment be destroyed ... there shall not be peace in Ireland'.[8]

A central Protestant Defence Association founded at Hillsborough, County Down, Ulster, in October 1867, held its first meeting in Dublin in February 1868, attended by 50 peers, 20 honourables, 46 baronets and knights, 36 members of Parliament, 127 deputy lieutenants and lords-lieutenant, 17 privy councillors, 360 JPs and more than 500 others.[9] A resolution was passed to the effect that 'the Protestants of Ireland, from their social position, wealth, intelligence and loyalty are entitled to as ample consideration and protection of their interests as any other class of Her Majesty's subjects in the realm and ... that in all legislation affecting their property, liberty or religion Ireland shall be dealt with not as a separate country but as an integral part of the United Kingdom'.[10]

A special Ulster Defence Association was also formed. But the relationship between the movement's aristocratic element and the Orangemen was uneasy, even though the Earl of Enniskillen, the Orange Lodge's Grand Master, had taken part in the Dublin meeting. The radical streak in the Orange Society's activity was represented by William Johnston of Ballykilbeg House, the Grand Master of County Down, who, in March 1868, was sentenced to a month's imprisonment for marching, in defiance of the Party Processions Act, from Newtonards to Bangor at the head of a crowd of twenty to thirty thousand with beating drums, orange flags and a band playing the 'Protestant Boys' and other provocative tunes.

Though educated opinion in Ulster disliked the Act under which Johnston had been sentenced, it did not condemn the sentence itself. And the Protestant

Defence Association, whose meetings were at this time, as the *Freeman's Journal* put it, 'as plentiful as blackberries'[11] with at least twenty-five branch associations all over Ireland, was to go out of its way to dissociate itself from the Orange Society altogether, even though the Earl of Enniskillen was a pillar of both organizations.[12]

Nevertheless, it was with the radical Orangemen that the real vitality of the movement lay, and when Johnston was released from prison in April special trains were run to Belfast for the celebrations, and the Reverend Drew declared that the government 'might trample on their hearts if they dared, but they never should crush or trample on the Orangemen of Ireland'.[13] At another celebration meeting the following month the resentment felt by rank and file Orangemen for the upper-class conservatives was particularly marked. Such conservatives, said Johnston, liked their votes very much but they disliked the name of Orangemen. They had used the Orangemen for thirty years and it was 'now time to put their members of Parliament through their catechism'.[14] In June 1868 the Grand Lodge of the Institution further reiterated the determination of Orangemen and Protestants that they would 'never surrender their civil and religious rights' purchased by the blood and treasure of their ancestors.[15] And when in July the Earl of Enniskillen, concerned to keep the Orange and conservative elements together, called a meeting in his ancestral town, he issued a Nelson-like summons 'expecting that every Protestant from 14 to 60, whether he be an Orangeman or not, will be at his post in Enniskillen to protest against meditated attacks'.[16]

But all the brave words which had seemed to create such a belligerent mood and atmosphere came to nothing when in due course Gladstone, having fought and won an election on the question of Disestablishment of the Irish Church, proceeded, early in 1869, to pass the Act through Parliament. As late as February 1869 one Ulster clergyman was boasting that he would put his house, glebe, church and schools under the protection of two thousand Orangemen against all comers, even including Her Majesty's Home Secretary.[17] But the general tone was one of impotence and bitterness. A speaker at one Protestant Defence Association commented with some foresight that the government 'should beware lest they made Protestant Fenians'.[18] And a manifesto issued by the Grand Orange Lodge, sensing correctly that even more fundamental changes than Church Disestablishment would one day be in store, laid down that as it was by virtue of the third article of the Act of Union that the Imperial Parliament was constituted and invested with legal authority, so 'upon the cancelling of that Act their functions as a Parliament would be extinguished'.[19] In other words, Protestant Ulstermen might not only one day have to look after themselves but would have the self-proclaimed constitutional right to do so.

This was inaccurate constitutional doctrine since the British Constitution recognizes only one unalterable legislative principle, namely that Parliament can always legislate to supersede earlier legislation. But it was to become a sincerely and widely held point of view that must be appreciated if later Ulster attitudes are to be understood.

For the time being, however, the impression left by the crisis was the dangerous one that all the talk of the Ulstermen and other Irish Protestants was mere bombast.

'Many in their ignorance,' Johnston had said in the course of the crisis, 'had talked of an Orange revival, but Orangeism never was dead and was undying.'[20] This was true in so far as the society permanently kept alive the rather aggressive Protestant solidarity of the labourers and dock workers of North-East Ulster. But it was outside events and the interests of more important parties alone which gave the society political significance. Thus it was not again until the great Land League crisis of 1881 and the signs of government 'weakness' in the Kilmainham Treaty that the Orange Society once more began to assume a prominence it had lacked throughout the seventies.

In July 1882 the society obtained an important new recruit in a wealthy Protestant landlord of County Cavan, a major in the militia and a Tory Member of Parliament for his county, Edward Saunderson. He had become an Orangeman, he announced, because the state of the country for the past two years – the years of the Land League – had been 'simply unbearable'. Having asked himself whether there was any organization capable of dealing with this condition of anarchy and rebellion, he had decided that there was only one 'not afraid to face and cope with it and that was the Orange organization'. But he had also come to the conclusion that the organization could be much improved by more discipline. It needed training in the use of the arms which many of them possessed and they should adopt a uniform. Then: '... If England in a moment of infatuation, determined to establish Home Rule ... they would take up arms and ask the reason why ...'.[21]

The following year Lord Arthur Hill, Orange Grand Master of County Down, was also asserting that tens of thousands of loyal Irishmen 'with stout hearts and strong arms were ready to defend to the death if necessary' their principles, calling for the combination of all Protestant Unionists whether originally Liberal or Conservative in one political party.[22]

Early in 1884, with the prospect of the extended franchise making a Home Rule Bill possible, Saunderson proclaimed that 'every Protestant was as ready to fight today as his ancestors were two hundred years ago', and boasted that the Orange Institution could concentrate fifty thousand men at any given point in Ulster at the shortest possible notice. He was in contact with foreign armament firms obtaining quotations for rifles with which to supply an Orange army.[23] To a crowd of twenty thousand Orangemen celebrating the anniversary of the Boyne on 12 July 1884, some with their drums stained with the blood of their wrists after the fury with which they had been beating their traditional tattoo, he declared that the organization had made more progress in the past three or four years than the most sanguine Orangemen would have thought possible.[24] But perhaps because Saunderson was such a jaunty likeable Irishman, so wealthy, a favourite in London drawing-rooms and, after all, a major only in the militia, with little real experience of soldiering, no one in the sophisticated world of British politics took his threats of action very seriously. It was not until after the General Election of 1885 which gave the balance of power to the Irish party in the House of Commons that a new significance was given to such militaristic vocabulary by support from a source which had hitherto treated it with little respect.

As late as 16 November 1885 Lord Randolph Churchill, the young Tory radical, had been writing of the 'foul Ulster Tories who have always ruined our party'.[25] During the election of 1885 the Orangemen had delivered their most violent and successful attacks against their fellow conservatives in Ulster, suspecting a betrayal to Parnell. The prospect of the Conservatives trimming with Catholic Irish nationalism had long been the Orangemen's bogey. But this was now largely dispelled by the political evolution in ondon, when Gladstone, faced with the results of the election, finally came out for Home Rule and the Conservatives nailed their colours then and for the next thirty-five years to the anti-Home Rule mast.

At the prospect of a Home Rule Bill the tension in Ulster and among Irish Protestants generally had risen immediately. On 1 December 1885 at a great Orange soirée in Dublin William Johnston stated plainly: '... the day that any Government brings into the House of Commons a Bill to separate Ireland from England and to dissolve the legislative Union, the Orange Volunteers would be mustered in Ulster under able and experienced officers, and if the bill proceeded further and received the Royal Assent there would be at once a civil war in Ulster ...'.[26] It was hardly surprising that Lord Randolph Churchill for the Conservatives now decided that 'the Orange card was the one to play'.[27] The Loyal and Patriotic Union, formed in Ireland in the summer of 1885, began to spread branches into England. In January 1886, the Ulster Loyalist anti-Repeal Union was formed and at its first meeting, symbolically at Dungannon, on 1 February 1886, one Orangeman called for an appeal to Germany if that to England should fall on deaf ears.[28]

At the New Year Churchill had met Saunderson and discussed the situation, and a month later, a few days before proceeding to Belfast for an organized campaign against Home Rule, he made a significant speech in his own constituency at Paddington. He declared that England could not leave the Protestants of Ireland in the lurch and that there were hundreds and thousands of English hearts – 'aye, and English hands' – that would stand by them.[29] He also made an astonishing statement, the arrogance of which was to underlay much of the English Conservative philosophy towards

Ireland for the next thirty-five years. 'The Protestants of Ireland,' said Churchill, 'on such an occasion as this, and in a national crisis such as this, are the only nation which is known to the English people in Ireland.'[30]

In February he crossed to Belfast and reassured the Ulstermen that 'in the dark hour there will not be wanting to you those of position and influence in England who are willing to cast their lot with you – whatever it may be'.[31] Ulster, he said a little later, 'would fight, and Ulster would be right'.

Appearances seemed to bear him out. The *Belfast News-Letter* declared that though the Loyalists did not want civil war they were not afraid to resort to it 'rather than submit to be ruled by boycotters and moonlighters exercising legislative functions in an Irish Parliament which would be the laughing stock of the civilized world'.[32] Advertisements appeared in the paper, asking for twenty thousand rifles and for competent men 'who must not be in receipt of pensions to instruct in military drill'.[33] As the second reading of the Home Rule Bill was argued out in the Commons, reports began to come in of enrolments of Orange volunteers between eighteen and sixty, and of drilling with and without arms, from various parts of North-East Ulster.[34] On 8 May 1886 Major Saunderson declared to a large and enthusiastic meeting of the Loyal and Patriotic Union in Dublin that 'there could only be one appeal left, and that was an appeal which they unquestionably intended to make and that appeal was to their own strong right arms'.[35] There was talk of Lord Wolseley and a thousand British officers putting themselves at the service of the Orangemen; of Lord Charles Beresford saying he would resign from the Navy rather than lead it against Ulster; of a supposed Ulster army of two army corps, an active one of thirty-eight thousand men, and a reserve of twenty-eight thousand. There was even a proposal for an Ulster convention and a solemn covenant.[36]

Home Rulers continued to dismiss all this as, in the last resort, 'all bunkum and bounce', as one Irish member put it. '... They have no intention whatever of fighting,' he said.[37] And he was echoed everywhere on the government benches. Labouchère described the advertisement for Snider rifles in the Ulster papers as 'a game of brag'. The whole thing, he said, was 'arrant humbug'.[38] They had not fought over Disestablishment and they would not fight now. 'A manufactured thing, a good deal of bluster and a good deal of bunkum,' Sir Charles Russell called it all.[39] T. D. Sullivan, the Irish member for College Green, also taunted the Ulstermen with their behaviour at the time of Disestablishment and went on to call their historical bluff. 'Their talk,' he said, 'about the battle of the Boyne was as great a fraud as their talk about Ulster.... Why, the Irish Protestants at the Battle of the Boyne represented only one eighth of King William's Army, and as an Irishman he was almost ashamed to say they were the least effective part of it.'[40]

It was as well perhaps that Home Rulers should enjoy the joke while it lasted. They were making the classical political mistake of thinking that reason rather than power would eventually decide the issue. In fact, the Home Rule Bill was rejected on its second reading on 8 June 1886 before the seriousness of such preparations could be put to the test. Certainly they never reached anything like the magnitude or level of organization that was to be achieved twenty-five years later. But what was important for the future was not just the precedent, but the firm establishment in the Home Rule mind of the conviction that this was all *only* bluff. The belief became part of standard Home Rule dogma.

This confidence was not based only on wishful thinking. Honourable men, it was felt, would see that the Ulster case did not stand up to rational scrutiny, and that all reasonable safeguards which Ulstermen or other Irish Protestants might require had been met in the proposals of the Home Rule Bill. Gladstone in introducing the bill devoted far more attention to what seemed to him a greater problem than that of Ulster, namely the decision whether or not to retain Irish members in the imperial legislature, which he had finally resolved in the negative. On Ulster he merely mentioned that a number of suggestions had been made, including one for the exclusion of part of Ulster from the operation of Home Rule, none of which had seemed to warrant inclusion in the bill, though he offered to keep an open mind on them in committee.[41] The confidence with which he was able to approach the problem undoubtedly derived partly from the fact that, as a result of the election, the Nationalists were actually in a majority of one – seventeen seats as opposed to sixteen – for the nine counties of Ulster: Antrim, Armagh, Down, Derry, Tyrone, Fermanagh, Donegal, Cavan and Monaghan. Given a belief in the elementary working principles of democracy it was unthinkable that certain minority objections in these counties should be allowed to wreck the proposal for the whole of Ireland. As one Liberal Ulsterman declared, it was virtually impossible 'to draw a plan of even a section of a county in the whole of Ulster in which section there would not be comprised persons of all the religions of Ireland'.[42] Statistics indeed seemed to make nonsense of the idea that Ulster should have any special say. The percentages of population over the entire province were fifty-two per cent Protestant and forty-nine per cent Catholic. In the counties of Antrim and in parts of Down and Armagh there was a concentration of Protestants which outnumbered Catholics there in the proportion of five and a half to two. Over the rest of Ulster, however, Catholics actually outnumbered Protestants by two to one.[43]

It was therefore not surprising that Lord Randolph Churchill in making his famous remark about the Orange card should, while hoping that it would prove the ace of trumps, have also expressed a fear that it might turn out to be the two.*[44] As regards any special treatment for Ulster, Saunderson him-

---

* It may be noted that Lord Randolph was only echoing, however unconsciously, a magistrate of the 1790s, who had also referred to the Orangemen as 'a rather difficult card to play' (Lecky, *History of Ireland in the Eighteenth Century*, vol. iii, p. 437).

self, speaking proudly as an Irishman, indignantly rejected the idea. 'We are prepared to stand or fall,' he declared, 'for weal or woe, with every loyal man who lives in Ireland.'[45] Except in fact for Joseph Chamberlain, who first seriously put forward a proposal for local autonomy of part of Ulster in a letter to *The Times* on 14 May 1886, no one on either side of the House entertained a partition of Ireland as a serious possibility at all.

Parnell himself made the most effective case against a separate legislature for Ulster. It would not be giving 'protection' to Irish Protestants for there would be as many as 400,000 Protestants left outside. Moreover, since in Ulster there was actually a majority for the Nationalists, the first action of any Ulster Parliament would be to unite with the Dublin Parliament. On the other hand, if a special Parliament were created simply for the concentration of Protestants in North-East Ulster alone it would entail abandoning to an even greater extent those Irish Protestants on whose behalf the exclusion was invoked, for seven-twelfths of all Irish Protestants lived outside the area.[46] He went on, in handsome terms, to express his positive objections as an Irish nationalist to any such measure. 'We cannot,' he said, 'give up a single Irishman. We want the patriotism, the talents and the work of every Irishman to ensure that this great experiment shall be a successful one. The best system of government should be the resultant of what forces are in that country.... The class of Protestants will form a most valuable element in the Irish legislature of the future, constituting, as they will, a strong minority, and exercising ... a moderating influence in making laws.... We want all creeds and classes in Ireland.... We cannot consent to look upon a single Irishman as not belonging to us.'[47]

To encourage Irish Protestants to respond to such an appeal significant concessions had been made in the framing of the bill. Care had been taken to ensure for them greater representation than their numbers alone warranted, in acknowledgement of their special position and influence. The Irish Parliament was to consist of two 'orders' which would normally sit together as one chamber. The upper order would consist of twenty-eight representative Irish peers, together with seventy-five members with a special property qualification, elected only by voters with higher property qualifications than normal. The two Houses could on the demand of either, vote and sit separately, and in this case either could put a veto on legislation initiated by the other for a limited period. In other words the Irish Protestants, including the Protestant Ulstermen – for theirs would be primarily the interests represented in the upper order – would not only be guaranteed an inbuilt influence in the single chamber Parliament but would also have a suspensory power if the majority in that single chamber initiated any legislation which seemed to threaten their freedom or interests. Assuming that the same attitude of cooperative goodwill towards constitutional safeguards were to prevail in the Irish as in the Westminster Parliament and the same disposition to make them work sensibly, these were as fair safeguards as any Irish Protestant could reasonably expect, who was prepared to accept the democratically expressed will of the majority. But the men of Ulster were not primarily concerned with democratic reasoning, nor in the long run with the interests of other Irish Protestants. They were thinking, as Irish history had trained them to think, in terms of their own interests, and they were convinced that these demanded that there should be no Home Rule for Ireland. The real questions were whether they would have the strength and determination to defy the British constitution if the time ever came when the Crown in Parliament were to grant Home Rule; and how far the British Conservative Party would be prepared to go in helping the Ulstermen in that defiance.

5
Parnell's Fall

Home Rule had really only acquired a true dynamic force in the mid-eighties under Parnell. It was easy for this to fade again in face of rebuff or the distraction of other matters. History written from a later separatist premise has sometimes implied that the eventual Irish disillusionment with Home Rule arose from the inadequacy of the national demand Home Rule made. But from 1886 to the passing of a Home Rule Act in 1914 few, apart from the usual tiny minority of Fenians, ever suggested that Home Rule was an inadequate national demand. All the public emphasis was the other way: that it was totally adequate. The real truth was that even for such a limited national demand, there was not, when things turned difficult, the enthusiasm to make it a cause of overriding, compelling urgency.

Certainly, the Irish Parliamentary Party and their full-time professional and amateur adherents had nailed their colours unequivocally to the Home Rule mast. And the people followed and voted for it because it was the only political avenue there was. But it became a cause of routine orthodoxy, not of burning enthusiasm. After all, there was no real prospect of Home Rule's success for nearly two decades after the failure of Gladstone's second bill, and yet Ireland was quieter during most of that time than ever before in her history; such disturbances as occurred centred as usual around the land and not around the national issue at all.

In fact, so unexciting did the political avenue become that even intellectual interest in nationalism began to turn more and more down non-political avenues altogether – into a study and attempted revival of Gaelic, the 'national' language, and Gaelic sports, into an interest in being Irish and culturally different for its own sake, as an escape from the monolithic advance of European materialist culture. In the Irish language, in Irish literature and a new Irish theatre many sought an 'Irishness' which as a personal characteristic would give them more dignity than any political creed. Of course, even this new development was the activity of a minority, just as political 'Irishness' had been. Most people, as throughout Irish history, remained interested only in their material relationship with the land. This, however, was becoming tolerable at last.

When the House of Commons rejected Gladstone's first Home Rule Bill on its second reading, the Land War itself was by no means over, though in retrospect it is possible to see that the path of development down which the Land Act of 1881 had set the land system was irreversible. There remained, however, technical problems which were to cause severe recurrences of disorder and repression, though never on such a scale as had masked the days of the Land League. Though the principle, at least, of security of tenure had been won, it was soon to be replaced as the chief agrarian issue by that of actual ownership. The peasant wanted to become not just the secure tenant, but the owner of the soil. The financial terms on which he was to do so under land-purchase arrangements, including whether or not such sale through land-purchase arrangements was to be made a compulsory obligation on the landlord, were to become a new source of agrarian dispute in Ireland. Even after a further Land Purchase Act of 1886, only 73,868 holdings altogether out of a total of something like 500,000 had come under land-purchase arrangements since the idea had been first introduced. And it was not until the Land Purchase Act of 1903, to be followed by another even more comprehensive, in 1909, that really large-scale transfers of ownership from tenant to landlord took place.

Meanwhile, however, many difficulties of the old rent-paying tenant-landlord relationship survived to give trouble. Though the Land Act of 1881 had been a success in its most important aspect – the control of rents – there was one major flaw in it as a solution to the land problem, quite apart from the arrears detail which had had to be cleared up after Kilmainham. This flaw in the rent-fixing arrangements under the Act was that they made no allowance for bad harvests and for the consequent variable ability of tenants to pay even the new fixed rents. The years immediately after the Land Act saw good harvests, but when prices turned down again in the mid-eighties tenants were once again faced with the age-old dilemma of being unable to pay their rents in bad times, and thus vulnerable to the most terrible fate which could threaten the Irish peasant: eviction.

By the time this further renewal of the land crisis developed, Parnell's political mind was concentrated on the Home Rule issue, which was in a state of deadlock. After the heroic failure of the bill he had fallen back on one of his chief political tactics, which was to do nothing when there seemed nothing very obvious to do. It was also a time in his life when personal considerations, centring round his clandestine life with his English mistress in the south of England, pulled strongly against his involvement in day-to-day Irish matters. Captain O'Shea, husband of Parnell's mistress, whatever his attitude to the liaison may have been in the past, and whatever his reason may now have been, had decided to try to break it up and was putting strong pressure on his wife to leave Parnell.[7]

A political consideration was that, since on the Home Rule front Parnell had achieved the remarkable success of bringing one of the two political parties respectably on to his side, he was unwilling to involve himself in a land situation to any degree, which by its lack of respectability might prejudice that alliance. He therefore took a guarded and equivocal attitude to the land war, which in this second phase was run almost entirely by John Dillon and Parnell's own one-time acolyte, the journalist William O'Brien.

Dillon and O'Brien's offensive weapon, which epitomized this phase of the land war, was the so-called Plan of Campaign, an ingenious device by which tenants on estates where evictions were being carried out calculated what they could afford to pay in rent, offered this to the landlord, and if it was refused paid the money into a fund which was then used to defend and protect those threatened by eviction. The stir which this bitter and violent campaign, lasting several years, caused in the life of the country and on the British political scene was out of proportion to the actual number of holdings involved, which were only 116. Of these the landlords on sixty gave in at once, and on twenty-four more after a struggle; on fifteen they held out and won, while on the remaining seventeen the disputes were still unsettled by 1893.[2] But the political impact was considerable. The campaign was resisted by the new Conservative Chief Secretary for Ireland, Arthur Balfour, with unexpected toughness and severity, and Dillon, O'Brien and their henchmen, who often included parish priests, more than once landed in prison where they enjoyed no special privileges as political prisoners and were even forced to wear convict clothes.

As usual the land war had a two-way significance as regards Irish nationalism. On the one hand it showed how the everyday issue of the land, a social issue, took precedence in Irishmen's minds over the political national issue. No one, after all, took to violence or incurred prison sentences in protest against the rejection of Home Rule. On the other hand the bitterness of each phase of the land war consolidated emotional feeling against the government and indirectly strengthened general 'national' feelings. The Plan of Campaign was organized by the party organization, the National League, whose overall demand for Home Rule was strengthened by the bitterness aroused.

In such circumstances Home Rule might indeed have continued the dynamic it had developed in 1886 but for other special factors which intervened. One was the conscious Conservative policy of 'killing Home Rule by kindness', that is to say, combining coercive toughness against agrarian disorders with real concessions such as further Land Purchase Acts (in 1891 and 1896) and – a truly revolutionary measure for Ireland – the Local Government Act of 1898. This for the first time gave the Irish people a direct share in their own administration, taking local government power out of the hands of the old property-controlled grand juries and placing it in the hands of elective county councils. And though such measures did not in the end succeed in killing Home Rule they certainly did much to sap its

immediate vitality. But a surprise event did more than Conservative policy
to cause Home Rule to fade as a dynamic issue. This was the loss to the
Irish Parliamentary Party by his death in 1891 of Charles Stewart Parnell,
as the result of a most dramatic development.

Parnell's love affair with Katharine O'Shea had been going on since before
the days of the Kilmainham Treaty. Their relationship had undoubtedly by
the late eighties acquired in all but name that depth and significance of a
true marriage which Parnell himself liked to claim for it. She had borne
him two more children after the first child which had died in infancy soon
after his release from Kilmainham, and in their letters the two old-established
lovers liked to address each other as husband and wife. The only trouble
with this 'marriage' of Parnell was that his wife was married to someone
else for eight of the nine years it lasted, and that, since early in 1886 at any
rate, her legal husband had been trying to get her to give her lover up. It
was very typical of Parnell, and illustrative of that natural haughtiness which
he often turned to such effective use in politics, that neither of these facts
seems to have worried him unduly and he therefore assumed that they need
worry no one else. It seems certain, admittedly, that Katharine O'Shea convinced Parnell early on that O'Shea was a complaisant husband and her
marriage with him one in name only. A complicating factor was the need
to keep the situation concealed from an old rich aunt of Mrs O'Shea's, a
Mrs Benjamin Wood, who intended to leave her a fortune. It is possible
that Katharine O'Shea may have successfully concealed from Parnell for
some time after 1886 the fact that Captain O'Shea was by then insisting on
the affair being broken up. But even if Parnell could have pleaded the total
complaisance of Captain O'Shea it was a situation unlikely to commend
itself to the moral outlook of either Liberal nonconformist England or of
Catholic Ireland.

Early in 1886 O'Shea seems to have got wind of charges then being prepared in certain Conservative quarters and subsequently to be ventilated in
The Times newspaper, to the effect that Parnell had written a clandestine
letter of sympathy to the Phoenix Park murderers after that gruesome event
in 1882,* assuring them that his denunciation of them had been merely for
show. Thereafter, O'Shea developed something of a frenzy in his efforts to
get his wife and Parnell to separate. This seems to substantiate the contention
that his chief objection to the affair was fear of the loss of the Wood fortune,
for if he already dreaded Mrs Wood getting wind of her favourite niece's
intimate association with Parnell – and we know he did – how much more
disastrous would have been the consequences if she had discovered that
such an intimate association was with an accessory after the fact to a particularly appalling political murder?

---

* See above, p. 383.

In 1889 the rich aunt, Mrs Wood, died. Later that year O'Shea brought proceedings for divorce. He cited only the period from 1886, thus making Parnell look particularly guilty, however much complaisance may or may not have been an earlier feature of the affair, for letters produced in court proved clearly that ever since that date O'Shea had been trying to persuade his wife to leave Parnell.

Parnell's personal standing with the British and Irish public had been particularly high when the divorce action broke; his fall now was to be all the greater. Only a year before he had been personally cleared of the Phoenix Park charges by a specially-appointed Government Commission. The allegedly incriminating letter, which had been reproduced in *The Times*, was found to have been forged by a nationalist journalist, Richard Piggott, a man at one time of some consequence in near-Fenian quarters but whom personal insolvency had increasingly obliged to exploit nationalism for financial advantage.

Right up to the hearing of the divorce case Parnell seems to have been confident that its revelations could do him no harm, and during the year that had elapsed between the serving of the divorce papers and the action's hearing he had continually reassured his colleagues and associates that it would not affect his political career. His confidence seems to have been based at least partly on his conviction of the utter moral propriety of his own behaviour. Partly, however, it was also based on the belief that O'Shea could be bought off, for Mrs Wood had duly bequeathed Mrs O'Shea the expected fortune. But the Wood family had disputed the will and at the last minute neither Mrs O'Shea nor Parnell could lay their hands on the necessary £20,000 which O'Shea seems to have been demanding.

The humiliating details of deception and dissimulation by Parnell – false names and other ruses traditional in such triangular situations – duly emerged in the courts. Parnell to the end maintained a defiant confidence that by character and political strength he could brazen the thing through. In this he proved wrong and received the only major political setback of his life, though if he had lived it is not inconceivable that he would have been proved right in the end.

For a moment, even so, it seemed that his strength might triumph. Immediately after the result of the divorce case the Irish party passed a unanimous vote of confidence in Parnell's leadership. But then something happened to turn the name of Mrs O'Shea into more than a mere cause of scandal in Irish history. Gladstone, though he personally had almost certainly known of the liaison between Mrs O'Shea and Parnell for many years, was made aware of such strong feeling of revulsion over the divorce details from his nonconformist supporters in the country that he issued a statement of the most profound importance. Parnell's continued leadership of the Irish Parliamentary Party, he said, was likely to render his own leadership of the Liberal

Party 'almost a nullity'. In other words, the Irish must choose between Parnell's continued leadership of the Irish party and the party's continued alliance with Gladstone in the cause of Home Rule.

Frightened by this the party, after a long and agonizing debate full of mutual invective in Committee Room 15 of the House of Commons, went back on its original unanimous decision and voted 45–29 against Parnell's continued leadership. Though Parnell refused to accept this result, nominal leadership of the majority of the party now passed to Justin McCarthy, a pleasant but uncommanding figure more at ease in literature than politics. The most effective character on the anti-Parnell side had been Tim Healy. Healy it was who in reply to a Parnellite supporter's interjection that Gladstone seemed to be the master of the party, called out viciously in front of Parnell, 'Who is to be the mistress of the party?'

Blows were nearly struck in Committee Room 15 and certainly were struck in the succession of bitter by-election battles that soon followed in Ireland between Parnellite and anti-Parnellite nationalists. Much of the newly mobilized national energy of the Home Rule movement now drained away into this dismal and vindictive quarrel between the two halves of the great national party which Parnell had brought so high.

Having, in his day, fought the House of Commons to a standstill on behalf of Ireland, Parnell was suddenly now at bay in his own country, taking on the greater part of his own party and the enormously powerful political influence, previously on his side, of the Catholic Church. His principal tactic had been from the first one of breath-taking arrogance, but of the sort that might have been expected of him, and well designed to appeal again to his earlier allies, the 'hillside' men and so-called 'ribbon-Fenians'. He seized on that aspect of Gladstone's statement which could be expected to divert attention from his own personal behaviour and indignantly challenged on behalf of Ireland the right of any English politician to lay down to Irishmen who should or should not be their leader, simultaneously vilifying any Irishmen who might slavishly acquiesce in such dictation. At the same time, he magnificently confused the issue by suddenly purporting to reveal that when he had stayed at Gladstone's home at Hawarden in Yorkshire some months earlier and had discussed with the Grand Old Man the terms of the next Home Rule Bill which a Liberal government would introduce when next returned to power, these had turned out to be humiliating to Ireland and a retreat on the provisions of the 1886 bill.

The obvious retort to this – and one that was made by Healy and co. – was to ask why such an important fact had not been revealed before, and Gladstone himself issued a denial of the conversations as recounted by Parnell. But drawing once again on the full force of his political strength, Parnell swept such objections and all references to his personal conduct aside, and continued to try and fight on the ground of his own choosing, namely, whether or not the Liberal alliance should be supported if the price was to be English dictatorship on terms detrimental to a good Home Rule Bill. It was a political manoeuvre and *tour de force* of astonishing daring but of no avail. Making the laborious journey to Ireland via Euston and Holyhead from Brighton where he lived with the former Katharine O'Shea, now his legal wife, he campaigned week after week in support of his own candidates in three consecutive by-elections, all of which he decisively lost. At one of them lime was thrown in his eyes. He fought on more savagely than ever.

On Sunday, 27 September 1891, he spoke at a meeting in pouring rain in County Galway, bareheaded and with one arm, crippled by rheumatism, in a sling. The change of clothes which Katharine Parnell had packed for him was somehow mislaid and he sat about for several hours in his wet suit. He then went to Dublin where he spent a few days before leaving for England on Wednesday, 30 September, saying he would be back on 'Saturday week'. He was a few hours out in his forecast. He died at Brighton with his wife by his side on 10 October, and his body was brought into Kingstown harbour on Sunday morning, 11 October, and buried in Glasnevin cemetery. The chances of Home Rule for the next twenty years were buried with him.

The split in the party caused by the O'Shea divorce was damaging enough while Parnell was still alive. But he was at least a political giant, a man who, so long as he remained upon the scene, might have achieved anything. With his sudden death, which shocked both friends and enemies equally, as if all recognized the profound change in the quality of political life it heralded, the dispute between them degenerated into a squalid and sterile internecine warfare that lasted the better part of ten years. Most of the energies which needed to be devoted to the Home Rule cause, if it was to be pursued successfully in the extremely difficult English political situation of the day, were turned inwards in this self-consuming Irish quarrel. And the dynamic of the relatively new nationalist movement which had survived the rejection of the first Home Rule Bill with such self-confidence failed to develop properly under the effects of such an apparently insatiable cancer.

The period that followed the death of Parnell in 1891 is often described as a political vacuum. In one sense this is accurate. Politically, there had been only two giants in Ireland in the nineteenth century: O'Connell and Parnell. Now Parnell was gone, and it was not so much the split in the party that was the cause of the vacuum after his death as the fact that there was no man on either side of the split to make Home Rule the vital issue Parnell could have continued to make it.

What is unsatisfactory about the vacuum description is the argument for which it has sometimes been made the premise: namely, that the Parliamentary Party was itself now a meaningless and vacuous institution and its final demise inevitable. This was by no means so. Home Rule remained the only viable national ideal for the vast majority of the Irish people and the party's collapse when it came many years later was in fact quite sudden and, until 1916, not even seriously expected. It was the men who proved inadequate – not the cause.

6

Second Home Rule Bill: Orangemen at Play

The level to which political passions in Ireland descended after the Parnell split may be gauged from a sermon preached at Roundwood, County Wicklow, by the parish priest just before the General Election of 1892.

'Parnellism,' he told his flock, 'is a simple love of adultery and all those who profess Parnellism profess to love and admire adultery. They are an adulterous set, their leaders are open and avowed adulterers, and therefore I say to you, as parish priest, beware of these Parnellites when they enter your house, you that have wives and daughters, for they will do all they can to commit these adulteries, for their cause is not patriotism – it is adultery – and they back Parnellism because it gratifies their adultery.'[1]

At the election only nine 'Parnellite' nationalists were elected (under the leadership of John Redmond), against seventy-one 'anti-Parnellites'. But the disarray of the Home Rule party was to be far greater than these figures suggest. For among the anti-Parnellites themselves personal rivalries, jealousies and animosities soon brought about a further inward dispersal of political energies. Among the anti-Parnellites there were to be Healyites, Dillonites and O'Brienites, all at first precariously kept together under the compromise leadership of the literary figure Justin McCarthy.

Faction fighting at Irish fairs had been a perennial feature of Irish national life. Soon this was proceeding on a national scale. The internal political partisanship it bred was felt more keenly than the national cause itself. This correspondingly began to go by default, though that it could do so was in itself evidence of a lack of coherent nationalism widely felt. There was almost certainly more truth than most nationalists would have admitted in the words of the Irish peer Lord Muskerry, who, speaking in 1893 from the experience of seventeen years' residence among tenant farmers in the south-west of Ireland, contended that they had no particular desire for Home Rule. 'Why should they,' he added, 'under the present system of land confiscation?' Discounting the pejorative bias in his definition of the land purchase revolution there was some sense in the remark.

Yet so long as Gladstone himself was alive and leader of the Liberal Party, it was impossible for Home Rule to become a wholly remote issue. He personally was totally committed to it in a way no other Liberal leader was ever to be again, and when he formed his last government in August 1892 at the age of eighty-three it was the major issue with which he concerned himself.

His second Home Rule Bill was similar in its limitations on Irish sovereignty to that of 1886. In a special preamble it declared the Westminster Parliament to be supreme; decisions on foreign affairs, trade, customs and excise and all ability to form military or naval forces were specifically removed from the proposed domestic Irish Government's powers. This time there were to be two separate chambers in the Parliament, each with a veto over the other. One chamber, the Legislative Council, created to help protect minority Protestant rights, was to be elected from a special 'constituency', as Gladstone called it, composed of electors with a special property qualification, and was to consist of 48 members. The other chamber, elected by the normal electorate, was to be the Legislative Assembly, consisting of 103 members from the usual constituencies. The chief difference between this bill and that of 1886 was that this time Irish members, to the number of 80, were to be retained at Westminster, partly as an outward manifestation of the supremacy of the Imperial Parliament, and partly as a means of allowing the Irish some say in imperial affairs.

All the old arguments for and against Home Rule were put forward on both sides. The Unionists said that the safeguard for the Protestant minority allegedly contained in the Legislative Council was quite inadequate. Though the special 'constituency' to elect it was to consist of only one in six of the total electorate, the qualification for this – a £20 rating value – was only half that of the common juror and his verdicts were often of a notoriously 'national' tinge. One Unionist claimed that the Legislative Council would in fact be composed of that very class of tenant farmer who was 'most under the influence of the Roman Catholic clergy'. It would, he claimed, be 'a priests' house'.[2]

But, as before, the chief argument against the bill was that it represented the thin end of the wedge of separation. As in 1886, the Unionists used the very feebleness of the bill's appeal to Irish national aspirations as an argument against any likelihood of it proving a permanent settlement. 'You told them,' said the Conservative leader Balfour, 'that they are a nation and that they deserve the treatment of a nation, and now you put them off with a constitution which does not only not make them a nation, but which puts them immeasurably below the smallest self-governing colony in this empire. How can you expect that they ... are really content with the measure of Home Rule you put before them?'[3]

The Irish, however, as in 1886, again insisted that though they might wish for changes in certain details, they regarded the satisfaction of national demands in the bill as adequate and demanded no more. Thomas Sexton, one of the ablest of the anti-Parnellites, delivered a eulogy of Gladstone, saying that he had secured beyond all change the gratitude of the Irish people. The first Home Rule Bill, he said, 'had been accepted by the Irish party and by the Irish people and their race throughout the world as the basis of a permanent settlement', and the present bill was 'on the whole a better plan than that of 1886 ...'. 'The supremacy of the Imperial Parliament,' he conceded, 'exists and cannot be altered.'⁴ Michael Davitt, who now sat in Parliament for Cork N.E., confirmed this view: 'The overwhelming majority of the Irish people and the Irish race abroad, as well as at home, accepted the Bill of 1886 as a satisfactory settlement of the Irish question and would have acted loyally upon that acceptance if the bill had become law. I assert the same of this bill now before the House. I go further and say that thirteen million of the Irish race, scattered round this world, will accept the bill as a pact of peace between Ireland and the Empire to be honourably upheld on both sides.' And later in his speech he called the bill 'an honourable and lasting compact between the people of Ireland and Great Britain'.⁵

Redmond, for the nine Parnellites, was expected to be more intransigent on the national issue. But he, too, made clear, on the first reading of the bill, that its severe limitations to what might be thought normal national aspirations were accepted by the Irish people. He went so far as to state categorically his willingness 'to accept a measure of this kind, based on the validity of the Act of Union and acknowledging the supremacy of the Imperial Parliament ...' adding, 'We have never asked for the curtailment of the Imperial Parliament under a Home Rule scheme.'⁶ On the second reading Redmond said candidly that he did not expect the bill, if passed, to be 'absolutely final or immutable', but thought that the constitutional principle involved would be a success and, because a success, would involve some development.

The leader of the anti-Parnellite group, Justin McCarthy, reinforced the solemnity of his own acceptance of the bill in similarly realistic terms. 'Although,' he said, on the second reading, 'no generation can pretend to bind all future generations – for the time may come when the whole constitution of these countries may be changed – all we say is this, that so far as our foresight will enable us to look into the future, we do believe that the measure when duly improved in committee, will be, for all events for our time, a final settlement of the Irish question.'⁷ And on the third reading, after the committee stage, he was if anything even more emphatic: 'I do not believe,' he said, '... that there will ever be the slightest desire on the part of the Irish people to break away from the principle of this great settlement.'⁸

Some Unionists undoubtedly were genuinely convinced that such statements were made only for the benefit of an English audience. But every Irish politician knew that for remarks made in the House of Commons he was answerable not so much to Westminster as to Ireland itself. No Irish politician would have dared give such categorical assurances on such an emotive issue if they had not substantially represented the Irish public opinion of the day.

On the third reading Redmond, for the small group of Parnellites, was less enthusiastic than he had been at first. He was deeply disappointed by alterations to financial provisions of the bill which had been made in committee. 'As the bill now stands ...' he said, 'no man in his senses can any longer regard it either as a full, a final or a satisfactory settlement of the Irish National Question. The word "provisional" has, so to speak, been stamped over every page of the bill' and he drew attention to the fact that a gathering of his own party in Dublin had come to the same conclusion.[9] However, the gathering of his own party, the National League, had voted overwhelmingly for support of the third reading and the small extent to which even their limited dissatisfaction was representative of public opinion can be partly gauged from the position of their Independent Home Rule Fund at the time. This stood at only £2,516 in August 1893 and was increasing at the rate of about £12 a fortnight at the time of the bill's rejection.[10]

John Dillon, by virtue of his vigorous activity in the land war, in both its Land League and Plan of Campaign phases, had at least as much right to speak for belligerent nationalism as Redmond. He maintained a diametrically opposite view on the question of the bill's finality: '... this bill,' he said in answer to Redmond, 'so far from settling nothing, is a great Charter of liberty to the people of Ireland, and they will accept it in that sense'. Finality, he said, was an impossible thing to accept with any law but '... if by finality we are to mean, as I think we ought to mean, that the people of Ireland ... would accept it, if passed into law, in good faith as a settlement of the National claims of Ireland, I say I believe they would.... We accept the supremacy of this [the Imperial] Parliament, and I am not aware that any considerable section of the Irish people wish to deny it.'[11]

Not only the branches of the National Federation bore him out. The *Freeman's Journal* expressed its confirmation of this point of view most fulsomely.

'Beyond all question,' it wrote, 'the bill will give to Ireland the substance of all that her patriots fought for through the long centuries.'[12]

This was of course a travesty of the truth. Who could possibly imagine that Tone, Lord Edward Fitzgerald, Emmet, Davis, O'Connell, Mitchel, Stephens, Allen, Larkin and O'Brien would have accepted the supremacy of the Westminster Parliament as a satisfactory final settlement of the Irish National Question? Yet the writer not only confidently assumed that the statement was reasonable but also correctly, that almost everyone else would think so too. A woolly imprecision still remained one of Irish nationalism's salient characteristics.

Meanwhile, other 'patriotic' Irishmen, the Protestant minority with their special concentration in the north-east corner of Ulster, were anything but content with this 'national' status envisaged for them.

The mobilization of Ulster opinion had this time been organized on a far more impressive scale than in 1886. In the spring of 1892, even before Gladstone had taken office again, but when it seemed probable that he would soon do so, an 'Ulster Unionist Convention', consisting of delegates elected from the electoral rolls of every district in the province, was summoned to Belfast. The convention met in a special wooden pavilion constructed in three weeks on the plains beside the Botanical Gardens, Belfast, on Friday, 17 June 1892. It was to be a landmark in Ulster history. The main streets were decked with flags and bunting; hotels and all other available accommodation were booked up days beforehand, and crowds poured into the city by every train and steamer.[13]

Four thousand of the twelve thousand delegates who attended were tenant farmers, and most of the rest businessmen. Few came from the landed classes, who were nevertheless well represented among the four hundred or so leading Unionists on the platform. The whole convention met under the chairmanship of the Duke of Abercorn. Above the platform were the arms of Great Britain and the words of the Poet Laureate:

> One with Great Britain, heart and soul
> One life, one flag, one fleet, one throne.

All around the walls of the pavilion hung numerous shields and appropriate mottoes, including an unfortunate quotation from the Gladstonian Liberal Lord Spencer, dating from before his leader's conversion to Home Rule. This ran: 'We feel like the Americans when the integrity of their country was threatened, and if necessary we must shed blood to maintain the strength and salvation of the country.'

A number of resolutions were passed by the convention. The first asserted Ulster's status as an integral portion of the United Kingdom and declared that the convention met 'to protest in the most unequivocal manner against the passage of any measure that would rob us of our inheritance in the Imperial Parliament, under the protection of which our capital has been invested and our homes and rights safeguarded'.

A second resolution expressed a determination to have nothing to do with a Parliament 'certain to be controlled by men responsible for the crime and outrage of the Land League, the dishonesty of the Plan of Campaign and the cruelties of boycotting, many of whom have shown themselves the ready instruments of clerical domination'.

A third resolution had a more positive inference. The attempt, it declared, to subject Ulster to a Parliament run by such men would 'inevitably result in disorder, violence and bloodshed such as have not been experienced in this century' and the convention resolved to take no part in the election of or the proceedings of such a Parliament, which they would repudiate. When the Duke of Abercorn, with upraised arm, declared 'We will not have Home Rule', the whole audience sprang to their feet and cheered for several minutes. But the greatest cheers of all were reserved for another speaker who in trumpet tones pronounced, 'As a last resource we will be prepared to defend ourselves.' At this, in the words of *The Times'* man on the spot, 'the feelings of the spectators appeared to lose all control'. It was not surprising that after attending such an impressive and enthusiastic gathering he should conclude emphatically that these were 'men to be reckoned with'.[14]

Their political opponents took them less seriously. Shortly before the convention Colonel Saunderson, the parliamentary leader of the Ulstermen, whose activities had earned him a place in Mme Tussaud's as long ago as 1888,[15] invited the Gladstonian Liberal, Sir William Harcourt, over to Belfast to see for himself the stuff of which the Ulstermen were really made. Harcourt had declined in bantering tones.

> I understand [he wrote] that your June review is rather in the nature of a preliminary review with a regard to future contingencies than an immediate call to arms with a view to instant hostilities. ... When your hypothetical insurrection is a little more advanced and war is actually declared, I may perhaps take advantage of your offer and solicit a place as spectator on your staff. I do not know if your plan of campaign contemplates a march upon London against the Crown and Parliament; if so, I might meet you half-way at Derby, which was the place where the Liberals of the last century encountered the 'loyal and patriotic' Highlanders who disapproved of the 'Act of Settlement' and resolved to resist it. ... I presume that might be the point where the rebel army would effect its junction with the ducal contingent from Chatsworth under the command of the Lord-Lieutenant of the county ...[16]

The Duke of Devonshire, as a prominent southern Irish land-owner, though unable to be present at the convention had expressed his total sympathy with its objects. But it was to be many years yet before the combination of the Ulstermen with the English upper classes and Conservative Party were to turn this sort of joke, so typical of the Liberals' attitude for so long, against them.

As Gladstone went ahead with his bill the Protestant Ulstermen exercised their verbal licence to the full. Their forefathers, proclaimed Colonel Saunderson in December 1892, held the walls of Derry; they would hold the gates. Their opponents wished them to leave those gates ajar; but they would have no Home Rule of any kind or any description. They rejected the policy of Home Rule not simply as Protestants but as Irishmen. ...[17] And in January 1893, at a great meeting in Belfast under the auspices of the Ulster Convention League, the Grand Master of the Belfast Orangemen, Dr Cane, while thanking God that they still had the House of Lords, reminded his audience that they also still had their own right arms and that if ejected from the Union 'they would carve out for themselves their new destiny'.[18] It was, he said, going to be quite different from the Church Disestablishment crisis, for on that issue Protestants had been divided and now they were united.

In Parliament, too, from the beginning the Ulster Unionists stated their position without equivocation. In the debate on the queen's speech in the House of Lords, the Marquess of Londonderry made it clear that he thought the men of Ulster would be justified in shedding blood 'to resist the disloyal Catholic yoke'.[19] Saunderson's own harangue in the Commons on the occasion of the bill's first reading contains an almost prophetic note.

'You have,' he said – conveniently forgetting his allies in the House of Lords for the sake of rhetorical effect – 'the power, I admit, to pass your Home Rule Bill and to create this Dublin Parliament and this government, but you have not the power to make us obey it.' The statement was greeted with a laugh, from the Home Rule benches. 'Allow me to tell them,' Saunderson cried, 'that before the Army of Great Britain is employed to shoot down the Irish loyalists you must have a British majority at your back.' What would happen, he asked, if Dillon, Healy and O'Brien started 'issuing orders, perhaps to Lord Wolseley, to march with the Army of the Curragh to shoot down Ulstermen? It requires,' concluded Saunderson, 'an imagination far greater than mine to conceive such a possibility.'[20]

Saunderson's implication that a purely British majority exclusive of Ireland, and not just an overall United Kingdom majority, was necessary for Home Rule before it could be constitutionally acceptable was to become an important part of anti-Home Rule doctrine. But it was a curious one for Unionists to employ whose chief constitutional tenet was after all that Ireland was indistinguishably merged in the Union.

As the bill proceeded through its various stages in the House of Commons the temperature in Belfast continued to rise. The appeal by a Derry Justice of the Peace to the men of Belfast 'to strike the note at the proper time and unfurl the flag, and call upon their fellow Loyalists to arm'[21] was hardly necessary. In Belfast, William Johnston holding up an open Bible received from a vast audience a vociferous and solemn pledge against Home Rule. Saunderson himself initiated an Ulster Defence Union and began to receive both arms and many offers of armed support from England. A general officer wrote to *The Times* demanding that the position of army officers should be made clear in the event of a conflict of loyalties in any possible civil war. One retired cavalry officer told Saunderson that he would advise his three sons to resign their commissions at once in such an event. Further shapes of things to come were outlined when Balfour, the Conservative leader, visited Belfast to watch a march past of some eighty thousand Ulster Loyalists. In words which were to be echoed with even greater force by another Conservative leader nearly twenty years later, Balfour declaimed:

'I do not come here to preach any doctrines of passive obedience or non-resistance. You have had to fight for your liberties before. [A Voice: 'And will again!' – cheers.] I pray God you may never have to fight for them again. I do not believe you will ever have to fight for them, but I admit that the tyranny of majorities may be as bad as the tyranny of Kings and that the stupidity of majorities may be even greater than the stupidity of Kings ... and I do not think any rational or sober man will say that what is justifiable against a tyrannical King may not under certain circumstances be justifiable against a tyrannical majority.'[22]

It would be hard to formulate a more succinct derogation of the whole principle underlying parliamentary democracy.

The Ulster Defence Union had made plans for an Ulster Assembly of six hundred delegates to be elected from among its own Unionist members. These six hundred were then to elect a council of forty to which would be added Ulster members of Parliament and Ulster peers as *ex officio* members making something very like a provisional government.[23]

'If,' word had gone out from the Orangemen of Belfast, 'If, which God forbid, we are forbidden to advance in the way of legislative union, then we most earnestly and solemnly desired to do as our fathers did, and, with trust in the God who inspired men to battle for truth and light, it will be our duty to take the path of self-reliance and insist on their right to carve out the future for ourselves.'[24] And the Orangemen resolved that they would resist an Irish Parliament and its new executive 'by every means in our power ... we will not recognize their officers, nor obey their laws, nor pay the taxes which they may pretend to impose ... come weal, come woe, we will stand by the Legislative Union if we have to fight over again the Battle of the Boyne.'[25]

What made it easier to laugh off rather than take too seriously this theoretically ugly situation was the knowledge that, though the bill was likely to pass in the House of Commons, it was certain to be rejected in the House of Lords. The contingency for which such theoretical preparations were being made was itself theoretical and remote. The statement made the previous year by a Belfast Unionist to the effect that Mr Gladstone had no more power to pass Home Rule than he had to install waterworks on the moon was not altogether a ludicrous one.[26]

The 1893 Home Rule Bill eventually occupied more parliamentary time than any other bill in the history of the century – eighty-two days altogether compared with forty-seven for the Reform Bill. Four hundred and thirty-nine speeches were made for it in the Commons and nine hundred and thirty-eight against. It passed the House of Commons on its third reading in the early morning of 2 September by a majority of 34. Everyone knew that

the Lords would reject it, which they did after four nights' debate in the
early morning of 9 September by 419 votes to 41. The margin in favour in
the Commons itself had been far too small for Gladstone to feel confident
enough to go to the country on the issue, and he did not dissolve Parliament.
Soon afterwards, however, he retired from the Liberal leadership, giving
place to Lord Rosebery whose dislike for Home Rule in the prevailing political situation was barely concealed. Gladstone did not die until 19 May 1898.
By then Home Rule as a real prospect as opposed to a political slogan had
already disappeared from view for the foreseeable future. But on the occasion of Gladstone's death John Dillon paid a well-deserved tribute to that
great Englishman who while he 'loved his own people as much as any
Englishman that ever lived ... acquired that wider and greater gift, the power
of understanding and sympathizing with other peoples'.[27] It was a dimension
of patriotism which had escaped and was to continue to escape every other
major English statesman who concerned himself with Ireland. For the
absence of it in future England was to pay dearly.

7
Nationalists at Ease

The relative complacency with which news of the Lords' rejection of the Home Rule Bill was received in Ireland epitomized the lack of urgency which was soon a characteristic of the Home Rule movement. One might perhaps have expected some prepared, even menacing, reaction to this blow at national aspirations, a display of resentment at least analogous to that of the Ulstermen when they regarded *their* rights as threatened. Some Irish speakers in the Home Rule debate had indeed hinted darkly at the violence that might follow if Ireland's wishes were thwarted. But absolutely nothing of the sort occurred. The branches of the National Federation sent in their congratulations to their parliamentary representatives and to Gladstone and his Liberals on their performances.[1] The *Freeman's Journal* reminded its readers that defeat in the Lords had been the forerunner of every great measure of reform that had ever taken place. It raised a laugh by singling out from the enormous hostile majority of peers Lord Hadley, who had returned to London after two and a half years shooting big game beyond the Zambesi to pass judgement on the Irish people.[2] Hopes were pinned, fairly unrealistically, on the results of the next General Election.

This took place in the summer of 1895 and, in the words of Gladstone's disciple John Morley, a third Home Rule Bill was 'expressly, deliberately before the electors in the very forefront of our programme'.[3] The result was an overwhelming Conservative victory and the Conservatives were to remain in office for ten years. Yet while accepting that 'Home Rule in 1895 had lost the enormous headway it made between 1886 and 1892' the *Freeman's Journal* still saw 'no grounds for despondency', and in an even self-congratulatory tone noted from the election results that Ireland itself was 'as much for Home Rule in 1895 as in 1892, and even more so'.[4]

The same note of papery optimism was to be sustained in the face of discouraging realities for many years, imparting a certain artificiality to the concept of the cause itself. The blunt truth had been stated by Redmond, who himself much later was to pay for forgetting its implications. They were, he said, in 1894, 'face to face with the ruin of the Home Rule cause . . . any measure of autonomy must be hung up till the English cared to give it'.[5]

With no alternative but to accept this state of affairs Irish politicians in-creasingly talked as if the real state of affairs were somehow different. All that was needed, said William O'Brien in 1895, was for Redmond to re-unite with the Irish party and 'the Irish party would use their victory to-morrow not for the purpose of trampling over or upon any of their fellow countrymen but for the purpose of pressing all good and honest Irish nationalists into one solid phalanx under the old flag to prove to England that the spirit of Irish nationality might be conciliated but never could be conquered or subdued'.[6]

The anniversary of the centenary of the rebellion of 1798 at the very nadir of the parliamentary party's fortunes in 1898 proved further what flights of fancy could do with Home Rule even if politicians themselves remained earthbound.

Arrangements for the centenary were in fact made by an Executive Com-mittee brought into being by the IRB, which flickered into apparently in-nocuous life for the occasion. President of the committee was the aged literary Fenian John O'Leary, long considered harmless enough to be allowed to live in Ireland, as indeed was now the old chief himself, James Stephens, whose permission to return to Ireland had been obtained from the govern-ment by Parnell himself shortly before his death.[7] Stephens, however, who was to survive Parnell by ten years, was only allowed to return on condition that he took no part in public life, and it was the incumbent 'President of the Irish Republic' in the person of F. J. Allan who figured on the Executive Committee of the '98 Centenary Celebrations with O'Leary. Clubs with evocative names were formed to help: Wolfe Tone clubs in many cases, but others were named after Father Murphy, Oliver Bond, Lord Edward Fitz-gerald, Napper Tandy, the Sheares brothers, Michael Dwyer and other heroes of a hundred years before.

The Nationalist Parliamentary Party, both Parnellites and anti-Parnellites as they still were, were soon in on the performance. The spirit of their par-ticipation was typified early by J. Jordan, the MP for Fermanagh, S., who declared at Belfast in June: 'Let them ungrudgingly celebrate the centenary of '98, and, inspired with the principles of the heroes of that time, let them too with constitutional weapons in their hands perform deeds of daring for the full enfranchisement of their native land.'[8] He was greeted with loud cheers. John Dillon said that 'every advance . . . made in asserting the liberty of Ireland or of any other nationality has been a triumph for the principles of the United Irishmen'.[9]

But to claim that most of the humble and bewildered peasants of a hundred years before had died asserting the liberty of Ireland or the purity of Irish nationality was an unjustifiable stretch of the historical imagination. Further, to equate the cause with which the United Irishmen tried to inspire the peasantry with the Parliamentary Party's own sophisticated brand of limited nationality known as Home Rule was little better than a historical confidence trick. It was one which the party practised shamelessly.

J. F. K. O'Brien, the victor of Ballyknockane barracks in 1867, declared to Irishmen in London in June 1898 that the struggle for Irish liberty which was carried on in the present generation was the same struggle in which the men of '98 were engaged, and it was their duty to carry on the struggle in the best way they could as long as life remained to them.[10]

The respectable *Freeman's Journal* equally blandly declared that wherever a croppy's grave was known, faithful hands would 'strew it with the flowers of an Irish summer', and eulogized Wolfe Tone as 'the grandest of Ireland's heroes'.[11]

In Dublin a great demonstration took place in memory of Tone himself. The day was virtually regarded as a bank holiday. Many establishments, as the *Freeman's Journal* reported, gave their employees 'the opportunity of fulfilling what to them was a patriotic duty'.[12] Dillon, the anti-Parnellite Party's Chairman, was present together with Redmond, leader of the Parnellite group, and eleven other MPs. Green banners were on display, one carrying the slogan 'Remember '98, '48, '65, '67'. The Dublin Trades Association all took part in the procession – coal labourers, book-binders, poulterers, gentlemen's bootmakers, etc. – and the pawnbrokers' assistants in particular 'made a very good turn out'. John O'Leary presided over the laying of a foundation stone for a memorial in St Stephen's Green, recalling that he himself had been in the dock thirty-three years before. The poet Yeats made a surprisingly cliché-ridden speech about the inextinguishable fire of patriotism rising like smoke from the breasts of the peasantry. Later, together with Maud Gonne, a beautiful Protestant upper-class Irish girl who had identified herself with extreme nationalist politics, and F. J. Allan of the IRB, Dillon, Redmond and other national and municipal figures, Yeats attended the Lord Mayor's banquet.

At Sligo William O'Brien cried: 'Let us prove by our lives and our actions that the fight of the men of '98 is not over yet. Let us show the world once more that the core and essence of the Irish question is this – that the relations between this country and our English rulers are the relations of civil war just as real as if it were carried on with firearms.' His words were greeted with loud cheers.

Dillon, speaking on Oulart Hill, claimed to sound a realistic note. 'Times have changed,' he warned, 'and the pikes which your forefathers used in the battle of Oulart ... would now be of little avail in your hands.... Why,' he added, 'they could drop shells here from the sea on us under modern conditions!' But his conclusion that they must not forget the principles of the men of '98 and that 'a free Ireland, a free nation, the mistress of her own destinies is the only complete and true monument to the memory of these men' combined oddly with the realities of those Home Rule Bills he was sincerely able to regard as a final settlement of the Irish national question.

This sort of double talk was eventually to rebound on the party in several ways. In the first place it enabled the party to deceive itself and by unending self-indulgence in such pseudo-heroics to believe that it embraced as much national vigour as it supposed. Second, it sickened those who saw through the intellectual dishonesty and thus sent some of the Nationalist Party's supporters off in search of other leaders. Third, while reviving talk of the principles of the United Irishmen and the Fenians as clichés, it gave them renewed currency without being able to ensure that they would always remain mere clichés.

At the end of August 1898 there appeared a small item of news to the effect that a man named H. H. Wilson had been released from Portland Gaol. This man whose release had been granted as part of a centenary amnesty had been serving a life sentence for his role in an unsuccessful dynamiting campaign organized from America in the early 1880s. He was a small, rather insignificant figure, prematurely aged at forty by the harshness of a prison life which had driven at least one of his fellow conspirators mad but which he had endured with spirit unbroken. He must have seemed at the time a very minor figure in the mythological hierarchy then being evoked. He was soon to emigrate to America again. Yet he was to constitute one of the few tenuous links eventually binding the centenary proceedings to reality. Even his real name was not then known for Wilson was a pseudonym he had adopted for his dynamiting operations fifteen years before. As Thomas J. Clarke he was to be the first signatory on the proclamation of an Irish Republic in 1916.

In 1900 the party became technically re-united under the new chairmanship of John Redmond. But personal quarrels between the leading figures continued, and the reunion was of small immediate benefit to the cause of Home Rule because, as Redmond himself had said, this was now entirely dependent on the English political scene. The Conservatives who returned to office for a second consecutive term in 1900 were unaffected by the reunion, while the Liberals after the death of Gladstone came swiftly to regard Home Rule much more as an embarrassing electoral liability than a noble cause.

In Ireland, 'national aspirations' – in so far as preoccupation with the Land Purchase revolution left time for any – lived a life of the imagination, partly within the otherwise increasingly sterile clichés of the Home Rule cause and partly in new forms altogether.

8
Growth of National Consciousness

Although Home Rule so soon became politically impracticable and remote, the idea itself had produced an atmosphere in which national consciousness in its own right began to grow. The movement which came generally to be known as the Irish Ireland movement or Irish revival is often regarded as a reaction from the apathy caused by the party's political ineffectualness after the Parnell split. But it would be truer to say that it coincided in the first place with the first waves of enthusiasm for the Home Rule movement and later continued to flourish on its own account as the political aim lacked lustre and receded.

Arthur Griffith himself, at this time an obscure young compositor but in thirty years to become first President of an 'Irish Free State', was one of the very few young men of this period eventually to look for actual political alternatives to Home Rule, but his national consciousness stemmed originally from the Home Rule movement when Home Rule seemed a close probability.

Already at the time of the introduction of the second Home Rule Bill he was writing newspaper articles on 'Notable Graves Round Dublin', and joining Celtic literary societies with his friend William Rooney.[1]

Earlier still, a Gaelic Athletic Association had been founded by a prosperous civil service crammer named Michael Cusack, under the patronage of Archbishop Croke of Cashel. It was the Archbishop himself who had defined the association's aims as being to remedy 'a parlous state of national pastimes and the consequent decline in national virility' and to replace tennis, croquet, cricket, polo, 'and other foreign and fantastic field sports' by Gaelic football and hurley. The association had actually held its first meeting at Thurles in County Tipperary in November 1884, before even the introduction of the first Home Rule Bill. By 1889 it had achieved a membership of over fifty thousand,[2] spreading a simple pride in Irish-consciousness for its own sake over large areas of the countryside.

It was also two years before Parnell's death – when in fact Parnell was at the height of his reputation – that a young poet, W. B. Yeats, born of a

Protestant family in County Sligo, made an accurate analysis of something else then happening in Ireland. 'A true literary consciousness – national to the centre – seems gradually to be forming...' he wrote. 'We are preparing likely enough for a new literary movement like that of '48 that will show itself in the first lull in politics.'[3]

Yeats was referring to a series of books, revealing the largely forgotten wealth of Irish historic legend and folk tales, that had begun to make an appearance. The earliest and perhaps most important of all these was by a Unionist discoverer of legendary Irish history, Standish O'Grady, who had published his *History of Ireland: Heroic Period 1* as long ago as 1878. A two-volume collection of folk tales was published in 1887 by Lady Wilde, mother of Oscar, who in her youth had been a fierce poetess of Duffy's paper *The Nation* under her pen-name Speranza. Her mood now was gentle and nostalgic for an Irish culture that seemed, with the language itself, to be dying away. Yeats himself published in 1888 his own collection of such tales and was about to give a remarkable impetus to the new movement he foresaw.

His father was an Irish artist, a Protestant, who had lived off and on in London, and was permanently settled there by the end of the eighties. But Yeats himself had spent many holidays with his grandparents and an uncle in County Sligo. There his inquiring imaginative nature found a new world in the ancient outlook of the common people. He was particularly fascinated by their relationship with the 'dim kingdom' of ghosts and fairies. Even among the fisherfolk of Howth, County Dublin, where his father had had a house for a time, Yeats had found stories to excite him. In Sligo, short-cuts to the dim kingdom were all about him. Though he had become a friend of the old literary Fenian John O'Leary and had even in 1888 assisted in a publication of Young Ireland verse, his political nationalism was always perfunctory rather than deeply felt. Spiritual Irish nationalism was what engaged him. Poetically idealistic, and apprehensive before the growing shadow of vulgarity and commercialism which he saw as the advancing shape of the modern world, he delved enthusiastically for something better into '...that great Celtic phantasmagoria whose meaning no man has discovered and no angel revealed'.*[4] Others were soon to take the plunge with him and find many other things besides ghosts and fairies, including ancient heroes.

It may seem improbable that such an esoteric venture could have made a contribution to the development of Irish nationalism. Yeats looked not to Tone and Emmet for inspiration, but to a little bright-eyed old man named Paddy Flynn living in a one-man cabin in Sligo, whose stories – remote

---

* The real pioneer of this romantic therapeutic view of Celtic legend had been the English poet Matthew Arnold, whose Oxford lectures 'On the Study of Celtic Literature' were published in 1867. For a first-class account of the origins of the whole Celtic historical and literary revival and its political implications see the first two chapters of William Thompson, *The Imagination of an Insurrection* (New York, 1967).

indeed from the green flag and the stones of Westminster – would begin with words like:

'One night a middle-aged man, who had lived all his life far from the noise of cabwheels, a young girl, a relative of his, who was reported to be enough of a seer to catch a glimpse of unaccountable lights moving over the fields among the cattle, and myself were walking along a far western sandy shore.'[5] Such stories Yeats published in an English magazine edited by W. E. Henley, the *National Observer*, and these were in 1893 collected into a volume called *The Celtic Twilight*. 'Perhaps,' he wrote of Paddy Flynn in the introduction, 'the Gaelic people shall by his like bring back again the ancient simplicity and amplitude of imagination.'[6] It is in this early stirring of Gaelic imagination that Yeats is historically important.

The cultural personality of the ordinary Irish people – in so far as it was any longer different from that of the English – had remained submerged beneath the outer veneer of respectable Irish life for much of the nineteenth century. It was almost as if invisible penal laws had been in effect, acting this time not against the popular religion but against the popular culture of the country. To most of the Irish gentry the Irish peasant, when he had not been a dangerous nuisance, was a joke. One important aspect of the literary renaissance and the much wider Irish Ireland movement of which it became a part was that it took the Irish peasant and his family seriously as people. And though this was done in a deliberately apolitical manner it inevitably helped to produce a climate in which an Irishman could feel new self-respect for being Irish.

It is easy to forget how much of what the world now finds the special charm and delight of Irish personality had to be pointed out to the world in the nineties by Yeats and the literary friends with whom he was soon working. Hitherto, for intelligent people the Irish peasant had been chiefly characterized by the Punch cartoon or the stage Irishman with his 'Begorrahs' and sly unreliability and fondness for liquor. And though there was often more truth in the stage Irishman than many Irishmen were prepared to admit – Yeats's Sligo man after all was called Paddy and died of drink[7] – yet the inaccuracy of the caricature lay in what was left out: the seriousness and innocence of a different way of life, inherited through many centuries from the ancient Gaelic world and preserved by isolation in poverty much as Gaelic clothing and butter and even people had sometimes been preserved in Irish bogs.

In 1890 a first book had appeared by another collector of folk tales who was soon to exercise a far greater influence on thought and style in Ireland than Yeats. This book was *Beside the Fire*, by Douglas Hyde, whom Yeats had met years before in the late 1870s when Hyde was a student at Trinity and even then a member of the 'Society for the Preservation of the Irish Language'. Yeats had been struck by the peasant quality of the dark young man's face, with his vague serious eyes and high cheekbones, and had found himself wondering how he had managed to get into Trinity.[8] In fact Hyde was the fairly well-to-do son of a Protestant clergyman of County Roscommon where in his youth Irish had been widely spoken and where he had learnt it fluently from the peasantry among whom he had grown up. His easy access to and delight in both spoken and written Gaelic tradition was of immense value now in helping to bring that tradition to life. He even wrote songs and poems in Irish himself and, according to Yeats, while Hyde was still a quite unknown student in Dublin, his songs were being sung by mowers and reapers from Kerry to Donegal.[9]

Hyde had sent Yeats what Yeats regarded as the best story for his own collection, *Fairy and Folk Tales*, published in 1888. Now Hyde's *Beside the Fire* and his *Love Songs of Connacht*, published in 1893, shed a new illumination on the Gaelic world. Half a century later it was to these two volumes of Hyde's that at least one Irishman who had been young at that time looked back as marking a new epoch.[10]

In 1892 Yeats, who had returned to live in Ireland, founded with Hyde the National Literary Society. At one of its early meetings – before Gladstone's second Home Rule Bill had been introduced – Hyde delivered what was to become a famous lecture under the title of 'The Necessity of De-Anglicizing Ireland'. Despite its title it was intended to be a wholly non-political lecture. Hyde addressed its appeal to all Irishmen – to 'everyone, Unionist or Nationalist, who wishes to see the Irish nation produce its best'.[11] But though his appeal to Unionists was sincerely meant – an equivalent to Davis's 'Gentlemen, you have a country' appeal to the Dublin historical society over fifty years earlier – he was, in the context of the time, even less likely to be sympathetically received by Unionists than Davis. It is a measure of Hyde's essential political naïvety that he can seriously have supposed that in a lecture employing phrases like, 'this awful idea of complete Anglicization',[12] he could attract the Unionist gentry of the day. His strictures against 'West Britonism', that half-culture, neither Irish nor English, which dominated Ireland, extended to almost every aspect of everyday life: music – where the song of the harp was to replace 'Ta-ra-ra-boom-de-ay'; anglicized surnames and Christian names, among which Patrick was to be replaced by Padraig and Charles by Cahal; and even clothing. Deploring 'English second-hand trousers', Hyde recommended in their place the clean worsted stockings and knee breeches of the past, and a more universal use of wholesome Irish tweed.[13] Only in the work of the Gaelic Athletic Association did he find any cause for self-congratulation in Ireland, remarking that the GAA had done more for Ireland in the past five years than all the speeches of politicians.[14] He even went so far in his enthusiasm to recommend that the 'warm green-striped jerseys' of the association should replace altogether in common usage the 'torn collars and ugly neckties hanging away' of the average male.[15] Cranky and even slightly absurd as some of this sounds today, its tone was to be taken up eagerly by a small but enthusiastic minority, making possible the Gaelic League founded in the following year and the whole movement which followed. That such ideas were now capable of capturing the idealism of young people in Ireland was the point of significance.

Hyde's severest strictures were reserved for those Irishmen indifferent to 'the loss of our language', by which he meant Irish. Even before the Parnell split Hyde had been criticizing the Nationalist Party for 'attempting to create a nation on the one hand and allowing to be destroyed the very thing that would best differentiate and define that nation'.[16]

When, fifty years earlier, Davis, as part of a political movement, had tried to inculcate an interest in things Irish, one salient fact of Irish life had been very different. Half the population had still spoken Gaelic as its first language. But since then the population had been almost halved by starvation and emigration and the use of Irish had been rapidly dying out. As a normal feature of everyday life it was now confined largely to the western and north-western seaboards, with some pockets on the southern coast, though a few old men and women could still be found even round Dublin and in the central counties to testify to its comparatively recent decay elsewhere. Perhaps the most significant feature of the language situation was that even where it was remembered and could be spoken the Irish peasantry themselves discountenanced it as something to be ashamed of. English was the language by which you got on in life. Hyde himself was once talking in Irish to a girl in County Sligo when her brother came in and started sneering at her for speaking Irish, at which she immediately broke into English.[17] On another occasion he had evidence of an even more unconscious rejection of the language. After talking some time in Irish to a Mayo boy who kept answering him in English he said:

'Nach labhrann tu Gaedlig?' ('Don't you speak Irish?')

To which the boy had replied:

'Isn't it Irish I'm speaking?'

Hyde said, no, it was not Irish but English he was speaking.

'Well, then,' said the boy, 'that's how I spoke it ever.'[18]

The story was also told of a couple of earnest Gaelic Leaguers who had been painstakingly teaching their parlourmaid Irish and only discovered when she left to get married that she had been brought up in an Irish-speaking district but preferred English because it was more respectable.[19]

Hyde was, of course, no pioneer in his interest in the language. Even in the mid-eighteenth century Irish Protestant gentlemen had been proud to associate themselves with their country's Gaelic past and traditions. Ever since the middle of the nineteenth century, when those few people who cared had realized that the Irish language and the quality of mind that went with it was vanishing, there had been clubs and societies for studying and preserving it. Smith O'Brien before his death in 1864 had lent his support to one of these. But at the beginning of the nineties, with Home Rule still apparently a real possibility, and with a new respect for the Gaelic mind quickening under Yeats's and others' interest, the climate for the foundation of a new society to propagate the language was particularly favourable. As early as 1891 the Professor of Irish in the Catholic priests' training college at Maynooth, Father Eugene O'Growney, who published a popular Irish grammar, had been corresponding not only with Hyde but also with a civil servant from Ulster, John MacNeill – soon dutifully calling himself Eoin – over their common enthusiasm for Irish. In July 1893, originally as a result of a suggestion from MacNeill, the three founded the Gaelic League with the declared object of preserving the national language of Ireland and extending its use as a spoken language. Hyde became the Gaelic League's President. He was to remain, like Yeats, essentially not a politically-minded man, but one for whom a cultural rather than political Irish nationalism seemed to open the way to a whole new spiritual emancipation. But he was to generate a warm and popular affectionate enthusiasm both for himself and his ideas, which were to permeate much of middle-class Ireland, and girls were before long to appear at Gaelic League festivals with his Irish *nom de plume* – An Craoibhin Aobhinn ('the pleasant little branch') – inscribed on the bands of their hats, almost as if he were some democratic politician.

Though the Gaelic League took some years to spread widely over Ireland and was always confined largely in its activity to the towns, it was to play a most significant part in widening and strengthening the Irish consciousness of many a middle-class and lower-middle-class Irishman. It had 58 branches by 1898; 200 by 1901; 600 by 1903; and 900 by 1906, with a total membership of 100,000.[20] By that time it could claim to have enforced the teaching of Irish in three thousand schools and to have enlisted the enthusiasm of some quarter of a million Irish men and women in learning Irish. With its language classes, its monthly and weekly magazines, its summer schools, music and poetry festivals and prizes, it was not unreasonable to describe it, as one contemporary observer did, as 'the only National University that Ireland possesses'. (The official National University of Ireland was not founded until 1909 and the Gaelic League could rightly claim to have played an important part in bringing this into being.)

The Gaelic League became the urban counterpart of the Gaelic Athletic Association. And though non-political in motive it could not help having an oblique political influence. Those to whom it appealed were primarily Nationalist party voters whatever they may have thought of the Nationalist party politicians, and the League gave backing to that vote by teaching that Irishness was in itself something to be proud of rather than provincially ashamed of.

A whole respectable way of looking at Ireland was in fact created by the

Gaelic League. Snobbishness was a powerful political factor in the Ireland of the turn of the century. It prospered particularly in the small county towns where real distinctions of wealth and birth were so small that only a competition in snobbishness could seem to provide them.[21] The Gaelic League and the Irish Ireland movement in general now attacked the conventional small-time snob, the 'seonin' (shoneen) or sycophant who tried to demonstrate his personal superiority by apeing the manners and attitudes of his English-oriented 'betters'. The League countered such snobbery with a new version by which it became respectable and praiseworthy to aspire to different-Irish-standards. Occasionally it even managed to get the best of both worlds, as when the League magazine, *An Claideamh Soluis*, wrote: 'We condemn English-made evening dress, but evening dress of Irish manufacture is just as Irish as a Donegal cycling suit. Some people think we cannot be Irish unless we always wear tweeds and only occasionally wear collars.'[22]

Much of the later mass support for the Sinn Fein movement, to which the success of the Gaelic League indirectly contributed, can be explained by the opportunity it extended to a snobbishly afflicted middle and lower-middle class independently to assert a new social self-respect.

As the Irish Ireland movement grew in popularity it attracted many different individual prophets, often crying alone in what was still something of a national wilderness, often warring with each other or with the Gaelic League, but always sharing a freshness and independence of mind in looking beyond stale political cliché, to new things Irish.

One of the most original and astringent of these new voices was that of an Irish journalist, D. P. Moran, who published his views in a new weekly paper, the *Leader*, which he edited from 1900. The gist of Moran's purposefully shocking argument was that it was now very doubtful if there was such a thing as an Irish nation at all, and that if there was to be one – as he thought there should be – drastic action along the lines of the Gaelic League's principles, only more so, was immediately necessary. 'There are,' he wrote, 'certainly some traits to be found in Ireland which stamp her as a distinct race even yet, but they characterize her torpor and decay rather than her development.'[23] If her energies were to be revived Ireland must start by becoming bilingual, for the language was the great basic link with nationality. She could move on from there towards the separation of national personality which must be her goal. If she was not prepared to do this then she might just as well accept what was already almost a historical *fait accompli*, namely that she was English, or at least West British. Anywhere between these two positions was humbug, and humbug rather than England was Moran's enemy.

What had passed for national sentiment for so long Moran dismissed with devastating scorn and historical perception. The wave of emotive public opinion which had backed the Land League he saw correctly as being inspired chiefly by materialism. From whom, he asked, could one get any rational expression of that nationality about which all talked so loudly? Irish nationality had been 'stuck on a flag of green' and Irishmen had pursued this instead of the different Gaelic civilization which had once been the only true meaning of nationality in Ireland. Irishmen had gone in for clatter and claptrap which they miscalled nationality, playing the fool throughout the century like a lot of hysterical old women. The nineteenth century, he said, had been mostly a century of humbug. 'We are sick of "Irish National" make-believes and frauds.' Turning from the general to the particular he castigated the Irish Parliamentary Party – each section of which had for ten years been calling themselves 'Nationalists' while accusing the others of being 'West British'. 'It began gradually to dawn upon the average mind,' he wrote, 'that, as there was practically no difference between A and B but a cry Irish Nationality, Irish Nationality must be made of a very cloudy substance indeed.'[24]

While Irish parliamentary politics flowed unevenly but monotonously on in the foreground of Irish life, Irish opinion was being subtly conditioned by these other forces in the background. There was nothing particularly coherent about such conditioning except that it was concerned with something different from what had gone on before, and with Irishness. But inasmuch as attention and energies were being focused on something different, and Irish at a time when the Irish Parliamentary Party remained doggedly fixed on the same old goal of Home Rule, a potential detachment from the party was growing all the time beneath the surface.

In 1897 Yeats, together with the forty-four-year-old widow of an ex-Governor of Ceylon, Lady Gregory, who lived in County Sligo, and a thirty-eight-year-old wealthy eccentric neighbour of hers from County Galway, Edward Martyn, had founded the Irish National Theatre which was soon to make the name of the Abbey Theatre, Dublin, famous all over the world. Moran early dismissed all such activities with cynical contempt. 'The birth of the Celtic note,' he wrote in 1899, 'caused a little stir among minor literary circles in London, but much less in Ireland itself, where the "Irish national" demand for *The Mirror of Life, The Police Gazette* and publications of a like kind, showed no signs of weakening.'[25]

Easy as it was to disparage the literary renaissance and even the new Irish theatre as untypical fringe activity, they had many repercussions on a wide range of Irish opinion. Lady Gregory's researches among the Sligo peasantry had revealed particularly a living tradition not only of ghosts and fairies but of the ancient Gaelic heroes. Thus, hearing from a centenarian how the hero Cuchulain fought with and slew his own son, she received in parenthesis a physical description of his love, Grania, as if the narrator had actually known her: 'Grania was very small, only four feet.'[26] And together with these living traditions she had found among the Gaelic-speaking peasantry an ancient love of country stemming from far beyond the days of the green flag. Indeed, she went so far as to write, 'Love of country is, I think, the real passion.'[27] Her popularizations of the legends of Cuchulain and other heroes, though they met with the disapproval of some scholars, did much to make available to anyone who might want to adopt it a new Gaelic warrior pride.

By unleashing Cuchulain and Finn and other Gaelic warrior chiefs from the mists of heroic mythology, Lady Gregory's and Yeats's and Hyde's primary objectives were those of literature and art. But the national myth had had to subsist so long on noble failures like Tone and Emmet that these new figures from the Gaelic past, combining in their remoteness even more convincingly god-like attributes with superior military prowess, proved irresistible to those looking to the national myth for intoxication. When Lady Gregory collaborated with Yeats on his play *Caitlin ni Houlihan* for the Abbey they created a model for an entire renewal of patriotic Irish thought. This story about Humbert's landing at Killala in 1798 ended with a famous line after an old woman, Caitlin no Houlihan, tragic and symbolic figure of Ireland, had called at a peasant's cottage to summon him to join the rebels. Just after she had left, the peasant's brother came in and, on being asked if he had seen an old woman going away down the path, gave the reply: 'I did not, but I saw a young girl and she had the walk of a Queen.' When many years later Yeats was to ask himself, 'Did that play of mine send out Certain men the English shot?' the answer was 'Yes' – perhaps more obliquely than Yeats would have liked to think, but 'Yes' all the same.[28]

> Know that I would accounted be
> True brother of a company:
> That sang, to sweeten Ireland's wrong.

he had written. And so he should be accounted.

Paradoxically, as part of his motivation in the literary renaissance, Yeats quite soon engaged in a battle against the claims of conventional patriotism and on behalf of true art. 'All the past,' he complained later, 'had been turned into a melodrama with Ireland for blameless hero and poet; novelist and historian had but one object: that we should hiss the villain.'[29] The trouble was of course, as he admitted, that there really had been victim and villain however different in form. His battle against clichés old and new was eventually to prove a losing one, and in the first decade of the twentieth century he drifted further and further away from the renaissance's nationalist implications. A personal complication for him, apart from his friendship with O'Leary, was the romantic attachment he had formed for Maud Gonne, the beautiful daughter of an Irish Unionist colonel, with whom he had collaborated in the '98 centenary celebration. Converted to an ardent nationalism by O'Leary, Maud Gonne had been confirmed in it by the relief work she carried out with passionate zeal among the distressed and often still starving peasantry of the west of Ireland in the nineties. In her honour Yeats dutifully maintained a patriotic and even political involvement, at least until painfully released by her marriage to an active member of the IRB, John MacBride, in 1903. But the primary object of his own energies was always aesthetic: that new kind of Ireland which he optimistically discerned in May 1899 as rising up amid the wreck of the old 'and in which the national life was finding a new utterance'.[30]

Moran, for all his gibes at Yeats, had the same aspiration. Having made the point that the Irish people did not hate England – 'the genius of our country is far more prone to love than hate' – Moran concluded in 1899: 'The prospect of such a new Ireland rising up out of the foundations of the old, with love and not hate as its inspiration, has already sent a great thrill through the land.'[31]

However imperfectly such aspirations from different quarters might be realized, the significant point was that new thoughts and emotions were thrilling certain people in Ireland, and the most thrilling thing about them was that they were new. Beside this excitement the political stalemate in which Home Rule found itself seemed less important.

Of course, the Irish Ireland movement and the Gaelic League themselves appeared to have limitations to many. A powerful school of Irish academics poured scorn on the whole idea of reviving the language. Trinity College, where this school was centred, had turned down Hyde for its Professorship of Irish two years after the foundation of the Gaelic League on the grounds that he knew only 'baboon Irish'.[32] John Mahaffy, the Vice-Provost of Trinity, vigorously though unsuccessfully tried to prevent Irish being incorporated into secondary school education in 1901, while even John Dillon himself opposed it as a compulsory subject for the new National University of Ireland in 1909.[33]

Even for its supporters the Gaelic League cannot always have been wholly inspiring. George Moore, the novelist, grandson of the independent-minded Member of Parliament for County Mayo in the days of the Pope's Brass Band, found himself caught up in the new movement for a time. He has left one memorable portrait of Hyde through the droop of whose moustache, he says, 'the Irish frothed like porter, and when he returned to English it was easy to see why he wanted to change the language of Ireland'.[34]

Moreover, the Gaelic League and the Irish Ireland movement, though influential, were all minority movements. To the great majority of the people of Ireland during these years the prospects and terms of land purchase in the countryside and the hard living conditions in the towns were the dominating

considerations of everyday life. But for all their faults and limitations they
were minority movements whose character slipped, often unnoticeably, into
the national ethos. As a result, when in 1911 Home Rule once again became
a practical possibility, the sensitiveness of Irish national opinion, though it
had developed virtually no new political demands, was much greater than
a quarter of a century before.

Many individual and often unconnected voices helped to produce this
change in the Irish national mood. Some were even Unionists who, by their
moderate and reasonable paternalist approach to the encouragement of
Irish self-reliance and a share in administration, inevitably made Home Rule
seem all the more reasonable and in the long run irresistible. The Local
Government Act of 1898 itself contributed to this effect, establishing elected
County Councils in Ireland, and thus taking the administration of local
affairs out of the hands of the property-qualified grand juries and the local
gentry. And the initiative for the great Land Purchase Act of 1903 (the
Wyndham Act, so-called after the Irish Chief Secretary of the day) came
first from a group of Unionist landowners headed by a Colonel Shawe Taylor
and the Earl of Dunraven.

One particular Unionist had encouraged in agriculture something of an
Irish Ireland outlook almost approaching the philosophy of D. P. Moran.
This was Sir Horace Plunkett, an Irish Protestant landowner and farmer who
had spent some years ranching in the United States. In 1889 he had begun
an Irish cooperative movement in agriculture known as the Irish Agricultural
Organization Society, which by 1903 had eight hundred branches with a
membership of eighty thousand representing some 400,000 persons.[35] Its
secretary was a Protestant Nationalist, an Irish poet and painter called
George Russell (his *nom de plume* was 'AE') who, apart from running the
Society efficiently, blurred the spiritual, political and economic interests of
Ireland into something like a mystical quest for what he called the 'national
soul'.

Plunkett in 1895 had taken the initiative from which eventually the Dunraven Land Conference and other changes of climate in Ireland were to
spring. He wrote a letter to the Irish press suggesting that a committee
should be formed during the parliamentary recess of Irish Members of
Parliament of both sides and all shades of political opinion who might have
the interests of Ireland at heart. 'We Unionists,' he wrote, 'without abating
one jot of our Unionism, and Nationalists, without abating one jot of their
Nationalism, can each show our faith in the cause for which we have fought
so bitterly and so long, by sinking our party differences for our country's
good, and leaving our respective policies for the justification of time...'

This was strange talk of 'our country's good' from a Conservative of the
late nineteenth century. And more orthodox Unionists certainly looked at it
askance. After all, this collaboration of Irishmen of all classes and creeds

for Ireland's sake was the very goal which the United Irishmen and the nationalists of the 1840s had always striven for.

Significantly, the majority of the parliamentary nationalists did not now like it either. For it set up a sort of Unionism as an alternative goal to the pure formula of Home Rule in which the party had a vested interest. The party similarly disliked Sir Horace Plunkett's Irish Agricultural Organization Society. Town shopkeepers and suppliers of farmers' credit in the party felt themselves threatened by the commercial rivalry of the cooperative societies and agricultural banks. The Nationalist Party, a quarter of a century earlier under Parnell, had been the radical force in Ireland. Now it was in many respects an alternative Irish Establishment to the Vice-Regal Lodge and Dublin Castle. And it is in the nature of all establishments that they can be toppled.

When Plunkett's campaign led in 1902 to the creation by the government for the first time of an Irish Department of Agriculture, with a partly elected Council of Agriculture to decide agricultural policy for different Irish localities, he regarded this as a new moral force in Ireland and talked of the 'reconstruction of Irish life' and 'organized self-help' like the Irish Ire-landers.[36] Redmond, who when split from the rest of the party had taken part in Plunkett's Recess Committee, now turned unashamedly against him. He described Plunkett with almost incredible unfairness as having an 'undisguised contempt for the Irish race'.[37] What rankled was the suggestion that anything but Home Rule might be the answer to Ireland's problems. But with Home Rule politically in the doldrums it was inevitable that national feeling, if it had any vitality at all, should switch much of that vitality into some of the many various channels now available. The party became increasingly aware that an enthusiasm of which it should have had the monopoly was going elsewhere. 'An effort must be made,' wrote John Dillon to Redmond in 1906, 'to put some life into the movement. At present it is very much asleep, and Sinn Feiners, Gaelic League etc. etc. are making great play.'[38]

This reference to 'Sinn Feiners' was to a small section of the new national mood which had actually switched into an alternative political organization altogether.

9
Arthur Griffith
and Sinn Fein

An essay written by Douglas Hyde just before the turn of the century described 'a blackness on the sun of Ireland' – a dark cloud, like a great crow choking and smothering the people of Ireland, breathing poison from its beak, sucking away the courage of the people and putting fog and cold into their hearts. This crow was the English mind and 'the Englishing of Ireland'. It was to be slain by a bow whose arrow was the Irish language, its archer the Gaelic League. The Irish people would then 'stand without chains on body or mind, free in the presence of God...'.[1]

In the essay, Hyde translated some Irish verse which expressed an ancient tradition constant in Irish folk legend through centuries of sorrow and misfortune:

> There is a change coming, a big change
> And riches and store will be nothing worth,
> He will rise up that was small eyed,
> And he that was big will fall down.
>
> The time will come, and it's not far from us,
> When strength won't be on the side of authority or law,
> And the neck will bend that was not bent,
> When that time comes it will come heavily ...

The essay was called 'The Return of the Fenians'.

But in recalling this legend of Finn and his warriors coming down from the North to destroy the enemies of Ireland, Hyde did not mean to appeal to the ideals of 1865 and 1867. He was using it as an allegorical summons to spiritual renewal through the language and ennobling standards of ancient Gaeldom. With such open abandon did he express his theme, concluding with a final cry of '...And the time is not far off', that clearly no possibility of a political interpretation can have entered his mind. That it should have been possible thus to talk of Fenians, without apparently suggesting any attempt to revive the republican separatist spirit of thirty years before, shows how remote that spirit itself had then become. Inevitably attempts were soon made to revive it together with other legends from the glorious past.

Irish history was then quite untaught both in the so-called National Board Schools and in private education. For those who in the new Irish Ireland climate suddenly began to discover their history, all periods, even quite recent ones, easily became mythological. Among the many individuals who in the nineties discovered Irish history in this manner were two middle-class young women of Protestant stock from Ulster, Alice Milligan and Anna Johnston (the latter writing under the name of 'Ethna Carberry'). In 1896 they started a monthly magazine in Belfast called the *Shan Van Vocht*, the name of the legendary old woman who was Ireland. 'Ireland dear,' wrote Alice Milligan in an ode for 6 October, the anniversary of Parnell's death, and dedicated 'to the memory of the dead and the cause that shall not die',

> Ireland dear! through the length of my childhood lonely,
> Throughout the toilsome hours of my schooling days,
> No mention of thee was made unto me, save only
> By speakers in heedless scorn or in harsh dispraise ...

In this childhood which she had spent in an Orange district of Ulster, Alice Milligan had often been brought in from play of an evening by a nurse's threat that if she stayed out the Fenians would get her:

> An army of Papists grim
> With a green flag o'er them,
> Red-coats and black police
> Flying before them.

> But God (who our nurse declared
> Guards British dominions)
> Sent down a deep fall of snow
> And scattered the Fenians.

The child had dropped asleep romantically sympathizing with the rebels and

> Wondering if God,
> If they prayed to Him
> Would give them good weather.

Anna Johnston, Alice Milligan's literary colleague, also dreamt of the Fenians, romanticizing them in the same golden terms as Cuchulain, Conor MacNessa, Finn and the other heroes of ancient legend. She wrote a poem about the *Erin's Hope*, the boat-load of square-toed Irish Americans who in reality had sailed belatedly across the Atlantic to join the fiasco of '67, unable to find a welcome the whole length of the Irish west coast.

> A sail! a sail upon the sea – a sail against the sun!
> A sail, wind-filled from out the West! our waiting time is done;
> Since sword and spear and shield are here to free our hapless One!

The distinction between myth and reality had always been vague in Irish history. But from this sort of thing it was to be a short step to living out mythology in the present.

The Irish Republican Brotherhood, clinging to the antique dogma of the 1860s that only physical force could help Ireland, was by the mid-1890s virtually moribund. Such vitality as the IRB had preserved after its reorganization in 1873 under Charles Kickham had been deflected to other fields than those of violent national revolution. Some Fenians had gone into the Parliamentary movement; others had diverted their energies into the Land League activity of the late seventies and early eighties. Still others, clinging almost desperately to violent action as an instrument of policy, had joined the Invincibles, the secret society which had killed Lord Frederick Cavendish in Phoenix Park. During the 1880s the IRB's one notable activity had been an attempt to secure control of the newly-founded Gaelic Athletic Association. Inasmuch as this was successful however, it led to a temporary but sharp decline in the GAA's membership, for the clergy, who were far more influential than the IRB, discouraged membership which fell in consequence from 52,000 in 1889 to 5,446 in 1892. But when the Brotherhood's influence on the direction of the GAA waned, membership revived, and Archbishop Croke was in 1895 again able to give it his support.[2]

The effectiveness of the Parliamentary Party under Parnell, and the apparent near-success, at least until mid-1893, of Home Rule as the national goal, made the Brotherhood seem more and more of a museum piece. Its continued existence was known to the police and watched though not taken seriously by anyone as a threat to the constitution. As if to stress the museum quality, John O'Leary and James Stephens himself were to be found harmlessly on view in Dublin. A Supreme Council of the IRB remained technically in being however, a nominal apparatus of radical extremists, fanatically devoted to a safely theoretical cause.

This reserve of individuals had played some part in Parnell's last campaign of 1891 when, deprived suddenly of his usual sources of support, he had turned back to 'the hillside men'. But the IRB's cause – that of the green flag to be carried to victory through shot and shell over the British Army – necessarily remained a near-theological rather than a practical issue, something to be argued about rather than engaged in.

That a revival of interest in such theology should form part of the generally awakening interest in things Irish was inevitable. But one young man whose interest had been thus aroused, John MacBride, whose family came from Ulster, though he had been born in County Mayo, was soon disillusioned by what he found in the IRB. Such energy as there was in the organization in the early nineties seems, by his own account at any rate, to have been supplied largely by himself. '... The older men were doing then what they are doing now,' he wrote in 1902 to John Devoy, the old Fenian who ran

Clan-na-Gael, the Irish extremist organization in America. 'Sitting on their backsides and criticizing and abusing one another.'[3]

The IRB's link with Clan-na-Gael and with that organization's financial resources in the States was the one feature that gave it any continuing significance. But that the cause of 'physical force' in Ireland, for which it stood, should ever again become a serious practical consideration seemed at this time beyond the bounds of possibility. Even in 1898 when under Fred Allan the IRB stirred itself into some activity to organize the centenary celebrations of that year, the qualities it revealed had not been very impressive. John Daly, a recently released Fenian, wrote to Devoy that summer: 'I would like to tell you something about how Mr Fred is running things on this side, but ... I must let it stand over.... I can't or won't play in with the chaps that run or work the rings.... And in truth I think it's nearly all rings now and rot and humbug ...'[4]

By 1896 John MacBride had left Ireland to seek a living for himself in South Africa. Besides being a member of the IRB he had also been a member of the Celtic Literary Society, the members of which had contacts with Alice Milligan and Anna Johnston of Belfast, in whose monthly they published verse and articles. In the Celtic Literary Society MacBride had become a friend of the nationally minded compositor and journalist named Arthur Griffith, and early in 1897 he had persuaded Griffith to come out to the Transvaal to join him.

There Griffith, after working for a short time as a journalist, took a job as a machine supervisor in a gold mining company in Johannesburg and with MacBride helped to organize the Irish '98 centenary celebrations in that town. When Griffith gave up his job and returned to Dublin later in the year, he decided with his other friend from the Celtic Literary Society, William Rooney, to found a newspaper.[5] The characteristic note which this paper struck immediately was very much in line with the sort of republican ideology Griffith had learned from MacBride. It took the name of Mitchel's paper the *United Irishman*, and the leader in the first issue of 4 March 1899 proclaimed its acceptance of 'the Nationalism of '98, '48, and '67'.

Both Griffith and Rooney were soon to become sworn members of the Irish Republican Brotherhood and their paper at first largely reflected its ideals in the context of the new Irish Ireland climate. It was only gradually in the years to come that Griffith evolved a different political position from that of the IRB.

The *United Irishman*, written at first almost entirely by Rooney and Griffith, set itself up as a watchdog of iconoclastic militant nationalism. It was not only the Parliamentary Party that was attacked – either directly, or by implication with the use of quotations from Mitchel, Meagher, Davis and James Fintan Lalor. The Gaelic League itself was assailed for preaching that nationality was 'not a thing of rights, arms, freedom, franchises and brotherhood' but a thing of 'singing and lute-playing, of mystic prose and thrice mystic poesy' and for its insistence on 'no politics'.[6] Yeats, who had been saying that he believed the work of Ireland was to lift up its voice for spirituality, ideality and simplicity in the English-speaking world, was told by the *United Irishman* that *it* believed nothing of the kind. 'The work of Ireland', it declared, 'is to uplift itself.'[7] Anyone reading the early issues would reasonably have supposed that the paper was preaching a thinly disguised Fenianism. 'Not a local legislature – not a return to "our ancient constitution" – not a golden link . . .' ran a prominently displayed quotation from Mitchel. 'But an Irish Republic One and Indivisible.' One early issue contained an article on the continuity throughout history of the Fenian spirit ('Fenianism is the Irish incarnation of . . . Delenda est Carthago. Read Britannia for Carthago . . .') and there were occasional snippets of news about old Fenians, particularly about the attempts of the released dynamiter Clarke to settle down in regular employment.[8]

But though letters and articles striking an old-fashioned military and insurrectionary note continued to appear in the *United Irishman* for several years, a potential development from the old cliché-ridden attitudes began to emerge in 1899 with increasingly insistent proposals from correspondents, taken up with interest by the editor, for some new 'National Organization' to coordinate the activities of those who thought as the *United Irishman* did. There were a number of small 'national' societies in existence, most of them remnants of groups that had come into being to help celebrate the rebellion of 1798, though many of these had quickly disintegrated.[9] Societies with names like the Robert Emmet '98 Club, the Oliver Bond Young Men's Club and the Old Guard Union were, together with Rooney and Griffith's old Celtic Literary Society, all at home in the *United Irishman's* pages. A tentative plan for some new comprehensive organization was first formulated in the *United Irishman* of 16 September 1899 by a correspondent, George Morton Griffith, a nationalist who was no relation of the paper's editor. Because constitutionalism was so deeply ingrained in the public's attitude, his argument ran, any such new party would have to sit in Parliament, but should do so, sworn to support Irish revolutionary principles and backed by an extreme party at home, which would be organizing and advising people for armed revolt. 'An Irish Party in Parliament,' the letter continued, 'need not necessarily be "Constitutional" except in so far as it was politic for them to be so.'

Arthur Griffith, who in an earlier issue had specifically declared that 'the era of constitutional possibilities for Irish nationality ended on the day Charles Stewart Parnell died',[10] merely called for the names and addresses of those who were interested in forming any new organization. And in the following week other correspondents continued to press for some sort of amalgamation of existing societies.

'What we want now,' wrote one of them, 'is a policy and an organization which will take practical steps to preserve our Irish nationality, foster our industries, protect our commerce and keep our people at home. If we wait for these things until the present warring parliamentarians have made Ireland a Nation, the country will be either a grass farm or a desert.'[11]

In the end the organization came before the policy and outside events gave the impetus for its foundation.

In the Transvaal in 1899 the Boer farmers were up in arms against the British Empire. Griffith's friend John MacBride, who had remained there, now helped to form and became second-in-command of a small 'Irish Brigade' of men of Irish origin in the Transvaal – mainly Americans – pledged to fight for the Boers.*[12] Opinion in Ireland, as in much of Liberal Britain, was strongly pro-Boer. On 10 October 1899 an Irish Transvaal Committee was formed in the offices of the Celtic Literary Society at 32 Lower Abbey Street, Dublin, with Maud Gonne in the chair, and a resolution sending congratulations to MacBride was seconded by Griffith. A green flag, gold-fringed with a harp in the centre inscribed 'Our Land – Our People – Our Language', was also sent, and before the end of the year was waving over the Irish Brigade camp among the Boers besieging Ladysmith.[13]

A short-term policy for this embryo 'national organization' represented by the Transvaal Committee was immediately available: a campaign against recruitment for the British forces. It issued a poster carrying such slogans as: 'Enlisting in the English Army is Treason to Ireland', and 'Remember '98. Remember the Famine. Think of the ruined homes, of the Emigrant Ships'.[14]

Much of the committee's activity met with superficial popular support. In November 1899, when Griffith and Maud Gonne visited Cork on behalf of the committee, the horses were removed from their carriage by the crowd who themselves dragged them in triumph from the railway station to the Victoria Hotel.[15] In December, Dublin Castle, aggravated by the temporary success of the anti-recruiting campaign, banned a Sunday meeting of the Transvaal Committee, which decided to go ahead with it. A horse-drawn brake containing Maud Gonne, Arthur Griffith and the Chairman of Dublin's tiny Irish Socialist Republican Party, an ex-British Army man himself, named James Connolly, drove into Beresford Square, Dublin, in defiance of the ban. A riot took place and James Connolly was later arrested and given a fine of £2 – paid by Maud Gonne – for driving a licensed vehicle, 'he not being a licensed driver'.[16] Griffith was sent sprawling by mounted police, who attempted to capture a child's Boer flag from the brake. At one time he was

* The Commander was a Colonel Blake, a former US army officer. The figure for the Brigade's numbers (1,000) in the *United Irishman* of 7 October 1899 is certainly an exaggeration. See below, p. 434.

seen waving both the flag and a police sword before hurling both into the crowd.[17]

A Frenchman who was in Dublin at the time of the early Boer victories wrote: 'The crowds would thrill with excitement, and men, radiant with delight, would stop in the streets to express to utter strangers the pleasure that the news gave them.'[18] But such reactions should probably be understood more as an Irish conditioned emotional endorsement of standard Liberal views on the war than as a reasoned expression of hatred for England. Irish regiments in the British Army served with honour in the war on many occasions. The Inniskillins, the Connaught Rangers and the Dublin Fusiliers all fought the Boers with particular distinction and the latter suffered heavy casualties. English music-hall songs, 'Bravo, Dublin Fusiliers' and 'What do you think of the Irish now?' duly signalized the fact. One of the actions in which MacBride's pro-Boer Irish Brigade took part was at Nikolson's Nek, a Boer victory where considerable numbers of the Royal Irish Fusiliers were among the captured.[19]

The pro-Boer Irish Brigade itself, of which MacBride himself took charge after its commanding officer had been wounded, played, by comparison with these Irishmen in the British Army, a totally insignificant part in the war. It existed only for one year, from September 1899 to September 1900, when it was disbanded by the Boers and the men gave themselves up to the Portuguese frontier post at Kamati.[20] They had fought in about twenty battles altogether, including Colenso, Spion Kop and Ladysmith, but had suffered no more than a total of eighty casualties of whom only seventeen had been killed.[21] Irish casualties among the British forces ran into thousands. Mac-Bride, who personally seems to have fought with gallantry and was thrown from his horse by a shellburst at Colenso, and slightly wounded at the battle of the Tugela river, later estimated his brigade's casualties at some thirty per cent of the total force.[22] This suggests that this 'Irish Brigade' in contrast with that of the British Army, which was a full brigade in the military meaning of the term, did not number much more than three thundred men altogether, although the *United Irishman* had at different times suggested that it consisted of between 1,000 and 1,700.[23] A second pro-Boer Irish brigade formed under the command of a 'Colonel' Lynch, who had originally gone to South Africa as a correspondent for the American magazine *Collier's Weekly*, was composed largely of Afrikaners, Germans and Frenchmen, built round a small nucleus of Irish. It was disbanded after three months and saw no fighting.*[24] Lynch later became a Nationalist member of Parliament.

Irish public opinion itself, for all the readiness of a respectable Dublin crowd to cheer Boer victories or a Dublin mob to riot in favour of the

---

* A Captain O'Donnell on the staff of de Wet, the Boer commander, is quoted in *United Irishmen*, 30 August 1902, as saying that the Irishmen involved on the Boer side numbered '500 and double that number of Irish-Afrikanders'.

Transvaal Committee, was by no means so clear-cut as appearances suggested. When in April 1900 Queen Victoria visited Dublin, the 'Famine Queen', as Maud Gonne described her in an issue of the *United Irishman*, seized by the police the week before, she received a friendly reception. The *United Irishman* itself had to admit that she was 'frantically cheered' in some quarters though it maintained that this was only done 'by those who look to her for their bread and butter'.[25] Where elsewhere there were silent people on the pavement there were 'cheering toadies in hired windows'. The Transvaal Committee tried to organize a demonstration that evening protesting that 'the loyalist pageant in the streets today in no wise reflects the sentiment of the people of Dublin'. A charge by Irish policemen dispersed it before its torchbearers could leave the building. Connolly was brought to the ground and Griffith struck by a baton.

The complex state of Irish public opinion on the national issue presented Griffith with a more serious obstacle than any police baton. He had already been given a devastating proof of the unpopularity of the simple neo-Fenian conclusions he and his friends drew from the Boer War situation. In February 1900 a parliamentary by-election had come up in the constituency of South Mayo where MacBride had been born. The Transvaal Committee nominated MacBride as an independent nationalist candidate against the orthodox candidate of the Parliamentary Party. John O'Leary and the recently released Fenian John Daly sat with Griffith on MacBride's election committee. In the *United Irishman* Griffith published a stirring version of 'The Wearing of the Green'.

> From land to land throughout the world the news is going round
> That Ireland's flag triumphant waves on high o'er English ground.
> In far-off Africa today the English fly dismayed
> Before the flag of green and gold borne by MacBride's brigade ...
>
> With guns and bayonets in their hands, their Irish flag on high
> As down they swept on England's ranks out rang their battle-cry:
> 'Revenge! Remember '98! and how our fathers died!
> We'll pay the English back today,' cried fearless John MacBride.
>
> They'll raise the flag of Emmet, Tone, and Mitchel up once more
> And lead us in the fight to drive the tyrant from our shore ...[26]

When the election result was announced it was found that MacBride had been defeated by the Parliamentary Party's candidate by a majority of over five to one in a campaign in which only twenty-five per cent of the electorate voted. The figures were: O'Donnell 2,401; MacBride 427.[27]

As the theme of the need for some new national organization was raised again in the columns of the *United Irishman* one correspondent, while himself enthusiastic, added a further realistic note:

Are the people of Ireland ready [he asked] to help in establishing such a confederation as that proposed? I fear not. ... In the very neighbourhood in which I reside poor men and women are to be found to whom it would be dangerous to say a word derogatory of England's invincibility. They have relatives among the Fusiliers etc. who are at present fighting in South Africa, and they are proud of the fact.[28]

But Griffith, hard-working, courageous, often oblivious of personal discomfort and uninterested in his material advancement, tenacious and single-minded almost to a fault, was not a man to be deterred from what he had decided was the right path, by lack of popularity. On 30 September 1900, with the Irish Transvaal Committee as a nucleus, he formed in its rooms in Lower Abbey Street an organization called Cumann na Gaedheal to unite a number of existing open national societies. This in turn was to be the nucleus of his later party known as Sinn Fein.

No clear agreed policy for the new organization was as yet evolved. The objects of Cumann na Gaedheal were listed as (a) diffusing a knowledge of Ireland's resources and supporting Irish industries; (b) the study and teaching of Irish history, language, music and art; (c) the encouragement of Irish national games and characteristics; (d) the discountenancing of everything leading to the Anglicization of Ireland. Membership was open to all who pledged themselves 'to aid to the best of their ability in restoring Ireland to her former position of sovereign independence'. But what precisely was meant by that – the sovereign independence of Grattan's Parliament under a Crown shared with England, or something more revolutionary after the style of 1798 – was not specified. Meanwhile, an article in the current issue of the *United Irishman* on the 'Use of the Pike and Bayonet in Warfare' drew attention to the uselessness of the pike.[29]

When the first Convention of the new organization was announced for 25 November 1900 – the anniversary of the execution of the Manchester martyrs – it was stressed by Griffith that it was in fact 'no new affair. ... It is merely a combination of a number of existing National bodies working heretofore locally on the broad principles enunciated by Tone and Davis.'[30] He then made plain that he was not just indulging in the traditional vague lip service to such heroes now claimed by virtually all Irish patriots. Cumann na Gaedheal, he wrote, 'come to insist on the difference between the ideals of '98, '48 and '67 and those which in our time are sought to be identified with them'.[31] John MacBride, who had just returned from South Africa, expressed a wish to join the new organization, and when the Convention met was elected Vice-President. John O'Leary was President. Rooney and Griffith took an active part in the proceedings.

Not surprisingly the new organization made little impact. It had little specifically to offer. Articles about some curiously unspecified future war continued to appear in the *United Irishman*, in one of which an offensive–defensive war was envisaged of attacks on the enemy in Ireland by exceedingly mobile forces who would live off the land. And where a gesture could be made Cumann na Gaedhael made it. It attended the funeral of James Stephens when he died at last in Dublin on 29 March 1901. But then so did the Lord Mayor – though he trimmed by not coming 'in state' – and even the Irish Parliamentary Party passed a resolution of regret – 'for American consumption' commented Griffith's paper sourly.[32] It was true that political gestures had been two a penny in Ireland for years. What Cumann na Gaedhael in particular wanted was not political gestures but political ideas. Before it could develop any, Griffith's friend and collaborator, William Rooney, died suddenly at the age of twenty-seven. It is an indication of how undeveloped Griffith's own political ideas were at this stage that he could write later, in describing the setback entailed by this relatively obscure young man's death, that 'for a time it seemed as if the blow would be a fatal one'.[33] Among those who attended Rooney's funeral was another relatively obscure young man of literary bent, an executive of the Gaelic League called P. H. Pearse, who occasionally contributed to the *United Irishman*.[34]

All the movement really amounted to at this early stage was an untypical but articulate dissatisfaction with the incompleteness and inadequacy of Home Rule as an expression of Irish nationalism. As Rooney had said: 'Home Rule might be an improvement in this state of affairs but it would not be nationhood.'[35] The chief difficulty Griffith and his contributors and the thirty thousand odd Irishmen who subscribed to the *United Irishman* had to contend with, was that for the vast majority of their countrymen Home Rule meant nationhood enough.[36]

Griffith first worked away at basic principles, trying to establish a suitable national anthem ('A Nation Once Again', 'Let Erin Remember . . .', 'God Save Ireland'), trying to define who was an Irishman and who was not. A long discussion took place in the *United Irishman* between those who said that only 'Gaels' were true Irishmen and those who maintained with Davis that 'Irish' and not 'Gael' was the key word. Supporters of the latter view quoted Davis's verse:

> Yet start not, Irish-born man,
> If you're to Ireland true,
> We heed not race, nor creed, nor clan,
> We've hearts and hands for you.[37]

On the other hand, one correspondent even maintained that a large body of the non-Gaelic population of Ireland would have to be deported from the new Ireland, though he recognized that individuals of the settler race might in exceptional cases be admitted if they had proved themselves 'in touch with the Gael'.[38] He could hardly do anything else. Tone, Mitchel, Parnell and others of his heroes all fell into this category.

Griffith, in his editorial judgement on the matter, was more consistent and logical. Again, he could hardly afford not to be, for though he was himself 'Gaelic' in the sense that he was Catholic, his grandfather had been a convert to the religion and he came from a family of Ulster Protestant farmers.[39] Griffith now defined an Irishman as one who accepts Ireland as his country and is ready to do a man's part for her; 'such a man, whatever his creed, is our brother and the Gael of a hundred generations who accepts the Empire is our enemy, did he belong to our creed a thousand times.'[40]

Griffith, while priggish almost to the point of absurdity on occasion about lapses from severe Irish Ireland standards, and resenting strongly, for instance, the guying of an Irish peasant on stage as a man in a battered hat or the singing of 'Phil the Fluter's Ball' at a concert, was free of a racial view of Irish nationality even in his attitude to the language.*

'Ireland is truly no longer the Gaelic Nation of the fifth or the twelfth or even the eighteenth century ...', he wrote. 'The Gael is gone, the Dane is gone, the Norman is gone, and the Irishman is here.... And he turns to the language of the Gaels, not because the Gael spoke it, but because it was moulded and formed in Ireland, and is therefore fitter for an Irishman than any other.'[41]

There was little tendency to shirk the essentially synthetic nature of the work ahead. 'We are nation-makers,' a *United Irishman* correspondent had written.[42] But how practically was the nation to be made when the bulk of the nation did not think nationally in this extreme sense at all, and when even those who did think nationally were concerned mainly for cultural and spiritual renewal and not political nationhood?

Griffith remained a member of the IRB, and in the early part of 1902 the *United Irishman* still had no newer policy to offer than a 'National Brigade' and a plea for drilling in Cumann na Gaedheal.[43] Meanwhile, it vigorously supported the work of the Gaelic League in the language revival and encouraged Irish industry, recalling the self-reliance preached by Young Ireland and embodied twenty years before in the motto of the Cork exhibition as Sinn Fein (Ourselves Alone).[44]

However, on 26 October 1902 at the third annual convention of Cumann na Gaedheal a practical policy which had been periodically advocated before in Irish history was officially adopted as the national organization's programme. It was contained in a resolution of Griffith's which ran: 'That we call upon our countrymen abroad [Irish Americans] to withhold all assistance from the promoters of a useless, degrading and demoralizing policy until such time as the members of the Irish Parliamentary Party substitute

---

* He was less free from bigotry on other matters, giving evidence of anti-semitic feeling more than once in the *United Irishman*. See, e.g., the issues of 9 September 1899 and 23 September 1899. When in 1900 his prediction that the Boer capital of Pretoria would never fall proved false he ascribed its capitulation without a shot to 'masonic influences' (Lyons, *Griffith*, p. 43).

for it the policy of the Hungarian deputies and refusing to attend the British Parliament or to recognize its right to legislate for Ireland, remain at home to help in promoting Ireland's interest and to aid in guarding its national rights.'[45] 'The "Hungarian Policy",' added Griffith, 'is the policy for Ireland to pursue, so long as she is unable to meet and defeat England on the battlefield.'[46]

There was nothing new in such a tactic, though it had not been revived for some time. The proposal that Irish Members of Parliament should withdraw from Westminster and sit in Ireland with other representatives as a National Parliament had first been made in *The Nation* of 19 November 1842.* The idea had been elaborated by O'Connell as a proposed Council of Three Hundred, inevitably hedged about with devices for circumventing the Convention Act, which then made any such activity in Ireland illegal. A general analogy between Ireland and the European nationalist movements developing under the Austrian Empire had also been made by Davis and the Young Irelanders in the 1840s. After the Fenian rising of 1867 the nationalist paper *The Irishman* had expressly recommended imitation by the Parliamentary party of the action of the Hungarian Deputies of 1861 in withdrawing from the Imperial Parliament and returning home.† Parnell and Michael Davitt had discussed such a course of action in 1877.‡ But then as now, when Griffith put it forward, the policy failed totally to recommend itself to the only people in a position to carry it out: the Parliamentary Party itself. In such circumstances it was bound to remain a rather academic proposal and, though it met with a welcome from supporters of Cumann na Gaedheal, little was heard of it again for almost another year after November 1902. The leadership of Cumann na Gaedheal remained theoretically Fenian with John O'Leary still President, and Thomas Clarke (then settled in New York), John Daly, Maud Gonne and John MacBride as Vice Presidents.§ Articles enjoining the patriotic citizen to practise route marching and drill continued to appear in the *United Irishman* well into 1903.

The executive of Cumann na Gaedheal to which Griffith had been elected met every Saturday and Griffith himself was invariably present. Apart from its routine work in trying to keep alive the spirit of the various affiliated clubs and 'national' societies, it also tried to discourage recruitment for the British forces and the police by counselling local authorities not to give jobs to men who had served in them.[47] Occasionally it ventured more boldly still into the field of public affairs. In April 1903 it passed a resolution calling on all public bodies in Ireland which professed to be National to reject with

* See above, p. 39.
† See above, p. 354.
‡ See above, p. 371.
§ Maud Gonne and John MacBride married in February 1903. The marriage was not a success and MacBride was reported to be drinking heavily later that same year. They eventually separated. (See Yeats, *Correspondence* (London, 1954), pp. 412–14.)

contempt any proposal to welcome King Edward VII to Ireland when he paid his proposed visit in the summer. 'To the Irish Nationalist,' wrote Griffith, 'the King is as foreign as the Akond of Swat, but, unlike that potentate, he claims to be the sovereign of this country.'[48]

Next month the Cumann na Gaedheal executive decided to call a conference to stimulate protest against the king's visit, and on 20 May 1903 a 'National Council to uphold National self-respect' on the occasion issued a letter calling for public support. As well as Griffith and the Fenian John Daly, Yeats and Lady Gregory's eccentric neighbour from County Galway, Edward Martyn, were among the signatories.[49]

This National Council met for the first time in Dublin on 6 June 1903 and held a public meeting on 2 July. Edward Martyn, a wealthy unmarried middle-aged landlord, who collected impressionists and had been opposed even to Home Rule as late as 1887, was in the chair.[50] A resolution of protest against the passing of loyal addresses to the king was passed, and a fortnight later as a result of the campaign the Dublin Corporation decided by a very small majority not to vote one.

This was about the limit of the National Council's achievement for the time being. The king and queen's visit to Ireland turned out to be an outstanding success, in marked contrast with their reception as Prince and Princess of Wales eighteen years before in 1885. They visited Dublin, where they walked in the streets, Belfast, Derry, Galway, the west coast and the Catholic seminary at Maynooth. 'No sovereign,' wrote the Nationalist *Cork Examiner*, 'visiting our shores, ever met with anything like the hearty good will, the honest, unaffected welcome extended by the people of all classes – in every part of the country.... This fortnight ... has made history, has provided materials for nation building....'[51]

It was to be a long time before any idea of nation-building other than one based on the concept of King and Country was to receive popular support in Ireland. The National Council, together with Cumann na Gaedheal, which still maintained a separate existence, was out of tune with the national mood. A few days after the royal departure, it published its Constitution, the first principle of which was that it should consist only of members opposed to British rule in Ireland. It elaborated a rather vague progressive political programme, including the abolition of slums, but there was no mention of the 'Hungarian policy'.[52]

However, in the New Year, 1904, a series of articles by Griffith began to appear in the *United Irishman*, entitled 'The Resurrection of Hungary'. At often tedious length and with some dubious historical interpretation they recounted the steps by which the Hungarians forty years earlier, using methods analogous to the Irish revival on a cultural level, and by political withdrawal of their representatives from the Imperial Parliament to their native land, had won for themselves the concession of a dual monarchy.

What was really most interesting about these articles was not what they taught so remorselessly about the history of the remote Hungarians, but an excursion which they began to take in the twenty-seventh article of the series into the history of Ireland itself. For Griffith thereby began to divert his readers' attention to a political model nearer home: the Protestant national movement of the late eighteenth century.

Again, in considerable detail he recounted how the patriots of that era had won 'legislative independence' for Ireland by forming themselves into Volunteer companies which put extra-parliamentary pressure on the government. Meeting in Dungannon, Griffith reminded his readers, the Volunteers had declared that 'the claim of any body of men rather than the King, Lords and Commons of Ireland to make laws to bind this kingdom is unconstitutional, illegal and a grievance'.[53] Sweeping aside the entirely different historical conditions of the eighteenth century, Griffith now proclaimed the Volunteers' goal as the political objective for twentieth-century Ireland 'We must retrace our steps,' he wrote, 'and take our stand on the Compact of 1782.' The tactic to be employed was that of the Hungarian deputies, or, as Griffith now conceded, again coming rather belatedly nearer home for his example, that proposed by O'Connell in his idea for a Council of Three Hundred. Griffith recommended that an Irish Parliament should be called consisting of the 103 members at present chosen for Westminster, with the addition of elected delegates from the County Councils, Corporations and Rural District Councils. A second or upper house with a discretionary power to delay legislation should be nominated from recognized bodies devoted to science, the arts, agriculture and industry. Griffith also adopted O'Connell's idea of independent civil arbitration courts to supersede the normal processes of law. Summing up his own personal position carefully, he declared: 'We hold that the subsistence of the connection between this country and Great Britain in any form is not for our country's good, but we recognize the existence of a large mass of our countrymen who believe ... that provided the countries retain each their independence, and exist co-equal in power, the rule of a common sovereign is admissible.'[54]

Here at last was some new thinking for the present – if based on an old style. An alternative both to Fenianism and the Parliamentary Party was being proposed. And when letters of support for the new policy began to come in to the *United Irishman*, recommending that Griffith himself should play the leader of such a new movement, he declared that he personally could not accept the link with the Crown without being untrue to his convictions. He took his stand, he said, with Tone, Mitchel and Emmet. Another member of the Brotherhood, his old friend John MacBride, actually expressed his scepticism of the proposed policy, pointing out that it would fail to appeal widely to the average Irishman who was only too willing to fit into the established order as it was. 'It is the ambition of every small farmer,' he wrote, 'to have a son in the clergy or in the police and sometimes both.... Today,' concluded the Major, 'the protest would end in smoke unless armed men were prepared to back it.'[55]

Griffith's articles, 'The Resurrection of Hungary',[56] reproduced as a pamphlet, sold something under thirty thousand copies in three months, most of these presumably to the converted since this was about the figure for the circulation of the *United Irishman*.[57] 'It would be pleasant,' wrote a contemporary later who had been one of Griffith's earliest supporters and a contributor to the *United Irishman*, 'to record that Mr Griffith's pamphlet sounded a trumpet-call which awakened a slumbering Ireland.... Nothing of the sort happened.'[58]

Although one man who knew Griffith at this time has written that behind all his composure and seriousness there was 'a very real jollity',[59] it is difficult to resist the impression from Griffith's writing that he was sometimes narrow-minded and lacking in humour and that his one great characteristic was his relentless doggedness. At the time of the appearance of the Hungarian articles he was engaged in a quarrel with Yeats from which he emerges poorly as a puritanical critic of J. M. Synge's play *The Shadow of the Glen*, and he was later strongly to disapprove of *The Playboy of the Western World*. Yeats, fast growing disillusioned with the political side of the Irish revival, had already accused Griffith of that 'obscurantism' of the politician 'who would reject every idea which is not of immediate service to his cause'.[60] But it is this very obscurantism, a determination to persist in working out and maintaining an alternative ideal for Irish nationalism to that so success-fully promoted by the Parliamentary Party, that gave him ultimately his historical importance. And already, slowly, barely perceptibly, there were some signs that he was influencing opinion if not events.

The National Council put up a few candidates at selected local elections. They had a little limited success, but more important was the reflection of their recently proclaimed policy in a meeting of the General Council of County Councils, consisting of delegates from all the elected county councils of Ireland, which met in Dublin in January 1905. This, said Griffith, was the most pregnant gathering of representative Irishmen since the Irish Volunteers had met in the church of Dungannon, and certainly in their resolution calling for a Home Rule Parliament they echoed almost exactly the words of that meeting of 1782, adding that 'the claim of any other body of men to make laws for or govern Ireland is illegal, unconstitutional and a grievance intolerable to the people of the country'.[61]

From May 1905 Griffith's new policy generally began to be called the 'Sinn Fein' rather than the 'Hungarian' policy. The suggestion for the new name had been made to him by a young woman named Mary Butler, late in 1904, though the words had long been fairly commonly used as a motto for Irish self-reliance and had in fact been the early motto of the Gaelic League.[62] The first National Council Convention met on Tuesday, 28 November 1905, under the slogan Sinn Fein and with Edward Martyn in the chair. It seemed later to a supporter, looking back on the occasion, to have been a forlorn affair.[63]

Indeed contemplating now this relatively obscure and slightly cranky organization, with its eccentric president, Edward Martyn, who retained his position until 1908 when he retired to devote himself wholly to literature, and the dogged but rather gauche journalist, Arthur Griffith, who was its tireless overseer, it seems almost incredible that within seventeen years the course of Irish history should have been irrevocably altered in its name. Within seventeen years the journalist was to be president of an Irish Free State, with its own flag, its own army and as full a control of all its internal and external affairs as the Dominion of Canada. To almost no one at the time could such an achievement have seemed remotely possible, except possibly to Griffith himself.

It has been stated by an early supporter of Sinn Fein that Griffith did not expect to see Sinn Fein enjoy a political success with the electorate in his own lifetime,[64] but this underrates that rather blinkered persistence which was partly responsible for Sinn Fein's ultimate success. 'I have no doubt,' he wrote in October 1906 in his new paper, *Sinn Fein*, which replaced the *United Irishman* that year, 'of the acceptance of the Sinn Fein policy as the policy of all Ireland in the near future, and no doubt of its ultimate triumph'.[65] Yet, for all his confidence, that triumph was to come about in a way which even he cannot possibly have foreseen.

The actual political significance of Sinn Fein in these early days can best be gauged if it is seen as a minority of a minority – the political offshoot of an Irish-Ireland movement which had itself preferred to turn its back on politics. Even some Irish Irelanders treated it as a joke, like Moran with his reference in *The Leader* to Griffith's 'green Hungarian Band' and 'Mr Martyn's excellent troupe of broad comedians'.[66] Its impact in the open political arena was negligible. Apart from its minor successes in local elections for the Dublin Corporation it achieved nothing which could be seen openly as a threat to the Parliamentary Party. It contested only one by-election in the entire period, early in 1908, when it reached what was to seem for years the zenith of its success.

The political situation was then particularly favourable to Sinn Fein. The impotence of the Nationalist Party at Westminster had been recently clearly demonstrated anew. For after the General Election of 1906 the Liberals found themselves with such a large majority that they could safely ignore the Irish demand for Home Rule altogether. They had gone into the election with a wary assurance that they would not grant Home Rule without further reference to the electorate, and they proposed if returned to power

only to introduce a bill for devolution or decentralization of some administrative powers from Westminster to Dublin. Redmond had tacitly accepted
this procedure for Home Rule by instalments.[67] It was an election pledge
which the Liberals were scrupulous in observing when they found themselves
returned to power with an enormous majority. Tepidness towards Home
Rule had seemed to pay off with the electorate.

There can be little doubt that, on the tactical level, even for the Irish party,
the instalment procedure towards Home Rule was an intelligent one, for each
new step forward made the next both easier to ask for and easier to concede.
But Home Rule nationalism was by now an emotive issue or it was nothing,
for social and economic changes were already proceeding on their own
account with the Land Purchase Acts. If the national issue was to be raised
at all it had to be raised sufficiently emotively to satisfy a minimum national
self-respect. It now seemed for a moment as if the Parliamentary Party had
lost sight of this fact.

The Liberals' Devolution Bill when it came provided for a so-called Irish
Council of 106 members, 82 of whom would be elected and the rest nominated by the government. This Council was to have no law-making or tax-
raising ability whatever. Its sole function was to take over administrative
control for Ireland of eight of the forty-five government departments, the
most important of which were those of Education, Local Government, Public
Works, Agriculture and the Board created by Balfour for helping with the
backward districts of Ireland and known as the Congested Districts Board.
It offered a small sop to Irish national feeling only in so far as it proposed
to hive off into Irish control some of the administrative functions of the
unpopular Dublin Castle.

Augustine Birrell, the Liberal Chief Secretary for Ireland, introducing
the bill went out of his way to belittle its scope in an unashamed effort to
appease English critics of Home Rule. He virtually took credit for the fact
that the bill did not contain 'a touch or a trace, a hint or a suggestion of
any new legislative power or authority ...' and the Government Front
Bench actually cheered their opponent Balfour when he conceded that the
bill could not lead to a larger policy.[68]

Redmond, though naturally in these circumstances approaching the bill
warily, seemed tentatively favourable at first. He admitted that the one
important question to decide was the effect it would have on the prospects
for Home Rule and that this must be decided by a National Convention of
the party organization, which was now called the United Irish League. His
own personal answer was inclined to be 'that its enactment would be an aid
and not a hindrance to Home Rule'.[69]

The National Party newspaper, the *Freeman's Journal*, and the *Cork
Examiner*, expressed a similar view at first.[70] But it soon became clear that

the party was underestimating the sense of disappointment in the constituencies. The branches of the United Irish League preparing for the Party Convention gave the bill a very bad reception.[71] When Griffith, for Sinn Fein, described it as an insult, he was more in tune with public opinion in Ireland than at any time since the Boer War. He called for an implementation of the Sinn Fein policy by a withdrawal from Westminster. At a private meeting of Nationalist Members of Parliament a small group of five actually put forward a resolution to this effect, though they were quickly voted down and three of them eventually resigned from the party.

Faced by the evident strength of feeling at the United Irish League Convention the Parliamentary Party rapidly retracted its tentative welcome for the bill. A resolution expressing Griffith's view that the bill was an insult was unsuccessful, but a unanimous resolution was passed that the party should reject it. The Government was left with no alternative but to drop it.[72]

That the Parliamentary Party had been to some extent losing its grip on its supporters had been noticed by John Dillon, a less complacent political observer than most within the party, almost a year before.* But he tended to put the trouble down to organizational difficulties and particularly shortage of funds. He had little real fear of Griffith himself.[73]

'I have always been of the opinion,' he had written to Redmond in September 1906, 'that this Sinn Fein business is a very serious matter and it has been spreading pretty rapidly for the past year. But if the party and movement keep on right lines it will not become very formidable, because it has no one with any brains to lead it.'[74]

Now the party had shown signs of wavering from 'right lines' over the Irish Council Bill and, though it had been quickly put back on them, the voice of Sinn Fein had at least been clearly heard in the moment of shocked silence. It was in this favourable climate that Sinn Fein was enabled early in 1908 to challenge the party outright in a by-election at North Leitrim. The sitting Nationalist Party member, a young man named Charles Dolan, an effective orator if a bit long-winded,[75] had been one of the small group in the party which had proposed withdrawal from Westminster. He resigned and now offered himself for re-election in his constituency as a Sinn Fein candidate. It was a straightforward fight with the new party candidate.

Dolan and Sinn Fein were overwhelmingly defeated, winning just over a quarter of the total poll. It is a measure of the political insignificance of Sinn Fein hitherto that this was regarded by Griffith as something of a triumph. Tim Healy agreed with him that it meant a new political era was beginning.[76] They were both wrong in the short term. But in the sense that a more serious alternative to the party than Fenianism was now on the political map they were right.

* See above, p. 437.

In 1909, however, the year after the North Leitrim by-election, political developments at Westminster began to take a favourable turn for the Irish Nationalist Party, with the prospect of a head-on clash between the Commons and the House of Lords, and the need of the Liberals for Irish Nationalist support. After the election of 1910, holding the balance between the two great English parties in the Commons, the Nationalists were once again in a position to force the Liberals to commit themselves to a new Home Rule Bill. And though the powers of the House of Lords had to be dealt with first, this was in any case an essential preliminary to the passing of a Home Rule Bill. Suddenly it seemed as if the prospects for Home Rule and the Nationalist Party had never been so bright and Ireland warmed to both.

Griffith, who recognized frankly that in this developing situation such support as had been slowly coming Sinn Fein's way was slipping back to the party, accepted what he called a 'self-denying ordinance' in order to give Redmond a fair chance and full freedom to secure Home Rule by his own methods. If, however, the Parliamentary Party were to fail, he said, 'Sinn Fein must be ready to form the rallying centre of a disappointed nation.'[77] As to the goal of Home Rule itself, Griffith and Sinn Fein accepted it, not – as the party and the majority of the country were prepared to do – as a final settlement of the national question but as a stepping-stone to national independence under a Dual Monarchy of the 1782 pattern. 'Sinn Feiners,' Griffith said in 1912, 'desired as much as any other section to see Home Rule established – not as a national settlement but because it might be used to Ireland's advantage.'[78] And on this basis of giving Redmond a free hand Sinn Fein virtually stood down and ceased from political activity.[79]

Of far greater importance all along than Sinn Fein's practical impact had been its position as a rallying point for all radical, dissatisfied and potentially disappointed individual nationalists in Ireland. The hybrid nature of its support with an overlap of poets, eccentrics, members of the Irish Republican Brotherhood, politically-minded Gaelic Leaguers and frustrated parliamentarians had been the movement's chief characteristic. Many lone wolves with a romantic or dogmatic or otherwise obsessional love of Ireland that had been born of Irish history, but frustrated in the present, gravitated towards Sinn Fein. And as with every movement that attracts rebels there were those who put into their love of Ireland obscure psychological motivations of their own.

Among the more extreme of such figures were some drawn from what would normally have been thought of as the Protestant ascendancy. Maud Gonne was one of these. Another woman from the same upper-class background was Constance Gore-Booth, born of a land-owning Protestant family that had lived for centuries in County Sligo. After breaking away from her family in fairly traditional style by going to art school first in London and then in Paris, she had married an attractive Polish Count named Markievicz and returned to live in Ireland at the beginning of the century. She had already met Yeats when he had visited the Gore-Booth family house, Lissadell, in County Sligo. There a Master of the Sligo Hunt had once described her as the equal of any good rider, man or woman, he had ever known,[80] and Yeats himself was to write of her:

> When long ago I saw her ride
> Under Ben Bulben to the meet
> The beauty of her countryside
> With all youth's lonely wildness stirred ...

Her intellect was not great and her artistic talent was no better than second rate, but it was this spirit of the hunting-field, and a lonely wildness that endured beyond all the physical ravages of time, which she was to carry into Irish nationalist politics.

Constance Markievicz had contributed money to that Irish theatre which Yeats and Lady Gregory founded at the Abbey. Her own and her husband's interest in painting had led her into Irish Ireland circles principally through George Russell, the painter and poet 'A.E.' who worked for Sir Horace Plunkett. But she was still attending fashionable receptions at Dublin Castle as late as 1904.[81] It was not until 1908 when she was in her fortieth year that she plunged suddenly into Irish nationalism, having accidentally found a copy of Griffith's *Sinn Fein* lying about a hall in which she was rehearsing some amateur theatricals.[82] She read an article about Robert Emmet who until then she had vaguely thought a Fenian.[83] She now made up for lost time with a vengeance. She joined Maud Gonne's national women's organization Daughters of Ireland (Inghinidhe nah Eireann) and before the end of 1908 was earning her own mention in Griffith's paper *Sinn Fein* for her nationalist activity.[84] At the fifth annual convention of what was now called the Sinn Fein Organization in 1909 she was elected to its council.[85] 'Ahland' was the manner in which, in her upper-class accent, Constance Markievicz always pronounced her country's name, but it was Caitlin ni Houlihan she now followed for the rest of her life with a dedication which ironically was eventually to earn her Yeats's bitter condemnation.[86]

Another wayward individual Protestant early drawn towards Sinn Fein, though he spent much of his life out of Ireland altogether, was a tall bearded figure from the glens of Antrim named Roger Casement. Casement had won some renown in the consular service for a devastating report published in 1904 on Belgian atrocities in the Congo. He, too, was to sacrifice himself in the cause of Caitlin ni Houlihan, to whom he had long been in thrall. It was, he said, soon after the Congo report was published in 1904, his sensitiveness to oppression as an Irishman that had made him take up the cause of the Congo native so insistently.[87] Early in 1905 he contributed an article to Griffith's *United Irishman* about his father who had helped the

Hungarian patriot, Kossuth.[88] Later the same year he was recommending in a private letter that the Irish Parliamentary Party, instead of hanging uselessly about Westminster, should come back to Ireland and form a National Executive with prime minister, ministers, etc. and 'create a confident reliant National mind in the country'.[89] But of course he recognized that there was not the slightest likelihood of such a thing happening. And before returning to consular service, this time in South America, in the autumn of 1906, he expressed admiration for Griffith in what otherwise seemed to him a bleak outlook for Irish national consciousness.[90]

Casement liked to insist that his address while abroad on consular service was not 'British Consulate' but 'Consulate of Great Britain and Ireland';[91] and he turned his mind frequently to the prospects which a nationalist Ireland might hope to have in the field of foreign relations. 'I am trying,' he had written in August 1905 to a young man he was befriending, 'to get some representative Irishmen interested in "foreign policy" and if we can succeed in getting a commercial agency into existence it will be a beginning. France will be our first field of effort ...'[92] Two years later, in 1907, in a letter to the same young man, he was saying that he wanted to see Ireland have her own team in the Olympic Games.[93]

This young man was a fellow Ulsterman, named Bulmer Hobson, whom Casement had first met at a Gaelic League festival in Antrim in 1904, and with whose prospects and material welfare he was to concern himself intermittently for the rest of his life. Hobson had come under the influence, while still at school, of Alice Milligan and Anna Johnston and their monthly magazine, the *Shan Van Vocht*. He had early declared his support for Griffith and had on his own account started up a number of nationalist-minded organizations, together with another young Ulsterman from the Falls Road area of Belfast, Denis McCullough.

Both McCullough and Hobson became sworn members of the IRB and represented in it a new wave which tried to reanimate the organization. This, in John MacBride's long absence abroad, had sunk back into inactivity under the dead hand of the older and longer-established members.[94] Together in 1905 they founded so-called Dungannon clubs, named after the meeting place of the Volunteers of 1778, and soon engaged as a full-time organizer for these another young man, Sean MacDermott, from County Leitrim, who had been earning his living in Belfast as a bar-tender and tram conductor.[95] All these young men found a natural rallying point in Griffith's activity in Dublin, culminating in the organization which became Sinn Fein.

In fact, for the greater part of the first decade of the century Griffith, though he himself left the IRB in 1906, acted far more than the IRB as a rallying point for active republican thinking, as well as for those more inclined towards his own slowly evolving ideas. In the early days the *United Irishman* had received substantial subsidies to enable it to keep going from

John Devoy's republican Clan-na-Gael in America,[96] and John MacBride had written to Devoy at that time: 'The *United Irishman* at present supplies the place of organizers in Ireland and is at least equal to a dozen.'[97] The Fenian representation on Cumann na Gaedheal and the National Council was always strong, and Hobson who for a short time in 1905 edited a new paper called *The Republic* was proud to declare himself simultaneously a Sinn Feiner.[98] Another young republican, an organizer for the IRB named Sean T. O'Kelly, one day to be President of the first internationally recognized Irish Republic, worked as Honorary Secretary on the National Council's executive in 1907.[99]

In the North Leitrim by-election in 1908 the principal organizer on behalf of the Sinn Fein candidate, Dolan, was the young man whom Hobson and McCullough had brought into the IRB and made an organizer of the Dungannon clubs, Sean MacDermott.[100] After the by-election defeat MacDermott continued to be described as a 'Sinn Fein organizer', and as such he lectured at a National Council meeting attended by the old dynamiter Tom Clarke, recently returned from America to live in Ireland.[101]

Clarke, Griffith's paper announced, had set up in business as a tobacconist and was acting as an agent for a special Irish stamp, sales of which were to help finance a new project for a Sinn Fein daily paper to replace the weekly.[102] Many other names besides MacDermott's and Clarke's, all to play vital parts in the near future of Ireland – Cosgrave, Cathal Brugha, the brothers Patrick and Willie Pearse, the O'Rahilly – are to be found associated with Sinn Fein activity at this time. A rather imprecise association of men, whose dedication to a fuller independence than Home Rule seemed more important than their differences about what exactly that independence was to be, or how it was to be achieved, was in being under the name Sinn Fein. It was an imprecision which was never wholly sorted out and which ultimately was to prove disastrous.

In 1909, as Griffith withdrew into political inactivity to give Redmond a chance with Home Rule, the republican elements associated with Sinn Fein expressed themselves as more and more dissatisfied. By August 1909 Hobson 'was considering whether or not he should throw the whole thing up'.[103] Another young Ulster IRB man, named Patrick McCartan, a former medical student and friend of Hobson and McCullough, was writing to Devoy in the States in March 1910 that 'things here are in a queer mess and nobody knows what to make of it all ... the Executive, the Resident Executive and other humbugs will be gravely elected by the frequenters of the club where the children will be taught to break Ireland's chains with their song.... McCullough, Countess Markievicz talk of the advisability of all clearing out of it and leaving them to go their own way.' Others on the executive, he said, including the IRB man Sean T. O'Kelly, 'all trimmed when they attended the meetings.... So you see there is not much hope.'[104]

What was interesting was the tacit admission that the only source of hope for republicans, if there was to be any, was Griffith and his organization. In 1911 an IRB paper, *Irish Freedom*, edited by Bulmer Hobson, was started in order to preach a traditionally outspoken and active line. But the IRB was not in itself strong or even confident enough to make a political impact on its own; it needed some other organization to work through. Griffith's, which had seemed so promising, was now in the light of his own new position disappointing. But if not round Griffith, where could they rally effectively? For the time being there seemed no answer.

Meanwhile, for the average citizen the IRB was popularly thought to have become defunct years ago. Both it and Sinn Fein's momentary flash in the pan seemed irrelevant. All eyes in Ireland were turned on Westminster where at last, after nearly twenty years, the people's representatives seemed set to win Home Rule. After such a long time in which Home Rule had been remote, it came suddenly into very sharp focus and in the new atmosphere of Irish-consciousness seemed all the more worth winning.

10

Asquith and the Third Home Rule Bill

The Liberal Party approached Home Rule in 1910 in a quite different spirit from that in which it had launched the first Home Rule Bill in 1886 and the second in 1893. The idealistic sense of crusade with which Gladstone had invested the issue had largely disappeared. Home Rule had become more a question of political arithmetic: 272 Unionists opposed by 272 Liberals, in a House of Commons which also contained 42 Labour and 82 Irish Nationalists, equalled Home Rule.* It was as crude as that. The fact does much to explain a certain lack of total determination in pressing the issue home, which finally proved fatal to it. The Liberals, subconsciously at least, were prepared for some compromise from the start.

Though Irish Home Rule had continued after 1893 to be theoretically one of the party's basic philosophical tenets, a policy of disengagement from any practical concern with it had been deliberately adopted in 1899, ironically by Gladstone's son Herbert, then the Liberal Chief Whip.[1] He had taken careful soundings of the party on his appointment to that post and found a general disposition to regard Home Rule as an electoral handicap. An official policy of 'stand and wait' was formulated, giving, as Herbert Gladstone put it, 'plenty of scope for individual divergencies. The flag might be nailed by some, while others might to some extent dissociate themselves from the question.'[2] The party had gone into the election of 1900 publicly declaring that it would 'let that question sleep awhile'.[3]

But after the Liberal defeat of 1900 the difficulty of papering over differences on a matter so close to the party's soul had become evident. The internal debate was fought out in the open in a manner that permanently sapped some of the Liberals' vigour on the whole issue. Positions within the party ranged across a wide spectrum. Rosebery, the former leader who had succeeded Gladstone as prime minister, for a short time now emerged from retirement to call for 'a clean slate' in Liberal policies and an abandonment of 'the fly-blown phylacteries of the past', by which he meant principally Home Rule. The new leader, Campbell Bannerman, a strong

* The figures are those for the second of the 1910 elections.

Home Ruler, equated Rosebery's clean slate with 'a white sheet' and declared that Liberal policy should be based on principles and not on electoral expediency.[4] Somewhere in the middle, but inclining more to the anti-Home Rule position of Lord Rosebery, had been Henry Herbert Asquith, the ambitious son of a small Yorkshire woollen manufacturer, and member for East Fife since 1886. Gifted with an effortless intellectual mastery of most subjects to which he turned his mind, Asquith had attained the post of Home Secretary in Gladstone's last government. By 1910 he was fifty-eight, in the prime of life for a politician.

As far back as September 1901 Asquith had publicly declared that Liberals should never again take office if they were dependent on the Irish members for a majority in the House of Commons.[5] In February 1902 he actually became a vice-president of Lord Rosebery's Liberal League, founded to promote the ex-premier's anti-Home Rule views, and he explained to his constituency chairman in East Fife that since the Home Rule policy had proved a failure the Liberals must dissociate themselves from all obligation to a third Home Rule Bill if returned to office.[6] In rather typical fashion he added that the party did still have an obligation to find ways of reconciling Ireland to the British Empire and of relieving the pressure of business on the Imperial Parliament at Westminster, but that these goals could only be arrived at 'by methods which carry with them, step by step, the sanction and sympathy of British opinion'.[7] It was this cautious 'step by step' principle that finally became the agreed Liberal policy for the 1906 election, with the reluctant acquiescence of the leader, Campbell Bannerman.

'If we are to get a majority in the next House of Commons,' Asquith had written to Herbert Gladstone shortly before that election, 'it can only be by making it perfectly clear to the electors that ... it will be no part of the policy of the new Liberal government to introduce a Home Rule Bill in the new parliament.'[8]

And it was on this understanding that the Liberals had gone before the electorate and triumphed. The abortive Irish Council Bill of 1907 was the only step taken towards Irish Home Rule during the four years' Liberal government that followed.* In 1908 Campbell Bannerman died and Asquith became prime minister. And when, after two successive general elections in 1910 with almost identical results, the Liberals were left dependent for their parliamentary majority on the Irish, it was ironically Asquith who introduced to the House of Commons the third Home Rule Bill in April 1912.

But if not really a Home Ruler by conviction, Asquith was by temperament, ambition and intellectual aptitude a politician of great skill and intelligence. A living embodiment of the principle that politics is both the art of the possible and the art of the unavoidable, he took in his stride the

* See above, p. 454.

realization that with the Liberals dependent on Irish support for a majority in the House of Commons the time had come for some substantial measure of Home Rule. 'Solvitur ambulando', or 'taking it on the curve', as he himself put it on two different occasions, was the cardinal principle of his political technique. Applied to the issue of Home Rule this inevitably meant a shallower level of commitment than that of the Irish nationalist who saw in Home Rule the final resolution of seven centuries of discord. But having satisfied himself that there was no possibility of a workable compromise on Home Rule to be obtained by agreement with the Conservatives, Asquith was prepared to assume towards the issue an uncompromising dedication, at least until such time as the need for compromise might or might not enforce itself.[9]

In one essential respect Asquith was in a much stronger position to carry Home Rule than Gladstone had ever been. The power of the House of Lords permanently to veto any bill had been removed the year before. This vital constitutional change, first demanded by the need to pass the Liberal 'People's Budget' of 1909 and now enshrined in the Parliament Act of 1911, had been the result of two years' mounting constitutional crisis involving two general elections in 1910. Throughout the crisis, Irish support for the Liberals in the House of Commons had been the decisive factor, and the implications for Home Rule of the abolition of the Lords' veto had never been far from Irish nationalists' minds. Though the two elections of 1910 had been fought by the Liberals on the specific issues of the Budget and the Lords' veto, Asquith, as part of a political bargain with the Irish, had to give them a clear public commitment to Home Rule, and he did this at the Albert Hall on 10 December 1909. Liberal policy, he there declared, was 'a policy which, while explicitly safeguarding the supremacy and indefectible authority of the Imperial Parliament, will set up in Ireland a system of full self-government in regard to purely Irish affairs'.[10] He had kept further pronouncements on the subject to the minimum in the course of the two elections, and 1911 had been occupied chiefly with the passage of the Parliament Bill.

But now in 1912 the Irish Nationalists were to be finally rewarded for their two-year-long support. As a result of the Parliament Act any bill rejected by the House of Lords could, if passed through the Commons again in two more consecutive sessions, automatically qualify for the royal assent and become law regardless of the Lords. Theoretically there was now nothing to stop the Liberals, with their Irish-based majority in the Commons, from passing a Home Rule Bill.

It was this very seeming inevitability that was to put such desperate vigour into the anti-Home Rule cause. A sense of unfairly imposed impotence dominated the opposition. If Asquith, the Liberals and the Irish Nationalists were theoretically in an unassailable position, the anti-Home Rulers became determined that it should not be theory alone that counted. Two important political factors lent them dynamism and strength. One was the urgent need for the Conservative Party to unite firmly on a good electoral issue after their embarrassing internal divisions over tariff reform. The other was the extent of the organization already in being in North-East Ulster dedicated to practical opposition to Home Rule at all costs.

Organized practical opposition to Home Rule from Ulster already had a long history. Naturally, the peaks of such organization had been achieved at moments when the danger seemed the greatest, that is to say, at the time of the two abortive Home Rule Bills of 1886 and 1893. Once those specific dangers were past, there had been a tendency for activity to lapse and intense emotion to wane, though the Orange Lodges ensured the permanence of at least a nucleus organization. However, in the first decade of the twentieth century a more subtle danger had appeared for the die-hard Unionists of Ulster, which had led to the construction of a permanent defensive organization on a more sophisticated political basis than that merely of the Orange Lodges. This danger was the appearance among Unionists themselves of a movement favouring the 'devolution' of at least some statutory powers to an Irish body, a proposal which looked to die-hard Unionists very much like a proposal for Home Rule by instalments.

This 'devolution' idea took shape under the aegis of the Irish Reform Association, a body sponsored by the Earl of Dunraven, a liberal-minded Unionist landlord who in 1903 had played a prominent part in negotiations leading to the great Land Purchase Act of that year. The Reform Association's plans eventually came to nothing, but the crisis to which they gave rise in 1904 sounded the alarm for all orthodox Unionists.

Through a misunderstanding the Under-Secretary of the day, Sir Anthony Macdonell, a Catholic whose brother was a member of the Nationalist Party, involved Dublin Castle more deeply and more sympathetically with the Reform Association's plans for devolution than the Chief Secretary, George Wyndham, intended. When this became apparent there was an explosion of wrath in the Unionist Party and though Wyndham publicly dissociated himself from the project he was eventually compelled to resign. The whole incident touched a most sensitive nerve in the Ulster Unionist temperament, already alerted by such conciliatory measures as the Local Government Act of 1898, the increasingly generous land-purchase arrangements and other aspects of 'killing Home Rule by kindness'. A suspicion was excited of 'softness towards Irish nationalism on the part of the adminstration', and the fear aroused that Ulster Unionists might be taken in the rear while facing the orthodox Home Rule enemy in front.

Within two days of the breaking of the devolution crisis of 1904, two Ulster Unionist Members of Parliament had declared it 'an opportune moment to revive on a war footing for active work the various Ulster Defence Associations'.[11] The practical consequence was the establishment in March

1905 of an Ulster Unionist Council. 'Consistent and continuous political action' was to be the watchword.[12] Thus when, in 1911, after the passing of the Parliament Act, the real crisis and the real enemy had to be faced in circumstances of grim finality, the Protestants of Ulster were prepared and an effective organization was in being and active.

It was an organization incomparably more professional than anything that had been seen in 1886 or 1893. In November 1910, even before the results of the second election of that year were known, the Ulster Unionist Council had opened an armament fund.[13] Colonel Saunderson, the colourful leader of the Ulster Unionists in the two previous crises, had died in 1906. His place had been taken for a few years by the English Conservative Walter Long, MP for Dublin South. But in the first General Election of 1910 Long had been returned for a London seat and the Ulster Unionists had to look round for another leader. Their choice fell on the senior Member for Dublin University, a Southern Irishman who enjoyed wide renown as the leading advocate of his day, who had been Solicitor General in the last Conservative government. His name was Sir Edward Carson.

Carson was fifty-five in 1910, and though something of a hypochondriac was then at the peak of those powers which had brought him such success and wealth at the bar. Courage, single-mindedness, clear-sightedness and determination, but above all an unquestionable and unflinching honesty of purpose, were his salient characteristics. Descended on both sides of his family from Protestant settlers who had first come to Ireland two centuries before, he was an Irishman whose devotion to the country of his birth was as great as his devotion to its union with the rest of the British Isles. 'It's only for Ireland that I'm in politics,' he said on one occasion, and on another: 'It's only for the sake of the Union that I am in politics.'[14] The two were indistinguishable in his mind and formed a single emotion. 'Heaven knows,' he said a few weeks after his wife died in 1913, 'my one affection left me is my love for Ireland.'[15]

He believed in order and discipline and firm government, and thought that administration of such things by the British Parliament through Dublin Castle was in the best interests of his country. But he was no blind reactionary. While a student at Trinity College, Dublin, he had spoken in the Historical Society's debates in favour of women's rights and the abolition of capital punishment.[16] And when nearly twenty years later he allowed his name to go forward as a candidate to represent his old college in Parliament objections were raised to him on the grounds that he was tainted with liberalism.[17] When he was finally elected it was as a Liberal Unionist.

Carson's work at the bar in Ireland, where he made his name and had been Crown Prosecutor before moving to England, had confirmed in him a natural distaste for the lawlessness and disorder with which all attempts to change the social and political *status quo* in Ireland were inevitably associated. On circuit in the eighties at the height of the Plan of Campaign* he had shown some personal courage in expressing his disdain for the mob at Mitchelstown on a day when three people were killed there by the RIC. Yet he did not allow his dislike of his country's popular movements to warp his attitude towards the people themselves. 'We welcome,' he once declared, curiously echoing something Parnell had once said, 'aye and we love, every individual Irishman, even though opposed to us.'[18] Though a Protestant he was a staunch defender, in an Irish rather than a Protestant way, of Catholic claims for university education. 'Honourable Members in their hearts,' he said on one occasion in the House of Commons, 'are afraid of something or other connected with the Catholic religion which they will not suggest and which they will not explain. I ask, what is this fear of a Catholic University? ... Do you think that the Catholics of Ireland will be worse off with the enlightenment of a university education than they are now when they are deprived of it?'[19]

It was only because Carson believed passionately that Irishmen would be worse off with Home Rule that he so steadfastly opposed it. When, in his speech against Home Rule in a debate in the Commons in February 1911, he said that he had first most earnestly and thoroughly considered whether it might be of any benefit to Ireland, it was impossible not to believe that he spoke the truth.[20] The worst that can be said of him as an Irishman is that, unlike Parnell, he over-readily identified Ireland with the interest of his own class.

Carson was incapable of taking up something he did not intend to go through with. Hints during 1910 of certain Conservative inclinations to compromise on Home Rule had exasperated him and, though they came to nothing, it was a possible failure of determination that he saw as the principal menace to the anti-Home Rule cause. 'I wish I could be in Ulster,' he wrote to Lady Londonderry in January 1911, '... to know whether men are desperately in earnest and prepared to make great sacrifices.'[21] And later that year, appalled by the Conservative leadership's attitude of resignation towards the Parliament Bill, he wrote to James Craig, Member of Parliament for East Down and the most active member of the Ulster Unionist Council: 'What I am very anxious about is to satisfy myself that the people over there really mean to resist. I am not for a mere game of bluff, and, unless men are prepared to make great sacrifices which they clearly understand, the talk of resistance is no use.'[22] In this respect Craig was his man.

Son of a self-made whisky millionaire, James Craig had been a founder member of the Belfast Stock Exchange as a young man and had then fought with gallantry and been wounded and taken prisoner in the Boer War. Affection for his home background in Ulster and for the Empire which he had helped to see through the testing time of the war provided the simple emotional inspiration for this solid upright man of independent means when

* See above, p. 407.

he decided to enter politics in 1903. It was a vision not in any way complicated, as was that of Carson, the Southern Irishman, by thoughts for the rest
of Ireland. Now that the testing time had come for Ulster itself, as Craig
saw it, he devoted all his energies and considerable cool organizing ability
to what he saw as Ulster's cause, and filled the role of Carson's principal
lieutenant.

It was Craig who arranged the first big Ulster demonstration of the new
anti-Home Rule epoch at his own home of Craigavon just outside Belfast
on 23 September 1911, six months before the bill was introduced. Here, after
a wet morning, the sun suddenly came out and Carson spoke to an awed
crowd of some fifty thousand Orangemen and Unionists assembled on the
lawns in front of the house. It was his first big speech to the Protestants of
Ulster as their leader in the new crisis and he began as he intended to go on.

'I now enter into compact with you,' he declared, 'and with the help of
God you and I joined together ... will yet defeat the most nefarious conspiracy that has ever been hatched against a free people.'

He proceeded to outline how to do this:

'We must be prepared, in the event of a Home Rule Bill passing, with such
measures as will carry on for ourselves the government of those districts of
which we have control. We must be prepared ... the morning Home Rule
passes, ourselves to become responsible for the government of the Protestant
Province of Ulster.'[23]

His audience had also begun as they intended to go on. At least one of the
contingents of Orangemen who had marched the two miles out from Belfast
to Craigavon that day in columns of four, particularly impressed people by
their order and discipline. They had already been practising drill.

It was soon discovered that an authorization to drill could be obtained
quite legally from a JP, provided the object was to help maintain the rights
and liberties of the United Kingdom's constitution.[24] From the beginning of
1912 more and more licences for drilling were applied for and by the time of
the next great Ulster demonstration at Balmoral, a suburb of Belfast, on
9 April 1912, two days before the Home Rule Bill was introduced, there was
a distinctly military flavour to the proceedings. Over 100,000 men, it was
reckoned, marched past a saluting base in columns while a Union Jack, said
to be the largest ever made, flew from a ninety-foot flagstaff in the centre of
the grounds. Carson must have been deeply reassured by what he saw. His
one fear was still that people would think they did not mean business. His
own mind, he wrote privately, was implacably made up for 'very drastic
action in Ulster'.[25] At a private dinner a fortnight before the Balmoral demonstration he had been introduced by Craig to Lord Roberts, who, though
retired, was the senior Field Marshal of the British Army. 'I hope,' wrote
Carson significantly, 'something will come of it.'[26]

At the same time, the most significant feature of the whole Balmoral

demonstration was the presence on the saluting base of the new leader of the
Conservative opposition in the House of Commons, himself a Scot of Ulster
descent, Andrew Bonar Law. 'There will not be wanting help from across
the Channel when the hour of battle comes,' Law had said on arrival in
Ulster the day before, and, as an Ulster Scot, he had spoken of the possible
need for Ulster to be prepared to face a Bannockburn or Flodden.[27] At Balmoral itself he reassured his vast audience that the Conservative Party regarded their cause as the cause not of Ulster alone but of the Empire. The
Conservatives, he declared, 'would do all that men could do to defeat a
conspiracy as treacherous as had ever been formed against the life of a great
nation'.[28] From this moment onwards there could be little doubt that the Conservatives intended to identify themselves at least as much as twenty years
before with the extra-parliamentary force gathering in Ulster. Bonar Law
said himself that they were 'even more in earnest than before'.[29]

Two days later, on 11 April 1912, Asquith introduced the new Home Rule
Bill in the House of Commons.

The principle of Home Rule had already been much debated since the new
Parliament's inauguration in 1911. For although the first major business to
concern this Parliament had been the veto of the House of Lords and the
passage of the Parliament Bill, it had been impossible to argue about that
without at the same time discussing the first immediate result which the
removal of the veto was likely to lead to: namely, Home Rule for Ireland.
Even in the Debate on the king's speech in February 1911 which had not
mentioned Ireland at all, one Unionist member had threatened civil war if a
Home Rule Bill were to go through.[30] Another Unionist member in the same
debate, asserting that Ulster could not be coerced, had cried prophetically:
'Try it. Call out the British troops to compel Ulster and see what happens!'[31]

To understand the intensity of passion and fury which the prospect of
Home Rule for Ireland unleashed among Conservatives during the years
1911–14 it is necessary first to realize that the pattern of the British Constitution which is taken for granted in the second half of the twentieth
century was not yet quite consolidated. Indeed, it was the events of these
years which finally consolidated that pattern. What is assumed today to be
part of the essential working of the constitution was then in the hazier area
of doubt and imprecision which characterizes all formative periods. One
essential element in today's constitution, the supremacy of the Commons
over the Lords, was after all, in 1911, still being debated, and only introduced
as a new feature at the end of that year. Even the role of the monarch seemed
less firmly circumscribed than it is today. Nothing in fact illustrates better
the slightly different constitutional climate of that time than that it should
have been possible for one of the leading legal figures of the day, Carson
himself, to make the following bitter joke and consider it nothing but a joke.

'Apparently,' he wrote in the middle of 1912, after reading an article in the *Spectator* which maintained that the royal assent to a bill was a formal, automatic affair, 'if the King was asked to sign a bill for the abolition of the monarchy he must as a constitutional sovereign obey!'[32]

This would not be questioned today, but such a possibility seemed then preposterous to Conservatives like Carson who could write of the king: 'I am told he is saturated with the idea of "constitutionalism" which he translates into doing everything his PM tells him. What a good King!'[33]

However, even such a disappointingly constitutional sovereign as George V was to try to assert himself before the crisis was out.

Only if this subtly different constitutional climate of the day is appreciated can the indignation of the Conservatives, and their feeling that the normal limits of constitutional action had been virtually suspended, be fairly understood. By modern constitutional conventions Asquith's political behaviour, if adroit, was scrupulously correct. At the same time, to some people it was questionable; to others, actually 'a conspiracy'. Asquith in his own political interest had used his Irish support to remove the Lords' veto. He had then paid the price for such support in the form of a Home Rule Bill which had not been the main issue of either election but against which the Lords were now impotent. This was the substance of the charge against the government.

'They have sold the Constitution,' Bonar Law told his Ulster audience. 'They have sold themselves and they thought they could sell you, but you were not theirs to sell. Under such circumstances, in order to try to force this calamity upon you ... it would not be by government at all, it would be by tyranny, naked and unashamed, and tyranny not the less real because the tyrants have usurped their power not by force, but by fraud.'[34] When later in the summer Bonar Law addressed a giant Unionist meeting at Blenheim in England he deliberately paraphrased Balfour's famous words of twenty years before, which he had carefully studied, about the tyranny of parliamentary majorities being as bad as the tyranny of kings.* 'There are things stronger than parliamentary majorities,' was the way he now put it, adding, 'I can imagine no length of resistance to which Ulster will go, in which I shall not be ready to support them ...'[35] Law had already told the king himself at a dinner at Buckingham Palace in the course of a conversation which made the king blush: 'They may say your assent is a purely formal act and the prerogative of veto dead. That was true as long as there was a buffer between you and the House of Commons, but they have destroyed that buffer and it is true no longer.'[36]

Both in the preliminary discussion of Home Rule during the passage of the Parliament Bill, and in the early debates on the new Home Rule Bill itself, argument concentrated less than on the two previous occasions on the old question of real Irish intentions and the danger of ultimate separation. In

* See above, p. 420.

the first stages there was some repetition of the familiar quotations from Parnell and other Nationalists still members of the House, suggesting that there were no final bounds to the measure of Irish freedom to which nationalists aspired. And though many were prepared to treat such remarks as the necessary exaggerations of a bygone political age, Carson made a neat point when he complained: 'We are always being told we must trust the Irish Nationalist members. But on what ground? Upon the ground that we ought not to believe a single word they ever said.'[37] On the other hand, whatever they might have said in the past, Redmond, Dillon, O'Brien and co. had now publicly committed their careers to a nationalism which fully accepted the overriding supremacy of the Imperial Parliament. In his very first speech in the new Parliament of 1911 Redmond, as Irish leader, had once again declared that a Home Rule incorporating this principle would be a final settlement and had pledged his countrymen to accept it as such.[38]

In general, many fundamental changes had taken place in the Irish situation in the previous twenty years, and both sides tried to argue from them to their advantage. Perhaps the most powerful new argument was that used by Carson when he said that there was now hardly a single special Irish grievance left for an Irish Parliament to deal with, as they had all been dealt with by the Imperial Parliament.[39]

Inasmuch as the vast majority of Irishmen were now owners of their farms, that there was since 1909 a Catholic University and since 1898 representative local government, there was undoubtedly much truth in this. But typically, coming from a man of Carson's class, such a view left out of account all the emotional residue of earlier suffering and the consequent really very modest demand for some national self-respect under the name of limited Home Rule.

The transformation of the atmosphere of Ireland could equally well be used to argue, as Winston Churchill did, that it was now very much safer to give Ireland Home Rule. The Irish question, said Churchill, no longer presented itself in the same 'fierce and tragic guise.... Rebellion, murder and dynamite, these have vanished from Ireland.'[40] At the same time, the success of self-government conferred on South Africa seemed to augur well for Ireland.

The practical workings of the 1898 Local Government Act were cited as evidence by both sides. A Unionist complained that 'even in the appointment of doctors the test has been one not of fitness for the post, but one of religion or being a good nationalist', to which Redmond's brother, Willie, replied indignantly that the proportion of local jobs given to Protestants in Catholic areas was very much fairer than the proportion of jobs given to Catholics in Protestant areas.[41] However, the weight of argument soon shifted away from the desirability of Home Rule for the greater part of Ireland. This, reluctantly, came to be virtually accepted as inevitable. The argument concentrated on whether or not, in the special circumstances in which the Home Rule Bill had been introduced, it was allowable to override the objections of 'Ulster'.

The bill itself was in general principle much the same as the two previous Home Rule Bills. It set up an Irish legislature with an Irish executive for purely domestic Irish affairs, while reserving for the Imperial Parliament all matters affecting the Crown, peace and war, the army, navy, international treaties, the imposition of most taxation in the first instance, and even for a period of six years control of the Royal Irish Constabulary – though control of the Dublin Metropolitan Police was to pass to the Irish immediately. The total supremacy of the Imperial Parliament over such an Irish Parliament was clearly stated and repeatedly emphasized by Asquith.

'We maintain,' he declared, '... unimpaired, and beyond the reach of challenge or question, the supremacy, absolute and sovereign, of the Imperial Parliament.'[42]

There were those Unionists who maintained that such legalistic supremacy would mean nothing. Balfour said it was like Kings of England continuing to call themselves Kings of France for several hundred years after they had been driven out of that country.[43] It was pointed out that such power existed equally over the Parliaments of the Dominions though no one would ever dream of trying to exercise it. But this was not on the whole a much debated issue, for the simple reason that the supremacy of the Imperial Parliament was something the Irish had no difficulty in accepting.

Redmond's support for the bill in Parliament was immediately echoed and confirmed by almost all Irishmen not only in Ireland but all over the world. The *Freeman's Journal* – the Nationalist Party paper – finding this Home Rule Bill 'the greatest, boldest and most generous of the three', forecast Irish reaction correctly when it declared that 'Ireland under this Bill, trusted and liberated, armed with all the powers necessary to the full development of her aspirations and her resources, will warmly reciprocate so splendid an invitation for final reconciliation between her and the people of England.'[44] Unanimous resolutions congratulating Redmond and the party poured in from branches of the United Irish League (the Party organization), from Irish local authorities and from prominent Irish Nationalists in all parts of the United States and Australia, including Patrick Egan, former Treasurer of the Land League. Although in the general chorus of approval there were criticisms of some financial details of the bill, no voice was raised, except by the tiny Sinn Fein and Republican minority in Ireland and the extremists in America, to criticize the principle of the Imperial Parliament's supremacy or

* Items in the bill singled out for favourable comparison with earlier bills were: the use of the term 'parliament' rather than 'legislature', as previously; immediate control of the Judicial Bench and the Dublin Police; and the provision of a financial subsidy instead of, as previously, the demand for a financial contribution.

to say that in terms of the aspirations of Irish nationalism the bill was inadequate. A vast National Convention in Dublin passed a unanimous resolution welcoming the bill 'as an honest and generous attempt to settle the long and disastrous quarrel between the British and Irish nations'.[45] And when in January 1913 the bill passed its third reading by a Commons majority of 110, tar barrels and bonfires blazed in celebration of the Home Rule 'Triumph' all over Ireland and innumerable bands pumped out the strains of 'A National Once Again'.

But already there were unmistakable indications that such rejoicing was premature. Victory over the bill's Unionist opponents in Parliament was not what mattered so much as the possible action such opponents might take outside Parliament to prevent the bill becoming law under the procedures of the Parliament Act.

The chief rational argument with which anti-Home Rulers backed their increasingly menacing protest was that Home Rule had never been properly submitted to the electorate at the second election of 1910. It was true that the Liberals had done much at the time to avoid mentioning what was still thought of as a potentially embarrassing political issue. Only some 84 of the 272 successful Liberal candidates in England, Scotland and Wales had actually mentioned Home Rule at all in their election addresses, and these 84 did not include, significantly, the Prime Minister, the Chancellor of the Exchequer, the First Lord of the Admiralty, the Home Secretary, or the Chief Secretary for Ireland.[46] Asquith, fighting on the Lords' veto and wanting to keep Home Rule as much in the background as possible, had presented it, when compelled to refer to it at all, rather as a technical adjustment to the administrative arrangements for the United Kingdom than a concession to Irish national feeling. He had noticeably refrained from reasserting the Liberals' commitment to it until a good number of the election results of December 1910 were declared.* However, it was also true, as Ramsay Macdonald among many other supporters of the government pointed out, that if the Liberals had not presented Home Rule as an issue at the election the Conservatives certainly had.[47] Almost every Conservative candidate had been at pains to stress that if the Liberals won on their main issue of the Lords veto, the way would then be open for them to pass Home Rule without further hindrance. 'He who gives a vote for the Parliament Bill,' the renowned constitutional lawyer Dicey had declared, 'most assuredly gives a vote for Home Rule for Ireland.' Though the Liberals could reasonably be censured for political cowardice, it could not reasonably be said that the British public had been unaware of the Home Rule question during the election. Reason, however, was fast fading into the background, and emotion was increasingly the spur to action.

The expressions 'Ulster' and 'coercing Ulster' had already assumed such

---

* Election results were then declared over a period of some weeks.

emotive force that it is necessary now to remind oneself of the facts behind them. The nine provinces of Ulster contained, according to the 1911 census, 886,000 Protestants of all sects, and 690,000 Catholics. Though it is roughly reasonable to regard the Protestants as Unionists and the Catholics as Home Rulers, this was not literally quite so. A more accurate idea of the Ulster population's feelings can be obtained from election figures. On the basis of the second General Election of 1910 these gave a total of 103,367 Unionist votes and 94,073 Home Rule votes over the whole province. Looked at by other democratic standards: five of the nine Ulster counties had Nationalist Home Rule majorities and the other four Unionist Rule majorities; while the distribution of Ulster's elected representatives in the House of Commons was, immediately after the 1910 election, sixteen Home Rulers to seventeen Unionists, but, after a by-election in Londonderry South early in 1913, seventeen Home Rulers to sixteen Unionists. There was thus actually a technical democratic majority of one in favour of Home Rule over the whole of Ulster. None of these figures seem to assert any very obvious right to special treatment by the Unionists of Ulster, given the fact that Ulster was itself only a minority of the whole unit of Ireland. (In the rest of Ireland by the 1911 census there were some 250,000 Protestants to 3,000,000 Catholics.)

But since democracy can never provide precise mathematical justice, an essential part of its successful functioning is the spirit in which it deals with those minorities which it inevitably overrides. In the British Constitution an unwritten safeguard is provided for minorities in parliamentary constituencies since each representative represents as well as he can, compatibly with his own conscience, those who compose the minority against him equally with those who vote for him. It could be argued that, in the Irish situation, regard for minorities had to be abnormally acute just because religious differences made it difficult for this spirit to be applied in the normal way. If a substantial minority cared principally for its Protestant religion it might reasonably be doubted whether the conscience of a predominantly Catholic Parliament and Executive could be rigorously exercised in its favour.

There were, it is true, special safeguards built into the Third Home Rule to give the Protestants of Ulster disproportionate consideration. Apart from the overriding supremacy of the imperial legislature there was to be an Upper House or Senate whose members would be nominated, and over-representation of Ulster in the Lower House together with a provision by which both Houses should sit and vote together if there were a dispute between the two. None of these safeguards, however, could provide the sort of absolute certainty Ulster Protestants wanted. They did not want reassurance. They simply did not want to be in a situation in which they needed reassurance. They did not want any new arrangement at all. The political mentality of the Protestant Irishmen of the North had been conditioned long ago by a self-perpetuating fear and mistrust of Catholics. And such mistrust had been consciously activated by Conservative political interests for the past quarter of a century. Moreover, even if there were no genuine grounds at all for the Protestant's religious and economic fears, there would always be a psychological loss involved for Ulster Protestants in a Home Rule Ireland – the loss of that status identified by Lecky when he wrote of the penal law era, that 'the most worthless Protestant, even if he had nothing else to boast of, at least found it pleasing to think that he was a member of a dominant race'.[48]

There was an almost indistinguishable overlap of the irrational and the rational, of emotion and reason in the Ulster Protestant attitude. One of the reasoned arguments much used in support of the basic emotion was that if special treatment in the form of Home Rule was justified for Catholic Ireland, which was after all a minority of the United Kingdom, then Ulster Protestants who were a minority of Ireland were equally justified in seeking special treatment. But this argument could soon be reduced to an absurdity of democratic Chinese boxes. For there was also a Catholic minority within the Protestant minority within the Catholic majority. In any democracy which is to function effectively there must come an arbitrary point at which minorities must accept a majority decision they dislike. Since five of the nine counties had a Nationalist majority, and four of them a Protestant one, a possible arbitrary dividing point might reasonably be said to have existed there. This would have left the five counties of Donegal, Monaghan, Cavan, Tyrone and Fermanagh to go to a Home Rule Ireland and the other four to be allowed to remain within the United Kingdom as the majority of their inhabitants demanded.

Given the fact that the vast majority of Irish nationalists were in any case prepared to accept considerable qualifications to their 'nationalism', involving identification on many points with the rest of the United Kingdom, such a solution was, at that time, in terms of logic and reason, probably the best and most equitable that could have been devised. But logic and reason were not the prime movers on either side of the Irish situation. It was not only Ulster Protestants but Catholic Nationalists whose fundamental attitude was emotive: Home Rule itself was for the Irish nationalist a strange compromise between reason and emotion. William O'Brien, who now sat in the House of Commons at the head of a small group of independent Home Rule MPs had conveyed well the confused nature of such a compromise in his moving speech on the first reading of the Home Rule Bill. The Bill involved, he had said, 'a certain degree of renunciation, by Irish nationalists of the old school, of those dreams, perhaps only dreams, but dreams that came in the youth of some of us as the blood in our veins'. And he asked, reasonably, for a parallel sacrifice on the part of Unionists.

If much of the emotive dream was being sacrificed in the permanent limitations of the Home Rule Bill, a bare minimum had to be retained if any illusion of that dream's fulfilment were to survive. The dream had been about Ireland as a country, and the indispensable part of that dream, even for Home Rulers, was that the country should still be Ireland as a whole. Thus, though in a purely reasonable and logical atmosphere the exclusion of the four counties of Derry, Down, Armagh and Antrim from the operation of the Home Rule Bill might have seemed an intelligent solution, anyone who really understood the nationalist element in Home Rule or comprehended the emotive sacrifice of which O'Brien had spoken could have seen that to exclude any part of Ireland permanently was simply not an acceptable possibility.

Gladstone might well have understood this. Unfortunately, neither for Asquith nor for the rest of the Liberal Cabinet was understanding of or identification with the deep feelings behind Home Rule an important motivation. Home Rule for them was merely a reasonable political necessity. They worked within the framework of reason. Therefore, presented from the start with 'Ulster's' obstruction to the whole principle of the bill, they moved gradually towards the logical point of compromise, regardless of the fact that it could never be acceptable to their Irish nationalist allies. This point of compromise involved the exclusion of some part of Ulster, presumably at least the four predominantly Protestant counties of Derry, Down, Antrim and Armagh.

Winston Churchill, First Lord of the Admiralty, perhaps because of the identification of his father with the Ulster Unionist cause in 1886, had been in favour of some such compromise even before the framing of the 1912 Bill. Lloyd George had backed him, but they had been over-ruled by Asquith and the rest of the Cabinet. It was not in the nature of Asquith's political skill to compromise before he had to. And yet Asquith's own pre-disposition to compromise on Home Rule was so long established that his position was weak from the start. It was a fair enough gibe when F. E. Smith, the brilliant Conservative Front Bench lawyer, said that it had always been Asquith's policy to drop Home Rule whenever he had had the chance of carrying it independently of the Irish. 'His haste in dropping it,' Smith added, 'is only equalled by the celerity with which he takes it up again as soon as he sees he cannot live as a Minister without the votes of the Irish party.'[49]

He was probably relieved to hear Bonar Law himself, as early as the first reading of the bill, hint at a reasonable point of compromise with a reference to Ulster 'or if you do not like to hear it called Ulster, of the north-east corner'.

In fact the broad lines of some eventual 'reasonable' solution were soon being aired. On 2 May 1912 W. G. Agar-Robartes, the Liberal Member for St Austell, on the second reading of the bill said that he thought there was only one solution to the problem and that was to leave Down, Derry, Antrim and Armagh out of the Home Rule scheme.[50] Just over a month later he introduced an amendment along these lines. The government opposed it, but the debate was useful to them in revealing something of the opposition's hand. For Bonar Law spoke in favour of the amendment and so did Carson though he declared that he could not make it his terms for Home Rule. He could not, he said, in the first place leave out Tyrone and Fermanagh from any such exclusion, and secondly he personally had to insist that he thought Home Rule would be disastrous for the rest of Ireland. But what the debate at least indicated was that Bonar Law would settle for exclusion on some terms. Since Carson's strength in Ulster, though increasingly effectively organized, was ultimately dependent on his support from Bonar Law and the Conservatives, this meant that he too would probably in the long run be prepared to settle for exclusion. He had even enumerated his minimum terms: the six counties of Derry, Down, Antrim, Armagh, Tyrone and Fermanagh. The government knew now at least that there was a safety valve.

Meanwhile Carson, ably assisted by Craig, set about further strengthening his practical position in Ulster. He was still worried that people in England did not seem to care in the same way as the people of Ulster cared, and a dramatic campaign to convey the depth and intensity of Ulster feeling was planned for the autumn of 1912. This centred round a 'Solemn League and Covenant' to resist Home Rule to be inaugurated in Belfast Town Hall, on 28 September, which was declared 'Ulster Day'. For ten days beforehand meetings were held all over Ulster, at which men paraded with wooden dummy rifles to fife and drum while Carson, F. E. Smith and other prominent Unionist orators addressed them, carrying unanimously time and time again the single resolution: 'We will not have Home Rule!'

On 28 September itself, in Belfast all shipyards and factories were closed and the day was devoted to the formal solemn ceremony of the signing of the covenant. After religious services in the churches, in which the hymn 'O God Our Help In Ages Past' epitomized the air of crisis, a procession headed by Carson and the faded yellow silk banner said to have been William III's at the battle of the Boyne marched through the streets to Belfast Town Hall, escorted by a guard of honour of 2,500 men in bowler hats, carrying walking sticks.[51] At the Town Hall Carson himself, with a silver pen, was the first to sign the pledge to refuse to recognize any Home Rule Parliament's authority. For the rest of that day tens of thousands streamed into the hall to desks arranged down a third of a mile of corridors to add their signatures. Many signed in their own blood. Within a few days it was found that 218,206 Ulstermen altogether had signed the Covenant while 228,991 women had signed a parallel declaration supporting them.

'Lions led by asses' was how the Liberal press had jeered at what it called the 'brayings of civil war' two years before.[52] But though there were still many English Liberals and Irish Nationalists who comforted themselves that

Carson was bluffing, Carson was not bluffing. Ulster Day and the Covenant made clear the area on which he was in deadly earnest. 'We will not have Home Rule' was the essence of the message. The unspoken accent was on the 'We'.

On New Year's Day 1913, Carson, in the House of Commons, moved an amendment to the Home Rule Bill to exclude all nine counties of Ulster and he was supported by Bonar Law. Though government supporters tended to dismiss the amendment as a 'wrecking amendment' designed merely to make things difficult for the bill as a whole, it was an important debate inasmuch as it once again suggested that both English parties were prepared to compromise in the long run. Bonar Law for his part declared that if Asquith were first to submit the Home Rule Bill to the electors and the electors were to approve, then he would no longer stand in its way.[53] And though the Ulstermen dissociated themselves from this viewpoint it proved that the Conservatives attached importance to seeming reasonable. Churchill, for the government, now declared: 'We shall not be found wanting if an opportunity occurs to grasp the prize of a settlement by consent and agreement. We recognize that such a settlement would involve real sacrifices from both parties.'[54] A fortnight later Asquith on the bill's third reading said: '... if we could meet the case, so far as it is founded on justice, *or even apprehension*, of those counties without doing injustice to Ireland as a whole we should be most glad and delighted to do so'.[55] And though he went on to say that exclusion of those four counties would violate the principles of democratic government, he had nevertheless opened up the possibility of *some* acceptable formula involving those counties.

Craig himself defined the Ulster position clearly. 'We all know,' he said, '... the vast majority of our fellow countrymen who are Nationalists in the South and West of Ireland will have Home Rule if this Bill becomes law, and we shall not have power to stop it. All we propose to do is to prevent Home Rule becoming law in our own part of the country.'[56]

To which William O'Brien replied that the nationalists were prepared to go to almost any lengths to meet the Ulstermen, 'with one exception – that is, the partition of our country'.[57]

The lines of battle were becoming clear.

11

Ulster Volunteers

The Ulstermen were taking no chances. In January 1913 the Ulster Unionist Council decided to raise an Ulster Volunteer Force of one hundred thousand men between the ages of seventeen and sixty-five. Organization of this force on a county basis through the machinery of the Orange Lodges and the Unionist clubs was soon proceeding fast. Drilling took place in Orange Halls usually with dummy wooden rifles ('one and eightpence in pitch pine, and one and sixpence in spruce' according to one advertisement),[1] but at the same time genuine rifles were beginning to appear from England, purchased by wealthy supporters of the movement.

By June 1913 recruiting for the Ulster Volunteer Force was ahead of expectations, and in that month Carson's private dinner with Lord Roberts of eighteen months before finally bore fruit. Roberts obtained for the Ulster Volunteer Force the services, as its commander, of a retired English General of the Indian army, Sir George Richardson. When Richardson arrived in Belfast in July to take up his post he found he had already fifty thousand men at his disposal. An efficient Headquarters Staff was organized, headed by another ex-Indian Army officer, Colonel Hacket Pain. It employed among others Captain Wilfrid Spender, who had recently secured his release from His Majesty's service, having been the youngest and one of the most brilliant staff officers in the British Army. At a review of fifteen thousand well-trained Volunteers at the Balmoral grounds near Belfast in September, Richardson took the salute with F. E. Smith acting as his galloper. 'Does anyone suppose,' Smith had asked in the House of Commons earlier that year, 'that any of us enjoy the prospect of playing a part for which so many of us are not obviously suited? I myself am a middle-aged lawyer, more at home, and I may perhaps add, more highly remunerated, in the law courts than I am likely to be on the parade ground.'[2]

Three days before, Carson had written to Bonar Law from Craigavon, saying that things were shaping towards a desire to settle on terms for the exclusion of Ulster. 'A difficulty arises, as to defining Ulster,' he wrote. 'My own view is that the whole of Ulster should be excluded but the minimum would be the six plantation counties, and for that a good case could be made.... Everything here,' he added, 'is going on splendidly ...'[3]

Meanwhile, Nationalists with what today seems unbelievable complacency treated the Ulster Volunteer Force as a joke. The *Freeman's Journal* much enjoyed itself in June 1913 when some 1,800 rifles labelled electrical plant had been seized on arrival at Belfast. The paper headlined its story 'The Orange Farce' and 'Playing At Rebellion'.[4] Redmond himself was convinced that Carson was bluffing.

If Carson had been defying a government uncompromisingly determined to pass its own Home Rule Bill as it stood and to enforce without question what would then become the law of the land, it might have been reasonable to dismiss Carson's actions as bluff. But his position was by no means so isolated. In the first place, it was already clear that the Protestant Ulstermen were no longer trying to deny Home Rule to most of Ireland and were prepared to settle on the basis of some sort of Ulster exclusion. Second, there had been unmistakable signs that the government were prepared to be less than adamant. All Carson had to do was to remain adamant himself. The real bluff was the government's, and Carson was calling it. Redmond, it could be argued, should have been doing the same.

Redmond, however, does not seem to have become seriously alarmed about the way things were going until September 1913 when, while resting at Parnell's old shooting lodge of Aughavanagh in the Wicklow mountains, he read in *The Times* a most singular letter from a recently retired member of the Liberal Cabinet, Lord Loreburn.[5] Loreburn had been Asquith's Lord Chancellor until a year before, had helped draft the Home Rule Bill and had hitherto been one of its most uncompromising supporters. Now he wrote to *The Times* that in view of the Ulstermen's preparations ministers should be 'willing to consider proposals for accommodation', and he urged a conference to find a means of settlement by consent.

Lord Loreburn was not the only august personage who had been doing such thinking. The king, deeply concerned by the distressing constitutional prospect before him and unable altogether to suppress a personal sympathy for the Protestant Ulster point of view, had been taking the initiative to bring the two British parties together. As a result of conversations between Churchill and Bonar Law when both were staying at Balmoral in September 1913, two secret meetings took place a few weeks later between Asquith and Bonar Law. In the course of these they discussed their respective positions with remarkable frankness.[6]

By this time Redmond had been thoroughly alerted not only by reports of the Churchill–Law conversations, but also by a speech by Churchill himself at Dundee on 9 October 1913 in which he declared that Ulster's claim for special consideration, if put forward with sincerity, could not be ignored by the government. Clearly the aspect of the Home Rule Bill that concerned the satisfaction of Irish national aspirations was being lost to view. Redmond replied a few days later that 'Irish nationalists can never

be assenting parties to the mutilation of the Irish nation; Ireland is a unit. . . .
The two nation theory is to us an abomination and a blasphemy."[7]

Signs of anxiety and restlessness began to appear in Ireland itself. The
Bishop of Donegal wrote to Redmond of 'a growing apprehension on the
part of a good many Catholics and Nationalists in the North of Ireland. . . .
If anything special is attempted for Ulster by the Government you will have
a most troublesome business in hand . . .'[8]

On 17 November 1913 Redmond received Asquith's account of his meeting with Bonar Law. Law, Asquith said, had proposed 'the total and permanent exclusion of Ulster from the bill – Ulster to mean an area to be
settled by agreement and discussion'.[9] Asquith – or so he told Redmond –
had flatly rejected this and suggested administrative autonomy for Ulster
within Home Rule, a solution which at this stage was the furthermost limit
of Irish Nationalist concession, preserving as it did the integrity of Ireland
but conferring what was sometimes known as Home Rule within Home Rule.
Law had turned this down. The conversation had been reported to the
cabinet and in the course of cabinet discussion Lloyd George had proposed
the exclusion of an area of Ulster (to be specified) for a period of five years
after which, unless the Westminster Parliament decided otherwise, the area
would be brought automatically into the jurisdiction of an Irish Parliament.
But quite apart from any objections Carson might have to this, Asquith had
told the cabinet that he did not think many English Home Rulers let alone
the Irish could accept this. To Redmond, Asquith had confided that the
government believed the Ulstermen to have something like five thousand
rifles and that anything up to thirty per cent resignations among army
officers must be expected, if the army were ordered to put down insurrection
in Ulster.[10]

Asquith had not been altogether frank with Redmond. There had in fact
been two meetings with Bonar Law, and Asquith seems only to have informed Redmond of the second. Perhaps this was because at the first meeting
Asquith had said to Law, when each leader was discussing his own recalci-
trant wing, that though people usually spoke of the Liberals as being
dependent on the Irish it was really the other way round.[11] The Nationalists,
said Asquith, were powerless without the support of the Liberal Party, and
if he or the government decided on any course which commanded the support of their own party, the Nationalists would have no choice but to accept
it. This must have been encouraging to Law, indicating that in the long run
the Liberals were not altogether averse to leaving the Irish in the lurch. If
the Irish had known of the remark, they might have been able to make
more effective plans on their own account accordingly.

It was at the second meeting between Bonar Law and Asquith that the
proposal for some form of exclusion for some part of Ulster was discussed
in detail. But at this point Asquith's version of what was said differs rather

from Bonar Law's, and both differ from the version Asquith gave Redmond. Law thought that Asquith had said he would definitely propose to the cabinet the exclusion of either four or six counties – probably six – on the basis that only a plebiscite by the area excluded could bring them under an Irish Parliament. According to Law, Asquith said he thought he could carry his cabinet and his own party with him on this.[12] In Asquith's own notes of this conversation, though the substance of the proposal was the same, namely the exclusion of six Ulster counties with a plebiscite alone capable of bringing them into a Home Rule Ireland, he committed himself to no more than saying he would report the substance of this proposal to the cabinet, and, if they approved, sound out the Nationalist leaders.[13] He did, however, tell Bonar Law that 'I might probably be able to carry my own cabinet and party with me, in any form of settlement that in the end I pressed upon them.'[14] Needless to say, Asquith gave Redmond no inkling either of this last remark or of his preparedness to consider what amounted to the permanent exclusion from the Home Rule Bill of six Irish counties.[15]

Over the next few months Redmond made it increasingly clear that he could not accept any form of permanent exclusion of 'Ulster', and insisted that any offer at all should first come from the Conservatives. However, he received a number of indications that he was in an increasingly weakening position. In an interview with Lloyd George on 25 November he was told that, though the cabinet agreed that for tactical reasons no proposals should be made 'for the present', nevertheless, 'under certain circumstances, if no offer were made', Churchill, Haldane, Sir Edward Grey and possibly he, Lloyd George himself, might resign.[16] Asquith seemed to give Redmond some temporary reassurance when he told him on 2 February 1914 that he and his cabinet colleagues were all firmly opposed to the exclusion even temporarily of any part of Ulster.[17] It would, said Asquith, be 'most disastrous' for Ireland; he himself favoured concessions in the form of some local autonomy for Ulster within Home Rule, with the addition of a right of appeal by the majority of Ulster members in the Irish Parliament direct to the Imperial Parliament.[18] However, by March 1914 Asquith had succeeded in persuading a most reluctant Redmond to agree that the government should initiate proposals for Ulster after all. In spite of what Asquith had said about even temporary exclusion being disastrous, the offer was to be a form of exclusion.

The proposal was that any Irish county should have the right to opt itself out of the Home Rule Act by plebiscite for a period of six years. After six years, if the Imperial Parliament had not in the meantime made other provision, such county should come under Home Rule. This was basically the same proposal which Lloyd George had made to the cabinet a few months earlier, and which Asquith had then described as very doubtful because of its probable unacceptability to the Irish and even many English

Home Rulers. The point about the six-year period was that it would enable another General Election to be held, the result of which could determine that the opted-out county continued to remain out. Redmond's reluctant consent was obtained on the firm understanding that this should be the very last concession the Nationalists would be asked to make, and that if the offer was rejected by the opposition then the government would pass the bill as it stood.

In thus accepting even as a remote probability the principle of permanent exclusion Redmond can now be seen to have made a disastrous move. A number of painful but just tolerable concessions had been open to him, and he had already shown himself prepared to make them. Unfortunately, none of these, which included additional representation for Ulster Protestants in a Home Rule Parliament, and 'Home Rule within Home Rule', were relevant since there could be no question of their satisfying Ulster Protestants. It was only in fact within the notion of 'exclusion' that any conceivable area of agreement lay. But if the Nationalists were to remain true to their principle of one Ireland, there was virtually no possibility of agreement in this area at all.

The one inalienable nationalist principle Redmond had laid down was that Ireland must remain a single unit. It was just possible to reconcile with this principle some temporary exclusion which could provide a psychological breathing space for the more apprehensive Ulster counties, after which they would automatically be included under the new Irish Parliament. But the period of six years now envisaged allowed a British General Election to intervene, after which new Westminster legislation might alter the arrangement altogether. To reconcile this concession with the 'one Ireland' principle it was necessary to convince oneself that after six years' exclusion Ulster Protestants would find themselves so attracted by the shining example of a Dublin Parliament that there could be no prospect of a newly-elected Westminster Parliament wanting to continue the exclusion. It could also be argued that even if further continuation of exclusion were to be legislated for it could not, in the nature of the British constitution, ever be permanent; but to regard the 'one Ireland' principle as safeguarded by such a hypothetical possibility of unity in the remote future came close to the absurd.* After so long, no finalization of an Irish national demand, however moderate, could afford to be absurd. Redmond had allowed the opening of a tiny but fatal breach in his whole position.

Quite apart from nationalist theory, the 'one Ireland' principle was a very practical down-to-earth consideration for hundreds of thousands of Catholic

---

* This, of course, is what the various governments of the twenty-six counties have done since 1921. Because they, in their minds, regard Ireland as one country, they regard the nationalist principle of one Ireland as at least theoretically maintained. They have not therefore countenanced further direct action of the sort that brought them to power.

Nationalists living in those Ulster counties which might be excluded. It says much for Redmond's political personality that, with the help of the leader of the Ulster Nationalists, Joe Devlin, he should have been able to get them to agree to a proposal involving any exclusion at all, even temporary. But he was under no illusion about the extent to which he was straining loyalties. The strain was increased to the very limit by an additional painful twist. Whereas the original proposal, to which Devlin had got his supporters to agree, was for a three-year exclusion, Redmond had finally had to accept a cabinet demand that the proposed period of temporary exclusion should be extended to six years. It is hardly surprising that in finally giving his consent to Asquith's proposal Redmond should have insisted that this must be the Nationalists' last concession.[19]

But once the government had thus breached their own position Carson was on strong ground. Some months previously he had got the southern Unionists to agree, with considerable reluctance, that he should settle for the best possible terms he could get for Ulster alone. And although there were inevitable difficulties for Bonar Law with his extreme right wing over this abandonment of the southern Unionists, the Conservative Party's effectiveness depended not on its extreme right wing but on the alliance between Law and Carson. Now that the government and Redmond had bowed before their threat sufficiently to offer them the principle of exclusion of four Ulster counties, they could feel confident of obtaining better terms still.

On 9 March 1914, under the processes of the new Parliament Act, the second reading of the Home Rule Bill took place for the second time round, having suffered its first rejection in the House of Lords. Carson dismissed the government's offer with contempt.

'We do not want,' he said, 'sentence of death with a stay of execution for six years.'

Incomprehensibly, no one pointed out that the whole point of the six years was that it gave a new British Parliament a chance to review its situation and thus grant a virtually permanent reprieve. A few days later, on 19 March, Carson stalked indignantly out of the House altogether and left for Belfast. People speculated on whether or not he had gone to proclaim the Ulster Provisional Government.

The British Government had pledged themselves to Redmond that this would be their last offer to Ulster. Now they were obliged to see that the Home Rule Bill when passed should be enforced as law. The firmness of their resolve was about to be put to the test.

12

The Liberal Nerve
Begins to Fail

Would the government 'coerce' Ulster? This was the usual form in which the question was put. Over and over again Conservative spokesmen in the House of Commons and elsewhere asked the government if they seriously thought of using British troops to 'coerce' Ulster. Even Liberals came to accept the term as convenient jargon. But it was an emotive term, putting the prospect of government action into a false pejorative light.

In the first place, the implication was that the province of Ulster was solidly against Home Rule. But a narrow majority of its parliamentary representatives were actually for it. And even among the voters themselves in the most Protestant parts of Ulster – those four counties to which the government was prepared to offer exclusion – there was a sizeable proportion of Home Rulers to Unionists.* Then again: the term 'coercion' in Irish history had hitherto been a highly respectable one, meaning special legislation to enforce the rule of law. But now that the very people who had continually called for it in the past were being required to obey the law, coercion had become a term of abuse. If the Home Rule Bill, under the processes of the Parliament Act, passed through three successive sessions of the House of Commons, and received the royal assent, it would become the law of the land. Any attempt to refuse to recognize the authority of the Irish Parliament which the law set up would have been a disturbance of law and order. Only if force were to be used to suppress the Ulster Unionist Council and the Ulster Volunteer Force before they had broken the law could reasonable exception be taken to coercion, and even so there is always an area in which authority is entitled to assert itself in order to prevent a breach of law. 'Coercion of Ulster' meant virtually no more than the maintenance of law and order.

In fact it was not illegal to drill or even, up to December 1913, to import arms (provided certain technical import regulations were complied with). It might have been said with accuracy that some of the public speeches of Carson, Craig and other Ulster leaders were an incitement to disobey the

* About 5:8 on votes cast, but unopposed returns increased the unionist proportion.

law in certain circumstances, and at one stage their prosecution was considered. But Redmond and the other leaders of the Irish Nationalist Party were against such prosecution. It was distasteful for them that the final recognition of Irish nationalism by a British Government, which had so often used legal restraint to suppress nationalists in the past, should itself be marked by the prosecution of fellow Irishmen. Moreover, there was nothing that Carson and the others had said in this vein that had not been said with equal force by Bonar Law and other Conservative leaders.

We now know that the preparations of the Ulster Volunteer Force to make the law of the land unenforceable were, by March 1914, so well advanced that the government would have been wholly justified in striking against the entire organization at this stage. As early as July 1913 the staff of the Ulster Volunteer Force had been seriously considering advice that it should not wait for the Home Rule Bill to become law before acting. An unsigned paper in the Unionist Council records the belief that the British Army, though hating its duty, would probably fight a Provisional Government of Ulster.[1] 'They, the Government,' this paper continued, 'will probably wait as long as they dare in the hope of things quietening down, and at the last suddenly move 20,000 to 30,000 men into Ulster – secure railways, bridges, etc., and reinforce weak police posts. If they are allowed to do this (and with the help of the Navy they could certainly do it in two days) I do not see how you can hope to get your men out and concentrate them in suitable positions. *Must you give up the enormous advantage of the first move?*'

Certainly by March 1914 the Ulster Volunteer Force, consisting by now of the 100,000 figure originally envisaged, had got itself on to a war footing. With the help of a British movement for the support of Ulster, founded the year before and now vigorously activated by the eminent proconsular figure of Lord Milner,* a number of half-pay and reserve officers from the British Army were recruited to take command of some of the regiments of the Ulster Volunteer Force.[2] This, with its highly efficient transport and communications corps, medical corps, intelligence corps and a Special Section with its own uniform, already had the makings of a real army. It had no artillery, but did have six machine guns, and although it was short of rifles – of which Asquith's estimate of five thousand at this stage may not have been far wrong – plans were already laid to remedy this defect in a most spectacular manner. Finally, some time early in 1914, a 'No. 1 Scheme' of action was adopted involving, along the lines of the advice given, 'a sudden, complete and paralysing blow' to be struck simultaneously at all railway communications by which troop or police reinforcements might be brought into Ulster, all telegraph and telephone lines and all depots of artillery, ammunition and other military equipment.[3]

But perhaps the Ulster Volunteer Force's most effective asset of all was

---

* Elgar and Kipling were among Milner's supporters in London.

the state of mind of much of the officer class of the British Army. The attitude which the army might take if called upon to act against Ulster Unionists in support of a law passed to appease Irish nationalism had long been a subject of speculation and debate. The improbability of the army obeying orders to shoot down Ulster 'loyalists' had been raised as a spectre as long ago as the earlier Home Rule debate of 1886. Ever since 1910 the question had never been far from the public mind.

The British Army was, of course, theoretically quite detached from politics. Yet the officer class was of an undeniably Conservative cast of mind, and as individuals most officers had undoubted sympathies with the Protestant Ulster point of view. Was it right, people asked, and if right feasible, to put such a strain on the professional officer's devotion to duty as to ask him, in the peculiarly new situation that emerged from the combination of the Parliament Act and the Home Rule Bill, to act against all his individual instincts? It is, of course, exactly the ability to do this, to obey legal orders to the exclusion of all personal feeling, that underlies the whole philosophy of a reputable officer corps and of all professional military mystique. The curious spectacle was now to be witnessed of those very people who normally set such store by the self-denying spirit of discipline in the call of duty, making excuses for a different line of behaviour when it suited their own interests to do so.

The king himself had posed the question to his Prime Minister in September 1913 when he had asked Asquith:

'Will it be wise, will it be fair to the Sovereign as head of the Army, to subject the discipline, and indeed the loyalty of his troops, to such a strain?'

It might have been replied without *lèse-majesté* that the only meaning words like discipline or loyalty had at all lay in their demand for submission to all personal strain within the limits of the law. This is certainly the meaning the sovereign and other senior officers had been accustomed to give them when personal feelings imposed a strain on the rank and file. Any Irish soldier employed, say, on enforcing an eviction in Ireland, who had pleaded personal feelings for absenting himself from duty, would have received short shrift.

One senior officer in particular now had no qualms whatever about suiting his concept of military honour to his own individual beliefs. This was no less than the Director of Military Operations at the War Office himself, Sir Henry Wilson, an Irishman from a well-to-do family that had lived in County Longford for more than two hundred years, and who was implacably opposed to Irish nationalism. In the circumstances a professional military man in such a responsible position might have been expected to do everything in his power to ease the strain on the army and ensure that it should keep its professional role strictly separate from its private feelings. International tension was gathering and it was more essential than ever in the national interest to keep the army an integrated disciplined force. But the feelings of sympathy for Ulster which Wilson shared with most army officers were too much for him. These were undoubtedly sincere and deep, and it never seems to have occurred to him that it intriguing, as he now did continually with both the leaders of the Conservative opposition and the Ulster leaders to try and deprive the government of the army's assistance in maintaining the law in Ulster once the Home Rule Bill had passed, he was doing anything but what was right.

The troops on whom the government would have to depend if necessary for the enforcement of the law in Ulster consisted of two infantry divisions and two cavalry brigades. A substantial part of these forces were quartered in the old military camp at the Curragh, a large grassy plain in County Kildare, in the centre of Ireland. On 14 March 1914 Churchill, challenging Carson's rejection of the government's offer, denounced in a public speech at Bradford the so-called Ulster Provisional Government as 'a self-elected body, composed of persons who, to put it plainly, are engaged in a treasonable conspiracy', and declared that the moment had come to 'go forward together and put these grave matters to the proof'.[4] On the same day the army council sent to the commander-in-chief in Dublin, Sir Arthur Paget, instructions for the tightening up of security on barracks, arms depots and government stores in the North which it declared were particularly liable to attack. Conceivably, intelligence of the UVF's 'No. 1 scheme' for pre-emptive action had come its way. Four days later, on 18 March, Paget came to London in answer to a summons to give details of his plans. On 20 March he returned to Ireland with amplified orders for the disposal of forces to meet an Ulster threat. It seems virtually certain that, although these further orders involved the movement of troops to certain key points such as rail junctions, they were solely of a precautionary nature and that no 'plot' as was alleged by Conservatives existed to deny Ulstermen the expression of their legal democratic rights.[5] Movements of warships to Northern Ireland waters were to coincide with the troop movements.

Sir Arthur Paget, who brought these orders back to Ireland early on the morning of 20 March, had waived aside an offer to have them put in writing, and this fact was partly to determine what followed. Paget was an expansive, not particularly clever, officer of the old school of sociable army men, fond of hunting and gardening and much given to reminiscing at table about his campaigns in Africa and Burma. Immediately on his return to Dublin he coloured his explanation to his senior officers of what was about to happen with his own vivid imaginings. 'The whole place would be in a blaze tomorrow' was a phrase of his which one eye-witness of that early morning conference remembered.[6]

Nothing could have been better calculated suddenly to inflame the anxieties of officers who for months past had been concerned about their likely role in any future development of the Ulster crisis. What made things much worse was Paget's clumsy handling of an even more important aspect of the situation. While at the War Office in London the day before, he himself had brought up the possibility that some of his officers might be unwilling to participate in action against 'Ulster'.[7] What was he to do about this? It seems an odd question for any self-respecting commander to have posed about his senior officers. But it is an indication of the abnormal atmosphere of the time that it was not regarded as unreasonable, and Paget was given a matter-of-fact answer. Officers domiciled in Ulster, he was told, might be exempted from taking part in operations there and allowed temporarily 'to disappear'. Any other officer unwilling to serve would be dismissed the service.[8] Though these instructions had been given him at his request for his own guidance he made the foolish mistake, on arrival in Dublin, of immediately placing before those officers not domiciled in Ulster the alternatives of either agreeing to serve there in the forthcoming movements which would set the whole place 'in a blaze' or being dismissed the service. He asked them to make their choice. When General Sir Hubert Gough, Commander of the Cavalry Brigade at the Curragh, notified Paget that he and fifty-nine of his other officers chose, in these circumstances, the alternative of dismissal from the service, the incident popularly known as 'The Mutiny at the Curragh' had begun.*

It was, of course, no mutiny in the strict sense of the word, for Gough and his colleagues had disobeyed no orders: they had merely been asked to make their choice by their commanding officer and had done so.[9] Yet the effect was exactly the same as if there had been a mutiny, for the entire reliability of the British Army in Ireland was now in question. In fact the 'mutiny' was far worse than the action of Gough and the fifty-nine other officers indicated. For, on the alternatives being placed before officers of the infantry regiments in Ireland, the majority had also at first immediately expressed their preference for dismissal. Only the impeccable example of the officer commanding the fifth division, Sir Charles Fergusson, finally persuaded them to refrain from making their attitude public and eventually, often 'with a bad grace', to re-think their position.[10] Nor was the unreliability of the officers confined to Ireland. When General Gough was summoned to London to explain himself, General Douglas Haig, the Commander-in-Chief at Aldershot, also came up to the War Office to warn his administrative superiors of the strong feeling among the officers of his command in favour of Gough.[11] He told the government that the only way to quieten unrest in the army was to issue an unequivocal statement to the effect that the army

---

* The number of officers involved in this section of the incident is often given as fifty-seven, as this was the figure cited in an official telegram, afterwards published in a White Paper from Paget to Seely, the Secretary of State for War.

would not be used to coerce Ulster, a line of argument in which Sir Henry Wilson enthusiastically supported him. The resignation of every officer in the Aldershot command could be expected, Haig warned, if Gough were punished.[12] A junior officer named Archibald Wavell, who found himself disturbed by much of this as improper, heard in the War Office of the possibility of 'wholesale resignations in the army', including that of Wilson, unless a pledge were given that the army would not be used against Ulster.[13]

To all intents and purposes the government had a major army mutiny on their hands. In a disastrous attempt to make out that things were not as bad as they were, they virtually condoned it. There was talk of 'misunderstanding', of a misinterpretation of the type of action intended against 'Ulster'. Gough was actually able to return to Ireland 'reinstated' in his command, carrying a document from the Chief of the Imperial General Staff which guaranteed him that the troops under his command would not be 'called upon to enforce the present Home Rule Bill on Ulster' and that he could assure his officers to that effect.[14] He was naturally welcomed back to the Curragh by his officers as a conquering hero.

The paragraphs in this document explicitly guaranteeing Gough that the army would not be called upon to enforce the Home Rule Bill on Ulster had in fact been added subsequently to the cabinet's approval of the rest of the document, by the Secretary of State for War, Seely, and the Chief of the Imperial General Staff, Lord French, acting on their own initiative. When this amplified text became known it spelt out the extent of the government's climb-down far too embarrassingly, and both Seely and French had to resign, while Asquith himself took over the office of Secretary of State for War along with the premiership. But the original document that Asquith and the Cabinet had approved was, with its accepted reinstatement of Gough and its reference to the resignations arising from 'misunderstanding' alone, quite enough to justify Gough's triumphal return from such a stand. Asquith repudiated in the House of Commons the guarantee not to use the army to enforce a Home Rule Bill in the name of maintaining law and order, but the personal guarantee to Gough was never specifically withdrawn, and he continued to hold it in a solicitor's office in Dublin. The government's humiliation, for all Asquith's face-saving gestures, had been sufficient for Gough never to have to make use of it.

The net result of the incident was that the army was shown to be too unreliable for Asquith ever to risk getting so close to mutiny again by putting 'these grave matters to the proof'. From this moment onwards Redmond's defeat on the issue of one Ireland was assured. Politically, the deadlock continued, but the one sure means of resolving it, the eventual use of force to prevent the Ulster Volunteer Force interfering with the rule of law when the Home Rule Act was passed, was no longer available, and both Carson and Asquith knew it. Carson's future negotiating position was virtually impregnable. As if to emphasize their 'Ulster' triumph, a month later, on 25 April 1914, long-laid plans for a mass importation of arms for the Ulster Volunteer Force came to fruition. A highly efficient mobilization of the force round the ports of Larne and Bangor physically prevented His Majesty's police and customs officers in the areas from interfering with the operation, while 24,600 rifles and some three million rounds of ammunition, secretly purchased in Germany by a former army officer named Crawford, were landed and dispersed throughout Ulster with total success.*

Certain bitter lessons from all this were beginning to be learned in the rest of Ireland.

Looking back many years later, one of the strangest phenomena of the time is the virtual paralysis with which Redmond and the Nationalist Party seem to have been afflicted when faced with such unmistakable evidence of the government's increasing reluctance and inability to support them. Redmond in particular seemed to accept with little more than wistful disappointment the series of *faits accomplis* with which he was presented and his own increasing impotence in the situation.

Partly this was due to his own political personality. Long years in Parliament had made of him an exemplary House of Commons man, unprepared as Parnell had been to make use of Parliament rather than be used by it. He no longer found it so easy to look beyond Parliament to Ireland as Parnell and O'Connell had both done. He seemed to feel himself almost as much a prisoner of the parliamentary deadlock as Asquith himself. For all the warnings that had already been given him of uneasiness in Ireland about the increasing concessions, he seems to have been slow to appreciate that new political forces were capable of arising there. And when the strength of these began to develop, though they were not basically hostile to him, they caught him by surprise.

But a quite different reason for the party's virtual impotence at the time was the fact that attention in Ireland was by no means solely focused on Home Rule. A separate and more down-to-earth issue altogether, in the form of labour troubles in Dublin, held the scene almost equally with the constitutional issue of Home Rule. Amazing as it now seems, when John Dillon in Dublin wrote to T. P. O'Connor in England at the time of the crucial Bonar Law–Asquith conversations in the autumn of 1913, he could say that 'the Ulster question and the cabinet appear dim and distant and of minor importance'.[15] His mind was dominated by the bitter labour dispute which since August 1913 had seen some twenty thousand of the desperately

---

* For this exact figure of rifles see Stewart, *Ulster Crisis*, pp. 244–9. The *total* number of rifles in the possession of the Ulster Volunteer Force by July 1914 was a little over forty thousand. At the time of the Second Home Rule Bill in 1893 Crawford had had a plan to kidnap Gladstone from the front at Brighton and take him to a lonely Pacific island.

poor workers of Dublin locked out by employers, most of these employers being – and the fact is not insignificant for the future – ardent Home Rulers.

The labour troubles in Ireland were the climax to years of activity in the trade union field by a wild and dynamic organizing genius named James Larkin. Born in 1876 in the Liverpool slums, the son of a poor Irish emigrant family, Larkin had worked in the docks there, had become an active socialist and been elected General Organizer for the National Union of Dock Labourers. Extending his work first to Belfast in 1907 and then to Dublin in 1908, he had organized the dockers and carters there, become involved in many successful and some unsuccessful strikes and disputes all over Ireland, and in December 1908 founded the Irish Transport and General Workers' Union. He became its General Secretary and in his preface to the new union's first rule book castigated the 'soulless, sordid money-grubbing propensities of the Irish capitalist class', and with talk of 'the land of Ireland for the people of Ireland' held out hopes that all Irish men, women and children might one day 'become entitled to the fullness of the earth and the abundance thereof'.[16] He made enemies not only among capitalists, but also among rival trade unionists, as well as many politicians of the United Irish League, and the supporters of Sinn Fein, whose founder Arthur Griffith denounced him futilely as the representative of English trade unionism in Ireland.[17] All sensed in him, rightly, an independent, restless force dangerous to all carefully prescribed modes of thinking. His one concern, manically displayed through a powerful ego, was to organize effectively for their own welfare the wretched urban working classes of Ireland. Now that the tenant farmer increasingly flourished as an owner-occupier under the operation of the Land Purchase Acts, this urban poor had inherited something of the role of the national down-trodden.

The poverty and squalor of much of Dublin in the early years of the twentieth century appalled all who encountered it. A government report issued in 1914 assessed that of a Dublin population of 304,000, some 194,000, or about sixty-three per cent, could be reckoned 'working classes'. The majority of these working classes lived in tenement houses, almost half of them with no more than one room to each family.[18] Thirty-seven per cent of the entire working class of Dublin lived at a density of more than six persons to a room; fourteen per cent in houses declared 'unfit for human habitation'.[19] The only water supply for houses that sometimes contained as many as ninety people was often a single tap in the outside yard, where were also usually two lavatories, often used by passers-by coming in off the street. Human excreta lay scattered about the yards and in some cases in the passages of the houses. 'We cannot conceive,' wrote the committee who presented this report, 'how any self-respecting male or female could be expected to use accommodation such as we have seen.'[20] Of the non-tenement houses in which the rest of the working-class population lived, they wrote that some 'scarcely deserve the name of house, and could be more aptly described as shelters'.[21] They usually had no lavatory of their own. The death rate in Dublin was higher than many other large centres of population of the United Kingdom, largely due to the tuberculosis which flourished in such conditions.[22] In all the principal towns of Ireland, in fact, the death rate was much in excess of that in the great towns of the rest of the United Kingdom, being highest of all in Wexford, Galway and Cork.[23]

The report on Dublin housing reproached the Dublin Corporation for 'a want of firmness in the enforcement of the ordinary Public Health Laws with regard to housing', and it also pointed out that three members of the corporation, Aldermen O'Reilly and Corrigan and Councillor Crozier, owned substantial blocks of tenement houses and actually received rebates of tax on them though some of the property was classed as unfit for human habitation.[24] Again, in looking for underlying reasons why some of the Dublin working class were soon to diverge politically from the policies of the Nationalist Party, it may not be insignificant that the Corporation at this time was solidly Nationalist, and Messrs O'Reilly, Corrigan and Crozier were enthusiastic supporters of Home Rule.

It was against a background of such conditions that Larkin had been more or less successfully building and giving strength to an organized labour movement in Ireland. Though his aim, like that of any labour leader, was to raise the workers' standard of living, particularly that of the unskilled workers whose rates of pay in Ireland were well below the average of those in England, his main battle concerned the actual organization of his union and the need to establish a firm foothold for it in the leading areas of employment. His attempt was equally firmly combated by the employers – mostly Home Rule Nationalists who, with the introduction of the Home Rule Bill, were anticipating political mastership in their own house.

Larkin, lion-hearted and personally erratic, was assisted in his work by two remarkable lieutenants of different character from himself. One was a clever and less heroic but well-balanced young tailor named William O'Brien (no connection of the Nationalist MP), who supplied the movement with much of the level-headedness and administrative efficiency which Larkin lacked. The other was James Connolly, born of a poor Irish family in Edinburgh in 1868.

Connolly's father had been an Edinburgh Corporation manure carter without any prospects except continuing poverty and the fear of losing his job. At the age of fourteen his son, the young James Connolly, had enlisted in the British Army, in the King's Liverpool Regiment, and remained in it for nearly seven years.[25] He spent almost all this time stationed in Ireland, and though it is a period about which he was afterwards reticent, it was also the period of the eighties when the land agitation was at its height and clearly helped to crystallize in his mind that identification of Irish national feelings with the interests of the working class which was always to the forefront of his thinking.

Connolly was personally made in a heroic mould, like Larkin, but was thoughtful as well as a man of action, pondering deeply from an early age the intolerable conditions of the nineteenth-century working class. He had soon been drawn towards Marxism and the socialist groups then proliferating in Britain. After his army service he had returned to Scotland and worked for the Scottish Socialist Federation and the Independent Labour Party with which it was affiliated. Supporting himself and a young family by casual labour, and for a time rather unsuccessfully as a cobbler, he was desperately poor, and in 1895 answered an advertisement for a post as paid organizer to a 'Dublin Socialist Club'. The following year in Dublin he himself helped to found the Irish Socialist Republican Party, the first manifesto of which appeared under a slogan of Desmoulins', 'The great appear great because we are on our knees', and which called for the establishment of an Irish Socialist Republic 'based upon the public ownership by the Irish people of the land and instruments of production, distribution and exchange'.[26] Once again as in Fenian times the heroic national ideal of an Irish Republic was being tinged with notions of international socialism.

The essentially twin nature of Connolly's political thinking, as simultaneously nationalist and socialist, was already clear. He was under no illusions about pure emotional nationalism. Writing in Alice Milligan's paper, *Shan Van Vocht*, he declared: 'If you remove the English army tomorrow and hoist the green flag over Dublin, unless you set about the organization of the socialist republic, your efforts would be in vain.... England would still rule you to your ruin, even while your lips offered hypocritical homage at the shrine of that freedom whose cause you betrayed.'[27] In a way it was a modern version of what Fintan Lalor (whom he had read thoroughly) had taught, with the urban working class increasingly replacing the now quite prosperous farmer. The implications for Irish nationalism were the same: that it had small substance unless the welfare of the people were bound up with it.

But though Connolly had contacts with all the other fringe groups active in Ireland at the turn of the century and figured prominently in at least one incident in the days of the Irish Transvaal Committee,* the Irish Socialist Republican Party did not flourish, and in 1903 Connolly emigrated with his family to America where he stayed seven years. On his return in 1910, practical rather than theoretical developments in the Irish labour movement were under way under the inexorable pressure of Larkin's personality. Connolly, whose return had been largely made possible by Larkin and O'Brien, threw in his lot with them. In 1911 he was appointed Belfast organizer of the Irish Transport Workers' Union.

* See above, p. 443.

Subsequent dramatic events, together with bitter internecine disputes in the Irish labour movement, have had the effect of making Connolly seem the major labour figure in twentieth-century Irish history. He was certainly a thinker of greater magnitude than Larkin, and as an individual more personally sympathetic. But the fact that Connolly was to be cut off in his prime and win an Irish martyr's crown in 1916, while Larkin, accidentally missing the heroics, was to live on to 1948 through years of Irish disillusion, political quarrelling, and personal identification with Soviet Communism, should not blind one historically to the other fact that it was Larkin who first effectively brought the old incoherent national emotions into Irish twentieth-century labour relations. He reactivated to some extent in the urban scene that incoherent national extremism which the Land Purchase Acts and the other successes of the Nationalist Parliamentary Party had laid to rest in the countryside. The lasting significant effect of this was to be extremely limited, but as a very small minority influence it was to play some part in events in which the actions of only a very small minority were to count decisively.

In the *Irish Worker*, a paper which Larkin had founded in 1911 and which had a regular circulation figure some ten times higher than Griffith's *Sinn Fein*, Larkin regularly attacked the nationalist failings of the Parliamentary Party, describing them as 'hypocrites, trading under the cloak of religion and hiding under the mantle of Nationality'.[28] In a public speech in Dublin in May 1913 he had spoken of his union's plans in words that conjured up the days of the United Irishmen and the Fenians: 'We are going to make this a year to be spoken of in the days to come. In a few days we are going to start a new campaign in which Sergeants, Captains and Commanders will require a discipline of a very high order.... There is a great dawn for Ireland.'[29] He cited Emmet and Tone as worthy models for the Dublin workers.[30] And when, in August 1913, threatened by a Larkin-organized strike on the Dublin trams, the tramway owner William Walter Murphy, a millionaire former Nationalist MP, started dismissing union members and thus provoked a strike which in turn provoked a general lock-out by the employers, Larkin defied the police to prevent him from holding a banned meeting in O'Connell Street with the following words:

'I am going into O'Connell Street on Sunday. I am going there, alive or dead, and I depend on you to carry me out if I am dead.... Remember the old song about the meeting by the river, with pikes on your shoulders by the rising of the moon. I would ask you to meet me at the old spot in O'Connell Street and you men come on ...'[31]

By that Sunday a warrant was out for Larkin's arrest, but after hiding in the house of Constance Markievicz he appeared disguised in a beard on the balcony of the Imperial Hotel and was, after a few words, carried out, alive, by the police. A street riot followed in which the police used their batons with considerable brutality, injuring some four hundred people and killing at least one. A lecturer at Dublin University named Thomas MacDonagh, who was also a poet, was present that day and saw sometimes three policemen attack a single individual. He saw them baton an old woman with a shawl over her head and attack a small man who had lost his hat and who had to fly for refuge inside the railings of the Metropole Hotel. 'There was continual rapping of batons on people's heads ... you could hear from the cries and shrieks that the same thing was happening opposite the Metropole and opposite the Post Office.'[32]

Since this brutality on 31 August 1913 has its place in subsequent national mythology it needs to be remembered that the individual policemen involved had names like MacGrath, Murphy, Ryan, McCarthy, O'Connor and O'Rorke.[33] But the riot did have a traumatic effect on the atmosphere of Dublin. Violence now became more and more part of the everyday order of things as the strike and lock-out continued and clashes took place between 'scab' workers protected by police and union pickets. Eventually, after repeated talk of the need for the workers to form a self-defensive force on their own, a so-called 'Irish Citizen Army' was officially formed on 23 November 1913.

The idea had first been vaguely mooted by Larkin himself as long ago as 1908,[34] but since during the early months of the lock-out Larkin was mostly either in gaol or in England trying to rally support from British labour, responsibility for the Citizen Army's organization largely fell on Connolly, as Larkin's deputy at Liberty Hall, the Union's Dublin headquarters. The Citizen Army's title expressed aspirations rather than reality, for it consisted only of a few hundred workers who were drilled periodically with hurley-sticks and wooden shafts on the recreation ground Larkin had purchased for the union at Croydon Park, Dublin. The drilling took place under the supervision of an unlikely figure, Captain Jack White, son of a much-honoured British general, who had won particular fame for his relief of Ladysmith during the Boer War. White, an ardent enthusiast for Home Rule, had been one of the originators of the Citizen Army scheme, referring to it at first as a Civic Guard. By its very name and existence the Citizen Army attracted many wayward aspirations beyond its practical purpose of a strikers' defence force. This was evidenced by a telegram which Sir Roger Casement, one of the many individuals increasingly anxious over the fate of Home Rule, sent to one of the inaugural meetings early in November 1913. He supported the 'drilling scheme' as a step towards the foundation of a corps of national volunteers.

Larkin himself continued to identify the cause of the workers with the national cause of Ireland. A government inquiry – in which the employers had been legally represented by the Independent Nationalist Member of Parliament, Tim Healy – failed to bring the two parties together. Eventually, at the end of January 1914, beaten by lack of funds and the failure to raise sufficient support from the rest of the United Kingdom's Union and Labour movement, Larkin had to acquiesce in a return to work under terms which secured no gains for the union and were even humiliating to it, though the employers' declared aim of breaking the union remained equally unachieved. But in spite of what amounted to a defeat, Larkin's voice was raised in increasingly powerful national strains.

When in March 1914 the offer was made to Carson of the exclusion of some Ulster counties, the Parliamentary Committee of the Irish Trades Union Congress, of which Larkin was Chairman, recorded its 'emphatic protest' against the partition as 'a national disgrace'.[35] And speaking at the Congress he declared: 'I claim we have an opportunity given us of achieving much in the near future of our beloved country, to work for, and if needs be to die, to win back, in the words of Erin's greatest living poet, for Caitlin ni Houlihan her four beautiful fields.'[36] And as the government's weakness before Carson became clearer and clearer Larkin wrote in the *Irish Worker* in July 1914: 'We can only say that if the workers of Ireland stand idly by whilst they are being betrayed, they get what they want and only that. Our fathers died that we might be free men. Are we going to allow their sacrifices to be as naught? Or are we going to follow in their footsteps at the Rising of the Moon?'[37]

By that time similar feelings of exasperation in other classes in Ireland, less drastically expressed, had made themselves felt and Redmond had had to take account of them.

13

Volunteers and Home Rule

Within the loose conglomeration of extreme national thinkers who had gravitated round Arthur Griffith's Sinn Fein, there was of course little surprise at the way in which Redmond and the Nationalist Party were apparently being entrapped into betrayal even of their own limited nationalist principles by the deadlock in English politics. Whether or not, like Griffith and his closer followers, the extremists stood for total Irish independence under the Crown, or whether, like the members of the Irish Republican Brotherhood, they stood for total Irish independence in the form of a republic, they had always seen Home Rule as, at best, only a means to an end. They inevitably became increasingly restless now as even the prospect of Home Rule began to recede before Asquith's appeasement of Ulster. But, more significant for the future, wider sections of public opinion, still resolutely pro-Redmond, were becoming restless too, and thus for the first time for over thirty years gave the fringe elements of extreme nationalism an access to, and a meaningful contact with, ordinary mass Irish opinion.

Griffith himself, though he had accepted an inactive role for Sinn Fein while the Home Rule Bill was before Parliament, thus dismaying many IRB and other extremists who regarded him as a rallying point, took a strong stand immediately the prospect of a compromise involving partition became clear. He wrote in his paper *Sinn Fein* on 21 February 1914, before Redmond had agreed to Asquith's county-option offer to Carson: 'The Irish leader who would connive in the name of Home Rule at the acceptance of any measure which alienated for a day – for an hour – for one moment of time – a square inch of the soil of Ireland would act the part of a traitor and would deserve a traitor's fate.'[1]

The mass rank-and-file supporters of the Parliamentary Party would not have used such strong language. They remained faithful to Redmond as a man doing his best for Ireland in extremely difficult circumstances. Yet they had already by that date joined with Griffith and other even more extreme national elements to form an organization which expressed alarm about the fate of the Home Rule Bill and a determination to stand fast in the face of further pressure for concessions. This was a body designed to counterbalance the Ulster Volunteers. It was called the Irish National Volunteers and was formally founded in Dublin on 25 November 1913 as an organization quite unconnected with the Parliamentary Party as such, though party supporters joined it. By the end of 1913 the Irish National Volunteers had achieved only a moderate membership of some ten thousand. But the partition offer to Carson in March 1914, and his rejection of it, followed by the Curragh incident and its implications, led to a very rapid rise in membership of the Volunteers during the next few months so that, by May, it was reckoned that over a hundred thousand men had been enrolled.*[2] This was actually a slightly higher figure than the estimated strength of the Ulster Volunteers Force at this time, though as military bodies there was otherwise little comparison between the two. The Irish Volunteers, while often drilling enthusiastically under former British Army instructors, had very few arms and achieved nothing like the same degree of military organization or efficiency as the Protestant Ulstermen.

The way in which the Irish Volunteers had come into being itself indicated a new tentative merging of separate patterns within Irish nationalist opinion. The first moves towards the formation of such a body had been made locally at Athlone in the centre of Ireland in October 1913.

This fact is even today little known, because the men who made these initial moves had no connection with those others who, some weeks later, first organized the movement on a national scale and later still won for themselves places in the national mythology. But the fact remains that several weeks before the official foundation of the national Volunteer movement, the idea of forming a nucleus of Volunteers to defend if necessary the Home Rule Bill in the same way as Carson's Ulstermen were preparing to attack it, had already been discussed and acted on in Athlone.

On 11 October a general parade of 'about a thousand' men, calling themselves the Midland Volunteer Force,† was held at Fair Green, Athlone, under a Mr Paddy Downing, who supervised the arrangements from a spirited charger.[3] A local newspaper commented reasonably that the only surprising thing was that no such action had been taken before.[4] A more ambitious parade with bugles, drums and fifes but no other weapons than sticks was held on 22 October 1913 when it was estimated, possibly optimistically, that five thousand men, including many British Army reservists, paraded in twenty companies with company commanders and a General Officer Commanding.[5] On a route march through the town afterwards there

---

* The police estimate of the Irish Volunteer numbers as given in Parliament by the Secretary of State for Ireland, Augustus Birrell, was eighty thousand but this was almost certainly an underestimate. (Hansard, H.C. Debates, 5th series, vol. 63, col. 764.)

† A contemptuous reference to the Midland Volunteer Force, implying that they were a figment of imagination, was made by Michael O'Rahilly (The O'Rahilly) in his *The Secret History of the Volunteers* (Dublin, 1915). See F. X. Martin (ed.), *The Irish Volunteers 1913–1915* (Dublin, 1965), p. 76.

was much singing of patriotic songs and simultaneous cheering of Redmond and the men of '98, '48 and '67. A prospectus issued by the Organizing Committee, whose chairman was an Athlone man named M. D. Hayes, opened: 'As Loyal Irishmen to our King and Country, the objects of the Midland Volunteer Force must enlist your sympathy and approval.'⁶ And when a Westmeath Warrant Officer in the British Army wrote from India in the following month asking to be enrolled in the force, the secretary, himself a Catholic Ulsterman, elaborated: 'We are simply banded together to give encouragement and help if necessary to the Catholics of Ulster in their struggle against the gross tyranny and intolerance of the rabid Orangeism of the north-east corner of Ulster.'⁷

It is clear, however, that the organizers of the Midland Volunteer Force had no great organizing ability, for in spite of their expressed hopes that the movement would spread to other Midland and Western towns, it developed no substance until quite different men began to develop the idea from Dublin some weeks later. The prime movers among these were Eoin MacNeill, the professor who had founded the non-political Gaelic League twenty years before, Bulmer Hobson, the active young man who had recently done so much to rejuvenate the Irish Republican Brotherhood, and Michael O'Rahilly, well-to-do heir of a Kerry clan and known as The O'Rahilly, who had been an enthusiastic nationally-minded Gaelic Leaguer for many years but was not a member of the IRB.

The O'Rahilly was then running the Gaelic League magazine *An Claideamh Soluis* and, having recently decided to re-style it, had asked MacNeill to write an editorial for the first issue of the new series. He suggested that it should be on some wider subject than mere Gaelic pursuits. MacNeill complied with an article entitled 'The North Began' in which he advocated that Home Rulers should imitate the example which Carson's Volunteers were setting them from the four Ulster Counties of Derry, Down, Antrim and Armagh.⁸

'There is nothing', MacNeill wrote, 'to prevent the other twenty-eight counties from calling into existence citizen forces to hold Ireland for the Empire. It was precisely with this object that the Volunteers of 1782 were enrolled, and they became the instrument of establishing Irish self-government...'⁹

Hobson had spotted the article and immediately went first to The O'Rahilly, and then with him to MacNeill to ask him if he would head a committee to bring such an organization into being. MacNeill agreed and Hobson, with the help of his young friends in the Irish Republican Brotherhood, then successfully set about organizing such a committee which formally inaugurated the Irish Volunteers under MacNeill's presidency just over three weeks later. Though a report of the meeting did not seem to warrant inclusion on the main news page of the Nationalist Party's newspaper it was, as reported on another page, a success and some three thousand people joined the Volunteers at once.

Hobson and other young members of the secret IRB like Sean MacDermott had done much to give the Volunteer organization its initial momentum, but its importance as they themselves appreciated derived from the non-extremist support it attracted. Two well-known followers of Redmond became officers of the committee, while many other party loyalists, untroubled by their new association with men of more extreme views like Griffith or Casement, gave it immediate encouragement and support. Of the thirty men who formally constituted the Provisional Committee twelve were – unknown, of course, to most people – members of the IRB, while three of the others were later to join it.[10] Of the four officers of the Provisional Committee who signed an appeal to the public on behalf of the Volunteers in December 1913 none were IRB members. The document ended with an appeal 'to every Irishman who believes in a self-respecting, self-reliant Ireland to do his part in equipping the first National Army of Defence established in Ireland since the great days of Grattan'.[11] The Gaelic title of the Volunteers was Oglaigh na hEireann, Army of Ireland, and the uniform cap badge was to bear the letters FF, standing for Fianna Fail, the mythical warrior band of Fionn Mac Cumhail. 'Are we to rest inactive,' the opening manifesto asked, 'in the hope that the course of politics in Great Britain may save us from the degradation openly threatened against us. . . . In a crisis of this kind, the duty of safe-guarding our own rights is our duty first and foremost. They have rights who dare maintain them.'[12] The manifesto had been written by MacNeill. The wonder only was that Redmond himself had not already undertaken some such Irish move to give himself manoeuvrability in his increasingly constricted political situation in England.

In spite of the fact that a number of prominent Redmond supporters were identified with the Volunteers from the start, the attitude of the official party and Redmond himself to the new organization had been ambivalent, not to say apprehensive.

'Redmond does not like this thing,' wrote an Irish MP close to the leader to whom a loyal party man in Cork had written for guidance. 'Neither,' he added, 'does Devlin, but they are loath to move at present. . . . Dillon is much more against it. It could not be controlled, and if the army met some day and demanded an Irish Republic where would our Home Rule leaders be?'[13]

This hypothesis must have seemed far-fetched at the time, particularly as MacNeill went out of his way to stress to Redmond that he had always been one of his supporters and pledged himself against any use of the Volunteer movement to weaken the party.[14] But certainly the Volunteers were an indication to Redmond that not only was he falling into an increasingly isolated position in the English political deadlock, but also that there was a danger of the situation in Ireland partly slipping out of his control too.

Dillon, not so sure as some of his colleagues that the movement would 'fizzle out', told Redmond, 'We must watch it.'[15] As they watched, it became clear that, with the situation at Westminster and in Ulster deteriorating, it was not fizzling out at all. There was only one thing for the party to do: itself to take control of the Volunteers.

This was not inherently difficult. Most of the rank-and-file Volunteers by the early summer of 1914 were Redmond's supporters anyway. It was true that some of the resolutions and messages of support that streamed in for him from all over Ireland carried anxious undertones as the spectre of partition emerged. But these were loyally expressed, as in a resolution from Clonakilty which approved and endorsed all the party's actions, simply singling out especially its stand of 'no more concessions'.[16] There was no doubt that the country, gritting its teeth, was solidly behind Redmond. It was a foregone conclusion that having once decided to get control of the Volunteers he would easily be able to do so. But the manner in which he eventually did so antagonized the original committee and caused difficult self-searching among its extremist members. For, exasperated by several weeks of inconclusive negotiations with MacNeill, who was not a particularly efficient man and did not keep his colleagues fully informed, Redmond on 9 June 1914 simply presented the committee with an ultimatum to co-opt an equal number of his own nominated representatives on to the committee of the Volunteers.

It was under the influence of Hobson himself that the majority of the committee finally agreed to accept Redmond's demand. Hobson argued sensibly that any split would be disastrous to the whole concept of national unity embodied in the Volunteers, and that in any case if there were a split Redmond would command by far the largest section of the one hundred thousand odd members.[17]

Hobson's attitude involved him in bitter recriminations with his IRB colleagues. Tom Clarke, who otherwise greatly admired his ability, gave him 'a very unpleasant time indeed'.[18] He was accused of 'selling-out', and dismissed from any connection with the paper *Irish Freedom*.[19] John Devoy in America, who was appalled by the development, also dismissed Hobson as a correspondent for the Clan-na-Gael paper, the *Irish American*.[20] With his income gone, Hobson actually thought for a time of leaving the national movement to its own devices and even getting out of Ireland altogether.[21] But largely thanks to Casement's intervention on his behalf, Devoy reinstated him, and Hobson returned to the inner councils of the IRB only to clash once again with his colleagues in a much graver crisis two years later.

There can be little doubt that quite apart from the realities of the situation which were all in favour of Redmond, to keep the Volunteer movement intact was the best policy for those members of the IRB who hoped to use it from within for their own purposes. For the first time since the days of the

Land League the extreme republican element in Irish nationalist politics was in association, if under cover, with a large body of Irish public opinion. It was an elementary tactical consideration for the IRB to preserve that link at all costs.

Even in recent years, with the rejuvenation of the IRB by the activities of men like Hobson, MacDermott and the father figure of Tom Clarke recently returned from America, there had been little focus for their enthusiasm once they had become disillusioned with Griffith's Sinn Fein. Hobson, that 'Napoleon', as his patron, Roger Casement, had once dubbed him, had done what he could.[22] Helped by the new-found national enthusiasm of Constance Markievicz he had founded in 1909 a nationally-minded boy scout movement called Fianna Eireann. The paper *Irish Freedom* started in 1911, which appeared first under Patrick McCartan's and then Hobson's editorship, had boldly and publicly preached the IRB's traditional republican creed, but to little apparent effect. Of the Fianna Eireann, it declaimed: 'The Fianna have not begun one day too soon to prepare for the final struggle ... come it will, and that before the boys of the Fianna are full grown men.'[23] And again a few months later an editorial declared: 'The work we have to accomplish is to establish an independent Irish Republic here in this country.'[24] But there was nothing to indicate that such rhetoric was in any different category from that with which Ireland had long been familiar, and the paper had a small circulation. The note of bombast sounded by Major John MacBride on, of all occasions, the Battle of Sydney Street in East London, was of typical unreality. Noting scathingly that two armed men with revolvers had been able to hold up 1,500 soldiers armed with magazine rifles and a Gatling gun for twelve hours, MacBride commented: 'The whole business should put heart into the younger generation of Irishmen', and, asked what lesson he learned from the event, he replied: 'As to that it is the lesson I learned on the battlefields of South Africa – that the English army is of very little account as a fighting force.'[25]

Irish Freedom consistently carried with approval remarks such as that 'no National Movement could ever be successful if it could not rely on the ultimate backing of the sword', and that 'the only thing which would fire the imagination of the young people was the ideal of an Irish republic, the means to it, physical force'.[26] But the uncomfortable fact of Irish life remained, as it had done ever since the republican creed had been first propounded in the 1790s, that the idea of an Irish republic to be achieved by physical force did not fire the imagination of many young people at all, however much some believed that it should.

One new voice making itself heard in the columns of *Irish Freedom*, while not actually adding anything new to the old creed, at least succeeded in imparting to it a new note of dedication and passion. This was Patrick Pearse, Gaelic League poet and schoolmaster, son of a Birmingham stone-mason and an Irish mother, who since 1908 had been running a nationally minded school for boys called St Enda's at Rathfarnham on the outskirts of Dublin. The boys were partly taught in Irish and the rooms in the school had the names of Irish heroes round the walls; Emmet even had a room to himself. Pearse was not yet a member of the IRB but had many friends who were. Beginning a series in *Irish Freedom* entitled 'From a Hermitage' in June 1913, he wrote: 'This generation of Irishmen will be called upon in the near future to make a very passionate assertion of nationality. The form in which the assertion shall be made must depend on many things, more especially on the passage or non-passage of the present Home Rule Bill.'[27]

One immediate limited national task which the re-animated IRB had set itself was to erect the Wolfe Tone Memorial for which John O'Leary had laid the foundation stone in St Stephen's Green as long ago as the anniversary celebrations in 1898, but which had never been completed. Tom Clarke became president of the new executive committee of which Sean MacDermott was secretary. But it was Pearse who, at a ceremony at Tone's grave in June 1913, delivered a strikingly unequivocal oration:

'We have come here,' he said, 'not merely to salute this noble dust and pay our homage to the noble spirit of Tone. We have come to renew our adhesion to the faith of Tone; to express once more our full acceptance of the gospel of Irish Nationalism which he was the first to formulate in worthy terms ... his voice resounds throughout Ireland calling to us from this grave when we wander astray following other voices that ring less true...' And he concluded: 'When men come to a graveside they pray; and each of us prays here in his heart. But we do not pray for Tone – men who die that their people may be free have no need of prayer. We pray for Ireland that she may be free, and for ourselves that we may free her. My brothers, were it not an unspeakable privilege if to our generation it should be granted to accomplish that which Tone's generation, so much worthier than ours, failed to accomplish! To complete the work of Tone.... And let us make no mistake as to what Tone sought to do. We need not re-state our programme; Tone has stated it for us: "To break the connection with England, the never-failing source of all our political evils ..." '

A very small crowd accompanied Pearse and Clarke to Bodenstown.

The tiny Irish Republican Brotherhood and their friends were well aware of their isolation. 'Ten years ago,' declared *Irish Freedom* in October 1913, 'the Parliamentary Party was losing its grip on the country.... Today the Parliamentary Party controls more thoroughly than ever the daily press and the public mind in Ireland.'[28] And earlier the same year an American correspondent had written to John Devoy of Clan-na-Gael, the IRB's counterpart in America: 'The dark side of the prospect here and overseas is not so much what Lloyd George, Redmond and Ryan propose, but the fact that there and here the Irish people accept and applaud their betrayal of everything national they once professed to advocate. It is not so much the apostasy of the platform demagogues as that of the people that disgusts ...' He added hopefully that he didn't believe that at heart the Irish people had lost 'the old manly spirit of '98, '48 and '67 but publicly they give no sign that it still lives'.[29]

Given the historical facts of '98, '48 and '67 it was hardly surprising that the spirit should be difficult to find in 1913, for it was something mythical that was being sought rather than something which had actually existed. The task of Irish republicans, though they seldom recognized this, consisted in having to turn myth into reality. It was to be Patrick Pearse's own special contribution to Irish nationalism that by acknowledging unashamedly the mythical and even mystical nature of the Republic he paradoxically brought it closer to reality.

But it was not until after the foundation of the Volunteers that Pearse or any other of the new aspiring extremists had a framework within which to become effective. Until that date both he and more down-to-earth republicans had had to admit that they were an unrepresentative handful working in an Irish void. The two-thousand-odd members of the Irish Republican Brotherhood, which was the total for the entire United Kingdom at the time,[30] had to content themselves with manipulating influence inside extra-political bodies like the Gaelic Athletic Association, making the occasional individual convert to their own doctrines, and, on the initiative of Hobson in 1913 who appreciated the opportunities opened up by Carson's example, taking part in a small amount of secret ritualistic drilling.[31] In any case, it was only the younger men in the organization, together with the recently returned Clarke, who were at all active. The older and controlling members of the Supreme Council, men like Fred Allen, 'almost stifled all activities' and were even opposed to the publication of *Irish Freedom* and reluctant to give it IRB funds.[32] One example of the conversion of one individual recruit to republican doctrines serves to illustrate how insignificant and ineffective a force the Irish Republican Brotherhood had long been even as a propagandist in its own cause. In June 1911, to protest against the visit to Ireland of George V in the year of his coronation, public meetings were held by a specially organized committee of extreme nationalists in which some members of the IRB were prominent. The campaign did not prevent the royal visit from being a popular success, but at one of the Dublin meetings a young teacher of mathematics and Irish, Eamon de Valera, found himself listening for the first time to advocacy of an Irish Republic. The idea had not come his way before. He went home approving of it but thinking it had little chance of success.[33] He joined the Irish Volunteers on the night of its inauguration on 25 November 1913.

The ineffectual isolation of the IRB was revolutionized by the foundation of the Volunteers. A quite new perspective for IRB men and other extreme nationalists now opened up. Pearse himself, speaking at the inaugural meeting, declared, 'The history of the last hundred years in Ireland might be described as a hopeless attempt of a mob to realize itself as a nation. Today we have an opportunity of rectifying the mistakes of the past. We go back therefore to the policy of the Volunteers [of 1778]...'[34] Before the month was out he was moving unashamedly beyond the constitutional aims of eighteenth-century nationalism into those realms of national mysticism which he was to make peculiarly his own.

'I have come to the conclusion,' he wrote, 'that the Gaelic League, as the Gaelic League, is a spent force; and I am glad of it.... The vital work to be done in the new Ireland will be done not so much by the Gaelic League itself as by men and movements that have sprung from the Gaelic League or have received from the Gaelic League a new baptism and a new life of grave.... [The Gaelic League] was a prophet and more than a prophet. But it was not the Messiah.... I am not sure that there will be any personal and visible Messiah in this redemption: the people itself will perhaps be its own Messiah, the people labouring, scourged, crowned with thorns, agonizing and dying to rise again immortal and impassible.' He concluded this article: '...We must accustom ourselves to the thought of arms, to the use of arms. We may make mistakes in the beginning and shoot the wrong people; but bloodshed is a cleansing and a sanctifying thing, and the nation which regards it as the final horror has lost its manhood. There are many things more horrible than bloodshed, and slavery is one of them.'[35]

This must have seemed very unreal stuff to any average rank-and-file members of the Volunteers who may have read it. Even the IRB members were thinking in more mundane terms of using the organization as a cover for their own activities. By April 1914 they had been able to convince John Devoy of Clan-na-Gael that this was seriously feasible and sums from Clan-na-Gael were being taken back for the Volunteers by IRB visitors to America.[36]

'You may have some doubts as to our personnel,' Devoy was told by The O'Rahilly (who though not an IRB member was close to the IRB's councils). 'Dismiss them. The men at the wheel are straight thinkers and include all the advanced and sincere men who are interested in nationality.... The objects of the men who are running this movement are exactly the same as yours.'[37]

Not all the 'advanced' men were nearly so sanguine. Thomas Ashe, an IRB man, wrote to Devoy a few weeks later that though MacDermott and others were 'doing their utmost to keep them [the Volunteers] straight' their chances were not good because of the preponderating majority of Redmondite supporters in the movement. And he quoted a letter he had had from a correspondent to the effect that 'They [the Volunteers] comprise outside a few good men, all the frauds that ever lived in this blessed country and you know how numerous they are'.[38] However, Tom Clarke was able to write in May to Devoy, "Tis good to be alive in Ireland in these times', drawing attention incidentally to difficulties the Volunteers were experiencing from another quarter altogether, namely the Larkinite Citizen Army. These, he wrote, had been largely inspired 'by a disgruntled fellow named O'Casey . . . '.*[39] But, he concluded, 'Liberty Hall is now a negligible quantity here'. He added that Mrs Clarke had just presented a new badge to the women's organization of the Volunteers the Cuman na Mban. It consisted of orange and green on the wings with white in the centre. It was a quite novel symbol, the significance of which had to be explained before they adopted it unanimously.

Yet Clarke's confidence in the IRB's ability to maintain its influence with the Volunteer movement was severely shaken by Redmond's take-over. Hobson undoubtedly kept the cooler head for he saw that without Redmond the Volunteers were nothing.

The notion is sometimes held that it was the IRB who secured such arms as the Irish Volunteers were able to obtain by August 1914 and indeed, given their under-cover role and ulterior motives, one might have expected this to be so. But it was not so. Before the foundation of the Volunteers the IRB using Clan-na-Gael funds had purchased a few rifles for such drilling as took place under Hobson's influence. Considering that there was then no ban on the importation of arms into Ireland and that advertisements appeared in *Irish Freedom* from gunsmiths offering Mauser magazine rifles in perfect order from 30s and Lee Enfield magazine rifles in perfect order at £2 17s 6d, this represented no very great achievement.[40] Indeed, given the basic IRB belief in the need for an ultimate resort to arms, and given Clan-na-Gael financial resources, one might have expected a stock of rifles to be laid up at least against some such eventuality as the formation of a Volunteer corps. But virtually nothing of this sort was done.

After the foundation of the Volunteers an arms sub-committee was set up and The O'Rahilly was charged by this committee to inquire into the possibility of purchasing arms from the Continent.[41] But this did not lead to the positive results one might have expected from the IRB's theoretical professional revolutionary role behind the scenes. The government had not made things easier by banning in December 1913, soon after the Volunteers had come into existence, the import of arms into Ireland, but it is with just such a situation that professional revolutionaries claim to be able to deal. The truth seems to be that the IRB at this stage was still a very amateurish organization.

The real initiative in procuring arms for the Volunteers came from a quite different group of people, and these may certainly be labelled enthusiastic amateurs.[42] They were a collection of individual Anglo-Irish Home Rulers, drawn largely from the upper and upper-middle classes and mainly resident in London. Their contact with the Volunteers in Ireland was Sir

* O'Casey was Sean O'Casey, the playwright.

Roger Casement, the distinguished consular official who was a friend and patron of Bulmer Hobson and was on the Volunteer Provisional Committee. But neither the Committee nor Hobson were responsible for the first steps in getting the Volunteers their one sizable batch of arms. The initiative was Casement's own, and the operative factor his friendship with the sixty-seven year-old widow of the famous English historian, J. R. Green, then living in Westminster.[43]

Alice Stopford Green had long lived in London but had been born in Ireland where, a daughter of the Protestant Archdeacon of Meath, she had spent the first twenty-five years of her life. Her studies of Irish history, made while helping her husband with his researches, had led her to a quasi-mystical view of Irish nationality. She saw in its full realization the payment of a sort of debt to history and to the memory of the Irish dead. In fact her wish to see this realization in the near future had sometimes led her in her writings to perceive it prematurely in the past.[44]

Mrs Green had been corresponding since 1904 with Casement when he had first written to her on behalf of the Congo Reform Association.[45] Neither she nor Casement was a revolutionary, as were, at least in intent, the young men of the IRB. But both shared a sympathy for a more profound concept of Irish Nationality than that to which the Parliamentary Nationalist party, with its pragmatic political outlook, gave currency. And like Casement, Alice Stopford Green was in principle a supporter of Griffith's Sinn Fein, though she found the Ireland of those days a depressing place to live in.[46] By 1913 she and Casement were addressing each other in correspondence in affectionate mock-heroic terms such as 'My dear Woman of the Three Books' or 'My dear Knight of the Island', and in the warm but rarefied atmosphere of this relationship there now prospered a most romantic conspiracy.

The other participants were all friends and acquaintances of Mrs Green. They consisted of the Hon. Mary Spring Rice, daughter of Lord Monteagle and cousin of an English Privy Councillor then British Ambassador in Washington; Erskine Childers, an English Liberal born in Ireland who had volunteered for the British Army in the Boer War and been Clerk to the House of Commons for fifteen years, and his American wife, Mary; Conor O'Brien, a Sinn Fein supporter who was a cousin of Mary Spring Rice and a grandson of the Smith O'Brien of 1848; and Darrell Figgis, a young writer and literary journalist who lived in London but spent the winter months on the isle of Achill off the west coast of Ireland and was also a supporter of Sinn Fein. The one thing all these people had in common was a passionate belief that Ireland should be in a position to defend her constitutional rights against every threat in the probable event of the Home Rule Bill becoming law. The decision to purchase arms was made in London, and the money to finance it was largely raised there.

Early in May 1914 Casement had gone to London with MacNeill to open the first phase of negotiations with Redmond over his participation in the Volunteer movement. They had found Redmond determined to get complete control of the movement and at the same time mistrustful of some of the Volunteer Provisional Committee, notably of Patrick Pearse.⁴⁷ Lunching next day at Mrs Stopford Green's house at 30 Grosvenor Road, Westminster, where the young writer Darrell Figgis was also a guest, they discussed the situation and reasoned that the best way in which they could counter-balance Redmond's otherwise inevitable dominance of the Volunteer movement was by independently securing the arms the Volunteers were longing for. They were being forced to drill with wooden rifles, and broom handles. Figgis, who had known something of The O'Rahilly's preliminary inquiries, suddenly offered to go at once to the Continent and buy them.

'That's talking!' cried Casement, walking across the room from the window where he had been staring out at the Thames, and now placing his hand on the table in a rather characteristic melodramatic gesture.⁴⁸

The decision was taken. The arrangements were to be made known to as few people as possible.

Just over a fortnight later Figgis went to Hamburg with Erskine Childers, who was a more ardent Home Ruler than most Liberals, in advocating not just the Home Rule Bill but full Dominion status for Ireland. He now offered his twenty-eight-ton white yacht, the *Asgard*, for the arms shipment.⁴⁹ He was an experienced seaman who as long ago as 1903 had written an excellent spy novel about sailing off the German North Sea coast, called *The Riddle of the Sands*. In Hamburg Childers and Figgis agreed to purchase 1,500 single-shot Mauser rifles and some 45,000 rounds of ammunition from a German firm.

Arrangements for the secret landing of this cargo in Ireland were necessarily complex and depended on the careful synchronization of an elaborate time-table. Details of the purchase were made known in June 1913 to Hobson who, keeping the knowledge very much to himself, assumed responsibility for the landing procedure. His plan, agreed with Casement and Childers in Dublin at the end of June, was that half the guns and ammunition should be brought into Howth harbour at twelve noon on Sunday, 26 July.⁵⁰ The remainder were to be brought the same day by another yacht, Conor O'Brien's *Kelpie*, to be landed at Kilcoole in County Wicklow. (Because both O'Brien's nationalism and his yacht were well known and therefore might be suspect, his cargo was to be transferred at sea before landing to another yacht belonging to a Dublin surgeon.) It was a hazardous plan, for the *Kelpie* and the *Asgard* had to sail for the Continent on 29 June and 2 July respectively, and from then on until the date of the Irish rendezvous were virtually out of touch with Hobson. Neither yacht had engines or radio. Each had first to keep a precise rendezvous on 12 July with Figgis who was bringing the cargo by tug from Hamburg to the Roetigen lightship in the North Sea on that date. The eventual arrival of the cargo precisely to synchronize with the landing arrangements in Ireland was also essential. For ever since the gun-running by the Ulster Volunteers at Larne three months before, the authorities had been keenly on the look-out for further such operations both North and South, but particularly South.

In the end the whole affair was a dazzling success, as brilliant a feat in its small amateur way as the much larger and more professional gun-running at Larne three months before. The rendezvous at the Roetigen lightship and the transfer of arms from Figgis's tug to the two yachts took place like clock-work, though Mary Spring Rice, who, with the two Childers, a young British Army man named Shepherd and two Donegal fishermen, formed the crew of the *Asgard*, found herself wondering if they would ever get their nine hundred rifles stowed into the tiny yacht.[51] Together with the heavy am-munition boxes these filled the saloon and the cabin and blocked the passage and the companion hatch. The possible effects of such extra weight in the event of bad weather caused anxiety. But Childers's one thought was to take everything; in the end he had to jettison only three ammunition boxes which had been kept on deck because there was no room for them below. In the *Kelpie* too, which had loaded up just before the *Asgard*, the rifles were stacked so high in the saloon that there was barely room to crawl over the bundles and nowhere to sit. In fact the reason why Childers in the *Asgard* found himself with rather more than half the total of 1,500 to carry was that the *Kelpie* could take no more than 600.

It was as well that Childers was an expert seaman. Thirty-six hours before the rendezvous at Howth the *Asgard* hit the worst storm in the Irish Sea since 1882. It was as well too that he was a man of both dash and resolution. For it had been agreed with Hobson that if the coast was clear at Howth a motorboat should emerge from the mouth of Howth harbour before the appointed time as a signal that all was well. The *Asgard* cruised up and down that Sunday morning just outside Howth waiting for the signal for two hours. No motorboat appeared. Childers finally decided to go in all the same. The *Asgard* sailed into Howth harbour at the very moment that the vanguard of a thousand Volunteers, mobilized by Hobson to land the arms, appeared at the other end of the jetty.

Hobson's stage management of the reception arrangements had been brilliant.[52] He had let only very few people into the secret of what was afoot, among them Tom Clarke, and some of his young friends in the IRB, such as Sean MacDermott. At the end of the previous month he had arranged for the Volunteers to undertake a series of weekly Sunday route marches to different destinations round Dublin. These had attracted some attention from the police at first, but after two or three weeks had come to be accepted as routine. The march out to Howth on Sunday, 26 July, therefore, attracted no particular attention and few even among the Volunteers – who included Arthur Griffith – knew the object of the exercise. A contingent of the youth movement, the Fianna, under a young man named Sean Heuston, accompanied the column. A number of taxis ostensibly taking young men and their girls to the coastal resort for the day had set out ahead under the leadership of a young IRB member, Charles Burgess, usually known in the Irish version of his name as Cathal Brugha.

The unloading of the *Asgard* was accomplished in about half an hour, and those rifles which had not been dispatched in the taxis with the ammunition were carried back towards Dublin rather unmilitarily – some on right shoulders, some on left – but in triumph, by the Volunteers.[53] Coastguards had spotted the landing but, overwhelmingly outnumbered, had not interfered. The police had, however, notified Dublin Castle. At Clontarf on the way back the Volunteers found themselves confronted and halted by a body of police reinforced by a military detachment of the King's Own Scottish Borderers.

The Assistant Police Commissioner in charge, named Harrell, was there on his own initiative. It was a delicate situation, for although in the light of the arms ban of the previous year the actual landing had been illegal, the legal position about forcibly removing the arms once landed from those in possession of them was less clear. The Ulster Volunteers were after all parading freely with arms through the streets of Belfast at this time and no attempt was being made by the law to interfere with them.

It was in fact afterwards found by a Royal Commission that Harrell in trying to disarm the Volunteers had acted with technical illegality.[54] In any case, some uncertainty was clearly apparent in Harrell's behaviour at the time. For after a first attempt by the police to take the Volunteers' rifles a fracas developed and Harrell let himself become involved in an argument with Figgis and the poet Thomas MacDonagh, under cover of which most of the Volunteers managed to slip away with their rifles across the fields. Only nineteen rifles were lost. But that was not the end of the incident.

By about half past four in the afternoon, both Volunteers, triumphant with their rifles, and the police, largely thwarted in their attempt to disarm them, had dispersed. Only the detachment of the King's Own Scottish Borderers remained at Clontarf for another hour or so: a hundred men in all carrying a hundred rounds of ammunition per man.[55] During the argument between Harrell and Figgis and MacDonagh they had been given the order to load, and had never subsequently been ordered to unload. While now waiting for orders to move off they were surrounded by a jeering and hooting bunch of civilians, angry with them for the part they had played in the incident.

A small crowd, continuing to scoff and jeer, eventually followed the soldiers back the three miles or so into Dublin, and there were moments en route when the rear ranks made lunges at the crowd with their bayonets. In Dublin the Sunday evening crowds following them through the streets began to grow. As the soldiers, making for their barracks, turned off O'Connell

Street on to one of the Quays by the Liffey named Bachelor's Walk – the site of a tram terminus and a particularly busy place of congregation on Sunday evenings – stones, bottles and other missiles were thrown. The senior officer present, who had not been at Clontarf but had come out to join the returning column, ordered the rearguard to wheel and face the crowd. He did not know that the men's rifles were already loaded.

Detailing five or six men to load and be ready to fire he then stepped out and raised his hand for silence so that he could address the crowd. Immediately a shot rang out, and this was followed by a volley. A man of forty-six, a woman of fifty and a boy of eighteen were killed, the latter by a shot fired through a simultaneous bayonet wound. Thirty-eight people were wounded, fifteen of them seriously, and one of these later died.

Appalling as the incident was, the emotive shock it caused in Ireland carried a special significance. It seemed almost that the southern Irish were being massacred for trying to assert their rights to Home Rule. In fact, what had happened was that for a few moments a tired, frustrated and exasperated local soldiery, jeered at for two hours and recently subject to a bombardment of stones and bottles, had too easily surrendered to a vague impression that there had been an order to fire. No soldier fired more than two rounds.[56] Within a fortnight a government commission concluded that the action of the police and troops had been 'tainted with illegality' and specifically censured the troops for lack of control and discipline. This does not exactly square with a picture of tyrannical repressive government.

Yet the significance of Bachelor's Walk was that it connected easily in the Irish mind with other bloody events which had been repressive in the past, and which had themselves been worked into a national myth. A relatively small single incident, it was not the only thing at the time to evoke the national myth. Below the surface of mass opinion the whole political situation, suggesting an English compromise at the expense of Ireland, was beginning to work on the emotive undertones of Irish history which ran through every Irishman.

'Bachelor's Walk' came as a climax to a period of extreme political tension. For there had been absolutely no progress with the attempt to solve the deadlock over 'Ulster'. The Government's offer to Carson – made with Redmond's and the majority of the Irish people's reluctant consent – still stood, giving the option to any Irish county that so wished to opt itself out of the jurisdiction of an Irish Home Rule Parliament for a period of six years. After this, unless the Westminster Parliament were in the meantime to legislate otherwise, it would automatically fall back within the Irish Parliament's jurisdiction. But if the offer still stood, it also still stood rejected. Carson's minimum terms – which he had not yet had to formulate precisely – were the total exclusion from an Irish Parliament for ever of the six Ulster counties of Derry, Antrim, Armagh, Down, Tyrone and Fermanagh. On this there could be no meeting point, for Redmond had already stretched the One-Ireland principle to the then endurable limit, if not beyond it.

In fact the deadlock was far worse than it had ever been before. For in a last-minute desperate effort to solve it the king had persuaded Asquith and the Conservative, Ulster and Irish Nationalist leaders to agree to attend a conference at Buckingham Palace. This sat from 21–24 July. Though the personal atmosphere of the conference was civilized it broke down at once over the area of Ulster to be excluded. On this no agreement could be reached. The even more difficult question of the extent of time for which any such area was to be excluded was never even discussed.

Two days later the arms for the southern Volunteers sailed into Howth in the *Asgard* and their successful arrival was followed by the traumatic news of Bachelor's Walk.* Under the mechanism of the Parliament Act the Home Rule Bill would shortly have to come up to be passed into law. In the North, more determined and efficiently organized to resist a Home Rule Act than ever, the Ulster Volunteer Force waited.

In this highly critical situation, events elsewhere were to rescue the government from their dilemma of having committed themselves to an agreed 'final settlement' of the Irish question while yet being unwilling to carry it out. On the same day, 24 July, on which Asquith informed the Commons of the breakdown of the Buckingham Palace Conference, he also had to tell them of the Austrian ultimatum to Serbia. The greatest international crisis in European history began to overshadow even the complexities of Ireland.

---

* The other consignment of arms transported in Conor O'Brien's yacht *Kelpie* was delayed because of a broken maintail in the yacht *Chotah*, to which it was to be transferred off the coast of County Wicklow. The six hundred rifles were eventually successfully landed without incident at Kilcoole, County Wicklow on the night of 1 August 1914.

14

Volunteers and the European War

The political deadlock in which the outbreak of war found the Irish problem had been virtually unchanged for months. But the atmosphere pervading it now changed almost overnight.

Towards the end of June the government had introduced, with Redmond's agreement, via the House of Lords, an Amending Bill to the Home Rule Bill. This incorporated the offer of county option for Ulster which Carson had already rejected when outlined by Asquith just before the Curragh crisis. But the offer had to be formally rejected if conciliation were to be seen to be done, and the Lords was the place where the government might most conveniently learn the worst at once. The Lords in fact amended the Amending Bill to exclude positively all nine counties of Ulster until such time as, voting in one block by plebiscite, they might vote themselves into the jurisdiction of an Irish Parliament. Given the small but unmistakable majority of Protestant inhabitants over Catholic, this proposal meant that all nine counties would be excluded from an Irish Parliament for any foreseeable future and virtually for ever. It was thus not conceivably acceptable to Redmond.

However, the willingness to compromise had to be placed fully on record, and, with this ominous prologue already performed, the Amending Bill was now due to come to the House of Commons. An indication of the terms on which the Conservatives and Carson might finally be induced to settle was revealed to Redmond through private intermediaries on 2 July.[1] The proposal was the positive exclusion of a geographical area of Ulster consisting of Antrim, Down, Derry, Tyrone, North and Mid Armagh, North Fermanagh and Derry City until such time as this area might vote itself under the rule of a Home Rule Parliament. Though this was, of course, a considerable improvement on the Lords' intransigent stand, releasing not only the three predominantly Catholic counties of Donegal, Cavan and Monaghan but also some Catholics in Armagh and Fermanagh, it still meant that substantial numbers of nationalists would be voted out of the Irish Parliament virtually for ever.

There was, of course, no guarantee that Carson and Bonar Law would be able to get their own followers to agree to such terms, but from a nationalist point of view they were in fact better than the form of partition which, some years later, Ireland had to settle for. Redmond might even have been able to improve on them marginally in negotiation. This can, however, be no valid argument for suggesting that in the context of that time Redmond should therefore have settled for them.

It would have been impossible for him to do so. The exclusion of Tyrone, where Catholics were in a small minority over Protestants, for any time at all, and the exclusion even of the predominantly Protestant parts of Ulster virtually for ever, stretched the already overstretched principle of One Ireland beyond endurance.

The failure of the Buckingham Palace Conference merely formalized this deadlock. But in terms of the parliamentary time-table the Amending Bill was still due to be offered in the House of Commons. In accordance with Redmond's agreement with Asquith, since the Tories were rejecting the offered conciliation, the Home Rule Bill was to go through as it stood, under the Parliament Act. As a very last concession and after persuasion by Asquith, Redmond and Dillon reluctantly agreed to let the county option proposal in the Amending Bill be put forward *without* the six-year time limit.[2]

But in the end the Amending Bill never came up in the House of Commons at all. In the six days before Redmond's final concession and the date due for the bill's introduction the European crisis deteriorated sharply. Moreover, the intervening episode in Ireland of the Howth gun-running and the shooting on Bachelor's Walk inevitably made Redmond's hold over his party in the light of this latest concession more difficult, though his ability to hold it was not in question. But for comfort's sake the bill was postponed for two days, due finally to be introduced on the afternoon of Thursday, 30 July 1914.

That very morning Asquith was sitting in the cabinet room with a map of Ulster, polishing up his speech for the afternoon, when a telephone call came from 'of all people in the world' Bonar Law to suggest a meeting with Carson in Law's house, Pembroke Lodge, Kensington. Law had sent his car for him. The Prime Minister got in, half wondering if he were being kidnapped by a section of the Ulster Volunteers.[3] Nothing so desperate was in store for him, though the meeting was not without drama.

Law and Carson proposed that in the interests of a united national front in the European crisis the introduction of the Amending Bill should be postponed to avoid the bitterness of public controversy. After consultation with his cabinet colleagues and Redmond, Asquith accepted this in principle. The procedure they agreed on among themselves was that Home Rule should become law and be placed on the statute book, but simultaneously with a Suspensory Act which would prevent it coming into force until a new Amending Bill could be introduced later. For an invaluable moment at least, a sudden calm settled over the wholly unsolved Irish problem.

When Grey, the Foreign Secretary, spoke to the House of Commons in sombre terms on 3 August 1914 he was able to say that 'the one bright spot in the very dreadful situation is Ireland. The position in Ireland – and this I should like to be clearly understood abroad – is not a consideration among the things we have to take into account now.'

Redmond then took a political gamble. 3 August was a Monday and he had not been in touch with his colleagues Dillon and Devlin in Ireland since the previous Friday, though he had clearly given the question of what he should say some thought over the weekend. The Prime Minister's wife, Margot Asquith, even wrote to him on the Saturday evening appealing to him to offer the Volunteers to the government, and, though he would not normally have taken much notice of such advice, it seems to have fitted in with the way in which his mind was moving.[4] He may even have read a letter from Darrell Figgis who had played such an important part in the arming of the Volunteers to date, which appeared in the *Freeman's Journal* of Saturday, 1 August, suggesting that the government should give arms to the Volunteers for the defence of Ireland.[5] At any rate, while Gray was speaking in the House, Redmond consulted one Irish member, John Hayden, about whether he should speak in this sense and received an encouraging reply. Another member, however, T. P. O'Connor, to whom he also spoke, thought that the bitter feeling over Bachelor's Walk made support for such a line in Ireland too problematical.[6] However, Redmond took the chance.

He knew that his authority in Ireland was immense. He was determined to do all he could to get the Home Rule Act on to the statute book in spite of the outbreak of war. The essence of the Irish nationalism for which he and the vast majority of the Irish people stood was that, individual as it was, it was a part of a wider family relationship with the rest of Great Britain. That family was now threatened with one of the greatest crises in her history and Redmond, re-emphasizing Ireland's individual claim to be a self-respecting member of that family, spoke for her as such.

'... In past times,' he said, 'when this Empire has been engaged in these terrible enterprises, it is true ... the sympathy of the Nationalists of Ireland, for reasons to be found deep down in the centuries of history, has been estranged from this country. Allow me to say, sir, that what has occurred in recent years has altered the situation completely. I must not touch and I may be trusted not to touch on any controversial topic; but this I may be allowed to say, that a wider knowledge of the real facts of Irish history has, I think, altered the views of the democracy of this country towards the Irish question, and today I honestly believe that the democracy of Ireland will turn with the utmost anxiety and sympathy to this country in every trial and every danger that may overtake it.'[7]

He told the government that they could take their troops out of Ireland tomorrow and that the coasts of Ireland would be defended by Irishmen of the Irish Volunteers, in conjunction he hoped with the Ulster Volunteers of the North.

The speech was welcomed with such relief and enthusiasm in the House of Commons that the references to the workings of Irish history may not have received the attention they deserved.

Outside the House of Commons it was a gamble which, in the short term and in the light of the calculations on which it had been taken, came off triumphantly. Except inevitably for the very small minority, consisting of IRB men, supporters of Sinn Fein and some of the other extreme nationalists in the original committee of the Volunteers, Redmond's attitude as expressed in the House of Commons speech was welcomed and applauded with enthusiasm throughout Ireland. But that it had been a risk was something Redmond himself was well aware of. Only two days before, he had received a letter from Colonel Maurice Moore, the Inspector General of the Volunteers and a staunch supporter of Redmond's, which said that should there be any hesitation on the part of the government in getting the king to sign the Home Rule Bill then Irish reservists should be told not to join up.[8] On returning to his room in the House of Commons after his speech on the 3rd, Redmond actually found a telegram awaiting him from the Volunteers in Derry which ran: 'Army and Naval Reserve met, decided refuse join colours until assured that King will sign Home Rule Bill.'[9]

Colonel Moore's letter had argued: 'This is the only pressure we can exert against a combination of the two English parties ...'[10] Redmond had merely decided to make the pressure a moral one rather than aggressively direct. Part of his calculation had been that a generous gesture of goodwill from Irish nationalists would prove more effective than any threat in enabling Asquith to get Home Rule onto the statute book. And certainly many Tories were deeply impressed by his attitude[11].

The element in his calculation which reckoned that Irish opinion would support him was confirmed at once. Colonel Maurice Moore sent immediate congratulations from Dublin. For over a week messages of endorsement and support continued to flow in to Redmond from individuals, local government bodies and local organizations of the Volunteers all over Ireland.[12]

On the main part of Redmond's calculation, that he could bring Asquith to place Home Rule on the statute book, there were to be some unpleasant moments when it seemed as if Asquith might be prevaricating. The Prime Minister had, in the war situation, many grave considerations that might reasonably be pleaded as more urgent. The opposition leaders, Law and Carson, while agreeing in the interests of national unity not actively to oppose the placing of Home Rule on the statute book, refused to acquiesce in it in any way, even given the assurance of an accompanying Suspensory

Act. Without Redmond's constant pressure and insistence that if Home Rule were not passed Ireland would once again become as grave an element in the situation as ever before, Asquith might well have found it more convenient to continue to evade the issue. But Redmond had plenty of evidence to support him. Already by the beginning of September Colonel Maurice Moore, the Volunteers' Inspector General, was complaining that the government had not taken a single step to help the Volunteers implement Redmond's offer. They had been offered neither rifles, money, officers nor any plans whatever for integration in the defence system.

Ten days later a correspondent wrote to the *Freeman's Journal*: 'Irishmen are beginning to have grave doubts.... A generous enthusiasm has been met by neglect. And another opportunity, greater perhaps than any before it, of treating Ireland with confidence and respect has been rejected.'[13]

However, Redmond had kept something in reserve. He had hitherto restrained his natural inclinations to encourage Irish recruiting until the *quid pro quo* he had bargained for was forthcoming. And within a week of the *Freeman's Journal*'s bitter comment the situation was transformed by Asquith's decision to put the Home Rule Act on the statute book immediately. Although the entire Conservative opposition walked out of the House of Commons in protest, on 18 September 1914 the Home Rule Act received the royal assent. It was accompanied by an act simultaneously suspending it for twelve months or until the end of the war, whichever were the longer period – and in the light of the then recently won Battle of the Marne there seemed indications, as the *Freeman's Journal* put it, that the war would 'last for a much less time' than twelve months.[14]

The net effect of the passing of the Home Rule Act was simply to shelve the problems of Ulster to be argued about again when peace returned. Yet it seemed a great landmark at the time. Even in retrospect it must be accounted as psychologically a great political victory for Redmond, for it meant that when Ulster did come to be argued about all over again, Redmond and the Nationalists would be theoretically in possession. Concessions from them would seem more remarkable concessions, and at the same time the enthusiastic participation of Ireland in the war effort would have conditioned English opinion even more favourably towards Irish sensibilities.

At the time, the passing of the Home Rule Act was indeed regarded as a major triumph at Westminster and in Ireland. After returning from the House of Lords to hear the Clerk of the Crown proclaim the royal assent, one Nationalist member produced a miniature green flag with a golden harp in the centre and carried it aloft into the Chamber. Cheers were followed by the singing of 'God Save the King' in which people in the gallery joined. At the end of it a Labour member cried out: 'God Save Ireland!' to which Redmond replied: 'God Save England too!'[15] For a few moments, forgetting the awkward realities that lay concealed by the Suspensory Act and the projected Amending Bill, it seemed a fitting climax to Redmond's long and selfless parliamentary career of thirty-four years.

All Ireland joined in the sense of triumph. Though Dublin itself received the news relatively quietly, in most parts of the country there were bonfires, street illuminations and bands playing 'A Nation Once Again' and 'God Save Ireland', while local bodies of Volunteers paraded proudly with their rifles. In Wexford tar barrels blazed on, among other places, Vinegar Hill. In the celebrations at Charleville, County Cork, it was noted that for the first time in living memory the words 'God Save the King' were heard on a Nationalist platform, and as the speaker uttered them a great outburst of cheering arose from the assembled multitude.[16] The *Freeman's Journal* itself, which saw 'the opening of an era of freedom, happiness and prosperity such as Ireland has not experienced for more than a hundred years', carried a banner headline crying IRELAND'S DAY OF TRIUMPH across all seven columns of its centre page.[17] On the opposite page there was a drawing of the old Irish Parliament House headed AT LAST! OUR OWN AGAIN! accompanied by sketches of Emmet, Napper Tandy, Lord Edward Fitzgerald, Grattan, Wolfe Tone, James Stephens, Butt, Davitt, O'Connell and Parnell, as if every thread that had ever appeared in the complex pattern of Irish nationalism had somehow been happily tied up at last. Indeed, that day's leader commented: 'Yesterday the charter of Ireland's freedom was signed.'[18]

Nor were the grounds for such feeling purely emotional. The very fact that Carson and the Tories had preferred to walk out of the House of Commons rather than witness the event seemed some proof that a real change had taken place. Hitherto in Irish history it had been the Irish who walked out of the House of Commons frustrated, either because they were ordered to; or because it was the only gesture left to them in a situation in which they were politically impotent. Now it seemed to be the Tories who were demonstrating their impotence.

In retrospect all this can easily be seen to have been an illusion. Within a few months the Tories were part of the government and Carson himself a member of the cabinet. Within a few years Redmond's triumph had turned to ashes. But things looked very different from Ireland at the time. Even though there were in the background disturbing features which made many feel that all might still not be well, it was the sense of Home Rule triumph which dominated the foreground.

Some ill omens might have been discerned in the very words with which Asquith, hoping vainly to avoid a scene in the House of Commons as the Home Rule Bill passed onto the statute book, sought to ingratiate himself with Carson and Bonar Law. He agreed that 'it might be said that the Ulstermen had been put at a disadvantage by the loyal and patriotic action they had undertaken' and continued: 'I say, speaking again on behalf of the Government, that, in our view, under the conditions which now exist ...

that employment of force, any kind of force, for what you call the coercion of Ulster is an absolutely unthinkable thing ... that is a thing we would never countenance or consent to.'[19] This did not augur well for the future of a united Ireland. Ever since the affair at the Curragh such an admission had been implicit in the situation, but it had never been made openly and voluntarily by the government before.

A further disappointment was the government's neglect of Redmond's offer of the Volunteers for the defence of Ireland. No move at all had yet been made or was ever to be made by the War Office to incorporate them in the defence forces. But with Home Rule on the statute book Redmond generously accepted the government's part of the deal as fairly completed, and proceeded to embark in Ireland on a recruiting campaign for the British Army. He had already, the day before the royal assent, issued a manifesto urging full cooperation by Ireland with the war effort. It was, he said, the most serious war in the Empire's history, 'a just war provoked by the intolerable military despotism of Germany.... It is a war for high ideals of human government and international relations, and Ireland would be false to her history, and to every consideration of honour, good faith, and self-interest, did she not willingly bear her share in its burdens and its sacrifices.'[20]

He returned to Ireland at the end of the week and on Sunday, 20 September 1914, while motoring to his house, Parnell's old shooting lodge of Aughavanagh in County Wicklow, happened to hear that a parade of East Wicklow Volunteers was being held at Woodenbridge on the way. He stopped and made them a short impromptu address. He was not going to make a speech, he said. But the words he did use were to have a far-reaching result.

This war, he said, was 'undertaken in defence of the highest principles of religion and morality and right, and it would be a disgrace for ever to our country, and a reproach to her manhood, and a denial of the lessons of her history, if young Ireland confined her efforts to remain at home to defend the shores of Ireland from an unlikely invasion, and shrunk from the duty of proving on the field of battle that gallantry and courage which has distinguished our race all through its history'.[21] He urged the Volunteers to go on drilling so that they could eventually account themselves as men in the firing line wherever that might be.

Although, as when he spoke in the House of Commons six weeks earlier, he had virtually consulted no one before speaking, he had gauged the mood of Irish opinion exactly. What he said was wholly in line with what the majority of the people of Ireland were thinking, and the recruiting figures from Ireland were soon to show it. Dillon, who was less enthusiastic about the war than Redmond in terms of international policy, though not in terms of Ireland's identification with the rest of Britain, made no objection at the time to this speech as he had made none to the earlier one, and indeed he was to support it and elaborate it on public platforms over the months to come. The only people who did object were a small caucus of the Volunteers comprised mostly, as one might have expected, of the IRB men, Sinn Fein supporters and other advanced nationalists who still wanted to think traditionally of England's war being Ireland's opportunity. Twenty members of the committee, including most of those who had given the Volunteer movement its original impetus, resigned. Under Eoin MacNeill they formed a new splinter body of Volunteers. The vast majority of the rank and file stayed in the main organization with Redmond.

Out of a total of some 188,000 Volunteers altogether at the time of the division, only some 13,500 had over four weeks later declared their allegiance for MacNeill.[22] The secessionists, who were widely regarded as a clique of almost unknown cranks (MacNeill was the only name among them widely known at all), were immediately popularly dubbed the 'Sinn Fein' Volunteers. Their official title was the 'Irish Volunteers', while the main body under Redmond continued to be known as the Irish National Volunteers, or simply National Volunteers to make the distinction clearer.

It so happened that in the face of this impertinent challenge Redmond was able to display immediate confirmation of the very wide support he commanded in Ireland over the attitude he had expressed at Woodenbridge. Asquith himself had come to Dublin that week to help celebrate the passing of the Home Rule Act, and a public meeting took place on the day after the MacNeill breakaway before a packed audience of three thousand people in the Round Room of the Mansion House with another one thousand overflowing into the supper room. Both Asquith and Redmond received long standing ovations, while five hundred Volunteers, who had marched through O'Connell Street to the Mansion House with rifles and bayonets, proudly acted as marshals at the meeting. When Redmond claimed that in proportion to population Ireland had a larger quota serving in the firing line than any other part of the United Kingdom (and the large number of Irish regiments already figuring in the casualty lists bore him out), he was particularly loudly cheered.[23] John Dillon seconded the vote of thanks to Asquith in words that showed no misgivings about Redmond's recruiting appeal. 'We have now got an opportunity,' said Dillon, 'and we shall avail ourselves of the opportunity of proving to the people of Great Britain and of Britain's Empire that the friendship of Ireland is worth the price.... England will learn and learn in her hour of need that Ireland never broke faith in her history.' He promised that Ireland would be 'united in our determination to prove ourselves brave and efficient friends to the British Empire and to England in this struggle'.[24] He too was cheered to the echo.

In fact, only in Dublin itself was the split in the Volunteers even of minor significance at the time. Slightly under one-third of the five Volunteer battalions there went with MacNeill into the Irish Volunteers.[25] But in the county of Dublin as a whole, only 210 out of a total of 3,719 Volunteers opted for MacNeill and the proportion was similar for other parts of the country.[26] Resolutions supporting Redmond and his attitude and repudiating the minority poured in, usually unanimously, from all over Ireland.[27] Even where a special effort was made by an individual Volunteer of outstandingly strong convictions to persuade his colleagues to join MacNeill the results were not far different. At a drill meeting at Larkill, Eamonn Ceannt, a member of the IRB, addressed the Volunteers in this strain but only managed to persuade fifteen out of seventy to go with him.*[28]

The impression has often been given that Redmond's pro-recruiting speech at Woodenbridge left the minority Irish Volunteers as the only active group in Irish nationalist opinion. This is a travesty of fact and of the whole character of Irish nationalist history. The vast majority of Irish nationalist opinion – those whose nationalism found expression in the idea of Home Rule – remained as nationalist and active as before, behind Redmond's policy of support for the Imperial war effort. The long-term result of this was inevitably that the cream of the Volunteer movement was eventually drawn off into the British Army, and the majority Volunteer movement at home gradually lost its vitality. Even by the early autumn of 1914, at the time of the split, many of the best of the Volunteer drill instructors, who had mainly been ex-British Army men on the Reserve, had been recalled as reservists. Other enthusiastic Volunteers were naturally among the first to leave to enlist in the British Army. But for a time even at home the Redmond National Volunteers remained strong and active, certainly putting the activities of the small body of obscure secessionists into the shade for the time being, and demonstrating that Redmond's attitude had in no way bewildered or confused the majority of nationalists.

A new Committee of the National Volunteers was immediately elected, with Redmond as President and Colonel Maurice Moore Inspector-General in 'Supreme Command of the Military Council'.[29] At a vast review of these Volunteers at Wexford on 4 October 1914, when long lines of National Volunteers, very many of them fully armed and in uniform, stretched for some miles into the countryside to welcome Redmond on his arrival by road into the town, he told them confidently not to worry about any future Amending Bill to the Home Rule Act but to trust the party as they had trusted it four years before.[30] Also on the same Sunday the indomitable Republican Mac-Bride addressed the Volunteers of the Colley and Carlingford districts in County Cork. But when he made a reference to the Irish party leaders as the 'so-called leaders' and described them as 'recruiting sergeants for the British

---

* The mathematics professor, Eamon de Valera, managed to persuade a majority of his company to follow him into the Irish Volunteers under MacNeill, but these 'thirty or forty' men soon dwindled to 'seven' at subsequent parades. Lord Longford and T. P. O'Neill, *Eamon de Valera* (London, 1970), p. 23.

Empire', the bulk of the audience rose in their seats, gave three cheers for Redmond, and marched out of the hall leaving only about a dozen behind.[31] On the same day in Limerick, while some 1,200 of the National Volunteers held a route march and review, what was described as 'the Sinn Fein' company could only muster 150 men.[32]

On the following Sunday, 11 October, Redmond held a review at Waterford of four thousand armed Volunteers, many in uniform and with their 'bayonets glinting in the sun', while there were other parades the same day at Athy and Naas and manoeuvres in the north of County Dublin.[33] It was also the twenty-third anniversary of Parnell's death, and some eight hundred National Volunteers, almost all armed, had acted as a guard of honour at the cemetery. A small group of MacNeill's Irish Volunteers had been to the cemetery earlier with rifles and in uniform, but their claim to speak for Ireland was further disputed when they found themselves in embarrassing disagreement even with Larkin's Citizen Army which had also paraded with rifles and in uniform at Parnell's grave. Larkin, who found himself prevented by the Irish Volunteers from speaking at an Irish Volunteer meeting in Parnell Square, though he insisted that he had been invited to do so, held a rival meeting at which he called out derisively in the direction of MacNeill's men: 'Nice rebels they are – they're not fit to run an ice-cream shop!'[34] It was a turbulent day for Larkin altogether, for later that afternoon some five hundred National Volunteers tried to march through his meeting and found their way barred by Citizen Army men flourishing swords and bayonets.[35]

In fact, for some weeks it looked as if the split in the Volunteers, far from weakening Redmond and the bulk of the Volunteer body, had given them new power and energy. 'The Volunteers are at last getting down to business ...' wrote the *Freeman's Journal* on 15 October. 'The departure has ended the reign of the do-nothings and made for the men of action.' A well-produced weekly paper, the *National Volunteer*, was started. The National Committee of the Volunteers, meeting at their offices in 24 Parnell Square, reaffirmed their objects as being 'to train, equip, and arm a Volunteer force for the defence of Ireland and the advancement and presentation of Irish rights and the maintenance of Irish self-government'.[36] On the following Sunday Redmond held another review, this time of some five thousand Volunteers at Kilkenny, which the local reporter described as 'a Citizen Army sprung into existence to safeguard Irish rights'.[37] Many of the Volunteer companies were in uniform and carried rifles and bayonets; the cheering crowds which welcomed Redmond beneath triumphal arches waved Irish flags, and numerous bands played national airs. 'The Union of 1800 is dead ...' declared Redmond in his speech. 'A new era has arisen in the history of our country ... we have won at last a free Constitution.'[38] The same afternoon Joe Devlin was presenting colours to the First Derry Regiment of National Volunteers in Derry, describing them as part of that 'Irish National

Army which had come into being to help the Irish party win Home Rule and help them maintain it once it had been won'.[39]

In this phase of Irish history it is necessary to free one's mind not only of the knowledge of what was to happen in Ireland in 1916 and after, but also of the knowledge of how the Great War was to develop. The confidence and enthusiasm with which Redmond and the vast majority of Irish nationalists in the National Volunteers could view the future in these late months of 1914, and even well into 1915, must be seen in the light of the European war as it then appeared. No one then knew that the war was going to last four years. No one could fully imagine the scale of the slaughter or the magnitude of the cataclysm in which Europe was involved. It was even still quite reasonable to think that the war might soon be over. What had hitherto been a war of rapid movement was only beginning to settle into the bloody stalemate of the trenches, and no one yet knew that it was a stalemate. As Sunday after Sunday reviews of several thousand armed National Volunteers were held in different parts of Ireland to be addressed by the Nationalist Party leaders[40] their political position seemed logical and vigorously optimistic.

Dillon in November made crystal clear the purpose for which the Volunteers were in existence when he said: 'If the army does not enforce the new law [i.e. Home Rule] which gives liberty to Ireland – the army which was only too willing to enforce the old bad law at the slightest hint from the government – Ireland will enforce it herself.'[41] And Redmond himself in December 1914, addressing some ten thousand National Volunteers on parade with arms on Limerick racecourse with the national flag of the gold harp on the green background flying above them, declared: 'The discipline and the unity of the Irish Party ... and the National Organization ... were never as necessary as they will be in the interval between now and the assembling of the Irish Parliament.'[42]

The logic of the position was straightforward: Home Rule, which was the form of nationalism the vast majority of the Irish people wanted, was law; it was law as it stood without any amendment and law for the whole of Ireland. This law was merely suspended either for twelve months, or if the war was by then not over, for a further period to be fixed by the king in Council, but in no case lasting longer than the end of the war. Thus once the initial twelve months were up, as Redmond himself put it in the middle of 1915, a Home Rule Parliament could come into existence before the end of the war but could not be delayed one hour longer.[43] When, in September 1915, this original twelve months did expire, the suspension of Home Rule was continued only for another six months or until the end of the war if that were to come sooner.

An as yet unspecified Amending Bill to the law was also provided for, but this it was hoped would be a matter for mutual agreement between all parties after discussion. Meanwhile, the Volunteers were a physical guarantee both that the law would be enforced and that, in the amendment to be agreed, nothing unacceptable to Irish national opinion such as the permanent partition of Ireland could be introduced. The Nationalist MP John Hayden, speaking for his leader to a parade of National Volunteers in Westmeath in March 1915, spelt this out:

'We desire to say,' he declared, 'when the Amending Bill comes forward that if it be unsatisfactory, and if we wish to reject it, we have behind us not only the sense and feeling of the people, but that we have also behind us a determined, united and disciplined body of Irishmen who are prepared to back us up at any hazard. If that is done, then I say you need not be afraid of anything in connection with this Amending Bill.'[44]

Redmond himself was optimistic that agreement on the terms of the Amending Bill would be achieved. But he, too, stressed that if an unacceptable Amending Bill should be forthcoming, possibly from a Conservative government, then the National Volunteer Force, 'if such a contingency should arise, will stand at the back of the civil organization and see that no successful attempt is made to filch from us the rights we have won'.[45]

And the party newspaper, the *Freeman's Journal*, urging an improvement in the arming and organization of the National Volunteers, wrote in a leading article:

'The National Volunteers will be the great rampart of defence against any attempt to defeat or delay Home Rule or to impair the guarantees of national autonomy contained in the Act to which the King has appended his sign manual.... Now is the time to take steps to make the National Army an effective weapon in the hands of the Nation's leaders ...'[46]

But apart from this sanction what grounds were there for optimism? What made Redmond suppose that there could be any more agreement over North-East Ulster in a future Amending Bill than there had been in the total deadlock reached in July 1914? It was an essential part of his whole policy that in addition to the new physical sanction of the National Volunteer Force there was simultaneously a moral sanction which had entirely altered the situation since July 1914. This was the moral sanction built up by nationalist Ireland's participation in the war.

Redmond had fought hard, often in the teeth of War Office and regular Army Unionist dislike of southern Irish nationalists, to give a specifically Irish National flavour to Ireland's contribution to recruiting. There had been a tendency at first to disperse southern Irishmen, who wanted to enlist, into English regiments rather than let them concentrate in their own units. This was in marked contrast to the treatment given to the Ulster Volunteer Force who were at once allowed to form their own Ulster Division of the British Army with distinctive badges and emblems. But eventually, thanks to Redmond's pressure, there was formed, in addition to the regular 10th Irish Division stationed at the Curragh, a third Irish Division (the 16th) with headquarters in Cork and Tipperary. Nevertheless, its commanding officer, General Sir Lawrence Parsons, a Unionist Irishman, though proud of his family's opposition to the Union in 1800 and its support of Catholic emancipation, was reluctant to allow the use of specific Irish badges and pedantically adamant against Redmond's wish to refer to the Division under the nostalgic Irish title of 'the Irish Brigade'.[47] These influences had acted as a slight brake on Irish recruiting fervour after the initial enthusiasm of the first few weeks of the war. Nor had some of the speeches made in favour of recruiting in the North by die-hard Unionists there helped recruiting in the rest of Ireland. Carson promised those whom he encouraged to enlist that he would see that those Ulster Volunteers left behind would be effectively reorganized and kept in being. 'I promise you,' he said, 'that they will be strong enough and bold and courageous enough to keep the old flag flying while you are away. We are not going to abate one jot or tittle of our opposition to Home Rule, and when you come back, you who go to the Front to serve your King and Country, you will come back just as determined as you will find us at home.'[48]

General Richardson, commander of the Ulster Volunteer Force, based his appeal for recruits unashamedly on Protestant Ulster's obligation to a British Army which, in the Curragh episode, 'came to the help of Ulster in the day of trouble and they would do so again'.[49]

But in spite of such provocation, and thanks both to Redmond's persistence over the Irish division and to the undoubted extent to which his own feeling about the duty of Irish nationalists to engage in the imperial war effort was genuinely reflected in the Irish nation, the recruiting figures were by the autumn of 1915 such that even the dour anti-nationalist Lord Kitchener had to describe them as 'magnificent'.[50] By that date there were already in the British Army 132,454 Irishmen, of whom 79,511 were Catholics and 52,943 were Protestants. Of these only some 22,000 had been serving when war broke out and a further 30,000 had been called up as reservists. Since the outbreak of war, altogether 81,408 Irishmen had volunteered as recruits, 27,412 of these being Ulster Volunteers and 27,054 being National Volunteers. The appalling casualty lists teemed with the names of great Irish regiments: Royal Irish Fusiliers, Munster Fusiliers, Dublin Fusiliers, Inniskilling Fusiliers, Royal Irish Rifles, the Leinster Regiment, the Irish Guards and Connaught Rangers. Irishmen had won seventeen VCs in the first thirteen months of the war. The first of the three great Irish Divisions, the 10th, was fighting with great gallantry at Gallipoli (though typically the War Office was reluctant to have the Irish identified by nationality in its despatches).

All of this had undoubtedly made a deep impression on reasonable Unionist opinion, and Redmond's, Dillon's and the rest of the leadership's assumption that this in itself would alter the old Unionist attitude when it came to an Amending Bill to accommodate Ulster seemed logical and reasonable. The Unionist paper, the *Birmingham Post*, wrote at the end of October 1915 that there was no doubt that the population of Ireland as a whole was 'heart and soul with England and their allies in this war' and concluded: 'Not that she has not sent more, but that she has sent, and freely sent, so many men is the most recent miracle of Ireland.'[51]

In such a climate the party's confidence remained high. John Dillon declared at a big review of National Volunteers in Belfast in March 1915 that men like the Irish VC Michael O'Leary were 'fighting for Ireland and for Ireland's rights as truly as any Irish Brigade ever fought on the fields of Flanders in the past. It is their deeds that will stand to us in the struggle that may yet be before us when we have ... to take up the threads of Irish politics when the war is over.'[52] And after a vast review of 27,000 National Volunteers from all parts of Ireland, almost all armed and many with rifles and even bayonets, held in Phoenix Park on Easter Sunday 1915, Dillon told the Convention that followed: 'We look forward to the day when we have to resume those arguments about the Amending Bill and when the National Volunteers may be again summoned to the capital, and shall march not 20,000 but 50,000 or 100,000 all armed and drilled and disciplined through the streets of Dublin. Then I think it will become manifest ... that Ireland free and indivisible must be conceded. That is my idea of the object of the National Volunteers.'[53]

'Given,' declared Redmond that summer of 1915, 'Given these two things – Ireland doing her duty to herself in the war and Ireland doing her duty to herself in keeping her political and military organizations intact ... there is nothing more certain in this world than that as soon as the war ends Ireland will enter into the enjoyment of her inheritance.'[54]

But there was in this twin moral and physical sanction a fatal flaw already beginning to be revealed but which, in the nature of the way in which things unfold in time, could still not be seen quite clearly. The very enthusiasm with which national Ireland asserted her moral claim by sending recruits to the British Army automatically weakened her physical sanction by depleting the strength of the National Volunteers. Supplying an élite for one purpose she deprived herself of an élite for the other. And simultaneously the moral fervour at home was directed rather to the fight overseas than into the state of preparedness at home. For a relatively short period of time the physical drain could have been tolerable. But the removal of the British Army reservists on the outbreak of war had deprived the Volunteers of almost all their best training instructors. By early 1915 the drain was beginning to tell. National Volunteer parades began to appear noticeably thinned by the departure for the Front of so many men of the very type who would have been keenest to turn out for such parades. The review of 27,000 Volunteers at Easter 1915 was virtually the last at which the National Volunteers made a big impression. By the end of 1915, though their nominal roll was still over 100,000, it was as far as members still in Ireland were concerned largely nominal, composed often of totally passive nationalists or even Unionists who had often joined on the outbreak of war as an expression of Irish-tinged Imperial patriotism.

Nevertheless, Nationalist politicians continued to talk as if the sanction of the National Volunteers were still a real factor. Greeted by 150 National Volunteers with rifles and fixed bayonets at a United Irish League Convention at Thurles in August 1915, Dillon argued boldly that 'the 30,000 odd National Volunteers who had left for the front would soon be back, trained and gallant soldiers, and that ... in the final struggle ... if it should be forced upon us, the fact of having a large force of determined organized Volunteers, stiffened by soldiers who have returned from the front, will be a deciding element in the result'.[55]

But it was in the nature of the horror still not fully unfolded in Europe that very many of those thirty thousand would not come back. The cause was coming to have to depend more and more on the moral obligation which Ireland had earned from England. The relevant question became increasingly: would England keep faith? In spite of the provocative statements of die-hard Ulstermen and certain other disconcerting developments in the course of 1915, the general inclination among Irishmen was still to answer that she would.

'Does anyone imagine that Belgium's scrap of paper will be honoured and Ireland's solemn treaty with England repudiated?' asked Joe Devlin at a meeting in Donegal in August 1915. And he added optimistically: 'The Amending Bill, and the Government which proposed it as a basis of common agreement are things of the past.'[56] Exclusion, he maintained, had been put forward as a tactical move in the fight against Home Rule, but now that Home Rule was on the statute book 'the tactical value of exclusion has practically ceased to exist'.[57] And he supported this extremely dubious thesis with the much more tenable argument that the events of the war had considerably mollified the attitude of many English and Irish Unionists with regard to Home Rule.

And yet there were also indications to make Irish nationalists doubt such an optimistic view of England's intentions. One could be found in that very change of government to which Devlin alluded. For, when a coalition had been formed in June 1915 in an attempt to secure a more successful prosecution of the war, not only that English champion of North-East Protestant Ulster, the Conservative leader Bonar Law, had been brought into the cabinet, but Carson himself, in the high post of Attorney General. It was true that Asquith had also offered an unspecified post to Redmond. The Prime Minister had even strenuously urged him to accept it after Redmond had immediately, and with nation-wide approval from Ireland, turned it down. But lack of consideration for the effect in Ireland of Carson's appointment inevitably revived memories of Asquith's own rather ambivalent identification with Irish nationalism in 1914 and earlier. Quite apart from which it seemed unthinkable that Carson and Bonar Law, in such positions of power, would permit the passage of any Amending Bill which contained less than their last demands of 1914. And these, Irish nationalists had already found totally unacceptable.

A further indication that, for all Ireland's participation in the war effort, her national susceptibilities might still not figure particularly high in the priorities of the British Government, was the attempt by Asquith under pressure from his new Tory coalitionists to appoint to the office of Lord Chancellor of Ireland no less a person than J. H. Campbell, Carson's fellow Unionist representative for Dublin University, and one of his most fanatical supporters from before the war. Campbell was actually supposed to have signed the Ulster Covenant in his own blood. He had certainly declared in 1914 that though civil war might be the path of danger, it was also the path of duty, and no other alternative was left to the loyalists of Ulster.[58] As the *Manchester Guardian* of 1915 put it, he was an 'antagonist of everything Nationalist Ireland stood for'.[59] And yet this was the man Asquith proposed for the office which would have to issue writs for an Irish Parliament – a man solemnly pledged to oppose in arms the existence of any such Irish Parliament at all. Thanks to a stubborn stand by Redmond, Asquith was eventually forced to drop the proposal, but the fact that the proposal could have been made produced a profound impression on Ireland. The Bishop of Killaloe, Dr Fogarty, a staunch supporter of the party, wrote to Redmond of 'a great revulsion of feeling' in the country. 'Home Rule is dead and buried,' he wrote bitterly, 'and Ireland is without a national party or national press. What the future has in store for us God knows...'[60]

The bishop was being a little premature in his bitterness. Party leaders like Dillon and Devlin were still laying great emphasis on the need to keep the National Volunteer organization strong as a sanction for Home Rule, and in August another cleric, the Dean of Cashel, declaimed: '... strong and commanding in the British Senate as is the voice of John Redmond, its power will be immeasurably intensified when it re-echoes the thunder of 100,000 Volunteer rifles....' His appeal for the filling up of the ranks of 'the National Army' actually led to a number of Cashel men handing in their names for drill.[61]

But the Bishop of Killaloe's bitter comment revealed at least a growing wariness and political sensitiveness where Irish nationalists had little to build on but trust, and the foundations of that trust suddenly began to seem uncertain. The periodically repeated rumours of the introduction of a conscription scheme which might include Ireland further increased this sensitiveness. Irish nationalist pride insisted that the very considerable contribution Ireland

was making to the Imperial war effort should be honoured for what it was –
a spontaneous and voluntary gesture with conscious political implications
for the future of Home Rule. To ride roughshod over this, turning such
contribution into a mere legal obligation exacted ultimately by force from
Westminster at a time when an indigenous Irish Parliament was actually on
the statute book, seemed not only an insult recalling all the other insults
Ireland had received from Britain in the past but also a direct threat to Home
Rule itself. In December 1915 the party summed up the attitude of the whole
of Ireland when it passed a resolution declaring that 'any attempt to bring
into force a system of compulsory service will meet with our vigorous
resistance'.[62]

The conscription threat also had one other important effect. An RIC intelligence report from Limerick was not unrepresentative in stating that
opposition to conscription brought a number of recruits to MacNeill's small
secessionist group of Irish Volunteers in the form of farmers' sons of military
age 'who believed that by becoming Sinn Feiners they would not be compelled to serve in the army'.[63]

Indeed, in the climate of mild uneasiness generated by the advent of the
Coalition Government at a time when the potential strength of the National
Volunteers had been dispersed in Flanders and elsewhere, often for ever, the
small rump of the original Volunteer organization, known since the split of
a year before as the Irish Volunteers or, by the public, 'Sinn Fein Volunteers', began to attract some attention in its own right.

15
The 'Sinn Fein' Volunteers

By far the most important characteristic of the Irish (or 'Sinn Fein') Volunteers was something quite unknown not only to the public at large in Ireland (in any case little interested in them at this date) but also unknown to the very great majority of the Irish Volunteers themselves. This was the fact that they were secretly under the control of that small group of young men who, with the former dynamiter Tom Clarke, had recently been re-animating the near-defunct Irish Republican Brotherhood.

In August 1914, very soon after the outbreak of war, the grandiloquently titled Supreme Council of this tiny secret society had met and had taken, in principle, the decision to apply the long classic separatist doctrine that England's difficulty was Ireland's opportunity.[1] They pledged themselves sometime in the course of the war to rise in arms for an Irish republic totally independent of Britain. When taken, this decision might reasonably have been regarded as of a largely academic nature, for to the overwhelming majority of the Irish people it would have seemed impractical and childish nonsense.

Although the IRB under Hobson's and MacDermott's guidance had been largely responsible for the successful foundation of the National Volunteer movement, the movement had soon grown into something much too big for them. Its strength and its wide popular support came almost entirely from those who saw in the Home Rule Bill an adequate satisfaction of national aspirations. Redmond's demand for control of the movement merely ratified a *fait accompli*, the assumption by his supporters of a new militancy in their determination to defend a Home Rule Act.

It had been Bulmer Hobson's argument at the time of the party take-over that the IRB's one chance of making any impact at all was by keeping the foothold it had acquired in popular opinion, and his acceptance of Redmond's nominees had been based on this. His argument was reasonable in the context of the time. But the outbreak of war changed everything in the Irish situation. Since the vast majority of the Volunteer movement supported the British war effort under Redmond's leadership, the IRB was unlikely to be able to use that movement as it stood to implement the decision they had just taken to strike at Britain. Thus although the split of the Volunteers in September 1914 – brought about by the original committee

members' rejection of Redmond's recruiting drive – left only some thirteen
thousand men, or less than a twelfth of the whole Volunteer movement,
under any sort of IRB control, these thirteen thousand were at least a more
compact force for the IRB to be able to manipulate.

Not that the vast majority of the thirteen thousand had then any inkling
of the direction in which they were to be manipulated. Their President, Eoin
MacNeill, had a clear idea of what *he* considered the purpose of the Irish
Volunteers. It was not so very different from that envisaged by the National
Volunteers, namely to be sure that there would be an effective force available
to insist on the implementation of Home Rule at the end of the war.[2] The
chief difference between his view and that of the Nationalist Parliamentary
Party leaders was one of tactics. He and most of his supporters in the Irish
Volunteers simply thought it unwise to commit Irishmen to the war effort
without being sure that Home Rule would be implemented. They feared that
their potential strength would be dissipated in the British Army – a fear
which by the latter part of 1915 was beginning to look well founded.

Bulmer Hobson, who had resigned from the Supreme Council of the IRB
after the appointment of Redmond's nominees, but remained a member of
the organization, had more than an inkling of the Supreme Council of the
IRB's theoretical decision to start an insurrection. But he may well have
thought at first that the likelihood of it being put into practice was remote.
Events certainly showed that he was on the alert against any attempt to
implement it which he thought unreasonable. His own views were basically
those of MacNeill.

MacNeill considered that the only justification for an actual rising lay in a
reasonable chance of positive military success and of this he saw no possibility
whatsoever. He specifically rejected the thesis which the military schoolmaster Patrick Pearse, a member of the IRB since 1913 and now in its inner
councils, consistently proclaimed to the effect that a blood sacrifice, however
hopeless its chances of military success, was necessary to redeem Ireland
from her loss of true national pride, much as Jesus Christ by his blood
sacrifice had redeemed mankind from its sins.[3] Sometimes this mystical
dedication to bloodshed of Pearse, personally one of the gentlest and tender-
hearted of men as events were soon to prove, seemed to reach heights of near-
insanity. Writing in December 1915 of the Great War which had then lasted
sixteen months, he declared: 'It is good for the world that such things should
be done. The old heart of the earth needed to be warmed with the red wine
of the battlefields.'[4]

For MacNeill the only circumstance other than a real chance of military
success which would justify the Volunteers' use of physical force would be if
an attempt were made to disarm them. Otherwise they must simply preserve
their strength to defend Ireland's legal rights at the end of the war. 'If,' he
wrote in a private memorandum in February 1916, 'we can win our rights

by being ready to fight for them but without fighting, then it is our duty to do so and we shall not be ashamed of it ... the Irish Volunteers, if they are a military force, are not a militarist force, and ... their object is to secure Ireland's rights and nothing else but that.'[5]

But MacNeill and the bulk of the Volunteers he commanded were unknowingly a tool in the hands of the IRB. In May 1915 the executive of the IRB formally appointed a 'Military Committee' of three to plan the insurrection on which they had decided. This consisted of Patrick Pearse, the St Enda's schoolmaster, Joseph Plunkett, a twenty-four-year-old poet and sometime editor of the literary *Irish Review*, and Eamonn Ceannt, a thirty-three-year-old employee of the Dublin Corporation who had been a founder member of the Gaelic League. All three of them had already had some discussion of insurrectionary plans together. These were mainly the brainchild of the poet Plunkett, and were to cover the whole of Ireland. In September 1915 Tom Clarke, together with Sean MacDermott, who had been imprisoned for a time under the Defence of the Realm Act for his anti-recruiting activities, were co-opted on to this committee which became known as the 'Military Council'.[6]

The extreme secrecy with which the IRB plan for a rising was elaborated, and the extent to which it represented the work of a minority inside a veritable Chinese box of other minorities, is evidenced by the fact that until September 1915 not even the full Supreme Council of the IRB knew of the existence of the military committee. It had been formed only on the authority of a smaller executive. When it is considered that the whole IRB itself was only a tiny minority within the 'Sinn Fein' Volunteers, the extent to which the Dublin rising of 1916 was unrepresentative of the people of Ireland can be properly gauged.

Pearse, in addition to his key position in the IRB's military council, also held the post within MacNeill's Volunteer organization of Director of Operations. Ceannt was appointed to the headquarters staff of the Volunteers in August 1915 as Director of Communications. Director of Training was another poet, Thomas MacDonagh, who was to be co-opted on to the military council for the insurrection at the last moment in April 1916. But though other members of the IRB held positions on the General Council of the Volunteers, Pearse, Plunkett and Ceannt were the only members of the headquarters staff who knew what was really being planned for the Irish Volunteers. Other members of the IRB, like Bulmer Hobson and The O'Rahilly were, together with MacNeill himself, until the very eve of the insurrection quite in the dark, like the vast majority of the thirteen thousand Volunteers they commanded.

The Volunteers had virtually had to reorganize themselves from scratch after seceding from the main organization in September 1914. It is an indication of how lacking in identity the rank and file must have felt at first that their own newspaper, the *Irish Volunteer*, carried as late as three weeks after the split a leader maintaining that in the war Ireland was 'as warmly on England's side as Belgium'.[7] Only in the following week did the *Irish Volunteer* become representative of the minority view and a new Volunteer paper, the *National Volunteer*, make its appearance to continue representation of the majority. The formal reorganization of the minority body of the Volunteers itself took place at a Convention at the end of October 1914, when some 160 delegates were addressed by their president Eoin MacNeill. He declared that their new Volunteer force might 'yet be the means of saving Home Rule from disaster and of compelling the Home Rule Government to keep faith with Ireland without the exaction of a price in blood'.[8] And it was not until the last week of December 1914 that a scheme for the military reorganization of these secessionist Irish Volunteers was published.[9] In spite of the understandable pride taken in the successful landing of some 1,500 rifles at Howth and Kilcoole earlier in the year, the outbreak of war had made that success virtually irrelevant, for there was now no difficulty in obtaining rifles at all, provided the money for them could be found. The Irish Volunteer executive even announced in November 1914 that it was 'anxious that it should be generally understood that rifles and ammunition are available for all duly affiliated Volunteer companies and that rifles would be despatched by return against a remittance from the Company's treasurer'.[10] Again in July 1915 Pearse himself proclaimed that there were quite enough arms and that it was only a question of the Volunteers paying for them.[11]

But the Irish Volunteers themselves were a pathetically small body of men. There was no sign of an increase in their numbers as month followed month after the split, though a London journalist gave it as his opinion at the end of November 1914 that papers like Griffith's *Sinn Fein* and the *Irish Worker* (now edited by James Connolly) were 'producing some effect among a credulous and ignorant peasantry in the South and West'. The next month, however, Griffith's paper was suppressed by the government as was the IRB paper *Irish Freedom*. Griffith replaced *Sinn Fein* by *Scissors and Paste*, composed chiefly of excerpts from British and neutral sources, sometimes containing German wireless news, and of quotations from Grattan, Davis and Parnell. It too was banned in March 1915. It is difficult to say in retrospect to what extent such papers, though their circulation was very small, were in fact preparing the ground for eventual shifts in opinion. The news of their suppression may have been as effective as anything in their content in encouraging new thoughts about the government and the Imperial war effort. Certainly there was little reflection of their influence in an access of numbers to the Irish Volunteers.

But as early as the beginning of December 1914 John Dillon was sounding an alarm that 'Sinn Fein' – by which he meant the Irish Volunteers, for

Griffith had virtually no political organization at this time – needed to be taken seriously. It was, he said, 'a most critical period in the history of the national movement'[12] and police intelligence reports from County Cork early in 1915 said the Irish Volunteers were beginning to 'assume an importance altogether out of proportion to their numbers'.[13]

It was some time before the 'Sinn Fein Volunteers', as they were by now almost universally called, made any effective impact on the public as a military body. And they were not popular. At one of their very first appearances as a separate force in Galway in October 1914, when about forty of them attempted to march through the town with dummy rifles, they had been much booed and jeered by a local crowd, including men on leave from the Connaught Rangers who had been among the first troops into Belgium with the British Expeditionary Force.

It was not in fact until August 1915 that the Irish Volunteers made any very obvious impression at all compared with the main body of Volunteers under Redmondite leadership. The occasion was the funeral of the old Fenian Jeremiah O'Donovan Rossa who after a long, stormy and not always dignified life in Irish-American politics had died in America. The IRB seized on the occasion to manufacture a large public national demonstration out of his funeral rather as Stephens had done with the funeral of the Young Irelander, McManus, over fifty years before. And though Redmond's National Volunteers claimed actually to have the largest numerical representation at the Rossa funeral on 1 August 1915, it was the Irish Volunteers who supervised the marshalling of the crowds and the arrangements generally and who alone appeared not only in uniform – as did the National Volunteers – but also armed with rifles – as the National Volunteers did not.[14] The poet, Thomas MacDonagh, now a 'Commandant-General' in the Irish Volunteers, took charge of the funeral arrangements while the mathematics teacher, Eamon de Valera, promoted from Captain to Commandant in the Volunteers in March 1915, supervised the arrival of seventeen special trains. Over Rossa's grave a guard of honour of Irish Volunteers actually fired their rifles in a solemn last military salute and Patrick Pearse gave a stirring oration, claiming to be speaking on behalf of a new generation that had been 're-baptized in the Fenian faith and that has accepted the responsiblity of carrying out the Fenian programme'. He pledged hate to English rule in Ireland and concluded: 'Life springs from death; and from the graves of patriot men and women spring living nations. The Defenders of this Realm ... think that they have pacified Ireland ... but the fools, the fools, the fools! – they have left us our Fenian dead, and while Ireland holds these graves, Ireland unfree shall never be at peace.'[15]

The fact that Rossa in his latter years had been a supporter of Redmond's United Irish League, and had actually been on the platform to welcome Redmond to New York on the occasion of his last visit there, was of no consequence to Pearse who was busy myth-making. What, however, was of interest, as if almost suggesting a growing willingness to listen to myths on the part of people normally concerned with the reality of politics, was the fact that the *Freeman's Journal*, the party paper, printed Pearse's speech without comment.

Sir Mathew Nathan, the intelligent and well-informed Under-Secretary at Dublin Castle who was the real man in charge of day-to-day administration in Ireland during the not infrequent absences in England of the Chief Secretary, Augustine Birrell, wrote even before the funeral: 'I have an uncomfortable feeling that the Nationalists are losing ground to the Sinn Feiners and that this demonstration is hastening the movement.'[16] And yet the Irish Volunteers' numbers had actually dropped off since the end of 1914,[17] in spite of the employment by the IRB of regular organizers like Sean MacDermott and Ernest Blythe working regularly on a salary provided by Clan-na-Gael funds from America. In fact, Irish Volunteer numbers showed no regular increase until after the Rossa funeral and then only at an average rate of a few hundred a month right up to the Rising of April 1916 itself.[18] This relative failure to attract much support is all the more remarkable, given the drop in emigration from Ireland which had taken place since the beginning of the war.* None of the new stay-at-home population seemed yet attached to the Irish Volunteers in any significant quantity. Recruitment for the British Army on the other hand was proceeding at the rate of over six thousand per month.†

As for Griffith's political organization proper, Alderman Kelly, one of its representatives on the Dublin Corporation, declared frankly in October 1915 on the anniversary of Thomas Davis's death that Sinn Fein was 'on the rocks' and that he did not see what could be done about it. It had kept the light of nationality alive for the past eight or ten years, he claimed, and without it there would be no Volunteers of any kind, yet 'We are now left in this position that we cannot pay the rent or taxes of these premises' (the headquarters at 6 Harcourt Street, Dublin).[20]

Nevertheless, the 'Sinn Fein' Volunteers, and even the hundred-or-so strong Irish Citizen Army of James Connolly with whom they were usually on bad terms because of their refusal to give any priority to labour problems, could hardly help increasingly attracting some attention, however contemptuous, as the other active Volunteers became absorbed by the British Army.

On 19 September Pearse led some 1,500 Volunteers, 600 of whom were armed, through the streets of Dublin and out into manoeuvres at Stepaside, the scene of one of the Fenian victories of 1867.[21] On 6 October James

* Only 8,176 Irishmen had emigrated to countries other than Britain in 1915 compared with 19,267 in 1914 which itself had seen the first annual increase in population since 1851.[19]

† Official figures, *Freeman's Journal*, 2 July 1915. There were 71,494 Irish Catholics alone from Ireland in the armed forces by 20 June 1915 – 49,247 Protestants.

Connolly and his minute Irish Citizen Army, with the Countess Markievicz in uniform as one of his lieutenants, even carried out a mock attack on Dublin Castle.[22] When the anniversary of the Manchester Martyrs' death came round in November that year it was the Irish Volunteers who organized the celebrations.[23] The fact that the reprieved companion in arms of 'the noble-hearted three', Edward O'Meagher Condon, the man who had in fact first shouted the immortal 'God Save Ireland' from the dock, was still alive, and had been a staunch supporter of Redmond for many years and an optimistic enthusiast for the Home Rule Act, troubled Pearse and his colleagues no more than had the United Irish League affiliations of O'Donovan Rossa.* They were working quite consciously with historical myth in a climate that was becoming subtly favourable to it.

The mounting pressure from Conservative quarters in England, as the war situation deteriorated, for a system of conscription which might well include Ireland sharpened the edge of the Volunteers' activity. And under the threat of conscription, they began to receive some support not only from parish priests but also indirectly from at least one member of the Roman Catholic hierarchy. When some Irish emigrants, trying to leave Liverpool for the United States, were attacked as shirkers by the mob and given white feathers, the Bishop of Limerick, the Most Reverend Dr O'Dwyer, wrote publicly in protest: 'It is very probable that these poor Connacht peasants knew little or nothing of the meaning of war.... They would much prefer to be allowed to till their own potato gardens in peace in Connemara.... Their crime is that they are not ready to die for England. Why should they? What have they or their forbears ever got from England that they should die for her? Mr Redmond will say: "A Home Rule Act is on the Statute Book." But any intelligent Irishman will say: "A Simulacrum of Home Rule with an express notice that it is never to come into operation".'[24]

'Any intelligent Irishman' was a gross exaggeration, but it was an exaggeration with a grain of substance in it which any intelligent Irishman would recognize. There was something of a vacuum in Ireland, with the better part of Volunteers off at the war and the attention of most of Ireland directed outwards into Flanders. And in this prevailing situation it was easy for both the Citizen Army and 'the Sinn Fein Volunteers' to acquire an exaggerated significance.

Their opposition to recruiting for the British Army, their insistence on an Irish patriotism which did not, like that of the majority of Ireland, involve identification with the Empire's war effort, made many Unionists in particular indignant at the liberty of action allowed them. But the Chief Secretary, Augustine Birrell, acting in close cooperation with Redmond and John Dillon, consistently refused to yield to the clamour to have them suppressed.

---

* He died in America the following month. (*Freeman's Journal*, 8 April 1915, 17 December 1915.)

Redmond and Dillon continued rightly to advise Birrell that these extremist forces represented only a minute proportion of Irish opinion and that so delicate were Irish sensibilities that the only danger lay in making martyrs of them. It is to Birrell's credit that he learnt to understand clearly the peculiar nature of an Irish nationalism which, for reasons of history, could so easily be stimulated into something far more extreme than it was. Under Redmond's and Dillon's guidance he correctly saw it as the main task of his wartime secretaryship to prevent emotive influences from unsettling that mass patriotic nationalism which had consolidated into the demand for Home Rule.

Thus, in spite of occasional Unionist outbursts, it became quite a common sight to see the Irish Volunteers and men of Connolly's Citizen Army marching through the streets of Dublin in their uniforms with rifles on their shoulders or wheeling in mock attacks on public buildings. There was not necessarily any sinister objective in all this. The Volunteers' Director of Organization, Patrick Pearse, had written publicly in May 1915 when calling for more recruits that military action was not envisaged by the Irish Volunteers in the near future. 'But,' he had continued, 'what if Conscription be forced upon Ireland? What if a Unionist or a Coalition British Ministry repudiate the Home Rule Act? What if it be determined to dismember Ireland? What if it be attempted to disarm Ireland?'

These seemed the objects for which the Irish Volunteers were parading. If they chose to think them of primary concern while most people gave priority to the war, then that was their business, if faintly ridiculous. The great majority even of this minority of the Volunteers saw it much this way too. They could be accused of excessive zeal but they were proud of it, proud to be emphasizing the priority of the green flag over the Union Jack rather than waving them both simultaneously. The fact that there was an immediate serious practical purpose in this activity was known only to a handful of men in the inner conclave of the IRB. And since this did not even include Eoin MacNeill, the actual President of the Volunteers, it is hardly reasonable to blame the government Chief Secretary for having known only very little more. What they did know did not seem to substantiate serious fears.

The government and Birrell had in fact known since the beginning of the war that there was some apparently hare-brained scheme to bring about an Irish rebellion. They had learnt of it through messages intercepted between the German Embassy in Washington and the German Government in Berlin, the code of which had been broken by the British Admiralty.[25] The scheme appeared to centre round the old ex-Fenian John Devoy, who presided over the extreme nationalist American organization, Clan-na-Gael, and the curious figure of the British Consular official from the Glens of Antrim, Sir Roger Casement.

16
Casement in Germany

On the same day at the beginning of July 1914 as Erskine Childers had sailed in the *Asgard* to collect his share of the arms shipment for Howth, Casement who had done so much to set the event in motion had sailed for America to try to procure more arms.* He was followed a few days later by a letter from Eoin MacNeill dated 7 July, describing him as the 'accredited representative of the arms sub-committee' of the Irish Volunteers.[1]

On arrival in New York on 19 July he immediately got in touch with John Devoy, head of the secret revolutionary directory of Clan-na-Gael. Casement and Devoy had never met before, though they had corresponded occasionally, and Casement was a subscriber to the newspaper of which Devoy was the editor, the *Gaelic American*. But they knew something of each other through their mutual friend, Bulmer Hobson, and this friendship was to make for awkwardness at their first meeting. Devoy was courteous, but explained that Casement's part in allowing Redmond's nominees on to the Volunteer Committee made him unacceptable to Clan-na-Gael. Casement felt too tired to attempt a full justification of his and Hobson's point of view that evening. But the next day he wrote a long explanatory letter to Devoy which Devoy showed to the other members of the revolutionary directory. 'All,' wrote Devoy afterwards, 'were impressed by the downright sincerity of the man.'[2]

The other prominent members of the revolutionary directory were Judge Dan Cohalan of New York and Joe McGarrity, a naturalized Irish-American of Philadelphia who had made a fortune in the liquor trade. Casement was soon in touch with them. He had also within a few hours of arriving in New York been accosted in the street with a hard-luck, down-and-out story by a clever, disreputable young Norwegian sailor, named Adler Christensen, whom he 'befriended'.[3]

Little attempt seems to have been made to do anything very practical about securing supplies of arms for Volunteers from America. Large public meetings were held at which money was raised and Irish-American morale boosted. This was the sort of thing that had been going on happily in America

* He sailed from Ireland to Glasgow on 2 July and from Glasgow to Montreal on 4 July.

at varying pitches of intensity for more than fifty years. Casement, though he had explicitly said to Devoy that what was wanted were arms and not dollars,[4] spoke at meetings, contacted public men outside revolutionary circles, published pamphlets and wrote letters to newspapers. At this period of his life he was a man easily distracted from the main task in hand by the bustle of his own activity.

But in any case the need to arm the Volunteers was becoming obscured by the larger shadow rapidly spreading over Europe. And the week which brought to Casement and McGarrity, desperate with excitement in Philadelphia, the wonderful news of the safe landing of the rifles at Howth also brought word that Europe was at war.

The war with Germany was something which Casement had expected though he had not expected it to come so soon. He was clear in his mind how it could be turned to what he saw as Ireland's advantage. In an article published in the magazine *Irish Review* in July 1913 he had already opposed the orthodox view that Ireland and Britain must stand or fall together in the event of war with Germany. The very opposite was the case, he maintained. A war with Germany in which England was defeated might bring about Ireland's separation from England and her establishment as an independent sovereign state: an independent Ireland would be a guarantee for Germany of the freedom of the seas from British control. This view had penetrated to the IRB and Devoy through Casement's friend Hobson as early as 1910 and 1911. In March 1914 Devoy had shown a Casement memorandum to this effect to the German ambassador.

Devoy again got in touch with the German ambassador in New York on the outbreak of war and gave him the message he had received from the IRB in Ireland to the effect that they intended to take advantage of the war to bring about an armed rebellion, and that they wanted arms. Soon afterwards the idea that Casement should go to Berlin in person to facilitate German cooperation was in the air.

Much later Devoy criticized Casement severely for his 'utter impracticability' and described him as an 'honest but visionary' meddler.[5] The impression has thereby grown up that Casement's mission to Germany was a self-styled one, not really endorsed by the revolutionary bodies either in Ireland or America. But this is incorrect.

It is not clear at what date the idea that Casement should go to Germany was first broached. On Sunday, 2 August, Casement and Devoy were riding together in an open carriage at a meeting held to protest against the shooting of the civilians at Bachelor's Walk. A press photographer rushed up to the carriage and before Casement could turn his face away had clicked the shutter of his camera. Casement was very worried because he thought the wide publication of his photograph might prejudice his chances if he should undertake any secret mission in the future. But he did not then say anything

more definite to Devoy.⁶ Certainly the two main points which he eventually
went to Germany to try and secure (a German declaration of sympathy with
Irish national aims, and the formation of an Irish Brigade from prisoners
of war) were agreed as objectives between himself and Devoy within a
matter of weeks. On 14 September Casement wrote from 'c/o John Devoy'
to Joe McGarrity:

'I saw a friend yesterday. They are keen for it – keener now than ever
before as they realize its moral value to their case. Also the other matter
you and I discussed I put forward, and that too they like and think can
be done – they will discuss and let me know.'⁷

On 18 September von Papen, then German military attaché in Washington,
wrote to Casement: 'As a result of our last interview I repeated yesterday
the cabled request concerning formation of a special Brigade ...'⁸

An emissary from the IRB had been in New York and had discussed
Casement's mission. He was Dr Patrick McCartan, editor of the IRB paper
Irish Freedom, and, after his return, the following letter in a simple general
code was sent from Dublin:

My dear Sister,
    You will be anxious to hear that I arrived safely without even being
questioned ...
    Things look fairly good regarding the establishment of the Mission which
we all discussed. ... The Fathers here think Father Rodgers should go to
Rome at once as he can do most there. They say a capital of five thousand
would be useless. It must be at least twenty-five thousand and better fifty
thousand. Better they think have as few converts as possible along as they
would be safer on the foreign Mission.... Father Rodgers [sic] must rush
the Superior into making the public statement we spoke of. It will clear the
air considerably.... Urge to go at once.
                                              Your fond sister,
                                                          Mary.⁹

Casement's mission to Germany was thus clearly approved by both the
IRB in Ireland and Devoy.

On 3 October Devoy wrote in a letter to McGarrity describing 'Rory's
[Casement's] trip' as 'the most important step we have yet taken'.¹⁰

On 15 October Casement, having washed his face in buttermilk to try
to give himself a fair complexion,¹¹ and travelling on a borrowed American
passport in the name of James Landy, sailed in the Norwegian ship *Osker II*
for Germany via Norway. He was accompanied by the young Norwegian,
Adler Christensen.

Christensen claimed to have a wife called Sadie living in Philadelphia,
habitually used make-up, was soon to be in trouble with the Berlin police,
admitted later to spying for the American Government and was finally
thought by Casement himself, after a warning received from John Devoy, to

be quite possibly in the pay of the British Government.[12] Whatever Christensen's later affiliations, and money seems always to have been his only interest in forming them, there is no doubt at all that at this stage he had decided that his interests lay primarily in being loyal to Casement. When the ship on which they sailed was stopped on the High Seas by the British Navy and detained for two days at Stornaway, Christensen did not give him away, although it is tempting to suspect that he had something to do with the 215 dollars stolen from Casement during the voyage.[13] And again when, after arriving safely in Oslo, the British Ambassador to Norway, Findlay, made a reasonable enough attempt to capture Casement by suborning Christensen, Christensen remained loyal. In fact Christensen was probably the type of man quite commonly thrown up in wars, who considers himself sharp enough to play both sides off against each other in his own interest. From long entanglement in such a game he probably sincerely thought himself to be on whatever side he happened to be getting money from at the moment.*

Historically Christensen is of interest only in showing the amateurish and makeshift nature of the Irish revolutionaries' practical arrangements. Casement was indeed, as Devoy later pointed out, a very poor conspirator, but that is as much a reflection on Devoy and the IRB themselves who, after all, claimed to be professional conspirators whereas Casement did not, and who should therefore have chosen a more suitable agent than Casement for carrying out 'the most important step' they had yet taken. Devoy later said that Casement's 'impracticability' in Germany had necessitated his being by-passed in negotiations between the revolutionaries and the Germans. But as late as 12 November 1915 Devoy wrote to the Germans:

'We have the fullest confidence in Sir Roger Casement; there has never been since he went to Germany any lack of confidence in him on our part. ... Sir Roger Casement has authority to speak for and represent the Irish Revolutionary Party in Ireland and America.'[14]

A few days earlier Devoy had been complaining to McGarrity that it was Casement who was by-passing *him* and that he was 'much disappointed that Casement did not write' and that he was 'evidently not to be considered any more ...'.[15] There is no evidence until 10 February 1916 of Devoy taking any initiative with the Germans independently of Casement. Then he did so for two very good reasons apart from any personal impatience with him. The first was that he was passing on a message of the IRB to the effect that they were definitely on the point of rising in Ireland and he knew that Casement was opposed to such a move. Casement had informed him as long

---

* The Irish KC Serjeant Sullivan, who defended Casement later at his trial for treason, in old age thought he remembered being told by the British Director of Prosecutions that the compromising Casement diaries of which the British Government made some use both before and after Casement's trial were bought from Christensen who had stolen them from Casement in the course of this journey. (Personal interview with author.)

ago as 20 June 1915 that 'a "rising" in Ireland would be a futile form of force ... and a crime too so I never have and shall not counsel that'.[6] The second reason was that Casement had written to McGarrity on 20 December 1915 to say that he was too ill to act as envoy any more, and that no more instructions should be sent to him.

Whether the revolutionaries in America and in Ireland subsequently liked to admit it or not, Casement was the only permanent direct link that was ever forged with their 'gallant allies in Europe'.*

What had happened in the thirteen months in Germany before Casement had virtually opted out of his mission through illness? The stagnation which was to settle over the mission did not make itself apparent at once. Three weeks after his arrival, on 20 November, 1914, the German Government issued the following official statement:

> ... The Imperial Government formally declares that under no circumstances would Germany invade Ireland with a view to its conquest or the overthrow of any native institutions in that country. Should the fortune of this great war, that was not of Germany's seeking, ever bring in its course German troops to the shores of Ireland, they would land there, not as an army of invaders to pillage and destroy, but as the forces of a Government that is inspired by good-will towards a country and a people for whom Germany desires only a national prosperity and national freedom.

Casement had written the Declaration himself. 'It breaks new ground in Europe and clears the air,' he wrote to McGarrity the next day, adding that he was spending money faster than he had expected, and that he badly needed a fur coat. '... I got nearly frozen to death going to the battle front in a motor-car 200 miles at a high rate of speed ...' He added cryptically: 'I have not seen the poor friends yet. They are still scattered but are being brought to one place.'[17]

This referred to what he saw as the second main objective of his mission, the organization of an Irish Brigade from British prisoners of war. And it was on this point that, in an attempt to turn into reality the ideal of Irish nationality for militant independent Irishmen, the mission broke down.

The Germans never concealed from Casement that their chief interest in the cause of Irish freedom was in its possible military advantage to themselves. They knew nothing about Ireland and Irish nationality, and therefore at first naturally accepted the Devoy–IRB–Casement interpretation at its face value. And, on the strength of that, it was not unreasonable to expect that many Irishmen captured with the British armies would be ready to change sides and fight against their 'traditional enemy'. The Central Powers knew something of the incipient disloyalty of oppressed nationalities, and a Czech Legion of several thousand men was to be fighting on the allied side

---

* Words of Republican Proclamation of 1916.

before the end of the war. Although the way to Ireland itself was blocked
to any large force so long as the British Navy controlled the seas, a successfully organized Irish Brigade in Europe might, they imagined, very possibly
encourage a situation in Ireland which would force the British to withdraw
a substantial number of troops from the Western Front.

Soon after Casement's arrival the Germans started collecting all Irish
prisoners of war together into a separate camp at Limburg. And on 3
December 1914, Casement, a dignified bearded consular figure with a hat and
an umbrella, went down there for the first time, accompanied by a German
prince who had been educated at Harrow,[18] to talk to the simple country
boys of Munster and Connaught.

Those among the prisoners who had imagined themselves to be fighting
for anything had imagined themselves to be fighting in the cause of Ireland
against Germany and had received some remarkably unpleasant treatment
from the Germans in the process. Their curious visitor now suggested to
them that they should come out and fight in the cause of Ireland *with* Germany instead. He went there again on 4 December and again on the 6th and
again – there were now about two thousand Irishmen in the camp altogether
– on 6 January 1915. At the same time he had been negotiating at the
German Foreign Office a treaty laying down the conditions on which an
Irish Brigade was to be raised and employed. Its members were to be Volunteers, equipped and fed but not paid by the German Government; they were
to have Irish officers; to fight under the Irish flag alone, to fight solely in
the cause of Ireland and under no circumstances to be employed for any
German end, and in the event of a German naval victory, to be landed on
the Irish coast with a supporting body of German officers and men.[19] This
treaty which was a distinct diplomatic achievement for Casement was signed
by himself and the German Secretary of State at the German Foreign Office
on 27 December 1914. But by this date he must already have suspected
that it was a dead letter.

He himself later tried to minimize the bad reception he got from the
prisoners of war (the 'poor friends' or 'poor brothers' as he called them in
letters to McGarrity) and certainly the very most of this reception was later
made, possibly to the extent of some invention, by his enemies. But even
Casement himself only claimed that he had a friendly reception from 'more
than half' the fifty men he talked to on 6 January, adding that 'only some
of the men (a very few) showed any sign of unfriendliness'.[20] A letter he
wrote to Father J. T. Nicholson, an Irish-American priest whom Devoy
sent over later in January to help with recruiting for the Brigade, probably
gives a clearer hint of what went on. 'I will not,' wrote Casement, 'return
to Limburg to be insulted by a handful of recreant Irishmen.... I cannot
meet insults from cads and cowards with insults. I can only avoid the cads
and cowards.'

At any rate the figures speak plainly enough. He returned to Berlin in January with only one man out of the two thousand Irishmen at Limburg committed. This man was Sergeant Timothy Quinlisk of the Royal Irish Regiment, whom Casement noted in his diary as looking a rogue.*

Faced with Casement's utter failure to bring about the one thing to which they really attached importance, the Germans naturally began to revise their view of him and the Irish situation as he and his friends had painted it. Their disillusionment must have been accelerated by Casement's own behaviour. It was not only that the Berlin police were receiving unsavoury reports about this man, Christensen's, moral character. Casement himself, humiliated by his experience with the prisoners of war, desperately aware of the sudden futility of his presence in Germany, now set about trying to deceive himself that he was doing some good there by building up into what he imagined was a superb propaganda story his account of the British Minister in Oslo's, Mr Findlay's, attempt to capture him on his way through to Berlin. His voluminous writings on this subject reveal a mind temporarily unbalanced. In view of the deep shock not only to his pride from the failure with the Irish Brigade but to all he had ever believed in about Ireland, this temporary loss of balance is understandable. He sought as far as possible to shift the blame for his predicament on to the cynicism of the Germans, but their failure to keep up their enthusiasm after the immediate failure of the Brigade was reasonable enough.

'I am at the end of my tether,' he wrote in June 1915, 'because I see no way out. I have been in that frame of mind for months. . . . The truth was forced on me in January and February that I had misjudged greatly and made a mistake.'

He would have liked to return to America,[21] but the British Navy controlled the seas. He remained in Germany 'a virtual prisoner'. In the circumstances he did the only thing possible. Encouraged by the persuasions of Father Nicholson, the Irish-American priest at Limburg, and the reports of Sergeant Quinlisk† and two other prisoners, Kehoe and Dowliing, who had since committed themselves, he embarked on a final attempt to make the Irish Brigade a reality. He knew that only by making the Irish National movement a military reality could he get the Germans interested in it again.

In a post-mortem on this second attempt which he wrote on 30 June, he said: 'I had to go on for so much depended on the possibility of the Agreement coming off' [i.e., the treaty signed on 27 December 1914 which, with only three men in the Brigade, naturally had remained unpublished] . . . 'but I went on like a man going to execution *because I had lost faith*† . . . . They

---

* He was to be shot by the IRA in 1920 for an attempt to betray Michael Collins to the British.
† Casement's italics.

[the Germans] want a show of physical force.... Now a "rising" in Ireland would be a futile form of force – more futile even than de Wet's in South Africa – and a crime too so I never have and shall not counsel that. But a force here on the Continent, under our flag, allied with these armies would give us the right to share in the fight and its results ...'

He knew now that he could not get an effective force together from British prisoners of war, but he hoped to get a sufficient nucleus to persuade the Germans to publish the treaty and then with the help of Devoy and McGarrity in America to raise a force of Irish Americans who would come to Germany and join it (for America had not yet entered the war on the allied side). After everything that Irish Americans had been saying they were prepared to do for the last fifty years or so this was not altogether unrea-sonable, and Casement pointed this out in a very strong letter to McGarrity written on 29 April 1915, which he held back for ten days because he knew it might cause trouble but eventually posted on 10 May. After outlining his plan he wrote:

I want help. I am here alone. I want officers. I want men. I want a fighting fund.... I came here for one thing only, to try and help national Ireland – and if there is no such thing in existence then the sooner I pay for my illusions the better.... This will be really a test – probably a final one – of the sincerity of Irish nationality. So far the mass of the exponents of Irish nationality have con- tented themselves for over a century with words not deeds. When the moment came to fight there were either no fighters or no guns.... Unless the Irish in Ireland and most of all in America – where they are free and can act as they will – come forward now and give effective proof of their patriotism then they may bury the corpse of Irish nationality for ever, for no one will want to look at the stinking carcase any longer.... While we are saying that a German victory over England will bring Ireland freedom, we, the most vitally concerned in that result, are not fighting for Ireland, or for Germany – but many thousands of Irishmen *are* fighting ... in the ranks of the British army.... The action so far taken by Irish Americans is contemptible – they have talked – floods of talk – but they have not even contributed money,* much less attempted any overt act for Ireland.... If today, when all Europe is dying for national ends, whole peoples marching down with songs of joy to the valley of eternal night, we alone stand by idle or moved only to words, then are we in truth the most contemptible of all the peoples of Europe.

The hysteria in this letter is that of a man shocked by the truth. At the end of it Casement drops a hint that if no help is forthcoming he will go out alone and face the English as a form of expiation. Perhaps it was this

---

* This, of course, was untrue. A typewritten account sheet found among McGarrity's papers shows that the Clan-na-Gael Treasurer handed over to John Devoy between 31 August 1914 and 2 April 1917, 98,297 dollars for the 'Home Organization' (i.e. IRB). Casement himself had up to this time been financed with some four thousand dollars of Irish-American money.

mood which, just over a year later, enabled him to face the appalling sentence, delivered by a twitching judge with black cap clumsily awry,[32] with a self-assurance and courage that impressed all who watched him.

Casement failed in his renewed effort to form a nucleus of the Brigade large enough to persuade the Germans to publish the treaty. In the end only fifty-five men were collected altogether from among the prisoners of war in Germany and one Irish American, John McGooey, came from the States to join them. The IRB, responding to Casement's request for officers relayed by Devoy, sent in October via the States and escorted by Christensen an ex-British NCO and Irish Volunteer instructor called Robert Monteith, to take command of the sad contingent. The fifty-five were kept at Zossen, seventeen miles from Berlin, 'practically as prisoners of war'. They went out on occasional route marches, sometimes pathetically accompanied by Casement, who had always been a great walker. But they were not allowed to carry rifles as Casement proposed, because, in the words of the German general who turned down the suggestion, they consisted 'of individuals proving themselves addicted to drink and opposing the laws of military discipline ... and good order'.[33] Certainly Monteith records one incident in which they came to blows with their German 'allies', and on 22 February 1916 he wrote to Casement to say that he had had to pay out 143·50 Marks (about £8) for 'blankets which some of the boys made away with'.[34] Monteith stood by them loyally in his book published fifteen years later, but when in April 1916 there was some question of sending the Irish Brigade to Ireland to take part in the Rising and Casement asked Monteith to draw up a list of the men in it who could be trusted, Monteith listed eleven, not including Quinlisk. One of the eleven turned king's evidence against Casement after he had landed with him in Ireland from a German submarine.

Thus, out of the two thousand or so Irishmen at Limburg, ten at most proved to be true Irish nationalists in the sense in which the leaders of the 1916 Rising meant the word. And perhaps the proportion of one in two hundred even over-represents the number of such nationalists in Ireland itself at the same time that rising was made.

For a few more months Casement, wandering restlessly round Germany, continued to have some hope of filling up the Brigade with Irish Americans. On 26 October 1915 he wrote to McGarrity: 'If we can get two hundred all told and two officers we have a chance here.'

Monteith, permanently at Zossen, was a great stand-by to him, for his conscience was troubled by the situation of the fifty-five men whom he had called out to commit treason with him in a gamble to convince the German Government, which had failed. Their treason he saw was utterly pointless.

In December he accepted defeat. 'Send no more,' he wrote to McGarrity after the one man from America, McGooey, had arrived. He added that he was trying to get the fifty-five men of the Brigade sent to the East, Syria, where they could fight with the Turks. And the failure to bring off even that mad-cap scheme was a fitting conclusion to the whole disastrous enterprise.

'Write instructions,' he concluded, 'to Monteith now, not to me. I am too sick.... Monteith is very good.... Meantime M. will send the old man [Devoy] news.'

Four days later, on Christmas Eve 1915, he was signing off altogether.

'Better not write me again as I fear I shall not be able to attend to it.... I can never forget all your careful work and thought and kindness, may He keep you still to see some hope dawn on the cause you have so faithfully worked for. You were worthy of a far better agent here than poor broken me. What I did may have been good but I can do no more now I fear all the rest of my days, for the seat of power is giving way ...'

But meanwhile the 'military council' of the IRB in Dublin had been hoping for German help.

17
The Dublin Rising, 1916

On Easter Sunday, 23 April 1916, John Dillon, who had gone over to Dublin for the parliamentary recess, wrote to Redmond, who had stayed in London:

'Dublin is full of the most extraordinary rumours ... you must not be surprised if something very unpleasant and mischievous happens this week.'[1]

The issue of the *Freeman's Journal*, the party paper, which appeared the next day, Monday, 24 April, was a routine one and fairly dull. Its first leader was about a by-election pending in Queen's County between two Home Rule Nationalists standing on an identical policy of loyalty to Redmond, and competing simply because no candidate had been selected for the constituency by the party convention. Only two items in the paper hinted at unusual events and both were mysteriously imprecise. One concerned the arrest of a prominent member of the Tralee Irish Volunteers, a Mr Austin Stack, on a charge of importing arms from Germany. The other reported that a collapsible boat with arms and ammunition had been found on Currahane strand, County Kerry, and that a stranger of unknown nationality had been arrested in the vicinity and conveyed under escort to Dublin.[2] Only later that day was it announced that the stranger was Roger Casement, and by that time the people of Dublin themselves had been caught up in extraordinary events.

The next issue of the *Freeman's Journal* to appear bore the comprehensive dates 26 April to 5 May, and its first leader began:

'The stunning horror of the past ten days in Dublin makes it all but impossible for any patriotic Irishman who has been a witness of the tragedy enacted in our midst to think collectedly or write calmly of the event.'

The event which took not only the ordinary population of Dublin but most of the rank and file of the Irish Volunteers wholly by surprise had started in an almost dreamlike way on Easter Monday morning, while devotees of the *Freeman's Journal* were still calmly perusing the leader about the election in Queen's County.

Around noon a number of odd things had begun to happen in Dublin. A party of some hundred or so Irish Volunteers and Citizen Army men marching through the streets of the city, as they had been in the habit of doing for months past – and attracting particularly little attention on a Bank Holiday when more normal holiday-makers had gone to the races – stopped opposite the General Post Office in O'Connell Street, then turned and ran into the building.* Within a few minutes, flourishing revolvers and even firing some shots into the air, they had cleared out both customers and officials. Soon two flags were flying from the buildings: one the traditional green flag with the gold harp, with the words 'Irish Republic' now inscribed on it in gold; and the other a new flag strange to most people, a tricolour of orange, white and green. The Post Office had become the headquarters of the new 'Republic'.

A little later, amazed by-standers saw Patrick Pearse emerge on to the steps of the portico and read a proclamation from 'the Provisional Government'. This stated that in the name of God and of the dead generations, from which Ireland 'received her ancient tradition of nationhood', she was summoning her children to her flag and striking for her freedom.[3] The proclamation spoke of the long usurpation of Ireland's right to control her own destinies by 'a foreign people and government', and stated most inaccurately that in every generation the Irish people had asserted their right to national freedom and sovereignty, adding 'six times during the past three hundred years they have asserted it in arms'. It referred to 'gallant Allies in Europe' who were supporting Ireland, thereby blandly dismissing the fact that the flower of Ireland's manhood had been fighting those allies in Europe for the past twenty months. Indeed, almost within the hour Irish men of the 3rd Royal Irish Rifles and the 10th Royal Dublin Fusiliers, themselves the product of the most recent British Army recruiting drive in Ireland, were the first to move against this self-styled republic in the Post Office.[4] Small wonder that Pearse's words fell among a largely uninterested crowd and that the principal sounds to greet them were not cheers but the crash of breaking glass as a Dublin mob, taking advantage of the absence of the police, began to loot the fashionable shops in O'Connell Street.[5] The proclamation was signed by Clarke, MacDermott, MacDonagh, Pearse, Ceannt, Plunkett and James Connolly.

Meanwhile, the 'Republic' had already drawn first blood. A party of Volunteers had set out before noon on an audacious expedition to blow up the large ammunition dump at the Magazine Fort in the Phoenix Park. They had skilfully tricked the sentry, gaining entry by pretending to pursue a football, and after wounding another sentry and taking the rest of the guard prisoner, cut the telephone wires and successfully placed a gelignite charge in part of the fort. They had, however, been unable to find the key to the main ammunition dump, for it had been taken by the officer in charge to

* O'Connell Street was then officially Sackville Street, but already popularly known by the name which it assumed officially on the creation of the Irish Free State.

Fairyhouse Races for the day. The subsequent explosion was not very great and did little important damage. The Volunteers made off with some captured rifles, but as they were hurrying away spotted a boy leaving the fort to give the alarm. He was the seventeen-year-old son of the Fort's commandant, who was then away in France, serving with an Irish regiment. The boy was shot with a revolver before he could reach a telephone and died within twenty-four hours.[6]

Another early casualty had been an unarmed middle-aged constable of the Dublin Metropolitan Police, named O'Brien. He had been on the gate of Dublin Castle when men of the Irish Citizen Army had appeared and tried to gain entrance. In the best traditions of the force he put up his hand, and was shot dead.[7] The party entered the Castle yard and, after throwing into the guardroom a home-made bomb which failed to explode, made the six soldiers they found there prisoner. Unknown to the Citizen Army men this was the only guard in this part of the Castle at all and the usual substantial garrison normally to be found round the corner in Ship Street mustered twenty-five men. The traditional seat of British rule in Ireland for many centuries lay within the rebels' power. Undoubtedly the news of its capture would have produced a psychological shock throughout Ireland. But almost inexplicably the Citizen Army men seem to have taken fright at their easy early victory and, evacuating the Castle itself, preferred to occupy some buildings opposite. More blood began to flow as they were engaged there by men of the Royal Irish Rifles and the Dublin Fusiliers who reached the Castle in the early afternoon.[8]

Over much of Dublin it was still quite difficult to appreciate that a coordinated attempt at rebellion had broken out. A young Irish writer, emerging an hour later for lunch from the National Gallery where he worked as registrar, knew nothing of what had happened until, approaching St Stephen's Green, he noticed crowds standing about in curiously silent inquiring attitudes as if there had been an accident. Physically, what had happened was that the 'Sinn Feiners' (detachments of the Irish Volunteers and the Irish Citizen Army plainly acting in harmony for once) had occupied some two dozen strong points – including St Stephen's Green – throughout the city, dominating barracks, railway stations, key approaches, and other prominent public thoroughfares. From the Post Office Pearse, now calling himself Commandant-General of a joint Irish Republican Army, exercised a rather static command with Connolly, Clarke and Plunkett. Commandant Thomas Mac-Donagh, the poet and university English lecturer, had occupied Jacob's Biscuit Factory behind Dublin Castle. A Citizen Army group to which Countess Markievicz, wearing green uniform and flourishing a revolver, was attached, had occupied the park in St Stephen's Green. There they had dug themselves in, until, coming under fire from the dominating Shelburne Hotel, they recognized that their position was militarily unsound and withdrew to the large distinguished building on the further side of the Green which was the College of Surgeons.

Among several other prominent positions occupied and fortified were the Four Courts under Edward Daly, the nephew of an old Fenian of '67, and Boland's Flour Mills, under the mathematics professor, Eamon de Valera, whose outposts commanded the main road into Dublin from the harbour of Kingstown, along which government reinforcements from Britain might be expected.

Although a quite ambitious plan for a more general rising had at one time been envisaged, involving other parts of Ireland and a more extensive and mobile occupation of Dublin itself, a whole sequence of misunderstandings, muddles and unfortunate disasters prevented it ever being put seriously to the test. Basically the pattern of the rebellion which unfolded over the next five days was that 'the Irish Republican Army' remained in most of the positions it had occupied on Easter Monday, inflicting what casualties it could – and these were sometimes substantial – on Irishmen and others in the British Army, who, backed by heavy artillery fire, inexorably closed in on them and eventually forced them to surrender. Any close study of the activity that took place during these five days in the epic headquarters of the rebellion, the General Post Office, reveals that apart from a brief moment in the afternoon of Easter Monday when Volunteer riflemen shot down and killed four Lancers of a detachment trying to make their way down O'Connell Street, its occupants did almost nothing at all under increasingly accurate shell-fire until they eventually tried to evacuate the burning building on Friday. Though some sixteen of the garrison were wounded, including James Connolly by a bullet in the ankle, none were killed until this attempted sortie on the Friday, when The O'Rahilly was one of those who fell, as they made a dash down Moore Street. In the meantime Pearse, Clarke, Plunkett and Connolly talked away the days, encouraging the men, issuing occasional over-confident dispatches about other parts of Ireland rising and German help being on the way, even once speculating among themselves on the advisability of appointing a German prince King of Ireland after the war, but always supremely confident that the assumption on which they had allowed the Rising to go ahead was justified.[9] This assumption was that success or failure was irrelevant and that it was the action itself which would stir old slumbering fires of fierce nationalism within the hearts of the Irish people, and eventually make the new green, white and orange flag now flying defiantly from the roof of the Post Office the flag of a truly national Ireland.

'We thought it a foolish thing for four score to go into battle against four thousand, or maybe forty thousand,' protested an ancient Gaelic hero in a play Pearse wrote late in 1915.[10]

'And so it is a foolish thing,' had come the super-heroic response. 'Do you want us to be wise?'

For years Pearse had been pining to see the mystical 'red wine of the battlefield' on Irish soil.[11] He gave the rank and file of the Volunteers no chance to challenge the rhetorical question of his play. But even Pearse, planning insurrection on the assumption that wisdom was irrelevant, had taken steps to make it as effective as he could. When, however, a series of events in the few days before the Rising caused it to be not only less effective than he and the IRB could make it, but downright disastrous, neither he nor the IRB were particularly worried. When at Liberty Hall on Easter Monday morning Connolly was assembling his men for the march to the Post Office, he told his friend William O'Brien: 'We are going out to be slaughtered.' O'Brien asked him if there were any chance of success at all. 'None whatever,' replied Connolly.[12]

In the interval between the funeral of O'Donovan Rossa in August 1915 and Easter Monday 1916 the Irish Volunteers had shown a slight but perceptible increase in their numbers for the first time since their split with the main body. This was due to a combination of practical and political factors. Among these were: the growing awareness that Redmond's own Volunteers were becoming ineffective as they were drained off to the war; the simultaneous feeling that the prospect of Home Rule, like the prospect of an end of the war itself, was receding into obscure mists of time in which a British Government might find it easier not to keep faith; the retention of a higher proportion of young farmers' sons on Irish soil than usual, owing to the halt in normal emigration; and the growing Irish determination that the threatened Conscription Act should never be applied to Ireland. The Conscription Act finally went through in January 1916. It was totally opposed by Redmond and the Irish party and in fact excluded Ireland. But the threat of an extension of conscription to Ireland was thereafter always present, and now that the main parliamentary battle on the subject had been won, such a threat was very much easier to implement quickly.

Yet, in these circumstances, the remarkable fact was not so much that the numbers of MacNeill's followers slightly increased but that they did not increase more significantly. According to police intelligence reports the increase was some 3,800 in eight months from August 1915 to April 1916.[13] But the British Army was able to obtain from Ireland over three times that number of recruits in the same period, 1,827 of them in the single month ending 15 April alone.[14] Though the Irish Volunteer parades became better attended and their and the Citizen Army's activity increasingly noticeable, resulting in a particularly good turn out both in Dublin and Cork for St Patrick's Day, 17 March 1916, they were still also noticeably out of tune with the vast mass of public opinion in the country. An Irish Volunteer of the time from Ennscorthy, County Wexford, has recorded how the farmer who lent him and his companions a hay-loft for drilling ran a serious risk in obliging them, because of their unpopularity.[15] Ernest Blythe, one of the principal Volunteer organizers of the day, has written of the 1914–15 period: 'The attitude of the majority of the people towards the Irish Volunteers and their independent nationalist stand was one of incredulity, suspicion or dour hostility.'[16] On 22 March 1916 an anti-Sinn Fein demonstration took place in Tullamore, when fourteen Irish Volunteers were besieged by a hostile mob in the local Sinn Fein hall. Feeling that they were inadequately protected by the police they fired revolvers to keep the mob away, and when the police moved in to disarm them resisted arrest, wounding a Sergeant Aherne seriously.[17]

The professions of the young men finally arrested in the Tullamore case give a useful cross-section of the social stratum from which the Irish Volunteer rank and file of the day were drawn. They consisted of a clerk, a barber's assistant, an apprentice, a malt-house workman, a blacksmith's assistant, a drayman, a painter, a cycle mechanic and a labourer.[18] Local police elsewhere described the Volunteers as being composed principally of shop assistants, artisans and, in the country districts, of small farmers' sons, while an English eye-witness of the occupation of the Post Office in Dublin a month later – who, incidentally, had the nerve to go in and ask for stamps before the Republic could be officially proclaimed – also commented on the fact that the rebels seemed drawn from the poorer classes. 'There were no well-dressed men amongst them,' he explained a few days later to fellow Englishmen, totally bewildered by events, 'although the Sinn Fein movement has within it a great number of better-class people.'[19] In other words they were of the same class as those who for twenty months had been dying in Flanders and at the Dardanelles, though as yet unrepresentative of them.

A marching song written some years earlier had recently become popular with the Irish Volunteers. The words had a rather artificial stagey ring, characteristic of the histrionic attitude the Volunteers often seemed to embody.

I'll sing you a song, a soldier's song,
With a cheering rousing chorus
As round our blazing camp-fires we throng
The starry heavens o'er us.
Impatient for the coming fight
And as we watch the dawning light
Here in the silence of the night.
We'll chant the soldier's song.

Soldiers are we, whose lives are pledged to Ireland,
Some have come from the land across the sea . . .*

---

* Written in 1907 by Peader Kearney. The tune had been composed by his friend Paddy Heaney. (O'Dubghaill, *Insurrection Fires*, p. 227.)

It was called 'The Soldier's Song' and though still almost unknown to most of the country was, within six years, to become the National Anthem of Ireland.

But although in this pre-Rising period the 'Sinn Feiners' were unrepresentative and even unpopular, the delicacy of national sensitivity in the prevailing situation was shown at the end of March when a public meeting was held in Dublin to protest against the ordered deportation of some ten Sinn Fein organizers from Ireland. The idea of banishment from Ireland was an ugly one in many Irish minds, and the hall was full and an overflow meeting was held outside it. It was this emotional area in Irish minds, with roots deep in Irish history, that Pearse and other members of the IRB's military council were determined to affect. Myth and reality had interacted on each other throughout Irish history. With a personal courage amounting almost to mania, Pearse and his fellow conspirators set out to turn the myth into reality by living it out in cold blood.

Up to a week before the Rising Eoin MacNeill, the nominal head of the Volunteers, had had no knowledge that it was being planned. He had, however, had certain misgivings, derived largely from the writings and utterances of people like Pearse and Connolly that some such action might one day be contemplated. Therefore in the middle of February 1916 he had made a deliberate point of attacking the living myth theory.

We have to remember [he wrote, in a memorandum designed to lay down the policy for the Irish Volunteers] that what we call our country is not a poetical abstraction, as some of us, perhaps all of us, in the exercise of our highly developed capacity for figurative thought, are sometimes apt to imagine – with the help of our patriotic literature. There is no such person as Caitlín Ní Uallachain or Roisin Dubh or the Sean-bean Bhoct, who is calling upon us to serve her. What we call our country is a concrete and visible reality. Now we believe that we think rightly on national matters ... if we are right nationally, it is our duty to get our country on our side, and not to be content with the vanity of thinking ourselves to be right and other Irish people to be wrong. As a matter of patriotic principle we should never tire of endeavouring to get our country on our side. ... I do not know at this moment whether the time and circumstance will yet justify distinct revolutionary action, but of this I am certain, the only possible basis for successful revolutionary action is deep and widespread popular discontent. We have only to look around us in the streets to see that no such condition exists in Ireland. A few of us, a small proportion who think about the evils of English government in Ireland are always discontented. We should be downright fools if we were to measure many others by the standards of our own thoughts.

I wish it then to be clearly understood that under present conditions I am definitely opposed to any proposal that may come forward involving insurrection. I have no doubt at all that my consent to any such proposal at this time and under these circumstances would make me false to my country besides involving me in the guilt of murder.[20]

Bulmer Hobson, who shared these views with MacNeill and was particularly anxious about Pearse's intention, had been instrumental in getting MacNeill to draw up the memorandum. After it had been discussed with the Volunteer leaders at MacNeill's house, Pearse categorically denied that he was planning an insurrection or that his view of the Volunteers' function was any different from their publicly declared defensive aims. In fact Pearse was lying, for the date for the Rising had already been decided on as Easter Sunday 1916. It had been notified as such to Devoy in America on 5 February and subsequently passed to the Germans. Another deception of MacNeill by Pearse concerned the labour leader James Connolly.

Since the beginning of the war Connolly, who became the outstanding Irish labour figure after Larkin's departure for America in October 1914, had been writing more and more outspoken denunciations of the British Government and of the recruiting campaign in Ireland, and hinting more and more openly at the need for someone in Ireland to rise in arms against Britain while the war lasted. He had, as early as 9 September 1914, been present at a meeting in the Library of the Gaelic League in Dublin at which the desirability of a rising was discussed, together with important members of the IRB such as Clarke, Pearse and Ceannt, and another outsider, Arthur Griffith. But it seems that the IRB members at this meeting did not let Connolly or other outsiders into the full secret of their own decisions or of their contacts already made with the Germans through Devoy.[21] Connolly appears to have had little real knowledge of the IRB's existence at the time, and, as the war continued, he became more and more impatient with and even contemptuous of the Volunteers. The IRB told him nothing of their own appointment of a secret Military Council and he judged the Volunteer organization at its face value.

Larkin's paper, the *Irish Worker*, had been suppressed in December 1914, and Connolly who had been editing it started a successor, the *Worker*, which in turn was suppressed after its sixth issue in February 1915. Thereafter he printed and published the *Workers' Republic* with his own plant at the Transport Workers' Union headquarters in Dublin, Liberty Hall, also the headquarters of the hundred or so strong Citizen Army. Across the front of Liberty Hall hung a bold banner proclaiming: 'We Serve Neither King nor Kaiser – but Ireland'. In itself it was an expression of sentiment which MacNeill would have found unexceptionable. But towards the end of 1915 MacNeill was being made increasingly anxious by talk of Connolly's intention to bring out the Citizen Army in a rising on its own account.[22]

The two utterly different temperaments of Connolly and MacNeill were illustrated in the respective issues of the *Workers' Republic* and the *Irish Volunteer* for Christmas Day 1915. Connolly, after reminding his readers of the price Wolfe Tone had paid for inaction at Bantry Bay in 1796, concluded with the words:

The Kingdom of Heaven [Freedom] is within you.

The Kingdom of Heaven can only be taken by violence. Heavenly words with a heavenly meaning.

Christmas Week, 1796; Christmas week, 1915 – still hesitating.[23]

Connolly's frequent attacks in the *Workers' Republic* on the Volunteers for their lack of aggressiveness not only alarmed MacNeill and irritated many rank-and-file of Volunteers but also caused considerable anxiety to Pearse and his fellow IRB manipulators behind the scenes. They began to fear that Connolly would be as good as his printed word and start an individual insurrection with the tiny Citizen Army which would prematurely wreck their own plans.

On 19 January 1916 Connolly disappeared for three days, and his whereabouts remained unknown even to his closest friends. When he reappeared at Countess Markievicz house on 22 January he seemed like a man with a load off his mind. The next issue of the *Workers' Republic* carried a new solemn determined note, the reason for which was not disclosed. He had in fact spent the three days in conclave with Pearse and the other IRB leaders, and had been made party to the secret of the Rising. He was himself appointed a member of the IRB's military council. He knew now that an insurrection was on for Easter Week.*

But Pearse used this incident to lull MacNeill's suspicions still further. A short while earlier, at the official request of the official Volunteer executive, MacNeill had arranged a private meeting with Connolly at which he heard him at first hand put forward his view that an immediate insurrection was necessary, and declare that whether or not the Volunteers came out the Citizen Army would fight in Dublin. Pearse, who was present at this meeting, assured MacNeill afterwards that he agreed with his point of view and that he would persuade Connolly to abandon his project. 'Very shortly afterwards', that is to say, presumably just after Connolly had spent his three days in conclave with the Military Council of the IRB, Pearse told MacNeill that he had got Connolly to abandon his project.[24] Though this, unlike his earlier statement that he was of MacNeill's point of view, was literally true in the sense that Connolly had now abandoned his project of a *separate* rising, it was deliberate deception of MacNeill who was thus led for the time being at any rate to believe that no 'act of rash violence' was being planned. In any case, shortly afterwards MacNeill received further assurances not only from Pearse but also from Plunkett that no insurrection was being planned.[25] MacNeill's own concept of the Volunteers' purpose

---

* For many years it was generally thought that Connolly had been 'kidnapped' by the IRB and held forcibly during his three days' absence, but most recent evidence suggests that he took part in the secret meeting of his own free will. William O'Brien, one of Connolly's closest colleagues at Liberty Hall, became satisfied many years ago that Connolly had not been kidnapped (*Sunday Press*, 17 April 1955). See also a methodical analysis of the incident in O'Dubghaill, *Insurrection Fires*, pp. 109–115.

remained, so it appeared, the only accepted one, namely that they would only take to arms if an attempt were made by the government to disarm them or to introduce conscription.

However, MacNeill's anxieties did not stay lulled for long. Several instances had already come to his notice of military dispositions being made for the Volunteers by Pearse, without his own authority, and early in April he actually received through the post a letter from America (that had incidentally been opened by the censor) containing a review article to the effect that a rising aided by Germany was planned for Ireland in the early summer by an extremist group in the Irish Volunteers. MacNeill publicized the fact and strongly disclaimed any such thing in the last issue of the *Irish Volunteer* to appear, which was dated Saturday, 22 April 1916. But by then MacNeill's peace of mind had been shattered by other events, and within twenty-four hours both he and the majority of the Volunteers themselves were in a state of considerable turmoil.

On Wednesday, 19 April 1916, a Sinn Fein alderman at a meeting of the Dublin Corporation read out a document, allegedly stolen from Dublin Castle, detailing instructions for the arrest of the Volunteer leaders and other national figures and for the suppression of the Volunteer organization. MacNeill had been shown the document at the beginning of the week. Although the arrest of the leaders was in fact under consideration at Dublin Castle, and contingency plans for it had doubtless been prepared, it seems virtually certain that this particular document was a bogus one, prepared, possibly on the strength of some information received from the Castle, by Joseph Plunkett and Sean MacDermott. Though it was suspect in some quarters at once, it served its purpose at first so far as MacNeill was concerned, for he accepted it and its menacing implications for the Volunteers as genuine. The secret design of Pearse, Plunkett and the rest of the IRB's Military Council was that MacNeill should openly and unwittingly undertake for them a large part of their undercover mobilization for insurrection.

The defensive conditions in which MacNeill had always been prepared to consider some action for the Volunteers, namely an impending attempt to be made by the government to disarm them, now seemed fulfilled. He ordered the Volunteers to prepare themselves against suppression by the government. His orders for this were made out in consultation with the other members of the Volunteer executive but, in MacNeill's own words, 'neither then nor at any previous meeting was the policy of insurrection adopted or proposed in any form'.[26] On Thursday night, 20 April, MacNeill learnt for the first time that in addition to his own order, other orders had also gone out unknown to him which were 'only intelligible as parts of a general scheme for insurrection'.[27] Appalled, he, Bulmer Hobson and another member of the Volunteer executive, J. J. O'Connell, went round at midnight to Pearse's school, St Enda's, to confront him with what they had discovered and there for the first time Pearse admitted that a rising was intended. MacNeill told Pearse he would do everything in his power, short of informing the government, to prevent the rising and would issue countermanding orders. A few hours later, on Friday morning, Sean MacDermott came to MacNeill's house and told him for the first time that a large quantity of arms was about to be landed from Germany. MacNeill, who still believed on the strength of the Castle document that a government swoop on the Volunteers was in any case imminent, realized that with the arrival of the arms the die would be firmly cast and agreed to accept what looked like the IRB's *fait accompli*.

'Very well,' he finally said to Sean MacDermott. 'If that is the case I'm in with you.'[28]

From this moment onwards MacDermott, wishing doubtless to simplify the IRB chain of command in the Volunteers as the crisis approached, and assuming that MacNeill would prove no further trouble, began to suggest privately that MacNeill had resigned as Chief of Staff of the Volunteers. He had already been suggesting earlier in the week that MacNeill was sanctioning all the secret preliminary orders for the insurrection. But there was as little truth in the new report as in the earlier one, and MacNeill, in spite of his new awareness that so much had already been going on behind his back, does not seem to have doubted that he again held authority over the Volunteers.

To prevent any possible further disruption of the Rising's plans the IRB also took the precaution of neutralizing the one other man who it seemed might seriously make things awkward for them. On the Friday evening they kidnapped and held prisoner over the next few crucial days Bulmer Hobson, the man who a few years before had done so much to give their organization life. However, unpleasant surprises were still in store for them.

On the following morning, Saturday, 22 April, two Volunteers arrived in Dublin from the south-west of Ireland to see MacNeill with dramatic information. In the first place, they were able to enlighten him that the 'Castle Document' on the strength of which he had based his initial orders to the Volunteers to prepare for mobilization was a bogus one, designed to get him to do just that. More important still, they brought news that the arms ship on which the leaders were depending and on the strength of which he had reluctantly agreed to go into an insurrection with them had been captured by the British Navy and had sunk itself in Queenstown harbour. The 20,000 rifles and hundreds of thousands of rounds of ammunition Pearse was expecting were at the bottom of the sea. Roger Casement, a link between the insurrectionists and the Germans, had landed from a German submarine and had been captured almost immediately.

MacNeill at once sent messengers all over Ireland cancelling any orders the Volunteers might have received for special action. He also arranged for a notice to appear in the largest circulation Sunday newspaper, *The Sunday*

Independent, rescinding any orders that might have been issued to the Volunteers for Easter Sunday and forbidding every individual Volunteer from taking part in any parades, manoeuvres or other movements. On the very morning therefore of the day on which Pearse, Connolly and the rest of the military council had planned to come out in arms for an Irish Republic, they found the men they hoped to command paralysed by an order from their official leader telling them not to move.

This was a severe enough blow, but that caused by the capture and destruction of the arms ship had been even worse.

For almost a year now negotiations of a rather desultory and unprofessional sort had been going on between the IRB and the Germans for some form of military help. The situation had been rendered opaque by the fact that their chief resident representative in Germany was Casement, a man embittered since early 1915 by the failure of the Irish Brigade to fulfil his hopes, and by what he increasingly considered the cynical exploitation of the Irish cause by the Germans.

In April 1915 the IRB had sent Joseph Plunkett to Germany to make its first direct contact with Casement. He had taken a month getting there via neutral countries, but when he arrived had nothing to tell that Casement did not know or had not guessed already.[29] There was to be a rising some time before the end of the war and he had come to see what sort of military help was available. Casement himself was at this time already doubtful that any effective scheme of active cooperation with the Germans could be worked out.[30] The Germans after all had had their eyes opened to the limited appeal of Irish separatism by the failure of the Irish Brigade. And the thin, ailing, poetical Plunkett made a poor impression on them as a specimen of Irish revolutionary militancy.[31] However, Casement took Plunkett along to see the German General Staff, where he could personally put forward the IRB request for fifty thousand rifles with ammunition for the Irish Volunteers. The Germans turned this down, telling Plunkett in so many words that there were millions of Irish in the United States and he should get the arms from them.[32] When, about 25 June, Plunkett eventually left Germany, he took with him a message from Casement for Dublin to the effect that it was not going to be possible to get an Irish Brigade together, that Casement saw no way of getting German help and that he regarded his own mission as ended.[33] Whether Plunkett delivered this message and in what terms is not known.

Casement was left behind, admiring Plunkett personally for the effort he had made but feeling that he had done little but add to the ridicule of his (Casement's) own situation. For once he even saw the German position quite tolerantly. 'In our own land,' he wrote, 'they see only that no force exists, that talk expresses the extremity of Irish nationalism – and that if I represent anyone it must be a mighty small handful.'[34]

A renewal of the request for arms came in October 1915 through the German military attaché in Washington passing on a message of Devoy's. It was proposed that rifles and ammunition should be sent in submarines to the coast of Kerry, and Fenit pier in Tralee Bay was suggested as a suitable landing point.[35] But the German Admiralty informed the General Staff in December 1915 that submarines were not practical. And Casement wrote to New York later in the month that arms could not be supplied.[36] His efforts now were concentrated on getting the Germans to send the tiny group of the Irish Brigade to fight for the Turks, finally securing an assurance from the German General Staff to this effect on 4 January 1916.[37] They were to be sent to Syria. Three weeks later he retired for a 'nerve rest'[38] to a nursing home in Munich, leaving Robert Monteith, the ex-British NCO and Irish Volunteer instructor sent out via New York in October to help with the Irish Brigade, to take over in Berlin as a direct link for Devoy and the IRB with the German government.

But although Pearse and the military council were about this time perfecting their final arrangements for the Rising, they seem to have shown little sense of urgency or devotion to detail on the question of a supply of arms from Germany. It was something they were hoping for and for which they made provisions in their plans for the rising in other parts of Ireland than Dublin, and yet paradoxically something to which they hardly gave the detailed priority it might seem to have deserved.

On or about 5 February 1916 Devoy in New York received a coded message from the IRB in Dublin, brought personally across the Atlantic by a seaman named Tommy O'Connor, to the effect that an insurrection would break out in Ireland on Easter Sunday, 23 April. The decoded message was passed to the German Ambassador in Washington who in turn passed it on by radio to Berlin on 10 February.[39] Devoy sent a cable to Berlin confirming this and asking rather vaguely for arms to be delivered 'between Good Friday and Easter Sunday, Limerick West Coast'.[40] This was followed by a letter setting out the request in greater detail and specifying a need for 100,000 rifles, and for artillery, together with German officers and artillerymen.

Casement, still unwell in his nursing home at Munich, was visited there early in March by Monteith with news of the cable, and sent a memorandum back to Berlin stressing that the Germans must notify the Irish clearly about landing places and times before sending the arms. On 16 March he and Monteith went to the General Staff in Berlin, and on the next day to the German Admiralty to hear the arrangements made with Devoy: 20,000 rifles, 10 machine guns and 5,000,000 rounds of ammunition were to be sent, together with 55 men of the Irish Brigade. The ship was to be met off the Inishtookert lightship in Tralee Bay beween Friday, 20 April and Sunday, the 23rd, and the pilot boat meeting it was to show two green lights after dark. Devoy had sent a cable agreeing these details.[41]

Both Monteith and Casement were appalled by what they considered the inadequacy of German help in the circumstances. And yet they were in an awkward position, for the Rising was clearly going ahead, and even this amount of help would be better than nothing. After protesting to the Germans bitterly against the inadequacy of the arrangements, they concentrated on two objectives: first, to prevent the dispatch of the fifty-five members of the Irish Brigade, and second, secretly to get a message through to Dublin strongly urging that no rising should take place in the circumstances.

After some argument with the Germans, in which Monteith and Casement maintained that no more than twelve out of the fifty-five members of the Irish Brigade were reliable, the Germans finally agreed not to send them.[42] Casement also managed to persuade the German Admiralty to let one member of the Irish Brigade – the only Irish American to have joined it, named McGooey – over the frontier into Denmark to try and get a ship to Scotland and then to Ireland. His ostensible purpose was to tie up the final arrangements for the arms landing. His real instructions from Casement, however, were to say that Casement 'strongly urged "no rising" ...' and to 'get the heads in Ireland to call off the rising and merely try to land the arms and distribute them'.[43]

When the German General Staff heard of McGooey's departure they were furious, accusing Casement of sending him off to try and stop the Rising. No word of McGooey seems ever to have been heard again. If he had reached Ireland it seems possible that, though he would almost certainly not have deflected the leaders from their intention to start an insurrection, what he had to say might have had some material bearing on events, for he may also have carried the information that the arms ship had no wireless.*

Devoy's letter to the Germans suggested that Casement should remain in Germany as 'the accredited representative till the end of the war of the Irish Revolutionary Body'.[44] But Casement persuaded the Germans to let him go with the arms to Ireland together with two companions, Monteith and another member of the Irish Brigade named Bailey. They were to travel by submarine. Casement's hope was to get ashore in time to dissuade the leaders from going through with the Rising. If unsuccessful in this he would identify himself with what he knew to be a desperate cause.

Things were even more desperate than he knew. In spite of Devoy's

---

* In a letter intended for the leaders of the rebellion written by Casement in Germany in April but never delivered, he specified among much other information that the ship, 'carries no wireless, I believe'. He added that he had sent John McGooey, 'a Clan-na-Gael man from Chicago, to try and reach Dublin and tell them all this', on 19 March. (Casement to a friend of James Malcolm at Berne, 6 April 1916. McGarrity Papers, NLI.)

agreement to the arrangements with the Germans given in the middle of March, the IRB in Ireland seem to have been rather inconsequential about their arrangements for the arms landing. At the beginning of April they sent Joseph Plunkett's father, an elderly Papal Count, to Switzerland. Through the German Embassy at Berne on 5 April he transmitted a message to Casement in Berlin, reiterating that the Rising was fixed for Easter Sunday (evening), that the arms ship should arrive in Tralee Bay 'not later than dawn of Easter Monday' and that the dispatch of German officers was imperative. Casement tried desperately to convey to his mysterious informant that all was not well, but could make no contact. In any case, four days later the arms ship, a former ship of the British Wilson line captured by the Germans and renamed the *Libau* but disguised for this occasion as a Norwegian trawler, the *Aud*, had sailed for Tralee Bay. Three days later Casement, Monteith and Bailey set out on the same journey by submarine.

Meanwhile, incredibly it only now seems to have occurred to the Military Council in Dublin that if the ship arrived any time *before* Sunday, 23 April in the bracket of three days originally agreed, it would alert the British and seriously compromise the chances of the Rising starting undetected on the Sunday evening. They therefore at that late stage sent Plunkett's sister to America with a message which she delivered to Devoy on 14 April, five days after the *Aud* had sailed. It stated that on no account must the arms be landed before the night of Easter Sunday. Devoy sent the message to Berlin, but the Germans had in fact no way of communicating with the *Aud* since she was without wireless.

In these circumstances it might have been expected that the rebel leaders would at least inquire whether the *Aud* carried a wireless or not. At the very least it might have been expected steps would be taken to meet the ship on the three earlier days originally agreed in case she arrived earlier than Easter Sunday. No such steps were taken. The most charitable explanation is that the leaders, weighing the risk of the arms ship's early arrival against the possible loss of the arms, decided that the former was the most serious. Their top priority after all was the occurrence of the rebellion, not its military success. In fact the *Aud* arrived in Tralee Bay after a journey through the British blockade on the afternoon of Thursday, 19 April. She was even seen there by the pilot, who, having received orders to expect nothing until Sunday, merely wondered what ship she was and went home. She remained there nearly twenty-four hours without signal from the shore, whereupon the captain, feeling that he could not risk waiting there any longer, moved away. His luck then ran out for he was intercepted by the Royal Navy, escorted into Queenstown and there with some skill succeeded in scuttling his ship and its cargo, raising the German colours just before he did so.

On the early morning of the same day, Good Friday, Casement, Monteith and Bailey landed from their submarine in a rubber dinghy on Banna strand, County Kerry. The dinghy overturned in the water and they were soaked to the skin. After walking some distance Casement, exhausted, hid in some brambles on the site of an ancient fort while the others pressed on to Tralee to try to make contact with the Volunteers. Early in the afternoon he was found there with sand on his trousers and a used railway ticket from Berlin to Wilhelmshaven in his pocket by a sergeant and constable of the RIC. He spent that night in Tralee gaol from which he might possibly have been rescued by the Volunteers if their leader, Austin Stack, had not been under strict instructions not to take any premature action until the Rising broke out in Dublin. However, through a priest, who was allowed to visit him, Casement managed to get out a verbal message which was taken to Dublin by a Volunteer. Pearse heard it from the messenger himself the next day, Saturday. It ran simply: 'Germany sending arms, but will not send men.'[45] But Pearse, who up to the last moment seems to have been hoping not only for troops but also some naval and air diversion to help the Rising, knew by then that even the arms would not be coming, for the news of the sinking of the *Aud* had also reached him.[46]

The disasters and errors of judgement had not been all on one side. The British Government had known since early in the war a good deal about the movements and intentions of Roger Casement in New York and Germany.[47] Early in 1915 British Naval Intelligence had broken the German diplomatic code and had been intercepting messages between the Embassy in Washington and Berlin, including those from Devoy which retailed information about the projected rising. This information and its source seems never to have been passed as a matter of urgency directly to Dublin Castle.

The possibility of some German invasion of Ireland had naturally been in the minds of the administration in Dublin Castle in a routine way. They were well aware that splinter elements in Ireland, like the Irish Volunteers, besides opposing recruiting might in certain circumstances favour an insurrection with German support. But they were also aware of what a minute section of Irish opinion these splinter elements represented. They knew that the vast majority of the Irish population were loyal to the Crown and behind the imperial war effort. Still, they kept their ears open. As always in Irish history the government had informers in the Irish radical quarters of the day, but for the first time in Irish history these appear themselves not to have been really well informed.[48] Clearly the government was given no proper concept of the IRB's role or effectiveness at the time. An intercepted letter from Casement in Germany to MacNeill even made it appear that MacNeill himself was one of the most dangerous men they had to face. In these circumstances the Liberal Chief Secretary, Augustine Birrell, understandably saw as his paramount task the need to keep a balance between prevention of a nuisance and the inflation of nuisance value into something more important than it was.

In this he was much encouraged and supported by the Parliamentary Nationalist Party's leaders, Redmond, Dillon and Devlin. Unionists were often outraged at the latitude allowed to the anti-recruiting activities of the Irish Volunteers and the relative freedom with which they paraded and manoeuvred. But the party leaders, who had as much to lose as anyone at their hands, always insisted that the only real danger the Irish Volunteers presented was as potential martyrs. Thus, although there was sporadic suppression of the various splinter 'seditious' organs of the press and some prosecution and deportation of individuals under the Defence of the Realm Act, Birrell and his Under-Secretary, Sir Matthew Nathan, in amicable consultation with the Nationalist Party leaders, pursued what might be called a 'soft line' towards the small dissident minority. Though Birrell, as early as November 1914, had recognized 'the danger of a real street row and sham rebellion in Dublin',[49] his chief concern was not to turn this small minority into traditional Irish martyrs. What he could hardly be expected to know without better sources of information was that a small minority within this small minority was determined that it should turn itself into martyrs at all costs.

The third member of an administrative triumvirate at Dublin Castle was the new viceroy who had replaced Lord Aberdeen in 1915, Lord Wimborne, formerly Sir Ivor Churchill-Guest, who had been created a peer in 1910 to swell the Liberal minority in the House of Lords. Wimborne was more orthodox in his view of authority's responsibilities than Birrell or Nathan and more naturally sensitive to the insistence of the Southern Unionist leader, Lord Midleton, that something should be done about the Irish Volunteers. And it was Wimborne who, at the last moment, very nearly prevented the Rising from breaking out altogether.

In November 1915 Birrell, in reply to a remonstrance of Midleton's about the Irish Volunteers, said that they could not be disarmed nor could their parades be forbidden because to take notice of speeches made by crackbrained priests and other enthusiasts would only halt the growth of loyalty in Ireland. 'I laugh at the whole thing,' he added.[50]

On the other hand, both he and Nathan were quite aware that winter of the perceptible increase in the numbers of the Irish Volunteers. Nathan was the less cocksure of the two. In November 1915, with the possibility of conscription for Ireland looming, he even described the situation as 'bad and fairly rapidly growing worse'.[51] With what was, for that time, almost uncannily premature foresight, he actually told Birrell that the Nationalist Party had lost control of the country, and Lord Midleton that 'Sinn Fein' were edging out Redmond.[52] Given such an appreciation, the coolness with which the administration was able to receive some of the reports from informers, and, in a roundabout way, British intelligence in the early months of 1916, seems remarkable.

British intelligence certainly behaved almost casually with the knowledge at its disposal. In the middle of March both Nathan and Wimborne saw a report from the Inspector General of the RIC in which he stated that information had been received 'from an informant in Ireland to the effect that the Irish Volunteer leaders have been warned to be in readiness for a German landing at an early date'.[53] Nathan continued to insist that he did not believe that the leaders of the Volunteers meant insurrection.[54] A strong recommendation from the GOC Irish Command, General Friend, that the Volunteers ought to be proclaimed had been turned down the month before.[55] And Birrell wrote to Midleton at the end of March that 'to proclaim the Irish Volunteers as an illegal body would be in my opinion a reckless and foolish act and would promote disloyalty to a prodigious extent'.[56] Midleton replied that the Castle was shirking its responsibility, and though the charge was unfair, for Birrell and Nathan's policy was carefully thought out, their continued unruffled confidence in the developing circumstances was certainly surprising. Wimborne himself was becoming anxious and was relieved to hear that at least a number of Sinn Fein organizers were being banished from Ireland at the end of March, speculating personally whether 'Clarke, Connolly and others whom I don't remember' might not soon follow them.[57] In justification of Birrell's and Nathan it must be said that even the deportations caused nationalist ripples beyond mere Sinn Feiner circles. Dillon himself noted anxiously: 'To me it appears that the tension has been seriously increased.'[58]

The military continued to wish to play safe regardless of political considerations, and a proposal was made that the garrison in Ireland should be reinforced by one or more infantry brigades from England.[59] The officer in charge of Irish intelligence reported that there was undoubted proof that Sinn Fein Irish Volunteers were working up for rebellion, if ever they had a good opportunity.[60] Reports from informers inside the ranks of the Volunteers sometimes confirmed this, but others said that in spite of the impatience of some young men in the Volunteers, backed by Connolly and the Citizen Army, the leaders were against a rising at present. Nathan's nerve held. He had again been momentarily disconcerted after St Patrick's Day, 17 March, when uniformed Volunteers with rifles and bayonets had manoeuvred in the centre of Dublin and held up traffic for two hours.[61] But on 10 April he wrote to Lord French, now GOC Home Forces in Britain: 'Though the Volunteer element has been active of late I do not believe that its leaders mean insurrection or that the Volunteers have sufficient arms if the leaders do mean it.'[62]

A week later he was handed a letter from the general in charge of the defence of the South of Ireland which relayed information that a landing of arms and ammunition was expected on the south-west coast, and a rising fixed for Easter Eve. And two days later an informer reported that Mac-Donagh, the Volunteer Commandant, had said to his men: 'We are not going out on Friday [Good Friday], but we are going on Sunday.... Boys, some of us may never come back.'[63] A time had been fixed for a general Volunteer march out on Sunday.

All this naturally put even Nathan on his guard. Birrell was in London. Nathan saw that the police were in a state of alert. But on the Saturday morning he heard of the capture and sinking of the *Aud*, and also that the man who had been arrested the previous day after landing from a German collapsible boat was Sir Roger Casement. The news seemed immensely reassuring both to himself and to Wimborne. The military, too, shared the view that Casement was the key man in the business. When on Sunday morning they read in the *Sunday Independent* that all movements ordered for the Volunteers for that day had been cancelled, they drew the reasonable conclusion that such plans as there were for a rising had been totally ruined.

However, such overwhelming evidence now existed of the Irish Volunteers' connection with the German enemy that, after some insistence from Wimborne, Nathan agreed on Sunday morning to cable Birrell in London for permission to arrest them. At lunch he assured his host and fellow-guests that all danger of a rising had been averted with Casement's arrest and that they could go to Fairyhouse Races on the following day, Easter Monday, quite happily.[64]

But there was work to be done, for a load of gelignite had been stolen that morning and taken to Liberty Hall. A police raid to recover this had to be planned and dispositions made for the projected arrest of the Volunteer leaders when permission arrived from Birrell in London. A conference was held that Sunday evening with senior army and police officers and the viceroy himself. Wimborne pressed for the arrest of from sixty to one hundred of the leaders that very night (Sunday).[65] Nathan, however, insisted on waiting for permission from Birrell to arrive the next day.

Birrell sent it the next morning. Nathan was in his office making final practical arrangements with the Senior Intelligence Officer and the Secretary of the Post Office, having just told the latter that the telephone and telegraph services in south-western Ireland must be temporarily confined to naval and military use, when rifle fire rang out below the window. It was the policeman on the gate being shot dead by the Citizen Army. The Rising had begun.

The shooting of fellow Irishmen in more or less cold blood continued sporadically for the rest of the day. There was an unpleasant scene near Beggar's Bush barracks shortly after four in the afternoon. A detachment of what was confusingly called the Irish Volunteer Defence Corps, a reserve training body of the *British* forces, consisting of middle-class Irishmen over military age, returned at that time from a route march in the countryside where they had been oblivious of events in Dublin. They carried rifles but no ammunition. Some sniping was in progress round the barracks at the time. The rebels, seeing the reserve corps (known as the Gorgeous Wrecks, from the GR they wore on their arm bands) marching down the road towards them, understandably did not stop to ask questions but poured a withering fire into the khaki ranks. They killed five and wounded nine. A little later that evening the writer James Stephens witnessed the shooting by a Volunteer of a civilian trying to extricate his cart from a barricade the Volunteers had built at St Stephen's Green.[66] Stephens noted that at that moment the crowd's mood, which earlier in the day had been one of bewildered curiosity, was one of hate for the Volunteers. At just about the same time fifty miles away at Castlebellingham in County Louth, an Irish constable named McGee and an English grenadier guards officer named Dunville were shot when lined up against some railings with other prisoners by Volunteers under the command of a Belfast electrical engineer named John MacEntee. MacEntee himself had until only the year before been a supporter of Redmond's and trying to get a commission in the British Army.[67] The Irish constable, who had been shot at least twice, died within a few hours; the Englishman, though shot through the chest, subsequently recovered.

But the shooting of the defenceless was not to be confined to the rebel side. On the evening of the next day an Irish officer of the Royal Irish Rifles, who was by nature excitable and eccentric and who had been in the retreat from Mons and wounded at the Battle of the Aisne, arrested three journalists in the Dublin streets, Thomas Dickson, Patrick MacIntyre and the well-known pacifist Francis Sheehy Skeffington.[68] The next morning without any sort of trial and entirely on his own initiative he had them shot by a make-shift firing squad in the barracks yard. The firing squad did its work so badly that a second party had to be assembled a few minutes later to finish Sheehy Skeffington off.[69] Later in the week some civilians were killed by the military in a house in North King Street while prisoners in their custody.[70] Such incidents on both sides were not significantly representative of the character of either, only of the nature of the situation for which anyone initiating a cold-blooded insurrection in these circumstances must take responsibility.

The Catholic Church, of which Patrick Pearse was a devout member, sanctions violent rebellion only when the government is a tyranny, ruling by force against the will of the governed, and the insurrection is approved by the community as a whole. As MacNeill had already emphasized, by no stretch of the imagination could it be maintained that such a state of affairs prevailed in Ireland in 1916.*[71] But Pearse had transcended mundane Church teaching with a vision of morality which equated what he saw as Ireland's redemption with the work of the Redeemer himself. Since, as a good Catholic, he knew that in the last resort, whatever the Church's rules, the final judgement on his action lay elsewhere, he had no moral doubts. It was hardly a coincidence that the date of the Rising had been fixed for Easter.

Though opinion continued to harden against the Volunteers during the course of the week, particularly when the British Army's heavy shelling of rebel strongholds in Dublin caused increasing destruction and casualties, James Stephens, who kept a day-to-day record of impressions and events, noted that as late as Wednesday when the heavy shelling started there was a strong ambivalence in public feeling, a reluctance, particularly among men, to express much more than curiosity or astonishment at what had happened. One part of people's minds was even grateful that the Volunteers had managed to hold out for as long as two days and avoid total humiliation.[72] Women were on the whole more condemnatory, often saying that all the rebels ought to be shot. 'Civil war' was how a nurse in Dublin Castle typically thought of what was going on, and many of the emotions at work were those that invariably accompany civil war.[73] And yet at the same time there was something special about this one, for the same Irishman was sometimes on both sides at once. Myth and reality were themselves warring in Irish minds. It was the very development on which Pearse and Connolly with their conscious reactivation of the myth had been counting.[74]

Wednesday, 26 April, saw the Volunteers achieve their greatest military success of the rebellion. On that morning the first British reinforcements from England landed at Kingstown, welcomed as deliverers by the local population, and marched towards the centre of the city.[75] They were men of the Sherwood Foresters from the English midlands, few of whom had been in the army more than three months. Advancing down Northumberland Road towards Mount Street Bridge to cross the canal which rings the centre of the city at this point they ran into extremely effective fire from de Valera's outposts, and it was only after many hours of bitter fighting that they succeeded in crossing the canal. The Sherwood Foresters' casualties here were four officers killed and fourteen wounded and 216 other ranks killed or wounded, and these amounted to more than half the entire British Army casualties in the rebellion. The essentially static and defensive nature of the rebel command's psychology was, however, once again manifested in this situation, for although de Valera's men in the outposts round Mount Street base fought with great bravery against overwhelming odds, the headquarters

---

* Other theological conditions required are that the tyranny should be irremovable except by bloodshed, that its evil be greater than the effects of the revolt and that it should have serious probability of success.

battalion in Boland's Mills remained virtually inert throughout the engagement.

Such psychology undoubtedly made things easier for the Army Commander, General W. H. M. Lowe. It was his strategy to tie a cordon round the area in which the rebel strongholds were situated, and then methodically reduce this by artillery fire – supported by the gun-boat *Helga* on the Liffey – and infantry pressure. To many people the Army's progress seemed slow, but given the extent to which it had been caught off guard on the Monday, with less than two thousand troops in Dublin altogether, and the need to bring reinforcements not only from other parts of Ireland but from England, the plan was carried out with methodical efficiency.

By Thursday evening the words Irish Republic on the green flag above the Post Office had been scorched to a deep brown by flames.[76] The building was on fire and no longer tenable as rebel headquarters. The O'Rahilly led the sortie to establish new headquarters elsewhere, in which he was killed by machine-gun fire as he dashed with his men up Moore Street. Pearse and Connolly – now on a stretcher with his ankle broken – were the last to leave the building, and after a temporary halt in a grocer's they knocked their way through the walls of a number of buildings to a fishmonger's shop in Great Britain Street.[77] From there Pearse witnessed the shooting down in the street of a publican and his family trying to leave their burning house under a white flag. In the circumstances the sight was too much for this gentle man who had longed for red war in Ireland. In any case his work was done. He had shown that the myth could be made to live. Now, to ensure its survival there was need in his eyes only for that death, which in the words of the greater Myth in which he was also a believer, would confer eternal life.

Connolly, a very different kind of man from Pearse, subscribed to the same fundamental belief in surprisingly similar terms. '... In all due humility and awe,' he had written in an editorial in the *Workers' Republic* in February 1916, 'we recognize that of us, as of mankind before Calvary, it may truly be said "without the shedding of Blood there is no Redemption." '[78]

Blood had been shed but the Calvary image had still to be completed.

At 3.30 p.m. on Saturday, 29 April, Pearse, wearing his Volunteer uniform with its Boer War style slouch hat, surrendered to Brigadier General Lowe on the steps of the burnt-out Post Office, ceremonially handing over his sword. For the rest of that day and on the following Sunday morning Pearse's and Connolly's orders to surrender were carried round to the various isolated Volunteer strongholds by a nurse who had been in the Post Office during the week, Elizabeth O'Farrell, now under British escort. Some of these strongholds were still virtually untried and intact. A Volunteer posted in a window overlooking St Stephen's Green had not even fired a shot, and when the order for surrender came round on Sunday there was a cry from the garrison there: 'Surrender! We haven't started yet.'[79] Other garrisons, such as those in the

South Dublin Union Workhouse under Eamonn Ceannt, and in the Four Courts area under Edward Daly, were hard pressed after bitter fighting in which they had conducted themselves with chivalry and courage.

The rebel casualties were not particularly heavy: 64 killed altogether during the week.[80] But casualties among civilians were high from sniping and artillery fire. Civilian casualties altogether were at least 220 killed, and an unknown number in excess of 600 wounded.[81] Total casualties among all Crown forces were 134 killed or died of wounds and 381 wounded. The killed included 35 officers and men of Irish regiments,[82] 5 GR's and 17 Irishmen of the RIC and Dublin Metropolitan Police. Most of the police casualties occurred not in Dublin at all but at a fight near Ashbourne, County Meath, on Friday, when a party of forty RIC men under a chief inspector, on their way by motor-car to relieve the police barracks at Ashbourne which had been reported occupied by Volunteers, were skilfully ambushed by rebels under Volunteer Commandant Thomas Ashe. The fight lasted for five hours, and when the police had run out of ammunition they surrendered. Eight of them had been killed and fifteen wounded.[83] The same group of rebels had been moving fairly freely over both eastern County Meath and northern County Dublin during the week, raiding police barracks and disturbing communications. The fate of the rebellion was, however, totally unaffected by their activity or by the 'Battle of Ashbourne', and it was in a different though also tragic role that Commandant Ashe the next year was to make a contribution to the success of Irish republicanism.

Elsewhere in Ireland, thanks to the double disaster of the loss of the German arms ship and the conflicting orders of MacNeill and Pearse, the Volunteers' efforts were either of less significance still, or, in most cases, nil. The town of Enniscorthy was actually taken over by the local Volunteers for three days from early Thursday morning, 27 April, while the police sat in a state of uneasy siege in their barracks, but no fighting took place, and when the leaders of the rebels sent an offer of help to the beleaguered garrisons in Dublin James Connolly turned it down. After a military armoured train moving up from Wexford had sent them into a defensive position on Vinegar Hill the rebels, who numbered about six hundred altogether, surrendered unconditionally having barely fired a shot.[84] John MacEntee, one of the leaders in County Louth of the party which had shot Constable McGee, made his way to Dublin and pluckily joined the besieged Post Office three days before the surrender.[85] In County Louth his men had dwindled to fourteen as the news reached them of British troop movements in their direction.

In Limerick, an old centre of Fenianism, two bodies of Volunteers over a hundred strong had been mobilized on the Sunday before the outbreak but then disbanded on receipt of MacNeill's countermanding order. The next day they actually received another order, from Pearse this time, telling them to go into action all the same but, understandably perhaps in view of their own disarray and the known loss of the arms ship, they did not obey.[86]

In 'rebel' Cork which had seen a very strong turn-out of armed and uniformed Irish Volunteers on St Patrick's Day only a month before, there was a similar story. Over a thousand men were in fact successfully mobilized for Easter Sunday, their task being to hold the military forces in the area while the arms from the *Aud* were being distributed. They received the countermanding order and dispersed, only to receive another order from Pearse the next day telling them that the action in Dublin was on and that they were to carry out their original instructions. However, since in the course of these days they actually received no less than nine separate dispatches from Dublin altogether, some of them contradictory, they eventually decided to do nothing. After the Rising the IRB held an inquiry into this activity and found, perhaps rather leniently by strict military standards, that 'Cork could not have acted other than it did'.[87]

In Belfast 132 Volunteers were mobilized in the Falls Road. But no countermanding order was needed here to throw their plan into confusion. This had been worked out by Pearse and Connolly in Dublin and provided for them to cross Ulster without engaging in any action and, together with other Volunteers from Tyrone, join up with the larger bodies due to rise in County Galway. However, the Tyrone men when they heard this plan flatly refused to leave their own county and the plan disintegrated. The leader of the Volunteers in Ulster, refusing to commit the Belfast men alone, was thus driven into total inaction.[88] Ironically, he was none other than Denis McCullough, the young pioneer of the new IRB with Hobson a few years before, and by right of his position as President of the Supreme Council technically, under the IRB constitution, 'President of the Irish Republic'. But Pearse, in taking on responsibility for the Fenian myth through the secret Military Council had appropriated this title for himself, although whether or not with McCullough's acquiescence is not clear.

In Galway, Liam Mellows, one of the Sinn Fein organizers who had been deported by Nathan and Birrell the previous month but who had made his way back to Ireland in disguise, managed to mobilize a thousand or so men. They had no more than sixty rifles and 350 shotguns between them and had been particularly dependent on the anticipated arms from the *Aud*. Some even carried pikes in the '98 tradition. They captured one police barracks and its five Irish policemen but failed to capture another defended by a similar handful. They cut some telegraph wires and uprooted some railway lines but eventually, after moving for some days desultorily round the county, harassed by troop movements and even some shells from a warship in Galway bay, dispersed on receiving news of the insurrection's collapse in Dublin.[89] Their failure was reminiscent of similar Fenian activity in 1867.

Except for the factual element of defeat the same could by no means be said of the rising in Dublin as a whole. Ineffectual as it had been in terms of military achievement, mustering altogether only about 1,500 rebels unsupported and even strongly condemned by the populace, it had brought about the only serious and disciplined fighting that had ever been conducted by Irishmen in single-minded pursuit of Wolfe Tone's aim of a totally independent Irish Republic. Something quite new had happened in Irish history. The centre of Dublin lay in ruins to prove it. Although the rebellion had come as a shattering surprise to ninety-nine per cent of Irishmen of all classes and political beliefs, being unexpected even by most of those who carried it out, such an event could not leave any nationally-minded Irishman's attitude to events in the future unaffected.

18

Executions and Negotiations

On the Sunday afternoon of 30 April as the last group of organized rebels,
under MacDonagh at Jacob's Biscuit factory, were about to surrender, still
almost intact as a fighting force, Birrell wrote his last report before resignation to Asquith. 'It is not an *Irish* rebellion,' he summarized. 'It would be
a pity if *ex post facto* it became one, and was added to the long and melancholy list of Irish rebellions.'[1]

It now seems astonishing that the danger should have been so accurately
predicted – and not only by Birrell – and yet the very action most likely to
enhance it was allowed to take its course. The same day Dillon wrote to
Redmond in London, from Dublin: 'You should urge strongly on the
government the *extreme* unwisdom of any wholesale shooting of prisoners.
The wisest course is to execute *no one* for the present. This is the *most
urgent* matter of the moment. If there were shootings of prisoners on any
large scale the effect on public opinion might be disastrous in the extreme.
So far feeling of the population in Dublin is against the Sinn Feiners. But a
reaction might very easily be created.'[2] A little further on in his letter he
repeated: 'Do not fail to urge the government not to execute any of the
prisoners. I have no doubt that if any of the well-known leaders are taken
alive they will be shot. But, except the leaders, there should be no court-
martial executions.'

Perhaps this preparedness to accept as inevitable the executions of some
leaders shows that even Dillon underestimated the infinitely precarious
balance of feeling in Ireland. Redmond, in London, clearly did. He saw
Asquith at once and thought he was doing the right thing by securing agreement that while 'the real ring-leaders' would have to be dealt with 'in the
most severe manner possible' the rest would be treated with leniency.[3] Two
days later, however, when definitely informed by Asquith that some executions would be necessary, he did make a protest.[4] On the same day, 3 May
1916, Pearse, MacDonagh and Clarke were shot at dawn in a yard at Kilmainham gaol.

A priest was allowed to give Holy Communion to them a few hours before
the executions. Assuming that the established custom in such matters would
be observed, the priest who attended Pearse and MacDonagh reassured

them that he would be close to them in their last moments even though they would be unable to see him because of their blindfolds. The thought made them happy.[5] But the military refused to allow it, and ordered the priest to leave the building so that he was not with them when the time came.

Probably Pearse, MacDonagh and Clarke were in too great a state of spiritual and patriotic exaltation to be much affected by this cruelty, but it was symbolic of the military's insensibility in such a highly sensitive situation. The insensibility with which they were now allowed to proceed seems all the more curious for the fact that Sir John Maxwell himself, who had arrived as Commander-in-Chief in Ireland at the end of Easter Week with full military powers, clearly had some appreciation of the delicacy of the atmosphere, and was prepared to receive at least advice from Dillon.[6] But his awareness was accompanied by that arrogance often inseparable from even high military intelligence. In later refusing the right of burial in consecrated ground for Pearse's body he was able to write brusquely: 'Irish sentimentality will turn these graves into martyrs' shrines to which annual processions will be made which will cause constant irritation in this country.'[7] He seems to have thought that quick-lime would be enough to dispel 'Irish sentimentality'. But it had failed in the case of Allen, Larkin and O'Brien and many others. He can hardly have supposed that when Pearse himself spoke of 'the fools' leaving extreme nationalists their Fenian dead, he was thinking literally of their corpses.

On 4 May four more executions after courts-martial were carried out – on Joseph Plunkett, Edward Daly, Michael O'Hanrahan and William Pearse, Patrick's younger brother. All were allowed to see priests shortly before their execution, and this time, it seems, the priests were allowed to stay with them to the last, though military clumsiness was not entirely absent. One of the men was brought to Confession in handcuffs and unable to remove his hat until they were unlocked.[8]

Plunkett, however, had been allowed to marry the girl he was engaged to by the light of a candle with a warder for witness in the prison chapel in the early hours. He at least, the elegant tubercular poet who had walked about the General Post Office during the Rising with a bangle on his wrist and a Mauser at his belt[9] could properly be described as one of the leaders. As a member of the IRB's military council he had helped draft the original plans for an insurrection and had signed the Proclamation of the Republic.[10]

Daly had had nothing to do with the planning of the rebellion though he was the son of an old Fenian, and had merely carried out his military duties as a Volunteer Commandant under orders. He had, however, done so in effective fashion from his command in the Four Courts area, and since the government knew nothing about the IRB's manipulation of the Volunteers it was not unreasonable for them to suppose him a leader.

The same could just be said of Michael O'Hanrahan, a literary man who had been a clerk at Volunteer headquarters. But if leading Volunteers were going to be executed on these grounds alone the indications were of a massive number of executions to come.

Willie Pearse seems to have been shot for no other reason than that he had taken part in the rebellion as a Volunteer and was Pearse's brother. Though devoted to his brother he had known nothing of his schemes for turning blood-red poetic fantasies into reality. But the military seem to have thought they had already been lenient enough for that particular day – which, by their own lights, they were. Simultaneously with the announcement of these four executions, they revealed that seventeen other courts-martial sentences of death, which had been confirmed, had been commuted to penal servitude.

Asquith, the Prime Minister, was himself uneasy, but not uneasy enough. As so often throughout the history of the Union, responsible English statesmen even when compelled to take Ireland seriously still accorded her a secondary priority. Thus, though even on 3 May Asquith told Redmond that he had given the War Office orders from the start 'to go slowly', and that he was himself shocked by the news of the first three executions, he would not absolutely promise that there would be no more, merely expressing that as 'his desire and intention'.[11] Now four more men had been executed. Nor was Asquith the only man to be weak or mistakenly flexible in a disastrously deteriorating situation. Redmond himself told Asquith that he would probably resign if there were any more executions.[12] Asquith told him that he had wired Maxwell that there should be no more. But Asquith's wire went unrespected. Redmond did not resign.

The next day, 5 May, another man, John MacBride, was executed. Though he had taken part in the rebellion and was a rank-and-file member of the IRB with some two thousand others, he, like almost all of them, had absolutely no prior knowledge of the plans for the rebellion. His well-known predilection for drink preserved him especially from any confidence on the part of the leadership. He had, however, led an Irish Brigade – composed mainly of Americans – against the British in the Boer War.* Unlike another Irishman, Arthur Lynch, who had done the same and later renounced his separatist views and become an MP, MacBride, who had enjoyed since 1911 the post of water bailiff to the Dublin Corporation, had remained true to 'the cause'. It is difficult not to think that he was shot partly as a simple act of revenge by the military for an offence for which the common law had long forgiven him, though he had continued to wage war in speech against the British, urging his hearers at a Manchester Martyrs' commemoration at Kilkenny in 1909 to 'do all in your power to prevent your countrymen from entering the degraded British Army'.[13] Undoubtedly, too, he had refused to show any signs of contrition at his court-martial. He had, he

* See above, pp. 443–4.

told the court, stared down the barrels of British rifles far too often in the past to be afraid of death.[14] And thus it may be assumed he bore himself at the end. He, too, in the words with which Yeats was soon to express his emotion at these strange events, had 'resigned his part in the casual comedy. ... A terrible beauty is born.'

Anyone with any sense of the workings of Irish history, particularly if also aware of that ambivalence which had underlain many attitudes even of downright hostility to the rebellion while it was going on, could have foretold what the long-term effect of these wholly unpredictable day-by-day executions was likely to be. Already a Capuchin Father noticed that the feeling among the working classes of Dublin was becoming 'extremely bitter' over the executions, 'even amongst those who had no sympathy whatever with the Sinn Feiners, or with the rising'.[15] Before long, as one Irishwoman was later to put it, the Irish people began to feel that they were 'watching a stream of blood coming from beneath a closed door'.[16] The fact that on the same day as MacBride's death the commutation of death sentences on two other Irish Volunteers, including William Cosgrave, was announced was not the fact that counted.

And yet even now, for most people the whole situation was immensely complicated and opaque. British statesmen and military men were not in the habit of thinking of Ireland in the light of the workings of past history. General Maxwell, with only the government's incomplete and over-simplified knowledge of the background to the rebellion at his disposal, saw it primarily as a German manoeuvre in the Great War which was at that moment going badly for England. Quite incorrectly, but sincerely, he thought that the Germans had inspired the rebellion and that what seemed like Casement's attempt to land with German arms to lead it was the corner-stone of the enterprise.[17] After all, the Republican Proclamation which Pearse had read out to such an apathetic audience from the front of the Post Office had actually mentioned with pride support from the Germans as 'gallant allies in Europe'.

Now every indication was that the vast majority of the Irish people found the thought of such support repellent. Some 90,000 Catholic Irish had joined the British Army from Ireland since the beginning of the war and far more had already died in the war than had died fighting the British Government in the past hundred years. Elements of seven Irish regiments had taken part in the suppression of the rebellion itself and there had, of course, been other Irishmen in non-Irish regiments.* Some of the sharpest fighting in Easter Week had been between the Royal Irish Regiment and the rebels at the South Dublin Union, and between the Dublin Fusiliers and the rebels at the barricades in Cabra Road. In his order of the day of 1 May

---

* For instance, among the Lancers, who had been the first military casualties of the rebellion. (*Rebellion Handbook*, p. 56.)

1916 Maxwell had singled out for praise 'those Irish regiments which have so largely helped to crush this rising'.[18] He may well have felt he had a duty to his own Irishmen to fulfill in enforcing at least some of the rigour of the law.

Moreover, in addition to pressure from Asquith and the Home Rule Nationalists to stop the executions, Maxwell was also under strong pressure in the opposite direction from Unionists. A memorial presented by 763 'influential' people in Dublin protested against any interference with the discretion of the C-in-C in Ireland and the operation of martial law.[19] Altogether, by his own lights, Maxwell was by no means unreasonable in the circumstances of the time in thinking he was being lenient in shooting only fifteen rebels over the period of nine days beginning on 3 May and commuting other death sentences to penal servitude. But where Irish nationalism was concerned nothing could be safely judged only by the light of reason, as Redmond and Dillon were well aware. And it was on this factor that Pearse in particular had been counting.

On Saturday, 6 May, no other executions were announced. Instead, eighteen death sentences were commuted to penal servitude and only two of these sentences as severe as life, one of which was that passed on Constance Markievicz. Dillon crossed to London that night with a draft resolution for the Irish party in his pocket condemning the insurrection, but protesting 'in the most solemn manner against the large number of military executions ...' continuing, '... We solemnly warn the government that very serious mischief has been done by the excessive severities.... And that any further military executions will have the most far-reaching and disastrous effects on the future peace and loyalty of the Irish people.'[20] Redmond had already told Asquith of a cable received from the president of the Irish League of New York, a loyal supporter of Redmond's and of the British war effort, saying that the first executions had revolted the American Irish who had condemned the rebellion itself.[21]

On Sunday the 7th there were rumours of more executions pending the next day. Redmond sent an urgent message to Asquith 'at his place in the country'. Asquith sent what he called 'a strong telegram' to Maxwell saying that he hoped the shootings, except in some quite exceptional cases, would stop. The next day Cornelius Colbert, Edmund Kent (Eamonn Ceannt), Michael Mallin and Sean Heuston were shot.

Colbert, a clerk in a bakery and yet another of the rebellion's poets, had been an active organizer of the Fianna Eireann, the nationalist boy scouts. Heuston, a railway clerk, another prominent figure in the Fianna, had held the Mendicity Institution bravely for three days during the Rising. He was shot sitting on a soap box.[22] Ceannt, a Dublin Corporation clerk, had been a member of the IRB's military committee since its inception in May 1915 – though the authorities had no such precise information – and one of the signatories of the proclamation; he had also been the commander of the garrison in the South Dublin Union. Mallin, a silk weaver with five children, had been second-in-command of Connolly's Citizen Army and in charge of the St Stephen's Green garrison during Easter Week.

Connolly himself was tried and sentenced to death the next day, 9 May, Maxwell noting laconically, in reply to Asquith's feeble demurs, that though his bullet wound had fractured the ankle bone he would recover 'in ordinary circumstances' in three months. He informed the Prime Minister that Connolly would be shot at dawn on 11 May. Sean MacDermott would be shot at the same time. 'They will be the last,' Maxwell conceded.[23]

Meanwhile, however, on 9 May Thomas Kent, a Cork Volunteer who had resisted an attempt to arrest him at his home near Fermoy two days after the rebellion in Dublin was over and had killed a policeman, was shot in Cork.

On 11 May, in a last desperate attempt to prevent further executions, Dillon moved the adjournment of the House of Commons. Bitterly he seems to have sensed that it was too late and that untold damage was already done. He who with Redmond stood to lose his whole political future from the rebellion showed how the executions had already begun to affect him. He lost control of himself and cried out to a hostile House:

I say I am proud of their [the rebels] courage and if you were not so dense and stupid, as some of you English people are, you could have had these men fighting for you ... it is not murderers who are being executed; it is insurgents who have fought a clean fight, however misguided, and it would have been a damned good thing for you if your soldiers were able to put up as good a fight as did these men in Dublin ...[24]

Even Asquith himself was now disturbed, if only by his own ineffectualness, and announced, while knowing quite well that Connolly and MacDermott were to be executed on the following day, that he was going to Dublin to investigate the future.

In the early morning of 12 May Connolly, after receiving Holy Communion, was put on a stretcher and taken by ambulance from Dublin Castle to Kilmainham. There in the yard he was placed in a chair and gripping the arms of it held his head high to the end.[25] Sean MacDermott had written to his family, '... you ought to envy me. The cause for which I die has been rebaptized during the past week by the blood of as good men as ever trod God's earth. ... It is not alone for myself I feel happy, but for the fact that Ireland has produced such men.'[26]

Many of them expressed in their last words the same confidence that their deaths were a sort of triumph, thus retrospectively at least subscribing to Pearse's theory of the blood sacrifice. 'People will say hard things of us now,' Pearse himself had written to his mother two days before his execution, 'but we shall be remembered by posterity and blessed by unborn generations. You too will be blessed because you are my mother.'[27] Sean Heuston wrote to his sister, a Dominican nun, 'If you really love me, teach the children the history of their own land and teach them the cause of Caitlin ni Uallachain never dies.'[28] Ceannt, who expressed resentment that Pearse had surrendered so early, nevertheless accepted that Pearse's ultimate objective had been achieved. 'Ireland has shown she is a Nation,' he wrote the day before he died. '... And in the years to come Ireland will honour those who risked all for her honour at Easter in 1916.'[29]

Meanwhile, no one knew for certain that the volley of the firing squad which had killed Connolly had been the last. Courts-martial were proceeding. Death sentences continued to be announced though simultaneously with their commutation to penal servitude. But this was no guarantee that executions were over. Seven commuted death sentences had been announced the day before Connolly and MacDermott were shot, among them one on Edward de Valera, the rebel Commandant of Boland's Mills – one of the many examples of Redmond's successful personal intervention with Asquith.*[30]

Eight more commuted death sentences were announced a few days afterwards. There had been over 3,000 arrests altogether, a number of them irrelevant, and though nearly 1,000 men and women were released within six weeks, more than 1,500 prisoners had been taken across the Irish Sea by 10 May. 1,867 were eventually interned there altogether, either in criminal prisons or at a special camp at Frongoch in Wales.[31]

On 30 May the findings of a court-martial on John MacNeill, who had been arrested a month earlier, were announced. The man who had known nothing of the planning of the rebellion and had done everything in his power, short of betraying his comrades, to prevent it once he had discovered what was afoot, was sentenced to life imprisonment and sent to Dartmoor.

In the special Irish situation an extremely tense and sensitive emotional atmosphere had been created by these measures, though in any normal situation they might indeed have seemed lenient on the part of a hard-pressed government in time of war. But even so it cannot be said that they need inevitably, in themselves, have led to the pronounced swing round of public opinion to the rebels' way of thinking which took place. They merely created a needlessly favourable climate for such a transformation.

Other influences less noble than martyrdom or even patriotism, which even before 1916 had helped to create a very slight shift of opinion towards

---

* It has often been said that de Valera, who was born of an Irish mother and a Spanish father in America and lived there until he was two, was saved as a result of American diplomatic intervention. But there is no evidence for this and de Valera was not technically an American citizen. See Alan J. Ward, *Anglo-American Diplomatic Relations* (London, 1969), pp. 117–18. Gwynn states that Redmond stressed to Asquith de Valera's American extraction.

extreme Irish nationalism, were now accentuated. As one witness before the Royal Commission of Inquiry into the rebellion put it, the country people were doing extremely well with their farms and were 'fat and prosperous'. 'A great many farmers' sons,' he added, had been 'joining the Sinn Fein movement, and ... using it as a kind of umbrella in excuse for not fighting.'[82] Extreme nationalism made it patriotic as well as advantageous not to want to join up. Now, with the British Army's need for men growing more and more desperate and the possibility of an extension of conscription to Ireland, the ideals of young heroes like Sean Heuston and Con Colbert undoubtedly offered some who might not normally have been drawn to Irish patriotism a happy conjunction of patriotism with self-interest.

Even so, these were all no more than conditioning factors in the situation, though conditioning factors, after so much Irish history, of particular force. The really decisive factor would be such political action as the British Government might now decide to take. The omens for a successful political manoeuvre could hardly be good in the atmosphere provoked by the manner of executions and deportations, but clearly something new had to be done, and quickly. The whole future of England's relationship with Ireland, which only eighteen months before had seemed about to be so happily resolved after seven centuries, now hung more precariously than ever in the balance.

In the prevailing political circumstances it is difficult to see that Asquith had any chance of success. He was already personally on the defensive within his own Coalition Government. That government contained men like Walter Long, Lord Selborne and Lord Lansdowne, the corner-stone of whose political faith was their opposition to Home Rule. It had for several months even contained Carson himself who had resigned only to be able to put pressure on Asquith more effectively. In a coalition situation Asquith had no parliamentary need to placate Redmond and the Irish nationalists, who were in any case themselves politically ham-strung by their patriotic commitment through Redmond to the war effort. But Asquith did need to placate the Unionists. Thus from now on almost every action he took almost inevitably made the situation worse, even those which in themselves were right.

His personal visit to Ireland on the eve of Connolly's and MacDermott's execution was a case in point.

In announcing his decision to go he had declared that the government recognized that the system under which Ireland was governed had 'completely broken down', and that what was essential was the creation 'at the earliest possible moment of an Irish government responsible to the Irish people'.[83] In other words, by their rebellion, republicans had brought the reality of Home Rule nearer. This was in itself already something to make that vast majority of the population who were Home Rulers look on the republicans with less hostility, and to begin a blurring of distinction between the two. The very importance of a visit from the Prime Minister at such a time, with non-republican feeling deeply disturbed by the executions, also lent importance to the republicans. Asquith even visited rebel prisoners in gaol in Dublin, finding them 'very good-looking fellows with such lovely eyes',[34] and the effect of his visit on them was, according to their gaolers, instantaneous. He had scarcely left the prison when, the warders maintained, the rebels who had been hitherto despondent and in tears began 'insulting their guards, throwing up their caps and shouting victory'.[35]

After his return to London he told the House of Commons that there was now 'a unique opportunity for a new departure for a settlement of outstanding problems'.[36] He had used the same phrase the day before in writing to one of his ministers and asking him to accept special responsibility for finding 'a permanent solution', by which he meant some way of immediately implementing Home Rule which would be acceptable to all. The minister who accepted this challenge was David Lloyd George.[37]

Not all the omens were bad. The Unionists through influential personalities of their press – Garvin of the *Observer* and Northcliffe of the *Daily Mail* – had expressed a willingness to go back to the Ulster deadlock of 1914 and see if some practical acceptable compromise could not be found.[38] Moreover, there was a direct reason why all British patriots should want to resolve the Irish difficulty now that the rebellion had shown that the passage and suspension of the Home Rule Act in 1914 had been inadequate. This reason was the need to placate public opinion in the United States of America, which country was then still neutral in the Great War, but sorely needed as an ally.

At the end of Easter Week the British Ambassador in Washington had been able to write that American public opinion had been on the whole totally opposed to the rebellion. Nineteen days later, however, after the executions, he was reporting a dangerous change.[39] He was substantiated by other observers. One Home Ruler had written to Redmond three days earlier from Vermont: 'The present wave of fury sweeping through Irish America originated with the executions and not with the rising ... pro-Ally Irishmen, who were calm and sorrowful at the rising ... have become hysterical during the protracted week of executions.'[40] Another Irishman reported from Chicago on 24 May that where the ' "Irish Rebellion", so-called' had excited only contempt and derision, after the executions 'a feeling of universal sympathy among the entire American people sprang into action at once'.[41]

In Ireland itself the same very sharp transformation of opinion which Dillon and others had already noted was continuing. 'It would really not be possible to exaggerate the desperate character of the situation here,' Dillon, who had returned to Dublin, wrote to Redmond while Asquith was still there. 'The executions, house-searching throughout the country, whole-

sale arrests ... *savage* treatment of prisoners, including a very considerable
number of those who had no more sympathy with Sinn Fein than you have,
have exasperated feeling to a terrible extent.'⁴² And Redmond himself was
already entertaining, in the absence of some settlement, 'very grave doubts
as to the future of the Irish party'.⁴³ Personally he was in a very depressed
state. His son had just left for the Front and he repeatedly talked of the
possibility of retiring from politics altogether.⁴⁴

It was therefore in an atmosphere of some urgency that Lloyd George
began his work. The known force of his own personal ambition made it
likely that, having accepted the task, he would do his utmost to succeed.
Typically, he did too much. Taking care to keep Carson and Redmond apart,
but conferring with each individually and giving favourable reports of his
discussions with each to the other, he succeeded in obtaining an initial
agreement between the two which looked like early success.

The same concessions in principle which had been made by each side
before the war still stood. That is to say, the Ulster Unionists conceded
the principle of Home Rule for the rest of Ireland if they themselves were
excluded; the Nationalists conceded the principle of exclusion for a limited
time of those Ulster counties with Protestant majorities. The difficult points
at issue were still those which had brought the Buckingham Palace Conference to deadlock and which had been put into cold storage by the device
of passing the act but with a suspensory act. These points concerned both
area and time. The Ulster Unionists held out for exclusion of all nine
counties of the province on a permanent basis. The Nationalists could only
accept the exclusion of the four majority Protestant counties (Derry, Antrim,
Down and Armagh) and only on a temporary basis. It was this deadlock
which, in a fashion typical of his personal political technique, Lloyd George
soon appeared to be overcoming.

The solution which both Redmond and Carson agreed to recommend to
their supporters was as follows: Home Rule was to be put into operation
at once for twenty-six of Ireland's counties, while the other six, in Ulster
(Derry, Antrim, Down, Armagh, Tyrone and Fermanagh) would be excluded.
This involved a final concession by Carson that not the whole province of
Ulster but only six counties would be excluded; Donegal, Cavan and
Monaghan were to be 'surrendered' to Home Rule. Similarly, the proposal
demanded from Redmond the concession that the two Ulster counties of
Tyrone and Fermanagh, each of which had Nationalist majorities, would
be surrendered to the Unionists. Each leader now agreed to recommend
these concessions to his supporters. In neither case was it anything like a
foregone conclusion that he would be able to force them through. The
really crucial point, however, on which ultimately any such agreement would
have to stand or fall, was the question of whether such exclusion was going
to be temporary or permanent. And on this a curious vagueness supervened.

What had happened was that Lloyd George by keeping the two negotiators apart had allowed each to receive a different impression and believe that the other had agreed to what he wanted. For good measure Lloyd George told Redmond, who had insisted that no further concessions should be demanded of the Nationalists, that he 'placed his life upon the table and would stand or fall by the agreement come to'.[45] In the agreement the provisional nature of the exclusion arrangement was indeed outlined. But this was done in ambiguous terms which might have made negotiators less desperate for a settlement than Redmond and Dillon suspicious. The exclusion of the six counties was to remain in force for the duration of the war and up to one year thereafter, but, if Parliament had not by that time made further permanent provision for the government of Ireland, the arrangement was to continue in force until it had. An Imperial Conference was also to be called at which the permanent settlement of the Irish question should be considered.[46]

All this was undoubtedly interpreted by the Nationalist leaders as meaning that the exclusion was to be only temporary. Yet, even so, and even with the self-sacrificing support of Joe Devlin, the Belfast Nationalist leader, and the sanction of a threat of resignation from Redmond, the leaders only just succeeded in getting the very reluctant agreement of the Ulster Nationalists, and thereafter that of the party as a whole, to the temporary abandonment of the substantial Nationalist minority in Ulster with its actual majority in two counties. Carson had an equally difficult time in getting his supporters in Ulster to agree to 'the clean cut' – the surrender to Home Rule of Donegal, Cavan and Monaghan with their substantial Protestant minorities. He had, however, as a result of his meetings with Lloyd George, a written assurance in his pocket of which the Nationalists were in total ignorance and without which he would have accomplished nothing. This assurance ran: 'We must make it clear that at the end of the provisional period Ulster does not, whether she wills it or not, merge in the rest of Ireland.'*[47]

It seems improbable that a man even of Lloyd George's consummate political guile could have kept the discrepancy in the proposal concealed for long. He presumably thought there was a chance of keeping it concealed long enough to be able eventually to convince Redmond and Dillon of the need to accept a *fait accompli*. But Redmond and Dillon had already strained their supporters' loyalty to the absolute limit. The dénouement came abruptly without their having to consider the possibility of trying to strain it even further.

Though Carson stuck loyally to his new position, a massive opposition to the whole scheme for putting Home Rule into operation at all was now mounted by the English Conservative Party and many of its leaders inside the coalition cabinet. 'They are all in it,' Lloyd George wrote disarmingly

* Clearly, in this letter, Lloyd George meant by 'Ulster' only the six counties.

to Dillon, 'except Balfour, Bonar Law and F. E. Smith. Long has behaved in a specially treacherous manner. He has actually been engaged clandestinely in trying to undermine the influence of Carson in Ulster.... He told them there was no war urgency, no prospect of trouble in America.... I could not think it possible that any man, least of all one with such pretensions of being an English gentleman, could have acted in such a way.'[48]

But Lloyd George, without any such pretensions, was hardly acting better and both doubtless were doing what they thought best. Long had many other English gentlemen to support him. Lord Selborne at least resigned from the cabinet at the prospect of having to be a party to the immediate implementation of Home Rule. Bonar Law had to bow before the Conservatives of the Carlton Club, who were unable to give him their support for the proposals. On 11 July Lord Lansdowne, another member of the cabinet, finally forced Lloyd George's hand when he stated in the House of Lords that in his view any proposed alteration to the Act of 1914 would be 'permanent and enduring'.[49]

The cat was now out of the bag. If Lord Lansdowne's views (and Walter Long's) did not represent those of the cabinet then Asquith would have to have their resignations. But on the defensive as he already was in his own cabinet for his conduct of the war, and with the high hopes with which the Battle of the Somme had begun a fortnight earlier disappearing into the mud, Asquith was in no position to face the break-up of his government. On 22 July Redmond was informed of the cabinet's decision that the proposed settlement was to be permanent. Two days later, in the House of Commons, Redmond, marking the collapse of the negotiations, accused the government of entering on a course which 'is bound to do serious mischief to those high Imperial interests which, we were told, necessitated the provisional settlement of this question ... they have taken the surest means to accentuate every possible danger and difficulty in this Irish situation'.[50]

Asquith wrote a wretched private letter to Redmond: 'My dear Mr Redmond, I am more afflicted than I can say (in the midst of many other troubles and worries) by the breakdown of the negotiations.... I think it is of great importance (if possible) to keep the negotiating spirit alive ...'

There was in fact at that very moment something Redmond might have persuaded Asquith to do which could at least temporarily have ameliorated the disastrous situation. But ironically even Redmond himself was not sufficiently attuned to the new mood in Ireland to perceive what this was. He seems to have accepted from the first days of May that Roger Casement would have to be executed as the rebels' chief contact with Germany. And, though much had changed since those first May days, it does not seem to have occurred to him that this attitude to Casement might need to be adjusted to that change.

On 29 June, after a trial in which the prosecutor was F. E. Smith, a man who had himself organized armed resistance to the Crown only two years before, Casement was convicted of high treason and condemned to death. There can, of course, be no doubt that, legally, the verdict against Casement was correct, for all the ingenious word-play with the ancient statute under which he was tried, indulged in by his advocate, Serjeant Sullivan, a consti- tutional Irish Nationalist of some spirit. Casement's own eloquent plea that he owed allegiance only to his country Ireland was, as he well knew, technically irrelevant, and even less eloquent than it might have been if he had not only a few years before felt sufficiently a liege man of George v's, however Irish, to accept a knighthood from him. His argument, too, that he had in fact come to try to put a stop to the rising, though perfectly true, was nothing like so convincing as he seemed to think it, for if the German help which he had worked for had been forthcoming he would have wanted the rising to proceed. He had conspired with the king's enemies in time of war and had tried to turn the king's soldiers against him. He had done so for the loftiest of reasons and in full knowledge of the risk he ran. That he was a courageous, sincere and even noble, if disturbingly lonely man is unques- tionable. It is equally unquestionable that no shadow of legal injustice was done to him at his trial, however personally distasteful and discredit- able F. E. Smith's role may appear. Whether or not, in the light of the earlier executions and Irish and American reaction to them and particularly in the deteriorating atmosphere after the collapse of the Lloyd George negotiations, it was politic to proceed with the death sentence was a different matter.

The fact that, after the rejection of Casement's appeal, the cabinet with due deliberation could come to a unanimous decision that it was right to execute him, may now seem incredible. On the very day after Asquith had written his pathetic 'negotiating spirit' letter to Redmond it even reaffirmed this decision. Once again a British government which boasted as one of its unalterable principles the connection with Ireland was to show that it had no true contact with Ireland at all.

Admittedly, some members of the cabinet had had their doubts about the matter, and had for a time seized at a most curious straw – a diary of Casement's – to try to get them out of their difficulty. When it proved inade- quate they put it to a less creditable use.

By some means, which to this day have not been authoritatively established, this diary of Casement's came into the government's possession, possibly sold to them by the disreputable sailor, Adolf Christensen, whom Casement had adopted as his servant companion.* Ninety-five per cent of the material of these diaries consisted of humdrum recordings of day-to-day movements and occurrences. But the remaining five per cent appeared to indicate unmis- takably a compulsive and obsessional homosexual activity of a promiscuous

* See above, p. 541.

nature, crudely described. A certain amount of circumstantial evidence exists to suggest that Casement may indeed have been a repressed or even a practising homosexual. It has also been suggested that the compromising passages were forged interpolations introduced by the British Intelligence Chief Admiral Hall (who undoubtedly showed the diaries to the press and influential people even before the trial). While this suggestion is not wholly impossible the authenticity or otherwise of the diaries is of less immediate concern to the historian than the further uses to which they were now put.

The government seems first to have tried to use the diaries officially to get Casement's defence lawyers to plead insanity on his behalf. Serjeant Sullivan properly refused to look at them, though one of his juniors did so, and the issue did not figure at the trial. Even after Casement's conviction, but before his appeal had been heard, some members of the cabinet, including incidentally Lord Lansdowne, thought it would be better to confine Casement as a criminal lunatic on the strength of the diaries rather than let him be 'canonized as a martyr both in Ireland and America'. But when a medical report had been received on the diaries to the effect that their author was 'abnormal but not certifiably insane', pages from the 'black' diaries were circulated and used to discourage sympathy for Casement in the minds of those urging the government for a reprieve. Among those so affected, to their discredit, were the Archbishop of Canterbury and John Redmond.[51]

On 3 August, just after nine in the morning, Casement, pinioned in the traditional fashion, was taken to the execution shed at Pentonville to be hanged. After a month's instruction he had been received into the Roman Catholic Church the day before, and the priest who had given him his first and last Communion that morning was allowed to remain with him to the end. The priest wrote afterwards: 'He marched to the scaffold with the dignity of a prince and towered over all of us ...'[52]

His last request to his cousin, Gertrude Bannister, had been 'don't let me lie here in this dreadful place – take my body back with you and let it lie in the old churchyard in Murlough Bay'.[53] A request for his body was made at once by Miss Bannister to the Home Office, but the British Government did not feel able to give it up again for another fifty years. Roger Casement, as predicted, became the sixteenth martyr of Easter Week at once.

Yeats was soon to write with more truth than accuracy (for Casement, of course, had been hanged):

> Oh but we talked at large before
> The sixteen men were shot,
> But who can talk of give and take,
> What should be and what not
> While those dead men are loitering there
> To stir the boiling pot?

You say that we should still the land
Till Germany's overcome;
But who is there to argue that
Now Pearse is deaf and dumb?
And is there logic to outweigh
MacDonagh's bony thumb?

How could you dream they'd listen
That have an ear alone
For those new comrades they have found,
Lord Edward and Wolfe Tone,
Or meddle with our give and take
That converse bone to bone?

It was the failure to achieve a settlement in the new situation created by the actions of Pearse and his companions that was now the real turning-point in the Nationalist Party's future. The suspicion that had lain over Home Rule ever since it had been placed on the statute book, and which had been aggravated when Carson and Smith had joined the government, and allayed only by the confident reassurances of Redmond, was now openly confirmed. It was not to go through. The Parliamentary Party were revealed in this last opportunity as unable to win Home Rule after all without permanently partitioning Ireland. In the new atmosphere created by the rebellion, the demand for Home Rule was now too firm to be disappointed much longer.

As early as June, T. P. O'Connor had been telling Lloyd George that the executed men were already passing into legend, with their scrupulously upright characters, their devoted Catholicism and in many cases their abstinence from drink. He recounted the story of a little girl who was said to have asked her mother for a new hat and, when the mother refused, to have prayed to 'St Pearse' until the mother relented.[54] The fact that the story was being told was what was significant. While martial law persisted masses for the dead men's souls were increasingly becoming a form of political demonstration in support of their ideals.

In September 1916 Dillon made a considered survey of the political situation in Ireland. After admitting that the party had been losing its hold on opinion unawares ever since the formation of the coalition, he wrote that its strength was now entirely of a negative character, due to the fact that there was no alternative either in leadership or policy. 'But,' he continued, 'enthusiasm and trust in Redmond and the party is *dead* so far as the mass of the people is concerned.'[55]

There was, however, an alternative leadership with an alternative policy. It was not immediately available. The bulk of it was in British prisons. But at this emotional moment in Irish history it could have had no more favourable starting-point.

Part Five

Ourselves Alone

Rebellion to De Valera's Election at Clare (July 1917)

It is sometimes said that it was the Dublin rebellion of 1916 and the subsequent executions which dramatically swung Irish majority opinion away from the goal of constitutional Home Rule nationalism in favour at least of a Fenian republican separatism to be achieved, if necessary, by bloodshed. This is a most misleading oversimplification. There is a sense in which that turned out to be the sequence of events, though whether Irish majority opinion was ever in favour of bloodshed to achieve nationalist aims is highly questionable. But certainly that sequence of events was no simple product of cause and effect.

It was neither the Fenian tradition nor Griffith's Sinn Fein which the rebellion and the executions immediately stimulated but the Home Rule movement itself. This fact is of the greatest importance in understanding the hybrid and even confused nature of much Irish opinion over the next few years. It is often forgotten that in the first by-election fought in Ireland after the rebellion – more than six months later, in the very representative nationalist constituency of West Cork in November 1916 – a man describing himself as a Sinn Feiner came easily bottom of the poll to two rival Home Rule candidates.* There can be little doubt that if the Home Rule Act as passed by Parliament had been put into effect immediately after the rebellion, it would have remained, at least for the foreseeable future, the measure of Irish nationalism which the vast majority of Irish nationalists were content to settle for. What the rebellion and the executions did was to give the demand for Home Rule a new and desperate urgency which, when frustrated by Lloyd George's post-rebellion manoeuvres, burst its bounds.

The thinking of the vast majority of Irish nationalists in the late summer of 1916 went something as follows: A Home Rule Act for all Ireland,

* See below, p. 594. The contest was between an unofficial United Irish League candidate (pro-Redmond, pro-Home Rule), an All-For-Ireland League candidate (anti-Redmond, pro-Home Rule) and an unofficial All-For-Ireland League candidate who declared himself a Sinn Feiner, though opposed to physical force. (*Irish Independent*, 11, 15 November 1916.)

without any mention of separate treatment for any Ulster county, had been passed by Parliament and signed by the king two years before. Ireland's contribution to the war effort and not least her repudiation of the 1916 rebellion, which had been partly suppressed by Irish troops, gave her a moral right to have the Home Rule Act put into legal effect forthwith. (It had, after all, been agreed in 1914 to suspend it only for twelve months, or, if the duration of the war were longer, only until its end. Few had thought it would last so long.) The shedding of blood in the common cause was taken to have redeemed Ireland from any Amending Bill. But the only response her sacrifice had elicited from the government was an actual diminution of the Home Rule Act involving the exclusion of six Ulster counties and the repudiation of the basic nationalist idea of an undivided Ireland. In other words all the government offered was a simple return to the pre-war situation. Ireland's gesture for the common cause might just as well never have been made. Reasonable, however, as the Home Rule case might seem morally, it was wholly out of touch with current political reality. Ulster Unionists, as a result of the coalition, had a far stronger control over the government than they had ever had in 1914. And the susceptibilities or even the moral rights of Irish nationalism were not considerations in which they were interested. The only future for Irish nationalism in fact now lay in coming to terms with this reality one way or the other – either by accepting it with the sacrifice of six counties it entailed, or by working out clearly and precisely what contesting it would involve and deciding to accept that or not as the case might be. Very few Home Rulers had yet done this.

Meanwhile, Redmond's own continued preparedness to accept, for a 'temporary' phase, an exclusion of six Ulster counties strained far more seriously than ever before the ties of loyalty binding the movement to him as its leader. Indignant protests against the whole principle of partition now poured in from responsible local bodies and authoritative moderate nationalists all over Ireland. Disapproval came too from the many staunch Southern Unionists it threatened to isolate. The *Irish Times*, the leading organ of Unionist opinion in Ireland, while saying that the situation was so difficult that Home Rule must wait until the end of the war, had totally rejected the idea of a divided Ireland as any sort of possible solution. Unionists, it said, accepted that the Home Rule Act was on the statute book and realized they must accept the inevitable; they were 'patriotic Irishmen and intended to live in their country unless and until they were driven out by intolerable misgovernment'. But,

If we are to have self-government, Ireland must be a self-governing unit. That instinct is implanted deeply in the heart of every thoughtful Irishman, Unionist or Nationalist. In the first place the country is too small to be divided between two systems of government. In the next place, the political, social and economic qualities of North and South complement one another; one without the other must be miserably incomplete. For Southern Unionists ... the idea of the dismemberment of Ireland is hateful. ... In a word, the permanent partition of our country is inconceivable.[1]

If these were the feelings of Southern Unionists, those of Irish Nationalists of every description can well be imagined. As an orthodox Home Ruler had written, 'a thrill of horror and amazement' had been felt throughout the land at the new exclusion proposals.[2] He said that it was Redmond's lack of contact with opinion in Ireland that had already made possible 'the unholy alliance of Sinn Fein and Liberty Hall', but insisted that, should he now fail to save his reputation as leader, 'there are men enough left in Ireland still to carry on the constitutional fight, who, with God and justice on their side will act with courage and refuse at any cost, all and every invitation to compromise'.

Just over a week later this correspondent wrote again to the *Irish Independent* saying that the formation of some new organization in Ireland was imperative, and the following day another correspondent also called for a national organization for those Nationalists who had 'lost confidence in the leaders of the so-called Nationalist party'.

An 'Anti-Partition League' was formed and, on the day of Casement's execution, at the beginning of August 1916, it changed its name to the Irish Nation League. But there were as yet no new leaders to lead these newly-impassioned Home Rulers, some of whom in their anger were already beginning to enlarge their concept of what Home Rule should mean to 'Colonial Home Rule', or a position analogous to that of Canada or Australia within the Empire. Without leaders and without any precise new policy, a stronger popular nationalist spirit than ever before was now abroad. Spontaneous searching for a new policy and new methods began to take place at the grass roots of the old movement. 'People are beginning to think and act for themselves,' wrote the *Galway Observer*, unconsciously evoking again Davis's old slogan of Sinn Fein. And the *Mayo News*, independently and without any need of help from Griffith or Sinn Fein, said of the Nationalist Party that they 'would have been much better employed in the last month cutting turf at home than promenading in the House of Commons'. Indeed, the paper thought it might well be better for Ireland not to send her representatives there at all but rather to 'take a lesson from the Covenanters by binding our Parliamentary representatives to form themselves into a National Council to promote National interests without any regard to the antics of the Westminster Parliament'. The new Irish Nation League, said the paper, would have to decide whether or not Irish representatives should sit at Westminster.[3]

Throughout this new ferment Redmond had remained silent, and when

he did finally choose to break his silence it was on 6 October, the anniversary
of Parnell's death, a day inevitably evoking some comparisons with that
earlier Home Rule leader's firmness and intransigence. Redmond's speech
was embarrassingly unimpressive. He referred to his vigorous critics as
'about the vilest excrescence that ever yet appeared in the body politic in
Ireland', and at the end of his speech ostentatiously tore up a list of questions
that had been handed to him and threw the fragments on the floor.⁴ In what
now seems an almost unbelievable failure to gauge the mood of the moment
he complacently confided: 'Now I will tell you a secret about myself.
For the last six weeks or two months I have been practically out of public
life. I have been lying in the purple heather and trying to entice the wily
trout out of the water, and trying to circumvent the still more wily grouse.
I have really seen little of the newspapers.'⁵ He seemed totally unaware that
the time had gone by when he could live off political capital like that. Three
weeks later the expanding Irish Nation League promulgated in Dublin its
constitution and objectives. Its first aim was 'to secure the National self-
government of Ireland without any partition of the nation', and its provisional
constitution declared that Irish MPs should 'if called on to do so, withdraw
from Westminster'.

And yet some indication of the size of the political capital which Redmond
and the old Parliamentary Party had accumulated over so many years was
demonstrated the following month in the by-election at West Cork, the
first since the rebellion. The result was actually a gain for the pro-Redmond
candidate over the other (independent) Home Ruler, the narrow victory being
made possible by the intervention of the self-styled Sinn Feiner. The significance of the result in the light of later developments undoubtedly lies in the
strength revealed of Home Rule nationalism whether or not discontented
with Redmond. In the course of the by-election the anti-Redmond candidate
– F. J. Healy, one of Tim Healy's brothers – powerfully expressed the
nature of anti-Redmond Home Rule sentiment at that time. Speaking of the
150,000 Irish soldiers (90,000 of them Catholics) who up to that date had
served in the war, he declared: 'I glory in their fame. I take pride in their
glory; but was it fair for a man who boasts himself leader of the Irish people
not to tell these men on their way to Flanders, "I have blown the bugle for
you, and when you come back, your country will have shrunk from thirty-
two counties to twenty-six."?'⁶

Such representative indignation was easily enough expressed. It was less
easy to see how the British Government could ever be persuaded to revert
to that thirty-two county concept on which every Home Rule Bill had been
based. It became less easy than ever the following month when, in a political
crisis over the conduct of the war, Asquith was ousted as Prime Minister
by Lloyd George, the very man who had given Carson the pledge of permanent six-county exclusion. Carson himself entered the government. Walter

Long, the staunch Ulster Unionist supporter, became Colonial Secretary, and Curzon, Milner and Bonar Law, all of whom had urged Ulster resistance to the point of defiance of the constitution in 1914, became members of the War Cabinet.

Later in December the new Prime Minister, as a Christmas gesture of goodwill designed to encourage the Americans to enter the war, released those 560 rebellion prisoners who had not been specifically sentenced by court-martial, but were being held in Britain without trial. They were all back in Ireland by Christmas Day. Their release caused no great stir in Ireland though there were some cheers for them at the quayside and on arrival at their homes. Among those few who had been held in Reading gaol and who looked wan and sickly as a result was Arthur Griffith, the founder of the pre-war Sinn Fein organization. Most of the internees had been held at a camp at Frongoch in Wales, and were in good health. Among them was a young man of twenty-seven from West Cork named Michael Collins, of whom few people in Ireland had ever heard. He was disappointed to find that in Clonakilty, the town nearest his home, only two people wanted to shake him by the hand.[7]

Collins had started his career as a clerk in the British Civil Service and had lived in London for nine years until the beginning of 1916, latterly working as a bank clerk for an American company in the City. He had become a London member of the IRB in 1909, and, having got wind of the coming rising, and not wishing to be conscripted in England under the new Conscription Act, had returned to Ireland in January 1916. He had taken part in the Rising and had been in the burning Post Office with the leaders to the end. In a letter from his prison camp at Frongoch in Wales a few months later, while expressing personal admiration for some of the leaders, especially Connolly and MacDermott, he strongly criticized the actual conduct of the Rising as being 'bungled terribly' and suffering from 'a great lack of very essential organization and cooperation'.[8] He was himself, within four years, to become the most effective organizer of armed rebellion in Irish history.

The political climate to which the prisoners returned had changed dramatically since that day eight months before when they had been marched off to the Dublin quays, sometimes to the jeers, sometimes merely to the curious stares of the Irish people. But the returning men themselves could present as yet no clear-cut offer of leadership. Their views as to future policy varied considerably. They included exponents of the orthodox constitutional Sinn Fein doctrine of pre-war days as preached by Griffith; they included Irish Volunteers who had simply obeyed orders at Easter, but whose views were more accurately represented by MacNeill than by the signatories of the Republican Proclamation; they also included other Volunteers, many of them under-cover members of the IRB like Michael Collins, who were determined to bring about an Irish Republic at all costs. They had virtually no organization at all, apart from such reorganization of the IRB as had taken place at Frongoch with Collins's participation and that was by definition secret and aloof. Collins himself now became Secretary of the National Aid Association, a body which Tom Clarke's widow Katherine had organized on the prisoners' behalf while they were away and which provided a further temporary framework in which extremists could work. But nothing like a coherent political organization yet existed to coordinate the new mood.

However, an opportunity for political action very soon presented itself. J. J. O'Kelly, the old Member of Parliament for Roscommon who had first sounded out Parnell for John Devoy, had died. A by-election was due there at the beginning of February 1917. A candidate to stand against Redmond's man in the constituency was found in Count Plunkett (a Papal count), father of that Joseph Mary Plunkett who had been executed after the rebellion and of two other sons then in English gaols. The Count had himself just suffered the indignity of being expelled from the Royal Dublin Society for his sons' activities. It shows the confused and blurred nature of Irish nationalist opinion at this time that the man who defended him staunchly at the Royal Dublin Society and led the unsuccessful vote against expulsion was a supporter of his Redmondite opponent in the by-election.[9] Griffith, Collins and other returned prisioners threw themselves energetically into the election to try to capture anti-Redmond Home Rulers' votes for Plunkett.

Plunkett stood on no very clear policy at all, stating frankly that his claim on them was 'as the father of his dead boy and his two sons who were suffering penal servitude'.[10] Griffith was unable to persuade him to declare that if elected he would refuse to attend at Westminster and it was in fact urged on Plunkett's behalf, at one election meeting at least, that his return would not only be good for Ireland but for the Irish party's influence on English politics.[11] The nearest thing to a policy for Ireland that was put forward on his behalf was the argument that he would be the ideal man to represent Ireland at the International Peace Conference which would follow the war.[12] But the bulk of dissident Nationalist votes were concerned about only one thing: namely, voting *for* a man who would not accept the partition of Ireland in any form whatever, and *against* a party which had shown itself too easily duped into doing so.

A number of practical factors were to Plunkett's disadvantage. His opponent, the party candidate, was a local man well known in the constituency. Moreover, Plunkett himself, who had been deported after the rebellion, remained in England sick until only a few days before polling. It was here that the energy put into his campaign by Griffith and Collins and other recently released Irish Volunteers stood him in good stead. They had bad weather to contend with and much of the constituency was snow-bound. But there was a noticeable enthusiasm at many of Plunkett's meetings and the opinion on the eve of the poll was that he would win.

He won, but the size of his majority amazed everyone. He received almost twice as many votes as Redmond's man. It was only at a celebration rally after the result that Plunkett declared that he had been considering whether or not to represent the people of Roscommon 'in a foreign parliament', but had decided that his place was beside them in their own country, 'for it is in Ireland that the battle of Irish liberty is to be fought'. How exactly it was to be fought, no one was too particular to inquire. At the conclusion of the rally, the crowd sang Davis's old song: 'The West's Awake'.[13] Press comment throughout Ireland was to the effect that the writing was now on the wall for Redmond's party. Nevertheless, there was still no proper organization with which to oppose him. 'There now exists,' wrote Collins at about this time, 'a wilderness – ripe for any advancement along the road to salvation.'[14]

There were certainly some signs that the IRB itself was at work. On Easter Monday 1917 a Republican flag (the orange, white and green tricolour) was flown at half-mast over the ruins of the GPO, and many holiday-makers passing down O'Connell Street raised their hats to it or waved handkerchiefs. Small posters reproducing the wording of the 1916 Republican Proclamation appeared all over the city with the words at the bottom: 'The Irish Republic still lives.' The Dublin mob responded with a certain amount of haphazard stone-throwing at police and troops.[15] But if the party were going to be challenged on a nation-wide scale, and if that mass opinion which had shown itself ready to be wooed away at the Roscommon by-election was to be successfully wooed all over Ireland, something much more effective and politically mature than this sort of activity had to be devised.

Ten days after Easter an 'Irish Assembly' was convened by Count Plunkett at the Dublin Mansion House. Over 1,200 delegates attended, and sixty-eight public bodies were represented, together with forty-one of Griffith's Sinn Fein clubs. The dominating note struck was the need to submit Ireland's case to the Peace Conference at the end of the war and to form some sort of organization for the next General Election. However, the most that could be practically agreed about such a future organization was that an organizing committee should be formed to establish it. At the same time there was an affirmation proclaiming Ireland a separate nation and asserting her right to freedom from all foreign control and denying the authority of any foreign parliament in Ireland.

This was, of course, taking the Irish national demand far beyond the Home Rule Act on the statute book. It might reasonably have been wondered how a British Government, which would not even agree to implementing that act without excluding six Ulster counties, was going to be brought to accept a far wider measure of independence without the same exclusion.

But the prevailing mood was not one to be precise about the future. In so far as doubts arose, they were generally silenced by the notion that an international Peace Conference summoned to conclude the war for the rights of small nations would impose its will on Britain to give Ireland the freedom she demanded. Certainly there was a total refusal to accept publicly even the possibility that physical force against the British Government might be required.

The *Irish Independent*, Ireland's biggest daily newspaper, which while deploring the rebellion and standing for Home Rule had long dissociated itself from Redmond, loosely referred to the men who had met in the Assembly as 'what is now known as the Sinn Fein party'. But a party organization and, more important, detailed policy, still had to be constructed. Meanwhile, the *Independent* itself gave an example of the prevailing mood of imprecise and optimistic thinking among nationalists. For it too extended its own national aims from the limited Home Rule of the act on the statute book to 'Colonial Home Rule' on the Canadian or Australian pattern. Again, it was not made clear how a British government which could not accept the lesser measure without partitioning the country could ever be brought to accept the greater. The paper was even less precise than Sinn Fein, going so far as to repudiate specifically the nearest thing the new 'Sinn Fein' grouping had to a constructive policy, namely that of abstention from Westminster. Plunkett had now declared this to be an indispensable commitment for all members of such new organization as might form his committee.

In this imprecise and optimistic national mood a further electoral test now presented itself – a by-election at Longford. Here the candidate chosen by Plunkett's committee, with the organizing experience of the Roscommon election behind them, was not even one who was able, as Plunkett had been, to put in an appearance at the last moment. For he was Joe MacGuinness, at the time a prisoner serving penal servitude in Lewes gaol for his part in the rebellion, and his name went before the electorate in the simple slogan: 'Put him in to get him out!'

MacGuinness, a Longford IRB man, had no wish to let his name go forward in the election at all. He felt that to do so would be to compromise the traditional republican attitude of contempt for parliamentary methods. And his refusal to stand was backed up by almost all his fellow-prisoners in Lewes gaol.[16] Michael Collins, however, in the interests of strengthening the Republican hold over the developing political movement, blandly ignored MacGuinness's refusal and went ahead with the election campaign on his behalf. Collins's preoccupation as a Republican at this time was with the need to preserve the new political movement from the relatively moderate ideas of Arthur Griffith, with whom he had been having some 'fierce rows'.[17] He now implored his only supporter among the prisoners in Lewes, Thomas Ashe, the rebel commander in the fight at Ashbourne in 1916, not to let them think that 'Master A.G. is going to turn us all into eighty-two-ites'.*

In fact, many old-style Sinn Fein devotees worked hard together with Griffith and Collins in the Longford election. Collins himself made use of his IRB control over the re-forming Volunteers to provide a body of enthusiastic campaign workers to rival the Redmond party machine. But perhaps the most decisive and, for the future, a most significant intervention on Mac-Guinness's behalf came from another quarter. It came in the form of a letter to the press on the eve of polling day from the Archbishop of Dublin, Dr W. J. Walsh himself. The Archbishop solemnly warned anyone who thought that partition had been abandoned as practical policy by the politicians that he was living in a fool's paradise.[18] Between two candidates, one of whom represented Redmond and the other of whom was in Lewes gaol, there could thus be little doubt as to who the Archbishop preferred. The new movement, embryonic, imprecise and even self-contradictory as it might be, now had all the indispensable respectability of the Catholic Church behind it.

The electrifying result of the by-election after a recount was that MacGuinness had won by thirty-eight votes over the Redmond candidate. Flags, illuminations, bonfires, blazing tar barrels and the singing of national songs took place all over Ireland in celebration of the victory.

A few days later the British Government and Redmond made one more attempt to reach an agreement over the Irish national demand. Redmond's political manoeuvrability had now been considerably circumscribed by the prevailing mood in Ireland. Clearly he could no longer afford to consider partition on any terms, and when the first half of Lloyd George's new offer proved to be one again involving exclusion of the six north-west counties of Ulster – to be reconsidered after a period of five years – Redmond had no alternative but to reject it out of hand. But the second instalment of Lloyd George's offer broke new ground. It had actually originated in a proposal of Redmond's.

Redmond, in rejecting partition this time, had let it be known that in his view the only hope was some sort of conference or convention at which Irishmen of both North and South should by themselves work out their own solution. Picking up this suggestion Lloyd George declared that if such a convention could reach 'substantial agreement' then he would accept whatever the terms of that substantial agreement might be. It was a tailor-made Lloyd George formula, combining surface plausibility with apparent concession while throwing the onus of success on to other shoulders than his own. Appearances were then of particular importance to Lloyd George, for with the United States at last entering the war in April 1917, it was urgently necessary, as the British Ambassador in Washington constantly reminded

*i.e., believers in the 1782 Constitution of King, Lords and Commons of Ireland.

him, to make the American contribution effective by showing that the war really was one for the sanctity of engagements and the independence of small nations.[19]

But beneath the surface plausibility, the chances of success for the convention, which was to meet in Dublin from July 1917 to April 1918, never looked bright. From the start, the two positions which needed to be reconciled – those of the Ulster Unionists and of all Irish nationalists – were totally irreconcilable. The government had driven Redmond up to and possibly beyond his farthest practical limit of concession long ago in 1914; it was now virtually impossible that he could carry Irish opinion with him on any form of exclusion of Ulster counties, however limited in time and place. At the same time, with Carson and so many other staunch Unionists in the government, the government was less than ever in any position to force any further concession from the Ulster Unionists beyond the abandonment of the three Ulster counties they had so reluctantly agreed to in 1916.*

The only possible room for manoeuvre left lay between the Nationalists and the Southern Unionists. The Southern Unionists did not want partition, partly on patriotic principle, and partly out of self-interest, for they did not wish to find themselves overwhelmingly isolated in a Catholic Ireland. It was Redmond's one remaining hope that if he could reach agreement with their leader, Lord Midleton, Southern Unionists themselves might bring pressure on the Ulster Unionists to abandon their inflexible attitude. Alternatively, it was possible that if agreement were reached between Redmond and the Southern Unionists, Lloyd George might interpret this as sufficiently close to 'substantial agreement' to put pressure himself on the Ulster Unionists to close the final gap.

But before the convention could get down to its deliberations a further event occurred to make them seem blighted.

Another by-election was pending, this time in East Clare, and another of the 1916 prisoners was selected as the Sinn Fein candidate to stand against Redmond's man there. This prisoner was the last of the surviving commandants of Easter Week, Eamon de Valera, whose death-sentence had been commuted to twenty years' imprisonment. The very day after it was announced that he would be standing, de Valera was included in an amnesty along with the 117 remaining other prisoners of Easter Week – an amnesty granted as a gesture of goodwill by the Lloyd George Government to create a favourable climate for the convention.[20]

This time, often to their amazement, the released prisoners received a rapturous welcome in Ireland. They were escorted through the streets of

---

* In fact, in the same month in which Carson joined the government, Lloyd George and the rest of the cabinet had been prepared to put Home Rule for all Ireland into effect at once with the sole proviso of a further review of the situation in five years' time. The proposal was vetoed by Carson; Lloyd George promptly dropped it.

Dublin by enthusiastic crowds, cheering and waving small orange, white and green tricolours.[21] The *Westmeath Independent* noted that 'Sinn Fein, whatever it may ultimately end in, for the present has caught the fancy of the country. Sinn Fein clubs are springing up as mushrooms.'

One specific thing at least which 'Sinn Fein' stood for was made clear by de Valera, who got down to electioneering in East Clare the day after his return. It was not himself they were supporting, he declared, but the principle for which he stood – the complete independence and liberty of Ireland.[22] Both he and MacNeill who campaigned for him totally repudiated Lloyd George's 'Convention'. How precisely 'Sinn Fein' intended to bring Ireland's complete independence and liberty about was left vague. De Valera's opponent in Clare, a popular local man named Lynch, in fact challenged him to say whether he was for the policy of revolution or for what was known as constitutional Sinn Fein. What, he demanded, was his alternative to a programme involving violence? And a speaker campaigning for Lynch in Ennis chided the Sinn Feiners with the 'audacity' of asking the electors to endorse a policy that was not yet formulated. But that, of course, was a large part of 'Sinn Fein's' attraction. The disgruntled electors themselves were not too clear where they wanted to go, and audacity was about all they demanded.

Griffith, speaking at a Westmeath Sinn Fein Convention during the Clare election, made the chief issue whether to seek for Ireland's independence at the inevitable post-war Peace Conference or in the English Parliament. This, he said, would be the main issue at the next general election.[23] The idea of appealing above the British Government's head to an International Peace Conference was indeed a sweepingly idealistic one suitable to the prevailing Irish mood. But de Valera, electioneering in Clare, kept even vaguer options open. They were not dependent on the Peace Conference alone, he said at Corofin on 1 July, '... they expected something good from it, but while waiting they would be able to do a good deal in making John Bull uncomfortable'.[24] Some days later, however, he complained that his opponents were trying to frighten the voters by saying he meant to lead the young men into an abortive rebellion and declared that the formation of a representative National Council to select delegates to the Peace Conference was the immediate political task. He told how a voter had said to him,

'Mr de Valera, I would vote for you but for fear you are going out in rebellion in a week or two!'

He replied: 'Can anyone be so stupid as to believe that?' adding that there was no fear of another Easter Week as it had accomplished its purpose.[25] The policy of abstention from Westminster was little mentioned.

The tall, austere, bespectacled figure of the young de Valera quickly impressed the Clare electorate personally, though almost all they knew about him was his record in the rebellion of the year before. Additional glamour attached to him from two small incidents during the campaign. Once narrowly escaping a collision between his motor-car and a runaway horse and trap, he jumped out and gave chase and captured the animal. On another occasion he gave prompt assistance to the occupants of a trap whose restless horse was threatening to overturn them.[26]

Two special features of the campaign were remarked. The first was the conspicuous number of young and middle-aged priests attending de Valera meetings; it was to one of these that an English correspondent heard an old farmer put the question: 'Is there another rising in the air, Father?' To which the priest replied with great seriousness: 'God forbid, Pat! We want no more bloodshed and we won't have it.'[27]

The second feature of de Valera's campaign was the excellence of the Irish Volunteer organization which supported him. On polling day Sinn Fein had a large number of motor-cars at its disposal and Volunteers from other districts entered the constituency to help escort Sinn Fein voters to the polls – a precaution which paid off, for a number of attacks with sticks and stones were made by Redmond's supporters on the occupants of Sinn Fein cars, and the *Irish Independent* reckoned there would have been bloodshed but for the Sinn Feiners' restraint.

The most optimistic Sinn Fein forecasts of the result were that from the electorate of eight thousand de Valera might get a majority of about one thousand. Such would have been a remarkable victory indeed. In fact the result was a landslide, giving de Valera a majority of almost three thousand over the Redmondite candidate.*

The *Cork Examiner* described it as the most surprising result since the ballot had been instituted. De Valera, appearing on the steps of the courthouse at Ennis in Volunteer uniform, told the huge crowd waving Republican flags: 'You are worthy descendants of the Claremen who fought under Brian Boru, with the same spirit in your hearts today that your fathers had a thousand years ago!'

In paying a tribute to those who had helped organize the campaign, he echoed the sort of ambivalent language that O'Connell had employed on the occasion of another famous Clare election. Of the Volunteer effort he said they had showed they could have a little military organization, and 'these habits of discipline and organization were worth more for a nation than anything else'.[28]

In Dublin the news of the result was received with wild enthusiasm. Handkerchiefs were waved, walking-sticks and hats flung in the air, and motor

---

* The figures were: de Valera   5,010
                       Lynch   2,035
                                   ───────
                       S.F. majority 2,975
Eighty-seven per cent of the electorate voted.

and horse traffic brought to a standstill.[29] The rejoicings throughout the rest of Ireland were, according to the *Irish Independent*, 'unprecedented in the history of Irish political contests'.[30] Symbolic of the deep emotional springs that were touched by the event was a pietistic visit by Carlow Sinn Feiners to the croppies' grave there.*[31]

* See above, p. 103.

2
The New Sinn Fein
(July 1917–April 1918)

Precision about the exact political future was still comfortably avoided. In personally pinning his colours to an Irish Republic, de Valera seemed to do so undogmatically.

'Until the Irish people declare that another form of government is more suitable,' he said at Mullingar soon after his victory, 'the Irish Republic is the form of government that the Sinn Feiners will give allegiance to.'[1] And though Redmondite Nationalists might complain with reason that when 'asked to say in simple words how the Irish Republic is to be raised on the ruins of the British Empire, he takes refuge in vague and impalpable generalities',[2] his argument that for Ireland's case to be heard at the Peace Conference she should first claim total independence seemed reasonably flexible to many old Home Rulers. The dominant political note of the day after the East Clare election was that Ireland was declaring for 'independence' not by revolution but by resort to the Peace Conference. As to what 'independence' itself actually meant to most new Sinn Fein supporters a writer in the *Irish Independent* of 14 July 1917 was accurate in saying that at that time 'Dominion Home Rule within the Empire would be accepted with practical unanimity by Nationalists and possibly a substantial section of Unionists would also vote for it'. The correspondent of the *Westminster Gazette*, analysing the East Clare election result, wrote that while the young genuinely did want total independence, the older voters did not think it feasible but had been content to vote for it, arguing that 'the more they ask for the more likely they are to get "Colonial Home Rule", a phrase now common in the mouths of moderate Irishmen everywhere – even in Unionist circles'.[3] He added that the Sinn Fein policy of abstentionism from Westminster hadn't really worried moderates at all, because the Irish party at Westminster had proved so totally ineffective against a combination of the two British parties anyway. He predicted, incidentally, that there would be no split between the de Valera–Volunteer type of Sinn Fein and the Griffith–Plunkett type until after the end of the war.

And if any moderate Irishman, disillusioned with Redmond, should momentarily raise an eyebrow at the way in which young men at the end of Sinn Fein meetings increasingly arranged themselves in military formations and marched off in fours singing national songs into the countryside, he could find reassurance enough in de Valera's definition of the reconstructed Volunteer body's task, namely that they would be 'the best protection that England could not come and rob them' of their rights.' This was, after all, the very purpose behind the mass Volunteer movement of 1914 in which all ardent Home Rulers had joined after the Curragh mutiny. And when at the beginning of August 1917 Colonel Maurice Moore again presided over an Irish National Volunteer Convention of 176 companies in Dublin, he called for a healing of the split of three years before and a reconciliation with the Irish Volunteers, implying that it was logically one movement again. The reality of his contention received some substantiation from the British Government ten days later when the Irish National Volunteer headquarters in Parnell Square, Dublin, were raided together with Catholic halls all over the country, and the rifles and other arms in them seized. The arms of the Ulster Volunteer Force in the North were, of course, not touched, and the *Irish Independent* remarked: 'This fact like the immunity enjoyed by the UVF in the past is setting people furiously to think.' If there was to be one law for the Unionist and a different law for the Nationalist, it seemed all the more logical for all Nationalists to be in the same boat.

The result of yet another by-election, this time in Kilkenny, declared just before the raids, had shown a further consolidation of the new nationalist front. The Sinn Fein candidate, William Cosgrave, had been fairly confidently expected to win, but even so it had hardly been expected that his victory, which turned out to be a two-to-one majority, would be so decisive, and once again there were enthusiastic celebrations in many parts of Ireland involving Volunteer parades and the singing of national songs in which the song of the 1916 rebels, 'The Soldiers' Song', increasingly figured.

The increasing efficiency and self-confidence of the newly reconstructed Volunteers was indeed beginning to disconcert the authorities. Predictable counter-measures were set in motion by them with the inevitable result of increasing their prestige among all Nationalists still further. Arrests for drilling began. Austin Stack, the commandant of the Tralee Volunteers, who, faithfully observing orders, had failed to rescue Casement from his police cell in the town the year before, was arrested and sentenced to two years' hard labour for wearing Volunteer uniform at a demonstration at Ardfert on the first anniversary of Casement's execution. Three thousand Volunteers of whom two hundred were on bicycles and three hundred on horses had attended the ceremony and the road from Tralee to Ardfert had been thronged all day, with orange, white and green colours visible everywhere. Sean MacEntee, the former Redmond supporter sentenced to death

after the rebellion, was now court-martialled for a recent speech at Drogheda
in which he, however, maintained he had simply advocated peaceful means
to obtain a Republic, telling the meeting that Ireland's status would be
recognized at the Peace Conference and that any further resort to violence
and rebellion would not be necessary.[5] Also re-arrested at this time, for a
speech at Longford, was Collins's associate, Thomas Ashe, who after his
release with all the other 1916 prisoners in June had been elected President
of the Supreme Council of the IRB.[6] By the middle of September 1917 there
were over thirty such Volunteers, or Sinn Fein prisoners, in Mountjoy gaol
serving sentences from six months to two years for drilling or making so-
called seditious speeches.

The Volunteers were controlled, in so far as they were centrally controlled
at all, by their own executive which included Collins and the reconstituted
IRB machinery. But more often than not they acted with local individual
spontaneity, and they now lent assistance to the new political movement in
a form even more valuable than the practical organization they had been
supplying at elections. They began to provide martyrs. For the repression
they invited from the authorities aroused old emotional springs of Irish
nationalism at the very moment when the mass of public opinion might
otherwise have paused and wondered whether there really was anything
coherent enough to follow in the new leaders after all. A number of contemporary political commentators had already noted that Sinn Fein's failure
to produce a really positive national policy was giving rise to serious second
thoughts.[7] But it was at this very moment that something happened to swing
sympathy towards Sinn Fein more markedly than ever before.

The prisoners in Mountjoy gaol, curiously perhaps in view of the Sinn
Fein insistence that there was no need for a further resort to arms, were
demanding for themselves treatment as 'prisoners of war'. An explanation
was that since no such special status as 'political prisoner' was recognized
by the authorities, 'prisoner of war' was the only recognizable status by
which they could be distinguished from common criminals. The prison
authorities adhered strictly to their own regulations which recognized no
distinction between anyone sentenced by the courts and placed in their
custody. The Volunteer prisoners, however, refused to work or wear prison
clothes and eventually, after some smashing of cell windows and organized
singing of national songs, resorted to the old suffragette weapon of the hunger
strike. The prison authorities again applied their own regulations and began
what was officially described as 'artificial' or forcible feeding. Some forty
prisoners were soon being subjected to the procedure. Large protest meetings
were addressed in Dublin by de Valera, by Cathal Brugha, recovered from
his wounds of Easter week, and by Griffith who did not hesitate to make
clear in the course of them that he had disapproved of the rebellion.[8]

The warders in Mountjoy were not brutal, but did their duty. The practice of regulation forcible feeding involved the strapping of a prisoner to a chair at the elbows and below the knees, the placing of an eighteen-inch rubber tube either via the mouth, or if the prisoner refused to open his mouth, via the nostrils down his throat and the pumping of two eggs beaten up in a pint of warm milk into the stomach by some twenty to thirty strokes of a stomach pump.[9] The whole business took between five and ten minutes. The prisoner usually vomited at first when the tube went down his throat. If fed through the nostrils, the nose and throat invariably bled.

Austin Stack, then the official leader of the prisoners in Mountjoy, thus described at the time what happened to him personally on Tuesday, 25 September, at the hands of the doctor in charge that day. This doctor was by all accounts more than usually maladroit.

He got the tube down eventually. I was unable to see as water was running from my eyes, and with the pain and a kind of vomiting I could not see what was going on. When he took up the tube I vomited about a quarter of a pint of liquid. I thought I had been fed then; when the doctor came again and asked me to open my mouth I said, 'What for? Haven't I been fed?' He said : 'No, not yet.'

While the doctor made another attempt, Stack thought he 'seemed to be using more force than skill, grinding his teeth practically'. His finger reached down his throat almost to his neck. When the operation had been completed Stack heard a warder call out. 'Ashe next'.[10]

Thomas Ashe had spent fifty hours the previous week deprived of his boots, bed and bedding as a punishment for insubordination. However, the prison medical officer had passed him as fit: '... fit for close confinement, fit for scale punishment no. 1 and 2. Also deprivation of mattress, fit for restraint in handcuffs, waist belt, muffs, restraint jacket or jacket in splints.'[11] Ashe had first been forcibly fed on Sunday, the 23rd, when like every other prisoner he found the experience very unpleasant and painful. He told the doctor he was sorry to see him reducing a noble profession to the level of an executioner. Stack had given orders to the prisoners not to resist the operation physically. The only struggle was between the doctor and the tube. When Ashe was released from the chair after following Stack on Tuesday, 25 September, he felt ill and weak and another doctor, meeting him on his way back to his cell, allowed him to be released at once to the Mater Hospital. Within hours he was dead.

At the autopsy a bruise was found on his neck, presumably evidence of the clumsiness of the feeding doctor's exertions. Grazes and scratches also found on his cheeks were probably caused when his beard was shaved after death. The coroner's jury – which contained a number of Unionists – eventually found that Ashe had died of heart failure and congestion of the lungs, and condemned forcible feeding as 'inhuman and dangerous'.[12] Every detail of what had been done to Ashe and was being done to the other prisoners could be read by the public in the inquest reports in the newspapers.

Arrangements for Ashe's funeral were made by Michael Collins and the IRB through their cover organization, the long-standing Wolfe Tone Memorial Committee, and the occasion was made one in the tradition of the great patriotic funerals of the past: T. B. McManus, Parnell and Rossa. In fact it was generally admitted that the funeral was even more impressive than Parnell's. After Ashe's body had lain in state the day before in the City Hall, from which troops were removed for the first time since the rebellion and replaced by Volunteer guards in uniform, and where last respects were paid to Ashe by a large Volunteer contingent headed by de Valera and a group of the Citizen Army led by Constance Markievicz, the funeral took place at Glasnevin cemetery on 30 September 1917.

Almost all Dublin was in mourning, and a procession estimated at between 30,000 and 40,000 followed the coffin through the crowded streets, the hearse itself being flanked by Volunteers in uniform with rifles reversed. Immediately behind it came about 150 clergy, then 8,000 members of the Irish Transport Workers' Union, 10,000 members of various trades bodies, 9,000 Irish Volunteers, most of them in uniform and, of some significance in denoting the unanimity of the reaction of Irish Nationalist opinion to Ashe's death, a large body of the Irish National Volunteers, previously Redmond supporters, under Colonel Moore. Constance Markievicz led a Citizen Army contingent, wearing full uniform with a revolver in her belt. Orange, white and green colours were extensively worn, even by the Dublin Fire Brigade. At the cemetery three volleys were fired over the grave by a Volunteer firing party and Collins delivered the only funeral oration. It was a very short one. After a few words in Irish he said, 'Nothing additional remains to be said. That volley which we have just heard is the only speech which it is proper to make over the grave of a dead Fenian.'[13]

The efficiency and order displayed throughout the proceedings were remarkable evidence of Collins's organizing ability. The various Volunteer tingents from many parts of Ireland drilled freely and marched in military formations to and from their various assembly points in defiance of all the regulations and regardless of the presence of the police. A film taken of the volleys fired over the graveside by the Volunteers was developed in motors on the way back to the city and was on view in Dublin the same night. The whole event testified strikingly to the growing power, both emotional and material, of the new movement.

The day of the funeral de Valera, speaking at Ennis, recalled the dead man's role at Ashbourne the year before and allowed himself to strike his most belligerent note since his release. Nothing but freedom, he said, would satisfy the Irish people and they were ready to perish one after the other rather than submit to be conquered. 'I feel as certain as I stand here that I shall see, before my day comes, Ireland free!'[14]

All commentators agreed that a new and much-needed stimulus had been given to the Sinn Fein movement. 'The circumstances of his [Ashe's] death and funeral', wrote the London *Daily Express*, have made 100,000 Sinn Feiners out of 100,000 constitutional nationalists.' The *Daily Mail* remarked that a month earlier Sinn Fein, despite its success at the by-elections, had been a waning force. 'It had no real practical programme, for the programme of going farther than anyone else cannot be so described. It was not making headway.... Sinn Fein today is pretty nearly another name for the vast bulk of the youth of Erin.'

Because of the war and the abrupt drop in emigration, there was a far higher proportion of that youth in Ireland than there had been for generations.

While the Volunteers grew bolder in public – 1,500 of them parading and marching through Cork with officers and many of the rank and file wearing uniforms and bandoliers – the political half of the movement set out to give itself a more plausible coherence at a great convention in Dublin at the end of October 1917. It was attended by about two thousand people, including delegates from over a thousand Sinn Fein clubs. All it really revealed was a commendable degree of professional skill in political management. Where a contest had been anticipated between de Valera, Count Plunkett and Griffith for the presidency of the new Sinn Fein organization which was here formally constituted, all the public saw was a display of brotherly sweetness and light as both Plunkett and Griffith stood down by agreement in de Valera's favour. The formal Sinn Fein constitution revealed itself as no more free of unresolved ambiguities than the movement had been since its inception. But it was to Sinn Fein's advantage to offer as vague and wide a political platform as possible. Thus, while it was known that Sinn Fein stood for 'total independence' and de Valera himself and many of his Volunteer comrades for a Republic, the wording of the new constitution was designed to placate moderates when it declared that Sinn Fein aimed 'at seeing the international recognition of Ireland as an independent Republic, and, having achieved that status, the people might by referendum, choose their own form of Government, when they would deny the right of the British, or other foreign Government to legislate for Ireland'.

A further aim was 'to make use of every available means to make impotent the power of England to hold Ireland in subjugation by military force or otherwise'. This significantly produced one of the few discordant notes in the meeting.

One of the several priests present moved an amendment to this part of the constitution to the effect that after the words 'every available means' should be added the words 'which in the judgement of the National Council are deemed legitimate and effective'. As the rule stood, he said, it might cover anything 'from pitch and toss to manslaughter' and they did not want Sinn Fein sullied by 'any crime or outrage'.[15]

This touched on the most awkward area in the minds of many who, while prepared to vote for Sinn Fein, feared that some of the Volunteer activists in the movement would lead Ireland into fresh violence. Another priest seconded the amendment, saying it was a slander to say, as some people did, that they were a secret society.

Now the movement had just benefited from a great access of public support, largely thanks to the discipline and organizing ability of a secret society deep in the heart of it, though this fact was, of course, unknown to all but a handful in that convention hall. And Collins and other IRB men and Volunteers had no squeamishness whatever about any methods that might be required to win an Irish Republic. But the majority of the Convention's opinion was almost certainly behind the sense of the two priests' amendment. For when voting took place for the twenty-four members of the Sinn Fein executive council MacNeill, who had opposed the rebellion of the year before and believed that the Volunteers should resort to violence only in their own defence, easily headed the poll by more than two hundred votes over his closest rival, the more uncompromising Cathal Brugha. Collins, himself not yet widely known, only just scraped on to the council in twenty-fourth place.[16]

De Valera's first major political task therefore was to placate the moderate majority in his movement while leaving as free a hand as possible to those who gave that movement effectiveness and practical organization. Now in the cooperative mood of this first convention the two priests' amendment presented him with no very severe test. He declared righteously that they were not going to truckle to anyone who insinuated such things as that they were really a secret society.[17] And inasmuch as de Valera himself now saw no need for the IRB, and declined to remain a member of it after the rebellion, this was an honest expression of intent, though he must have known something of the extent of Collins's activity and have been aware of its value to the movement.

He kept a wary option open, however, on the use of violence itself, adding that 'available means' meant 'justly available in the minds of all Irishmen'. Cathal Brugha followed him in reply to the amendment. Brugha also disapproved of further use of the IRB, on the grounds that now that there was an open Republican party, with its open Republican army (the Volunteers), secrecy was unnecessary and dangerous. But he was in fact as implacable in his belief in unsanctioned violence as any Fenian who had ever sworn allegiance to an Irish republic, as his record the year before proved. Nevertheless, he now echoed the overall mood of the conference by saying that they did not intend to meet English rule by assassination.[18] The Sinn Fein

Convention concluded in an impressive display of superficial unanimity with the Chairman, Griffith, maintaining that they would never break the moral law, and a tumult of cheering greeting MacNeill's election to the Council at the head of the poll.

A few days later de Valera was telling a meeting at Baillieboro' that there were no differences in Sinn Fein. 'They were all out for one and the same thing – to get international recognition for a free and independent Republic. The methods ... were any methods and means in accordance with the moral law and the will of the Irish people.' On the question of physical force he maintained that Irishmen had a perfect right to arm and defend themselves against any attempt to impose conscription on Ireland:

Nothing would please John Bull better than that they should put it into their minds that physical force in any shape or form was morally wrong. ... As to the word 'constitutional', they had no Constitution of Ireland. The English Constitution was not theirs and they were out against it. What he understood as Constitutionalism was that they should act in accordance with the will of the Irish people and the moral law. Their movement was constitutional in that sense.[19]

With such skilled ambivalence did the new movement more or less successfully conceal for the time being its crucial discrepancies.

As a self-sufficient organization the Volunteers held a convention of their own, at the same time as the Sinn Fein Convention. Further to convey an impression of unified identity for the whole Sinn Fein movement, de Valera was elected President of the Volunteers as well as of Sinn Fein, while Brugha, Sinn Fein's Vice-President, was made Chief of Staff. But the unity was far more apparent than real. Brugha himself was a split personality in his dual role. For all his moderation towards a Sinn Fein Convention he was always to regard the Volunteers as an instrument for wresting an Irish Republic from England by physical force. Furthermore Collins, with identical views, was now officially made the Volunteers' Director of Organization. And utilizing the IRB network which Brugha thought redundant, Collins was increasingly to become the effective force in the central control of the Volunteers, placing other competent activists in key posts.

A letter for which Collins and the Volunteer Executive had been responsible a few months earlier caused some embarrassment when it came to light in the late autumn of 1917, inducing a critical priest from Wexford to raise that question which, he said, every man and woman in Ireland should ask themselves, namely: 'What does Sinn Fein stand for?'

'The principle duty of the executive,' this Volunteer executive letter dated 22 May 1917 had declared, 'is to put them [the Volunteers] in a position to complete by force of arms the work begun by the men of Easter Week ...'. the Volunteers are notified that the only orders they are to obey are those of their own executive.' They were reminded that in the past the conjunction of Fenianism with constitutional politics had led to the abandonment of physical force as a policy and were warned to join Sinn Fein only in order to propagate the principles of their own organization which was the only one to which they owed allegiance.[20]

De Valera applied himself to this difficulty with that evergrowing combination of dexterity and single-minded integrity which was to be his particular political talent. He pointed out with technical correctness that the letter had not been written by the present executive and that he had himself been in Lewes gaol at the time, but then added typically that there was in fact nothing in that document that he himself would not put his name to and that it was Sinn Fein's own policy to proclaim that only sovereign independence would satisfy the aspirations of the Irish people.[21] The need to discuss the crucial issue of physical force was thus somehow obviated.

Within the Volunteer movement itself there was little doubt both among the organizers and the younger and active rank and file that physical force would in the proper time be used to assert Ireland's sovereign independence. Sinn Feiners who were not Volunteers were sneered at.[22] To reassure opinion de Valera would himself point out in public that the Volunteers were a completely distinct and separate organization from Sinn Fein, as if this and his own dual role somehow clarified rather than obscured the political future. But the truth was that the situation carried real dangers. The Volunteers themselves, drilling, studying manuals of British field tactics, starting up their own local companies quite independently of any central organization, even unashamedly shocking the local Sinn Fein supporters by their audacity, were going their own way from early 1917 onwards, sometimes unamenable even to their own executive's discipline in Dublin.[23]

De Valera's attempt to reassure public opinion over the opaqueness of the political future was by no means wholly successful. The Irish correspondent of the *Westminster Gazette* commented that any Irish Parliament would split into several groups and that 'of the Sinn Fein voters at elections there are a large number who deprecate under any circumstances, barring attempted conscription, a resort to armed force'.[24] Cardinal Logue warned that 'an agitation ill-considered and Utopian' had sprung up and was spreading, and that if persevered in it would 'entail present suffering, disorganization and danger and is sure to end in future disaster, defeat and collapse'.[25] To redress the balance de Valera strove to win over more constitutional Nationalists by saying that though some who lived for their national interests might still feel bound up with the British Empire, this was no reason not to agree to differ about ways and means with other Nationalists and still march shoulder to shoulder with them.[26] But *The Times* noted that in Mr de Valera's 'scholastic hands' Sinn Fein was losing much of its political force.[27] And a correspondent wrote to the *Irish Independent* warning of the consequences of Sinn Fein trying to win Irish independence on the field of battle, saying that it could not be done, but would bring upon Ireland 'dire misfortune and untold horrors, and ruin and devastation, and the demon of civil strife'.[28]

From the beginning of 1918 raids for arms by independent groups of Volunteers began to be reported from different parts of the country. At the end of January a stud farm near Bansha in County Tipperary was raided by about twenty masked men calling for 'arms for the Irish army', but otherwise behaving in a scrupulously correct manner, taking neither valuables nor money and apologizing to the owner's secretary.[29] A month later more masked men – including one of Count Plunkett's surviving sons – cleared the armoury and one thousand rounds of ammunition from Rockingham House near Boyle. Other Volunteers had long been buying or stealing individually British service rifles from individual British (often Irish) soldiers. In February 1918, a new activity loosely carried out under the auspices of Sinn Fein but recalling more ancient aspects of the Irish struggle began to disturb many moderates in the movement.

In the name of necessary precautions against famine, parties of men in the countryside, but particularly in the west of Ireland, began driving cattle off private grass land and commandeering it in the name of the Irish Republic and ploughing it up for food cultivation. Compensation was offered to the landlord and was often agreed, but where there was a dispute the last word tended to lie with whoever could produce the bigger battalions. Ironically, one such dispute took place on the land of the first ever President of Sinn Fein, Edward Martyn, the friend of Yeats and Lady Gregory, at Tulyra in County Galway. Martyn got an injunction from the courts to prevent local Sinn Feiners ploughing up his land after he had freely offered them one field which they had turned down as unsuitable.[30] Evidence that there were stronger, more independent forces at work in this activity than those merely of the Sinn Fein political movement was revealed when the Standing Committee of Sinn Fein, after conceding that most cattle drives were 'no doubt justifiable', declared that some had taken place without due regard to the circumstances and that 'foolish or indiscreet action' was to be deplored. By the end of the month County Clare had to be declared a special military area and the town of Ennis itself was under curfew with troops lining the streets.

Not only the government but the local Sinn Fein Executives themselves tried, increasingly in vain, to keep things under some sort of control. But a lawlessness reminiscent of the old days of the Land League or even the Defenders was soon rife in that part of Ireland. Offences up before the Clare Grand Jury at the beginning of March included cattle-driving, raids for arms, ploughing-up of poor people's land, firing into houses and intimidation. Two men in Kerry were even arrested under the old Whiteboy Act. And a man living with his wife and child in a remote part of County Roscommon woke to find that a warning grave had been dug on his land.[31]

Though some of this activity gained crude popular support for the movement and sympathy for the Volunteers in the countryside – crudest when, as
in a few cases, individuals were actually able to help themselves to land –
the growing signs of anarchical violence were an embarrassment to Sinn Fein
and a liability to its attempts to woo moderate but disgruntled Home Rulers.
At the beginning of March the headquarters staff of the Volunteers had
directed not only that the raiding of houses for odd guns was strictly prohibited but that Volunteers should not take part in cattle drives as such
because these were 'neither of a national or a military character'.[32] A week
later Collins himself, speaking in County Longford, expressly stated that the
raids on homesteads by Sinn Fein or Volunteers were not only not sanctioned but carried out in direct opposition to the leaders. But the rest of his
reproof was hardly an assurance to the moderates. If, he said, the Volunteers
wanted arms they would not have to resort to such methods of raiding farmhouses for useless old shotguns and rusty weapons.[33] Drilling and the acquisition of arms by more sophisticated means in fact proceeded apace. Raids
unauthorized by headquarters also recurred from time to time.

All this activity led to a substantial increase in the number of arrests made
for offences such as illegal drilling, unlawful assembly, raiding for arms and
cattle-driving. Prisoners in court who were almost always members of the
Volunteers usually refused to recognize the court's authority, declaring that
they were soldiers of the Irish Republic, and generally disrupting proceedings
by singing the 'Soldiers' Song', smoking and refusing to remove their hats.
In the middle of March two of Collins's key men in the organization, Oscar
Traynor and Richard McKee, received three months' hard labour for illegal
drilling.

That the organization itself was continuing both to recruit successfully
from the numbers of young men in the country who in more normal times
might have been emigrating, and to increase its efficiency, was displayed convincingly at three more by-elections that took place in the early part of 1918.
These also served to give some indication of the degree of success Sinn Fein
was having in winning over disgruntled Home Rule supporters, though their
results represented something of a check to its hitherto annihilating progress.

The electors in fact, if they were beginning to see reasons for disillusionment with Sinn Fein's lack of constructive policy or alarm at its anarchical
tendencies, were in something of a dilemma. For the only political alternative,
the old Nationalist Party, had done nothing to restore its fortunes in the
Convention summoned by Lloyd George, which had made no relevant progress and was soon to founder totally in disaster. The negotiations themselves had run a predictably calamitous course. Quite apart from the inbuilt
irreconcilability of the two chief attitudes to be negotiated, the total boycott
of the Convention by Sinn Fein had further seriously undermined its plaus-

ibility from the beginning. However, Redmond by great perseverance did succeed finally in reaching agreement with Midleton and the Southern Unionists. But he achieved it only at the price of new concessions over a Home Rule government's power to impose taxes. At a time when opinion was moving beyond the concept of Home Rule altogether a further diminution by Redmond himself even of such Home Rule as was at least on the statute book seemed preposterous. Moreover, Redmond had risked the concession without any categorical assurance from Lloyd George that the government would back the Nationalist and Southern Unionist agreement against the Ulster Unionist demand for permanent exclusion. The furthest Lloyd George had gone was to say that if in the end the only opposition to Home Rule for all-Ireland came from the Ulster Unionists then he would 'use his influence with his colleagues ... to accept the proposal and give it legislative effect'.[94]

Once again, it was a palatable Lloyd George formula without substance. The Prime Minister's 'colleagues' when he gave that assurance included Carson and Bonar Law. More and more Redmond seemed manoeuvred out of the political ring altogether. We now know that the Ulster Unionists in the Convention had all along had a definite assurance from the government through Carson that they were not to be bound by any majority vote and that 'without their concurrence no legislation was to be founded on any agreement between the other group in the Convention'.[95] In other words Lloyd George's promise of legislation on 'substantial' agreement allowed substance only to the Ulster Unionists. Any new ground that might have been opened up by the Convention had really been cut from under it from the beginning. It finally collapsed altogether in April 1918. Midleton, the Southern Unionist leader, afterwards asserted that the Southern Unionists would never have participated in the Convention at all if he had realized that it was thus committed in advance to Partition.

Redmond, humiliated and defeated, did not live to see the Convention's formal closure. After a short illness and an operation for gallstones he died in London in March 1918, a saddened and bitterly disappointed man, confronted with the ruin of all his patient hopes. Staunch and generous-hearted, he had brought the cause of a popular and practical Irish nationalism inherited from O'Connell, Butt and Parnell to an apparent triumph in the Home Rule Act of 1914 and had seen his triumph turn to ashes.

The immediate effect of his death was to cause a by-election in Waterford – the second of three which Sinn Fein had had to fight in the early part of 1918.

None of these three by-elections could be said to provide a particularly representative cross-section of the country as a whole. And since Sinn Fein lost all three of them they drew consolation from that fact. All three defeats were at the hands of the old Home Rule Nationalist Party, but two were in

Ulster where that party's organization had for obvious defensive reasons long been more vigorous than in other parts of Ireland. Sinn Fein, on the other hand, had to build an organization from scratch there, which it did as in the 1917 by-elections by bringing in large numbers of Volunteers from Dublin and the South. On polling day in the South Armagh by-election in February there were twenty Sinn Fein motor-cars operating whose drivers carried special licences authorizing them 'to drive and use a motor-car in the performance of the duty assigned to him. In the name of the Irish Republic – Signed Eamon de Valera, 31st Jan. 1918.'[36]

At the last election in South Armagh there had been a Unionist vote of 1,600 there. This time the Unionist candidate withdrew, and since the Sinn Fein candidate, the IRB man Patrick McCartan, lost by 1,019 to the Nationalist in a not greatly reduced poll, it was not unreasonable to deduce that possibly the Nationalist had won only thanks to the Unionist vote, and certainly that Sinn Fein had not done badly in the circumstances.

The same sort of deduction could reasonably be made in the other two by-elections. The second defeat, in Waterford, the seat made vacant by John Redmond's death, was inflicted by his son, who campaigned in British uniform with a black armband for his father on his left arm. Not only could he command in that constituency the strongest personal loyalties of the old party but he could be reasonably sure of the greater part of the three to four hundred estimated Unionist voters in Waterford. Moreover, like all the by-elections fought before the General Election in 1918, it was fought before the extension of the franchise to all men of twenty-one and over and to women of thirty – so that Sinn Fein did not have the advantage of its undoubted wide support among the young.

De Valera, Griffith and Darrel Figgis of the Howth gun-running adventure bore the brunt of the campaigning for Sinn Fein in Waterford. De Valera made the tart point that there was little likelihood of the Parliamentary Party obtaining Colonial Home Rule when they had failed to get 'even the miserable Bill that is at present on the statute book'.[37] Captain Redmond's main line of attack was that Sinn Fein meant 'anarchy and destruction'. When de Valera charged him with being an English officer Redmond replied that he was an Irish officer and that anyway he had a high regard for English officers who fought for their country but none for a hybrid American who would not fight for the Stars and Stripes.[38]

There was a certain amount of violence in the election, the Sinn Fein candidate being hit on the head with a stick by a soldier when travelling on an outside car with de Valera and having to have his wound dressed in hospital. De Valera himself had a large block of wood thrown at him on one occasion and a number of Volunteers were severely beaten up. Captain Redmond won by 478 votes in a total poll of just over 2,000.[39]

Taking into account the Unionist votes, the old franchise and the personal element in this constituency, it was by no means a decisive defeat for Sinn Fein. And when the Mayor of Kilkenny hoisted the municipal flag over the Town Hall there to celebrate Redmond's victory, the local Volunteers in a confident counter-demonstration seized the building, hoisted the orange, white and green tricolour in its place and held the building for a day. Equally indicative of an old order changing was the actual hauling down at Balting-lass of a green flag hoisted there to celebrate the Nationalist victory and its burning amid the cheers of the crowd.

A further defeat for Sinn Fein in the Ulster constituency of East Tyrone was hardly regarded as a setback for they had not even intended to contest the election at first, but on deciding to test the strength of Sinn Fein support there won over 1,200 votes in a poll of about 3,000. The following Sunday a body of about five hundred Volunteers carried out manoeuvres in the Dublin mountains quite unhindered and undismayed.

The recent by-elections demonstrated that Sinn Fein, while not perhaps gaining democratically and even causing a certain number of second thoughts among potential supporters, was still a very vital political force. If its strength lay perhaps more in the enthusiasm of the Volunteers than in its electoral policies, from now on things were to be made easier for it by the British Government.

3
Conscription Crisis to General Election (December 1918)

By April 1918 the disaster suffered by the British armies in France as a result of the German March offensive was the War Cabinet's chief preoccupation. The situation was desperately serious and replacements for the extremely heavy casualties were imperative. The cabinet understandably began to reconsider whether conscription should not, after all, now be extended to Ireland. The decision to do this was announced on 9 April.

The predictable effect was to unite the whole of nationalist Ireland against the measure, and strengthen Sinn Fein, the newest political force in the field, with all the vigour of the new protest. The blurring of all nationalist feeling into a Sinn Fein image – the very objective for which de Valera and others had been striving for the past nine months – was now virtually achieved in a matter of days.

Lloyd George, incredibly, offered as a sop to such sentiment a simultaneous Home Rule Bill on the partition principle. Never perhaps had British insensitiveness to Ireland been more blatantly illustrated. The effect was to add insult to injury on a gigantic scale. The very words with which the Prime Minister chose to introduce this part of his measure rang with the bitterest irony in former Home Rulers' ears after what had happened in the past four years.

'When the young men of Ireland are brought into the fighting line,' he declared, 'it is imperative that they should feel they are not fighting for establishing a principle abroad which is denied to them at home.'[1]

This had been the essence of Redmond's case and of many tens of thousands of his followers in supporting the war effort and volunteering for the British Army. Now the British Government, having rejected that case, when the Irish were enlisting voluntarily, was prepared to concede it in order to purchase their agreement to compulsion.

As the Irish bishops under Cardinal Logue immediately declared in unanimously condemning conscription: 'Had the Government in any reasonable time given Ireland the benefit of the principles which are declared to be at stake in the war, by the concession of a full measure of self-government, there would have been no occasion for contemplating forced levies from her now.'[2] Local public bodies from all over Ireland condemned conscription as 'unjust', 'tyrannous', 'fatuous' and 'insane'. On 16 April, the day on which the new Conscription Bill passed through Parliament, the Irish Nationalist Party left the House of Commons in a body in protest and returned to Ireland. Such a leaf out of the Sinn Fein abstentionist book could hardly fail to add to the credit of Sinn Fein plausibility.

On 18 April an unprecedented type of conference took place at the Mansion House, Dublin, at which all sections of nationalist opinion were represented: Devlin and Dillon for the Nationalist Party, de Valera and Griffith for Sinn Fein, Healy and William O'Brien for the dissident element in the old Home Rule Party and three representatives for Labour. After adjourning to consult personally with the Catholic hierarchy which was simultaneously meeting at Maynooth, the Conference issued the following unanimous declaration: 'The attempt to enforce conscription will be unwarrantable aggression which we call upon all true Irishmen to resist by the most effective means at their disposal.'[3] The Catholic hierarchy themselves issued a statement saying that conscription thus enforced was 'an oppressive and inhuman law' and that the Irish people had a right to resist it by all means consonant with the law of God.[4]

In such an atmosphere a greater degree of tolerance at least inevitably developed in the attitude of moderate Sinn Feiners towards the activities of the Volunteers. The first two Volunteers had in fact been killed in a raid for arms on a police hut in County Kerry four days after the announcement of conscription for Ireland.[5] Near Dublin masked men held up a motor-car in which a load of 250 lb. of gelignite was being transported and removed it. In Tipperary on the initiative of a local Volunteer, Dan Breen, raids on private houses were stepped up in spite of all the headquarters executive's previous orders. 'We generally went at night and asked for the arms,' he wrote afterwards. 'Those who would have liked to refuse knew they dare not. Many others gave them willingly, and some even sent us word to call for them.'[6] In County Cork a young Volunteer named Liam Lynch, who was to become one of the most uncompromising militant republicans of the next few years, though he had not in fact committed himself to the Republic until after the 1916 rising, chose this moment of the conscription crisis to give up his regular job and devote himself entirely to preparation for an eventual armed struggle.[7]

When canvassing for the next pending by-election began early in May – a contest between Sinn Fein and the party in East Cavan which broke the temporary alliance achieved over conscription – the Volunteers were out in force in support of the Sinn Fein candidate who was Arthur Griffith himself. One thousand Volunteers paraded in the town of Cavan and two thousand in Kilnaleck at the very start of the campaign which did not promise to be anything like a walk-over. Not only was the old Nationalist Party well-organized as in all Ulster constituencies, but there were reckoned to be some 1,000–1,500 Unionists out of an electorate of 9,000, many of whom in the absence of a Unionist candidate would cast an anti-Sinn Fein vote for the party. But political circumstances were strongly in Griffith's favour. With the conscription crisis at its height it was a bad moment for the party to try to make an issue of the British Parliament's importance to Ireland as against the Sinn Fein policy of abstention and an appeal to an eventual Peace Conference. More important, the British Government once again played into Sinn Fein's hands, for when polling day came in the middle of June Griffith himself, together with most of the other new leaders, including de Valera, was again in prison in England.

The *Manchester Guardian* appears to have got wind of what was about to happen when on 12 May a new Viceroy, Lord French, and a new Chief Secretary, Short, arrived in Dublin to take up their appointments. It wrote that the government was preparing for 'some very evil work in Ireland. . . . If not restrained it will within a few short weeks undo, and much more than undo, all the progress which has been made since Mr Gladstone first undertook the work, in the pacification of Ireland.' It went on to say that the government was about to produce an Ireland 'more ungovernable except by main force, more exasperated in feeling, more alienated than any with which this country has had to deal since the Rebellion of 1798'.[8]

The prediction was soon to come horrifyingly true.

Within five days of his arrival, French, the new Viceroy, issued a sensational proclamation declaring that there was in Ireland a 'German Plot', and that Sinn Fein had been found to be in treasonable communication with the German enemy. Drastic measures, the proclamation insisted, would have to be taken to put down 'this German Plot, which measures will be solely taken against that Plot'. Seventy-three of the leading Sinn Fein political activists, including Griffith and de Valera, were arrested during the night.

It was an indication of how far the government was out of touch with Irish opinion, at this critical stage, to think that the majority of the Irish people would be convinced by such reasoning. In fact, of course, the effect was highly favourable to Sinn Fein, for the immediate conclusion drawn was that the government had struck at Sinn Fein because they were the really powerful force in the anti-conscription movement. While it must be remembered that, from the British point of view, this action took place at perhaps the most critical point in the whole war, with the German armies driving forwards in an offensive that was within days to have Rheims half-encircled and constitute a menace to Paris itself, yet even the most loyal government supporters found the allegation of a plot hard to swallow. Wimborne, the replaced Viceroy, made no secret in the House of Lords of his scepticism, and when the government responded to various challenges by producing its evidence the plot looked thinner than ever. Much of the 'evidence' consisted of a repetition of the long-known contacts between the 1916 rebels with Germany before the rebellion; and those details which were concerned with communications on Irish affairs between the German Embassy in Washington and Berlin *after* April 1916 all referred to dates on which de Valera and all the other Sinn Fein leaders had been in English gaols or internment camps. The only direct evidence adduced personally against de Valera was a public speech he had made in which he had said the Volunteers must be ready to take advantage of any German invasion of *England*.

There was, however, one additional item of evidence that did seem relevant. In the second week of April a member of Casement's pathetic Irish Brigade, named Dowling, had been picked up on the west coast of Ireland after landing from a German submarine in a collapsible boat. He had brought a message from the Germans intended for the Sinn Fein leaders, inquiring about their plans and offering assistance. Dowling had been arrested before the message could be delivered. In fact, though some individual Volunteers knew of Dowling's pending mission, the mission itself was clear enough evidence that de Valera and his colleagues were *not* in contact with the Germans, for the essence of the message was that the Germans were in the dark. But used in conjunction with earlier events and de Valera's public statements, the government, perhaps understandably, thought it provided an adequate excuse to try to stifle the whole Sinn Fein movement. More subtle acquaintance with the emotive factor in Irish history might have made them weigh more carefully the long-term disadvantages of such action.

From this moment onwards Sinn Fein began to make further electoral advances. Polling in the East Cavan by-election took place on 19 June. The fact that the Sinn Fein candidate, Griffith, was now in gaol, though the government had announced that none of the prisoners would be tried, was of course a great additional asset to him. The Sinn Fein campaign organizers had been confidently expecting to win by a majority of 500. There was a high poll. When the result was announced, Griffith had a majority of 1,204. Again, bonfires blazed that night on the surrounding hills and all over Ireland.

The arrests had also brought about one other result that was to have great importance for the future. Advance warning of the impending arrests given by a nationalist-minded detective at Dublin Castle, named Kavanagh, had reached Michael Collins. Collins had passed it on to the Sinn Fein Executive, which had been meeting that night in their headquarters at 6, Harcourt Street, Dublin. Most of the leaders decided to accept arrest, correctly assessing that this would work politically to Sinn Fein's advantage.[9] Only those who were thinking militarily rather than politically about the future decided to avoid arrest and these included Collins himself, his close IRB friend

Harry Boland and Cathal Brugha. The result was to give the surviving organization of Sinn Fein a more militant and uncompromisingly republican leadership beneath the surface – an influence not in itself weakened by a personal rivalry which was to develop between Brugha and Collins.

It was from this moment onwards that Collins, now 'on the run' though he made occasional appearances in public at political meetings,[10] began to assert a dominant control of the 'underground' organization of the movement, equal to that of de Valera and Griffith in the political field. The continuing strength of the organization in the country was manifested when, in spite of a proclamation at the beginning of July declaring Sinn Fein, the Irish Volunteers and even the Gaelic League dangerous organizations, Sinn Fein meetings continued to be held defiantly throughout the country. The police sometimes interfered and made arrests and sometimes took notes. When the military raided a Sinn Fein Hall at Charlestown, County Mayo, and removed a large tricolour flying from an upper storey, the newspaper report of the incident concluded: 'Shortly afterwards another flag was hoisted in the same position and remains there.'[11]

Arrests and sentences multiplied and with them the popular prestige of Sinn Fein and the Volunteers, now seen more and more generally, however imprecisely, as one movement. Crowds outside the courts invariably shouted 'Up the rebels!' or waved tricolour flags. A cinema was prevented from showing the film of Ashe's funeral or the scenes in Dublin when the rebel prisoners had returned from England the year before.[12] The proprietor of a concert party was sentenced to two years' imprisonment by a court-martial for singing 'seditious songs', which term was used indiscriminately to include 'Wrap the Green Flag round me, boys' (an exile's song of the American Civil War), 'God Save Ireland' and 'The Soldiers' Song'. As a Sinn Fein spokesman declared to a group of journalists at the beginning of October 1918, there were by then five hundred people in Ireland imprisoned under the Defence of the Realm Regulations on charges ranging from singing a song written seventy years before to presenting their names in Irish when accosted by a policeman. But Sinn Fein's growing power was demonstrated most forcibly in a more effective field.

The success of the anti-conscription campaign had made the government temporarily abandon the idea of immediately implementing conscription for Ireland. But with the legal power to do so now in their possession they kept the threat of it permanently in the background, to Sinn Fein's continued advantage. The decision not to enforce it immediately had been conditioned perhaps less by sensitiveness to Irish susceptibilities than by a sudden change of fortunes in the war. For the Germans, who had been on the Marne at the end of May, were by the end of June being driven back in the retreat which was to bring them to sue for an armistice on their own frontiers a few months later. And, though the full scale of the allied success was not yet known, as an experiment a new voluntary recruiting campaign was instituted in Ireland, with the aim of raising fifty thousand new recruits there. The campaign got into full swing early in August with well-known Nationalist MPs in uniform, such as Arthur Lynch (once condemned to death for his part in raising a pro-Boer Irish Brigade in the South African war) and Stephen Gwynn, speaking to large meetings. Sinn Fein organized an efficient and systematic counter-campaign to reduce the meeting to chaos and prevent the speakers from being heard.

Historical hindsight now leads us to take the political success of Sinn Fein at this period so much for granted that it is instructive to note the difficulties with which it still had to contend in order to achieve that success. This last recruiting campaign is a case in point. The meetings were, more often than not, successfully broken up by small organized groups of articulate Sinn Feiners operating from strategic positions in the crowd.[13] But though the authorities got nowhere near their target of fifty thousand recruits, it is revealing to note the success they did have. Even during 1917 when disappointment with the Home Rule failure was so rapidly breathing life into the new movement the British Army, without any particular campaign at all, had managed to secure 14,013 voluntary recruits from Ireland.[14] Now, in the peculiarly unfavourable atmosphere produced by the conscription threat, the German plot and the arrests of the leaders in addition to the systematic campaign against recruiting so efficiently managed by Sinn Fein, it succeeded in getting more than eleven thousand recruits in eleven weeks.[15] The weight of nationalist opinion of the old Redmondite school was still by no means contemptible. And it now became the principal task of Sinn Fein to win over as much of it as possible in the General Election announced for December 1918.

The calling of this election in an immediate post-war atmosphere entailed many adverse conditions for Sinn Fein, including the arrest of consecutive Sinn Fein Election Directors and the censorship of part of the Sinn Fein manifesto. But in another respect the speed with which the election was called acted in Sinn Fein's favour. Very many soldiers on leave or otherwise separated from the units had not received their postal voting papers by the close of the poll, even though this was extended for soldiers for a further fortnight after the rest of the electorate had voted. In London, for instance, it was reckoned that by the end of that fortnight only about one-third of the soldiers' votes there had been cast and this was thought to have been typical of the rest of the country.[16] The figure for Ireland was often even lower. In North Wexford only one-sixth of the absent voters cast their votes; in south County Dublin one-fifth.[17] And it seems probable that many of the Irish soldiers' votes would have been for the old Nationalist Party rather than Sinn Fein, still often thought of as 'pro-German'. The torpedoing of the Holyhead mail boat in the last few weeks of the war by a German submarine with the loss of over four hundred Irish lives had not added to the popularity of being thought pro-German. Although on Armistice night itself in Dublin there had been nothing worse than wordy discussions between those wearing orange, white and green colours and other celebrating crowds, two nights later the Sinn Fein headquarters in Harcourt Street, Liberty Hall and the Mansion House were attacked by hostile crowds, many of whom were Irish soldiers, and the rooms in Harcourt Street were totally wrecked, after which troops were temporarily confined to barracks. The premises had been wrecked, admitted Harry Boland, one of Collins's closest collaborators who had been inside the building at the time, but they had not wrecked Sinn Fein.[18] And the subsequent election campaign was to prove him right.

Sinn Fein was also much favoured in the election by the greatly enlarged new register which almost trebled the previous Irish electorate.* For the first time the vote had been extended to all males over twenty-one without other qualification and to women over thirty. A higher proportion both of young people and of poor people were voting than ever before – the numbers of young men being in any case swelled by the virtual suspension of emigration during the war.

Another telling factor was that in the course of the election campaign itself Sinn Fein was already revealed as the winning party. Not only did a number of prominent Nationalists of the old school publicly come down in its favour, such as William O'Brien and Colonel Maurice Moore of Redmond's National Volunteers, but in no fewer than twenty-six constituencies the Nationalist Party failed to muster even sufficient enthusiasm to raise a candidate. And these twenty-six constituencies representing nearly a quarter of the total Irish electorate had thus gone to Sinn Fein even before polling day. The manifesto, for all the mutilations of the censor, made clear that Sinn Fein stood for an Irish Republic and that its elected candidates, refusing to attend at Westminster, would form a national assembly in Dublin, which would appeal to the Peace Conference. However, probably what most Sinn Fein voters were voting for was simply the greatest measure of independence, without partition of the country, which Ireland could get. If pressed, in the manner of modern opinion polls, as to what they thought they would actually be prepared to settle for, the majority would probably have replied: 'Dominion Home Rule', as a minimum. If asked the awkward question: 'How did they expect the British Government to concede this without the exclusion of six Ulster counties?' they would probably have given the Sinn Fein reply: 'By an appeal to the Peace Conference.' The one thing they were certainly not voting for was an attempt to win sovereign independence by force of arms or a campaign of terrorism. This was a goal

* The Irish electorate was now 1,931,588 compared with 698,098 on the old register. Some 800,000 of the new voters were reckoned to be women. (*Irish Independent*, 5 December 1918.)

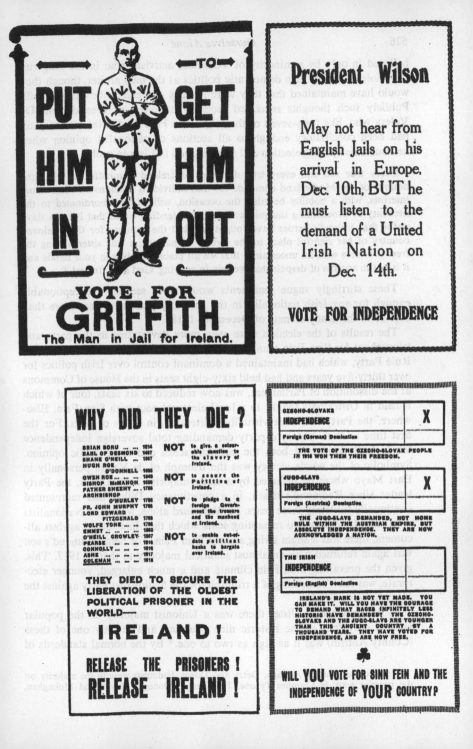

believed in only by a minority of Volunteer activists, who in the long run
saw violence rather than democratic politics as the final arbiter, though they
would have maintained that they were thereby expressing the national will.
Publicly such thoughts remained tactfully unvoiced or even denied. De
Valera who, like forty-seven of the other Sinn Fein candidates, was in gaol,
had been conciliatory enough to all sections of nationalist opinion when
he issued his opening election call from his cell in Lincoln gaol.

Every true son and every true daughter of Ireland is mindful of what the
honour of the Motherland demands ... that individual opinions and individual
interests, with a nobility befitting the occasion, will all be subordinated to the
necessity of proclaiming unequivocally to an attending world that it is no slave
status that Ireland's heroes have fought for, but the securing for their beloved
country of her rightful place in the family of nations, a true sister among the
free. It is thus with no uncertainty that we all place ourselves in your hands and
it is not in accents of despair that we join in praying 'God save Ireland.'[19]

These stirringly vague sentiments would have seemed unexceptionable
enough for any Irish nationalist in the past fifty years and were more than
ever so in the heady climate of December 1918.

The results of the election were even more devastating to the party and
triumphant for Sinn Fein than anyone had expected. The Nationalist Home
Rule Party, which had maintained a dominant control over Irish politics for
over thirty-five years and had held sixty-eight seats in the House of Commons
at the dissolution of Parliament, was now reduced to six seats, four of which
it held in Ulster only thanks to a local electoral pact with Sinn Fein. Elsewhere, the Party had been virtually obliterated, in terms of seats. For the
first time in Irish history a party demanding total sovereign independence
for Ireland dominated both the political scene and Irish public opinion.
Symbolic of the whole victory was the triumph of de Valera personally in
East Mayo where he defeated by a large majority John Dillon, the Party
leader since Redmond's death, in a constituency Dillon had represented
continually for thirty-three years. In Waterford alone, where the Nationalists
won one of the only two remaining seats which they had fought against all-
comers, there was a slight swing against Sinn Fein. For here Redmond's son
was again returned with an almost identical majority to that of 1917. This,
given the prevailing Sinn Fein climate and a much enlarged, younger electorate, was itself something of a triumph for the Nationalist Party against the
overwhelming trend.

In the province of Ulster there was a Unionist majority on the popular
vote in only four of the historic nine counties, and in only one of these
(County Antrim) was it as high as two to one.* By the normal standards of

---

* In Counties Antrim, Armagh, Derry and Down, Unionists were in the majority on
the popular vote; in Counties Tyrone, Fermanagh, Donegal, Cavan and Monaghan,

democracy this could hardly be said to justify such special treatment for six counties as would invalidate the nationalist principle for which the rest of the country had overwhelmingly voted. This seemed particularly so when such special treatment would itself create a much larger (Nationalist) minority within those six counties than the Unionists of those six counties represented within the whole of Ireland.

As to the overall result, suggestions made at the time and since that a low poll indicated considerable Nationalist abstentions and thus gave a misleading impression of Sinn Fein ascendancy cannot be upheld. The poll of seventy-three per cent in constituencies where there was a contest was around the average for Irish general elections in the past.[20] Thus, given the known low figure on the postal vote (which certainly did favour Sinn Fein) the percentage of ordinary voters may even be said to have been a little higher than usual. And though there was some disfranchisement owing to Sinn Fein candidates having been returned unopposed in 25 of the 105 constituencies, unopposed returns had long been a normal feature of Irish elections. There had been 63 of them in the last election in 1910, almost all returning members of the Nationalist Party. In short, Sinn Fein had taken over the party's place. There was, however, one important detail about the results that is often overlooked, but which held significance for the future. Though Sinn Fein, with a popular vote of 485,105, had won nearly all the Nationalist seats, 237,393 Nationalists, voting for the Nationalist Party, had still voted against Sinn Fein and an Irish Republic.[*21]

Nevertheless, the results were sensational. And when they became fully known one of those priests who had for the past two years been so active in the new movement, Father Michael O'Flanagan, a Vice-President of Sinn Fein, declared: 'The people have voted for Sinn Fein. What we have to do now is to explain to them what Sinn Fein is.'[22]

This would have been easier if Sinn Fein itself had known more precisely. The ambiguity of the movement, particularly where the role of Collins, Brugha and the other militant Volunteers was concerned, was largely concealed, and totally unresolved. Moreover, little thought seemed to have been given to the one aspect of the Irish situation which had hardly changed since the summer of 1914: namely, the British Government's refusal to include in any concept of Irish nationalism the six north-east counties of Ulster.

Meanwhile, Harry Boland, Collins's lieutenant, and an IRB man tried to

---

Nationalists (either Sinn Fein or the old Nationalist Party) were in the majority on the popular vote. In all these counties except Fermanagh the majority on the popular vote reflected the majority in terms of parliamentary seats. Fermanagh returned one Unionist and one Nationalist seat.

* The total anti-Republican vote, including Unionists, was 557,435 or a distinct majority over Sinn Fein. This latter figure, though, is not of great significance for the vast majority of Nationalist voters would almost certainly have voted Sinn Fein rather than Unionist.

persuade those who had voted Nationalist to accept Sinn Fein henceforth, saying that their differences were only in method and not in principle.[23] But the force of this depended rather on the extent to which Nationalists felt obliged to apply principles to methods.

4

Sinn Fein in a Vacuum
(January–May 1919)

The whole emphasis of the victorious Sinn Fein movement as the year 1919 opened was on the hope of securing Ireland's right to self-determination from the forthcoming Peace Conference. The American President, Woodrow Wilson, was expected to be the dominating figure at the Conference and he had long made clear his own special concern for the rights of small nations. Thus it was with a sense of righteousness and respectability that the majority of the Irish people now faced the future under the leadership of Sinn Fein. The paper *New Ireland* declared: 'If Irishmen today wish to prevent recourse to armed rebellion they should throw themselves whole-heartedly into the present Sinn Fein movement.'[1]

A sense of emotional inheritance from earlier historic attempts to assert Ireland's identity was fed by the presence in gaol of thirty-four or nearly half of her newly-elected representatives. And at one of the many meetings soon being held to protest against this fact, Harry Boland provided an answer to that question that might be in some supporters' minds as to what action could be taken if Ireland's case was not admitted to the Peace Conference after all. There were, he declared, twenty-five million Irishmen in America and they would insist on President Wilson's ideas being carried out.[2]

Meanwhile, the government disregarded all protests and the prisoners remained in gaol. Only Count Plunkett was immediately released and allowed to return to Ireland.

On the other hand, the authorities did stop the pursuit of those members of Sinn Fein who had escaped their net at the time of the 'German plot' the year before. Almost their last attempt was made on Collins himself on 6 January 1919 when he was addressing a prohibited protest meeting at Dunmanway in County Cork. Police and soldiers charged the crowds with batons and fixed bayonets but Collins escaped. He had, quite unknown to the authorities, just been helping to re-organize the very militant Cork Volunteers into three separate brigades.[3] The next day he appeared, with other Irish MPs who were still at large, in the Dublin Mansion House to make arrangements for the projected summoning of an Irish National Assembly or Dail Eireann. The authorities did not interfere and in fact released after three hours one of the wanted men they happened to have picked up in Cork that morning.[4] In the Mansion House that day the representatives pledged themselves 'to accept nothing less than complete separation from England in settlement of Ireland's claims', and to abstain from Westminster.[5]

The tense but reserved atmosphere of the beginning of a long duel now settled over Ireland as people waited to see both what Sinn Fein and the British Government would do next. About Sinn Fein itself the correspondent of the sympathetic London *Daily News* reported from Sligo that the two distinct movements within it were drawing further and further apart. The 'physical force men', he said, were supremely contemptuous of the main body with its 'moral force' programme and still preached their secret doctrine of fifty years before. 'They are never in the ascendant except at times of extraordinary national emotion,' he wrote with historical accuracy. 'Such a time it is only too plain to see we are rapidly approaching now.'[6] What this correspondent probably did not know, what no outsider had as yet fully realized, was the extent to which in Dublin itself the physical force men had inextricably entangled themselves in the main body.

All over the world international delegates were now being appointed to the Paris Peace Conference due to open on 20 January, but there was no official place for any from Ireland. In fact, though de Valera, Griffith and Plunkett were selected by Sinn Fein to represent Ireland there, the chances of the rest of the diplomatic world taking Sinn Fein as seriously as they took themselves were not bright. All the great powers at the Conference were specifically pledged against interference in each other's internal affairs, and by international law Ireland was unquestionably an internal affair of Britain's. It was with the minorities of the *defeated* powers that the Conference was prepared to concern itself.

The day after the Peace Conference opened, Dail Eireann, the first representative Irish political assembly since the demise of 'Grattan's Parliament' in 1800, met at the Dublin Mansion House. All other Irish MPs returned at the General Election, whether Sinn Fein or not, had been invited to attend, but only one took the trouble even to send a refusal.* Carson's name was actually called out on the roll call to some laughter. All observers commented favourably on the dignity and decorum with which the rather colourless proceedings were conducted. The London *Daily Mail* observed patronizingly of the brief speeches, which were almost entirely in Irish: 'Speaking in a difficult language, and one to which the orator is not born, is a great shortener of political proceedings.'[7]

The official Constitution of the Dail was announced. It provided itself

* A Unionist, Sir Robert Woods.

with full legislative and executive powers and a cabinet consisting of a Prime Minister, or President of the Dail, and other ministers to be nominated by him. These ministerial offices were soon to be filled – though the names were not immediately made public – by, among others, de Valera (Prime Minister or President), Arthur Griffith (Home Affairs), Count Plunkett (Foreign Affairs), John MacNeill (Industry), Cathal Brugha (Defence), Constance Markievicz (Labour), William Cosgrave (Local Government) and Michael Collins (Finance). The elevation of Brugha to the rank of Minister automatically promoted his former Deputy, Richard Mulcahy, an IRB man who had fought with Ashe at Ashbourne in Easter Week, to be the new Volunteer Chief of Staff.

It all sounded impressive enough, but it was not taken very seriously in London or, always, in Dublin. Even the normally sympathetic *Manchester Guardian* lapsed into sarcasm: 'One fancies that the Ministers of Finance, Home Affairs and all the other dignitaries will be hard put to it to find an outlet for any executive capacity they may possess.'[8]

The Dail also issued an Irish Declaration of Independence in which it linked the Irish Republic voted for by the electorate in December 1918 with that 'proclaimed in Dublin on Easter Monday, 1916, by the Irish Republican Army, acting on behalf of the Irish people'.[9] Further business included the unanimous adoption of a so-called Democratic Programme containing vaguely socialistic phrases which claimed to emanate from 'our first President, Padraic Pearse', but were more truly an acknowledgement to the memory of Connolly.[10] In addition there was a message to the free nations of the world asking for recognition of Ireland's national status, mentioning 'her last glorious resort to arms in 1916' and referring to an 'existing state of war between England and Ireland' which could only be ended when 'Ireland is definitely evacuated by the armed forces of England'.[11] It all reads rather hollow fifty years later, when the armed forces of England have still not evacuated Ireland; and it was hollow then.

At these first sessions of the Dail, Cathal Brugha presided in the absence of de Valera in gaol. He quoted Wolfe Tone to the effect that those wanting to save the country would have to do so 'without the help of those who looked to the foreigner',[12] thus ignoring the fact that looking to the foreigner in the form of the statesmen of the Peace Conference and the American electorate was the major part of Sinn Fein's official policy at that time. How in fact the Dail's noble-sounding declarations were to be made to bear any relation to reality was, as the *Freeman's Journal* reasonably pointed out, the question which dominated all other issues – that, and 'whether it is seriously proposed to take measures to give them practical effect'.[13] The real answer to the latter part of the question came that same week, though its full significance was as yet unappreciated.

On 19 January, two days before the Dail met, two RIC men who had

discovered a party of Volunteers drilling on Three Rock Mountain, Rathfarnham, County Dublin, had been knocked down as they attempted to
intervene and left bound and gagged while the Volunteers made off with
their equipment. A few days later the constables were sitting as interested
spectators of the Dail proceedings in the Mansion House.[14] They were more
fortunate than two of their colleagues in County Tipperary, Constables
McDonnell and O'Connell, who, escorting a cart carrying gelignite to a
quarry at Soloheadbeg, were set upon by masked Volunteers and shot dead
with revolvers at point-blank range. The Volunteers stripped the bodies of
their rifles and ammunition and made off with these and the gelignite. The
names of the chief participants in the attack were Dan Breen, Seumas
Robinson, Sean Treacy and Sean Hogan, and they had taken the action
entirely on their own initiative.[15]

The two Irish constables, both Catholics, one a widower with four children,
were very popular locally and had never had any connection with political
prosecutions. Their deaths aroused widespread indignation and horror, and
there was a poignant moment at the inquest when one of McDonnell's
sons asked if they had been given any time to surrender the explosives or
had had a dog's chance.[16] The coroner's jury extended its sympathy to the
relatives in their bereavement and a Tipperary priest immediately proclaimed
in church that no good cause would be served by such crimes which would
bring on their country disgrace and on themselves the curse of God.[17]
Another said that no one would deplore the crime more than the leader
of the Sinn Fein movement.[18] The action was condemned as a crime at masses
throughout Tipperary the following Sunday and the Archbishop of Cashel
in Thurles Cathedral proclaimed it an offence against the law of God. He
added: 'We pray that we may be spared a recurrence of such a deed.' In
St Michael's Church, Tipperary, another cleric, Monsignor Ryan, cried:
'God help poor Ireland if she follows this deed of blood!'[19]

Nevertheless, in spite of an offer of £1,000 reward, the killers were able
to vanish without trace until an even more sensational appearance three
months later.

The south riding of Tipperary was immediately declared a military area.
Thus the precedent was set for a pattern of cause and effect that was soon
to exercise a profound political influence. For military restrictions involving
the closing of fairs and markets, personal searches, traffic delays and other
frustrations inevitably diverted much of the original indignation at the outrage itself into more conventional anti-government channels. The pattern
was to repeat itself with cumulative effect throughout 1919, and to a large
extent solve Sinn Fein's recurring political problem for it, of how to retain
popular support in the absence of any positive political success. In fact, for
those in Sinn Fein who had always secretly intended to try to obtain a
republic by popular revolution, to create this pattern may well have been a

deliberate tactic, although clear evidence of such Machiavellian design is limited.* Certainly their objects were often more successfully served by the British authorities' reaction to Volunteer exploits than by the military results of such exploits themselves.

Another act of violence took place a few days later in County Cork when an attempt was made to disarm some soldiers near their camp at Macroom. One soldier was seriously injured, a fact which caused much distress in the town, where relations between the military and civilians had always been good. The local RIC Inspector even rejected the suggestion that the Sinn Fein organization could have been responsible in any way for the raid and attributed it to 'persons whose evil instincts are apt to manifest themselves in times of marked political excitement'.²⁰ He was partly right: the raid had been carried out on the local initiative of one of the Cork Brigades, though it was one of those which Collins had just reorganized.†²¹

A pro-Sinn Fein priest had said of the Tipperary killings that 'the leaders of the popular movement were far too logical and God-fearing to countenance such crimes'.²² This reflected a widespread belief among many moderate Sinn Fein supporters at the time, and even among observers generally unsympathetic to Sinn Fein. There was a particle of truth in it inasmuch as these particular actions had been the responsibility of local Volunteers. But the belief that the leaders were incapable of countenancing such actions was, as events were soon to show, sadly astray, however superficially plausible.

At all elections up to and including the General Election of 1918 it had been constantly repeated, even by former rebels of Easter Week, that further resort to rebellion was unnecessary. Only during the conscription crisis had it been held that the Volunteers would have a right, along MacNeillite lines, to defend themselves if attacked and to prevent conscription from being enforced. But the question of taking offensive action against police and soldiers in Ireland in order to establish an Irish Republic had never been before the Irish people and if it had been at the General Election of 1918 it would have been decisively rejected. The only specific methods proposed by Sinn Fein for establishing the Irish Republic had been an appeal to the Peace Conference combined with the passive resistance involved in abstention from Westminster and the creation of a National Assembly in Ireland. In 1917, when the Sinn Fein constitution had spoken of 'every available means' to make English power impotent, de Valera himself had defined these as being 'means justly available in the minds of all Irishmen' and, a little later, means 'in accordance with the moral law and the will of the Irish people'.‡ Now the will of the Irish people had never been sounded on the issue of shooting policemen and soldiers by surprise, and the highest

---

* For some evidence see below, p. 642.
† See above, p. 629.
‡ See above, pp. 610–11.

dignitaries of the Catholic Church were continually to proclaim it as contrary to the moral law.

At a later stage in the dramatic events which were now unfolding de Valera was to state that he had only to look into his own heart to know the will of the Irish people. He was as yet too circumspect to assume responsibility for the national will quite so unequivocally and his exact position at this time on the question of violence is therefore obscure, but many of his colleagues felt no such restraints. It is a recognized principle that a revolutionary may, with honour at least, assume responsibility for interpreting the national will even against apparent national wishes, provided he sincerely and selflessly believes it to be in the national interest to do so. Of the honour, sincerity, selflessness and patriotism of men like Brugha, Collins and others of this time who were about to lead the Irish people against their will, but with some spectacular results into the most effective rebellion in their history, there can never be the slightest doubt. And the same may be said of the vast majority of those who followed them. Such men, passionately conscious of the long injustice to Irish dignity in the past, must personally be granted a wholly moral motive. The more general moral validity of their actions can only be tested by the quality of the results they achieved and by consideration of whether or not better or as good results might not have been achieved another way. They were brave men, and to expose themselves to the risk of such a test more than physical courage was required. Many of them were devout Catholics, and, to them, it was a risk which might entail eternity.

Perhaps for some such reason there was at the time, and has been in retrospect, an attempt to give the whole operation the appearance of a democratic sanction from the start. Much of this was made possible by the cloak of ambiguity which shrouded the whole movement. Men like Collins and Brugha, and indeed a large proportion of Dail Eireann, were at the same time democratic representatives elected on one understanding, and also members of a clandestinely directed organization, the Volunteers, or even of a wholly secret organization within that organization, the IRB, operating on another understanding. The fact that the general public vaguely gave Sinn Fein, the Volunteers and Dail Eireann all one identity, made self-deception easier.

Brugha and Collins each had dual identities both as Dail Eireann ministers and as directors of the Volunteers. Since they were undoubtedly democratic representatives of the people on one count, it was possible to argue that being in fact only one man each, they were equally so on the other. Brugha's duality in this respect was particularly important at the very beginning because while de Valera, the Volunteers' nominal President and President of the Dail, was still in gaol, he, the Volunteers' far more active Chief of Staff, was the Dail's Acting President.

Thus in his role as Chief of Staff of the Volunteers Brugha sanctioned as early as 31 January 1919 a directive issued to all Volunteers by Piaras Beaslai, the editor of the Volunteers' secretly-distributed journal, *An t Oglach* ('The Soldier'). This told Volunteers throughout Ireland that the authority of the nation was behind them as the Army of Ireland, that Dail Eireann as the national authority claimed that right which every theologian recognized as belonging to every free national government to inflict death on the enemies of the State, and that enemies of the State were soldiers or policemen of the British Government whom every Volunteer was entitled 'morally and legally ... to slay ... if it is necessary to do so in order to overcome their resistance'.[23] No public statement to this effect was issued by Dail Eirean or any of the leaders of Sinn Fein.

Further sanction of the national authority, and thus, by implication, of the Irish people for such actions was alleged to be available in a phrase which Dail Eireann had used in its message to the free nations of the world. This, in drawing attention to the British Government's refusal of Ireland's national demands, had described the relations existing between the two countries as 'a state of war'. This was now interpreted by Beaslai and Brugha as meaning that a state of war had been declared. Beaslai also stated later that until January 1921 no Deputy of the Dail ever objected to the activity of the Volunteers.[24] But whatever Beaslai might say at the time or later, the theologians he invoked did not support him. There could be no shortage of them in Ireland, and throughout the so-called War of Independence from 1919 to 1921 Cardinal Logue himself, the three archbishops and the entire hierarchy, together with the vast majority of parish priests, condemned bloodshed by the Volunteers as crimes and offences against the law of God. Moreover, even if it could be argued that the Dail had, however tacitly, permitted such activity, it could not conceivably be argued that the war policy thus had the democratic sanction of the Irish people. If such a drastic change in policy were to be introduced by popular representatives without further consultation with the electorate, only a most exceptional change of the circumstances could, democratically, justify it. But the only change of circumstances that in fact took place between 14 December 1918 and 31 January 1919 was a relaxation of measures against those Sinn Fein MPs who were at large, permission for Dail Eireann to sit in public and the killing of two Irish policemen on routine duties by Volunteers in Tipperary.

Writing seven years later Beaslai tried to maintain that 'as far as the situation could be said to have been forced in the direction of bloodshed it was forced solely by the violence of the British Government.'[25] If by 'violence' in this context is meant physical brutality and bloodshed the statement cannot possibly be substantiated. Of the twelve civilian deaths at the hands of Crown forces that took place in Ireland between June 1916 and the end of

January 1920 only two could conceivably be described as evidence of brutality: one death from a bayonet wound in the search of a Sinn Fein hall and the other 'while trying to escape'. Three of the others resulted from failures to answer the challenge of military sentries, two from panicky misapprehension by police and soldiers that they were under attack (at a time when they were continually under attack) and three were those of Volunteers actually engaged in attacking the police or military with firearms at the time. One man was also killed in a party driving cattle off another man's land, after the police had given repeated warnings and even fired over the crowd's heads; another while committing a burglary. In the same period sixteen police or ex-policemen and soldiers were killed, almost all in cold blood.

If, however, by 'British Government violence' is meant the refusal to take any notice at all of the Irish people's political demand for self-determination as expressed democratically in the General Election of 1918, the refusal to make any alternative political offer by way of amends, the refusal at first even to release those representatives who had been in gaol when elected – then the classical case for terrorism by the weak against the strong can reasonably be made. But it still cannot be said that the policy of terrorism was the will of the Irish people. Throughout 1919 members of popularly-elected bodies, such as urban and rural district councils, often supporters of Sinn Fein, were to express condemnation or at least dislike of what was being done by the Volunteers. It was only when condemnation and dislike for what the British Government were to do by way of retaliation began far to exceed this, that popular acquiesence in what was in reality the open rebellion of a small minority materialized. What was enacted between 1919 and 1921 was a rebellion started in the Fenian tradition of 1916, but much more subtly conducted and gradually acquiring as it developed much of that active mass political support which had always eluded separatist movements in the past.

None of this was clear at the beginning of 1919. The grim niceties required for the rationalization of terrorism were conducted behind the scenes. The Volunteer paper *An t Oglach* was a secret publication and, as for the Dail itself, no word was heard from it one way or the other about the killings at Soloheadbeg or the attack at Macroom.

Apart from its hitherto apparently abortive attempts to get into the Peace Conference, the first official exercise of autonomous power which Sinn Fein displayed was a decree banning hunting in Ireland until the political prisoners were released. The 'decree' was, for obvious non-political reasons, not altogether popular in the Irish countryside, but it was treated seriously largely because of the ability of local bodies of Volunteers to enforce it. Some hunts respectfully asked Sinn Fein to rescind the decree but to no avail. Those hunts which did try to meet encountered bands of men armed with sticks and revolvers, and a horse of the Ward Hunt was actually grazed by a bullet.[26] By the end of January hunting had been brought to a standstill for the season.

Most of the prisoners, however, remained in prison. A few in poor health were released, for the death from influenza in Usk prison at the end of 1918 of the Volunteer Richard Coleman had alerted the government to the ever-present dangers of martyrdom. Of the rest, those who were free owed their liberty not to the government but either to their own ingenuity or to that of Michael Collins and Harry Boland. At the time of the Dail's first public session Collins and Boland had secretly gone over to England and at the beginning of February pulled off a spectacular coup by personally helping de Valera and two others to escape from Lincoln gaol with a duplicate key.*

The success did much to raise the morale of all supporters of Sinn Fein in the absence of positive political achievements. And the British Government, which might easily have diminished the impact by announcing the release of all prisoners anyway, delayed another month before doing so, thus, as so often in its dealings with Irish public opinion, getting the worst of all possible worlds.

Politically the escape of de Valera concentrated attention on Sinn Fein's future action. It was a matter with which de Valera had been much concerning himself while in prison. As the most sophisticated political mind in the movement he was well aware of the potential stalemate with which Sinn Fein was confronted and, being a politician rather than a revolutionary, he had come to a political conclusion. In the light of the total failure so far of the Peace Conference idea he would go to America to mobilize what was still Ireland's greatest single asset on the international scene: the vast wealth and influence of the twenty-five million or so men and women of Irish blood who lived there. His decision dismayed Collins and Boland and the other leaders of the Volunteers and it was only with some reluctance that he eventually agreed to go to Ireland for a period first.[27] There, at a secret hide-out, he gave an interview to an American correspondent in the form of a long written answer to a single question: 'Do you believe that the statesmen in Paris will force England to do justice to Ireland?' In his reply de Valera made it clear that he was pinning his hopes on the influence of President Wilson and the United States.[28]

A few days later he issued a St Patrick's Day message to the Irish people on what might have struck some as a distinct note of bathos. To save the Irish language, he said, was the special duty of that generation. The ultimate

---

* Collins's and Boland's names were answered to in the Dail on 21 January and their presence published in the newspapers, but this was a device to conceal their absence. The official Dail record was subsequently amended to accord with the truth. (Beaslai, *Collins*, vol. 1, p. 256.) The other prisoners to escape with de Valera were Sean McGarry and Sean Milroy.

winning of sovereign independence was not in doubt: '... should we fail, a future generation will succeed. But the language, that must be saved by us or it is lost for ever.'[29] And Joe McGrath, an IRB man and one of the internees who had contrived his own escape from prison in England, was hardly more inspiring when he told his audience in a St Patrick's Day speech: 'As to the future ... be patient for a little while.' Dail Eireann, he assured them, was working in committees day and night.[30]

Evidence of night work of a different sort had just appeared at an inquest on a monumental mason named Pearson, the father of a British soldier, who was shot dead in his house in Dublin for refusing to give up a couple of rifles and some ammunition he kept there. A woman in the house revealed how at least some Sinn Fein supporters were made in these times. Finding herself confronted by one of the masked raiders holding a revolver she had called out to him: 'Don't shoot! ... I am a Sinn Feiner, don't shoot for mercy's sake!'[31]

A more impressive raid for arms was carried out a few days later when about thirty men tied up the guard at Collinstown military aerodrome just outside Dublin and got away with no less than seventy-two rifles and bayonets without a shot being fired.[32] The raid had been organized by Collins whose vital role behind the scenes does not yet seem to have been suspected by the authorities, for he was moving uninhibitedly about Dublin until the end of March. When the body of another prisoner who had died of influenza in Gloucester gaol, just before the general amnesty, arrived in Dublin, Collins met it at the railway station with about five hundred other Volunteers, many in uniform, and personally helped to carry the coffin.[33]

A further boost to nationalist moral came at the end of March when, as a result of another skilfully planned operation by Collins, twenty prisoners including Beasli, the editor of the Volunteer paper *An t Oglach*, climbed over the wall of Mountjoy gaol with a rope ladder in broad daylight and escaped, to the delight of passers-by, through the Dublin streets. But, though such events might hearten or cause alarm, as the case might be, politically they did not bring an Irish Republic any nearer. It was to the political sphere that most Sinn Fein supporters still looked for success, and there none seemed forthcoming.

The political offensive of Sinn Fein proceeded on two fronts: in America, where Irish opinion was being mobilized both in Congress and outside, with the help of Patrick McCartan, Sean MacDermott's old IRB friend, who was now Sinn Fein's 'Ambassador' to the States; and in Paris, where Sean T. O'Kelly, also an IRB man from pre-war days, had set himself up at the Grand Hotel, Boulevard des Capucines, as Sinn Fein's man knocking on the door of the Peace Conference.* In Paris Kelly worked extremely hard, maintaining a wide range of press contacts and delivering, along with copies

* Sean T. O'Kelly became first President of the Republic of Ireland in 1949.

of the Dail's Declaration of Independence, letters to all the Conference delegates in which he asked for Ireland's case to be heard at the earliest possible moment. Very few even troubled to reply. The rules of the Conference also allowed the Secretariat to receive outside petitions, and such as were of political interest were to be summarized and distributed to all the delegates. This procedure was, of course, something of an anti-climax after Sinn Fein's confident election assurances that Ireland would be able to walk into the Conference by the front door, but it was only one of the many devices at the indomitable Kelly's command.

Most hope of all attached to President Wilson personally. But Wilson too failed to reply to Kelly's early attempts to see him, adjourning in any case to the States soon after Kelly arrived in Paris. There were, however, hopes of better treatment on his return, because while in the States Wilson was subjected to intensive pressure by the Irish lobby to get Ireland admitted to the Conference. On 22 February a great Irish Race Convention sitting in Philadelphia had demanded 'Irish Freedom' and the House of Representatives had passed a resolution urging the Peace Conference to consider Ireland's claim to self-determination favourably. As Griffith's paper *Nationality* put it: '... even if Wilson had simply been trying to avoid embarrassment in Paris he couldn't avoid the embarrassment which the question "What about Ireland?" would cause him in America.' Griffith announced that he was inclined to give Wilson 'a chance to make good'.[34] And Wilson himself seemed partially to encourage such thinking when he declared in Boston: 'It seems as if the settlements of this war affect directly or indirectly every small nation in the world.... We set this nation up to make men free, and we did not confine our conception and purpose to America; and now we will make men free.'[35]

He returned to Paris where the persistence of Kelly – later joined by Gavan Duffy, grandson of the patriot of 1848 – in presenting the Irish case, was beginning to have some effect at least on the world's press and international opinion generally. Part of the weakness of the Irish position was that this was a conference of victors in a war in which many of the Sinn Fein leaders, including Kelly himself, had appeared at least neutral or even friendly to the losing side. The Republican Proclamation of 1916 had openly described the Germans as 'gallant allies in Europe'. Kelly clearly found this aspect of the situation awkward at times, and once replied quite inaccurately to a foreign correspondent that the only help given to Germany during the war came from Casement 'acting entirely on his own'.*[36] The old Redmondite supporters really had a far better right to argue the case for Irish admission, and indeed a memorial signed by 140 officers, including two Generals, had

---

* Casement's mission to Germany with, among other objects, that of raising an Irish Brigade, to fight against the allies, was a collective decision of both Clan-na-Gael and the IRB. (See above, p. 540.)

petitioned King George V to have the claim of the Irish nation heard at the Conference. It is uncertain whether Kelly also judiciously applied this line of argument, but certainly he was soon reaping the benefit of it. The French newspaper *La Gazette* reminded its readers of the strength of Ireland's claim with the statement that 'the green flag of Erin' had floated above every major battlefield of the Great War and only yesterday her sons had been dying in the service of France and her allies.[37]

In the end, however, it was not to be any sort of eloquence nor even the claims of justice which were to be decisive at the Conference but the pragmatic demands of power politics. Lloyd George, at the head of his Unionist-dominated Coalition, had no intention of allowing Ireland to be considered as anything but an internal affair of the British Government. President Wilson, for all the embarrassing pressures of Irish-American influence, which were strengthened by the arrival in Paris of a special three-man American Commission for Irish Freedom to urge Ireland's case, had no intention of adding a major break with the British Government to his other international troubles. The furthest he was prepared to go when speaking to members of the American Commission was to express his own personal understanding of Ireland's claim while reserving the position of the President of the United States. And although this American Commission paid an important visit to Ireland in May to confer with de Valera on the whole question of securing international recognition at the Conference, de Valera himself was being forced to speak before long of 'our apparent defeat in Paris'.[38]

Sinn Fein, it seemed, would have to turn to other channels.

5

Michael Collins and Others
(April–December 1919)

Another in the series of systematic assassinations of Crown agents by the Volunteers, which was to mark the next two years in Ireland, had taken place in Westport on the night of 31 March. At a few minutes to eleven, a former Inspector of the RIC called Milling, now a Resident Magistrate, had just gone into his drawing-room to put his clock on to the new summer-time before retiring, when four revolver shots were fired at him in the old White-boy or Land League style through the window, shattering the glass and hitting him in the abdomen. He died next morning, murmuring to a RIC man who had been summoned to his death-bed: 'They have got me at last.' Milling had become particularly unpopular in the previous year when he had sent Volunteers to prison for unlawful assembly and drilling and had been under police protection ever since. A week before he had helped send two men to prison for cattle-driving.[1]

The deed seems to have been the work of local men acting without sanction from the Dublin executive headquarters, though it could conceivably have been ordered by the IRB. Many local activists were at this time afraid that inactivity would lead to a decay in the Volunteer organization and one of them has written: 'It was saved mainly because a minority of officers and men vigorously agitated the policy of action, argued its feasibility and more or less convinced or coerced General Headquarters into giving it a reluctant sanction.'[2] One of those at General Headquarters who almost certainly required very little persuasion along these lines was Michael Collins. He had made his own attitude towards future action clear in a revealing scene at the end of March.

On de Valera's return to Ireland, Collins, on his own and Harry Boland's initiative, had issued public notices to the effect that the President would make an official entrance into Dublin 'at the gates of the City' where he was to be received by the Lord Mayor and escorted to the Mansion House. The last person to be so received had been the British monarch Queen Victoria, nineteen years before. Understandably the authorities banned the proposed ceremony. But Collins insisted that it should go ahead and de

Ourselves Alone

Valera prepared a fairly militant speech for the occasion.[3] Many Sinn Fein supporters were apprehensive of bloodshed and a meeting was called of the Sinn Fein executive, in whose name Collins had announced the ceremony. He had even attached the signature of the Honorary Secretary to the notice without consulting him. After some protest had been made at this high-handedness Collins rose and, admitting full responsibility, announced that the decision had been taken nominally by Sinn Fein but in reality by 'the proper body, the Irish Volunteers'. He said, according to one who was present, that

> the sooner fighting was forced and a general state of disorder created through the country, the better it would be for the country. Ireland was likely to get more out of a state of general disorder than from a continuance of the situation as it then stood. The proper people to take decisions of that kind were ready to face the military, and were resolved to force the issue. And they were not to be deterred by weaklings and cowards.*

On this occasion he was over-ruled, but within the Volunteer organization itself he was not so easily hampered. Only a few weeks later he was to write to a Volunteer Brigade commander: 'When you ask me for ammunition for guns which have never fired a shot in this fight, my answer is a simple one. Fire shots at some useful target or get to hell out of it.'[4] The day before the shooting of Milling at Westport, a constable had been seriously wounded by a Volunteer with a revolver in Cork.

The Westport killing was received with horror and widespread indignation throughout Ireland. The jury at the inquest found that Milling had been 'foully murdered' and a public meeting held in Westport condemned the outrage unanimously as did the Westport Urban District Council. The Archbishop of Tuam described it as a dastardly crime and the perpetrator, if not insane, 'a criminal of the first order'. The *Irish Independent,* which had supported Sinn Fein at the General Election, wrote in a leader entitled 'Cowardly Crimes' that the killing had been 'indefensible' and 'morally

---

* This eye-witness account is that of Darrell Figgis, *Recollections of the Irish War* (London, 1927), p. 243. His book was written, according to the publisher, some two to three years after this incident and since Figgis says that Collins's 'words on this occasion are too well printed on my memory ever to be forgotten', they may reasonably be regarded as substantially correct. Figgis, who had played a part in the events leading up to the Howth gun-running (see pp. 507–8) and in electioneering activities for Sinn Fein from 1917 until his arrest at the time of the 'German plot' in May 1918, was a self-opinionated and difficult man and, as his end was to show, to some extent personally unstable. His book has often been discredited by extremists partly because he was one of the first to oppose them. However, his analysis of the general trend within the Sinn Fein movement between 1919 and 1921 has much to recommend it and is substantiated by other evidence (see below, *passim*). Figgis committed suicide in Bloomsbury in 1925 after the death, following an abortion, of a London dancing teacher with whom he had been living for two years. His wife had shot herself in the Wicklow Mountains the year before. (*The Times*, 23, 28, 30 October 1925.)

wrong' and that it could 'only bring odium on the whole country and do irreparable harm to the national cause'.[5]

A week later a Constable O'Brien was shot dead in Limerick when a party of some twenty men rescued a Volunteer named Byrne in his pyjamas from a hospital where he was being treated under guard. In the mêlée, however, Byrne was himself shot by one of the police and died a few days later. In moving a resolution of sympathy with Byrne's mother and simultaneously paying a tribute to Constable O'Brien of the RIC, a speaker at the Limerick Board of Guardians repudiated 'English' statements that Sinn Fein had had knowledge of 'recent murders'. 'They would not tolerate,' he said, 'the murder of any man. They were prepared to meet their enemies by open day and would not hide themselves or act as assassins.'[6]

Even at this point in time, after the General Election, after all the sense of betrayal over Home Rule, after all earlier Irish history, the British Government, by some form of settlement which would have acknowledged the nationalist principle of a united Ireland, could almost certainly have driven a wedge between the vast majority of moderate Sinn Fein opinion and the extremists within the movement who were determined to force a bloody revolution at all costs. But the political realities of the time make such speculation irrelevant. Not only were the British Government and the British Parliament dominated by men with strong ties of loyalty to the anti-national minority in North-East Ulster, but Britain had just emerged triumphant and apparently unweakened from the greatest test of her strength in history and was as yet in no psychological mood drastically to re-think Irish policy. The government therefore took the only action it thought necessary: repression. This made it easier for Volunteer extremists to convince their moderate Sinn Fein supporters that the fight for nationalist principles was indeed as brutal and violent as Fenians had always said it must be.

The local sense of outrage at the Soloheadbeg killings in County Tipperary in January had been to some extent blunted by the subsequent imposition of military restrictions. The same thing now happened in Westport and in Limerick, which were both immediately proclaimed military districts. Whereas the funeral of Constable O'Brien had been sympathetically attended by some Sinn Fein supporters, that of the Volunteer Byrne took place down streets menacingly lined by British troops with fixed bayonets and armoured cars, and a military aircraft even flew overhead.[7] By the next day in addition to Tipperary, Westport and Limerick (both City and County), much of County Cork including the city, County Roscommon and County Kerry were under military rule. In Limerick, where the military restrictions on fairs, markets and social functions and the need of permits for movement caused much resentment, a particularly serious situation developed and a General Strike was called for a few days. On one occasion a thousand citizens who had left the town without permits to watch a football match were prevented from legally returning at night by the military. Most, however, had filtered back by their own devices the following morning, thus re-arousing all the traditional scorn for authority as well as resentment. Sympathetic farmers sent eggs, butter, milk and bread into the beleaguered city from the surrounding countryside.[8]

Such crude displays of British military strength disconcerted many otherwise moderate nationalists who had a more acute sense of Irish history than the British Government. The *Irish Independent* which, while pro-Sinn Fein, deplored the shootings, stressed that military measures were no way to deal with them.[9] Henry Harrison, the former Nationalist MP who had been an ardent supporter of Parnell's and had served with distinction and gallantry in the 16th Irish Division in France, wrote a significant letter to *The Times* on 23 April. Constitutionalism, he wrote – by which he meant the Home Rule movement – had achieved its success only to be robbed of its fruits by unconstitutional action on the part of the two great English political parties acting as accomplices. There would soon, he said, be nothing but counsels of despair. When he came to lay aside his uniform, his duty to Ireland would override all other loyalties, and if the betrayal of constitutionalism were finally consummated he would betake himself to 'such courses (if any) as may seem most expedient for helping Ireland's cause, whether or not the law allows or the Constitution warrants'.[10]

Robert Lynd, the correspondent of the *Daily News*, reported that 'even the soldiers who fought for the allies as they return home are becoming converted by the thousand into Sinn Feiners'.[11] One such was a young man of twenty-one from West Cork named Tom Barry, who had been in the British Army in Mesopotamia and who was soon to apply to join the Volunteers, or, as they were beginning to be called in the countryside, the Irish Republican Army. He had had no nationalist ideas at all before the war. Within two years he was to become one of the most skilled guerrilla commanders in Ireland.[12]

A feeling of separateness from Britain, which, up to now, the Fenians and Sinn Fein had had to argue and which Harrison and most Nationalists had always denied, was being created and visibly consolidated by the British Government with its refusal to offer Ireland anything but military force.

It was at this sensitive moment that the American Commission for Irish Freedom arrived in Ireland to see de Valera. They were to prove of considerably more value to the Irish republican cause in Ireland than they had been in Paris. For the week-long journeying of its three delegates about the country in the company of the Irish leaders, with many unabashed speeches calling for an Irish Republic on platforms where the tricolour waved with the Stars and Stripes, did much to convey the impression that the power of America was behind the cause, and to rally popular opinion when there was in fact little else with which to rally it. The Commission even managed to provoke a few incidents with the British authorities which rallied opinion still further.

On the afternoon of 12 May they attended in the Dublin Mansion House a private meeting of Dail Eirann which they addressed. Collins and Robert Barton – the latter had escaped from Mountjoy gaol some weeks before – were among the Dail representatives present, and though they withdrew up a long ladder into an adjoining building at the end of the proceedings, a large force of police and soldiers came raiding for them shortly afterwards.[13] To some extent at least the authorities were by now aware of Collins's importance. When, later that evening, guests began to arrive for an official public reception by the Lord Mayor for the American Commission, they found the building surrounded by troops in full field equipment with steel helmets and fixed bayonets and an armoured car pointing its machine-gun at the crowds. The delegates themselves, accompanied by de Valera and the Archbishop of Cashel and the Bishop of Killaloe, were actually prevented from entering for a time while the vain search continued. The reception was eventually allowed to take place, but as the London *Star* commented: 'A more maladroit exhibition could not well be conceived ... What a story they have got for American platforms...'

They had another from Westport, County Galway, where the military with fixed bayonets and an armoured car held the Commission up for one and a half hours outside the town and refused to allow them to enter. MacNeill, who was with them, was manhandled out of the way and moved off at the point of the bayonet. At the meetings which the Commission were allowed to hold in their progress through Galway, Mullingar, Athlone and other towns, Volunteers regulated the enthusiastic crowds.[14]

'Three weeks ago,' wrote the *Irish Times* when they left, 'none save fools and fanatics believed in the possibility of an Irish Republic. Today a large number of Irish Nationalists hope, and a still larger number fear, that in the near future an Irish Republic may come to birth from the grotesque union of British folly and American sentiment....'[15]

When the delegates called on Dr Walsh, the Archbishop of Dublin, to say farewell, he was able to say to them that they had had an experience of 'the kind of government under which we are living in Ireland'.[16]

In vain did the government's supporters as well as its opponents look to it for a policy. There was silence. 'Some solution must be found,' *The Times* had cried on 16 April, 'for the condition of Ireland is poisoning the broader currents of our Imperial and external policies.' And on 2 May the paper had sounded an eleventh-hour note of desperation in its plea that 'If there ever was a moment when it was vital that the Government should understand the situation in Ireland it is now. Most people agree that something should be done and done quickly.'

On May 22 came the first political pronouncement the government had made on the Irish question since the General Election. It came from Carson's old Galloper, Lord Birkenhead, now Lord Chancellor, hardly an auspicious source. He said that when the Peace Treaty was finally signed the government would consider what to do about the Home Rule Act. Meantime, he continued, the only proper policy for Ireland was any degree of force that might be necessary to maintain order there. For, he contended, with what was an absurd exaggeration, even if an exaggeration of a certain truth, the great majority of the Irish people were in a state of open rebellion.

The slow rebellion that the extremist Republicans were developing under the name of Sinn Fein was indeed gradually getting under way. And yet for all the rally of national sentiment in face of British activities, when, on 13 May 1919, two more RIC constables were shot dead in a daring rescue of a Volunteer prisoner from a train at Knocklong station, County Tipperary, many moderates felt dismayed, and the strongest condemnation was forthcoming from the Church at once. The parish priest of a locality in which the two constables had served declared that murder was murder, however much people might attempt to cloak it with a political motive. And Dr Harty, the Archbishop of Cashel who had been confronted with British bayonets outside the Mansion House in Dublin a few days before, denounced what he called 'the deplorable occurrence' at Knocklong as 'a crime against the law of God and a crime against Ireland'. He asked the young men of the country 'not to stain the fair name of their native land by deeds of bloodshed'. It was, he said, no use to appeal to the fact that the British Government had been committing outrages in Ireland: two wrongs did not make a right.[17] The inquest jury conveyed an ambivalence suggestive of the resentment which British military measures were creating. While expressing sympathy for the relatives of the dead policemen it added a rider that 'the Government should cease arresting respectable persons, thereby causing bitter exasperation among the people'.[18]

As far as the respectability of the arrested person in this instance was concerned, he was Sean Hogan, a Volunteer who had been present at the Soloheadbeg killings. He had been rescued by his former comrades in that venture, Dan Breen, Seumas Robinson and Sean Treacy with help from other local Volunteers. Breen later wrote that he had to fire at once on this occasion because otherwise the constables would have shot their prisoner as they had done in the Limerick hospital. Though Breen was himself severely wounded he again successfully disappeared with the others into the countryside, getting help from local people and being passed along the Volunteer network.[19] He and his comrades had again carried out the exploit on their own initiative.

The true attitude of the Dail representatives to these displays of Volunteer initiative cannot easily be discerned. Many Dail members, of course, being themselves Volunteers or even IRB men, had no scruples about such action for in their eyes all police and military could legitimately be treated as enemies. We have Beaslai's word that no voice was raised against such action in the Dail in 1919, and yet not all the representatives there can have felt at ease, particularly in view of the persistent condemnation of the Church. Eoin MacNeill clearly had to resort to self-deception in order to accept it. When asked about the shooting of policemen in an interview with the *Glasgow Herald* at the end of May he replied: 'As to the shooting of policemen, in all cases, as far as I know, these acts were committed in resistance to policemen engaged on purely repressive activities.'[20]

It is hard to see how the two local constables guarding a load of gelignite on its way to blasting operations at Soloheadbeg in January could have been regarded as engaged on repressive activities, or the two policemen caught at Knocklong guarding, in the normal course of duty, one of the Soloheadbeg killers. The raids for arms were easier to justify. MacNeill had been in favour of a defensive role for the Volunteers since before 1916. If they did not get arms now where they could, he told the *Glasgow Herald*, they would be 'overridden'.

But if such public utterances on the awkward subject were rare from the Dail 'Government' we do know what the attitude of the Sinn Fein executive was at this time. Collins castigated it in a letter on 17 May – five days after he had attended the Dail addressed by the American Commission. 'The position is intolerable,' he wrote, '– the policy now seems to be to squeeze out anyone who is tainted with strong fighting ideas or, should I say I suppose, ideas of the utility of fighting.' And the next day he wrote again: 'We have too many of the bargaining type already. I am not so sure that our movement or part of it at any rate is fully alive to the developing situation. It seems to me that official S. F. is inclined to be ever less militant and ever more political and theoretical. . . . It is rather pitiful and at times somewhat disheartening. At the moment I'm awfully fed up, yet 'tis in vain etc.'[21]

The last words were an evocation of the joking doggerel with which Wolfe Tone had often completed entries in his diary: 'Yet 'tis in vain for soldiers to complain!' Collins indeed embodied much of the dash and charm of Tone's fearless spirit, combining with these qualities considerably greater military effectiveness. From his own point of view he was soon to set the situation to rights.

Working from offices in Dublin, some secret, some not (one of the former in the first school started by Patrick Pearse, St Ita's) Collins not only supervised the organization of Volunteer brigades throughout the country, but built up a formidable active élite in the capital itself, ably assisted by the Volunteer Chief of Staff, Richard Mulcahy, together with a Chief Intelligence Officer, Liam Tobin, and what later came to be known as 'the Squad' of expert gunmen. At the same time Collins appeared openly at sessions of the Dail between January and September 1919, functioning in his other role of Minister of Finance, and relying on information from his increasingly subtle intelligence system to give him warning of raids on the Mansion House. During a Dail session in April, when his face appeared respectably in the newspapers,[22] he actually spent part of one of the nights inspecting British secret reports and documents inside the headquarters of the Dublin detective force, whither he had been conducted by a detective of the political section, working as a double agent in Collins's service. This man, Edward Broy, together with other double agents, James Kavanagh, Patrick Macnamara and David Neligan, Irishmen who had decided that loyalty to Ireland could no longer be identified with loyalty to the Crown they served, were to provide the heart of an intelligence system which was totally to reverse the traditional eighteenth- and nineteenth-century pattern by which the informers were on the government side. Collins was even at a later date to enrol the services of an English officer working for British Military Intelligence in Dublin Castle.[23]

A less easily determined force complementing Collins's underground revolutionary apparatus was what his British opponents called the Sinn Fein 'terror' in Ireland. The label 'Sinn Fein' in this context is confusing, but at a distance of fifty years the term 'terror' can be stripped of its pejorative content. Intimidation is an instrument of which the most high-minded nationalist revolutionaries have always made use as a means of ensuring that the often inert mass of the population should at least not hinder those operations conducted, according to the revolutionaries, on its own behalf. It was inevitably to figure prominently in these years in Ireland where it had historical roots going back to the agrarian secret societies of the eighteenth and nineteenth centuries, and had manifested itself most recently in the days of the Land League. Threatening letters, the infliction of cruel wounds, firing through windows of houses or at the person had intermittently been a feature of Irish rural life for agrarian purposes for two centuries. They became easily applied by individuals to new political objectives which also had to be pursued in secret.

So much history of what came to be known as the Irish War of Independence has been in terms of hagiography that the extent to which the intimidation of ordinary people – as opposed to the attacks on policemen, soldiers and officials – played a useful part is often omitted. The relative ease with which men like Breen or the killer of the magistrate Milling and Constable O'Brien of Limerick were able to remain undetected is evidence not only of reluctance to cooperate with the law for patriotic reasons but also of more self-interested motives. The fear of what might happen to a man who contravened the law of secret societies was a folk-tradition which rural Irishmen were inclined to respect, and of which they were not infrequently reminded.

A transgressor had his ears cut off with a pair of shears as late as January 1920 and a girl had the calf of her left leg shot off by two masked men the following month.[24] And though these punishments – probably for simple agrarian offences – would have been disapproved of by most Volunteers they created a climate from which they benefited. The Volunteers themselves usually preferred more direct methods, shooting the culprit cleanly and tying a label marked 'Spy – killed by IRA' to the corpse. Dozens of Irishmen were to die such deaths at the hands of their fellow-countrymen before the 'war of independence' was over.

Though physical violence against non-conforming individuals was not threatened in the name of the Volunteers or IRA on any scale until the second half of 1919, and did not assume significant proportions until the years 1920–21, some fear of intimidation at least played a part from the start. 'There is more terrorism,' wrote the Unionist *Daily Telegraph* at the end of May 1919, 'than in the worst days of the Land League. People are compelled to fall into line with the Sinn Feiners or they could neither trade nor buy the necessities of life.'[25] The paper may well have been exaggerating, but that a boycott was in force could not be disputed.

The boycott – that mildest but in some ways most effective of all agrarian weapons – had been decreed by no less a man than de Valera himself, when, in addressing the Dail in April, he described the RIC as 'spies in our midst' and went on, somewhat in the tradition of Charles Stewart Parnell:

... these men must not be tolerated socially as if they were clean healthy members of our organized life. They must be shown and made to feel how base are the functions they perform, and how vile is the position they occupy. To shun them, to refuse to talk to them, or have any social intercourse with them or to treat them as equals, will give them vividly to understand how utterly the people of Ireland loathe both themselves and their calling ...[26]

This was no incitement to violence in itself, but de Valera knew enough of rural Ireland, as Parnell had done, to know that there would be men in the countryside who saw to it that such a boycott was enforced. Later in the year a poster was to be found, placed close to where two policemen had been shot dead in County Clare, proclaiming: 'Shun all policemen and spies! Three cheers for the IRA!' and in the next two years apart from numerous executions of 'spies' there were to be many cases of women who had their heads shaved or were otherwise maltreated for consorting with Irish police or British soldiers.[27] Even though such action may often have been taken by local individuals independently of Collins and Headquarters, the atmosphere these actions produced certainly made conditions for more significant operations easier. From several counties in the south and west of Ireland the RIC were to report by the end of 1919 that degrees of Sinn Fein terrorism accounted for total lack of cooperation between the population and the police. '... Even persons upon whom outrages have been committed,' said the report from County Galway, 'are not disposed to give the police any information which might lead to the discovery of the perpetrators of the outrages, fearing that by so doing further outrages would be committed on themselves or their property ...'[28]

But the most potent force of all operating in favour of Collins and the other militants was undoubtedly the British Government itself. The embittered Home Rulers and other moderates who had largely voted Sinn Fein into power had been offered nothing in response to their challenging demand for a radical new policy. The government had tacitly admitted they had none to give and, responding to the activity of the extremists, sent steel-helmeted troops and armoured cars, adding to the political injury the insulting presence of an unwanted military authority in the streets. Gradually, reluctantly, the moderates were brought to acknowledge the fact that in an extreme situation there was little place for moderation.

But the process in the middle of 1919 was only just beginning and Collins, confronted by the caution of the political forces of Sinn Fein, was sometimes in despair. His bitterness against the Sinn Fein executive in the middle of May had been partly caused by an inadvertent public revelation on its part that its secretary, Harry Boland, had left the country.[29] For, having refused to accept the deputy whom Boland left behind, they had insisted on electing a less belligerent figure in his place. Up to that point Collins had managed to keep Boland's departure a secret for five weeks. Boland had in fact left Ireland to prepare the way physically and politically for de Valera's clandestine departure for the United States. And early in June de Valera was successfully spirited out of the country by Collins and arrived in New York on 11 June. Collins may by now have been partly relieved to see him go.

De Valera's own view at this moment of the best methods by which to pursue the goal of the Republic was, as often when an issue was delicate, obscure. On the one hand he was still technically President of the Volunteers, as well as the President of the Dail: and he was ready enough publicly to proclaim that the men of the tiny minority of 1916 had been 'justified in regarding themselves as genuine representatives of the nation'.[30] His official position with the Volunteers could be said to have been effectively taken over by the Minister of Defence, Cathal Brugha, but he knew well enough the sort of extremism for which both Brugha and Collins stood. On the other hand, his very insistence on going to America at all made it clear that he was thinking primarily in terms of a political rather than a guerrilla solution. He was in fact to remain in America for eighteen months, from June 1919 until December 1920. During this time the situation in Ireland changed dramatically and irrevocably.

6
The Campaign of Killing
(1919–20)

A grim process, brilliantly master-minded by Collins, of systematic terror against Irish police and detectives began on 24 June 1919. An Inspector of the RIC named Hunt was shot dead in the back in the main square of Thurles in broad daylight. There was a large crowd passing through the square at the time on its way back from a race meeting, but it made no attempt to help the dying man and the assailant disappeared into it with ease. He was never caught. Hunt had recently been assiduous in directing the law against the Volunteers and on the two previous Sundays had broken up Sinn Fein meetings, seizing from one of them a Republican flag.

However, the jury at the inquest did not accept the view that such activities warranted a death sentence. They found a verdict of wilful murder and passed a vote of condolence to the Inspector's family.[1] The Archbishop of Tuam denounced 'this shocking crime' as 'a most grave violation of the law of God' and said that the man who committed it would one day 'also be called before the Judgement Seat of God, and will meet his victim face to face for his punishment through eternal life'.[2]

The very day of Hunt's death – though before it was known – the archbishop had been one of the signatories of a statement issued by the entire Irish hierarchy from Maynooth. This had castigated the irritations of military rule and the denial of political rights to the Irish people.* 'The existing method of Government cannot last,' this statement had run. '... We have the evils of military rule exhibited at our doors. In this ancient civilizing nation, the people are not permitted to rule themselves through men of their own choice.' The acts of violence which the hierarchy 'deplored' sprang, they said, 'from this cause and this cause alone'.[3]

Now too in the archbishop's condemnation of the deed at Thurles there was a note which for all his abhorrence made some justification of such things easier: 'For all this,' he said, 'there is only one solution: let the

---

* Piaras Beaslai MP, Lawrence Ginnell MP, J. J. Clancy MP and Constance Markievicz MP had all been arrested or given sentences that month.

military domination of Ireland cease at once. Let the people of Ireland choose for themselves the Government under which they are to live . . ."[4]

At this time in the middle of 1919 there was an unresolved ambivalence in the minds of the Irish people. On the one hand they were being roused by government policy into a national political front such as had only been equalled in Irish history by O'Connell's movement for Repeal of the Union. Readers of the Nationalist Party paper, the *Freeman's Journal*, read headlines like 'Free Use of the Baton in Kilmallock'; 'Women Suffer'; 'Glen of Aherlow Aroused by Troops, Aeroplanes etc.'[5] and reacted indistinguishably from those who had voted Sinn Fein rather than Nationalist at the election. The very appearance in the towns and villages of large numbers of soldiers with rifles and bayonets evoked associations of an ancient land war that went deeper than any political frustration. On the other hand the bloodshed caused by the actions of the Volunteers in provoking the government was disliked and deplored.

In the long run, in the light of history, there could be no doubt on whose side the Irish people would come down in a simple contest of brutality between the government and the Volunteers. In the absence of any realistic policy but repression from the government they were bound to come down, for all their early misgivings, on the side of the Volunteers. In this the policy of Collins and the other extremists in the Sinn Fein movement succeeded brilliantly. They won their battle against the moderates in Sinn Fein by making moderation irrelevant.

The Archbishop of Tuam had concluded his pronouncement on the killing of Inspector Hunt with the words: 'We humbly implore God to grant us soon that liberty for which we and our fathers before us have prayed and longed. We ask Him at long last to grant us peace – peace from the blighting rule of the stranger, and peace from that baneful influence of deeds of violence.'

The only answer came from Dublin Castle. It immediately banned the entire Sinn Fein organization in Tipperary and even the Gaelic League itself. From Lloyd George and the government, euphoric over the Peace Treaty which they had just formally concluded at Versailles, there came no vestige of a new policy for Ireland.

Unionists were now more than ever desperately aware that some attitude other than either repression or the old proposal for the exclusion of six Ulster counties was required. A group headed by Sir Horace Plunkett formed in June 1919 an Irish Dominion League demanding Dominion Home Rule for all Ireland. The minority in Ireland, they declared, had no right to deny the fundamental right of the Irish people to see the unity of their country preserved.[6] English Conservatives, like Garvin of the London *Observer*, commented that it was 'no longer enough for the Ulster Covenanters to say "We won't have it." That pre-war formula is as dead as King

William.... Mere "won't have it" is what the vast majority of the United Kingdom won't have."[7] He recommended an Ulster government sub-autonomous to Dublin.

But for Irishmen the only Conservative voice that seemed relevant was that of Carson, and with some reason considering how many of his staunch supporters were in the government.* And what Carson now said was: 'We will have nothing to do with Dominion Home Rule, or any other Home Rule.... We avoid it as a thing unclean, we fling it back at them.'[8]

Carson knew well enough that the government would have to offer something eventually, but he was determined that the sacrosanct position he had built up for the exclusion of six counties of Ulster should not be tampered with. Bargaining from immense strength he actually called for a Repeal of the Home Rule Act and said that if there were an attempt to impose it he would summon his provisional government and call out the Ulster Volunteers.[9]

Talk like this made many moderates in Ireland feel that for all Sinn Fein's apparent shortcomings there was still nothing to support but Sinn Fein. After all, the respectable illusion that the Irish Republic might still somehow be implemented by moral pressure and by the abstentionist policy of self-reliance was still formally maintained. Announcements of the Dail 'Government's' establishment of Arbitration Courts for land disputes, of commissions of investigation into the country's economic resources and above all the launching of an ambitious Republican Loan of which £250,000 was to be raised with de Valera's help in the United States and another £250,000 in Ireland itself, had an impressive ring.

Collins himself, as Minister of Finance, was in charge of the loan. Many people thought at the time that the target was absurdly high for, having no idea of his extraordinary role behind the scenes, they were quite unaware of his exceptional administrative ability or organizing powers. Within a year he was able to announce the closing of the loan at a figure of more than £357,000 for Ireland itself.[10]

That pressure was sometimes used to help raise this money seems undeniable, for when lists of subscribers periodically fell into the hands of British Intelligence they even included the names of well-known Unionists.[11] But even though the IRB and Volunteer network which was Collins's principal concern made organization and collection easier, the technical business of successfully lodging the money in hiding-places and various bank accounts which would escape the scrutiny of persistent British attempts to locate it, at a time when Collins himself was continually on the run, was a masterly

---

* In addition to Bonar Law, Birkenhead and Walter Long, all the law officers of the Crown in Ireland were Ulster "Covenanters".

achievement. It seems all the more so given the extent and far-reaching impact of his other activities and responsibilities at the time.

The Volunteers were now coming more under the control of Collins and General Headquarters in Dublin, though it was in the nature of the situation that much flexibility had always to be left to individual initiative in the field. Through able organizers whom he himself appointed and sent out, like Ernie O'Malley, a young red-headed middle-class Catholic of literary tastes, or through dedicated young local commanders with whom he was in touch, like Liam Lynch from Cork, the energy and spirit of individual groups of Volunteers was slowly harnessed to a potential guerrilla force, with some counties, like Cork itself, active enough to provide as many as three brigades. In active areas like Cork such brigades contained at first about 3,500 Volunteers though their nominal strength at least was to grow greater.* The vast majority of these men, however, at all times through the next two years continued simultaneously to lead apparently normal everyday lives in the towns and countryside.

At this time, in the middle of 1919, their activities still had a desultory quality. 'We are still so to speak in the trenches,' the secret Volunteer paper *An t Oglach* had put it in May, 'but our "trench raids" and active operations against the enemy are growing more and more frequent, and are usually attended with brilliant success.' Though sometimes lethal, these operations also sometimes recalled the more ineffectual efforts of the Fenians. Thus in August a police hut in East Clare was besieged for over an hour by an unknown number of men with rifles and revolvers and successfully defended by six members of the RIC who had actually been in bed at the start of the attack.[12] Two days before, however, another barracks in Clare had been captured and two of the constables shot dead. The Bishop of Galway described their deaths as wilful murder and the ordinary citizens who composed the coroner's jury had no hesitation in confirming his judgement with a verdict to the same effect. There were sympathetic crowds at the constables' funeral.[13]

But again the pattern that had established itself at Westport and Limerick and in Tipperary was repeated. The whole of Clare was immediately proclaimed a military district and by the end of August 1919 some seven thousand troops were on the move throughout the county day and night. There was a ten o'clock curfew with lights out half an hour later. Significantly, when shots were fired at night through the window of a man who had been working for a relative under police protection, and the man's fifteen-year-old

---

* O'Donoghue, *No Other Law*, p. 36. By 1921 brigades were organized in divisions. The size of divisions varied greatly. The First Southern Divisions under Lynch numbered nominally 33,550, a quarter of the entire nominal strength of the IRA. The 3rd Southern Division numbered 6,000 which was much nearer the average size (ibid., p. 334).

son was killed, the coroner's jury, in a verdict that was treated with some scepticism, pinned the blame on the military.*

In Dublin Collins began systematically dealing out death to those Irishmen in the 'G' (detective) division of the Dublin Metropolitan Police whom his intelligence network told him were becoming well-informed about Volunteer activities.[14] He organized small units of skilled young gunmen who, filled with the highest patriotic motives, became proficient at liquidating both their fellow-countrymen and agents sent from England in the public streets. On 31 July 1919 an unarmed Irish detective sergeant named Smyth, a man with seven children, was shot in the back just outside his home in Dublin by one such group. 'You cowards,' he cried, understandably failing to appreciate the risks his assailants themselves incurred, and he turned and faced them. They fired again and continued to fire until he was within fifteen yards of his house, hitting him five times in all.[15] He was to die some weeks later.

A few days after the attack the Corporation of Dublin carried a motion condemning recent outrages and the Lord Mayor, Laurence O'Neill, who had done much to fight for better gaol treatment for Sinn Fein prisoners, strongly associated himself with the Bishop of Galway's use of the term 'murder'. 'There was,' he said, 'no justification for murder and outrage.'[16] It was a generally representative view at the time. The Westmeath County Council ten days later passed a resolution condemning 'in the strongest terms our language can afford the murders and outrages that are occurring in various parts of the country'. These were, it said, engineered by the dangerous parts of society. One of the speakers said that 'a storm of indignation should go forth from the elected representatives of the people. The instigators of those crimes are no acquisition to any political party or organization.'[17]

It did not yet seem to occur to the bulk of Sinn Fein supporters that it was precisely the elected representatives of the people – or an all-important element in them – who were applying the policy of 'murder and outrage' without popular sanction. On the very day of the Westmeath resolution, one such representative, who was still referred to in the newspapers as Mr M. Collins MP, gave a remarkable demonstration of his own extraordinary sangfroid as a revolutionary. For while Detective Sergeant Smyth lay dying in hospital Collins appeared at a Sinn Fein Congress at the Mansion House on 21 August, and, speaking as Minister of Finance, in a lucid detailed speech which was publicly reported, described the purpose and methods of

* The affair remains a mystery. The Army afterwards held an inquiry and found that the shots could not have been fired by any of the troops then stationed in the district. A year later such an inquiry would itself have been treated with scepticism. But at this stage it cannot be so easily dismissed. The Army had suffered no casualty here and the fact that the bullets by which the boy was killed were military is hardly conclusive evidence in the circumstances of the time. The connection with the man under police protection and the Land League style of the murder may, or may not, be significant. (*Clare Champion*, 30 August 1919.)

collection of the Republican Loan. On it, he said, the whole constructive policy of Dail Eireann depended. The money was to go to a Consular Service, to Irish fisheries, afforestation, the encouragement of industry, and the establishment of a national civil service and arbitration courts.

'Even if nothing comes of this moment', he said, '– which is impossible – the loan will be redeemed by the next Irish Government even as today we are redeeming the Fenian bonds.'[18]

Earlier in the summer when a search had been made for him at the Mansion House, Collins had escaped up a rope ladder, and this time he presumably took careful precautions when entering and leaving the building. Two days later he was writing to his sisters: 'For the moment . . . things are settled enough, but I am looking forward to the winter for significant happenings.'[19] On 12 September he had Detective Constable Daniel Hoey shot dead in the street outside police headquarters in the middle of Dublin. It had been a spectacular day, for only a few hours before the government had finally given an answer to the urgent question of what it was going to do about Ireland. It had suppressed and declared illegal Dail Eireann.

Hoey had taken part in the raid on the Mansion House that had followed the decision, but Collins had escaped through a skylight. A few hours later the detective's body slumped on to the pavement, hit by revolver bullets. He was unarmed and all that was found in his pocket was money and some religious emblems, for he was a devout Catholic.[20] His was the third death of a member of the Crown forces that week and the sixth in less than six weeks.

One of the other casualties had been a soldier killed in Fermoy, County Cork, in a daring assault on a party of troops marching to church on Sunday, 7 September. This raid had been formally authorized by Collins and the Volunteer GHQ in Dublin, although on condition that there should be no casualties.[21] It was brilliantly executed by Liam Lynch, revealing guerilla professionalism of which he was one of the earliest Volunteer exponents. The eighteen men of the King's Shropshire Light Infantry in the church party were swiftly overpowered and thirteen of their rifles loaded into waiting motor-cars which were immediately driven off. Military vehicles which took off in pursuit found roads blocked by fallen trees which had been sawn through during the night and held back by ropes until the escaping raiders were safely past. Only one detail of the operation had gone awry, for in the scuffle one of the soldiers had been shot dead and three others seriously wounded.

The jury at the subsequent inquest unanimously expressed horror and condemnation for 'this appalling outrage in the midst of a peaceable and civil community, between whom the most friendly feelings have always existed', but they did not find a verdict of murder because the raid's intention had clearly been to get the rifles and the killing had been unpremeditated.[22]

For this oversight, in spite of their additional expression of sympathy with the dead man's relatives, they were made to pay a heavy price. That night undisciplined troops broke out of barracks and did considerable damage in the town, smashing shop windows and particularly attacking the house of the foreman of the jury.[23] Just as Lynch's raid had indicated the sophisticated guerrilla technique which the Volunteers were eventually to develop in the countryside on a considerable scale, so this reprisal by the military fore-shadowed a new pattern of violence that was to impress itself on Ireland with such profound long-term effects in the following year.

The official reaction to Lynch's Fermoy raid was predictable. Both Sinn Fein and the Volunteer organization were banned in the Cork district. Equally predictably, this decision had the opposite effect to that intended, for it emphasized an identification of the two elements in the new national move-ment at a time when a division could have been exploited. Thus, de Valera, commenting from New York a few days later, was able to say of the sup-pression of Sinn Fein in Cork that 'the English are ... seeking to goad the people into open rebellion in the field'.[24] What was really happening was that the Volunteers were goading the government into goading the people into rebellion – a process in which, much aided by the government itself, they were eventually to be successful.

For the time being, however, though Volunteer successes were enjoyed and applauded when they were achieved without bloodshed, those that caused casualties were still regarded by the Irish people with considerable reserva-tion, if not dismay. Most of the victims after all were fellow Irishmen. A few days before the Fermoy raid a RIC Sergeant named Brady had been shot dead while on patrol duty in Tipperary. He left eight children and a widow, a simple Catholic Irishwoman who broke down pitifully at the funeral service, sobbing violently and calling out over and over again: 'Mur-dered by the roadside! Murdered by the roadside!'[25]

The following Sunday the local priest, with this and the recent systematic killings of Irish policemen in Dublin and elsewhere in mind, cried in an impassioned outburst:

'Who has authorized a small band of unknown, ignorant persons to meet in secret and decide that the life of a fellow human being may be taken law-fully.... The Irish people will not approve of bloodshed, and the freedom of martyred Ireland will not be achieved by midnight assassination.'[26]

A month later, on 19 October 1919, another Catholic Irishman of the RIC, Constable Downing, was shot in the stomach and killed in a Dublin street at 2 a.m. He was shot on Collins's orders and with the sanction of the 'Minister of Defence', Cathal Brugha, who, when Sinn Fein had been seek-ing democratic support, had declared that Ireland's freedom would never be won by assassination.* Three weeks later Brugha and Collins had a detective officer named Wharton shot in the back at night on the corner of

* See above, p. 610.

St Stephen's Green, Dublin, though his severe wounds did not prove fatal. Wharton had been prominent in a number of prosecutions of the Volunteers. On 1 December, again on the orders of Brugha and Collins, another detective of the political 'G' Division named Barton, an Irishman from County Kerry, was shot in the back and killed. The coroner's jury found a verdict of 'wilful murder' and added: 'We consider his death a loss to the citizens of Dublin and we condemn these outrages.' The Lord Mayor of Dublin, Larry O'Neill, a good nationalist, again publicly associated himself with the verdict, expressing his 'abhorrence of this terrible crime' and describing the dead detective as 'an asset to the city of Dublin'.[27]

When, dismayed by this slaughter of their best detectives, Dublin Castle sent for a particularly intelligent Inspector from Belfast named Redmond, Collins had him shot and killed in Dublin on 21 January 1920. Meanwhile, in his other capacity as a senior 'Minister' of the Dail, he had been issuing prospectuses for the Republican Loan, one of which ran: 'You can restore Ireland's Health, Her Beauty and Her Wealth: Subscribe today To the Irish National Loan.'[28]

In the countryside, too, the campaign against 'the enemy' continued bloodily. Another RIC constable had been killed when opening the door of a barracks to a Volunteer raiding party in County Meath at the end of October, an act which brought down the curse of God upon the perpetrator from the Bishop of Meath in Mullingar Cathedral.[29] The 'barracks' at Ballivor, County Meath, where this constable was shot, like very many of the six hundred or so 'barracks' in Ireland, was simply an ordinary two-storey house in the village street. It is understandable how such deeds, since sanctified into deeds of heroism, struck very many Irishmen at the time quite otherwise. This was long before any Irishman had been killed in a reprisal, and no Black and Tan had yet set foot in Ireland. When in December yet another RIC constable was shot dead by Volunteers in County Cork, in implementation of the doctrine long received from headquarters in *An t Oglach*, the Cork Corporation denounced the killing unanimously as a 'cowardly and disgraceful murder'.

That many Irishmen needed to be persuaded by the Volunteers to think differently about such things was as clear to the Volunteers now as it had been to them in the more rarefied atmosphere of 1916. Notices to 'Shun All Policemen as Spies and Traitors', signed 'A Soldier of the IRA (Irish Republican Army)' were appearing and were not to be taken lightly.[30] In Toomevara, County Tipperary, that autumn a notice naming for boycott a family 'which had done injury to three soldiers of the Irish Republic', and instructing that 'they must not be greeted or sat next to in Church', threatened punishment for non-compliance.[31] What punishment in the name of the Irish Republic meant in this sense was illustrated in Clare when an Irishman who had been in the British Army was appointed schoolmaster at

Knockjames. Notices were sent round to the parents of the local children reading: 'Keep your son from Knockjames, otherwise you will have reason to regret it. By Order of the Irish Republican Army.' The attendance was thus successfully reduced from forty-five children to sixteen, but one of the fathers who defied it received three hundred shot-gun pellets in both thighs, the groin and the lungs, in a manner that recalled the punishment of those who had always defied secret societies in Ireland.[32] The Judge who tried the case in which the victim applied for compensation voiced the common illusion of most Irishmen of the time. He said he was glad to believe that the perpetrators of such deeds got no sympathy whatsoever from 'any politician in this country. I would despair of my country,' he continued, 'if I thought the men elected to representative positions would or could for one moment sanction such outrages.'[33]

Elected representatives of the Irish people were sanctioning more lethal outrages than that against equally innocent people, but when in December Cardinal Logue, the Catholic Primate of All Ireland, was moved to speak out formally against the long sequence of killings in Dublin and elsewhere he, too, found it difficult to face the real truth:

Holy Ireland, the land of St Patrick, shall never be regenerated by deeds of blood or raised up by the hand of the midnight assassin .... It is hard to believe that the intelligent and reasonable members of any Christian political party could sanction or sympathize with crime.... Among the body of the people those crimes inspire horror, contempt and reprobation. Their sympathies are with the unfortunate and innocent victims, not with the cowardly assassins.[34]

Even as the Cardinal was writing this address the men to whom he indirectly referred – Collins, Mulcahy and Brugha among others – had perfected plans on which they had long been working for a most daring assassination of no less a person than the Viceroy, Lord French, himself. His car was attacked at Ashtown, County Dublin, in broad daylight on 19 December 1919. The attack failed because those who lay in ambush for him, including Dan Breen, directed most of their fire against the wrong car in a small convoy of two and Collins was furious at the mistake.[35] The Archbishop of Dublin described the attack on French as 'an appalling attempt at murder'.[36]

The popular Dublin newspaper, the *Irish Independent*, concurred in the condemnation. Two days later a group of Collins's men armed with revolvers went to the editorial building where, after the editor had been informed of their disapproval of his comment and had been told that he would be shot if he stirred, the entire printing machinery of the paper was dismantled and destroyed.[37]

Patriotic motives must again be emphasized for Collins and others whom the Church, most responsible Irishmen and many ordinary Irishmen and women then regarded as murderers, though unaware of their identities. The

Volunteer leaders and their followers were acting in the pure Fenian tradition, setting out to redeem Ireland's past sufferings and redress her present wrongs by extreme methods because in their eyes these alone seemed appropriate to the extremity of the sufferings and the wrongs. There can be no doubt that their actions were immoral by the standards of the Church at the time, and were often by any standards vile. There can be no doubt that, like all revolutionaries, they had cynically exploited democratic processes to give the Irish people what they judged good for them rather than what the Irish people wanted. But for them these charges were irrelevant. For them the end alone would justify the means.

While de Valera's attitude to Collins's campaign of violence was further obscured by his long absence in America, the attitude of Arthur Griffith at this time, a man who believed in moral force and had disapproved of the 1916 rebellion, and whose moderating political influence on the movement Collins had feared two years before, must also remain something of a mystery. Griffith was now Acting President or Prime Minister of the underground 'Government' in de Valera's absence. We know that on at least one occasion, in 1919 when warned of an act of violence by Volunteers planned in Cork, Griffith intervened successfully with Collins to prevent it.[38] He must have known clearly enough who was having policemen shot down in the Dublin streets, or other Irishmen fatally ambushed on country roads or in their villages. It must still be guesswork to what extent he questioned the need for these things, or was worried by the condemnations of the Church and of secular organs of pro-Sinn Fein opinion. Perhaps, in spite of these, he justified such deeds by straightforward revolutionary logic. His own preoccupation was to establish a genuinely Sinn Fein or self-reliant Irish administration, with an independent national economy and judicial system. He was no pacifist. He had after all begun his nationalist career as a Fenian and had even remained a member of the IRB until 1906. His conversion to moral force had been more from consideration of the impracticability of physical force than from any moral conviction. He had the essential political gift of pragmatic adaptability. As 1919 proceeded it became clear that, with the activity of Collins and the country Volunteers, what had seemed foolishly impractical and therefore irrelevant before 1914, or even in 1916, might no longer be so. Since the total separation of Ireland from England in one form or another was his paramount concern, he may not have found it so difficult to adjust reservations about means to the consistency with which his one end could be kept in view.

That Griffith and others in the leadership felt some unease at the prevailing situation, however, and considered that it needed some form of regularization was indicated by the decision in August 1919 that the Volunteers should take an oath of allegiance to the Irish Republic and Dail Eireann. Reciprocally, members of the Dail, who surprisingly had not yet made a formal undertaking of this sort, also took the oath. From then onwards, though the Volunteers still remained in fact under the control of their own organization and were directed, in so far as they were directed from the centre at all, by Collins rather than any cabinet decision, it was at least easier to say legalistically that the Volunteers were now the official army of the Irish Republic. Moderate men could regard what was being done as 'responsible'. The Irish Republican Brotherhood, of course, which Collins also directed, remained responsible to no one but itself.

Collins was opposed to the Volunteers taking the Dail oath, maintaining that the ordinary Volunteer oath to the Republic was sufficient. He eventually agreed to the formality on the understanding that a separate Volunteer executive should remain in being as an advisory body to the Ministry of Defence.[39] But he seems to have been in no hurry to see the decision implemented in the Volunteer units up and down the country. Some of these treated the oath to the Dail, as he must have guessed they would, with extreme suspicion. Collins's organizer, O'Malley, who found himself swearing in brigade officers to Dail allegiance as late as the middle of 1920, could not take the whole thing too seriously when one of them pointed out that the headquarters staff had had no authority from the Volunteers themselves to hand over control of them to the Dail. 'The Dail might go wrong and accept less than a Republic,' this Brigade Commander objected. '... I suppose the Headquarters staff might go wrong also?' They both just laughed.[40]

There seems to have been nothing exceptional about O'Malley administering the Dail oath to the IRA so long after the formal decision had been arrived at. It was not until nearly a year after that decision, on 16 July 1920, that Collins officially notified brigade commandants that the oath was to be taken, and it was a week later that the oath itself and the order to administer it was issued as a general instruction from GHQ in Dublin.[41]

The truth is not only that Collins, with his special position of control over the inner mechanism of the Volunteers, could be virtually a law unto himself whatever he might undertake formally for the comfort of political elements in the movement, but also that the Volunteers or IRA were by no means very tightly even under his or GHQ's control.

Officers from active areas such as Cork would visit Dublin for conferences with Collins at GHQ from time to time and good officers like Liam Lynch would do their best to make the link a real one. It was in their interests to do so for GHQ was a central source of arms, ammunition and information. But the military situation did not permit easy contact and made it a necessity to delegate much initiative to local areas. No senior GHQ officers from Dublin visited Cork, the most heavily engaged county of all, after August 1919.[42] As to the political sanction that was supposed to lie behind GHQ, Liam Lynch himself had once written revealingly that: 'The Army has to hew the way for politics to follow.'[43]

The execution of civilian 'spies' and informers which was to become a feature of IRA activity in the following year was theoretically only to be carried out with sanction from Collins's GHQ. But as a leading guerrilla commander of the next year has pointed out, this was seldom sought although a certain local nicety was observed in ascertaining that the victim was the correct one.[44] IRA commandants would often reply to GHQ directives that local conditions made them inadvisable or impossible to carry out. Even lower down the chain of command a spirited local independence was to be the keynote of much IRA activity. One Volunteer, on being told by a superior that the legitimacy of his raids on the post office mails was in doubt and that there would have to be an IRA inquiry, refused to attend it. When told he would be forcibly taken to it, he replied that he would shoot to kill if an escort was sent. He therefore asked his own battalion commander either explicitly to sanction or call off the next mail raid.[45]

Such a state of affairs, an extension into politics of the whole Irish historical tradition of local secret societies, was to have significant political repercussions. The notion that the IRA was in anything but propagandist theory 'the constitutional army of Dail Eireann' was a myth.* For it, in the end, Ireland and Collins himself were to pay dearly.

At the latter end of 1919 the public attitude to the sporadic killings which, with the anti-police boycott, was still the chief activity of the Volunteers, continued ambivalent. On the one hand, there was a mounting dislike of the bloodshed on the part of the mass of moderate Nationalists who had voted Sinn Fein. On the other hand, there was also a mounting loathing of the military rule to which Volunteer activity gave rise, and this inevitably, given the whole background of Irish history, was directed not against the Volunteers who were the cause of these measures, but against the government which ordered them. The petty discomforts and insults of the military presence, to be read or heard about, if not experienced personally, acted as a continual goad to a sensitively conditioned Irish pride. Moreover, the enormity of the political insult which Ireland was experiencing in receiving, after the General Election and all the turmoil of the past few years, let alone the rest of Irish history, no further political acknowledgement of her national feelings at all, was something which festered daily in Irish minds. Not only

---

* For an example of the propaganda put out to this effect see the following passage from an interview given by de Valera to the *Neue Züricher Zeitung* on 3 May 1921:

Question: 'What is the position of the Republican Government towards the Army?'

De Valera: 'The Republican Army is the constitutional military arm of the Government of the Republic. It can be employed only where and in what manner this civil government prescribes. Its officers are under the control of and removable by the civil government. The Army is, therefore, a regular national defence force.' (Macardle, *Irish Republic*, p. 931.)

had many of her democratic representatives been arrested but the suppression at last of Dail Eireann itself in August 1919 had made the political impasse seem more hopeless than ever. Stories from Mountjoy gaol, where in October the Lord Mayor found thirty-nine Sinn Fein prisoners in handcuffs in solitary confinement, after refractory attempts to assert their political status, simply inflamed the national sense of political frustration, though most people probably shared the Lord Mayor's condemnation of Volunteer killings equally with his indignation at the prisoners' treatment.

The release of the Mountjoy prisoners later in the month after a successful hunger strike seemed like a national political victory in the absence of any other, particularly since only two days before, the government had prevented the annual convention of Sinn Fein from meeting with a display of armoured cars and lorry-loads of steel-helmeted troops in the Dublin streets. When, on 25 November 1919, the government suppressed Sinn Fein itself as a political organization throughout the country, Arthur Griffith was able to say with some substance to an interviewer: 'The English Government in Ireland has now proclaimed the Irish nation, as it formerly proclaimed the Catholic Church, an illegal assembly.' The old Nationalist Party newspaper, the *Freeman's Journal*, described the action as 'Nation-Baiting'.[46]

The confused popular attitude to the actions of the Volunteers was, however, well illustrated in a debate in the Clare County Council in December 1919. Tipperary North-East County Council had already passed a resolution placing on record horror at the outrages, saying they were acts of 'irresponsible persons with whom no responsible person could have the slightest sympathy'. It called on all public bodies 'to bring the perpetrators of such crimes to justice'. The Clare County Council met to decide whether or not to adopt this resolution itself. All the members were nationalists, either supporters of the old party or of Sinn Fein. One Nationalist Party supporter who wanted the resolution adopted said there was no man in the room who wanted to see an Irish Republic more than he did – 'If I saw an Irish Republic in the morning', he said, '– our own steamers leaving the Liffey, and being saluted by other Nationalities, I would die happy!' But outrages, he insisted, acted against Ireland's best interests. His chief Sinn Fein opponent who suggested that the resolution should simply be marked 'Read' argued that, if the government would grant Ireland self-determination, 'I have no doubt in saying it, in six months' time there will be no such thing as ... shooting at persons, or no such thing as outrages of any kind'. He spoke of the government as dealing out 'persecution and legalistic outrage' instead of justice and freedom. The Chairman summed-up by saying that nobody liked violence and the honest people of Clare did not like it, but the actual wording of the resolution played into the hands of Ireland's enemies. It was decided by a 9–5 vote simply to mark the resolution 'Read'.[47]

Just over a week later the government, speaking through no less a person

than the Prime Minister, offered Ireland for the first time since the General
Election something other than 'persecution and legalistic outrage' or simple
enforcement of the *status quo.* Lloyd George had already announced at the
beginning of the month that he hoped soon to make 'a real contribution
towards settling this most baffling of all problems'.[48] Now, speaking on 22
December 1919 in the House of Commons, he outlined proposals for a new
Home Rule Bill which he intended to introduce the following year.

It is possible now to see that in the context of the time this was at least
an attempt to think up something new. What seems astonishing, if it is to be
viewed at all as a genuine attempt to meet the wishes of the people of
Ireland rather than simply an attempt to safeguard the wishes of the Protestants of North-East Ulster, is that its authors should not have realized that
it would be the similarity of the proposal to what had already been rejected
which would make the impact on popular opinion, rather than the new
aspects.

In the first place, what was unchanged was the proposal to separate or
partition North-East Ulster from the rest of Ireland. Instead, however, of
excluding this area from Home Rule, it was to be given its own Home Rule
legislature, subordinate to Westminster. Another innovation, important in
the light of later events, was that the exact area of North-East Ulster to be
partitioned from the rest of Ireland was to be determined by taking the six
counties as a basis only and ironing out where practicable Catholic and
Protestant communities one side or other of the border, thus producing 'an
area as homogeneous as it is possible to achieve under these circumstances'.*[49]
But it was the fact of partition that made the impression. This was particularly in the light of the bill's second major defect for nationalists, for the
actual measure of Home Rule to be given both Parliaments of Ireland was
virtually the same as in the 1912–14 period, as if nothing had happened
in the interval to enlarge the concept of Irish national aspirations.

Some attempt to respect the concept of a united Ireland was met in a
proposed Council of Ireland with twenty members from each Parliament
which was to have the power, *without reference to Westminster,* to unite
the two Parliaments. But all the minor virtues of the proposed bill were
totally eclipsed by what seemed to all parties its major defects. The majority
of the Irish people – whom after all it was intended to placate – did not
want it because they regarded it doubly as an offence to their national
feelings. The southern Irish Unionists did not want it, partly on patriotic
principles, and partly because it isolated them from the rest of the Protestant
community of Ireland and reduced their representation to insignificance. The
Protestants of North-East Ulster did not want it, because they wished to

---

* This proposition, foreshadowing the later Boundary Commission, was dropped
when the bill made its appearance.

remain bound by the closest ties with Westminster. Given the geographic compactness of their strength they could still refuse to acknowledge, unlike southern Unionists, that the majority of the Irish people had any right to determine their own future.* The *Irish Times* summed up Lloyd George's proposal as follows:

> Its principle is hateful alike to Unionist and Nationalist. They know that national ideals and the ancestral spirit of a common patriotism cannot persist in a divided country. They know that the fantastic homogeneity which the Government proposes for the Ulster Unionists would be an excrescence on the map of Ireland, and would be ruinous to the trade and industry of the Northern Protestants. ... We yearn for peace, but in Mr Lloyd George's proposal we see not peace but a sword.[50]

This last forecast at least was soon proved accurate. Before the next year was out Ireland had become engulfed in horrors unsurpassed since the Rebellion of 1798.

---

* Though the proposal had no friends at all in Ireland, the northern Protestants eventually accepted it reluctantly as at least safeguarding what they regarded as the legitimate privacy of their interests. In 1920 it became the basis of the Government of Ireland Act (see p. 714) which, supplemented by the Free State Agreement Act and the Treaty provides the constitutional basis for the present Government of Northern Ireland. The six-county state has in fact turned out far better for northern Protestants' private interests than its leaders of the day immediately visualized. It has suited a strong strain of local self-sufficiency and independence which has always been present in the Ulster Protestant character and which, as seen above (Part Two) even manifested itself for a short time in favour of Irish nationalism. This strain's expedient identification with Unionism, and with leaders of a landed class who often became more English than Ulster in their attitudes, has sometimes obscured its essentially independent character. This may be observed today in conflict with its own leadership. It is part of the southern Irish nationalists' argument that this strain would realize itself more fully in a wholly Irish context.

7

Enter Black and Tans (1920)

The last means of assessing with some reasonable accuracy the real attitude of popular opinion to the Volunteers' campaign of violence took place in the middle af January 1920, with the municipal elections of that month.* These were fought under a new system of proportional representation, recently introduced by the government to give full weight to the views of minorities in Ireland, and were therefore unusually accurate. In the overall picture Sinn Fein which, though banned, was represented by individual candidates, swept the polls. It won control of eleven out of the twelve cities and boroughs of Ireland. An analysis of the actual votes, however, shows a different picture of attitudes to the campaign of violence.

Even if it can be assumed that all Sinn Fein voters were in favour of the killings, which was by no means the case, they were in terms of actual seats in a minority of more than two to one in all Ireland. 550 seats were won by Sinn Fein, as opposed to 1,256 by Unionists, Nationalists (of the old Party), Labour, Municipal Reformers and Independents. If it is supposed that some Labour voters were in favour of violence at this stage they may be taken as cancelled out by those Sinn Fein voters who disapproved of it, though there was probably a greater number of the latter. Even omitting the four north-east counties of Ulster, where the Unionist vote was of course disproportionately high, there were in the twenty-eight counties of nationalist Ireland only 572 Sinn Fein seats as opposed to 872 seats won by other parties. On the simple issue of self-determination or even the Republic itself, both Labour and Nationalist could have been reckoned with Sinn Fein in an overwhelming majority over the other parties, but on the issue of violence they must be counted with the opposition, as the debate in the Clare County Council had indicated.

None of this, however, was of much concern to Collins and the other men who were conducting the campaign of violence. Like all revolutionaries they had a larger view of democracy than one governed by mere voting processes and were only interested in the latter inasmuch as they could

* The County Council Elections of May 1920, and the General Election of 1921, in which every one of the parliamentary seats in twenty-six counties were uncontested, can hardly be said to have been fought under representative democratic conditions.

be of use to them. On the day after the final municipal election results were announced, Collins had Assistant Commissioner Redmond of the Dublin police shot dead in the back about forty yards from the Russell Hotel in the centre of the city. In Thurles, County Tipperary, an unarmed constable named Finnegan, a native of Galway with twelve years' service in the RIC, was shot in the groin and killed a few yards from the house where he had lived with his wife and two small children. In both cases the coroner's jury brought in verdicts of wilful murder.[1] This brought the total number of Irish police killed since the General Election of 1918 to fourteen, while over twenty others had been wounded.

Perhaps the most remarkable feature of this campaign of killing to date, backed as it was by an intense social boycott of those who were spared, was that the police had so far not retaliated in any undisciplined form. In general, in fact, the police morale had held remarkably well. When, in the country-side, patrols or barracks were attacked the police almost always refused to surrender and fought bitterly, often driving off superior numbers of their fellow-countrymen after a fight of several hours – though the real numbers of the attackers were usually far fewer than the police in the elation of triumph or the humiliation of defeat tended to claim. But on the night in January on which Constable Finnegan was shot in Thurles, an incident took place which was to establish a sinister new pattern of events and add a whole extra dimension of hopelessness to the already desperate situation in Ireland.

About half an hour after Constable Finnegan had been brought into his house in great pain, the quiet of the town was shattered by the noise of breaking glass and the firing of volley after volley in the streets. The police had gone on the rampage. A scene was enacted that was soon to be repeated so often in most parts of Ireland that it would seem as if there had never been a time when such things did not happen. People barred their doors and windows in a state of terror as they listened to what sounded like a pitched battle being conducted in the streets. Certain houses were selected for special attention, in particular that of the President of the local Sinn Fein club, where every pane of glass in the porch was smashed and bullets were sent crashing into the upstairs bedrooms, riddling the walls and the furniture. By good luck no one in the house was hurt, and when a little later a dozen police arrived looking for the owner he, fortunately for him perhaps in the light of later events elsewhere, had made good his escape. The offices of the local newspaper, the *Tipperary Star*, had its windows smashed with rifle butts and hand-grenades were thrown in, one of which burst on the editor's desk. In Thurles Cathedral the following Sunday the Archbishop of Cashel and the officiating clergy at all other masses vigorously condemned both the killing of Constable Finnegan and the subsequent 'orgy of violence' by the police as 'most grave violations of the law of God'.[2]

Such clerical denunciations of violence which continued manfully were now to lose some of their force by increasingly having to be projected in two opposite directions. They expressed the grave deterioration in affairs graphically, but the moral guidance they bestowed seemed more and more remote from what was actually happening. Thus, writing soon after the killing by the military of a woman and child in Limerick, an event which itself followed the shooting in the face there of an RIC sergeant and the imposition of new military restrictions, Cardinal Logue addressed himself in a Lenten Pastoral Letter to his flock as follows:

Not within living memory can we find in Ireland such calamitous conditions as exist at present ... a military regime rivalling in severity even that of the most pitiless autocracy, vindictive sentences ... arbitrary arrests more frequent than in pre-revolutionary France, deportations such as raised a wild cry of reprobation against the Germans when in military occupation of Belgium; these and similar acts of power cannot fail to create exasperation, recklessness, despair and general disorder. On the other side ... lawlessness and crime, such as any man guided by God's law must regret and reprobate.

These crimes, he said, were the work of 'a few irresponsible desperate hot-heads, probably the emissaries or dupes of secret societies.... We should never forget that however oppressive and intolerable conditions may appear, they cannot justify crime.... Crime can never aid us in the assertion of our rights.' And the Archbishop of Dublin echoed the Cardinal when he said that 'the end, no matter how noble, does not justify immoral means'.[3]

As the hierarchy were thus pronouncing, news came in of the killing of a woman of sixty-one in Enniscorthy after a pathetically ineffectual raid for arms there by some young Volunteers in masks who had felt they ought to do something in that district to emulate what was being done elsewhere.[4]

From March 1920 routine killings of both Crown servants and – by one party or another – ordinary citizens began to appear in the newspapers with a monotony which was soon to dull the senses. While Dublin acclimatized itself to the routine of a curfew and night raids by soldiers searching for suspects and documents, while police were shot in the counties of Kilkenny, Limerick and Tipperary, it was in the city of Cork that the shooting of a District Inspector named MacDonagh sparked off events which confirmed the newest pattern of trouble in Ireland. Once again the police got out of hand.

That same night, 11–12 March 1920, they took to the streets, firing volleys at random, and smashed up the Sinn Fein and Thomas Ashe clubs, breaking furniture and crockery and wrenching patriotic pictures from the walls. They also raided and damaged the house of a Sinn Fein alderman and that of a number of other Sinn Fein supporters.

At the next meeting of the Cork Corporation the Sinn Fein Lord Mayor, Tomas MacCurtain, spoke out. He said that there had been an attempt to conceal the fact that it was police firing in the streets that night and to suggest that this had been done by civilians. It was policemen, he said, who fired the shots and the responsibility should be fixed on them for shooting at people's property and putting the lives of citizens in danger. 'When nobody was around policemen fired shots all over the place. There could not be anything like peace in the city if this thing went on.'[5]

Two nights later an attack took place in the streets of Cork on a local alderman, Professor Stockley. Superficially it looked like a standard attempt by one of the Volunteer assassination squads: two men in civilian clothes came up to the Professor and fired at him with revolvers at close range. But the curious thing was that Stockley was a Sinn Fein supporter.

Amazingly the bullets passed through his coat leaving him unharmed, and the next day, at a meeting appropriately of the Public Health Committee of the Cork Corporation, he was congratulated on his marvellous escape. MacCurtain, the Lord Mayor, said the time was approaching when they would have to take steps to defend their rights and the lives of the citizens and their property. He said that they would ask those in charge of the forces in Cork to withdraw altogether and let the Corporation take over control of the city, and he pointed out that the usual police patrol had been operating in the street in which Stockley was shot at.

The night of this speech, an authentic Volunteer assassination squad was at work. An Irish Constable named Murtagh, a man with twenty-four years' service in the RIC who had just returned from attending the funeral of another constable shot in Tipperary, was himself shot dead in the streets of Cork. Two hours later a party of men armed with rifles but with blackened faces and wearing civilian clothes arrived at the Lord Mayor's house and demanded entrance. The police had often searched the house in the past and were familiar with its layout. Two men rushed straight upstairs to Mac-Curtain's bedroom and shot him at point-blank range in his pyjamas. Members of the household who tried to cry for help from the upstairs windows were fired at from the streets. A short time later a party of soldiers which had heard nothing of this event arrived at the house with orders to arrest MacCurtain and found him dead. Though there was a police barracks, which would have heard the shooting, only a few hundred yards away from the house, no police from there came near the house for several hours.

Attempts were immediately made by the British authorities to say that MacCurtain had been murdered by IRB fanatics on his own side for being insufficiently enthusiastic about the campaign of violence. But this theory, though perhaps not quite so inherently impossible as Irish sources have sometimes suggested, cannot stand up to the evidence of the inquest, combined with a knowledge of the previous deliberations in the Cork

Corporation. Few people in Cork or Dublin were in a moment's doubt about the real authors of the crime and the coroner's jury, though indulging a certain poetic licence, was substantially correct in returning a verdict of wilful murder against David Lloyd George, Lord French (the Viceroy), Ian Mac-Pherson (the Chief Secretary), District Inspector Swanzy of the RIC, and unknown members of the same force.

At MacCurtain's funeral, Irish Volunteers, who had stood guard over the body as it lay in state in the cathedral during the night, made all the practical arrangements and controlled the immense crowds with efficiency in the total absence of the police from the streets throughout the day. At the cemetery there was a roll of muffled drums, the Last Post was sounded and three volleys were fired by Volunteers over the grave, sending, in the words of the *Freeman's Journal*, 'their message of defiance in ringing echoes through the Glen of Glasheen. The echoes,' continued the paper, 'came from the hillside where stands the birthplace of the brothers Sheares'.*[6]

When Professor Stockley had so narrowly escaped the same fate as Mac-Curtain a few days before he had noticed one significant thing about his would-be assassins. They had talked, he said, 'like strangers'.[7]

For some time now the campaign against the police had begun to show results that were even more important than the number of dead and maimed. Individual members of the RIC had begun to prefer discretion to valour and to resign from the force. With them went an indeterminable number of others who felt a conflict of Irish loyalties in the present situation. This last factor may well have been exaggerated in propaganda both at the time and since, but for whatever reason a substantial number of resignations were taking place. The Recorder of a Crown court in February 1920 commented on the fact that they appeared to be going on 'to an extraordinary degree'.†[8]

The important consequence was that to fill the gap the authorities started recruiting for the RIC in England as well as Ireland. This had been going on since December 1919 and by 15 April 1920 some four hundred English recruits had been obtained in this way.[9] There was a shortage of the traditional dark bottle-green uniforms of the RIC – a fact which indicates that the force was being expanded as well as filled up – and at an inquest in April on a young man shot dead by the police it was noticed that 'Constables Grey and Hardwicke had khaki trousers'.[10] Thus there came into being the first consignment of what were soon to be known all over Ireland and go down to history as the Black and Tans.

The term seems first to have been applied to a group of RIC operating from a police station near Upperchurch, County Tipperary, and was adapted from the name of a local pack of hounds.[11] It began to come into regular popular usage in the late summer of 1920, although there were at that time

* For the Sheares brothers see above, pp. 100 and 46.
† Even so, only about ten per cent of the RIC had resigned by August 1920.

only some 1,200 such new recruits in the force. There were eventually to be about 7,000 of them altogether, the greater part recruited after 1 November 1920.[12]

The Black and Tans were supplemented by a new specially-raised Auxiliary Division of the RIC which was brought into being on 27 July 1920. The Auxiliaries were eventually to reach 1,500 in numbers, though only just over 500 of them had arrived in Ireland by the end of September 1920.[13] In some ways this Auxiliary Division, which permitted its members to wear either the traditional dark RIC uniform or army officers' service dress without badges of rank, with dark Glengarry caps, and which was to hunt rebels in motorized packs across the Irish countryside, qualified even more aptly for the term Black and Tans.[14] All the new forces were often referred to in tones equally expressive of hatred, contempt and healthy respect as 'the Tans'. And as such they have gone into Irish myth.

It has so often been stated that the Black and Tans were the sweepings of English gaols that it is necessary to re-state some facts about them and the conditions under which they were recruited. Appeals for recruits to the regular RIC were originally addressed to men who had been demobilized from the British Army and they had to supply, together with the name of their regiment, their army discharge and 'character'. No man was eligible with less than a 'good' character.[15] Their pay was to be £3 10s a week, rising to £4 15s. Only about 4,400 of them were recruited in England, Scotland and Wales which means that perhaps as many as a third were recruited in Ireland, mainly presumably from North-East Ulster.[16] The majority were not active in Ireland for more than eight months.

The members of the Auxiliary Division of the RIC, or 'Cadets' as they were officially called, had to be ex-officers of the army and also supply full particulars of their service. They were paid £1 a day plus allowances and had a month's leave a year. They were, as things turned out, to fight in Ireland for slightly under a year, most of them for not more than nine months.

In both cases the period was to be quite long enough. The Black and Tans left an indelible imprint on Anglo-Irish relations. Yet the new members of the old RIC and the members of the new Auxiliary Division were probably neither better nor worse than most battle-conditioned young men at the end of a long war. The large contingent of Englishmen among them, who were to prove the most callous, knew and cared little about Ireland, where they found themselves immediately not only unpopular and the object of an intense social and economic boycott but also in extreme physical danger, liable to be shot at as individuals or in groups at any hour of the day or night by civilians indistinguishable from other civilians who did not shoot at them. Whereas in 1919 thirteen policemen and one soldier had been killed by the Volunteers, in 1920 Crown casualties were to be much more than ten times that number – 182 police and 50 soldiers killed and 387 wounded altogether.

The anxiety and resentment which such conditions inevitably provoked in individuals strained even the traditional discipline of the British Army beyond breaking-point on occasions. It is not surprising that temporarily recruited men, subject to the less rigid discipline of a police force whose traditions they hardly shared, should increasingly take the law into their own hands, and when they saw the dead or mutilated bodies of their comrades brought into police stations and heard their cries of pain, want to wreak their vengeance on the locality, in their frustration at being unable to get at the real culprits. The vengeance they took as the year 1920 pursued its brutalizing course was increasingly savage.

Historically, what was to be important was that this vengeance, usually exacted from people quite innocent of the act that had provoked it, further consolidated national feeling in Ireland. It made the Irish people feel more and more in sympathy with fighting men of their own who were engaging a force actually composed increasingly of Englishmen. But so much emotive propaganda has been made, both at the time and since, out of reprisals, that it is necessary to remember that they were reprisals for things that had been done to the police, and that the majority of the personnel of the RIC remained, to the end, Irish. The increasingly brutal behaviour of the police, and the very rough Black and Tan reprisal campaign which was soon to develop, grew out of a situation in which an Irishman could have a shotgun discharged into his knee simply for joining the RIC or be killed while sitting drinking in uniform in a bar, or, having been shot in the back while on routine patrol, be finished off while lying on the ground asking for mercy.[17] These things all happened before any Black and Tan campaign had started in Ireland and at a time when all attacks on the police were abhorred and vigorously denounced both by local priests and also by bishops of the Church that represented the vast majority of the people of Ireland.

'Who are the police?' asked the national-minded Bishop of Cork, Dr Cohalan, in March 1920. 'They are Irishmen doing their duty,' and added with a confidence that was sadly misplaced: 'I am satisfied that the National Organization which the country has accepted and which it supports has no responsibility for these outrages.'[18] He pronounced their perpetrators to be outside the moral law.

The police at Thurles in County Tipperary who included some of the first constables in dark tunics and khaki trousers and who had suffered a number of casualties in March were already dealing out sterner medicine. In the last two days of the month a group of about six of them with blackened faces visited the houses of two young men from families of well-known national sympathies and shot them dead.[19] Apart from MacCurtain, the Lord Mayor of Cork, these were the first civilians to be murdered in retaliation. It was fifteen months since the campaign of killing had been begun against the police.

While the RIC which was already developing along these dangerous lines was being expanded by an influx of newly demobilized Englishmen, the government announced new public appointments for Dublin. The post of Chief Secretary was given to Sir Hamar Greenwood, a Canadian and a Coalition Liberal, who came to Ireland, in his own words, 'a life-long Home Ruler ... full of sympathy with Home Rule aspirations'. He seemed almost unaware of the deteriorating situation he was facing. The day on which he made this well-meaning statement, which time was so swiftly to render fatuous, was a typical one. The body of an Irishman named Foley, a former soldier in the Irish Guards who had later joined the RIC, was found in a yard in Kerry with hands tied and eyes bandaged, struck by twenty-six bullets – one of the 'spies' executed by the IRA to discourage the others.[*20] A man who had been interned for a time after 1916 as a rebel was shot dead by the police in Dundalk with less ceremony. In Milltown-Mallbay, County Clare, the funeral took place of three men who had been shot dead the day before when restless police and military had fired into a crowd. The crowd had been celebrating the release from Mountjoy gaol of seventy prisoners who had beaten the authorities with a ten-day hunger strike. This seemed an unmistakable national victory in which all Irishmen could join without reservation, some evidence at last that the government could be made to give in to moral pressure.

In the fortnight before Greenwood actually took up office the pace of events quickened horribly. Two Irish RIC constables were shot down as they walked out of Mass on Sunday in County Clare; a detective was shot by Collins's men in Dublin, bullets being fired into his stomach as he lay on the ground; two police were shot by masked men in County Cork; a man was shot by the military in Arklow, a police barracks in Tipperary was captured and its armoury ransacked, while another in County Dublin successfully beat off an attack. Two new nation-rallying hunger-strikes took place; one of 160 prisoners who had been deported to Wormwood Scrubs in London, and another of seventy-four prisoners in Belfast gaol.

For all this Lloyd George and the British Government had nothing to offer but the new team in Dublin and the 'Partition' or Government of Ireland Bill which was winding its way, unwanted and irrelevant, through the House of Commons. Those selected to assist Home Ruler Sir Hamar

---

* Collins had already had a number of such spies executed, including, in Cork, a man named Quinlisk, a former member of Casement's Irish Brigade, who had unquestionably been trying to betray Collins to the authorities for money. Others such as J. C. Byrne, alias Jameson, and Fergus Molloy, an RASC pay clerk, seem to have been professional agents of the British Government. (See Beaslai, *Collins*, vol. i, pp. 329–410.)

Greenwood included General Sir Nevile Macready who was made Commander-in-Chief of the Army in Ireland, and another regular army officer, General H. H. Tudor, who was put in charge of the RIC.

Macready, a son of the great Irish actor ('I have never considered myself in any way an Irishman,' he said), had taken part in the last battle in which the British Army had fought in red coats, at Tel-El-Kebir, and had a meritorious professional army career which, while it did not dispose him to think well of natives generally or indeed of any sort of people who gave trouble, had inculcated certain standards of decent behaviour. When he had been officially in Dublin and Belfast during the pre-war Home Rule crisis he had despised and disliked Birrell, as he did most politicians, but had scrupulously maintained the view that it was the British Army's duty to fight Carson and the Ulster Volunteers if called upon to do so.[21] Like many professional soldiers of the period he took an exaggeratedly straightforward view of complex problems and now as C.-in-C. of some fifty thousand troops in a country where many districts were to be under military rule, he hardly exercised an influence for enlightenment where subtler minds than his found themselves at a loss for policy.

A few months later the military hierarchy in Dublin was joined by a brash and fanatical adherent of the old imperialist school, the forty-year-old Brigadier-General Crozier, who was given command of the Auxiliary Division of the RIC. Brought up in Ireland in a classically Unionist tradition, Crozier had fought in a British square against the Hausa in West Africa, believed that military executions should be carried out by machine-gun fire, as being 'easier, more humane, less exacting and more accurate than a firing squad', and, having at one time been excessively addicted to alcohol, had taken the pledge eight years before. The eccentric violence of his irascible personality within its conventional framework led to clashes with Macready and Tudor over attempts of his to discipline his often undisciplinable Auxiliaries and he was to resign before the year was out and end up curiously, smarting under his experiences, an advocate of justice to Ireland.[22]

This, then, was the face the British Government presented in 1920 to the IRA and to the Irish people between whom it increasingly made no distinction, thus rendering them indeed increasingly indistinguishable. One young Irishman of this time was to write later: 'What probably drove a peacefully-inclined man like myself into rebellion was the British attitude towards us: the assumption that the whole lot of us were a pack of murdering corner boys.'[23]

Not only the RIC but the IRA too was developing its organization and extending its operations.

Collins in Dublin, taking great personal risks and cycling about the city without disguise on the principle that the absence of disguise was the best disguise for a 'wanted' man, had further perfected his intelligence system and was usually aware of most moves the authorities intended to make before they made them. Through his contacts not only in the police but in the post office and other services he kept a continuous check on official correspondence, even seizing on one occasion with the aid of armed men the entire Viceregal and Dublin Castle mailbag. Nor was his systematic liquidation of troublesome government agents confined to detectives and spies.

A Resident Magistrate of some experience, named Alan Bell, an Irishman of sixty-two from King's County, who as a young man in the RIC had helped investigate the hidden workings of the Land League, was appointed to try to locate the growing Republican Loan in the labyrinth of 'cover' bank accounts in which Collins had concealed it. Travelling to his office just after 9 a.m. on a Dublin tram, reading his newspaper, Bell suddenly found two young men standing beside him as the tram stopped at a routine halt. 'Come on, Mr Bell,' said one of them. 'Your time has come.' He was so aghast that he appeared unable to do or say anything. There was a moment of terrible suspense and anxiety in the crowded tram as everyone looked at each other in bewilderment. Nobody said a word. Then one of the young men spoke again: 'Ah, come on,' he said, and he and his companion with the aid of some other young men who came down from upstairs forced Bell out of the tram and along the pavement to where, while he stood erect and apparently unperturbed, they shot him dead. His killers, who were undisguised and were described as 'respectable young men', walked calmly away in a group and dispersed after a hundred yards or so. Of two passengers who came forward to try to do something for Bell, one had the use of only one arm. They called out, 'Is there nobody then to help us?' But nobody dared come forward.[24] The Irish half of the Republican Loan was successfully closed later that year at £357,000.

In the countryside the Volunteers, or IRA, began to move towards more ambitious operational methods. *An t Oglach* had announced at the beginning of 1920 that the period in the trenches was over and that a continuous policy of guerrilla war was now to be applied: 'Surprises, ambushes, raids on their fortified positions, sniping at their stragglers, capturing of their arms and equipment, interruptions of their communications.'[25] This sort of thing often sounded more impressive in theory than in practice. Sniping at stragglers, for instance, meant in reality shooting Irishmen emerging from Mass or cycling absent-mindedly along a country road. When two policemen (both Irishmen) were shot dead from their bicycles in this fashion in April, their comrades from Nenagh set fire to two creameries in the locality and the Volunteers, for all their military talk, were unable to do anything to prevent or even harass the reprisal. The Bishop of Ardagh and Clonmacnoise, speaking of what the Volunteers were doing, said that in fact it was nonsense for them to talk of being at war with the enemy;[26] and this was

true in more than just the moral sense in which he meant it. Nothing like
a coherent fought-out action between two bodies of troops had yet taken
place, or was really ever to do so, and the continual assaults with rifle and
bomb against local police stations, though occasionally successful, were
still continually beaten off. Nearly two-thirds of the raids made on occupied
police barracks during the year were unsuccessful.[27]

Such attacks had, however, at least led to garrisons being withdrawn from
a considerable number of small isolated outposts and, in an action in many
ways more impressive than some of the attacks themselves, on the night of
3–4 April 1920 over 150 of such posts were simultaneously burned all over
Ireland together with income tax offices in sixteen different counties. Such
action showed at least a remarkable ability to coordinate a plan on a
national level where serious opposition was not a factor. There were to be
repeat performances on a smaller scale in the following month and by the
end of the year 510 unoccupied 'barracks' in Ireland had been destroyed
altogether.[28] Also, evidence of something more than mere bravado was the
capture in June and successful concealment for over a month of the British
Commander of the forces in the South, Brigadier-General Lucas.

Lucas was surprised by Liam Lynch and some of his men while fishing
with other British officers on the River Blackwater. A nation-wide search in
which all means, including aircraft, were deployed failed to reveal the
General, and he only emerged again after loosening a bar over the window
of a room in which he was being held. He had spent the month 'on the run'
like his captors. He was reported as calling them 'delightful people', saying
he had been treated as a gentleman by gentlemen.[29] This was handsome
of him since he had a slight wound on his forehead as he faced the press,
caused when the military lorry which had picked him up wandering along
a road had later run into an ambush and, in the firing in which he participated, a bullet had grazed his head. Two soldiers in the lorry were killed.

One of the few army reprisals of the time had taken place after Lucas's
capture. Many shops in the town of Fermoy were attacked; plate-glass
windows were smashed; the local Sinn Fein hall was wrecked and damage
done to the town was generally estimated at several thousand pounds. No
one, however, was killed. This, in the grim daily balance sheet of the time,
was a gain compared with what was then happening, for instance, in Bantry.
For the police there were conducting what the *Freeman's Journal* described
as 'a reign of terror', beating up citizens with little concern for the niceties
of questioning procedure and incidentally shooting dead a crippled Sinn
Fein supporter named Cornelius Cowley.

The Bantry RIC had themselves just been through a particularly unpleasant time. On 12 June one of their number, Constable King, a native of
County Galway, had been cycling unarmed and in civilian clothes along
the road to Glengariff when he had been attacked and wounded by masked

men with revolvers. He managed to escape to a neighbouring house where he hid in a cupboard, but on being discovered was dragged out, and had his head blown off by his captors. His body was thrown on to a dungheap in the yard outside. Just over a week later another member of the Bantry force, Constable Brett, a Waterford man with thirty years' service in the RIC, had been shot and killed three miles outside the town.

Similar patterns of outrage and reprisal were establishing themselves as a routine feature of Irish life. In County Limerick where, after a five-hour siege, the RIC barracks at Kilmallock – last attacked by the Fenians in 1867 – was utterly destroyed and a sergeant and a constable were killed and six other constables wounded, hundreds of townspeople fled from their homes immediately in anticipation of reprisals, because a fortnight before, after the shooting of two constables in Limerick City itself, the RIC had run amok in the streets, felling people with rifle butts, breaking ribs, firing into houses, and shooting one man dead.[30] Those policemen who killed civilians in reprisals in this way were hardly ever brought to justice, any more than were those civilians who killed the police.

As well as the more spectacular outrages and reprisals dozens of smaller but equally painful examples interrupted everyday life over the greater part of Ireland, each one exacerbating the state of bitterness and apprehension in which people on both sides anticipated the next. Either soldiers or police might be involved. The burning of creameries on which the livelihoods of so many ordinary people in the Irish countryside depended could follow a small incident. Hugh Martin, the correspondent of the English liberal *Daily News*, reported that summer how on the afternoon of 22 July 1920 a number of young Volunteers attacked a girl of eighteen who was milking her father's cows, cut off her hair with a pair of shears and left her bound hand and foot in a field because she had been walking out with English soldiers. A few hours later the nearby cooperative creamery – one of the finest in Ireland – was burned to the ground. 'It is not difficult to understand the point of view of the soldiery,' wrote Martin. 'Here was a cowardly assault upon a woman, intended to insult the King's uniform. As usual, no official redress was possible.... Let it be known that a group of creameries will be wiped out for every outrage that occurs, and the community may be induced to stop the outrages.'[31] But, as he pointed out, the flaw in this argument was that the community could not stop the outrages even if it wanted to.

The frustration of knowing that there was no way of getting at the guilty was often responsible for the disproportionate scale of many reprisals. Thus when a few weeks later two Black and Tans were set upon in a Limerick park, robbed of their arms and tied humiliatingly to a tree, some thirty or forty of their comrades wrecked a number of streets in the city in a desperate attempt to obtain retribution of some sort.[32] In such an atmosphere the frontiersman's law of a life for a life soon came to seem like a natural right.* The real responsibility lay with a government which had let the political atmosphere deteriorate to such a pitch.

Politically indeed the most striking feature of the whole summer of 1920 lay less in the growing daily series of deaths and acts of violence, to which Ireland was becoming sickeningly accustomed, than in the extent to which king's writ was not only failing to run over large tracts of the country but was actually being replaced by the writ of the underground Dail Eireann. In this, of course, the IRA played a major part by asserting the Dail's writ where necessary by force.

Between 15 April and 8 June it had been possible to introduce the Sinn Fein courts of Arthur Griffith's concept together with Volunteer police patrols in twenty-one of the thirty-two counties of Ireland. The *Irish Bulletin*, a Sinn Fein propaganda sheet of considerable journalistic ability, run by two Volunteers, Desmond Fitzgerald and Frank Gallagher, with assistance from the former Home Rule gun-runner Erskine Childers, now an ardent Republican, made the most of this astonishing fact, so much more palatable for international and British home consumption than the killings of policemen which made it possible. By the middle of June the *Irish Bulletin* was able to report that eighty-four arrests of criminals in twenty-four counties had been made by Republican police in the past thirteen days. Both Republican Arbitration Courts and Criminal Courts met and performed their functions quite openly under Volunteer guard in those parts of the South and West of Ireland where Crown authority had temporarily vanished.

Perhaps the most spectacular feat of all had been to bring to Republican justice three men who had carried out a highly successful bank robbery at Millstreet in County Cork the year before. They had got away with some £20,000 and it had been assumed by many at the time that this raid by masked men had been simply one more example of the way in which the Volunteers were prepared to exploit patriotic motives for lawless ends. But Liam Lynch, the zealously ascetic Commandant of Cork No. 2 Brigade, in whose area the robbery had been carried out, had been determined to track them down as inexorably as he tracked the RIC or the British Army. He and his men eventually recovered almost all the money, which he faithfully returned to the banks concerned and, having arrested the thieves, brought them before a Republican court. They were sentenced to terms of fifteen, ten and eight years' deportation from Ireland, a sentence increased in the case of the first

* A curious echo of this summer's events in Ireland took place in June in India where some two hundred men of the Connaught Rangers mutinied at Jullundur in the Punjab. They had their own grievances and seized on the disturbing reports in letters from home to make a national protest and to refuse to soldier any more for England. The mutiny did not become very serious, the ring-leader was eventually shot by firing squad and several other mutineers were sentenced to long terms of imprisonment. See T. P. Kilfeather, *The Connaught Rangers* (Tralee, 1969).

man to twenty years when it was found that he had returned soon afterwards with a list of names for 'execution' in his pocket. This time he was escorted across the Irish Sea by a Republican armed guard.[33]

Other work of the Republican police at this time involved the enforcement of licensing laws, the suppression of illicit stills, arrests for house-breaking, cattle-stealing, drunkenness, 'riotious behaviour' and even on one occasion the apprehension of a bookmaker caught absconding with £67 12s from Barrastown Races in County Tipperary.[34] Methods of interrogation were sometimes rough and ready and at least once included flogging. Punishment was always a difficult problem for the Volunteer police because they had to contend with the anomaly that a rival system of justice was continually trying to arrest them and release their prisoners. Nevertheless, sentences of imprisonment were sometimes imposed – for instance, for breach of a Sinn Fein Land Court finding in County Galway. The guilty were described as being removed 'to an unknown destination'. When some prisoners serving a three-week term on an island off the west coast were rescued by the RIC they refused to accept their release on the grounds that they were loyal citizens of the Irish Republic.[35] Fear of still direr Republican punishment if they accepted their freedom at the hands of the police may have had something to do with it. In other cases sentences included fines – for example, twice the amount stolen from an old-age pensioner – banishment from the province, or, in the case of some land-hungry men who had levelled the walls of a Galway land-owner, the rebuilding of the walls.

There had been an understandable tendency on the part of the agrarian poor and the landless to try to take advantage of the prevailing chaos to improve their position, and a good part of the Sinn Fein court activity was concerned with such operations or disputes over land. The courts respected the rights of property and a Unionist peer, Lord Monteagle, went so far as to praise in the House of Lords the high standards of justice and equity that were dispensed there. Simultaneously, a Sinn Fein Land Commission held inquiries in many parts of the country to determine what might legitimately be done by proper authority to assist genuine cases of land hunger and hardship.

One special activity of Volunteer or Republican police had been to patrol polling stations and protect ballot boxes when Local County Council Elections took place at the beginning of June 1920. The results were, as expected, an overwhelming victory for Sinn Fein. County Council after County Council now declared their allegiance to Dail Eireann, withholding payments of rates and taxes from the Local Government Board wherever practically possible. The Meath County Council carried a resolution thanking the Volunteers for their efficiency in the elections and allowing them expenses, and also resolved that the Republican tricolour should be hoisted above the Council Chamber in place of the old green flag. In Sligo prayers invoking success for the Republic were recited in Irish and a speaker advised the new local Scholarship Committee to see that no policemen's children were allowed to compete. Roscommon County Council extended congratulations to the Irish Republican Army on its success in the field 'and the many fortresses it had captured'. Copies of the resolution were ordered to be sent to 'the Commander-in-Chief of the IRA'.[36]

When, in July and again in August 1920, sessions of the underground Dail were held in Dublin and most members were able to participate, in spite of the incessant military raids and searches which made day and night so irksome to ordinary citizens, the claim that there was an alternative government in Ireland with real authority was able to look quite plausible and impressive. The Dail laid down limitations on rent, declared religious tests for employment illegal, announced an Economic Commission for Ireland and made emigration from Ireland without special sanction illegal. Within the country, the important British rail communications system was severely hampered by an edict ordering train-drivers, guards and firemen not to work trains carrying troops or police. Some complied with straightforward patriotic enthusiasm. For others perhaps, as in the days of agrarian secret societies, faced by two rival systems of authoritarian law, it was a question of acquiescing most easily with the one which claimed to be on your side. There were, however, also those who had to be persuaded and there were a number of cases of engine-drivers and guards who were stripped and tarred by the IRA as a punishment for defying the edict or seized and frightened into signing a document that they would never do so again.[37]

On the whole, what might so easily have been just a pretentious illusion – the notion of a genuine 'Ourselves Alone' or Sinn Fein government operating simultaneously and in many ways more effectively than the king's writ – was by the late summer of 1920 something of a reality. That this was possible was due to the violent campaign against authority conducted by the Volunteers, or IRA. It was a fact which inevitably blurred still further such reservation as Griffith and other moderates may have had about the campaign of violence itself. Their own policies had been brought to fruition because of violence; it was difficult any longer to dissociate the one from the other. And it became easy for Sinn Fein moderates to forget the extent to which their political activity took place on sufferance from the IRA.

In another important respect, too, the members of the Dail were living in an illusion. They claimed, of course, to be a Parliament for All Ireland, but considerable areas of North-East Ulster were not represented in the Dail at all and regarded the claim with abhorrence. The fact was unpleasantly emphasized in the summer on a number of occasions when members of Carson's Ulster Volunteers in the North, inflamed and exasperated by accounts of events in the South, took the law into their own hands and exacted vengeance from the minority of Sinn Fein Irishmen who lived among them.

In June there had been appalling scenes of anarchy in Derry when at least nine people were killed in two days. The Dail in its partial success found itself glossing too easily over the fact that the really important obstacles to realization of an All-Ireland nationalism not only remained as intractable as ever but was actually being made more intractable still by events. In the wake of this illusion came a semi-parochial view of nationalism concentrating too easily on twenty-six counties of Ireland instead of thirty-two.

The Dail's confidence of that summer was reflected at an important conference which took place in Dublin between senior IRA officers from the country and Collins and Brugha. Some of the officers pressed for a campaign in England of counter-reprisal for reprisals in Ireland. The final directive issued was that the guerrilla campaign should be slowed down so that the civil administration could be allowed to develop.[38] But the pace of the guerrilla war was determined not by directives from Dublin but by what was actually happening in the countryside. And with the inauguration of the Auxiliary Division of the RIC at the end of July, and a continuing influx of Englishmen into the RIC, the war was to be speeded up rather than slowed down. There had been 556 more Irish resignations from the RIC between 1 May and 31 July 1920 and their places had been taken by over eight hundred more Black and Tan recruits. The British Government was not prepared to see the royal writ in Ireland superseded so easily.

8

Murder by the Throat (1920)

In the summer of 1920 the situation, from the British Government's point of view, looked bad on every count. Politically there was no longer even an attempt to make progress; the discredited Government of Ireland Bill had to continue to serve as a panacea. But militarily, too, the position was humiliating. The least that might have been expected of a government that had decided not to compromise with political demands was that its authority should be effective. But the government's authority was plainly not effective. The royal writ no longer ran in many parts of Ireland. The RIC, for all its numerical strengthening over the 10,000 mark by the Black and Tan element, was increasingly confined to barracks and depots, unable, in face of the campaign of slaughter, to continue usefully that steady day-by-day patrolling by small groups or individuals which is the essence of effective police work. General Macready had some 50,000 troops, mostly of British regiments, at his disposal, but troops are notoriously bad at police work, a fact which was demonstrated all too plainly in Cork at the beginning of August. For there, at a meeting in the Town Hall, troops captured not only five senior officers of Cork No. 1 Brigade IRA, but also Liam Lynch himself, apparently without realizing the importance of their find. Lynch gave a false name, but some of the other IRA men did not even do that. Four days later all were released with the exception of Terence MacSwiney who was held, presumably for prestige reasons, in his capacity as Lord Mayor. The troops were unaware that he was also OC Cork No. 1 Brigade, thinking that what they had surprised was a Republican court in session.

But if the government could no longer effectively police the country, they also could not hope to keep it effectively under military control with only 50,000 troops and without the benefit of martial law. Although military restrictions were in force in the disturbed areas and courts-martial had taken over the work of the normal courts, the penalties they applied were often in the circumstances amazingly light. At a time when any policeman was liable to be shot dead by any civilian at any time, sentences for illegal possession of a revolver and ammunition had hitherto never been more than two years' imprisonment, even when the prisoner proudly proclaimed himself 'a soldier of the Irish Republic'. Often they were as little as six months. Similarly, large numbers of Volunteers were readily identifiable and might easily have been interned even though no individual charge could be preferred against them. But though the government had powers to intern without trial under the Restoration of Order in Ireland Act 1920 it had not yet taken them and no internment camp had yet been opened. In fact, if the authorities had simply arrested in a body the chief mourners at the funeral of Tomas Mac-Curtain in March they would have apprehended some of the important men engaged in Collins's headquarters operations in Dublin: Richard McKee, Peader Clancy, Gearoid O'Sullivan and Frank Thornton were all there openly and even photographed in the procession.[1]

What in fact was happening was that the government was earning all the political opprobrium of a tough policy with very few of its attendant military benefits. Sir Henry Wilson, Chief of the Imperial Staff, was exasperated by the illogicality of the situation. 'I don't see any determination or driving power in the Cabinet,' he wrote in his diary on 28 June. 'I really believe that we shall be kicked out.'[2] Slowly, cumbrously, over the next few months and particularly after the arrival of the first companies of the Auxiliary Division of the RIC, the government was in fact to grow effectively tougher and re-establish at least some of its lost control. But the price was to be a still bloodier contest and a proportionate further deterioration in the general Irish situation. Meanwhile, humiliated like the government they represented and in considerably greater physical danger, the RIC and particularly the Black and Tan element increasingly exercised a tough and vindictive initiative of its own.

On the night of 20 July a motor-car bringing four Irish constables of the RIC back from Galway Assizes was brought to a halt by trees felled across the road three miles outside Tuam. A volley of shots was fired into it from behind a hedge and a Constable Burke of Birr, and a Constable Carey of Skibbereen were shot dead, the other two being overpowered, blindfolded, disarmed and told to return to Tuam. At about three o'clock in the morning the patrols which had been out looking for the ambushers returned to the police barracks and, after viewing the bodies of their dead comrades, marched fully armed into the streets of Tuam and started firing into windows, wrecking shops, rushing into houses and dragging the occupants from their beds with threats to shoot them. No one in fact was killed. 'We are going to give you more mercy than you or some of your chums showed to my comrades,' a constable said to a young electrician named Neville whom he dragged out into the street. But Neville, a Sinn Fein supporter, hardly felt reassured when he saw ten to fifteen police there with their rifles raised and heard one of them say, 'Have you made an Act of Contrition? If not, make it.' They contented themselves with marching him to the barracks for questioning and firing shots over his head. Meanwhile, terrified inhabitants, confined to their houses by cries of 'Get back or you'll be shot', and huddled on the stairs or in the backs of houses, recited the Rosary and listened to the smashing of glass, the firing of shots and the dull thuds of hand-grenades in the streets outside. The Town Hall, the most prominent shops and some houses were set ablaze by the police with cans of petrol.

There seem to have been no Black and Tans among the police on this occasion. So much efficient propaganda about reprisals was made on behalf of the Sinn Fein cause that it can now be too easily forgotten that a strong element of civil war was involved in the events of 1920–21; it accounted for much of the peculiar savagery. The effect of reprisals, however, was much the same whoever committed them and was simply further heightened as English Black and Tans increasingly came to carry them out. As the *Galway Express* put it after these first reprisals at Tuam: 'When they throw petrol on a Sinn Feiner's house, they are merely pouring paraffin on the flames of Irish nationality.'[3]

From a Sinn Fein point of view this was in itself a strong argument in favour of ambushes. From the government point of view it was an equally strong argument in favour of the need to keep reprisals in check. But although the police were, admittedly, technically more difficult to discipline than the Army, the government seems to have awoken slowly to the political consequences of reprisals, concentrating at first on the wholly irrelevant point that while deplorable they were understandable. They did not seem understandable to the innocent people who usually suffered from them. And the vile incident that often provoked them quickly got lost sight of in the subsequent much more spectacular outburst. Though the Archbishop of Tuam castigated equally the 'murder' of the constables and the wrecking of the town as crimes, there could be little doubt how the inhabitants of Tuam and every other nationalist Irishman who read of the events would weigh the two crimes in the political balance. And when a few days later in Thurles a Sergeant Mulhern of the RIC was shot dead going in to Mass by two men who had been waiting for him with revolvers inside the porch, it was the subsequent reprisal which in the national situation easily became the greater event. The atmosphere round Thurles became tenser still when a few days after Mulhern's death an ambush took place near the village of Upperchurch a few miles away and two Black and Tans were badly wounded. A family of four in Upperchurch then experienced what was soon to become the standard type of Black and Tan raid.

Roused from their beds at two o'clock in the morning by a battering of rifle butts on the door, they opened it to be faced by a group of police, some wearing ordinary dark uniforms and others khaki, several of them also with blackened faces or wearing masks in imitation of similar raiding parties of the IRA. The family was ordered out of the house clutching their clothes while the roof was set ablaze. They moved towards the stable, but the police fired at them and the young man of the family received two flesh wounds.

'After this,' he recounted later, 'we dashed for the stable. We prayed for God's protection. The house was blazing, but we could do nothing. There were a few minutes silence that appeared to be ages and we thought our assailants had withdrawn. I made a move to put on my clothes when suddenly a man wearing police uniform rushed in. He flashed a light upon me, put it out again and then fired at point blank range.' The young man fell over backwards but had not been hit. The policeman, apparently thinking him dead, went out again, and a few minutes later there was the sound of a motor lorry driving away with a firing of shots and 'loud yells like the whoops of savages'.[4]

In Limerick innocent people were less lucky. A small boy was shot dead by reckless firing in the streets, and a young man who was an epileptic was killed while having tea. Limerick suffered again at the end of August when Collins had a District Inspector Wilson shot in Templemore, County Limerick. Wilson was particularly popular with his men and an area of the city was badly wrecked when the police ran amok there the next day. A young Sinn Fein supporter named Patrick Lynch was taken from his house by police and shot dead. It was the beginning of an appalling fortnight. At the weekend no fewer than seven policemen and one army officer were killed in ambushes in different parts of Ireland, one of them being the District Inspector Swanzy whom the Cork jury had indicted for the murder of MacCurtain. Swanzy was shot dead in his home town of Lisburn, County Antrim. It was an Orange town and forty houses of Catholics were burned down in revenge. During this same week, in riots in Belfast triggered off by events in the South, twenty people were killed and eighty-seven wounded.[5]

Even in nationalist Ireland there was still strong disapproval of the attacks on the police which provoked these reprisals. The IRA made it a dangerous sentiment to express. But there were brave men who spoke out what was on their consciences. Thus, in County Kildare the foreman of a jury at an inquest on a RIC constable killed near Naas, tactfully directed by the Coroner to give an innocuous verdict of 'slugs fired by person or persons unknown', said he could not agree to that. It was murder, he said, and not less so because it had a political motive. He would rather go down in his coffin than have the taint of murder on his soul.[6] Braver still were a coroner's jury in County Carlow the following month, who in their verdict on two RIC sergeants named Delaney and Gaughan killed near Tullow, actually dissociated themselves from a policy of attacking the police.[7] It was safer for the Church to say such things. At Mass in Longford at the beginning of September the Most Reverend Dr Hoare, referring to the killing of two more police, indignantly denied the excuse that all this was part of a war. 'We are not at war,' he cried. 'If we are, it should be declared or waged by the public and competent authority and not by a few individuals.'[8]

But increasingly it was horror at the reprisals and the special moral indig-

nation aroused by acts of lawlessness committed by the forces of law themselves which dominated public opinion not only in Ireland but in liberal
England too. It became easier to think of the ambushes and even the individual killings as acts of revenge for the ruthlessness which the authorities
let loose with the Black and Tans. By September 1920 reprisals were already
routine. In fact, in that month more than twenty police of the RIC were shot
dead in singles or in groups, in ambushes on country roads or in the towns
in which they were stationed, bringing the total of RIC deaths for 1920
alone to over a hundred, with 170 wounded. Only a few of those killed
were English Black and Tans, the majority being Catholic Irishmen like
Constables Keefe and Downey, shot leaving a pub where they had been
having a drink in County Clare, both men who were well-liked locally. Constable Downey had already sent in his resignation from the force.[9] But it was
the chain of reprisals, in which civilians were killed and creameries burned
down that affected opinion and were effectively publicized by the *Irish
Bulletin*.

At Balbriggan (County Dublin) on 21 September a Head Constable
Burke was shot down in daylight in the streets. Burke had been popular as
an instructor at the nearby Black and Tan recruits' depot at Gormanstown
and lorry-loads of Black and Tans arrived in Balbriggan during the night,
and again during the following day, setting fire to shops and houses, firing
rifles and throwing hand-grenades indiscriminately, generally terrorizing the
inhabitants under cover of a search for the culprits and shooting and bayoneting two citizens to death in their nightshirts. Their corpses, declared an
eye-witness, looked 'as if they had been killed not by human beings but by
animals'.[10] A sight hitherto associated with the flight of Belgian and French
refugees before the German invaders was thus seen within twenty miles of
the Irish capital as women and children fled from the blackened ruin of their
homes with belongings on perambulators and hand-carts in anticipation of
another visit from the Black and Tans during the night.

A phenomenon not seen in Ireland since the terrible summer of 1798 now
made its appearance, as a regular sunset exodus took place from small towns
and villages which were anticipating reprisals, and people slept out at night
in hedgerows and beside haystacks and in old barns just as Thomas Cloney
had described them as doing in County Wexford over a century before.*
When as many as four police were killed at once in one ambush at Dineen
in County Clare,† the towns of Miltown Malbay, Lahinch and Ennistymon
experienced the full force of RIC and Black and Tan fury. The wife of the
local Secretary of the Irish Transport and General Workers' Union was
driven from her house in the middle of the night with her baby in her arms,

---

* See above, p. 100.
† Only one of those killed was an Englishman; the others came from Counties Cork,
Roscommon and Sligo.

while her husband was kept behind and shot and then cremated in the blazing ruins of his own house. Another civilian was killed for trying to help a neighbour whose house had just been set fire to. An eye-witness wrote:

You never saw anything so sad as the sight in the sandhills that morning. Groups of men and women, some of them over seventy years, practically naked, cold, wet, worn-looking and terrified, huddled in groups on the wet grass. I met two mothers with babies not three weeks old, little boys, partly naked, leading horses that had gone mad in their stables with the heat, and then when we got near the village a group of men standing round the unrecognizable corpse of Salmon [the civilian who had tried to put out his neighbour's blaze], distracted people running in all directions looking for their friends with the awful thought haunting them that the burned corpse might be some relative of their own. Oh, it was awful! Every evening since then there is a sorrowful procession out of the village. The people too terrified to stay in their houses sleep out in the fields.[11]

Similar scenes followed a few days later the wrecking and burning of houses in Trim, County Meath, by Black and Tans after the RIC barracks there had been captured in an IRA attack and destroyed. This time some refugees spent the night in a Protestant churchyard. The next day the army itself took reprisals in Mallow, County Cork, after the death of a sergeant in a raid on the barracks there. The attack had been carried out with much resource by Lynch and O'Malley who smuggled themselves and their men unobserved into the town in the course of the night, and hid in the Town Hall until daybreak. While they waited O'Malley told his men the story of the wooden horse of Troy.[12] They captured thirty rifles and two Hotchkiss machine-guns in the raid and the subsequent wrecking and firing of the town, which they witnessed impotently from the hills around, and which involved the destruction of property belonging to Unionists and Sinn Feiners alike, lasted for three and a half hours.

By the end of September 1920 there were still only just over five hundred members of the new Auxiliary Division of the RIC in Ireland, but they had quickly made an effective impact.[13] Their role was envisaged from the start as more mobile than that of the regular RIC and Black and Tans with whom, because of the similar mixture of uniforms, they tended to be indiscriminately labelled. Divided into companies of about a hundred men each they were distributed as independent units to different bases in particularly disturbed areas, and from these they emerged periodically in their Crossley tenders or motor lorries, asserting their presence by a liberal discharge of ammunition in a search for trouble. By the spring of 1921 there were to be fifteen such companies altogether, three in County Cork, three in Dublin itself and one each in Counties Kerry, Clare, Tipperary, Kilkenny, Meath, Roscommon, Sligo and Longford – an indication of the areas of Ireland where the IRA operated as an effective force.[14] The first mobile company to be thus installed took up residence in Macroom Castle which was commandeered for them in October 1920.[15]

The introduction of the Auxiliaries matched a new development in the style of operation of the IRA. At the end of May two senior officers of the Limerick IRA, who had themselves just successfully crossed about thirty miles of open country, armed, in broad daylight, by judicious selection of resting-places and avoidance of the towns, came to the conclusion that there was no reason why a larger body of armed men should not be able to move about the countryside in a similar fashion.[16] This notion of an active service unit, or flying column, was then put into practice in East Limerick and the principle enthusiastically adopted and advocated to other IRA brigade areas by Collins at GHQ in Dublin. The flying column, a nucleus of about thirty-five men on full-time active service for specific periods, supplemented where necessary by part-time IRA men who otherwise continued with their normal civilian lives, now became the chief offensive weapon of the IRA. Probably no more than about three thousand men took part in such flying columns altogether, though the full nominal strength of the IRA in 1921 was 112,650.[17] But with the RIC Auxiliary garrisons increasing simultaneously and new Black and Tan recruitment for the regular RIC force being stepped up dramatically, the 'war' was to take on a new ferocity, with, as usual, the ordinary Irish population suffering in the middle.

The illusory calm in some districts in which it had appeared that the royal writ had been successfully replaced by that of Dail Eireann was shattered as the Auxiliaries and other Black and Tans asserted their presence more and more aggressively. Republican courts were raided and broken up and had to retreat to the shadows. Places which had seen no police other than those of the IRA for weeks were suddenly jolted back to the reality of a more regular authoritarian government as a lorry-load of Auxiliaries came to a halt in the main street: Englishmen who regarded the Irish as hostile natives, firing off their rifles at random to show it. Thus at Moycullen in County Galway a Crossley tender full of Auxiliaries, trailing a Republican flag behind it in the dust, arrived one Sunday just as the congregation was leaving Mass. The men were herded into a field at revolver point and told that an unpopular land agent was being reinstated in his house and that if anyone touched him, six Republicans would be killed. At Athenry in the middle of the night a lorry-load arrived firing shots and forced a number of people in their night clothes to call off their boycott of the police. These abrupt reminders of the realities of power began to have their effect and a number of IRA officers wrote to GHQ in Dublin in October saying that they were hard pressed in their localities. The police boycott had to be called off in Ballaghdareen, Dungarvan, Arklow and many other places. One IRA man wrote of 'a great falling-off and loss of confidence, as if a kind of terror were slowly creeping in'.[18]

Members of the government began themselves to feel a new and fatal confidence. 'We are going to break up this murder gang,' declared Winston Churchill at Dundee on 16 October. 'That it will be broken up utterly and absolutely is as sure as that the sun will rise tomorrow morning.... Assassination has never changed the history of the world and the Government are going to take good care it does not change the history of the British Empire.'[19]

But assassination continued. Whenever an ambush took place families now automatically fled from their homes in anticipation of the inevitable reprisals, and further to complete the analogy with 1798 the Black and Tans started stripping civilians and flogging them with straps and whips to obtain information about the IRA. Twenty civilians were so dealt with on one day in County Clare in October.[20] They took, too, to the cropping of the heads of known women Sinn Fein supporters in retaliation for the same treatment which the IRA had long been inflicting on Irish girls rash enough to fall for policemen. And a sixteen-year-old boy was reported to have been half-hanged at a farmhouse near Angharan.[21]

Feelings grew more and more savage on both sides. Attempts on the part of decent RIC officers to exercise discipline over their men grew more and more ineffectual. 'I have never seen men in such anger,' declared one, describing how he had been totally unable to restrain his own men as the body of an Irish Detective Inspector shot in an ambush at Tobercurry, County Sligo, was brought into their barracks. A constable who had been in the ambush with him was wandering about with shotgun pellets in his face while in an adjoining room another constable was moaning with pain as he lay there with the calf of his leg blown off. That night four heavy lorries entered Tobercurry crowded with men who loosed-off volleys of rifle fire and, smashing their way with sledge-hammers into groceries and other stores, looted and wrecked them and later destroyed two local creameries.[22]

Again, however valiantly the Roman Catholic clergy might continue to maintain that the ambushes were as wrong as the reprisals – the Bishop of Kildare categorically insisted that they were worse[23] – it was the reprisals that seemed to ordinary people the wrong that mattered. Even the Bishop of Achonry, writing to the parish priest of Tobercurry to sympathize with the people in their ordeal, while conventionally condemning the ambush as 'a shocking atrocity' clearly found his sympathies torn by the situation.

That bad government is primarily responsible is only too true [he wrote]. But ... for myself and for my priests who know our young men so well and admire them for their sobriety, for their virtue and for their sensitiveness to honour's reproach, the bitterest ingredient in the cup of sorrow which is ours is the thought that these fine fellows, so stainless and pure in most ways, will, under the delusion that they are doing a service to their country, imbrue their hands in the blood of a brother, and speed the bullet that leaves wife without husband, the child without the father.... These boys allege that they must obey orders. What does that mean? It must mean that they are in the grip of some secret organization which arrogates the authority to impose its will, no matter whether the thing proposed is right or wrong.[24]

A few days later one of these 'boys', Sean Treacy, who had been with Breen at Soloheadbeg and Knocklong and had since been OC of No. 3 Tipperary Brigade, was cornered and shot down in a daylight gun battle in Dublin. He easily became a hero as legendary as Cuchulain and an ancient Irish lament was adapted to commemorate his death: '...Our lovely Sean is dead and gone, Shot down in Talbot Street.'*

Not only in Ireland but in England, too, it was the horror of the reprisals that increasingly counted. And it could be convincingly argued that it was right and proper that it should. The violence was after all the product of the government's failure to solve the political problem in a manner acceptable to the majority of the Irish people. Having chosen instead simply to assert its authority, it was intolerable by any recognized standards of civilized government that that authority should itself be asserted by lawless methods. This was the point on which the government's critics seized to the exclusion of all others, however much they might also deplore the methods of the IRA.

Excessively heartened perhaps by premature hopes of success with the 'murder gang' the government continued to be slow to appreciate the political threat thus developing on its own flank. Lloyd George after all was a Liberal Prime Minister and he led a coalition partly dependent on Liberal support in the country. But he concentrated at first simply on the point that the police had been 'unendurably provoked'. 'There is no doubt,' he said at Caernarvon in October, 'that at last their patience has given way, and there has been some severe hitting back. But take the conditions...'[25] He argued that civilians in Ireland shot at the police without warning so that it was no wonder the police shot fast.

Though a perfectly fair point, it was not the one that was relevant politically. Aside from the moral issue that no civilized government should exercise its authority by uncivilized methods, what mattered politically was that in Ireland the conflict was being daily regarded more and more in the purely nationalistic terms in which the extremists had always painted it. Every day aggravated still further the original difficulty of achieving a political solution.

By 1921 the authorities were fully alive to the dangers of lawlessness by the Crown forces and were to make considerable efforts to impose discipline. These were at least partly succcessful. There were no more of the large-scale undisciplined reprisals of the sort that had caught the headlines in the summer and autumn of 1920 and reached their climax in December 1920 with the burning down by a company of Auxiliaries of a large part of the

---

* He had shot his way out to safety a few weeks earlier when trapped in a raid on a Dublin house together with Dan Breen.

centre of Cork.* Reprisal killings by Crown forces on the other hand continued ruthlessly, either by men with blackened faces dragging individuals
from their beds in the middle of the night or in the traditional form of men
shot 'trying to escape'. Yet considering the very sharp intensification of the
conflict which took place in 1921 the government attempt at least to impose
discipline cannot be ignored.

In the first three months of 1921, some 208 Black and Tan RIC and 59
Auxiliaries were dismissed as unsuitable; a further 28 RIC and 15 Auxiliaries
were removed from the force as a result of prosecutions and in addition a
total of 24 more RIC and Auxiliaries were sentenced by court-martial.[26]
Some of the sentences awarded were even quite severe and included five years'
imprisonment for assault, stealing a bottle of whisky and demanding two
bottles of whisky and a bottle of stout with intent to steal, or three years for
stealing clothes and a piece of jewellery to the total value of £10.[27] Only one
successful prosecution for murder was, however, instituted against an
Auxiliary for the deliberate killing by the side of the road of a priest, Canon
Magner, and a civilian, which was witnessed by an Army officer. The
Auxiliary was found guilty but insane. In another court-martial of three
Auxiliaries for the murder of two men in the Dublin suburb of Drumcondra,
the accused were found not guilty in a verdict that seemed seriously at
variance with the disclosed facts.†[28] But even so, such measures revealed a
change of attitude from the latter part of 1920 when General Macready had
on one occasion said to an interviewer that it was only human that the police
should act on their own initiative, adding: 'Punishment for such acts is a
delicate matter, inasmuch as it might be interpreted as setting at naught the
hoped-for effect of the training the officers have given the men.'[29] Sir Hamar
Greenwood had made the unfortunate statement in the House of Commons
about the same time that he had yet to find one authenticated case of members of the Auxiliary Division being accused of anything but the highest
conduct.[30]

One means by which more discipline was eventually achieved was the
substitution of a policy of 'official' for unofficial reprisals – the destruction by
the military of houses near the scenes of ambushes when it was thought that
their owners could have given the authorities warning of what was being
planned. This, however, was a double-edged device. In the first place it
appeared to add to the reprisal policy since unofficial reprisals by no means

---

* The results of an official inquiry into the burning of Cork by General Strickland
were never published – in itself a conclusive enough indictment of the Crown forces.
Though making some injudicious statements at the time about the fire being caused by
accident, Sir Hamar Greenwood virtually conceded later in the House of Commons
that the Crown forces were responsible.

† One of the Auxiliary officers found not guilty was a captain who had beaten and
tortured Ernie O'Malley when he was captured for a time under the false name of
Stewart. He eventually escaped. (O'Malley, *On Another Man's Wound*, pp. 246–8.)

692 Ourselves Alone

ceased and all thereby tended to seem official. Second, though official reprisals may have made some of the Crown forces feel better, they hardly diminished the sense of indignation on the part of the house-owners who were thus presented with the alternative of the destruction of their house or their own 'execution' by the IRA as spies if they gave information to the authorities. And although General Strickland, Commander of the Forces in the South, maintained that this factor was taken into account, the probability of being given much benefit of doubt by the forces on the spot in the circumstances of the time must have been remote.[31] The owners' sense of indignation was echoed by all who read about or saw pictures of such things in the newspapers.

This was the all-important effect of all reprisals, however caused. They consolidated a real sense of national struggle, confirming the point separatists had always tried to make but which had never before seemed much more than interpretative fantasy, that it was the Irish people on one side and the forces of England on the other. Blackened houses, wrecked creameries, the corpses of innocent civilians were constant visible symbols of the total bankruptcy of British Government policy in Ireland. And to fight against such things seemed now, more and more, the only policy Ireland herself required.

Encouraged by the undoubted superficial success of the autumn campaign Lloyd George tended to lean on it heavily for comfort. Like any good politician he kept open such other options as there seemed to be, but these were few. This was not entirely his own fault. His whole political nature was of the sort that was happiest with as many options open as possible. But as Liberal leader of a Coalition Government in which the Conservative, pro-Ulster and anti-Irish Nationalist element was the dominating one, he was a prisoner of the political situation into which his own skill and ambition had manoeuvred him. Nor was this his only problem. The curiosity of the Union had always been that it maintained its own subordinate miniature government in Dublin Castle and the men in charge there now, with certain exceptions among the civil servants, were simple militarists of the old school with whom the Chief Secretary Greenwood was happy to identify himself.

When the first tentative suggestion of a peace move from a private Irish source close to Griffith reached Lloyd George in October 1920, his natural political instinct to explore it had to be tempered by consideration not only for the Unionists in his own cabinet but also for the die-hard element in the Castle on which he was, with his present policy, so dependent.

The peace move came through a businessman named Moylett who before one of his private business journeys to London had been to see Griffith to ask if he could help. Griffith had said that the first necessity was to get the British Government to recognize Dail Eireann. Moylett, stressing that he was acting solely on his own initiative, had consultations in London with one of Lloyd George's civil service secretaries and with H. A. L. Fisher, the

Minister who headed the Cabinet Committee on Ireland. He returned to say that Lloyd George might be prepared to meet three or four men nominated by the Dail in a conference in which both the Republic and the Union would be 'left outside the door', like coats to be assumed again by the two parties if necessary as they left. As this implied partial recognition of the Dail Griffith was much moved.[32] Collins was notified of the tentative moves and approved, though an event that was about to occur suggests that he did not attach great importance to them. Moylett returned to discuss the possible calling of a truce between the two armed sides.

Meanwhile, Lloyd George in public made the most of the government's new-found confidence. On 9 November he delivered himself of the momentous announcement that he had 'murder by the throat'. Within a fortnight Collins had given him a terrible answer.

Just after nine o'clock on the morning of 21 November 1920 in a well-planned operation he sent his 'execution' squads to different parts of the city of Dublin, including the Gresham Hotel in O'Connell Street, and had twelve British officers, all but one of them members of a counter-terrorist network, shot dead in bedrooms and on landings, some of them in front of their wives. Only one 'mistake' seems to have been made, on a harmless veterinary officer sitting up in bed reading his newspaper in the Gresham. All the gunmen except one escaped.* Two Auxiliaries who had happened to be passing one of the houses where the bloodshed was in progress and had stopped to investigate were also seized and shot out of hand – the first casualties the Division had suffered. It was only the beginning of a day that was to be known as Bloody Sunday.[33]

A Gaelic football match was to be played that afternoon at the Dublin ground of Croke Park between Dublin and Tipperary. In the circumstances of the time, it was not unreasonable of the authorities to have surrounded the ground, intending a search for IRA gunmen in the crowd. The move had indeed been planned anyway some days before.[34] On the other hand, in the emotional climate of that day it was a fatal move. Nothing could illustrate better the futility of substituting firmness for a political policy; for in such a situation even the right moves made by authority were inevitably wrong. Whether or not shots at Croke Park were first fired from the crowd cannot now be ascertained with certainty, but in the light of contemporary evidence it seems unlikely. It seems more likely that some of the RIC may have thought they were. They were in any case in an ugly mood after the events of the morning. What is certain is that Auxiliaries and RIC opened fire on the crowd, killing twelve civilians including a woman, a child and a Tipperary forward. The same night two of Collins's most valued Dublin Brigade IRA men, Richard McKee and Peadar Clancy, who had been picked up in a raid

---

*The captured IRA man, Frank Teeling, who had been wounded by Auxiliaries, was tried and sentenced to death but escaped from prison.

twenty-four hours before, were killed by Auxiliaries in the guard room at Dublin Castle. With them and also killed was a harmless Gaelic Leaguer from the West of Ireland named Clune, a man quite unconnected with the IRA who had happened to be in Vaughan's Hotel, a known nationalist rendezvous which was raided the same night.

Whether the deaths of the three men were acts of vengeance for what had happened that morning or were really, as Dublin Castle put out, the result of an attempt to escape cannot now be stated with absolute certainty. General Sir Ormonde Winter, Chief of British Intelligence, maintains that they were indeed attempting an escape and claims that he convinced a sceptical Sir John Anderson, then one of the Under-Secretaries at the Castle, that this was so.[35] But Winter was a notorious 'hard-liner' at the time and the fact that writing over thirty years later he had still not discovered that Clune was not an IRA man makes him seem at best a cursory assessor of evidence. All that can be said for certain is that it seems improbable that the innocent Clune at least would have inculpated himself so easily and that if an attempt to escape did take place something may have happened to make the prospects of the three men seem desperate indeed. Though their bodies were riddled with bullets their faces did not bear marks of torture and brutality as popular myth has often asserted.* Collins, in a typical gesture, took an appalling risk of capture when he was one of those who went to view them in the Pro-Cathedral after they had been given up by the authorities, and even helped carry a coffin at the Requiem Mass next day.[36]

The loss of the fourteen officers in Dublin was a severe blow to the authorities' new-found confidence. Although Lloyd George tried to keep a line open to Griffith through Moylett even after 21 November,[37] the events of that day temporarily put an end to further discussion of a truce. The only terms that would have been politically acceptable at such a moment required the exception of Collins from any amnesty and such an exception was unthinkable to Griffith or anyone on the Irish side. The deadlock was made all the more grim and complete when a week later the authorities received from a different quarter another shattering blow to their prestige. Two lorry-loads of the company of Auxiliaries stationed at Macroom Castle ran into a well-laid ambush position prepared by Tom Barry and the West Cork Flying Column on a lonely site of bogland and rocks near Kilmichael. It was the Auxiliaries' first major engagement and a terrible one.

After a savage fight at close quarters in which three IRA were killed and,

---

* Edward MacLysaght, *Master of None* (private MS. shown to the author in 1954). 'I am bound to say,' writes MacLysaght, 'that the statement which was afterwards made to the effect that their faces were so battered as to be almost unrecognizable and horrible to look at is untrue ... I remember those pale dead faces as if I had looked at them yesterday. They were not disfigured.' The MS. was written in 1951. Clune had been an employee of the MacLysaght family.

according to Barry, the Auxiliaries made use of notorious 'false surrender' tactics, the entire convoy was wiped out, and seventeen of the eighteen Auxiliaries were killed. The eighteenth was so severely wounded that he was in hospital for long afterwards.* Some of the Auxiliaries' bodies were afterwards found to have wounds inflicted after death and the first British officer on the scene after the fight said that although he had seen thousands of men lying dead in the course of the war, he had never before seen such an appalling sight as met his eyes there. The doctor at the inquest, an Irishman, said that there was no doubt that some of the injuries had been inflicted after death.[38]

The government made full propaganda use of the injuries, even going so far as to state that the corpses of the 'Cadets' had been mutilated 'by axes'. Bayonets were certainly used in the fight and, since moments before and after death are not immediately ascertainable in hand-to-hand fighting, they may well have accounted for some of the 'mutilation' on both counts.† That some bayoneting may even have taken place deliberately after death is not impossible, since irregulars in action often have to make up with primitive emotion for the steadier nerve acquired by professionals in long training. Barry concedes that the morale of the column was so disturbed by the fight that to reassert discipline he had to drill them in the road for five minutes afterwards among the corpses and blazing lorries.[39] In any case the matter is irrelevant, given the other horrors of guerrilla warfare and reprisal in which Ireland was then engulfed‡ The fact that the government still thought that effective points could be scored against the IRA by propaganda was what was revealing, disclosing further its total failure to come to grips with the Irish situation in any meaningful way.

In any case, as far as the propaganda war was concerned the government had long been left far behind by Sinn Fein. Two other events of that autumn had already been turned into symbolic evocations of Ireland's martyrdom and her spirit of defiance. One had been the first British execution of an

* Barry, *Guerilla Days in Ireland*, pp. 34–46. Barry states that the only survivor never recovered consciousness, but he can be seen sitting up in bed with a bandage round his head in the *Freeman's Journal*, 17 January 1921.

† Survivors of an ambush in County Clare two months later said that the wounded had been bayoneted in the road by the IRA. (*Irish Times*, 25 January 1921.)

‡ The victory was celebrated in a cynical rhyme which perhaps conveys more of the true atmosphere of the period than a heroic bowdlerized version beginning 'Hurrah for the boys of Kilmichael' which also exists. The former runs:

'On the 28th day of November
Outside of the town of Macroom,
The Tans in their big Crossley tenders
Were hurtling away to their doom.
For the lads of the column were waiting
With hand-grenades primed on the spot
And the Irish Republican Army
Made sh—t of the whole f—ing lot.'

Irishman in the post-war period, that of Kevin Barry, an eighteen-year-old medical student caught with a revolver beneath an army bread lorry in Dublin after a raid on its armed escort. One of the soldiers had been shot dead. Barry was found guilty of murder by court-martial, and executed by the common hangman in Dublin, in spite of pleas for mercy from all sides on account of his youth. An affidavit of his to the effect that he had been beaten by British officers in the course of interrogation made a considerable impact on public opinion. By contrast the fact that the soldier he had shot was as young as himself made virtually none.

The other event also concerned a courageous individual, but in a manner which uniquely concentrated attention from all over the world on the spirit and determination of Irish militants. Terence MacSwiney, the Lord Mayor of Cork, arrested in August in Cork Town Hall at the IRA conference which his military captors had mistakenly supposed to be a Republican court, had displayed a spirit as brazen as it was courageous by immediately going on hunger-strike in protest against the British Government's interference with elected civic functionaries. He had been deported to Brixton prison in London where his hunger-strike continued.

In previous hunger-strikes of the period, in Mountjoy gaol earlier in the year and in 1919, and in Wormwood Scrubs also in 1920, the government had given in after ten days or so when the hunger-strikers had appeared close to death, being naturally unwilling to create martyrs. In the case of MacSwiney the government had announced early, with a certain amount of courage of its own, that it did not intend to surrender to moral blackmail. What it had underestimated, however, was both the physical courage of MacSwiney and the length of time it took a resting man to die of hunger. After a fortnight of MacSwiney's hunger-strike it was assumed that he was on the point of death and public opinion not only in Ireland, but in Britain and much of the rest of the world, focused on the lonely suffering figure of this defiant Irishman in his British cell. He became an easily graspable symbol of the entire political situation in his country. And so he remained for a further fifty-nine days.

The British Government, unnerved by MacSwiney's stand, gave some credence to the story that he was being brought secret supplies of nourishment. The prison authorities even sent the contents of the hand basin in which he had cleaned his teeth to a laboratory for analysis.[40] There was a rumour that the priest who visited him brought food concealed in his beard. On 24 October 1920, after a seventy-three-day hunger-strike, MacSwiney died. Another IRA hunger-striker died in Cork gaol a few hours later, while yet another had died there the week before.

These deaths, and MacSwiney's moving funeral attended by vast crowds in Cork, made a profound impression on all observers of the Irish scene. Of all the many individual incidents that had made the year 1920 so extraordinary in the history of Ireland, none seemed to convey so solemnly the message that whatever resources of civilization the British Government might continue to summon to its aid in the form of police or military reinforcements, there was at last a force in Ireland which could not be deflected from its notion of Irish freedom and which would never give in.

It was against this background of hardened attitudes that the last phase of the struggle was to take place.

9
War and Truce (1921)

The so-called 'Anglo-Irish war' or 'War of independence' can be divided into three phases.

The first, which had run from January 1919 to the beginning of March 1920, had consisted largely of cold-blooded attacks by Volunteers on individual Irish policemen carrying out their duties as unprovocatively as was consistent with their carrying out their duty at all. During this time more than twenty serving or former members of the RIC were killed and over forty wounded. Perhaps the most remarkable feature of this whole phase had been the way in which the RIC morale held firm. Only towards the end had the strain begun to tell. Resignations took place, though not yet numbering more than five per cent of the original force.* More important: among the new English recruits in particular the urge for undisciplined vengeance had begun to assert itself.

This was the phase in which the extreme Fenian element in the new Sinn Fein movement, personified by Collins, gained domination over the political non-revolutionary element for which the country had voted. By the spring of 1920 the country found itself committed to a violent rebellion against British rule for which it had given no sanction. In the nature of the situation, as Collins had foreseen, the country was left with little option but to support the rebellion.

The second phase of the 'war' had run from March 1920 to October 1920. In it a strange two-faced anarchy had established itself in Ireland. As the government's law and order broke down under the continuing pressure of the Volunteers, a rebel law and order grew up as an alternative. Reciprocally, the conventional forces of law and order had increasingly resorted to lawlessness to assert themselves, a process further accelerated by the arrival of Black and Tan recruits and the Auxiliaries. However, by October 1920 there were still only approximately 1,500 Black and Tans in Ireland and a little over 500 Auxiliaries.

It was from October 1920 onwards that the really considerable reinforcement of the RIC by the Black and Tan element took place, averaging nearly a thousand recruits each month from November 1920 to March 1921, by

* They were never more than about thirty per cent altogether.

which time the Auxiliary Division had reached its full strength of 1,500.[1] And with the increase in government forces not only was the alternative rebel administration forced underground again but, with a corresponding development in IRA techniques principally by the flying columns, the 'war' entered its third and harshest phase.

Crown casualties – soldiers and police – for the first nine months of 1920 had been 125 killed and 235 wounded. For the next nine months, to 11 July 1921, there were some 400 killed and 700 wounded.[2] By late 1920 the government had stopped trying to give full official civilian casualties as there was little possibility of making them realistic. The number of IRA casualties – technically 'civilian' – was for obvious reasons unobtainable. It was almost equally impossible to keep track of those civilians shot either accidentally or intentionally by Crown forces, or of the so-called 'spies' and other non-cooperators with the Irish Republic shot by the IRA. But one of the last sets of figures on specific casualties which the government did release in 1920 carried an emotive patriotic note: ex-servicemen killed by the IRA during the year (all serving members of the police) had been forty.[3] The government were also able to reveal the number of civilians killed in 1920 when failing to halt in response to a military challenge: 41 killed and 43 wounded.[4]

Civilian casualties for the six and a half months' conflict in 1921 were higher to an appalling extent. The *Freeman's Journal*, simply by going through its files, reckoned that there were 707 civilians killed from all causes between 1 January and 11 July 1921, and 756 wounded.[5] It would almost certainly be no exaggeration to say that well over a hundred of these dead were 'spies' shot by the IRA: seventy-three were shot between 1 January and 1 April alone.[6] Perhaps an even larger number were deliberately killed by Crown forces in cold blood. Many civilian casualties, particularly in Dublin, were also caused accidentally in the course of fusillades between the Crown forces and the IRA.

'The long drawn out struggle is reaching its final stages and Ireland is winning,' Dail Eireann had proclaimed when setting its ban on emigration in 1920. 'All that is needed is a little more patience and then a bracing up for a final tussle.' In 1921 the final tussle began in earnest.[7] The form the fighting took during the last phase was similar in kind to that in the earlier phases, only considerably intensified. Sometimes the IRA were winning and sometimes not. Limerick provided an example of its fluctuating fortunes. A Limerick flying column had carried out a successful ambush of twenty men of the Lincolnshire regiment at Glencurrane just before Christmas, killing four of them and depriving the rest of their arms and equipment after they had surrendered. But at Christmas, when a number of Limerick IRA men rashly attended a dance at Caherguillamore House, the place was surrounded by Black and Tans and Auxiliaries, and five IRA were killed and over forty others arrested. A month later the flying column destroyed a convoy of Black and Tans at Dromkeen, killing nine of them.[8]

An equally successful ambush had taken place at Ballinalee in County Longford two days earlier when the IRA commandant, a blacksmith named Sean MacEoin, forced eighteen RIC and Auxiliaries to surrender after a three-quarters of an hour fight in which three police were killed. In County Clare at Sixmilebridge six police were killed.

On the other hand, the IRA suffered severe reverses early in the year in County Cork where, on 28 January at Peake, on 15 February at Mourne Abbey, and again on 20 February at Clonmult, parties were surprised and surrounded, with the total loss of seventeen dead and twenty captured, the high ratio of dead to captured leading some to surmise that prisoners had been shot after surrender.[9] By contrast, although it was maintained by survivors of the Sixmilebridge ambush that the IRA had bayoneted wounded men in the road, the behaviour of MacEoin at Ballinalee had been chivalrous. He had delayed his withdrawal after the ambush to care for the wounded police and had himself whispered an Act of Contrition to a dying District Inspector.[10] Chivalry on the part of either side in this conflict was rare enough to be worthy of note. In June Sean Moylan of the Cork IRA was revealed at his court-martial as having saved the lives of wounded after an ambush when some of the men in his column had wanted to shoot them. Discipline was often difficult to enforce in the brigades, partly because of the lack of regulation punishment.[11] 'If you shoot them, then I'll shoot you,' Moylan had cried to his men. The President of the Court said that in something like five thousand cases he had tried in Ireland this was one of the few instances of chivalry by the IRA.[12] But there were others apart from MacEoin's, and two army officers released after being held for five minutes by the South Mayo Flying Column were treated 'with every courtesy and consideration', being told that they were lucky they were regulars and not Black and Tans, in which case they would have had 'other treatment'.[13]

Many senior IRA officers were in fact anxious to behave as correctly as possible as belligerents, partly perhaps to ease nagging doubts about the morality of what they were doing. Doubts were not even always unconscious. One man who had been out in what he called 'a good stand-up fight' in Easter Week had written to GHQ the year before saying that quite candidly ambushes seemed to him too much like murder.[14] And the Catholic Church continued to give no mercy. 'The misguided criminals,' declared the Bishop of Tuam after an ambush at Heaford, County Galway, in January, expressing sentiments which must have been echoed by many of his flock, 'the misguided criminals who fired a few shots from behind a wall and then decamped are guilty of a triple crime ... knowing as they must know the nature of the reprisals that are likely to follow an ambush, they came from outside to do a foul and craven deed, and then having fired these few

cowardly shots, they beat a hasty retreat, leaving an unprotected and innocent people at the mercy of uniformed forces.'[15] And in his Lenten Pastoral
for 1921 the Bishop of Cork stated categorically that Dail Eireann could not
be held to constitute a sovereign state. What, he asked, in words which
before long were not to seem nearly so ridiculous as they were now intended
to be, what if Connaught or Munster suddenly declared itself a Republic, did
that give it the solemn right to be so regarded and to declare war?'[16]

Yet nothing perhaps conveys more clearly the profound and rapid change
brought about by the intensified conflict of these months than the fact that
only a short time after this pronouncement by a prominent member of the
hierarchy, other members, including Cardinal Logue, Dr Walsh, the Archbishop of Dublin, and Dr Gilmartin, the Archbishop of Tuam, were prepared
to associate themselves with an appeal for an Irish White Cross relief fund in
a General Committee on which stood the names not only of prominent
Unionists but that of Michael Collins himself.[17] 'The Irish White Cross,' concluded the appeal, 'believes that the names of those who have associated
themselves with it will justify and give confidence in the appeal for funds.'
In answering a question in the House of Commons some time before, Sir
Hamar Greenwood had already given Collins's name as that of the Commander-in-Chief of the IRA.

As both the number and size of ambushes increased, so for all their horror
did their status. The idea that there was a sort of war going on in Ireland
took root with all sides. Birkenhead, the Lord Chancellor, was to refer to it
as 'a small war'. And the acknowledgement was itself a victory for the IRA
of some political significance. For it automatically implied that there was a
nation fighting this war in a sense in which no Englishman had ever quite
acknowledged the Irish nation before. Thus the very scale of the IRA
activity, whether militarily successful or not, won preliminary ground for
that negotiation which would one day surely have to come.

In detail it was a vile and squalid war. As the *Irish Times* wrote in
February, for those whose sense of horror recent events had not blunted, the
daily newspaper had become a nightmare. An item such as the killing of an
RIC Inspector and his wife outside Mallow station and the subsequent
shooting by Black and Tans and Auxiliaries of three railwaymen when
searching the station had become routine. Women were now killed frequently, not just through careless firing on the part of the Crown forces but
increasingly as the result of IRA operations. A woman passenger on a train
was killed along with five other civilians when the IRA ambushed the Cork–
Bantry train at Upton in February. On two consecutive days in May women
were killed in ambushes in County Galway and County Tipperary: a Mrs
Blake, the wife of a District Inspector with whom she was travelling, and a
Miss Barrington, the friend of another on her way back with him and others
from a game of tennis.

Many more martial occasions were, of course, also recorded in these months of 1921: at Glasdrummon in County Leitrim where six soldiers of the Beds. and Herts. Light Infantry were killed and one captured; at Clonbanin in County Cork where (under Sean Moylan) a British colonel and three other soldiers were killed; in County Kerry where another train was ambushed, this time killing an officer and six other ranks; at Crossbarry where not only did Tom Barry and his flying column successfully ambush a convoy of nine military lorries but fought their way out of a massive attempt to encircle them afterwards; at Tourmakeady in County Mayo where another column after killing four also escaped subsequent encirclement. One of the hottest fights for a police barracks in the whole war resulted in March in the capture of the building at Rosscarbery in County Cork by Barry's column; the RIC garrison were specially commended by Dublin Castle for their defence. At Rathmore in County Kerry in May, nine RIC were ambushed and killed when going out to bring in the body of an eighty-year-old Irishman shot by the IRA as a spy and left on the road. At Clonmore, County Kerry, in June, four RIC were killed, and at Carrowcennedy in County Mayo, six more were killed the next day. These last two bloody victories were won by the IRA without loss to themselves though seven out of the ten men they killed on those two days were Irishmen.

But it was less the regular police and military casualties inflicted in these operations and in the many smaller ambushes that took place continually during the same period, than the endless daily series of individual killings on both sides, that emphasized the horror from which there seemed no escape. The bodies of 'spies' bearing some cautionary message such as 'Tried by court martial and found guilty – All others beware – IRA' were found littered throughout the four fields of Ireland. Sometimes they would actually be British officers. A Captain Thomson of the Manchester Regiment had already been found blindfolded and shot near Bishopstown in November 1920.[18] In County Galway in February 1921, the above message was found attached to the bodies of three unarmed privates of the Oxford and Bucks. Light Infantry. More often they would be ordinary Irishmen, labourers or farmers of all ages, though one boy on the day in March when two such 'spies' were shot at Thurles was simply left tied up with the label 'Too Young To Be Shot. Keep Your Mouth Shut' attached to him.

Callousness and brutality on one side was being continually duplicated by the other. A single day in February which saw a man shot dead by civilians in the streets of Enniscorthy – one of many shot in these times for little other reason than that he was an ex-British soldier – a labourer named Fabray shot dead by the IRA for filling up a trench dug by them in the road near his home, and the body of the managing director of a catering company, a JP for twenty-three years, found with an envelope pinned to him reading 'Beware of the IRA', also saw two nationalists taken from their homes in

Drogheda and shot by Black and Tans, and two young Dublin men who had
previously been taken to the Castle for questioning found fatally shot with
badly beaten faces behind a wall in the suburb of Drumcondra.[19]

Young Irishmen seized by Crown forces in vengeance seem often to have
been selected almost at random. Similarly, the IRA definition of a spy was
often a most general one. 'Convicted Spy. The penalty for all who associate
with Auxiliary Cadets, Black and Tans and RIC – IRA Beware' was the
notice found on the body of a well-known Cork business man.[20] There was
no discrimination of class among the victims by either side. A Galway
councillor was taken from his bed by Black and Tans and shot after an
ambush; the body of the Postmaster of Navan who had been unfortunate
enough to catch some Black and Tans looting was discovered some time later
floating down a river; a Cork JP of seventy, a member of Plunkett's
Dominion Home Rule League, was taken from his house and shot dead by
Black and Tans for making an affidavit in favour of IRA men captured in
Cork.[21] Sir Arthur Vicars, a prominent Unionist of Listowel, was taken from
his house by the IRA after breakfast and shot in his dressing-gown.[22]

The *Manchester Guardian*, a paper friendly to the Irish cause, described
Vicars's death as one of the most horrible in the black recent records of
crime and counter-crimes in Ireland, though it was difficult to see why it was
any worse than most of the others except that the victim was a member of
the upper classes.[23] The Black and Tans were reputed to have killed an
Irishman in East Limerick by trailing him along the road from the back of
a Crossley tender.[24] On one occasion the IRA actually seized from Cork
South Infirmary the unconscious figure of a former recruiting-sergeant whose
execution they had already bungled and shot him again outside.[25]

On another they were to stop a car carrying an officer of the Worcester
Regiment and three ladies near Dublin, take the officer out, shoot him, and
then when they found they had not done the job properly, make one of the
ladies drive him and them up into the Dublin mountains where they shot
him again.*[26]

An eighty-year-old Protestant clergyman, Dean Finlay, was shot by the
IRA apparently for no other reason than that his house was about to be
commandeered by the Auxiliaries,[27] but for good measure the house was
subsequently burned as well. A man who had been on the jury which found
the RIC guilty of MacCurtain's murder was taken and shot dead by Black
and Tans to help him prove his point still further. 'The whole country runs
with blood,' the *Irish Times* had written. 'Unless it is stopped and stopped
soon every prospect of political settlement and material prosperity will perish
and our children will inherit a wilderness.'[28]

Only in North-East Ulster and particularly Belfast did the bloodshed
assume a serious sectarian character and this had been aggravated by the

* See below, p. 715.

creation towards the end of 1920 of a new special police force, the Ulster Special Constabulary, with its 'A' (full-time) members some 2,000 strong and 'B' (one night a week reserve) 'Specials' recruited from among Carson's old Ulster Volunteer Force. The hope was to control the murderous rioting that had tended to break out in the North so easily in reaction to events in the South. But even such martinets as Sir Nevile Macready and Sir Henry Wilson took alarm at the thought of giving such men armed authority at such a time. 'Simply inviting trouble,' Wilson called it, '. . . to arm a lot of "Black North" on the chance of their keeping order is childish and worse.' And Macready replying to him said that it had been suggested that such constables should accompany the military to act as guides as to who was bad and who was good. 'This just shows what you and I know, what they are driving at,' he commented. He said he would on no account allow the military to go with special constables, 'unless the latter are under full control of the police'.[29]

The anti-Catholic nature of much of the violence that followed in the North, thus justifying Wilson's and Macready's worst fears, led in turn to retaliation against individuals particularly in the Catholic areas of Ulster, and in the second quarter of 1921 there was a noticeable increase in the number of spies and other undesirables shot dead who were also Protestants. But it was officially declared by IRA headquarters in Dublin, for what such a declaration might be worth, that no one was to be attacked just because he was a Protestant.

Similarly, for what it might be worth, Erskine Childers's Sinn Fein Publicity Department made an announcement to counter a rumour that the IRA would prevent Trinity College Sports Week from being held that summer. 'We desire to state expressly that the IRA do not send threatening letters,' this announcement ran. 'Any person receiving such a thing might safely rest assured that whether they emanate from an anti-Irish body or from private individuals they do not come from the source from which they purport to come.'[30] 'Safely' was the operative word. What, for instance, were the citizens of Waterford to make of a communication signed by the 'Brigade Commandant and Brigade Quartermaster IRA Brigade Head-quarters Waterford' which ran: 'A levy is being made throughout the area, with the sanction of the proper authorities, to help in the work of arming and equipping the IRA. You will be expected to contribute a fair amount.'[31] Was this to be regarded as not being a genuine communication from the IRA? Or, alternatively, at a time when bodies were found daily with 'Beware the IRA' pinned to them, was this not a threat? In either case few Waterford citizens would have felt that they could safely disregard it.

Moreover, the apprehensions about Trinity Sports Week had some foundation in fact. A girl of twenty-one had been killed ten days before when shots were fired from the street at a cricket match being played in Trinity College

Park between the Gentlemen of Ireland and the Military.[32] The *Irish Times*, which now subordinated its traditional dogmatic Unionism to a personal sense of horror at what it had to record daily, commented: 'The increasing callousness with which these things are read is hardly less dreadful than the growing helplessness with which they are watched.'[33] In the previous three days twenty police and soldiers had been killed in four incidents in different parts of the country, two of the soldiers being boys of the Hampshire Regiment's band who died when a land-mine was exploded in the road beneath them near Youghal.[34]

Dublin itself had increasingly become a scene of violent action, and by the summer of 1921 street ambushes of the Auxiliaries and the military, with bombs and hand-grenades thrown at passing lorries, had become everyday occurrences. Collins had formed an Active Service Unit for the city itself headed by a special élite known as 'The Squad'. Casualties among civilians in the street including many women and children were frequent. Between 1 January and 4 June 1921 there were 147 street attacks on Crown forces in Dublin, as a result of which 46 civilians were killed and 163 wounded. These figures included known IRA casualties, but the majority were ordinary Dublin citizens, several of them women and children.[35]

Sometimes a pitched battle would take place in the street, as on the morning of 14 March when a company of Auxiliaries surrounded 144 Brunswick Street in the supposition that Dail Eireann was in session there. They were briskly engaged by the IRA from neighbouring houses – a fact which seemed to confirm the supposition – and there were casualties on both sides and among passing civilians.[36]

Twice the IRA in Dublin attempted something more ambitious than executions and ambushes. On the first occasion, on an evening in February, an attempt was made by a bogus telephone call to lure Crown forces into a trap at Amiens Street railway station around which 165 IRA armed men were waiting for them. The telephone call was, however, suspected by the Auxiliaries who merely arrived warily to probe the railway line and surrounding streets with searchlights. The IRA eventually withdrew.[37]

On the second occasion, on 25 May, a large party of over a hundred IRA entered by day the celebrated eighteenth-century Dublin Customs House which was the headquarters of the Local Government Board and thus virtually of the British civil administration in Ireland, and successfully set fire to it. They were, however, surrounded by troops and Auxiliaries before they could escape and five were killed and seventy taken prisoner. One of those who watched the Customs House burn from O'Connell Street was the old parliamentarian, John Dillon. His thoughts were bitter and very different from the triumphant note immediately struck by Childers in the *Irish Bulletin*. But perhaps his description catches the true flavour of the time more exactly.

The whole scene [wrote Dillon the next day] was one of the most ... tragic I have ever witnessed. A *lovely* summer afternoon, the crowds of *silent* people, afraid to express any opinion, and the appalling sight of the most beautiful [building] of Ireland [of] our period of greatness, wantonly and deliberately destroyed by the youth of Ireland as the latest and highest expression of idealism and patriotism.[38]

But compared with other expressions of idealism and patriotism that had taken place in recent months in Ireland it was an almost noble event.

Corresponding with the increase in fighting there had gone undoubtedly a vicious increase in the callousness with which both sides fought. On the government side the callousness was partly official. It was at the beginning of the year that official reprisals were first carried out by the Army: the burning of six houses at Midleton, County Cork, after an ambush there. It was also announced then that henceforth civilian hostages would be carried in convoys liable to ambush. Martial law had been decreed for the Cork area in December and extended on 5 January 1921 to Counties Clare, Kilkenny, Roscommon and Waterford. The power to intern without trial throughout the country had also been taken at last and by the end of January 1921 there were 1,463 civilians interned in camps at Ballykinlar and elsewhere.[39] The Chief Secretary, Sir Hamar Greenwood, was careful to announce that they would be given prisoner-of-war treatment without prisoner-of-war *status*.

The distinction was important. The IRA, while breaking – for what it was worth – the first rule of war by fighting in civilian clothes, claimed to be belligerents and, if captured in arms, entitled to honourable treatment as prisoners of war. The British Government, on the other hand, under their new martial law regulations, were preparing to execute all rebels taken in arms.

In February the first executions since the hanging of Kevin Barry in November took place by firing squad in Cork. Seven IRA men were shot in Cork Barracks that month. A priest who was present to the last with a group of six of them, shot in batches of two at quarter of an hour intervals, described them as going to their deaths like schoolboys.[40]

The old Parliamentary Nationalist T. P. O'Connor, who still sat for Liverpool in the House of Commons, made the obvious point that at this stage in Irish history the judicial shooting by the British Government of six young Irishmen, the youngest of whom was nineteen and the eldest twenty-three, could hardly lead to an improvement in the situation. In fact, the bitterness in Ireland was already so great that the executions did not, as in 1916, stir new emotions, but rather simply hardened those that already held sway.

The executions provoked IRA retaliation. An elderly lady, a Mrs Lindsay of Coachford, County Cork, a Unionist Irishwoman, had given warning to

the authorities of an ambush being prepared in her locality. It was her information which led to the arrest of those IRA men who were shot in Cork
barracks. She had meanwhile been kidnapped by the IRA as a hostage and
when the sentences were carried out in Cork barracks she was herself shot
dead. Her execution as 'a spy' did not prevent further reprisals being taken
by the IRA the next day on six unarmed soldiers who were shot dead in the
streets of Cork.[41]

Collins at headquarters in Dublin had not been informed of the Cork No.
1 Brigade's initiative in shooting Mrs Lindsay, and indeed, nearly two months
later, Erskine Childers was in a state of some embarrassment on the subject.
Another Irishwoman of a different class, Kitty Carrol, had also been shot by
the IRA apparently because she had disobeyed a Republican police injunction to stop distilling illicit whisky.[42] 'Shall we,' wrote Childers to Collins on
2 May 1921, 'say (a) the execution of women spies is forbidden, and that
Kitty Carrol was not killed by the IRA? Or (b) Kitty Carrol was killed in
contravention of orders by the IRA, and that (c) Mrs Lindsay is now in
prison for giving information to the enemy?' Mrs Lindsay, unknown to
Childers, had then been dead for seventy-nine days.[43]

Another of the very many 'executions' of which headquarters was not
informed was that of a British officer, Captain Compton-Smith, captured as
a hostage, again by Cork No. 1 Brigade, and shot when four more IRA
prisoners were executed by firing squad in Cork at the end of March.
Compton-Smith had been a popular officer in his locality and was liked even
by his captors; Collins wrote afterwards that he would have tried to prevent
his death if he had known what was happening.[44]

On these occasions certain prescribed conventions were correctly complied with by the IRA, such as the returning of rings and money and the
delivery of a last letter to the next of kin. In fact, in the case of another
hostage executed by the IRA, District Inspector Potter of the RIC, the
receipt of such things was his wife's first notification of what had become of
him since he was taken prisoner in an ambush. There could be no clearer
evidence of the brutalizing atmosphere of the time than the fact that even
the sensitive O'Malley, by now Officer Commanding the 2nd Southern
Division IRA, seems to have felt relatively resigned to what he regarded as
his duty to shoot three British officers whom he captured while out for a
country walk in June. As with similar ceremonies in Cork barracks, com-
pliance with the niceties of procedure protected those involved from serious
doubts.

One of the officers remarked to O'Malley that some banks they saw on the
way down to the churchyard wall in the dawn would make stiff banks for
hunting. 'There's not much hunting now,' said O'Malley, who was then just
twenty-four. 'None of us want to do it,' he told them, 'but I must think of our
men.' He tied handkerchiefs round their eyes and shook hands with them

and his Quarter-Master, Dan Breen, finished them off with a revolver as they lay twitching on the grass beside the road after the volley.[45]

The scene was in its macabre and wistful way a small indication of how much things in Ireland had changed since Breen and Treacy had shot the unfortunate Constables McDonnell and O'Connell at Soloheadbeg in January 1919. Something very like a formal state of war had by now indeed come about and was accepted as such by both sides and by the Irish people. In this acceptance the old fantasy proclaimed since the days of Strongbow that the Irish were fighting England for their freedom at last became a sort of reality. The Republicans had drawn the Irish people into their view of history. Whether all this should have been started was one thing; but after this there could be no going back.

A quite genial young Black and Tan looking back later on his service in Ireland was to write: 'It has been said that no one can serve two masters, yet the common folk of Ireland were forced to do so.'[46] In one way this was true. The ordinary small farmer might at any moment be called out from his house by revolver-carrying IRA to dig trenches across roads for the sabotage of police and military transport, and a day later be forced out at bayonet point by the police and military to fill them in again. But the small Irish farmer had been in that sort of situation off and on since the days of the earliest agrarian secret societies. It was the continuity of Irish history that was being enforced with its emphasis on some sort of Irish 'freedom'.

Thus, while there was for the Irish people that year much suffering and personal hardship as they tried to pursue their daily round, there was also sometimes a certain fateful elation in the air, a whiff of ancient legend.

IRA men found themselves becoming folk-lore in their own lifetime. It was not only the dead Sean Treacy who was sung about. O'Malley heard his own name in song at dances he attended.[47] In the countryside people could see in the flying columns the ghosts of the Fenians or those of the old Celtic warriors of legend, made suddenly flesh and blood. And inconvenient as they might often be, they were in a tradition they had been brought up to revere. Ancient emotions about land and the depredations of 'the stranger' going back beyond the famine and the penal laws, beyond even the great O'Neill and the battle of Kinsale, emotions that had lain so deep so long that they had lost coherence in all but poetry, found what seemed plausible everyday expression in the leather-gaitered, trench-coated, rifle and bandolier-slung figures of the flying columns. And the lorry-loads of Glengarry-capped Auxiliaries, firing their rifles and revolvers and yelling in their English accents as they jumped down into the road, were the 'English enemy', who were always supposed to have been there, and were now made flesh and blood too. Even the old homely enemy, the police, had become invading Black and Tans. In a curious way these grim and horrible times were for some also a fairy tale come true. 'Many of us,' wrote O'Malley, 'could hardly see ourselves for the legends built up around us.'[48]

In the towns, too, among the middle classes, thanks partly to the rhetorical nationalism which the old Parliamentary Party had always kept alive and even more to the Irish revival of the early part of the century which had given it substance, there was a quite well-formed reserve of national con-sciousness to draw on as the times grew harder. So that what as late as 1919 had often seemed mere rhodomontade or plain murder on the part of the Volunteers, acquired under the pressure of events something of the heroic aura they awarded themselves. It increasingly escaped people's attention that the change from a political impasse into a national struggle had been manipulated without their own consent. 'We were becoming almost popular,' wrote O'Malley. 'Respectable people were beginning to crawl in to us, neutrals and those who thought they had best come over were changing from indiffer-ence or hostility to a painful acceptance with the knowledge that some kind of a peace settlement would be made.'[49] In the circumstances, for all the routine denunciation of the Church it was now easily forgotten that much of what was being done by the 'National Army' was as vile as what was being done by the small murder gangs of Black and Tans.

Often in fact it was a problem to tell their work apart. When the Lord Mayor and ex-Lord Mayor of Limerick, George Clancy and Michael O'Callaghan, were murdered by masked men bursting into their houses on the same night in March 1921, Collins himself had an inquiry initiated to make sure that the deed had not been done by IRA extremists critical of Clancy's and O'Callaghan's rather unagressive attitude to the struggle.* In this case it was the king's men who fired the bullets. But their work was no more squalid than that of some of the IRA men who dealt with spies and traitors. Among the latter might be people as relatively innocuous as process-servers who continued to try to earn their livings by serving writs issued by the royal courts, or simply, as at Tormanbarry in July, a young man who refused to help dig an IRA trench. His body was found riddled with bullets.[50]

Paradoxically, throughout this final bitter stage of the conflict between the Crown forces and the IRA there had run a continuing undercurrent of talk of peace. It was not just that in the horrific circumstances of the time a longing for peace on the part of ordinary people could hardly be ignored. Real tentative possibilities for negotiation existed in the background through-out these months and even accounted for much of the ferocity of the struggle as both sides manoeuvred up to the very last moment for a better negotiating position.

* The British also held an inquiry which unlike Collins's absolved the forces of the Crown. There seems little doubt, however, that the murderers were Black and Tans or Auxiliaries or both. Mrs O'Callaghan, who herself struggled with the raiders, cer-tainly believed this to be so. (See Dail Eireann Official Report on the Treaty between Great Britain and Ireland, Dublin, 1922, p. 60.)

In this manoeuvring the advantage was really with the IRA. Anything short of their total annihilation by the Crown forces was going to leave them in a position of advantage. For the government to negotiate with them at all was to undermine much of the attitude it had adopted towards them throughout, to recognize at least some substance in what they stood for and acknowledge them as representatives of the Irish nation. To this extent, though Sir Hamar Greenwood might talk manfully as late as May 1921 about fighting on 'until the last revolver had been plucked from the hand of the last assassin', the government were engaged in a losing battle.

Militarily, the British Army, by a series of large sweeps and the use of flexible columns of their own, were proving increasingly troublesome to the IRA's flying columns, who were also short of arms and ammunition. It is not true, as was later alleged, that Lynch came up to Dublin in July to tell Collins the Southern Brigades could not continue the fight; but Barry was certainly in Dublin that summer making clear the shortage of ammunition to Collins and others, and there is no doubt that life for the IRA was becoming more difficult and unpleasant.[51] Collins himself was later reported to have said privately that the IRA that summer were within three weeks of defeat. If he did so it was in the middle of a night charged with emotion when he would personally have wished to convince himself of the impossibility of facing renewed fighting.[52] The essential truth of the time, militarily, is that though the IRA did not have the same control of parts of Ireland they had had in the middle of 1920, they were now more experienced and better organized, and to have beaten them would have required a far greater British military effort than any yet seen in Ireland.

Subsequent experience of regular forces with guerrilla movements enjoying support from their own people – in Palestine, Cyprus and Algeria – suggests that a military victory is never possible in such circumstances. Once such guerrillas have been able to establish themselves effectively at all there can only be a political solution. British public opinion in 1921, deeply disturbed about the violence in Ireland and the apparently inevitable lawlessness of Crown forces in the prevailing conditions, would have been most reluctant to see further repression on the inevitably gigantic scale required. In this sense the IRA won a victory by forcing political negotiation. The question was: what sort of political solution could there be?

De Valera had returned from America at the end of 1920. Though he had made much effective propaganda for the Republican cause and had raised over £1 million for the Republican Loan, his eighteen months in the States had not been an unqualified success. Thinking only of Ireland, he had become uncomfortably entangled in the always essentially American character of Irish-American politics and there had been unfortunate quarrels and recriminations involving himself and John Devoy and Irish-American politicians.

He had failed to secure the recognition of the Irish Republic, which had been one of his ultimate aims. But he returned to Ireland at an opportune moment.

The political side of the movement had necessarily been eclipsed by the military, as military activity intensified. But military activity was, after all, for political ends. The time was approaching when the effectiveness of the IRA would have to be translated back into political terms and some political leadership, now admittedly carried far beyond the official moderation of 1918, would have to reassert itself.

Only de Valera, Griffith and Eoin MacNeill had so far seemed to have public political stature in the Republican movement. And both Griffith, who had been Acting President while de Valera was away, and MacNeill, had been arrested by the Castle authorities in a rather futile gesture after Bloody Sunday in November. Apart from the need for some political figure of stature who was physically free, nothing indicated more clearly the need for de Valera's return than the extent to which on arrival he revealed himself as partly out of touch with the situation in Ireland. When he met the Dail in January he argued for a certain cooling-off in IRA activity, a holding action rather than continued aggressiveness, in order not only to quieten some of the doubts international opinion might have about guerrilla methods but also to ease the burden on the people of Ireland. Clearly he had little understanding of the practical situation in the countryside where the IRA could hardly have disengaged even if they had wanted to. Nor did he appreciate the extent to which political considerations within the movement had long had to cede place to military. He did something to bridge the gap between the two spheres when in a press interview in March he was the first political leader openly to accept responsibility for the IRA's activity in public, insisting that it was not 'a praetorian guard' but 'the national army of defence'.[53] The very fact that there had been no such statement before showed the need for political leadership to assert itself. Above all, political leadership was necessary to handle the inevitably delicate nature of preliminary overtures for peace.

These had continued simultaneously with the intensification of the conflict, even after Bloody Sunday and the Kilmichael ambush of November 1920. At Dublin Castle the Under-Secretary, Sir John Anderson, and the Assistant Under-Secretary, Sir Alfred ('Andy') Cope, were both favourably disposed to the idea of a settlement and encouraged any serious intermediaries who presented themselves. In December an Australian cleric, the Archbishop of Perth, had acted as go-between for Anderson with Griffith in prison and there had seemed a momentary likelihood of official negotiations starting. Griffith, with Collin's approval, made his only conditions a mutual cessation of armed activity, a moratorium on arrests and permission for the Dail to meet. The proposal broke down on Lloyd George's last-minute insistence that

there must first be a surrender of arms by the IRA. Both Griffith and
Collins firmly asserted that while they were for peace on honourable terms
there could be no question of capitulation.[54]

But Cope in particular persisted in his optimism and on de Valera's
secret return to Ireland the British Cabinet took an important step. Though
they had in fact wished to prevent his return to Ireland if possible, once he
was there they decided not to arrest him unless some definite criminal charge
could be proved against him. In other words, a line to those behind the IRA
was to be kept open.[55]

In April 1921 a further independent effort to get peace moves going was
undertaken by Lord Derby, who had just completed a two-year term as
British Ambassador in Paris. He visited Dublin, staying at the Shelbourne
Hotel under the name of 'Edwards' in what he imagined to be a disguise
afforded by unaccustomed horn-rimmed glasses. He was taken to see de
Valera. He had previously seen James Craig, who had now taken over leadership of the Ulster Unionists in the North on Carson's retirement. But Derby
had disappointingly little to offer beyond goodwill, and de Valera played
the whole move down. Determined not to give away negotiating points
before negotiation started, he stuck to the position assumed by Griffith and
Collins at the time of the visit of the Archbishop of Perth: an equal truce
and no preliminary conditions. Lloyd George defined the British Government's attitude in the House of Commons on 21 April. The government, he
said, was ready to meet representatives of the Irish people 'for the purpose
of discussing any proposals which offer the prospect of reconciliation and
settlement, subject only to the reservations that the strategic unity of the
Empire must be safeguarded, and that Ulster must not be coerced. Every
facility of safe conduct for a meeting of members of the Dail would be
granted' with the exception of three or four members accused of serious
crime. (Among them obviously men like Collins and Mulcahy.) Pressed,
Lloyd George stated that if such three or four were found to have been
guilty of serious crime they would be subjected to the law of the land.[56] It
was not clarified whether or not there would be a truce in the fighting while
such negotiations took place.

The exception of men like Collins from an amnesty was obviously unthinkable to the Dail as Lloyd George knew already from his contacts with
the businessman Moylett and the Archbishop of Perth. But if there were
to be negotiations he had after all to condition his predominantly Conservative supporters to the idea by easy stages. Besides, he was himself in a
personally embarrassing position. He had continually referred to the people
he would have to negotiate with as murderers and needed time in which
to shift his ground at least with some show of political dignity. It was a
difficulty in which he was not alone. 'Surrender to a miserable gang of
cowardly assassins, like the human leopards of West Africa,' Winston

Churchill had said at Dundee in October 1920, 'would be followed by a passionate repentance and a fearful atonement.'[57] A clear indication, however, that the personal position of Collins and others was not the important point lies in a message which he transmitted to de Valera via Lord Derby just before he delivered his speech in the House of Commons. Was it so, Derby asked, that those controlling the Irish movement would not consent to meet the Prime Minister unless the principle of complete independence was first conceded? To which de Valera replied, again through Derby, most typically and significantly with another question. Was it so, de Valera asked, that Lloyd George would not consent to negotiate unless the principle of complete independence was first surrendered?

Thus months before these two gifted practitioners of the political arts were to meet, the first issue between them was clearly defined: were negotiations to take place without commitment on either side or must at least the integrity of the British Empire be first proclaimed as non-negotiable? If, of course, it were not to be so proclaimed as non-negotiable, then it could be said that it was theoretically negotiable. And in that case the Irish would have won a major victory right at the start.

The end, when it came, came almost suddenly. It took place in the aftermath of a major political change in Ireland which the IRA for all its effectiveness elsewhere had been quite powerless to prevent.

Under the Government of Ireland Act 1920 elections were held in May 1921 for the first time for the two new Parliaments thereby created: those for Northern and Southern Ireland. The Dail decided to accept the electoral machinery for the Southern Parliament as its own. There were 128 constituencies in the new twenty-six-county area, four of which were Trinity College seats to which four Unionists were returned unopposed. These four members actually met as the Parliament of Southern Ireland and then adjourned. In the other 124 constituencies Sinn Fein candidates were returned unopposed and constituted themselves the Second Dail. In the six counties of the new Northern Ireland a more normal election was held for the Northern Parliament – though there was intimidation against the united Sinn Fein–Nationalist coalition.* The result was that forty Unionists and twelve Nationalists were returned to the Northern Parliament.

The partition of Ireland – the very issue over which Sinn Fein had deprived the old Nationalist Party of its mass support in the first place – was now, after two and a half years of bloodshed which the Church condemned as murder, the loss of some fifteen hundred lives and much material destruction throughout Ireland, a more unalterable fact than it had ever been in the whole previous nine years it had been under consideration. The area thus apparently lost to Irish nationalism was larger than that involved in the final

---

* In the South, Dillon, the leader of the old Nationalist Party, though still strongly opposed to Sinn Fein, had decided not to oppose it in any constituency.

offer to Redmond at the time of the Buckingham Palace Conference in 1914.*

De Valera, the Dail and the IRA were at the time so deeply involved in maintaining their own Republican integrity both in face of the authorities' ruthless physical pressure and Lloyd George's peace manoeuvres that the full force of what was really a major defeat, questioning the validity of the entire policy of the past two and a half years, does not seem to have struck them. But it must have been a factor at some level of consciousness impelling them to bring Irish nationalism back once again from the field of battle to that of political negotiation. For whatever the IRA might prove capable of in the South it was clearly never going to achieve the All-Ireland nationalism which had been the Sinn Fein party's original *raison d'être*.

In fact there were at this stage – though this is often forgotten today – two unusual indications that the leaders of the Ulster Unionists in the North were not wholly indifferent to aspirations for a united Ireland. These can be taken to have been based on self-interest rather than ideology, for at this time it was by no means a foregone conclusion in Ulster Unionist minds that the Six-County State which they had not wanted would be a viable political and economic entity. The Government of Ireland Act in accordance with Lloyd George's original proposals provided for a Council of Ireland to consist of twenty representatives each from the Northern and Southern Parliaments and with the right by agreement to unite the functions of the two Parliaments on any matters within their powers, even including the union of the two Parliaments' powers altogether without further reference to Westminster.

Carson himself, just after announcing on 25 January 1921 that for reasons of health he would be unable to assume the Ulster leadership in the new Parliament, had made a significant statement at Torquay on the 30th.

'There is no one in the world,' he said, 'who would be more pleased to see an absolute unity in Ireland than I would, and it could be purchased tomorrow, at what does not seem to me a very big price. If the South and West of Ireland came forward tomorrow to Ulster and said – "Look here, we have to run our old island, and we have to run her together, and we will give up all this everlasting teaching of hatred of England, and we will shake hands with you, and you and we together, within the Empire, doing our best for ourselves and the United Kingdom, and for all His Majesty's Dominions will join together", I will undertake that we would accept the handshake.'[58]

It was the spirit of this statement that Craig, Carson's successor, took up in an election speech at the beginning of May. Pointing out that the Council of Ireland provided automatic machinery for a meeting with de Valera, he

* See above, p. 513.

said it would be the first duty of his colleagues and himself 'to select a band
of men to go down or wait here for the others to come up, to meet in
council under the Council of Ireland'.[59] Three days later he proved with
some personal courage that this was not mere electioneering. He went to
Dublin and, strongly encouraged by Cope to believe that good could come
of the venture, entrusted himself to an IRA escort which brought him to
de Valera at a secret meeting-place in Dublin. In fact both de Valera and
Craig had been led to believe by Cope that the other wanted the meeting
and nothing came of it. As a result de Valera now felt more convinced than
ever that it must be the British Government's responsibility to solve the
Ulster problem.[60] Perhaps he did not sufficiently appreciate that by recipro-
cating something of the Ulster Unionists' tentative gestures he could have
made it easier for the British Government to do so.

Instead, in conformity with previously declared policy, when the Northern
Parliament came into being after the election at the end of May the Dail
declared an economic boycott of Ulster goods. The slight predisposition in
the new circumstances on the part of Ulster Unionists to show at least some
awareness of their political weakness where the South was concerned was
thus further blighted; and the daily bloodshed made traditional sectarian
embitterment between Protestants and Catholics a more formidable factor
than ever.

But Cope's efforts to secure peace negotiations continued assiduously. On
22 June a party of the Worcestershire Regiment, acting on a tip-off, surrounded the villa in the Dublin suburb of Blackrock in which de Valera was
hiding. The soldiers were clearly unaware of any higher political directive
that de Valera was not to be arrested, and were proud of their capture.
However, after three or four hours in a prison cell he was, on the intervention of Cope, suddenly transferred to the relative splendour of an officer's
room in Portobello barracks whence he was released in some bewilderment
the next day.

Just before his release de Valera witnessed from his window what his
official biographers describe as 'the funeral of a British officer killed in an
ambush in the Dublin mountains'. In fact this was the officer who had been
taken from a car by the IRA and clumsily shot in front of three lady companions, one of whom had been made to drive him further up into the
Wicklow mountains for the *coup de grâce*.* Remonstrated with by his captors, de Valera replied that ambush techniques were permissible to a nation
which only had stone walls and hedges to protect it against tanks.†[61] That
a kindly, civilized politician could use such an argument in the circumstances, and that it could be simultaneously both relevant and irrelevant,

---

* See above, p. 703.
  † The dead officer was from the same regiment – the 2nd Worcestershire – as the
soldiers who had effected de Valera's capture.

was an indication of the terrible pass to which the political situation in Ireland had degenerated.

The very day of de Valera's arrest King George v made a speech at the formal opening of the Northern Parliament. It reflected plain human dismay at the situation in a tone far transcending the stately occasion at which it was delivered:

I appeal to all Irishmen to pause, to stretch out the hand of forbearance and conciliation, to forgive and forget, and to join in making for the land they love a new era of peace, contentment and goodwill.... May this historic gathering be the prelude of the day in which the Irish people, North and South, under one Parliament or two ... shall work together in common love for Ireland ...

The speech had been prepared on the advice of General Smuts – then in London for the Imperial Conference – and with Lloyd George's approval, by Sir Edward Grigg, the Prime Minister's Private Secretary. It was a good deal more conciliatory than the draft which the Irish Office in Dublin had originally provided,[62] and it moved public opinion throughout the British Isles.

Two days later Lloyd George sent a letter to de Valera, now conveniently free again, asking him 'as the chosen leader of the great majority in Southern Ireland' and 'in the spirit of the King's words' to attend a conference in London.[63]

De Valera replied that he would consult 'such principal representatives of our nation as are available' and would consult with 'certain representatives of the political minority in this country' (by which he meant the Unionists). He was thus in fact already indirectly negotiating with Lloyd George by his choice of words, refusing to be drawn into a preliminary acceptance of partition or his own role as a mere representative of the South.

Griffith and Barton were released from prison to attend the consultation. Craig – also already negotiating by taking his stand firmly on the *status quo* in the North – refused to attend the conference. But the Southern Unionists, led by Lord Midleton, did so, and it was through their influence and the further conciliatory efforts of General Smuts that a truce was eventually arranged between the IRA and the government forces. It was agreed at the Dublin Mansion House on 8 July at a meeting which General Macready attended with some wariness, bringing a revolver in his pocket and being taken aback to be greeted by Larry O'Neill, the Lord Mayor, as if he were his 'long-lost brother'.*[64]

The truce which was to end all aggressive acts and provocative displays of force by either side was to come into force at noon on 11 July and was terminable at seventy-two hours' notice.

---

* The truce, though officially announced by the British on the evening of 8 July, was not formally agreed as to terms until 9 July.

Though operations by the Crown forces virtually ceased from the time of the truce conference, activity by the IRA continued up to the very last moment. On the day of the conference two spies were shot dead, one near Cashel and another near Tullamore, the latter bearing the slogan 'sooner or later we get them. Beware of the IRA.' The execution of a third man, a railway ganger, on the morning of Saturday, 9 July, was witnessed by a boy who heard him crying, 'Murder!' as he was forced to kneel beside the railway line and told to say his prayers. A girl had all her hair cut off at Wexford the same day, while threatened with a revolver, for 'spending all her time with Black and Tans'. Four unarmed soldiers were kidnapped in the streets of Cork on the night of Sunday, 10 July, and three of them were found blindfolded and shot dead in a field near a cemetery the next morning.

The last Black and Tan murder seems to have been that of a Cork JP, a supporter of Plunkett's Dominion Home Rule who had made an affidavit on behalf of IRA prisoners in Cork gaol. He was taken from his house and shot dead 'by armed men' on the night of Sunday, 10 July. The last of the 'enemy' to die at the hands of the IRA on the very last morning of this war of independence were, like the first in January 1919, two Irish Catholic policemen: Sergeant King, shot off his bicycle by two undisguised men in the street of Castlerea, and Constable Clarke shot dead in Skibbereen. The former had seen twenty-three years' service, the latter thirty-four years' service with the RIC.[65] Whereas the killing of Constables MacDonnell and O'Connell at Soloheadbeg had shocked the Irish nation, the deaths of Sergeant King and Constable Clarke barely caused the flicker of an eyelid except among those who mourned them. And too many people in Ireland were now mourners for much thought to be given to them.

That these last IRA actions were hardly those of irregular irresponsible individuals is indicated by the fact that as soon as the truce came into force, over most of Ireland where violent death had long been as routine as the rising-up and the going-down of the sun, there was in almost unearthly fashion suddenly a total absence of killing. Day after day at first there came the stunned realization that in this respect at least the truce was not being violated.* Only in the North was the truce welcomed in grim fashion. In Belfast ten people were killed and a thousand Catholics driven from their homes. It was a salutary reminder that for all the terrible events of the past two and a half years, the nature of that problem which had brought them about in the first place was quite unchanged. But with unarmed Auxiliaries and Black and Tan mixing freely with the people in the Dublin streets

---

* After four months of truce the British Government had complained of 595 breaches of the truce by the IRA altogether but none of them involved murder. 150 of them were concerned with the disputed issue of whether or not the terms permitted the IRA to drill publicly. 206 were concerned with the kidnapping of individuals but in over 150 of these cases the release of the victims was quickly secured by the IRA's truce liaison officers. (Hansard, H.C., 5th series, vol. 148, col. 389.)

and leather-gaitered men of the IRA coming down from the hills like heroes, the relief was too great for this to be widely remembered. It seemed almost more to the point that 'Mick' Collins had been offered £10,000 for his memoirs by an English publisher.[66]

10

Treaty (1921)

The responsibility of the leaders of the Republican movement was now awesome. They had to emerge from the blend of euphoric fantasy and day-to-day realism in which they had lived for the past five years and render account not only to the Irish people whom they had brought along with them but also, in their own view at any rate, to the past generations of Irish history. For the first time they faced the British Government as Redmond and Dillon had had to face them: round the negotiating table.

What were the realities with which they were confronted?

The truce had been a victory and a defeat for both sides. With it both sides acknowledged that they would prefer to fight no more. Inasmuch as the British Government were by far the stronger party and had always before been able to crush armed Irish rebellion, this represented a unique Irish victory. The government was treating its opponents as nominal equals. On the other hand they were not equals, and both sides knew it.

Far from having been able to drive the British out of Ireland, the IRA had been unable, as Mulcahy, the Chief of Staff, was soon to remind it, to drive them out of anything more than 'a fairly good-sized police barracks'.[1] If it came again to a mere test of strength – and contingency plans for the introduction of 250,000 British troops and even a blockade of Ireland were being discussed[2] – the IRA could never physically win. Moreover, in the sort of war the IRA had been fighting, a truce was much more harmful to their future capabilities than it was to that of regular professional forces. Key men had to come out into the open; the highly-strung tension on which so much of the successful morale of underground warfare depends was relaxed; and a population overwhelmed by relief automatically became less ready to resume the burdens of a war in which they had always been the chief sufferers. To offset this physical imbalance a most important political factor operated in favour of the Irish. The Irish leaders were unquestionably now representative of the vast majority of the Irish people, and British public opinion would only have been prepared to see the government's superior might made use of under certain circumstances.

This was really the strongest card in the Irish hand. Provided the terms they held out for did not seem outrageous to British public opinion, the

government would have to forgo its physical advantage and submit to
them.

There were two points around which all discussion of terms revolved. The
first was the question of allegiance to the British Crown, carrying within
it the very real issue of British security from some future enemy's attack
through Ireland. The second was the question of North-East Ulster. The
Crown in itself had never in the past been an important issue one way or
the other in the priorities of the vast majority of Irishmen, concerned as
they were with their everyday grievances. Attempts by political theorists
like Tone and his Fenian descendants to make republicanism a panacea for
those grievances had been ineffectual. The two great mass movements which
had effectively sought to deal with grievances on the level of national aspirations, those of O'Connell and Parnell, had had no difficulty in acknowledging loyalty to the Crown. Those national aspirations which survived the
resolution of practical grievances, reinforced by the cultural movement at
the beginning of the century, continued to be expressed as far as the great
majority of the people were concerned in the Home Rule movement. And
this continued to accept without question the constitutional role of the
Crown. Indeed, it would have been extraordinary if it had not done so.
One of the great traditions of nationalism to which all Irish nationalism
looked back, that of the Protestant colonists of the eighteenth century, had
been based on a nominally independent Crown, Lords and Commons of
Ireland – the Crown being shared with England. And it was this model
which Arthur Griffith, now to head the Irish delegation to London, had
realistically accepted as the only feasible one for the twentieth century.

Griffith's notion of the scale of autonomy required by Ireland had been
far greater than that of the Home Rulers who formed the mass of Irish
opinion, but on the question of the Crown itself there had been no dispute
with them. Equally, the great majority of those who had voted for a Republic
in 1918 had done so not as doctrinaire republicans but in the belief that to
bid for a Republic was the most effective way of securing the largest measure
of freedom the government could be forced to grant. Few of them then, or
three years later, seriously believed that a British Government, whose prime
concern for centuries had been the threat to Britain's security presented by
an independent Ireland, would allow Ireland to abandon all form of nominal
allegiance to the Crown. From the point of view of British public opinion,
all-important to the negotiations, abandonment of the Crown could not be
seen as a reasonable demand.

On the other hand, the leaders of the Irish delegation to London were in
a peculiar difficulty as a result of their own rise to the position of negotiators
for the Irish people. For they represented not only the Irish people but at
the same time a minority clique of republican dogmatists who had been the
active spearhead of the most recent phase of the nationalist movement. The

Republic for such people had become a Holy Grail, a sanctified symbol by which the suffering of the Irish people throughout history was to be redeemed – something inviolable and remote, and certainly not just a means to a political end. Anyone negotiating for Ireland at this moment was in the difficulty of simultaneously representing the Irish people and also representing this unrepresentative minority.

On the question of North-East Ulster there should have been no such complicating factor. This was after all the issue which had brought the mass of Irish opinion into support of minority republicanism in the first place. Only on a point of emphasis was there a difference of attitude. Since it was the all-embracing symbol of the Republic which was vital to out-and-out republican activists, the detail of North-East Ulster tended to assume a secondary position, whereas it was in fact, and always had been, the most important issue.

The early stages of the negotiations were handled by de Valera who, as the subtlest political mind on the Irish side, was well aware of all delicate considerations. He had once declared that he himself was no doctrinaire republican. He could not, however, ignore the fact that influential people both in the IRA and in his own ministry were doctrinaire republicans – among the latter Austin Stack and Cathal Brugha. De Valera was found at his desk by Griffith one day during this period, working out on paper what seemed like some geometric problem of right angles and curves and positions marked A, B, C and D. He explained that he was trying to devise some means by which he could get out of 'the strait-jacket' of the Republic and bring Brugha along with him.[3] To General Smuts in Dublin in July 1921 he had said – according to Smuts – 'If the status of a Dominion is offered me, I will use all our machinery to get the Irish people to accept it.'[4] And he had already admitted to Casement's brother, Tom, 'that a Republic was out of the question'.[5]

De Valera was in fact offered the status of a Dominion almost immediately but with fundamental reservations, most important of which was that the position of the six counties under the Parliament of Northern Ireland would remain as it was under the Government of Ireland Act. According to Lloyd George, de Valera replied with a demand for Dominion status inclusive of the North, with issues such as facilities for the British navy and air forces to be negotiated later between the two governments; alternatively, he demanded total independence for the rest of Ireland. On being told that these alternatives were unacceptable and meant the end of the truce, he turned very pale and demanded a respite for discussion in Dublin, which was granted. He asked Lloyd George not to publish the proposals and counter-proposals since this, he said, in a significant phrase, 'would increase my difficulties'.[6]

The Dail, on de Valera's recommendation, unanimously rejected the

British proposals, but with the air thus cleared he re-established contact with Lloyd George and after much haggling over terminology eventually accepted an invitation to a conference on terms which were without any pre-conditions whatever. They did not imply the sovereign independent status for the Irish delegates which de Valera had doggedly tried to establish. On the other hand, they did not imply any Irish obligation to the British Empire either. The invitation, which followed further conciliatory intervention by George v, asked him to come 'with a view to ascertaining how the association of Ireland with the community of nations known as the British Empire can best be reconciled with Irish national aspirations'.⁷ The Conference began in London on 11 October.

On the Crown the Irish from the start adopted the ingenious compromise de Valera had worked out by geometry for Cathal Brugha's benefit and which he now called External Association. The actual use of the word 'external' came to him one morning after his first meetings with Lloyd George when he was tying his bootlaces in his house in Dublin.⁸ The term meant the voluntary association of an independent sovereign state with the British Empire, the membership of such association creating a special link with the Crown which was to be the head of the association.

Ironically, this was one day to become the standard constitutional pattern by which the British Empire or Commonwealth was enabled to survive, permitting African and Indian nationalist states to become wholly independent sovereign states while still linked to Britain. In 1921, however, such a formula seemed totally unacceptable to any British Government as disruptive of the Empire, and though it was to be presented over and over again by the Irish delegates it was always to be flatly rejected. Persistence with it did, however, successfully lead by way of compromise to at least a remarkable obfuscation in terminology of that allegiance the British regarded as indispensable. In any case the obvious Irish tactics were to break with the British, if break they must, not on the Crown – unimportant as it was to the Irish people as a whole and important to the British – but on Ulster.

On Ulster the Irish were on much stronger ground. Few people in Britain or Ireland liked partition. The Unionists as well as the Nationalists in the South were opposed to it. If a British Government were prepared, as they were, to give a form of Dominion status to the vast majority of the Irish people, why, it might be asked, should that status not apply to the whole of their country, including those sections of that vast majority who lived among a relatively small anti-nationalist minority in the north-east? The nationalists had after all already committed themselves in a statement of de Valera's to the principle of some autonomy within an Irish state for that minority. It was extremely unlikely that British public opinion would want to incur all the moral opprobrium and embarrassment of all-out war in Ireland for the sake of preventing that, particularly if further safeguards were to be given to Britain's security by the grant of special facilities to the British Navy in Irish ports.

It is easy now to see that the Irish delegation should have stuck rigidly to this position in their negotiations, making further concessions on the Crown, and on other matters if necessary, but on no account abandoning the basic principle of national unity for the preservation of which the Irish people had first called upon their party. We know now that given the evolutionary development of the British Empire that was to take place within even the next ten years, the widening of an Irish Dominion's internal powers and the eventual extension of its constitutional status would have presented no great difficulties and certainly would have involved no all-out war. But even without hindsight, to say this is to leave a number of vital contemporary factors out of account.

In the first place there was the simple personal factor. Lloyd George headed the British team, the 'Welsh wizard' by the lowest standards, and, by the highest, one of the most brilliant political manipulators of all time. Behind him were two men also of political stature in any age: Birkenhead and Winston Churchill. Only de Valera at the head of the Irish delegation might have been a match for Lloyd George, who had already paid him the compliment of saying that arguing with him was like trying to pick up mercury with a fork.* But for reasons which people have interpreted differently de Valera this time decided not to go to London. His enemies have said that it was because he knew there must be a compromise which would incur such odium among republicans in Ireland that he did not wish to be tainted by it. But this is wholly unjust.

It was indeed because de Valera knew there must be compromise that he remained in Ireland, but not in his own self-interest. By remaining in Ireland he was able to retain manoeuvre for two political situations at once. First, he was well positioned for the inevitable game of bluff needed to secure an acceptable compromise in London, with himself advantageously appearing an inflexible symbol of the Republic. Second, he was ready to deal with the delicate political situation that would arise at home with out-and-out republicans when the inevitable compromise on the Crown (embodied, he hoped, in some form of external association) went through. It was an example of the whole Republican movement's weakness as representative of Ireland in this crisis that the more important political problem should have appeared to arise not across the negotiating table in London but in the reaction to what happened in London among dogmatic republican circles in Ireland. For this reason, above all, Ireland's best player was, as Griffith put it, kept among the reserves.' And self-imprisoned in the slight unreality of that

---

* 'Why doesn't he use a spoon?' was de Valera's riposte. See Frank Pakenham (new Lord Longford), *Peace by Ordeal*, London, 1935, p. 84. This fine work is the best account of the Treaty negotiations in detail.

Dublin situation de Valera inevitably applied to the negotiations in London something of its unreal perspective.

The other Irish negotiators, in addition to Griffith, were: Michael Collins, who had accepted the role most reluctantly, but whom the British, it could be assumed, would regard as representative of the hard-line IRA – and who conversely might be expected to lend a certain republican respectability to any necessary compromise in the minds of the IRA; Robert Barton, chosen partly for his economic interests, but also because as an ex-English public schoolboy and a land-owner he understood the background and mentality of men like Churchill and Birkenhead in the British delegation; E. J. Duggan, a solicitor who had acted as an intelligence front in Dublin for Collins in the past two and a half years, and George Gavan Duffy who had been a Sinn Fein representative in Paris. Erskine Childers, who had helped make such a brilliantly effective job of Sinn Fein's propaganda, was the delegation's secretary. The members of the delegation were defined in their credentials as 'plenipotentiaries', but they agreed to keep in touch with Dublin and also to submit the complete text of any draft treaty about to be signed with the British to Dublin and await a reply before signing.[10]

The full, complex, and detailed negotiations which led to the eventual signing of the so-called Anglo-Irish Treaty on the early morning of 6 December 1921 need not concern us. In the context of seven centuries of Irish history, or, more narrowly, in the context of a century and a half of different forms of Irish nationalism, what is important is what the negotiators brought back and why.

That as negotiators they were outclassed is undeniable. Their own private political difficulties in Dublin were certainly a handicap. But then the British delegation had an analogous handicap with many of their own party rank and file, of whom they were far in advance, in dealing with 'murderers' and assassins at all. The British, particularly Lloyd George, simply handled their own difficulties more subtly and skilfully.

The chief mistake the Irish delegation made was to allow the two all-important issues of the Crown and Ulster to become confused. They did not sufficiently single out Ulster as the issue on which to challenge the British to renew the war. This was largely because, though the unity of Ireland was more important than the issue of allegiance, to the people of Ireland in general, the issue of allegiance was of equal importance to the minority of republican dogmatists whom the delegates also represented. In the event they fought both issues either simultaneously or alternatively and lost over both. In terms solely of the tactics which the situation seemed to demand it is amazing to find that as late as ten days after the conference had begun the Irish were writing to de Valera through Childers for instructions as to which issue to give most weight to: Ulster or the Crown. When Griffith indicated that his natural inclinations were to offer concessions on the

Crown, de Valera wrote back that there could be 'no question of our asking the Irish people to enter an arrangement which could make them subject to the Crown, or demand from them allegiance to the British King. If war is the alternative we can only face it. . . .'[11]

It was to be de Valera's weakness throughout that, staying in Dublin where even External Association presented a problem, he should have been able to feel that he had made all the compromise necessary by (*a*) being prepared to give up the actual word 'Republic', and (*b*) by conceding a recognition of the Crown as head of the Commonwealth with which Ireland was to be associated. After Griffith had expostulated at de Valera's interference with the delegation's power of manoeuvre over the Crown, de Valera became less inclined to make further suggestions, and the dangers of future misunderstanding were enhanced by distance. The possibility that might have been open had the delegation felt wholly free to offer concessions on the Crown was revealed to Griffith by Lloyd George, who said that provided he had Irish reassurances on the Crown he would 'smite the Die-Hards and would fight on the Ulster matter to secure "essential unity"'.[12] And a few days later Griffith told de Valera that if Ulster proved unreasonable the British Government were prepared to resign rather than go back to war against the South.[13]

There were two difficulties. The first was that Griffith and Collins had only limited freedom of manoeuvre on the Crown. The second was that in the stage in the negotiations after Sir James Craig had shown himself uncomfortably intransigent towards any change in the 1920 *status quo*, Lloyd George had introduced a subtle device to try to get himself off both the Belfast and the Dublin hooks simultaneously. The device was a Boundary Commission which, along the lines of his original proposal for the Government of Ireland Bill,* would sit and adjust the borders in accordance with the wishes of the inhabitants. If this were to mean what it said, it could only mean that large areas of Counties Tyrone and Fermanagh, together with other areas of County Derry, South County Down and South County Armagh would be transferred to a Dublin government in return for small reverse border indentations in the Counties of Donegal, Cavan and Monaghan. On the grounds that any border adjustment of this sort would probably make the Northern Government politically and economically unviable, Griffith had privately agreed to accept it as a temporary solution of the Ulster difficulty when Lloyd George said that what he wanted was reassurances with which to calm his own right wing. When in the last hours of the negotiations, after it had seemed that they would break down altogether over the question of the oath, and the Irish delegates, on referring themselves to Dublin, had been sent back again with instructions to break on Ulster, Lloyd George suddenly produced Griffith's agreement to the Boundary

* See above, p. 664.

Commission, the delegates found they did not have Ulster to break on, only the Boundary Commission.[14] And to break on that would in the circumstances have come even more unreasonably from Griffith – who had agreed to it privately – than from Craig. It was a superb piece of political manoeuvre on the part of Lloyd George.

The very title of the agreement which the delegates brought back from London – 'Articles of Agreement for a Treaty Between Great Britain and Ireland' – announced a new era in Irish history, a change as fundamental in its way as that brought about by the arrival of the Norman barons seven centuries before. The use of the word 'Treaty' conferred a status Ireland had never before been granted.

'Who are our Ambassadors? What treaties do we enter into?' Sir Lawrence Parsons had exclaimed, deploring the hollowness of the Irish 'Nation' of Grattan's Parliament, 130 years before. Now she had a Treaty with the country that had disputed her nationality so long. By this document Ireland was given the constitution and status of Canada and the other Dominions 'in the community of nations known as the British Empire'. (As Collins was to point out, this automatically made the other Dominions guarantors of Ireland's status.) She was to be styled the Irish Free State – a literal translation of the Irish word *Saorstat* which Dail Eireann had been using as the Irish for Republic over the past two and a half years.

The 'representative of the Crown in Ireland' – a last-minute improvement secured by Collins over the word 'Governor-General' – was to be appointed and to act in accordance with the practice of the Canadian Governor-General. The oath to be taken by Members of the Parliament was set down in Clause 4 of the Treaty, and since it was to dominate the future of internal Irish politics for the next six years, is worth studying in full. In many ways it was a masterpiece of ingenuity, a compromise as brilliantly calculated to satisfy equally two diametrically opposed interpretations as any compromise of words could be.

'I ...,' the oath began, 'do solemnly swear true faith and allegiance to the Constitution of the Irish Free State as by law established ...' (Not, it may be noted, allegiance to the king.) It went on: '... and that I will be faithful to H.M. King George v, his heirs and successors by law, in virtue of the common citizenship of Ireland with Great Britain and her adherence to and membership of the group of nations forming the British Commonwealth of Nations.'[15] There was on a purely literal interpretation no oath to the king. The fact that 'allegiance' was subtracted from faithfulness where the king was concerned may even be said to have made this point emphatically. The faithfulness sworn was in respect of 'common citizenship' with Great Britain, and of Ireland's membership of the Commonwealth. The very use of the word 'Commonwealth' rather than the then current usage 'Empire' was in itself a mark of deference to Irish Republican susceptibilities. The phrase 'common citizenship' could be interpreted in two ways. In one interpretation it could be made to mean that Irish Free State citizens were still automatically subjects of H.M. King George V as English citizens were, and as Irishmen hitherto always had been. In another interpretation it could be made to seem that common citizenship specifically excluded subjection and was something voluntarily entered into by Irishmen with this Treaty. The whole past history of the close intermingling of the people of the two islands in their everyday lives made this a not undignified decision.

Amazing as it may now seem, Ireland was largely to destroy herself, to know again two rival reigns of terror – by government (though an Irish one this time) and by civilian guerrillas – to read again of executions by the roadside and in barracks yards, to see many more of her fine buildings consumed in flames and the highest hopes of those who had believed in Irish freedom for so long turned to ashes – all on the issue of whether or not the Treaty which contained this oath was a betrayal of all she had been struggling for.

On the question of Ulster, so much more fundamental to the concept of Irish nationalism, there were two major items. First, though the Treaty and the constitutional status similar to Canada's were conferred on Ireland as a whole, the powers of the Government of Northern Ireland established the year before were to remain unaffected until one month after the ratification of the Treaty by Act of Parliament. If within that month the Government of Northern Ireland so asked, then Northern Ireland was to continue to be excluded from the powers of the Free State. Second, if that happened – and everyone knew that it would – then a Commission was to sit to 'determine in accordance with the wishes of the inhabitants, so far as may be compatible with economic and geographic considerations, the boundaries between Northern Ireland and the rest of Ireland'.

Except for such adjustments as this Boundary Commission might give rise to, this was basically no improvement on the 'temporary' partition of the six counties to which Redmond had reluctantly agreed. Purely theoretically it might be said that since the six counties now had autonomy from Westminster, a sort of constitutional lip-service was thereby paid to the Irish nationalist principle. But in practice, given the known two-thirds anti-nationalist majority in the North, autonomy put paid to the national hopes of those who lived there more finally than subservience to Westminster had ever done. The Boundary Commission alone seemed to give some chance of a reprieve. For if the border were thus re-aligned then large tracts of Tyrone and Fermanagh at least and some parts of Derry, Armagh and Down would presumably be allotted to the Free State, and the question would inevitably arise as to whether 'Northern Ireland' could reasonably continue as a viable political and economic unit if so truncated. This was the hope to which Collins in particular clung, enabling him to convince himself that in the end the Treaty would not be found to have destroyed the All-Ireland principle. Just before the Treaty was signed Collins had an interview with Lloyd George in which the British Prime Minister allowed Collins to think that he too interpreted the significance of the Boundary Commission in this sense – i.e. in the sense that it would transfer large areas to the nationalist South.[16]

The constitutional status of Canada permitted Ireland to raise her own military and naval defence forces, but other clauses in the Treaty gave the British forces certain rights and facilities in four Irish ports. Some recognition, however, of the special strategic relationship between Britain and Ireland had always been made by Sinn Feiners and these rights could hardly be said to constitute a violation of Irish nationality in the circumstances.* Unquestionably the Treaty did not give Ireland the Republic many people had been fighting for. But hopes of getting that had been tacitly abandoned by entering into negotiations at all. Soon after they had begun in fact Collins had admitted in a private letter that Dominion status, though nowhere near a finalized solution, was 'the first step'. More than this could not be expected.[17] And de Valera himself had earlier made the same compromise. What the Treaty unquestionably did do was to end Ireland's old relationship with England for ever. And that for the vast majority of Irishmen and women after all they had gone through in the past two and a half years, after all their forefathers had gone through in seven centuries, was not a bad start. Ireland at last could now look to herself for salvation.

Of the five Irish signatories to the Treaty – Griffith, Collins, Duggan, Barton and Duffy – none had liked its compromises, but the first three had thought its advantages far outweighed its disadvantages. The essence of their position was that it gave, in Collins's phrase, the freedom to achieve freedom.

In London Collins, essentially a realist for all the extreme republican position from which he had started as a young man, had successfully adjusted fantasy to reality. Practical by temperament, he was able to maintain the adjustment on return to Ireland. The reality after all was greater than the majority of Irish nationalists only a few years before would have dreamt possible. On the other hand, Collins knew quite well the sort of mood he had to answer to among his former comrades. In the night hours in which the Treaty had been signed in London Churchill had noticed that Collins

---

* Nevertheless, there were extremists who so interpreted it and not even supporters of the Treaty, of course, liked the idea. Curiously, these rights, which constituted a difficulty between Britain and Ireland for eighteen years, were abandoned by the British Government in April 1938, a year before the outbreak of the Second World War in which they were to be so badly needed.

at one point looked as if he were going to shoot someone, 'preferably himself'. On his arrival by boat in Dublin on 8 December his first words to his intelligence agent Tom Cullen, who was first across the gangway, were: 'Tom, what are our fellows saying?' 'What is good enough for you is good enough for them,' came the reply.[18]

With Barton and Duffy the emphasis in their attitude to the Treaty was different. They had been appalled by its compromises, but thought them better than the alternative which was a breakdown, bringing, if not the 'terrible war' which Lloyd George threatened, at least a sterile and dangerous deadlock in which the Irish would have lost all advantage. (Collins, in whose political interest it was to play up the threat of war, in fact rather played it down.) Erskine Childers, the Secretary to the delegation, affected perhaps by the remorselessness of his own propaganda in the later phases of the military struggle, was by now an ascetically severe and dogmatic Republican, and had long been casting a baleful eye on the way things were going in London. Just before the end of the negotiations Collins had described Childers's advice and inspiration as being 'like farmland under water – dead. With a purpose, I think – with a definite purpose. Soon he will howl his triumph for what it is worth.'[19]

The remark is a good example of how Collins, realistic about the negotiations, was equally realistic about the potential political crisis over his shoulder in Dublin – in fact he had already once described Dublin as 'our over-riding difficulty'.[20]

Childers, uninhibited by any need to face the personal alternatives of signature or commitment to war, did much to reinforce the grievous doubts which de Valera himself felt when he first read the Treaty's details as outlined in the evening papers of 6 December. For the plenipotentiaries, though they had returned to Dublin to discuss with de Valera Britain's final offer on 3 December, when it was regarded by all as unacceptable, had signed, without further reference back, a Treaty that was only marginally improved.

The technicalities which have been endlessly argued over in Ireland ever since as to whether the plenipotentiaries really had full powers or whether they should have again referred back to Dublin before signing (which according to their original instructions they should have done) or whether the instructions were contradictory to their plenipotentiary status, are not in themselves nearly so important as they have sometimes been made to seem. They are important inasmuch as de Valera personally felt them to be important. He was in any case tensely prepared for the political situation he knew he would have to face over the inevitable compromise. Rightly or wrongly, he saw himself in Dublin as the central figure in control of the most delicate part of the political situation. And if that seems a parochial and dogmatic view in the context of the great drama being played out in terms of the lives of ordinary Irish people in London, it must be said that a dogmatic narrowness of view amounting at times to a sense of total unreality had long been one of the weaknesses of the Fenian and Republican movements. When, through what he regarded as a disregard of the technical arrangements he had made, he found himself by-passed in his control, an understandable personal resentment was added to what in any case was his own disappointment with the actual terms.

But that his own idea of what the minimum acceptable terms should have been were not in themselves so different from what were accepted could be immediately seen from the so-called 'Document No. 2' which he produced as an alternative in the great debate in the Dail that was inaugurated on 14 December 1921. For Document No. 2 did not mention the word 'Republic', though it spoke of the 'Sovereign Irish Nation', and inasmuch as it associated Ireland 'for purposes of common concern' with the British Commonwealth it recognized 'for the purposes of the Association ... His Britannic Majesty as head of the Association'. The fact that such a formula had been consistently turned down by the British negotiators from the very first hardly seemed to figure in his considerations. But in many ways the most remarkable feature of Document No. 2 was that on the most important question of all, that of Ulster, it actually accepted the provisions of the Treaty.[21]

The emotion with which de Valera and his supporters in the Dail now opposed Griffith and Collins and their supporters in debate was something which far out-reached the significance of the literal points on which they differed. Given the comradeship in difficult and dangerous times they had shared so long, and the courageous unanimity – unique in the history of Irish revolt – with which they had appeared to face the British Government, given the major national victory achieved by the removal of British rule from twenty-six of the thirty-two counties of Ireland, and the challenge that remained of vindicating the nationalist principle over the other six, it seems amazing that the movement should now have split as it did, so suddenly and ferociously. Part of the explanation of the intensely emotional character of this split must lie in the simple release of tension that automatically followed a period so long fraught with suppressed fears and anxieties on both the purely human and political levels. Individual personal rivalries and jealousies, too, that had long had to be restrained or concealed, could now leap out into the open.* Closer to the heart of the matter was the removal of the need for what had often been unnatural unanimity. There had always been moderates and extremists in the movement though the difference had been fairly efficiently concealed. More important: there had always been realists and fantasists and this difference was now often revealed clearly

---

* Cathal Brugha in a bitter and embarrassing speech in the Treaty Debate made little attempt to conceal his jealousy of Collins, whose nominal superior he had been in the IRA as Minister of Defence. He implied absurdly that Collins had merely been a publicity seeker and that his reputation had been largely forged in the newspapers.

for the first time as some of the toughest of the extremists in the past – Commandants of the IRA like MacEoin, of Ballinalee, and Mulcahy the Chief of Staff – followed Collins, the toughest of them all, in support of the Treaty. The women had perhaps the best reason to cling to fantasy: Mrs Pearse, mother of Padraic and Willie, Mrs Clarke, widow of Tom, Miss Mary MacSwiney, sister of Terence, and Mrs O'Callaghan, widow of the murdered Mayor of Limerick, all were passionate opponents of the Treaty. It was a struggle between those who were prepared to come down to earth from the loftiest flights of Irish nationalism and those who were not. And this, of course, was where the Irish people who had never been up there but had allowed their fate to be taken over by republican fantasists almost without realizing it, now suffered from being represented by an esoteric clique, which had to resolve its own contradictions in public.

The Dail in the end approved the Treaty by 64 votes to 57, a result which led to a number of near-theological political adjustments. De Valera resigned as President or Prime Minister and went into opposition to Griffith who took his place. The Treaty stipulated that a Provisional Government chosen by the Parliament of Southern Ireland was to implement its terms and produce the Constitution of the Irish Free State. But the mystical Republic continued in being for a time both in the minds of the supporters as well as of opponents of the Treaty. The Army, the pro-Treaty Mulcahy asserted in the last words of the entire twelve-day debate, remained the Army of the Republic.

The members of Dail Eireann were also nominally members of the so-called Southern Parliament, except for one man who represented only an Ulster constituency and therefore was only a member of the Dail. A momentary ghostly overlap of Parliaments thus became possible as the four Southern Unionists who alone had attended the Southern Parliament's one previous meeting joined pro-Treaty Dail members to elect a Provisional government. An even more curious ghostly overlap of governments thus came into being. This Provisional government had for form's sake to have a different leader from that of the fading Republic. Thus Collins, who retained his post as Minister of Finance in Griffith's government, became Chairman of the Provisional government with Griffith as his closest collaborator. Other ministers of Griffith's still Republican government became simultaneously ministers of Collins's Provisional Free State government: men like William Cosgrave, Kevin O'Higgins and Richard Mulcahy. Constitutionally the Irish Republic was disappearing like the Cheshire Cat in *Alice in Wonderland*.

But, of course, there were hard realities, and the chief of them was the Army.

11
Nemesis (1922–3)

It is more than likely that had the Republican movement been a genuine democratic political movement there would have been, as de Valera stoutly maintained there was, and as all hoped there would prove to be, a proper constitutional way of resolving its internal political differences. But the movement which had been outwardly democratic from 1917 to the General Election of 1918 had since been entirely taken over by violent undemocratic forces from within. Nothing in all the Treaty debate rang more hollow than the continued protestations on both sides that members' only responsibility was to their constituents. Collins himself, of all people, actually proclaimed: 'I would not be one of those to commit the Irish people to war without the Irish people committing themselves to war.'[1] And Kevin O'Higgins chose this moment to 'acknowledge as great a responsibility to the 6,000 people who voted against me in 1918 as to the 13,000 people who voted for me'.[2]

But, of course, it was the Volunteers, the 'Army', acting quite regardless of the people's approval, who had brought about the situation in which there was a Treaty to be debated at all. And not illogically, many of them failed to see why they should be any more responsible to the people now than they had been in the past two and a half years. The IRA had never been very respectful of its nominal allegiance to Dail Eireann and had often been remarkably independent even of its own headquarters leadership. The IRA was now better armed than ever before; its ranks were swelled by new eager young warriors anxious to emulate their elders; its veterans were flushed with what felt like victory over the British, and enjoying the public adulation which easily came their way. The IRA was the effective force in the country whatever happened on the political level.

For many of the most idealistic IRA leaders – men like Liam Lynch and Ernie O'Malley – the Republic may indeed have been a symbol, but it was a symbol which was solemn and very real. 'It is a living tangible thing,' declared Liam Mellows, the 1916 Galway leader, during the Treaty debate. 'Something for which men gave their lives, for which men were hanged, for which men are in gaol, for which the people suffered and for which men are still prepared to give their lives.'*[3] Even if only a word it was one which

---

* Mellows had been in America for most of the past three years. His words have a prophetic note in view of later events.

many men had sanctified with all they held most dear and to de-sanctify it was to betray themselves.

Pro-Treaty IRA men were just as agonized by the denial of something inside themselves which support of the Treaty required, none more so than Collins himself. One detail in the complex situation, however, made things easier: the continuing apparatus of the secret Irish Republican Brotherhood. Though in most ways superseded by the larger underground apparatus which Collins had developed in the IRA itself, the nucleus of the secret society still existed and Collins himself controlled it. He was able to throw it behind the Treaty with double advantage. First, it gave him a loyal organizational network within the IRA with which to rally material support to his side. Second, it enabled Republicans, even Collins himself, to feel that the establishment of the Free State was a temporary strategic requirement in continued pursuit of the still inviolate mystical Republic. With this factor in their favour Collins, Mulcahy and the Provisional Government were able to carry about half the IRA with them in support of the Treaty, arming them, giving them uniforms and, with a certain amount of ambiguity of Republican terminology, transferring them simultaneously into a Free State Army.

Roughly speaking, the IRA split down the middle, with units conforming to the pro- or anti-Treaty dispositions of their commanders. And since the IRA was officially taking over barracks from the evacuating British forces, pro- and anti-Treaty troops became distributed at random all over the country. Sometimes they occupied different premises in the same town, confronting one another in uneasy rivalry made all the more bizarre by the persisting comradeship of former times.

In March the anti-Treaty faction began to organize itself as a separate force. It repudiated its nominal allegiance to the Dail and in a press interview Rory O'Connor, who had been Director of Engineering in the old IRA and now headed the anti-Treaty section, left no doubt as to where the responsibility for future events was to lie. Asked if there were any government in Ireland to which he gave his allegiance, he responded, 'No.'

'Do we take it we are going to have a military dictatorship then?' went on his questioner.

'You can take it that way if you like.'[4]

The civil war which was soon to follow has often been popularly blamed on de Valera, but the responsibility was not his. His anti-Treaty attitude undoubtedly gave a coherence and a political point of focus to anti-Treaty opinion in the country. But anti-Treaty opinion inside the IRA, which was what was to bring about the civil war, organized and consolidated itself independently. It looked not to de Valera but to its own leaders.

On the night of 13 April O'Connor, supported by a new independent IRA executive including Liam Lynch, Ernie O'Malley, Sean Moylan and other battle-scarred combatants of the 'Tan war', occupied and set up military headquarters in the Four Courts, Dublin. Interviewed again by the press, O'Connor repeated that the IRA now had no political connections, merely adding that 'If the army were ever to follow a political leader, Mr de Valera is the man.' Independent gunmen had long been able to think that they were the only true guardians of Ireland's destiny and, with their occupation otherwise gone, saw no reason now to relinquish their sacred charge. Collins himself was now at the mercy of the very system he had created.

Politically de Valera still hoped to effect a compromise that would prevent civil war. He had prophesied its dangers clearly enough in near-hysterical words at Thurles in March, when he said that those who wanted to complete the work of the past four years would have to wade through the blood of Irish soldiers and even of members of the Irish Government to do so. It seems he meant this as a warning, though it sounded like a threat. Psychologically, de Valera was in the same position on the anti-Treaty side as Collins was on the pro-Treaty side: both desperate to avoid a split but committed to making a split inevitable.

To Collins's own anxieties over the anti-Treaty IRA were added complications over the situation in the North. There, the news of the Boundary Commission clause in the Treaty had been received badly by Protestants and had animated the worst sort of traditional tension between Protestants and Catholics. It immediately became clear that Lloyd George (by a trick similar to that with which he had reassured both Redmond and Carson with opposite interpretations of a single clause in 1916) had allowed both Collins and Craig to take totally contradictory impressions of what the Boundary Commission was meant to do. 'I will never,' said Craig in January 1922, 'give in to any re-arrangement of the Boundary that leaves our Ulster area less than it is under the Government of Ireland Act', emphasizing that Lloyd George had given him reassurances to this effect. Collins replied equally emphatically that there could be no dispute as to the fact that 'very large areas' in Tyrone, Fermanagh, Down, Derry and Armagh had been unquestionably understood as being involved in the agreement with the British delegation.[5] It was on this understanding that he had been able to convince himself that the Treaty did not at least make impossible the essential national unity of Ireland.

Rioting on a serious scale now broke out in the North. Neither pro- nor anti-Treaty IRA there hesitated to support in arms the Catholic minority or cease to regard the North as national territory. The recently-created force of Ulster A and B specials did not hesitate to support the Protestants. In three weeks in February 138 casualties were reported from Belfast, of whom ninety-eight were Catholics. Thirty people were killed there in a single night. Catholic refugees streamed south of a border that began to look as if it were not going to be changed after all.

Collins's own personal position was extremely ambivalent. Technically bound by the Treaty to regard the northern area as outside the Free State's powers, he could not possibly bring himself to stand by and watch Irish nationalists subjected to violence because they were Irish nationalists. What, after all, had he been fighting for all these years? He therefore found himself in the ambiguous position of being on the verge of civil war with anti-Treaty IRA in the South, while virtually recognizing no differences in the IRA in the North and even supplying them with arms regardless of whether they were anti-Treaty or not. In a meeting with Craig in London he had done what he could by negotiation, calling off the Dail's Ulster boycott in return for Craig's promise to reinstate expelled Catholic shipyard workers in Belfast. But the disagreement over the Boundary Commission left him in an appalling state of frustration. 'I am really and truly having an awful time,' he wrote in January to the Irish girl in County Longford to whom he was engaged, 'and am rapidly becoming quite desperate. Oh Lord, it is honestly frightful.' And after Craig's uncompromising statement on the Border, 'This is the worst day I have had yet – far, far the worst. May God help us all.'[6]

Events in the North and the South interacted upon each other disastrously. A year before, at the time of the Northern Ireland election and at the height of the conflict between British forces and the IRA, there had been a preparedness by Northern leaders to consider some eventual cooperation with the South and some gesture towards the principle of a united Ireland.* It had been inspired more by pragmatic doubts about 'Northern Ireland's' future viability than by consideration for the South's susceptibilities, but it had been a positive attitude. Now there was only a cold and self-preserving shutting of the mind to everything but the ancient principle, rooted in fear, of 'What we have, we hold'.

The change had started as a negotiating position at the time of the opening of the Treaty talks in London. Craig had correctly understood that it was in his tactical interest to take the firmest possible stand on 'the rock of Ulster' as planted in the new Government of Ireland Act. To a large extent his tactics had succeeded and he now only had the Boundary Commission to fight, with Northern Ireland Protestant opinion solidly behind him, expressed in the new Parliament which had had nearly a year's viable existence. With its assistance he had created his own para-military force of some 25,000 A and B Specials, many of them fanatical Orangemen from Carson's old Ulster Volunteer Force, and had introduced a Special Powers Bill giving him power to inflict flogging and the death penalty for unauthorized possession of arms. A feeling that the Six-County State of Northern Ireland was sacrosanct, and somehow part of the natural order of things, took root among Northern Protestants, though the British Government had been prepared to make it negotiable only a few months previously and were still nominally

* See above, pp. 714–15.

committed to adjust its form. Similarly, a sense of helplessness and desperation began to overwhelm northern nationalists, who, as the prospects of a
genuine Boundary Commission receded, saw their only support in the IRA.
In March, sixty people were killed in Belfast, and Craig appointed Sir Henry
Wilson, arch-enemy of Irish nationalism, as his adviser to help provide
law and order.

Rory O'Connor's anti-treaty republican headquarters in the Four Courts,
openly tolerated by Collins, further increased the Northern Protestants'
sense of threat and their determination to defend their new establishment. As
anti-Catholic riots continued, sometimes supported in ugly fashion by uniformed forces who were supposed to be preserving law and order, it seemed
to Irish nationalists both inside and outside the IRA that in the North
something like the Tan war was still in progress. By the middle of June,
264 people had been killed altogether in the six counties of Northern Ireland
since the signing of the Treaty – 93 of them Protestants and 171 Catholics.
Thousands of refugees streamed south to Dublin and a thousand even across
the water to Glasgow.[7]

This Northern situation made it even more imperative for Collins to try
to avoid the danger of civil war in the South and was a contributory factor
to a curious political event which now took place there. A general election
was due to give democratic status to the Provisional Government and its
new Constitution based on the Treaty. Collins and de Valera, in their mutual
anxiety to avoid civil war, worked out an electoral Pact by which the old
Sinn Fein party was to stand for election as one party on a single panel.
Candidates were to be distributed on the panel between the two sides in the
proportion of 64 pro-Treaty to 57 anti-Treaty, being the proportion in which
the vote had been distributed on the Treaty in the Dail. Candidates of other
parties, or independents, were of course free to stand as they chose, but the
panel would nevertheless undoubtedly result in a far greater number of anti-
Treaty candidates being returned than was representative of the true state
of opinion on the Treaty in the country. Furthermore, by the terms of the
Pact, it was provided that after the election there should be a Coalition
Government composed of five pro-Treaty Ministers and four anti-Treaty
Ministers.

In some respects the Collins–de Valera Pact actually increased Collins's
difficulties. For news of it was heard with alarm in London and at the same
time drove Craig in the North into an intransigent frenzy. He seized it as an
opportunity to denounce privately to the British Government the whole idea
of the Boundary Commission, feeling not without some justification that if
Collins and de Valera could agree politically, then the Treaty was being
undermined. Publicly, Craig declared that if the clause on the Boundary
Commission were now enforced it would lead to civil war.[8] On the Government side the evacuation of British forces from Southern Ireland was sus-

pended. Churchill declared that should a new Coalition Government such as might emerge from a Pact election set up a Republic in defiance of the Treaty it would produce a situation comparable to that which gave rise to the American civil war: 'We should no more recognize it than the Northern States of America recognized secession.'[9]

Collins's motives in agreeing to the Pact with de Valera – which strained his own relations with Griffith to the limit – were mixed. He was desperate to avoid civil war, partly for straightforward emotional reasons, partly because he wished to retain an effective unity with which to confront the situation in the North. In this sense he undoubtedly wanted, against all the odds, to try to reconcile two irreconcilable positions. On the other hand, he had always been the most practical realist of them all. And there was an element of strict realism in the de Valera Pact. The explanation which he gave to the British Government, namely that it was the only way of allowing Ireland to have an election at all, had good sense in it and may well have been his principal motivation. The split in the IRA and the dissociation of the anti-Treaty elements had led to conditions of increasing anarchy in the South over which the government had no control. It was not just that fusillades between pro- and anti-Treaty IRA forces, sudden and furious as hailstorms, though usually as harmless, swept the streets of towns like Sligo and kilkenny. Far more serious was the breakdown of law and order on an everyday detailed level over much of the area in which any local Brigade Commander was an anti-Treatyite.

Some of the lawlessness was honestly undertaken. Sean Moylan, for instance, commended once for his chivalry in action after an IRA ambush of British forces,* actually boasted proudly in the Dail that he had robbed nineteen Post Offices in one day in the neighbourhood of Kantark in March 1922. He told how he had 'collected' dog taxes with relish from pro-Treaty citizens and others, to clothe and provide food, tobacco and – 'We are not all Pussey footers' – a drink or two for his men. He would do it again, he said, because in doing such things he was 'standing up for and defending the Republic'.[10] It can be imagined what opportunities such a state of affairs provided also for those who were just standing up for themselves. In the three weeks from 29 March to 19 April, 323 Post Offices were robbed in the South of Ireland; and forty consignments of goods were seized from the Dublin and South-Eastern Railway between 23 March and 22 April, though in only thirty of the cases was the seizure even stated to be 'by order IRA'. When a big pro-Treaty meeting was held at Wexford on 9 April special trains were stopped by armed men and the crews forcibly prevented from running them; telephone and signal wires were cut and sleepers and rails removed.[11] Murders of former RIC men, ex-servicemen, or other individuals against whom old scores of one sort or another needed to be settled occurred

* See above, p. 700.

weekly, sometimes daily. There were constant forced levies of money from people too frightened to resist or to inquire too closely the exact nature of the cause to which they were contributing. All these activities to which it had been so easy to give a patriotic gloss in the days of the 'War of Independence' were resumed now in the anti-Treaty cause with even less punctiliousness than before. Not for nothing were the anti-Treaty forces becoming known as 'irregulars'.

It was difficult to think of an election taking place successfully in such an atmosphere. Ordinary public opinion in the country was overwhelmingly for the Treaty, but at the mercy of anti-Treaty men with revolvers who often had long training in the arts of intimidation. Prior to the Pact, de Valera himself, though he expressed disapproval of interference with political freedom of speech, used a number of constitutional excuses to try to have the election postponed, principally complaining that the electoral register which had not been revised since October 1918 was unfair. By the Pact Collins secured de Valera's and the political republicans' active participation in the election. For quite apart from any genuine hopes Republicans might have of a bold change of face on the part of Collins, it was obviously in their interest to take advantage of an election presented to them in such advantageous terms.

That a certain Machiavellian realism at least overlapped Collins's more emotional conflict of loyalties was shown by his electioneering behaviour. For although early in the campaign he addressed a number of meetings on behalf of the panel as a whole, speaking on the same platform as de Valera, yet on the eve of the poll itself, when the Pact had done its work and secured at least a coherent election, he made a speech in Cork which undermined the Pact's whole intention. A large number of independents and candidates of other parties had in fact presented themselves on nomination day to oppose the panel, and all were pro-Treaty. Now in this speech in Cork Collins advised his audience to vote not necessarily for the Sinn Fein panel but for the candidate they thought best. 'The country must have the representatives it wants,' he continued. 'You understand fully what you have to do and I call on you to do it.'[12]

Voting took place on 16 June and the results were declared on 24 June. A surprisingly high number of pro-Treaty candidates outside the panel had been elected: thirty altogether – without the four Unionists from Trinity College. Ninety-four out of the total of 128 members of the new Dail were for the Treaty. Collins made no move towards implementing the Coalition clause of the Pact, though de Valera waited for an invitation. Collins now had unmistakable democratic sanction for the Treaty.

Such clear expression of the people's will had been accomplished in the nick of time. For on 22 June there came a piece of news which transformed the entire post-Treaty situation.

Sir Henry Wilson, on returning by taxi to his house on the corner of

Eaton Place and Belgrave Place on the afternoon of 22 June, having just unveiled a memorial at St Pancras to the employees of the Great Eastern Railway Company who had lost their lives in the war, was attacked on his doorstep by two men with revolvers. He made a spirited attempt to defend himself with his sword but fell, mortally wounded by their bullets. His assailants were IRA men named Joseph O'Sullivan and Reginald Dunne and both had previously served in the British Army. O'Sullivan had lost a leg at Ypres and his consequent slowness in making a getaway led to the almost immediate capture of himself and his companion.

The killing had been carried out on the order of Collins, the last of the long series of such killings for which he had been personally responsible since 1919. Dunne and O'Sullivan, though they eventually revealed their own identity and membership of the IRA, said nothing of Collins. Whether or not their orders had been issued recently or had been given before the Treaty and the men were now acting on their own initiative in the light of Catholic suffering in Northern Ireland is still uncertain. It seems at least possible that Collins himself had issued the order expressly as a result of recent events in the North. He was anguished by what was happening there and at the extent to which his ability to act was hampered by his obligations to the Treaty. During the Tan war he had been opposed to the assassination of British political figures and there seems little reason why he should then have selected Wilson as an exception. He certainly now did what he could to save Dunne and O'Sullivan from the gallows, though to no avail. The question of responsibility for the deed at this time is however only of academic interest. What was important was its consequence.

Ironically, the British Government automatically put the blame on the anti-Treaty Republicans with their headquarters in the Four Courts. Their first instinct was to order General Macready, who was still in Dublin, to attack the building and force O'Connor's surrender. But sensibly advised by Macready that the result would be to unite pro- and anti-Treaty men solidly against the British and thus destroy all hopes for the Treaty, the government eventually issued an ultimatum to Collins and Griffith as heads of the Provisional Government to take action at last and do the job themselves. If they did not they would regard the Treaty as abrogated.

The Provisional Government's own relationship with the men in the Four Courts was at that moment particularly tense. The result of the election and the imminent assembly of the new pro-Treaty Dail had brought about a situation in which the anti-Treaty men would soon be forced to act if they wanted to make themselves effective. There was talk in O'Connor's executive about an immediate attack on the British, and of a move against the North. For several days there was tension while Collins played for time with the British demand, asking for proof of association between the Four Courts and Wilson's assassins. There at least he knew he was on strong ground.

Relatively trivial incidents set off the explosion. The Four Courts men 'commandeered' sixteen cars from a garage in Dublin, but the officer in charge of their operation was arrested by Collins's forces. The Four Courts men retaliated by kidnapping one of Collins's generals, 'Ginger' O'Connell. At 3.40 a.m. on the morning of 28 June Collins decided. He sent an ultimatum to the Four Courts to surrender within twenty minutes. There was no reply. At seven minutes past four, two field guns which Collins had borrowed from General Macready, opened fire on the building from across the Liffey. The government's soldiers wore the new green uniform of what was soon to be the Free State Army. They were so inexperienced that one of the gunners blew a hole in the banks of the Liffey on his own side.[13]

Most of the available shells were shrapnel and it took two days to reduce the building, though it was only a few hundred yards away, but on 30 June the Four Courts surrendered and the anti-Treaty IRA executive, including Rory O'Connor, Liam Mellows, Ernie O'Malley and a hundred others, were taken prisoner. O'Malley escaped, as he had once done from the British, and made his way south to join Liam Lynch, Seumas Robinson and other legendary IRA figures in a new war for the Republic on a line of resistance that ran roughly from Wexford to Limerick. South and west of that line had been all the most aggressive of the IRA Brigades which Collins had helped to organize against the British. Now they were organized against him.

The rest of the story has something of the quality of the last act of *Hamlet*.

There were other individual anti-Treaty IRA units installed in different buildings in Dublin. In the first serious fighting after the Four Courts surrender, the opposite side of O'Connell Street to that which had been destroyed in Easter Week was burned and battered to the ground. Out of one of the blazing buildings in which a group of anti-Treaty men had eventually surrendered there emerged after a pause, into the dust and rubble, a small dark man carrying a Thompson sub-machine gun. He had shaken off a St John's Ambulance man who tried to make him give himself up, and suddenly started firing.[14] It was Cathal Brugha. He was brought down in a hail of bullets, and died two days later. Altogether some sixty people were killed and three hundred wounded in the eight days' fighting in Dublin.[15]

Beaten in Dublin, the anti-Treaty IRA who began to be referred to simply as Republicans or, from the government side, 'irregulars', consolidated in the South. De Valera, temporarily an irrelevant figure, joined them, as did Erskine Childers whose virulent propaganda techniques were now effectively displayed against the Free State. For the Free State, Collins, liberated suddenly from the insidious toils of politics into the field of action, threw himself into the campaign with his old gusto. Though the Republican forces had the initial military advantage in the South, with many of the best brigades of the old IRA in arms, it was inevitably only a matter of time before the superior resources of the Free State, with the official machinery of government at its disposal, began to tell. Collins received considerable supplies of rifles from the British Government.* To the nucleus of the pro-Treaty sections of the old IRA he recruited new raw young Irish country boys, many of whom only learnt to load their rifles shortly before going into action,[16] together with ex-professional Irish elements from the British and even American armies and some former members of the RIC.

At the end of July 1922, units of the new Free State Army were sent round by sea to the South and West of Ireland and by 10 August Cork, the only large town occupied by Republicans, had fallen into Free State hands. From then on the Republicans were more and more forced to fight a guerrilla war of ambushes and flying columns in the countryside similar to that which they had fought against the British. The major difference now, however, was that the support of the ordinary people in the countryside could no longer be counted on and without such support a guerrilla movement is doomed. 'The Republic' and many of the dreams that had been made to go with it began to disappear from view in increasingly senseless acts of gunmanship and in the roar of flames of country houses burned as often as not in vindictive impotent rage as for any 'military' purpose. In the course of the fighting in July and August 1922 about five hundred men were killed on both sides.

Military success in any civil war is a bitter thing. In Ireland after the historic climax to seven hundred years which had just been achieved, victory seemed more than ever like self-destruction, and death ate into every triumph like acid. Though Cathal Brugha had made a savage attack on Collins in the Treaty debates his death caused him only sadness. 'Because of his sincerity,' he wrote, 'I would forgive him anything. At worst he was a fanatic though in what has been a noble cause.'[17]

One of the worst consequences of the Treaty for Collins had been his disagreement over it with his old friend and companion of happier days, Harry Boland. When the civil war fighting broke out Boland took the Republican side. 'Harry – it has come to this! Of all things it has come to this!' Collins wrote to him on 28 July 1922.[18] Three days later, in the middle of the night, Free State Army troops went to arrest Boland in the Grand Hotel, Skerries, where he was staying. The soldiers who came into his bedroom seem to have been nervous. Boland insisted on seeing the officer in charge of the raid and moved towards the bedroom door. A soldier fired, hitting him in the stomach. He died soon afterwards, asking to be buried beside Cathal Brugha. Collins passed the hospital that night. 'My mind went in to him lying dead there,' he wrote. '. . . I only thought of him with the friendship of 1918 and 1919.' A few days later he wrote, 'There is no one who

---

* 10,000 according to a British cabinet document of the time. (See Younger, *Ireland's Civil War*, p. 318.)

feels it all more than I do.' But Nemesis, of which he seems to have been unconscious, was at work. 'My condemnation,' he continued, 'is for all those who would put themselves up as paragons of Irish Nationality and all the others as being not worthy of concern."[19]

A week later, on 12 August 1922, the day after the Free State troops had taken Cork, a new and completely unexpected blow struck Ireland. Arthur Griffith, now Prime Minister of the new Free State Government, who had been spending a few days recovering from overwork in a Dublin nursing-home, suddenly collapsed and died. Collins, who, as Commander-in-Chief of the Free State Army, had been touring positions in the South and West, returned to Dublin for the funeral where he marched beside Mulcahy, MacEoin and other IRA heroes of the past, all in their new uniforms. Two of his men, Dunne and O'Sullivan, had just gone to the gallows for the killing of Sir Henry Wilson. 'Oh! Pray for our poor country,' wrote Dunne in his last letter.[20]

Ten days later Collins himself was dead.

He was killed in an ambush at Bealnamblath on the Macroom–Bandon road in his own home county of Cork. The ambush party, which had learnt of his presence in the neighbourhood quite accidentally that morning, had been waiting for him all day. They had just given up hope and were dispersing in the fading evening light when the convoy of a motor-cycle outrider, Collins's open touring Rolls, a Crossley tender and an armoured car drove up into the position. The fight, in which Collins took part with a rifle, lasted about half an hour and he was hit towards the end of it by a ricochet bullet in the back of the head.*

But Nemesis was only just beginning. Leadership of the Free State Government, which had just lost its two principal leaders, was now assumed by William Cosgrave and Kevin O'Higgins, both former Ministers of Griffith and earlier of de Valera. Saddled with their sudden responsibility, the one over-riding task in their own eyes seemed understandably to be to preserve the new State from disintegration at all costs and to restore law and order. Both had long been identified with the movement. Cosgrave had been out in Easter Week and condemned to death; O'Higgins, a young law student, had been imprisoned in 1918, and elected at the General Election. Earlier for a time he had been a member of the IRB. But both were less immediately entangled in the conflicting loyalties which had tortured Collins, and thus less concerned with reconciliation as an end in itself than he might have been if he had lived. They had the staunch support of Collins's old Chief of Staff, Richard Mulcahy, new Minister of Defence. Mulcahy obtained, through

---

* Forester, *Collins*, pp. 332–9. Many myths and suspicions have accumulated round the manner of Collins's death. This most recent account seems the best summary of all available evidence. Dr Oliver St John Gogarty carried out a post-mortem and confirmed the nature of the wound.

the new pro-Treaty Dail, emergency powers to set up military courts and Cosgrave specifically stated that the government were not going to treat rebels as prisoners of war. They offered an amnesty for surrender before a certain date and thereafter, armed with their emergency powers, set out to break the Republican guerrilla war of attrition with a sternness which was sometimes to cause even their supporters to gasp.

Unauthorized possession of a revolver was now punishable, as it had been in the final phases of the conflict with the British in martial law areas, by death. On 10 November Erskine Childers, who had been conducting Republican anti-Treaty propaganda with all his old single-minded zeal, was trapped by Free State troops and arrested in County Wicklow. He was armed with a revolver which had been given him by Collins as a token of comradeship in arms in other times. On the day he was tried by court-martial *in camera* it was suddenly announced by the government that four rank-and-file members of the Dublin anti-Treaty IRA who had been arrested at night under arms in the streets of Dublin had been shot by a firing squad.

The emergency powers had been granted two months before and these were the first executions under them. Mulcahy explained the decision to a shocked Dail. 'We are faced,' he said, 'with eradicating from the country the state of affairs in which hundreds of men go around day by day and night by night to take the lives of other men.'[21] Another Minister, Ernest Blythe, the old Sinn Fein organizer, who in his day had vigorously incited Volunteers to kill policemen in *An t Oglach*, declared that there was now no such thing in reality as a Republican movement but only a movement of anarchy; so-called Republicans were for the most part criminals and stern measures were essential to put down the 'conspiracy of anarchy'.[22] But Kevin O'Higgins, Minister for Home Affairs, gave a more ominous-sounding explanation of the four unknown men's execution, though none of the uneasy members of the Dail then picked him up on it. 'If,' said O'Higgins, 'If you took as your first case some man who was outstandingly active or outstandingly wicked in his activities the unfortunate dupes throughout the country might say, "Oh, he was killed because he was a leader", or, "He was killed because he was an Englishman."...'[23]

It was a common gibe among opponents of Erskine Childers that he was an Englishman, though his mother was Irish, and, having been brought up in Ireland, he had given many years of his life to the cause first of Irish Home Rule and then of a Republic. But even Griffith had jeered at him as an Englishman in the Dail. Now in O'Higgins's use of the term, though he did not name Childers, there was a sinister ring.

A week later Childers was taken from his cell and shot at dawn at Beggars Bush barracks. A week after that three more rank-and-file Republican IRA were executed, bringing the total number of executions for the month to eight. Even more shocking news was to come.

Ever since the surrender of the Four Courts in July the government had held in prison the hundred or so men captured there, including the members of the then Republican executive: Rory O'Connor, Liam Mellows, Joseph McKelvey and Richard Barrett. These men, of course, in the nature of things had no direct responsibility for what was being done now in November, though Mellows was in fact nominated 'Minister for Defence' in a new underground government which de Valera set up in agreement with the IRA in October. But it was a military and not a political situation in this period and the effective military personality was the Republican Chief of Staff, Liam Lynch. There was a particular poignancy typical of the Irish tragedy of the time about Rory O'Connor's imprisonment, for in the days of the fight against the British he had been the much loved and highly praised secretary of Kevin O'Higgins himself. O'Connor had even been best man at O'Higgins's wedding.

On 30 November 1922 Liam Lynch issued an order which the government captured, stating that all members of the government or members of the Dail who had voted the emergency powers were to be shot on sight. On 7 December two deputies were shot at as they were leaving their hotel for the Dail and one of them, Sean Hales, whose brother was actually a Brigade Commander on the Republican side, was killed. As a deterrent to more such shootings Mulcahy asked the rest of the cabinet to take an unprecedentedly severe form of action, to which after considerable discussion they agreed – O'Higgins, to do him justice, one of the last.[24] During the following night Rory O'Connor, Liam Mellows, Joseph McKelvey and Richard Barrett were woken in their cells and told to prepare themselves for death. They were shot without trial in the yard of Mountjoy gaol at dawn.

Altogether, in just over six months the new Free State Government executed seventy-seven Republicans by shooting, more than three times the number executed by the British Government in the two and a half years of the 'Anglo-Irish war'. Thirty-four of the Free State's executions were in the month of January 1923 alone. The executions ended when de Valera, speaking as political head of a movement whose one chance of success had appeared to rest on its military effectiveness, and whose military effectiveness had patently collapsed, issued with IRA agreement an order to dump arms. 'Soldiers of the Rearguard,' he told the 8,000 or so gunmen who were by May 1923 now the only free scattered remnants of the anti-Treaty IRA, 'other means must be sought to safeguard the nation's right.' There were also by then some 13,000 Republican prisoners, including Ernie O'Malley, who had been severely wounded. But one former hero was not among them. Liam Lynch, refusing stubbornly to face up to the realities of the Republicans' hopeless situation, had been killed in a running fight with Free State troops in the Knockmealdown mountains of Tipperary on 10 April 1923.

The last few months of the civil war, though they presented no serious threat to the political stability of the new Free State Government, presented a continuous and horrible threat to the peace and order of ordinary citizens' everyday lives. With only the newly-created police force, the unarmed 'Civic Guard', and a Free State Army of some 35,000 men it was often impossible to eliminate or even contain the small bands of irregulars who created for themselves fastnesses in mountainous country and descended from time to time to rob and terrorize and kill on behalf of the Republic. One of the many individuals murdered by the Republicans in this time was O'Higgins's own father. And in such an atmosphere, and in the atmosphere created by the government's ruthless severity, other things besides human values got lost sight of. For all the corpses and all the burned houses, the worst casualty of the civil war from the point of view of the ideals of Irish nationalism was the cause of One-Ireland.

In the first place such events in the South hardened a determination among the Protestants of North-East Ulster to retreat into the self-protected isolation offered by their border. The long tradition of fear and prejudice on which the division between the two sections of the population was based became still more deeply entrenched. O'Higgins himself expressed this aspect graphically and bitterly:

We had an opportunity [he said, referring to the North-East] of building up a worthy State that would attract and, in time, absorb and assimilate those elements. We preferred the patriotic way. We preferred to burn our own houses, blow up our own bridges, rob our own banks, saddle ourselves with millions of debt for the maintenance of an Army and for the payment of compensation for the recreations of our youth. Generally, we preferred to practise upon ourselves worse indignities than the British had practised on us since Cromwell and Mountjoy and now we wonder why the Orangemen are not hopping like so many fleas across the Border in their anxiety to come within our fold and jurisdiction.[25]

It was a reproof, however, which could have been extended to other Republicans besides those who now got called 'irregular'. On the question of national unity, O'Higgins put his faith in the Boundary Commission clause of the Treaty which still had to be implemented. Like Collins, he believed that the Commission's findings must lead to such a substantial adjustment of the Border in favour of the Free State that the remaining Northern Ireland territory would cease to be viable and eventual national unity be assured. It would be the ultimate vindication of the Treaty. But unlike Collins, O'Higgins was temperamentally inclined to trust the British Government.[26] If Collins had lived it is difficult to think that he would have accepted the disastrous collapse of the Boundary Commission principle with which the Free State were soon to be presented as a *fait accompli*.

The minds of O'Higgins and Cosgrave had in any case been seriously deflected from the Boundary Commission by the need to fight for the very existence of the infant Free State. Again, if Collins had lived this might not have happened, either because he would not have allowed it to or because he would have achieved the end of the civil war earlier. In fact it was not until 1924 that the Free State asked the British Government to constitute the Boundary Commission as prescribed.

Differences of opinion as to what exactly the Commission's function was to be had existed between North and South from the beginning, and Sir James Craig for the North had, of course, specifically repudiated it altogether in 1922. He now refused to nominate one of the three members of the Commission as stipulated by the Treaty – the other two to be nominees of the British and Free State Governments.

Craig was not a signatory of the Treaty. But the British Government was and thus found itself unable to honour its word. The clause was in fact reasonably precise, defining the Commission's function as being to determine the border 'in accordance with the wishes of the inhabitants, so far as may be compatible with economic and geographic conditions'. There could be no doubt that the inhabitants of large parts of Tyrone and Fermanagh, and smaller parts of Derry, South Down and South Armagh wished to be incorporated with their fellow nationalists in the Free State, while the inhabitants of a strip of East Donegal and North Monaghan wished to be incorporated in Northern Ireland. And with the reservation, accepted by the Treaty clause, that economics and geography laid down certain limitations, there was no practical reason why such a rearrangement of the Border should not be made. The clause had been instrumental in bringing the Irish to sign the Treaty. It could not simply be ignored.

The British Government therefore appointed an extra Commissioner of their own, reasonably enough in the circumstances an Ulsterman who was a close friend of Craig's named Fisher. The Free State Commissioner was to to be Eoin MacNeill, himself an Ulsterman from the Catholic and nationalist part of County Antrim. The other British nominee, the Chairman, was a South African judge, Mr Justice Feetham, a former protégé of Lord Milner's and therefore a man whose mind was cast politically in an imperial mould. Deadlock between Fisher, who wished to preserve as much of Northern Ireland as possible, and MacNeill, who wished the reverse, was inevitable and it would be Feetham's role to resolve it. He assumed the task in an atmosphere conditioned by statements from Birkenhead and Austen Chamberlain, both signatories of the Treaty, to the effect that the clause had been intended to consolidate the Northern Ireland Government's jurisdiction over the six counties, and to affect only a few parishes. A voice by which he was less likely to be influenced was that of the *Irish Independent* which declared that but for the Boundary Commission and the interpretation Collins and Griffith had placed on it the Treaty 'would never have received five minutes' consideration in this country'.

The Commission sat for a year during which MacNeill proved a most ineffectual advocate of the Collins' and Free State Government interpretation of its function. At the same time the Free State Government allowed itself to become curiously out of touch with what was transpiring. Finally, in November 1925, after an accurate leak to a newspaper had revealed that only very minor adjustments of the Border were intended and that these would actually include a transfer of territory in East Donegal from the Free State to Northern Ireland, MacNeill resigned in an embarrassingly late protest. It was Mr Justice Feetham's conclusion that the Commission could not recommend any adjustment of the order which would affect materially the political integrity of Northern Ireland.[27]

The Commission's findings were in fact never officially published or implemented. Instead, Cosgrave, O'Higgins and Ernest Blythe went to London and negotiated an amendment to the Treaty by which the Boundary Commission was revoked in its entirety in return for a revocation of the Free State's financial obligations to the United Kingdom under the Treaty. In a phrase which now seems curiously unfortunate, Cosgrave told the Dail he had got from the British what he wanted: 'a huge O'.[28]

The financial part of the transaction could legitimately be regarded as a success. But it was difficult for nationalists in Tyrone, Fermanagh, Derry, South Down and South Armagh not to feel that they had been sold. As for the eventual collapse of partition which had been so implicit to Collins in the Boundary Commission concept, that could be a hope no longer. All-Ireland unity had been abandoned more permanently than in any compromise Redmond had ever considered. In order to survive at all the movement had had to forsake for all practical purposes that very principle which had enabled it to claim the support of the Irish people in the first place.

This, surely, was the final act of Nemesis.

Epilogue

In his last message to the 'Soldiers of the Republic, Legion of the Rearguard', de Valera had assured them that their sacrifices and the deaths of their comrades had not been in vain, and that in a little time the civilian population who were now weary and needed a rest would recover and rally again to the standard. 'When they are ready,' he wrote, 'you will be, and your place will be again as of old with the vanguard.'[1]

This analysis of future events was to prove in one sense correct, though it was a prophecy to be fulfilled so much more in the letter than in the spirit that the heroic tone in which it was uttered has a hollow ring today. The divisions of the civil war continued to scar Irish political life for nearly half a century. In the course of that half century, Ireland, or rather the greater part of her, evolved into a totally independent sovereign republic, technically a realization of all the most extreme nationalist had ever dreamed of. Certainly it was a serious blemish that six counties of the North escaped the realization altogether. But a piece of political casuistry by which this Republic's constitution is made to apply theoretically to the whole of Ireland even enables some Irishmen to overlook that blemish and thus fosters the illusion that, on the issue of a united Ireland, Republicans have been able to do better than Redmond.

This achievement came about largely thanks to the political skill and perseverance of Eamon de Valera himself. He was to spend some thirty years tidying up the aftermath of the Treaty and bringing reality into line as far as possible, and on paper at least, with the aspirations with which the Republican movement had gone into the General Election of 1918. And on paper at least, with a literal consistency and a mathematical zeal transcending fanaticism, he can be said to have been successful.

After the end of the civil war in 1923, de Valera and the Republicans actually took no part in the official political structure for many years. They made use of the General Election for the Dail of August 1923 to establish that they were no insignificant force in public opinion, but their forty-four successful candidates (out of a total Dail membership of 153) refused to enter the Dail because to do so meant acceptance of the oath to the King. At this election, de Valera himself, standing for his old seat of Clare, was arrested by Free State troops while attempting to address his constituents at Ennis. He was held prisoner for nearly a year, though he had won the seat by an overwhelming majority. Later in 1924, though prohibited from entering the Six Counties by the Northern Ireland Government, he went to address an election meeting in Newry, was arrested and spent a month in Belfast gaol.

In the South, thanks to the stern single-mindedness and courage of men like Cosgrave, O'Higgins and Blythe, which won them many enemies, law and order was consolidated. Many Republicans chose to emigrate rather than stay where unemployment was high in what seemed the waste-land of their ideals and dreams. But there were still occasional acts of violence. One in 1927 had something of the epic horror of old. For on a Sunday morning in July of that year, while walking alone to Mass, Kevin O'Higgins was fired at with a revolver at point-blank range by a man who stepped out of a waiting motor-car. Turning and trying to run for cover from the bullets, as so many men had done in Ireland in the past eight years, O'Higgins was set upon by two other men who emptied their revolvers into him as he lay dying on the ground. His murderers were never caught and there is a mystery about them to this day.[2]

Also in 1927, de Valera, recognizing the sterility of leaving a sizable proportion of Irish public opinion disfranchised, caused a further split among Republicans by finally entering the Dail after all. He did so expressly to abolish the oath of allegiance, and took with him a new party he had formed: Fianna Fail (Warriors of Ireland). He got round the embarrassment of taking the oath himself after all this time by simply signing his name in the book as required while pushing away the Bible which lay beside it and declaring categorically that he was taking no oath. However, as the only physical requirement for the taking of the oath was the placing of his signature in the book, this secured him entry even though he insisted that all he had done was to contribute his autograph.[3]

The band of die-hard Republicans who regarded this entry into the Dail by de Valera as a betrayal continued to call their militant wing the Irish Republican Army which, surviving further internal disruptions, has thus continued its existence in Ireland as a clandestine and illegal organization, from the time of the Fenians to the present day.

In a General Election in 1933, de Valera's prophecy of ten years before began to be fulfilled as the Irish people, reacting against ten years' government by one set of men moved round to support him. They elected himself and Fianna Fail to power, and in 1937 he produced a new Constitution to replace that created by the Treaty. This was the Constitution of Eire (Ireland) which abolished the oath of allegiance and claimed sovereignty over all thirty-two counties while recognizing that in six of them the claim could not be implemented for the foreseeable future. It recognized as in Document No. 2 the king as Head of the Commonwealth. The office of king's representative in Ireland created by the Treaty and first occupied by the aged anti-Parnellite Parliamentarian Tim Healy was now abolished, and in a further acknowledgement of the continuity of Irish history Douglas Hyde, first President of the Gaelic League, was nominated first President of Eire.

The British Government, embarrassed by this unilateral re-styling of the Treaty, recognized that it made little real difference where its own essential interests were concerned. The new Constitution did not alter the former Free State's membership of the Commonwealth and the position of Northern Ireland remained in practice unaffected. Advantage was taken of the unfamiliarity of the term 'Eire' in English ears to make it apply, for British Government purposes, to the twenty-six counties only, though it was of course nonsensical to pretend that the six counties in the North were somehow not part of 'Ireland'. However, having already made what, to many Unionists, was 'the great surrender' in 1921, the British Government continued to make up for past intransigence with a cooperative attitude towards the new Ireland.

In the following year, 1938, the British Government even agreed to a further most important modification of the 1921 Treaty. This concerned the clauses permitting military and naval bases to British forces in certain areas of Ireland, specifically at Berehaven in Bantry Bay and at Cobh (Queenstown), the port of Cork. Rights to these bases were now abandoned. Since one of the chief arguments even against Home Rule and later against any attempt to take Ireland outside the British Empire had rested on the need for British bases in time of national emergency, there was something bitterly ironical about the timing of this generous-hearted concession. For within two years Britain was to be at war in the greatest crisis of her history and desperately handicapped by lack of the Irish bases from which to protect her western approaches against enemy submarines and aircraft. One line of reasoning might be to blame this handicap on the ineptitude of the Chamberlain government of the day. But it is at least as reasonable to blame the short-sighted Unionist imperialism of 1914. For it is not unlikely that if Home Rule for all Ireland had been allowed to progress beyond the statute book in 1914 the southern Irish bases would have been available to Britain in 1940 as a matter of course.

It was de Valera's skill and determination in keeping Eire neutral in the Second World War which more than any constitutional nomenclature signified the real degree of political independence that Ireland, or more than three-quarters of her, had at last achieved. By a further ironical twist of the sort in which Irish history abounds, it was while de Valera himself was temporarily out of office that 'Eire' finally received the sacred appellation of Republic and was taken outside the Commonwealth. The change was brought about as an internal political manoeuvre by a temporary coalition of the old pro-Treaty party (Fine Gael) and a new legal republican party (Clann na Poblchta) headed by Sean MacBride, son of John MacBride and Maud Gonne. In the British Government's Ireland Act of 1949 this further *fait accompli* was accepted with a good grace. But a valuable acknowledgement was made to past realities by the refusal, while accepting the Republic's sovereign and independent status, to treat citizens of that Republic as aliens. A further clause in the Act spelt out that the British Government would never consent to the placing of Northern Ireland outside the Crown's dominions without the consent of the Parliament of Northern Ireland.

Few Irishmen today would accept that what Irish nationalists have achieved represents a true fulfilment of that near-mystical ideal for which, in one form or another, Irishmen had striven for so long. Every mystical ideal is diminished by being translated into reality but the sense of diminishment in Ireland has been profound. One reason, in addition to the missing counties, is perhaps that the real substance of the aspirations that had made Irish history so tumultuous for a century and a half had already been achieved before the climax of these last years was reached.

What had kept the green flag flying throughout the period which Patrick Pearse saw as 'a hopeless attempt by a mob to realize itself as a nation'⁴ had been no doctrinaire concept of nationality but a much more simple human desire for a decent life, for an assurance of life at all, in the beautiful country in which Irishmen were born. The goal of 'freedom' was as vague as that and embraced a wide and diffuse political emotion. With the social revolution begun by the Land Acts and ending in the massive transfer of land-ownership through the long Land Purchase operation the greater part of this goal was quietly achieved. There remained only what might be called a debt to history, to be paid in the form of an award of that political self-respect which went with some form of Home Rule. For long years Irishmen had not been particularly insistent about this. And yet refusal to pay it, and a contemptuous refusal at that, stirred old memories and eventually led to an extraction of the debt after much bitterness and bloodshed in a compromise form of payment. In the course of this bitterness and bloodshed all the old emotions had been re-aroused.

James Connolly and other socialists had hoped to give the new nationalism a dynamic of its own, but socialism made little appeal to a nation of Catholic peasant proprietors with the traditions of an ancient Gaelic aristocracy deep in its folk memory. Even the cause of a united Ireland slumbered for nearly half a century before other, social grievances among the Catholic minority in Northern Ireland raised it again to embarrass not only the British Government, but this time the Republic too.

An incident from the battle of Fredericksburg early in the American Civil War epitomizes the emotion which once surrounded Ireland's old green flag.

Meagher's Irish Brigade with the Union army had been making repeated assaults on the Confederate positions across the Rappamahoch river but had been consistently repelled, and, in the course of the fighting, one of the Brigade's colour-bearers had fallen and with him the green flag. Its fall had been noted by an Irish Confederate soldier named Michael Sullivan, fighting opposite Meagher with the Georgia Irish Brigade. Under cover of darkness Sullivan returned to the spot, and after taking the green flag and wrapping it round his body under his shirt swam across the river to the Union lines. He was hit by a bullet in the thigh as he went, fired from Confederate outposts who supposed him to be a deserter.

On arrival in the Union lines Sullivan indeed gave himself up and asked to be taken to General Meagher to whom he presented the flag. Meagher had Sullivan's wound dressed and, though he was now technically a prisoner, offered to let him go a free man on Union soil. Sullivan, however, having done his duty to Ireland now wished to continue to do it to his adopted cause. He asked to be allowed to return to the Confederate lines. And this Meagher, against all the normal conventions of war, permitted him to do.[5]

Many other brave men tried to give the new tricolour flag and the notion of 'the Republic' the same sanctity, but much of the substance of that emotion was wasted in the bitterness of civil war and its aftermath. As a mere political formula the Republic had only been for a very short time an important reality of Irish life. Its final literal achievement could not help but be a sort of anti-climax.

This strange historical anti-climax has left us with certain facts which cannot be altered and must be lived with. The logical and reasonable solution to the Irish problem was Home Rule for all Ireland with special safeguards, and even a degree of internal autonomy for parts of North-East Ulster. But that solution itself passed from the realm of reality over fifty years ago. And though relatively few in Ireland had ever seriously wanted a republic and the literal rejection of allegiance to a British king had been historically of little urgency to the Irish people, yet these things became in this century symbols essential to an expiation of the past. For the majority of Irishmen today these symbols, in the light of that past, can only be permanently revered.

There is another phenomenon in Ireland today which is not natural to Ireland and yet which in fifty years has also acquired by right of survival a natural status. This is the concept of a 'Northern Ireland' whose problems can somehow be kept separate from those of the rest of Ireland. How these two unnatural realities – 'The Republic' and 'Northern Ireland' – can be re-adjusted in future to a new reality compatible with the unity of Ireland is a matter which is not yet the concern of the historian.

References

PART ONE

WHO WERE IRISHMEN?

1 Treaty Night

1 *Daily Express*, 7 December 1921. Other weather details from *The Times* and other contemporary newspapers.
2 6 April 1893. Hansard, H.C. Debates, 4th series, vol. 10, col. 1597.

2 Contradictions of Irish Nationality

1 William O'Brien and Desmond Ryan (eds.), *John Devoy's Post Bag*, 1871–1928, 2 vols., Dublin, 1948, 1953, vol. ii, p. 522. Letter to Dr Patrick McCartan, 7 February 1918.
2 C. F. N. Macready, *Annals of an Active Life*, London, 1924, p. 573.

3 Strongbow (1170) to the Ulster Plantation (1609)

1 Cited in A. G. Richey, *A Short History of the Irish People*, Dublin 1869, p. 367; from State Papers, Ireland, vol. ii, p. 562.
2 Richey, op. cit., p. 489.
3 W. E. H. Lecky, *History of Ireland in the Eighteenth Century*, 5 vols., London, 1892, vol. 1, p. 5.
4 Richey, op. cit., p. 481.
5 Cited Lecky, op. cit., vol. i, p. 6.
6 ibid., p. 9.
7 Minutes of evidence taken before a *Select Committee appointed to inquire into the Disturbances in Ireland in the last session of Parliament, May 1824*, p. 338. Evidence of the Reverend Michael Collins, parish priest of Skibbereen.
8 *United Irishman*, 30 August 1902.

4 Great Rebellion (1641) to Penal Laws (1703)

1 Edward MacLysaght, *Irish Life in the Seventeenth Century after Cromwell*, Dublin, 1939, p. 30.
2 Aidan Clarke, *The Old English in Ireland*, London, 1966, pp. 179–80.
3 Quoted by Isaac Butt, Hansard, H.C. Debates, 3rd series, vol. 228, col. 771, 29 March 1876.
4 Lecky, *History of Ireland in the Eighteenth Century*, vol. ii, p. 182. See also the phrase of a modern Irish poet, Seamus Heaney, in describing the figure of an Orange drummer on 12 July: 'He is raised up by what he buckles under.' (*Listener*, 29 September 1966.)
5 Diarmuid Murtagh, 'The Battle of Aughrim', in G. A. Hayes-MacCoy (ed.), *The Irish at War*, Thomas Davis Lectures, Cork, 1964, p. 61.
6 J. G. Simms, 'Land owned by Catholics in Ireland in 1688', in *Irish Historical Studies*, vol. vii, no. 27, March 1951, p. 189.

5 Majority Living (1703–1880)

1 Jonathan Swift, *A Short View of the State of Ireland*, Dublin 1727–8, p. 13. Cited in James Carty (ed.), *Ireland from the Flight of the Earls to Grattan's Parliament*, Dublin, 1951, p. 108.
2 Swift, op. cit., p. 12. Cited in Carty, op. cit., p. 108.
3 Swift, *Proposal for the Universal Use of Irish Manufacture*, cited Lecky, *History of Ireland in the Eighteenth Century*, vol. i, p. 181.
4 Cited in Lecky, op. cit., vol. i, p. 184.
5 *The Querist* (Question 132). Cited in Carty, op. cit., p. 109.
6 J. Bush, *Hibernia Curiosa, giving a general view of the Manners, Customs, Dispositions and co. of the inhabitants of Ireland*, London, 1764, pp. 31–2.
7 Lecky, op. cit., vol. ii, p. 39n.
8 Francis Plowden, *An Historical Review of the State of Ireland from Henry II to the Union*, 2 vols., London, 1803, vol. ii, p. 157.
9 De Latocnaye, *Promenade d'un Français dans l'Irlande*, 1797, pp. 88, 147, 167.
10 *Devon Commission Report Digest*, vol. i, p. 343.
11 Lecky, op. cit., vol. i, p. 363.
12 G. C. Lewis, *On Local Disturbances in Ireland*, London, 1836, p. 107.
13 Hansard, H.C. Debates, 3rd series, vol. 257, col. 1754.
14 Lecky, op. cit., vol. ii, p. 23.
15 *Select Committee 1824*, Minutes of Evidence, p. 25.
16 Lewis, op. cit., p. 14.
17 Cited in R. R. Madden, *The United Irishmen, their lives and times*, 7 vols., London, 1842–6, vol. i, p. 26.

18 Bush, op. cit., p. 136.
19 Lecky, op. cit., vol. ii, p. 165.
20 Lewis, op. cit., p. 162.
21 *Select Committee 1824*, pp. 129, 135–6, 249.

6 *Minority Politics, Eighteenth Century*

1 Lecky, *History of Ireland in the Eighteenth Century*, vol. ii, p. 54.
2 Speech and address on motion for Declaration of Independence, 1782. Lecky, op. cit., vol. ii, pp. 300–1.
3 Lecky, op. cit., vol. ii, p. 217.
4 Lecky, op. cit., vol. ii, p. 284.
5 ibid., p. 313.
6 Cited in Plowden, *An Historical Review* . . ., vol. ii, pp. 296–7.
7 Lecky, op. cit., vol. iii, p. 7.

PART TWO

THE FIRST IRISH REPUBLICANS

1 *Ireland and the French Revolution*

1 For a summary of Grattan's arguments see Lecky, *History of Ireland in the Eighteenth Century*, vol. iii, p. 135.
2 Charles Bowden, *A Tour of Ireland*, London, 1791, p. 158.
3 ibid.
4 See the speech of Fitzgibbon, Attorney-General, in the Irish House of Commons, 31 January 1787. Cited in Plowden, op. cit., vol. ii, p. 156.
5 Letter dated Dublin, 4 August 1763. B.M. Add MSS 32, 950, f. 123.
6 Francis Plowden, *A Short History of the British Empire*, 1792–3, London, 1794, p. 240.
7 Brother Laurence Dern, *Ahimon Rezon, or Help to a Brother*, Belfast, 1782, p. 3.
8 Plowden, op. cit., p. 276.
9 ibid.
10 Thomas MacNevin, *Leading State Trials, 1794–1803*, London, 1844; trial of James Weldon, pp. 297–347.

2 *Wolfe Tone and Samuel Neilson*

1 Lecky, *History of Ireland in the Eighteenth Century*, vol. iv, p. 235.

2 R. R. Madden, *The United Irishmen, their lives and times*, 1st series, vol. ii, p. 221.

3 Madden, op. cit., p. 276.

4 William Theobald Wolfe Tone (ed.), *Life of Theobald Wolfe Tone*, 2 vols., Washington, 1826, vol. i, p. 26.

5 Tone, op. cit., pp. 27–8.

6 ibid., pp. 36–7.

7 ibid., p. 43.

8 ibid., p. 36.

9 R. B. McDowell, *Irish Public Opinion, 1750–1800*, London, 1944, pp. 93–4.

10 Tone, op. cit., p. 140.

11 *Report from the Committee of Secrecy to the House of Commons*, London, 1797, p. 5.

12 Tone, op. cit., p. 140.

13 *Report from the Secret Committee of the House of Commons*, Dublin, 1798. Appendix IV. The authorship of the paper as quoted is anonymous. Evidence in D. A. Chart (ed.), *The Drennan Letters*, Belfast, 1931, p. 54, suggests it was probably the work of William Drennan, a radical doctor of medicine who was to be prominent in the early aspirations of the United Irishmen.

14 Tone, op. cit., p. 52.

15 ibid., p. 142.

16 ibid., p. 147.

17 ibid., p. 149.

18 ibid., p. 150.

19 ibid., p. 143.

20 *Report of the Committee of Secrecy to the House of Commons*, London, 1797, Appendix II, p. 46.

21 *Report from the Secret Committee of the House of Commons*, Dublin, 1798, Appendix V, p. 110.

22 ibid.

3 United Irishmen and Defenders

1 Tone (ed.), *Life of Theobald Wolfe Tone*, vol. 1, p. 55.

2 ibid., p. 158.

3 ibid., p. 163.

4 ibid., p. 164.

5 ibid., p. 168.

6 ibid., pp. 115–16.

7 ibid., p. 175.

8 ibid., p. 208.

9 W. J. MacNeven and T. A. Emmet, *Pieces of Irish History*, New York, 1807, p. 35.

10 Tone, op. cit., p. 202.

11 ibid., p. 203.

12 ibid., p. 247.

13 *The Times*, 14 November 1792.

14 Tone, op. cit., p. 179.

15 *The Times*, 1 October 1792.

16 ibid., 8 January 1793.

17 ibid., 9 January 1793.

18 ibid., 30 January 1793.

19 ibid., 20 February 1793.

20 ibid., 22 February 1793.

21 See an account of the trial of two Defenders, Lawrence O'Connor and Michael Griffin, in Walker's *Hibernian Magazine* for November 1795, p. 433. This source is given by Lecky, *History of Ireland in the Eighteenth Century*, vol. iii, p. 391. The first part of the trial is reported in the magazine's previous issue for October 1795.

22 Lecky, op. cit., vol. iii, p. 387.

23 *The Times*, 8 June 1793.

24 *Report of the Secret Committee of the House of Lords*, Dublin, 1793.

25 Plowden, *An Historical Review of the State of Ireland*, vol. ii, pp. 389–91.

26 Tone, op. cit., p. 97.

27 MacNeven and Emmet, op. cit., p. 47.

28 *Report from the Secret Committee of the House of Commons*, Dublin, 1798, p. 99.

29 ibid., p. 101.

30 See R. B. McDowell, 'Proceedings of the Dublin Society of United Irishmen', in *Analectica Hibernica*, no. 17, Dublin, 1949, pp. 3ff.

31 MacNeven and Emmet, op. cit., p. 67.

4 French Contacts

1 Lecky, *History of Ireland in the Eighteenth Century*, vol. iii, p. 103.

2 ibid., vol. iii, p. 104.

3 Thomas Moore, *The Life and Death of Lord Edward Fitzgerald*, 2 vols., London, 1831, p. 170.

4 Quoted in Frank MacDermot, *Wolfe Tone*, London, 1939, pp. 141–2.

5 Lecky, op. cit., p. 234, n. 1.

6 *Report from the Secret Committee of the House of Commons*, Dublin, 1798, p. 226, Appendix XXII. This incident is also described in Tone (ed.), *Life of Theobald Wolfe Tone*, vol. i, p. 117.

7 Tone, op. cit., p. 116.

8 Cited in MacNeven and Emmet, *Pieces of History*, p. 72.

9 Tone, op. cit., p. 114.

10 ibid. For Tone's own vindication of his later action in the light of his agreement, see ibid., pp. 125–6.

11 For this and subsequent details, see MacNevin, *Leading State Trials, 1794–1803*, pp. 274 ff.

12 MacNeven and Emmet, op. cit., p. 108.

5 Defenders and Orangemen

1 *The Times*, 22 March 1794.

2 ibid., 21 March 1794

3 ibid., 28 May 1794.

4 Lecky, *History of Ireland in the Eighteenth Century*, vol. iii, p. 218.

5 ibid., p. 387.

6 ibid., p. 385.

7 MacNevin, *Leading State Trials*, p. 387.

8 ibid., p. 313.

9 Walker's *Hibernian Magazine*, October 1795, pp. 351 ff.

10 MacNevin, op. cit., p. 319.

11 ibid., p. 303.

12 ibid., pp. 472–3.

13 ibid., p. 319.

14 ibid., p. 350.

15 ibid., p. 392.

16 ibid.

17 ibid., p. 467.

18 ibid., p. 380.

19 ibid., p. 466.

20 ibid., p. 423.

21 Plowden, *An Historical Review of the State of Ireland*, vol. ii, p. 548. The threat was quoted by Grattan in the Irish House of Commons.

22 Lecky, op. cit., vol. iii, pp. 430–31.

23 *Walkers Hibernian Magazine*, November 1795, p. 430.

24 ibid., p. 433.

25 Cited in Moore, *Fitzgerald*, vol. i, p. 274.

26 *Report of Committee of Secrecy* (printed 6 June 1799), House of Commons Report, vol. xliv.

27 Lecky, op. cit., p. 447.

28 J. T. Gilbert, *Documents Relating to Ireland*, 1795–1804, London, 1893, p. 153.

29 Gilbert, op. cit., p. 150.

6 Bantry Bay

1 Tone (ed.), *Life of Theobald Wolfe Tone*, vol. ii, p. 94.
2 Gilbert, *Documents*, p. 170.
3 Tone, op. cit., vol. i, p. 130.
4 Lecky, *History of Ireland in the Eighteenth Century*, vol. iii, p. 498.
5 Tone, op. cit., vol. i, p. 133.
6 ibid., vol. ii, p. 107.
7 ibid., p. 50.
8 ibid., p. 97.
9 For emigrés generally, see Lecky, op. cit., vol. iii, pp. 523–6.
10 Tone, op. cit., vol. ii, p. 92.
11 ibid., p. 152.
12 For a full account of Arthur O'Connor's life see Frank MacDermot, 'Arthur O'Connor' in *I.H.S.*, XV, no. 57 (March 1966), pp. 48–69. The family were not as Gaelic in origin as they sounded, being descended from rich London merchants called Connor who had settled in Cork several generations before.
13 See depositions by soldiers and letters between General Coote and Pelham in the summer of 1797. B.M. Add. MSS. 33104, 318–27.
14 Lecky, op. cit., vol. iii, p. 504.
15 ibid., vol. iii, p. 522.
16 ibid., p. 206.
17 ibid., p. 229.
18 MacDermot, *I.H.S.*, vol. xv, no. 57, March 1966, pp. 54–5.
19 MacNeven and Emmet, *Pieces of Irish History*, p. 187.
20 ibid.
21 *Report from the Secret Committee of the House of Commons*, Dublin, 1798, Appendix VI, p. 114.
22 B.M. Add. MSS. 33104/331.
23 Tone, op. cit., vol. ii, p. 240.
24 ibid., p. 241.
25 ibid., p. 252.
26 Cited in T. Crofton Croker, *Popular Songs Illustrative of the French Invasion of Ireland*, London, 1845. The account of the expedition that here follows is taken principally from Tone, and Lecky, op. cit.; but see also works by Guillon, Gribayedoff, Hayes and Stuart Jones, listed in the Bibliography.
27 Tone, op. cit., vol. ii, p. 260.
28 E. H. Stuart Jones, *An Invasion that Failed*, Oxford, 1950, p. 175.
29 Lecky, op. cit., vol. iii, p. 541.
30 ibid.

31 ibid., pp. 542–3.
32 MacNeven and Emmet, op. cit., p. 189.

7 United Irishmen in Trouble

1 Lecky, *History of Ireland in the Eighteenth Century*, vol. iv, p. 29.
2 ibid., p. 31.
3 ibid., p. 33.
4 ibid., p. 34.
5 Samuel MacSkimmin, *Annals of Ulster*, London, 1906, p. 47.
6 Lecky, op. cit., vol. iv, p. 32.
7 Cited in Charles Dickson, *Revolt in the North*, Dublin, 1960, p. 106.
8 ibid., pp. 112–13.
9 Lecky, op. cit., p. 45.
10 Sir J. F. Maurice (ed.), *The Diary of Sir John Moore*, London, 1904, vol. i, p. 284.
11 Lecky, op. cit., vol. iv, p. 208.
12 Maurice (ed.), *Diary of Sir John Moore*, vol. i, p. 287.
13 *Secret Committee*, Dublin, 1798, Appendix IX, p. 120.
14 ibid., Appendix VIII, p. 118.
15 Dickson, op. cit., p. 240. Information of James MacGuckin.
16 B.M. Add. MSS. 38759.
17 Lecky, op. cit., vol. iii, p. 430.
18 Cited in McDowell, *Irish Public Opinion 1750–1800*, p. 239.
19 Private letter dated Dublin 30 June 1797, B.M. Add. MSS. 38759.
20 De Latocnaye, *Promenade d'un Français dans l'Irlande*, p. 286.
21 Lecky, op. cit., vol. iv, p. 90.
22 ibid., p. 96.
23 ibid., p. 77.

8 New French Preparations

1 Tone (ed.), *Tone*, vol. ii, p. 414.
2 ibid., p. 416.
3 ibid., p. 420.
4 ibid., pp. 422, 424.
5 ibid., pp. 455–6.
6 ibid., p. 458.
7 *Report from the Secret Committee of the House of Commons*, Dublin, 1798, Appendix XIV, p. 147.
8 Plowden, *An Historical Review of the State of Ireland*, vol. ii, p. 566. The Reverend J. B. Gordon, *History of the Rebellion in Ireland 1798*, London, 1803, pp. 31–3.

9 *Report of the Secret Committee of the House of Commons*, Dublin, 1798, Appendix XVI, p. 168.

10 Lecky, *History of Ireland in the Eighteenth Century*, vol. iv, p. 252.

11 Tone, op. cit., vol. ii, p. 473.

12 ibid., pp. 471–2.

13 Moore, *Fitzgerald*, vol. ii, p. 84.

9 Repression 1798

1 James Caulfield (ed.), *The MSS and Correspondence of James, First Earl of Charlemont*, 2 vols., London, 1891–4, vol. ii, p. 301.

2 ibid., p. 304.

3 ibid., p. 306.

4 Coote to Pelham, 9 July 1797. B.M. Add. MSS. 33104. At a court-martial in Belfast in May, a sentence of 1,500 lashes had been pronounced on Private Thomas Redmond of the Galway Militia. *Report of Secret Committee of House of Commons*, Dublin, 1798, p. 291.

5 R. M. Young, *Ulster in '98*, p. 17.

6 Maurice (ed.), *Diary of Sir John Moore*, vol. i, p. 271.

7 James Alexander, *Some Account of the ... Rebellion in Kildare ... Wexford*, Dublin, 1800, p. 28.

8 ibid., p. 28.

9 Roger McHugh (ed.), *Carlow in '98*, Memoirs of William Farrell, Dublin, 1949, p. 75.

10 Maurice (ed.), *Diary of Sir John Moore*, vol. i, p. 294.

11 Mary Leadbeater, *The Leadbeater Papers*, 2 vols., London, 1862, vol. i, p. 227.

12 Thomas Cloney, *A Personal Narrative of those Transactions ... in Wexford ... 1798*, Dublin, 1832, p. 14.

13 B.M. Add. MSS. 41192.

14 Gordon, *History of the Rebellion in Ireland*, p. 62.

15 *Report of the Trial of Henry and John Sheares*, Dublin, 1798, p. 179.

16 ibid., p. 75.

17 ibid., p. 91.

18 McHugh (ed.), op. cit., p. 82.

19 ibid., pp. 82–3.

20 Gordon, op. cit., p. 86.

21 McHugh (ed.), op. cit., p. 90.

22 Gordon, op. cit., p. 92.

23 The following details of her experience are extracted from *The Leadbeater Papers*, pp. 227ff.

24 *McHugh* (ed.), op. cit., p. 95.

25 Charles Ross (ed.), *Correspondence of Charles, First Marquis of Cornwallis*, 3 vols., London, 1859, vol. iii, p. 357.

26 ibid., vol. iii, p. 359.
27 Gordon, op. cit., p. 100.
28 Lecky, op. cit., vol. iv, pp. 336–7. Lecky himself gives the loyalist losses for this action as only nine killed. However, *A History of the Rebellion in Ireland in the year 1798*, a competent factual compilation printed by W. Borrowdale in 1806, gives the figure of twenty-seven dead.
29 Cited in Charles Dickson, *The Wexford Rising in 1798*, Tralee, 1955, p. 16.
30 B.M. Add. MSS. 33104 and *Report of Secret Committee of House of Commons*, Dublin, 1798, Appendix XXIX.
31 Gilbert (ed.), *Documents 1794–1803*, p. 124.
32 ibid., p. 131.
33 Tone (ed.), *Tone*, vol. ii, p. 484.
34 ibid., p. 491.
35 Moore, *Fitzgerald*, vol. ii, pp. 112–18.

10 Rebellion in Wexford

1 B.M. Add. MSS. 32335.
2 B.M. Add. MSS. 41192.
3 B.M. Add. MSS. 37308.
4 ibid.
5 Dickson, *Wexford Rising*, pp. 21–2.
6 Edward Hay, *History of the Insurrection of 1798*, Dublin, 1842, p. 46.
7 Cloney, *Personal Narrative*, p. 98.
8 Wheeler and Broadley, *The War in Wexford*, London, 1910, p. 48.
9 Gordon, *History of the Rebellion*, pp. 104–5.
10 ibid., p. 106.
11 Account of an eye-witness named Peter Foley recorded by Luke Cullen and cited in Dickson, op. cit., pp. 51–6.
12 ibid., p. 53.
13 Cited in Dickson, op. cit., p. 55.
14 Wheeler and Broadley, op. cit., pp. 85–6.
15 Patrick F. Kavanagh, *A Popular History of the Insurrection of 1798*, London, 1898, p. 299. (An eye-witness account of the author's paternal grandfather.)
16 B.M. Add. MSS. 38102.
17 Gordon, op. cit., Appendix III, p. 373. Evidence at the trial of Andrew Farrall.
18 ibid., p. 168.
19 ibid.

20 *History of the Rebellion in Ireland in the Year 1798* (printed by W. Borrowdale, 1806), p. 78.

21 B.M. Add. MSS. 41192 (Letter of Lady Sunderlin dated 3 July 1798).

22 Charles Jackson, *A Narrative of the Sufferings and Escape of Charles Jackson*, 1799, p. 23.

23 *History of the Rebellion* (Borrowdale, 1806), p. 78.

24 Gordon, op. cit., p. 266.

25 Cloney, op. cit., p. 47.

26 Kavanagh, op. cit., pp. 341–2.

27 Charles Jackson, op. cit., p. 21.

28 The carefully calculated conclusion of Dickson, *Wexford Rising*, p. 34.

29 Cloney, op. cit., p. 20.

30 *History of the Rebellion* (Borrowdale, 1806), p. 102. For fuller extracts from Mrs Brownrigg's diary see Wheeler and Broadley, op. cit.

31 Dinah Goff, *Divine Protection through Extraordinary Dangers . . . during the Irish Rebellion of 1798*, London, 1857, p. 9.

32 Goff, *Divine Protection*, pp. 13–14.

33 Cited in Dickson, op. cit., pp. 115–16.

34 Cloney, op. cit., p. 39.

35 Gordon, op. cit., p. 272.

36 Cited in Dickson, op. cit., p. 255.

37 ibid., p. 242.

38 Luke Cullen, MSS. cited in Dickson, op. cit., p. 260.

39 Gordon, op. cit., pp. 363–4.

40 Thomas Hancock, *The Principles of Peace . . . during the Rebellion of 1798*, London, 1826, p. 105.

41 Cited in Dickson, op. cit., p. 268.

42 Gordon, op. cit., pp. 366–7.

43 Wheeler and Broadley, op. cit., p. 173.

44 John Jones, *An Impartial Narrative of . . . Engagements . . . during the Irish Rebellion of 1798*, Dublin, 1799, p. 42.

45 Extract from a Letter from a Gentleman in Ireland (B.M. Tracts relating to Ireland). Letter dated 1 August 1798.

46 ibid.

11 Collapse of United Irishmen

1 Letter of W. Wellesley Pole, Captain of Bally Fin Yeomanry, dated 24 August 1798. B.M. Add. MSS. 37308, f. 167.

2 ibid.

3 Ross (ed.), *Cornwallis Correspondence*, vol. ii, p. 355.

4 Maurice (ed.), *Diary of Sir John Moore*, vol. i, p. 311.

5 B.M. Add. MSS. 37308, 167.

6 Gordon, *History of the Rebellion*, p. 269.

7 Ross, op. cit., vol. ii, p. 369.

8 Jackson, *Narrative*, p. 21.

9 Diary of Captain Hodges, English Militia Officer, B.M. Add. MSS. 40166. Entry for 15 October 1798.

10 Sir Jonah Barrington, *Personal Sketches*, 2 vols., London, 1827, vol. i, p. 276.

11 MacNeven and Emmet, *Pieces of Irish History*, p. 189.

12 ibid., p. 196.

13 ibid., p. 189.

14 ibid., p. 221.

15 ibid.

16 Alexander, *Account of Rebellion in Kildare*, p. 95.

17 Ross, op. cit., vol. ii, p. 387.

18 ibid., p. 352.

19 ibid., p. 377.

20 Cited in Dickson, *Revolt in the North*, p. 121.

21 Tone (ed.), *Tone*, vol. ii, p. 511.

22 Cited in Dickson, op. cit., pp. 221–2.

23 ibid.

24 ibid., p. 135.

25 Lecky, *A History of Ireland in the Eighteenth Century*, vol. iv, p. 288. This work was first published in 1884.

26 Cited in Dickson, op. cit., pp. 222–4 and 227–31.

27 Hancock, *Principles of Peace*, p. 131.

28 ibid., p. 133.

12 The French Landing

1 Details of French decisions at this time from Edouard Guillon, *La France et l'Irlande Pendant La Révolution*, Paris, 1888, which is based on the French national archives. See particularly pp. 321 ff.

2 Guillon, op. cit., p. 368.

3 ibid., p. 369.

4 L. O. Fontaine, *Notice Historique de la Descente des Français en Irlande*, Paris, 1801, p. 4. Fontaine was the third senior French officer in the expedition. Further details of the French arrival and subsequent events from *A Narrative of What Passed at Killala* (1801) by an eyewitness (i.e. the Bishop of Killala, J. Stock). The diary of another French officer who took part in the landing, Capitaine Jobit (*Analecta Hibernica*, no. 11, edited by Nuala Costello), is also factually interesting and largely substantiates other accounts, although it is animated by strong personal resentment against Humbert. The same edition of

Analecta Hibernica contains a diary covering the first ten days of the landing by a local Protestant clergyman.

5 Stock, *A Narrative of What Passed at Killala*, pp. 34–5.

6 ibid., p. 16.

7 Sir Herbert Taylor, *Impartial Relation of the Military Operations by an Officer*, Dublin, 1799, Appendix.

8 Stock, op. cit., p. 10.

9 Cited from *Dublin Journal*, 18 September 1798, in an article in the *Dublin Review*, vol. 121, no. 23.

10 Guillon, op. cit., p. 303.

11 Stock, op. cit., p. 96.

12 ibid., p. 103.

13 W. H. Maxwell, *History of the Irish Rebellion in 1798*, London, 1845, pp. 255–62, extracts from the Bishop of Killala's day-to-day diary.

14 Taylor, op. cit., p. 59.

15 ibid., p. 58.

16 ibid, p. 67.

17 Fontaine, op. cit., p. 34.

18 ibid., p. 36.

19 ibid., p. 37.

20 B.M. Add. MSS. 40166. Diary of Captain Hodges.

21 Fontaine, op. cit., pp. 41–2.

22 Maxwell, op. cit., p. 261.

23 Stock, op. cit., p. 145.

24 ibid., p. 163.

25 Sir Richard Musgrave, *Memoir of the Different Irish Rebellions*, Dublin, 1801, p. 480.

26 C. W. Vane (ed.), *Memoir and Correspondence of Viscount Castlereagh*, 12 vols., London, 1848–53, vol. 1, pp. 400–3, 406–9, Musgrave, op. cit., p. 464, Appendix XXI, 10 (letter of the Postmaster of Rutland Island written the day after the expedition arrived).

27 Musgrave, op. cit., p. 466.

28 ibid., p. 465.

29 Vane (ed.), op. cit., vol. i, p. 407. (A first-hand account by the Adjutant himself.)

30 ibid.

31 Ross (ed.), *Cornwallis Correspondence*, vol. iii, p. 338.

32 Details of the French fleet from Guillon, op. cit., p. 407. Sir John Warren in his dispatches quoted in the *Annual Register* for 1798 (Appendix, pp. 144–6) seems to have exaggerated the French gun strength.

33 Dispatches of Sir John Warren, *Annual Register*, 1798, Appendix, pp. 144–6.

34 Tone (ed.), *Tone*, vol. ii, p. 346. Commentary by the Editor. Tone's son,

seems to have got the account of his father's part in the action from returning French officers.

35 Historical Manuscripts Commission. Charlemont MSS., 2 vols., vol. ii, p. 337.

36 ibid.

37 An account by the bystander himself, Sir George Hill, given in a letter written the same day (see Lecky, *History of Ireland in the Eighteenth Century*, vol. v, p. 76n.). It seems more likely to be true than the story told by Tone's son that Hill viciously unmasked him while at breakfast with other French officers (Tone, op. cit., vol. ii, p. 348).

38 *State Trials*, XXVII, col. 616.

39 ibid., cols. 617–18.

40 ibid., col. 621.

41 ibid., col. 624.

42 Historical Manuscripts Commission. Dropmore MSS., vol. iv, p. 370.

43 ibid., p. 374.

44 *State Trials*, XXVII, col. 626.

45 Tone (ed.), op. cit., vol. ii, p. 370.

PART THREE

THE UNION

1 The Making of the Union

1 B.M. Add. MSS. 40166. Diary of Captain Hodges.

2 Leadbeater, *Leadbeater Papers*, p. 269.

3 ibid., p. 275.

4 B.M. Add. MSS. 40166. Diary of Captain Hodges.

5 ibid.

6 29 November 1798. Historical MSS. Commission. Laing MSS., vol. ii, p. 466.

7 Buckingham to Grenville, 11 March 1799. Historical MSS. Commission. Fortescue MSS., vol. iv, p. 497.

8 Historical MSS. Commission. Charlemont MSS., vol. ii, p. 348.

9 Lecky, *History of Ireland in the Eighteenth Century*, vol. v, p. 154.

10 Cited in McDowell, op. cit., p.244.

11 Author's italics. Quoted Lecky, op. cit., vol. v, p. 158.

12 ibid., pp. 148–9.

13 Charlemont to Hartley, 14 May 1799. Charlemont MSS., vol. ii, p. 351.

14 Lecky, op. cit., vol. v, p. 268.

15 ibid., pp. 415–16.

16 Duigenan to Castlereagh, 20 December 1798. Vane (ed.), *Castlereagh Correspondence*, vol. ii, p. 52.

17 Vane (ed.), op. cit., vol. ii, p. 48.

18 Castlereagh to Portland, 2 January 1798. Vane (ed.), op. cit., vol. ii, p. 81.

19 ibid., pp. 79, 328, 339.

20 Lecky, op. cit., vol. v, p. 202n.

21 Clare to Castlereagh, 16 October 1798. Vane (ed.), op. cit., vol. i, p. 393.

22 Cornwallis to Portland, 5 December 1798, ibid., vol. ii, p. 35.

23 Troy to Castlereagh, 24 December 1798, ibid., p. 61.

24 Lecky, op. cit., vol. v, p. 250.

25 ibid., p. 236.

26 Charlemont to Halliday, 25 January 1799. Charlemont MSS., vol. ii, p. 344.

27 ibid., p. 345.

28 Lecky, op. cit., vol. v, p. 351.

29 ibid., p. 298.

30 Moore to Castlereagh, 27 June 1799. Vane (ed.), op. cit., vol. ii, p. 343.

31 Cooke to Castlereagh, 18 September 1799, ibid., p. 403.

32 Vane (ed.), op. cit., vol. iii, p. 344.

33 Lecky, op. cit., vol. v, p. 288.

34 Vane (ed.), op. cit., vol. iii, p. 340.

35 ibid., p. 220.

36 Lecky, op. cit., vol. v, p. 237.

37 ibid., pp. 412–13.

2 Robert Emmet's Fall and Rise

1 Vane (ed.), *Castlereagh Correspondence*, vol. iii, pp. 366, 379, 381.

2 Lecky, *History of Ireland in the Eighteenth Century*, vol. v, p. 337.

3 Leon O'Broin, *The Unfortunate Mr Robert Emmet*, Dublin and London, 1958, p. 47.

4 ibid., p. 53.

5 ibid.

6 Madden, *The United Irishmen, Their Lives and Times*, 3rd series, vol. iii, p. 88.

7 ibid., p. 304.

8 ibid., pp. 97–8.

9 Details quoted from Thomas Emmet's diary by O'Broin, op. cit., pp. 56–7.

10 ibid.

11 Madden, op. cit., vol. iii, p. 304.

12 For this, and all other details of the failure, see the account which Emmet himself wrote for his brother on the eve of execution, but which was retained by the British authorities. Madden, op. cit., vol. iii, pp. 127–35.
13 ibid.
14 O'Broin, op. cit., p. 106.
15 Madden, op. cit., vol. iii, p. 132.
16 ibid., pp. 303–5.
17 ibid., pp. 312–16.
18 ibid., p. 134.
19 M. MacDonagh, *The Viceroy's Post Bag*, London, 1904, p. 413.
20 Madden, op. cit., vol. iii, p. 246.

3 The Failure of the Union

1 For earlier comparisons see above, p. 22.
2 Minutes before *Select Committee Inquiring into the Disturbances in Ireland*, 1824, p. 300 (5 June 1824).
3 Hansard, H.C. Debates, 3rd series, vol. 85, col. 753.
4 *Select Committee*, 1824, p. 126.
5 Cited in J. E. Pomfret, *The Struggle for the Land in Ireland*, Princeton, 1930, p. 8.
6 Kohl. Quoted P.S. O'Hegarty, *History of Ireland Under the Union*, London, 1952, p. 388.
7 Hansard, H.C. Debates, 3rd series, vol. 304, col. 1790.
8 De Latocnaye, *Promenade d'un Français dans l'Irlande*, p. 146.
9 *Select Committee*, 1824. MCSMFW
10 *Select Committee on State of Ireland*, 1825, p. 48.
11 R. D. Edwards and T. D. Williams, *The Great Famine*, Dublin, 1956, p. 127.
12 *Select Committee Inquiring into Disturbances in Ireland*, 1824. Minutes before House of Lords, p. 131.
13 R. B. O'Brien, *Thomas Drummond, Life and Letters*, London, 1889, p. 208.
14 Hansard, H.C. Debates, 3rd series, vol. 85, col. 751.
15 Select Committees of 1824, 1825; Devon Commission Report, 1845.
16 Minutes Before *Select Committee Inquiring Into Disturbances in Ireland* (5 June 1824), p. 361.
17 ibid., 17 June 1824, p. 437.
18 Edwards and Williams, op. cit., p. 252.
19 Hansard, H.C. Debates, 3rd series, vol. 85, cols. 1364–5.
20 ibid., col. 274.
21 ibid., col. 1363.
22 ibid., vol. 105, col. 1287.
23 ibid.

24 The best account of the famine is to be found in R. D. Edwards and T. D. Williams (eds.), *The Great Famine*. But it is a scholarly work not primarily concerned with narrative for its own sake. For the general reader there is also Cecil Woodham-Smith's *The Great Hunger*, in which good narrative and scholarship are combined.

25 Hansard, H.C. Debates, 3rd series, vol. 105, col. 300.

26 ibid., H.L. Debates, 3rd series, vol. 254, col. 1857.

27 ibid., H.C. Debates, 3rd Series, vol. 190, cols. 1357–8.

28 Angus Macintyre, *The Liberator*, London, 1965, p. 104.

4 Daniel O'Connell and Catholic Emancipation

1 John O'Connell (ed.), *The Life and Speeches of Daniel O'Connell*. Dublin, 1846, vol. i, pp. 23–4.

2 *The Nation*, 26 November 1844.

3 *The Nation*, 11 July 1846. Quoted by O'Hegarty, *History of Ireland under the Union*, p. 241.

4 9 September 1844. Quoted O'Hegarty, op. cit., p. 187.

5 Michael MacDonagh, *Daniel O'Connell and the Story of Catholic Emancipation*, London, 1929, p. 114.

6 ibid.

7 ibid., p. 115.

8 Michael Tierney (ed.), *Daniel O'Connell: Nine Centenary Essays*, Dublin, 1949, p. 133.

9 ibid.

10 James Reynolds, *The Catholic Emancipation Crisis in Ireland, 1823–9*, Yale, 1954, p. 96.

11 Tierney, op. cit., p. 138.

12 ibid., p. 122.

13 Reynolds, op. cit., pp. 141–2.

14 ibid., p. 140.

15 ibid., p. 148.

16 December 1824, ibid., p. 143.

17 ibid., p. 148.

18 ibid., p. 146.

19 ibid., p. 158.

20 ibid.

21 ibid.

22 ibid., p. 162.

23 MacDonagh, op. cit., p. 195.

24 ibid., p. 196.

5 *The Repeal Debate*

1 Hansard, H.C. Debates, 3rd series, vol. 22, col. 1093.
2 ibid., col. 1156.
3 ibid., col. 1178.
4 ibid., col. 1166.
5 ibid., col. 1188.
6 ibid., col. 1204.
7 T. W. Moody and J. C. Beckett (eds.), *Ulster Since 1800*, London, 1954, p. 34.
8 Hansard, H.C. Debates, 3rd series, vol. 22, col. 1204.
9 ibid., vol. 23, col. 246.
10 ibid., vol. 22, col. 1212.
11 ibid., col. 1195.
12 ibid., vol. 23, col. 70.
13 ibid., H.L. Debates, col. 303.
14 Angus Macintyre, *The Liberator*, London, 1965, pp. 164–5.
15 MacDonagh, *Daniel O'Connell and the Story of Catholic Emancipation*, p. 219.
16 ibid., p. 246.

6 *O'Connell and Davis*

1 MacDonagh, *O'Connell and the Story of Catholic Emancipation*, p. 250.
2 Sir James Graham, cited in Kevin Nowlan, *The Politics of Repeal*, London, 1965, p. 33.
3 Nowlan, op. cit., p. 51.
4 *The Nation*, 22 October 1842.
5 *The Nation*, 22 July 1842.
6 *The Nation*, 22 July 1843.
7 Charles Gavan Duffy, *Young Ireland*, London, 1880, pp. 373, 387–8.
8 Charles Gavan Duffy, *Thomas Davis: A Memoir*, London, 1890, p. 24.
9 D. O. Madden, *Ireland and Its Rulers*, pp. 247–51.
10 Duffy, *Davis*, p. 41.
11 Bolton King, *Mazzini*, London, 1902, p. 107.
12 An Address read before the Historical Society, Dublin, 26 June 1840.
13 Duffy, *Davis*, p. 84.
14 Quoted T. W. Rolleston (ed.), *Prose Writings of Thomas Davis*, London, 1889, p. 281.
15 Rolleston, op. cit., p. 194.
16 ibid., p. 160.
17 ibid., p. 162.

18 ibid., p. 155.
19 ibid., pp. 156–7.
20 ibid., p. 218.
21 ibid., p. 222.
22 *The Nation*, 22 October 1842.
23 ibid.
24 ibid., 25 March 1843.
25 ibid., 3 June 1843.
26 ibid., 17 June 1843.
27 ibid., 10 December 1842.
28 ibid., 25 March 1843.
29 ibid., 5 August 1843.
30 Duffy, *Davis*, p. 111.
31 ibid.
32 ibid., p. 114.

7 'Monster Meetings'

 1 *The Nation*, 4 February 1843.
 2 ibid., 19 November 1842.
 3 ibid., 25 March 1843.
 4 ibid., 22 April 1843.
 5 ibid.
 6 MacDonagh, *O'Connell and the Story of Catholic Emancipation*, p. 266.
 7 *The Nation*, 27 May 1843.
 8 Cited in Nowlan, *The Politics of Repeal*, p. 52.
 9 ibid., p. 55.
10 *The Nation*, 3 June 1843.
11 ibid., 17 June 1843.
12 ibid.
13 ibid.
14 ibid., 8 July 1843.
15 ibid.
16 ibid., 22 July 1843.
17 ibid., 29 July 1843.
18 ibid., 22 July 1843.
19 ibid., 29 July 1843.
20 ibid., 5 August 1843.
21 ibid., 12 August 1843.
22 ibid., 19 August 1843.
23 ibid., 26 August 1843.
24 British Museum Catalogue, 1872, c. 1. (10), (Ballads).

25 *The Nation*, 19 August 1843.
26 ibid., 26 August 1843.
27 ibid., 30 September 1843.
28 ibid., 16 September 1843.
29 ibid., 23 September 1843.
30 ibid.
31 ibid., 7 October 1843.
32 ibid., 30 September 1843.

8 Biding Time After Clontarf

 1 Duffy, *Young Ireland*, p. 371.
 2 *The Nation*, 14 October 1843.
 3 ibid., 2 December 1843.
 4 ibid., 28 October 1843.
 5 ibid., 11 November 1843.
 6 ibid.
 7 ibid.
 8 ibid., 28 October 1844.
 9 ibid.
10 ibid., 21 October 1843.
11 ibid.
12 ibid., 30 December 1843.
13 ibid., 17 February 1844, for attack on Catholics *not* resigning.
14 Duffy, *Young Ireland*, p. 519.
15 *The Nation*, 18 March 1848.
16 H.C. Debates, 3rd series, vol. 70, cols. 675–7.
17 *The Nation*, 30 December 1843.
18 ibid.
19 ibid., 17 February 1844.
20 ibid., 24 February 1844.
21 ibid., 2 March 1844.
22 ibid., 9 March 1844.
23 Duffy, *Thomas Davis: A Memoir*, p. 189.
24 *The Nation*, 2 March 1844.
25 ibid., 9 March 1844.
26 Clarke, *I.H.S.*, vol. iii, no. 9 (March 1942), p. 22.

9 O'Connell's Imprisonment and After

 1 Duffy, *Thomas Davis: A Memoir*, p. 190.
 2 *The Nation*, 9 March 1844.

3 ibid., 16 March 1844.
4 ibid., 23 March 1844.
5 ibid., 30 March 1844.
6 ibid., 6 April 1844.
7 ibid., 13 April 1844.
8 ibid., 1 June 1844.
9 ibid., 8 June 1844.
10 Duffy, op. cit., p. 230.
11 *The Nation*, 8, 22, 29 June 1844.
12 ibid., 8 June 1844.
13 ibid., 29 June 1844.
14 ibid.
15 ibid., 31 August 1844.
16 ibid.
17 ibid., 14 September 1844.
18 ibid.
19 Duffy, *Four Years of Irish History*, pp. 2, 22–3. Duffy sees no inconsistency in talking on the one hand of O'Connell's fading powers and yet attributing to him tactical skill and even genius 'to the last hour of his career' when accusing him of manoeuvring against Young Ireland (op. cit., pp. 120, 198). Modern historians have followed him in implying that by 1845 O'Connell had abandoned Repeal; e.g., Clarke, *I.H.S.*, vol. iii, no. 9, p. 22; Angus Macintyre, *The Liberator*, London, 1965, p. 277; Denis Gwynn, *Young Ireland and 1848*, Cork, 1949, p. 31. Gwynn describes O'Connell in 1844 as 'plainly worn out and weary of the burden of political leadership and agitation'. See also J. C. Beckett, *The Making of Modern Ireland*, London, 1966, p. 327.
20 W. J. O'Neill Daunt, *A Life Spent for Ireland*, London, 1869, p. 57.
21 ibid., p. 61.
22 *The Nation*, 14 September 1844.
23 ibid.
24 ibid., 20 July 1844.
25 W. J. Fitzpatrick, *Correspondence of O'Connell*, 2 vols., London, 1888, vol. ii, pp. 346–7.
26 *The Nation*, 14 September 1844.
27 ibid., 21 September 1844.
28 ibid.
29 Duffy, *Young Ireland*, p. 542.
30 Nowlan, *The Politics of Repeal*, p. 73.
31 ibid., p. 74.
32 ibid.
33 *The Nation*, 21 September 1844.
34 ibid., 28 September 1844.

35 ibid.
36 ibid.
37 ibid., 5 October 1844. For *Nation* optimism, 12 October 1844.
38 Fitzpatrick, op. cit., vol. ii, p. 331.
39 The letter is given in full in the Appendix to Fitzpatrick, op. cit., vol. ii, p. 434.
40 Duffy, *Thomas Davis: A Memoir*, pp. 249–50, 262.
41 ibid., p. 446.
42 Duffy, *Thomas Davis: A Memoir*, p. 244.
43 Duffy, *Young Ireland*, p. 578.
44 ibid., p. 589n.
45 ibid.
46 ibid.
47 *The Nation*, 30 November 1844.
48 ibid., 16 November 1844.

10 More 'Monster Meetings'

1 See, e.g., *The Nation*, 26 April, 3, 10, 24, 31 May, 7, 14 June, 2, 9 August, 27 September, 11, 18 October 1845.
2 ibid., 7 December 1844.
3 ibid., 14 December 1844.
4 ibid., 18 January 1845.
5 ibid., 29 March 1845.
6 Denis Gwynn, *Young Ireland and 1848*, Cork, 1949, p. 30.
7 *The Nation*, 29 March 1845.
8 ibid.
9 ibid., 26 April 1845.
10 ibid.
11 R. B. McDowell, *Public Opinion and Government Policy in Ireland, 1801–46*, London, 1952, p. 226.
12 *The Nation*, 26 April 1845.
13 Gwynn, op. cit., p. 34.
14 The criticism first came from an English Tory. Gwynn, op. cit., p. 41.
15 *The Nation*, 31 May 1845.
16 ibid.
17 ibid.
18 *The Pilot*, 28 May 1845.
19 *The Nation*, 31 May 1845.
20 ibid., 3 May 1845.
21 ibid.
22 ibid., 31 May 1845.
23 ibid.

24 ibid., 7 June 1845.
25 ibid., 29 March 1845.
26 ibid., 14 June 1845.
27 ibid.
28 ibid.
29 ibid., 12 July 1845.
30 ibid., 26 July 1845.
31 ibid., 2 August 1845.
32 ibid., 9 August 1845.
33 Duffy, *Young Ireland*, pp. 715ff.
34 Fitzpatrick, *Correspondence of O'Connell*, vol. ii, p. 363.
35 *The Nation*, 13 September 1845.
36 ibid., 20 September 1845.
37 ibid., 27 September 1845.
38 ibid.
39 ibid.
40 ibid.
41 ibid.
42 ibid., 4 October 1845.
43 ibid., 11 October 1845.
44 ibid.
45 ibid.
46 ibid., 18 October 1845.
47 ibid.
48 ibid., 15 November 1845.
49 ibid., 11 October 1845.
50 ibid., 25 October 1845.
51 ibid., 25 October 1845.
52 ibid.
53 ibid., 15 November 1845.

11 Repeal, Famine and Young Ireland

1 *The Nation*, 20 December 1845.
2 ibid.
3 ibid.
4 ibid.
5 See shipping columns of contemporary newspapers throughout the famine period *passim*, but particularly *The Nation*.
6 *The Nation*, 20 December 1845.
7 ibid.
8 Duffy, *Four Years of Irish History*, p. 116.

9 *The Nation*, 22 November 1845.
10 ibid.
11 Duffy, *Four Years of Irish History*, pp. 117–18.
12 ibid., p. 119.
13 *The Nation*, 31 January 1846.
14 ibid., 24 January 1846.
15 ibid., 14 February 1846.
16 ibid., 21 February 1846.
17 Duffy, *Four Years of Irish History*, pp. 10–11.
18 Duffy, *Four Years of Irish History*, p. 10.
19 *The Nation*, 21 February 1846.
20 ibid., 28 February 1846.
21 ibid., 24 January 1846.
22 ibid., 21 February 1846.
23 ibid.
24 ibid., 21 March 1846.
25 ibid., 4 April 1846.
26 ibid.
27 ibid., 16 May 1846.
28 ibid., 23 May 1846.
29 ibid., 30 May 1846.
30 ibid.
31 ibid., 13 June 1846.
32 ibid.
33 ibid.
34 ibid.
35 ibid., 20 June 1846.
36 ibid.
37 ibid.
38 ibid.
39 ibid., 27 June 1846.
40 ibid.
41 ibid.
42 ibid.
43 For this and all subsequent details of this part of the debate see *The Nation*, 18 July 1846.
44 ibid.
45 This and all subsequent details of this debate from *The Nation*, 1 August 1846.
46 Duffy, *Young Ireland*, p. 749.
47 ibid., p. 739.

12 The Irish Confederation

1 *The Nation*, 12 September 1846.
2 ibid., 29 August 1846.
3 ibid., 30 January 1847.
4 ibid., 26 December 1846.
5 ibid., 5 December 1846.
6 ibid., 7 November 1846.
7 ibid., 13 November 1847.
8 ibid., 20 February 1847.
9 ibid., 28 August 1847, 13 November 1847.
10 ibid., 6 November 1847.
11 ibid., 27 November 1847.
12 ibid., 17 July 1847.
13 *Irish Felon*, 1 July 1848, which contains a reprint of the letter Lalor wrote '... in the last week of January 1847 ... to a leading member of the Confederation'. See also Duffy, *Four Years of Irish History*, p. 474.
14 Duffy, op. cit., pp. 476–7.
15 Duffy, op. cit., p. 484.
16 *The Nation*.
17 *The Nation*, 1 January 1848.
18 Duffy, op. cit., pp. 487–8.
19 Duffy, op. cit., p. 494.
20 *United Irishman*, 12 February 1848.
21 ibid.
22 ibid., 15 March 1848.
23 *The Nation*, 5 February 1848.
24 Denis Gwynn, *Young Ireland and 1848*, Cork, 1949, p. 146.
25 Duffy, op. cit., pp. 504–5.
26 *The Nation*, 5 February 1848.
27 ibid.
28 ibid.
29 ibid., 18 September 1847.
30 ibid., 4 March 1848.
31 ibid.
32 Duffy, op. cit., p. 537.
33 ibid., p. 538.
34 ibid., p. 547.
35 ibid.
36 ibid., pp. 538–9.
37 *The Nation*, 11 March 1848.
38 *United Irishman*, 18 March 1848.
39 *The Nation*, 11 March 1848.

40 Cited in *United Irishman*, 11 March 1848.
41 ibid., 22 April 1848.
42 ibid., 8 April 1848. Quoted from the *Galway Vindicator*.
43 *The Nation*, 18 March 1848.
44 ibid., 11 March 1848.
45 ibid., 18 March 1848.
46 ibid.
47 Quoted, *United Irishman*, 29 April 1848.
48 ibid.
49 ibid.
50 *The Nation*, 15 April 1848; *United Irishman*, 29 April 1848.
51 *The Nation*, 25 March 1848.
52 ibid., 20 May 1848.
53 ibid.
54 Duffy, op. cit., p. 594.
55 ibid., pp. 595–6.
56 ibid., p. 597.
57 O'Brien's personal memorandum, quoted Gwynn, *Young Ireland*, p. 193.
58 *The Nation*, 27 May 1848.
59 *Irish Felon*, 24 June 1848.
60 Gwynn, op. cit., p. 193.
61 *Irish Felon*, 24 June 1848.
62 For this and the following details of Mitchel's imprisonment see Mitchel's own *Jail Journal*.
63 *The Irish Tribune*, 10 June 1848.
64 e.g. Gwynn, *Young Ireland*, p. 272.
65 Mitchel, *Jail Journal*, p. 53.
66 ibid., p. 124.
67 ibid., pp. 278, 284.

13 Smith O'Brien's 'Rising' 1848

1 *The Nation*, 15 April 1848.
2 Duffy, *Four Years of Irish History*, pp. 608–9.
3 ibid., p. 609.
4 Gwynn, *Young Ireland*, pp. 206–7, O'Brien's Memorandum.
5 Duffy, op. cit., pp. 617–18.
6 *The Nation*, 10 May 1848.
7 ibid.
8 ibid., 3 May 1848.
9 ibid., 10 May 1848.
10 *State Trials, Trial of Smith O'Brien*, vol. vii, cols. 877–8.
11 Gwynn, op. cit., p. 212.

12 ibid., pp. 212–13.

13 ibid., p. 213.

14 *The Irish Tribune*, 1 July 1848.

15 Letter from Joseph Brennan, a young man from Cork and a poet, *Irish Felon*, 8 July 1848.

16 *The Nation*, 17 June 1848.

17 ibid.

18 Duffy, op. cit., p. 624.

19 Duffy, op. cit., pp. 625–6.

20 Gwynn, op. cit., p. 228.

21 *State Trials, Trial of Smith O'Brien*, col. 110.

22 ibid., col. 111.

23 Gwynn, op. cit., p. 227.

24 *State Trials, Trial of Smith O'Brien*, col. 93.

25 ibid., Appendix A, col. 1096.

26 ibid., cols. 262 and 264.

27 Gwynn, op. cit., pp. 229–30, ibid.; Meagher's *Narrative*, p. 284; *State Trials, Trial of Smith O'Brien*, col. 264.

28 Verbatim quote by Maher in evidence, *State Trials, Trial of Smith O'Brien*, col. 264.

29 O'Brien's Memorandum, quoted Gwynn, op. cit., p. 230.

30 ibid., p. 282.

31 *State Trials, Trial of Smith O'Brien*, col. 97.

32 Meagher's *Narrative*, Gwynn, op. cit., p. 298.

33 ibid., p. 258. Also *Kilkenny Journal*, 29 July 1848.

34 Meagher's *Narrative*, Gwynn, op. cit., p. 280.

35 ibid., p. 286.

36 ibid., p. 288.

37 ibid.

38 *State Trials, Trial of Smith O'Brien*, col. 133.

39 Meagher's *Narrative*, Gwynn, op. cit., p. 289.

40 ibid., p. 290.

41 ibid., p. 291.

42 ibid., p. 292.

43 ibid., pp. 292–5.

44 O'Mahony's *Narrative*; see Michael Cavanagh, *Memoirs of Thomas Meagher*, New York, 1892, p. 273.

45 ibid., pp. 273, 275.

46 *State Trials, Trial of Smith O'Brien*, col. 138.

47 Meagher's *Narrative*, Gwynn, p. 304.

48 Michael Cavanagh, op. cit., p. 278.

49 O'Mahony's *Narrative*, Cavanagh, op. cit., p. 272; and Doheny, *Felon's Track*, p. 166.

50 *State Trials, Trial of Smith O'Brien*, col. 143.
51 ibid., col. 144.
52 Charles Kickham's *Narrative*, see Gwynn, op. cit., p. 316.
53 ibid., p. 233.
54 ibid., p. 316.
55 Cavanagh, op. cit., p. 258.
56 Magee's *Narrative*, Gwynn, op. cit., p. 320.
57 Kickham's *Narrative*, Gwynn, op. cit., p. 317.
58 ibid.
59 Duffy, op. cit., p. 664; Gwynn, op. cit., p. 253.
60 McManus's *Narrative*, Gwynn, op. cit., p. 312.
61 *State Trials, Trial of Smith O'Brien*, col. 162.
62 ibid., col. 163.
63 McManus's *Narrative*, Duffy, op. cit., p. 668.
64 ibid, p. 470.
65 *State Trials, Trial of W. S. O'Brien*, col. 72.
66 Father P. Fitzgerald, *Personal Recollections of the Insurrection at Ballingarry*, Dublin, 1862, p. 15.
67 McManus's *Narrative*, Gwynn, op. cit., p. 313.
68 McManus's *Narrative*, Duffy, op. cit., p. 683.
69 Fitzgerald, op. cit., p. 23.
70 *State Trials, Trial of Smith O'Brien*, col. 168.
71 ibid. Appendix A, col. 1089.
72 Duffy, op. cit., p. 686.
73 ibid., also *State Trials, Trial of Smith O'Brien*, col. 176–8.
74 *State Trials, Trial of Smith O'Brien*, cols. 180–83, 319.
75 ibid., cols. 170, 171.
76 ibid., col. 177.
77 Gwynn, op. cit., p. 319.
78 Fitzgerald, op. cit., p. 30.
79 *State Trials, Trial of Smith O'Brien*, Carrol's evidence, cols. 184–7.
80 McManus's *Narrative*, Duffy. op. cit., p. 688.
81 *Freeman's Journal*, 4 August 1848, cited *Kilkenny Journal*, 9 August, 1848.
82 Gwynn, op. cit., p. 234.
83 Fitzgerald, op. cit., p. 26.
84 *Kilkenny Journal*, 9 August 1848.
85 *Longford Journal*, 12 August 1848.
86 *Kilkenny Moderator*, 20 August 1848.
87 *Kilkenny Journal*, 4 November 1848.
88 Michael Doheny, *Felon's Track*, Dublin, 1914, *passim*. Ryan, *Fenian Chief*, p. 42.
89 *Freeman's Journal*, 10 October 1848.

90 Cited *Longford Journal*, 21 October 1848.
91 ibid., 28 October 1848.
92 John Mitchel, *Jail Journal*, p. 300.
93 James Stephens, *Reminiscences*, *Weekly Freeman*, 3 November 1883, cited in Ryan, op. cit., p. 69.
94 Cecil Woodham-Smith, *The Great Hunger*, London, 1962, p. 417.
95 Cited in T. F. O'Sullivan, *The Young Irelanders*, Dublin 1945, p. 188.
96 R. G. Athearn, *Thomas Francis Meagher: An Irish Revolutionary in America*, Colorado, 1949, pp. 120–22.
97 ibid.
98 ibid.
99 ibid., pp. 137, 139.
100 ibid., p. 166.

14 The Corpse on the Dissecting Table

1 *Kilkenny Journal*, 19 August 1848.
2 *Dublin Evening Packet*, 27 July 1848.
3 *Kilkenny Moderator*, quoted in *Dublin Evening Packet*, 3 August 1848.
4 ibid.
5 See, e.g., *Freeman's Journal*, 'Evictions on Lord Clonmel's Estates', 11 September 1848.
6 *Freeman's Journal*, 15, 18, 19, 28 August 1848.
7 See description by the Reverend James Maher of Carlow, *Freeman's Journal*, 25 September 1848.
8 W. J. O'Neill Daunt, *Ireland and Her Agitators*, London, 1867, p. 230.
9 John Savage, *Fenian Heroes and Martyrs*, p. 333.
10 Marcus Bourke, John O'Leary: *A Study in Separation*, Tralee, 1967, pp. 18–19. *Freeman's Journal*, 11 November 1848.
11 Bourke, op. cit., pp. 25–6.
12 Frederick Lucas, *The Tablet*, cited in J. H. Whyte, *The Independent Irish Party* 1850–59, Oxford, 1958, p. 80.
13 Whyte, op. cit., pp. 71–81.
14 See P. J. Corish, 'Political Problems, 1860–1878', in *A History of Irish Catholicism*, vol. v.
15 Cited J. H. Whyte, 'Political Problems 1850–1860', in *A History of Irish Catholicism*, vol. v.
16 Whyte, *The Independent Irish Party*, p. 88.
17 ibid., p. 108.
18 ibid.
19 ibid.
20 ibid., p. 115.
21 ibid.

22 ibid., p. 120.
23 ibid.
24 W. J. O'Neill Daunt, op. cit., p. 242.
25 A. M. Sullivan, *New Ireland*, London, 1877, p. 247.

15 Beginnings of the Fenian Movement

1 Sullivan, *New Ireland*, pp. 36ff.
2 ibid.
3 *Cork Constitution*, 4 November 1858.
4 ibid., 16 November 1858.
5 *Cork Examiner*, 29 November 1858.
6 See letter to the Lord Lieutenant, Lord Naas, from the priest, Father John O'Sullivan of Kenmare, dated 5 October 1858 in John Rutherford, *The Fenian Conspiracy*, 2 vols., London, 1877, vol. i, p. 118.
7 *Cork Examiner*, 10 December 1858.
8 *Clare Journal*, 14 March 1859.
9 ibid.
10 Lord Abercorn, 6 February 1866, Hansard, 3rd series, vol. 181, col. 68.
11 *Clare Journal*, 14 March 1859.
12 *Cork Examiner*, 14 March 1859.
13 See *Irishman*, 1 January 1859, in Belfast; *Irishman*, 8 January 1859, in Westmeath; *Irishman*, 26 February 1859.
14 *Westmeath Guardian*, 3 March 1859.
15 ibid.
16 *Irishman*, 12 February 1859; Sullivan, op. cit., pp. 201–2; *Cork Examiner*, 24 December 1858.
17 *Kilkenny Moderator*, 8 January 1859.
18 See, e.g., *Irishman*, 12 March 1859.
19 See letter from John O'Mahoney to O'Doheny, autumn 1856, cited in Ryan, *Fenian Chief*, pp. 51–3. Also Stephens himself, *Weekly Freeman*, 15 November 1883.
20 Cited in Ryan, op. cit., p. 48.
21 Ryan, op. cit., p. 56.
22 Stephens, Reminiscences, *Weekly Freeman*, 13 October 1882.
23 *The Tribune*, 17 November 1856.
24 ibid., 19 January 1856.
25 ibid.
26 Stephens, *Weekly Freeman*, 13 October 1882.
27 ibid.
28 ibid., 8 December 1883.
29 ibid., 1 December 1883.

30 ibid., 17 November 1883.
31 ibid., 15 November 1883.
32 ibid., 17 November 1883.
33 ibid., 3 November 1883.
34 ibid., 9 February 1884.
35 Ryan, op. cit., p. 84.
36 Stephens, Reminiscences, *Weekly Freeman*, 9 February 1884.
37 Joseph Denieffe, *A Personal Narrative of the Irish Revolutionary Brotherhood*, New York, 1904; William D'Arcy, *The Fenian Movement in the United States*, 1947, p. 2.
38 D'Arcy, op. cit., p. 5.
39 ibid., p. 8.
40 Denieffe, op. cit., p. 3.
41 ibid.
42 Cited in Ryan, op. cit., p. 62.
43 ibid.
44 Stephens, Reminiscences, *Weekly Freeman*.
45 Ryan, op. cit., p. 82.
46 Denieffe, op. cit., pp. 156–7.
47 Ryan, op. cit., p. 90.
48 Denieffe, op. cit., p. 22.
49 John O'Leary, *Recollections of Fenians and Fenianism*, vol. ii, p. 81.
50 Rutherford, *The Secret History of the Fenian Conspiracy*, pp. 62–5. Rutherford, a Unionist journalist from the West of Ireland, allowed his book to become full of small inaccuracies but he was clearly writing, in 1877, with much authentic material provided by the authorities at his disposal, and it is not nearly so worthless as nationalist sources have usually suggested. For an account of the IRB organization in 1880 see article by A. Chester Ives, the *New York Herald*, 12 August 1880. The article was based on information from first-hand sources. (See O'Brien and Ryan, *Devoy's Post Bag*, vol. ii, pp. 546–7.)
51 Ryan, op. cit., p. 279. O'Leary, op. cit., p. 65.
52 Cluseret, *Fraser's Magazine*, July 1872, new series, vol. vi, p. 54.
53 O'Leary, op. cit., vol. i, p. 123.
54 'Derivation of the Fenians', *Irish People*, 16 August 1865.

16 James Stephens at Work

1 Ryan, *Fenian Chief*, p. 159.
2 Ryan, op. cit., p. 160, from Denieffe, *Personal Narrative*, pp. 46ff.
3 Ryan, op. cit., p. 161.
4 ibid., p. 161.
5 ibid., p. 165.

6 William D'Arcy, *The Fenian Movement in the United States*, Washington, 1947, pp. 25, 27, 52.

7 *Irish People*, 5 March 1864.

8 O'Leary, *Recollections*, pp. 124, 148.

9 Ryan, op. cit., p. 175.

10 Regulations for Lent read in all Catholic churches in the Dublin diocese, Sunday 28 February 1859 – see, e.g., *Drogheda Argus*, 5 March 1859.

11 All details of McManus's funeral from *Freeman's Journal*, 11 November 1861.

12 ibid.

13 O'Leary, op. cit., p. 180.

14 Sullivan, *New Ireland*, p. 249.

15 e.g., 29 July 1866.

16 *Irish People*, 2 January 1864.

17 ibid., 13 February 1864.

18 ibid., 26 December 1863.

19 ibid., 9 April 1864.

20 D'Arcy, op. cit., p. 30.

21 ibid., p. 27.

22 ibid., p. 40.

23 ibid., p. 46.

24 ibid., p. 47.

25 Denieffe, op. cit., p. 91.

26 D'Arcy, op. cit., pp. 56–7.

27 ibid., p. 57.

28 John Devoy, *Recollections of an Irish Rebel*, New York, 1929, pp. 21, 25.

29 *Report of Dublin Special Commission for the Trial of T. F. Bourke*, 1867, p. 211.

30 *Report of Dublin Special Commission for the Trial of T. C. Luby*, 1865, pp. 141, 156, 221.

31 ibid., p. 148.

32 See, e.g., arrests in Belfast reported *Irish People*, 23 March 1864 and 3 May 1864.

33 D'Arcy, op. cit., pp. 46ff.

34 ibid., p. 72.

35 ibid.

36 ibid., pp. 74–5.

37 ibid, p. 87.

38 Ryan, op. cit., p. 208, gives the text of these letters.

39 Denieffe, op. cit., pp. 97ff.

40 *Report of Dublin Special Commission for the Trial of T. C. Luby*, 1865, p. 1043.

41 Munster News, quoted by *Irish People*, 16 September 1865.

42 ibid.

43 ibid.

44 ibid.

45 Ryan, op. cit., p. 207.

46 *Report of Dublin Special Commission for the Trial of T. C. Luby*, 1865, p. 182.

17 Stephens In and Out of Trouble

1 D'Arcy, *The Fenian Movement in the United States*, p. 79.

2 Sullivan, *New Ireland*, p. 257.

3 *Irish Liberator*, quoted in *Irish People*, 13 February 1864.

4 *Report of Dublin Special Commission for the Trial of T. F. Bourke and others*, pp. 601–11.

5 Ryan, *Fenian Chief*, p. 212.

6 D'Arcy, *The Fenian Movement in the United States*, p. 72.

7 ibid., p. 99.

8 ibid.

9 Ryan, op. cit., p. 212.

10 Sullivan, op. cit, p. 265.

11 D'Arcy, op. cit., p. 101.

12 Parliamentary Papers. Accounts and Reports, 1876, vol. lviii, pp. 495, 497, 499.

13 Ryan, op. cit., p. 216.

14 D'Arcy, op. cit., p. 114.

15 ibid., p. 139.

16 D'Arcy, op. cit., p. 159.

17 ibid., p. 166.

18 ibid., p. 165.

19 ibid., p. 169.

20 ibid., p. 214.

21 ibid., p. 218.

22 Cited in Ryan, op. cit., p. 247.

23 Massey's evidence at, for example, the trial of J. F. X. O'Brien, *Cork Examiner*, 20 May 1867. Also at the trial of T. F. Bourke, *Report of Dublin Special Commission*, p. 173.

24 Massey's evidence, *Cork Examiner*, 30 May 1867. Also Stephens' own statement, cited Ryan, op. cit., p. 249.

25 Ryan, op. cit., p. 249.

26 ibid., p. 252.

27 *Cork Examiner*, 30 May 1867. Massey's evidence at trial of J. F. X. O'Brien.

28 Ryan, op. cit., p. 244.

29 *The Times*, 29 April 1868. Trial of Richard Burke.
30 Trial of T. F. Bourke, *Report of Special Commission*, p. 169. Trial of J. F. X. O'Brien, *Cork Examiner*, 30 May 1867.
31 Officially confirmed in this designation, 15 February 1867, D'Arcy, op. cit., pp. 251–2.
32 Ryan, op. cit., p. 238.
33 ibid.
34 Article by Cluseret in *Fraser's Magazine*, July 1872, new series, vol. vi, p. 32.
35 ibid., p. 39.

18 *1867: Bold Fenian Men*

1 *The Times*, 29 April 1868, Trial of Richard Burke.
2 ibid., 30 April 1868, Trial of Richard Burke.
3 ibid.
4 Ryan, *Fenian Chief*, p. 239.
5 *Cork Examiner*, 24 May 1867, Trial of McClure. Evidence of Corydon.
6 See letter of Kelly from Ireland, 19 March 1867, D'Arcy, *The Fenian Movement in the United States*, pp. 240–41. See also evidence of Massey, *Report of Special Commission for Trial of T. F. Bourke*, etc., pp. 178–9; also Trial of J. F. X. O'Brien, *Cork Examiner*, 30 May 1867
7 Denieffe, *A Personal Narrative of the I.R.B.*, pp. 278–80.
8 *The Times*, 30 April 1868, Trial of Richard Burke.
9 ibid., Corydon.
10 *Report of Special Commission for Trial of T. F. Bourke*, etc., pp. 201, 501, 563–78.
11 Evidence of Massey, Trial of J. F. X. O'Brien, *Cork Examiner*, 30 May 1867.
12 *Report of Special Commission* 1867, Trial of Bourke, p. 535.
13 ibid., p. 502.
14 *Freeman's Journal*, 13 February 1867.
15 *Report of Dublin Special Commission*; Trial of T. F. Bourke, etc., p. 502.
16 ibid., p. 503.
17 ibid., p. 209.
18 *Freeman's Journal*, 15, 16 February 1867.
19 *Cork Examiner*, 12, 16 February 1867.
20 ibid., 30 May 1867. Trial of P. J. Condon.
21 ibid.
22 ibid.
23 ibid.
24 Cluseret, *Fraser's Magazine*, July 1872, p. 37.
25 ibid., pp. 38, 41.

26 ibid., p. 38.

27 These and subsequent details, *Cork Examiner*, 30 May 1867. Trial of P. J. Condon. Evidence of Massey.

28 The proclamation is given in full in *The Times*, 8 March, 1867.

29 Letter published in the *Irishman*, quoted *The Times*, 13 January 1868.

30 *Report of the Dublin Special Commission, 1867*, Trial of T. F. Bourke, etc., pp. 186–7.

31 *The Times*, 1 June 1867. *Cork Examiner*, 30 May 1867.

32 *The Times*, 15 July 1867.

33 *Report of the Dublin Special Commission*, 1867, pp. 244–50.

34 ibid.

35 ibid., pp. 154–5.

36 ibid., Trial of T. F. Bourke, etc., pp. 248–9. The Report here gives the figures as 'between 40,000 and 50,000', but Lennon was a fairly hard-headed man and we know from elsewhere (Trial of P. J. Condon, *Cork Examiner*, 30 May 1867) that 14,000 men were organized for Dublin. I am assuming that the larger figures were a mis-hearing.

37 ibid., p. 152.

38 ibid., p. 224.

39 ibid., p. 164.

40 This and subsequent details, *Report of the Special Commission*, Trial of T. F. Bourke, p. 221.

41 ibid.

42 *Drogheda Argus*, 9 March 1867.

43 *Cork Examiner*, 9 March 1867.

44 ibid.

45 ibid., 25, 27 May 1867.

46 *Report of Special Commission*, p. 271.

47 These and subsequent details, *Report of Special Commission*, pp. 288–92.

48 ibid., pp. 465–6.

49 J. J. Finnan, *Patriotic Songs*, Limerick, 1913, pp. 136–7.

50 *Cork Examiner*, 24 May 1867.

51 D'Arcy, op. cit., p. 243.

52 ibid., p. 245.

53 *The Times*, 4 November 1867. Trial of Colonel Warren.

54 ibid.

55 Listed among those named in *The Times*, 17 June 1867.

56 D'Arcy, op. cit., p. 246.

57 *The Times*, 14 November 1867.

58 D'Arcy, op. cit., p. 247.

59 *The Times*, 4 November 1867.

60 ibid., 15 June 1867.
61 ibid., 19 June 1867.

19 The Manchester Martyrs

1 Anthony Glynn, *High Upon the Gallows Tree*, Tralee, 1967, pp. 30–1. This competent compilation of the available facts is the most recent and extensive study of the Manchester Rescue.
2 Glynn, op. cit., pp. 94ff.
3 *The Times*, 2 November 1867.
4 Glynn, op. cit., p. 104.
5 ibid., p. 125.
6 *The Times*, 25 November 1867.
7 Hansard, H.C. Debates, 3rd series, vol. 230, col. 808.
8 *The Times*, 29 May 1867.
9 ibid., 27 May 1867.
10 ibid., 28 May 1867.
11 e.g., *The Times*, 23 May 1867.
12 ibid., 14 January 1868.
13 ibid., 11 January 1868.
14 ibid., 18 January 1868.
15 ibid., 14 January 1868 (Queen's evidence from Patrick Mullany).
16 ibid., 18 January 1868.
17 ibid., 14 January 1868.
18 ibid., 8 January 1868.
19 ibid., 14 January 1868.
20 ibid., 2, 6 January 1868.

PART FOUR

THE TRAGEDY OF HOME RULE

1 Beginnings of Home Rule

1 Parliamentary Reports, 1881, vol. lxxvii, 725.
2 ibid.
3 David Thornley, *Isaac Butt and Home Rule*, London, 1964, p. 25.
4 *The Times*, 23 January 1868.
5 ibid., 29 January 1868.
6 Quoted in *The Times*, 3 March 1868.
7 Evelyn Ashley, 'Mr Gladstone – Fragments of Personal Reminiscence' in *National Review*, vol. xxxi, no. 184, June 1898.

8 Hansard, H.C. Debates, 3rd series, vol. 191, col. 491.
9 ibid., col. 471.
10 ibid., col. 515.
11 ibid., col. 711.
12 ibid., col. 853.
13 ibid., col. 864.
14 ibid., col. 505.
15 ibid., col. 507.
16 ibid., vol. 304, col. 149.
17 ibid., vol. 199, col. 333.
18 ibid., col. 1761.
19 Thornley, op. cit., p. 92.
20 ibid., p. 112.
21 ibid., p. 127.
22 Parliamentary Papers, 1871, vol. xxxii, p. 14.
23 ibid., p. 369.
24 Thornley, op. cit., p. 71.
25 ibid., p. 18.
26 ibid., p. 71.
27 ibid., p. 154.
28 ibid., p. 161.
29 ibid., p. 168.
30 ibid., p. 179.
31 ibid., p. 215.
32 ibid., p. 230.
33 ibid., p. 81.
34 ibid., p. 251.
35 W. J. O'Neill Daunt's *Journal*, cited in Thornley, op. cit., p. 254.

2 *Parnell and the Land Crisis*

1 For biographical details, see Bibliography.
2 Michael Davitt, *The Fall of Feudalism in Ireland*, London and New York, 1906, p. 110.
3 William O'Brien and Desmond Ryan (eds.), *Devoy's Post Bag, 1871–1928*, vol. i, p. 269.
4 *Irish World*, 6 March 1880.
5 Quoted P. S. O'Hegarty, *A History of Ireland under the Union, 1801 to 1922*, London, 1952, p. 529.
6 John J. Horgan, *Parnell to Pearse*, Dublin, 1949, p. 39.
7 Hansard, H.C. Debates, 3rd series, vol. 233, col. 1049.
8 *The Times*, 13 April 1877.
9 N. D. Palmer, *The Irish Land League Crisis*, New Haven, 1940, p. 64.

10 Parliamentary Reports, 1881, vol. lxxvii, 275.
11 Palmer, op. cit., p. 93.
12 ibid., p. 105.
13 Thornley, *Isaac Butt*, p. 363.
14 O'Brien and Ryan (eds.), op. cit., vol. i, p. 312.
15 ibid., p. 268.
16 R. Barry O'Brien, *The Life of Charles Stewart Parnell*, 2 vols., London, 1898, vol i., p. 139.
17 *Devoy's Post Bag*, vol. i, p. 298.
18 ibid., vol. i, p. 325.
19 ibid., vol. ii, p. 40.
20 ibid., pp. 89–90.
21 Michael Davitt, op. cit., p. 119.
22 ibid., p. 113.
23 ibid., p. 131.
24 ibid., p. 153.
25 ibid., p. 154.
26 Palmer, op. cit., pp. 141–2.
27 Hansard, H.C. Debates.
28 ibid., vol. 253, col. 1715.
29 ibid., H.L. Debates, vol. 254, col. 1869.
30 Hansard, H.C. Debates.
31 *The Times*, 3 December 1880.
32 Quoted Palmer, op. cit., p. 120.
33 ibid., p. 171.
34 ibid., p. 168.

3 Parnell and Home Rule

1 Conor Cruise O'Brien, *Parnell and His Party, 1880–1890*, Oxford, 1957, p. 137.
2 Palmer, *The Irish Land League Crisis*, p. 205.
3 O'Brien, op. cit., p. 61.
4 ibid., p. 64.
5 ibid., p. 67.
6 Thomas Corfe, *The Phoenix Park Murders*, London, 1968, p. 176.
7 P. J. Tynan, *The Irish National Invincibles and Their Times*, New York, 1894, p. 272.
8 ibid., p. 444.
9 Corfe, op. cit., p. 142.
10 *Cork Examiner*, 8 June 1886.
11 ibid., 18 July 1886.
12 ibid., 1 July 1886.

13 ibid., 14 July 1886.

14 *Freeman's Journal*, 14 July 1886.

15 Hansard, H.C. Debates, 3rd series, vol. 304, cols. 1195–6.

16 ibid., col. 1330.

17 ibid., col. 1253.

18 ibid., vol. 306, col. 1173.

19 ibid., vol. 305, col. 1707.

20 ibid., cols. 627, 625.

21 O'Brien, op. cit., p. 67.

22 e.g., Leader in *The Times*, 9 June 1886.

23 *I.H.S.*, vol. viii, no. 31, p. 141.

24 Hansard, H.C. Debates, 3rd series, vol. 306, col. 683.

4 The Orange Card

1 Hansard, H.C. Debates, 3rd series, vol. 306, col. 388.

2 ibid., vol. 304, cols. 1081–2.

3 E. R. R. Green, 'The Beginnings of Industrial Revolution', in *Ulster since 1800* (edited T. W. Moody and J. C. Beckett), British Broadcasting Corporation, 1954, p. 37.

4 Parliamentary Papers, 1857–8, vol. xxvi, p. 10.

5 ibid., pp. 292, 270.

6 ibid., p. 180.

7 Quoted by Sir Charles Russell during the second reading of the first Home Rule Bill, Hansard, H.C. Debates, 3rd series, vol. 306, col. 63.

8 ibid.

9 *The Times*, 6 February 1868.

10 ibid., 7 February 1868.

11 ibid., 9 November 1868.

12 ibid., 10 July 1869.

13 ibid., 30 April 1868.

14 ibid., 8 May 1868.

15 ibid., 10 June 1868.

16 ibid., 20 July 1868.

17 ibid., 6 February 1868.

18 ibid., 5 February 1869.

19 ibid., 14 December 1868.

20 ibid., 15 July 1868.

21 Reginald Lucas, *Colonel Saunderson, M.P.*, London, 1908, p. 67.

22 *The Times*, 13 July 1883.

23 Lucas, op. cit., pp. 71, 101.

24 *The Times*, 14 July 1884.

25 Cited *I.H.S.*, vol. xvi, no. 62, September 1968, p. 167, fn. 39.

26 *The Times*, 2 January 1885.
27 W. S. Churchill, *Lord Randolph Churchill*, 2 vols., London, 1906, vol. ii, p. 59.
28 D. C. Savage, 'The Origins of the Ulster Unionist Party' in *I.H.S.*, vol. xii, no. 48, September 1961, pp. 194–5.
29 *The Times*, 15 February 1886.
30 ibid.
31 Cited in *I.H.S.*, vol. xii, no. 47, March 1961, p. 185.
32 *The Times*, 24 February 1886.
33 *I.H.S.*, vol. xii, no. 47, p. 201; *The Times*, 14 May 1886.
34 *The Times*, 12, 14, 25, 28 May 1886.
35 ibid., 8 May 1886.
36 *I.H.S.*, vol. xii, no. 47, p. 208.
37 Hansard, H.C. Debates, 3rd series, vol. 305, col. 659.
38 ibid., col. 1342.
39 ibid., vol. 306, col. 62.
40 ibid., vol. 305, col. 1353.
41 ibid., cols. 1053–4. The committee stage, of course, was never reached.
42 Sir Charles Russell.
43 Figures quoted by John Redmond from Parliamentary Return, Hansard, H.C. Debates, 3rd series, vol. 305, col. 970.
44 Churchill, *Lord Randolph Churchill*, vol. ii, p. 59.
45 Hansard, H.C. Debates, 3rd series, vol. 304, cols. 1385, 1395.
46 ibid., vol. 306, col. 1179.
47 ibid., col. 1180.

5 Parnell's Fall

1 *The Times*, 17 November 1890.
2 F. S. L. Lyons, *John Dillon*, London, 1968, p. 109.

6 Second Home Rule Bill: Orangemen at Play

1 *The Times*, 22 June 1892, quoting a report of the sermon in the *Irish Daily Independent* of 20 June 1892.
2 Hansard, H.C. Debates, 4th series, vol. 10, col. 1864.
3 ibid., 3rd series, vol. 364, cols. 1419–20.
4 ibid., cols. 1315–18.
5 ibid., 4th series, vol. 11, col. 44.
6 ibid., 3rd series, vol. 364, col. 1467.
7 ibid., cols. 1862–3.
8 ibid., 4th series, vol. 15, col. 1742.
9 ibid., 4th series, vol. 15, cols. 1504–6.

10 *The Times*, 10 August 1893, 13 September 1893.
11 Hansard, H.C. Debates, 4th series, vol. 15, cols. 1656–8.
12 *Freeman's Journal*, 12 September 1893.
13 These and subsequent details from *The Times*, 15, 17, 18 June, 1892.
14 ibid., 18 June 1892.
15 Lucas, *Saunderson*, p. 102.
16 ibid., pp. 180–1. Also *The Times*, 31 May 1892.
17 *The Times*, 20 December 1892.
18 ibid., 18 January 1893.
19 Hansard, H.C. Debates, 3rd series, vol. 363, col. 185.
20 ibid., col. 1338.
21 ibid., col. 550. Quotation of a report from the *Derry Sentinel*.
22 *The Times*, 5 April 1893.
23 ibid., 17 March 1893.
24 ibid., 3 March 1893.
25 William Johnston, MP.
26 *The Times*, 10 August 1892.
27 Quoted Lyons, *Dillon*, p. 190.

7 Nationalists at Ease

1 *Freeman's Journal*, 14 September 1893.
2 ibid., 9, 11, 12 September 1893.
3 ibid., 5 July 1895.
4 ibid., 19 July 1895, 25 June 1895, 31 July 1895.
5 Denis Gwynn, *Life of John Redmond*, London, 1932, p. 84.
6 *Freeman's Journal*, 22 July 1895.
7 A speculative but interesting comment on this action of Parnell's may be found in the Epilogue by Owen Dudley Edwards to Desmond Ryan's *Fenian Chief*.
8 *Freeman's Journal*, 7 June 1898.
9 ibid.
10 ibid., 9 June 1898.
11 ibid., 17, 29 June 1898.
12 These and subsequent details of this day from the *Freeman's Journal*, 15 August 1898.

8 Growth of National Consciousness

1 *United Irishman*, 12 October 1901.
2 See M. O'Dubghail, *Insurrection Fires at Eastertide*, Cork, 1966, p. 20; also David Greene, 'Cusack and the G.A.A.', in *The Shaping of Modern Ireland*, edited by Conor Cruise O'Brien, London, 1959.

3 Quoted – from *Representative Irish Tales* – by H. Krans, *W. B. Yeats*, London, 1905, p. 10. See also W. B. Yeats, *Autobiographies*, London, 1926, p. 245.

4 W. B. Yeats, *The Celtic Twilight*, London, 1893, p. 25.

5 ibid., p. 83.

6 ibid., p. 6.

7 ibid.

8 Yeats, *Autobiographies*, p. 267.

9 ibid., p. 268.

10 Myles Dillon, 'Douglas Hyde', in C. C. O'Brien (ed.), *The Shaping of Modern Ireland*, p. 51.

11 See reprint of lecture in *The Revival of Irish Literature*, London, 1894, p. 160.

12 ibid., p. 161.

13 ibid., p. 158.

14 ibid., p. 157.

15 ibid., p. 123.

16 Douglas Hyde, *Beside the Fire*, London, 1890, Preface, p. xlv.

17 *The Revival of Irish Literature*, pp. 137–8.

18 ibid.

19 George A. Birmingham (The Reverend J. O. Hannay), *An Irishman Looks at His World*, London, 1919, pp. 168–9.

20 O'Dubghail, *Insurrection Fires*, p. 27; Sydney Brooks, *The New Ireland*, Dublin, 1907, p. 27.

21 ibid.

22 Quoted in the *United Irishman*, 22 June 1901.

23 D. P. Moran, *The Philosophy of Irish Ireland*, Dublin, 1905, p. 2.

24 ibid., pp. 4, 96, 10, 13–14, 98.

25 ibid., p. 105.

26 Elizabeth Coxhead, *Lady Gregory*, London, 1963, p. 59.

27 ibid., p. 58.

28 Robert Brennan, *Allegiance*, Dublin, 1950, p. 11.

29 Yeats, *Autobiographies*, p. 254.

30 W. B. Yeats, 'The Literary Movement in Ireland', *Ideals in Ireland* (ed. Lady Gregory), London, 1901.

31 Moran, op. cit., pp. 108, 114.

32 Donal McCartney, 'Hyde, D. P. Moran and Irish Ireland', in F. X. Martin (ed.), *Leaders and Men of the Easter Rising: Dublin 1916*, London, 1966, p. 46.

33 Myles Dillon, 'Douglas Hyde', in C. C. O'Brien (ed.), *The Shaping of Modern Ireland*, pp. 55, 57.

34 George Moore, *Hail and Farewell*, London, 1937, p. 256.

35 Sir Horace Plunkett, *Ireland in The New Century*, London, 1905, p. 192.

36 ibid., pp. 228, 288.
37 ibid., pp. 310–11.
38 Lyons, *Dillon*, p. 288.

9 *Arthur Griffith and Sinn Fein*

1 Gregory (ed.), *Ideals in Ireland*, pp. 65–8.
2 Louis Marcus, 'The G.A.A. and the Castle', *Irish Independent*, 9–10 July 1964, cited by O'Dubhghail, *Insurrection Fires*, p. 20.
3 O'Brien and Ryan (eds.), *Devoy's Post Bag*, vol. ii, p. 347.
4 ibid., pp. 340–1.
5 In 1900. George Lyons, *Some Recollections of Griffith and His Times*, Dublin, 1923, pp. 9, 44.
6 *United Irishman*, 11 March 1899; 1 April 1899.
7 ibid., 3 June 1899.
8 ibid., 25 March 1899; 8 April 1899; 1 April 1899; 3 June 1899: 30 September 1899; 18 August 1900; 22 September 1900.
9 See letter from George A. Lyons, *United Irishman*, 23 September 1899.
10 *United Irishman*, 8 April 1899.
11 ibid., 30 September 1899.
12 ibid., 7 October 1899.
13 ibid., 14 October 1899; 30 December 1899.
14 ibid., 14 October 1899.
15 ibid., 18 November 1899.
16 ibid., 23 December 1899; Nora Connolly, *Portrait of a Rebel Father*, London and Dublin, 1935, p. 60.
17 George Lyons, op. cit., p. 24.
18 L. Paul-Dubois, *Contemporary Ireland*, London, 1908, p. 178.
19 *United Irishman*, 9 December 1899.
20 ibid., 16 March 1901.
21 ibid., 22 December 1900.
22 ibid., 16 March 1901.
23 ibid., 7 October 1899; 9 December 1899.
24 ibid., 1 September 1900; 31 January 1903.
25 ibid., 7 April 1900.
26 ibid., 24 February 1900.
27 ibid., 3 March 1900.
28 ibid., 6 October 1900.
29 ibid.
30 ibid., 17 November 1900.
31 ibid.
32 ibid., 6 April 1901.
33 ibid., 1 November 1902.

34 ibid., 18 May 1901.
35 ibid., 19 October 1901.
36 Circulation figures given in *United Irishman*.
37 ibid., 9 March 1901.
38 ibid., 30 March 1901.
39 Padraic Colum, *Arthur Griffith*, Dublin, 1959, p. 3.
40 *United Irishman*, 14 September 1901.
41 ibid., 15 February 1902.
42 ibid.
43 ibid., 18 January 1902.
44 ibid., 10 May 1902.
45 ibid., 1 November 1902.
46 ibid.
47 ibid., 28 February 1903.
48 ibid., 18 April 1903.
49 ibid., 6 June 1903.
50 Denis Gwynn, *Edward Martyn and the Irish Revival*, London, 1930, p. 63.
51 *Cork Examiner*, 3 August 1903. See also Horgan, *Parnell to Pearse*, p. 102, confirming this.
52 *United Irishman*, 8 August 1903.
53 ibid., 2 July 1904.
54 ibid.
55 ibid., 10 September 1904.
56 For other reactions to articles see ibid., 23 July 1904.
57 ibid., 18 February 1905.
58 George A. Birmingham, *An Irishman Looks at His World*, p. 43.
59 James Stephens, 'In the Morning of His Triumph', in *Arthur Griffith, Michael Collins, A Memorial Album*, Dublin, 1922.
60 *United Irishman*, 28 January, 4, 11 February 1905.
61 ibid., 21 January 1905.
62 ibid., 1 April 1905; facsimile of letter in Griffith's handwriting in W. G. Fitzgerald (ed.), *The Voice of Ireland*, Manchester, 1924. For earlier uses of the words Sinn Fein in Irish history see above pages of this book.
63 Article by Mary Butler in Fitzgerald (ed.), op. cit.
64 P. S. O'Hegarty, *The Victory of Sinn Fein*, Dublin, 1924, p. 30.
65 *Sinn Fein*, 17 October 1906.
66 *Leader*, 8 June 1907.
67 Denis Gwynn, *Life of John Redmond*, London, 1932, p. 115.
68 *Freeman's Journal*, 8 May 1907.
69 ibid.
70 ibid., 9 May 1907.
71 ibid., 15 May 1907.

72 ibid., 18 May 1907.
73 Lyons, *Dillon*, p. 288.
74 ibid., p. 289.
75 O'Brien and Ryan (eds.), *Devoy's Post Bag*, vol. ii, p. 359. He lived until 1965.
76 T. M. Healy, *Letters and Leaders of My Day*, 2 vols., London, 1928, vol. ii, p. 482; *Sinn Fein*, 29 February 1908.
77 *Sinn Fein*, 8 October 1910; 14 October 1911; 18 February 1911.
78 ibid., 27 November 1912.
79 'Standing down' and 'cessation of activity' were Griffith's own terms – see *Sinn Fein*, 7 October 1911.
80 Sean O'Faolain, *Constance Markievicz*, London, 1934, p. 29.
81 Jacqueline van Voris, *Constance de Markievicz*, Massachusetts, 1967, pp. 56, 51.
82 ibid., p. 58.
83 ibid.
84 *Sinn Fein*, 5 September 1908.
85 ibid., 4 September 1909.
86 See his poem : *On a Political Prisoner*.
87 Casement to Alice Stopford Green, 24 April 1904, N.L.I.
88 *United Irishman*, 25 February 1905.
89 Casement to Bulmer Hobson, 10 September 1905, N.L.I.
90 Casement to Alice Stopford Green, 8 September 1906, N.L.I.
91 Casement to Alice Stopford Green, 21 September 1906, N.L.I.
92 Casement to Bulmer Hobson, 10 August 1905, N.L.I.
93 Casement to Bulmer Hobson, 13 August 1907, N.L.I.
94 Bulmer Hobson, *Ireland Yesterday and Tomorrow*, Tralee, 1968, p. 35.
95 ibid., p. 8.
96 O'Brien and Ryan (eds.), *Devoy's Post Bag*, vol. ii, pp. 347, 350.
97 ibid., p. 350.
98 *Sinn Fein*, 2 February 1907.
99 ibid., 30 March, 1907.
100 ibid., 14 March 1908. *Sinn Fein*, 18 March 1908.
101 *Sinn Fein*, 18 March 1908.
102 ibid., 15 February 1908.
103 O'Brien and Ryan (eds.), op. cit., vol. ii, p. 383.
104 ibid., p. 390.

10 Asquith and the Third Home Rule Bill

1 For full details of these transactions see H. W. Macready, 'Home Rule and the Liberal Party 1899–1908', in *I.H.S.*, vol. xii, no. 52, September 1963, pp. 316–48.

2 ibid., p. 322.

3 ibid., p. 323.

4 ibid., p. 328.

5 ibid., p. 324.

6 ibid., p. 333.

7 ibid., pp. 333–4.

8 ibid., p. 342.

9 For some details of attempts, before the introduction of the third Home Rule Bill, to explore the possibility of a compromise with the Conservatives which might release the Liberals from their dependence on the Irish see Montgomery Hyde, *Carson* (London, 1953), pp. 277–80, and Roy Jenkins, *Asquith* (London, 1964), pp. 246–7. The attempts were conducted by Lloyd George.

10 Denis Gwynn, *Life of John Redmond*, London, 1932, p. 169.

11 Cited by F. S. L. Lyons 'The Irish Unionist Party and the devolution crisis of 1904–5', in *I.H.S.*, vol. vi, no. 21, March 1948, p. 10.

12 ibid., p. 13.

13 *Freeman's Journal*, 30 November 1910.

14 Hyde, *Carson*, pp. 158, 209.

15 ibid., p. 329.

16 ibid., p. 14.

17 ibid., p. 89.

18 ibid., p. 329.

19 ibid., p. 157.

20 Hansard, H.C. Debates, 5th series, vol. xxi, col. 1157.

21 Hyde, op. cit., p. 283.

22 ibid., p. 286.

23 ibid., p. 291.

24 A. T. Q. Stewart, *The Ulster Crisis*, London, 1967, p. 69.

25 Hyde, op. cit., pp. 310–11.

26 ibid.

27 *Belfast Evening Telegraph*, 9 April 1912.

28 ibid., 19 April 1912.

29 ibid., 9 April 1912.

30 Sir J. B. Lonsdale, MP for Mid Armagh and Member of the Ulster Unionist Council, Hansard, 5th series, vol. xxi, col. 89.

31 Ian Malcolm, MP for Croydon, Hansard, ibid., col. 1082.

32 Hyde, op. cit., p. 316.

33 ibid., p. 311.

34 *Belfast Evening Telegraph*, 10 April 1912.

35 Robert Blake, *The Unknown Prime Minister*, London, 1955, p. 130.

36 ibid., p. 133.

37 Hansard, H.C. Debates, 5th series, vol. 36, col. 1437.

38 ibid., vol. 21, cols. 1103–6.
39 ibid., cols. 1156–7.
40 ibid., col. 1117.
41 ibid., cols. 1134, 1145.
42 ibid., col. 1424.
43 ibid., col. 41.
44 *Freeman's Journal*, 12 April 1912.
45 ibid., 24 April 1912.
46 Hansard, H.C. Debates, 5th series, vol. 22, col. 91; vol. 21, col. 1161.
47 See Macdonald's speech on Parliament Bill, Hansard, H.C. Debates, 5th series, vol. 25, col. 1380.
48 Lecky, *History of Ireland in the Eighteenth Century*, vol. ii, p. 182.
49 Hansard, H.C. Debates, 5th series, vol. 29, cols. 826–7 (7 August 1911).
50 ibid., vol. 37, col. 2162; see also vol. 39, col. 771.
51 For full details of the ceremony see Stewart, *Ulster Crisis*, pp. 61–6.
52 *Daily News*, quoted in *Freeman's Journal*, 21 December 1910.
53 Hansard, H.C. Debates, 5th series, vol. 46, col. 468.
54 ibid., vol. 46, col. 478.
55 ibid., cols. 2125–6. Author's italics.
56 ibid., col. 2150.
57 ibid., col. 2191.

11 Ulster Volunteers

1 Stewart, *Ulster Crisis*, p. 71.
2 Hansard, H.C. Debates, 5th series, vol. 46, cols. 2324–5.
3 Hyde, *Carson*, p. 339.
4 *Freeman's Journal*, 5 June 1913.
5 Gwynn, *Redmond*, p. 228.
6 For details see Blake, *The Unknown Prime Minister*, pp. 161–7.
7 Gwynn, op. cit., p. 232.
8 ibid., p. 231.
9 ibid., pp. 234–6.
10 ibid.
11 Blake, op. cit., pp. 161–2.
12 ibid., pp. 164–5.
13 Roy Jenkins, *Asquith*, p. 292.
14 ibid., p. 290.
15 Gwynn, op. cit., pp. 234–6.
16 ibid., pp. 237–8.
17 ibid., p. 250.

18 ibid., pp. 250–1.
19 ibid., pp. 267–73.

12 *The Liberal Nerve Begins to Fail*

1 Stewart, *Ulster Crisis*, pp. 119–20.
2 ibid., pp. 130–40. See also A. M. Gollin, *Pro-Consul in Politics*, London, 1964.
3 ibid., pp. 126–7.
4 *The Times*, 16 March 1914.
5 Two excellent authoritative accounts of these events are to be found in Sir James Fergusson, *The Curragh Incident* (London, 1964) and A. P. Ryan, *Mutiny at the Curragh* (London, 1956). The former, written by the son of one of the principal participants, is the more detailed, and, like the latter, admirably objective.
6 Fergusson, op. cit., p. 67.
7 ibid.
8 ibid., pp. 56, 69.
9 ibid., pp. 84, 88.
10 ibid., pp. 106–13.
11 ibid., pp. 145–6.
12 ibid., pp. 150–51.
13 ibid., pp. 125, 146–7, 153.
14 ibid., p. 152.
15 Lyons, *Dillon*, p. 335.
16 Emmet Larkin, *James Larkin*, London, 1968, pp. 56–7.
17 Quoted from *Sinn Fein*, 28 November 1908, in Larkin, op. cit., p. 57.
18 *Report ... Into the Housing Conditions of the Working Classes in Dublin*, Parliamentary Papers, 1914, vol. xix, p. 66.
19 ibid., p. 68.
20 ibid., pp. 68–9.
21 ibid., p. 70.
22 ibid., p. 69.
23 *Report on Local Government*, Parliamentary Papers, 1914, vol. xxxix, p. 628.
24 Parliamentary Papers, 1914, xix, p. 79, pp. 76–9.
25 C. Desmond Greaves, *The Life and Times of James Connolly*, London, 1961, pp. 14–20.
26 ibid.
27 ibid., p. 69.
28 *Irish Worker*, 11 May 1912. Quoted Larkin, op. cit., p. 74. For circulation figures see ibid., p. 71.

29 *Report of the Dublin Disturbances Commission,* Parliamentary Papers, 1914, vol. xviii, p. 647.
30 ibid., p. 645.
31 ibid., p. 647.
32 ibid., pp. 651–2.
33 ibid.
34 Larkin, op. cit., p. 53.
35 ibid., p. 160.
36 ibid., p. 155.
37 ibid., p. 162.

13 Volunteers and Home Rule

1 *Sinn Fein,* 21 February 1914.
2 Gwynn, *Redmond,* p. 307.
3 *Westmeath Independent,* 18 October 1913.
4 ibid.
5 *Freeman's Journal,* 26 September 1914; *Westmeath Independent,* 25 October 1913.
6 *Westmeath Independent,* 13 December 1913.
7 ibid., 18 October 1913.
8 Martin, *The Irish Volunteers,* p. 71.
9 ibid., p. 59.
10 ibid., pp. 33–40.
11 ibid.
12 ibid., pp. 119–20.
13 Horgan, *Parnell to Pearse,* p. 229.
14 ibid., pp. 228–9.
15 Lyons, *Dillon,* p. 350.
16 *Freeman's Journal,* 27 March 1914.
   (eds.), *Devoy's Post Bag,* vol. ii, pp. 456, 463, N.L.I.
17 Casement to Alice Stopford Green, 20 June 1914, Ryan and O'Brien (eds.), *Devoy's Post Bag,* vol. ii, pp. 456, 463, N.L.I.
18 Hobson to Casement, 30 June 1914, N.L.I.
19 Clarke to Devoy, 7 July 1914, N.L.I.
20 O'Brien and Ryan (eds.), op. cit., p. 456.
21 Hobson to Casement, 14 July 1914.
22 Casement to Alice Stopford Green, 8 September 1906, N.L.I.
23 *Irish Freedom,* December 1910.
24 ibid., August 1911.
25 ibid., January 1911.
26 Statements by Ernest Blythe and Cathal O'Shannon respectively, *Irish Freedom,* July 1912.
27 ibid., June 1913.

28 ibid., October 1913.

29 O'Brien and Ryan (eds.), op. cit., vol. ii, pp. 403–4.

30 Martin, op. cit., p. 15.

31 Hobson, *Ireland Yesterday and Tomorrow*, p. 43.

32 ibid., pp. 37–9; Martin, op. cit., p. 17.

33 Van Voris, *Constance Markievicz*, p. 82.

34 *Freeman's Journal*, 26 November 1913.

35 P. H. Pearse, *Political Writings and Speeches*, Dublin 1952, pp. 91–9.

36 O'Brien and Ryan (eds.), op. cit., pp. 425, 450, 466.

37 ibid., pp. 42–5.

38 ibid., p. 427.

39 ibid., p. 445.

40 *Irish Freedom*, July 1913.

41 Darrell Figgis, *Recollections of the Irish War*, London, 1927, pp. 10–11.

42 Martin, op. cit., p. 32. Gwynn, *Redmond*, p. 311.

43 See Bulmer Hobson's account in Martin, op. cit., pp. 32–3.

44 See A. S. Green, *Irish Nationality*, London, 1912.

45 Casement to Mrs A. S. Green, 24 April 1904, N.L.I.

46 Casement to Mrs A. S. Green, 24 August 1906, N.L.I.

47 Figgis, op. cit., p. 15.

48 ibid., p. 18.

49 F. X. Martin, *The Howth Gun-Running* (Dublin, 1964), p. 38. Figgis, *Recollections*, pp. 22–37.

50 Martin, *Howth Gun-Running*, p. 129.

51 Martin, *Howth Gun-Running*, pp. 79–80 (extract from Mary Spring Rice's diary).

52 ibid., pp. 128–63.

53 ibid., top photograph facing p. 150.

54 *Report of the Royal Commission on the circumstances connected with the landing of arms at Howth on 26th July 1914*, Parliamentary Papers, 1914–16, xxiv, p. 805. '... The proceedings of the police and military were tainted by fundamental illegality.'

55 These and other details of this event from *Royal Commission*, Parliamentary Papers, 1914–16, vol. xxiv, pp. 824–89 (minutes of evidence).

56 ibid., p. 892.

14 Volunteers and the European War

1 Gwynn, *Redmond*, p. 330.

2 Jenkins, *Asquith*, p. 321.

3 ibid., p. 323.

4 Gwynn, op. cit., p. 354.

5 *Freeman's Journal*, 1 August 1914.

6 Gwynn, op. cit., p. 355.

7 ibid., p. 356.

8 ibid., p. 353.

9 ibid., p. 357.

10 ibid., p. 353.

11 T. P. O'Connor to Dillon, quoted Lyons, *Dillon*, p. 357.

12 *Freeman's Journal*, 2 September 1914.

13 ibid., 12 September 1914.

14 ibid., 15 September 1914.

15 Gwynn, op. cit., p. 383; *Freeman's Journal*, 19 September 1914.

16 *Freeman's Journal*, 22 September 1914; *Irish Independent*, 23 September 1914.

17 *Freeman's Journal*, 19 September 1914.

18 ibid.

19 Quoted Gwynn, op. cit., pp. 380–81.

20 ibid., p. 385.

21 *Freeman's Journal*, 21 September 1914.

22 Breandán Mac Giolla Choille, *Intelligence Notes 1913–16*, Dublin, 1966, p. 175.

23 *Freeman's Journal*, 26 September 1914.

24 ibid.

25 *National Volunteer*, 24 October 1914.

26 ibid., 7 November 1914.

27 *Freeman's Journal*, 28, 29 September 1914; 7, 16, 17 October 1914.

28 ibid., 29 September 1914.

29 ibid., 1 October 1914.

30 ibid., 5 October 1914.

31 ibid.

32 ibid.

33 ibid., 12 October 1914.

34 ibid.

35 ibid.

36 ibid., 15 October 1914.

37 ibid., 18 October 1914.

38 ibid., 19 October 1914.

39 ibid.

40 See *Freeman's Journal* and *Irish Independent*, September 1914, *passim*.

41 *Freeman's Journal*, 19 November 1914.

42 ibid., 21 December 1914; *Irish Independent*, 20 December 1914. The former gives the numbers at this meeting as 14,000, the latter as upward of 12,000. Police reports placed them lower at about 5,000, Mac Giolla Choille (ed.), *Intelligence Notes*, p. 80.

43 *Freeman's Journal*, 18 March 1915.

44 ibid.

45 ibid., 26 August 1915.

46 ibid., 23 August 1915.

47 Gwynn, *Redmond*, pp. 397, 404–5, 407.

48 Quoted Gwynn, op. cit., p. 390.

49 ibid., p. 401. Also quoted by John Dillon, *Freeman's Journal*, 26 October 1914.

50 *Freeman's Journal*, 16 October 1915.

51 ibid., 29 October 1915.

52 ibid., 8 March 1915.

53 ibid., 4 April 1915.

54 ibid., 2 July 1915.

55 ibid., 4 August 1915.

56 ibid., 18 August 1915.

57 ibid.

58 Gwynn, op. cit., p. 274.

59 Quoted *Freeman's Journal*, 4 June 1915.

60 Gwynn, op. cit., pp. 431–2.

61 *Freeman's Journal*, 18 August 1915.

62 ibid., 22 December 1915.

63 Mac Giolla Choille (ed.), *Intelligence Notes*, p. 149.

15 The 'Sinn Fein' Volunteers

1 O'Hegarty, *Victory of Sinn Fein*, p. 18. The strength of the IRB in January 1914 was approximately 2,000. See Diarmuid Lynch, *The I.R.B. and the 1916 Rising*, Cork, 1957, p. 24.

2 See F. X. Martin, 'Eoin Macneill on the 1916 Rising', *I.H.S.*, vol. xii, March 1961, p. 226, particularly pp. 234–40.

3 Pearse, *Political Writings*, p. 91.

4 ibid., p. 216.

5 Martin in *I.H.S.*, vol. xii, pp. 236ff.

6 Lynch, op. cit., pp. 25, 102, 113, 131.

7 *Irish Volunteer*, 15 October 1914.

8 Martin, *Irish Volunteers*, p. 169.

9 ibid., pp. 170ff.

10 *Eire*, 17 November 1914.

11 *Irish Volunteer*, 20 March 1915; 10 July 1915.

12 *Freeman's Journal*, 5 December 1914.

13 Mac Giolla Choille (ed.), *Intelligence Notes*, p. 147.

14 *Freeman's Journal*, 2 August 1915; *National Volunteer*, 14 August 1915; *Irish Volunteer*, 7 August 1915.

15 Pearse, op. cit., pp. 133–7. Rossa: *Freeman's Journal*, 31 July 1915.

16 Leon O'Broin, *Dublin Castle and the 1916 Rising*, Dublin, 1966, p. 53.
17 Mac Giolla Choille (ed.), op. cit., p. 176.
18 ibid., p. 176. Also *Freeman's Journal*, 2 July 1915.
19 Official figures quoted in *Freeman's Journal*, 12 January 1916; see also *Freeman's Journal*, 11 May 1915.
20 ibid., 14 October 1915.
21 Mac Giolla Choille (ed.), op. cit., p. 224.
22 O'Broin, *Dublin Castle*, p. 53.
23 Mac Giolla Choille (ed.), op. cit., p. 224.
24 Dorothy Macardle, *The Irish Republic*, Dublin, 1951, p. 138; *Freeman's Journal*, November 1915.
25 *Documents Relative to the Sinn Fein Movement* (Cd 1108), 1921; Sir William James, *The Eyes of the Navy*, London, 1955, p. 43.

16 Casement in Germany

1 McGarrity Papers.
2 Devoy, *Recollections*, p. 411.
3 Casement's own word. See C. E. Curry (ed.), *Sir Roger Casement's Diaries*, Munich, 1922, p. 25.
4 Casement to Devoy, 21 July 1914. Devoy, *Recollections*, p. 411.
5 *Documents Relative to the Sinn Fein Movement*, 1921.
6 Devoy, op. cit., p. 417.
7 McGarrity Papers, N.L.I.
8 ibid.
9 Moloney Papers, N.L.I.
10 ibid.
11 Devoy, op. cit., p. 419.
12 See Desmond Ryan, *The Rising*, p. 18, footnote, and Casement's Brief to his Counsel, Casement microfilm (1) and Maloney Papers (Box 182), N.L.I.
13 Casement to McGarrity from Berlin, 21 November 1914, McGarrity Papers, N.L.I.
14 Herbert O. Mackey, *The Life and Times of Roger Casement*, Dublin, 1954, pp. 77–8.
15 McGarrity to Casement, 9 November 1915, McGarrity Papers, N.L.I.
16 See Memorandum by Patrick McCartan quoted in *Documents Relative to the Sinn Fein Movement* (C1108), 1921.
17 Casement to McGarrity, 21 November 1914, McGarrity Papers, N.L.I.
18 Fürst von Leiningen. Casement's Brief to Counsel, Casement microfilm (i) and Maloney Papers, N.L.I.
19 For facsimile copy of this treaty in Casement's handwriting see Denis Gwynn, *The Life and Death of Roger Casement*, London, 1930.

20 Brief to Counsel, N.L.I.
21 Letter to McGarrity, 23 March 1915.
22 See René MacColl, *Roger Casement*, London, 1956, p. 268.
23 Cited MacColl, op. cit., p. 190.
24 Moloney Papers, N.L.I.

17 *The Dublin Rising, 1916*

1 Gwynn, *Redmond*, p. 471.
2 *Freeman's Journal*, 23 April 1916.
3 For a full page facsimile of the proclamation see Macardle, *Irish Republic*, or Max Caulfield, *The Easter Rebellion*, London, 1964.
4 Sir John Maxwell's Dispatch. *Sinn Fein Rebellion Handbook*, Dublin, 1916, p. 93.
5 E. R. Dodds (ed.), *Journal and Letters of Stephen MacKenna*, London, 1936, p. 51.
6 *Rebellion Handbook*, pp. 29–30. Caulfield, *Easter Rebellion*, p. 70–4.
7 *Rebellion Handbook*, pp. 15, 17. Caulfield, *Easter Rebellion*, p. 2.
8 *Rebellion Handbook*, p. 93.
9 Desmond Fitzgerald, *The Memoirs of Desmond Fitzgerald*, London, 1968, pp. 140–1.
10 Patrick Pearse, *The Singer*, Dublin, 1915.
11 Patrick Pearse, *Political Writings*, p. 216.
12 Ryan (ed.), *Labour and Easter Week*, p. 21.
13 Mac Giolla Choille (ed.), *Intelligence Notes*, p. 176.
14 *Rebellion Handbook*, p. 154.
15 Robert Brennan, *Allegiance*, Dublin, 1950, p. 2.
16 Cited F. X. Martin, '1916 – Myth, Fact and Mystery', in *Studia Hibernica*, 1968, p. 98.
17 *Freeman's Journal*, 24 March 1916.
18 *Rebellion Handbook*, p. 193.
19 Roger McHugh, *Dublin 1916*, Dublin, 1966, pp. 81, 87.
20 F. X. Martin (ed.), *I.H.S.*, vol. xix, pp. 239–40.
21 Ryan, *Labour and Easter Week*, Dublin, 1949.
22 F. X. Martin (ed.), *I.H.S.*, vol. xii, p. 245.
23 Cited in Ryan (ed.), *Labour and Easter Week*, p. 13.
24 F. X. Martin (ed.), *I.H.S.*, vol. xii, p. 246.
25 ibid., p. 247.
26 ibid., p. 248.
27 ibid.
28 Eoin MacNeill, *Memoirs*, Dublin, 1935, p. 115.
29 Casement to McGarrity, 5 May 1915, 10 May 1915, McGarrity Papers, N.L.I.

30 ibid., 5 May 1915.
31 ibid., 20 June 1915.
32 ibid.
33 Casement's Brief to Counsel, 20 June 1915, N.L.I.
34 Casement to McGarrity, 30 June 1915, McGarrity Papers, N.L.I.
35 Karl Spindler, *The Mystery of the Casement Ship*.
36 Casement to McGarrity, 20 December 1915, McGarrity Papers (microfilm), N.L.I.
37 Diary of Casement entitled *The Last Page*, N.L.I. microfilm.
38 ibid.
39 Devoy, *Recollections*, p. 458.
40 *Documents Relative to the Sinn Fein Movement*, H.M.S.O. (Cmd. 1108), p. 9.
41 Casement, *The Last Page*, N.L.I. microfilm.
42 ibid.
43 ibid.
44 Devoy to German General Staff, 16 February 1916, McGarrity Papers, N.L.I.
45 MacColl, *Casement*, p. 212.
46 See German documents cited from microfilm at St Anthony's College, Oxford, by MacColl, op. cit., p. 199.
47 Admiral Sir William James, *The Eyes of the Navy*, London, 1955, pp. 43ff.
48 For some evidence of informers see Leon O'Broin, *Dublin Castle and the 1916 Rising*, Dublin, 1966, p. 81; and Mac Goilla Choille, *Intelligence Notes*, p. 278.
49 O'Broin, op. cit., p. 40.
50 ibid., p. 54.
51 ibid.
52 ibid., p. 55.
53 Mac Goilla Choille, op. cit., p. 278.
54 O'Broin, op. cit., p. 73.
55 ibid., p. 62.
56 ibid., p. 75.
57 ibid.
58 ibid., p. 72.
59 ibid., p. 70–1.
60 ibid., p. 74.
61 ibid., p. 70.
62 ibid., p. 73.
63 ibid., p. 85.
64 ibid., p. 87.
65 ibid., p. 88.

66 Stephens, *Insurrection in Dublin*, p. 18.
67 Rebellion Handbook, pp. 109–12; *Freeman's Journal*, 19 June 1916.
68 *Rebellion Handbook*, pp. 102–8.
69 ibid., p. 104.
70 ibid., p. 29.
71 Martin, '1916 – Myth, Fact and Mystery', in *Studia Hibernica*, no. 7, p. 108.
72 Stephens, op. cit., pp. 35–6.
73 ibid., p. 39.
74 McHugh, *Dublin 1916*, p. 97.
75 Max Caulfield, *Easter Rebellion*, p. 223.
76 ibid., p. 332.
77 ibid., p. 344.
78 Cited Greaves, *Connolly*, p. 319.
79 *Capuchin Annual*, 1966, pp. 232, 234.
80 Lynch, *I.R.B. and the 1916 Rising*, p. 143.
81 *Rebellion Handbook*, pp. 59–61. The death figure is a compilation of the cemetery interments resulting from the rebellion.
82 ibid., pp. 52–8.
83 ibid., pp. 112–15; also p. 57.
84 Brennan, *Rebellion Handbook*, pp. 178–9; Wells and Marlowe, *A History of the Easter Rebellion*, pp. 184–7; but see also Brennan, *Allegiance*, pp. 72–3.
85 Sean MacEntee, *Episode at Easter*, Dublin, 1966, pp. 107–35.
86 *Capuchin Annual*, 1966, pp. 353–68.
87 ibid., pp. 376–80.
88 ibid., pp. 382–4.
89 *Rebellion Handbook*, pp. 175, *Capuchin Annual*, 1966, pp. 324–6.

18 Executions and Negotiations

1 O'Broin, *Dublin Castle*, p. 121.
2 Gwynn, *Redmond*, p. 475.
3 ibid., pp. 475–6.
4 ibid., p. 480.
5 'Personal Recollections of the late Father Aloysius, O.F.M.', *Capuchin Annual*, 1966, p. 288.
6 O'Broin, op. cit., p. 130.
7 ibid., p. 139.
8 *Capuchin Annual*, 1966, pp. 304–5.
9 Martin, *Studia Hibernica*, no. 7, p. 10.
10 Lynch, *The I.R.B. and the 1916 Rising*, p. 25.
11 Gwynn, op. cit., p. 483.

12 ibid., p. 483.
13 *Rebellion Handbook*, p. 269.
14 T. M. Healy, *Letters and Leaders of My Day*, vol. ii, p. 563.
15 Lyons, *Dillon*, p. 379.
16 Countess of Fingall, *Seventy Years Young*, London, 1937, p. 375.
17 O'Broin, *Dublin Castle*, p. 141.
18 *Sinn Fein Rebellion Handbook*, p. 99.
19 O'Broin, op. cit., p. 132.
20 Gwynn, op. cit., p. 488.
21 ibid., p. 485.
22 *Capuchin Annual*, 1966, p. 306.
23 O'Broin, op. cit., p. 133.
24 Hansard, H.C. Debates, 5th series, vol. 82, cols. 935–51.
25 *Capuchin Annual*, 1966, p. 290; Greaves, *Connolly*, p. 34.
26 *Capuchin Annual*, 1966, p. 302.
27 O'Broin, op. cit., p. 136. (A letter which Maxwell did not allow to be sent.)
28 *Capuchin Annual*, 1966, p. 306.
29 ibid., p. 301.
30 Gwynn, op. cit., pp. 491, 502.
31 *Rebellion Handbook*, pp. 69, 87–91.
32 ibid., p. 182.
33 Gwynn, op. cit., p. 493.
34 Roy Jenkins, *Asquith*, p. 147.
35 Alison Phillips, *The Revolution in Ireland*, London, 1920, p. 108.
36 Gwynn, op. cit., p. 499.
37 Jenkins, op. cit., p. 448 (paperback).
38 Gwynn, op. cit., pp. 497–9.
39 ibid., pp. 500–501.
40 ibid.
41 ibid., p. 501.
42 Lyons, *Dillon*, p. 384.
43 ibid.
44 ibid., p. 385.
45 Gwynn, op. cit., p. 506.
46 For full headings of the draft proposals see Gwynn, op. cit., pp. 517–18.
47 Hyde, *Carson*, p. 403.
48 Lyons, op. cit., p. 396.
49 ibid., p. 401.
50 Hansard, H.C. Debates, 5th series, vol. 84, col. 1434.
51 Denis Gwynn, *The Life and Death of Roger Casement*, pp. 16–17.
52 René MacColl, *Roger Casement*, p. 296.
53 ibid., p. 293.

54 Cited Lyons, op. cit., p. 394.
55 ibid., p. 403.

PART FIVE

OURSELVES ALONE

1 Rebellion to de Valera's Election at Clare (July 1917)

1 *Irish Times*, 27 June 1916.
2 *Irish Independent*, 6 July 1916.
3 ibid., 14 August 1916.
4 ibid., 7 October 1916.
5 ibid.
6 ibid., 11 November 1916.
7 Margery Forester, *Michael Collins: The Lost Leader*, London, 1971, p. 61.
8 Rex Taylor, *Michael Collins*, London, 1958, pp. 77–8.
9 The O'Mahony, *Irish Independent*, 19 January 1917; 1 February 1917.
10 *Irish Independent*, 3 February 1917.
11 ibid., 31 January 1917.
12 ibid.
13 ibid., 6 February 1917.
14 Taylor, op. cit., p. 82.
15 *Irish Independent*, 10 April 1917.
16 Beaslai, *Collins*, vol. i, p. 152.
17 Sean O Luing, *I Die In A Good Cause: a study of Thomas Ashe*, Dublin, 1970, p. 122.
18 *Irish Independent*, 8 May 1917.
19 Gwynn, *Redmond*, pp. 543–5.
20 *Irish Independent*, 15 June 1917.
21 See, particularly for the return of Countess Markievicz, the contemporary news film included in Gael Linn's film *Mise Eire*, directed by George Morrison.
22 *Irish Independent*, 23 June 1917.
23 ibid., 25 June 1917.
24 ibid.
25 ibid., 9 July 1917.
26 ibid.
27 *Daily Mail*, 9 October 1917.
28 *Irish Independent*, 12 July 1917.

29 ibid.
30 ibid., 16 July 1917.
31 ibid.

2 *The New Sinn Fein (July 1917–April 1918)*

1 *Irish Independent*, 16 July 1917.
2 ibid., 14 July 1917.
3 ibid., 12 July 1917.
4 ibid., 17 July 1917.
5 ibid., 5 September 1917.
6 Sean O Luing, *I Die In A Good Cause*, p. 124.
7 *Irish Times*, 2 October 1917; *Daily Mail*, 15 October 1917.
8 *Irish Independent*, 25 September 1917.
9 All details of these proceedings from the inquest on Thomas Ashe reported in the *Irish Independent*, 28 September 1917–2 November 1917.
10 *Irish Independent*, 30 October 1917.
11 ibid., 9 October 1917.
12 ibid., 2 November 1917.
13 ibid., 1 October 1917; Beaslai, *Collins*, vol. i, p. 166.
14 *Irish Independent*, 1 October 1917.
15 ibid.
16 ibid., 26 October 1917.
17 ibid.
18 ibid.
19 ibid., 29 October 1917.
20 ibid., 26 November 1917.
21 ibid., 3 December 1917.
22 Ernie O'Malley, *On Another Man's Wound*, London, 1936, p. 57.
23 Dan Breen, *My Fight for Irish Freedom*, Dublin, 1950, pp. 6–10.
24 *Irish Independent*, 26 November 1917.
25 ibid.
26 ibid., 10 December 1917.
27 ibid., 12 December 1917.
28 ibid., 15 January 1918.
29 ibid., 25 January 1918.
30 ibid., 23 February 1918.
31 ibid., 26, 28 February; 4, 15, 19 March 1918.
32 ibid., 2 March 1918.
33 ibid., 9 March 1918.
34 Gwynn, *Redmond*, p. 579.
35 ibid., p. 568.
36 *Irish Independent*, 2 February 1919.

37 ibid., 20 March 1918.
38 ibid., 22 March 1918.
39 Election and post-election details, ibid., 16, 23, 24, 26 March 1918.

3 Conscription Crisis to General Election (*December 1918*)

1 *Irish Independent*, 10 April 1918.
2 ibid.
3 ibid., 19 April 1918.
4 ibid.
5 Richard Laide and John Browne.
6 Breen, *My Fight for Irish Freedom*, pp. 15–16.
7 Florence O'Donoghue, *No Other Law*, Dublin, 1954, pp. 8, 22–3.
8 *Manchester Guardian*, 13 May 1918.
9 Taylor, *Collins*, p. 93.
10 See, e.g., *Irish Independent*, 9, 14 December 1918.
11 ibid., 20 August 1918.
12 ibid., 29 August 1918.
13 David Hogan (Frank Gallagher), *The Four Glorious Years*, Dublin, 1953, pp. 34–8.
14 *Irish Independent*, 5 October 1918.
15 ibid., 31 October 1918.
16 ibid., 28 December 1918.
17 *Irish Times*, 28 December 1918.
18 *Irish Independent*, 14 November 1918.
19 ibid., 12 November 1919.
20 The total Irish electorate in December 1918, as given by *The Times*, was 1,937,245. There were, in the uncontested seats, 474,778 electors. This leaves a possible electorate of 1,462,467. Of these, 1,071,086 voted, making a percentage of seventy-three per cent (*The Times*, 4 January 1919 and 7 January 1919). For the abstention theory see *The Times*, 17 January 1919; also W. Alison Phillips, *The Revolution in Ireland*, London, 1923, pp. 152–3 and Edgar Holt, *Protest in Arms*, London, 1960, p. 168. Holt for some reason gives the poll in 1918 as sixty-nine per cent. A. J. P. Taylor, *English History 1914–1945*, Oxford, 1965, even less explicably gives it as sixty per cent (p. 154n.).
21 *The Times*, 4 January 1919.
22 P. S. O'Hegarty, *The Victory of Sinn Fein*, Dublin, 1924, p. 32.
23 *Irish Independent*, 31 December 1918.

4 Sinn Fein in a Vacuum (*January–May 1919*)

1 Cited in *Irish Independent*, 4 January 1919.
2 ibid., 7 January 1919.

3 O'Donoghue, *No Other Law*, p. 35; *Irish Independent*, 7 January 1919.
4 Sean O'Murthuile (John Hurley). ibid., 8 January 1919.
5 Margery Forester, *Michael Collins: The Lost Leader*, p. 97.
6 *Daily News*, 16 January 1919.
7 *Daily Mail*, 22 January 1919.
8 *Manchester Guardian*, 24 January 1919.
9 Macardle, *Irish Republic*, p. 273.
10 ibid., pp. 274–5.
11 ibid., p. 925.
12 *Irish Independent*, 22 January 1919.
13 *Freeman's Journal*, 22 January 1919.
14 *Irish Independent*, 21, 23 January 1919.
15 Breen, *My Fight For Irish Freedom*, pp. 34–40.
16 *Irish Independent*, 23 January 1919.
17 *Irish Times*, 24 January 1919.
18 *Tipperary Star*, 25 January 1919.
19 *Irish Times*, 27–8 January 1919.
20 *Irish Independent*, 27 January 1919.
21 O'Donoghue, *No Other Law*, pp. 44–5.
22 *Irish Independent*, 27 January 1919.
23 Beaslai, *Collins*, vol. i, pp. 274–5.
24 ibid., p. 277.
25 ibid., p. 276.
26 *Irish Independent*, 21 February 1919.
27 Beaslai, op. cit., pp. 269–70.
28 *Irish Independent*, 13 March 1919.
29 ibid., 17 March 1919; Beaslai, op. cit., p. 304.
30 ibid., 17 March 1919.
31 *Irish Times*, 12 March 1919.
32 *Irish Independent*, 21 March 1919.
33 *Irish Times*, 12 March 1919. The prisoner who had died was Pierce McCann.
34 *Nationality*, 21 February 1919.
35 *Irish Independent*, 26 February 1919.
36 ibid., 4 March 1919.
37 Cited ibid., 22 March 1919.
38 *Freeman's Journal*, 2 June 1919.

5 Michael Collins and Others (*April–December 1919*)

1 *Irish Times*, 2 April 1919; *Mayo News*, 20 March 1918, 28 June 1919.
2 O'Donoghue, *No Other Law*, p. 44.

3 Lord Longford and T. P. O'Neill, *Eamon de Valera*, London, 1970, p. 90.

4 On 17 May 1919. Taylor, *Collins*, p. 105.

5 *Irish Independent*, 1 April 1919.

6 ibid., 10 April 1919.

7 ibid., 10–11 April 1919.

8 ibid., 22–3 April 1919.

9 ibid., 23 April 1919.

10 ibid.

11 *Daily News*, 31 May 1919.

12 Tom Barry, *Guerrilla Days in Ireland*, Cork, 1950, pp. 1–2, 5.

13 Forester, *Collins*, p. 102.

14 *Irish Independent*, 12 May 1919.

15 *Irish Times*, 10 May 1919.

16 *Irish Independent*, 12 May 1919.

17 ibid., 16 May 1919.

18 ibid., 21 May 1919.

19 Breen, *My Fight for Irish Freedom*, pp. 83–105.

20 *Glasgow Herald*, 31 May 1919.

21 Forester, op. cit., pp. 103–4.

22 *Irish Independent*, 11 April 1919.

23 Taylor, *Collins*, pp. 126–8 and p. 130.

24 *Freeman's Journal*, 14 February 1920.

25 *Daily Telegraph*, 31 May 1919.

26 Denis Gwynn, *De Valera*, p. 77.

27 Seven such cases between 31 July and 5 October 1920 alone, taken from police records, are given in 'I.O.' (Major C. J. Street), *The Administration of Ireland, 1920*, London, 1921, pp. 234–5. There were many others.

28 ibid., pp. 64–7.

29 Forester, op. cit., pp. 103–4.

30 Longford and O'Neill, op. cit., p. 90.

6 The Campaign of Killing (1919–20)

1 *Freeman's Journal*, 25 June 1919; *Irish Times*, 26, 27 June 1919; *Tipperary Star*, 21, 28 June 1919.

2 *Irish Times*, 30 June 1919.

3 *Freeman's Journal*, 25 June 1919.

4 *Irish Times*, 30 June 1919.

5 *Freeman's Journal*, 16 June 1919.

6 ibid., 28 June 1919.

7 *Observer*, 13 July 1919.

8 *Freeman's Journal*, 14 July 1919.

9 ibid.

10 Taylor, *Collins*, p. 286.

11 Sir Ormonde Winter, *Winter's Tale*, London, 1955, pp. 299–300.

12 *Irish Times*, 4 August 1919.

13 *Freeman's Journal*, 6, 9, 15 August 1919.

14 Beaslai, *Collins*, pp. 302–4, 333–5.

15 *Freeman's Journal*, 11 August 1919.

16 ibid., 12 August 1919.

17 *Irish Times*, 22 August 1919.

18 *Freeman's Journal*, 22 August 1919.

19 Forester, *Collins*, p. 123.

20 *Freeman's Journal*, 15, 16 September 1919.

21 O'Donoghue, *No Other Law*, p. 48.

22 *Irish Times*, September 1919 (Inquest proceedings). For an inside account of the raid see O'Donoghue, *No Other Law*, pp. 48–54, in which the number of rifles taken is given as fifteen.

23 ibid.

24 ibid., 12 September 1919.

25 ibid., 9 September 1919.

26 ibid.

27 *Freeman's Journal*, 1 December 1919.

28 As published, for instance, in the *Killarney Echo*, 20 September 1919. This and other papers, notably the staid Nationalist *Cork Examiner*, were suppressed by the authorities for a few issues for publishing such advertisements.

29 *Freeman's Journal*, 3 November 1919.

30 *Irish Times*, 27 September 1919.

31 ibid., 16 September 1919.

32 *Clare Champion*, 25 October 1919.

33 ibid., 25 October 1919.

34 *Irish Times*, 22 December 1919.

35 Taylor, *Collins*, p. 106.

36 *Irish Times*, 22 December 1919.

37 Breen, *My Fight For Irish Freedom*, pp. 143–4.

38 O'Hegarty, *The Victory of Sinn Fein*, pp. 46–8.

39 Macardle, *Irish Republic*, pp. 304–5.

40 O'Malley, *On Another Man's Wound*, p. 145.

41 See captured document quoted in court-martial proceedings, *Irish Times*, 22 October 1920. Also O'Donoghue, *No Other Law*, pp. 42–3.

42 O'Donoghue, op. cit., p. 35.

43 ibid., p. 86.
44 Barry, *Guerrilla Days in Ireland*, p. 100.
45 See captured document cited in the trial of Sean Morrisey, *Irish Times*, 22 October 1920.
46 *Freeman's Journal*, 27 November 1919.
47 *Clare Champion*, 13 December 1919.
48 *Freeman's Journal*, 8 December 1919.
49 *Irish Times*, 23 December 1919.
50 ibid.

7 Enter Black and Tans (*1920*)

1 *Irish Times*, 22, 26 January 1920.
2 ibid., 22, 26 January 1919.
3 *Freeman's Journal*, 16 February 1920.
4 ibid., 26 February 1920.
5 *Cork Examiner*, 17 March 1920.
6 *Freeman's Journal*, 23 March 1920.
7 *Cork Examiner*, 19 March 1920.
8 *Freeman's Journal*, 26 February 1920.
9 ibid., 15 April 1920.
10 ibid., 16 April 1920.
11 ibid., 31 July 1920.
12 Hansard, H.C., 5th series, vol. 139, col. 238; vol. 140, col. 436.
13 *Freeman's Journal*, 28 September 1920.
14 Parliamentary Papers, H.C., 1922, Cmd. 1618, XVII, p. 785.
15 *Freeman's Journal*, 19 March 1920.
16 Hansard, H.C., 5th series, vol. 153, col. 257.
17 *Freeman's Journal*, 27, 12, 18 March 1920.
18 ibid., 15 March 1920.
19 *Tipperary Star*, 3 April 1920.
20 *Freeman's Journal*, 17 April 1920.
21 General Sir Nevile Macready, *Annals of an Active Life*, London, 2 vols., 1924.
22 Brigadier F. P. Crozier, *Impressions and Recollections*, London, 1930; *Ireland For Ever*, London, 1932.
23 Edward Maclysaght, *Master of None* (MS. of an autobiography shown to the author in 1954).
24 Inquest details. *Irish Times*, 27 March 1920.
25 ibid., 31 March 1920.
26 *Freeman's Journal*, 20 April 1920.
27 H. of C., 1922, XXIX, Cmd. 1534, pp. 398–9.
28 ibid.

29 *Freeman's Journal*, 5 August 1920.
30 *Irish Times*, 31 May, 2 June 1920.
31 Hugh Martin, *Insurrection in Ireland*, London, 1921, pp. 69–70.
32 ibid.
33 O'Donoghue, *No Other Law*, pp. 63–5. *Freeman's Journal*, 16 June 1920.
34 *Freeman's Journal*, 4 June 1920.
35 *Freeman's Journal*, 9 June 1920.
36 *Irish Times*, 21, 23 June 1920.
37 *Freeman's Journal*, 20 July 1920. *Irish Times*, 10 August 1920.
38 O'Malley, *On Another Man's Wound*, p. 168.

8 Murder by the Throat (1920)

1 Florence O'Donoghue, *Tomas MacCurtain*, Dublin, 1958, photograph facing p. 202.
2 Callwell, *Wilson*, vol. ii, p. 246.
3 *Galway Express*, 24, 31 July 1920.
4 *Tipperary Star*, 2 August 1920.
5 *Irish Times*, 4 September 1920.
6 ibid., 23 August 1920.
7 ibid., 11 September 1920.
8 ibid., 7 September 1920.
9 ibid., 1 October 1920.
10 *Freeman's Journal*, 22 September 1920.
11 ibid., 11 October 1920.
12 See O'Malley, *On Another Man's Wound*, pp. 189–94; O'Donoghue, *No Other Law*, pp. 99–101.
13 *Irish Times*, 28 September 1920.
14 ibid., 20 April 1921.
15 James Gleeson, *Bloody Sunday*, London, 1962, pp. 56–78.
16 D. O'Hannigan (one of the IRA officers concerned), 'Origins and Activities of the First Flying Column', in J. M. MacCarthy (ed.), *Limerick's Fighting Story*, Tralee, pp. 85–7.
17 O'Donoghue, *No Other Law*, p. 334.
18 Hansard, H.C., 5th series, vol. 135, cols. 507–8 (captured IRA documents).
19 *Irish Times*, 18 October 1920.
20 ibid., 19 October 1920. Also see *Galway Observer*, 9, 23 October, 13 November 1920.
21 Hansard, H.C., 5th series, vol. 135, col. 544.
22 *Irish Times*, 2, 7 October 1920.
23 ibid., 1 October 1920.

24 ibid., 13 October 1920.
25 ibid., 11 October 1920.
26 ibid., 20 April 1921.
27 ibid., 1 April 1921.
28 ibid., 13, 16 April 1921.
29 *Freeman's Journal*, 25 September 1920.
30 *Irish Times*, 21 October 1920.
31 For General Strickland's statement, *Evening Standard*, January 1921.
32 *Irish Times*, 16 November 1965. Three articles based on Moylett's papers appeared on that date and on 15 and 17 November 1965.
33 For a detailed description of all these events compiled from contemporary newspapers and other sources, see James Gleeson, *Bloody Sunday*.
34 Forester, *Collins*, p. 172, where the diary of a Castle official, Mark Sturgis, is cited.
35 Winter, *Winter's Tale*, p. 323.
36 Forester, op. cit., p. 174.
37 *Irish Times*, 16 November 1956.
38 ibid., 12 January 1921.
39 Barry, *Guerrilla Days in Ireland*, p. 46.
40 Callwell, *Diaries of Sir Henry Wilson*, vol. ii, p. 265.

9 War and Truce (1921)

1 Hansard, H.C., 5th series, vol. 133, col. 1582; vol. 139, cols. 2245, 2384.
2 31 March 1920 to 14 April 1921 ibid., vol. 140, cols. 16, 1277. 1 January 1919 to 31 May 1921 ibid., vol. 143, col. 2172. Also White Paper cited *Irish Times*, 4 March 1921. Casualties 1 January 1921 to 11 July 1921 see *Freeman's Journal*, 12 July 1921, citing official sources.
3 Hansard, H.C., 5th series, vol. 140, col. 1277.
4 ibid., vol. 135, col. 2447.
5 *Freeman's Journal*, 12 July 1921.
6 Holt, *Protest in Arms*, p. 241 and see newspapers passim.
7 Cited *Irish Times*, 4 February 1921.
8 MacCarthy (ed.), *Limerick's Fighting Story*, pp. 107–28.
9 *Irish Times*, 1, 15, 21 February. For Mourne Abbey see O'Donoghue, *No Other Law*, pp. 135–6; for Clonmult see Barry, *Guerrilla Days*, pp. 78–86. Barry has an interesting account (pp. 78–86) of a successful IRA break-out from a similar trap at Burgatia House, Rosscarberry, in the same month. In this the Crown claimed six IRA dead but there were in fact none. See also *Irish Times*.
10 For Sixmilebridge see *Irish Times*, 25 January 1921. For MacEoin, see *Irish Times*, 8 August 1921.

11 See captured IRA document, asking for GHQ guidance on this point, cited *Irish Times*, 28 February 1921.

12 *Irish Times*, 6 June 1921.

13 ibid., 7 May 1921.

14 See Hansard, H.C., 5th series, vol. 135, col. 508.

15 *Irish Times*, 25 January 1921.

16 ibid., 7 February 1921.

17 See advertisement, *Irish Times*, 14 March 1921.

18 *Irish Times*, 26 November 1920.

19 ibid., 10 February 1921.

20 ibid., 16 February 1921.

21 ibid., 12 July 1921.

22 ibid., 15 April 1921.

23 ibid., 20 April 1921.

24 O'Malley, *On Another Man's Wound*, p. 316.

25 *Irish Times*, 21 February 1921.

26 *Irish Times*, 20 June 1921.

27 ibid.

28 ibid., 14 March 1921.

29 MacCready, *Annals*, vol. ii, pp. 488–9.

30 *Irish Times*, 13 June 1921.

31 ibid., 22 April 1921.

32 ibid., 4 June 1921.

33 ibid.

34 ibid., 1 June 1921.

35 ibid., 18 June 1921.

36 ibid., 15 March 1921.

37 Captured IRA document dated 7 February 1921, cited in *Irish Times*, 26 March 1921.

38 Cited in Lyons, *Dillon*, p. 467.

39 *Freeman's Journal*, 12 July 1921.

40 *Irish Times*, 1 March 1921.

41 ibid., 1, 2 March 1921.

42 ibid., 29 April 1921.

43 Winter, *Winter's Tale*, p. 302.

44 Beaslai, *Collins*, vol. ii, p. 193.

45 O'Malley, op. cit., pp. 328–32.

46 Douglas V. Duff, *The Rough with the Smooth*, London, 1940, pp. 79–80.

47 O'Malley, op. cit., p. 311.

48 ibid.

49 ibid., p. 326.

50 *Irish Times*, 16 April 1921; 6 July 1921.

51 O'Donoghue, *No Other Law*, p. 173.

52 In Downing Street to Sir Hamar Greenwood after the signing of the Treaty. L. S. Amery, *My Political Life*, 3 vols., London, 1953, vol. ii, p. 230. Greenwood was Amery's brother-in-law.

53 Longford and O'Neill, *De Valera*, p. 121.

54 T. P. O'Neill (ed.), Introduction to Frank Gallagher, *The Anglo-Irish Treaty*, London, 1965, pp. 21–4.

55 Longford and O'Neill, *De Valera*, pp. 115–16.

56 Hansard, H.C., 5th series, vol. 140, cols. 2044–5.

57 *Irish Times*, 18 October 1920.

58 ibid., 31 January 1921.

59 ibid., 4 May 1921.

60 Longford and O'Neill, *De Valera*, p. 123.

61 ibid., p. 125.

62 Sir Harold Nicolson, *King George V*, London, 1952, pp. 348–54.

63 Macardle, *Irish Republic*, p. 471.

64 MacCready, *Annals of an Active Life*, p. 572.

65 *Irish Times*, 11, 12 July 1921. *Freeman's Journal*, 12 July 1921.

66 *Irish Times*, 16 July 1921.

10 Treaty (1921)

1 Dail Eireann Official Report, Treaty Debates, p. 143.

2 For the figure of 250,000 see Sir Geoffrey Shakespeare, *Let Candles Be Brought In*, London, 1949, p. 88.

3 O'Hegarty, *The Victory of Sinn Fein*, p. 87.

4 Nicolson, *George V*, p. 356.

5 Forester, *Collins*, p. 196. The source is a diary entry of Tom Casement's, dated 14 June 1921.

6 Nicolson, op. cit., p. 351.

7 Pakenham, *Peace by Ordeal*, p. 88.

8 Longford and O'Neill, *De Valera*, p. 139.

9 ibid., p. 143.

10 ibid., pp. 149–50.

11 ibid., pp. 152–3.

12 ibid., p. 157.

13 Pakenham, *Peace By Ordeal*, pp. 315–16.

14 ibid., pp. 218, 299–300.

15 For text of Treaty see Macardle, *Irish Republic*, pp. 953–8.

16 Forester, *Collins*, pp. 249–50. Source: a Collins minute of the interview. In the Dail Debate on the Treaty, Collins declared it as his belief that the way in which the Treaty dealt with the problem of the North-East

would bring it under an Irish Parliament. Dail Eireann Official Report, p. 35.

17 Taylor, *Collins*, p. 163.
18 Forester, op. cit., p. 260.
19 Taylor, *Collins*, p. 175.
20 ibid., p. 165.
21 For Document No. 2 see Macardle, *Irish Republic*, pp. 959–63.

11 Nemesis (1922–3)

1 Dail Eireann Official Report, Treaty Debate, p. 34.
2 ibid., p. 46.
3 ibid., p. 229.
4 Cited Macardle, *Irish Republic*, p. 678.
5 ibid., pp. 658–60.
6 Forester, *Collins*, pp. 287–8.
7 ibid., pp. 729–30.
8 Forester, *Collins*, p. 306. Hansard, H.C., 5th series, vol. 154, col. 2149.
9 ibid.
10 Dail Eireann Official Report, 28 April 1922, p. 340.
11 ibid., 26 April 1922, pp. 256–7. Report by Richard Mulcahy.
12 Macardle, op. cit., p. 721.
13 Calton Younger, *Ireland's Civil War*, London, 1968, p. 318.
14 Taylor, *Collins*, p. 235.
15 Macardle, op. cit., p. 754.
16 Calton Younger, op. cit., p. 401.
17 Taylor, *Collins*, p. 236.
18 ibid., pp. 238–9.
19 Forester, *Collins*, p. 329.
20 ibid., p. 332.
21 Dail Eireann Official Report, vol. i, p. 2264.
22 ibid., p. 2274.
23 ibid., p. 2267.
24 T. de Vere White, *Kevin O'Higgins*, paperback ed., Tralee, 1968, p. 131.
25 ibid., pp. 206–7.
26 ibid., p. 203.
27 For MacNeill's statement and Feetham's views see Macardle, op. cit., pp. 886–7.
28 ibid., p. 892.

Epilogue

1 Macardle, *Irish Republic*, p. 858.

2 For a reasoned speculation about their identity see T. P. Coogan, *Ireland Since the Rising*, London, 1966, pp. 261–2.
3 ibid., p. 65.
4 *Freeman's Journal*, 26 November 1913.
5 For this story see *Freeman's Journal*, 28 March 1914.

Select Bibliography

The following is a selection from the sources consulted for *The Green Flag*. It has been divided into periods corresponding with the parts of the book, with occasional comments for the convenience of those who wish to pursue further reading.

PARTS ONE *and* TWO

WHO WERE IRISHMEN? *and* THE FIRST IRISH REPUBLICANS

Beckett, J. C., *A Short History of Ireland* (London, 1952, 3rd edition, 1966)
Easily the best short history.

Beckett, J. C., *The Making of Modern Ireland, 1603–1923* (London, 1966)
Masterly account of the political, social and economic forces at work in Ireland between these two dates. General reading for the student perhaps more than the general reader.

Bowden, Charles, *A Tour of Ireland* (London, 1791)

Bush, J., *Hibernia Curiosa* (London, 1764)

Carty, James (ed.), *Ireland From the Flight of the Earls to Grattan's Parliament* (Dublin, 1951)

Caulfield, James (ed.), *The MSS and Correspondence of James, First Earl of Charlemont* (2 vols. London, 1891–4)

Chart, D. A. (ed.), *The Drennan Letters* (Belfast, 1931)

Clarke, Aidan, *The Old English in Ireland 1625–1642* (London, 1966)

Cloney, Thomas, *A Personal Narrative of Transactions . . . in Wexford . . . 1798* (Dublin, 1832)
Vivid memoirs published thirty years later of an articulate rebel drawn into the rising in Wexford.

Corkery, D., *The Hidden Ireland* (Dublin, 1925)

Croker, T. Crofton, *Popular Songs Illustrative of the French Invasion of Ireland* (London, 1845–47)

Croker, T. Crofton (ed.), *Memoirs of Joseph Holt* (London, 1838)

Curtis, E., *A History of Ireland* (London, 1936)
A distinguished scholar's work. Often given as the best general volume, but in fact not very readable. The twentieth century is only cursorily treated.

Dickson, Charles, *The Wexford Rising in 1798* (Tralee, 1955)

A thorough compilation of detailed incident from many sources, including hitherto unpublished manuscripts. Often fascinating, but the author's
eye is very close to the ground.

Dickson, Charles, *Revolt in the North* (Dublin, 1960)

A similar work covering '98 in Ulster.

Edgeworth, Maria (ed.), *Memoirs of R. L. Edgeworth* (2 vols., London,
1820)

Edwards, R. D. and Williams, T. D. (eds.), *The Great Famine* (Dublin, 1956)

The best account of the famine. An admirably scholarly work not
primarily concerned with narrative for its own sake.

Fontaine, L. O., *Notice Historique de la Descente des Français en Irlande*
(Paris 1801)

The author was the third senior officer in the French forces which
landed in Ireland in 1798.

Gilbert, J. T., *Documents Relating to Ireland 1784–1803* (Dublin, 1893)

Useful government letters of the time of the rebellion. Also the United
Irishmen's (O'Connor, MacNeven, Emmet) memoir on their transactions.

Goff, Dinah, *Divine Protection Through Extraordinary Dangers ... During
the Irish Insurrection of 1798* (London, 1857)

Gordon, the Reverend James, *History of the Rebellion in Ireland in the Year
1798* (London and Dublin, 1803)

Recommended, with good reason, by Lecky as the best contemporary
account of '98.

Gribayedoff, V., *The French Invasion of Ireland in '98* (New York, 1890)

Guillon, Edouard, *La France et l'Irlande Pendant La Révolution* (Paris,
1888)

Based on French national archives.

Hancock, Thomas, *The Principles of Peace ... during the Rebellion of 1798*
(London, 1826)

Hay, Edward, *History of the Insurrection of 1798* (Dublin, 1842)

A Catholic gentleman rebel of '98 publishing a personal account many
years later.

Hayes, Dr Richard, *The Last Invasion of Ireland* (Dublin, 1937)

Historical Manuscripts Commission, Fortescue MSS., Charlemont MSS.

Inglis, Brian, *The Story of Ireland* (London, 1956)

Jackson, Charles, *A Narrative of the Sufferings and Escape of Charles Jackson (1799)*

Jacob, Rosamund, *The Rise of the United Irishmen 1791–1794* (London,
1937)

Johnston, Edith M., *Irish History: A Select Bibliography* (Historical Association Pamphlet no. 73, 1969)

Excellent concise guide to further reading for serious students.

Jones, E. H. Stuart, *An Invasion that Failed* (Oxford, 1950)

Kavanagh, Patrick F., *A Popular History of the Insurrection of 1798* (London, 1898)

Latimer, William T., *Ulster Biographies* (London, 1897)

Latocnaye, De, *Promenade d'un Français dans l'Irlande* (1797)
> Also in a translation 'by an Englishman' entitled *Rambles Through Ireland* (1799).

Leadbeater, Mary, *The Leadbeater Papers* (2 vols., London, 1862)

Lecky, W. E. H., *History of Ireland in the Eighteenth Century.* Vols. 1–5 (London, 1892 Edition)
> One of the great historical works of all time, combining as it does readability with great scholarship and enabling the interested general reader to take long looks at original sources. A leisurely read, however.

Lecky, W. E. H., *The Leaders of Public Opinion in Ireland* (1883)
> Stimulating, though occasionally rather discursive sketches on Swift, Flood, Grattan and O'Connell.

Lewis, G. C., *On Local Disturbances in Ireland* (London, 1836)

MacDermot, Frank, *Wolfe Tone* (London, 1939)
> An excellent cool appraisal.

MacDowell, R. B., *Irish Public Opinion 1750–1800* (London, 1944)
> Admirable digest of the many strands of opinion in Ireland which helped form (1) the Volunteer movement and the first active display of Protestant Irish patriotism, (2) the radical movement which developed from that, and (3) the state of mind which accepted the Union.

MacHugh, R. J. (ed.), *Carlow in '98: Memoirs of William Farrell* (Dublin, 1949)

MacLysaght, Edward, *Irish Life in the Seventeenth Century after Cromwell* (Dublin, 1939)

MacNeven, W. J. and Emmet, T. A., *Pieces of Irish History* (New York, 1807)
> Indispensable first-hand memoirs of two of the leading United Irishmen written reasonably soon after the events they describe.

MacNevin, Thomas, *Leading State Trials 1794–1803* (London, 1844)

MacSkimmin, Samuel, *Annals of Ulster* (London, 1906)

Madden, R. R., *The United Irishmen, Their Lives and Times* (Three Series: 7 vols. London, 1842–6)
> Indispensable biographical detail on a mammoth scale, sometimes rather muddled in arrangement.

Maurice, Sir J. F. (ed.), *Diary of Sir John Moore* (London, 1904)

Maxwell, W. H., *History of the Irish Rebellion in 1798* (London, 1845)

Moore, Thomas, *The Life and Death of Lord Edward Fitzgerald* (2 vols. London, 1831)

Musgrave, Sir Richard, *Memoir of the Different Irish Rebellions* (Dublin, 1801)

Pakenham, Thomas, *The Year of Liberty* (London, 1969)
  Detailed, well-written modern account of the Rebellion of 1798 confined very largely to that year.
Plowden, Francis, *An Historical Review of the State of Ireland from Henry II to the Union* (2 vols. London, 1801)
Plowden, Francis, *A Short History of the British Empire 1792–3* (London, 1794)
Pomfret, J. E., *The Struggle for the Land in Ireland* (Princeton, 1930)
  An indispensable source book for an understanding of the land problem.
Report of Debates in the Parliament of Ireland in the Session of 1793 (Dublin, 1793)
Report of the Trial of Henry and John Sheares (Dublin, 1798)
Richey, A. G., *A Short History of the Irish People* (Dublin, 1869)
  Illuminating.
Ross, Charles (ed.), *Correspondence of Charles, First Marquis of Cornwallis* (3 vols. London, 1859)
Senior, Hereward, *Orangeism in Ireland and Britain 1795–1836* (London, 1966)
State Trials, Vol. XXVII
Stock, J., *A Narrative of What Passed at Killala* (London, 1801)
Swift, Jonathan, *A Short View of the State of Ireland* (Dublin, 1728)
Taylor, George, *A History of the Rebellion in the County of Wexford* (London, 1829)
Taylor, Sir Herbert, *An Impartial Relation of the Military Operations By An Officer* (Dublin, 1799)
Tone, William Theobald Wolfe, *Life of Theobald Wolfe Tone* (2 vols. Washington, 1826)
  Sometimes known as the Autobiography of Wolfe Tone. Invaluable and fascinating reading by any standards. Abridgements have also been published, but this full edition published by his son is the most rewarding.
Twiss, Richard, *A Tour in Ireland in 1775* (London, 1777)
Wheeler (H. F. B.) and Broadley (A. M.), *The War In Wexford* (London, 1910)
  Contains interesting extracts from contemporary documents.
Woodburn, J. B., *The Ulster Scot* (London, 1914)
Young, Robert M., *Ulster in '98* (London, 1893)

Newspapers and Periodicals

Daily Express
The Times
Annual Register 1798
Walkers Hibernian Magazine October, November 1795

Analecta Hibernica No. 11, No. 17
Historical Journal IV (1961)
Irish Historical Studies (I.H.S.)

> ii (March 1940): R. B. McDowell, 'The Personnel of the Dublin Society of United Irishmen'
>
> iii (March 1942): R. B. McDowell, 'United Irish Plans of Parliamentary Reform 1793'
>
> xi (September 1958): Maureen Wall, 'The rise of a Catholic Middle Class in eighteenth century Ireland'
>
> xiv (March 1964): J. C. Beckett, 'Anglo-Irish Constitutional Relations in the later eighteenth century'

Official Publications

Select Committee appointed to inquire into the Disturbances in Ireland in the last session of Parliament, May 1824
Devon Commission Report Digest 1847–8
Reports of the Secret Committees of Lords and Commons, Dublin, 1797
Report from the Secret Committee of the House of Commons, Dublin, 1798
Report from the Secret Committee of the House of Lords, Dublin, 1798
Report from the Committee of Secrecy to the House of Commons, London, 1799
Hansard House of Commons Debates

Manuscripts

B.M. Add. MSS. 32950, 33104, 38759, 41192, 32335, 37308, 38102, 40166 (Diary of Captain Hodges)

PART THREE

THE UNION

Ahern, James L., *Thomas Davis and his Circle* (Dublin, 1945)
Cavanagh, Michael, *Memoir of Thomas Meagher* (New York, 1892)
Cluseret, *Mémoires* (3 vols. Paris, 1887)
Corish, P. J. (ed.), *A History of Irish Catholicism*, Vol. V (Dublin, 1697)
Crilly, F. L., *The Fenian Movement: The Story of the Manchester Martyrs* (London, 1909)
D'Arcy, William, *The Fenian Movement in the United States* (Washington 1947)

> Indispensable to any study of Fenianism. Based on contemporary Fenian papers.

Daunt, W. J. O'Neill, *Personal Recollections of the Late Daniel O'Connell* (London, 1848)

Daunt, W. J. O'Neill, *A Life Spent For Ireland* (London, 1896)

Davis, Thomas Osborne, *An Address read before the Historical Society* (Dublin, 26 June 1840)

Davis, Thomas Osborne, *Literary and Historical Essays* (Dublin, 1846)

Denieffe, Joseph, *A Personal Narrative of the I.R.B.* (New York, 1904)

Devoy, John, *Recollections of an Irish Rebel* (New York, 1929)

> Interesting but not altogether reliable.

Doheny, Michael, *Felon's Track* (Dublin, 1914)

Duffy, Gavan, *Thomas Davis: A Memoir* (London, 1890)

Duffy, Gavan, *Young Ireland* (London, 1880, Final Revision, 1896)

Duffy, Gavan, *Four Years of Irish History* (London, 1883)

> Written some thirty years after the events they describe, these two books are based on many contemporary documents and are indispensable source-books, for all their distortions of emphasis, for the years 1840–48.

Edwards, R. D., and Williams, T. D. (eds.), *The Great Famine* (Dublin, 1956)

> The best account of the famine. An admirably scholarly work not primarily concerned with narrative for its own sake.

Fitzgerald, Father P., *Personal Recollections of the Insurrection at Ballingary in July 1848* (Dublin, 1862)

Fitzpatrick, W J., *Correspondence of Daniel O'Connell* (London, 1888)

Freeman, T. W., *Pre-Famine Ireland* (London, 1957)

Glynn, Anthony, *High Upon The Gallows Tree* (Tralee, 1967)

> Most recent and extensive study of the Manchester Rescue.

Gwynn, Denis, *Daniel O'Connell* (London, 1947)

Gwynn, Denis, *Young Ireland* (Cork University and London 1948)

> Based extensively on the Smith O'Brien papers and on Duffy's *Young Ireland* and *Four Years of Irish History* (q.v.) which are accepted at face value. Very useful, though sometimes a little lifeless in the connecting narrative.

Harman, Maurice (ed.), *Fenians and Fenianism* (Dublin, 1968)

Hone, Joseph, *Thomas Davis* (London, 1934)

MacDonagh, Michael, *Daniel O'Connell and the Story of Catholic Emancipation* (London, 1929)

Macintyre, Angus, *The Liberator: Daniel O'Connell and the Irish Party 1830–1847* (London, 1965)

McDowell, R. B., *Public Opinion and Government Policy in Ireland, 1801–1846* (London, 1952)

McDowell, R. B., *Social Life in Ireland, 1800–1845* (Dublin, 1957)

Madden, R. R., *The United Irishmen, their Lives and Times* (Three Series: 7 vols. London, 1842–6)

> Indispensable detail on a mammoth scale sometimes rather muddled in arrangement.

Mansergh, Nicholas, *The Irish Question 1840–1921* (London, 1965)
   Stimulating interpretative commentary for those with some knowledge of
   the background of these years. A complete revision of the author's *Ireland
   in the Age of Reform and Revolution* published in 1940.
Mitchel, John, *Jail Journal* (Dublin, 1913)
Moody, T. W. and Beckett, J. C. (eds.), *Ulster Since 1800* (London, 1954)
Moody, T. W., *The Londonderry Plantation* (London, 1939)
Moody, T. W., *Thomas Davis* (Dublin, 1945)
Moody, T. W. (ed.), *The Fenian Movement* (Cork, 1968)
   Radio Eireann Talks.
Norman, E. R., *The Catholic Church and Ireland in the Age of Rebellion*
   (London, 1965)
Nowlan, Kevin, *The Politics of Repeal* (London, 1965)
O'Bourke, Marcus, *John O'Leary: A Study in Separation* (Dublin, 1967)
O'Brien, C., *Economic History of Ireland from the Union to the Famine*
   (London, 1921)
O'Brien, R. Barry, *Thomas Drummond: Life and Letters* (London,
   1889)
O'Broin, L., *The Unfortunate Mr Robert Emmet* (Dublin and London,
   1958)
O'Faolain, Sean, *King of the Beggars* (London, 1938)
O'Hegarty, P. S., *History of Ireland Under the Union* (London, 1952)
   A helpful compendium by a former member of the Irish Republican
   Brotherhood.
O'Leary, John, *Recollections of Fenians and Fenianism* (2 vols. London,
   1896)
   Memoirs of one of the Fenian patriarchs, published many years later.
Pigott, Richard, *Personal Recollections of an Irish National Journalist*
   (Dublin, 1882)
*Report of the Dublin Special Commission for the Trial of T. F. Bourke and
   others* (1867)
*Report of the Dublin Special Commission for the Trial of T. C. Luby and
   others* (1865)
Reynolds, James, *The Catholic Emancipation Crisis in Ireland 1823–9* (Yale,
   1954)
Rolleston, T. W. (ed.), *Prose Writings of Thomas Davis* (London, 1889)
Ross, Charles (ed.), *Correspondence of Charles, First Marquis of Cornwallis*
   (3 vols. London, 1859)
Rutherford, J., *The Secret History of the Fenian Conspiracy* (2 vols. London,
   1877)
   The work of an intelligent Unionist journalist drawing on police records.
   Sometimes inaccurate, but by no means as black as some nationalists have
   painted it.

Ryan, Desmond, *The Fenian Chief* (Dublin, 1967)
　　Indispensable biography of James Stephens.
Ryan, Desmond, *The Phoenix Flame* (London, 1937)
Ryan, Desmond and O'Brien, William (eds.), *Devoy's Post Bag* (2 vols. Dublin, 1948, 1953)
Savage, John, *Fenian Heroes and Martyrs* (London, 1868)
State Trials:
　　Trial of Smith O'Brien
　　Trial of Thomas Meagher
Sullivan, A. M., *New Ireland* (2 vols. London, 1877)
Sullivan, T. D., *Recollections of Troubled Times* (Dublin, 1905)
Tierney, Michael (ed.), *Daniel O'Connell: Nine Centenary Essays* (Dublin, 1949)
Vane, C. W. (ed.), *Memoirs and Correspondence of Viscount Castlereagh* (12 vols. London, 1848–53)
Wallis, T. (ed.), *The Poems of Thomas Davis* (London, 1846)
Whyte, J. H., *The Independent Irish Party 1850–59* (Oxford, 1958)
Woodham-Smith, Cecil, *The Great Hunger* (London, 1962)
　　The best account of the famine for the general reader.
Woodward, E. L., *The Age of Reform: 1815–1870* (Oxford, 1938)

Newspapers and Periodicals
The Nation
The Pilot
The Irish Felon
The United Irishman
The Irish Tribune
Dublin Evening Packet
Kilkenny Journal
Kilkenny Moderator
Longford Journal
Freeman's Journal
Weekly Freeman
Cork Constitution
Cork Examiner
Clare Journal
Westmeath Guardian
Irishman
The Tribune
Irish People
Drogheda Argus
The Times

Official Publications

Select Committee appointed to inquire into the Disturbances in Ireland in the last session of Parliament, May 1824

Minutes Before House of Lords

Select Committee on State of Ireland, 1825

Report to the Lord Lieutenant on the escape of James Stephens: 1866, LXVII, 479

Hansard House of Commons Debates

Frazer's Magazine, 1872

Irish Historical Studies (I.H.S.)

> ii (March 1942): Clarke, R., 'The relations between O'Connell and the Young Irelanders'
>
> xvi (March 1969): Breandan Mac Giolla Choille, *Fenian Documents in the State Paper Office*

PART FOUR

THE TRAGEDY OF HOME RULE

Abels, Jules, *The Parnell Tragedy* (London, 1966)

Baker, Ernest, *Ireland in the last 50 years* (London, 1919)

Birmingham, George A., *An Irishman Looks at His World* (London, 1919)

Blake, Robert, *The Unknown Prime Minister* (London, 1955)

Bourke, M., *John O'Leary: A Study in Separation* (Tralee, 1967)

Brennan, Robert, *Allegiance* (Dublin, 1950)

Brooks, Sydney, *The New Ireland* (Dublin, 1907)

Brown, T. N., *Irish-American Nationalism* (Philadelphia and New York, 1966)

Carty, James, *Bibliography of Irish History, 1870–1911* (Dublin, 1940)

Carty, James, *Bibliography of Irish History, 1911–1921* (Dublin 1936)

> Both are indispensable to any serious student of the period.

Caulfield, M., *The Easter Rebellion* (London, 1964)

Churchill, W. S., *Lord Randolph Churchill* (2 vols. London, 1906)

Clarke, Thomas J., *Glimpses of an Irish Felon's Life* (Dublin, 1922)

Coffey, Diarmid, *Douglas Hyde, President of Ireland* (Dublin, 1938)

Colum, Padraic, *Arthur Griffith* (Dublin 1959)

Connolly, James, *Labour and Easter Week* (Introduction by William O'Brien. Dublin, 1949)

Corfe, Thomas, *The Phoenix Park Murders* (London, 1968)

Coxhead, Elizabeth, *Lady Gregory: a Literary Portrait* (London, 1966)

Curry, C. E., *Sir Roger Casement's Diaries* (Munich, 1922)

Curtis, L. P., *Coercion and Conciliation in Ireland, 1880–92* (Princeton and London, 1963)

Davitt, Michael, *The Fall of Feudalism in Ireland* (London and New York, 1904)

    Essential for the origins of 'the new departure'.

Devoy, John, *The Land of Eire* (New York, 1882)

Devoy, John, *Recollections of an Irish Rebel* (New York, 1929)

Duff, Charles, *Six Days to Shake An Empire* (London, 1966)

Duffy, Charles Gavan, *The Revival of Irish Literature* (London, 1894)

Ensor, R. C. J., *England, 1870–1914* (Oxford, 1936)

Fergusson, Sir James, *The Curragh Incident* (London, 1964)

Fox, R. M., *Jim Larkin* (London, 1957)

Gogarty, Oliver St John, *As I Was Going Down Sackville Street* (London, 1937)

Gogarty, Oliver St John, *It Isn't This Time Of Year At All* (London, 1954)

Gollin, A. M., *Pro-Consul in Politics* (London, 1964)

Greaves, C. Desmond, *The Life and Times of James Connolly* (London, 1961)

Gregory, Lady, *Ideals in Ireland* (London, 1901)

Gwynn, Denis, *Life of John Redmond* (London, 1932)

Gwynn, Denis, *The Life and Death of Roger Casement* (London, 1930)

Gwynn, Denis, *Edward Martyn and the Irish Revival* (London, 1930)

Gwynn, Stephen, *Redmond's Last Years* (London, 1919)

Hammond, J. L., *Gladstone and the Irish Nation* (London, 1938)

Harrison, H., *Parnell Vindicated* (London, 1931)

Haslip, Joan, *Parnell* (London, 1936)

Healy, T. M., *Letters and Leaders of My Day* (2 vols. London, 1928)

Henry, R. M., *The Evolution of Sinn Fein* (Dublin, 1920)

Hobson, Bulmer, *Ireland Yesterday and Tomorrow* (Tralee, 1968)

Hone, J. M., *The Life of George Moore* (London, 1936)

Hone, J. M., *W. B. Yeats 1865–1939* (London, 1962)

Horgan, John J., *Parnell to Pearse* (Dublin, 1949)

Hurst, Michael, *Parnell and Irish Nationalism* (London, 1968)

Hyde, Douglas, *Beside the Fire* (London, 1890)

Hyde, Montgomery, *The Trial of Roger Casement* (London, 1960)

Irish Times, *Sinn Fein Rebellion Handbook: Easter 1916*

    Invaluable contemporary documentation.

Jenkins, Roy, *Asquith* (London, 1964)

Jenkins, Roy, *Mr Balfour's Poodle* (London, 1954)

Larkin, Emmet, *James Larkin* (paperback edition, London, 1968)

Le Caron, Henri, *Twenty-Five Years in the Secret Service* (London, 1892)

Le Roux, L. N., *Patrick Pearse* (Dublin, 1932)

Le Roux, L. N., *Tom Clarke and the Irish Freedom Movement* (Dublin, 1926)

Lucas, Reginald, *Colonel Saunderson, M.P.* (London, 1908)

Lynch, D., *The I.R.B. and the 1916 Rising* (ed. F. O'Donoghue, Cork, 1957)

Lyons, F. S. L., *John Dillon* (London, 1968)
 A major biography in a thinly-covered field.

Lyons, F. S. L., *The Irish Parliamentary Party, 1890–1910* (London, 1951)

Lyons, F. S. L., *The Fall of Parnell, 1890–1901* (London, 1960)
 A fair-minded detailed analysis of the events which followed the Parnell divorce case.

Lyons, George, *Some Recollections of Griffith and His Times* (Dublin, 1923)

MacColl, R., *Roger Casement* (London, 1956)

MacDonagh, Michael, *The Home Rule Movement* (Dublin and London, 1920)

McDowell, R. B., *The Irish Convention, 1917–18* (London, 1970)

MacEntee, Sean, *Episode At Easter* (Dublin, 1966)

Mac Giolla Choille, B. (ed.), *Intelligence Notes, 1913–16* (Dublin 1966)

Mackey, H. O., *The Life and Times of Roger Casement* (Dublin, 1954)

MacManus, A. J. (pseud 'Ethna Carberry'), *The Four Winds of Erin* (Dublin, 1918)

MacManus, M. J., *Eamon de Valera* (Dublin, 1944)

Marreco, A., *The Rebel Countess* (London, 1967)

Martin, F. X. (ed.), *The Irish Volunteers, 1913–1915* (Dublin, 1963)

Martin, F. X. (ed.), *The Howth Gun-Running, 1914* (Dublin, 1964)

Martin, F. X. (ed.), *Leaders and Men of the Easter Rising: Dublin 1916* (London, 1967)
 Radio Eireann Talks.

Martin, F. X., *1916 – Myth, Fact and Mystery* in *Studia Hibernica* (Dublin, 1967)

Martin, F. X., *The 1916 Rising – A Coup d'Etat or a 'Bloody Protest'?* in *Studia Hibernica* (Dublin, 1968)

Moloney, W., *The Forged Casement Diaries* (Dublin, 1936)

Montieth, R., *Casement's Last Adventure* (Dublin, 1953)

Moody, T. W. (ed.), *The Fenian Movement* (Cork, 1968)

Moore, George, *Hail and Farewell* (3 vols. London, 1937)

Moran, D. P., *The Philosophy of Irish Ireland* (Dublin, 1905)

Nowlan, K. B. (ed.), *The Making of 1916* (Dublin, 1969)

Noyes, Alfred, *The Accusing Ghost or Justice for Casement* (London, 1957)

O'Brien, Conor Cruise, *Parnell and His Party, 1880–1890* (Oxford, 1957)
 An authoritative specialist work.

O'Brien, Conor Cruise (ed.), *The Shaping of Modern Ireland* (London, 1959)
 Radio Eireann Talks.

O'Brien, Nora Connolly, *Portrait of a Rebel Father* (London, 1935)

O'Brien, R. Barry, *The Life of Charles Stewart Parnell 1846-1891* (2 vols. London, 1898)

O'Brien, W., *An Olive Branch in Ireland* (London, 1910)

O'Brien, W., and Ryan, Desmond (eds.), *Devoy's Post Bag* (2 vols. Dublin, 1948 and 1953)

O'Broin, L., *Dublin Castle and the 1916 Rising* (Dublin, 1966)

O'Broin, L. *Augustine Birrell and Ireland* (London, 1969)

O'Casey, Sean, *Drums Under the Window* (London, 1945)

O'Connor, T. P., *Memoirs of an Old Parliamentarian* (London, 1929)

O'Connor, Uick, *Oliver St John Gogarty* (London, 1964)

O'Donnell, F. H., *History of the Irish Parliamentary Party* (2 vols. London, 1910)

O'Dubghail, M., *Insurrection Fires at Eastertide* (Cork, 1966)

O'Faolain, Sean, *Constance Markievicz* (London, 1934)

O'Hegarty, P. S., *The Victory of Sinn Fein* (Dublin, 1924)

O'Hegarty, P. S., *A History of Ireland Under the Union, 1801-1922* (London, 1952)

   A helpful compendium by a former member of the Irish Republican Brotherhood.

O'Leary, John, *Recollections of Fenians and Fenianism* (2 vols. London, 1896)

O'Shea, Katharine, *Charles Stewart Parnell* (2 vols. London, 1914)

   Invaluable letters.

Palmer, N. D., *The Irish Land League Crisis* (New Haven, 1940)

Paul-Dubois, L., *Contemporary Ireland* (London, 1908)

Pearse, P. H., *Political Writings and Speeches* (Dublin, 1952)

Plunkett, Sir Horace, *Ireland In The New Century* (London, 1905)

Redmond-Howard, L. G., *Six Days of the Irish Republic* (Dublin, 1916)

Ryan, A. P., *Mutiny at the Curragh* (London, 1956)

Ryan, D., *The Phoenix Flame: A Study of Fenianism and John Devoy* (London, 1937)

Ryan, D., *James Connolly, his life, work and writings* (Dublin, 1924)

Ryan, D., *The Rising: The Complete Story of Easter Week* (Dublin, 3rd ed., 1957)

Ryan, D., *Remembering Sion* (London, 1934)

Ryan, Mark, *Fenian Memories* (Dublin, 1945)

Sheehan, D. D., *Ireland Since Parnell* (London, 1921)

Singleton-Gates, P., and Girodias, M. (ed.), *The Black Diaries* (Paris, 1959)

Spindler, Karl, *The Mystery of the Casement Ship* (Berlin, 1931)

Stephens, James, *Insurrection in Dublin* (Dublin and London, 1916)

Stewart, A. T. Q., *The Ulster Crisis* (London, 1967)

   A fine objective study.

Sullivan, A. M., *New Ireland* (London, 1877)

Thompson, William, *The Imagination of an Insurrection* (New York, 1967)
      The first two chapters contain an excellent account of the origins of the Celtic revival and its political implications.

Thornley, David, *Isaac Butt and Home Rule* (London, 1964)

Tynan, P. J., *The Irish National Invincibles and their Times* (New York, 1894)

Van Voris, Jacqueline, *Constance de Markievicz* (Massachusetts, 1967)

Wells, Ware and Marlowe, *A History of the Irish Rebellion of 1916* (Dublin, 1918)

White, J. R., *Misfit* (London, 1930)

White, T. de V., *The Road of Excess* (Dublin, 1946)

Whyte, J. H., *The Independent Irish Party, 1850–59* (Oxford, 1958)

Whyte, J. H., 'Political Problems, 1850–1960' in Corish, P. J. (ed.), *A History of Irish Catholicism* (Dublin, 1967)

Wilde, Lady, (Jane Francesca Speranza), *Ancient Legends of Ireland* (2 vols. London, 1887)

Yeats, W. B., *Autobiographies* (London, 1926)

Yeats, W. B., *The Celtic Twilight* (London, 1893)

Yeats, W. B., *Correspondence* (London, 1954)

Yeats, W. B. (ed.), *Fairy and Folk Tales of the Irish Peasantry* (London, 1888)

Newspapers and Periodicals

United Irishman
Sinn Fein
Irish Freedom
The Leader
Irish Worker
Freeman's Journal
Weekly Freeman
Cork Examiner
Belfast Evening Telegraph
The Times
Irish World

Irish Historical Studies (I.H.S.)

   ix (September 1954): McCaffrey, L. J., 'Home Rule and the General Election of 1874'

   xii (March 1961): Savage, D. C., 'The Origins of the Ulster Unionist Party, 1885–6' ix (March 1955): Moody, T. W., 'Parnell and the Galway Election of 1886'

xvi (March 1968): Hawkins, Richard, 'Gladstone, Forster and the Release of Parnell 1882–8'

xvii (March 1970): Steele, E. D., 'Gladstone and Ireland'

xvii (March 1970): Boyce, D. G., 'British Conservative opinion, the Ulster Question, and the partition of Ireland 1912–21'

xiii (September 1963): McCready, H. W., 'Home Rule and the Liberal Party, 1890–1810'

xii (March 1961): Buckland, P. J., 'The Southern Irish Unionists and British Politics'

vi (March 1948): Lyons, F. S. L., 'The Irish Unionist Party and the Devolution Crisis of 1904–5'

xii (March 1961): Martin, F. X. (ed.), 'Eoin MacNeill on the 1916 Rising'

PART FIVE

OURSELVES ALONE

Barry, Tom, *Guerrilla Days In Ireland* (Cork, 1950)
 The author commanded an IRA Flying Column.

Beaslai, Piaras, *Michael Collins and the Making of a New Ireland* (2 vols. London, 1926)
 The author was editor of the secret Volunteer paper *An t'Oglach* and worked close to Collins 1919–21.

Bennett, R., *The Black and Tans* (London, 1959)

Breen, Dan, *My Fight For Irish Freedom* (Dublin, 1950)
 Experiences of a Volunteer 'gunman'.

Brennan, Robert, *Allegiance* (Dublin, 1950)
 The author was Sinn Fein Director of Elections 1918.

Bromage, M. C., *De Valera and the March of a Nation* (London, 1956)

Callwell, Major-Gen. Sir C. E., *Field Marshal Sir Henry Wilson, His Life and Diaries* (2 vols. London, 1927)

Carty, James, *Bibliography of Irish History, 1911–21* (Dublin, 1936)

Churchill, W. S., *The Aftermath* (Vol. V. of *The World Crisis*) (London, 1929)

Coogan, T. P., *Ireland Since The Rising* (London, 1968)
 Very useful as an objective up-dater.

Crozier, Brigadier F. P., *Impressions and Recollections* (London, 1930)

Crozier, Brigadier F. P., *Ireland For Ever* (London, 1932)

Dalton, Charles, *With the Dublin Brigade 1917–21* (London, 1929)

Duff, Douglas V., *The Rough With The Smooth* (London, 1940)

Ervine, St John, *Craigavon* (London, 1949)
> Extremely discursive but useful.

Figgis, Darrel, *Recollections of the Irish War* (London, 1927)

Fitzgerald, Desmond, *Memoirs* (London, 1969)

Forester, Margery, *Michael Collins: The Lost Leader* (London, 1971)
> Interesting personal papers of Collins.

Gallagher, Frank (pseud. David Hogan), *The Four Glorious Years* (Dublin, 1953)

Gallagher, Frank, *Days of Fear* (London, 1928)

Gallagher, Frank, *The Anglo-Irish Treaty* (edited with Introduction by T. P. O'Neill) (London, 1965)

Gleeson, James, *Bloody Sunday* (London, 1962)

Gwynn, Denis, *De Valera* (London, 1933)

Gwynn, Denis, *The Life of John Redmond* (London, 1932)

Gwynn, Denis, *The Life and Death of Roger Casement* (London, 1931)

Gwynn, Denis, *The Irish Free State* (London, 1928)

Henry, R. M., *The Evolution of Sinn Fein* (Dublin and London, 1920)

Holt, Edgar, *Protest In Arms* (London, 1960)

Kilfeather, T. P., *The Connaught Rangers* (Tralee, 1969)

Longford, Lord, and O'Neill, T. P., *Eamon de Valera* (London, 1970)
> Best biography of de Valera, written with his co-operation.

Lyons, F. S. L., *John Dillon* (London, 1968)

Macardle, Dorothy, *Irish Republic* (London, 1937: Dublin, 1951)
> Encyclopaedic account from committed Republican and anti-Treaty point of view of events 1916–25.

MacCarthy, J. M. (ed.), *Limerick's Fighting Story* (Tralee)

McCracken, J. L., *Representative Government in Ireland* (Oxford, 1958)

MacCready, Sir Nevile, *Annals of an Active Life* (2 vols. London, 1924)

McDowell, R. B., *The Irish Convention 1917–18* (London, 1970)

MacLysaght, Edward, 'Master of None' (private MS.)

Martin, Hugh, *Insurrection in Ireland* (London, 1921)

Neeson, E., *The Civil War in Ireland, 1922–1923* (Cork, 1967)

Neeson, E., *The Life and Death of Michael Collins* (Cork, 1968)

Nicolson, Sir Harold, *King George V* (London, 1952)

Nowlan K. and Williams T. D. (ed.), *Ireland In the War Years and After 1939–51* (Dublin, 1969)

O'Brien, William, *The Irish Revolution and How it Came About* (London, 1928)

O'Connor, Batt, *With Michael Collins in the Fight for Irish Independence* (London, 1929)

O'Connor, F., *The Big Fellow* (Dublin, revised edition, 1965)

O'Donnell, P., *The Gates Flew Open* (Cork, 1965)

O'Donoghue, Florence, *No Other Law (The Story of Liam Lynch and the*

Irish Republican Army 1916–1923) (Dublin, 1954)
   Valuable. The author was Lynch's intelligence officer.
O'Donoghue, Florence, *Tomas MacCurtain* (Dublin, 1958)
O'Hegarty, P. S., *The Victory of Sinn Fein* (Dublin, 1924)
O'Luing, S., *I Die In A Good Cause: A Study of Thomas Ashe* (Dublin, 1970)
O'Malley, Ernie, *On Another Man's Wound* (London, 1936)
   A work of literature, as well as of historical interest, by one of the IRA's
   leading fighters.
O'Neill, T. P. (ed.), *The Anglo-Irish Treaty*
   (See also Gallagher, Frank and Longford, Lord)
O'Sullivan, Donal, *The Irish Free State* (London, 1940)
Pakenham, Frank (now Lord Longford), *Peace By Ordeal* (London, 1935)
   Indispensable account of Treaty negotiations.
Parmiter, G. de C., *Roger Casement* (London, 1936)
Petrie, Sir Charles, *Life and Letters of Sir Austen Chamberlain* (London,
   1939)
Phillips, W. A., *The Revolution in Ireland* (London, 1923)
   Unionist history, bitter and astringent.
Pollard, H. B. C., *The Secret Societies of Ireland* (London, 1922)
Shakespeare, Sir Geoffrey, *Let Candles Be Brought In* (London, 1949)
Strauss, E., *Irish Nationalism and British Democracy* (London, 1957)
Street, C. J., (pseud. 'I.O.'), *The Administration of Ireland 1920* (London,
   1921)
Street, C. J., *Ireland in 1921* (London, 1922)
Taylor, A. J. P., *English History 1914–1945* (Oxford, 1965)
Taylor, Rex, *Michael Collins* (London, 1958)
   Interesting personal papers of Collins.
Ward, A. J., *Ireland and Anglo-American Relations, 1899–1921* (London,
   1969)
White, T. de Vere, *Kevin O'Higgins* (London, 1948)
Williams, T. Desmond (ed.),*The Irish Struggle* (London, 1966)
Winter, Sir Ormonde, *Winter's Tale* (London, 1955)
   Two chapters in this autobiography cover the author's time in charge
   of British Intelligence in Dublin Castle, 1920–21.
Younger, Calton, *Ireland's Civil War* (London, 1968)

OTHER SOURCES

Newspapers and Periodicals

Irish Independent
Irish Times
Daily Mail

Tipperary Star
Freeman's Journal
Mayo News
Clare Champion
Killarney Echo
Cork Examiner
Galway Express
Galway Observer

Official Publications

Hansard House of Commons Debates
Dail Eireann Official Reports:
　　Minutes of Proceedings 1919–21 (Dublin, 1921)
　　Treaty Debate (Dublin, 1922)
　　16–26 August 1921 and 28 February to 8 June 1922 (Dublin, 1922)
　　Parliamentary Debates: Vols. 1 and 2 (Dublin, 1922–3)
Documents relating to the Sinn Fein Movement; 1921 Cmd. 1108 XXIX 429
Arrangements governing the Cessation of Active Operations in Ireland
　　which came into force on 11 July 1921; 1921 Cmd. 1534 XXIX 427
Return showing the number of serious outrages in Ireland reported by the
　　Royal Irish Constabulary and the Dublin Metropolitan Police during the
　　months of October, November and December 1920; 1922 Cmd. 1165
　　XVII 807, 815
Outline of Terms on which Cadets of the Auxiliary Division of the Royal
　　Irish Constabulary were engaged; 1922 Cmd. 1618 XVII 785

Index

Shortt, Chief Secretary, 620

Sinn Fein (*see also* under Griffith), noted by Dillon, 436; Griffith's 'Hungarian' policy (1905), 452; political significance of, 453; and Devolution Bill, 455; candidate for North Leitrim defeated (1908), 455; gives Redmond a free hand, 456; and notion of Dual Monarchy of, 456; republican elements dissatisfied with, 459–60; reconstruction by de Valera (1917), 604; by-election successes and reverses (1917–18), 605, 615–17; Irish National Volunteers call for reconciliation with (Aug. 1917), 605; and political platform (Oct. 1917), 609–10; complications of separate identities of Volunteers and, 611–12; attempts to stop arms and other raids, 613–14; remain vital force after by-election defeats (1918), 615–16; effect of conscription on, 618; 'German Plot' and arrest of leaders of (May 1918), 620; militant members avoid arrest, 621–2; and Harcourt Street HQ wrecked, 624; General Election manifesto of (1918), 624; triumphs at General Election (1918), 626; and need to explain meaning of, 627; and attitude to Volunteer killings (1919), 633; bans hunting in Ireland, 636–7; and political offensive in Paris and America, 638–9; repudiates murder, 643; effects of military repression on, 644; Collins's castigation of, 647; banned in Tipperary (May 1919), 652; and analysis of votes at municipal elections (Jan. 1920), 666; and victories at County Council elections (June 1920), 679; elected candidates constituted as the Second Dail (May 1921), 713

Sixmilebridge, ambush at, 700

Skeffington, Francis Sheehy, shot dead, 567

Skibbereen, Co. Cork, 174, 259, 300

Sligo, pro-Union, 154; arrival of *Erin's Hope* at, 339

Smith, F. E., *see* Lord Birkenhead

Smith O'Brien, William (Liberal Member for Limerick): resigns commission of the peace, 205; joins Repeal Asso-

ciation, 215; swears to teetotalism, 223; and the '82 Club, 233; and 'Middle-Aged Ireland', 236; display of militancy, 247–8; imprisoned in Westminster, 249; forms Irish Confederation (Jan. 1847), 257; deprecates extremism, 262–3; charged with sedition, 267–8; approves Irish League, 271; in militant mood, 272–3; insists on constitutional methods, 275–6; goes to Kilkenny, 277–8; unable to raise support for action, 279–80; demands surrender of police at Mullinahone, 281–2; at barricade, 282–3; and start and finish of 'rising' at Ballingarry, 284–6; arrested at Thurles, 286; death sentence commuted to transportation, 287; pardon and return to Ireland of, 287–9

Smuts, General, 716, 721

Smyth, Detective, shot in Dublin, 655

Smyth, P. J., and orders to start Dublin insurrection (1848), 281, 282

'Soldier's Song, The' (later National Anthem of Ireland), begins to be sung, 553–4; spreading, 605

South Africa Bill, obstruction of (1877), 366

Southern Ireland Parliament: the Dail accepts electoral machinery of (1921), 713; and overlap of Parliaments in Provisional Government, 731

Southern Unionists: disapprove of partition, 592, 600; Redmond's hope of pressure on Ulster Unionists from, 600; and Midleton's reaction to Convention and partition, 615

South Mayo Flying Column, its courtesy, 700

Special Constabulary, *see* Ulster

Spender, Wilfrid, Captain, with Ulster Volunteers, 478

Spring Rice, *see* Rice

'Spies', execution of, 658, 662, 673, 702–4

'Squad', the, IRA élite, 706

Stack, Austin, 563, and forcible feeding in Mountjoy gaol, 606–7

Stepaside; capture of police barracks, 335

Stephen's Green, St, 550, 567

He just wanted a decent book to read ...

Not too much to ask, is it? It was in 1935 when Allen Lane, Managing Director of Bodley Head Publishers, stood on a platform at Exeter railway station looking for something good to read on his journey back to London. His choice was limited to popular magazines and poor-quality paperbacks – the same choice faced every day by the vast majority of readers, few of whom could afford hardbacks. Lane's disappointment and subsequent anger at the range of books generally available led him to found a company – and change the world.

'We believed in the existence in this country of a vast reading public for intelligent books at a low price, and staked everything on it'
Sir Allen Lane, 1902–1970, founder of Penguin Books

The quality paperback had arrived – and not just in bookshops. Lane was adamant that his Penguins should appear in chain stores and tobacconists, and should cost no more than a packet of cigarettes.

Reading habits (and cigarette prices) have changed since 1935, but Penguin still believes in publishing the best books for everybody to enjoy. We still believe that good design costs no more than bad design, and we still believe that quality books published passionately and responsibly make the world a better place.

So wherever you see the little bird – whether it's on a piece of prize-winning literary fiction or a celebrity autobiography, political tour de force or historical masterpiece, a serial-killer thriller, reference book, world classic or a piece of pure escapism – you can bet that it represents the very best that the genre has to offer.

Whatever you like to read – trust Penguin.